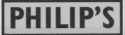

STREE

North Yorkshire

www.philips-maps.co.uk
First published in 2002 by Philip's,
a division of Octopus Publishing Group Ltd
www.octopusbooks.co.uk
Endeavour House,
189 Shaftesbury Avenue
London WC2H 8JY
An Hachette UK Company
www.hachette.co.uk

Third edition 2009,
Second impression 2012
NYOCA

978-1-84907-003-4 (pocket)

To the best of the Publishers' knowledge, the information in this atlas was correct at the time of going to press. No responsibility can be accepted for any errors or their consequences.

The representation in this atlas of a road, track or path is no evidence of the existence of a right of way.

Ordnance Survey and the OS Symbol are registered trademarks of Ordnance Survey, the national mapping agency of Great Britain.

Speed camera data provided by **PocketGPSWorld.com Ltd**

Post Office is a trade mark of Post Office Ltd in the UK and other countries.

Printed in China

Contents

II Mobile safety cameras

III **Key to map symbols**

IV **Key to map pages**

VI **Route planning**

X **Administrative and Postcode boundaries**

1 **Street maps** at 1⅓ inches to 1 mile

208 **Street maps** at 2⅔ inches to 1 mile

233 **Street map** of York at 5⅓ inches to 1 mile

234 **Index** of towns, villages, streets, hospitals, industrial estates, railway stations, schools, shopping centres, universities and places of interest

Digital Data

The exceptionally high-quality mapping found in this atlas is available as digital data in TIFF format, which is easily convertible to other bitmapped (raster) image formats.

The index is also available in digital form as a standard database table. It contains all the details found in the printed index together with the National Grid reference for the map square in which each entry is named.

For further information and to discuss your requirements, please contact philips@mapsinternational.co.uk

Mobile safety cameras

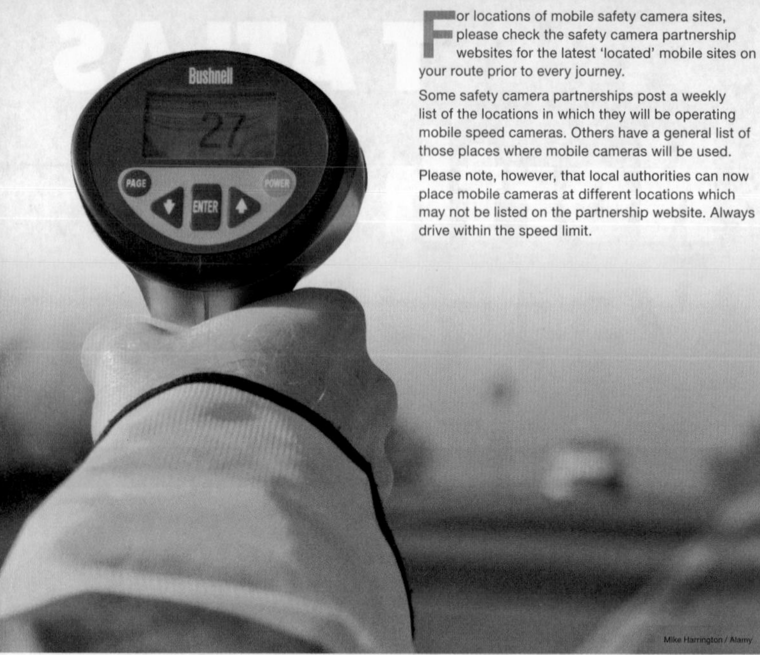

For locations of mobile safety camera sites, please check the safety camera partnership websites for the latest 'located' mobile sites on your route prior to every journey.

Some safety camera partnerships post a weekly list of the locations in which they will be operating mobile speed cameras. Others have a general list of those places where mobile cameras will be used.

Please note, however, that local authorities can now place mobile cameras at different locations which may not be listed on the partnership website. Always drive within the speed limit.

Mike Harrington / Alamy

Useful websites

Cumbria safety Cameras
www.cumbriasafetycameras.org

Durham Constabulary
www.durham.police.uk/durhamc/central_deps/operations/scu.php

East Riding safety camera partnership
www.eastriding.gov.uk/safetycamerapartnership

Lancashire Partnership for Road Safety
www.safe2travel.co.uk

South Yorkshire safety camera partnership
www.safetycamera.org/home

West Yorkshire safety camera partnership
www.safetycameraswestyorkshire.co.uk

Further information
www.dvla.gov.uk
www.thinkroadsafety.gov.uk
www.dft.gov.uk
www.road-safe.org

Key to map symbols

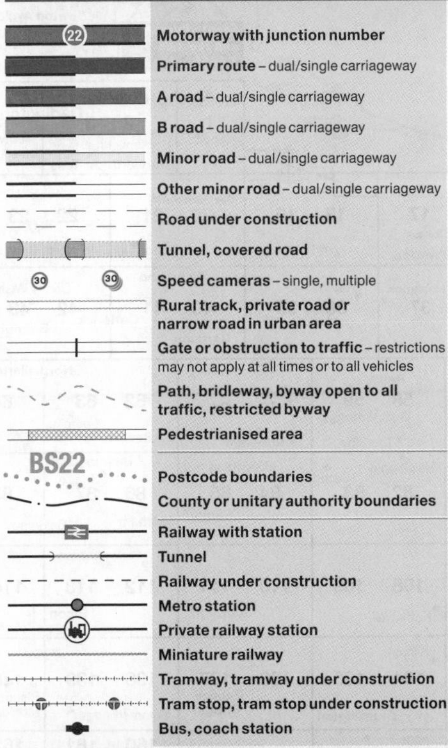

Motorway with junction number (22)	
Primary route – dual/single carriageway	
A road – dual/single carriageway	
B road – dual/single carriageway	
Minor road – dual/single carriageway	
Other minor road – dual/single carriageway	
Road under construction	
Tunnel, covered road	
Speed cameras – single, multiple	
Rural track, private road or narrow road in urban area	
Gate or obstruction to traffic – restrictions may not apply at all times or to all vehicles	
Path, bridleway, byway open to all traffic, restricted byway	
Pedestrianised area	
Postcode boundaries BS22	
County or unitary authority boundaries	
Railway with station	
Tunnel	
Railway under construction	
Metro station	
Private railway station	
Miniature railway	
Tramway, tramway under construction	
Tram stop, tram stop under construction	
Bus, coach station	

◆	Ambulance station
◆	Coastguard station
◆	Fire station
◆	Police station
✚	Accident and Emergency entrance to hospital
H	Hospital
+	Place of worship
i	Information centre – open all year
	Shopping centre, parking
P&R	Park and Ride, Post Office
⚑	Camping site, caravan site
	Golf course, picnic site
Church	Non-Roman antiquity, Roman antiquity
ROMAN FORT	

Univ	Important buildings, schools, colleges, universities and hospitals
	Woods, built-up area
River Medway	Water name
	River, weir
	Stream
	Canal, lock, tunnel
	Water
	Tidal water

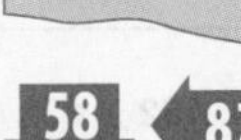

58 ◀ 87	Adjoining page indicators and overlap bands – the colour of the arrow and band indicates the scale of the adjoining or overlapping page (see scales below)
246	

The dark grey border on the inside edge of some pages indicates that the mapping does not continue onto the adjacent page

The small numbers around the edges of the maps identify the 1-kilometre National Grid lines

Abbreviations

Acad	Academy	Meml	Memorial
Allot Gdns	Allotments	Mon	Monument
Cemy	Cemetery	Mus	Museum
C Ctr	Civic centre	Obsy	Observatory
CH	Club house	Pal	Royal palace
Coll	College	PH	Public house
Crem	Crematorium	Recn Gd	Recreation ground
Ent	Enterprise		
Ex H	Exhibition hall	Resr	Reservoir
Ind Est	Industrial Estate	Ret Pk	Retail park
IRB Sta	Inshore rescue boat station	Sch	School
		Sh Ctr	Shopping centre
Inst	Institute	TH	Town hall / house
Ct	Law court	Trad Est	Trading estate
L Ctr	Leisure centre	Univ	University
LC	Level crossing	W Twr	Water tower
Liby	Library	Wks	Works
Mkt	Market	YH	Youth hostel

Enlarged maps only

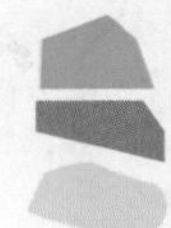

	Railway or bus station building
	Place of interest
	Parkland

The map scale on the pages numbered in green is 1⅓ inches to 1 mile
2.1 cm to 1 km • 1:47 620

0	½ mile	1 mile	1½ miles	2 miles
0	500m	1km	1½km	2km

The map scale on the pages numbered in blue is 2⅔ inches to 1 mile
4.2 cm to 1 km • 1:23 810

0	¼ mile	½ mile	¾ mile	1 mile
0	250m	500m	750m	1km

The map scale on the pages numbered in red is 5⅓ inches to 1 mile
8.4 cm to 1 km • 1:11 900

0	220yds	440yds	660yds	½ mile
0	125m	250m	375m	500m

IV

Key to map pages

113	Map pages at 1⅓ inches to 1 mile
221	Map pages at 2⅔ inches to 1 mile
233	Map pages at 5⅓ inches to 1 mile

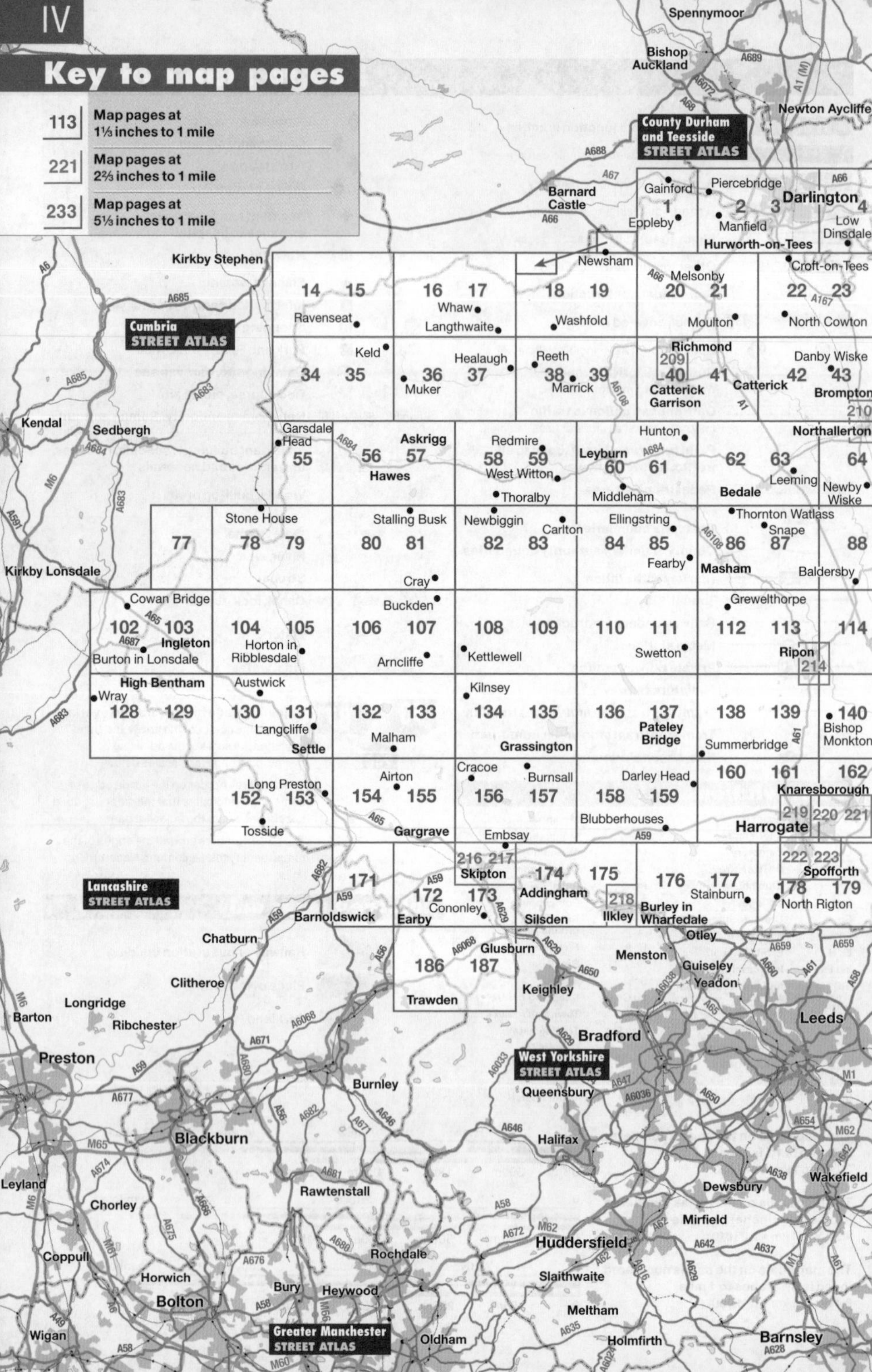

Spennymoor

Bishop Auckland

Newton Aycliffe

County Durham and Teesside STREET ATLAS

Barnard Castle

Gainford 1 Piercebridge 2 3 Darlington 4
Eppleby Manfield Low Dinsdale
Hurworth-on-Tees

Kirkby Stephen

Newsham

Cumbria STREET ATLAS

14 15   16 17   18 19   Melsonby 20 21   22 23
Ravenseat Whaw Washfold Moulton North Cowton
Langthwaite

Keld   Healaugh Reeth   Richmond 209 Danby Wiske
34 35   36 37   38 39   40 41   42 43
Muker Marrick Catterick Garrison Catterick Brompton
210

Kendal Sedbergh

Garsdale Head Askrigg   Redmire   Hunton   Northallerton
55   56 57   58 59   Leyburn 60 61   62 63 64
Hawes West Witton Middleham Bedale Leeming Newby Wiske

Thoralby

Stone House Stalling Busk Newbiggin Ellingstring Thornton Watlass
77   78 79   80 81   82 83   84 85   86 87 88
Carlton Fearby Snape
Cray   Masham Baldersby

Kirkby Lonsdale

Cowan Bridge Buckden Grewelthorpe
102 103   104 105   106 107   108 109   110 111   112 113 114
Ingleton Horton in Ribblesdale Swetton Ripon
Burton in Lonsdale Arncliffe Kettlewell 214

High Bentham Austwick Kilnsey
Wray 128 129   130 131   132 133   134 135   136 137   138 139 140
Langcliffe Malham Pateley Bridge Bishop Monkton
Settle Grassington Summerbridge

Airton Cracoe Darley Head 162
Long Preston 152 153   154 155   156 157   158 159   160 161 Knaresborough
Tosside Burnsall Blubberhouses 219 220 221
Gargrave Embsay Harrogate
222 223

216 217 Skipton 174 175   176 177   178 179
171 172 173 Addingham 218 Stainburn Spofforth
Barnoldswick Earby Cononley Silsden Ilkley Burley in North Rigton
Chatburn Wharfedale
Otley
Glusburn Menston Guiseley Yeadon
186 187 Keighley
Clitheroe Trawden

Longridge Ribchester
Barton
Preston Bradford Leeds

West Yorkshire STREET ATLAS
Burnley Queensbury

Blackburn Halifax Dewsbury Wakefield
Leyland
Chorley Rawtenstall Mirfield

Coppull
Horwich Rochdale Huddersfield
Wigan Bury Heywood Slaithwaite Barnsley
Bolton Meltham
Greater Manchester STREET ATLAS Oldham Holmfirth

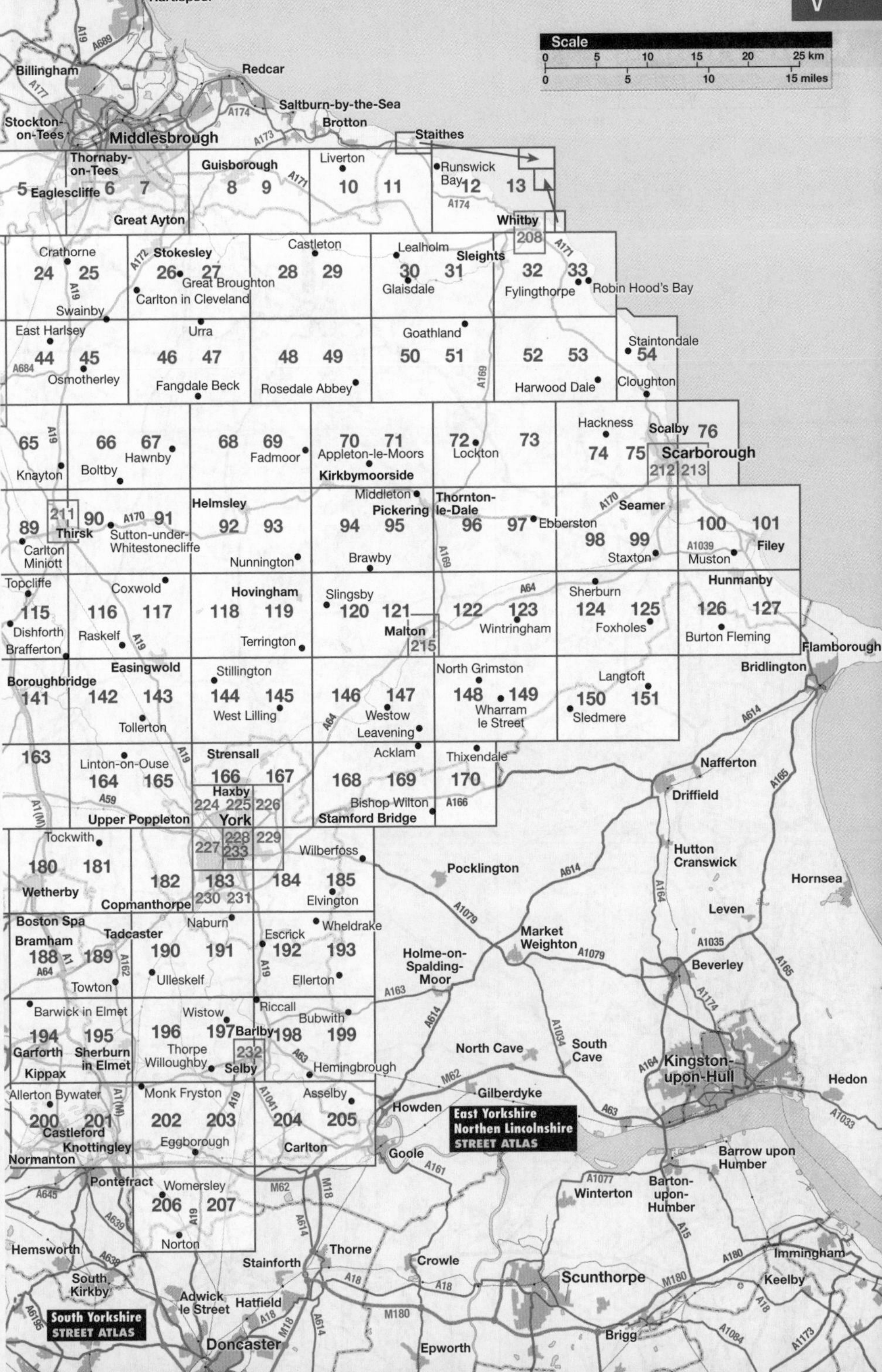
V
Scale
0 5 10 15 20 25 km
0 5 10 15 miles
Hartlepool
Billingham
Redcar
Saltburn-by-the-Sea
Brotton
Stockton-on-Tees
Middlesbrough
Staithes
Thornaby-on-Tees
Guisborough
Liverton
Runswick Bay
5 Eaglescliffe 6 7
8 9
10 11
12 13
Great Ayton
Whitby
208
Crathorne
24 25
Stokesley
26 27
Great Broughton
Carlton in Cleveland
Swainby
Castleton
28 29
Lealholm
30 31
Glaisdale
Sleights
32 33
Fylingthorpe
Robin Hood's Bay
East Harlsey
44 45
Osmotherley
Urra
46 47
Fangdale Beck
48 49
Rosedale Abbey
Goathland
50 51
52 53
Harwood Dale
Staintondale
54
Cloughton
65
Knayton
66 67
Hawnby
Boltby
68 69
Fadmoor
70 71
Appleton-le-Moors
Kirkbymoorside
72 73
Lockton
Hackness
74 75
Scalby 76
Scarborough
212 213
211
89 90 91
Thirsk
Carlton Miniott
Sutton-under-Whitestonecliffe
Helmsley
92 93
Nunnington
Middleton
Pickering
94 95
Brawby
Thornton-le-Dale
96 97
Ebberston
Seamer
98 99
Staxton
100 101
Muston
Filey
Topcliffe
115
Dishforth
Brafferton
Coxwold
116 117
Raskelf
Hovingham
118 119
Terrington
Slingsby
120 121
Malton
215
122 123
Wintringham
Sherburn
124 125
Foxholes
Hunmanby
126 127
Burton Fleming
Flamborough
Bridlington
Boroughbridge
141
Easingwold
142 143
Tollerton
Stillington
144 145
West Lilling
146 147
Westow
Leavening
North Grimston
148 149
Wharram le Street
Langtoft
150 151
Sledmere
163
Linton-on-Ouse
164 165
Upper Poppleton
Strensall
166 167
Haxby
224 225 226
York
227 228 229
233
Acklam
168 169
Bishop Wilton
Stamford Bridge
Thixendale
170
Nafferton
Driffield
Tockwith
180 181
Wetherby
182
Copmanthorpe
183
230 231
184
Wilberfoss
185
Elvington
Pocklington
Hutton Cranswick
Hornsea
Leven
Boston Spa
Bramham
188 189
Tadcaster
Towton
190
Ulleskelf
Naburn
191
Escrick
192
Wheldrake
193
Ellerton
Holme-on-Spalding-Moor
Market Weighton
Beverley
Barwick in Elmet
194 195
Garforth
Sherburn in Elmet
Kippax
Wistow
196 197
Thorpe Willoughby
Barlby
232
Selby
Riccall
198 199
Bubwith
Hemingbrough
North Cave
South Cave
Kingston-upon-Hull
Hedon
Allerton Bywater
200 201
Castleford
Knottingley
Normanton
Monk Fryston
202 203
Eggborough
Asselby
204 205
Carlton
Howden
Gilberdyke
East Yorkshire
Northern Lincolnshire
STREET ATLAS
Goole
Barrow upon Humber
Barton-upon-Humber
Winterton
Pontefract
Womersley
206 207
Norton
Hemsworth
Thorne
Stainforth
Crowle
Scunthorpe
Immingham
Keelby
South Kirkby
Adwick le Street
Hatfield
Doncaster
Epworth
Brigg
South Yorkshire
STREET ATLAS

Route Planning

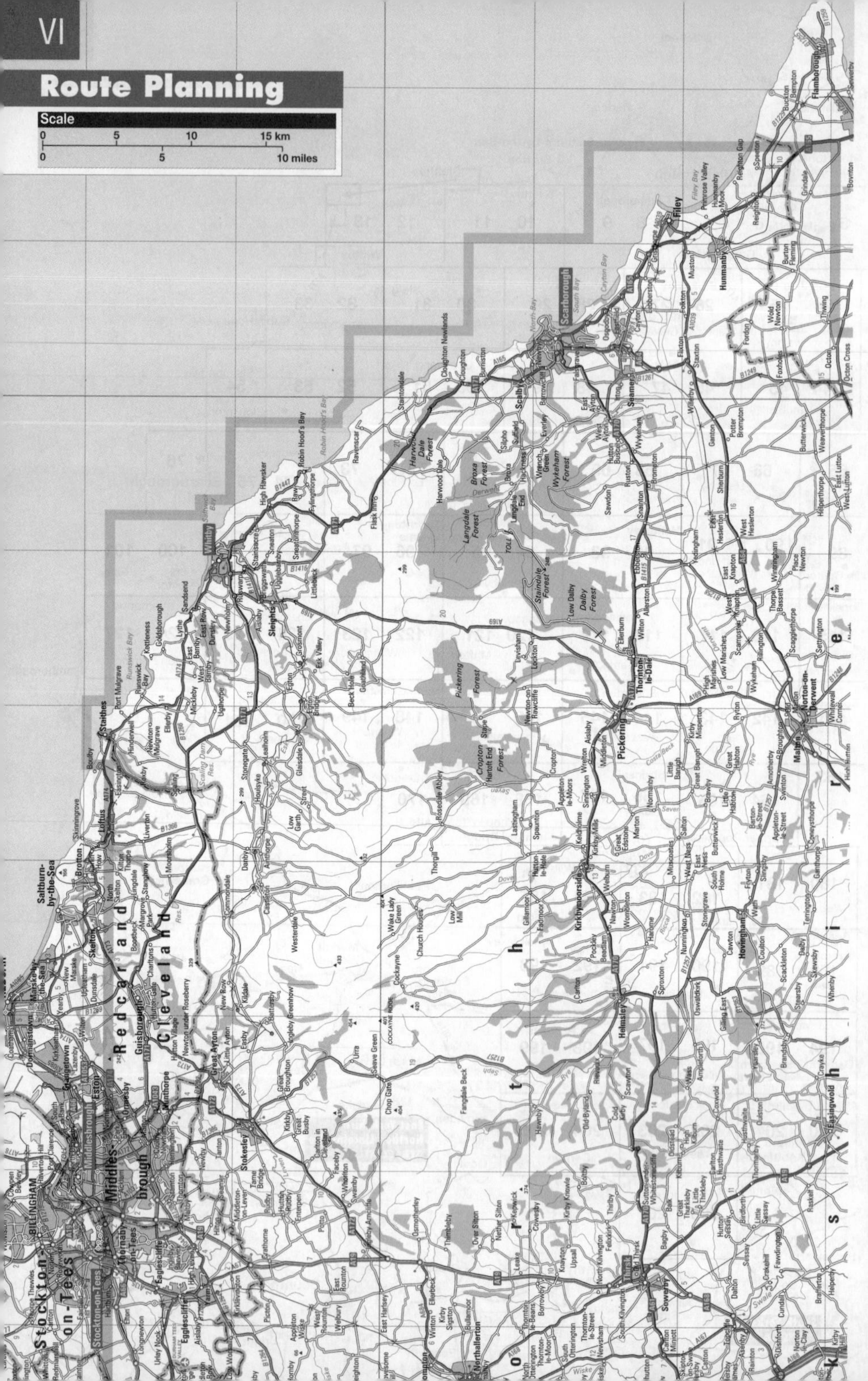
Scale
0 5 10 15 km
0 5 10 miles
Stockton-on-Tees
Middlesbrough
Redcar and Cleveland
Guisborough
Saltburn-by-the-Sea
Loftus
Staithes
Whitby
Robin Hood's Bay
Scarborough
Filey
Hunmanby
Flamborough
Seamer
Pickering
Thornton-le-Dale
Malton
Norton-on-Derwent
Kirkbymoorside
Helmsley
Hovingham
Easingwold
Thirsk
Sowerby
Stokesley
Great Ayton
Northallerton
Langdale Forest
Broxa Forest
Wykeham Forest
Dalby Forest
Pickering Forest
Cropton Forest
Harwood Dale Forest
Staindale Forest

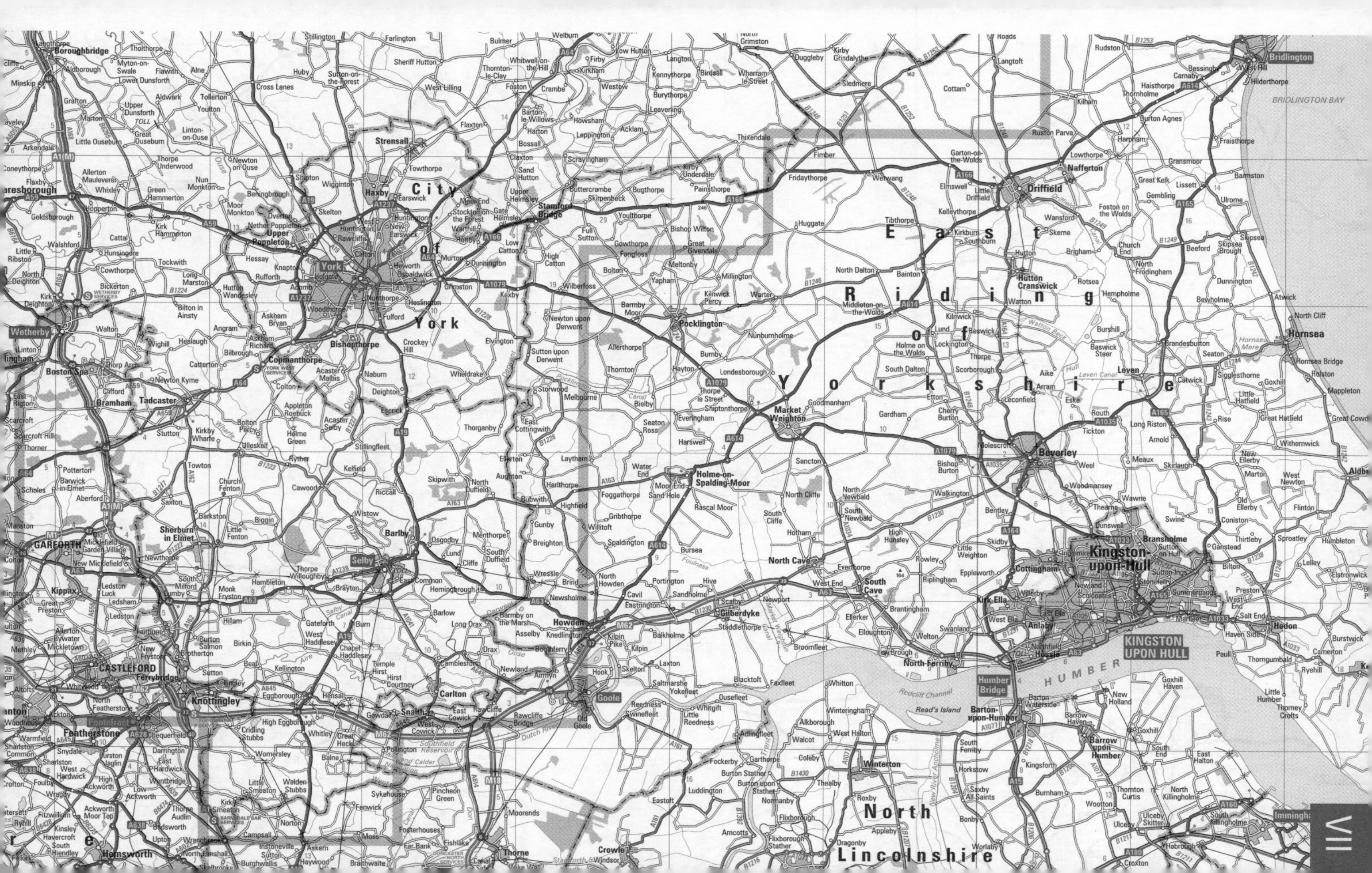
BRIDLINGTON BAY
Bridlington
Hornsea
Driffield
Nafferton
Beverley
Leven
Hedon
Kingston-upon-Hull
KINGSTON UPON HULL
HUMBER
Humber Bridge
Barton-upon-Humber
Barrow upon Humber
Immingham
East Riding of Yorkshire
North Lincolnshire
City of York
York
Haxby
Strensall
Stamford Bridge
Pocklington
Market Weighton
Holme-on-Spalding-Moor
North Cave
South Cave
Gilberdyke
Howden
Goole
Selby
Barlby
Bishopthorpe
Copmanthorpe
Upper Poppleton
Tadcaster
Sherburn in Elmet
Castleford
Knottingley
Featherstone
Garforth
Kippax
Wetherby
Boston Spa
Boroughbridge
Bramham
Carlton
Thorne
Winterton
Hemsworth
Snaith

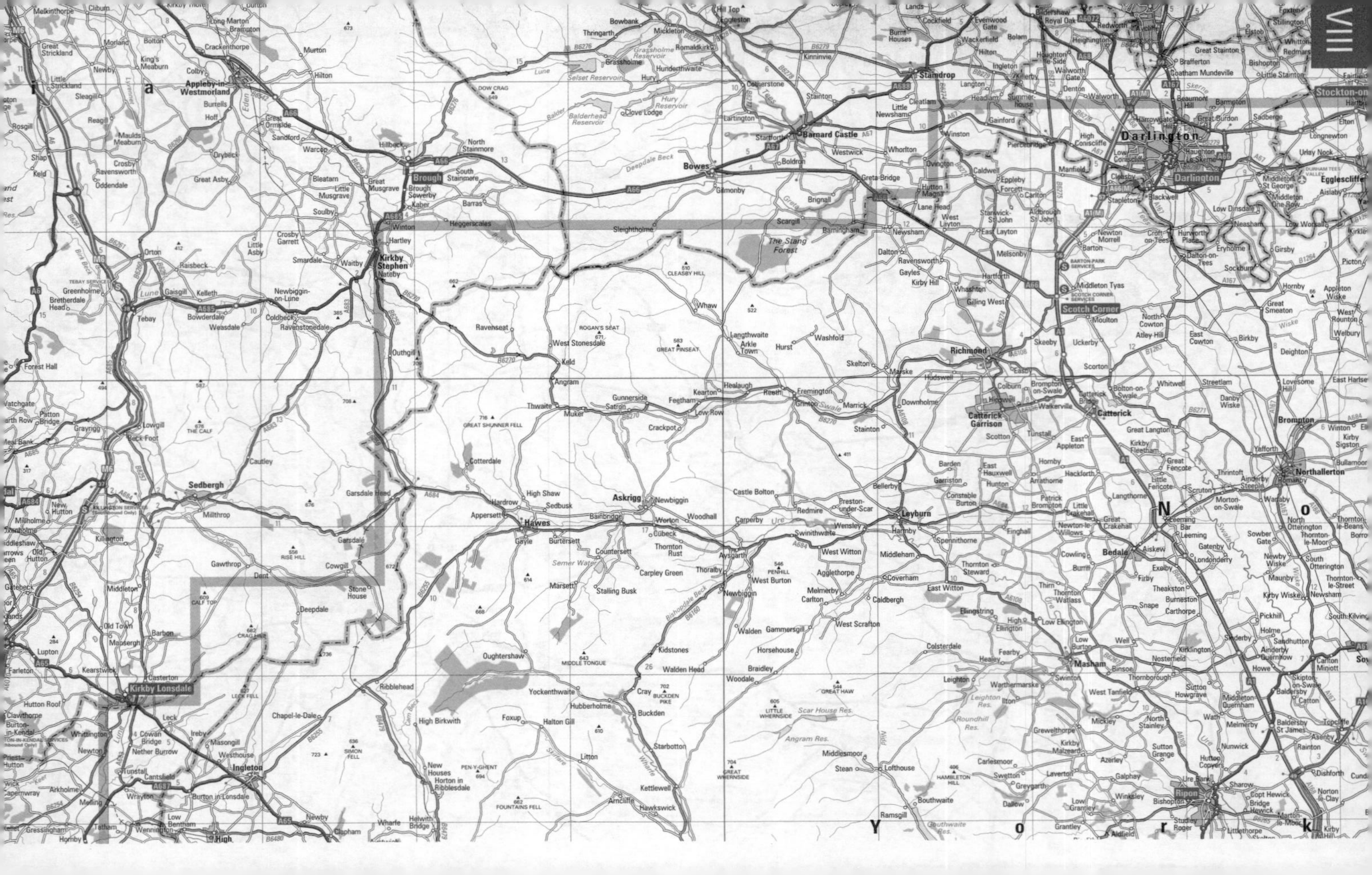
Appleby-in-Westmorland
Brough
Kirkby Stephen
Barnard Castle
Bowes
Staindrop
Darlington
Stockton-on
Scotch Corner
Richmond
Catterick
Catterick Garrison
Northallerton
Bedale
Leyburn
Masham
Ripon
Sedbergh
Hawes
Askrigg
Kirkby Lonsdale
Ingleton
The Stang Forest
Selset Reservoir
Grassholme Reservoir
Balderhead Reservoir
Hury Reservoir
Semer Water
Scar House Res.
Angram Res.
Leighton Res.
Roundhill Res.
GREAT SHUNNER FELL
ROGAN'S SEAT
GREAT PINSEAT
CLEASBY HILL
MIDDLE TONGUE
BUCKDEN PIKE
GREAT WHERNSIDE
LITTLE WHERNSIDE
GREAT HAW
PEN-Y-GHENT
FOUNTAINS FELL
SIMON FELL
CALF TOP
RISE HILL
THE CALF
HAMBLETON HILL
DOW CRAG
N
o
r
t
h
Y
o
r
k

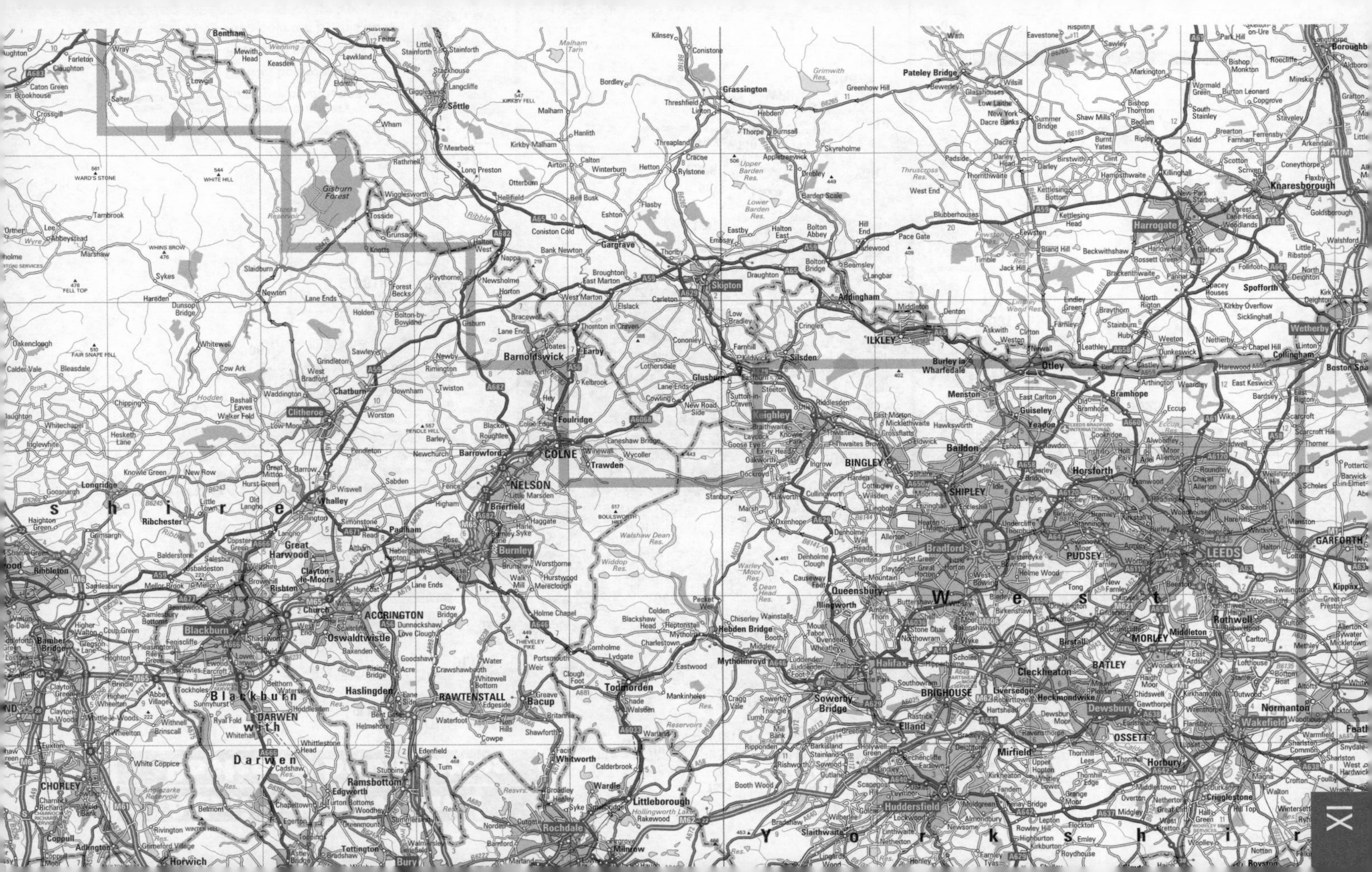
Pateley Bridge
Grassington
Settle
Bentham
Knaresborough
Harrogate
Wetherby
Spofforth
Otley
ILKLEY
Skipton
Keighley
BINGLEY
SHIPLEY
Baildon
Bradford
LEEDS
PUDSEY
Horsforth
Yeadon
Guiseley
MORLEY
BATLEY
Dewsbury
OSSETT
Wakefield
Normanton
Rothwell
Halifax
BRIGHOUSE
Elland
Huddersfield
Mirfield
Cleckheaton
Queensbury
Hebden Bridge
Todmorden
Littleborough
Rochdale
Barnoldswick
Gargrave
COLNE
NELSON
Burnley
ACCRINGTON
Clitheroe
Whalley
Great Harwood
Blackburn
DARWEN
Haslingden
RAWTENSTALL
Bacup
Ramsbottom
Longridge
Ribchester
CHORLEY
Horwich
West Yorkshire

Administrative and Postcode boundaries

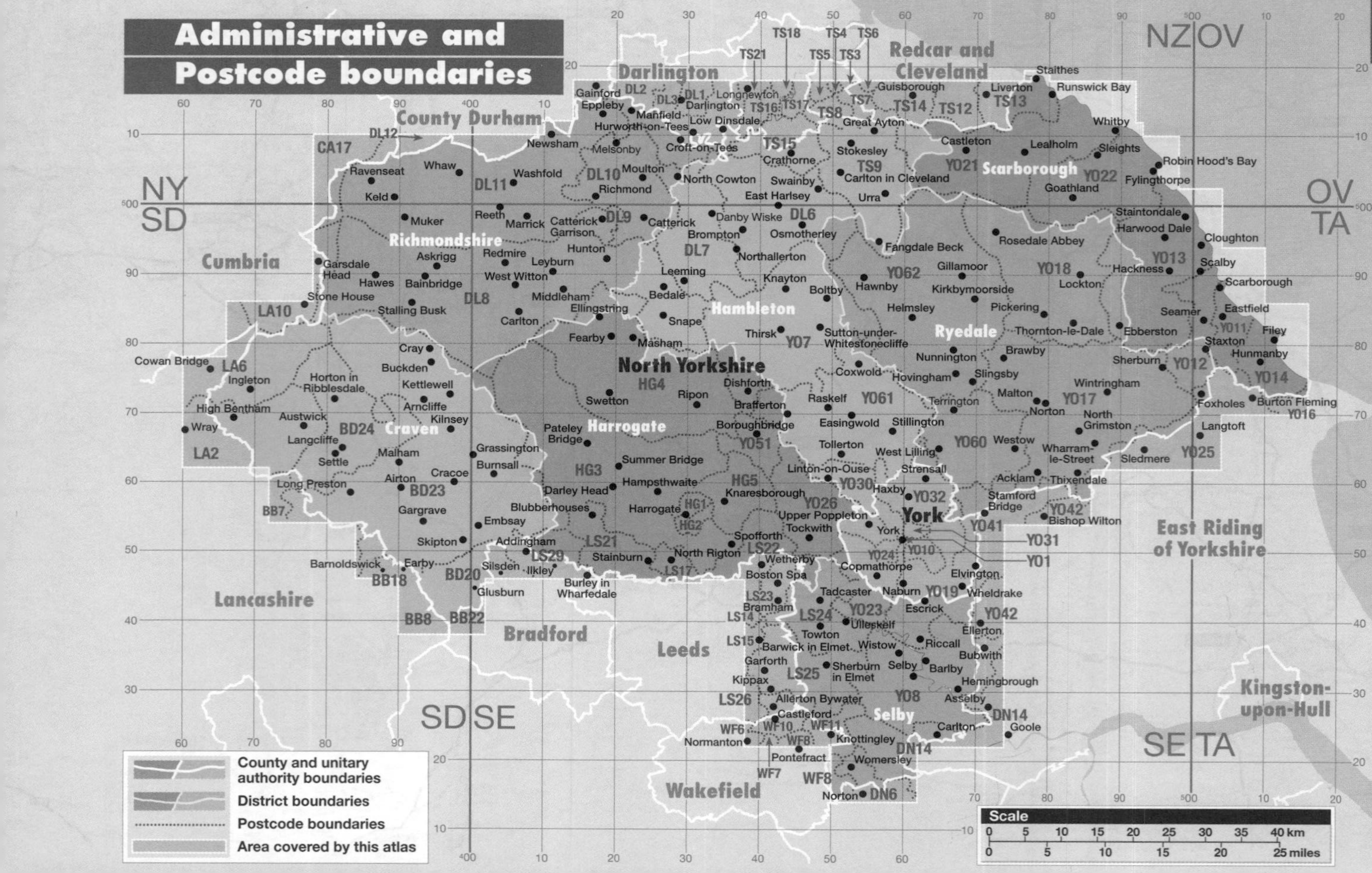

County Durham

Darlington

Redcar and Cleveland

Richmondshire

Hambleton

North Yorkshire

Scarborough

Ryedale

York

Harrogate

Craven

Selby

East Riding of Yorkshire

Kingston-upon-Hull

Leeds

Bradford

Wakefield

Cumbria

Lancashire

Scale

| 0 | 5 | 10 | 15 | 20 | 25 | 30 | 35 | 40 km |
| 0 | 5 | 10 | 15 | 20 | 25 miles |

Legend
- County and unitary authority boundaries
- District boundaries
- Postcode boundaries
- Area covered by this atlas

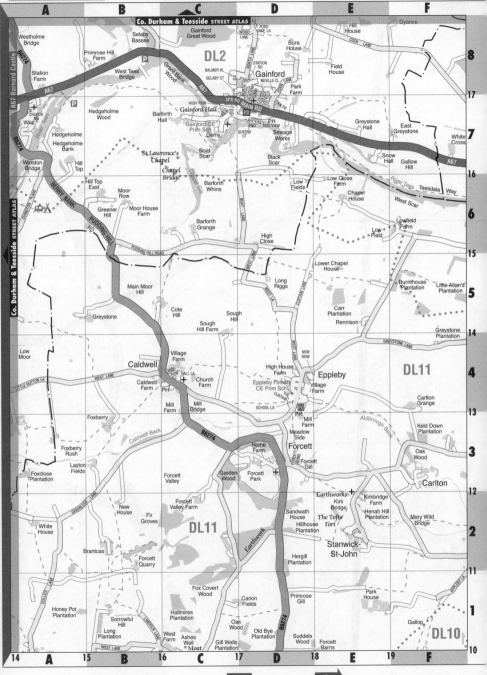

2

A B C D E F

8 17 7 16 6 15 5 14 4 13 3 12 2 11 1 10

Westholme Bridge
Selaby Basses
Gainford Great Wood
Hill House
Dyance
Primrose Hill Farm
DL2
Burn House
COCK LANE
Station Farm
West Tees Bridge
Grant Bank Wood
Gainford
Field House
A67 Barnard Castle
B6274
A67
BALMER HL
SELABY CT
STATION RD
NORTH LANE
NEVILLE CL
EDEN LANE
Park Farm
WOOD LANE
FORD DIKE LA
NORTH TR
ACADEMY GDNS
EDEN CREST
EDEN PK
HIGH ROW
SPA RD
MAIN RD
Gainford Hall
LOW RD
Hedgeholme Wood
Barforth Hall
CHURCH MS
Wks
River Tees
Gainford CE Prim Sch
Cemy
WATERS END
QUEENS CT
PH
TEES VIEW
Sewage Works
Greystone Hall
East Greystone
White Cross
Hedgeholme
Hedgeholme Bank
St Lawrence's Chapel
Boat Scar
Black Scar
Snow Hall
Gallow Hill
A67
Winston Bridge
Hill Top
Chapel Bridge
Chapel Gill
Hill Top East
Barforth Whins
Low Fields
Low Close Farm
River Tees
Teesdale Way
BERRY BANK
OVINGTON LANE
Moor Row
BOAT LANE
Chapel House
West Scar
Greener Hill
Moor House Farm
Barforth Grange
Lowfield Farm
PUDDING HILL RD
Low Field
High Close
PUDDING HILL ROAD
WEST LANE
Lower Chapel House
Long Riggs
Burnthouse Plantation
Little Allan's Plantation
Main Moor Hill
WEST LA
CURTAIN LANE
Cote Hill
Sough Hill
Carr Plantation
Greystone
Sough Hill Farm
Rennison
Greystone Plantation
GREYSTONE LANE
Low Moor
Village Farm
NEW ROW
Caldwell
High House Farm
Eppleby
DL11
HIGH ROW
HALL LA
Church Farm
LITTLE HUTTON LA
WEST LANE
Caldwell Farm
Eppleby Forcett CE Prim Sch
Village Farm
THE CURTAIN
PH
Carlton Grange
Mill Farm
Mill Bridge
SCHOOL LA
PH
Foxberry
Mill Farm
Aldbrough Beck
Keld Down Plantation
Caldwell Beck
Meadow Side
B6274
Home Farm
Forcett
Foxberry Rush
Oak Wood
FORCETT GDNS
Forcett Gill
Layton Fields
Foxclose Plantation
Garden Wood
Forcett Park
Forcett Valley
Carlton
Earthworks
Kirkbridge Farm
GREENLESS LANE
Forcett Valley Farm
Kirk Bridge
New House
Sandwath House
Henah Hill Plantation
Fir Groves
The Tofts Fort
Mary Wild Bridge
White House
DL11
Hillhouse Plantation
Earthwork
Stanwick-St-John
Brantcas
Forcett Quarry
Hergill Plantation
Fox Covert Wood
COLLIER LANE
Park House
APPLEBY LA
Carkin Fields
Primrose Gill
Honey Pot Plantation
Hallmires Plantation
Gallop
Sorrowful Hill
LIMEKILN LANE
Oak Wood
DL10
Long Plantation
West Farm
Ashes Well
Old Bye Plantation
B6274
Suddels Wood
Forcett Barns
WEST LANE
Moat
Gill Wells Plantation

14 A 15 B 16 C 17 D 18 E 19 F

20

2

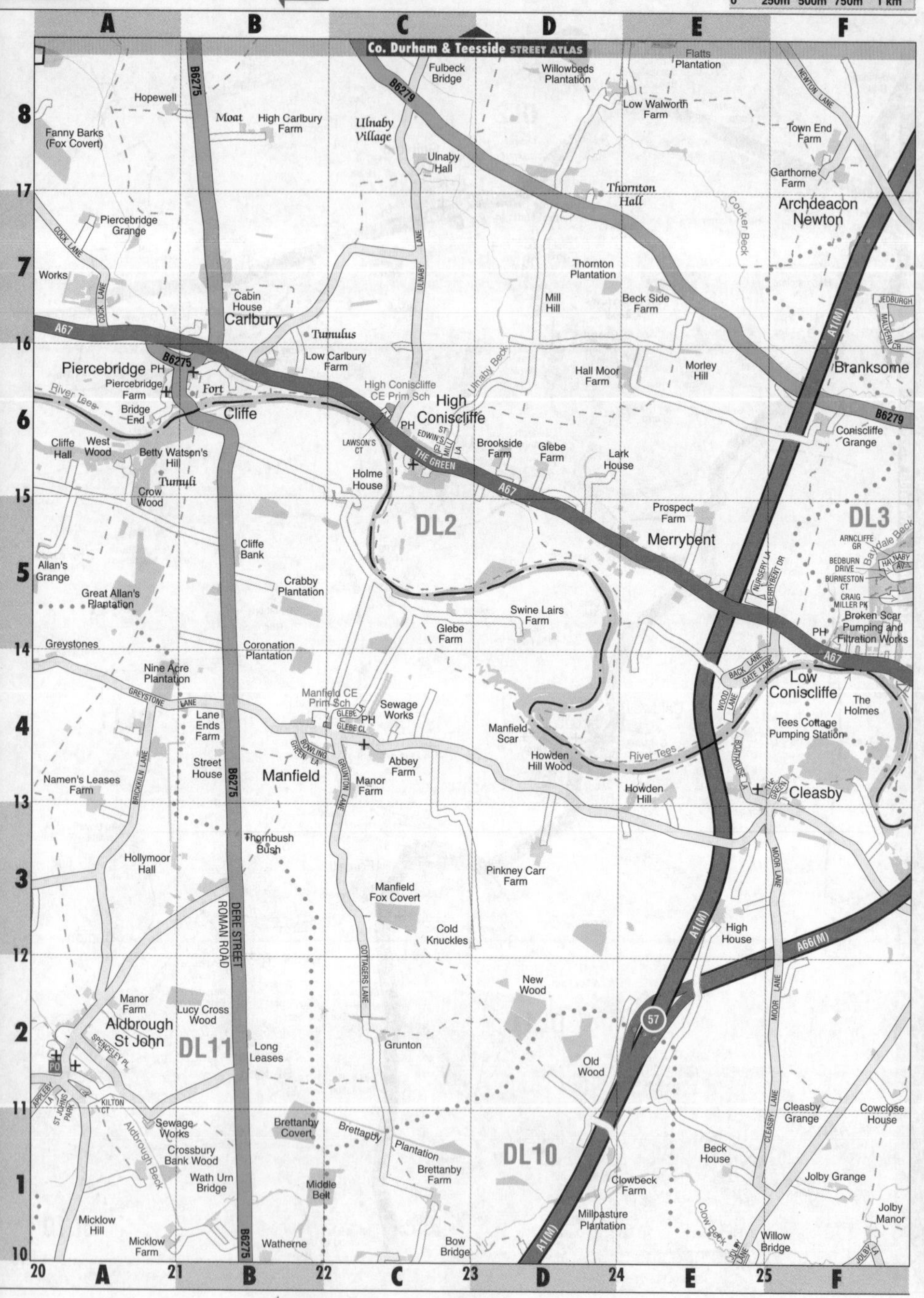

Scale: 1½ inches to 1 mile

0 ¼ ½ mile
0 250m 500m 750m 1 km

Co. Durham & Teesside STREET ATLAS

Row 8 / 17

Fanny Barks (Fox Covert)
Hopewell
B6275
Moat
High Carlbury Farm
Ulnaby Village
Ulnaby Hall
Fulbeck Bridge
Willowbeds Plantation
Low Walworth Farm
Flatts Plantation
Town End Farm
Garthorne Farm
Archdeacon Newton

Piercebridge Grange
Works
COCK LANE
Cabin House
Carlbury
Tumulus
DERE RD LANE
Thornton Hall
Thornton Plantation
Mill Hill
Beck Side Farm
Cooker Beck
A1(M)
JEDBURGH
MALTERN CR
Branksome

Row 16 / 6

A67
Piercebridge
Piercebridge Farm
PH
B6275
Fort
Bridge End
Cliffe
Low Carlbury Farm
High Coniscliffe CE Prim Sch
High Coniscliffe
ST EDWIN'S
PH
Ulnaby Beck
Hall Moor Farm
Morley Hill
B6279
Coniscliffe Grange

River Tees
Cliffe Hall
West Wood
Betty Watson's Hill
Tumuli
Crow Wood
LAWSON'S CT
THE GREEN
Holme House
Brookside Farm
Glebe Farm
A67
Lark House
DL2
DL3
ARNCLIFFE GR
BEDBURN DRIVE
BURNESTON CT
CRAIG MILLER PK
HALINBY AVE
Broken Scar Pumping and Filtration Works

Row 15 / 5

Allan's Grange
Great Allan's Plantation
Cliffe Bank
Crabby Plantation
Glebe Farm
Swine Lairs Farm
Merrybent
Prospect Farm
PINSENT DR
BACK LANE
GATE LANE
A67
PH

Row 14 / 4

Greystones
Nine Acre Plantation
GREYSTONE LANE
Coronation Plantation
Manfield CE Prim Sch
GLEB
GLEBE CL
Sewage Works
Manfield Scar
Howden Hill Wood
River Tees
WOOD LANE
Low Coniscliffe
Tees Cottage Pumping Station
The Holmes
MOOR LANE
BRANKSIDE DR

Namen's Leases Farm
BROOMHILL LANE
LANE ENDS FARM
Street House
BOWLING GREEN LA
B6275
Manfield
Abbey Farm
Manor Farm
Howden Hill
Cleasby

Row 13 / 3

Hollymoor Hall
Thornbush Bush
DERE STREET
ROMAN ROAD
COTTAGERS LANE
Manfield Fox Covert
Cold Knuckles
Pinkney Carr Farm
A1(M)
MOOR LANE

Row 12 / 2

Manor Farm
Aldbrough St John
Lucy Cross Wood
DL11
Long Leases
Grunton
New Wood
Old Wood
57
High House
A66(M)
Cleasby Grange
Cowclose House

Row 11 / 1

STAPLEY PL
KILTON CT
Sewage Works
Crossbury Bank Wood
Wath Urn Bridge
Brettanby Covert
Brettanby Farm
Brettanby Plantation
DL10
A1(M)
Beck House
CLEASBY LANE
Jolby Grange
Jolby Manor

Micklow Hill
Micklow Farm
B6275
Watherne
Middle Belt
Bow Bridge
Clowbeck Farm
Millpasture Plantation
Chow Beck
Willow Bridge
JOLBY LANE

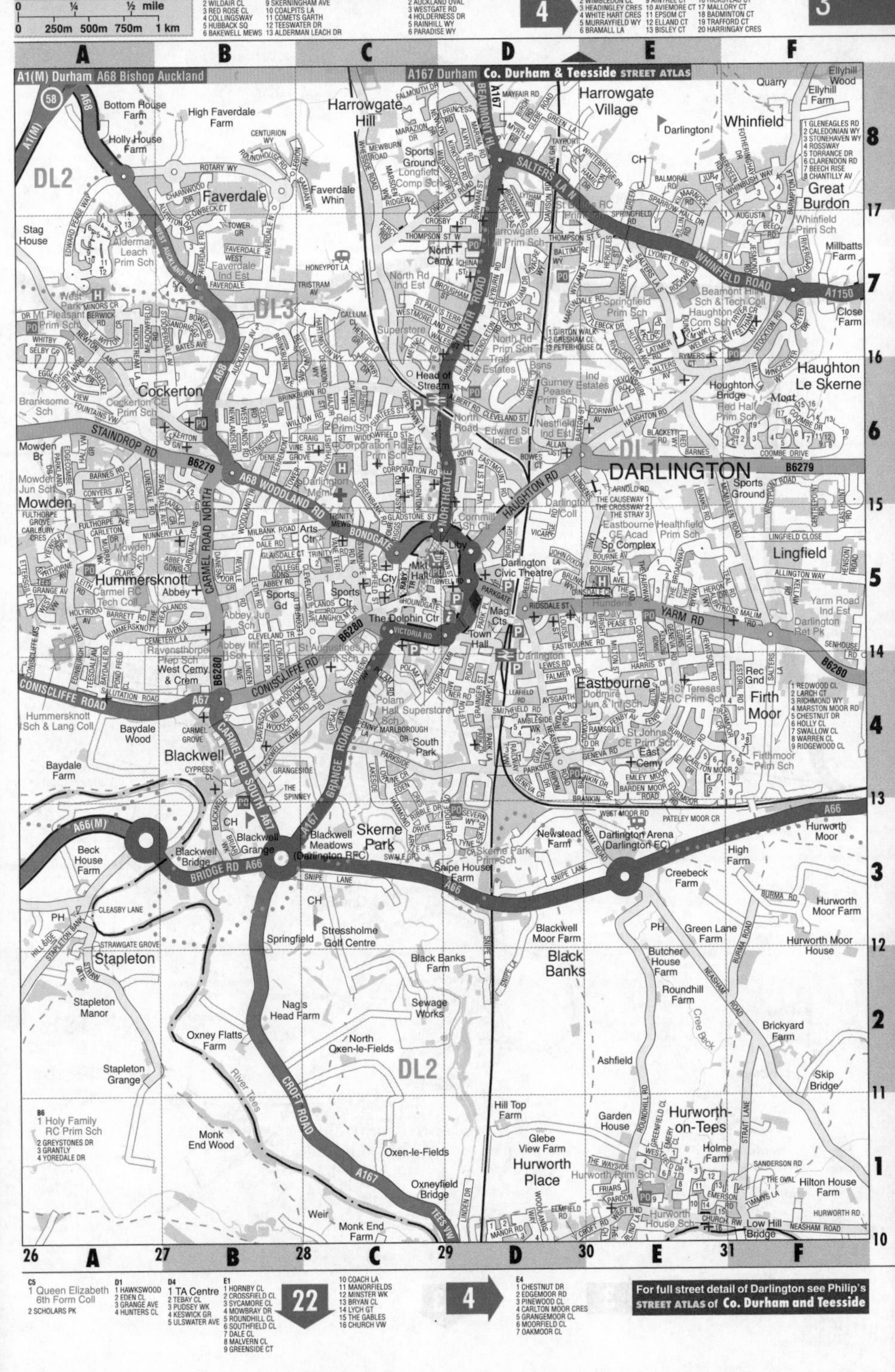

Scale: 1⅓ inches to 1 mile
0 ¼ ½ mile
0 250m 500m 750m 1 km
A7
1 SHORTHORN LA
2 WILDAIR CL
3 RED ROSE CL
4 COLLINGSWAY
5 HUBBACK SQ
6 BAKEWELL MEWS
7 HOLDERNESS DR
8 OLD FAVOURITES WALK
9 SKERNINGHAM AVE
10 COALPITS LA
11 COMETS GARTH
12 TEESWATER DR
13 ALDERMAN LEACH DR
14 JOHN FOWLER WY
B7
1 BRINKBURN DR
2 AUCKLAND OVAL
3 WESTGATE RD
4 HOLDERNESS DR
5 RAINHILL WY
6 PARADISE WY
7 LOCOMOTION LA
8 HONEYPOT LA
4
F6
1 AYRESOME WY
2 WIMBLEDON CL
3 HEADINGLEY CRES
4 WHITE HART CRES
5 MURRAYFIELD WY
6 BRAMALL LA
7 DEEPDALE WY
8 ANFIELD CT
9 AINTREE CT
10 AVIEMORE CT
11 EPSOM CT
12 ELLAND CT
13 BISLEY CT
14 CHEPSTOW CT
15 KEMPTON CT
16 HICKSTEAD CT
17 MALLORY CT
18 BADMINTON CT
19 TRAFFORD CT
20 HARRINGAY CRES
21 ROKER CL
3
A1(M) Durham A68 Bishop Auckland
A167 Durham Co. Durham & Teesside STREET ATLAS
Harrowgate Hill
Harrowgate Village
Whinfield
Faverdale
Great Burdon
DL2
DL3
DL1
Cockerton
DARLINGTON
Mowden
Hummersknott
Haughton Le Skerne
Lingfield
Eastbourne
Firth Moor
Blackwell
Skerne Park
Stapleton
Black Banks
Hurworth-on-Tees
Hurworth Place
1 GLENEAGLES RD
2 CALEDONIAN WY
3 STONEHAVEN WY
4 ROSSWAY
5 TORRANCE DR
6 CLARENDON RD
7 BEECH RISE
8 CHANTILLY AV
1 REDWOOD CL
2 LARCH CT
3 RICHMOND WY
4 MARSTON MOOR RD
5 CHESTNUT DR
6 HOLLY CL
7 SWALLOW CL
8 WARREN CL
9 RIDGEWOOD CL
1 GIRTON WALK
2 GRESHAM CL
3 PETERHOUSE CL
B6
1 Holy Family RC Prim Sch
2 GREYSTONES DR
3 GRANTLY
4 YOREDALE DR
26 A 27 B 28 C 29 D 30 E 31 F
C5
1 Queen Elizabeth 6th Form Coll
2 SCHOLARS PK
D1
1 HAWKSWOOD
2 EDEN CL
3 GRANGE AVE
4 HUNTERS CL
D4
1 TA Centre
2 TEBAY CL
3 PUDSEY WK
4 KESWICK GR
5 ULSWATER AVE
E1
1 HORNBY CL
2 CROSSFIELD CL
3 SYCAMORE CL
4 MOWBRAY DR
5 ROUNDHILL CL
6 SOUTHFIELD CL
7 DALE CL
8 MALVERN CL
9 GREENSIDE CT
22
10 COACH LA
11 MANORFIELDS
12 MINSTER WK
13 BRYAN CL
14 LYCH GT
15 THE GABLES
16 CHURCH VW
4
E4
1 CHESTNUT DR
2 EDGEMOOR RD
3 PINEWOOD CL
4 CARLTON MOOR CRES
5 GRANGEMOOR CL
6 MOORFIELD CL
7 OAKMOOR CL
For full street detail of Darlington see Philip's STREET ATLAS of Co. Durham and Teesside

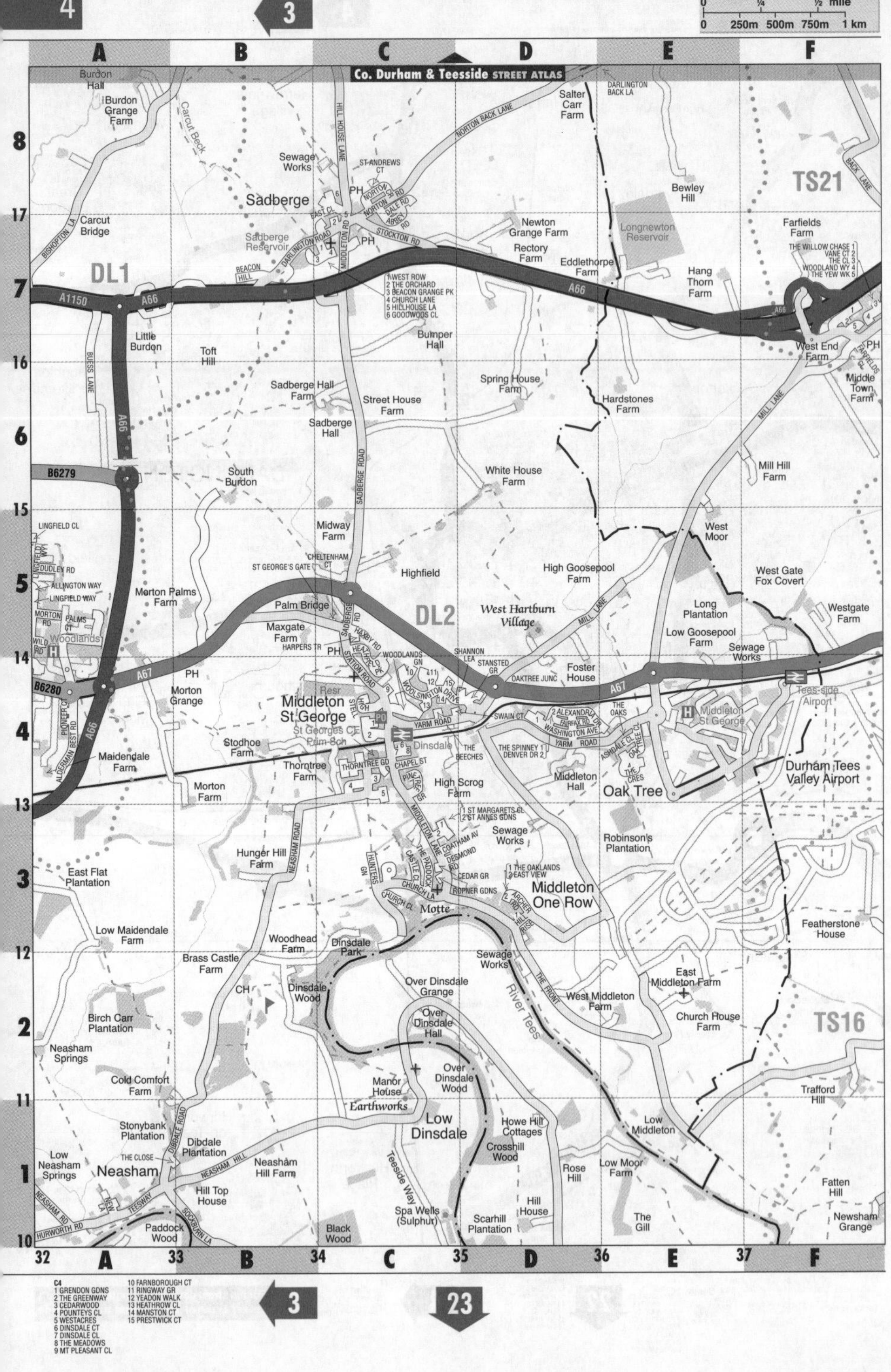

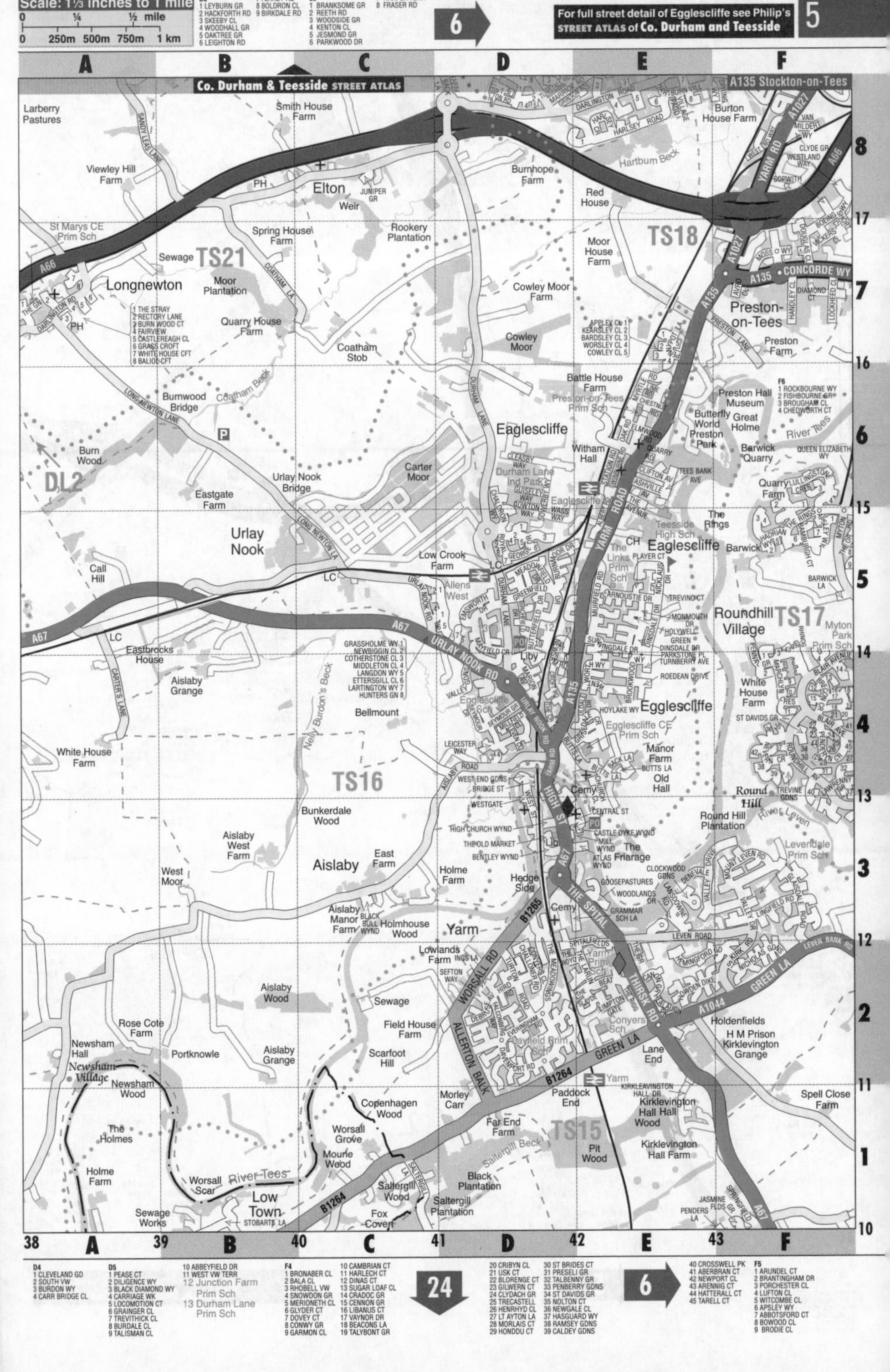

Scale: 1⅓ inches to 1 mile
0 ¼ ½ mile
0 250m 500m 750m 1 km
D8
1 LEYBURN GR
2 HACKFORTH RD
3 SKEEBY CL
4 WOODHALL GR
5 OAKTREE GR
6 LEIGHTON RD
7 FEARBY RD
8 BOLDRON CL
9 BIRKDALE RD
E8
1 BRANKSOME GR
2 REETH RD
3 WOODSIDE GR
4 KENTON CL
5 JESMOND GR
6 PARKWOOD DR
7 HARPER TERR
8 FRASER RD
6
For full street detail of Egglescliffe see Philip's STREET ATLAS of Co. Durham and Teesside
5
Co. Durham & Teesside STREET ATLAS
A135 Stockton-on-Tees
Larberry Pastures
Smith House Farm
Viewley Hill Farm
Elton
Weir
JUNIPER GR
Burnhope Farm
Red House
Hartburn Beck
Burton House Farm
St Marys CE Prim Sch
Sewage
TS21
Spring House Farm
Rookery Plantation
Moor House Farm
TS18
Longnewton
Moor Plantation
Cowley Moor Farm
Preston-on-Tees
1 THE STRAY
2 RECTORY LANE
3 BURN WOOD CT
4 FAIRVIEW
5 CASTLEREAGH CL
6 GRASS CROFT
7 WHITE HOUSE CFT
8 BALIOL CFT
Quarry House Farm
Coatham Stob
Cowley Moor
APPLEY CL 1
KEARSLEY CL 2
BARDSLEY CL 3
WORSLEY CL 4
COWLEY CL 5
Preston Farm
Burnwood Bridge
Battle House Farm
Preston-on-Tees Prim Sch
F6
1 ROCKBOURNE WY
2 FISHBOURNE GR
3 BROUGHAM CL
4 CHEDWORTH CT
Preston Hall Museum
Butterfly World Preston Park
Great Holme
River Tees
Burn Wood
DL2
Eaglescliffe
Witham Hall
Barwick Quarry
Carter Moor
Urlay Nook Bridge
Eastgate Farm
Durham Lane Ind Park
Quarry Farm
Urlay Nook
The Rings
Teesside High Sch
Eaglescliffe
Barwick
Call Hill
Low Crook Farm
Allens West
The Links Prim Sch
Eastbrocks House
TS17
Roundhill Village
Myton Park Prim Sch
Aislaby Grange
GRASSHOLME WY 1
NEWBIGGIN CL 2
COTHERSTONE CL 3
MIDDLETON CL 4
LANGDON WY 5
ETTERSGILL CL 6
LARTINGTON WY 7
HUNTERS GN 8
URLAY NOOK RD
White House Farm
Egglescliffe
Egglescliffe Sch
Bellmount
Egglescliffe CE Prim Sch
White House Farm
TS16
Manor Farm
Old Hall
Round Hill
Bunkerdale Wood
Round Hill Plantation
River Leven
Aislaby West Farm
The Friarage
Levendale Prim Sch
West Moor
Aislaby
East Farm
Holme Farm
Hedge Side
Aislaby Manor Farm
Holmhouse Wood
Yarm
Lowlands Farm
Aislaby Wood
Sewage
Yarm Prim Sch
Rose Cote Farm
Field House Farm
Conyers Sch
Holdenfields
H M Prison Kirklevington Grange
Newsham Hall
Newsham Village
Portknowle
Aislaby Grange
Scarfoot Hill
Layfield Prim Sch
Lane End
Newsham Wood
Copenhagen Wood
Morley Carr
Paddock End
Yarm
Kirklevington Hall Wood
Spell Close Farm
The Holmes
Worsall Grove
Far End Farm
TS15
Pit Wood
Kirklevington Hall Farm
Holme Farm
Mourie Wood
Saltergill Beck
Worsall Scar
River Tees
Low Town
Saltergill Wood
Black Plantation
Saltergill Plantation
Sewage Works
Fox Covert
A66
A67
A135
A1027
A1044
B1264
B1265
D4
1 CLEVELAND GD
2 SOUTH VW
3 BURDON WY
4 CARR BRIDGE CL
D5
1 PEASE CT
2 DILIGENCE WY
3 BLACK DIAMOND WY
4 CARRIAGE WK
5 LOCOMOTION CT
6 GRAINGER CL
7 TREVITHICK CL
8 BURDALE CL
9 TALISMAN CL
10 ABBEYFIELD DR
11 WEST VW TERR
12 Junction Farm Prim Sch
13 Durham Lane Prim Sch
F4
1 BRONABER CL
2 BALA CL
3 RHOBELL WY
4 SNOWDON GR
5 MERIONETH CL
6 GLYDER CT
7 DOVEY CT
8 CONWY GR
9 GARMON CL
10 CAMBRIAN CT
11 HARLECH CT
12 DINAS CT
13 SUGAR LOAF CL
14 CRADOC GR
15 CENNON GR
16 LIBANUS CT
17 VAYNOR DR
18 BEACONS LA
19 TALYBONT GR
24
20 CRIBYN CL
21 USK CT
22 BLORENGE CT
23 GILWERN CT
24 CLYDACH GR
25 TRECASTELL
26 HENRHYD CL
27 LT AYTON LA
28 MORLAIS CT
29 HONDDU CT
30 ST BRIDES CT
31 PRESELI GR
32 TALBENNY GR
33 PENBERRY GDNS
34 ST DAVIDS GR
35 NOLTON CT
36 NEWGALE CL
37 HASGUARD WY
38 RAMSEY GDNS
39 CALDEY GDNS
6
40 CROSSWELL PK
41 ABERBRAN CT
42 NEWPORT CL
43 ARENNIG CT
44 HATTERALL CT
45 TARELL CT
F5
1 ARUNDEL CT
2 BRANTINGHAM DR
3 PORCHESTER CL
4 LUFTON CL
5 WITCOMBE CL
6 APSLEY WY
7 ABBOTSFORD CT
8 BOWOOD CL
9 BRODIE CL

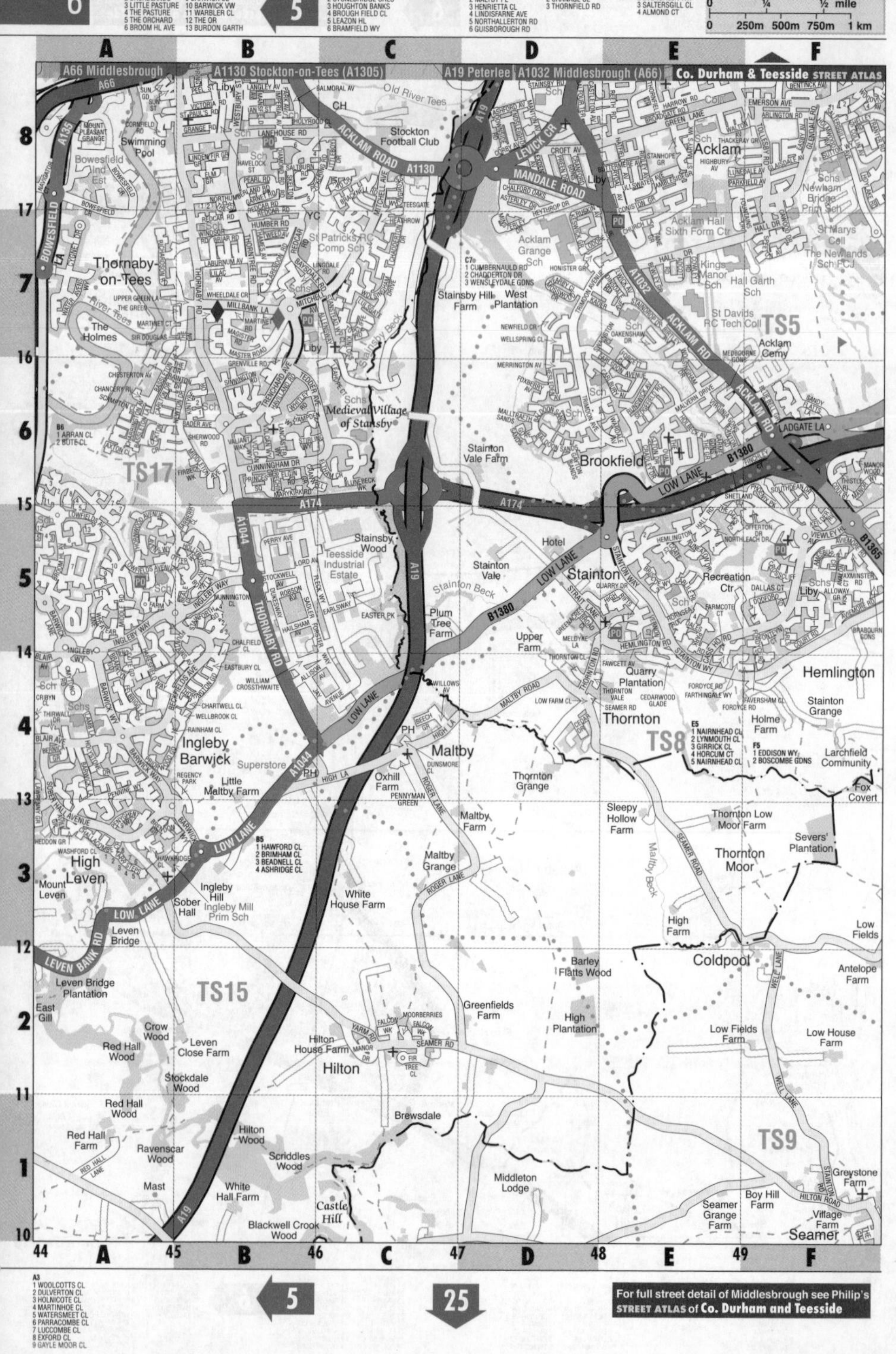

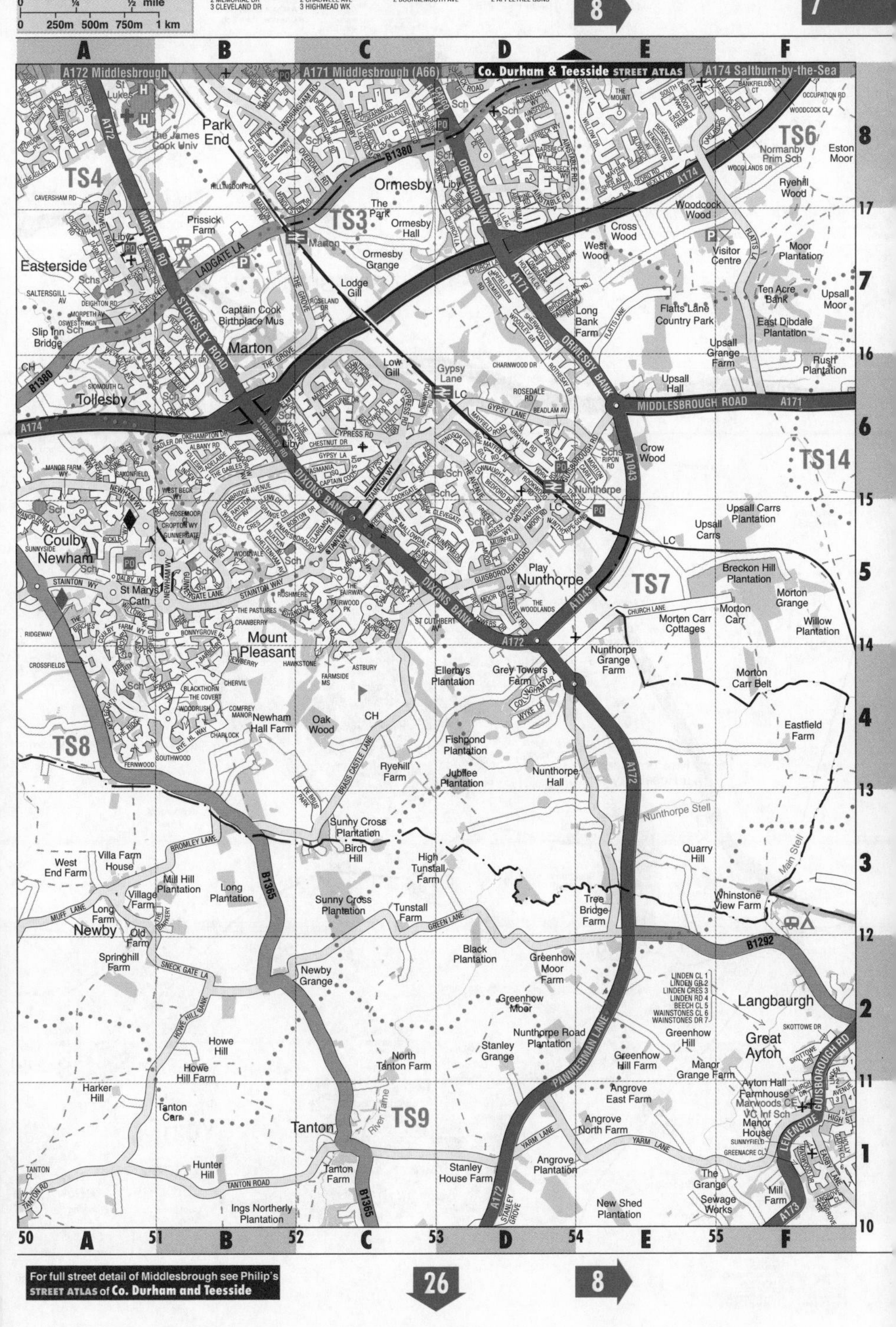

Scale: 1⅓ inches to 1 mile
0
¼
½ mile
0
250m
500m
750m
1 km
B6
1 THE WICKETS
2 MEMORIAL DR
3 CLEVELAND DR
B8
1 CHANTRY CL
2 CHADWELL AVE
3 HIGHMEAD WK
C8
1 MARTON GR
2 BOURNEMOUTH AVE
D8
1 DUNHOLM AVE
2 APPLETREE GDNS
8
7
A
B
C
D
E
F
A172 Middlesbrough
A171 Middlesbrough (A66)
Co. Durham & Teesside STREET ATLAS
A174 Saltburn-by-the-Sea
St Lukes
The James Cook Univ
Park End
TS4
Ormesby
The Park
Ormesby Hall
TS3
Prissick Farm
Marton
Ormesby Grange
Easterside
Lodge Gill
Captain Cook Birthplace Mus
Slip Inn Bridge
Marton
Tollesby
Low Gill
Gypsy Lane
TS6
Normanby Prim Sch
Eston Moor
Ryehill Wood
Woodcock Wood
Cross Wood
West Wood
Visitor Centre
Moor Plantation
Ten Acre Bank
Upsall Moor
Flatts Lane Country Park
East Dibdale Plantation
Long Bank Farm
Upsall Grange Farm
Rush Plantation
Upsall Hall
MIDDLESBROUGH ROAD
Crow Wood
TS14
Nunthorpe
Upsall Carrs Plantation
Upsall Carrs
Coulby Newham
St Marys Cath
Play
Nunthorpe
TS7
Breckon Hill Plantation
Morton Grange
Morton Carr
Morton Carr Cottages
Willow Plantation
Mount Pleasant
Nunthorpe Grange Farm
Ellerbys Plantation
Grey Towers Farm
Morton Carr Belt
Newham Hall Farm
Oak Wood
CH
Eastfield Farm
TS8
Fishpond Plantation
Ryehill Farm
Jubilee Plantation
Nunthorpe Hall
Sunny Cross Plantation
Nunthorpe Stell
Birch Hill
High Tunstall Farm
Quarry Hill
Main Stell
West End Farm
Villa Farm House
Mill Hill Plantation
Long Plantation
Village Farm
Long Farm
Newby
Old Farm
Sunny Cross Plantation
Tunstall Farm
Tree Bridge Farm
Whinstone View Farm
Springhill Farm
Newby Grange
Black Plantation
Greenhow Moor Farm
Greenhow Moor
Langbaurgh
Howe Hill
Howe Hill Farm
Nunthorpe Road Plantation
Stanley Grange
North Tanton Farm
Greenhow Hill
Greenhow Hill Farm
Great Ayton
Manor Grange Farm
Harker Hill
Tanton Carr
Angrove East Farm
Ayton Hall Farmhouse
Marwoods CE VC Inf Sch
Manor House
TS9
Tanton
Angrove North Farm
Hunter Hill
Tanton Farm
Stanley House Farm
Angrove Plantation
The Grange
Sewage Works
Mill Farm
Ings Northerly Plantation
New Shed Plantation
50
51
52
53
54
55
10
11
12
13
14
15
16
17
6
5
4
3
2
1
For full street detail of Middlesbrough see Philip's STREET ATLAS of Co. Durham and Teesside
26
8

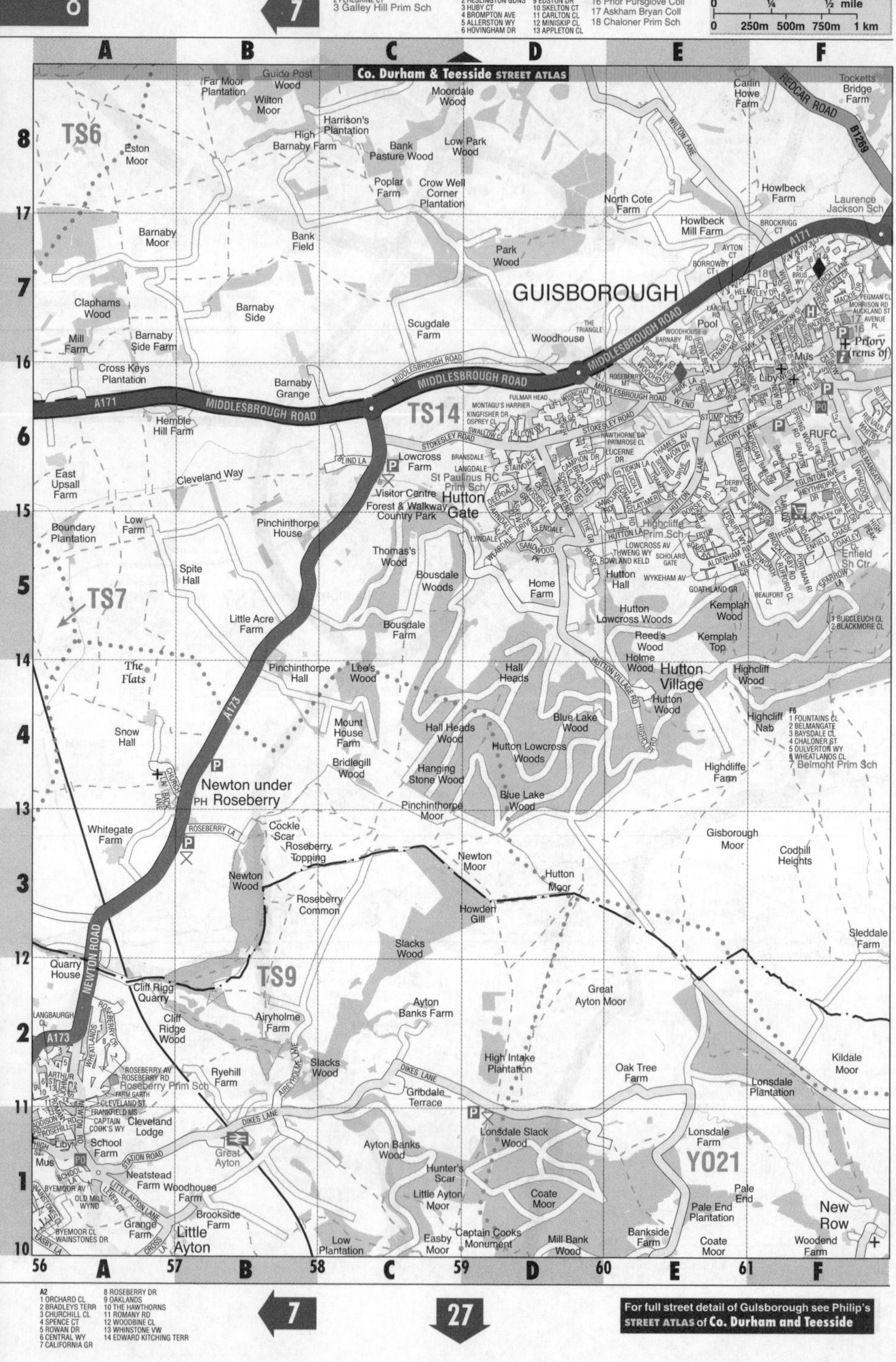

7

D6
1 REDWING RISING
2 PEREGRINE CT
3 Galley Hill Prim Sch

F7
1 WHELDRAKE CL
2 HESLINGTON GDNS
3 HUBY CT
4 BROUGHAM AVE
5 ALLERSTON WY
6 HOVINGHAM DR

7 MONKTON RISE
8 THIRLBY WY
9 EDSTON DR
10 SKELTON CT
11 CARLTON CL
12 MINISKIP CL
13 APPLETON CL

14 WOODALE CL
15 SLEIGHTS CT
16 Prior Pursglove Coll
17 Askham Bryan Coll
18 Chaloner Prim Sch

Co. Durham & Teesside STREET ATLAS

TS6

TS7

TS9

TS14

Y021

GUISBOROUGH

Guide Post Wood

Far Moor Plantation

Wilton Moor

Moordale Wood

Tocketts Bridge Farm

Carlin Howe Farm

Howlbeck Farm

Laurence Jackson Sch

Eston Moor

High Barnaby Farm

Harrison's Plantation

Bank Pasture Wood

Low Park Wood

North Cote Farm

Howlbeck Mill Farm

Poplar Farm

Crow Well Corner Plantation

Barnaby Moor

Bank Field

Park Wood

Claphams Wood

Mill Farm

Barnaby Side

Barnaby Side Farm

Scugdale Farm

Woodhouse

THE TRIANGLE

Pool

Cross Keys Plantation

Barnaby Grange

MIDDLESBROUGH ROAD

RUFC

Hemble Hill Farm

East Upsall Farm

Cleveland Way

Lowcross Farm

Visitor Centre Forest & Walkway Country Park

St Paulinus RC Prim Sch

Hutton Gate

Pinchinthorpe House

Boundary Plantation

Low Farm

Spite Hall

Thomas's Wood

Bousdale Woods

Home Farm

Hutton Hall

Hutton Lowcross Woods

Kemplah Wood

Kemplah Top

Little Acre Farm

Bousdale Farm

Reed's Wood

The Flats

Pinchinthorpe Hall

Lee's Wood

Hall Heads

Holme Wood

Hutton Village

Hutton Wood

Highcliff Wood

Highcliff Nab

Snow Hall

Mount House Farm

Bridleigill Wood

Hall Heads Wood

Hutton Lowcross Woods

Blue Lake Wood

Highcliffe Farm

F6
1 FOUNTAINS CL
2 BELMANGATE
3 BAYSDALE CL
4 CHALONER ST
5 DULVERTON WY
6 WHEATLANDS CL
7 Belmont Prim Sch

Newton under Roseberry

Hanging Stone Wood

Pinchinthorpe Moor

Blue Lake Wood

Gisborough Moor

Codhill Heights

Whitegate Farm

Cockle Scar Roseberry Topping

Newton Moor

Hutton Moor

Sleddale Farm

Quarry House

Langbaurgh

Cliff Rigg Quarry

Newton Wood

Roseberry Common

Howden Gill

Slacks Wood

Great Ayton Moor

Aryholme Farm

Cliff Ridge Wood

Ayton Banks Farm

High Intake Plantation

Oak Tree Farm

Kildale Moor

Lonsdale Plantation

Ryehill Farm

Slacks Wood

Gribdale Terrace

Lonsdale Slack Wood

Lonsdale Farm

Roseberry Prim Sch

School Farm

Cleveland Lodge

Great Ayton

Ayton Banks Wood

Hunter's Scar

Coate Moor

Bankside Farm

Pale End Plantation

New Row

Neatstead Farm

Woodhouse Farm

Little Ayton Moor

Captain Cooks Monument

Mill Bank Wood

Coate Moor

Woodend Farm

Grange Farm

Brookside Farm

Little Ayton

Low Plantation

Easby Moor

27

A2
1 ORCHARD CL
2 BRADLEYS TERR
3 CHURCHILL CL
4 SPENCE CT
5 ROWAN DR
6 CENTRAL WY
7 CALIFORNIA GR

8 ROSEBERRY DR
9 OAKLANDS
10 THE HAWTHORNS
11 ROMANY RD
12 WOODBINE CL
13 WHINSTONE VW
14 EDWARD KITCHING TERR

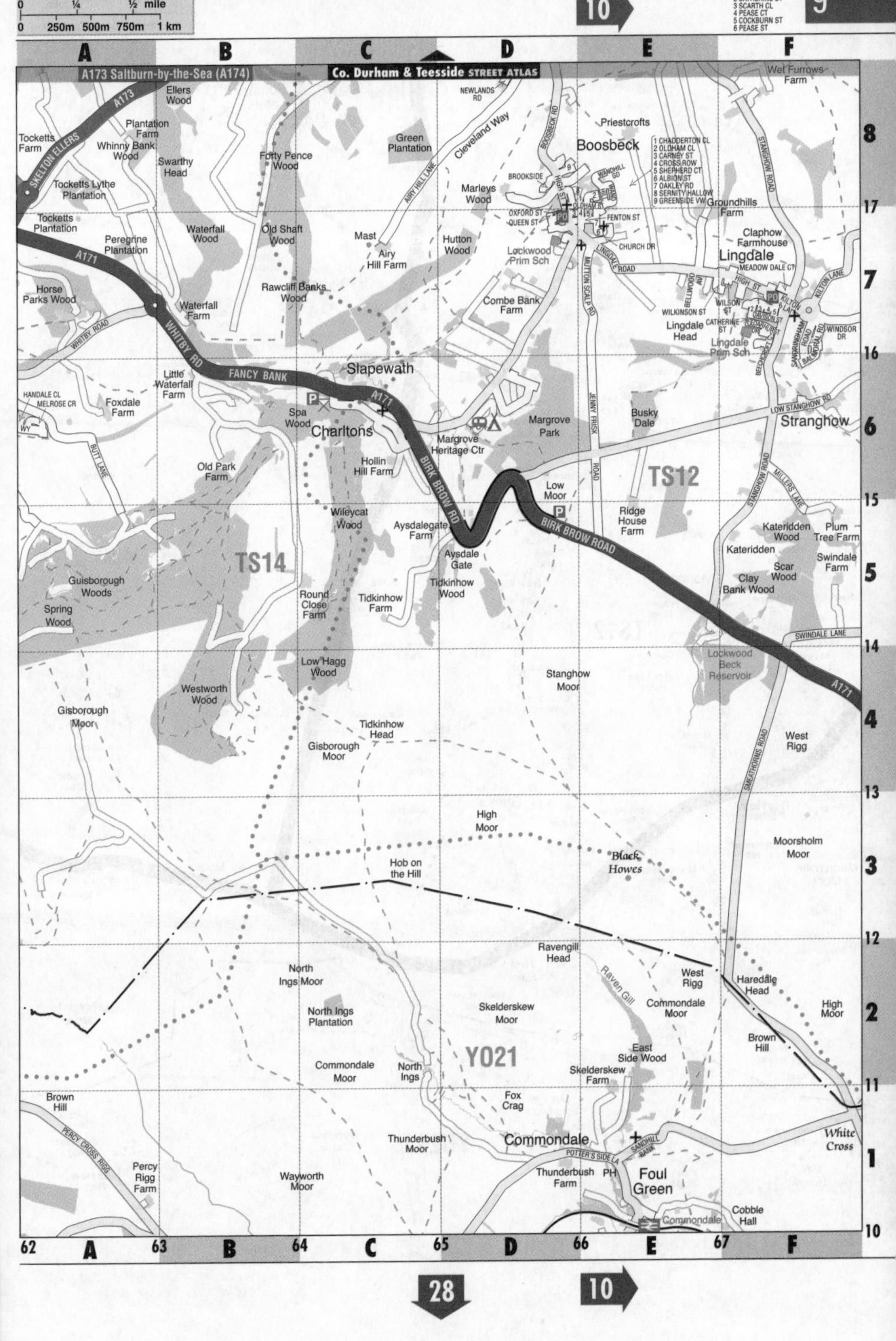

9

Scale: 1½ inches to 1 mile

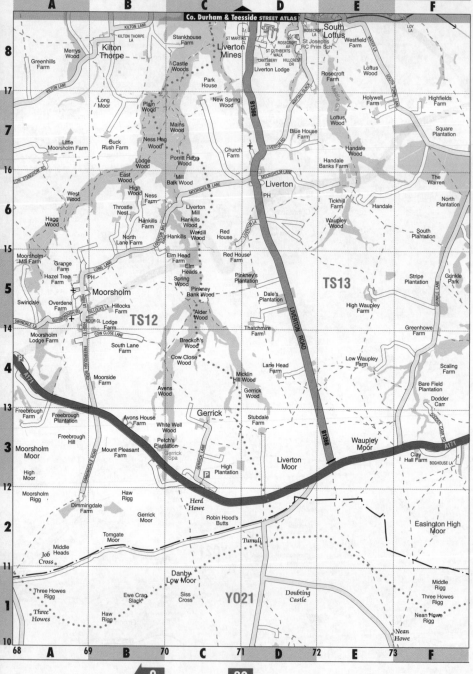

Co. Durham & Teesside STREET ATLAS

A B C D E F

8

17

7

16

6

15

5

14

4

13

3

12

2

11

1

10

68 A 69 B 70 C 71 D 72 E 73 F

Greenhills Farm
Merrys Wood
KILTON LANE
Kilton Thorpe
KILTON THORPE LA
Stankhouse Farm
ST MARTINS
Liverton Mines
St Josephs RC Prim Sch
South Loftus
LOY LA
Westfield Farm

Little Moorsholm Farm
Long Moor
Plain Wood
Park House
New Spring Wood
ST CUTHBERTS WALK
ANTSBERY DR
HILLCREST DR
Liverton Lodge
Rosecroft Farm
Loftus Wood

Buck Rush Farm
Ness Hag Wood
Mains Wood
Castle Woods
Church Farm
Blue House Farm
Loftus Wood
Handale Wood
Highfields Farm
Square Plantation

West Wood
East Wood
Lodge Wood
High Wood
Ness Farm
Porritt Ridge Wood
Mill Balk Wood
MOORSHOLM LANE
Liverton
PH
Handale Banks Farm
The Warren

Hagg Wood
Throstle Nest
Hankills Wood
Liverton Mill
Hankills Wood
Wardill Wood
Red House
Tickhill Farm
Waupley Wood
Handale
North Plantation

Moorsholm Mill Farm
Grange Farm
Hazel Tree Farm
North Lane Farm
Hankills
Elm Head Farm
Elm Heads
Spring Wood
Red House Farm
Pinkney's Plantation
Dale's Plantation
South Plantation
Stripe Plantation
Grinkle Park

Swindale
Overdene Farm
Moorsholm
HILLOCKS LA
Hillocks Farm
TS12
Pinkney Bank Wood
Alder Wood
TS13
High Waupley Farm
Greenhowe Farm

Moorsholm Lodge Farm
Lodge Farm
South Lane Farm
Breckon's Wood
Thatchmire Farm
Low Waupley Farm
Scaling Farm
Bare Field Plantation

A171
Moorside Farm
Cow Close Wood
Micklin Hill Wood
Larie Head Farm
Gerrick Wood
Dodder Carr

Freebrough Farm
Freebrough Plantation
Avons House Farm
White Well Wood
Gerrick
Stubdale Farm
Waupley Moor
Clay Hall Farm
BOGHOUSE LA
A171

Moorsholm Moor
Freebrough Hill
Mount Pleasant Farm
Petch's Plantation
Gerrick Spa
High Plantation
Liverton Moor

High Moor
Moorsholm Rigg
Dimmingdale Farm
Haw Rigg
Herd Howe
Easington High Moor

Gerrick Moor
Robin Hood's Butts
Tumuli

Job Cross
Middle Heads
Tomgate Moor
Danby Low Moor
Siss Cross
Y021
Doubting Castle
Middle Rigg
Three Howes Rigg

Three Howes Rigg
Three Howes
Ewe Crag Slack
Haw Rigg
Nean Howe Rigg
Nean Howe

Scale: 1⅓ inches to 1 mile

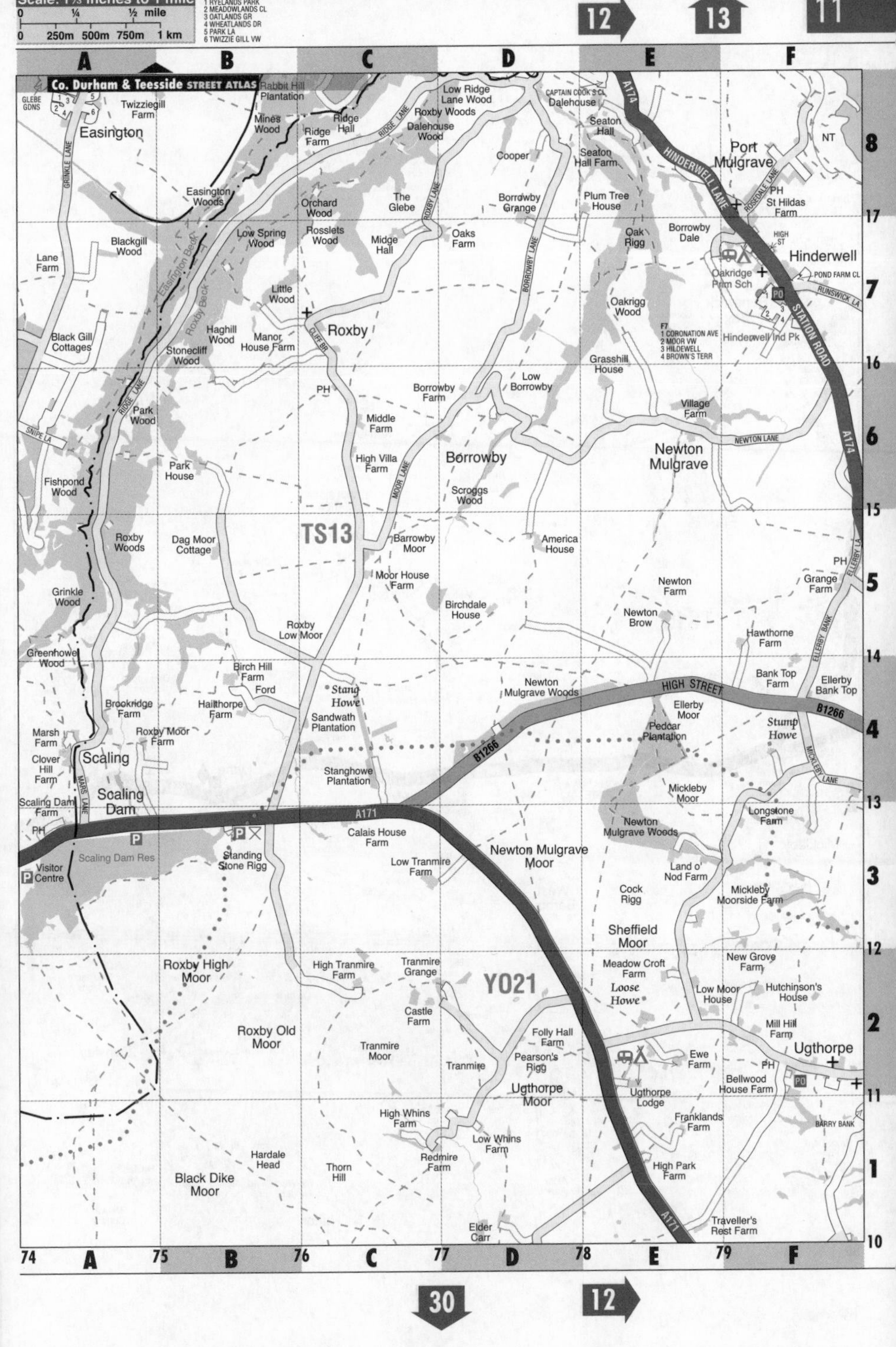

A8
1 RYELANDS PARK
2 MEADOWLANDS CL
3 OATLANDS GR
4 WHEATLANDS DR
5 PARK LA
6 TWIZZIE GILL VW
12
13
Co. Durham & Teesside STREET ATLAS
Easington
Twizziegill Farm
Rabbit Hill Plantation
Mines Wood
Ridge Farm
Ridge Hall
Low Ridge Lane Wood
Roxby Woods
Dalehouse Wood
CAPTAIN COOK'S CL
Dalehouse
Seaton Hall
Seaton Hall Farm
Port Mulgrave
HINDERWELL LANE
ROSEDALE LANE
St Hildas Farm
Hinderwell
POND FARM CL
RUNSWICK LA
STATION ROAD
Oakridge Prim Sch
Hinderwell Ind Pk
F7
1 CORONATION AVE
2 MOOR VW
3 HILDEWELL
4 BROWN'S TERR
Easington Woods
Orchard Wood
The Glebe
Borrowby Grange
Plum Tree House
Cooper
Blackgill Wood
Low Spring Wood
Rosslets Wood
Midge Hall
Oaks Farm
Oak Rigg
Borrowby Dale
Lane Farm
Little Wood
Roxby
Oakrigg Wood
Black Gill Cottages
Haghill Wood
Manor House Farm
Stonecliff Wood
Grasshill House
Low Borrowby
Borrowby Farm
Village Farm
Park Wood
Middle Farm
NEWTON LANE
Newton Mulgrave
SNIPE LA
Park House
High Villa Farm
Borrowby
Fishpond Wood
Scroggs Wood
TS13
Roxby Woods
Dag Moor Cottage
Barrowby Moor
America House
Moor House Farm
Newton Farm
Grange Farm
Grinkle Wood
Birchdale House
Newton Brow
Roxby Low Moor
Hawthorne Farm
Greenhowe Wood
Birch Hill Farm
Ford
Stang Howe
Newton Mulgrave Woods
HIGH STREET
Bank Top Farm
Ellerby Bank Top
Brookridge Farm
Hailthorpe Farm
Sandwath Plantation
Ellerby Moor
B1266
Stump Howe
Marsh Farm
Roxby Moor Farm
Pedcar Plantation
Clover Hill Farm
Scaling
Stanghowe Plantation
Mickleby Moor
MICKLEBY LANE
Scaling Dam
Scaling Dam Farm
A171
Longstone Farm
Calais House Farm
Newton Mulgrave Woods
Scaling Dam Res
Standing Stone Rigg
Newton Mulgrave Moor
Visitor Centre
Low Tranmire Farm
Land o' Nod Farm
Cock Rigg
Mickleby Moorside Farm
Sheffield Moor
Roxby High Moor
High Tranmire Farm
Tranmire Grange
YO21
Meadow Croft Farm
Loose Howe
New Grove Farm
Low Moor House
Hutchinson's House
Castle Farm
Mill Hill Farm
Roxby Old Moor
Tranmire Moor
Folly Hall Farm
Pearson's Rigg
Tranmire
Ewe Farm
Ugthorpe
Ugthorpe Moor
Ugthorpe Lodge
Bellwood House Farm
High Whins Farm
Franklands Farm
BARRY BANK
Low Whins Farm
Redmire Farm
Hardale Head
Thorn Hill
High Park Farm
Black Dike Moor
Elder Carr
Traveller's Rest Farm
30
12

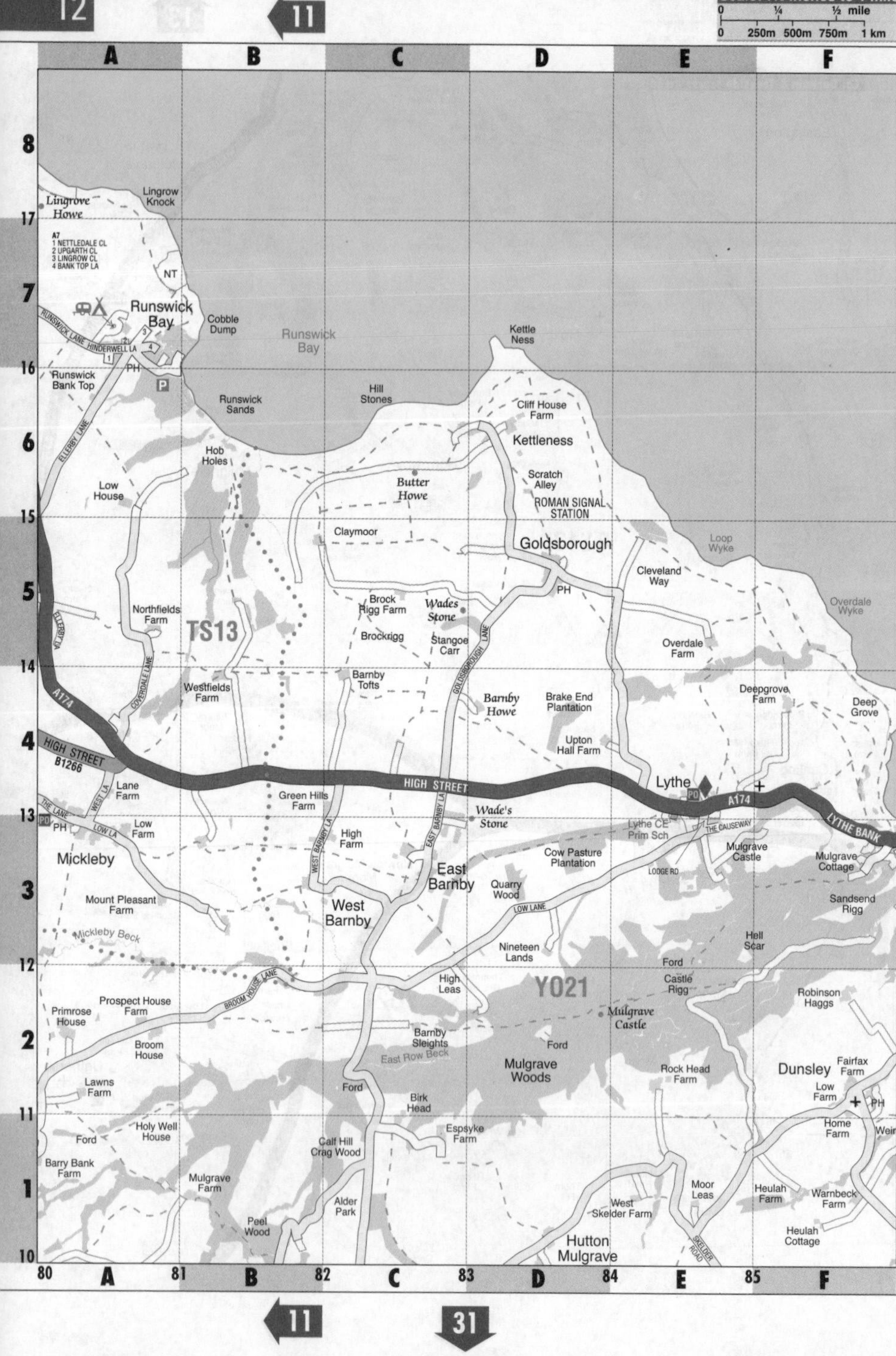

Scale: 1⅓ inches to 1 mile

0 ¼ ½ mile

0 250m 500m 750m 1 km

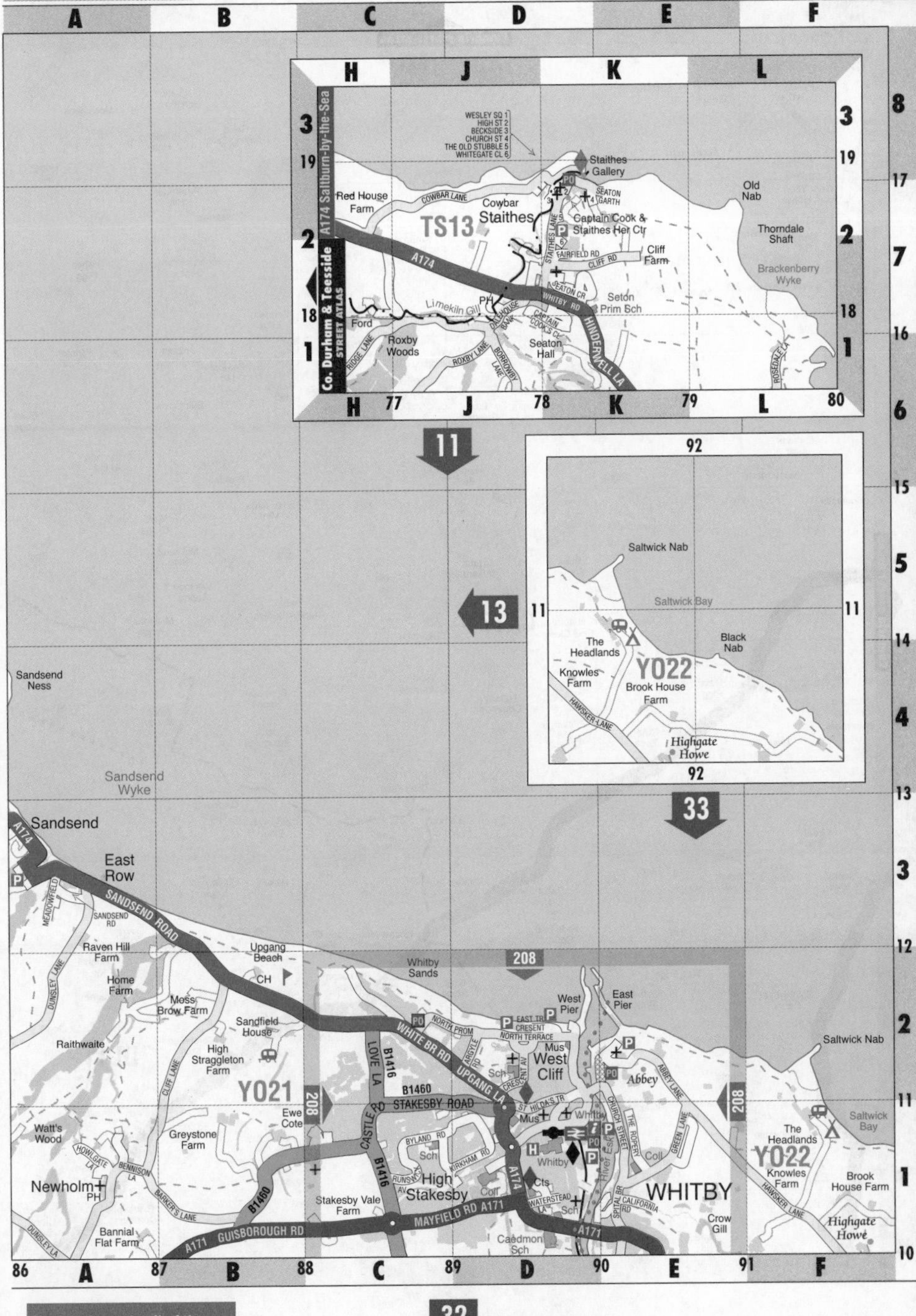

A B C D E F

8 H J K L

Co. Durham & Teesside STREET ATLAS — A174 Saltburn-by-the-Sea

WESLEY SQ 1
HIGH ST 2
BECKSIDE 3
CHURCH ST 4
THE OLD STUBBLE 5
WHITEGATE CL 6

Staithes Gallery

Red House Farm

COWBAR LANE

Cowbar

SEATON GARTH

Staithes

TS13

Captain Cook & Staithes Her Ctr

Old Nab

Thorndale Shaft

Brackenberry Wyke

A174

FAIRFIELD RD

CLIFF RD

Cliff Farm

Limekiln Gill

WHITBY RD

Seton CE Prim Sch

PH

Ford

Roxby Woods

ROXBY LANE

Seton Hall

HINDERWELL LA

H 77 J 78 K 79 L 80

11

92

Saltwick Nab

Saltwick Bay

11 11

The Headlands

Knowles Farm

YO22

Brook House Farm

Black Nab

Highgate Howe

92

13

33

Sandsend Ness

Sandsend Wyke

Sandsend

East Row

A174

SANDSEND ROAD

SANDSEND RD

Raven Hill Farm

Home Farm

Moss Brow Farm

Upgang Beach

CH

Whitby Sands

208

West Pier

East Pier

P

NORTH PROM

EAST TER

NORTH TERRACE

West Cliff

Mus

Saltwick Nab

Raithwaite

Sandfield House

High Straggleton Farm

WHITE BR RD

UPGANG LA

LOVE LA

Abbey

The Headlands

YO21

B1416

B1460

STAKESBY ROAD

CASTLE

A171

Watt's Wood

Ewe Cote

Greystone Farm

BYLAND RD

BIRKDAM RD

KIRKHAM

High Stakesby

Sch

Sch

YO22

Knowles Farm

Brook House Farm

Newholm

PH

HOMEGATE

BENNISON

CLIFF LA

B1460

Stakesby Vale Farm

MAYFIELD RD A171

H

Whitby

Sch

WATERSTEAD

CALIFORNIA

WHITBY

Highgate Howe

Bannial Flat Farm

DUNSLEY LA

A171 GUISBOROUGH RD

Caedmon Sch

A171

Crow Gill

86 A 87 B 88 C 89 D 90 E 91 F

For full street detail of the highlighted area see page 208.

32

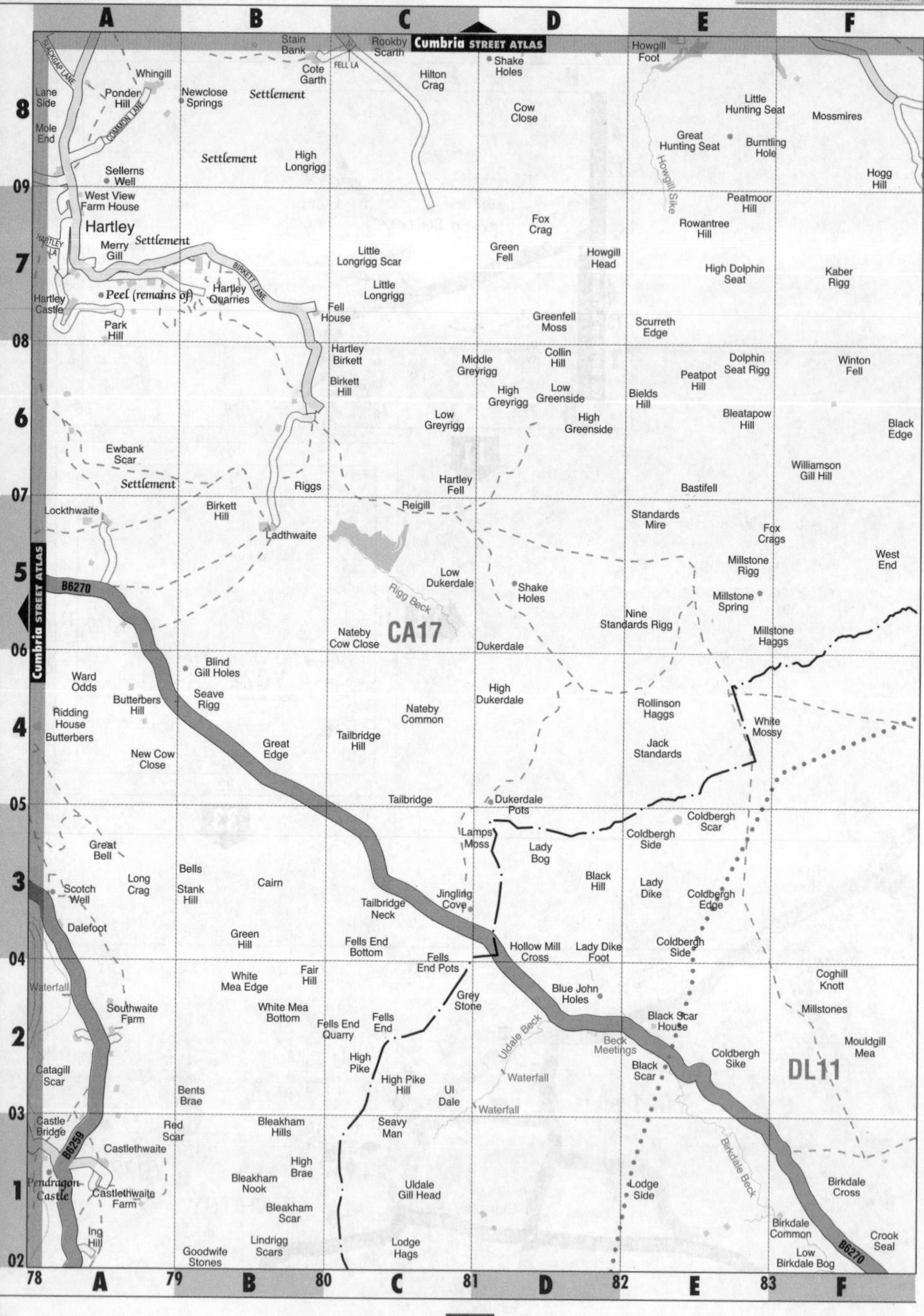

Scale: 1½ inches to 1 mile

Whingill
Stain Bank
Rookby Scarth
Howgill Foot

Lane Side
Ponder Hill
Newclose Springs
Cote Garth
FELL LA
Hilton Crag
Shake Holes

Mole End
Settlement
Cow Close
Little Hunting Seat
Mossmires

Sellerns Well
Settlement
High Longrigg
Great Hunting Seat
Burntling Hole

West View Farm House
Hogg Hill

Hartley
Peatmoor Hill

Merry Gill
Settlement
Little Longrigg Scar
Green Fell
Howgill Head
Rowantree Hill
Kaber Rigg

Hartley Quarries
Little Longrigg
High Dolphin Seat

Hartley Castle
Peel (remains of)
Fell House
Greenfell Moss
Scurreth Edge

Park Hill
Hartley Birkett
Middle Greyrigg
Collin Hill
Peatpot Hill
Dolphin Seat Rigg
Winton Fell

Birkett Hill
High Greyrigg
Low Greenside
Bields Hill
Bleatapow Hill

Ewbank Scar
Low Greyrigg
High Greenside
Black Edge

Settlement
Riggs
Hartley Fell
Williamson Gill Hill

Lockthwaite
Birkett Hill
Reigill
Bastifell

Ladthwaite
Standards Mire
Fox Crags

Low Dukerdale
Shake Holes
Millstone Rigg
West End

B6270
Nateby Cow Close
CA17
Dukerdale
Nine Standards Rigg
Millstone Spring
Millstone Haggs

Ward Odds
Blind Gill Holes
High Dukerdale

Butterbers Hill
Seave Rigg
Rollinson Haggs
White Mossy

Ridding House Butterbers
New Cow Close
Great Edge
Tailbridge Hill
Nateby Common
Jack Standards

Tailbridge
Dukerdale Pots
Coldbergh Scar

Great Bell
Lamps Moss
Coldbergh Side

Scotch Well
Long Crag
Bells Stank Hill
Cairn
Tailbridge Neck
Jingling Cove
Lady Bog
Black Hill
Lady Dike
Coldbergh Edge

Dalefoot
Green Hill
Fells End Bottom
Hollow Mill Cross
Lady Dike Foot
Coldbergh Side

Waterfall
White Mea Edge
Fair Hill
Fells End Pots
Grey Stone
Blue John Holes
Black Scar House
Coghill Knott

Southwaite Farm
White Mea Bottom
Fells End Quarry
Fells End
Uldale Beck
Beck Meetings
Black Scar
Coldbergh Sike
Millstones
Mouldgill Mea

Catagill Scar
High Pike
High Pike Hill
Ul Dale
Waterfall
DL11

Bents Brae
Waterfall

Castle Bridge
B6259
Red Scar
Bleakham Hills
Seavy Man

Castlethwaite
High Brae
Lodge Side
Birkdale Cross

Pendragon Castle
Castlethwaite Farm
Bleakham Nook
Bleakham Scar
Uldale Gill Head
Birkdale Common
Crook Seal

Ing Hill
Goodwife Stones
Lindrigg Scars
Lodge Hags
Low Birkdale Bog
B6270

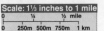

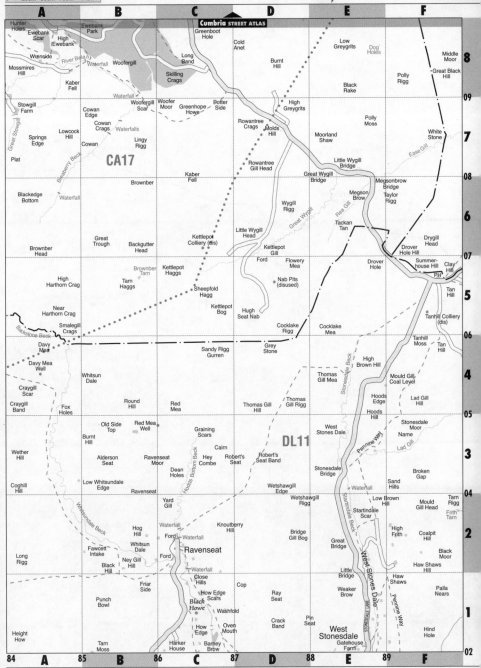

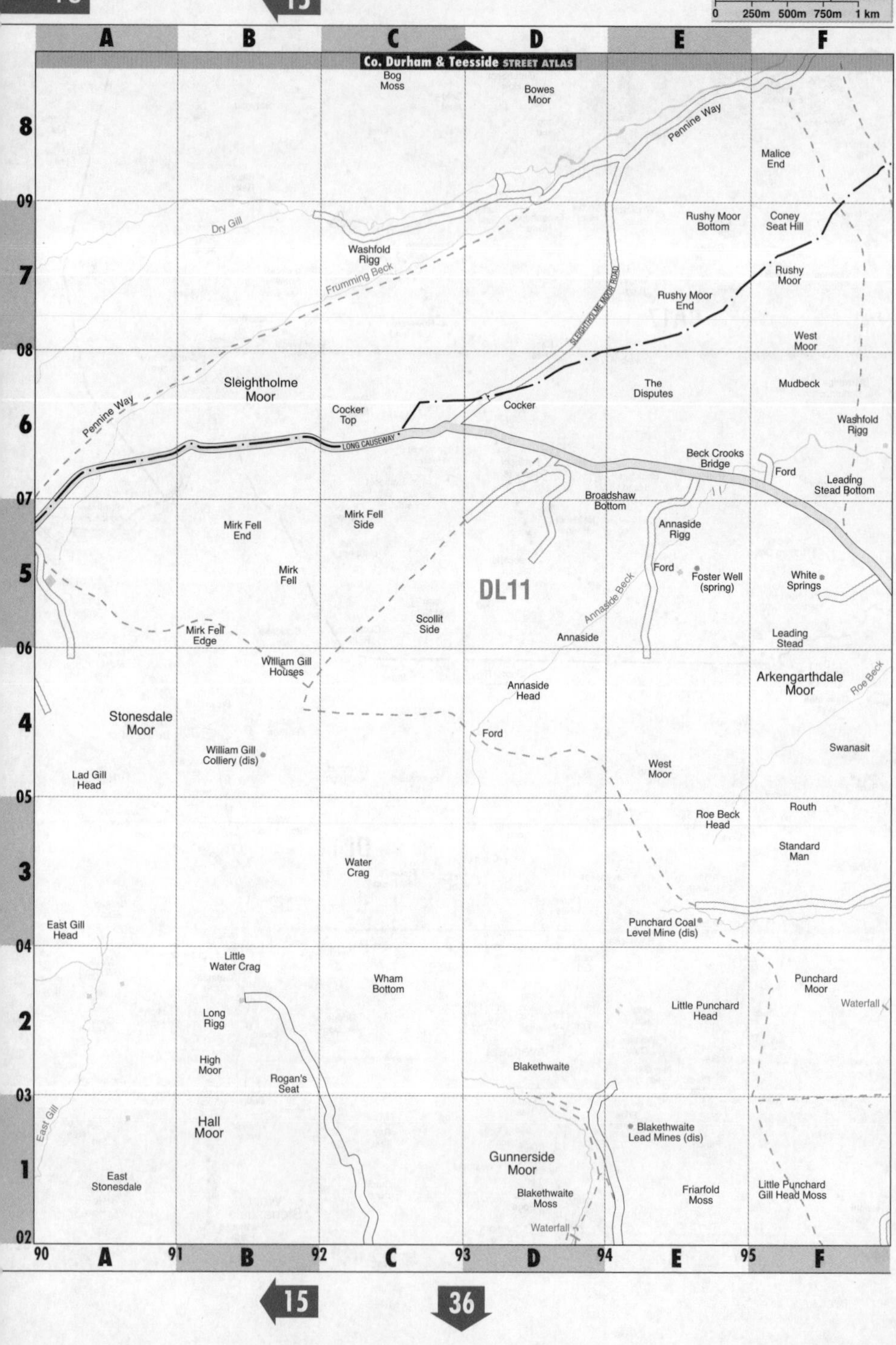

Scale: 1⅓ inches to 1 mile

0   ¼   ½   mile
0   250m 500m 750m 1 km

Co. Durham & Teesside STREET ATLAS

Bog
Moss

Bowes
Moor

Pennine Way

Malice
End

Dry Gill

Washfold
Rigg

Frumming Beck

Rushy Moor
Bottom

Coney
Seat Hill

Rushy
Moor

Sleightholme
Moor

Pennine Way

SLEIGHTHOLME MOOR ROAD

Rushy Moor
End

West
Moor

Cocker
Top

LONG CAUSEWAY

Cocker

The
Disputes

Mudbeck

Washfold
Rigg

Beck Crooks
Bridge

Ford

Leading
Stead Bottom

Broadshaw
Bottom

Mirk Fell
End

Mirk Fell
Side

Annaside
Rigg

Mirk
Fell

Ford

Foster Well
(spring)

White
Springs

DL11

Annaside Beck

Mirk Fell
Edge

Scollit
Side

Annaside

Leading
Stead

William Gill
Houses

Annaside
Head

Arkengarthdale
Moor

Roe Beck

Stonesdale
Moor

Ford

West
Moor

Swanasit

Lad Gill
Head

William Gill
Colliery (dis)

Roe Beck
Head

Routh

Water
Crag

Standard
Man

East Gill
Head

Punchard Coal
Level Mine (dis)

Little
Water Crag

Wham
Bottom

Punchard
Moor

Waterfall

Long
Rigg

Little Punchard
Head

High
Moor

Rogan's
Seat

Blakethwaite

East Gill

Hall
Moor

Blakethwaite
Lead Mines (dis)

Little Punchard
Gill Head Moss

East
Stonesdale

Gunnerside
Moor

Friarfold
Moss

Blakethwaite
Moss

Waterfall

Scale: 1⅓ inches to 1 mile

18

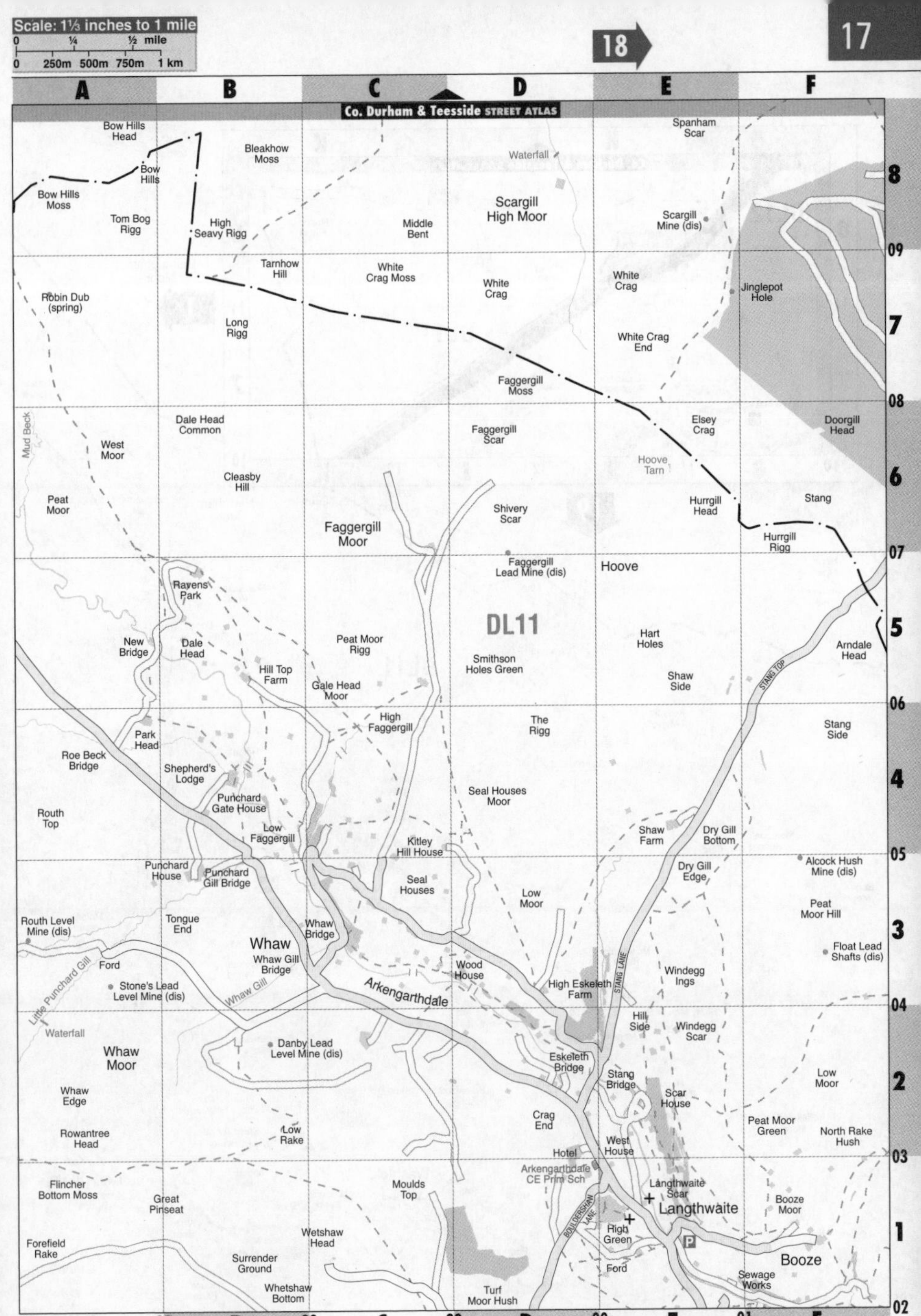

Co. Durham & Teesside STREET ATLAS
A
B
C
D
E
F
Bow Hills Head
Bow Hills
Bow Hills Moss
Tom Bog Rigg
Bleakhow Moss
High Seavy Rigg
Tarnhow Hill
Middle Bent
White Crag Moss
Scargill High Moor
Waterfall
Spanham Scar
Scargill Mine (dis)
White Crag
Jinglepot Hole
White Crag End
Robin Dub (spring)
Long Rigg
Faggergill Moss
Elsey Crag
Doorgill Head
Dale Head Common
Faggergill Scar
Mud Beck
West Moor
Cleasby Hill
Hoove Tarn
Hurrgill Head
Stang
Peat Moor
Faggergill Moor
Shivery Scar
Hurrgill Rigg
Faggergill Lead Mine (dis)
Hoove
Ravens Park
DL11
Hart Holes
New Bridge
Dale Head
Peat Moor Rigg
Arndale Head
Smithson Holes Green
Hill Top Farm
Gale Head Moor
Shaw Side
STANG TOP
High Faggergill
The Rigg
Park Head
Stang Side
Roe Beck Bridge
Shepherd's Lodge
Seal Houses Moor
Punchard Gate House
Routh Top
Low Faggergill
Shaw Farm
Dry Gill Bottom
Kitley Hill House
Punchard House
Punchard Gill Bridge
Dry Gill Edge
Alcock Hush Mine (dis)
Seal Houses
Low Moor
Peat Moor Hill
Routh Level Mine (dis)
Tongue End
Whaw Bridge
Whaw
Float Lead Shafts (dis)
Whaw Gill Bridge
Ford
Wood House
STANG LANE
Windegg Ings
Stone's Lead Level Mine (dis)
Whaw Gill
Arkengarthdale
High Eskeleth Farm
Little Punchard Gill
Hill Side
Windegg Scar
Waterfall
Whaw Moor
Danby Lead Level Mine (dis)
Eskeleth Bridge
Stang Bridge
Low Moor
Whaw Edge
Scar House
Crag End
Peat Moor Green
North Rake Hush
Rowantree Head
Low Rake
Hotel
West House
Arkengarthdale CE Prim Sch
Flincher Bottom Moss
Moulds Top
Langthwaite Scar
Booze Moor
Great Pinseat
BOULDERSHAW LANE
Langthwaite
High Green
Wetshaw Head
Forefield Rake
P
Booze
Surrender Ground
Ford
Sewage Works
Whetshaw Bottom
Turf Moor Hush
8
09
7
08
6
07
5
06
4
05
3
04
2
03
1
02
96
97
98
99
00
01

37

18

17

Scale: 1⅓ inches to 1 mile

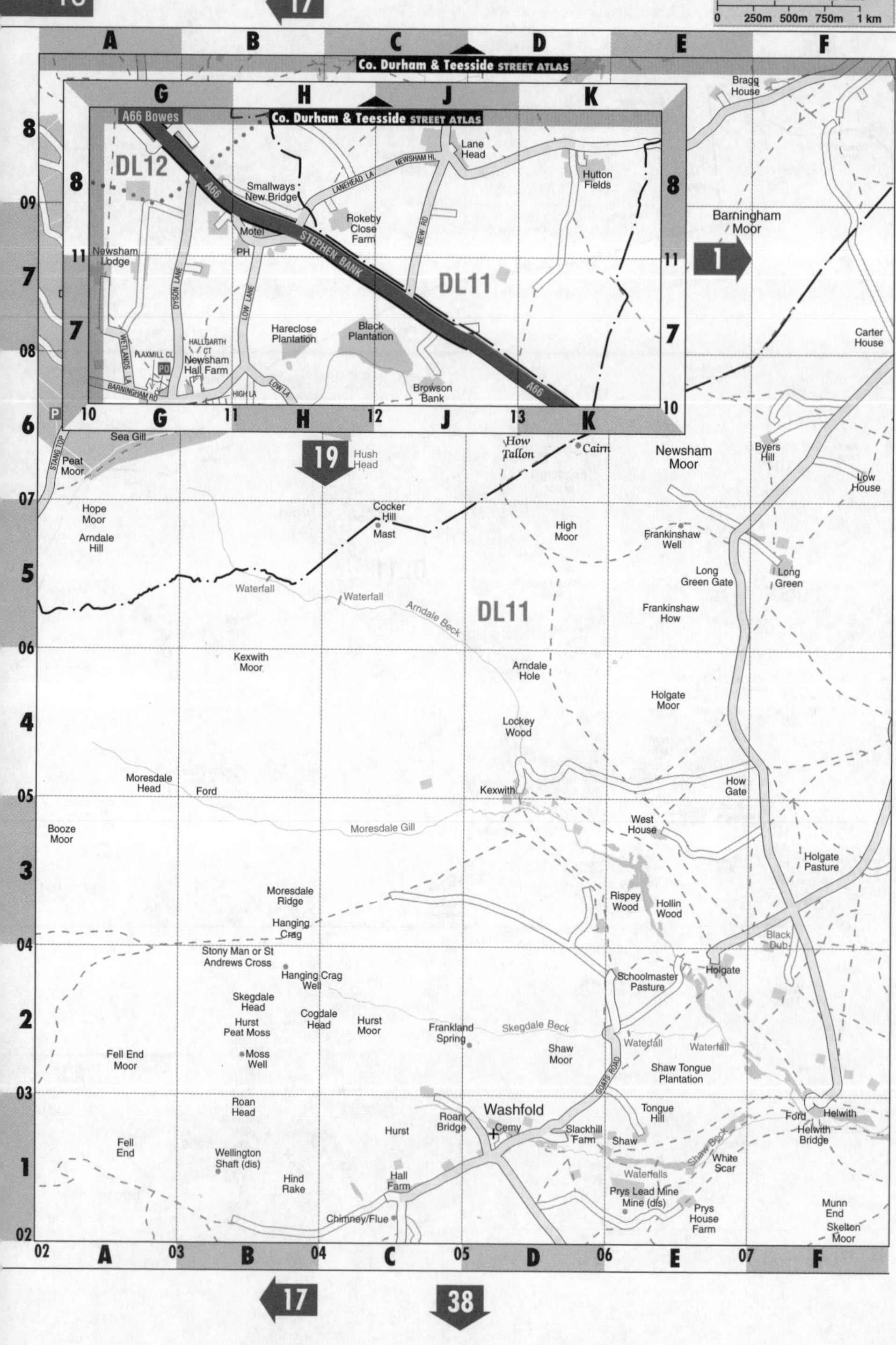

Co. Durham & Teesside STREET ATLAS
A66 Bowes
DL12
DL11
Newsham Lodge
Smallways New Bridge
Motel
PH
Rokeby Close Farm
Lane Head
Hutton Fields
Hareclose Plantation
Black Plantation
Browson Bank
Newsham Hall Farm
STEPHEN BANK
Bragg House
Barningham Moor
Carter House
Sea Gill
Peat Moor
Hush Head
How Tallon
Cairn
Newsham Moor
Byers Hill
Low House
Hope Moor
Arndale Hill
Cocker Hill
Mast
High Moor
Frankinshaw Well
Long Green Gate
Long Green
Frankinshaw How
Waterfall
Arndale Beck
Kexwith Moor
Arndale Hole
Holgate Moor
Lockey Wood
Moresdale Head
Ford
Kexwith
How Gate
West House
Booze Moor
Moresdale Gill
Holgate Pasture
Moresdale Ridge
Rispey Wood
Hollin Wood
Hanging Crag
Black Dub
Stony Man or St Andrews Cross
Hanging Crag Well
Schoolmaster Pasture
Holgate
Skegdale Head
Cogdale Head
Hurst Moor
Hurst Peat Moss
Frankland Spring
Skegdale Beck
Moss Well
Shaw Moor
Shaw Tongue Plantation
Fell End Moor
Roan Head
Washfold
Roan Bridge
Cemy
Slackhill Farm
Tongue Hill
Shaw
Helwith
Helwith Bridge
Hurst
Fell End
Wellington Shaft (dis)
Hind Rake
Hall Farm
Waterfalls
Shaw Beck
White Scar
Prys Lead Mine Mine (dis)
Prys House Farm
Chimney/Flue
Munn End
Skelton Moor
GOATS ROAD
STANG TOP

19
1

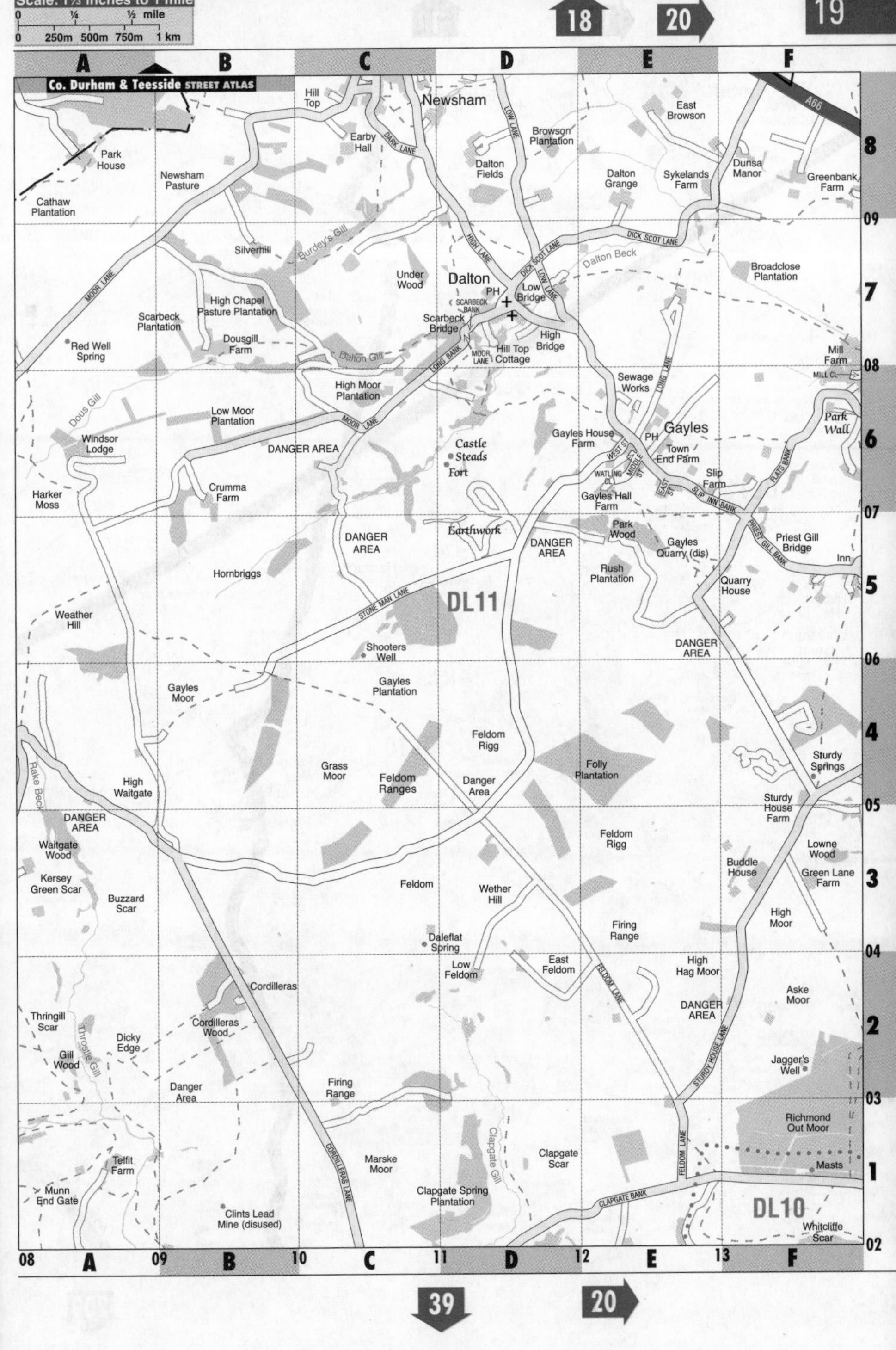
Scale: 1⅓ inches to 1 mile
0 ¼ ½ mile
0 250m 500m 750m 1 km
18
20
Co. Durham & Teesside STREET ATLAS
A B C D E F
8 09 7 08 6 07 5 06 4 05 3 04 2 03 1 02
08 09 10 11 12 13
A66
Newsham
Hill Top
Earby Hall
DARK LANE
LOW LANE
Browson Plantation
East Browson
Dalton Fields
Dunsa Manor
Greenbank Farm
Park House
Newsham Pasture
Cathaw Plantation
Dalton Grange
Sykelands Farm
DICK SCOT LANE
Burdey's Gill
Silverhill
HIGH LANE
Dalton Beck
Broadclose Plantation
MOOR LANE
Under Wood
Dalton
PH
Low Bridge
High Chapel Pasture Plantation
Scarbeck Plantation
SCARBECK BANK
Scarbeck Bridge
High Bridge
Red Well Spring
Dousgill Farm
Dalton Gill
LONG BANK
MOOR LANE
Hill Top Cottage
Mill Farm
MILL CL
LONG LANE
Sewage Works
Dous Gill
High Moor Plantation
Low Moor Plantation
Park Wall
Windsor Lodge
DANGER AREA
Castle Steads Fort
Gayles House Farm
Gayles
Town End Farm
WEST ST
MIDDLE ST
WATLING CL
EAST ST
Slip Farm
SLIP INN BANK
FLATS BANK
Harker Moss
Crumma Farm
Gayles Hall Farm
Earthwork
Park Wood
Gayles Quarry (dis)
PRIEST GILL BANK
Priest Gill Bridge
Inn
DANGER AREA
Hornbriggs
Rush Plantation
Quarry House
STONE MAN LANE
DL11
Weather Hill
Shooters Well
DANGER AREA
Gayles Moor
Gayles Plantation
Feldom Rigg
Folly Plantation
Sturdy Springs
Grass Moor
Feldom Ranges
Danger Area
Rake Beck
High Waitgate
Sturdy House Farm
DANGER AREA
Waitgate Wood
Feldom Rigg
Lowne Wood
Kersey Green Scar
Buddle House
Green Lane Farm
Buzzard Scar
Feldom
Wether Hill
High Moor
Daleflat Spring
Firing Range
Low Feldom
East Feldom
FELDOM LANE
High Hag Moor
Aske Moor
Cordilleras
Thringill Scar
DANGER AREA
Throstle Gill
Cordilleras Wood
Dicky Edge
Gill Wood
Jagger's Well
Danger Area
Firing Range
STURDY HOUSE LANE
Richmond Out Moor
CORDILLERAS LANE
Clapgate Gill
Telfit Farm
Marske Moor
Clapgate Scar
FELDOM LANE
Masts
Munn End Gate
Clapgate Spring Plantation
CLAPGATE BANK
DL10
Clints Lead Mine (disused)
Whitcliffe Scar
39
20

19
1

Scale: 1⅓ inches to 1 mile

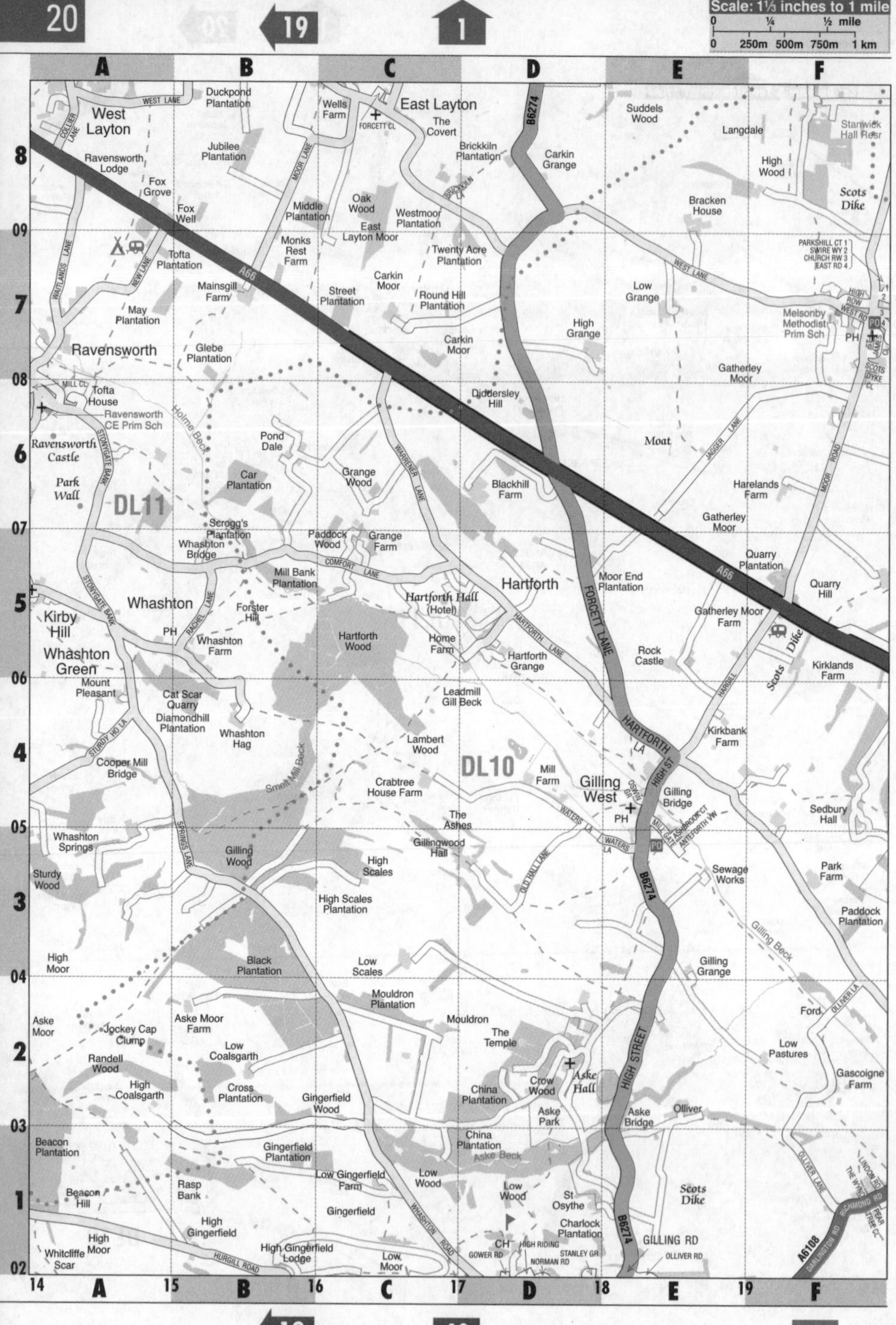

19
40
209

2
22
41
22

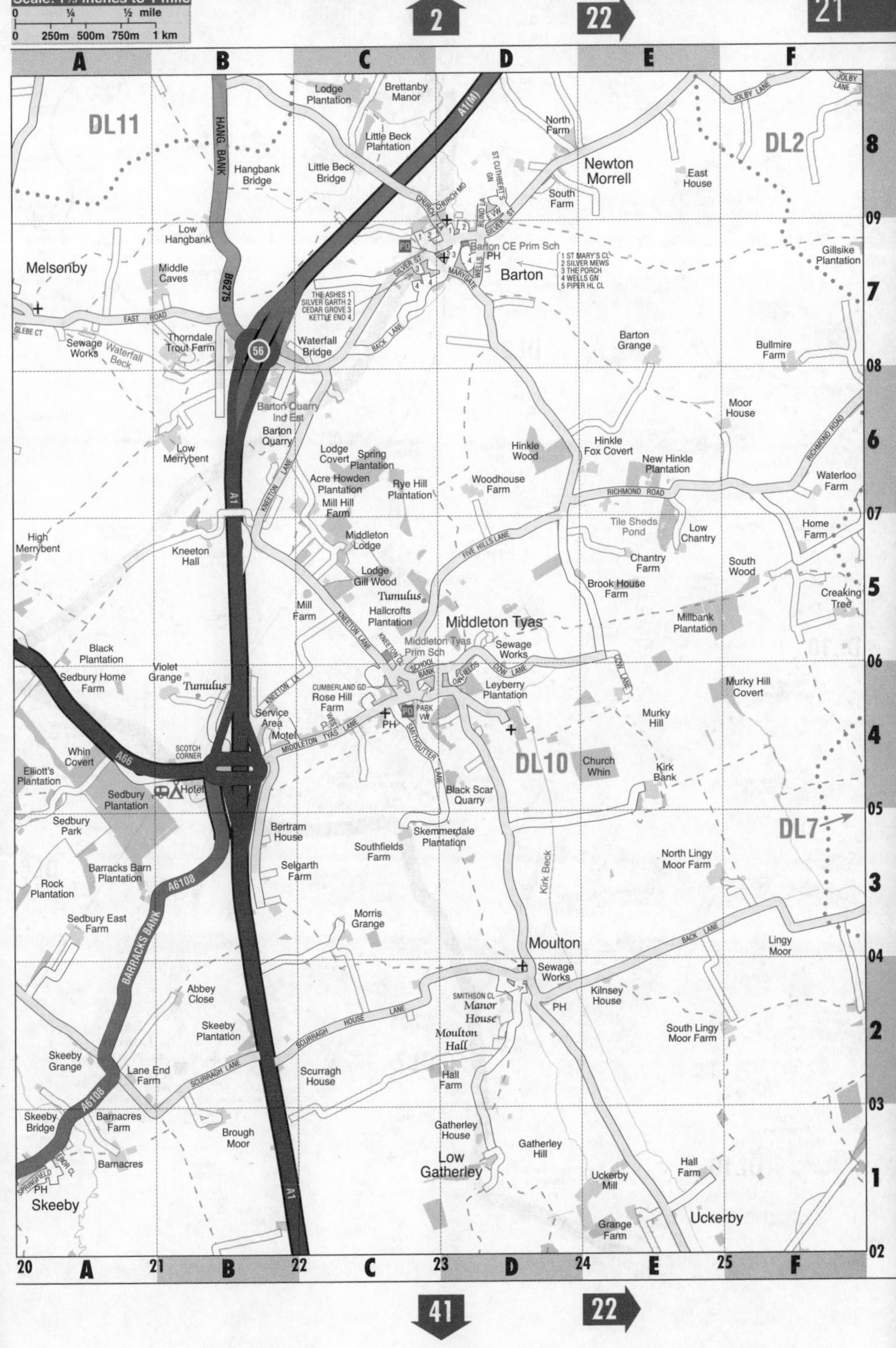
Scale: 1⅓ inches to 1 mile
DL11
DL2
DL10
DL7
Melsonby
Newton Morrell
Barton
Middleton Tyas
Moulton
Skeeby
Uckerby
Low Gatherley
Lodge Plantation
Brettanby Manor
Little Beck Plantation
Little Beck Bridge
Hangbank Bridge
Low Hangbank
Middle Caves
North Farm
East House
South Farm
Barton CE Prim Sch
1 ST MARY'S CL
2 SILVER MEWS
3 THE PORCH
4 WELLS GN
5 PIPER HL CL
THE ASHES 1
SILVER GARTH 2
CEDAR GROVE 3
KETTLE END 4
Gillsike Plantation
Thorndale Trout Farm
Sewage Works
Waterfall Beck
Waterfall Bridge
Barton Grange
Bullmire Farm
Barton Quarry Ind Est
Barton Quarry
Low Merrybent
Lodge Covert
Spring Plantation
Acre Howden Plantation
Mill Hill Farm
Rye Hill Plantation
Woodhouse Farm
Hinkle Wood
Hinkle Fox Covert
New Hinkle Plantation
Moor House
Waterloo Farm
High Merrybent
Kneeton Hall
Middleton Lodge
Lodge Gill Wood
Tumulus
Tile Sheds Pond
Low Chantry
Chantry Farm
Home Farm
South Wood
Brook House Farm
Creaking Tree
Mill Farm
Hallcrofts Plantation
Millbank Plantation
Middleton Tyas Prim Sch
Sewage Works
Black Plantation
Sedbury Home Farm
Violet Grange
Tumulus
Rose Hill Farm
Leyberry Plantation
Murky Hill Covert
Murky Hill
Service Area
Motel
Whin Covert
Elliott's Plantation
SCOTCH CORNER
Hotel
Sedbury Plantation
Church Whin
Kirk Bank
Sedbury Park
Black Scar Quarry
Bertram House
Skemmerdale Plantation
Southfields Farm
North Lingy Moor Farm
Barracks Barn Plantation
Rock Plantation
Selgarth Farm
Kirk Beck
Sedbury East Farm
Morris Grange
Lingy Moor
Sewage Works
Abbey Close
SMITHSON CL
Manor House
Kilnsey House
PH
Skeeby Plantation
Moulton Hall
South Lingy Moor Farm
Skeeby Grange
Lane End Farm
Scurragh House
Hall Farm
Skeeby Bridge
Barnacres Farm
Brough Moor
Gatherley House
Gatherley Hill
Barnacres
Hall Farm
Uckerby Mill
Grange Farm
A1(M)
A1
A66
A6108
B6275
HANG BANK
EAST ROAD
GLEBE CT
CHURCH LA
CHURCH MD
ST CUTHBERTS GN
BLIND LA
SILVER ST
MARYGATE
WELLS LA
BACK LANE
KNEETON LANE
RICHMOND ROAD
FIVE HILLS LANE
KNEETON CL
SCHOOL BANK
COW LANE
OAKFIELDS
CUMBERLAND GD
KNEETON LA
MIDDLETON TYAS LANE
PARK VW
SMITHGUTTER LANE
BARRACKS BANK
SCURRAGH HOUSE LANE
SCURRAGH LANE
JOLBY LANE
SPRINGFIELD
PO
PH
56
A B C D E F
8 7 6 5 4 3 2 1
09 08 07 06 05 04 03 02
20 21 22 23 24 25

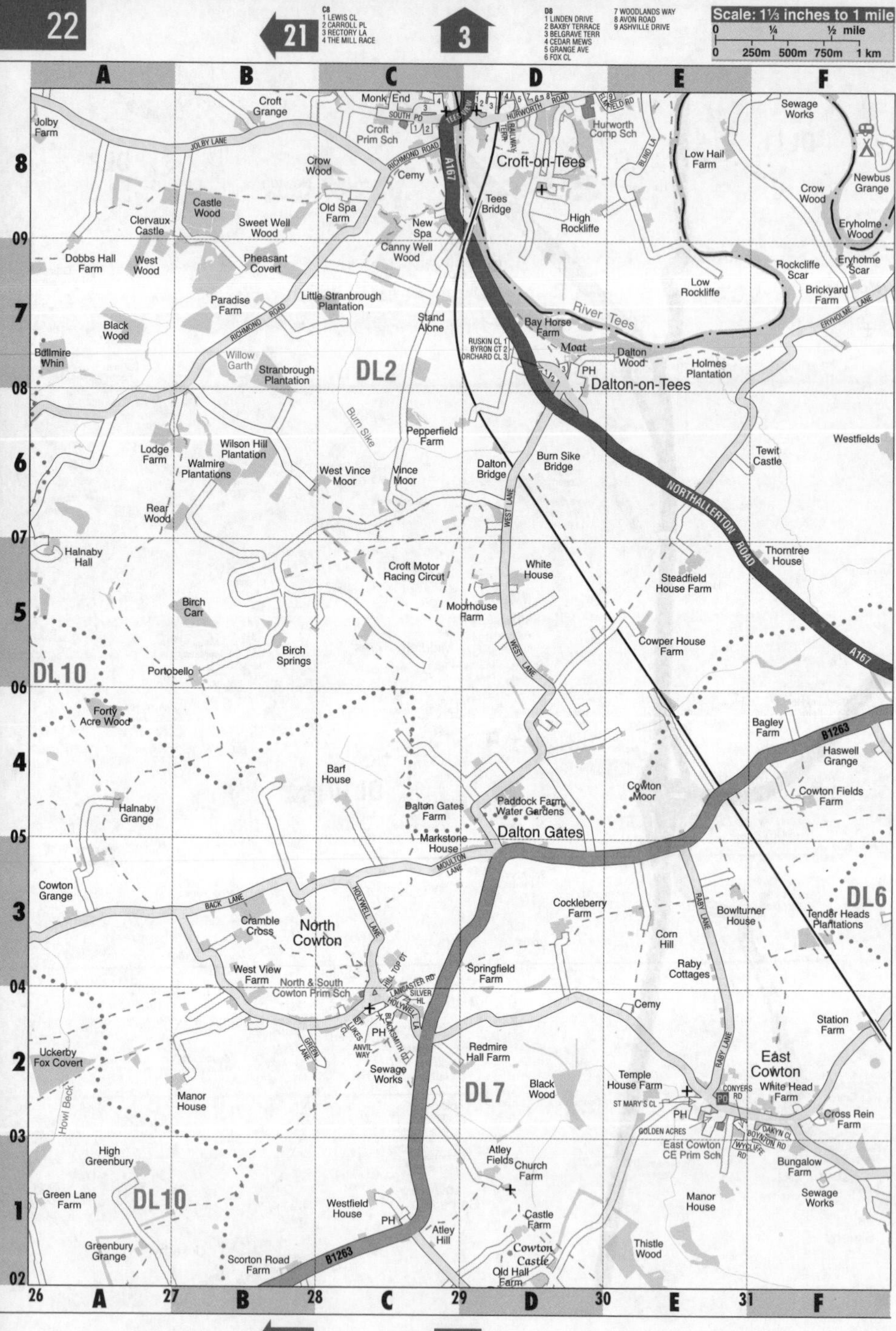

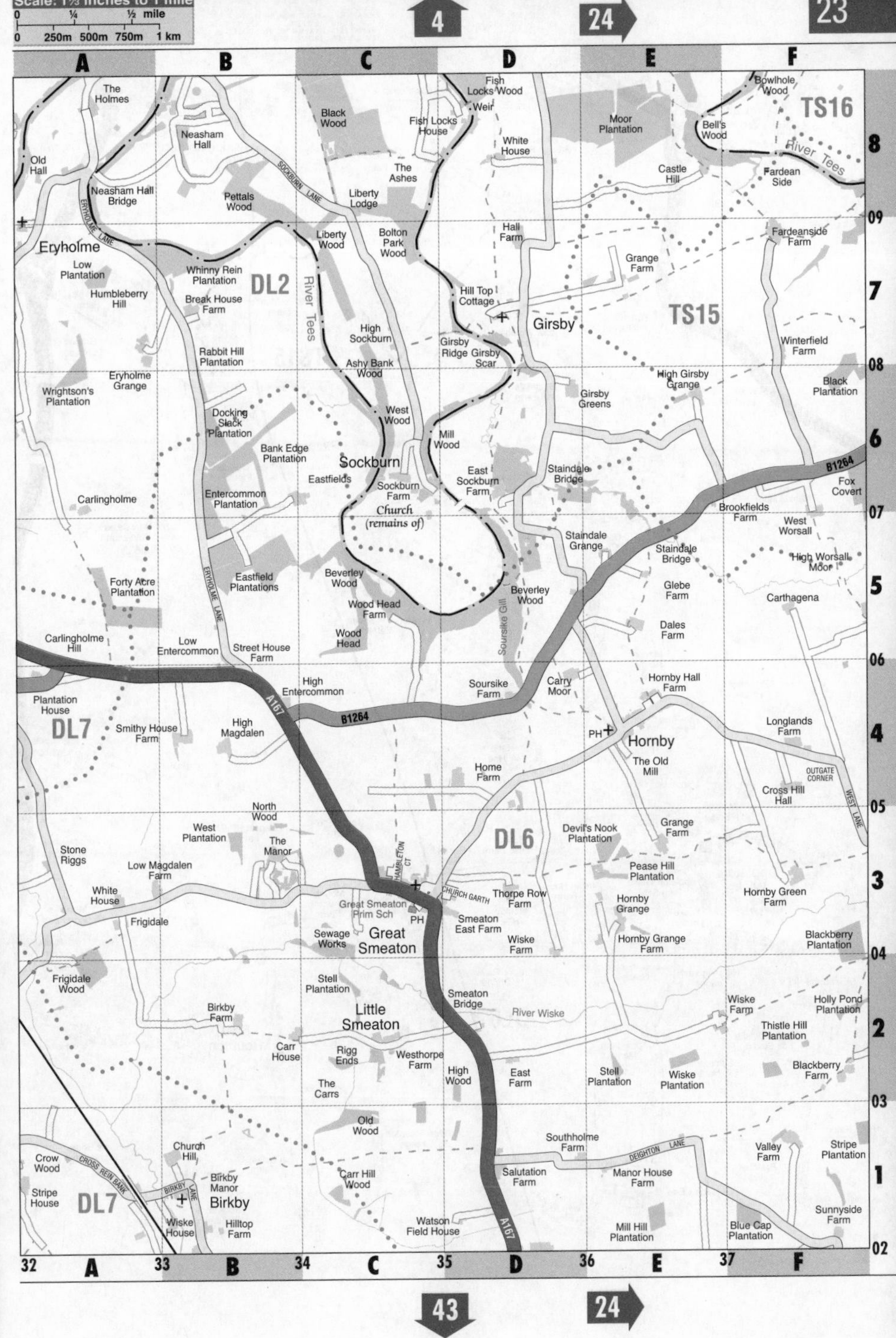
Scale: 1½ inches to 1 mile
0 ¼ ½ mile
0 250m 500m 750m 1 km
4
24
A B C D E F
The Holmes
Neasham Hall
Black Wood
Fish Locks Wood
Weir
Fish Locks House
White House
Moor Plantation
Bowlhole Wood
Bell's Wood
TS16
River Tees
Old Hall
Neasham Hall Bridge
SOCKBURN LANE
Pettals Wood
The Ashes
Liberty Lodge
Castle Hill
Fardean Side
Eryholme
ERYHOLME LANE
Liberty Wood
Bolton Park Wood
Hall Farm
Fardeanside Farm
Low Plantation
Whinny Rein Plantation
DL2
River Tees
Grange Farm
Humbleberry Hill
Break House Farm
Hill Top Cottage
TS15
Girsby
High Sockburn
Winterfield Farm
Rabbit Hill Plantation
Girsby Ridge
Girsby Scar
Ashy Bank Wood
Eryholme Grange
High Girsby Grange
Black Plantation
Wrightson's Plantation
Girsby Greens
Docking Slack Plantation
West Wood
Mill Wood
Bank Edge Plantation
Sockburn
Staindale Bridge
B1264
Eastfields
East Sockburn Farm
Fox Covert
Sockburn Farm
Carlingholme
Entercommon Plantation
Church (remains of)
Brookfields Farm
West Worsall
Staindale Grange
Staindale Bridge
High Worsall Moor
ERYHOLME LANE
Eastfield Plantations
Beverley Wood
Glebe Farm
Forty Acre Plantation
Beverley Wood
Carthagena
Wood Head Farm
Soursike Gill
Dales Farm
Wood Head
Carlingholme Hill
Low Entercommon
Street House Farm
High Entercommon
Soursike Farm
Carry Moor
Hornby Hall Farm
Plantation House
A167
B1264
DL7
Smithy House Farm
High Magdalen
PH
Hornby
Longlands Farm
The Old Mill
Home Farm
OUTGATE CORNER
Cross Hill Hall
WEST LANE
North Wood
West Plantation
The Manor
DL6
Devil's Nook Plantation
Grange Farm
Stone Riggs
HAMBLETON CT
Low Magdalen Farm
Pease Hill Plantation
White House
CHURCH GARTH
Thorpe Row Farm
Hornby Grange
Hornby Green Farm
Great Smeaton Prim Sch
PH
Smeaton East Farm
Frigidale
Sewage Works
Great Smeaton
Wiske Farm
Hornby Grange Farm
Blackberry Plantation
Frigidale Wood
Stell Plantation
Smeaton Bridge
River Wiske
Wiske Farm
Holly Pond Plantation
Birkby Farm
Little Smeaton
Thistle Hill Plantation
Carr House
Rigg Ends
Westhorpe Farm
High Wood
East Farm
Stell Plantation
Wiske Plantation
Blackberry Farm
The Carrs
Old Wood
Southholme Farm
DEIGHTON LANE
Valley Farm
Stripe Plantation
Crow Wood
CROSS REIN BANK
Church Hill
Birkby Manor
Carr Hill Wood
Salutation Farm
Manor House Farm
Stripe House
DL7
BIRKBY LANE
Birkby
Wiske House
Hilltop Farm
Watson Field House
A167
Mill Hill Plantation
Blue Cap Plantation
Sunnyside Farm
8
09
7
08
6
07
5
06
4
05
3
04
2
03
1
02
32 A 33 B 34 C 35 D 36 E 37 F
43
24

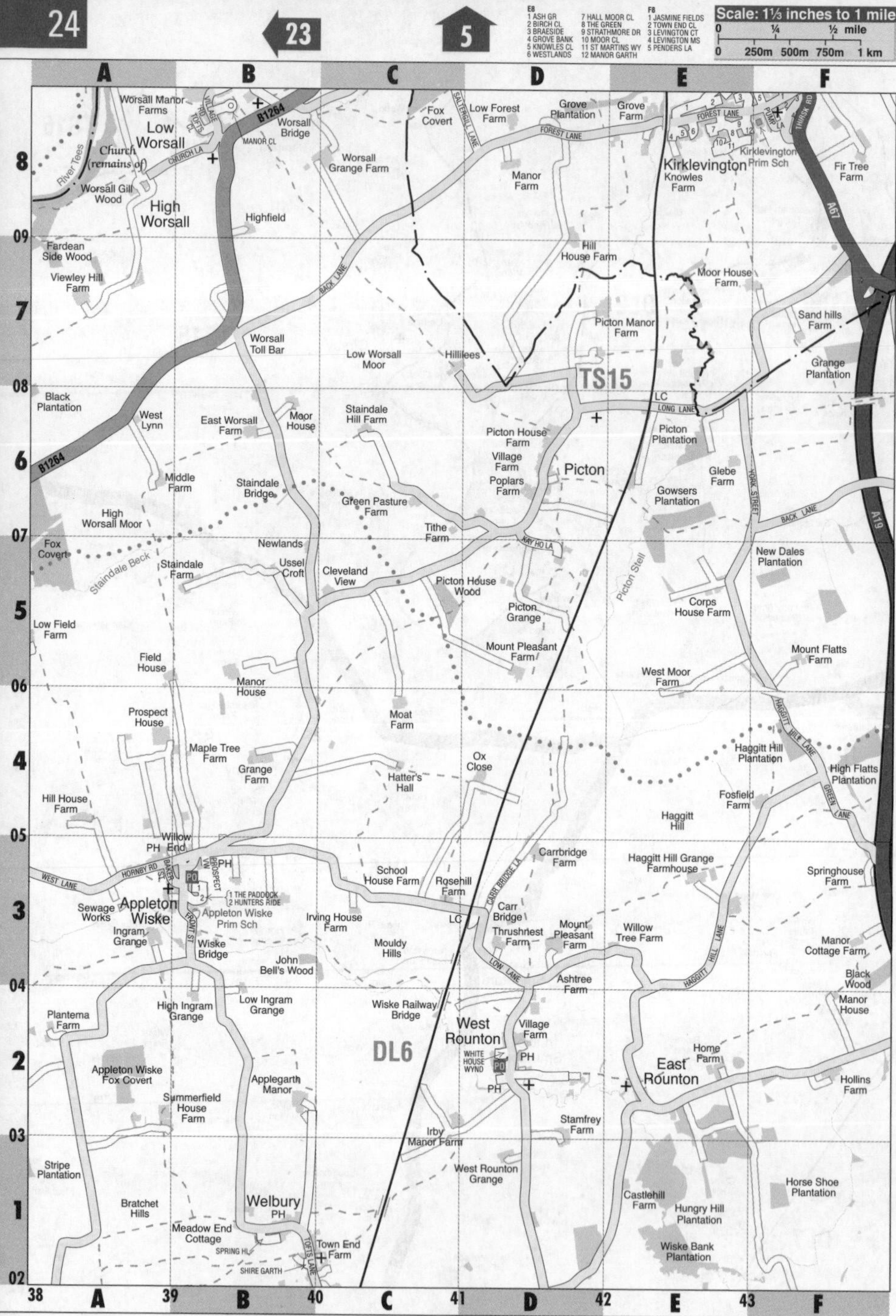

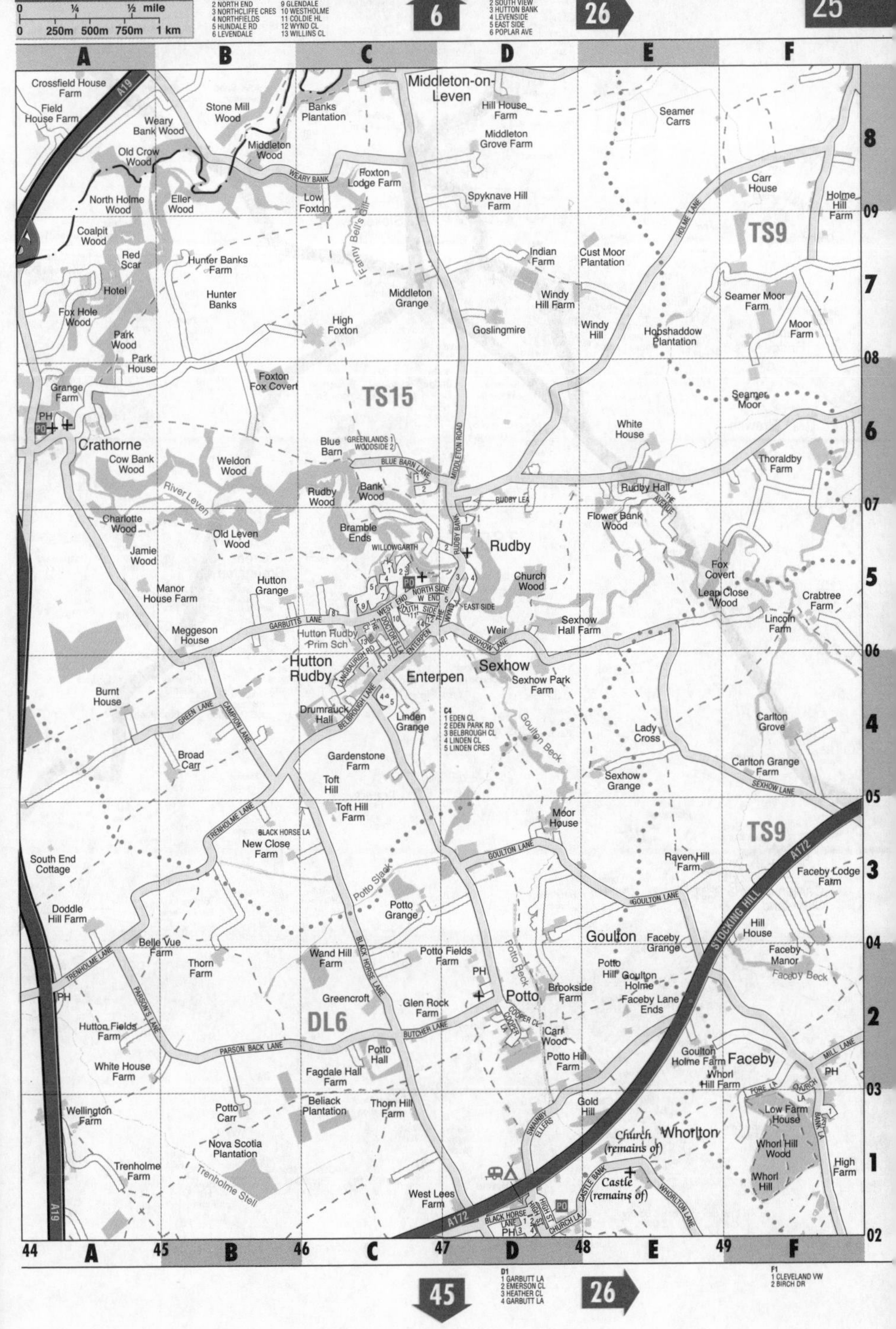

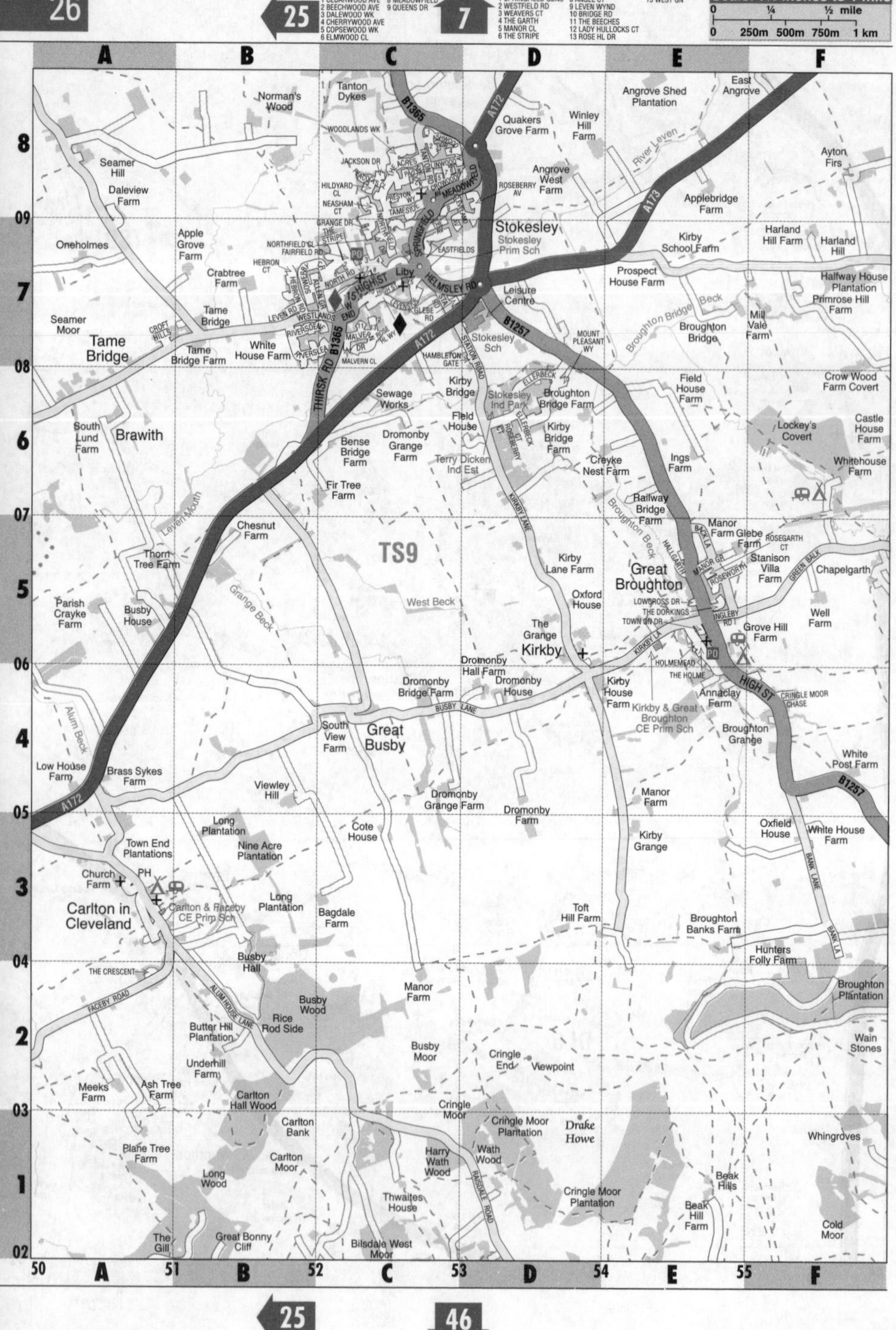

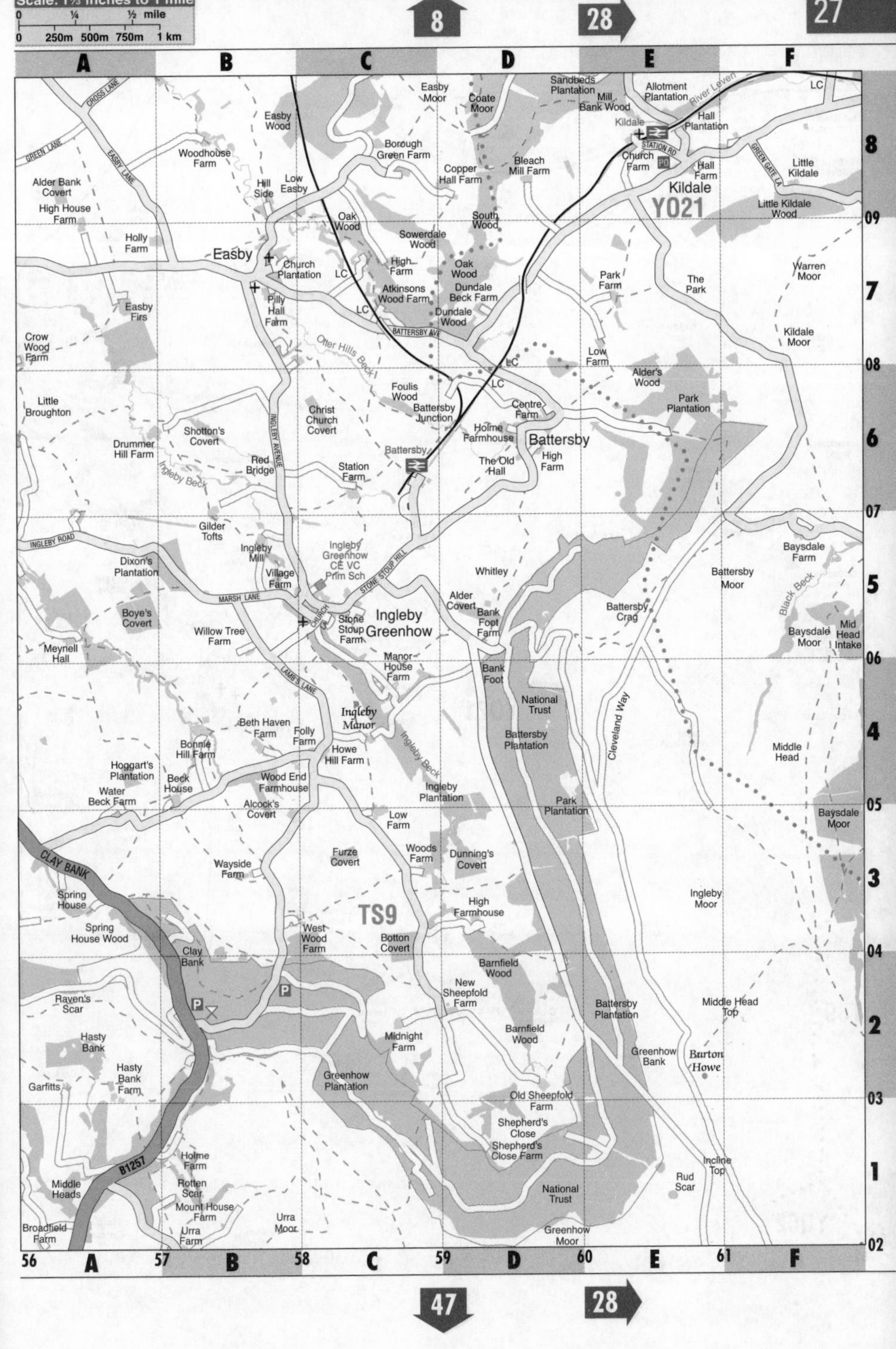
Scale: 1⅓ inches to 1 mile
8
28
Easby
Ingleby Greenhow
Battersby
Kildale
YO21
TS9
Cleveland Way
CLAY BANK
B1257
47
28

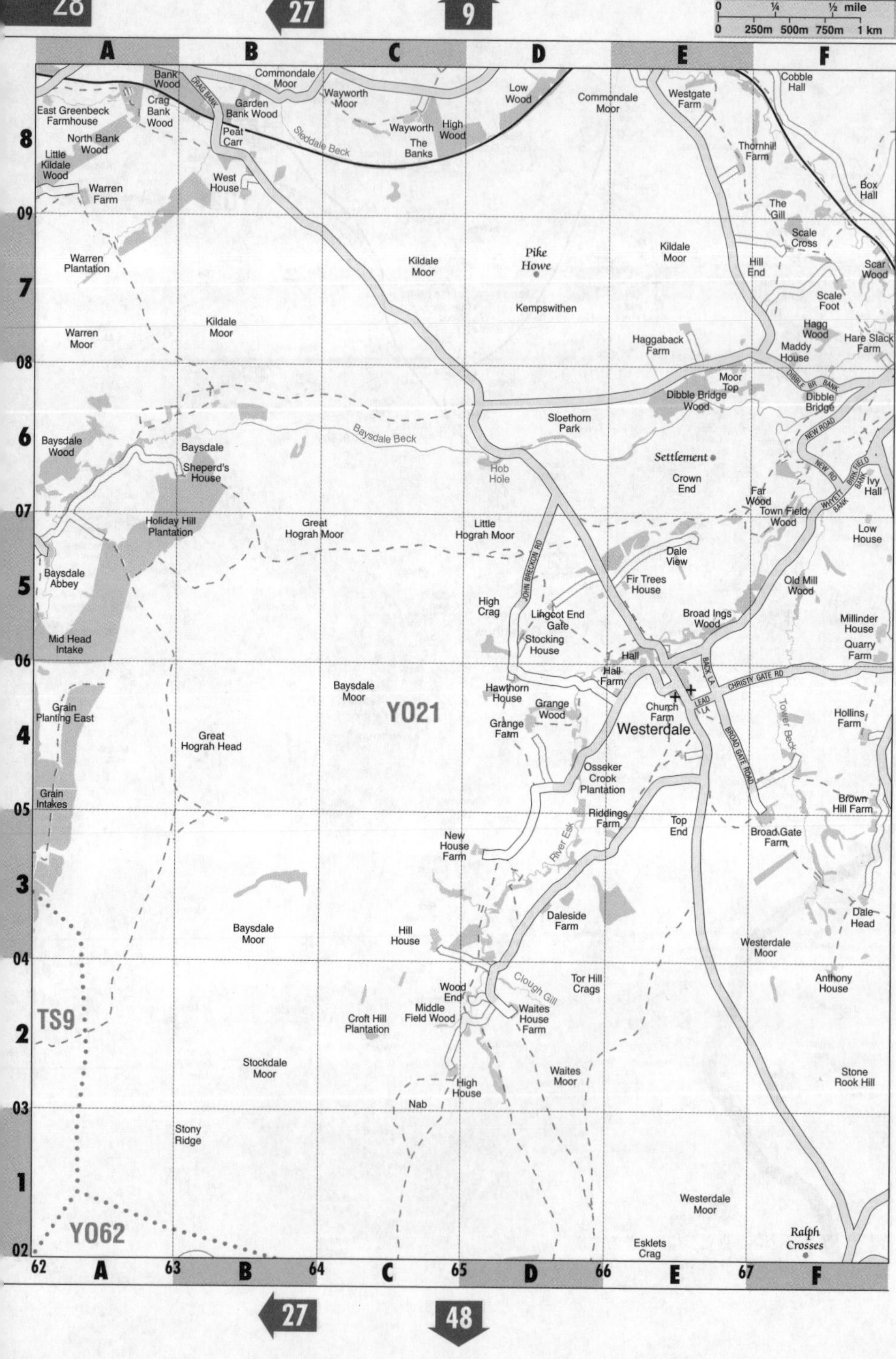

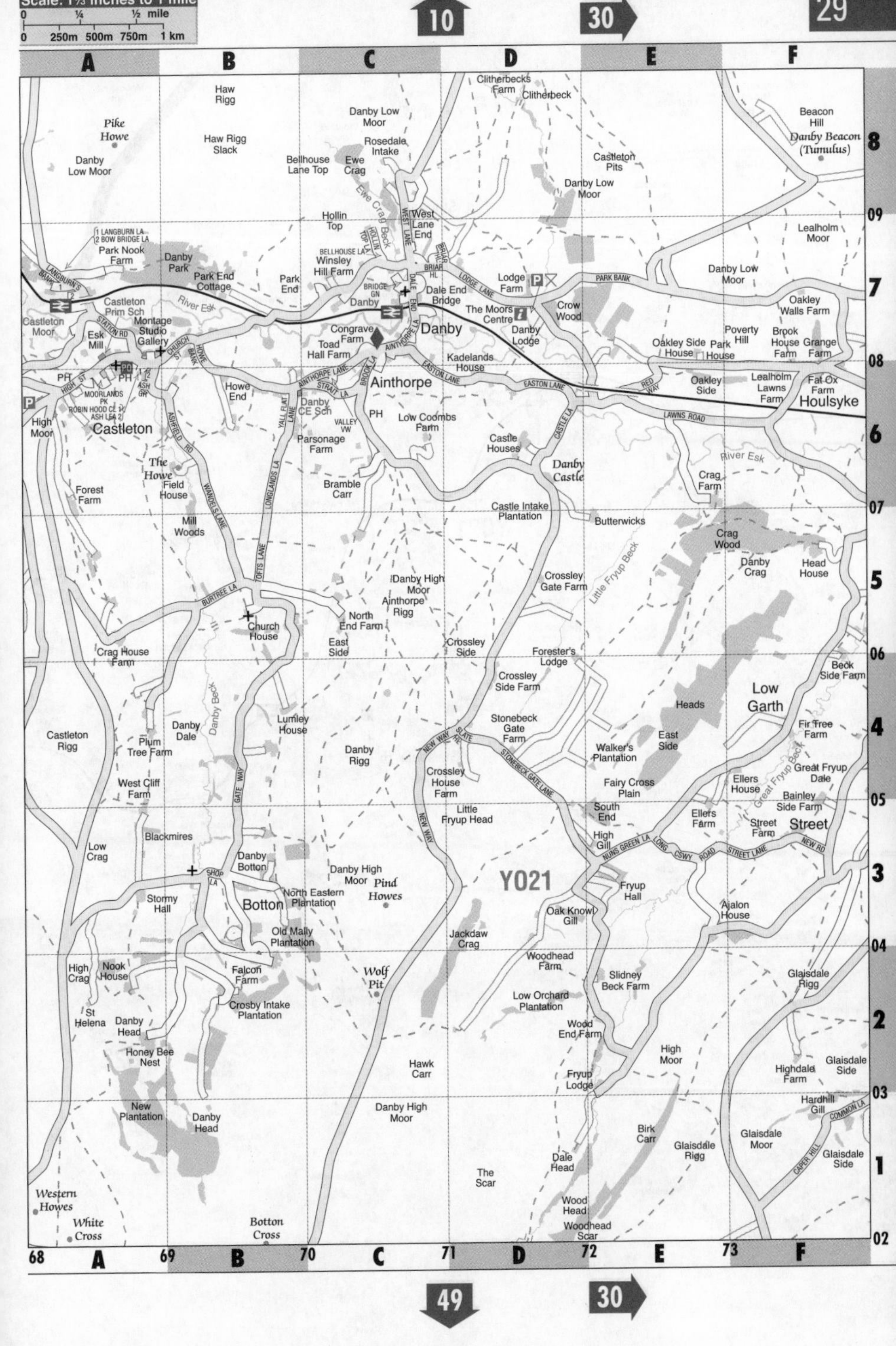
Scale: 1⅓ inches to 1 mile
10
30
Castleton
Danby
Ainthorpe
Botton
Houlsyke
Low Garth
Street
YO21
Danby Castle
Danby Beacon (Tumulus)
River Esk
49
30

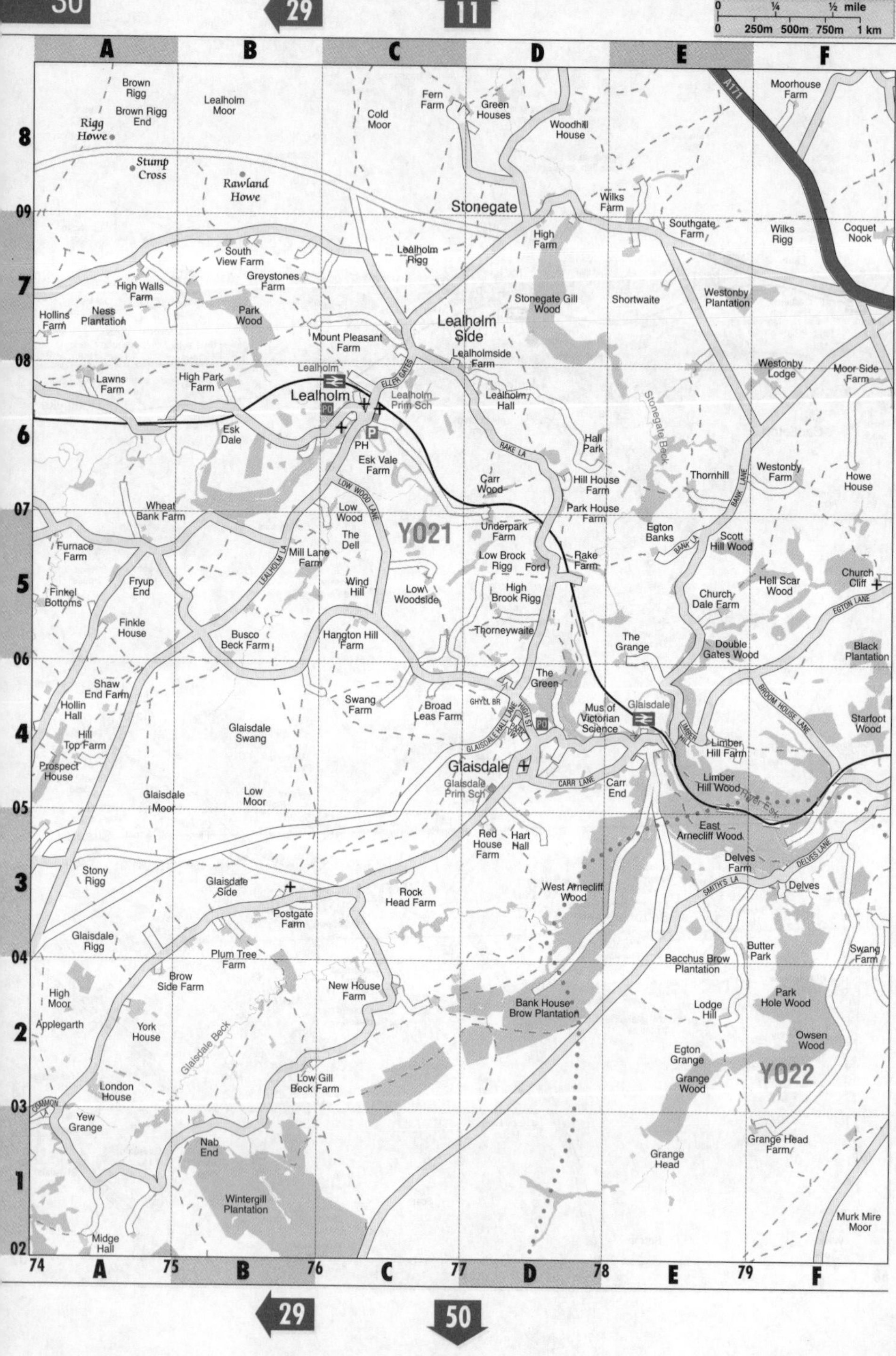

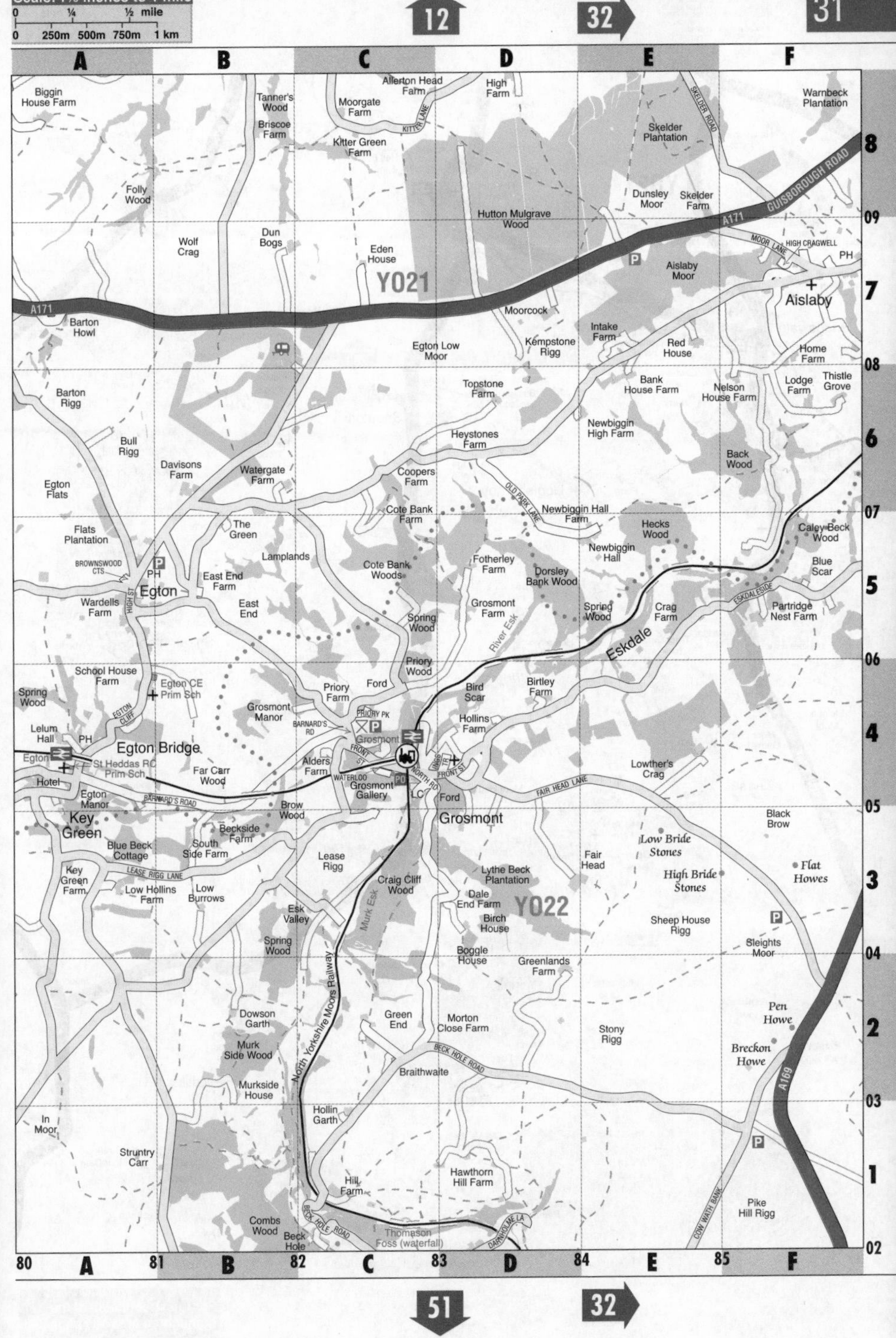
Biggin House Farm
Tanner's Wood
Briscoe Farm
Moorgate Farm
Allerton Head Farm
Kitter Green Farm
High Farm
Skelder Plantation
Warnbeck Plantation
Folly Wood
Dunsley Moor
Skelder Farm
Hutton Mulgrave Wood
GUISBOROUGH ROAD
A171
Wolf Crag
Dun Bogs
Eden House
YO21
HIGH CRAGWELL
MOOR LANE
Aislaby Moor
PH
Aislaby
Barton Howl
Moorcock
Kempstone Rigg
Intake Farm
Red House
Home Farm
Egton Low Moor
Barton Rigg
Topstone Farm
Bank House Farm
Nelson House Farm
Lodge Farm
Thistle Grove
Bull Rigg
Heystones Farm
Newbiggin High Farm
Davisons Farm
Watergate Farm
Coopers Farm
Back Wood
Egton Flats
Cote Bank Farm
OLD PARK LANE
Newbiggin Hall Farm
Hecks Wood
Caley Beck Wood
Flats Plantation
The Green
Lamplands
Cote Bank Woods
Fotherley Farm
Newbiggin Hall
Blue Scar
BROWNSWOOD CTS
PH
Egton
East End Farm
East End
Dorsley Bank Wood
Spring Wood
Crag Farm
ESKDALESIDE
Partridge Nest Farm
Wardells Farm
HIGH ST
Grosmont Farm
River Esk
Eskdale
School House Farm
Egton CE Prim Sch
Priory Farm
Ford
Priory Wood
Bird Scar
Birtley Farm
Spring Wood
EGTON CLIFF
Grosmont Manor
PRIORY PK
BARNARD'S RD
Hollins Farm
Lelum Hall
PH
Egton Bridge
Grosmont
FRONT ST
Egton
St Heddas RC Prim Sch
Far Carr Wood
Alders Farm
WATERLOO
Grosmont Gallery
PO
NORTH RD
FRONT ST
Lowther's Crag
FAIR HEAD LANE
Hotel
Egton Manor
BARNARD'S ROAD
Brow Wood
LC
Ford
Grosmont
Key Green
Beckside Farm
Black Brow
Low Bride Stones
Blue Beck Cottage
South Side Farm
Lease Rigg
Fair Head
LEASE RIGG LANE
Lythe Beck Plantation
High Bride Stones
Flat Howes
Key Green Farm
Low Hollins Farm
Low Burrows
Craig Cliff Wood
Dale End Farm
YO22
Esk Valley
Murk Esk
Birch House
Sheep House Rigg
Spring Wood
Sleights Moor
North Yorkshire Moors Railway
Boggle House
Greenlands Farm
Dowson Garth
Green End
Morton Close Farm
Stony Rigg
Pen Howe
Murk Side Wood
BECK HOLE ROAD
Braithwaite
Breckon Howe
Murkside House
A169
In Moor
Hollin Garth
Struntry Carr
Hawthorn Hill Farm
Hill Farm
COW WATH BANK
Pike Hill Rigg
Combs Wood
Beck Hole
BECK HOLE ROAD
Thomason Foss (waterfall)
DARNHOLME LA
A B C D E F
8 09 7 08 6 07 5 06 4 05 3 04 2 03 1 02
80 81 82 83 84 85

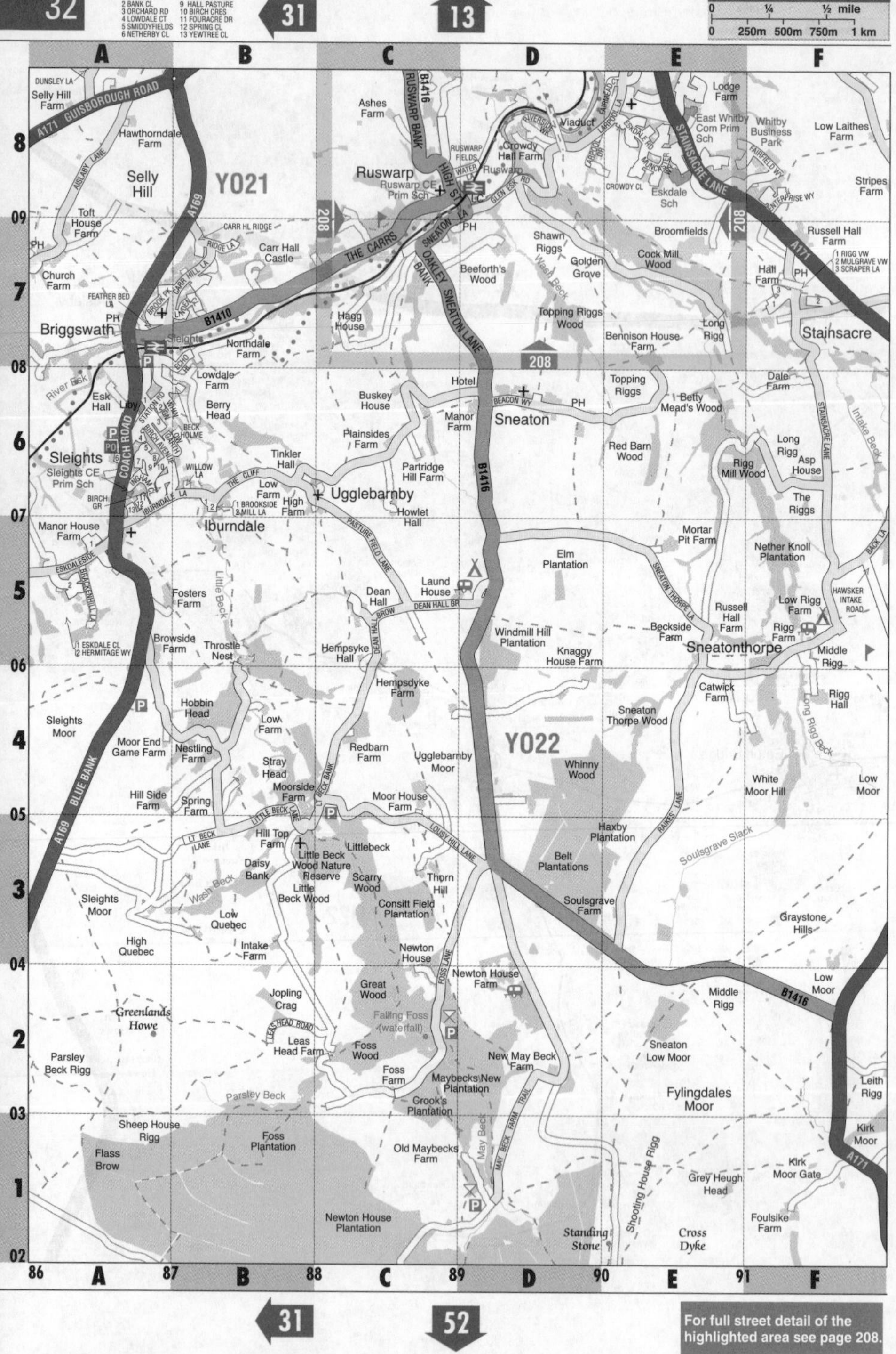
A6
1 THE AVENUE
2 BANK CL
3 ORCHARD RD
4 LOWDALE CT
5 SMIDDYFIELDS
6 NETHERBY CL
7 SELSTONE CR
8 NARROWFIELD
9 HALL PASTURE
10 BIRCH CRES
11 FOURACRE DR
12 SPRING CL
13 YEWTREE CL
31
13
Scale: 1⅓ inches to 1 mile
0 ¼ ½ mile
0 250m 500m 750m 1 km
A B C D E F
Selly Hill Farm
A171 GUISBOROUGH ROAD
Hawthorndale Farm
Selly Hill
YO21
Ashes Farm
B1416
RUSWARP BANK
Ruswarp
Ruswarp CE Prim Sch
HIGH ST
Viaduct
Crowdy Hall Farm
East Whitby Com Prim Sch
Lodge Farm
Whitby Business Park
Low Laithes Farm
Stripes Farm
STAINSACRE LANE
Eskdale Sch
Toft House Farm
Carr Hall Castle
THE CARRS
208
Shawn Riggs
Golden Grove
Broomfields
Cock Mill Wood
Russell Hall Farm
Church Farm
Beeforth's Wood
Hall Farm
Briggswath
B1410
Hagg House
Topping Riggs Wood
Bennison House Farm
Long Rigg
Stainsacre
Northdale Farm
Lowdale Farm
River Esk
Esk Hall
Berry Head
Buskey House
Hotel
Sneaton
Topping Riggs
Betty Mead's Wood
Dale Farm
Manor Farm
Plainsides Farm
Sleights
Sleights CE Prim Sch
COACH ROAD
Tinkler Hall
Partridge Hill Farm
Red Barn Wood
Long Rigg
Asp House
Rigg Mill Wood
Low Farm
Ugglebarnby
High Farm
Howlet Hall
The Riggs
Manor House Farm
Iburndale
Mortar Pit Farm
Nether Knoll Plantation
Elm Plantation
Fosters Farm
Dean Hall
Laund House
Low Rigg Farm
Russell Hall Farm
Rigg Farm
Beckside Farm
Windmill Hill Plantation
Sneatonthorpe
Middle Rigg
Browside Farm
Throstle Nest
Hempsyke Hall
Knaggy House Farm
Hempsdyke Farm
Catwick Farm
Rigg Hall
Sleights Moor
Hobbin Head
Sneaton Thorpe Wood
Low Farm
Moor End Game Farm
Nestling Farm
Stray Head
Redbarn Farm
Ugglebarnby Moor
YO22
Whinny Wood
White Moor Hill
Low Moor
Hill Side Farm
Spring Farm
Moorside Farm
Moor House Farm
Hill Top Farm
Littlebeck
Haxby Plantation
Daisy Bank
Little Beck Wood Nature Reserve
Scarry Wood
Thorn Hill
Belt Plantations
Soulsgrave Slack
Sleights Moor
Little Beck Wood
Consitt Field Plantation
Soulsgrave Farm
Graystone Hills
Low Quebec
High Quebec
Intake Farm
Newton House
Newton House Farm
Low Moor
Jopling Crag
Great Wood
Middle Rigg
B1416
Greenlands Howe
Falling Foss (waterfall)
Leas Head Farm
Foss Wood
New May Beck Farm
Sneaton Low Moor
Parsley Beck Rigg
Foss Farm
Maybecks New Plantation
Fylingdales Moor
Leith Rigg
Parsley Beck
Grook's Plantation
Sheep House Rigg
Foss Plantation
Kirk Moor
Flass Brow
Old Maybecks Farm
Kirk Moor Gate
Grey Heugh Head
Shooting House Rigg
Newton House Plantation
Foulsike Farm
Standing Stone
Cross Dyke
A169 BLUE BANK
A171
86 87 88 89 90 91
31
52
For full street detail of the highlighted area see page 208.

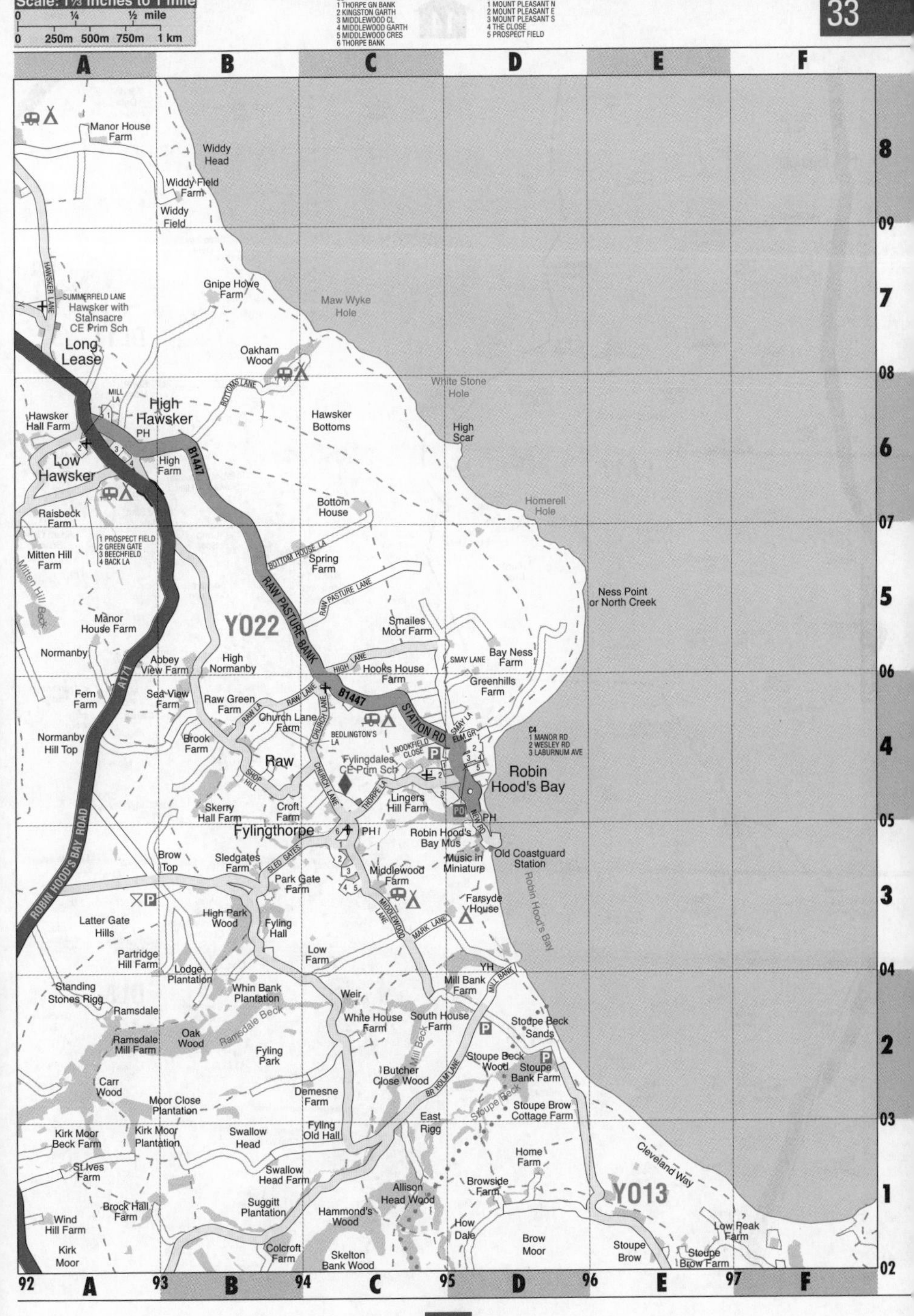

Scale: 1⅓ inches to 1 mile

0   ¼   ½ mile

0   250m 500m 750m 1 km

C3
1 THORPE GN BANK
2 KINGSTON GARTH
3 MIDDLEWOOD CL
4 MIDDLEWOOD GARTH
5 MIDDLEWOOD CRES
6 THORPE BANK

D4
1 MOUNT PLEASANT N
2 MOUNT PLEASANT E
3 MOUNT PLEASANT S
4 THE CLOSE
5 PROSPECT FIELD

14

Scale: 1½ inches to 1 mile

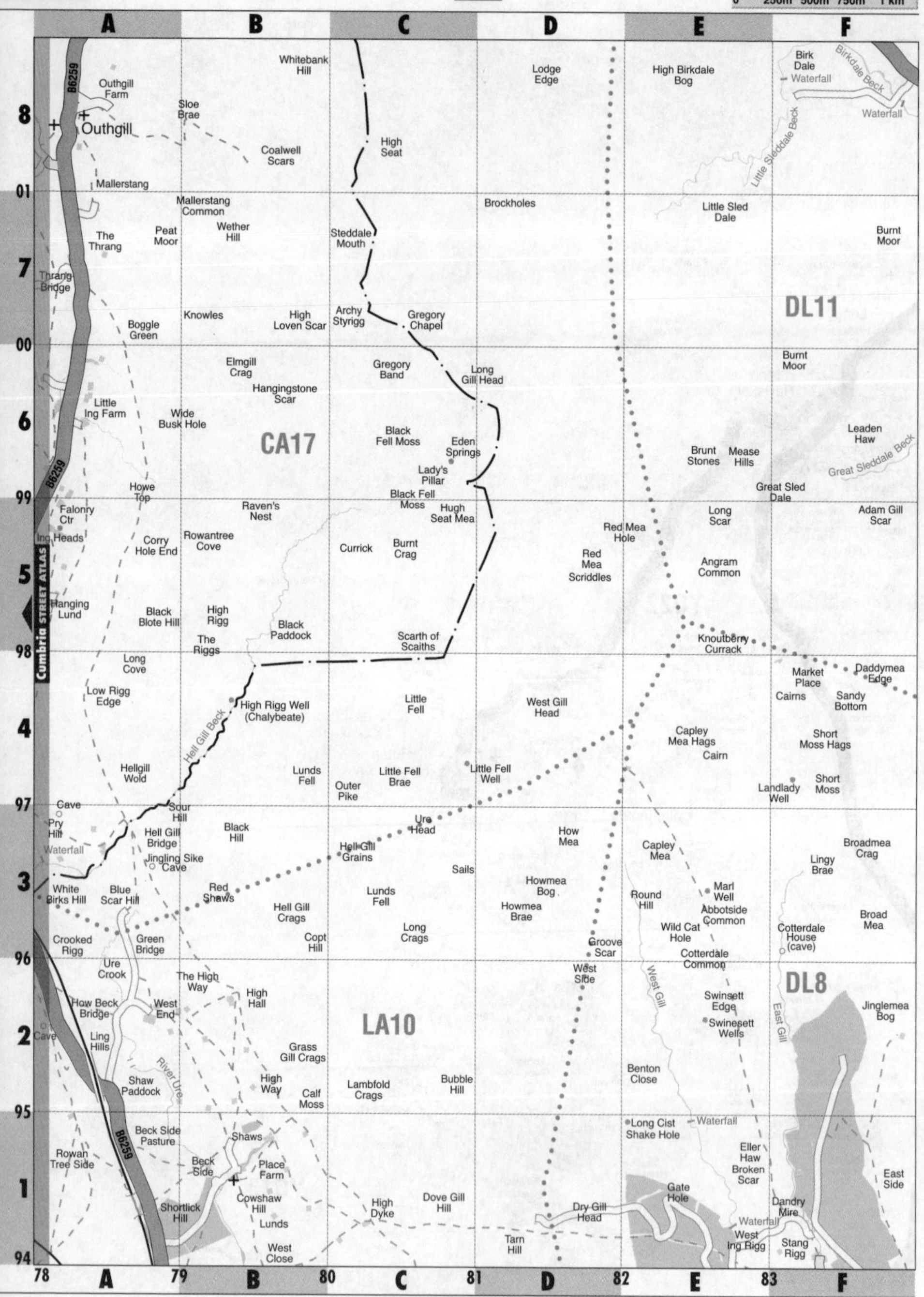

A B C D E F
Whitebank Hill
Lodge Edge
High Birkdale Bog
Birk Dale
Waterfall
Birkdale Beck
Outhgill Farm
Sloe Brae
Outhgill
B6259
High Seat
Coalwell Scars
Little Sleddale Beck
Mallerstang
Mallerstang Common
Brockholes
Little Sled Dale
Peat Moor
Wether Hill
Steddale Mouth
Burnt Moor
The Thrang
Thrang Bridge
DL11
Boggle Green
Knowles
High Loven Scar
Archy Styrigg
Gregory Chapel
Elmgill Crag
Gregory Band
Long Gill Head
Burnt Moor
Hangingstone Scar
Little Ing Farm
Wide Busk Hole
CA17
Black Fell Moss
Eden Springs
Leaden Haw
Brunt Stones
Mease Hills
Great Sleddale Beck
Lady's Pillar
Howe Top
Black Fell Moss
Great Sled Dale
Falonry Ctr
Raven's Nest
Hugh Seat Mea
Long Scar
Adam Gill Scar
Ing Heads
Corry Hole End
Rowantree Cove
Currick
Burnt Crag
Red Mea Hole
Red Mea Scriddles
Angram Common
Hanging Lund
Black Blote Hill
High Rigg
Black Paddock
Scarth of Scaiths
Knoutberry Currack
The Riggs
Long Cove
Market Place
Daddymea Edge
Low Rigg Edge
High Rigg Well (Chalybeate)
Little Fell
West Gill Head
Cairns
Sandy Bottom
Hell Gill Beck
Capley Mea Hags
Short Moss Hags
Cairn
Hellgill Wold
Lunds Fell
Little Fell Brae
Little Fell Well
Outer Pike
Short Moss
Landlady Well
Cave
Sour Hill
Pry Hill
Hell Gill Bridge
Black Hill
Ure Head
How Mea
Capley Mea
Broadmea Crag
Waterfall
Hell Gill Grains
Jingling Sike Cave
Lingy Brae
Sails
Howmea Bog
Marl Well
White Birks Hill
Blue Scar Hill
Red Shaws
Lunds Fell
Round Hill
Abbotside Common
Hell Gill Crags
Howmea Brae
Broad Mea
Wild Cat Hole
Cotterdale House (cave)
Crooked Rigg
Green Bridge
Long Crags
Copt Hill
Groove Scar
Cotterdale Common
Ure Crook
The High Way
West Side
DL8
How Beck Bridge
West End
High Hall
West Gill
Swinsett Edge
Jinglemea Bog
Swinesett Wells
East Gill
Cave
Ling Hills
LA10
Grass Gill Crags
River Ure
Benton Close
Shaw Paddock
High Way
Lambfold Crags
Bubble Hill
Calf Moss
Long Cist Shake Hole
Waterfall
Beck Side Pasture
Shaws
Rowan Tree Side
Eller Haw Broken Scar
Beck Side
Place Farm
East Side
Gate Hole
Cowshaw Hill
High Dyke
Dove Gill Hill
Dandry Mire
Shortlick Hill
Lunds
Dry Gill Head
Waterfall
West Close
Tarn Hill
West Ing Rigg
Stang Rigg
Cumbria STREET ATLAS
78 79 80 81 82 83
8 01 7 00 6 99 5 98 4 97 3 96 2 95 1 94

55

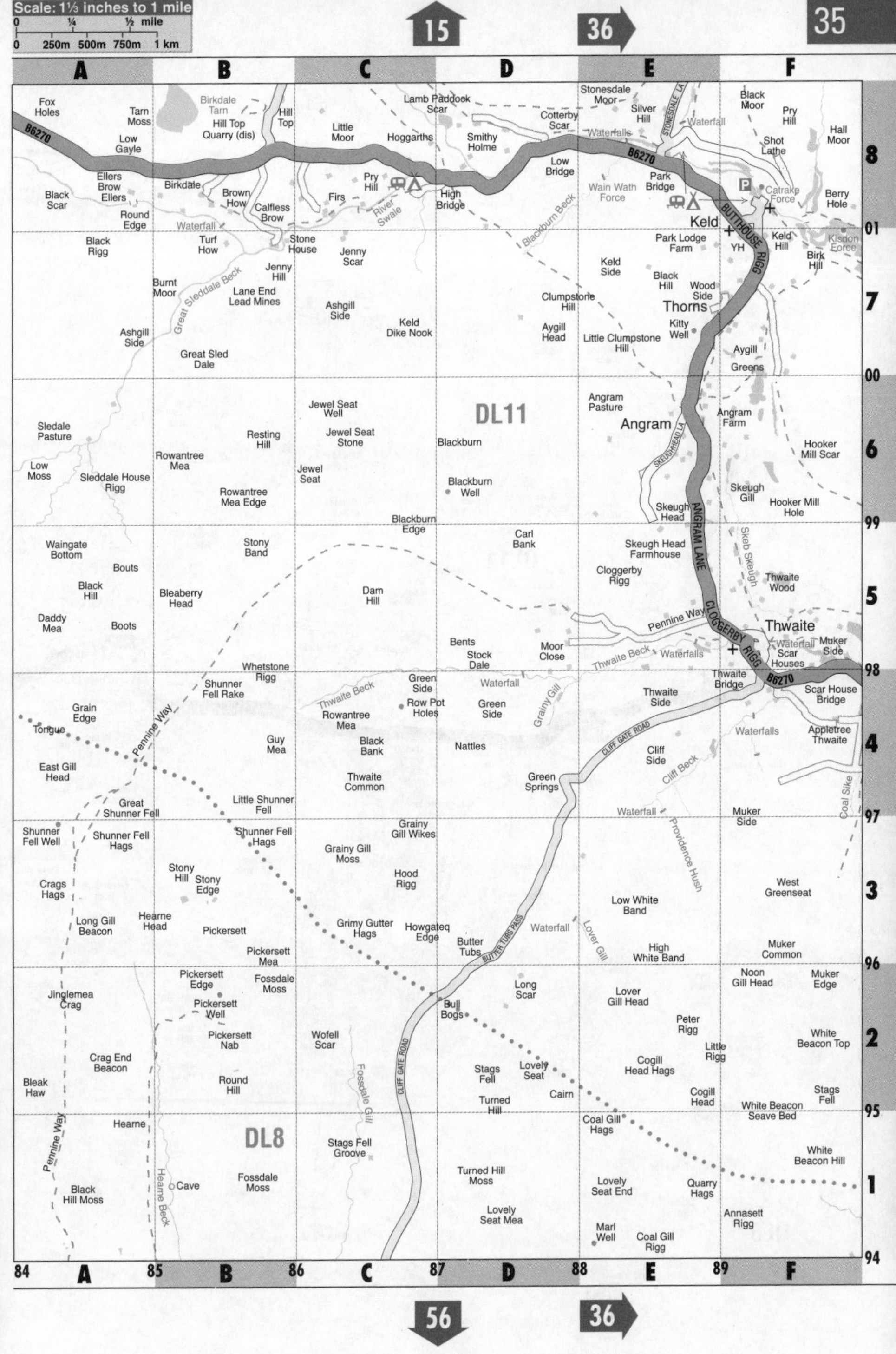
Scale: 1⅓ inches to 1 mile
15
36
A B C D E F
Fox Holes
Tarn Moss
Birkdale Tarn
Hill Top Quarry (dis)
Hill Top
Little Moor
Lamb Paddock Scar
Hoggarths
Smithy Holme
Stonesdale Moor
Cotterby Scar
Silver Hill
Waterfalls
Black Moor
Pry Hill
Hall Moor
Shot Lathe
Low Gayle
B6270
Ellers Brow Ellers
Black Scar
Birkdale
Brown How
Calfless Brow
Pry Hill
Firs
River Swale
High Bridge
Low Bridge
Wain Wath Force
Park Bridge
Catrake Force
Berry Hole
Round Edge
Waterfall
Keld
Butthouse Rigg
Black Rigg
Turf How
Stone House
Jenny Scar
Blackburn Beck
Park Lodge Farm
YH
Keld Hill
Kisdon Force
Birk Hill
Jenny Hill
Keld Side
Black Hill
Wood Side
Burnt Moor
Great Sleddale Beck
Lane End Lead Mines
Ashgill Side
Clumpstone Hill
Thorns
Kitty Well
Keld Dike Nook
Aygill Head
Little Clumpstone Hill
Aygill
Ashgill Side
Great Sled Dale
Greens
Jewel Seat Well
DL11
Angram Pasture
Angram
Angram Farm
Sledale Pasture
Resting Hill
Jewel Seat Stone
Blackburn
Skeugh Head La
Hooker Mill Scar
Rowantree Mea
Low Moss
Sleddale House Rigg
Jewel Seat
Blackburn Well
Skeugh Gill
Rowantree Mea Edge
Skeugh Head
Hooker Mill Hole
Blackburn Edge
Angram Lane
Carl Bank
Skeugh Head Farmhouse
Skeb Skeugh
Waingate Bottom
Stony Band
Cloggerby Rigg
Bouts
Thwaite Wood
Black Hill
Bleaberry Head
Dam Hill
Daddy Mea
Boots
Pennine Way
Thwaite
Bents
Moor Close
Muker Side
Stock Dale
Thwaite Beck
Waterfalls
Waterfall
Scar Houses
Whetstone Rigg
Thwaite Bridge
Shunner Fell Rake
Green Side
Waterfall
Thwaite Side
Scar House Bridge
Grain Edge
Thwaite Beck
Row Pot Holes
Green Side
Grainy Gill
Tongue
Rowantree Mea
Cliff Gate Road
Waterfalls
Appletree Thwaite
Guy Mea
Black Bank
Nattles
Cliff Side
East Gill Head
Thwaite Common
Cliff Beck
Green Springs
Coal Sike
Great Shunner Fell
Little Shunner Fell
Waterfall
Muker Side
Shunner Fell Well
Shunner Fell Hags
Shunner Fell Hags
Grainy Gill Wikes
Providence Hush
Grainy Gill Moss
Stony Hill
Stony Edge
Hood Rigg
West Greenseat
Crags Hags
Low White Band
Long Gill Beacon
Hearne Head
Pickersett
Grimy Gutter Hags
Howgateq Edge
Butter Tubs Pass
Butter Tubs
Waterfall
Lover Gill
Pickersett Mea
High White Band
Muker Common
Pickersett Edge
Fossdale Moss
Long Scar
Noon Gill Head
Muker Edge
Jinglemea Crag
Pickersett Well
Bull Bogs
Lover Gill Head
Pickersett Nab
Wofell Scar
Peter Rigg
White Beacon Top
Little Rigg
Crag End Beacon
Stags Fell
Lovely Seat
Cogill Head Hags
Bleak Haw
Round Hill
Fossdale Gill
Turned Hill
Cairn
Cogill Head
Stags Fell
White Beacon Seave Bed
Coal Gill Hags
Pennine Way
Hearne
DL8
Stags Fell Groove
White Beacon Hill
Black Hill Moss
Cave
Fossdale Moss
Turned Hill Moss
Lovely Seat End
Quarry Hags
Hearne Beck
Lovely Seat Mea
Annasett Rigg
Marl Well
Coal Gill Rigg
8 01 7 00 6 99 5 98 4 97 3 96 2 95 1 94
84 85 86 87 88 89
56
36

35
16

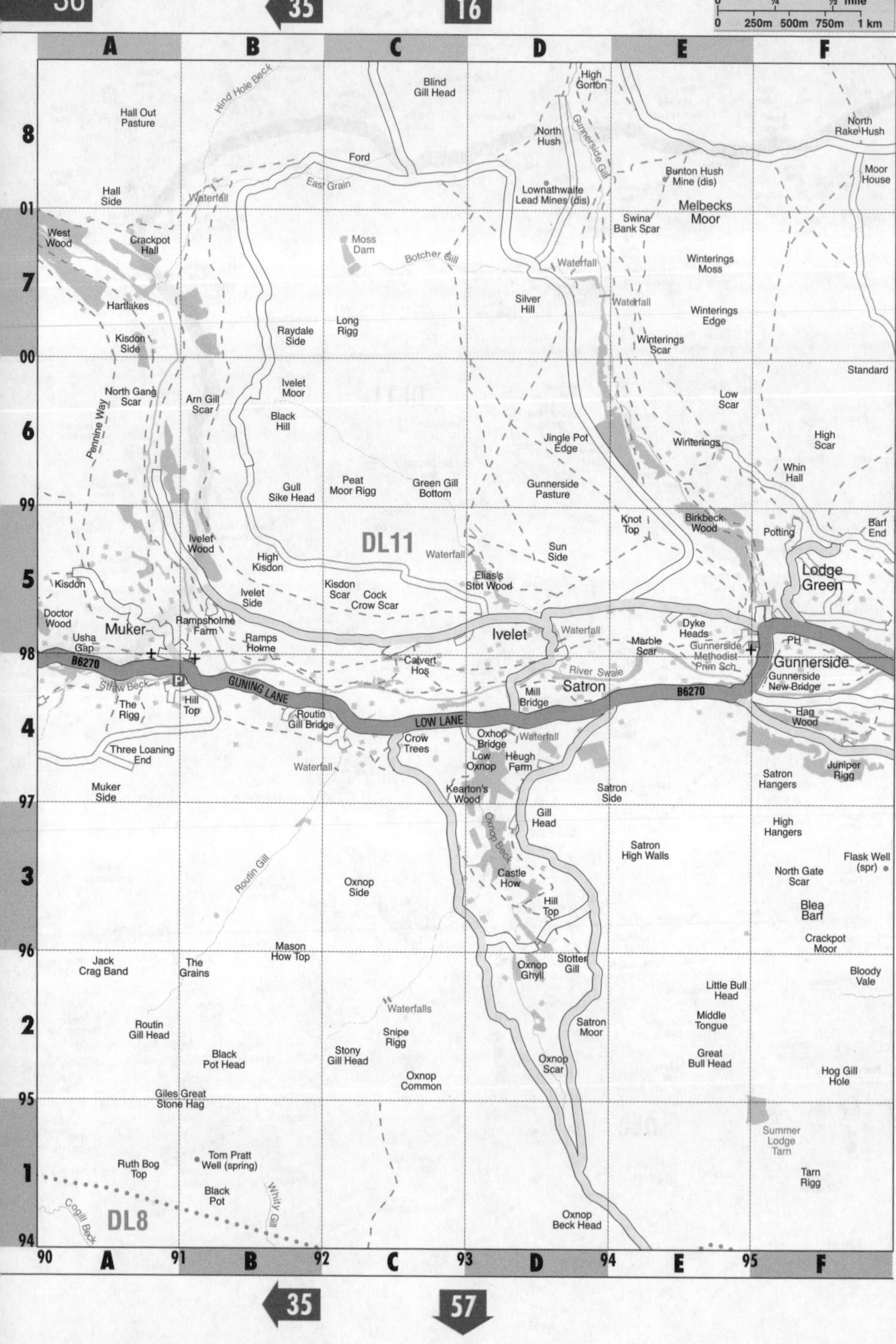
Scale: 1⅓ inches to 1 mile
0 ¼ ½ mile
0 250m 500m 750m 1 km
A B C D E F
8
01
7
00
6
99
5
98
4
97
3
96
2
95
1
94
90 91 92 93 94 95
Hall Out Pasture
Hind Hole Beck
Blind Gill Head
High Gorton
North Hush
Gunnerside Gill
North Rake Hush
Ford
East Grain
Bunton Hush Mine (dis)
Moor House
Hall Side
Waterfall
Lownathwaite Lead Mines (dis)
Melbecks Moor
Swina Bank Scar
West Wood
Crackpot Hall
Moss Dam
Botcher Gill
Winterings Moss
Silver Hill
Hartlakes
Long Rigg
Raydale Side
Winterings Edge
Kisdon Side
Winterings Scar
Standard
North Gang Scar
Arn Gill Scar
Ivelet Moor
Low Scar
Pennine Way
Black Hill
Jingle Pot Edge
Winterings
High Scar
Whin Hall
Gull Sike Head
Peat Moor Rigg
Green Gill Bottom
Gunnerside Pasture
Knot Top
Birkbeck Wood
Potting
Barf End
Ivelet Wood
DL11
Waterfall
Sun Side
High Kisdon
Lodge Green
Kisdon
Kisdon Scar
Cock Crow Scar
Elias's Stot Wood
Ivelet Side
Doctor Wood
Muker
Rampsholme Farm
Ivelet
Dyke Heads
Usha Gap
Ramps Holme
Marble Scar
Gunnerside Methodist Prim Sch
PH
Gunnerside
B6270
Calvert Hos
River Swale
Satron
Straw Beck
P
Hill Top
GUNING LANE
Mill Bridge
Gunnerside New Bridge
The Rigg
Routin Gill Bridge
LOW LANE
Hag Wood
Crow Trees
Oxnop Bridge
Three Loaning End
Low Oxnop
Heugh Farm
Juniper Rigg
Muker Side
Kearton's Wood
Satron Side
Satron Hangers
Gill Head
High Hangers
Oxnop Beck
Satron High Walls
Routin Gill
Flask Well (spr)
Castle How
North Gate Scar
Oxnop Side
Hill Top
Blea Barf
Crackpot Moor
Mason How Top
Jack Crag Band
The Grains
Oxnop Ghyll
Stotter Gill
Bloody Vale
Little Bull Head
Waterfalls
Routin Gill Head
Satron Moor
Middle Tongue
Snipe Rigg
Stony Gill Head
Black Pot Head
Great Bull Head
Oxnop Scar
Oxnop Common
Hog Gill Hole
Giles Great Stone Hag
Summer Lodge Tarn
Ruth Bog Top
Tom Pratt Well (spring)
Tarn Rigg
Black Pot
Whity Gill
Cogill Beck
DL8
Oxnop Beck Head

35
57

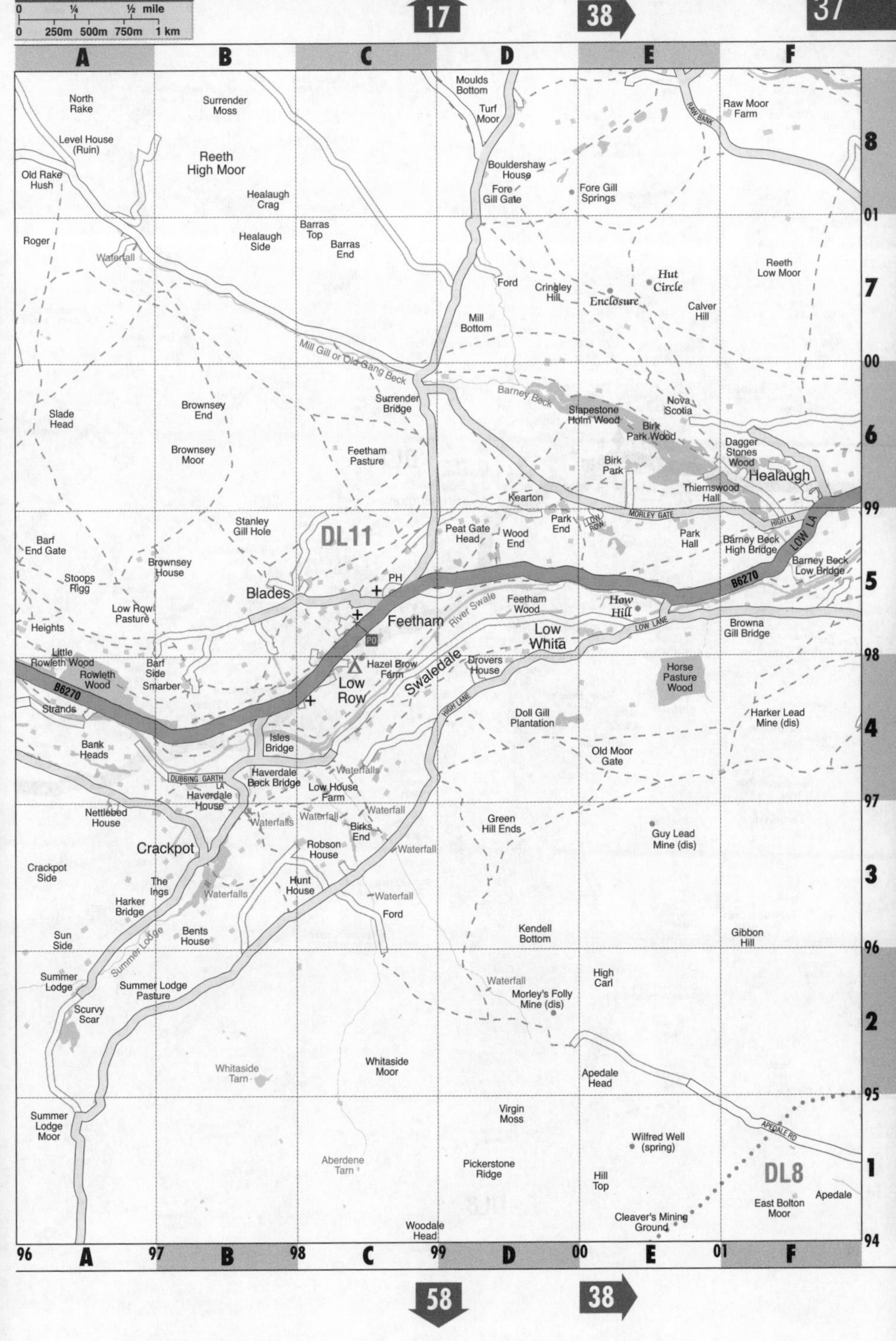
Scale: 1⅓ inches to 1 mile
0 ¼ ½ mile
0 250m 500m 750m 1 km
17
38
A B C D E F
North Rake
Surrender Moss
Moulds Bottom
Turf Moor
Raw Moor Farm
RAW BANK
Level House (Ruin)
Reeth High Moor
Old Rake Hush
Bouldershaw House
Fore Gill Gate
Fore Gill Springs
Healaugh Crag
Roger
Healaugh Side
Barras Top
Barras End
Waterfall
Ford
Cringley Hill
Enclosure
Hut Circle
Reeth Low Moor
Calver Hill
Mill Bottom
Mill Gill or Old Gang Beck
Barney Beck
Surrender Bridge
Slapestone Holm Wood
Nova Scotia
Slade Head
Brownsey End
Birk Park Wood
Brownsey Moor
Feetham Pasture
Dagger Stones Wood
Birk Park
Healaugh
Thiernswood Hall
Kearton
MORLEY GATE
HIGH LA
LOW LA
LOW ROW
Stanley Gill Hole
DL11
Peat Gate Head
Wood End
Park End
Park Hall
Barney Beck High Bridge
Barf End Gate
Brownsey House
Barney Beck Low Bridge
Stoops Rigg
PH
B6270
Blades
Feetham
River Swale
Feetham Wood
How Hill
Low Row Pasture
Heights
PO
Low Whita
LOW LANE
Browna Gill Bridge
Little Rowleth Wood
Hazel Brow Farm
Swaledale
Drovers House
Rowleth Wood
Barf Side
Smarber
Low Row
Horse Pasture Wood
B6270
Strands
HIGH LANE
Doll Gill Plantation
Harker Lead Mine (dis)
Bank Heads
Isles Bridge
Old Moor Gate
DUBBING GARTH LA
Haverdale Beck Bridge
Waterfalls
Low House Farm
Haverdale House
Nettlebed House
Waterfall
Waterfall
Green Hill Ends
Guy Lead Mine (dis)
Waterfalls
Birks End
Crackpot
Robson House
Waterfall
Crackpot Side
The Ings
Hunt House
Waterfalls
Waterfall
Harker Bridge
Ford
Sun Side
Bents House
Kendell Bottom
Gibbon Hill
Summer Lodge
High Carl
Summer Lodge
Waterfall
Summer Lodge Pasture
Morley's Folly Mine (dis)
Scurvy Scar
Whitaside Tarn
Whitaside Moor
Apedale Head
Summer Lodge Moor
Virgin Moss
APEDALE RD
Wilfred Well (spring)
Aberdene Tarn
Pickerstone Ridge
DL8
Hill Top
Apedale
East Bolton Moor
Cleaver's Mining Ground
Woodale Head
8
01
7
00
6
99
5
98
4
97
3
96
2
95
1
94
96 A 97 B 98 C 99 D 00 E 01 F
58
38

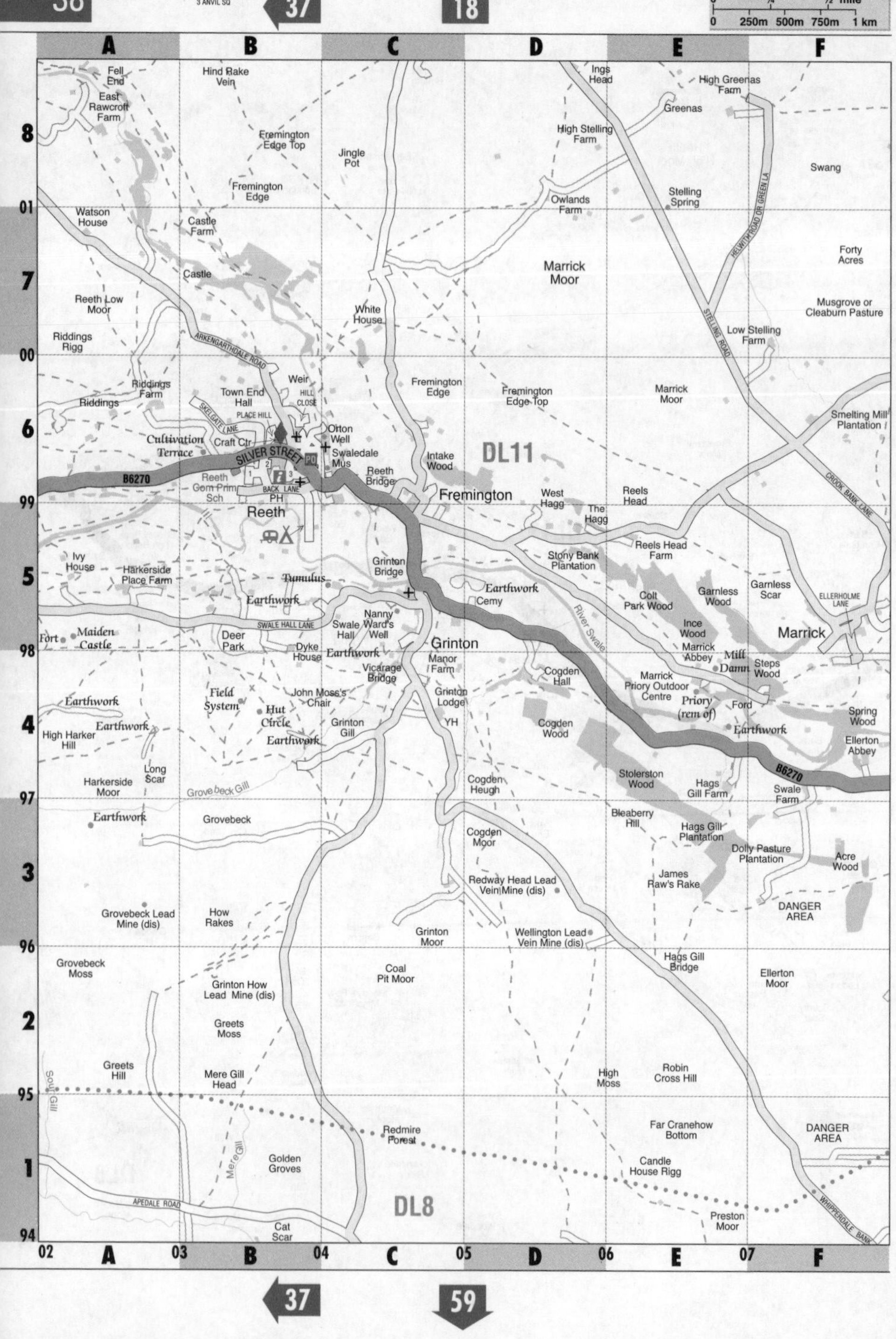

B6
1 QUAKER CL
2 LANGHORNE DR
3 ANVIL SQ
37
18
Scale: 1⅓ inches to 1 mile
0 ¼ ½ mile
0 250m 500m 750m 1 km
A B C D E F
8
01
7
00
6
99
5
98
4
97
3
96
2
95
1
94
02 03 04 05 06 07
Fell End
East Rawcroft Farm
Hind Rake Vein
Fremington Edge Top
Jingle Pot
Fremington Edge
Watson House
Castle Farm
Castle
Reeth Low Moor
Riddings Rigg
ARKENGARTHDALE ROAD
Riddings Farm
Riddings
Town End Hall
PLACE HILL
SKELGATE LANE
Weir
HILL CLOSE
Cultivation Terrace
Craft Ctr
Orton Well
SILVER STREET
PO
Swaledale Mus
B6270
Reeth Com Prim Sch
BACK LANE
PH
Reeth
Reeth Bridge
White House
Fremington Edge
Fremington Edge Top
Intake Wood
DL11
Fremington
Ings Head
High Greenas Farm
Greenas
High Stelling Farm
Owlands Farm
Stelling Spring
HELWITH ROAD OR GREEN LA
Swang
Marrick Moor
Forty Acres
Musgrove or Cleaburn Pasture
STELLING ROAD
Low Stelling Farm
Marrick Moor
Smelting Mill Plantation
CROOK BANK LANE
West Hagg
The Hagg
Reels Head
Reels Head Farm
Stony Bank Plantation
Ivy House
Harkerside Place Farm
Tumulus
Grinton Bridge
Earthwork
Earthwork
Cemy
River Swale
Colt Park Wood
Garnless Wood
Garnless Scar
ELLERHOLME LANE
Marrick
SWALE HALL LANE
Fort
Maiden Castle
Deer Park
Swale Hall
Nanny Ward's Well
Dyke House
Earthwork
Grinton
Manor Farm
Ince Wood
Marrick Abbey
Mill Dam
Steps Wood
Vicarage Bridge
Cogden Hall
Marrick Priory Outdoor Centre
Priory (rem of)
Ford
Earthwork
Field System
John Moss's Chair
Grinton Lodge
Hut Circle
High Harker Hill
Grinton Gill
YH
Cogden Wood
Spring Wood
Ellerton Abbey
Earthwork
Long Scar
Stolerston Wood
Hags Gill Farm
Swale Farm
Harkerside Moor
Grovebeck Gill
Cogden Heugh
Earthwork
Grovebeck
Bleaberry Hill
Hags Gill Plantation
Cogden Moor
Dolly Pasture Plantation
Acre Wood
James Raw's Rake
Redway Head Lead Vein Mine (dis)
DANGER AREA
Grovebeck Lead Mine (dis)
How Rakes
Grinton Moor
Wellington Lead Vein Mine (dis)
Grovebeck Moss
Coal Pit Moor
Hags Gill Bridge
Ellerton Moor
Grinton How Lead Mine (dis)
Greets Moss
Greets Hill
Mere Gill Head
High Moss
Robin Cross Hill
Soul Gill
Redmire Forest
Far Cranehow Bottom
DANGER AREA
Mere Gill
Golden Groves
Candle House Rigg
APEDALE ROAD
DL8
Cat Scar
Preston Moor
WHIPPERDALE BANK
37
59

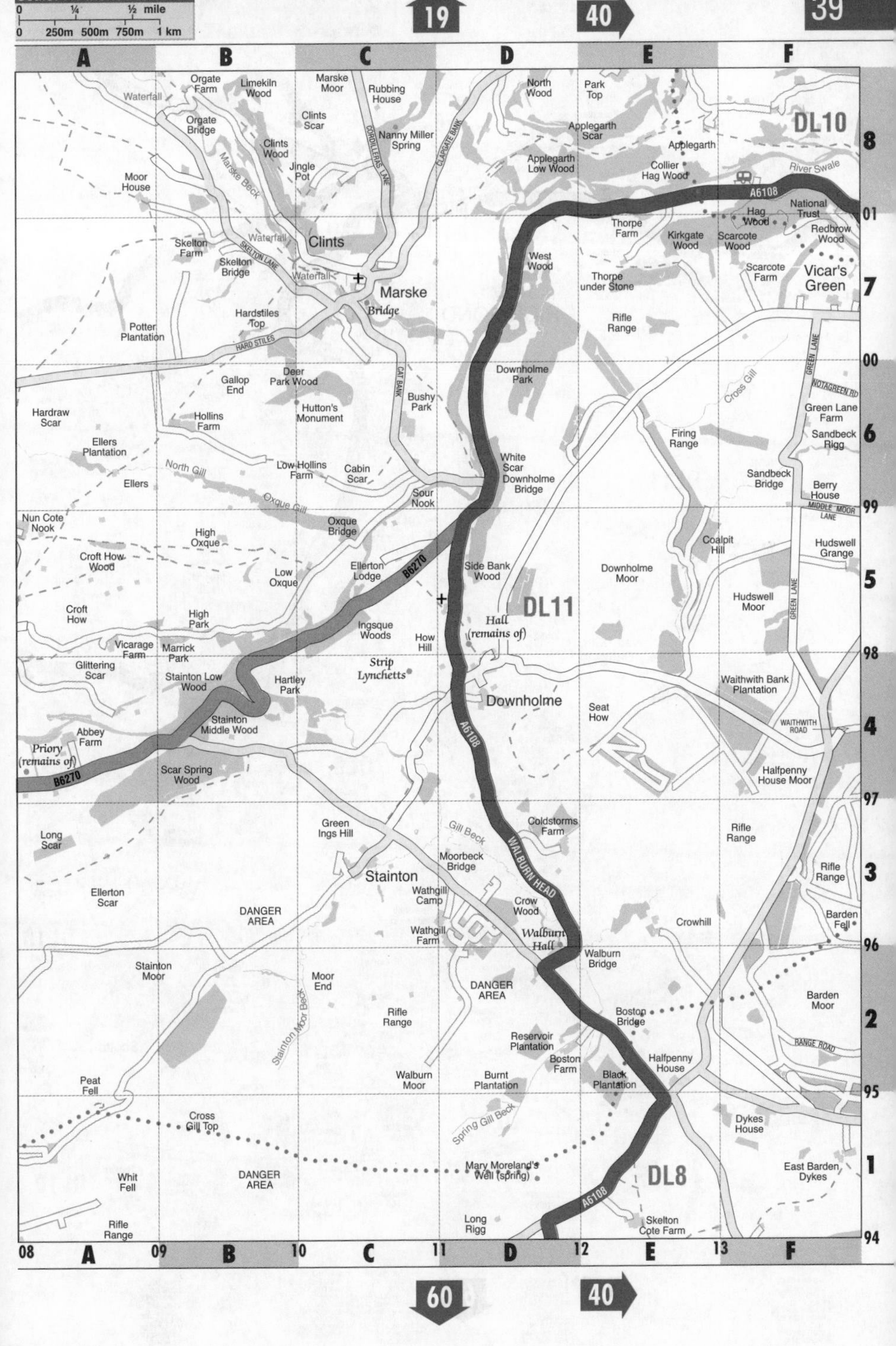

Scale: 1⅓ inches to 1 mile
0 ¼ ½ mile
0 250m 500m 750m 1 km
19
40
A B C D E F
Waterfall
Orgate Farm
Limekiln Wood
Marske Moor
Rubbing House
North Wood
Park Top
Orgate Bridge
Clints Scar
Nanny Miller Spring
CORDILLERAS LANE
CLAPGATE BANK
Applegarth Scar
DL10
Marske Beck
Clints Wood
Applegarth
Applegarth Low Wood
Collier Hag Wood
River Swale
Moor House
Jingle Pot
A6108
National Trust
Hag Wood
Thorpe Farm
Redbrow Wood
Kirkgate Wood
Scarcote Wood
Waterfall
Skelton Farm
Clints
SKELTON LANE
West Wood
Scarcote Farm
Vicar's Green
Skelton Bridge
Waterfall
Thorpe under Stone
Marske
Bridge
Potter Plantation
Hardstiles Top
Rifle Range
HARD STILES
GREEN LANE
CAT BANK
Downholme Park
Cross Gill
Gallop End
Deer Park Wood
NOTAGREEN RD
Hardraw Scar
Bushy Park
Hutton's Monument
Green Lane Farm
Hollins Farm
Firing Range
Sandbeck Rigg
Ellers Plantation
North Gill
White Scar
Downholme Bridge
Low Hollins Farm
Cabin Scar
Sandbeck Bridge
Ellers
Berry House
Sour Nook
Oxque Gill
MIDDLE MOOR LANE
Nun Cote Nook
Oxque Bridge
High Oxque
Coalpit Hill
Hudswell Grange
Croft How Wood
Ellerton Lodge
B6270
Side Bank Wood
Downholme Moor
Low Oxque
DL11
Hudswell Moor
Croft How
High Park
Hall (remains of)
Ingsque Woods
How Hill
Vicarage Farm
Marrick Park
Glittering Scar
Strip Lynchetts
Stainton Low Wood
Hartley Park
Waithwith Bank Plantation
Downholme
Seat How
Stainton Middle Wood
Abbey Farm
A6108
WAITHWITH ROAD
Priory (remains of)
Scar Spring Wood
Halfpenny House Moor
B6270
Green Ings Hill
Coldstorms Farm
Long Scar
Gill Beck
Rifle Range
WALBURN HEAD
Moorbeck Bridge
Stainton
Rifle Range
Ellerton Scar
Wathgill Camp
DANGER AREA
Crow Wood
Crowhill
Wathgill Farm
Walburn Hall
Barden Fell
Stainton Moor
Walburn Bridge
Moor End
DANGER AREA
Barden Moor
Boston Bridge
Rifle Range
Stainton Moor Beck
Reservoir Plantation
RANGE ROAD
Boston Farm
Halfpenny House
Peat Fell
Walburn Moor
Burnt Plantation
Black Plantation
Dykes House
Cross Gill Top
Spring Gill Beck
Mary Moreland's Well (spring)
DL8
East Barden Dykes
Whit Fell
DANGER AREA
A6108
Rifle Range
Long Rigg
Skelton Cote Farm
8
01
7
00
6
99
5
98
4
97
3
96
2
95
1
94
08 09 10 11 12 13
60
40

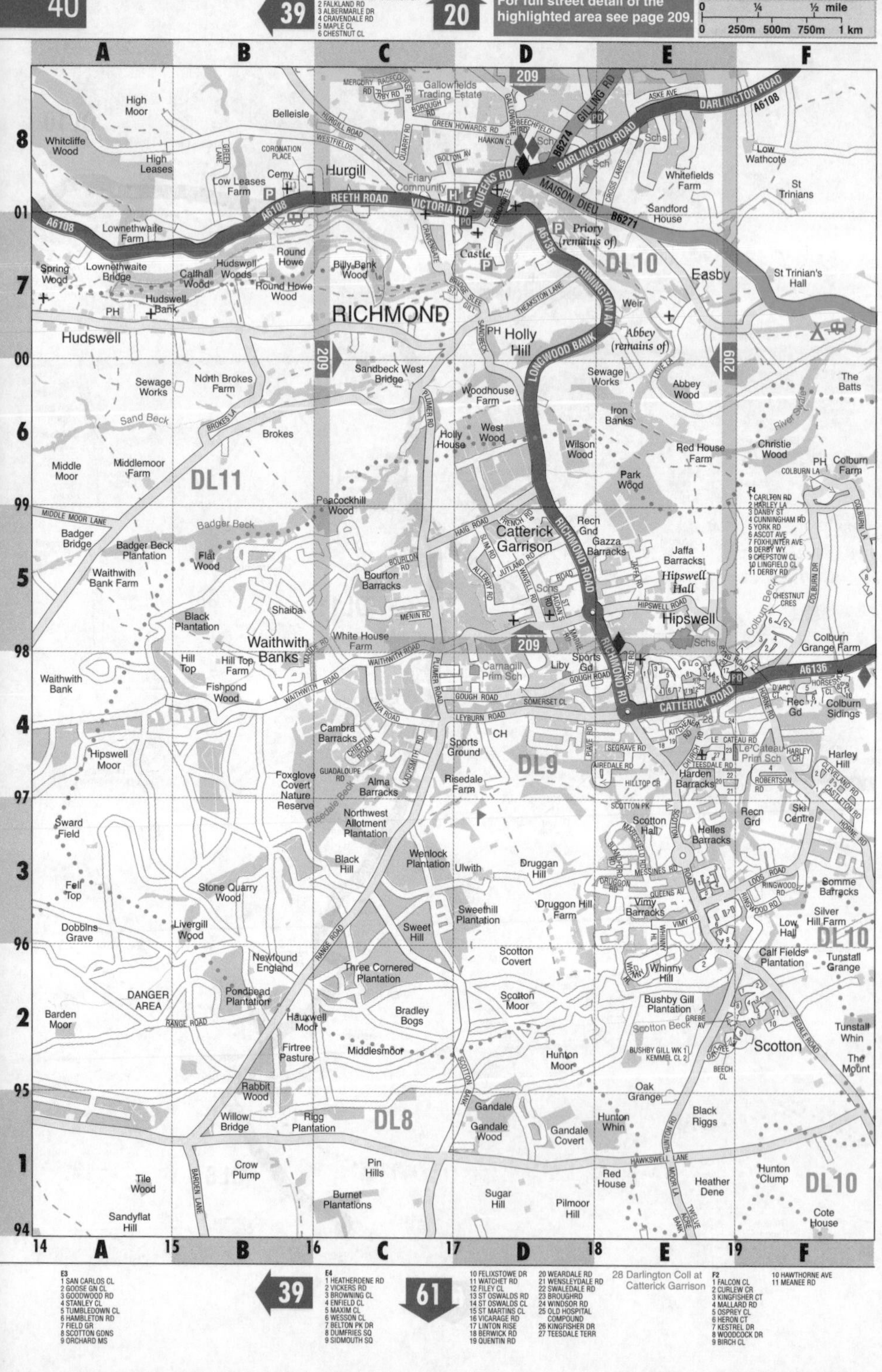

40
39
F5
1 WESTRIDGE CRES
2 FALKLAND RD
3 ALBERMARLE DR
4 CRAVENDALE RD
5 MAPLE CL
6 CHESTNUT CL
7 GRANGE RD
8 MANOR GR
20
For full street detail of the highlighted area see page 209.
Scale: 1⅓ inches to 1 mile
0 ¼ ½ mile
0 250m 500m 750m 1 km
A B C D E F
8
01
7
00
6
99
5
98
4
97
3
96
2
95
1
94
14 15 16 17 18 19
209
High Moor
Whitcliffe Wood
High Leases
Belleisle
HURGILL ROAD
WESTFIELDS
CORONATION PLACE
Low Leases Farm
Cemy
Hurgill
Gallowfields Trading Estate
GREEN HOWARDS RD
QUARRY RD
BOLTON AV
Friary Community
REETH ROAD
VICTORIA RD
QUEENS RD
A6108
A6108
Lownethwaite Farm
Spring Wood
Lownethwaite Bridge
Calfhall Wood
Hudswell Woods
Round Howe
Round Howe Wood
Billy Bank Wood
Castle
Hudswell Bank
PH
Hudswell
RICHMOND
BRIDGE ST
SLEE GILL
THEAKSTON LANE
GILLING RD
ASKE AVE
DARLINGTON ROAD
A6108
B6274
MAISON DIEU
B6271
CROSS LANES
Schs
Sch
Low Wathcote
Whitefields Farm
St Trinians
Sandford House
Priory (remains of)
A6136
RIMINGTON AV
DL10
Easby
St Trinian's Hall
Weir
Abbey (remains of)
Holly Hill
LONGWOOD BANK
Sandbeck West Bridge
Sewage Works
North Brokes Farm
Sand Beck
BROKES LA
Brokes
Sewage Works
Abbey Wood
LOVE LA
The Batts
River Swale
Woodhouse Farm
PLUMER RD
Holly House
West Wood
Iron Banks
Wilson Wood
Red House Farm
Christie Wood
PH
Colburn Farm
COLBURN LA
Middle Moor
Middlemoor Farm
DL11
Park Wood
MIDDLE MOOR LANE
Peacockhill Wood
Badger Beck
Badger Bridge
Badger Beck Plantation
Flat Wood
HAIG ROAD
Catterick Garrison
RICHMOND ROAD
Recn Gnd
Gazza Barracks
Jaffa Barracks
Hipswell Hall
F4
1 CARLTON RD
2 HARLEY LA
3 DANBY ST
4 CUNNINGHAM RD
5 YORK RD
6 ASCOT AVE
7 FOXHUNTER AVE
8 DERBY WY
9 CHEPSTOW CL
10 LINGFIELD CL
11 DERBY RD
Waithwith Bank Farm
Bourton Barracks
BOURLON RD
JUTLAND RD
WAVELL RD
ALLENBY RD
Schs
ST AIDAN'S RD
HIPSWELL ROAD
Hipswell
CHESTNUT CRES
COLBURN DR
Colburn Beck
Black Plantation
Shaiba
MENIN RD
White House Farm
Colburn Grange Farm
Waithwith Banks
Hill Top
Hill Top Farm
WAITHWITH ROAD
Carnagill Prim Sch
Liby
Sports Gd
Schs
Waithwith Bank
Fishpond Wood
GOUGH ROAD
SOMERSET CL
CATTERICK ROAD
A6136
Rec Gd
Colburn Sidings
LEYBURN ROAD
AVA ROAD
Cambra Barracks
CHIEFTAIN ROAD
CH
Sports Ground
KITCHENER RD
LE CATEAU RD
Le Cateau Prim Sch
HARLEY CR
Harley Hill
Hipswell Moor
GUADALOUPE RD
Foxglove Covert Nature Reserve
Alma Barracks
Risedale Farm
DL9
SEGRAVE RD
AIREDALE RD
HILLTOP CR
TEESDALE RD
Harden Barracks
ROBERTSON RD
CLEVELAND RD
CASTLETON RD
Risedale Beck
SCOTTON PK
Sward Field
Northwest Allotment Plantation
Scotton Hall
Helles Barracks
Recn Gnd
Ski Centre
Black Hill
Wenlock Plantation
Ulwith
Druggan Hill
MESSINES RD
LOOS ROAD
RINGWOOD RD
Somme Barracks
Fell Top
Stone Quarry Wood
DRUGGON RD
QUEENS AV
Vimy Barracks
VIMY RD
Dobbins Grave
Livergill Wood
Sweethill Plantation
Druggon Hill Farm
Low Hall
Silver Hill Farm
DL10
Sweet Hill
RANGE ROAD
Newfound England
Three Cornered Plantation
Scotton Covert
WHINNY HL
Whinny Hill
Calf Fields Plantation
Tunstall Grange
DANGER AREA
Pondhead Plantation
Scotton Moor
Bushby Gill Plantation
Barden Moor
RANGE ROAD
Hauxwell Moor
Bradley Bogs
Scotton Beck
GREBE AV
Scotton
RISEDALE ROAD
Tunstall Whin
Firtree Pasture
Middlesmoor
Hunton Moor
BUSHBY GILL WK 1
KEMMEL CL 2
BEECH CL
The Mount
SCOTTON BANK
Rabbit Wood
Oak Grange
Willow Bridge
Rigg Plantation
DL8
Gandale
Gandale Wood
Gandale Covert
Hunton Whin
HUNTON RD
Black Riggs
Crow Plump
Pin Hills
HAWKSWELL LANE
Tile Wood
BARDEN LANE
Red House
MOOR LA
Heather Dene
Hunton Clump
DL10
Burnet Plantations
Sugar Hill
Pilmoor Hill
TWELVE ACRE BANK
Sandyflat Hill
Cote House
E3
1 SAN CARLOS CL
2 GOOSE GN CL
3 GOODWOOD RD
4 STANLEY CL
5 TUMBLEDOWN CL
6 HAMBLETON RD
7 FIELD GR
8 SCOTTON GDNS
9 ORCHARD MS
39
E4
1 HEATHERDENE RD
2 VICKERS RD
3 BROWNING CL
4 ENFIELD CL
5 MAXIM CL
6 WESSON CL
7 BELTON PK DR
8 DUMFRIES SQ
9 SIDMOUTH SQ
61
10 FELIXSTOWE DR
11 WATCHET RD
12 FILEY CL
13 ST OSWALDS RD
14 ST OSWALDS CL
15 ST MARTINS CL
16 VICARAGE RD
17 LINTON RISE
18 BERWICK RD
19 QUENTIN RD
20 WEARDALE RD
21 WENSLEYDALE RD
22 SWALEDALE RD
23 BROUGHRD
24 WINDSOR RD
25 OLD HOSPITAL COMPOUND
26 KINGFISHER DR
27 TEESDALE TERR
28 Darlington Coll at Catterick Garrison
F2
1 FALCON CL
2 CURLEW CR
3 KINGFISHER CT
4 MALLARD RD
5 OSPREY CL
6 HERON CT
7 KESTREL DR
8 WOODCOCK DR
9 BIRCH CL
10 HAWTHORNE AVE
11 MEANEE RD

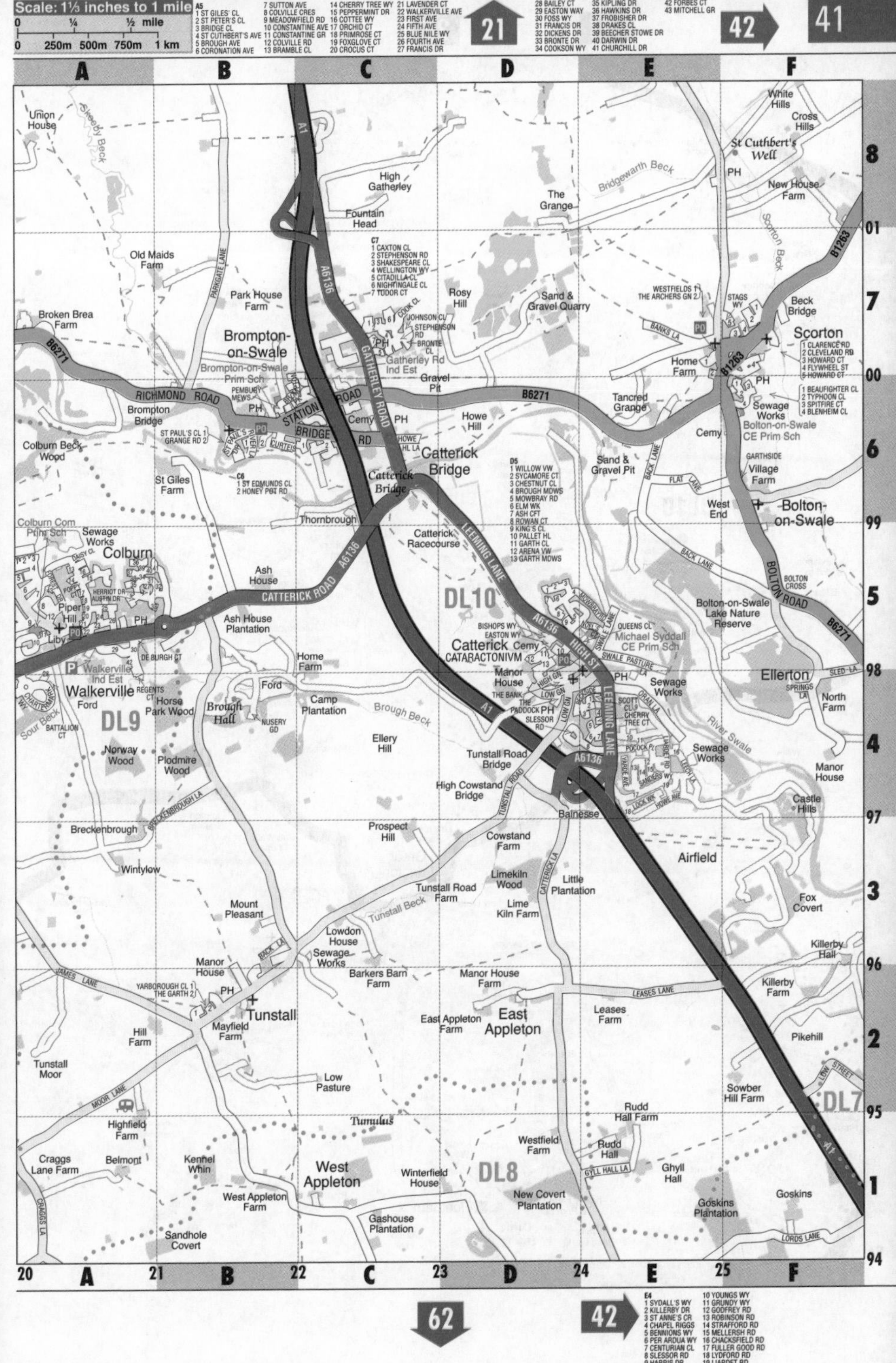

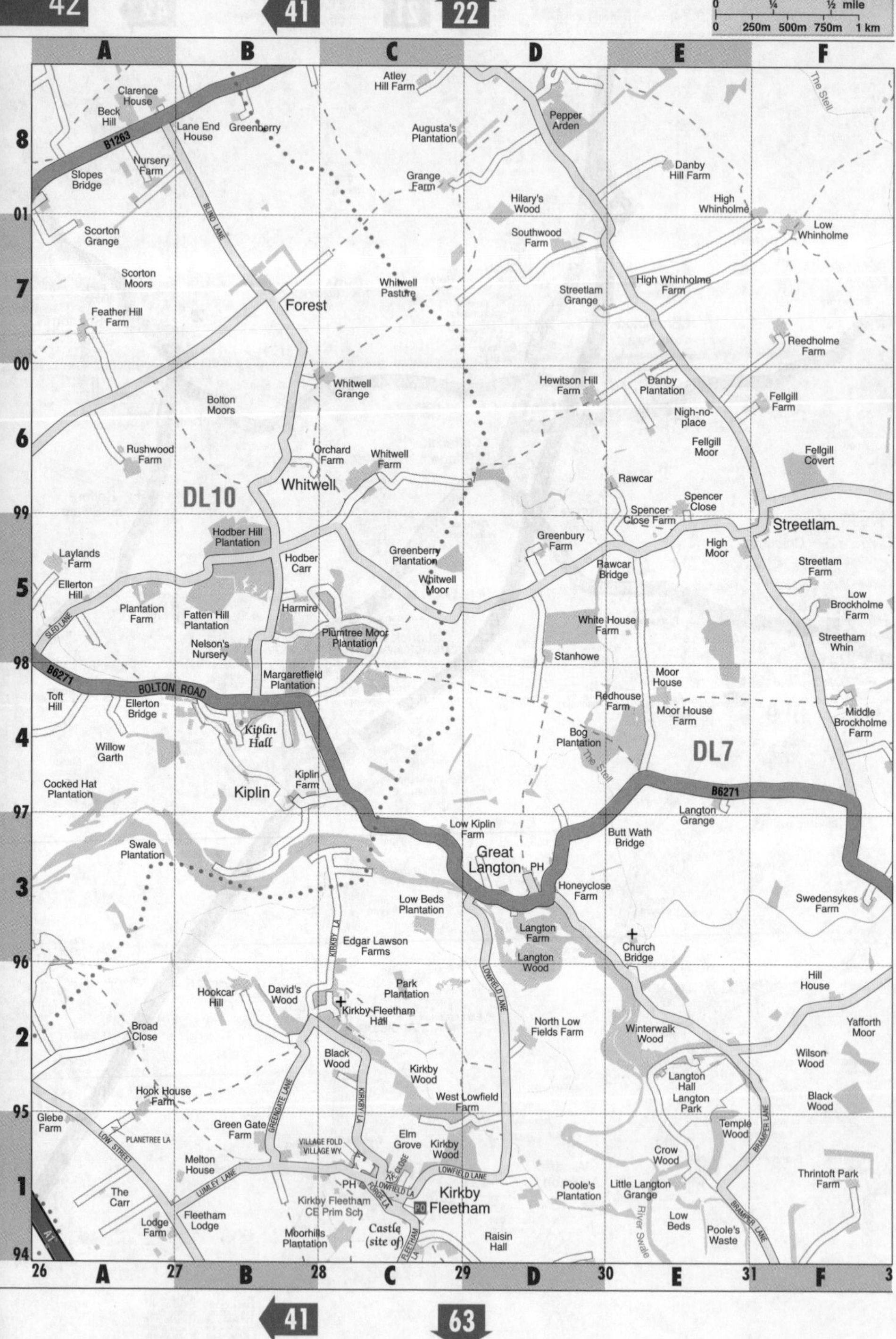

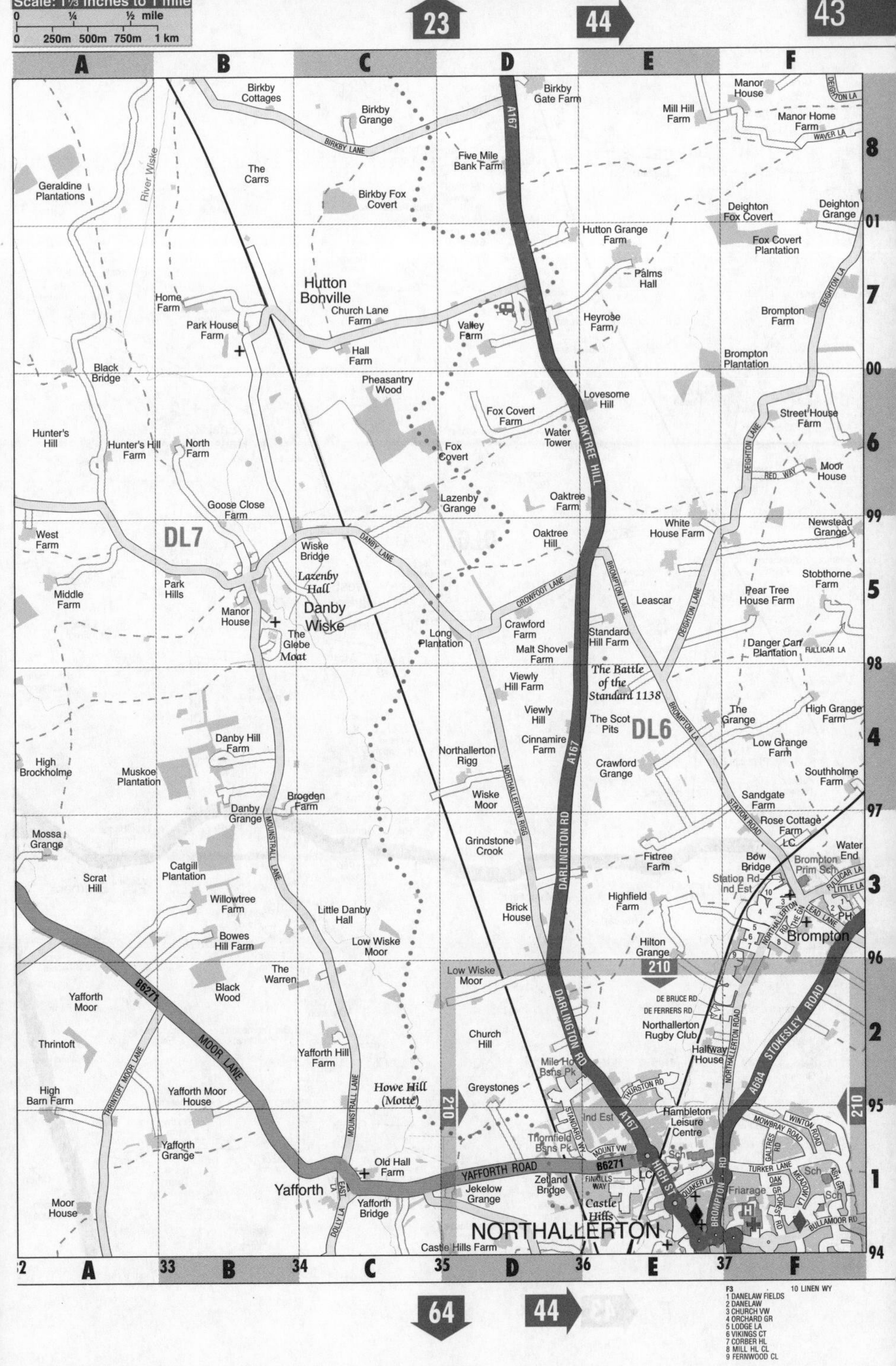
Scale: 1⅓ inches to 1 mile
0 ¼ ½ mile
0 250m 500m 750m 1 km
23
44
A B C D E F
Birkby Cottages
Birkby Grange
BIRKBY LANE
Birkby Gate Farm
A167
Manor House
Mill Hill Farm
Manor Home Farm
DEIGHTON LA
WAVER LA
Geraldine Plantations
River Wiske
The Carrs
Five Mile Bank Farm
Birkby Fox Covert
Deighton Fox Covert
Deighton Grange
Hutton Grange Farm
Fox Covert Plantation
Palms Hall
Hutton Bonville
Home Farm
Church Lane Farm
Park House Farm
Valley Farm
Heyrose Farm
Brompton Farm
DEIGHTON LANE
Hall Farm
Brompton Plantation
Black Bridge
Pheasantry Wood
Lovesome Hill
Fox Covert Farm
Street House Farm
Hunter's Hill
Hunter's Hill Farm
North Farm
Water Tower
OAKTREE HILL
Fox Covert
RED WAY
Moor House
Lazenby Grange
Goose Close Farm
Oaktree Farm
White House Farm
Newstead Grange
West Farm
DL7
Oaktree Hill
DANBY LANE
Wiske Bridge
BROMPTON LANE
Lazenby Hall
Park Hills
Middle Farm
CROWFOOT LANE
Leascar
Stobthorne Farm
Pear Tree House Farm
Danby Wiske
Manor House
The Glebe
Moat
Crawford Farm
Long Plantation
Standard Hill Farm
Danger Carr Plantation
FULLICAR LA
Malt Shovel Farm
Viewly Hill Farm
The Battle of the Standard 1138
BROMPTON LA
Viewly Hill
The Scot Pits
DL6
The Grange
High Grange Farm
Danby Hill Farm
Cinnamire Farm
Low Grange Farm
High Brockholme
Muskoe Plantation
Northallerton Rigg
NORTHALLERTON RIGG
Crawford Grange
Southholme Farm
Brogden Farm
Wiske Moor
DARLINGTON RD
Sandgate Farm
Danby Grange
MOUNSTRALL LANE
STATION ROAD
Rose Cottage Farm
LC
Mossa Grange
Grindstone Crook
Water End
Catgill Plantation
Fitree Farm
Bow Bridge
Brompton Prim Sch
Scrat Hill
Station Rd Ind Est
FULLICAR LA
LITTLE LA
Willowtree Farm
Highfield Farm
Little Danby Hall
Brick House
LEAD LANE
THE GN
PH
Bowes Hill Farm
Low Wiske Moor
Hilton Grange
Brompton
The Warren
Low Wiske Moor
210
Yafforth Moor
B6271
Black Wood
DE BRUCE RD
DE FERRERS RD
STOKESLEY ROAD
Northallerton Rugby Club
MOOR LANE
Church Hill
NORTHALLERTON RD
Thrintoft
THRINTOFT MOOR LANE
Yafforth Hill Farm
Halfway House
A684
Mile Ho Bsns Pk
High Barn Farm
Yafforth Moor House
MOUNSTRALL LANE
Howe Hill (Motte)
Greystones
THURSTON RD
Ind Est
Hambleton Leisure Centre
MOWBRAY ROAD
WINTON ROAD
STANDARD WY
Thornfield Bsns Pk
MOUNT VW
GALTRESS RD
Yafforth Grange
Old Hall Farm
YAFFORTH ROAD
Sch
TURKER LANE
Sch
ASH GR
Yafforth
EAST LA
Yafforth Bridge
Jekelow Grange
Zetland Bridge
FINKILLS WAY
HIGH ST
QUAKER LA
Friarage
OAK GR
FORREST RD
MEADOW LA
Moor House
DOLLY LA
Castle Hills
BROMPTON RD
BULLAMOOR RD
NORTHALLERTON
Castle Hills Farm
8 01 7 00 6 99 5 98 4 97 3 96 2 95 1 94
32 33 34 35 36 37
64
44
F3
1 DANELAW FIELDS
2 DANELAW
3 CHURCH VW
4 ORCHARD GR
5 LODGE LA
6 VIKINGS CT
7 CORBER HL
8 MILL HL CL
9 FERNWOOD CL
10 LINEN WY

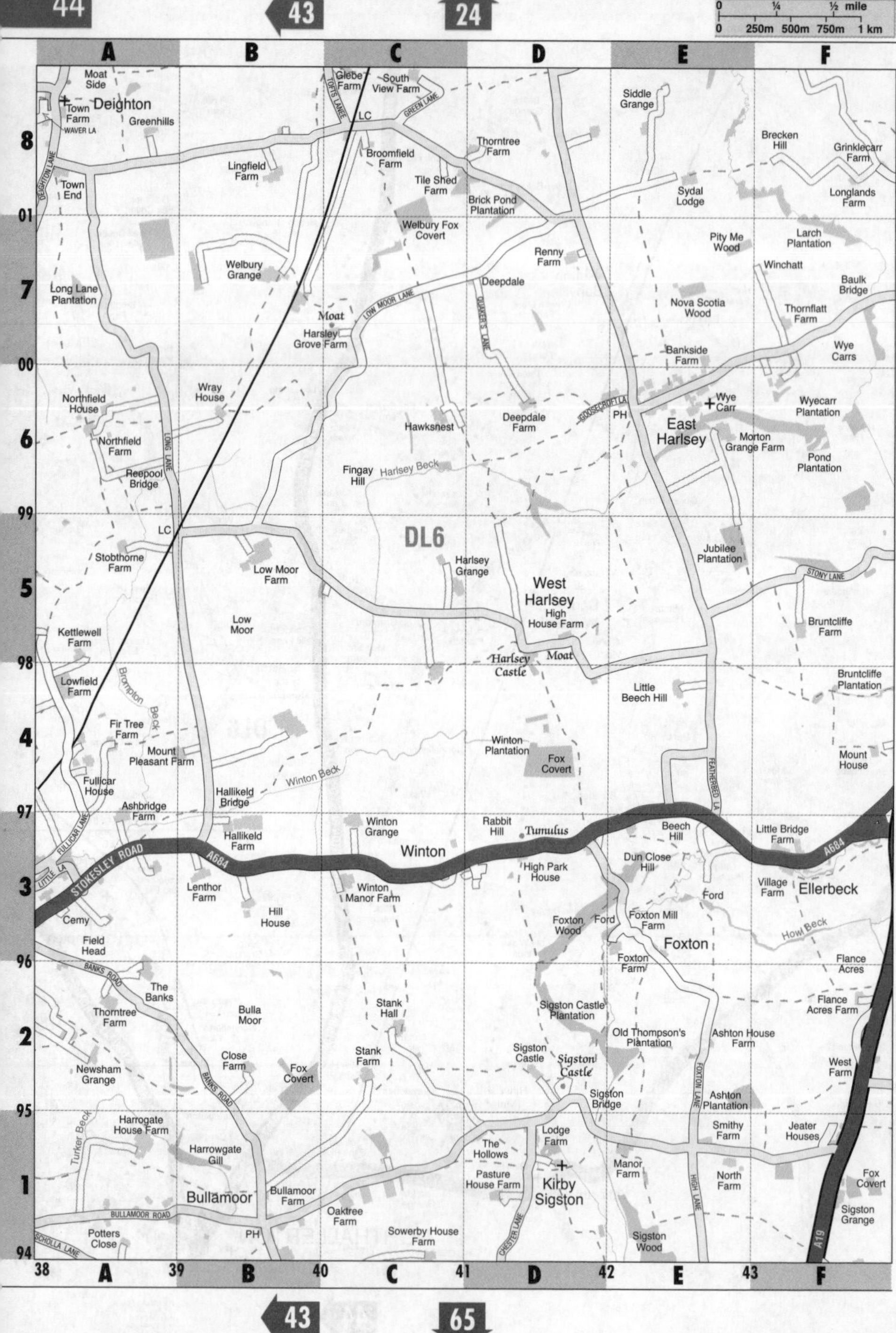

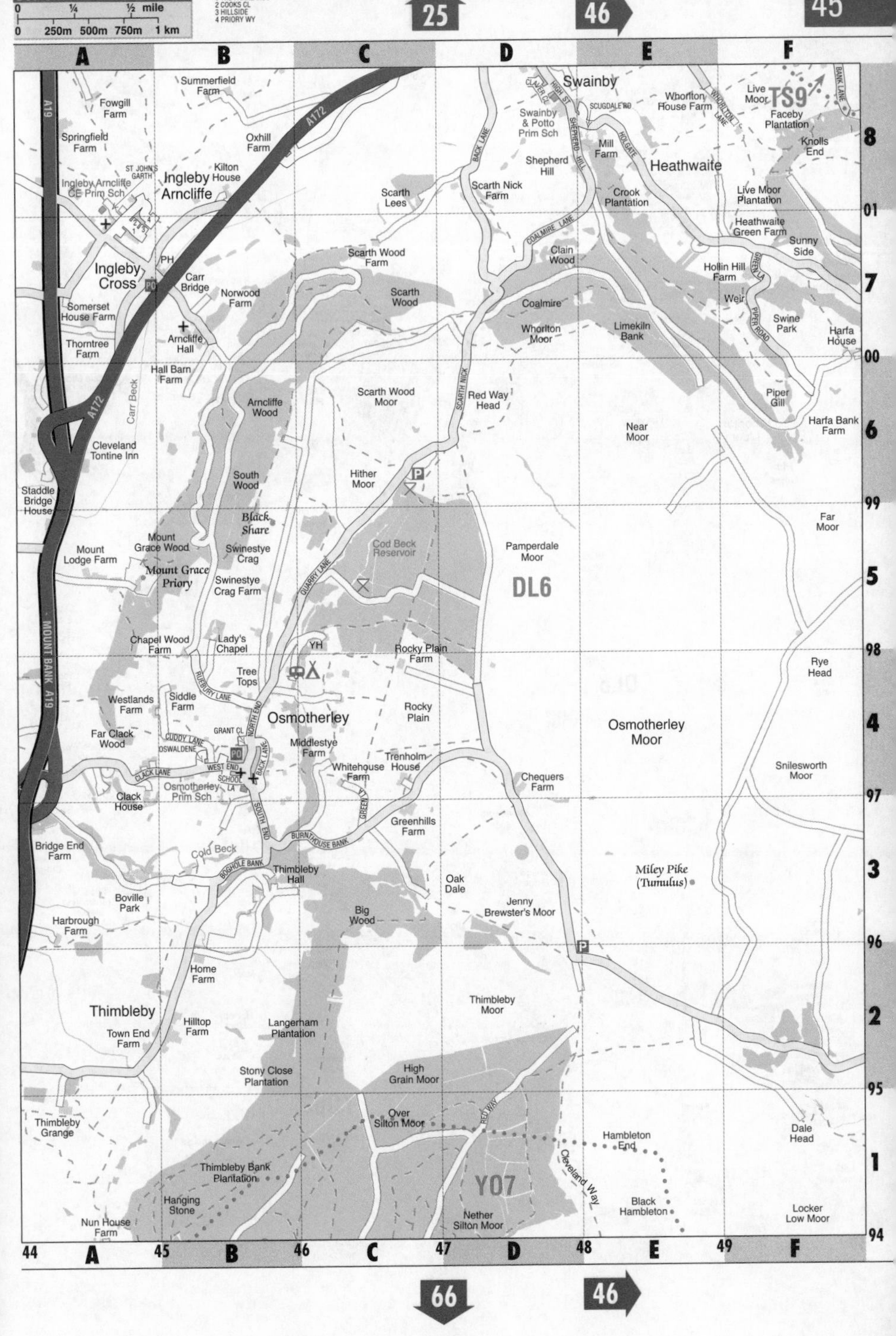
Scale: 1⅓ inches to 1 mile
0 ¼ ½ mile
0 250m 500m 750m 1 km
A7
1 THE PARKLANDS
2 COOKS CL
3 HILLSIDE
4 PRIORY WY
25
46
A B C D E F
Summerfield Farm
Fowgill Farm
Springfield Farm
Oxhill Farm
Kilton House
ST JOHN'S GARTH
Ingleby Arncliffe
Ingleby Arncliffe CE Prim Sch
A19
A172
Swainby
Swainby & Potto Prim Sch
HIGH ST
SHEPHERD HILL
SCUGDALE RD
HOLGATE
BACK LANE
Whorlton House Farm
WHORLTON LANE
Live Moor
TS9
Faceby Plantation
BANK LANE
Knolls End
Mill Farm
Shepherd Hill
Heathwaite
Scarth Nick Farm
Scarth Lees
Crook Plantation
Live Moor Plantation
Heathwaite Green Farm
Sunny Side
COALMIRE LANE
Clain Wood
Hollin Hill Farm
GREEN LA
PIPER ROAD
Weir
Swine Park
Harfa House
PH
Ingleby Cross
PO
Carr Bridge
Norwood Farm
Scarth Wood Farm
Scarth Wood
Coalmire
Whorlton Moor
Limekiln Bank
Somerset House Farm
Thorntree Farm
Arncliffe Hall
Hall Barn Farm
Carr Beck
Arncliffe Wood
Scarth Wood Moor
SCARTH NICK
Red Way Head
Piper Gill
Harfa Bank Farm
Near Moor
Cleveland Tontine Inn
South Wood
Hither Moor
P
Staddle Bridge House
Black Share
Far Moor
Mount Grace Wood
Mount Lodge Farm
Mount Grace Priory
Swinestye Crag
Swinestye Crag Farm
Cod Beck Reservoir
QUARRY LANE
Pamperdale Moor
DL6
MOUNT BANK A19
Chapel Wood Farm
Lady's Chapel
YH
Rocky Plain Farm
Rye Head
Tree Tops
RUEBURY LANE
Westlands Farm
Siddle Farm
NORTH END
Osmotherley
Rocky Plain
Osmotherley Moor
Far Clack Wood
CUDDY LANE
GRANT CL
OSWALDENE
BACK LANE
WEST END
Middlestye Farm
Trenholm House
Whitehouse Farm
Chequers Farm
Snilesworth Moor
CLACK LANE
SCHOOL LA
Osmotherley Prim Sch
Clack House
SOUTH END
GREEN LA
Greenhills Farm
BURNTHOUSE BANK
Bridge End Farm
Cold Beck
BOGHOLE BANK
Thimbleby Hall
Oak Dale
Miley Pike (Tumulus)
Boville Park
Big Wood
Jenny Brewster's Moor
Harbrough Farm
Home Farm
Thimbleby Moor
Thimbleby
Hilltop Farm
Langerham Plantation
Town End Farm
Stony Close Plantation
High Grain Moor
Thimbleby Grange
Over Silton Moor
RED WAY
Hambleton End
Dale Head
Cleveland Way
Thimbleby Bank Plantation
Hanging Stone
YO7
Black Hambleton
Locker Low Moor
Nun House Farm
Nether Silton Moor
8 01 7 00 6 99 5 98 4 97 3 96 2 95 1 94
44 45 46 47 48 49
66
46

45
26

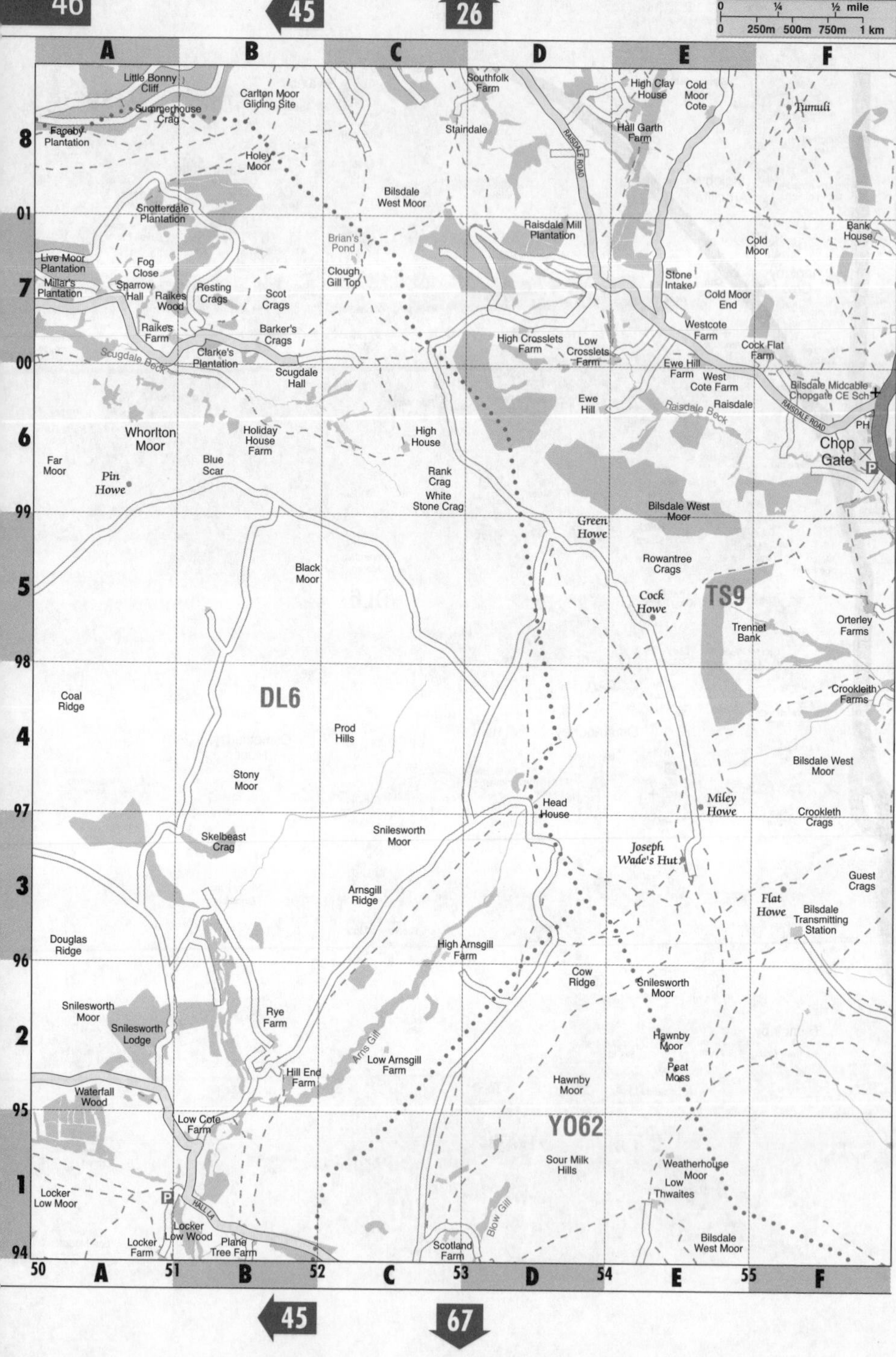
Scale: 1⅓ inches to 1 mile
0 ¼ ½ mile
0 250m 500m 750m 1 km
A B C D E F
8 01 7 00 6 99 5 98 4 97 3 96 2 95 1 94
50 51 52 53 54 55
Little Bonny Cliff
Summerhouse Crag
Faceby Plantation
Carlton Moor Gliding Site
Holey Moor
Southfolk Farm
Staindale
Bilsdale West Moor
High Clay House
Cold Moor Cote
Hall Garth Farm
Tumuli
RAISDALE ROAD
Snotterdale Plantation
Brian's Pond
Raisdale Mill Plantation
Cold Moor
Bank House
Live Moor Plantation
Fog Close
Millar's Plantation
Sparrow Hall
Raikes Wood
Resting Crags
Scot Crags
Clough Gill Top
Stone Intake
Cold Moor End
Raikes Farm
Barker's Crags
Westcote Farm
High Crosslets Farm
Low Crosslets Farm
Cock Flat Farm
Scugdale Beck
Clarke's Plantation
Scugdale Hall
Ewe Hill Farm
West Cote Farm
Bilsdale Midcable Chopgate CE Sch
Ewe Hill
Raisdale Beck
Raisdale
Whorlton Moor
Holiday House Farm
High House
PH
Chop Gate
Far Moor
Blue Scar
Rank Crag
White Stone Crag
Pin Howe
Bilsdale West Moor
Green Howe
Black Moor
Rowantree Crags
Cock Howe
TS9
Trennet Bank
Orterley Farms
Coal Ridge
DL6
Crookleith Farms
Prod Hills
Bilsdale West Moor
Stony Moor
Head House
Miley Howe
Crookleth Crags
Skelbeast Crag
Snilesworth Moor
Joseph Wade's Hut
Arnsgill Ridge
Guest Crags
Flat Howe
Bilsdale Transmitting Station
Douglas Ridge
High Arnsgill Farm
Cow Ridge
Snilesworth Moor
Snilesworth Moor
Snilesworth Lodge
Rye Farm
Hawnby Moor
Arns Gill
Low Arnsgill Farm
Peat Moss
Hill End Farm
Waterfall Wood
Hawnby Moor
Low Cote Farm
YO62
Sour Milk Hills
Weatherhouse Moor
Low Thwaites
Locker Low Moor
HALL LA
Blow Gill
Locker Low Wood
Locker Farm
Plane Tree Farm
Scotland Farm
Bilsdale West Moor

45
67

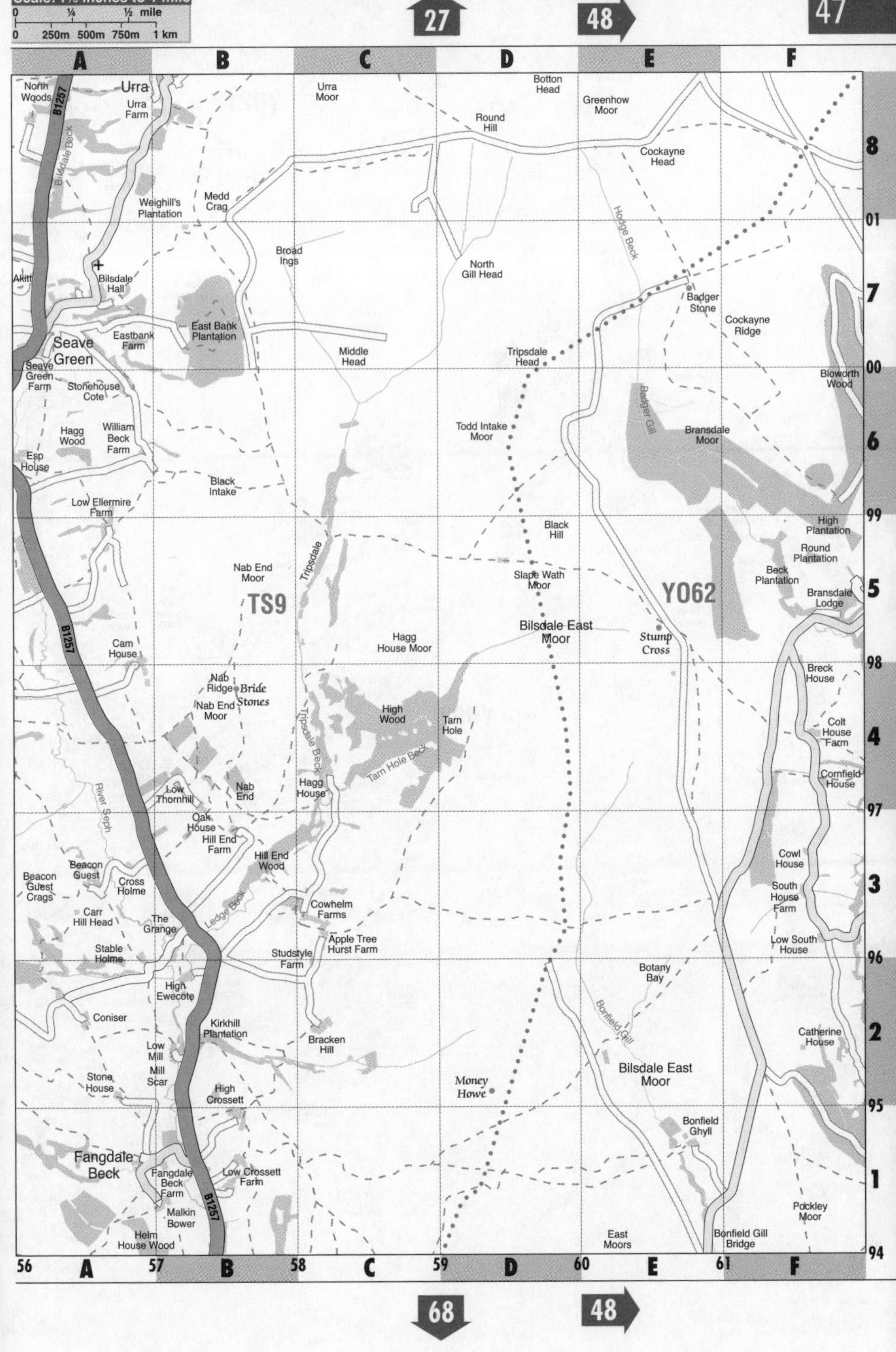
Scale: 1⅓ inches to 1 mile
0 ¼ ½ mile
0 250m 500m 750m 1 km
27
48
A B C D E F
North Woods
Urra
Urra Farm
B1257
Bilsdale Beck
Urra Moor
Botton Head
Greenhow Moor
Round Hill
Cockayne Head
Weighill's Plantation
Medd Crag
Hodge Beck
Broad Ings
North Gill Head
Akitt
Bilsdale Hall
East Bank Plantation
Badger Stone
Cockayne Ridge
Seave Green
Eastbank Farm
Middle Head
Tripsdale Head
Seave Green Farm
Stonehouse Cote
Bloworth Wood
Badger Gill
Hagg Wood
William Beck Farm
Todd Intake Moor
Bransdale Moor
Esp House
Black Intake
Low Ellermire Farm
Black Hill
High Plantation
Round Plantation
Nab End Moor
Tripsdale
Slape Wath Moor
Beck Plantation
Bransdale Lodge
TS9
YO62
Bilsdale East Moor
Cam House
Hagg House Moor
Stump Cross
Nab Ridge
Bride Stones
Nab End Moor
Breck House
High Wood
Tarn Hole
Tripsdale Beck
Tarn Hole Beck
Colt House Farm
River Seph
Low Thornhill
Nab End
Hagg House
Cornfield House
Oak House
Hill End Farm
Hill End Wood
Beacon Guest
Beacon Guest Crags
Cross Holme
Ledge Beck
Cowl House
Cowhelm Farms
South House Farm
Carr Hill Head
The Grange
Apple Tree Hurst Farm
Stable Holme
Studstyle Farm
Low South House
High Ewecote
Botany Bay
Coniser
Bonfield Gill
Kirkhill Plantation
Bracken Hill
Catherine House
Low Mill
Mill Scar
Stone House
Money Howe
Bilsdale East Moor
High Crossett
Bonfield Ghyll
Fangdale Beck
Fangdale Beck Farm
Low Crossett Farm
Malkin Bower
Pockley Moor
Helm House Wood
East Moors
Bonfield Gill Bridge
8
01
7
00
6
99
5
98
4
97
3
96
2
95
1
94
56
57
58
59
60
61
68
48

47
28

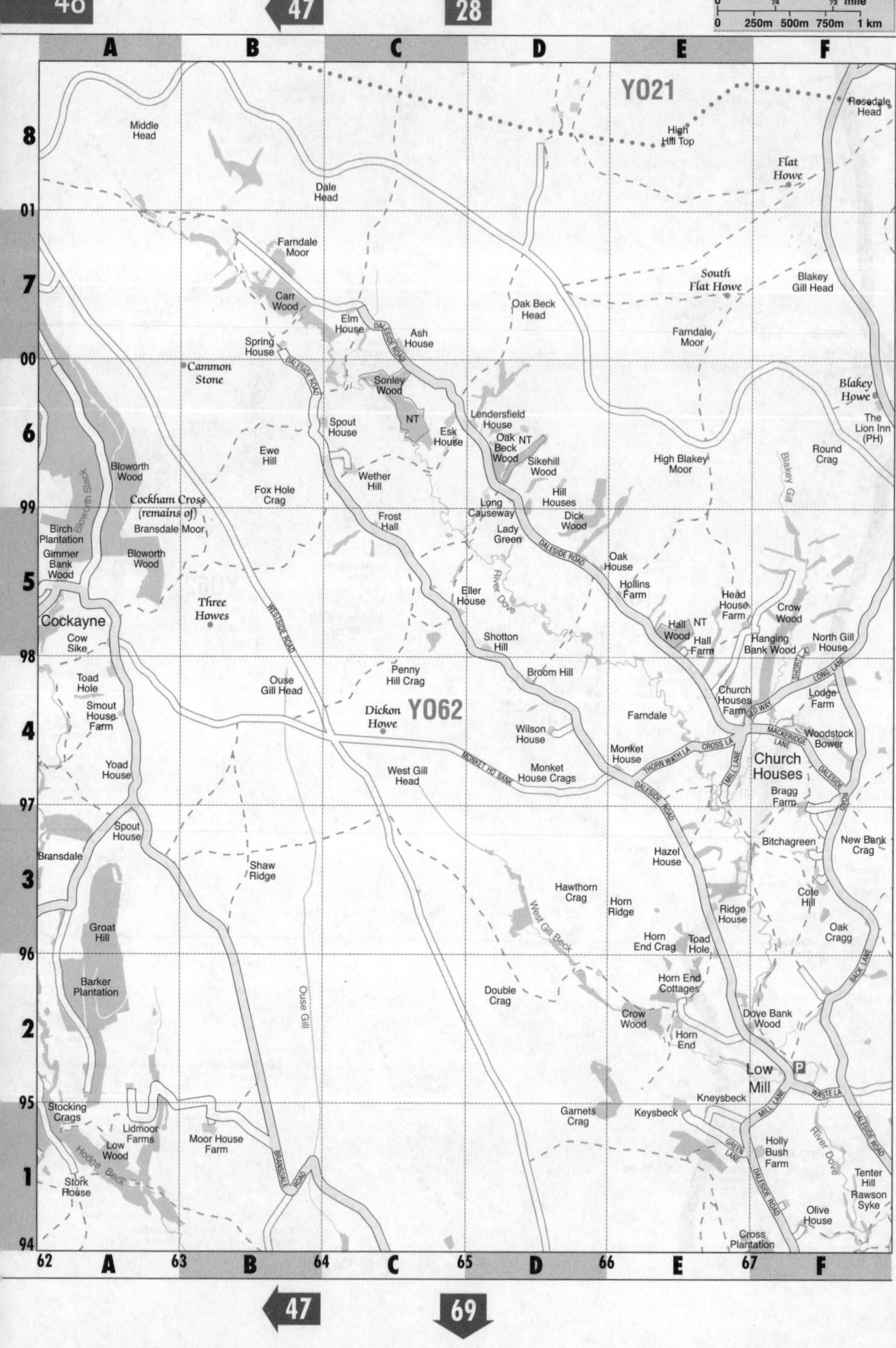
Scale: 1⅓ inches to 1 mile
0 ¼ ½ mile
0 250m 500m 750m 1 km
A
B
C
D
E
F
YO21
Middle Head
High Hill Top
Rosedale Head
Flat Howe
Dale Head
Farndale Moor
South Flat Howe
Blakey Gill Head
Carr Wood
Elm House
Ash House
Oak Beck Head
Farndale Moor
Spring House
DALESIDE ROAD
Cammon Stone
Sonley Wood
Blakey Howe
NT
The Lion Inn (PH)
Spout House
Esk House
Lendersfield House
Oak Beck Wood
Sikehill Wood
Round Crag
Ewe Hill
High Blakey Moor
Blakey Gill
Bloworth Wood
Wether Hill
Bloworth Slack
Cockham Cross (remains of)
Fox Hole Crag
Long Causeway
Hill Houses
Birch Plantation
Bransdale Moor
Frost Hall
Dick Wood
Gimmer Bank Wood
Bloworth Wood
Lady Green
Oak House
Hollins Farm
Head House Farm
Crow Wood
Three Howes
Eller House
River Dove
Cockayne
WESTSIDE ROAD
Hall Wood
Hall Farm
North Gill House
Cow Sike
Shotton Hill
Hanging Bank Wood
Toad Hole
Penny Hill Crag
Broom Hill
LONG LANE
Ouse Gill Head
Lodge Farm
Smout House Farm
Dickon Howe
YO62
Church Houses Farm
RED WAY
Farndale
Woodstock Bower
Wilson House
MACKERIDGE LANE
Monket House
THORN WATH LA
CROSS LA
Church Houses
Yoad House
West Gill Head
MONKET HO BANK
Monket House Crags
MILL LANE
Bragg Farm
Spout House
Bitchagreen
New Bank Crag
Bransdale
Hazel House
Shaw Ridge
Hawthorn Crag
Horn Ridge
Cote Hill
Groat Hill
West Gill Beck
Ridge House
Oak Cragg
Horn End Crag
Toad Hole
BACK LANE
Barker Plantation
Ouse Gill
Double Crag
Horn End Cottages
Crow Wood
Dove Bank Wood
Horn End
Low Mill
P
WASTE LA
Stocking Crags
Kneysbeck
Keysbeck
Garnets Crag
Lidmoor Farms
Moor House Farm
Low Wood
Hodge Beck
BRANSDALE ROAD
GREEN LANE
Holly Bush Farm
River Dove
Stork House
Tenter Hill
Rawson Syke
Olive House
Cross Plantation
8
01
7
00
6
99
5
98
4
97
3
96
2
95
1
94
62
63
64
65
66
67

47
69

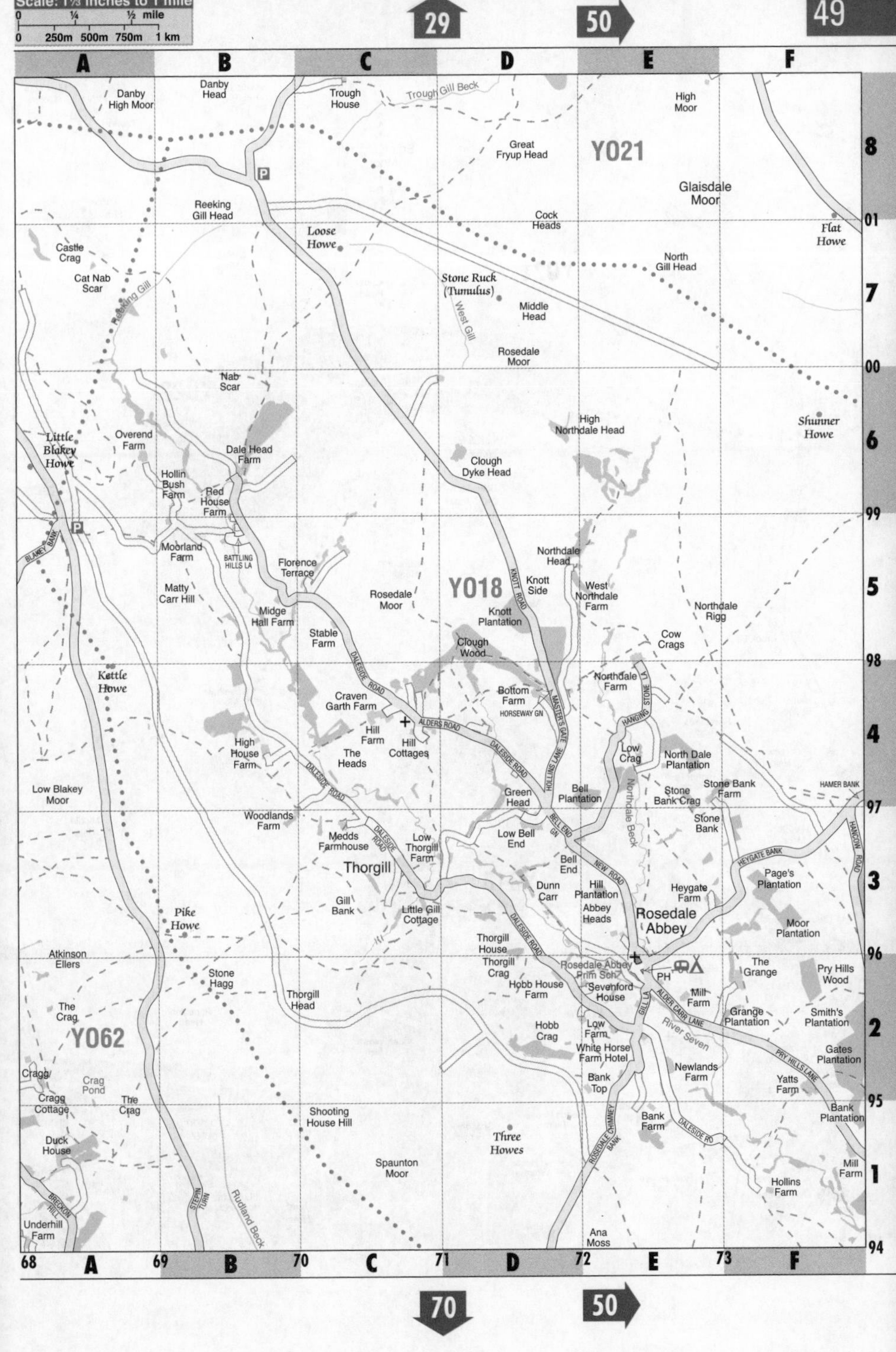
Scale: 1⅓ inches to 1 mile
0 ¼ ½ mile
0 250m 500m 750m 1 km
29
50
A B C D E F
Danby High Moor
Danby Head
Trough House
Trough Gill Beck
High Moor
Great Fryup Head
YO21
Glaisdale Moor
Reeking Gill Head
Cock Heads
Flat Howe
Loose Howe
Castle Crag
Cat Nab Scar
Reeking Gill
North Gill Head
Stone Ruck (Tumulus)
Middle Head
West Gill
Rosedale Moor
Nab Scar
High Northdale Head
Shunner Howe
Little Blakey Howe
Overend Farm
Dale Head Farm
Clough Dyke Head
Hollin Bush Farm
Red House Farm
Blakey Bank
Moorland Farm
Battling Hills La
Florence Terrace
Northdale Head
Knott Road
YO18
Knott Side
West Northdale Farm
Matty Carr Hill
Rosedale Moor
Northdale Rigg
Midge Hall Farm
Knott Plantation
Stable Farm
Clough Wood
Cow Crags
Daleside Road
Kettle Howe
Northdale Farm
Bottom Farm
Horseway Gn
Master's Gate
Craven Garth Farm
Hanging Stone La
Alders Road
Hill Farm
Hill Cottages
High House Farm
The Heads
Low Crag
North Dale Plantation
Hollins Lane
Low Blakey Moor
Green Head
Bell Plantation
Stone Bank Crag
Stone Bank Farm
Hamer Bank
Northdale Beck
Woodlands Farm
Stone Bank
Low Bell End
Bell End Gn
Medds Farmhouse
Low Thorgill Farm
Heygate Bank
Hancow Road
Bell End
New Road
Thorgill
Page's Plantation
Dunn Carr
Hill Plantation
Heygate Farm
Gill Bank
Little Gill Cottage
Abbey Heads
Rosedale Abbey
Pike Howe
Moor Plantation
Thorgill House
Atkinson Ellers
Thorgill Crag
Rosedale Abbey Prim Sch
PH
The Grange
Pry Hills Wood
Stone Hagg
Hobb House Farm
Sevenford House
Mill Farm
Thorgill Head
Alder Carr Lane
Grange Plantation
Smith's Plantation
The Crag
Gill La
River Seven
YO62
Hobb Crag
Low Farm
White Horse Farm Hotel
Gates Plantation
Pry Hills Lane
Cragg
Crag Pond
Newlands Farm
Bank Top
Yatts Farm
Cragg Cottage
The Crag
Shooting House Hill
Bank Farm
Bank Plantation
Rosedale Chimney Bank
Daleside Rd
Duck House
Three Howes
Spaunton Moor
Mill Farm
Hollins Farm
Breckon Hill
Stepin Turn
Rudland Beck
Underhill Farm
Ana Moss
8 01 7 00 6 99 5 98 4 97 3 96 2 95 1 94
68 69 70 71 72 73
70
50

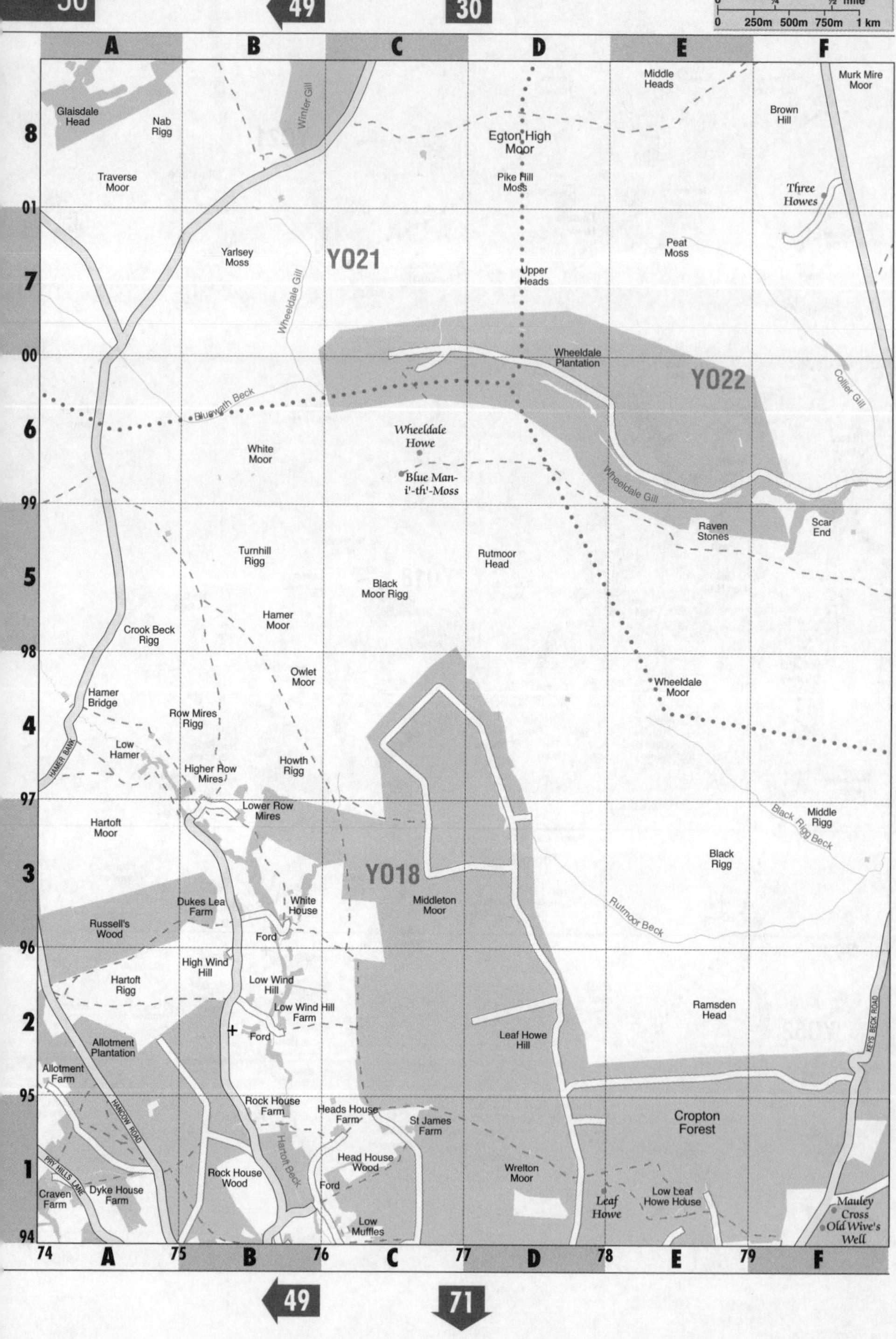

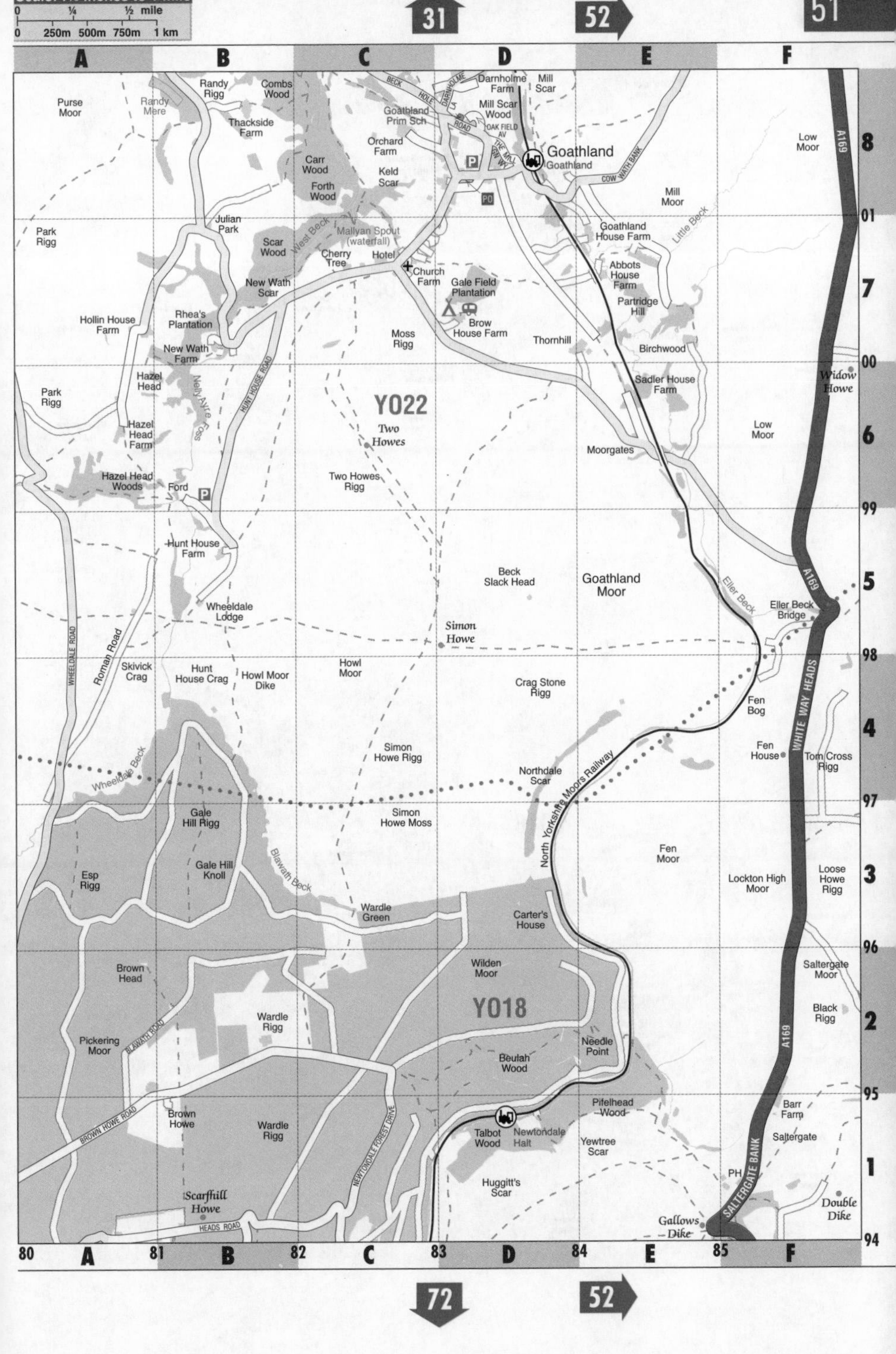
Scale: 1⅓ inches to 1 mile
0 ¼ ½ mile
0 250m 500m 750m 1 km
31
52
A
B
C
D
E
F
Purse Moor
Randy Rigg
Randy Mere
Combs Wood
Thackside Farm
Beck Hole
Darnholme La
Darnholme Farm
Mill Scar
Mill Scar Wood
Goathland Prim Sch
Oak Field Av
Orchard Farm
Carr Wood
Keld Scar
Forth Wood
Goathland
Cow Wath Bank
Low Moor
A169
Mill Moor
Park Rigg
Julian Park
West Beck
Mallyan Spout (waterfall)
Scar Wood
Cherry Tree
Hotel
Church Farm
Goathland House Farm
Little Beck
Abbots House Farm
New Wath Scar
Gale Field Plantation
Partridge Hill
Hollin House Farm
Rhea's Plantation
Brow House Farm
Moss Rigg
Thornhill
Birchwood
New Wath Farm
Hazel Head
Nelly Ayre Foss
Hunt House Road
Sadler House Farm
Widow Howe
Park Rigg
YO22
Hazel Head Farm
Two Howes
Low Moor
Moorgates
Hazel Head Woods
Ford
Two Howes Rigg
Hunt House Farm
Beck Slack Head
Goathland Moor
Eller Beck
Eller Beck Bridge
Wheeldale Lodge
Roman Road
Wheeldale Road
Simon Howe
Skivick Crag
Hunt House Crag
Howl Moor Dike
Howl Moor
Crag Stone Rigg
White Way Heads
Fen Bog
Simon Howe Rigg
Fen House
Tom Cross Rigg
Wheeldale Beck
Northdale Scar
North Yorkshire Moors Railway
Gale Hill Rigg
Simon Howe Moss
Fen Moor
Blawath Beck
Gale Hill Knoll
Esp Rigg
Lockton High Moor
Loose Howe Rigg
Wardle Green
Carter's House
Wilden Moor
Brown Head
Saltergate Moor
YO18
Black Rigg
Wardle Rigg
Pickering Moor
Blawath Road
Needle Point
Beulah Wood
Brown Howe Road
Brown Howe
Pifelhead Wood
Barr Farm
Talbot Wood
Newtondale Halt
Wardle Rigg
Newtondale Forest Drive
Yewtree Scar
Saltergate
Saltergate Bank
PH
Huggitt's Scar
Scarfhill Howe
Double Dike
Heads Road
Gallows Dike
8
01
7
00
6
99
5
98
4
97
3
96
2
95
1
94
80
81
82
83
84
85
72
52

51
32

Scale: 1⅓ inches to 1 mile

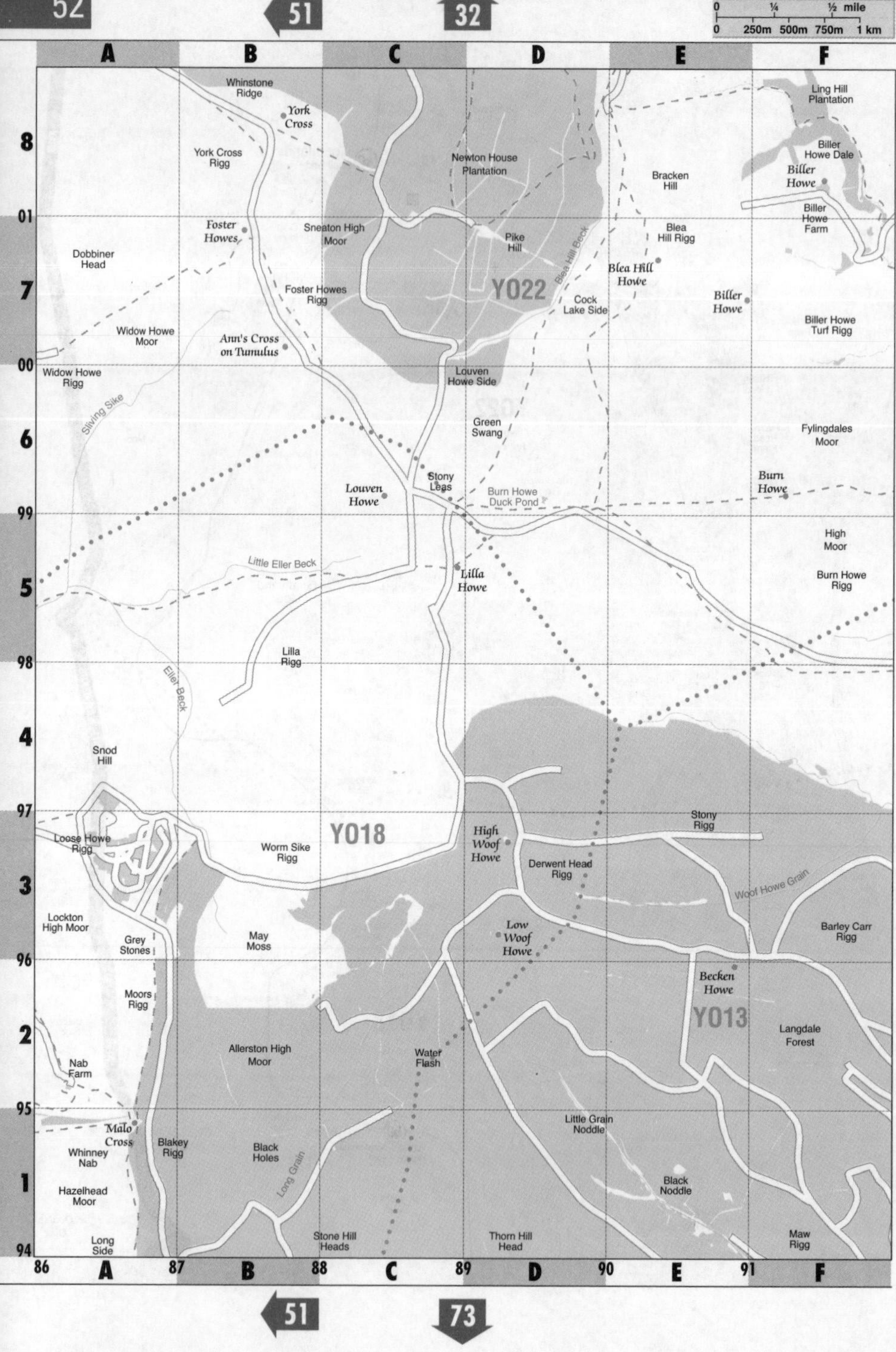
0
¼
½ mile
0
250m
500m
750m
1 km
A
B
C
D
E
F
Whinstone Ridge
York Cross
York Cross Rigg
Newton House Plantation
Ling Hill Plantation
Biller Howe Dale
Biller Howe
Bracken Hill
Biller Howe Farm
Foster Howes
Sneaton High Moor
Pike Hill
Blea Hill Rigg
Dobbiner Head
Blea Hill Beck
Blea Hill Howe
YO22
Foster Howes Rigg
Cock Lake Side
Biller Howe
Biller Howe Turf Rigg
Widow Howe Moor
Ann's Cross on Tumulus
Widow Howe Rigg
Louven Howe Side
Slaving Sike
Green Swang
Fylingdales Moor
Stony Leas
Burn Howe
Louven Howe
Burn Howe Duck Pond
High Moor
Little Eller Beck
Lilla Howe
Burn Howe Rigg
Lilla Rigg
Eller Beck
Snod Hill
Stony Rigg
Loose Howe Rigg
YO18
High Woof Howe
Worm Sike Rigg
Derwent Head Rigg
Woof Howe Grain
Lockton High Moor
May Moss
Low Woof Howe
Barley Carr Rigg
Grey Stones
Becken Howe
Moors Rigg
YO13
Langdale Forest
Allerston High Moor
Water Flash
Nab Farm
Malo Cross
Little Grain Noddle
Blakey Rigg
Black Holes
Whinney Nab
Long Grain
Black Noddle
Hazelhead Moor
Long Side
Stone Hill Heads
Thorn Hill Head
Maw Rigg
8
01
7
00
6
99
5
98
4
97
3
96
2
95
1
94
86
87
88
89
90
91

51
73

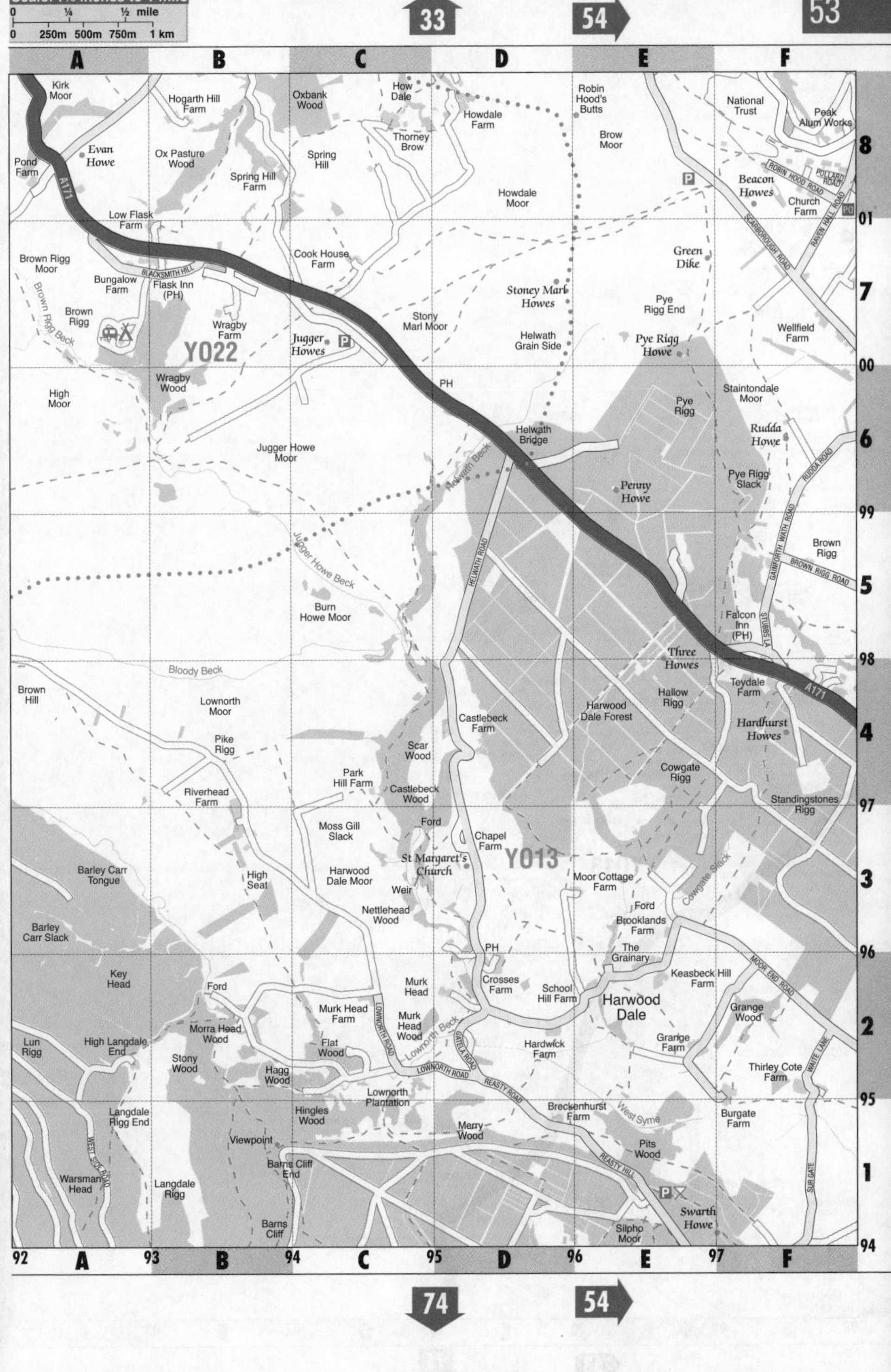
Scale: 1⅓ inches to 1 mile
0 ¼ ½ mile
0 250m 500m 750m 1 km
33
54
A B C D E F
Kirk Moor
Hogarth Hill Farm
Oxbank Wood
How Dale
Robin Hood's Butts
National Trust
Peak Alum Works
Evan Howe
Pond Farm
Ox Pasture Wood
Spring Hill
Thorney Brow
Howdale Farm
Brow Moor
Spring Hill Farm
Howdale Moor
Beacon Howes
ROBIN HOOD ROAD
POLLARD ROAD
Church Farm
RAVEN HALL ROAD
SCARBOROUGH ROAD
A171
Low Flask Farm
Brown Rigg Moor
Cook House Farm
Green Dike
BLACKSMITH HILL
Bungalow Farm
Flask Inn (PH)
Stoney Marl Howes
Brown Rigg Beck
Brown Rigg
Wragby Farm
YO22
Jugger Howes
Stony Marl Moor
Pye Rigg End
Helwath Grain Side
Pye Rigg Howe
Wellfield Farm
High Moor
Wragby Wood
PH
Staintondale Moor
Pye Rigg
Jugger Howe Moor
Helwath Bridge
Rudda Howe
RUDDA ROAD
Helwath Beck
Pye Rigg Slack
Penny Howe
GAINFORTH WATH ROAD
HELWATH ROAD
Jugger Howe Beck
Brown Rigg
BROWN RIGG ROAD
Burn Howe Moor
Falcon Inn (PH)
STUBBS LA
Three Howes
Bloody Beck
Brown Hill
Lownorth Moor
Hallow Rigg
Teydale Farm
Harwood Dale Forest
Castlebeck Farm
Hardhurst Howes
Pike Rigg
Scar Wood
Cowgate Rigg
Park Hill Farm
Riverhead Farm
Castlebeck Wood
Standingstones Rigg
Moss Gill Slack
Ford
Chapel Farm
YO13
St Margaret's Church
Barley Carr Tongue
High Seat
Harwood Dale Moor
Moor Cottage Farm
Cowgate Slack
Weir
Nettlehead Wood
Ford
Brooklands Farm
Barley Carr Slack
PH
The Grainary
Key Head
Ford
Murk Head
Crosses Farm
School Hill Farm
Keasbeck Hill Farm
MOOR END ROAD
Murk Head Farm
Harwood Dale
Grange Wood
Morra Head Wood
Murk Head Wood
Lun Rigg
High Langdale End
Flat Wood
Lownorth Beck
Hardwick Farm
Grange Farm
Stony Wood
LOWNORTH ROAD
GATELA ROAD
REASTY ROAD
Thirley Cote Farm
WAITE LANE
Hagg Wood
Lownorth Plantation
Breckenhurst Farm
West Syme
Burgate Farm
Langdale Rigg End
Hingles Wood
Merry Wood
Viewpoint
Pits Wood
WEST SIDE ROAD
Barns Cliff End
REASTY HILL
Warsman Head
Langdale Rigg
SUR GATE
Swarth Howe
Barns Cliff
Silpho Moor
8
01
7
00
6
99
5
98
4
97
3
96
2
95
1
94
92 93 94 95 96 97
74
54

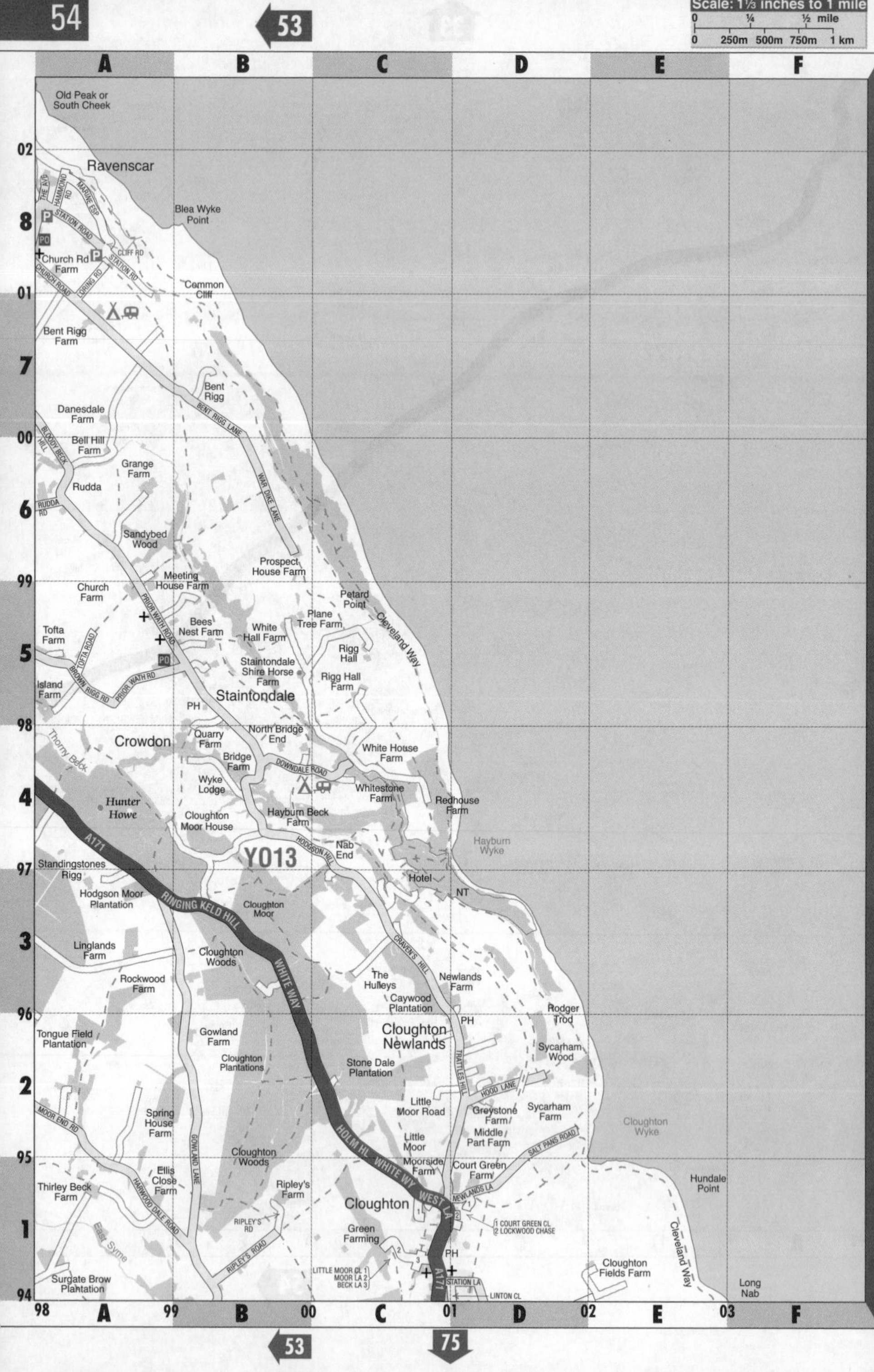
Scale: 1⅓ inches to 1 mile
0 ¼ ½ mile
0 250m 500m 750m 1 km
A B C D E F
Old Peak or South Cheek
Ravenscar
Blea Wyke Point
Church Rd Farm
Common Cliff
Bent Rigg Farm
Bent Rigg
Danesdale Farm
Bell Hill Farm
Grange Farm
Rudda
Sandybed Wood
Prospect House Farm
Meeting House Farm
Church Farm
Petard Point
Plane Tree Farm
Bees Nest Farm
White Hall Farm
Tofta Farm
Rigg Hall
Staintondale Shire Horse Farm
Rigg Hall Farm
Island Farm
Staintondale
Crowdon
North Bridge End
Quarry Farm
Bridge Farm
White House Farm
Wyke Lodge
Whitestone Farm
Hunter Howe
Redhouse Farm
Cloughton Moor House
Hayburn Beck Farm
Hayburn Wyke
YO13
Nab End
Standingstones Rigg
Hotel
NT
Hodgson Moor Plantation
Cloughton Moor
Linglands Farm
Cloughton Woods
The Hulleys
Newlands Farm
Rockwood Farm
Caywood Plantation
Rodger Trod
Tongue Field Plantation
Gowland Farm
Cloughton Newlands
Sycarham Wood
Cloughton Plantations
Stone Dale Plantation
Little Moor Road
Greystone Farm
Sycarham Farm
Spring House Farm
Middle Part Farm
Cloughton Wyke
Little Moor
Cloughton Woods
Moorside Farm
Court Green Farm
Hundale Point
Ellis Close Farm
Thirley Beck Farm
Ripley's Farm
Cloughton
Green Farming
East Syme
Thorny Beck
Surgate Brow Plantation
Cloughton Fields Farm
Long Nab
Cleveland Way
THE AVE
HAMMOND RD
MARINE ESP
STATION ROAD
CLIFF RD
STATION RD
CHURCH ROAD
LORING RD
BENT RIGG LANE
WAR DIKE LANE
BLOODY BECK HILL
RUDDA RD
PRIOR WATH ROAD
TOFTA ROAD
BROWN RIGG RD
PRIOR WATH RD
DOWNDALE ROAD
HODGSON HILL
CRAVEN'S HILL
A171
RINGING KELD HILL
WHITE WAY
TRATTLES HILL
HOOD LANE
SALT PANS ROAD
MOOR END RD
GOWLAND LANE
HARWOOD DALE ROAD
HOLM HL
WHITE WY
WEST LA
NEWLANDS LA
RIPLEY'S RD
RIPLEY'S ROAD
1 COURT GREEN CL
2 LOCKWOOD CHASE
LITTLE MOOR CL 1
MOOR LA 2
BECK LA 3
STATION LA
LINTON CL
PH
P
PO
02
8
01
7
00
6
99
5
98
4
97
3
96
2
95
1
94
98
99
00
01
02
03

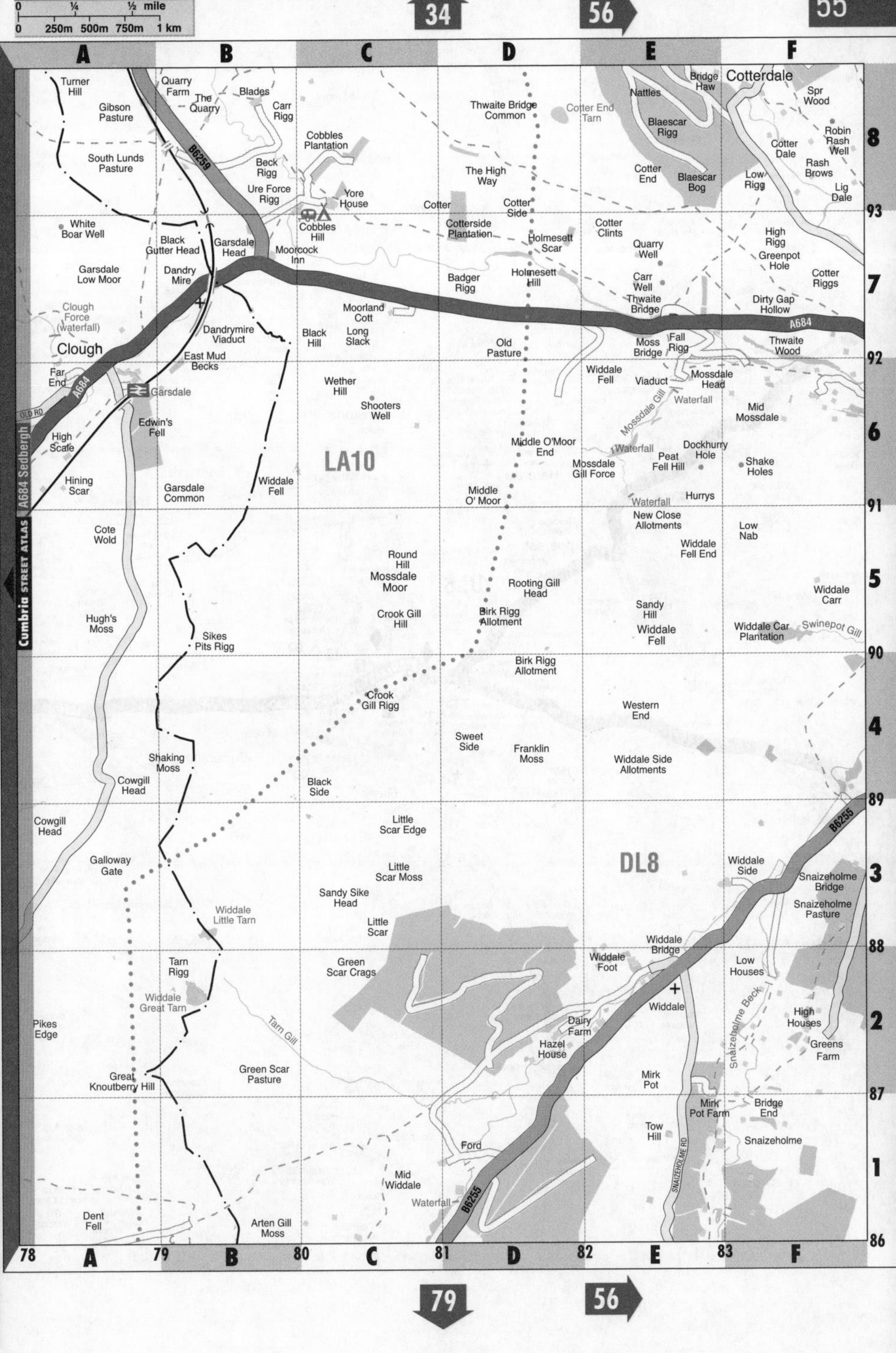
Scale: 1⅓ inches to 1 mile
0 ¼ ½ mile
0 250m 500m 750m 1 km
34
56
A
B
C
D
E
F
Turner Hill
Gibson Pasture
Quarry Farm
The Quarry
Blades
Carr Rigg
Thwaite Bridge Common
Cotter End Tarn
Nattles
Bridge Haw
Cotterdale
Spr Wood
Blaescar Rigg
Robin Rash Well
Cotter Dale
Cobbles Plantation
South Lunds Pasture
B6259
Beck Rigg
Ure Force Rigg
The High Way
Cotter End
Blaescar Bog
Low Rigg
Rash Brows
Lig Dale
Yore House
Cotter
Cotter Side
White Boar Well
Cobbles Hill
Cotterside Plantation
Cotter Clints
High Rigg
Black Gutter Head
Garsdale Head
Holmesett Scar
Quarry Well
Moorcock Inn
Greenpot Hole
Garsdale Low Moor
Dandry Mire
Badger Rigg
Holmesett Hill
Carr Well
Cotter Riggs
Clough Force (waterfall)
Moorland Cott
Thwaite Bridge
Dirty Gap Hollow
A684
Dandrymire Viaduct
Black Hill
Long Slack
Old Pasture
Moss Bridge
Fall Rigg
Thwaite Wood
Clough
East Mud Becks
Widdale Fell
Far End
Wether Hill
Viaduct
Mossdale Head
Garsdale
Shooters Well
Waterfall
Mid Mossdale
Edwin's Fell
Mossdale Gill
High Scale
LA10
Middle O'Moor End
Waterfall
Peat Fell Hill
Dockhurry Hole
Shake Holes
Mossdale Gill Force
Hining Scar
Garsdale Common
Widdale Fell
Middle O' Moor
Hurrys
Waterfall
New Close Allotments
Cote Wold
Low Nab
Widdale Fell End
Round Hill
Mossdale Moor
Rooting Gill Head
Widdale Carr
Crook Gill Hill
Birk Rigg Allotment
Sandy Hill
Hugh's Moss
Widdale Fell
Widdale Car Plantation
Swinepot Gill
Sikes Pits Rigg
Birk Rigg Allotment
Crook Gill Rigg
Western End
Sweet Side
Franklin Moss
Widdale Side Allotments
Shaking Moss
Cowgill Head
Black Side
B6255
Cowgill Head
Little Scar Edge
DL8
Widdale Side
Galloway Gate
Little Scar Moss
Snaizeholme Bridge
Sandy Sike Head
Snaizeholme Pasture
Widdale Little Tarn
Little Scar
Widdale Bridge
Tarn Rigg
Green Scar Crags
Widdale Foot
Low Houses
Widdale Great Tarn
Widdale
Snaizeholme Beck
Pikes Edge
Tarn Gill
Dairy Farm
High Houses
Hazel House
Greens Farm
Great Knoutberry Hill
Green Scar Pasture
Mirk Pot
Mirk Pot Farm
Bridge End
Tow Hill
Ford
Snaizeholme
Mid Widdale
SNAIZEHOLME RD
Dent Fell
Waterfall
Arten Gill Moss
78
79
80
81
82
83
86
87
88
89
90
91
92
93
1
2
3
4
5
6
7
8
A684 Sedbergh
Cumbria STREET ATLAS
OLD RD
79
56

55
35

Scale: 1⅓ inches to 1 mile

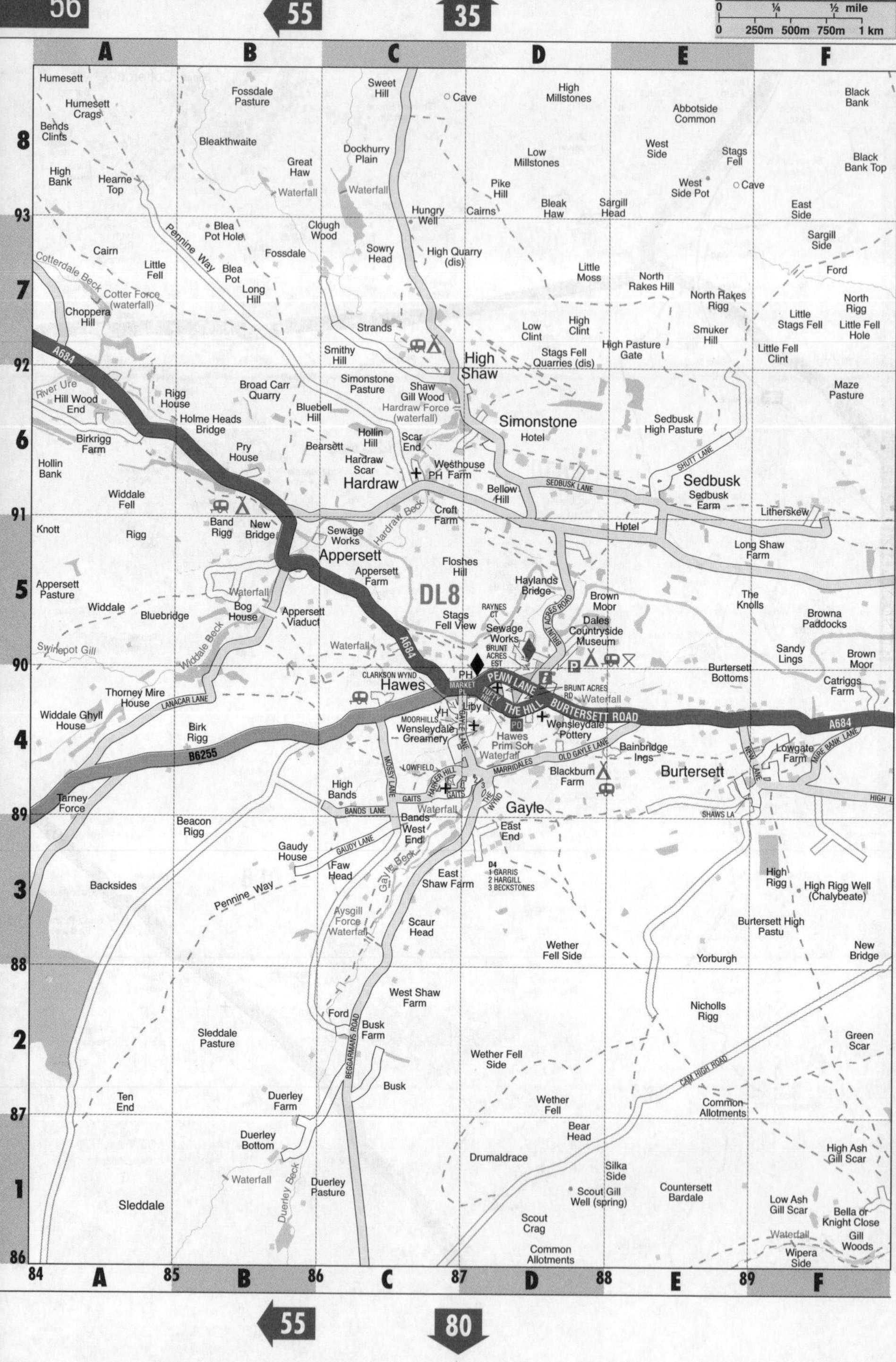
0 ¼ ½ mile
0 250m 500m 750m 1 km
A B C D E F
8 93 7 92 6 91 5 90 4 89 3 88 2 87 1 86
84 85 86 87 88 89
Humesett
Humesett Crags
Bends Clints
High Bank
Hearne Top
Fossdale Pasture
Bleakthwaite
Great Haw
Sweet Hill
Cave
Dockhurry Plain
Waterfall
High Millstones
Low Millstones
Abbotside Common
West Side
Stags Fell
West Side Pot
Cave
Black Bank
Black Bank Top
Pike Hill
Cairns
Hungry Well
Bleak Haw
Sargill Head
East Side
Sargill Side
Blea Pot Hole
Clough Wood
Pennine Way
Fossdale
Sowry Head
High Quarry (dis)
Cairn
Little Fell
Blea Pot
Long Hill
Little Moss
North Rakes Hill
North Rakes Rigg
Ford
North Rigg
Cotterdale Beck
Cotter Force (waterfall)
Choppera Hill
Strands
Low Clint
High Clint
Smuker Hill
Little Stags Fell
Little Fell Hole
A684
Smithy Hill
High Shaw
Stags Fell Quarries (dis)
High Pasture Gate
Little Fell Clint
River Ure
Hill Wood End
Rigg House
Broad Carr Quarry
Simonstone Pasture
Shaw Gill Wood
Maze Pasture
Holme Heads Bridge
Bluebell Hill
Hardraw Force (waterfall)
Simonstone
Sedbusk High Pasture
Birkrigg Farm
Pry House
Bearsett
Hollin Hill
Scar End
Hotel
Shutt Lane
Hollin Bank
Hardraw Scar
PH
Westhouse Farm
Sedbusk
Hardraw
Sedbusk Lane
Sedbusk Farm
Widdale Fell
Bellow Hill
Hardraw Beck
Croft Farm
Litherskew
Knott
Band Rigg
New Bridge
Rigg
Sewage Works
Hotel
Long Shaw Farm
Appersett
Floshes Hill
Appersett Farm
Haylands Bridge
Brunt Acres Road
DL8
Appersett Pasture
Waterfall
Brown Moor
The Knolls
Widdale
Bluebridge
Bog House
Appersett Viaduct
Raynes Ct
Stags Fell View
Sewage Works
Dales Countryside Museum
Browna Paddocks
Swinepot Gill
Widdale Beck
Waterfall
Brunt Acres Est
Sandy Lings
Brown Moor
Clarkson Wynd
PH
Penn Lane
Brunt Acres Rd
Burtersett Bottoms
Thorney Mire House
Hawes
Market Pl
Tufty Hill
The Hill
Waterfall
Burtersett Road
Catriggs Farm
Lanacar Lane
Liby
YH
Wensleydale Pottery
Widdale Ghyll House
Moorhills
Wensleydale Creamery
Gayle Lane
PO
Birk Rigg
Hawes Prim Sch
Waterfall
Old Gayle Lane
Bainbridge Ings
New Lane
Lowgate Farm
Mire Bank Lane
B6255
Mossy Lane
Lowfield
Harker Hill
Marridales
Blackburn Farm
Burtersett
Tarney Force
High Bands
Gaits
Gayle
Shaws La
High La
Bands Lane
Waterfall
Bands West End
East End
Beacon Rigg
Gaudy House
Gaudy Lane
Faw Head
Gayle Beck
D4
1 Garris
2 Hargill
3 Beckstones
The Wynd
Backsides
Pennine Way
East Shaw Farm
High Rigg
High Rigg Well (Chalybeate)
Aysgill Force Waterfall
Scaur Head
Burtersett High Pastu
Wether Fell Side
New Bridge
Yorburgh
West Shaw Farm
Ford
Nicholls Rigg
Beggarmans Road
Busk Farm
Sleddale Pasture
Green Scar
Wether Fell Side
Cam High Road
Busk
Ten End
Duerley Farm
Wether Fell
Common Allotments
Bear Head
Duerley Bottom
Drumaldrace
High Ash Gill Scar
Silka Side
Waterfall
Duerley Beck
Duerley Pasture
Scout Gill Well (spring)
Countersett Bardale
Sleddale
Low Ash Gill Scar
Bella or Knight Close
Scout Crag
Gill Woods
Waterfall
Common Allotments
Wipera Side

55
80

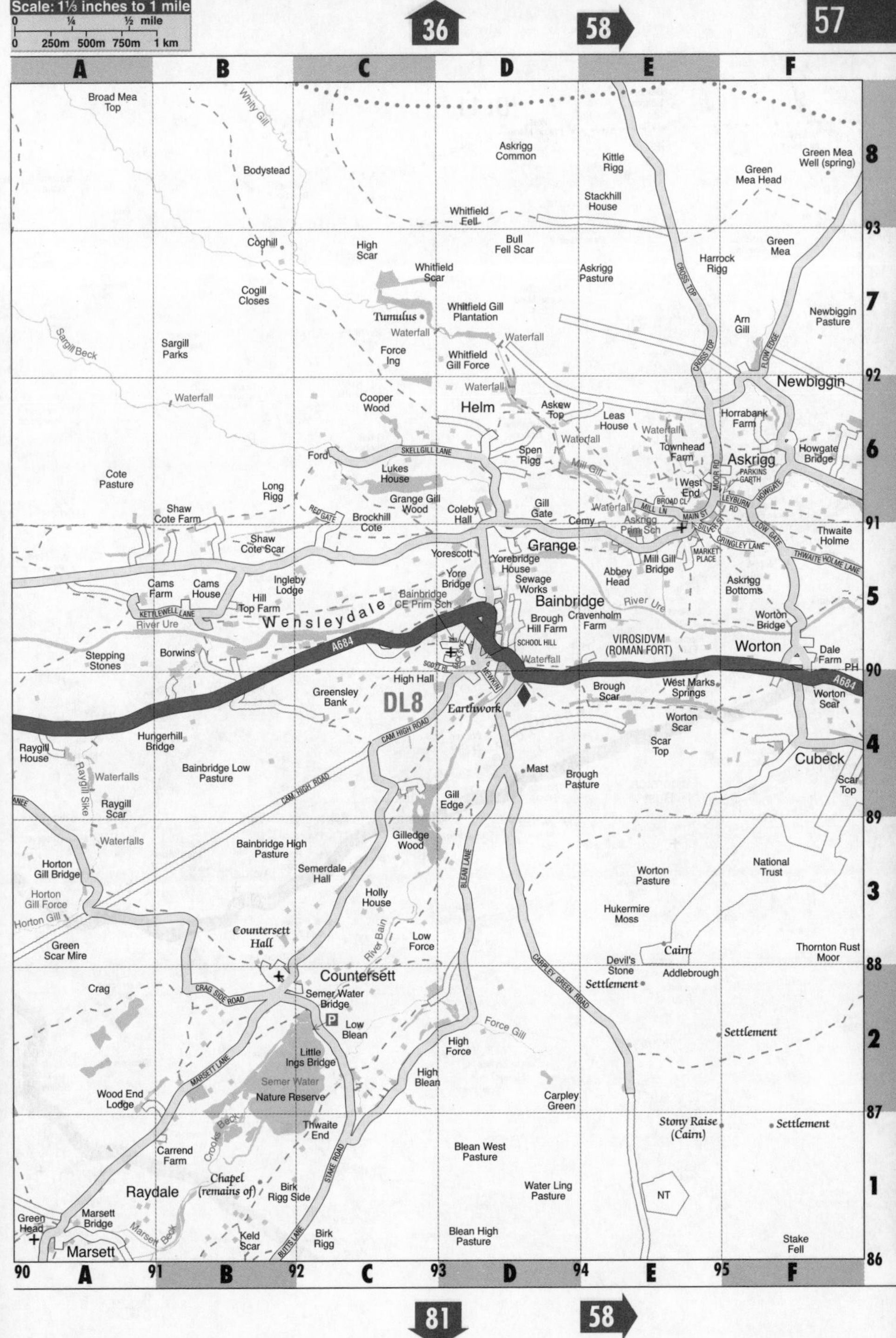
Scale: 1⅓ inches to 1 mile
0 ¼ ½ mile
0 250m 500m 750m 1 km
36
58
A B C D E F
8
93
7
92
6
91
5
90
4
89
3
88
2
87
1
86
Broad Mea Top
Whity Gill
Askrigg Common
Kittle Rigg
Green Mea Well (spring)
Green Mea Head
Bodystead
Stackhill House
Whitfield Fell
Bull Fell Scar
Coghill
High Scar
Green Mea
Harrock Rigg
Whitfield Scar
Askrigg Pasture
Cross Top
Cogill Closes
Tumulus
Whitfield Gill Plantation
Newbiggin Pasture
Arn Gill
Waterfall
Sargill Beck
Sargill Parks
Force Ing
Whitfield Gill Force
Flow Edge
Newbiggin
Waterfall
Cooper Wood
Helm
Askew Top
Leas House
Horrabank Farm
Skellgill Lane
Spen Rigg
Mill Gill
Townhead Farm
Askrigg
Howgate Bridge
Ford
Lukes House
Moor Rd
Parkins Garth
Cote Pasture
Long Rigg
Grange Gill Wood
Coleby Hall
Gill Gate
West End
Broad Cl
Mill Ln
Main St
Leyburn Rd
Howgate
Shaw Cote Farm
Red Gate
Brockhill Cote
Cemy
Askrigg Prim Sch
Silver St
Low Gate
Thwaite Holme
Shaw Cote Scar
Grange
Cringley Lane
Yorescott
Yorebridge House
Mill Gill Bridge
Market Place
Thwaite Holme Lane
Cams Farm
Cams House
Ingleby Lodge
Yore Bridge
Sewage Works
Abbey Head
Askrigg Bottoms
Kettlewell Lane
Hill Top Farm
Bainbridge CE Prim Sch
Bainbridge
River Ure
Wensleydale
Brough Hill Farm
Cravenholm Farm
Worton Bridge
School Hill
Virosidvm (Roman Fort)
Worton
Dale Farm
PH
Stepping Stones
Borwins
A684
Waterfall
Scott Pl
Newkin
High Hall
Brough Scar
West Marks Springs
Worton Scar
Greensley Bank
DL8
Earthwork
Worton Scar
Cam High Road
Scar Top
Raygill House
Hungerhill Bridge
Cubeck
Bainbridge Low Pasture
Mast
Brough Pasture
Scar Top
Raygill Sike
Waterfalls
Raygill Scar
Gill Edge
Waterfalls
Bainbridge High Pasture
Gilledge Wood
Blean Lane
National Trust
Horton Gill Bridge
Semerdale Hall
Worton Pasture
Horton Gill Force
Holly House
Hukermire Moss
Horton Gill
Countersett Hall
Low Force
River Bain
Cairn
Thornton Rust Moor
Green Scar Mire
Devil's Stone
Addlebrough
Countersett
Settlement
Crag
Carpley Green Road
Crag Side Road
Semer Water Bridge
Low Blean
Force Gill
Settlement
Little Ings Bridge
High Force
Marsett Lane
Semer Water
High Blean
Wood End Lodge
Nature Reserve
Carpley Green
Thwaite End
Stony Raise (Cairn)
Settlement
Crooks Beck
Carrend Farm
Stake Road
Blean West Pasture
Chapel (remains of)
Raydale
Birk Rigg Side
Water Ling Pasture
NT
Green Head
Marsett Bridge
Marsett Beck
Keld Scar
Butts Lane
Birk Rigg
Blean High Pasture
Stake Fell
Marsett
90 91 92 93 94 95
81
58

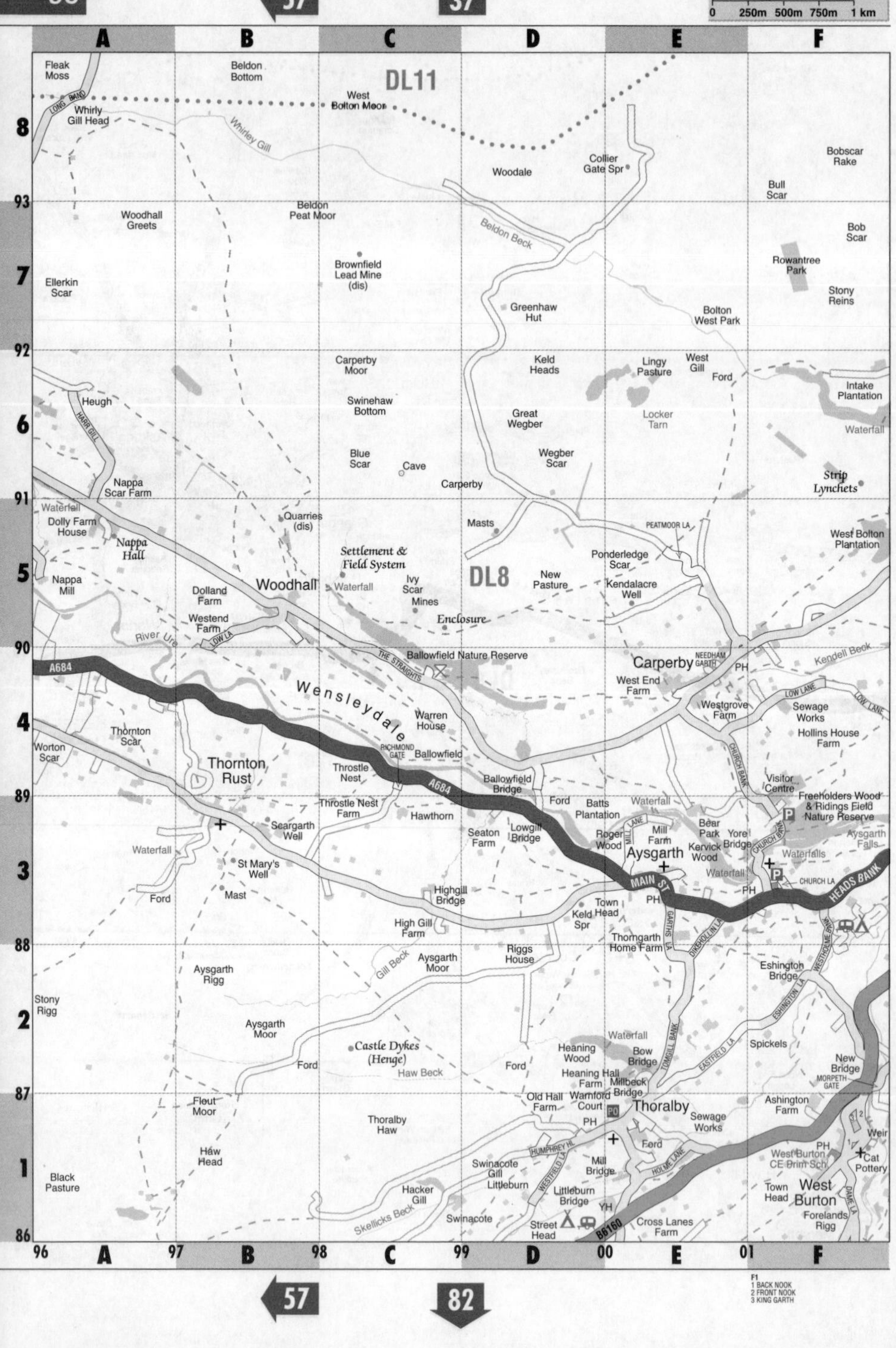

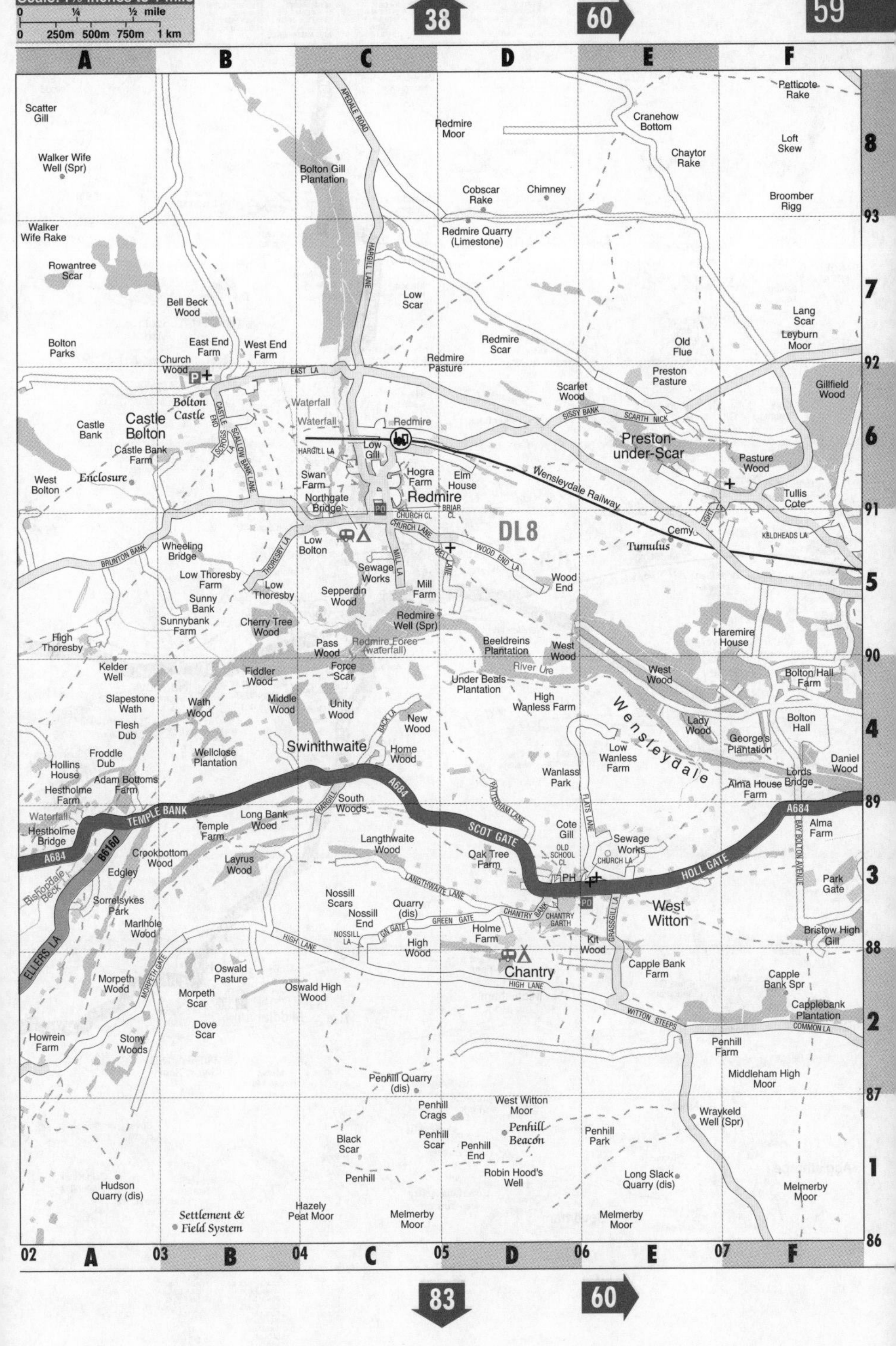
Scale: 1⅓ inches to 1 mile
38
60
83
60
Scatter Gill
Walker Wife Well (Spr)
Walker Wife Rake
Rowantree Scar
Bell Beck Wood
Bolton Parks
East End Farm
West End Farm
Church Wood
Bolton Castle
Castle Bolton
Castle Bank
Castle Bank Farm
West Bolton
Enclosure
Bolton Gill Plantation
Redmire Moor
Cobscar Rake
Chimney
Redmire Quarry (Limestone)
Low Scar
Redmire Scar
Redmire Pasture
Cranehow Bottom
Chaytor Rake
Petticote Rake
Loft Skew
Broomber Rigg
Lang Scar
Leyburn Moor
Old Flue
Preston Pasture
Gillfield Wood
Scarlet Wood
Preston-under-Scar
Pasture Wood
Tullis Cote
Waterfall
Redmire
Low Gill
Swan Farm
Hogra Farm
Elm House
Northgate Bridge
Wensleydale Railway
DL8
Cemy
Tumulus
Low Bolton
Wheeling Bridge
Low Thoresby Farm
Low Thoresby
Sunny Bank
Sunnybank Farm
Sewage Works
Sepperdin Wood
Mill Farm
Wood End
Cherry Tree Wood
Redmire Well (Spr)
Redmire Force (waterfall)
Pass Wood
Beeldreins Plantation
West Wood
Haremire House
High Thoresby
Kelder Well
Fiddler Wood
Force Scar
River Ure
Under Beals Plantation
Bolton Hall Farm
Slapestone Wath
Wath Wood
Middle Wood
Unity Wood
High Wanless Farm
Wensleydale
Bolton Hall
Flesh Dub
New Wood
Lady Wood
George's Plantation
Froddle Dub
Wellclose Plantation
Swinithwaite
Home Wood
Low Wanless Farm
Daniel Wood
Hollins House
Adam Bottoms Farm
Wanlass Park
Lords Bridge
Hestholme Farm
Alma House Farm
Waterfall
Hestholme Bridge
Long Bank Wood
South Woods
Temple Farm
Cote Gill
Sewage Works
Alma Farm
Crookbottom Wood
Langthwaite Wood
Oak Tree Farm
Edgley
Layrus Wood
PH
Park Gate
Bishopdale Beck
Sorrelsykes Park
Nossill Scars
Quarry (dis)
West Witton
Marlhole Wood
Nossill End
Holme Farm
Kit Wood
Bristow High Gill
High Wood
Chantry
Capple Bank Farm
Oswald Pasture
Morpeth Wood
Oswald High Wood
Capple Bank Spr
Morpeth Scar
Capplebank Plantation
Dove Scar
Howrein Farm
Stony Woods
Penhill Farm
Middleham High Moor
Penhill Quarry (dis)
West Witton Moor
Penhill Crags
Wraykeld Well (Spr)
Penhill Scar
Penhill Beacon
Penhill Park
Black Scar
Penhill End
Robin Hood's Well
Long Slack Quarry (dis)
Penhill
Hudson Quarry (dis)
Melmerby Moor
Hazely Peat Moor
Melmerby Moor
Melmerby Moor
Settlement & Field System
APEDALE ROAD
HARGILL LANE
EAST LA
CASTLE LA
SCALLOW BANK LANE
HARGILL LA
CHURCH CL
BRIAR CL
CHURCH LANE
MILL LA
WELL LANE
WOOD END LA
THORESBY LA
BRUNTON BANK
SISSY BANK
SCARTH NICK
LIGHT LA
KELDHEADS LA
BACK LA
A684
TEMPLE BANK
B6160
SCOT GATE
HOLL GATE
PATTERHAM LANE
FLATS LANE
OLD SCHOOL CL
CHURCH LA
BAY BOLTON AVENUE
LANGTHWAITE LANE
CHANTRY BANK
CHANTRY GARTH
GRASSGILL LA
GREEN GATE
GN GATE
NOSSILL LA
HIGH LANE
WITTON STEEPS
COMMON LA
ELLERS LA
MORPETH GATE
A B C D E F
02 03 04 05 06 07
93 92 91 90 89 88 87 86
8 7 6 5 4 3 2 1

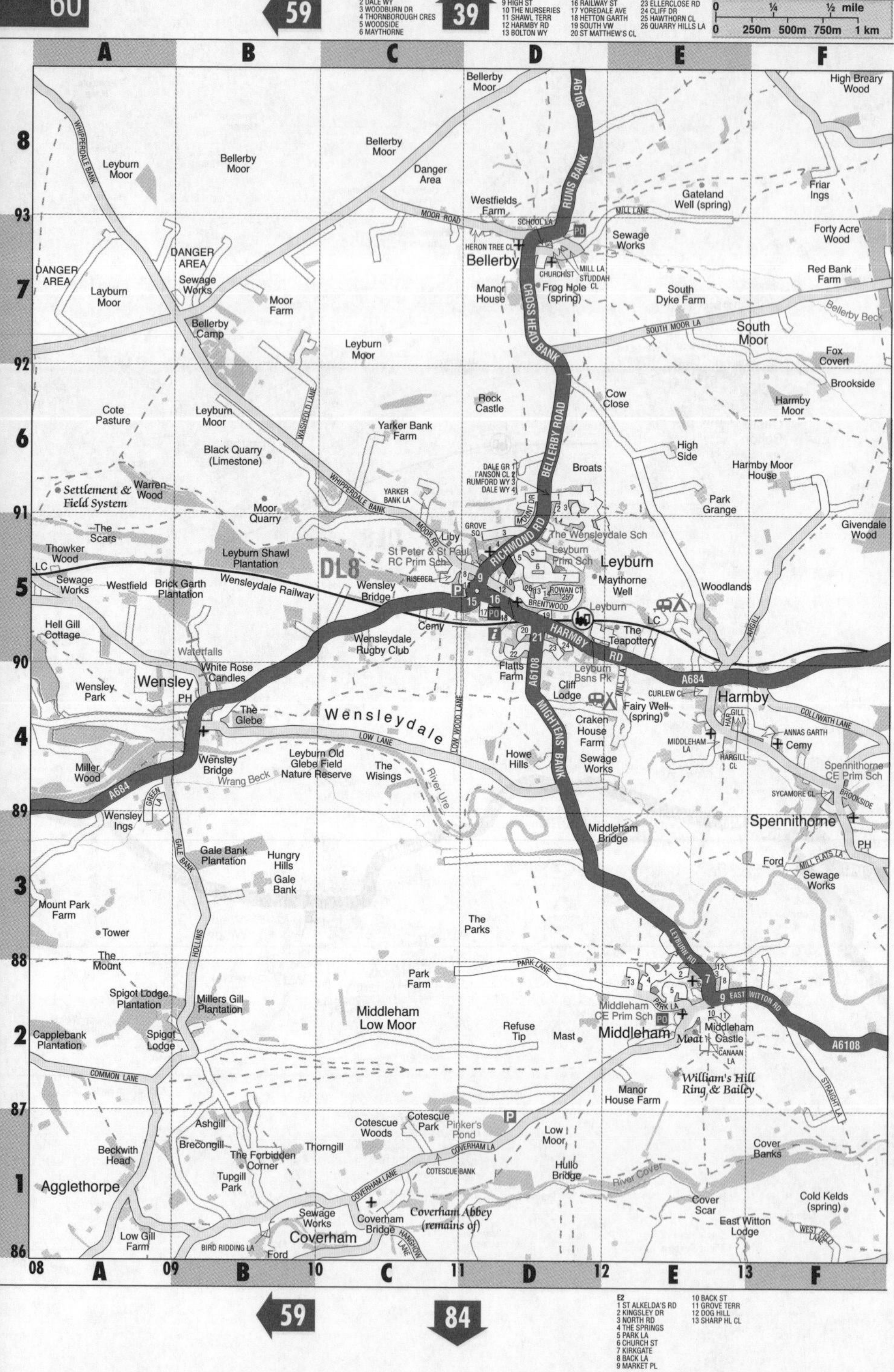

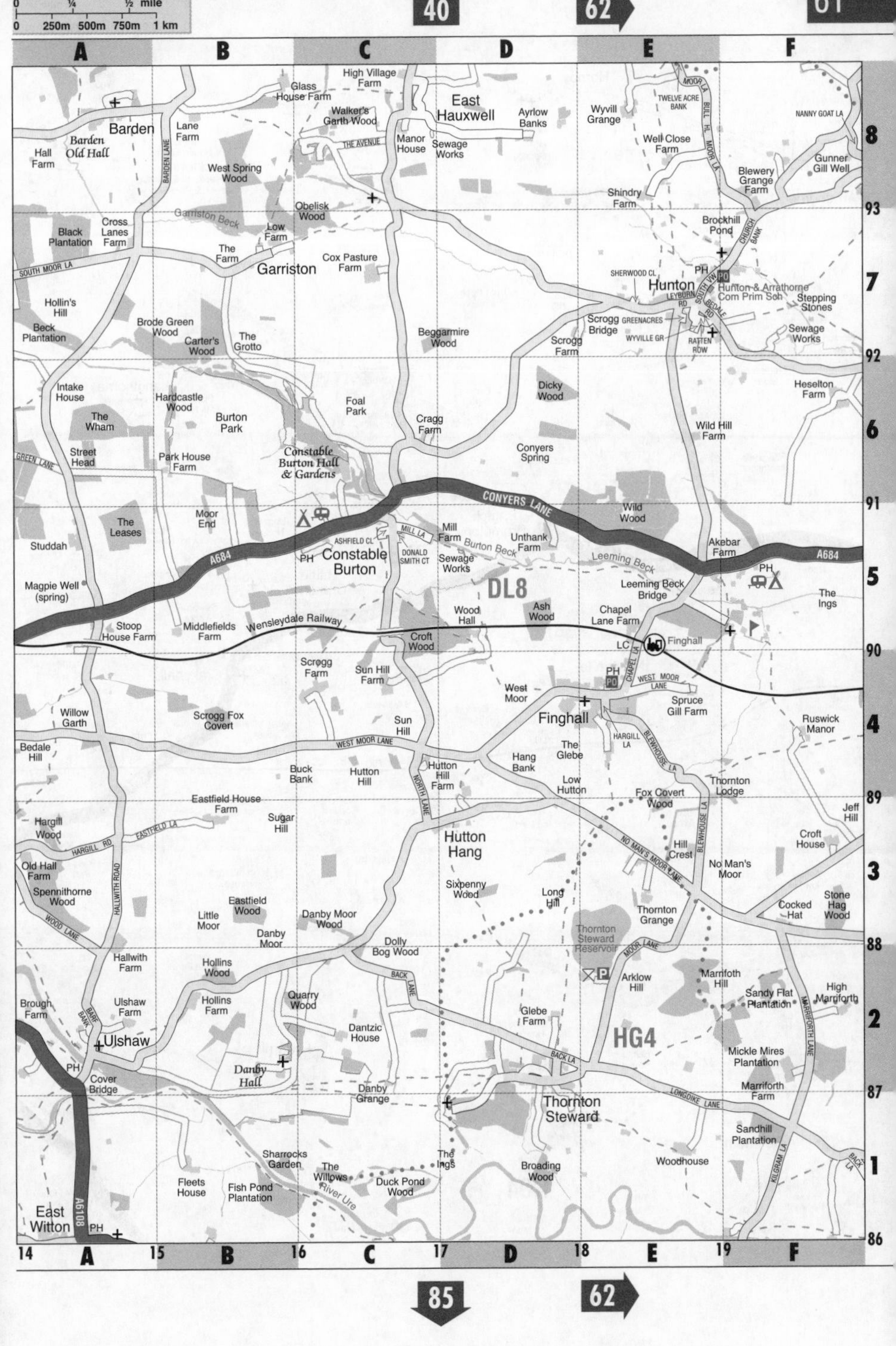
Scale: 1⅓ inches to 1 mile
40
62
Barden
Barden Old Hall
Hall Farm
Lane Farm
Glass House Farm
High Village Farm
Walker's Garth Wood
East Hauxwell
Ayrlow Banks
Wyvill Grange
Manor House
Sewage Works
West Spring Wood
Obelisk Wood
Garriston Beck
Black Plantation
Cross Lanes Farm
Low Farm
The Farm
Garriston
Cox Pasture Farm
Well Close Farm
Shindry Farm
Blewery Grange Farm
Gunner Gill Well
Brockhill Pond
Hunton
Hunton & Arrathorne Com Prim Sch
Stepping Stones
Sewage Works
Scrogg Bridge
Scrogg Farm
Hollin's Hill
Beck Plantation
Brode Green Wood
Carter's Wood
The Grotto
Beggarmire Wood
Intake House
Hardcastle Wood
Burton Park
Foal Park
Cragg Farm
Dicky Wood
Heselton Farm
Wild Hill Farm
The Wham
Street Head
Park House Farm
Constable Burton Hall & Gardens
Conyers Spring
CONYERS LANE
The Leases
Moor End
Wild Wood
Studdah
Constable Burton
Mill Farm
Sewage Works
Unthank Farm
Burton Beck
Leeming Beck
Akebar Farm
A684
DL8
Magpie Well (spring)
Wood Hall
Ash Wood
Leeming Beck Bridge
Chapel Lane Farm
The Ings
Stoop House Farm
Middlefields Farm
Wensleydale Railway
Croft Wood
Finghall
Scrogg Farm
Sun Hill Farm
West Moor
Spruce Gill Farm
Willow Garth
Scrogg Fox Covert
Sun Hill
Finghall
Ruswick Manor
Bedale Hill
WEST MOOR LANE
Buck Bank
Hutton Hill
Hutton Hill Farm
Hang Bank
The Glebe
Low Hutton
Thornton Lodge
Eastfield House Farm
Sugar Hill
Fox Covert Wood
Jeff Hill
Hargill Wood
Hutton Hang
Hill Crest
Croft House
Old Hall Farm
No Man's Moor
Spennithorne Wood
Sixpenny Wood
Long Hill
Eastfield Wood
Little Moor
Danby Moor Wood
Danby Moor
Thornton Grange
Cocked Hat
Stone Hag Wood
Thornton Steward Reservoir
Hallwith Farm
Hollins Wood
Dolly Bog Wood
Arklow Hill
Marrifoth Hill
Sandy Flat Plantation
High Marriforth
Brough Farm
Ulshaw Farm
Hollins Farm
Quarry Wood
Glebe Farm
HG4
Ulshaw
Danby Hall
Dantzic House
Mickle Mires Plantation
Cover Bridge
Danby Grange
Thornton Steward
Marriforth Farm
Sandhill Plantation
Sharrocks Garden
The Willows
The Ings
Broading Wood
Woodhouse
Fleets House
Fish Pond Plantation
Duck Pond Wood
River Ure
East Witton
A6108
85
62

61
41

Scale: 1⅓ inches to 1 mile

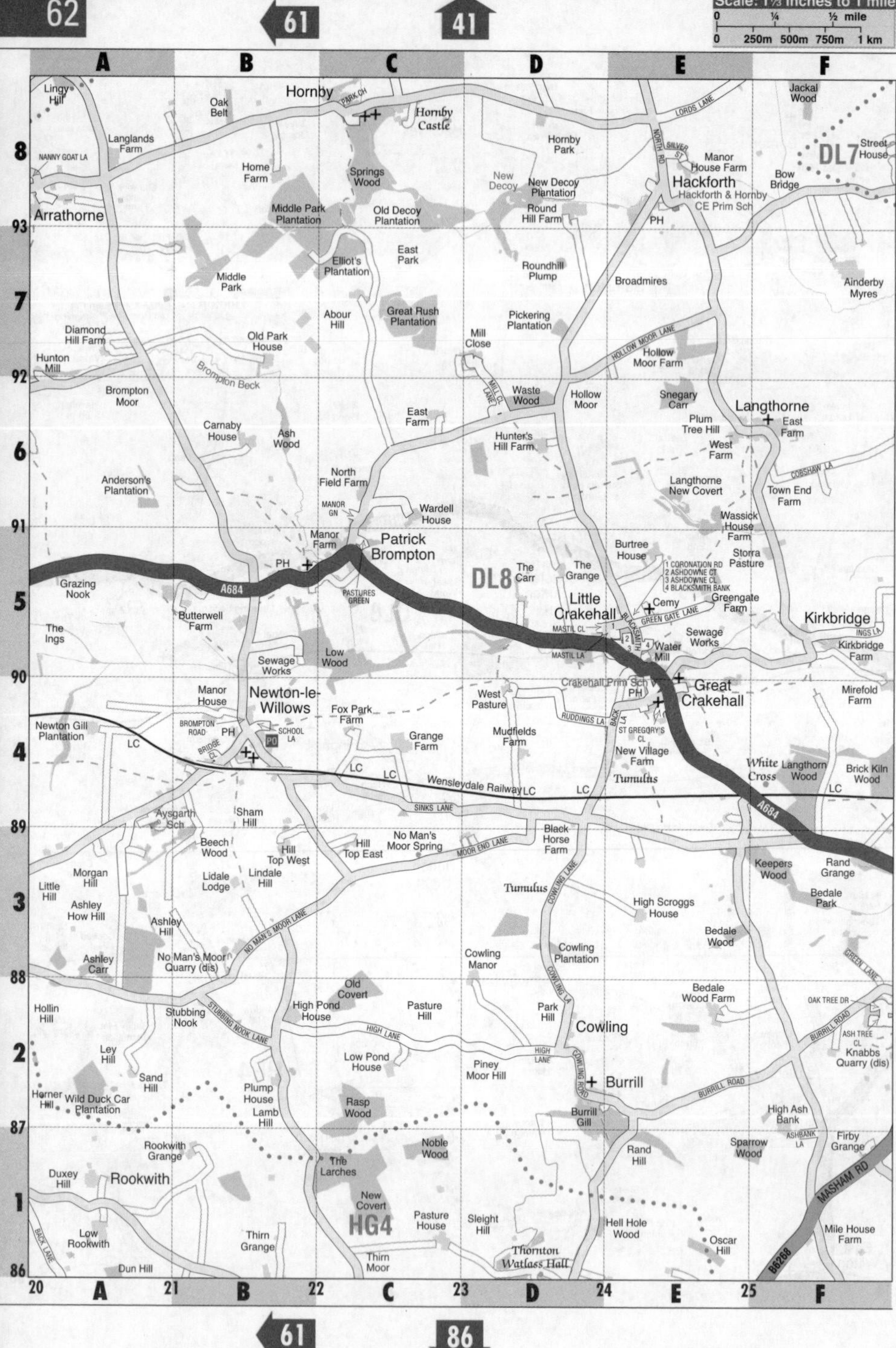

Hornby
Hornby Castle
Arrathorne
Hackforth
Hackforth & Hornby CE Prim Sch
Patrick Brompton
Newton-le-Willows
Little Crakehall
Great Crakehall
Langthorne
Kirkbridge
Cowling
Burrill
Rookwith
DL7
DL8
HG4
A684
B6268
Wensleydale Railway
Thornton Watlass Hall

61
86

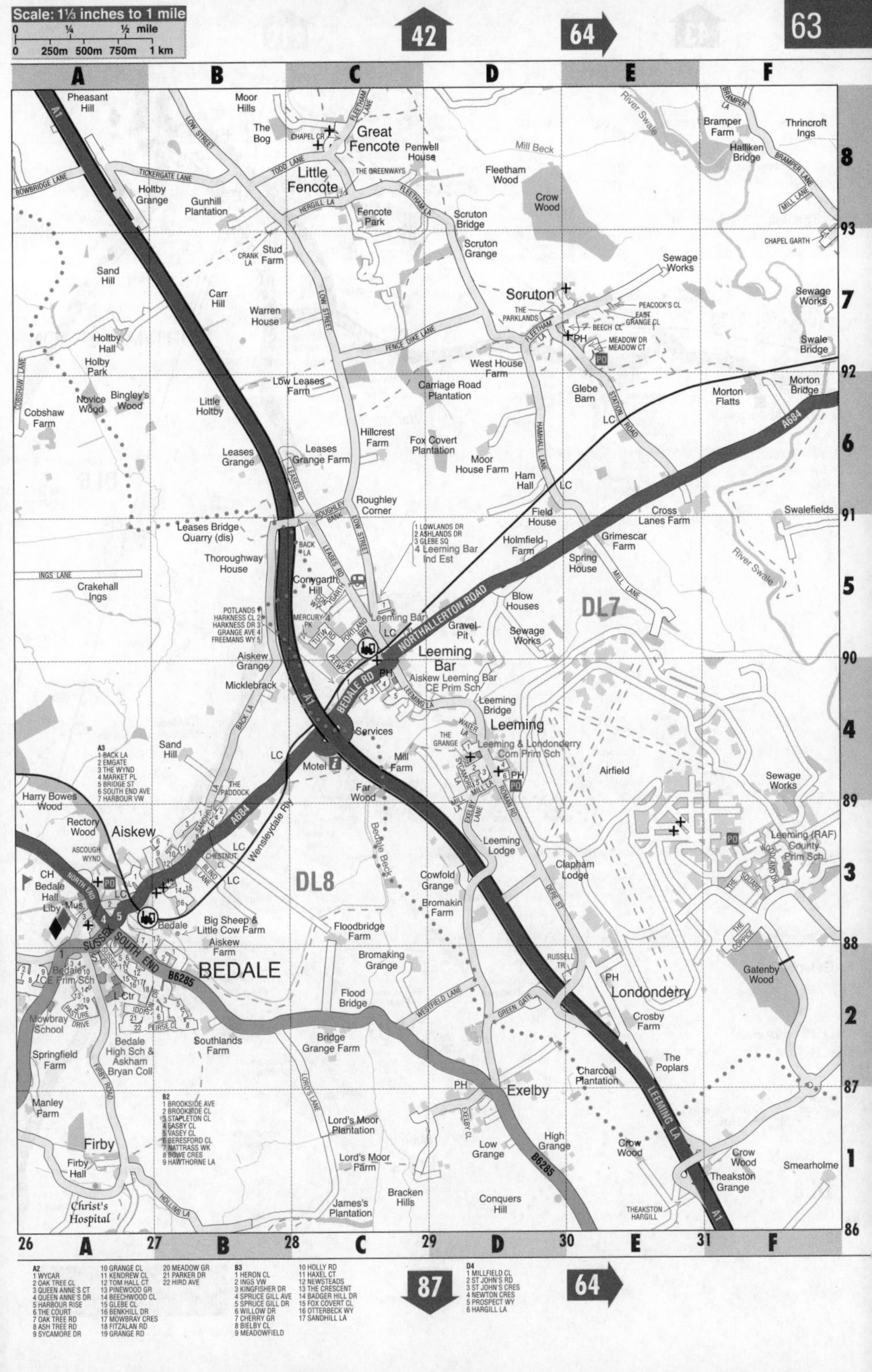
Scale: 1⅓ inches to 1 mile
0 ¼ ½ mile
0 250m 500m 750m 1 km
42
64
63
A B C D E F
Pheasant Hill
Moor Hills
The Bog
Great Fencote
Penwell House
Little Fencote
Holtby Grange
Gunhill Plantation
Fencote Park
Stud Farm
Sand Hill
Carr Hill
Warren House
Holtby Hall
Holby Park
Novice Wood
Bingley's Wood
Cobshaw Farm
Little Holtby
Low Leases Farm
Leases Grange
Leases Grange Farm
Hillcrest Farm
Roughley Corner
Leases Bridge Quarry (dis)
Thoroughway House
Crakehall Ings
Conygarth Hill
Aiskew Grange
Micklebrack
Mill Beck
Fleetham Wood
Crow Wood
Scruton Bridge
Scruton Grange
Scruton
West House Farm
Carriage Road Plantation
Fox Covert Plantation
Moor House Farm
Ham Hall
Field House
Holmfield Farm
Bramper Farm
Thrincroft Ings
Halliken Bridge
Sewage Works
Swale Bridge
Morton Bridge
Morton Flatts
Glebe Barn
Cross Lanes Farm
Grimescar Farm
Spring House
Swalefields
River Swale
DL7
Blow Houses
Gravel Pit
Leeming Bar
Aiskew Leeming Bar CE Prim Sch
Leeming Bridge
Leeming
Leeming & Londonderry Com Prim Sch
Airfield
Services
Motel
Mill Farm
Far Wood
Sand Hill
Harry Bowes Wood
Rectory Wood
Aiskew
CH
Bedale Hall
Liby
Mus.
Bedale
Big Sheep & Little Cow Farm
Aiskew Farm
BEDALE
DL8
Wensleydale Rly
Bedale Beck
Cowfold Grange
Bromakin Farm
Floodbridge Farm
Bromaking Grange
Flood Bridge
Leeming Lodge
Clapham Lodge
Leeming (RAF) County Prim Sch
Gatenby Wood
Londonderry
Crosby Farm
The Poplars
Charcoal Plantation
Crow Wood
Crow Wood
Theakston Grange
Smearholme
Exelby
High Grange
Low Grange
Conquers Hill
Bedale CE Prim Sch
L Ctr
Mowbray School
Bedale High Sch & Askham Bryan Coll
Springfield Farm
Southlands Farm
Bridge Grange Farm
Manley Farm
Lord's Moor Plantation
Lord's Moor Farm
Firby
Firby Hall
Christ's Hospital
Bracken Hills
James's Plantation
THEAKSTON HARGILL
A1
A684
B6285
NORTHALLERTON ROAD
BEDALE RD
LEEMING LA
1 LOWLANDS DR
2 ASHLANDS DR
3 GLEBE SQ
4 Leeming Bar Ind Est
POTLANDS
HARKNESS CL 2
HARKNESS DR 3
GRANGE AVE 4
FREEMANS WY 5
A3
1 BACK LA
2 EMGATE
3 THE WYND
4 MARKET PL
5 BRIDGE ST
6 SOUTH END AVE
7 HARBOUR VW
B2
1 BROOKSIDE AVE
2 BROOKSIDE CL
3 STAPLETON CL
4 EASBY CL
5 VASEY CL
6 BERESFORD CL
7 NATTRASS WK
8 BOWE CRES
9 HAWTHORNE LA
8 93 7 92 6 91 5 90 4 89 3 88 2 87 1 86
26 A 27 B 28 C 29 D 30 E 31 F
A2
1 WYCAR
2 OAK TREE CL
3 QUEEN ANNE'S CT
4 QUEEN ANNE'S DR
5 HARBOUR RISE
6 THE COURT
7 OAK TREE RD
8 ASH TREE RD
9 SYCAMORE DR
10 GRANGE CL
11 KENDREW CL
12 TOM HALL CT
13 PINEWOOD GR
14 BEECHWOOD CL
15 GLEBE CL
16 BENKHILL DR
17 MOWBRAY CRES
18 FITZALAN RD
19 GRANGE RD
20 MEADOW GR
21 PARKER DR
22 HIRD AVE
B3
1 HERON CL
2 INGS VW
3 KINGFISHER DR
4 SPRUCE GILL AVE
5 SPRUCE GILL DR
6 WILLOW DR
7 CHERRY GR
8 BIELBY CL
9 MEADOWFIELD
10 HOLLY RD
11 HAXEL CT
12 NEWSTEADS
13 THE CRESCENT
14 BADGER HILL DR
15 FOX COVERT CL
16 OTTERBECK WY
17 SANDHILL LA
87
D4
1 MILLFIELD CL
2 ST JOHN'S RD
3 ST JOHN'S CRES
4 NEWTON CRES
5 PROSPECT WY
6 HARGILL LA
64

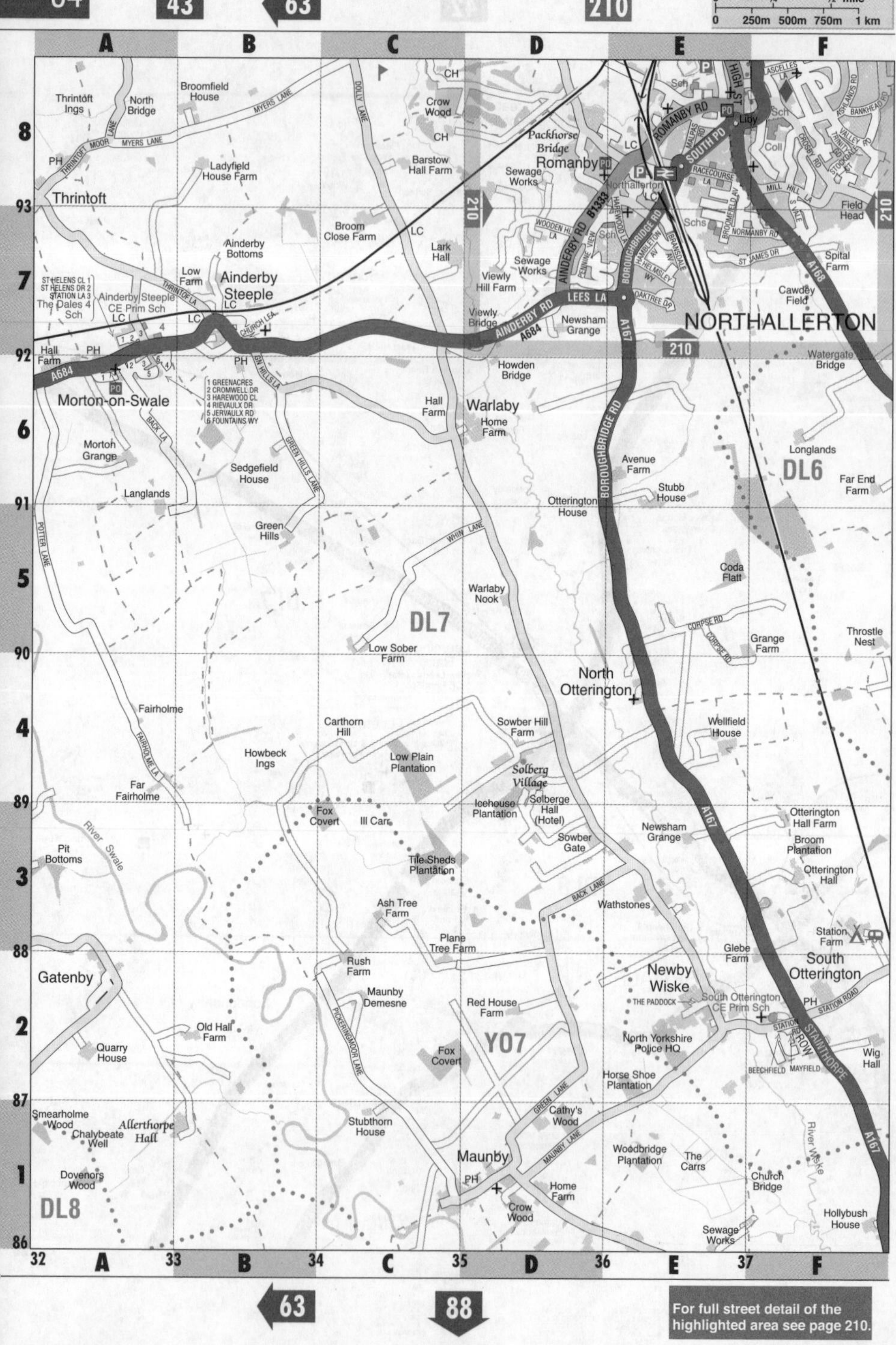

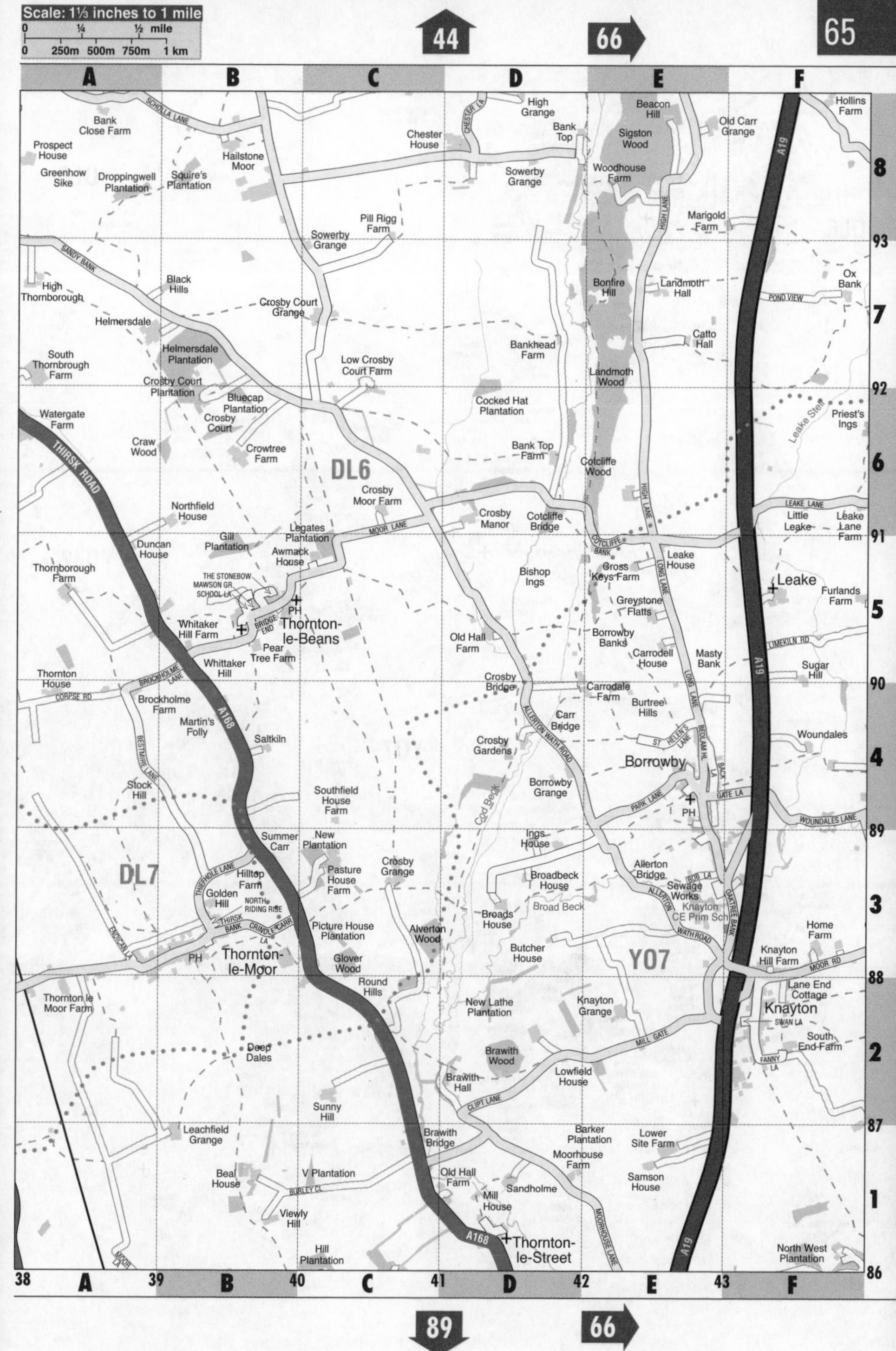
Scale: 1⅓ inches to 1 mile
0 ¼ ½ mile
0 250m 500m 750m 1 km
44
66
A B C D E F
8
93
7
92
6
91
5
90
4
89
3
88
2
87
1
86
38 39 40 41 42 43
Bank Close Farm
Prospect House
Greenhow Sike
Droppingwell Plantation
Squire's Plantation
Hailstone Moor
Scholla Lane
Chester House
Chester La
High Grange
Bank Top
Sowerby Grange
Beacon Hill
Sigston Wood
Woodhouse Farm
Old Carr Grange
Hollins Farm
A19
Pill Rigg Farm
Sowerby Grange
High Lane
Marigold Farm
Sandy Bank
High Thornborough
Black Hills
Crosby Court Grange
Bonfire Hill
Landmoth Hall
Pond View
Ox Bank
Helmersdale
Helmersdale Plantation
South Thornbrough Farm
Low Crosby Court Farm
Bankhead Farm
Catto Hall
Crosby Court Plantation
Landmoth Wood
Bluecap Plantation
Watergate Farm
Crosby Court
Cocked Hat Plantation
Priest's Ings
Leake Stell
Craw Wood
Crowtree Farm
Bank Top Farm
Thirsk Road
DL6
Cotcliffe Wood
Crosby Moor Farm
Northfield House
Crosby Manor
Cotcliffe Bridge
Leake Lane
Little Leake
Leake Lane Farm
Legates Plantation
Moor Lane
Gill Plantation
Duncan House
Awmack House
Cotcliffe Bank
Long Lane
Leake House
Gross Keys Farm
Thornborough Farm
The Stonebow
Mawson Gr.
School La
Bishop Ings
Leake
Furlands Farm
PH
Greystone Flatts
Bridge End
Whitaker Hill Farm
Thornton-le-Beans
Old Hall Farm
Borrowby Banks
Limekiln Rd
Pear Tree Farm
Whittaker Hill
Carrodell House
Masty Bank
Sugar Hill
Thornton House
Brockholme Lane
Corpse Rd
Crosby Bridge
Carrodale Farm
Brockholme Farm
Burtree Hills
Martin's Folly
A168
Carr Bridge
Allerton Wath Road
St Helen's Lane
Bedlam Hl
Woundales
Bestmire Lane
Saltkiln
Crosby Gardens
Borrowby
Back La
Stock Hill
Southfield House Farm
Borrowby Grange
Cod Beck
Park Lane
Gate La
Woundales Lane
Summer Carr
New Plantation
Ings House
DL7
Hilltop Farm
Pasture House Farm
Crosby Grange
Broadbeck House
Allerton Bridge
Bob La
Sewage Works
Thiefhole Lane
Golden Hill
North Riding Rise
Broad Beck
Knayton CE Prim Sch
Oaktree Bank
Home Farm
Thirsk Bank
Grindle Carr La
Picture House Plantation
Broads House
Allerton Wath Road
Endican La
Alverton Wood
PH
Thornton-le-Moor
Glover Wood
Butcher House
YO7
Knayton Hill Farm
Moor Rd
Round Hills
Lane End Cottage
Thornton le Moor Farm
New Lathe Plantation
Knayton Grange
Knayton
Swan La
Mill Gate
South End Farm
Deep Dales
Brawith Wood
Fanny La
Lowfield House
Brawith Hall
Clipt Lane
Sunny Hill
Leachfield Grange
Brawith Bridge
Barker Plantation
Lower Site Farm
Moorhouse Farm
Beal House
V Plantation
Old Hall Farm
Sandholme
Samson House
Burley Cl
Mill House
Viewly Hill
Moorhouse Lane
Moor La
Hill Plantation
Thornton-le-Street
North West Plantation
89
66

65
45

Scale: 1⅓ inches to 1 mile

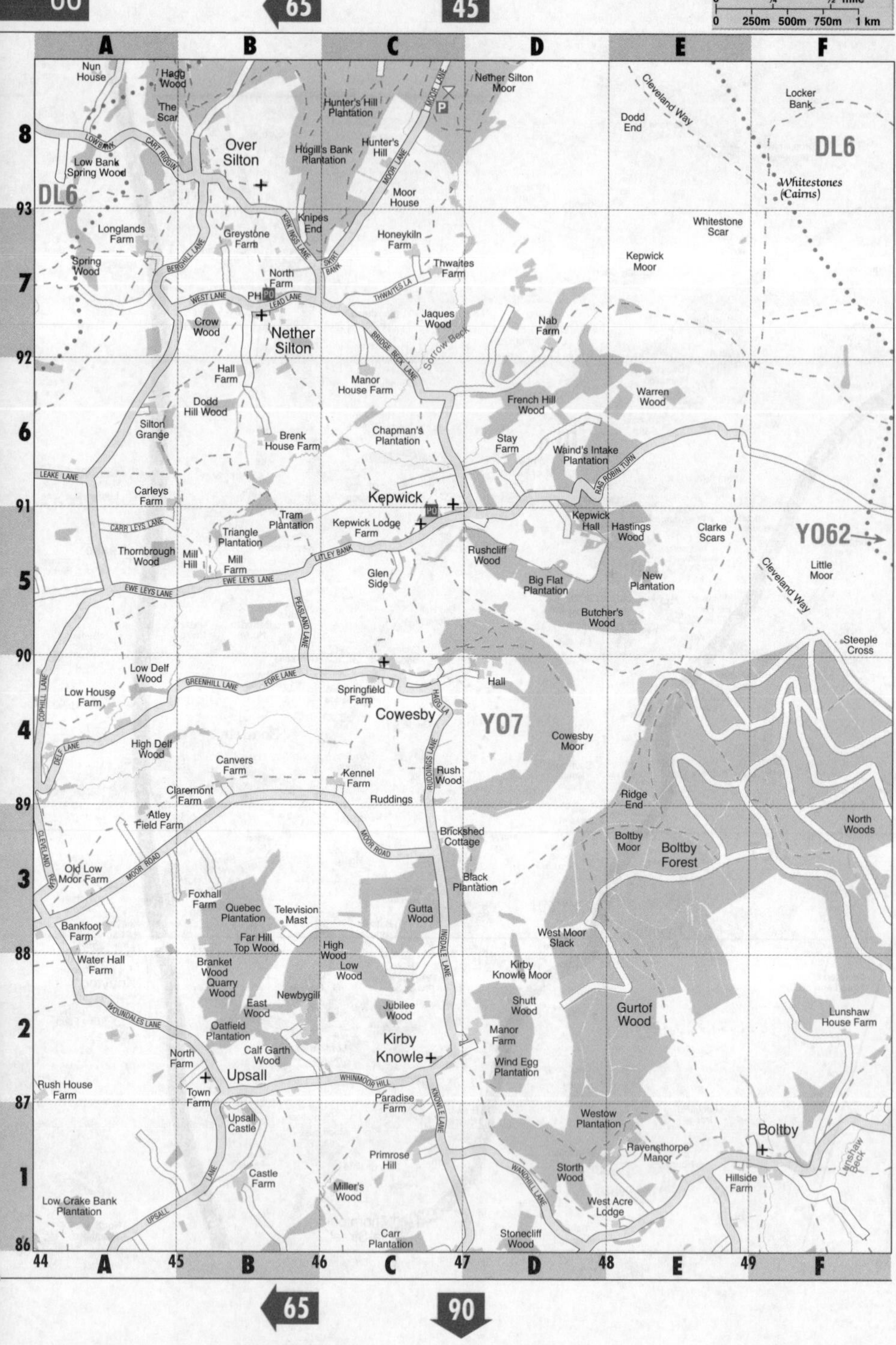

Nun House
Hagg Wood
The Scar
Over Silton
Low Bank Spring Wood
DL6
Longlands Farm
Spring Wood
Greystone Farm
North Farm
Nether Silton
Crow Wood
Hall Farm
Dodd Hill Wood
Silton Grange
Brenk House Farm
Carleys Farm
Thornbrough Wood
Mill Hill
Mill Farm
Triangle Plantation
Tram Plantation
Hunter's Hill Plantation
Hugill's Bank Plantation
Hunter's Hill
Moor House
Knipes End
Honeykiln Farm
Thwaites Farm
Jaques Wood
Manor House Farm
Chapman's Plantation
Kepwick
Kepwick Lodge Farm
Glen Side
Nether Silton Moor
Dodd End
Cleveland Way
Locker Bank
Whitestones (Cairns)
Whitestone Scar
Kepwick Moor
Nab Farm
French Hill Wood
Warren Wood
Stay Farm
Waind's Intake Plantation
Rushcliff Wood
Big Flat Plantation
Kepwick Hall
Hastings Wood
Clarke Scars
YO62
Little Moor
New Plantation
Butcher's Wood
Steeple Cross
Low Delf Wood
Low House Farm
High Delf Wood
Canvers Farm
Claremont Farm
Atley Field Farm
Old Low Moor Farm
Springfield Farm
Cowesby
Hall
YO7
Cowesby Moor
Kennel Farm
Rush Wood
Ruddings
Brickshed Cottage
Black Plantation
Ridge End
Boltby Moor
Boltby Forest
North Woods
Foxhall Farm
Quebec Plantation
Television Mast
Gutta Wood
Bankfoot Farm
Far Hill Top Wood
Water Hall Farm
Branket Wood
Quarry Wood
High Wood
Low Wood
West Moor Slack
Kirby Knowle Moor
Newbygill
East Wood
Jubilee Wood
Shutt Wood
Gurtof Wood
Lunshaw House Farm
Oatfield Plantation
North Farm
Calf Garth Wood
Kirby Knowle
Manor Farm
Wind Egg Plantation
Rush House Farm
Upsall
Town Farm
Paradise Farm
Upsall Castle
Westow Plantation
Boltby
Primrose Hill
Ravensthorpe Manor
Storth Wood
Castle Farm
Miller's Wood
Hillside Farm
Lunshaw Beck
Low Crake Bank Plantation
West Acre Lodge
Carr Plantation
Stonecliff Wood
Sorrow Beck
LOWBAN
CART RIGGIN
KIRK INGS LANE
MOOR LANE
SKIRT BANK
BERGHILL LANE
WEST LANE
LEAD LANE
THWAITES LA
BRIDGE BECK LANE
RAG ROBIN TURN
LEAKE LANE
CARR LEYS LANE
LITLEY BANK
EWE LEYS LANE
PEASLAND LANE
GREENHILL LANE
FORE LANE
HAGG LA
COPHILL LANE
DELF LANE
RUDDINGS LANE
MOOR ROAD
CLEVELAND REW
INGDALE LANE
WOUNDALES LANE
WHINMOOR HILL
KNOWLE LANE
WANDHILL LANE
UPSALL LANE
PH
PO
P
A B C D E F
8 7 6 5 4 3 2 1
93 92 91 90 89 88 87 86
44 45 46 47 48 49

65
90

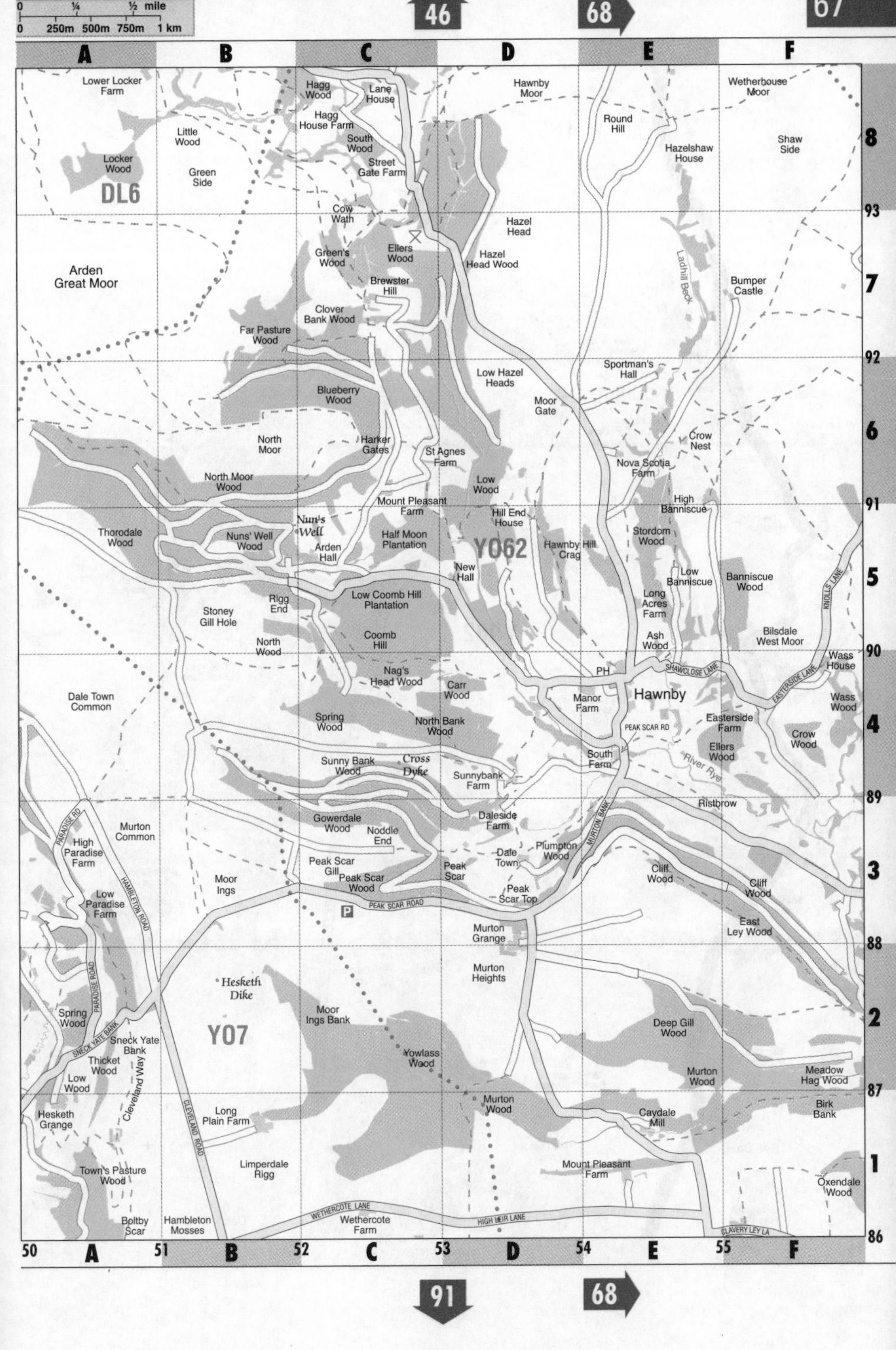

Scale: 1⅓ inches to 1 mile
0 ¼ ½ mile
0 250m 500m 750m 1 km
46
68
A B C D E F
Lower Locker Farm
Little Wood
Locker Wood
Green Side
DL6
Hagg Wood
Lane House
Hagg House Farm
South Wood
Street Gate Farm
Hawnby Moor
Round Hill
Wetherhouse Moor
Hazelshaw House
Shaw Side
Cow Wath
Green's Wood
Ellers Wood
Hazel Head
Hazel Head Wood
Arden Great Moor
Brewster Hill
Clover Bank Wood
Far Pasture Wood
Ladhill Beck
Bumper Castle
Low Hazel Heads
Sportman's Hall
Moor Gate
Blueberry Wood
North Moor
Harker Gates
St Agnes Farm
Crow Nest
Nova Scotia Farm
North Moor Wood
Low Wood
Mount Pleasant Farm
High Banniscue
Thorodale Wood
Nuns' Well Wood
Nun's Well
Arden Hall
Half Moon Plantation
Hill End House
YO62
Hawnby Hill Crag
Stordom Wood
New Hall
Low Banniscue
Banniscue Wood
Knolls Lane
Stoney Gill Hole
Rigg End
Low Coomb Hill Plantation
Long Acres Farm
Coomb Hill
North Wood
Ash Wood
Bilsdale West Moor
Nag's Head Wood
PH
Shawclose Lane
Easterside Lane
Wass House
Hawnby
Dale Town Common
Carr Wood
Manor Farm
Wass Wood
Spring Wood
North Bank Wood
Peak Scar Rd
Easterside Farm
Crow Wood
Ellers Wood
Sunny Bank Wood
Cross Dyke
Sunnybank Farm
South Farm
River Rye
Ristbrow
Paradise Rd
Murton Common
High Paradise Farm
Gowerdale Wood
Noddle End
Daleside Farm
Murton Bank
Hambleton Road
Dale Town
Plumpton Wood
Moor Ings
Peak Scar Gill
Peak Scar Wood
Peak Scar
Cliff Wood
Cliff Wood
Low Paradise Farm
Peak Scar Top
Peak Scar Road
P
East Ley Wood
Murton Grange
Paradise Road
Murton Heights
Hesketh Dike
Moor Ings Bank
Spring Wood
Sneck Yate Bank
Sneck Yate Bank
YO7
Deep Gill Wood
Thicket Wood
Yowlass Wood
Murton Wood
Meadow Hag Wood
Low Wood
Cleveland Way
Murton Wood
Hesketh Grange
Long Plain Farm
Cleveland Road
Caydale Mill
Birk Bank
Town's Pasture Wood
Limperdale Rigg
Mount Pleasant Farm
Oxendale Wood
Wethercote Lane
Wethercote Farm
High Weir Lane
Clavery Ley La
Boltby Scar
Hambleton Mosses
8 93 7 92 6 91 5 90 4 89 3 88 2 87 1 86
50 51 52 53 54 55
A B C D E F
91
68

67
47

Scale: 1⅓ inches to 1 mile

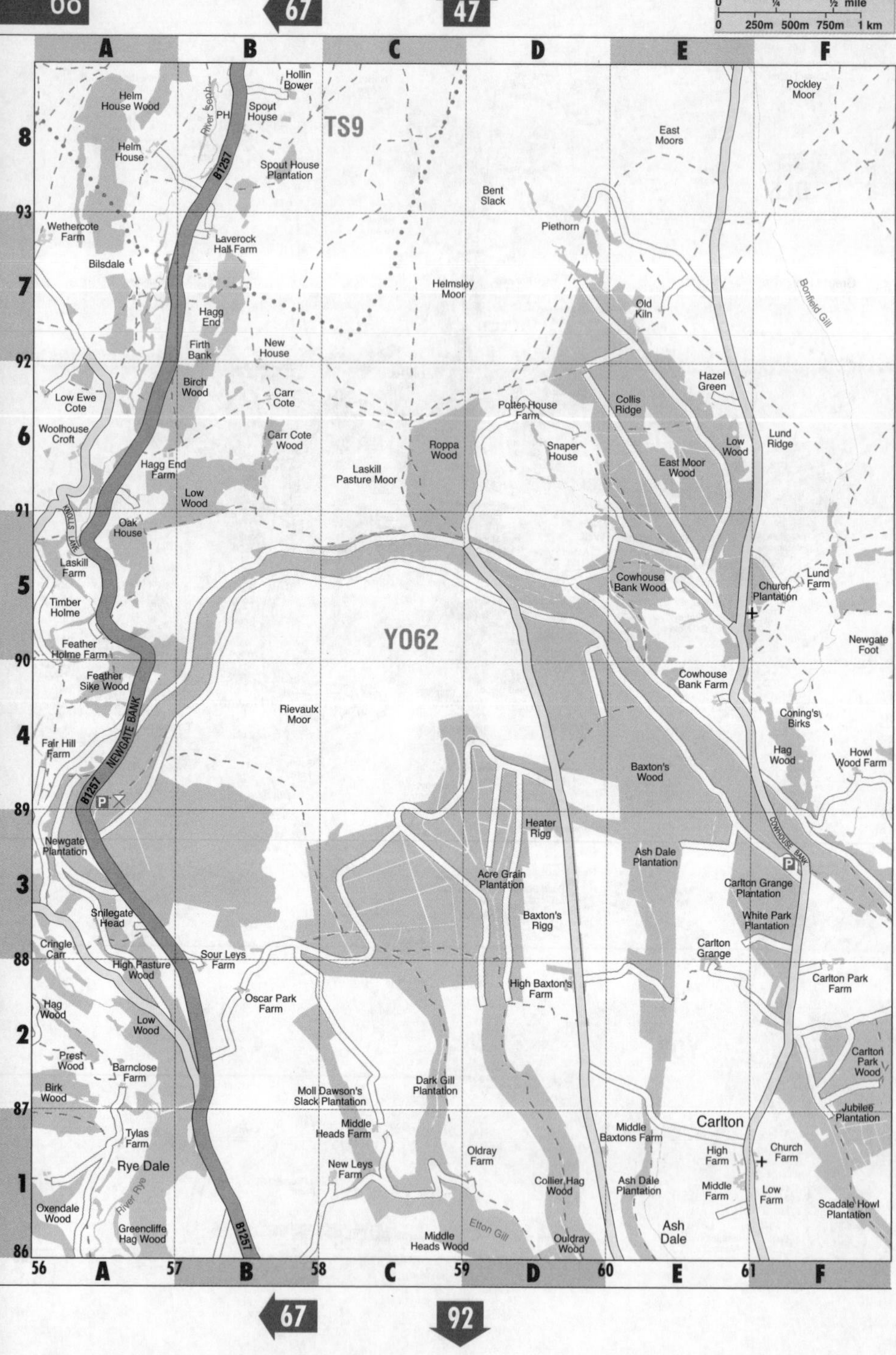
TS9
YO62
Helm House Wood
Helm House
Hollin Bower
Spout House
Spout House Plantation
PH
River Seph
B1257
Pockley Moor
East Moors
Bent Slack
Piethorn
Wethercote Farm
Laverock Hall Farm
Bilsdale
Helmsley Moor
Old Kiln
Bonfield Gill
Hagg End
Firth Bank
New House
Hazel Green
Low Ewe Cote
Birch Wood
Carr Cote
Potter House Farm
Collis Ridge
Woolhouse Croft
Carr Cote Wood
Roppa Wood
Snaper House
Low Wood
Lund Ridge
Hagg End Farm
Laskill Pasture Moor
East Moor Wood
Low Wood
Knolls Lane
Oak House
Laskill Farm
Cowhouse Bank Wood
Lund Farm
Church Plantation
Timber Holme
Newgate Foot
Feather Holme Farm
Cowhouse Bank Farm
Feather Sike Wood
Newgate Bank
Rievaulx Moor
Coning's Birks
Fair Hill Farm
Hag Wood
Baxton's Wood
Howl Wood Farm
Heater Rigg
Cowhouse Bank
Newgate Plantation
Ash Dale Plantation
Acre Grain Plantation
Carlton Grange Plantation
Baxton's Rigg
White Park Plantation
Snilegate Head
Cringle Carr
Sour Leys Farm
Carlton Grange
High Pasture Wood
High Baxton's Farm
Carlton Park Farm
Hag Wood
Oscar Park Farm
Low Wood
Prest Wood
Barnclose Farm
Carlton Park Wood
Birk Wood
Moll Dawson's Slack Plantation
Dark Gill Plantation
Jubilee Plantation
Middle Heads Farm
Carlton
Tylas Farm
Middle Baxtons Farm
Oldray Farm
High Farm
Church Farm
Rye Dale
New Leys Farm
Collier Hag Wood
Ash Dale Plantation
Middle Farm
Low Farm
Oxendale Wood
River Rye
Scadale Howl Plantation
Greencliffe Hag Wood
Etton Gill
Middle Heads Wood
Ouldray Wood
Ash Dale

67
92

Scale: 1⅓ inches to 1 mile

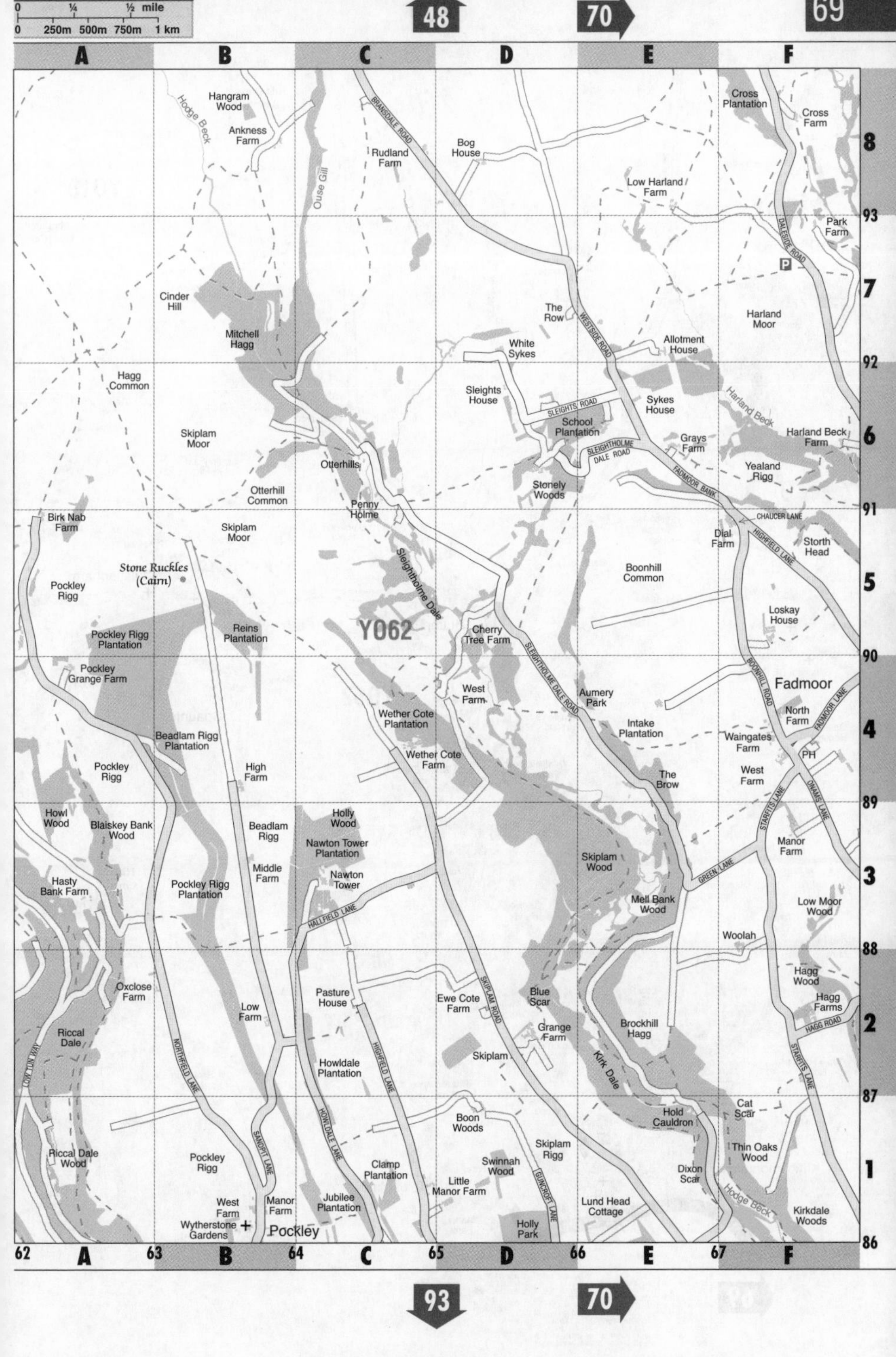
0
¼
½ mile
0
250m
500m
750m
1 km
48
70
A
B
C
D
E
F
Hangram Wood
Hodge Beck
Ankness Farm
Ouse Gill
BRANSDALE ROAD
Rudland Farm
Bog House
Cross Plantation
Cross Farm
Low Harland Farm
Park Farm
DALESIDE ROAD
Cinder Hill
Mitchell Hagg
The Row
WESTSIDE ROAD
White Sykes
Allotment House
Harland Moor
Hagg Common
Sleights House
SLEIGHTS' ROAD
School Plantation
Sykes House
Harland Beck
Skiplam Moor
Otterhills
SLEIGHTHOLME DALE ROAD
Grays Farm
Harland Beck Farm
Otterhill Common
Penny Holme
Stonely Woods
FADMOOR BANK
Yealand Rigg
Birk Nab Farm
Skiplam Moor
CHAUCER LANE
Dial Farm
HIGHFIELD LANE
Storth Head
Stone Ruckles (Cairn)
Sleightholme Dale
Boonhill Common
Pockley Rigg
YO62
Loskay House
Pockley Rigg Plantation
Reins Plantation
Cherry Tree Farm
SLEIGHTHOLME DALE ROAD
Pockley Grange Farm
BOONHILL ROAD
Fadmoor
West Farm
Aumery Park
Wether Cote Plantation
Intake Plantation
North Farm
FADMOOR LANE
Beadlam Rigg Plantation
Waingates Farm
PH
Pockley Rigg
High Farm
Wether Cote Farm
The Brow
West Farm
STARFITS LANE
ONAMS LANE
Howl Wood
Blaiskey Bank Wood
Holly Wood
Beadlam Rigg
Nawton Tower Plantation
Skiplam Wood
Manor Farm
Hasty Bank Farm
Pockley Rigg Plantation
Middle Farm
Nawton Tower
GREEN LANE
Mell Bank Wood
Low Moor Wood
HALLFIELD LANE
Woolah
Oxclose Farm
Pasture House
Ewe Cote Farm
SKIPLAM ROAD
Blue Scar
Hagg Wood
Hagg Farms
Low Farm
Grange Farm
Brockhill Hagg
HAGG ROAD
Riccal Dale
NORTHFIELD LANE
Howldale Plantation
HIGHFIELD LANE
Skiplam
Kirk Dale
LOW TUN WAY
STARFITS LANE
Boon Woods
Hold Cauldron
Cat Scar
HOWLDALE LANE
Riccal Dale Wood
Pockley Rigg
SANDPIT LANE
Clamp Plantation
Swinnah Wood
Skiplam Rigg
Thin Oaks Wood
Little Manor Farm
GUNCROFT LANE
Dixon Scar
Hodge Beck
West Farm
Manor Farm
Jubilee Plantation
Lund Head Cottage
Kirkdale Woods
Wytherstone Gardens
Pockley
Holly Park
8
93
7
92
6
91
5
90
4
89
3
88
2
87
1
86
62
63
64
65
66
67
93
70

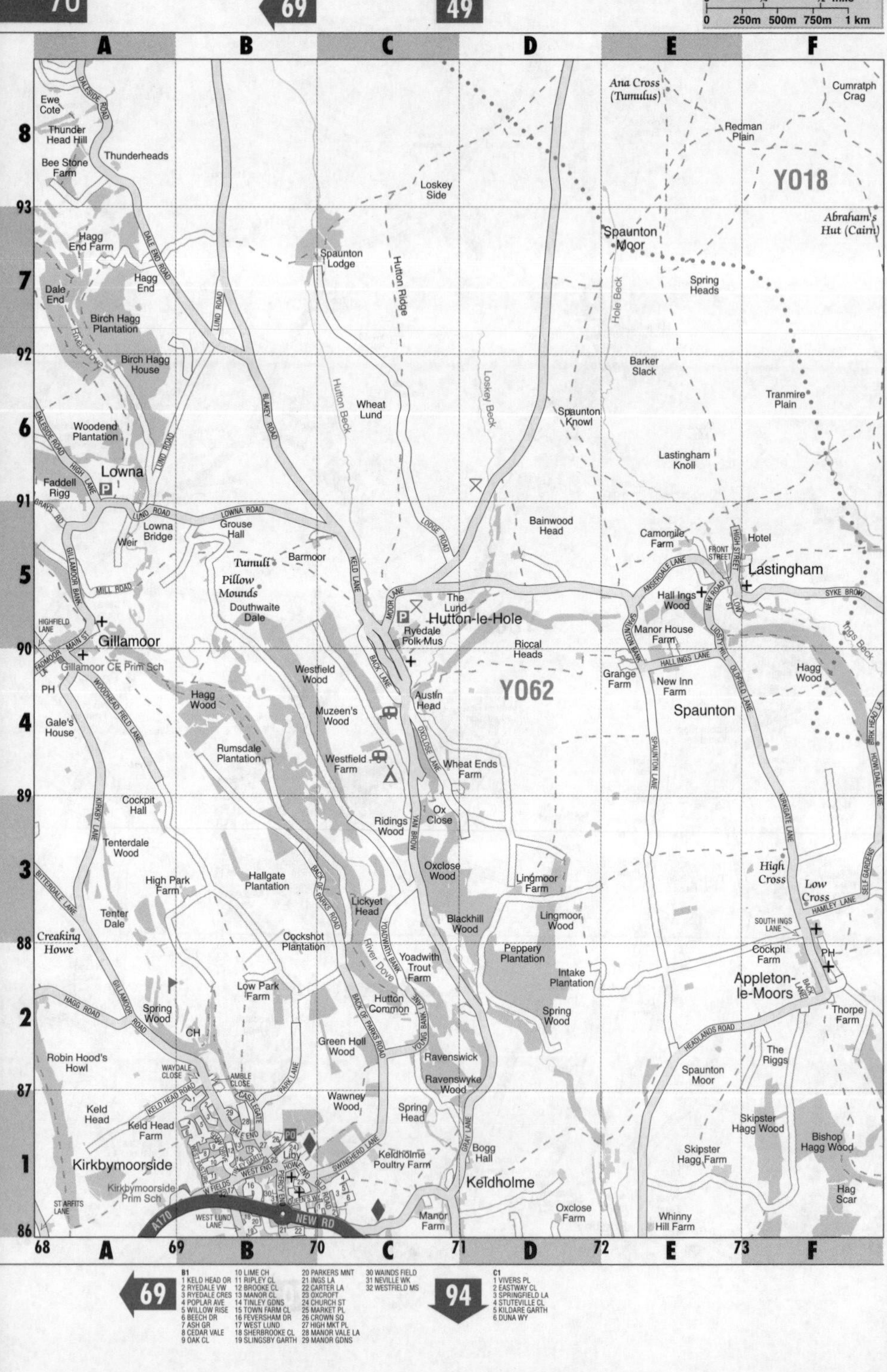

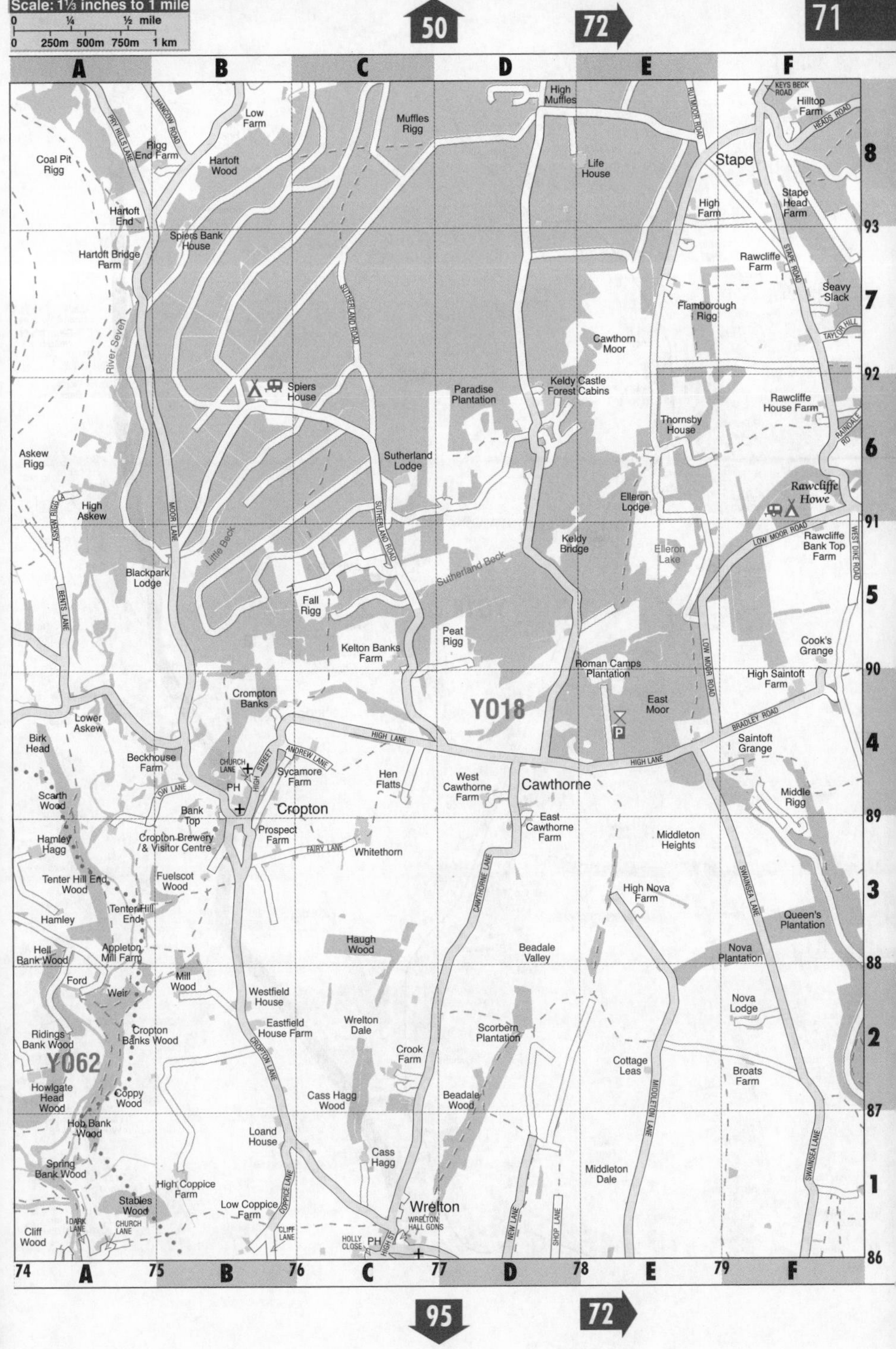
Scale: 1⅓ inches to 1 mile
0 ¼ ½ mile
0 250m 500m 750m 1 km
50
72
A
B
C
D
E
F
High Muffles
Low Farm
Muffles Rigg
Hilltop Farm
Coal Pit Rigg
Rigg End Farm
Hartoft Wood
Stape
Life House
Hartoft End
High Farm
Stape Head Farm
Spiers Bank House
Hartoft Bridge Farm
Rawcliffe Farm
Seavy Slack
Flamborough Rigg
Cawthorn Moor
Spiers House
Keldy Castle Forest Cabins
Paradise Plantation
Rawcliffe House Farm
Thornsby House
Askew Rigg
Sutherland Lodge
Rawcliffe Howe
High Askew
Elleron Lodge
Keldy Bridge
Elleron Lake
Rawcliffe Bank Top Farm
Blackpark Lodge
Fall Rigg
Peat Rigg
Kelton Banks Farm
Cook's Grange
Roman Camps Plantation
High Saintoft Farm
Crompton Banks
YO18
East Moor
Lower Askew
Birk Head
Beckhouse Farm
Sycamore Farm
Hen Flatts
West Cawthorne Farm
Cawthorne
Saintoft Grange
Middle Rigg
Scarth Wood
PH
Cropton
Bank Top
Prospect Farm
East Cawthorne Farm
Middleton Heights
Hamley Hagg
Cropton Brewery & Visitor Centre
Whitethorn
Tenter Hill End Wood
Fuelscot Wood
High Nova Farm
Tenter Hill End
Hamley
Queen's Plantation
Haugh Wood
Hell Bank Wood
Appleton Mill Farm
Beadale Valley
Nova Plantation
Ford
Mill Wood
Weir
Westfield House
Nova Lodge
Eastfield House Farm
Wrelton Dale
Scorbern Plantation
Ridings Bank Wood
Cropton Banks Wood
YO62
Crook Farm
Cottage Leas
Broats Farm
Howlgate Head Wood
Coppy Wood
Cass Hagg Wood
Beadale Wood
Hob Bank Wood
Loand House
Cass Hagg
Spring Bank Wood
Middleton Dale
High Coppice Farm
Stables Wood
Low Coppice Farm
Wrelton
Cliff Wood
PH
River Seven
Little Beck
Sutherland Beck
PRY HILLS LANE
HANCOW ROAD
RUTMOOR ROAD
KEYS BECK ROAD
HEADS ROAD
STAPE ROAD
TAYLOR HILL
RAINDALE RD
SUTHERLAND ROAD
MOOR LANE
LOW MOOR ROAD
WEST DIKE ROAD
BENTS LANE
HIGH LANE
BRADLEY ROAD
CHURCH LANE
HIGH STREET
ANDREW LANE
LOW LANE
FAIRY LANE
CAWTHORNE LANE
SWAINSEA LANE
MIDDLETON LANE
CROPTON LANE
COPPICE LANE
CLIFF LANE
NEW LANE
SHOP LANE
DARK LANE
CHURCH LANE
HOLLY CLOSE
HIGH ST
WRELTON HALL GDNS
8
93
7
92
6
91
5
90
4
89
3
88
2
87
1
86
74
75
76
77
78
79
95
72

Scale: 1⅓ inches to 1 mile

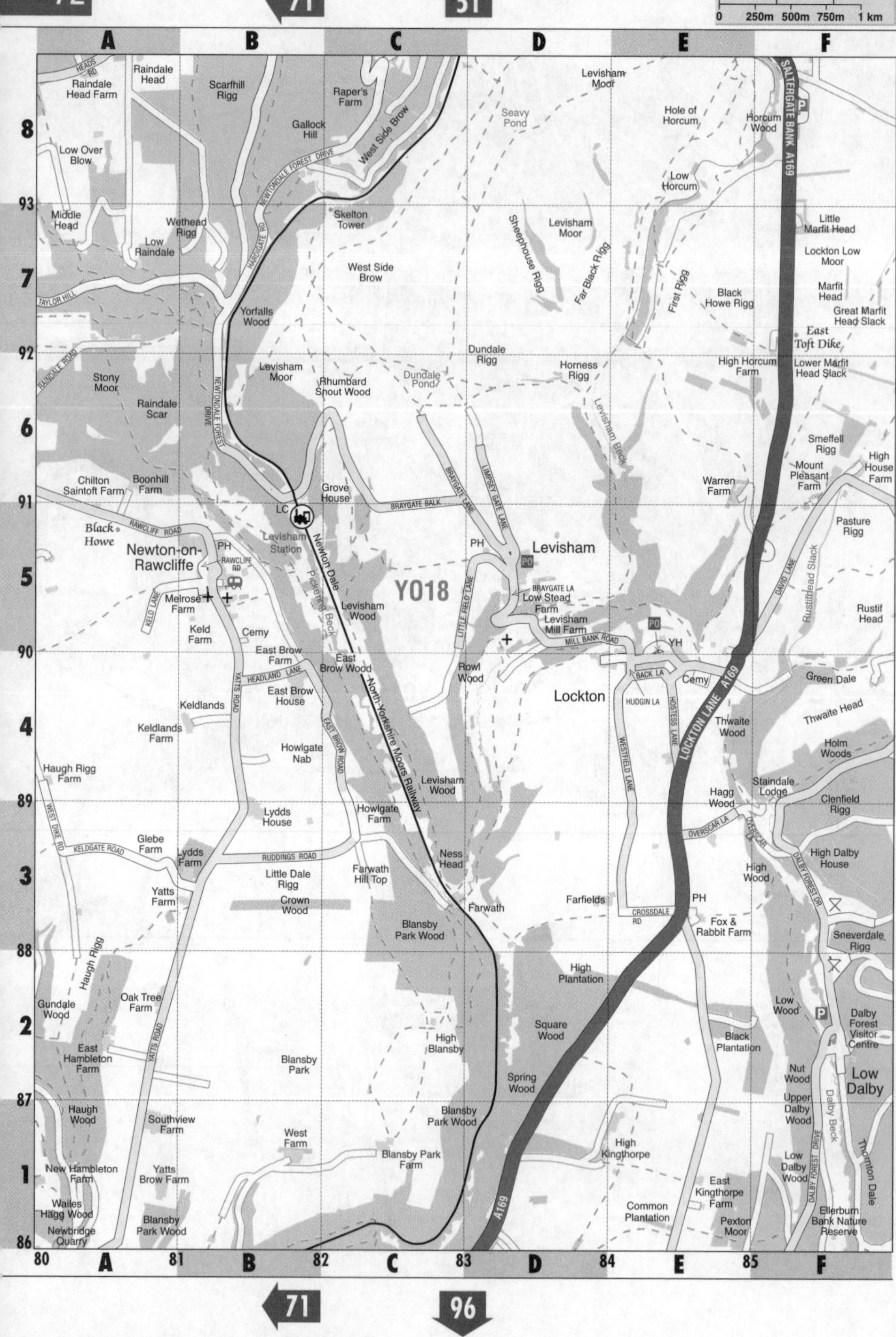
A
B
C
D
E
F
Raindale Head
Raindale Head Farm
Scarfhill Rigg
Raper's Farm
Gallock Hill
West Side Brow
Levisham Moor
Seavy Pond
Hole of Horcum
Horcum Wood
SALTERGATE BANK A169
Low Over Blow
Low Horcum
Middle Head
Wethead Rigg
Low Raindale
Skelton Tower
Levisham Moor
Sheephouse Rigg
Far Black Rigg
Little Marfit Head
Lockton Low Moor
West Side Brow
First Rigg
Black Howe Rigg
Marfit Head
Great Marfit Head Slack
TAYLOR HILL
Yorfalls Wood
East Toft Dike
Dundale Rigg
Horness Rigg
High Horcum Farm
Lower Marfit Head Slack
RAINDALE ROAD
Stony Moor
Levisham Moor
Rhumbard Snout Wood
Dundale Pond
Raindale Scar
NEWTONDALE FOREST DRIVE
Levisham Beck
Smeffell Rigg
Mount Pleasant Farm
High House Farm
Chilton Saintoft Farm
Boonhill Farm
Grove House
BRAYGATE BALK
BRAYGATE LANE
LIMPSEY GATE LANE
Warren Farm
Pasture Rigg
Black Howe
RAWCLIFF ROAD
LC
Levisham Station
Newton Dale
PH
Levisham
PO
Newton-on-Rawcliffe
RAWCLIFF RD
Pickering Beck
YO18
LITTLE FIELD LANE
BRAYGATE LA
Low Stead Farm
DAVID LANE
Rustithead Slack
KELD LANE
Melrose Farm
Keld Farm
Cemy
Levisham Wood
Levisham Mill Farm
MILL BANK ROAD
PO
YH
Rustif Head
East Brow Farm
East Brow Wood
Rowl Wood
BACK LA
Cemy
Green Dale
HEADLAND LANE
YATTS ROAD
East Brow House
Lockton
HUDGIN LA
HOSTESS LANE
LOCKTON LANE A169
Thwaite Head
Keldlands
Thwaite Wood
Keldlands Farm
Howlgate Nab
EAST BROW ROAD
North Yorkshire Moors Railway
WESTFIELD LANE
Holm Woods
Haugh Rigg Farm
Levisham Wood
Staindale Lodge
WEST DIKE RD
Lydds House
Howlgate Farm
Hagg Wood
Clenfield Rigg
OVERSCAR LA
OVERSCAR LA
Glebe Farm
KELDGATE ROAD
Lydds Farm
RUDDINGS ROAD
Ness Head
High Dalby House
DALBY FOREST DR
Little Dale Rigg
Farwath Hill Top
High Wood
Yatts Farm
Crown Wood
Farfields
PH
Farwath
CROSSDALE RD
Fox & Rabbit Farm
Blansby Park Wood
Sneverdale Rigg
Haugh Rigg
High Plantation
Gundale Wood
Oak Tree Farm
Low Wood
P
Dalby Forest Visitor Centre
Square Wood
Black Plantation
High Blansby
East Hambleton Farm
YATTS ROAD
Blansby Park
Spring Wood
Nut Wood
Low Dalby
Haugh Wood
Upper Dalby Wood
Dalby Beck
Blansby Park Wood
Southview Farm
West Farm
High Kingthorpe
Thornton Dale
Blansby Park Farm
Low Dalby Wood
DALBY FOREST DRIVE
New Hambleton Farm
Yatts Brow Farm
East Kingthorpe Farm
A169
Wailes Hagg Wood
Common Plantation
Ellerburn Bank Nature Reserve
Blansby Park Wood
Pexton Moor
Newbridge Quarry
8
93
7
92
6
91
5
90
4
89
3
88
2
87
1
86
80
81
82
83
84
85

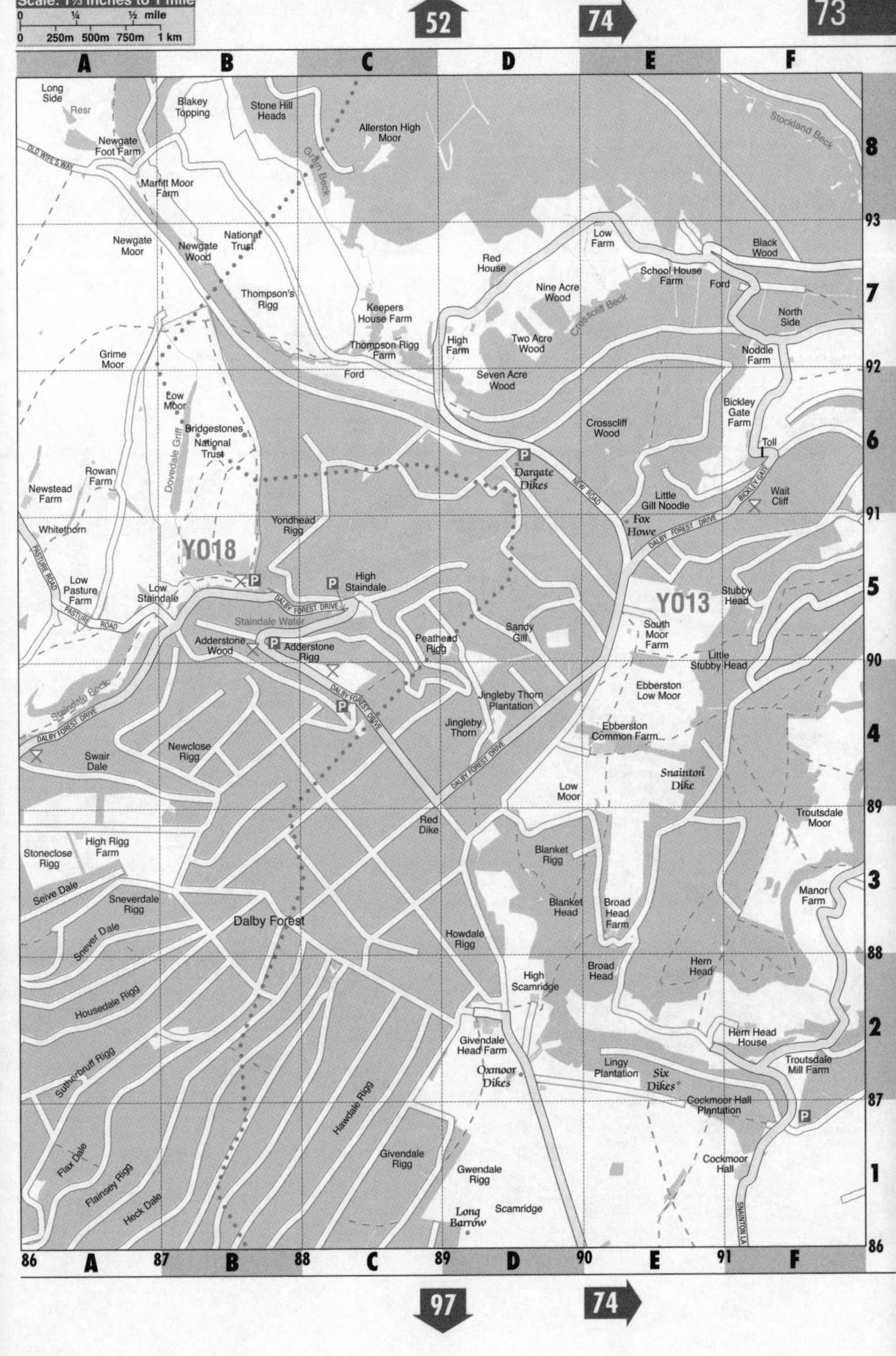
Scale: 1⅓ inches to 1 mile
0 ¼ ½ mile
0 250m 500m 750m 1 km
52
74
A B C D E F
Long Side
Resr
Blakey Topping
Stone Hill Heads
Allerston High Moor
Stockland Beck
Newgate Foot Farm
OLD WIFE'S WAY
Grain Beck
Marfitt Moor Farm
Newgate Moor
Newgate Wood
National Trust
Low Farm
Black Wood
Red House
School House Farm
Ford
Nine Acre Wood
Thompson's Rigg
Keepers House Farm
Crosscliff Beck
North Side
High Farm
Two Acre Wood
Thompson Rigg Farm
Noddle Farm
Grime Moor
Ford
Seven Acre Wood
Low Moor
Bickley Gate Farm
Dovedale Griff
Bridgestones National Trust
Crosscliff Wood
Toll
Rowan Farm
Dargate Dikes
NEW ROAD
Wait Cliff
Newstead Farm
Little Gill Noodle
BICKLEY GATE
Whitethorn
Yondhead Rigg
Fox Howe
DALBY FOREST DRIVE
YO18
PASTURE ROAD
Low Pasture Farm
Low Staindale
High Staindale
YO13
Stubby Head
Staindale Water
Sandy Gill
South Moor Farm
Adderstone Wood
Adderstone Rigg
Peathead Rigg
Little Stubby Head
Staindale Beck
Ebberston Low Moor
Jingleby Thorn Plantation
Jingleby Thorn
Ebberston Common Farm
Swair Dale
Newclose Rigg
Snainton Dike
Low Moor
Troutsdale Moor
Red Dike
Stoneclose Rigg
High Rigg Farm
Blanket Rigg
Seive Dale
Sneverdale Rigg
Blanket Head
Broad Head Farm
Manor Farm
Dalby Forest
Snever Dale
Howdale Rigg
Housedale Rigg
High Scamridge
Broad Head
Hern Head
Hern Head House
Givendale Head Farm
Sutherbruff Rigg
Oxmoor Dikes
Lingy Plantation
Six Dikes
Troutsdale Mill Farm
Cockmoor Hall Plantation
Hawdale Rigg
Givendale Rigg
Gwendale Rigg
Cockmoor Hall
Flax Dale
Flainsey Rigg
Heck Dale
Long Barrow
Scamridge
SNAINTON LA
8 93 7 92 6 91 5 90 4 89 3 88 2 87 1 86
86 87 88 89 90 91
97
74

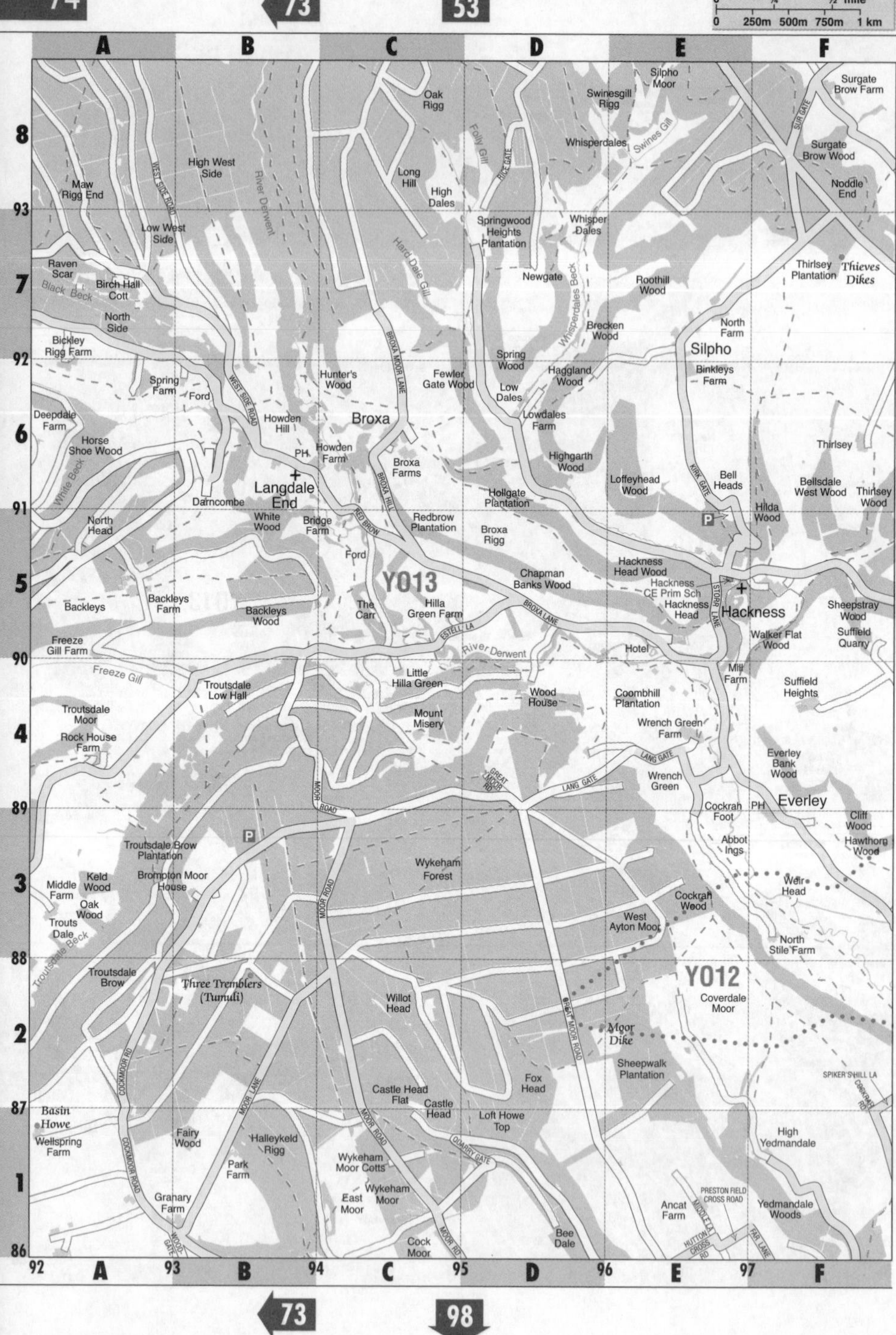

73
53

Scale: 1⅓ inches to 1 mile

0   ¼   ½   mile

0   250m   500m   750m   1 km

Column A

Maw Rigg End
Low West Side
Raven Scar
Black Beck
Birch Hall Cott
North Side
Bickley Rigg Farm
Deepdale Farm
Horse Shoe Wood
White Beck
Spring Farm
Ford
North Head
Backleys
Backleys Farm
Freeze Gill Farm
Freeze Gill
Troutsdale Moor
Troutsdale Low Hall
Troutsdale Brow Plantation
Rock House Farm
Middle Farm
Keld Wood
Oak Wood
Trouts Dale
Troutsdale Brow
Troutshire Beck
Basin Howe
Wellspring Farm
Cockmoor Rd
Fairy Wood
Granary Farm

Column B

High West Side
River Derwent
West Side Road
Howden Hill
Beck Back Road
Howden Farm
PH
Langdale End
Darncombe
White Wood
Bridge Farm
Ford
Backleys Wood
The Carr
Moor Road
Three Tremblers (Tumuli)
Brompton Moor House
Moor Lane
Halleykeld Rigg
Park Farm
East Moor
Wykeham Moor Cotts
Cock Moor
Moor Road

Column C

Oak Rigg
Long Hill
High Dales
Fairy Gill
Hard Dale Gill
Hunter's Wood
Broxa
Broxa Moor Lane
Broxa Farms
Broxa Hill
Red Brow
Redbrow Plantation
Hilla Green Farm
STELL LA
Little Hilla Green
Mount Misery
Wykeham Forest
Willot Head
Castle Head Flat
Castle Head
Wykeham Moor
Y013

Column D

Springwood Heights Plantation
Newgate
Buck Gate
Spring Wood
Fewler Gate Wood
Low Dales
Lowdales Farm
Hollgate Plantation
Broxa Rigg
Chapman Banks Wood
Broxa Lane
River Derwent
Wood House
Great Moor Road
Lang Gate
Moor Dike
Loft Howe Top
Fox Head
Bee Dale
Quarry Gate

Column E

Swinesgill Rigg
Silpho Moor
Swinss Gill
Whisperdales
Whisper Dales
Whisperdales Beck
Roothill Wood
Brecken Wood
Haggland Wood
Highgarth Wood
Loffleyhead Wood
Silpho
Binkleys Farm
Bell Heads
Hilda Wood
Hackness Head Wood
Hackness CE Prim Sch
Hackness Head
Hotel
Coombhill Plantation
Wrench Green Farm
Lang Gate
Wrench Green
Cockrah Foot
Abbot Ings
Cockrah Wood
West Ayton Moor
Black Moor Road
Coverdale Moor
Y012
Sheepwalk Plantation
Ancat Farm
Preston Field Cross Road
Hutton Lane

Column F

Surgate Brow Farm
Surgate Brow Wood
Sea Cut
Noddle End
Thirlsey Plantation
Thieves Dikes
North Farm
Thirlsey
Bellsdale West Wood
Thirlsey Wood
Hackness
Sheepstray Wood
Suffield Quarry
Store Lane
Walker Flat Wood
Suffield Heights
Mill Farm
Everley Bank Wood
Everley
PH
Cliff Wood
Hawthorn Wood
Weir Head
North Stile Farm
Spiker's Hill La
High Yedmandale
Yedmandale Woods
Fire Lane

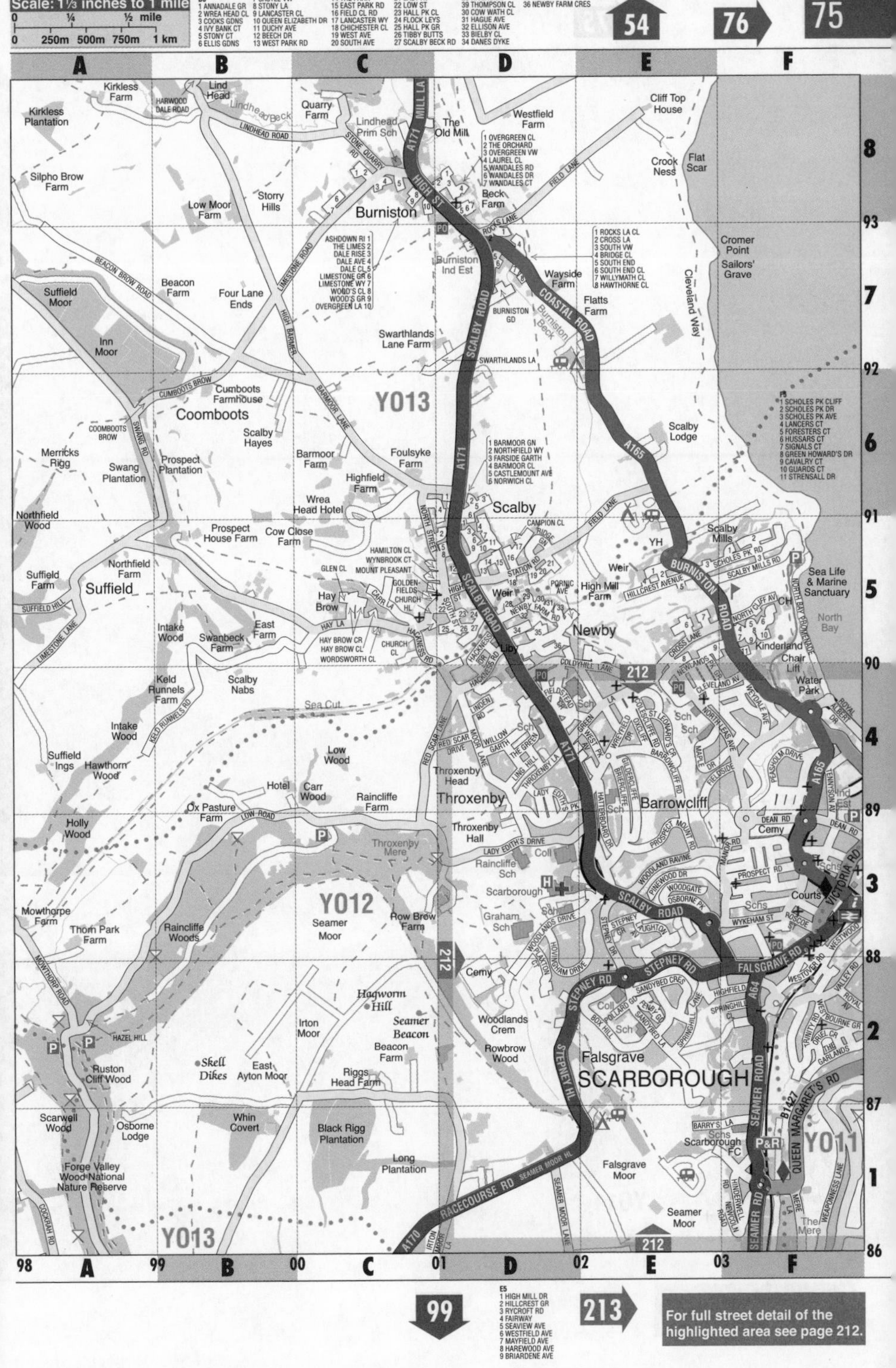
Scale: 1⅓ inches to 1 mile
0 ¼ ½ mile
0 250m 500m 750m 1 km
D5
1 ANNADALE GR
2 WREA HEAD CL
3 COOKS GDNS
4 IVY BANK CT
5 STONY CT
6 ELLIS GDNS
7 CASTLE VW
8 STONY LA
9 LANCASTER CL
10 QUEEN ELIZABETH DR
11 DUCHY AVE
12 BEECH DR
13 WEST PARK RD
14 THE PARK
15 EAST PARK RD
16 FIELD CL RD
17 LANCASTER WY
18 CHICHESTER CL
19 WEST AVE
20 SOUTH AVE
21 EAST AV
22 LOW ST
23 HALL PK CL
24 FLOCK LEYS
25 HALL PK GR
26 TIBBY BUTTS
27 SCALBY BECK RD
28 RIVERSIDE
29 THOMPSON CL
30 COW WATH CL
31 HAGUE AVE
32 ELLISON AVE
33 BIELBY CL
34 DANES DYKE
35 NEWBY FARM CL
36 NEWBY FARM CRES
54
76
A B C D E F
8 93 7 92 6 91 5 90 4 89 3 88 2 87 1 86
Kirkless Farm
Kirkless Plantation
Lind Head
Lindhead Beck
Quarry Farm
Lindhead Prim Sch
MILL LA
The Old Mill
Westfield Farm
Cliff Top House
Crook Ness
Flat Scar
1 OVERGREEN CL
2 THE ORCHARD
3 OVERGREEN VW
4 LAUREL CL
5 WANDALES RD
6 WANDALES DR
7 WANDALES CT
Silpho Brow Farm
Storry Hills
Low Moor Farm
Burniston
HIGH ST
Beck Farm
FIELD LANE
ROCKS LANE
ASHDOWN RI 1
THE LIMES 2
DALE RISE 3
DALE AVE 4
DALE CL 5
LIMESTONE GR 6
LIMESTONE WY 7
WOOD'S CL 8
WOOD'S GR 9
OVERGREEN LA 10
1 ROCKS LA CL
2 CROSS LA
3 SOUTH VW
4 BRIDGE CL
5 SOUTH END
6 SOUTH END CL
7 WILLYMATH CL
8 HAWTHORNE CL
Cromer Point
Sailors' Grave
Burniston Ind Est
Wayside Farm
Flatts Farm
Cleveland Way
BEACON BROW ROAD
Beacon Farm
Four Lane Ends
LIMESTONE ROAD
Suffield Moor
Inn Moor
BURNISTON GD
COASTAL ROAD
Swarthlands Lane Farm
SWARTHLANDS LA
SCALBY ROAD
CUMBOOTS BROW
Cumboots Farmhouse
Coomboots
YO13
BARMOOR LANE
F5
1 SCHOLES PK CLIFF
2 SCHOLES PK DR
3 SCHOLES PK AVE
4 LANCERS CT
5 FORESTERS CT
6 HUSSARS CT
7 SIGNALS CT
8 GREEN HOWARD'S DR
9 CAVALRY CT
10 GUARDS CT
11 STRENSALL DR
COOMBOOTS BROW
SWANG RD
Merricks Rigg
Swang Plantation
Prospect Plantation
Scalby Hayes
Barmoor Farm
Foulsyke Farm
1 BARMOOR GN
2 NORTHFIELD WY
3 FARSIDE GARTH
4 BARMOOR CL
5 CASTLEMOUNT AVE
6 NORWICH CL
A171
A165
Scalby Lodge
Highfield Farm
Wrea Head Hotel
Scalby
Northfield Wood
Prospect House Farm
Cow Close Farm
NORTH STREET
CAMPION CL
FIELD LANE
YH
Scalby Mills
SCHOLES PK RD
SCALBY MILLS RD
Sea Life & Marine Sanctuary
Suffield Farm
Northfield Farm
Suffield
HAMILTON CL
WYNBROOK CT
MOUNT PLEASANT
GLEN CL
GOLDEN FIELDS
CHURCH HL
STATION RD
Weir
PORNIC AVE
High Mill Farm
HILLCREST AVENUE
BURNISTON ROAD
NORTH BAY PROMENADE
SUFFIELD HILL
Hay Brow
CARR LA
HAY LA
HAY BROW CR
HAY BROW CL
WORDSWORTH CL
CHURCH CL
HACKNESS RD
NEWBY FARM RD
Newby
NORTH CLIFF AV
CH
North Bay
Kinderland
Intake Wood
Swanbeck Farm
East Farm
Liby
CROSS LANE
Chair Lift
Water Park
LIMESTONE LANE
Keld Runnels Farm
Scalby Nabs
COLDYHILL LANE
212
NEWLANDS PK
CLEVELAND AV
WEYDALE AVE
ROYAL ALBERT DR
Sea Cut
KELD RUNNELS RD
RED SCAR LANE
LINDEN RD
WILLOW GARTH
THE GREEN
FIELDSTEAD
GREEN LA
WREFIELD DR
ST LEONARD'S CR
BARROWCLIFF RD
NORTH LEAS AVE
MAPLE DR
FIELDSIDE
PEASHOLM DRIVE
TENNYSON AV
Intake Wood
Low Wood
RED SCAR DRIVE
MOOR LANE
LING HILL
THROXENBY LA
Suffield Ings
Hawthorn Wood
Hotel
Carr Wood
Throxenby Head
Raincliffe Farm
Throxenby
LADY EDITH'S PK
GILDERCLIFFE
BRIERCLIFFE
HATTERBOARD DR
Barrowcliff
Ind Est
Ox Pasture Farm
LOW ROAD
Holly Wood
Throxenby Hall
LADY EDITH'S DRIVE
PROSPECT MOUNT RD
MANOR RD
Cemy
DEAN RD
Throxenby Mere
Coll
Raincliffe Sch
WOODLAND RAVINE
PINEWOOD DR
WOODGATE
OSBORNE PK
PROSPECT RD
VICTORIA RD
Courts
YO12
Scarborough
Mowthorpe Farm
Thorn Park Farm
Raincliffe Woods
Seamer Moor
Row Brow Farm
Graham Sch
SCALBY ROAD
WOODLANDS DRIVE
STEPNEY DR
STEPNEY
WYKEHAM ST
ROSCOE ST
FALSGRAVE RD
WESTWOOD
MOWTHORP ROAD
Cemy
HOVINGHAM DRIVE
STEPNEY RD
SANDYBED CRES
HIGHFIELD
SPRINGHILL CL
WESTOVER RD
VALLEY RD
Hagworm Hill
Irton Moor
Seamer Beacon
Woodlands Crem
Coll
POLLARD GD
BOX HILL
SANDYBED LA
SPRINGHILL LANE
A64
TRINITY RD
WESTBOURNE GR
ORIEL CR
THE GARLANDS
HAZEL HILL
Ruston Cliff Wood
Skell Dikes
East Ayton Moor
Beacon Farm
Riggs Head Farm
Rowbrow Wood
STEPNEY HL
Falsgrave
SCARBOROUGH
SEAMER ROAD
QUEEN MARGARET'S RD
B1427
Scarwell Wood
Osborne Lodge
Whin Covert
Black Rigg Plantation
BARRY'S LA
Schs
Scarborough FC
P&R
YO11
Forge Valley Wood National Nature Reserve
Long Plantation
RACECOURSE RD
SEAMER MOOR HL
SEAMER MOOR LANE
Falsgrave Moor
HINDERWELL RD
NEWCOLN ROAD
MERE LA
WEAPONNESS LANE
COCKRAH RD
YO13
A170
IRTON MOOR LA
Seamer Moor
The Mere
SEAMER RD
98 A 99 B 00 C 01 D 02 E 03 F
99
E5
1 HIGH MILL DR
2 HILLCREST GR
3 RYCROFT RD
4 FAIRWAY
5 SEAVIEW AVE
6 WESTFIELD AVE
7 MAYFIELD AVE
8 HAREWOOD AVE
9 BRIARDENE AVE
213
For full street detail of the highlighted area see page 212.

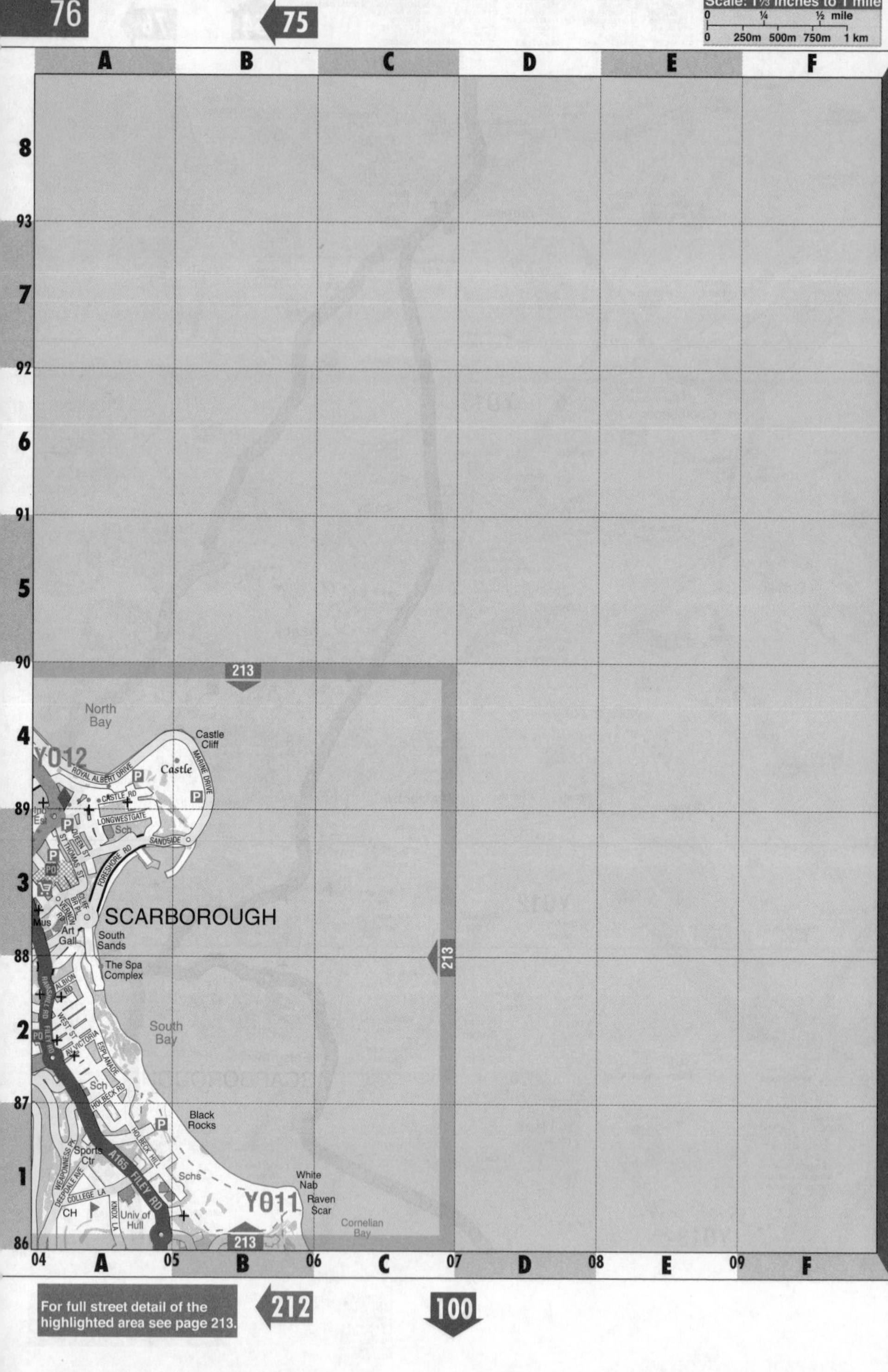

Scale: 1⅓ inches to 1 mile

| 0 | ¼ | ½ mile |
| 0 | 250m | 500m 750m 1 km |

North Bay

Castle Cliff

YO12

ROYAL ALBERT DRIVE

Castle

MARINE DRIVE

CASTLE RD

LONGWESTGATE

Sch

SANDSIDE

SCARBOROUGH

Mus

Art Gall

South Sands

The Spa Complex

South Bay

Sch

Black Rocks

Sports Ctr

A165

FLEET RD

COLLEGE LA

CH

Schs

Univ of Hull

YO11

White Nab

Raven Scar

Cornelian Bay

213

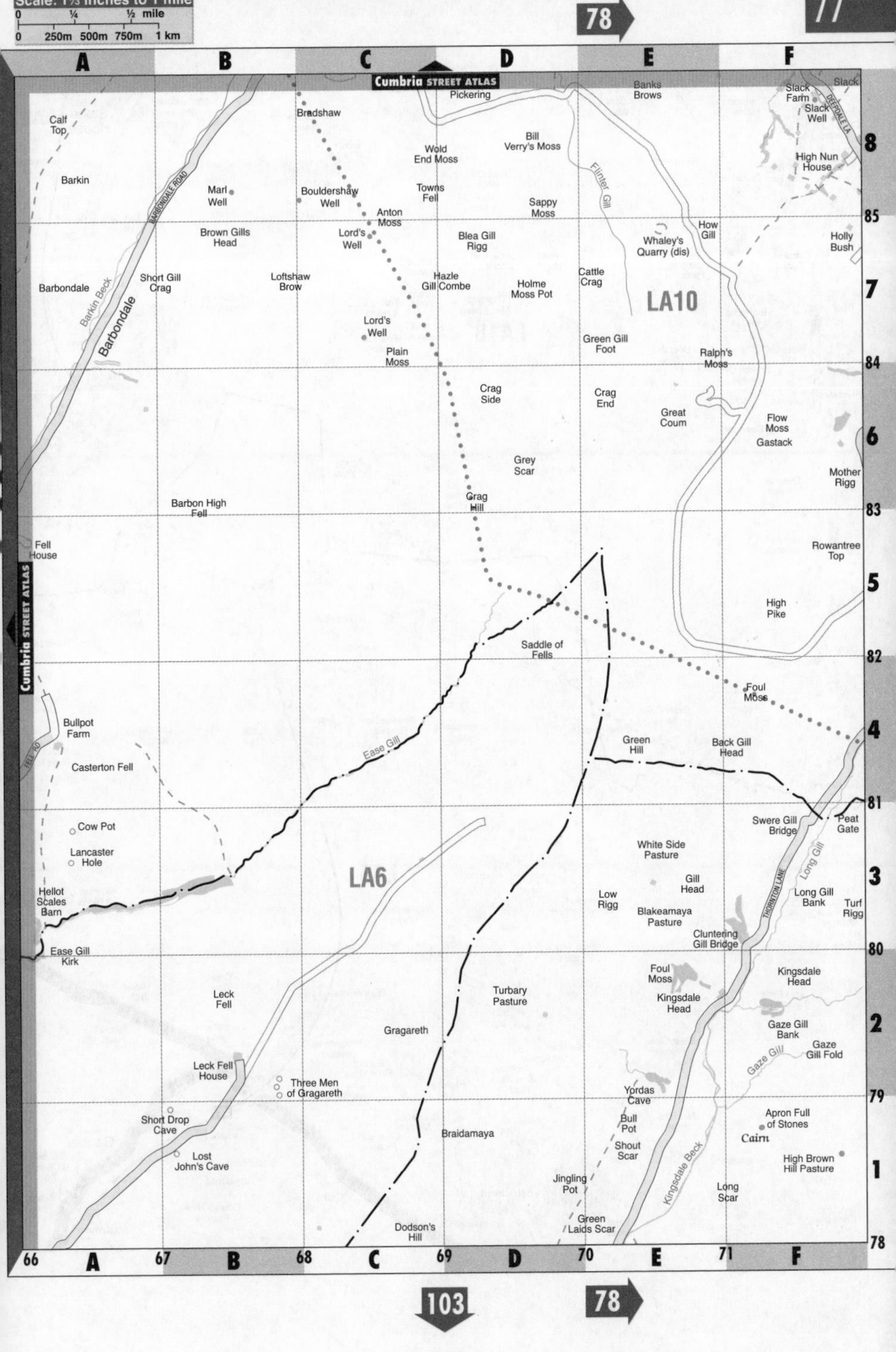
Scale: 1⅓ inches to 1 mile
0 ¼ ½ mile
0 250m 500m 750m 1 km
78
A B C D E F
Cumbria STREET ATLAS
Pickering
Banks Brows
Slack Farm
Slack
Slack Well
DEEPDALE LA
Calf Top
Bradshaw
Wold End Moss
Bill Verry's Moss
High Nun House
Barkin
BARBONDALE ROAD
Marl Well
Bouldershaw Well
Towns Fell
Sappy Moss
Flinter Gill
Anton Moss
Brown Gills Head
Lord's Well
Blea Gill Rigg
How Gill
Whaley's Quarry (dis)
Holly Bush
Barbondale
Barkin Beck
Short Gill Crag
Loftshaw Brow
Hazle Gill Combe
Holme Moss Pot
Cattle Crag
LA10
Barbondale
Lord's Well
Plain Moss
Green Gill Foot
Ralph's Moss
Crag Side
Crag End
Great Coum
Flow Moss
Gastack
Grey Scar
Mother Rigg
Crag Hill
Barbon High Fell
Fell House
Rowantree Top
High Pike
Saddle of Fells
Foul Moss
Bullpot Farm
Green Hill
Back Gill Head
FELL RD
Ease Gill
Casterton Fell
Swere Gill Bridge
Peat Gate
Cow Pot
White Side Pasture
Lancaster Hole
THORNTON LANE
Long Gill
LA6
Gill Head
Hellot Scales Barn
Low Rigg
Long Gill Bank
Turf Rigg
Blakeamaya Pasture
Cluntering Gill Bridge
Ease Gill Kirk
Foul Moss
Kingsdale Head
Leck Fell
Turbary Pasture
Kingsdale Head
Gaze Gill Bank
Gragareth
Gaze Gill
Gaze Gill Fold
Leck Fell House
Three Men of Gragareth
Yordas Cave
Apron Full of Stones
Short Drop Cave
Bull Pot
Cairn
Braidamaya
Shout Scar
Lost John's Cave
Kingsdale Beck
High Brown Hill Pasture
Jingling Pot
Long Scar
Green Laids Scar
Dodson's Hill
8 85 7 84 6 83 5 82 4 81 3 80 2 79 1 78
66 67 68 69 70 71
103
78

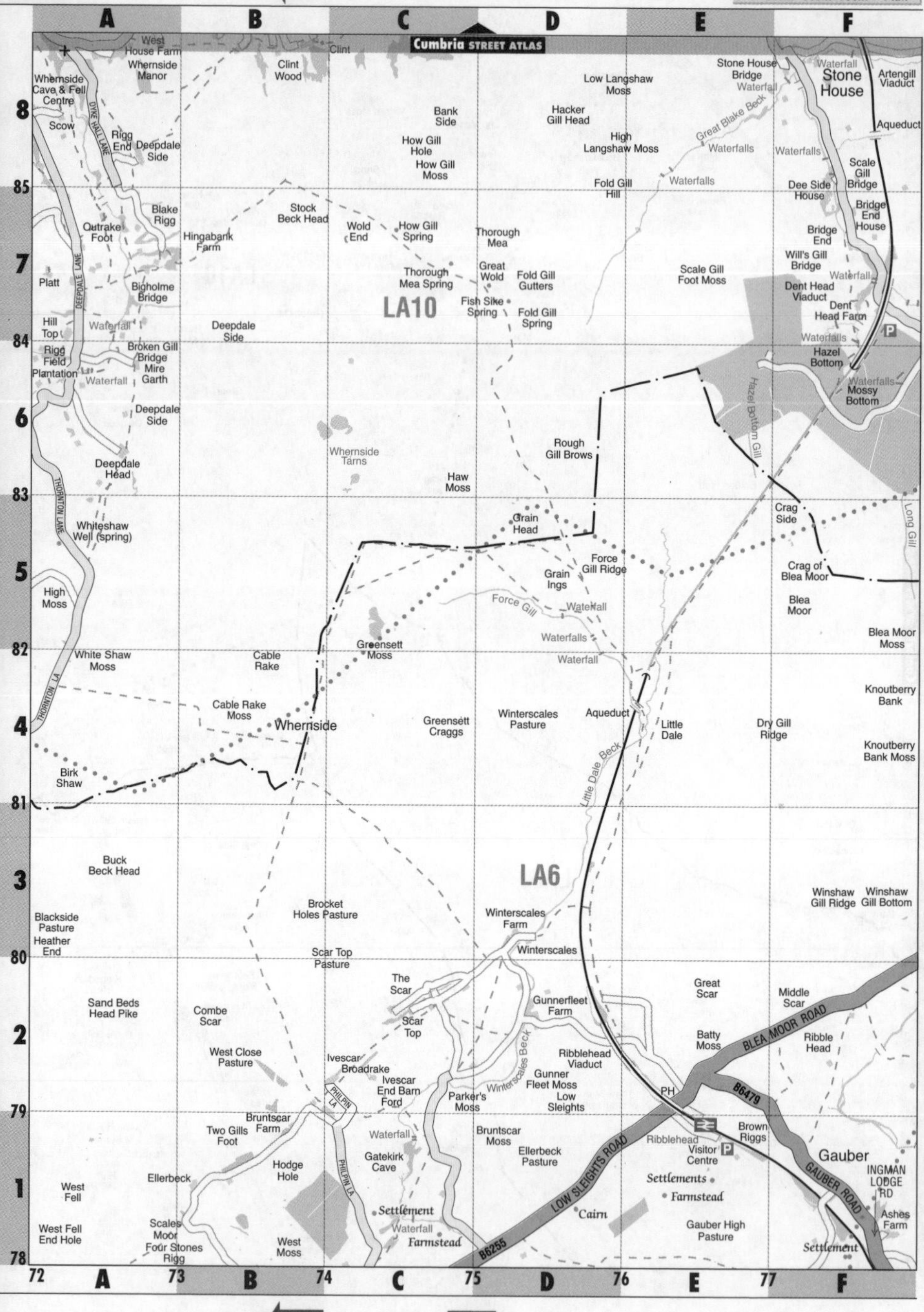

Scale: 1⅓ inches to 1 mile

0   ¼   ½ mile
0   250m 500m 750m 1 km

Cumbria STREET ATLAS

LA10

LA6

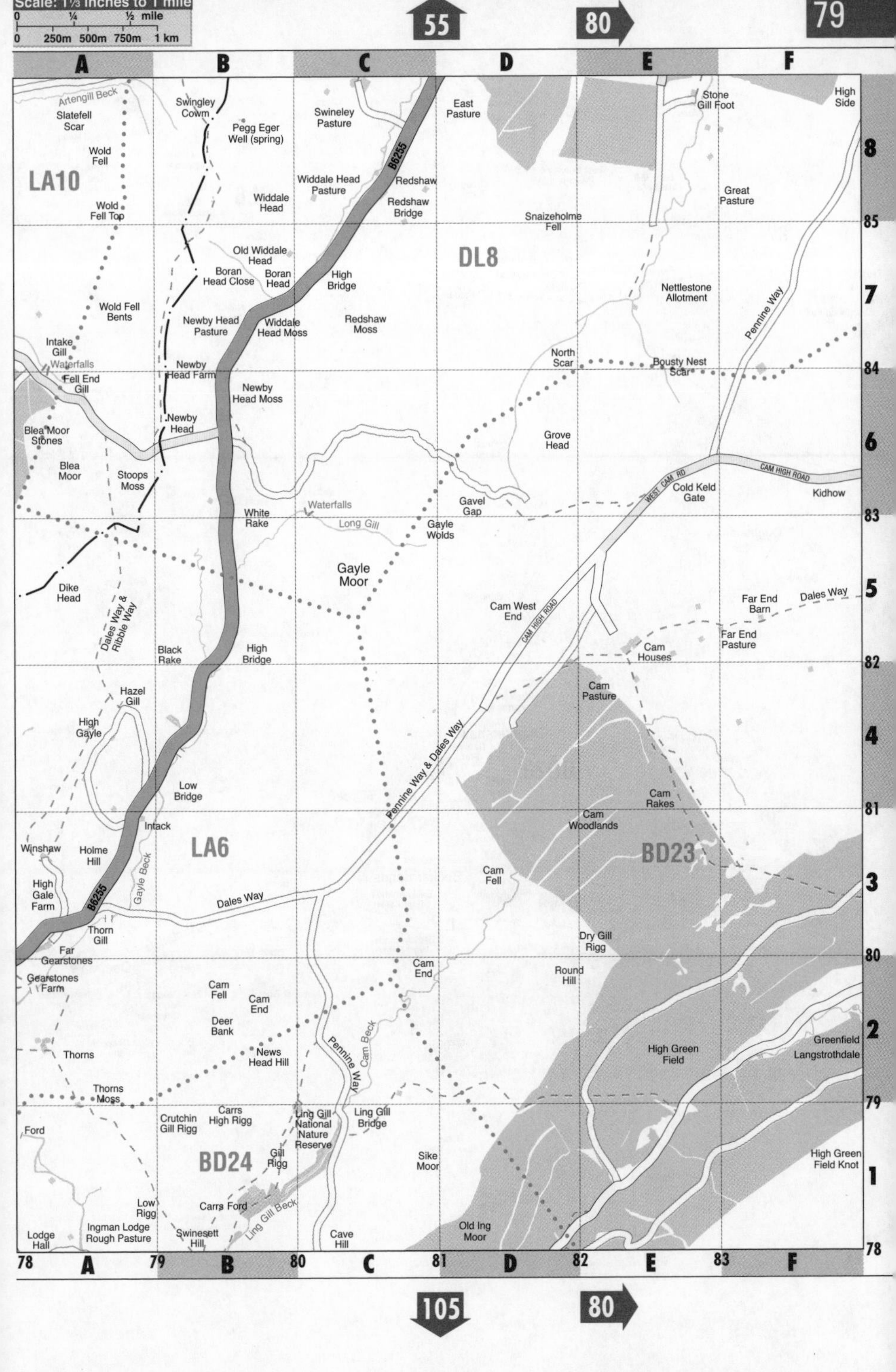
Scale: 1⅓ inches to 1 mile
0 ¼ ½ mile
0 250m 500m 750m 1 km
55
80
A B C D E F
Artengill Beck
Slatefell Scar
Swingley Cowm
Pegg Eger Well (spring)
Swineley Pasture
East Pasture
Stone Gill Foot
High Side
Wold Fell
LA10
Widdale Head Pasture
Redshaw
Widdale Head
Redshaw Bridge
Great Pasture
Wold Fell Top
Snaizeholme Fell
Old Widdale Head
Boran Head Close
Boran Head
High Bridge
DL8
Nettlestone Allotment
Wold Fell Bents
Newby Head Pasture
Widdale Head Moss
Redshaw Moss
Pennine Way
Intake Gill
Waterfalls
Fell End Gill
North Scar
Bousty Nest Scar
Newby Head Farm
Newby Head Moss
Blea Moor Stones
Newby Head
Grove Head
Blea Moor
Stoops Moss
Cold Keld Gate
CAM HIGH ROAD
WEST CAM RD
Kidhow
White Rake
Waterfalls
Long Gill
Gavel Gap
Gayle Wolds
Gayle Moor
Dike Head
Cam West End
CAM HIGH ROAD
Far End Barn
Dales Way
Dales Way & Ribble Way
Black Rake
High Bridge
Far End Pasture
Cam Houses
Cam Pasture
Hazel Gill
High Gayle
Pennine Way & Dales Way
Low Bridge
Cam Rakes
Cam Woodlands
Intack
Winshaw
Holme Hill
LA6
BD23
Gayle Beck
High Gale Farm
B6255
Cam Fell
Dales Way
Thorn Gill
Dry Gill Rigg
Far Gearstones
Gearstones Farm
Cam End
Round Hill
Cam Fell
Cam End
Deer Bank
Pennine Way
Cam Beck
High Green Field
Greenfield
Langstrothdale
Thorns
News Head Hill
Thorns Moss
Crutchin Gill Rigg
Carrs High Rigg
Ling Gill National Nature Reserve
Ling Gill Bridge
Ford
BD24
Gill Rigg
Sike Moor
High Green Field Knot
Low Rigg
Carrs Ford
Ling Gill Beck
Lodge Hall
Ingman Lodge Rough Pasture
Swinesett Hill
Cave Hill
Old Ing Moor
8 85 7 84 6 83 5 82 4 81 3 80 2 79 1 78
78 79 80 81 82 83
105
80

79
56

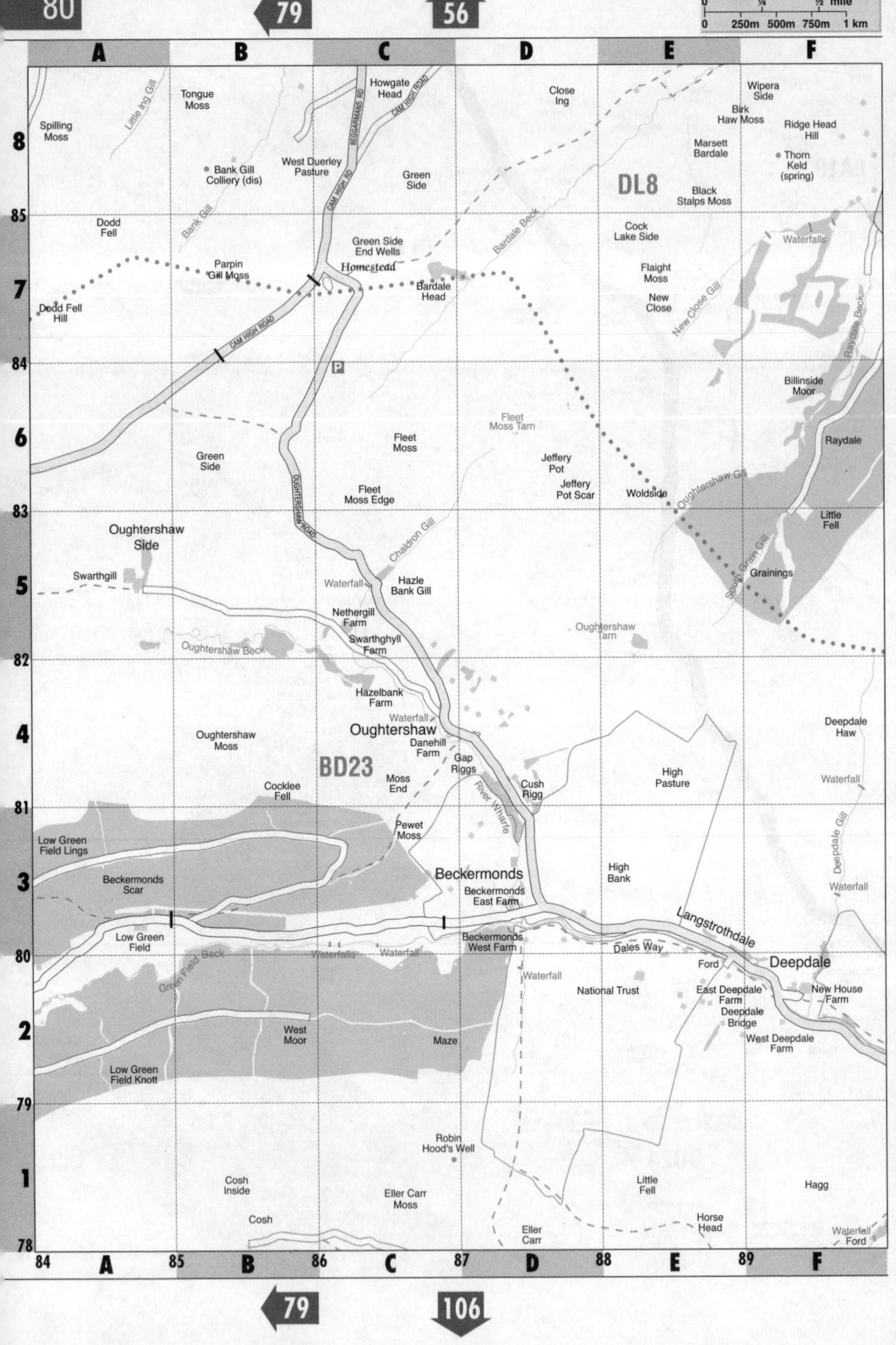
Scale: 1⅓ inches to 1 mile
0 ¼ ½ mile
0 250m 500m 750m 1 km
A B C D E F
Spilling Moss
Tongue Moss
Little Ing Gill
Howgate Head
BEGGARMANS RD
CAM HIGH ROAD
Close Ing
Wipera Side
Birk Haw Moss
Ridge Head Hill
Marsett Bardale
Thorn Keld (spring)
Bank Gill Colliery (dis)
West Duerley Pasture
Green Side
DL8
Black Stalps Moss
Dodd Fell
Bank Gill
Cock Lake Side
Waterfalls
Bardale Beck
Green Side End Wells
Homestead
Parpin Gill Moss
Flaight Moss
Bardale Head
New Close
New Close Gill
Raydale Beck
Dodd Fell Hill
CAM HIGH ROAD
Billinside Moor
Fleet Moss Tarn
Fleet Moss
Raydale
Green Side
Jeffery Pot
Jeffery Pot Scar
OUGHTERSHAW ROAD
Fleet Moss Edge
Woldside
Oughtershaw Gill
Little Fell
Oughtershaw Side
Chaldron Gill
South Grain Gill
Swarthgill
Grainings
Waterfall
Hazle Bank Gill
Nethergill Farm
Swarthghyll Farm
Oughtershaw Tarn
Oughtershaw Beck
Hazelbank Farm
Waterfall
Deepdale Haw
Oughtershaw
Oughtershaw Moss
Danehill Farm
Gap Riggs
BD23
High Pasture
Cocklee Fell
Moss End
Cush Rigg
Waterfall
River Wharfe
Pewet Moss
Low Green Field Lings
Deepdale Gill
High Bank
Beckermonds
Beckermonds Scar
Beckermonds East Farm
Waterfall
Langstrothdale
Low Green Field
Beckermonds West Farm
Dales Way
Green Field Beck
Waterfalls
Waterfall
Ford
Deepdale
Waterfall
National Trust
East Deepdale Farm
New House Farm
Deepdale Bridge
West Moor
Maze
West Deepdale Farm
Low Green Field Knott
Robin Hood's Well
Cosh Inside
Little Fell
Hagg
Ellercarr Moss
Cosh
Horse Head
Eller Carr
Waterfall Ford
8 85 7 84 6 83 5 82 4 81 3 80 2 79 1 78
84 85 86 87 88 89

79
106

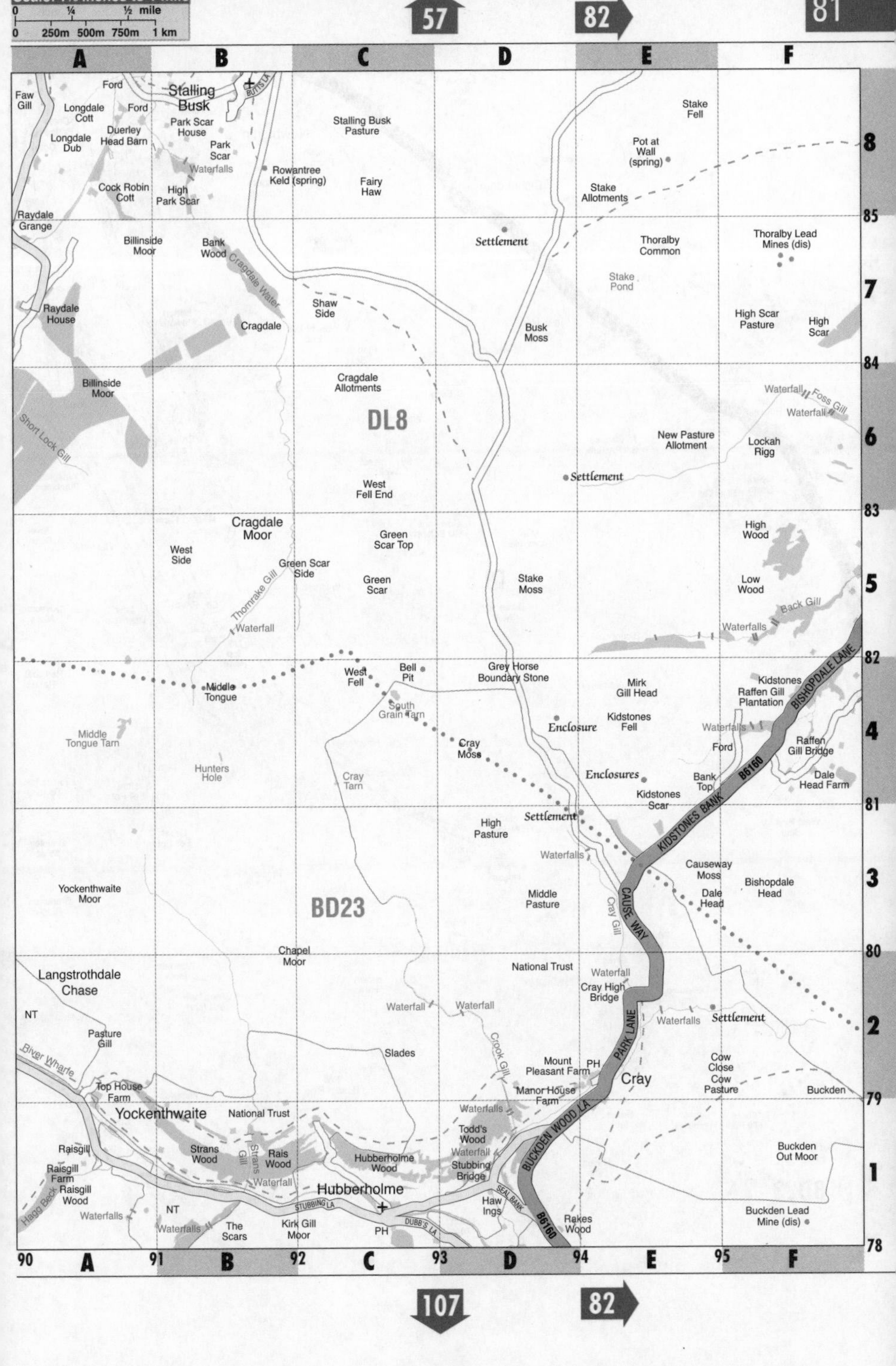
Scale: 1⅓ inches to 1 mile
0 ¼ ½ mile
0 250m 500m 750m 1 km
57
82
A B C D E F
Stalling Busk
Faw Gill
Ford
Longdale Cott
Longdale Dub
Duerley Head Barn
Park Scar House
Park Scar
Waterfalls
Rowantree Keld (spring)
Stalling Busk Pasture
Fairy Haw
Cock Robin Cott
High Park Scar
Raydale Grange
Billinside Moor
Bank Wood
Cragdale Water
Stake Fell
Pot at Wall (spring)
Stake Allotments
Settlement
Thoralby Common
Thoralby Lead Mines (dis)
Stake Pond
Raydale House
Cragdale
Shaw Side
Busk Moss
High Scar Pasture
High Scar
Billinside Moor
Cragdale Allotments
DL8
Short Lock Gill
Waterfall
Foss Gill
New Pasture Allotment
Lockah Rigg
West Fell End
Cragdale Moor
West Side
Green Scar Top
Green Scar Side
Green Scar
Stake Moss
High Wood
Low Wood
Thornrake Gill
Back Gill
Waterfalls
Middle Tongue
West Fell
Bell Pit
Grey Horse Boundary Stone
Mirk Gill Head
Kidstones Raffen Gill Plantation
BISHOPDALE LANE
South Grain Tarn
Enclosure
Kidstones Fell
Middle Tongue Tarn
Cray Moss
Ford
Raffen Gill Bridge
Hunters Hole
Cray Tarn
Enclosures
Bank Top
B6160
Dale Head Farm
Kidstones Scar
KIDSTONES BANK
High Pasture
Causeway Moss
Dale Head
Bishopdale Head
Yockenthwaite Moor
BD23
Middle Pasture
CAUSE WAY
Cray Gill
Chapel Moor
National Trust
Cray High Bridge
Langstrothdale Chase
NT
Pasture Gill
River Wharfe
Slades
PARK LANE
Crook Gill
Mount Pleasant Farm
PH
Cray
Cow Close
Cow Pasture
Buckden
Top House Farm
Manor House Farm
Yockenthwaite
Todd's Wood
BUCKDEN WOOD LA
Raisgill
Strans Wood
Strans Gill
Rais Wood
Hubberholme Wood
Stubbing Bridge
Buckden Out Moor
Raisgill Farm
Raisgill Wood
Hubberholme
SEAL BANK
STUBBING LA
DUBB'S LA
Haw Ings
Hagg Beck
Rakes Wood
Buckden Lead Mine (dis)
The Scars
Kirk Gill Moor
8 85 7 84 6 83 5 82 4 81 3 80 2 79 1 78
90 91 92 93 94 95
107
82

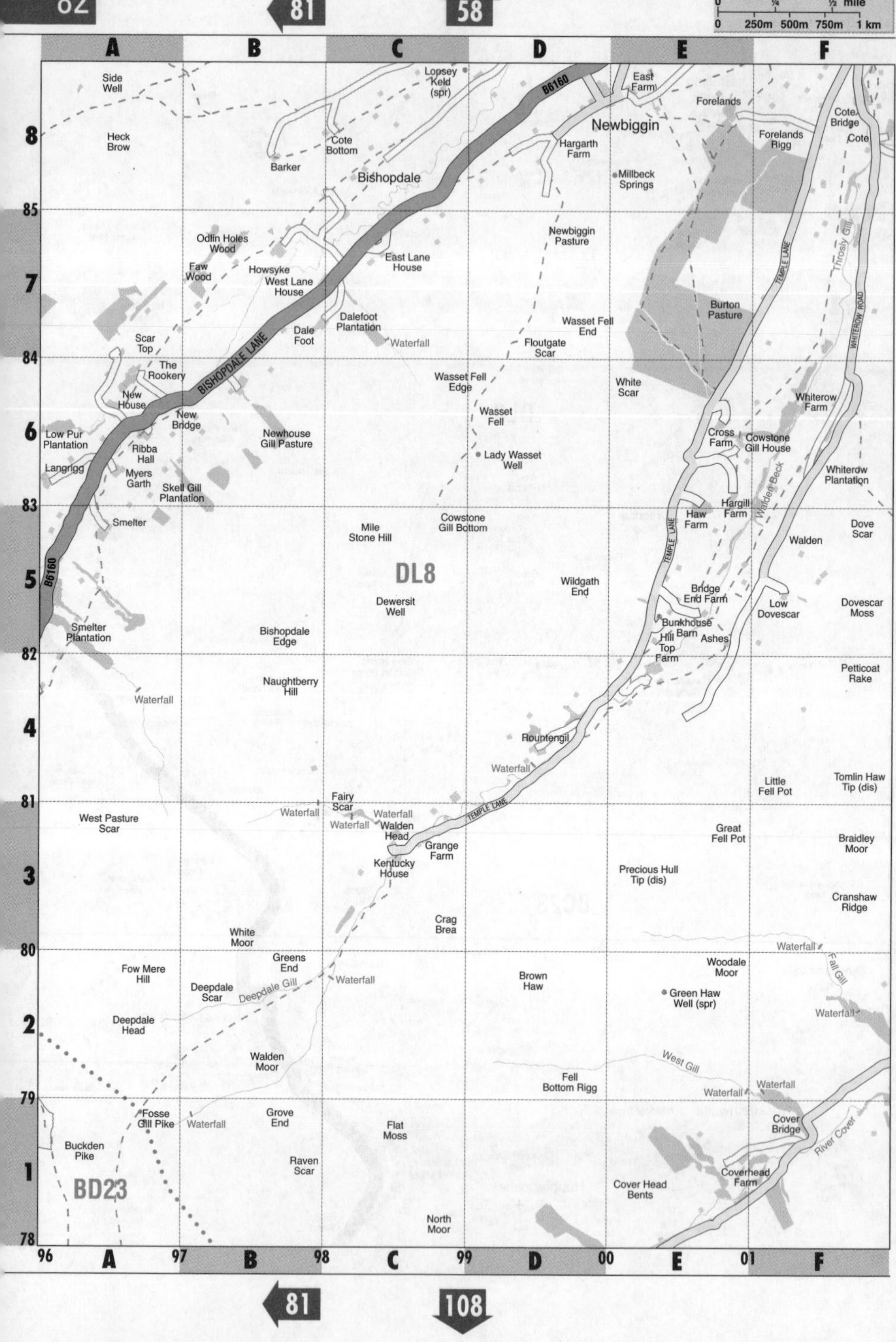

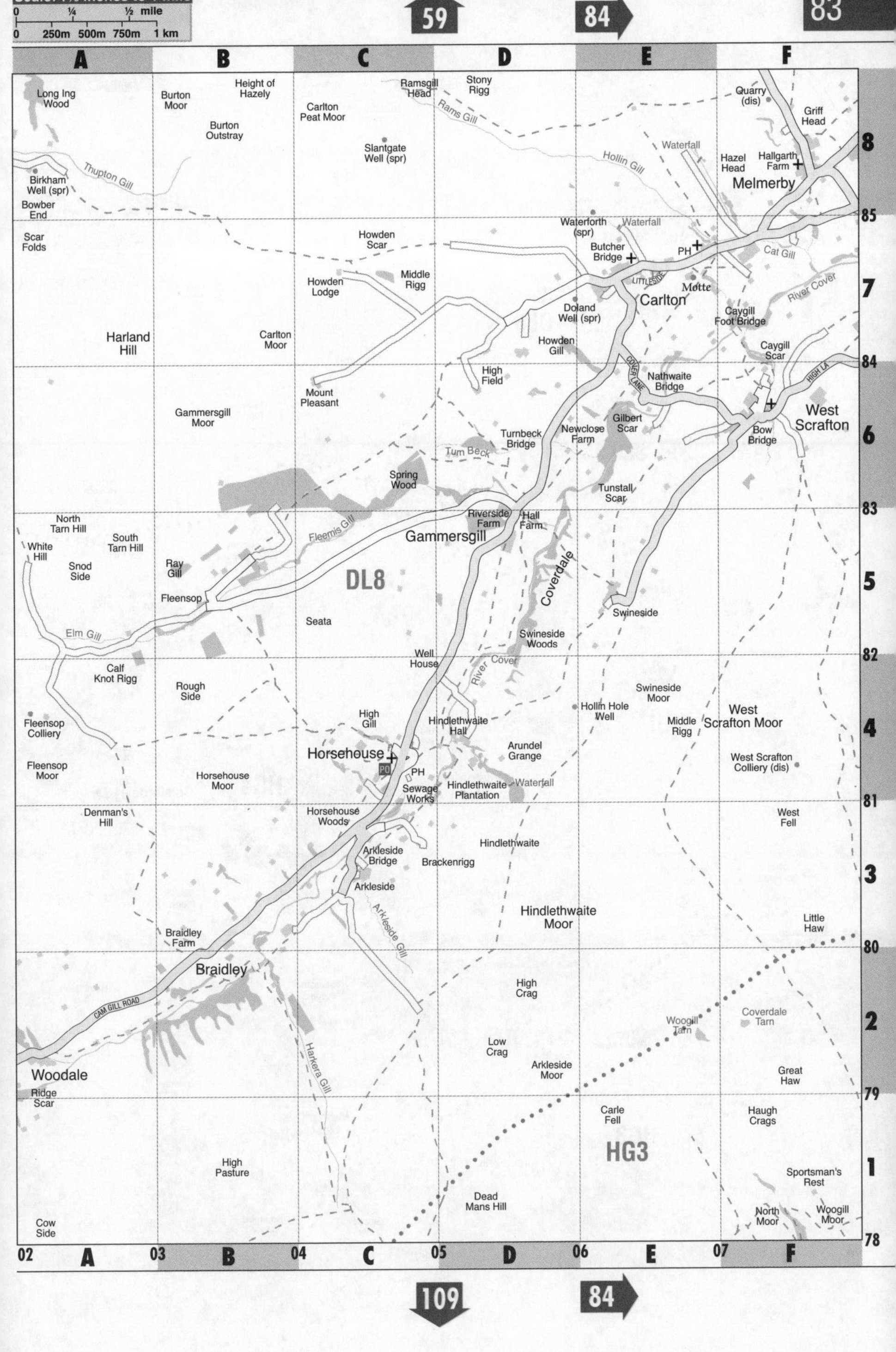

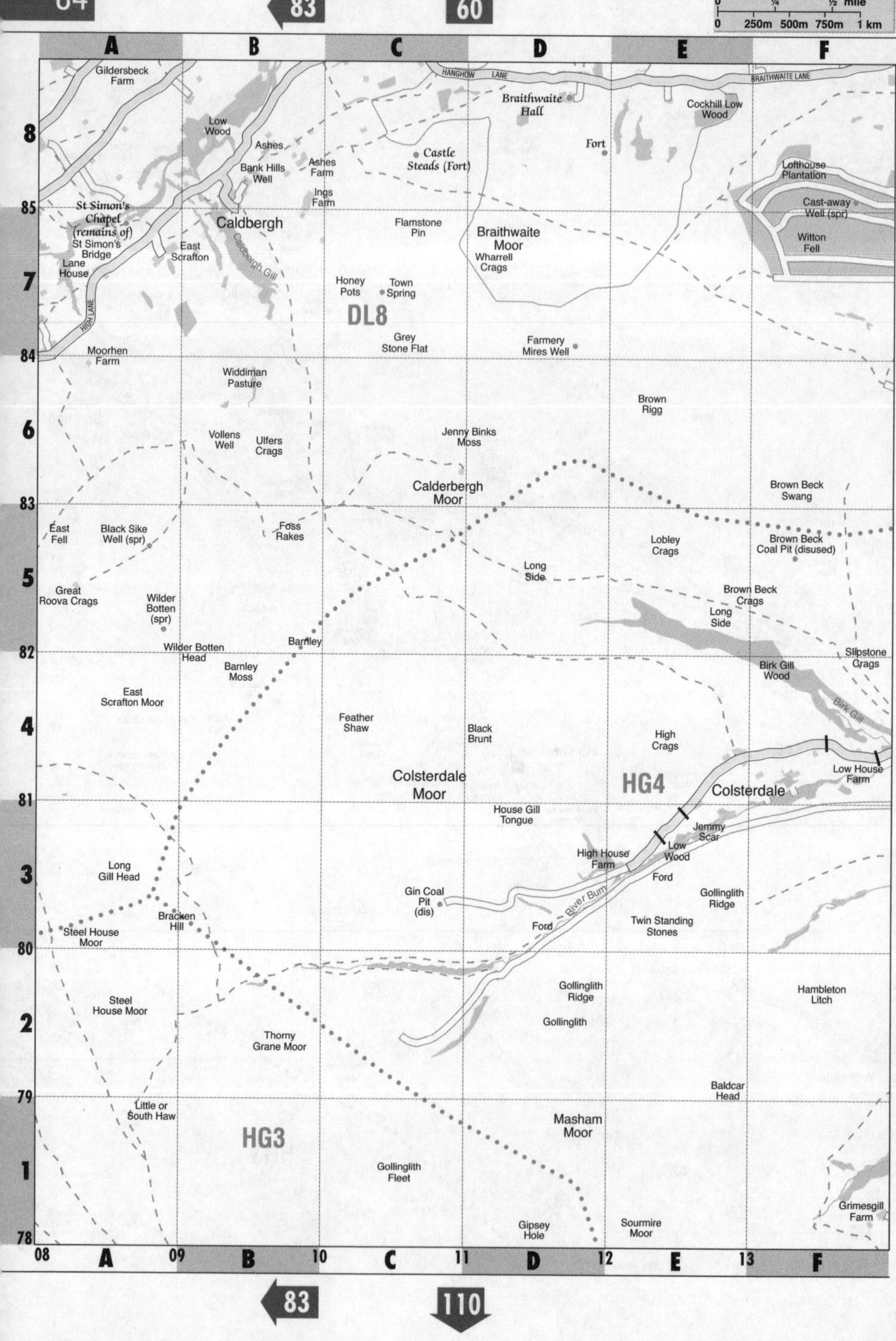

Scale: 1½ inches to 1 mile

0   ¼   ½ mile
0   250m 500m 750m 1 km

A **B** **C** **D** **E** **F**

Gildersbeck Farm

HANGHOW LANE

Braithwaite Hall

BRAITHWAITE LANE

Fort

Cockhill Low Wood

Low Wood

Ashes

Lofthouse Plantation

8

Ashes Farm

Castle Steads (Fort)

Cast-away Well (spr)

Bank Hills Well

Ings Farm

Witton Fell

St Simon's Chapel (remains of)

85

Caldbergh

Flamstone Pin

Braithwaite Moor

St Simon's Bridge Lane House

East Scrafton

Wharrell Crags

Caldbergh Gill

7

Honey Pots

Town Spring

DL8

Grey Stone Flat

Farmery Mires Well

Moorhen Farm

84

HIGH LANE

Widdiman Pasture

Brown Rigg

6

Vollens Well

Ulfers Crags

Jenny Binks Moss

East Fell

Black Sike Well (spr)

Foss Rakes

Calderbergh Moor

Brown Beck Swang

83

Lobley Crags

Brown Beck Coal Pit (disused)

5

Long Side

Brown Beck Crags

Great Roova Crags

Wilder Botten (spr)

Long Side

Slipstone Crags

Barnley

82

Wilder Botten Head

Barnley Moss

Birk Gill Wood

Birk Gill

East Scrafton Moor

Feather Shaw

Black Brunt

High Crags

4

Colsterdale Moor

HG4

Colsterdale

Low House Farm

81

House Gill Tongue

Jemmy Scar

High House Farm

Low Wood

Long Gill Head

3

Gin Coal Pit (dis)

Ford

River Burn

Ford

Gollinglith Ridge

Steel House Moor

Bracken Hill

Ford

Twin Standing Stones

80

Steel House Moor

Gollinglith Ridge

Hambleton Litch

2

Thorny Grane Moor

Gollinglith

Baldcar Head

79

Little or South Haw

HG3

Masham Moor

1

Gollinglith Fleet

Grimesgill Farm

78

Gipsey Hole

Sourmire Moor

08 **A** **09** **B** **10** **C** **11** **D** **12** **E** **13** **F**

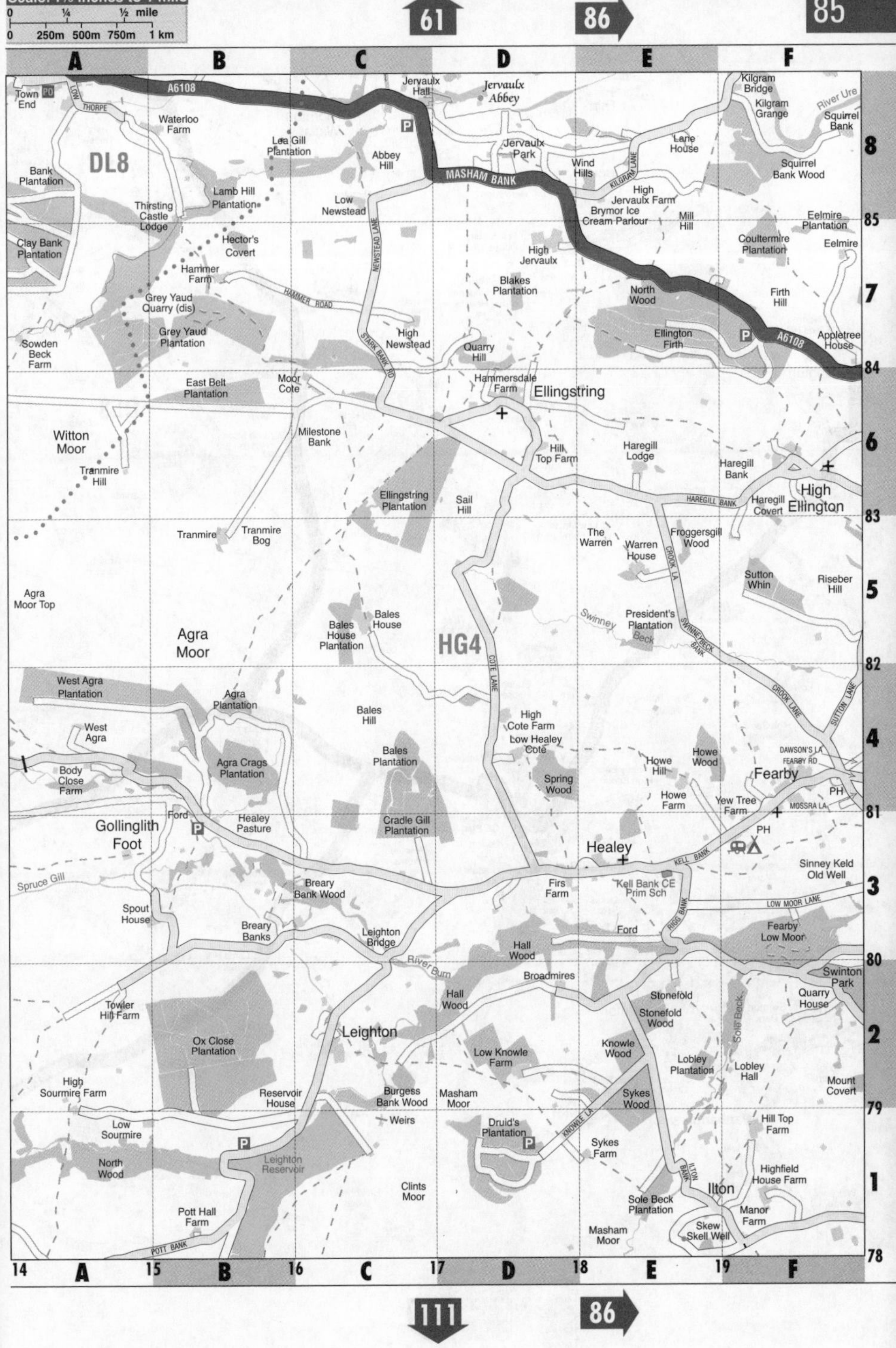
Scale: 1⅓ inches to 1 mile
0 ¼ ½ mile
0 250m 500m 750m 1 km
61
86
A B C D E F
A6108
Town End
Waterloo Farm
Lea Gill Plantation
Jervaulx Hall
Jervaulx Abbey
Kilgram Bridge
Kilgram Grange
River Ure
Squirrel Bank
DL8
Bank Plantation
Abbey Hill
Jervaulx Park
Lane House
Wind Hills
Squirrel Bank Wood
MASHAM BANK
KILGRAM LANE
Lamb Hill Plantation
Thirsting Castle Lodge
Low Newstead
High Jervaulx Farm
Brymor Ice Cream Parlour
Mill Hill
Elmire Plantation
Elmire
Clay Bank Plantation
Hector's Covert
NEWSTEAD LANE
High Jervaulx
Coultermire Plantation
Hammer Farm
HAMMER ROAD
Blakes Plantation
North Wood
Firth Hill
Grey Yaud Quarry (dis)
Grey Yaud Plantation
High Newstead
Quarry Hill
Ellington Firth
Appletree House
Sowden Beck Farm
STARK BANK RD
East Belt Plantation
Moor Cote
Hammersdale Farm
Ellingstring
Witton Moor
Milestone Bank
Hill Top Farm
Haregill Lodge
Haregill Bank
High Ellington
Tranmire Hill
Ellingstring Plantation
Sail Hill
HAREGILL BANK
Haregill Covert
Tranmire
Tranmire Bog
The Warren
Warren House
Froggersgill Wood
CROOK LA
Sutton Whin
Riseber Hill
Agra Moor Top
Swinney Beck
President's Plantation
Agra Moor
Bales House Plantation
Bales House
HG4
COTE LANE
SWINNEY BECK BANK
CROOK LANE
SUTTON LANE
West Agra Plantation
Agra Plantation
Bales Hill
High Cote Farm
Low Healey Cote
West Agra
Bales Plantation
DAWSON'S LA
FEARBY RD
Body Close Farm
Agra Crags Plantation
Howe Hill
Howe Wood
Fearby
Spring Wood
Howe Farm
Yew Tree Farm
PH
MOSSRA LA
Gollinglith Foot
Ford
Healey Pasture
Cradle Gill Plantation
Healey
KELL BANK
Sinney Keld Old Well
Spruce Gill
Breary Bank Wood
Firs Farm
Kell Bank CE Prim Sch
RIGG BANK
LOW MOOR LANE
Spout House
Breary Banks
Leighton Bridge
Hall Wood
Fearby Low Moor
River Burn
Broadmires
Swinton Park
Towler Hill Farm
Stonefold
Stonefold Wood
Sole Beck
Quarry House
Ox Close Plantation
Leighton
Low Knowle Farm
Knowle Wood
Lobley Plantation
Lobley Hall
Mount Covert
High Sourmire Farm
Reservoir House
Burgess Bank Wood
Masham Moor
Sykes Wood
Weirs
Druid's Plantation
KNOWLE LA
Hill Top Farm
Low Sourmire
North Wood
Leighton Reservoir
Sykes Farm
ILTON BANK
Highfield House Farm
Clints Moor
Ilton
Sole Beck Plantation
Manor Farm
Pott Hall Farm
POTT BANK
Masham Moor
Skew Skell Well
8 85 7 84 6 83 5 82 4 81 3 80 2 79 1 78
14 15 16 17 18 19
111
86

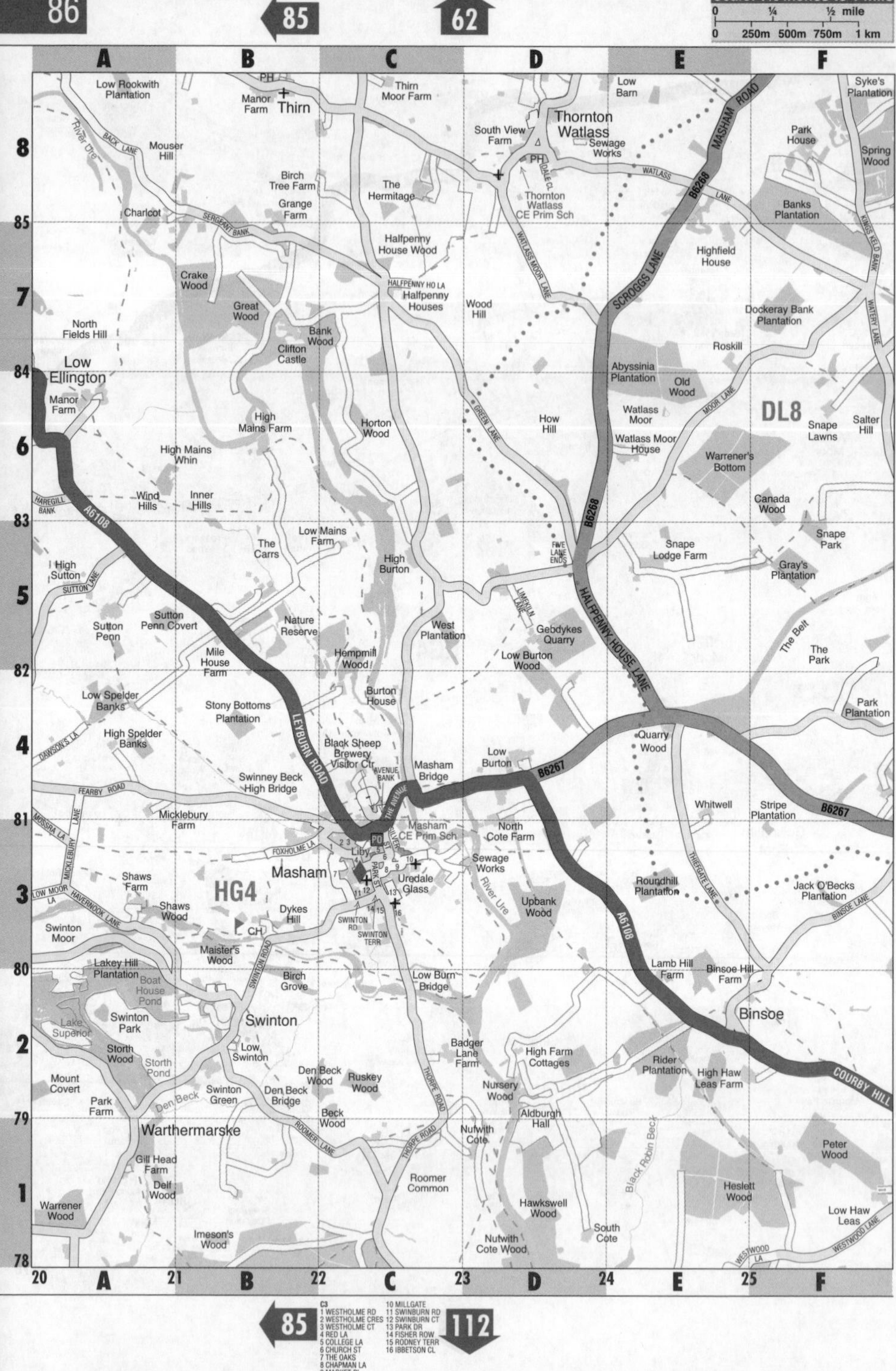
85
62
Scale: 1⅓ inches to 1 mile
0 ¼ ½ mile
0 250m 500m 750m 1 km
A B C D E F
8 85 7 84 6 83 5 82 4 81 3 80 2 79 1 78
20 21 22 23 24 25
Low Rookwith Plantation
PH
Manor Farm
Thirn
Thirn Moor Farm
Low Barn
Thornton Watlass
South View Farm
Sewage Works
MASHAM ROAD
Syke's Plantation
Park House
Spring Wood
River Ure
BACK LANE
Mouser Hill
Birch Tree Farm
The Hermitage
PH
DALE CL
Thornton Watlass CE Prim Sch
WATLASS
B6268
LANE
Banks Plantation
KINGS KELD BANK
Charlcot
SERGEANT BANK
Grange Farm
Halfpenny House Wood
WATLASS MOOR LANE
SCROGGS LANE
Highfield House
Crake Wood
HALFPENNY HO LA
Halfpenny Houses
Wood Hill
Great Wood
Dockeray Bank Plantation
WATERY LANE
North Fields Hill
Bank Wood
Clifton Castle
Roskill
Low Ellington
Abyssinia Plantation
Old Wood
MOOR LANE
DL8
Manor Farm
High Mains Farm
Horton Wood
GREEN LANE
How Hill
Watlass Moor
Watlass Moor House
Snape Lawns
Salter Hill
High Mains Whin
Warrener's Bottom
HAREGILL BANK
Wind Hills
Inner Hills
A6108
Canada Wood
B6268
Snape Park
Low Mains Farm
The Carrs
High Burton
FIVE LANE ENDS
Snape Lodge Farm
High Sutton
SUTTON LANE
Gray's Plantation
LIMEKILN LANE
Sutton Penn Covert
Nature Reserve
West Plantation
Gebdykes Quarry
HALFPENNY HOUSE LANE
Sutton Penn
The Belt
The Park
Mile House Farm
Hempmill Wood
Low Burton Wood
Low Spelder Banks
Stony Bottoms Plantation
Burton House
LEYBURN ROAD
Park Plantation
High Spelder Banks
Quarry Wood
DAWSON'S LA
Black Sheep Brewery Visitor Ctr
AVENUE BANK
Low Burton
B6267
Swinney Beck High Bridge
Masham Bridge
FEARBY ROAD
THE AVENUE
Micklebury Farm
Whitwell
Stripe Plantation
B6267
MOSSRA LA
MICKLEBURY LANE
Masham CE Prim Sch
North Cote Farm
PO
FOXHOLME LA
SILVER ST
Liby
Masham
PARK ST
Uredale Glass
Sewage Works
Shaws Farm
HG4
Roundhill Plantation
THIEFGATE LANE
Jack O'Becks Plantation
LOW MOOR LA
HAVERNOOK LANE
Shaws Wood
Dykes Hill
SWINTON RD
SWINTON TERR
River Ure
Upbank Wood
A6108
BINSOE LANE
Swinton Moor
CH
Maister's Wood
Lakey Hill Plantation
SWINTON ROAD
Birch Grove
Low Burn Bridge
Lamb Hill Farm
Binsoe Hill Farm
Boat House Pond
Lake Superior
Swinton Park
Swinton
Binsoe
Storth Wood
Storth Pond
Low Swinton
Badger Lane Farm
High Farm Cottages
Rider Plantation
High Haw Leas Farm
Mount Covert
Den Beck Wood
Ruskey Wood
THORPE ROAD
Nursery Wood
COURBY HILL
Park Farm
Den Beck
Swinton Green
Den Beck Bridge
Beck Wood
Aldburgh Hall
Warthermarske
ROOMER LANE
THORPE ROAD
Nutwith Cote
Black Robin Beck
Peter Wood
Gill Head Farm
Delf Wood
Roomer Common
Heslett Wood
Warrener Wood
Hawkswell Wood
Low Haw Leas
Imeson's Wood
Nutwith Cote Wood
South Cote
WESTWOOD LA
WESTWOOD LANE
85
112
C3
1 WESTHOLME RD
2 WESTHOLME CRES
3 WESTHOLME CT
4 RED LA
5 COLLEGE LA
6 CHURCH ST
7 THE OAKS
8 CHAPMAN LA
9 MARKET PL
10 MILLGATE
11 SWINBURN RD
12 SWINBURN CT
13 PARK DR
14 FISHER ROW
15 RODNEY TERR
16 IBBETSON CL

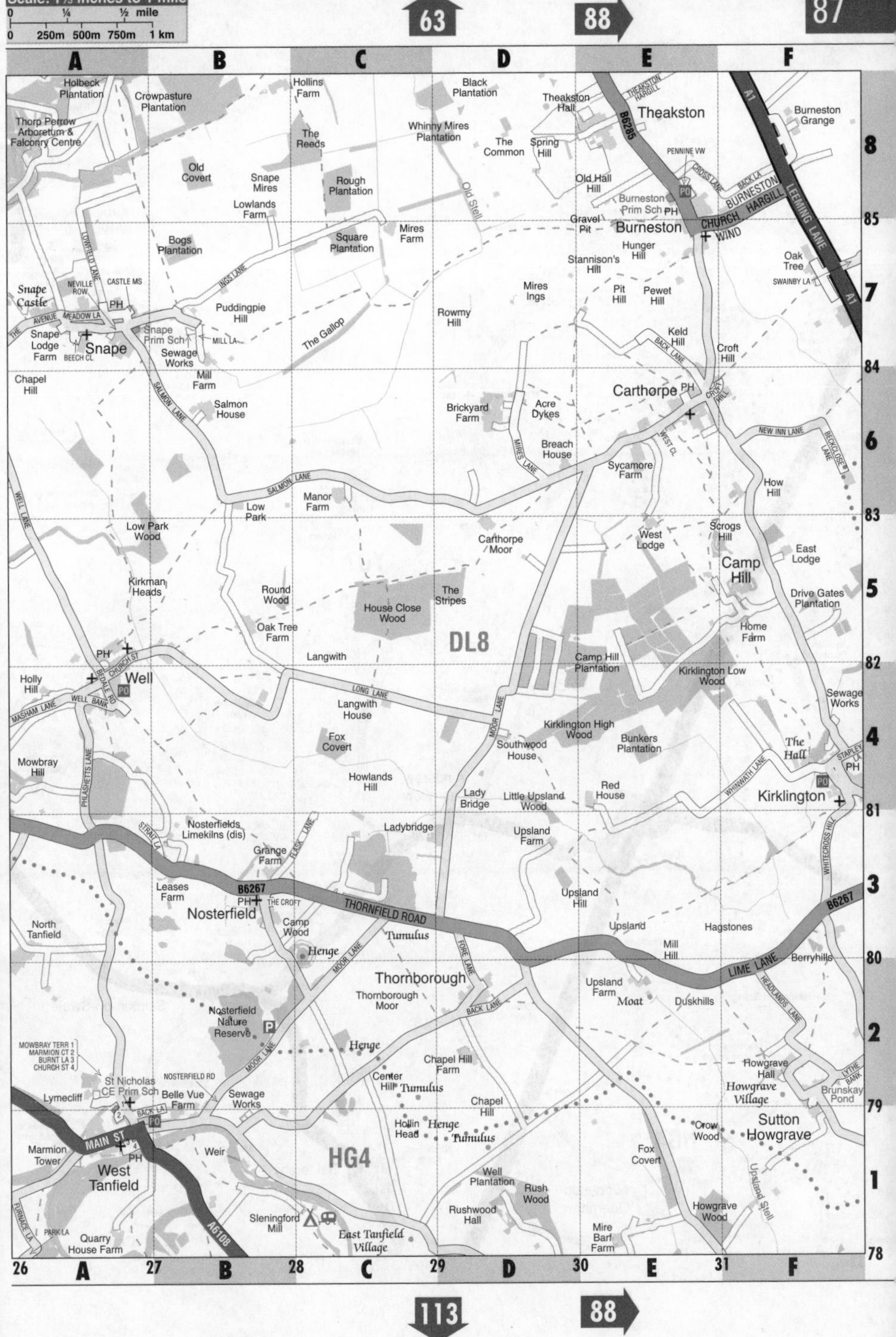
Scale: 1⅓ inches to 1 mile
0 ¼ ½ mile
0 250m 500m 750m 1 km
63
88
A B C D E F
Holbeck Plantation
Crowpasture Plantation
Thorp Perrow Arboretum & Falconry Centre
Hollins Farm
The Reeds
Black Plantation
Whinny Mires Plantation
Theakston Hall
Theakston
B6285
Burneston Grange
A1
The Common
Spring Hill
Old Covert
Snape Mires
Rough Plantation
Old Stell
Old Hall Hill
PENNINE VW
CROSS LANE
BACK LA
BURNESTON
LEEMING LANE
Lowlands Farm
Burneston Prim Sch
PH
Gravel Pit
Burneston
CHURCH HARGILL
WIND
Bogs Plantation
Square Plantation
Mires Farm
Hunger Hill
Stannison's Hill
Oak Tree
SWAINBY LA
LOWFIELD LANE
INGS LANE
Snape Castle
NEVILLE ROW
CASTLE MS
Mires Ings
Pit Hill
Pewet Hill
PH
Puddingpie Hill
Rowmy Hill
THE AVENUE
MEADOW LA
Snape Lodge Farm
Snape
BEECH CL
Snape Prim Sch
Sewage Works
MILL LA
The Gallop
Keld Hill
Croft Hill
BACK LANE
Chapel Hill
Mill Farm
SALMON LANE
Carthorpe
CROFT HILL
Salmon House
Brickyard Farm
Acre Dykes
WEST CL
NEW INN LANE
BECKCLOSE LANE
Breach House
MIRES LANE
Sycamore Farm
How Hill
WELL LANE
Low Park
Manor Farm
Low Park Wood
Carthorpe Moor
West Lodge
Scrogs Hill
East Lodge
Camp Hill
Kirkman Heads
Round Wood
The Stripes
House Close Wood
Drive Gates Plantation
Oak Tree Farm
DL8
Home Farm
PH
CHURCH ST
Langwith
Well
Camp Hill Plantation
Kirklington Low Wood
Holly Hill
BEDALE RD
WELL BANK
MASHAM LANE
LONG LANE
Langwith House
MOOR LANE
Sewage Works
Kirklington High Wood
Bunkers Plantation
The Hall
Fox Covert
Southwood House
STAPLEY LA
PH
Mowbray Hill
PHLASHETTS LANE
Howlands Hill
WHINWATH LANE
Kirklington
Lady Bridge
Little Upsland Wood
Red House
WHITECROSS HILL
Nosterfields Limekilns (dis)
FLASK LANE
Ladybridge
STRAIT LA
Upsland Farm
Grange Farm
Leases Farm
B6267
PH
THE CROFT
Nosterfield
THORNFIELD ROAD
Upsland Hill
B6267
North Tanfield
Camp Wood
Tumulus
Upsland
Hagstones
Henge
MOOR LANE
FORE LANE
Mill Hill
Thornborough
LIME LANE
Berryhills
Thornborough Moor
BACK LANE
Upsland Farm
Moat
Duskhills
HEADLANDS LANE
Nosterfield Nature Reserve
Henge
MOWBRAY TERR 1
MARMION CT 2
BURNT LA 3
CHURCH ST 4
MOOR LANE
Chapel Hill Farm
Howgrave Hall
LYTHE BANK
NOSTERFIELD RD
St Nicholas CE Prim Sch
Center Hill
Tumulus
Howgrave Village
Brunskay Pond
Lymecliff
Belle Vue Farm
Sewage Works
Chapel Hill
BACK LA
Sutton Howgrave
MAIN ST
Hollin Head
Henge
Tumulus
Crow Wood
Marmion Tower
PH
Weir
HG4
Fox Covert
West Tanfield
Upsland Stell
Well Plantation
Rush Wood
A6108
Sleningford Mill
Rushwood Hall
Howgrave Wood
FURNACE LA
PARK LA
Quarry House Farm
East Tanfield Village
Mire Barf Farm
8 85 7 84 6 83 5 82 4 81 3 80 2 79 1 78
26 27 28 29 30 31

113
88

87
64
Scale: 1⅓ inches to 1 mile

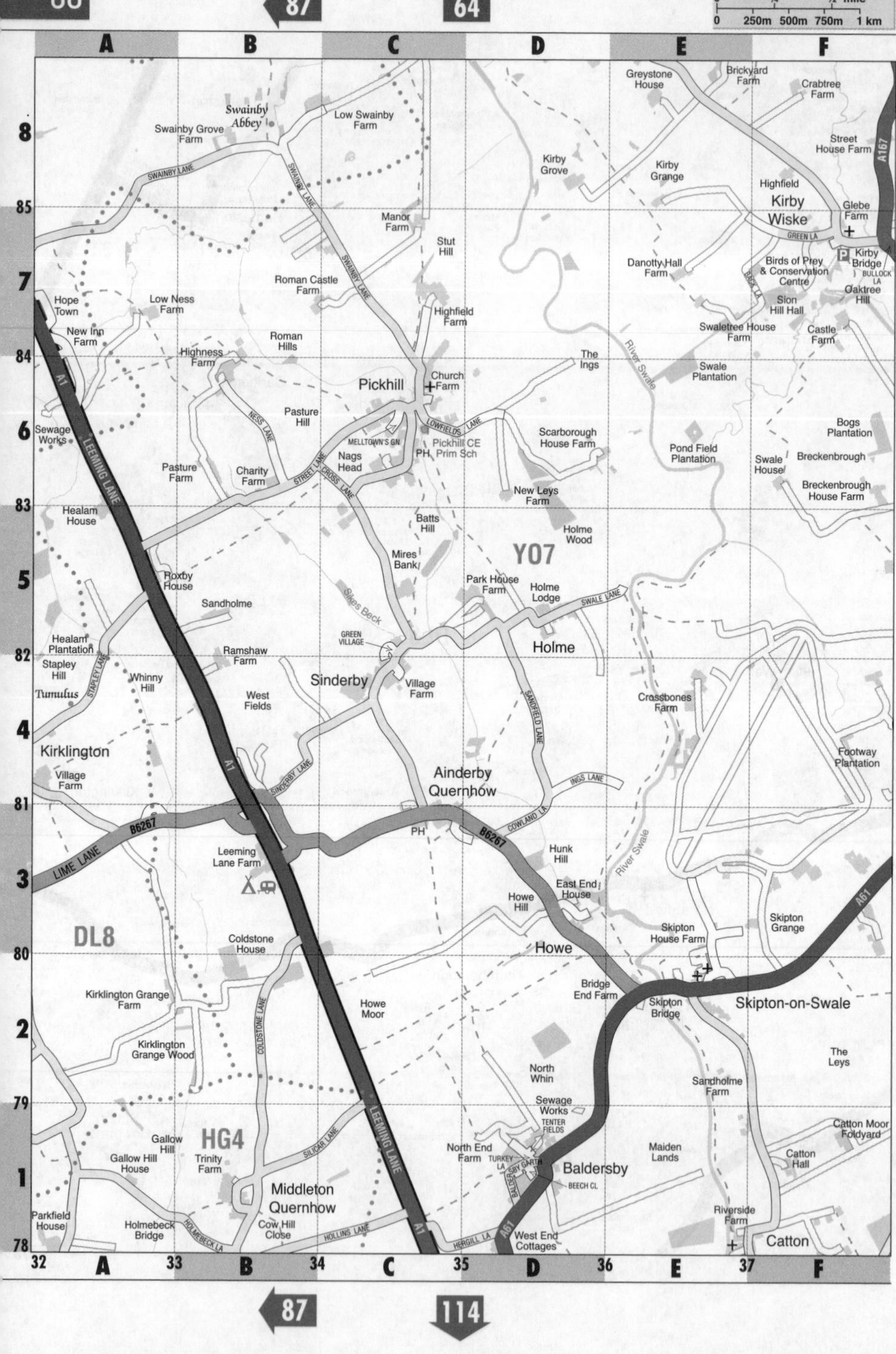
Swainby Grove Farm
Swainby Abbey
Low Swainby Farm
Greystone House
Brickyard Farm
Crabtree Farm
Street House Farm
A167
Kirby Grove
Kirby Grange
Highfield
Kirby Wiske
Glebe Farm
Manor Farm
Stut Hill
Danotty Hall Farm
Birds of Prey & Conservation Centre
Kirby Bridge
Oaktree Hill
Sion Hill Hall
Roman Castle Farm
Hope Town
Low Ness Farm
New Inn Farm
Highfield Farm
Swaletree House Farm
Castle Farm
Roman Hills
Highness Farm
The Ings
Swale Plantation
Pickhill
Church Farm
River Swale
Pasture Hill
Sewage Works
Scarborough House Farm
Bogs Plantation
Pickhill CE Prim Sch
Nags Head
Pond Field Plantation
Swale House
Breckenbrough
Pasture Farm
Charity Farm
Breckenbrough House Farm
New Leys Farm
Healam House
Batts Hill
Holme Wood
YO7
Mires Bank
Roxby House
Park House Farm
Holme Lodge
Sandholme
Sikes Beck
Healam Plantation
Green Village
Holme
Ramshaw Farm
Stapley Hill
Whinny Hill
Sinderby
Village Farm
Tumulus
West Fields
Crossbones Farm
Kirklington
Footway Plantation
Village Farm
Ainderby Quernhow
PH
Hunk Hill
Leeming Lane Farm
East End House
Howe Hill
Skipton Grange
DL8
Skipton House Farm
Coldstone House
Howe
Bridge End Farm
Skipton Bridge
Skipton-on-Swale
Kirklington Grange Farm
Howe Moor
Kirklington Grange Wood
The Leys
North Whin
Sandholme Farm
Sewage Works
Catton Moor Foldyard
Gallow Hill
HG4
North End Farm
Maiden Lands
Catton Hall
Gallow Hill House
Trinity Farm
Baldersby
Middleton Quernhow
Parkfield House
Holmebeck Bridge
Cow Hill Close
Riverside Farm
West End Cottages
Catton
A1
A61
B6267
Leeming Lane
Swainby Lane
Ness Lane
Street Lane
Cross Lane
Lowfields Lane
Swale Lane
Sandfield Lane
Ings Lane
Cowland La
Sinderby Lane
Stapley Lane
Lime Lane
Coldstone Lane
Silicar Lane
Holmebeck La
Hollins Lane
Hergill La
Green La
Bullock La
Melltown's Gn
Tenter Fields
Turkey La
Baldersby Garth
Beech Cl
A B C D E F
8 85 7 84 6 83 5 82 4 81 3 80 2 79 1 78
32 33 34 35 36 37
87
114

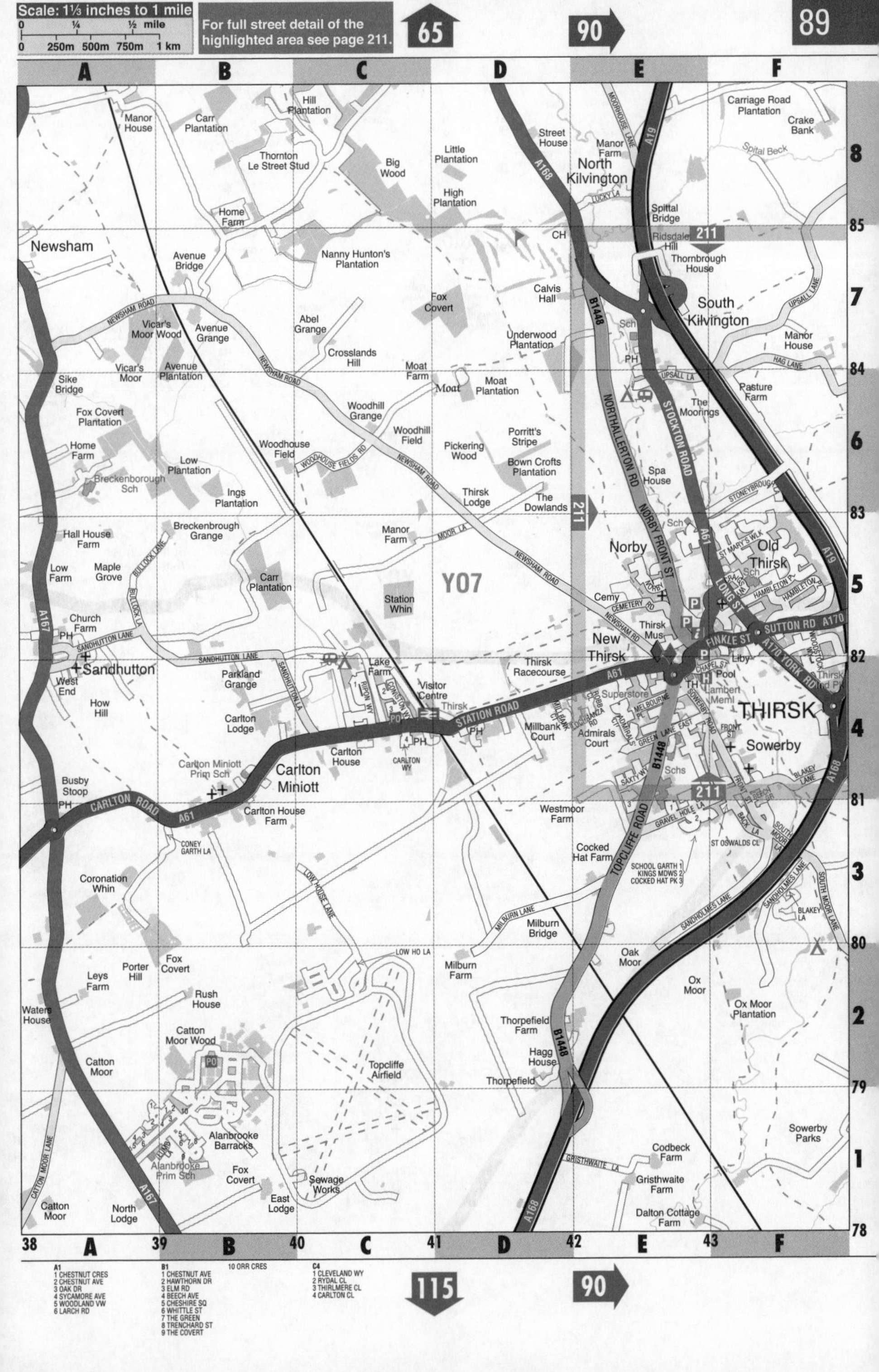
Scale: 1⅓ inches to 1 mile
0 ¼ ½ mile
0 250m 500m 750m 1 km
For full street detail of the highlighted area see page 211.
65
90
A B C D E F
Manor House
Carr Plantation
Hill Plantation
Thornton Le Street Stud
Big Wood
Little Plantation
High Plantation
Street House
Manor Farm
North Kilvington
Carriage Road Plantation
Crake Bank
Spital Beck
Spittal Bridge
Home Farm
Newsham
Avenue Bridge
Nanny Hunton's Plantation
CH
Ridsdale Hill
Thornbrough House
211
Fox Covert
Calvis Hall
South Kilvington
Upsall Lane
Newsham Road
Vicar's Moor Wood
Avenue Grange
Abel Grange
Crosslands Hill
Underwood Plantation
Manor House
Hag Lane
Vicar's Moor
Avenue Plantation
Sike Bridge
Moat Farm
Moat
Moat Plantation
Upsall La
Pasture Farm
Fox Covert Plantation
Woodhill Grange
The Moorings
Home Farm
Woodhouse Field
Woodhill Field
Pickering Wood
Porritt's Stripe
Bown Crofts Plantation
Northallerton Rd
Stockton Road
Low Plantation
Woodhouse Fields Rd
Breckenborough Sch
Spa House
Ings Plantation
Thirsk Lodge
The Dowlands
Stoneybrough
Breckenbrough Grange
Manor Farm
Moor La
Norby Front St
Hall House Farm
Norby
Old Thirsk
Low Farm
Maple Grove
Bullock Lane
YO7
Carr Plantation
Long St
Station Whin
Cemy
Cemetery Rd
Hambleton Pl
Church Farm
Sandhutton Lane
Thirsk Mus
New Thirsk
Finkle St
Sutton Rd
A170
York Rd
Sandhutton
Lake Farm
Thirsk Racecourse
Chapel St
Liby
Pool
West End
How Hill
Parkland Grange
Ripon Wy
Coniston Wy
Visitor Centre
Thirsk
Station Road
TH
Lambert Meml
THIRSK
Carlton Lodge
Millbank Court
Admirals Court
Superstore
Melbourne Pl
Green Lane East
Sowerby Road
Front St
Sowerby
Carlton Wy
Carlton House
Carlton Miniott Prim Sch
Carlton Miniott
Schs
Saxty Wy
Blakey Lane
Busby Stoop
Carlton Road
A61
Carlton House Farm
Westmoor Farm
Gravel Hole La
Back La
South Moor La
Coney Garth La
Cocked Hat Farm
St Oswalds Cl
School Garth 1
Kings Mdws 2
Cocked Hat Pk 3
Coronation Whin
Low House Lane
Topcliffe Road
B1448
Sandholmes Lane
South Moor Lane
Blakey La
Milburn Lane
Milburn Bridge
Low Ho La
Oak Moor
Porter Hill
Fox Covert
Leys Farm
Milburn Farm
Ox Moor
Rush House
Ox Moor Plantation
Waters House
Thorpefield Farm
Catton Moor Wood
Topcliffe Airfield
Hagg House
Catton Moor
Thorpefield
Alanbrooke Barracks
Alanbrooke Prim Sch
Sowerby Parks
Codbeck Farm
Catton Moor Lane
Fox Covert
Sewage Works
Gristhwaite La
Gristhwaite Farm
Catton Moor
North Lodge
East Lodge
Dalton Cottage Farm
A167
A168
A19
38 39 40 41 42 43
8 85 7 84 6 83 5 82 4 81 3 80 2 79 1 78
A1
1 CHESTNUT CRES
2 CHESTNUT AVE
3 OAK DR
4 SYCAMORE AVE
5 WOODLAND VW
6 LARCH RD
B1
1 CHESTNUT AVE
2 HAWTHORN DR
3 ELM RD
4 BEECH AVE
5 CHESHIRE SQ
6 WHITTLE ST
7 THE GREEN
8 TRENCHARD ST
9 THE COVERT
10 ORR CRES
C4
1 CLEVELAND WY
2 RYDAL CL
3 THIRLMERE CL
4 CARLTON CL
115
90

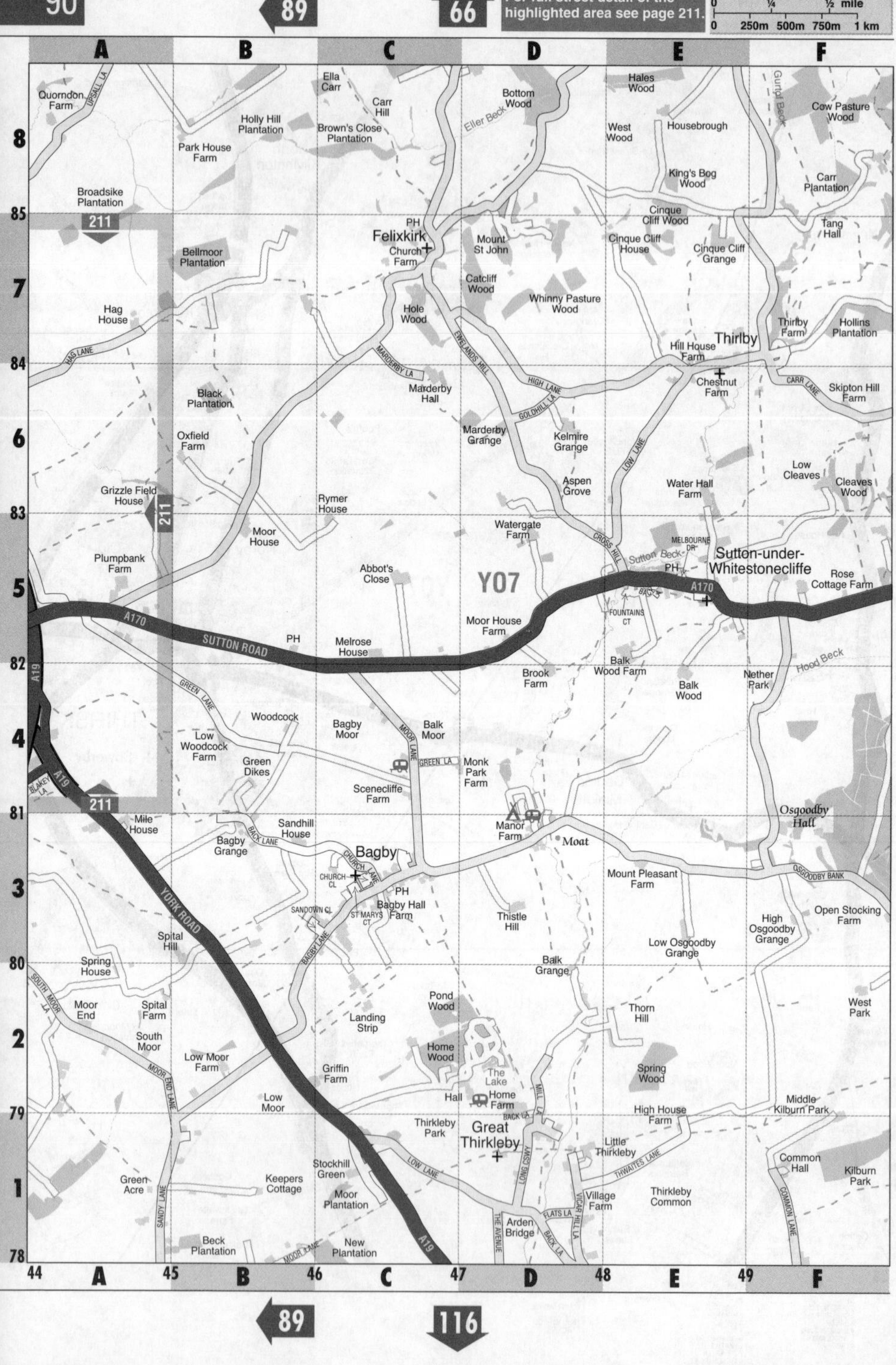

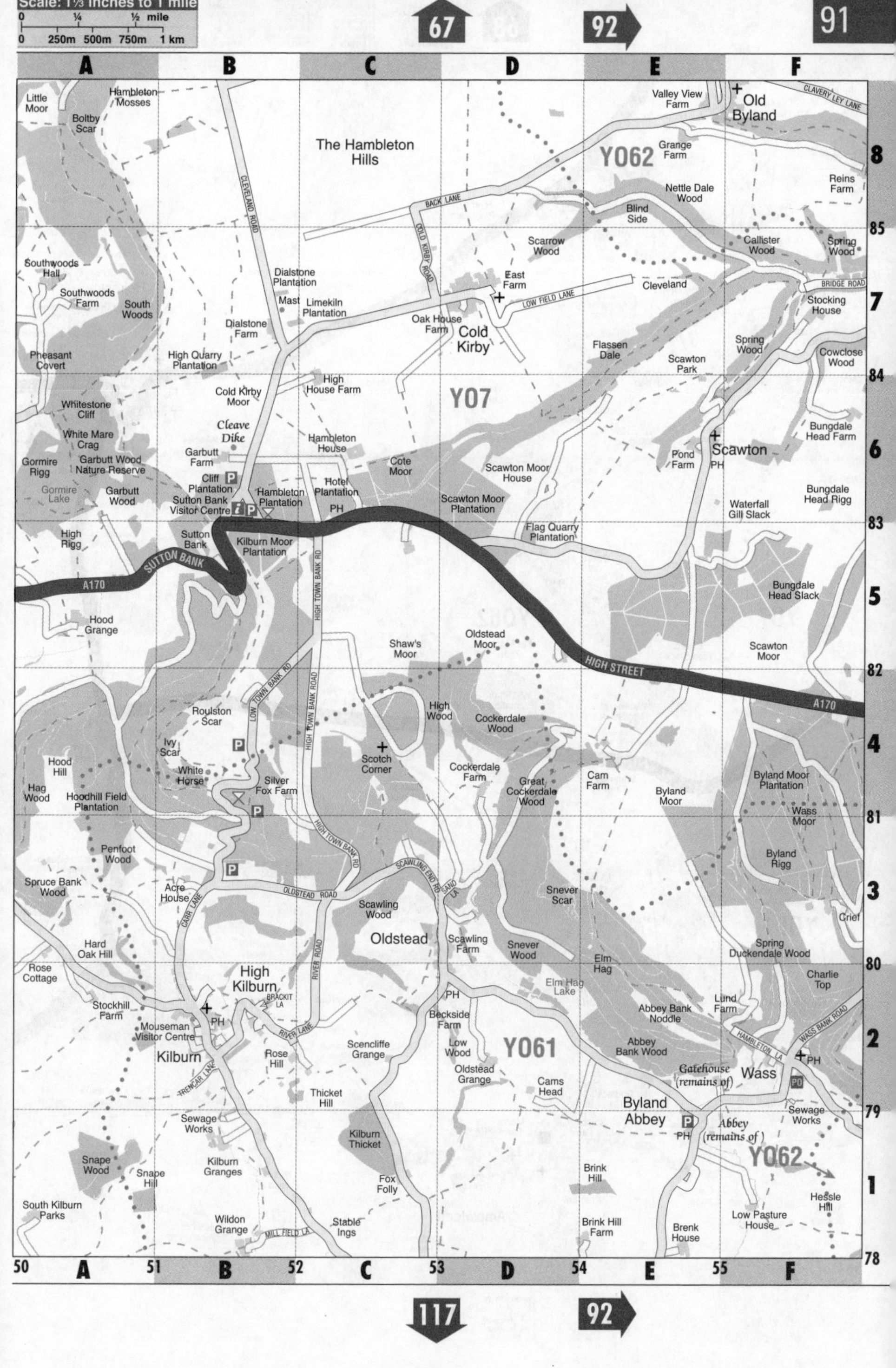
Scale: 1⅓ inches to 1 mile
0 ¼ ½ mile
0 250m 500m 750m 1 km
67
92
A
B
C
D
E
F
Little Moor
Hambleton Mosses
Boltby Scar
The Hambleton Hills
Valley View Farm
Old Byland
CLAVERY LEY LANE
Grange Farm
YO62
CLEVELAND ROAD
BACK LANE
Nettle Dale Wood
Reins Farm
Blind Side
COLD KIRBY ROAD
Scarrow Wood
Callister Wood
Spring Wood
Southwoods Hall
Southwoods Farm
South Woods
Dialstone Plantation
Mast
Limekiln Plantation
East Farm
LOW FIELD LANE
Cleveland
BRIDGE ROAD
Stocking House
Dialstone Farm
Oak House Farm
Cold Kirby
Flassen Dale
Spring Wood
Cowclose Wood
Pheasant Covert
High Quarry Plantation
Scawton Park
High House Farm
Cold Kirby Moor
YO7
Whitestone Cliff
Cleave Dike
Bungdale Head Farm
White Mare Crag
Hambleton House
Scawton
Garbutt Farm
Pond Farm
PH
Gormire Rigg
Garbutt Wood Nature Reserve
Cote Moor
Scawton Moor House
Cliff Plantation
Hotel Plantation
Bungdale Head Rigg
Gormire Lake
Garbutt Wood
Sutton Bank Visitor Centre
Hambleton Plantation
PH
Scawton Moor Plantation
Waterfall Gill Slack
High Rigg
Sutton Bank
Kilburn Moor Plantation
Flag Quarry Plantation
SUTTON BANK
HIGH TOWN BANK RD
A170
Bungdale Head Slack
Hood Grange
Oldstead Moor
Shaw's Moor
Scawton Moor
HIGH STREET
LOW TOWN BANK RD
HIGH TOWN BANK ROAD
Roulston Scar
High Wood
Cockerdale Wood
A170
Ivy Scar
Scotch Corner
Hood Hill
White Horse
Cockerdale Farm
Cam Farm
Byland Moor
Byland Moor Plantation
Hag Wood
Hoodhill Field Plantation
Silver Fox Farm
Great Cockerdale Wood
Wass Moor
HIGH TOWN BANK RD
Penfoot Wood
Byland Rigg
SCAWLING END RD
Spruce Bank Wood
Acre House
OLDSTEAD ROAD
SAND LA
Snever Scar
CARR LANE
Scawling Wood
Crief
Hard Oak Hill
Oldstead
Scawling Farm
Snever Wood
Spring Duckendale Wood
Rose Cottage
RIVER ROAD
Elm Hag
High Kilburn
Elm Hag Lake
Charlie Top
BRACKIT LA
PH
Stockhill Farm
Lund Farm
Beckside Farm
Abbey Bank Noddle
WASS BANK ROAD
Mouseman Visitor Centre
PH
RIVER LANE
HAMBLETON LA
Low Wood
YO61
Abbey Bank Wood
Kilburn
Rose Hill
Scencliffe Grange
PH
Gatehouse (remains of)
Wass
TRENCAR LANE
Oldstead Grange
Cams Head
PO
Thicket Hill
Byland Abbey
Sewage Works
Sewage Works
PH
Abbey (remains of)
Kilburn Thicket
YO62
Snape Wood
Kilburn Granges
Snape Hill
Brink Hill
Fox Folly
Hessle Hill
South Kilburn Parks
Low Pasture House
Wildon Grange
Stable Ings
Brink Hill Farm
Brenk House
MILL FIELD LA
8
85
7
84
6
83
5
82
4
81
3
80
2
79
1
78
50
51
52
53
54
55
117
92

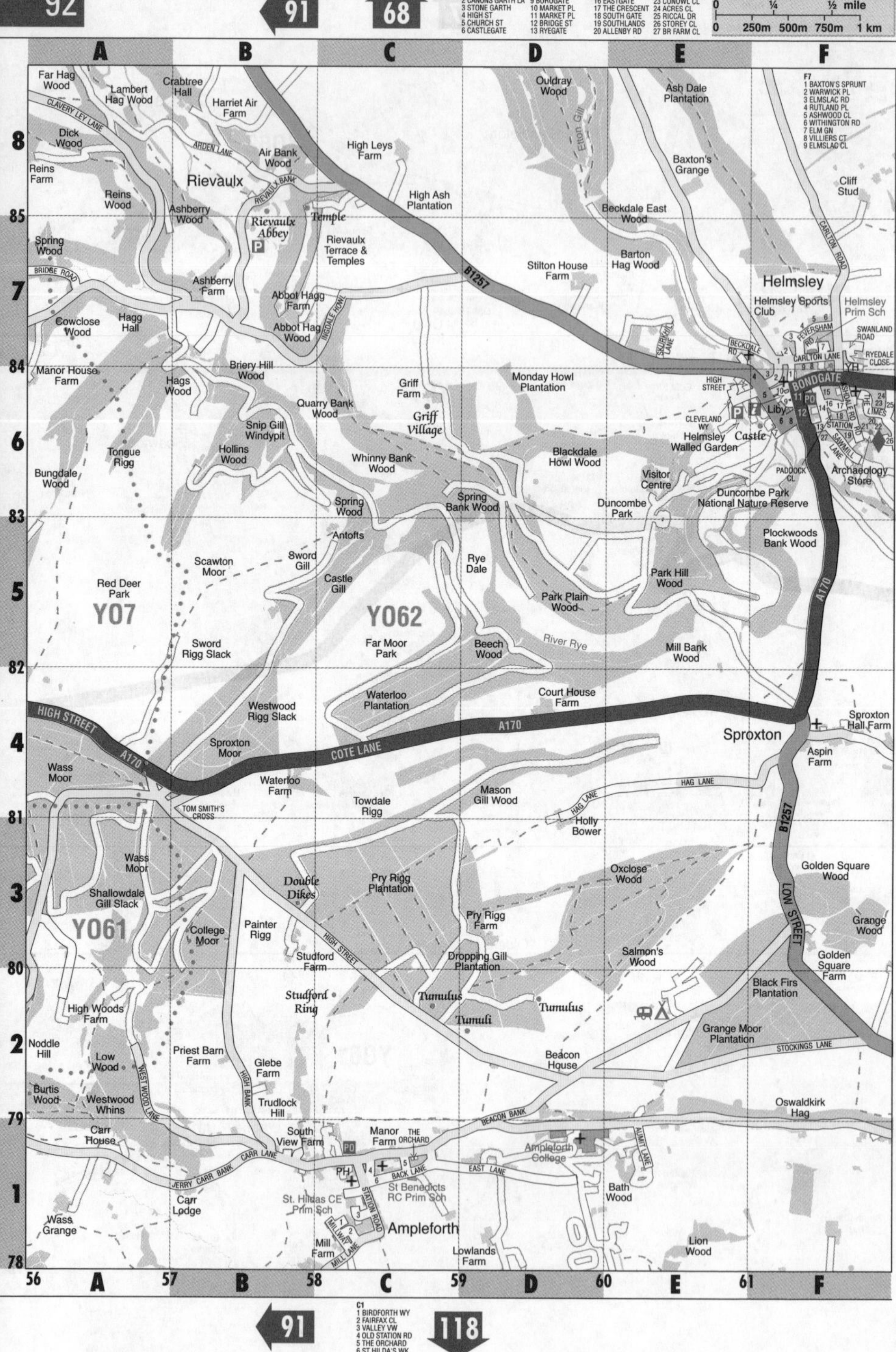

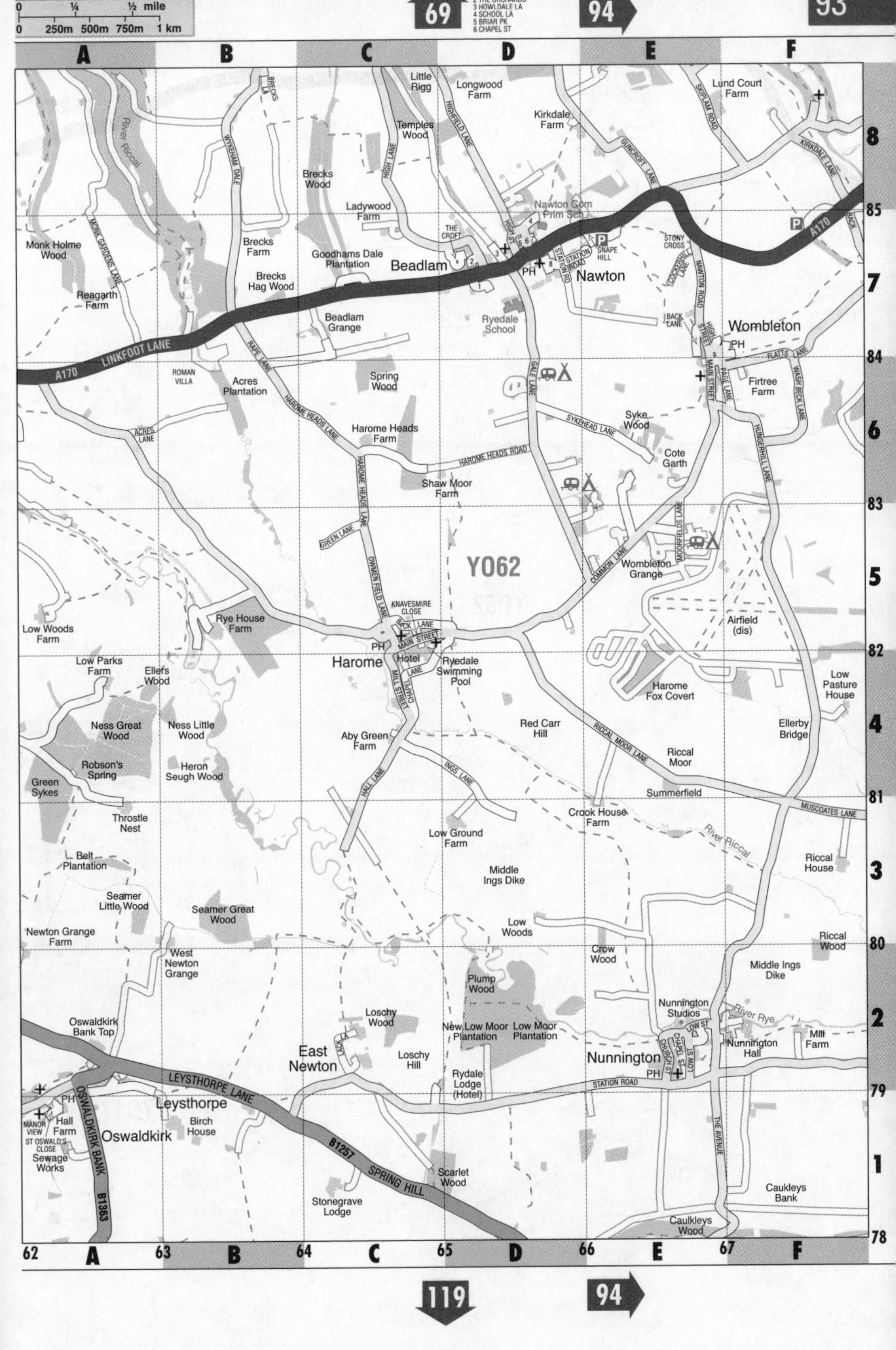

Scale: 1⅓ inches to 1 mile
0 ¼ ½ mile
0 250m 500m 750m 1 km
69
D7
1 BIRKLANDS
2 THE ORCHARDS
3 HOWLDALE LA
4 SCHOOL LA
5 BRIAR PK
6 CHAPEL ST
7 BELLABY PK
8 BECKETT CL
94
Little Rigg
Longwood Farm
Lund Court Farm
Kirkdale Farm
Temples Wood
Brecks Wood
Ladywood Farm
Nawton Com Prim Sch
Monk Holme Wood
Brecks Farm
Goodhams Dale Plantation
Beadlam
Nawton
Wombleton
Brecks Hag Wood
Reagarth Farm
Beadlam Grange
Ryedale School
A170
LINKFOOT LANE
ROMAN VILLA
Acres Plantation
Spring Wood
Firtree Farm
Syke Wood
Harome Heads Farm
Cote Garth
Shaw Moor Farm
YO62
Wombleton Grange
Rye House Farm
Airfield (dis)
Low Woods Farm
Harome
Hotel
Ryedale Swimming Pool
Low Parks Farm
Ellers Wood
Harome Fox Covert
Low Pasture House
Ness Great Wood
Ness Little Wood
Red Carr Hill
Ellerby Bridge
Aby Green Farm
Riccal Moor
Robson's Spring
Heron Seugh Wood
Green Sykes
Summerfield
Throstle Nest
Crook House Farm
Low Ground Farm
River Riccal
Riccal House
Belt Plantation
Middle Ings Dike
Seamer Little Wood
Seamer Great Wood
Low Woods
Riccal Wood
Newton Grange Farm
West Newton Grange
Crow Wood
Middle Ings Dike
Plump Wood
Nunnington Studios
River Rye
Oswaldkirk Bank Top
Loschy Wood
New Low Moor Plantation
Low Moor Plantation
Mill Farm
East Newton
Loschy Hill
Nunnington
Nunnington Hall
Rydale Lodge (Hotel)
LEYSTHORPE LANE
STATION ROAD
Leysthorpe
Hall Farm
Oswaldkirk
Birch House
MANOR VIEW
ST OSWALD'S CLOSE
Sewage Works
OSWALDKIRK BANK
B1257
SPRING HILL
Scarlet Wood
Caukleys Bank
Stonegrave Lodge
Caulkleys Wood
B1363
THE AVENUE
62 63 64 65 66 67
A B C D E F
78 79 80 81 82 83 84 85
1 2 3 4 5 6 7 8
119
94

93
70

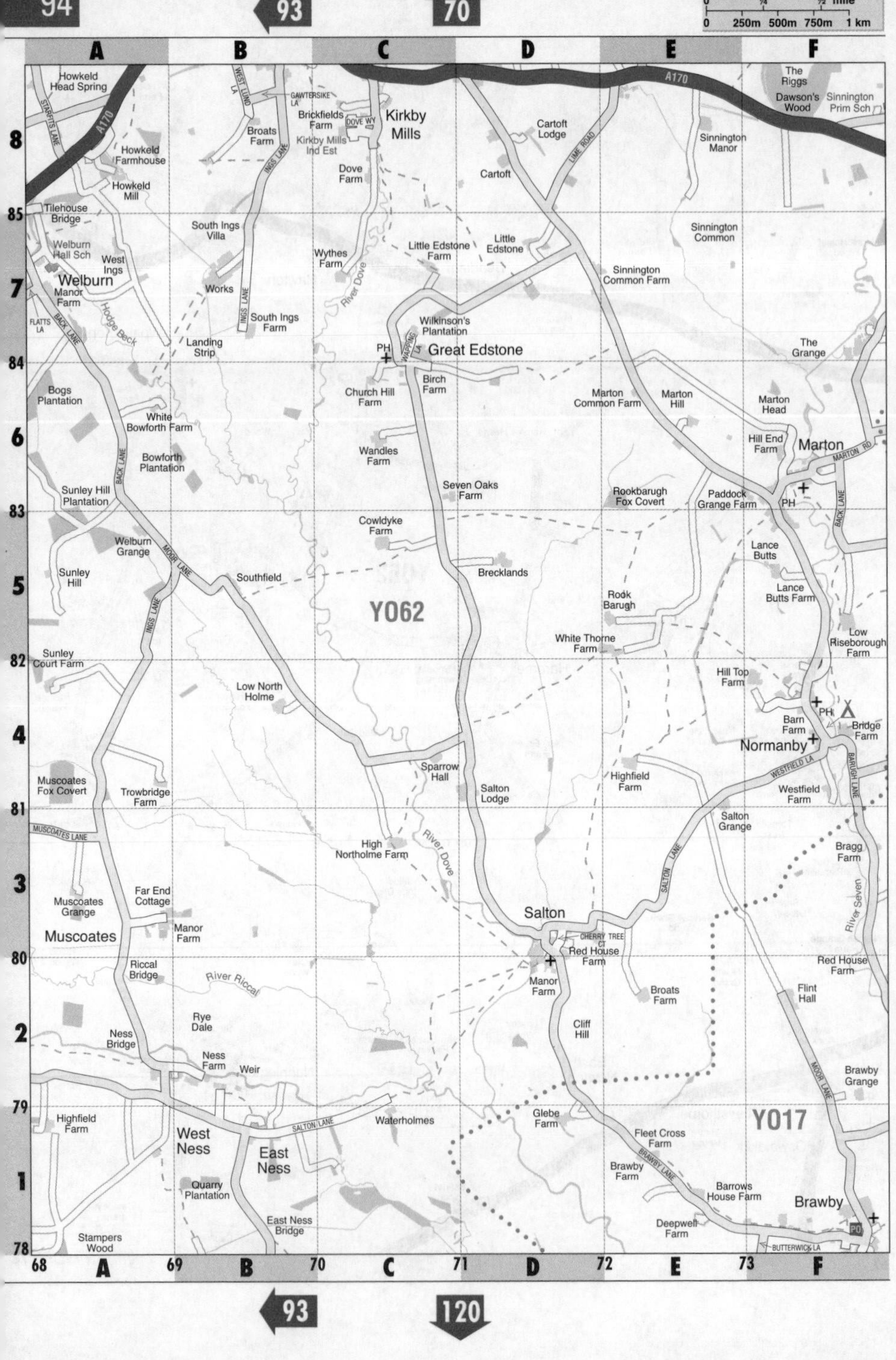
Scale: 1⅓ inches to 1 mile
0 ¼ ½ mile
0 250m 500m 750m 1 km
A170
Howkeld Head Spring
Howkeld Farmhouse
Howkeld Mill
Tilehouse Bridge
Welburn Hall Sch
West Ings
Welburn
Manor Farm
Hodge Beck
Bogs Plantation
White Bowforth Farm
Bowforth Plantation
Sunley Hill Plantation
Welburn Grange
Sunley Hill
Sunley Court Farm
Muscoates Fox Covert
Trowbridge Farm
Muscoates Grange
Far End Cottage
Muscoates
Manor Farm
Riccal Bridge
River Riccal
Rye Dale
Ness Bridge
Ness Farm
Weir
Highfield Farm
West Ness
East Ness
Quarry Plantation
East Ness Bridge
Stampers Wood
Broats Farm
South Ings Villa
Works
South Ings Farm
Landing Strip
Southfield
Low North Holme
Brickfields Farm
Kirkby Mills
Kirkby Mills Ind Est
Dove Farm
Wythes Farm
River Dove
Great Edstone
Church Hill Farm
Birch Farm
Wilkinson's Plantation
Wandles Farm
Cowldyke Farm
Seven Oaks Farm
Brecklands
YO62
Sparrow Hall
Salton Lodge
High Northolme Farm
Salton
Red House Farm
Manor Farm
Cliff Hill
Waterholmes
Glebe Farm
Little Edstone Farm
Little Edstone
Cartoft Lodge
Cartoft
Sinnington Manor
Sinnington Common
Sinnington Common Farm
The Riggs
Dawson's Wood
Sinnington Prim Sch
The Grange
Marton Common Farm
Marton Hill
Marton Head
Hill End Farm
Marton
Rookbarugh Fox Covert
Paddock Grange Farm
Lance Butts
Lance Butts Farm
Rook Barugh
White Thorne Farm
Low Riseborough Farm
Hill Top Farm
Barn Farm
Bridge Farm
Normanby
Highfield Farm
Westfield Farm
Salton Grange
Bragg Farm
River Seven
Red House Farm
Flint Hall
Broats Farm
Brawby Grange
YO17
Fleet Cross Farm
Brawby Farm
Barrows House Farm
Deepwell Farm
Brawby
STARFITS LANE
WEST LUND LA
GAWTERSIKE LA
DOVE WY
INGS LANE
LIME ROAD
WAPPING LA
BACK LANE
FLATTS LA
MOOR LANE
MUSCOATES LANE
SALTON LANE
CHERRY TREE CT
BRAWBY LANE
MARTON RD
WESTFIELD LA
BARUGH LANE
BUTTERWICK LA
PH
PO
A B C D E F
8 85 7 84 6 83 5 82 4 81 3 80 2 79 1 78
68 69 70 71 72 73

93
120

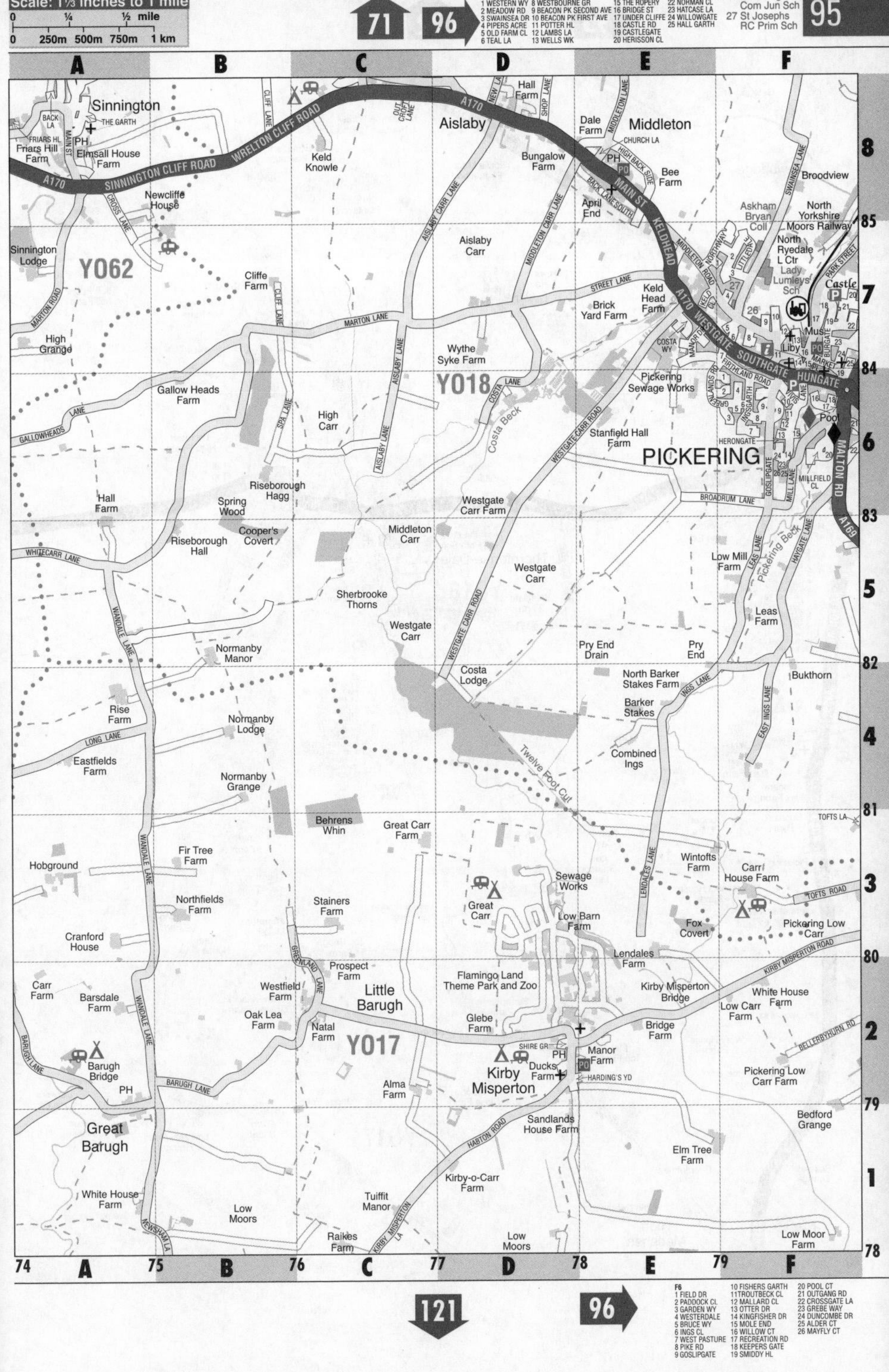
Scale: 1⅓ inches to 1 mile
0 ¼ ½ mile
0 250m 500m 750m 1 km
71
96
F7
1 WESTERN WY
2 MEADOW RD
3 SWAINSEA DR
4 PIPERS ACRE
5 OLD FARM CL
6 TEAL LA
7 ANCHORITE LA
8 WESTBOURNE GR
9 BEACON PK SECOND AVE
10 BEACON PK FIRST AVE
11 POTTER HL
12 LAMBS LA
13 WELLS WK
14 TRAIN LA
15 THE ROPERY
16 BRIDGE ST
17 UNDER CLIFFE
18 CASTLE RD
19 CASTLEGATE
20 HERISSON CL
21 ROSAMUND AVE
22 NORMAN CL
23 HATCASE LA
24 WILLOWGATE
25 HALL GARTH
26 Pickering Com Jun Sch
27 St Josephs RC Prim Sch
95
A
B
C
D
E
F
Sinnington
Friars Hill Farm
Elmsall House Farm
A170
SINNINGTON CLIFF ROAD
WRELTON CLIFF ROAD
Newcliffe House
Keld Knowle
Aislaby
Hall Farm
Middleton
Dale Farm
Bungalow Farm
Bee Farm
April End
Broodview
Askham Bryan Coll
North Yorkshire Moors Railway
North Ryedale L Ctr
Lady Lumleys Sch
Castle
Sinnington Lodge
YO62
Cliffe Farm
Aislaby Carr
Keld Head Farm
Brick Yard Farm
MAIN ST
KELDHEAD
WESTGATE
SOUTHGATE
HUNGATE
STREET LANE
MARTON LANE
High Grange
Wythe Syke Farm
YO18
Gallow Heads Farm
High Carr
Pickering Sewage Works
Stanfield Hall Farm
PICKERING
Mus
Liby
Pool
A169
MALTON RD
Costa Beck
Hall Farm
Riseborough Hagg
Spring Wood
Cooper's Covert
Riseborough Hall
Westgate Carr Farm
Middleton Carr
BROADRUM LANE
Low Mill Farm
Pickering Beck
Westgate Carr
Sherbrooke Thorns
Westgate Carr
Leas Farm
Normanby Manor
Costa Lodge
Pry End Drain
Pry End
North Barker Stakes Farm
Barker Stakes
Bukthorn
Rise Farm
Normanby Lodge
Eastfields Farm
Normanby Grange
Combined Ings
Twelve Foot Cut
Behrens Whin
Great Carr Farm
Fir Tree Farm
Hobground
Wintofts Farm
Carr House Farm
Sewage Works
Northfields Farm
Stainers Farm
Great Carr
Low Barn Farm
Fox Covert
Pickering Low Carr
TOFTS ROAD
TOFTS LA
Cranford House
Prospect Farm
Lendales Farm
Carr Farm
Barsdale Farm
Westfield Farm
Little Barugh
Flamingo Land Theme Park and Zoo
Kirby Misperton Bridge
White House Farm
Low Carr Farm
KIRBY MISPERTON ROAD
Oak Lea Farm
Natal Farm
YO17
Glebe Farm
Bridge Farm
Barugh Bridge
PH
Manor Farm
Ducks Farm
Kirby Misperton
Alma Farm
Pickering Low Carr Farm
Great Barugh
Sandlands House Farm
Bedford Grange
Elm Tree Farm
Kirby-o-Carr Farm
White House Farm
Low Moors
Tuiffit Manor
Raikes Farm
Low Moors
Low Moor Farm
WANDALE LANE
BARUGH LANE
HABTON ROAD
LENDALES LANE
INGS LANE
EAST INGS LANE
8
7
6
5
4
3
2
1
85
84
83
82
81
80
79
78
74
75
76
77
78
79
121
96
F6
1 FIELD DR
2 PADDOCK CL
3 GARDEN WY
4 WESTERDALE
5 BRUCE WY
6 INGS CL
7 WEST PASTURE
8 PIKE RD
9 GOSLIPGATE
10 FISHERS GARTH
11 TROUTBECK CL
12 MALLARD CL
13 OTTER DR
14 KINGFISHER DR
15 MOLE END
16 WILLOW CT
17 RECREATION RD
18 KEEPERS GATE
19 SMIDDY HL
20 POOL CT
21 OUTGANG RD
22 CROSSGATE LA
23 GREBE WAY
24 DUNCOMBE DR
25 ALDER CT
26 MAYFLY CT

95
72

Scale: 1⅓ inches to 1 mile

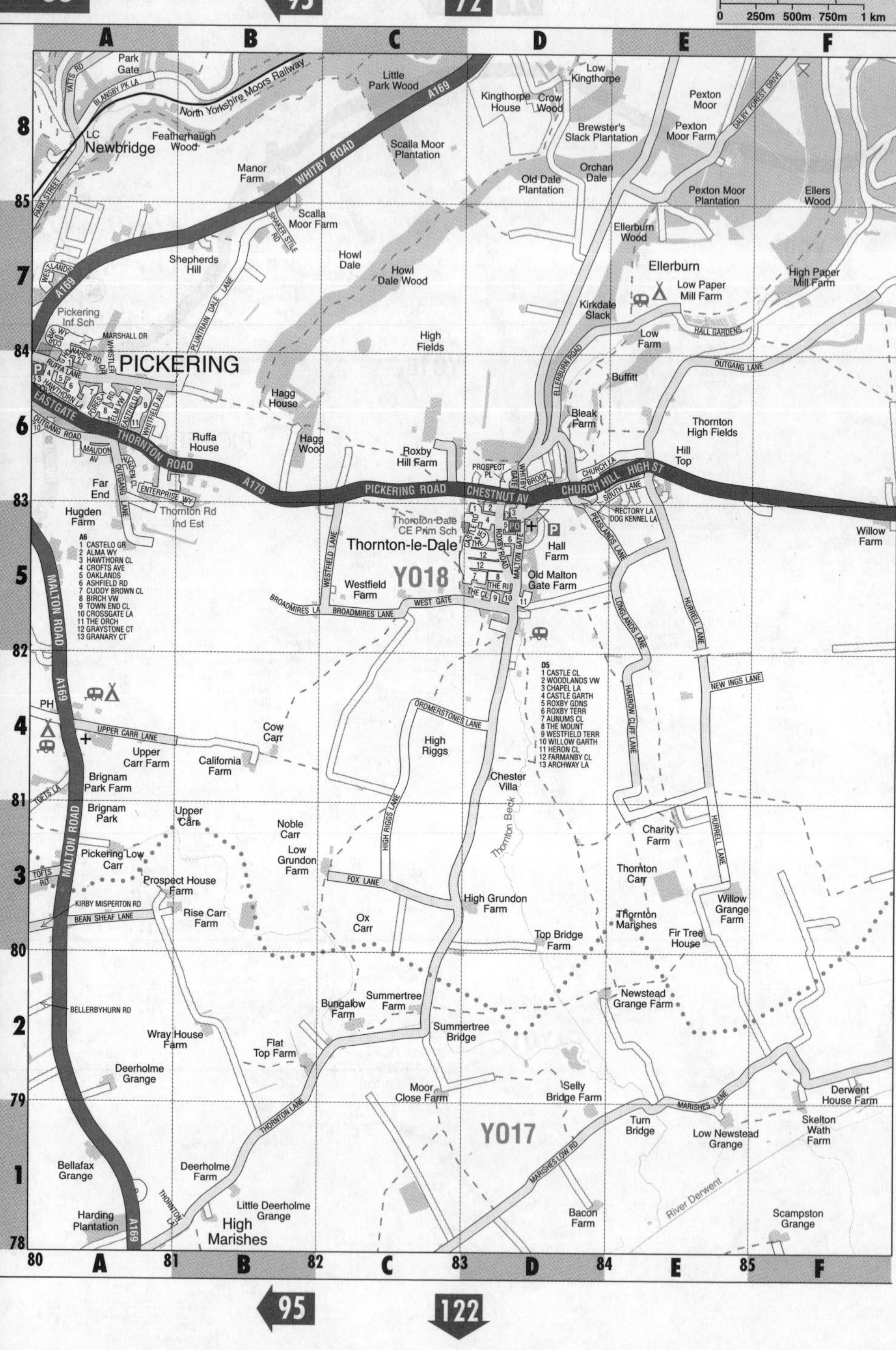
PICKERING
Newbridge
Thornton-le-Dale
Ellerburn
High Marishes
YO18
YO17
A169
A170
WHITBY ROAD
MALTON ROAD
THORNTON ROAD
PICKERING ROAD
CHESTNUT AV
CHURCH HILL
HIGH ST
EASTGATE
North Yorkshire Moors Railway
A6
1 CASTELO GR
2 ALMA WY
3 HAWTHORN CL
4 CROFTS AVE
5 OAKLANDS
6 ASHFIELD RD
7 CUDDY BROWN CL
8 BIRCH VW
9 TOWN END CL
10 CROSSGATE LA
11 THE ORCH
12 GRAYSTONE CT
13 GRANARY CT
D5
1 CASTLE CL
2 WOODLANDS VW
3 CHAPEL LA
4 CASTLE GARTH
5 ROXBY GDNS
6 ROXBY TERR
7 AUNUMS CL
8 THE MOUNT
9 WESTFIELD TERR
10 WILLOW GARTH
11 HERON CL
12 FARMANBY CL
13 ARCHWAY LA
Park Gate
Little Park Wood
Low Kingthorpe
Kingthorpe House
Crow Wood
Pexton Moor
Featherhaugh Wood
Scalla Moor Plantation
Brewster's Slack Plantation
Pexton Moor Farm
Manor Farm
Orchan Dale
Old Dale Plantation
Pexton Moor Plantation
Ellers Wood
Scalla Moor Farm
Ellerburn Wood
Shepherds Hill
Howl Dale
Howl Dale Wood
High Paper Mill Farm
Low Paper Mill Farm
Pickering Inf Sch
Kirkdale Slack
High Fields
Low Farm
HALL GARDENS
OUTGANG LANE
Buffitt
Hagg House
Bleak Farm
Thornton High Fields
Ruffa House
Hagg Wood
Roxby Hill Farm
Hill Top
Far End
Hugden Farm
Thornton Rd Ind Est
ENTERPRISE WY
Thornton Dale CE Prim Sch
Hall Farm
Willow Farm
Westfield Farm
Old Malton Gate Farm
BROADMIRES LA
BROADMIRES LANE
WEST GATE
WESTFIELD LANE
LONGLANDS LANE
HURRELL LANE
NEW INGS LANE
HARROW CLIFF LANE
ORMERSTONES LANE
UPPER CARR LANE
PH
Cow Carr
Upper Carr Farm
California Farm
High Riggs
Chester Villa
Brignam Park Farm
Brignam Park
Upper Carr
Noble Carr
Charity Farm
Low Grundon Farm
Thornton Beck
Pickering Low Carr
Prospect House Farm
FOX LANE
HIGH RIGGS LANE
Thornton Carr
High Grundon Farm
Willow Grange Farm
KIRBY MISPERTON RD
BEAN SHEAF LANE
Rise Carr Farm
Ox Carr
Thornton Marishes
Top Bridge Farm
Fir Tree House
Newstead Grange Farm
BELLERBYHURN RD
Summertree Farm
Bungalow Farm
Summertree Bridge
Wray House Farm
Flat Top Farm
Deerholme Grange
Moor Close Farm
Selly Bridge Farm
Derwent House Farm
MARISHES LANE
Turn Bridge
Low Newstead Grange
Skelton Wath Farm
THORNTON LANE
MARISHES LOW RD
Bellafax Grange
Deerholme Farm
Little Deerholme Grange
Bacon Farm
River Derwent
Scampston Grange
Harding Plantation
LC
PARK STREET
YATTS RD
BLANSBY PK LA
DALBY FOREST DRIVE
SHAKER STILE RD
PLUNTRAIN DALE LANE
ELLERBURN ROAD
PROSPECT PL
WHITBY GATE
BROOK LA
CHURCH LA
SOUTH LANE
RECTORY LA
DOG KENNEL LA
PEASLANDS LANE
CASTLE RD
ROXBY ROAD
MALTON GATE
THE CL
THE RI
MARSHALL DR
WARDS RD
WHISTLER DR
RUFFA LANE
HAWTHORN LA
FOREST RD
ELM VW
EASTFIELD RD
WHITFIELD AV
OUTGANG ROAD
MAUDON AV
HUGDEN CL
OUTGANG LANE
TOFTS LA
TOFTS RD
THORNTON
A
B
C
D
E
F
8
85
7
84
6
83
5
82
4
81
3
80
2
79
1
78
80
81
82
83
84
85

95
122

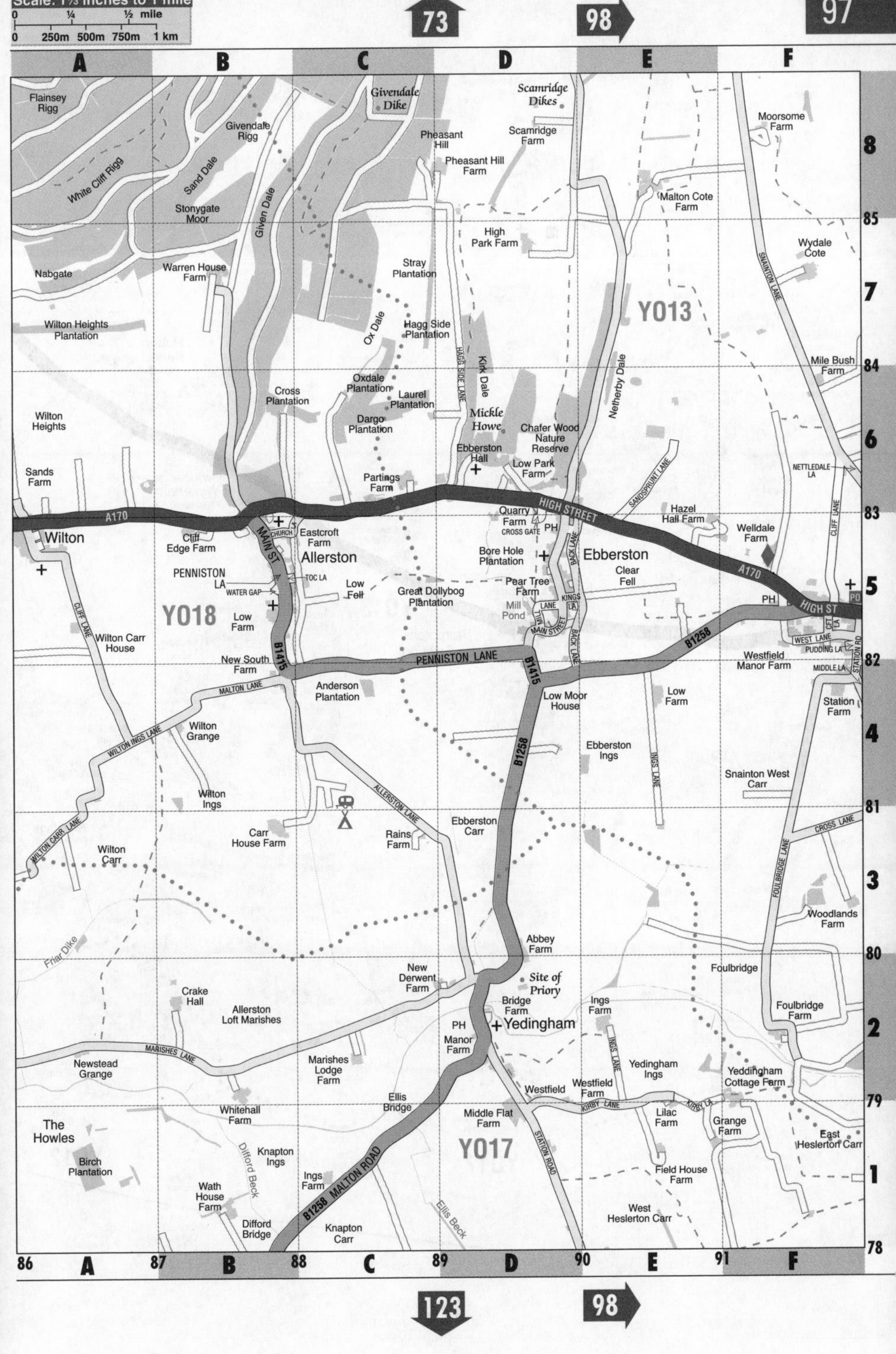
Scale: 1⅓ inches to 1 mile
0 ¼ ½ mile
0 250m 500m 750m 1 km
73
98
A B C D E F
Flainsey Rigg
Givendale Dike
Scamridge Dikes
Givendale Rigg
Sand Dale
White Cliff Rigg
Stonygate Moor
Given Dale
Pheasant Hill
Pheasant Hill Farm
Scamridge Farm
Moorsome Farm
Malton Cote Farm
High Park Farm
Wydale Cote
Snainton Lane
Nabgate
Warren House Farm
Stray Plantation
Y013
Wilton Heights Plantation
Ox Dale
Hagg Side Plantation
Hagg Side Lane
Kirk Dale
Mile Bush Farm
Netherby Dale
Cross Plantation
Oxdale Plantation
Laurel Plantation
Wilton Heights
Dargo Plantation
Mickle Howe
Chafer Wood Nature Reserve
Ebberston Hall
Low Park Farm
Nettledale La
Sands Farm
Partings Farm
Sandsprunt Lane
Cliff Lane
High Street
A170
Quarry Farm
PH
Cross Gate
Hazel Hall Farm
Welldale Farm
Wilton
Cliff Edge Farm
Church
Main St
Eastcroft Farm
Allerston
Bore Hole Plantation
Back Lane
Ebberston
Clear Fell
Penniston La
Toc La
Water Gap
Low Fell
Great Dollybog Plantation
Pear Tree Farm
Kings La
PH
High St
PO
Y018
Low Farm
Mill Pond
Lane
Main Street
Cft La
West Lane
Pudding La
Station Rd
B1415
Wilton Carr House
B1258
Westfield Manor Farm
Middle La
New South Farm
Penniston Lane
Malton Lane
Anderson Plantation
Low Moor House
Low Farm
Station Farm
Wilton Ings Lane
Wilton Grange
Ebberston Ings
Ings Lane
Snainton West Carr
Wilton Ings
Allerston Lane
Cross Lane
Wilton Carr Lane
Carr House Farm
Rains Farm
Ebberston Carr
Foulbridge Lane
Wilton Carr
Woodlands Farm
Friar Dike
Abbey Farm
New Derwent Farm
Site of Priory
Foulbridge
Crake Hall
Allerston Loft Marishes
Bridge Farm
Ings Farm
Foulbridge Farm
PH
Yedingham
Marishes Lane
Manor Farm
Newstead Grange
Marishes Lodge Farm
Yedingham Ings
Westfield
Westfield Farm
Yeddingham Cottage Farm
Ellis Bridge
Kirby Lane
Kirby La
Whitehall Farm
Middle Flat Farm
Lilac Farm
Grange Farm
The Howles
East Heslerton Carr
Y017
Station Road
Difford Beck
Knapton Ings
Birch Plantation
Field House Farm
Malton Road
Wath House Farm
Ings Farm
Ellis Beck
West Heslerton Carr
Difford Bridge
Knapton Carr
8 85 7 84 6 83 5 82 4 81 3 80 2 79 1 78
86 87 88 89 90 91
123
98

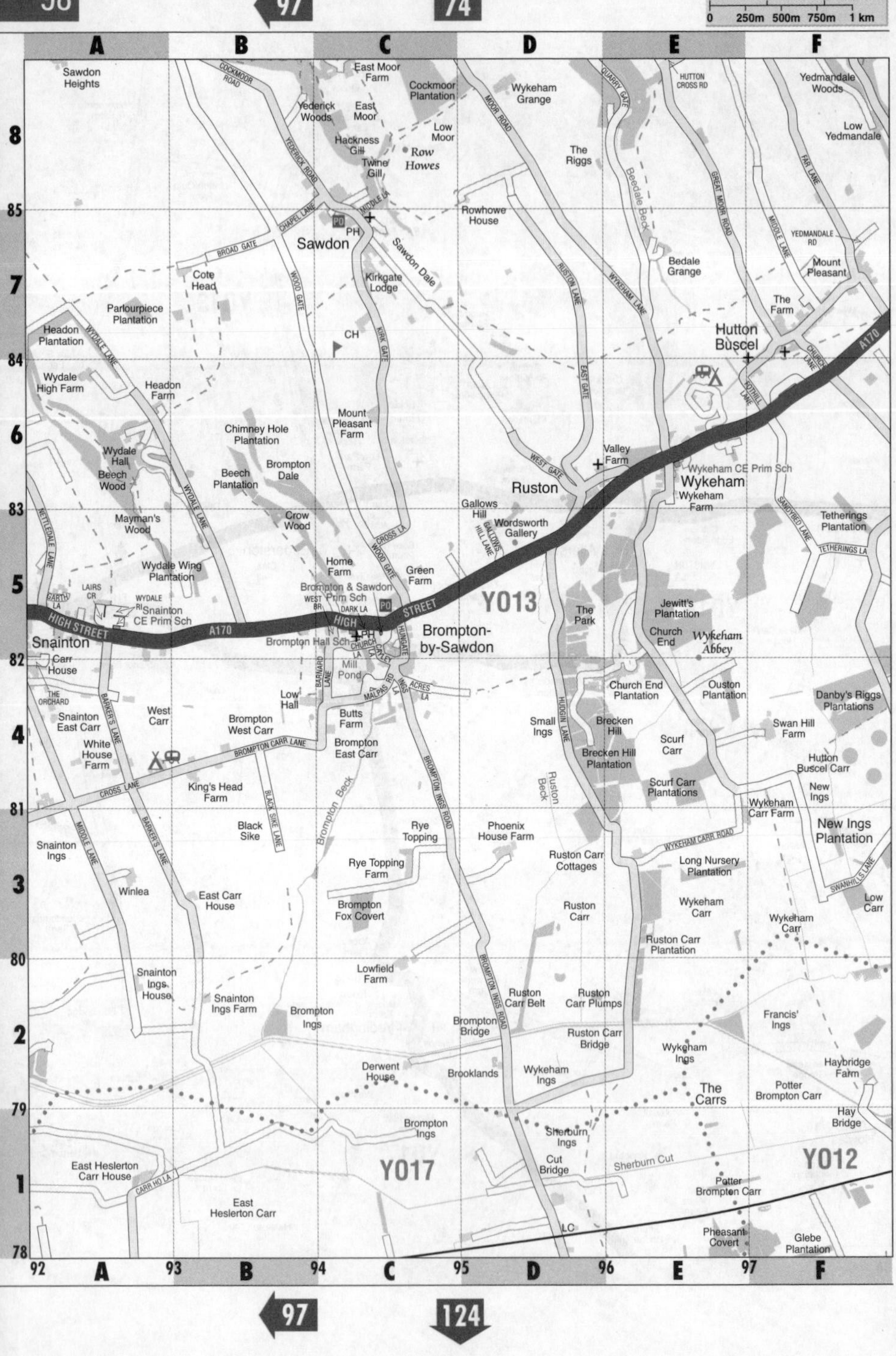

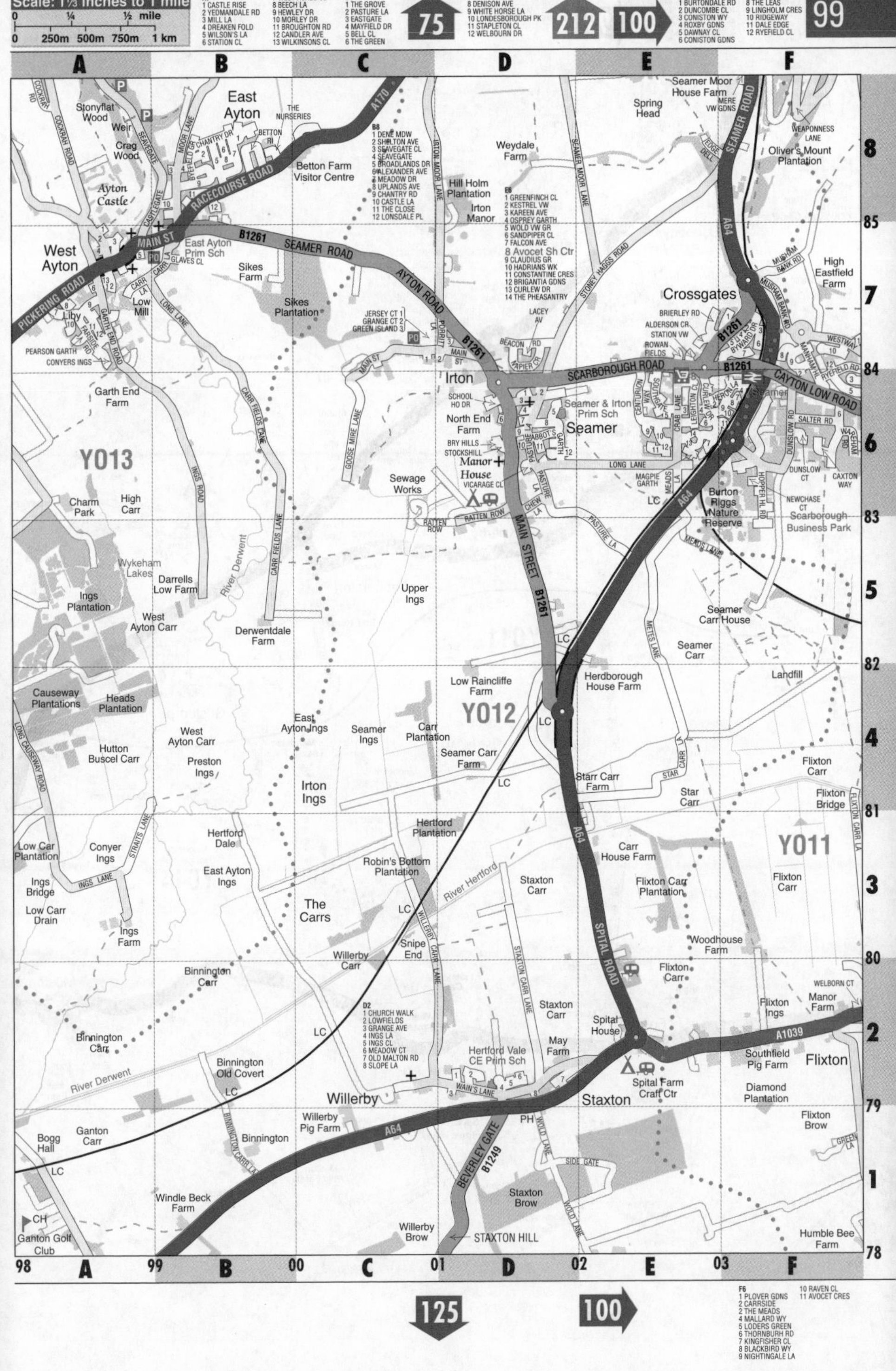
Scale: 1⅓ inches to 1 mile
0 ¼ ½ mile
0 250m 500m 750m 1 km
A7
1 CASTLE RISE
2 YEDMANDALE RD
3 MILL LA
4 DREAKEN FOLD
5 WILSON'S LA
6 STATION CL
7 WEST ACRES CL
8 BEECH LA
9 HEWLEY DR
10 MORLEY DR
11 BROUGHTON RD
12 CANDLER AVE
13 WILKINSONS CL
D6
1 THE GROVE
2 PASTURE LA
3 EASTGATE
4 MAYFIELD DR
5 BELL CL
6 THE GREEN
75
7 RAINFORD CL
8 DENISON AVE
9 WHITE HORSE LA
10 LONDESBOROUGH PK
11 STAPLETON CL
12 WELBOURN DR
212
100
F7
1 BURTONDALE RD
2 DUNCOMBE CL
3 CONISTON WY
4 ROXBY GDNS
5 DAWNAY CL
6 CONISTON GDNS
7 RYDALE CRES
8 THE LEAS
9 LINGHOLM CRES
10 RIDGEWAY
11 DALE EDGE
12 RYEFIELD CL
A
B
C
D
E
F
B8
1 DENE MDW
2 SHELTON AVE
3 SEAVEGATE CL
4 SEAVEGATE
5 BROADLANDS DR
6 ALEXANDER AVE
7 MEADOW DR
8 UPLANDS AVE
9 CHANTRY RD
10 CASTLE LA
11 THE CLOSE
12 LONSDALE PL
E6
1 GREENFINCH CL
2 KESTREL VW
3 KAREEN AVE
4 OSPREY GARTH
5 WOLD VW GR
6 SANDPIPER CL
7 FALCON AVE
8 Avocet Sh Ctr
9 CLAUDIUS GR
10 HADRIANS WK
11 CONSTANTINE CRES
12 BRIGANTIA GDNS
13 CURLEW DR
14 THE PHEASANTRY
Stonyflat Wood
Weir
Crag Wood
Ayton Castle
East Ayton
THE NURSERIES
Betton Farm Visitor Centre
RACECOURSE ROAD
A170
Hill Holm Plantation
Irton Manor
Weydale Farm
Spring Head
Seamer Moor House Farm
SEAMER ROAD
WEAPONNESS LANE
Oliver's Mount Plantation
West Ayton
MAIN ST
East Ayton Prim Sch
B1261
SEAMER ROAD
AYTON ROAD
Sikes Farm
Sikes Plantation
Low Mill
PICKERING ROAD
LONG LANE
STONEY HAGGS ROAD
SEAMER MOOR LANE
IRTON MOOR LANE
Crossgates
High Eastfield Farm
MUSHAM BANK RD
JERSEY CT 1
GRANGE CT 2
GREEN ISLAND 3
PORRITT LA
BEACON RD
LACEY AV
NAPIER CR
BRIERLEY RD
ALDERSON CR
STATION VW
ROWAN FIELDS
SCARBOROUGH ROAD
CAYTON LOW ROAD
WESTWAY
PEARSON GARTH
CONYERS INGS
Garth End Farm
Irton
SCHOOL HO DR
North End Farm
BRY HILLS
STOCKSHILL
Manor House
VICARAGE CL
Seamer & Irton Prim Sch
Seamer
LONG LANE
MAGPIE GARTH
SALTER RD
DUNSLOW CT
CAXTON WAY
YO13
Charm Park
High Carr
INGS ROAD
GOOSE MIRE LANE
Sewage Works
RATTEN ROW
MAIN STREET
CHEW LA
PASTURE LA
Burton Riggs Nature Reserve
NEWCHASE CT
Scarborough Business Park
MEADS LANE
Wykeham Lakes
Ings Plantation
Darrells Low Farm
River Derwent
CARR FIELDS LANE
Upper Ings
Seamer Carr House
West Ayton Carr
Derwentdale Farm
METES LANE
Seamer Carr
Landfill
LC
Causeway Plantations
Heads Plantation
Low Raincliffe Farm
Herdborough House Farm
YO12
East Ayton Ings
Seamer Ings
Carr Plantation
West Ayton Carr
Hutton Buscel Carr
Preston Ings
Seamer Carr Farm
STAR CARR LA
Flixton Carr
LONG CAUSEWAY ROAD
Irton Ings
Starr Carr Farm
Star Carr
Flixton Bridge
FLIXTON CARR LA
STRAITS LANE
Hertford Dale
Hertford Plantation
A64
YO11
Low Car Plantation
Conyer Ings
Robin's Bottom Plantation
Carr House Farm
East Ayton Ings
River Hertford
Staxton Carr
Flixton Carr Plantation
Flixton Carr
Ings Bridge
INGS LANE
Low Carr Drain
The Carrs
SPITAL ROAD
Ings Farm
WILLERBY CARR LANE
Snipe End
Woodhouse Farm
Willerby Carr
STAXTON CARR LANE
Binnington Carr
Flixton Carr
WELBORN CT
Manor Farm
Flixton Ings
Staxton Carr
Spital House
D2
1 CHURCH WALK
2 LOWFIELDS
3 GRANGE AVE
4 INGS LA
5 INGS CL
6 MEADOW CT
7 OLD MALTON RD
8 SLOPE LA
A1039
Binnington Carr
Hertford Vale CE Prim Sch
May Farm
Southfield Pig Farm
Flixton
Binnington Old Covert
River Derwent
WAIN'S LANE
Spital Farm Craft Ctr
Diamond Plantation
Willerby
Staxton
Willerby Pig Farm
PH
Flixton Brow
Bogg Hall
Ganton Carr
Binnington
BINNINGTON CARR LA
BEVERLEY GATE
B1249
WOLD LANE
SIDE GATE
GREEN LA
Windle Beck Farm
Staxton Brow
CH
Ganton Golf Club
Willerby Brow
STAXTON HILL
Humble Bee Farm
8
85
7
84
6
83
5
82
4
81
3
80
2
79
1
78
98
99
00
01
02
03
F6
1 PLOVER GDNS
2 CARRSIDE
2 THE MEADS
4 MALLARD WY
5 LODERS GREEN
6 THORNBURH RD
7 KINGFISHER CL
8 BLACKBIRD WY
9 NIGHTINGALE LA
10 RAVEN CL
11 AVOCET CRES

125
100

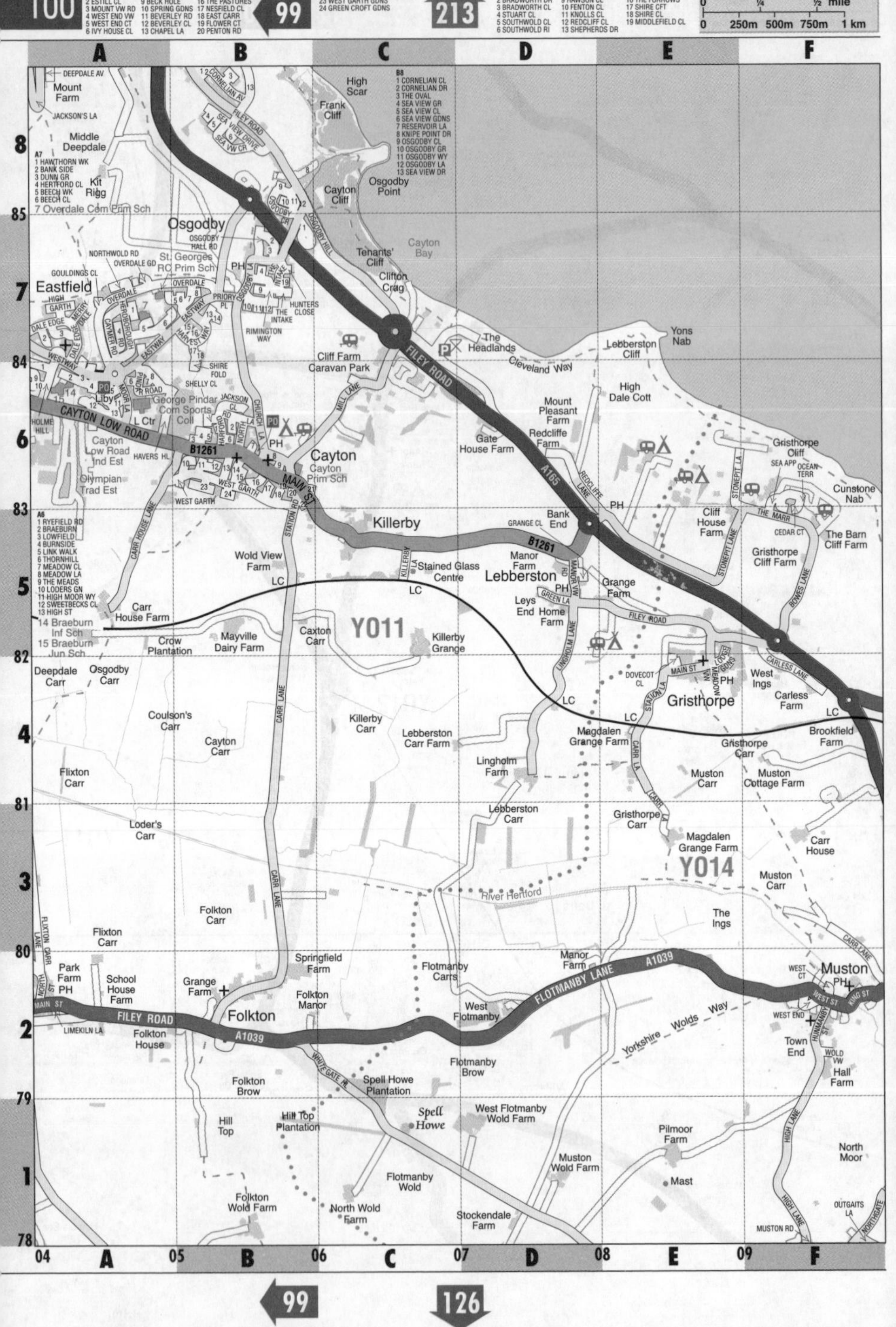
B6
1 FENWICK CL
2 ESTILL CL
3 MOUNT VW RD
4 WEST END VW
5 WEST END CT
6 IVY HOUSE CL
7 LODGE CL
8 LIMEKILN LA
9 BECK HOLE
10 SPRING GDNS
11 BEVERLEY RD
12 BEVERLEY CL
13 CHAPEL LA
14 GREEN PARK RD
15 GREEN PARK AVE
16 THE PASTURES
17 NESFIELD CL
18 EAST CARR
19 FLOWER CT
20 PENTON RD
99
21 EAST LEA VW
22 STANLEY CL
23 WEST GARTH GDNS
24 GREEN CROFT GDNS
213
B7
1 SEAVIEW AVE
2 BRADWORTH DR
3 BRADWORTH CL
4 STUART CL
5 SOUTHWOLD CL
6 SOUTHWOLD RI
7 SOUTHWOLD
8 SOUTHWOLD CRES
9 HAWSON CL
10 FENTON CL
11 KNOLLS CL
12 REDCLIFF CL
13 SHEPHERDS DR
14 PLOUGHMANS CT
15 WAIN CL
16 THE FURROWS
17 SHIRE CFT
18 SHIRE CL
19 MIDDLEFIELD CL
Scale: 1⅓ inches to 1 mile
0 ¼ ½ mile
0 250m 500m 750m 1 km
A B C D E F
DEEPDALE AV
Mount Farm
JACKSON'S LA
Middle Deepdale
A7
1 HAWTHORN WK
2 BANK SIDE
3 DUNN GR
4 HERTFORD CL
5 BEECH WK
6 BEECH CL
7 Overdale Com Prim Sch
Kit Rigg
CORNELIAN AV
FILEY ROAD
SEA VIEW DRIVE
SEA VW CR
High Scar
Frank Cliff
B8
1 CORNELIAN CL
2 CORNELIAN DR
3 THE OVAL
4 SEA VIEW GR
5 SEA VIEW CL
6 SEA VIEW GDNS
7 RESERVOIR LA
8 KNIPE POINT DR
9 OSGODBY CL
10 OSGODBY GR
11 OSGODBY WY
12 OSGODBY LA
13 SEA VIEW DR
Cayton Cliff
Osgodby Point
OSGODBY HILL
Osgodby
OSGODBY HALL RD
NORTHWOLD RD
OVERDALE GD
St. Georges RC Prim Sch
Cayton Bay
Tenants' Cliff
Clifton Crag
GOULDINGS CL
Eastfield
HIGH GARTH
DALE EDGE
OVERDALE
EASTWAY
PRIORY PL
THE INTAKE
HUNTERS CLOSE
RIMINGTON WAY
HARVEST WAY
SHIRE FOLD
SHELLY CL
WESTWAY
Cliff Farm Caravan Park
The Headlands
Cleveland Way
Yons Nab
Lebberston Cliff
High Dale Cott
Liby
George Pindar Com Sports Coll
JACKSON CL
CHURCH LA
MILL LANE
FILEY ROAD
Mount Pleasant Farm
Redcliffe Farm
Gate House Farm
HOLME HILL
CAYTON LOW ROAD
L Ctr
Cayton Low Road Ind Est
Olympian Trad Est
HAVERS HL
B1261
Cayton
Cayton Prim Sch
MAIN ST
WEST GARTH
A165
REDCLIFFE LANE
Gristhorpe Cliff
SEA APP
OCEAN TERR
Cunstone Nab
STONEPIT LA
THE MARR
CEDAR CT
Cliff House Farm
The Barn Cliff Farm
Gristhorpe Cliff Farm
A6
1 RYEFIELD RD
2 BRAEBURN
3 LOWFIELD
4 BURNSIDE
5 LINK WALK
6 THORNHILL
7 MEADOW CL
8 MEADOW LA
9 THE MEADS
10 LODERS GN
11 HIGH MOOR WY
12 SWEETBECKS CL
13 HIGH ST
14 Braeburn Inf Sch
15 Braeburn Jun Sch
CARR HOUSE LANE
STATION RD
Killerby
Bank End
GRANGE CL
B1261
Manor Farm
Lebberston
MANOR VW
GREEN LA
STONEPIT LANE
BOWES LANE
Wold View Farm
KILLERBY LA
Stained Glass Centre
Grange Farm
Leys End
Home Farm
FILEY ROAD
Carr House Farm
Crow Plantation
Mayville Dairy Farm
Caxton Carr
YO11
Killerby Grange
LINGHOLM LANE
DOVECOT CL
MAIN ST
MEADOW VW
LODGE GDNS
West Ings
CARLESS LANE
Carless Farm
STATION LA
Gristhorpe
Deepdale Carr
Osgodby Carr
Coulson's Carr
Cayton Carr
Killerby Carr
Lebberston Carr Farm
Magdalen Grange Farm
Brookfield Farm
Gristhorpe Carr
Flixton Carr
CARR LANE
Lingholm Farm
CARR LA
Muston Carr
Muston Cottage Farm
Loder's Carr
Lebberston Carr
Gristhorpe Carr
Magdalen Grange Farm
Carr House
YO14
Muston Carr
River Hertford
Folkton Carr
The Ings
FLIXTON CARR LANE
NORTH LANE
Flixton Carr
Springfield Farm
Flotmanby Carrs
Manor Farm
A1039
FLOTMANBY LANE
CARR LANE
Muston
WEST CT
KING ST
WEST ST
WEST END
Park Farm
School House Farm
Grange Farm
Folkton Manor
West Flotmanby
MAIN ST
FILEY ROAD
Folkton
LIMEKILN LA
Folkton House
A1039
Yorkshire Wolds Way
HUNMANBY ST
Town End
WOLD VW
Hall Farm
WHITE GATE HL
Spell Howe Plantation
Flotmanby Brow
Folkton Brow
Hill Top
Hill Top Plantation
Spell Howe
West Flotmanby Wold Farm
Pilmoor Farm
North Moor
HIGH LANE
Muston Wold Farm
Mast
Flotmanby Wold
Folkton Wold Farm
North Wold Farm
Stockendale Farm
OUTGAITS LA
NORTHGATE
MUSTON RD
8 85 7 84 6 83 5 82 4 81 3 80 2 79 1 78
04 05 06 07 08 09

Scale: 1½ inches to 1 mile

0	¼	½ mile

| 0 | 250m | 500m | 750m | 1 km |

Map grid columns: A B C D E F
Map grid rows: 8 85 7 84 6 83 5 82 4 81 3 80 2 79 1 78

The Wyke

Cloakhouse End

Newbiggin

Newbiggin Farm West Moat

Crayke House Farm

Filey Dams Nature Reserve

Beacon Hill

Swimming Pool

Allison Field Farm

KING HILL

MOUNT VW

North Moor

North Moor Farm

The Dams

Club Point

North Cliff

Cleveland Way

Filey Field

Filey Spa

North Cliff Ctry Park

Filey Brigg

Filey Sands

Filey Mus

LB Sta

Evron Centre

FILEY

Mill Farm

Muston Grange

Muston Sands

Lowfield Farm

Filey Golf Club

Filey Bay

SOUTH CLIFF DR

PH

Highlands Cl
Primrose Dr
Primrose Valley Rd

LAKESIDE

Hunmanby Sands

Primrose Valley

1 BACK SEA VW
2 THE CLOSE
3 HAWTHORN WY

SCARBOROUGH ROAD

MUSTON ROAD

MOOR ROAD

A165

A1039

Cemetery Way

Yorkshire Wolds Way

CHERRY TREE DR.

PINEWOOD AV

PLANE TREE WY

WOODDALE CL

Y014

B3

1 THE CROFT	19 LINTON CL	37 WEST VALE	55 BRIGG RD
2 ASHLEY CT	20 STATION AVE	38 RUTLAND ST	56 CLARENCE DR
3 QUEEN'S TERR	21 GRANVILLE RD	39 HINDLE DR	
4 LAUNDRY RD	22 CROMWELL AVE	40 FLOWER GARTH	
5 CHURCH ST	23 CLAREMONT	41 HALLAM CL	
6 ST OSWALDS CT	24 MITFORD ST	42 ST JOHN'S AVE	
7 RAVINE TOP	25 CLIFFORD'S TERR	43 BROOKLANDS	
8 BIRCH CL	26 THE AVENUE	44 BROOKLANDS CL	
9 CARLTON RD	27 CHAPEL ST	45 DORAN CL	
10 VICTORIA AVE	28 UNION ST	46 PADBURY CL	
11 WORMAN CRES	29 RAINCLIFFE AVE	47 CLARENCE AVE	
12 WEST RD	30 HOPE ST	48 SOUTHDENE	
13 PROVIDENCE PL	31 MURRAY ST	49 COOPER RD	
14 QUEEN ST	32 CARIGATE HL	50 PADBURY AVE	
15 REYNOLDS ST	33 BELLE VUE CRES	51 SOUTH CR CL	
16 MARINER'S TERR	34 BELLE VUE ST	52 MELVILLE TERR	
17 WHITKIRK PL	35 JOHN ST	53 CRESCENT HL	
18 WHISTON DR	36 WELFORD RD	54 SOUTH CR AVE	

A3

1 SANDPIPER CL	10 RIVELIN WY
2 TEAL CL	11 FEWSTON CL
3 CURLEW DR	12 COLLINGHAM WY
4 HAREWOOD DR	13 WASHBURN CL
5 SILVERWOOD AVE	14 WHARNCLIFFE PL
6 BURNSALL CL	15 MIDHOPE WY
7 LANGSETT AVE	16 EWDEN CL
8 LEYBURN PL	
9 BARDEN PL	

B4

1 LARCH GR	10 ELM CL
2 WILLOW CL	11 ALMOND GR
3 CEDAR GR	12 ASH GR
4 GROVE HILL RD	13 ASH RD
5 HORNDALE RD	14 GROVE RD
6 THORN TREE AVE	15 THE GARDENS
7 ALMOND CL	16 THE CROFT
8 ARNDALE WY	17 RAVINE HL
9 CHURCH CLIFF DR	18 CHURCH CL
	19 SYCAMORE AVE

Scale: 1⅓ inches to 1 mile

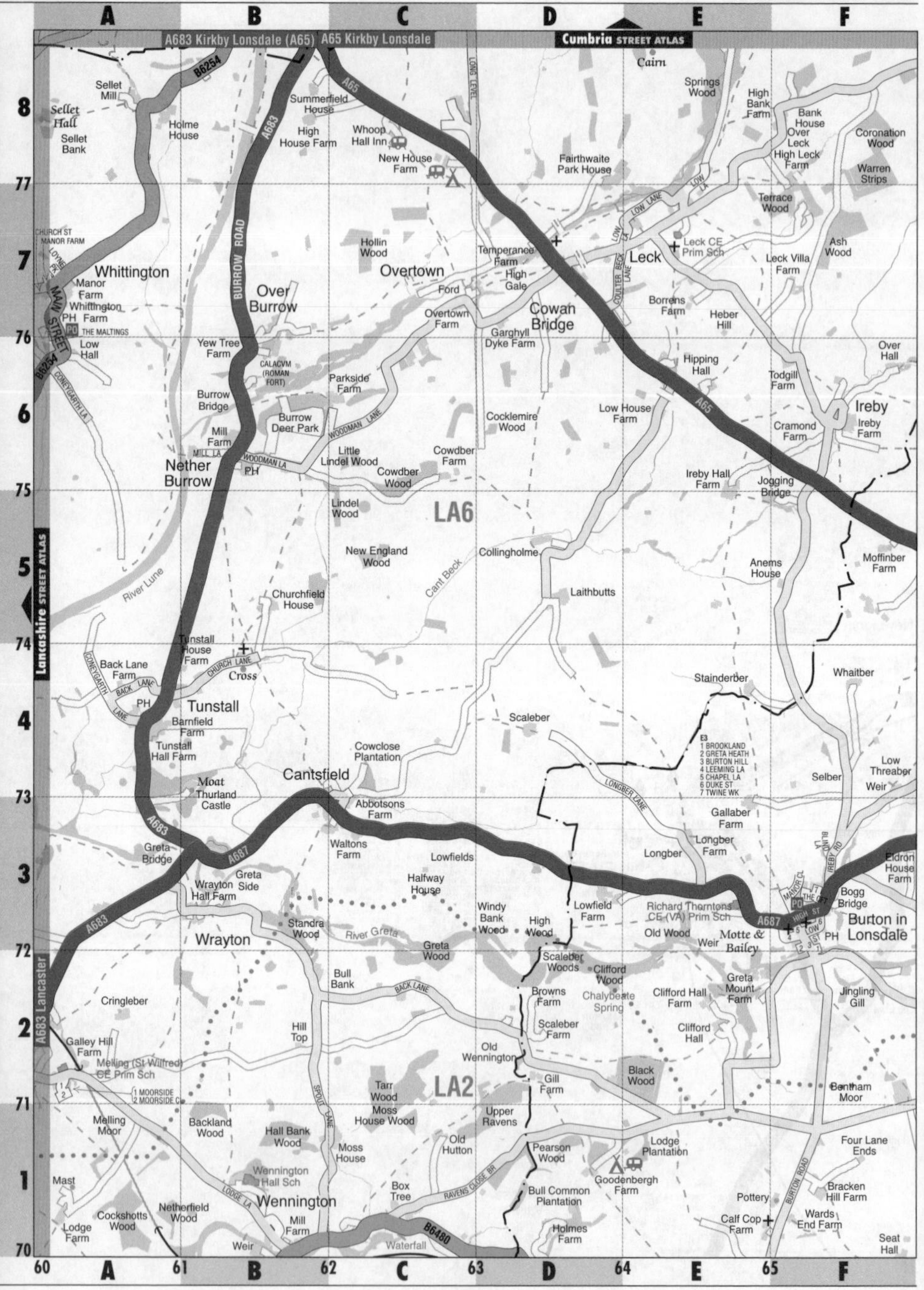
A683 Kirkby Lonsdale (A65)
A65 Kirkby Lonsdale
Cumbria STREET ATLAS
Lancashire STREET ATLAS
A683 Lancaster
Whittington
Over Burrow
Nether Burrow
Overtown
Cowan Bridge
Leck
Ireby
Tunstall
Cantsfield
Wrayton
Burton in Lonsdale
Wennington
LA6
LA2
Sellet Hall
Holme House
Summerfield House
High House Farm
Whoop Hall Inn
New House Farm
Fairthwaite Park House
Springs Wood
High Bank Farm
Bank House
Over Leck
High Leck Farm
Coronation Wood
Warren Strips
Terrace Wood
Ash Wood
Leck Villa Farm
Leck CE Prim Sch
Hollin Wood
Temperance Farm
High Gale
Borrens Farm
Heber Hill
Over Hall
Hipping Hall
Todgill Farm
Low House Farm
Cramond Farm
Ireby Farm
Manor Farm
Whittington Farm
THE MALTINGS
Low Hall
Yew Tree Farm
CALACVM (ROMAN FORT)
Parkside Farm
Garghyll Dyke Farm
Overtown Farm
Burrow Bridge
Burrow Deer Park
Cocklemire Wood
Mill Farm
Little Lindel Wood
Cowdber Farm
Cowdber Wood
Ireby Hall Farm
Jogging Bridge
Lindel Wood
New England Wood
Collingholme
Anems House
Moffinber Farm
Laithbutts
Churchfield House
River Lune
Cant Beck
Tunstall House Farm
Back Lane Farm
Stainderber
Whaitber
Barnfield Farm
Tunstall Hall Farm
Scaleber
Cowclose Plantation
Low Threaber
Selber
Weir
Moat
Thurland Castle
Abbotsons Farm
Gallaber Farm
Greta Bridge
Waltons Farm
Lowfields
Longber
Longber Farm
Eldron House Farm
Greta Side
Wrayton Hall Farm
Halfway House
Windy Bank Wood
High Wood
Lowfield Farm
Richard Thorntons CE (VA) Prim Sch
Bogg Bridge
Standra Wood
River Greta
Greta Wood
Old Wood
Motte & Bailey
Scaleber Woods
Clifford Wood
Greta Mount Farm
Jingling Gill
Bull Bank
Cringleber
Browns Farm
Chalybeate Spring
Clifford Hall Farm
Hill Top
Scaleber Farm
Clifford Hall
Galley Hill Farm
Melling (St Wilfred) CE Prim Sch
Old Wennington
Black Wood
Gill Farm
Bentham Moor
Tarr Wood
Moss House Wood
Upper Ravens
Melling Moor
Backland Wood
Hall Bank Wood
Old Hutton
Pearson Wood
Lodge Plantation
Four Lane Ends
Moss House
Wennington Hall Sch
Mast
Box Tree
Goodenbergh Farm
Bull Common Plantation
Bracken Hill Farm
Pottery
Netherfield Wood
Cockshotts Wood
Lodge Farm
Mill Farm
Calf Cop Farm
Wards End Farm
Holmes Farm
Seat Hall
Waterfall
Cairn
Cross
Ford
1 MOORSIDE
2 MOORSIDE C
E3
1 BROOKLAND
2 GRETA HEATH
3 BURTON HILL
4 LEEMING LA
5 CHAPEL LA
6 DUKE ST
7 TWINE WK
A65
A683
A687
B6254
B6480
BURROW ROAD
WOODMAN LANE
MILL LA
LONG LEVEL
LOW LANE
COULTER BECK LANE
CHURCH LANE
BACK LANE
CONEYGARTH LANE
LONGBER LANE
SPOUT LANE
LODGE LA
RAVENS CLOSE BR
BURTON ROAD
IREBY RD
BLIND LA
HIGH ST
MAIN STREET
CHURCH ST
A B C D E F
8 77 7 76 6 75 5 74 4 73 3 72 2 71 1 70
60 61 62 63 64 65

128

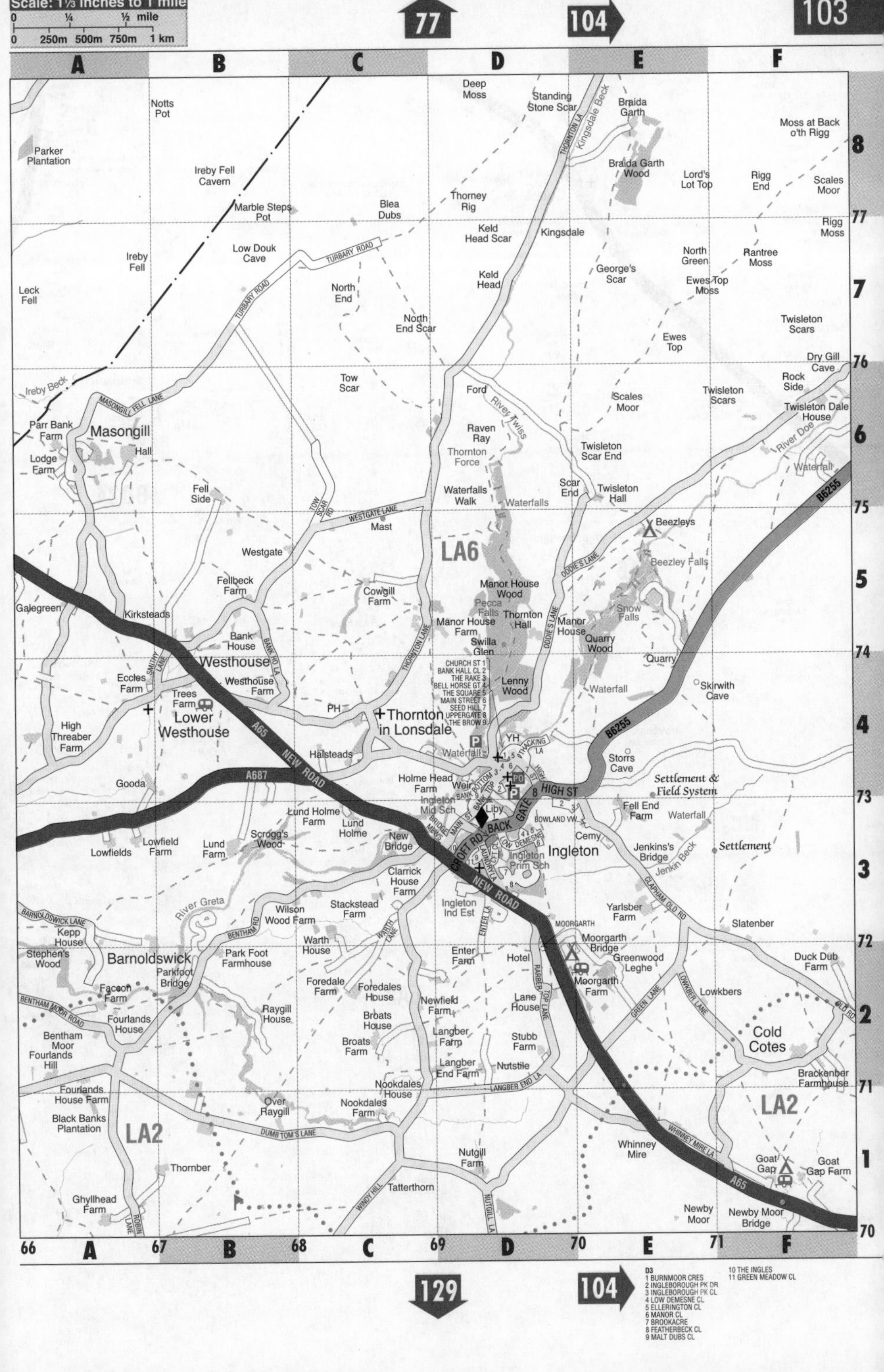

103
78

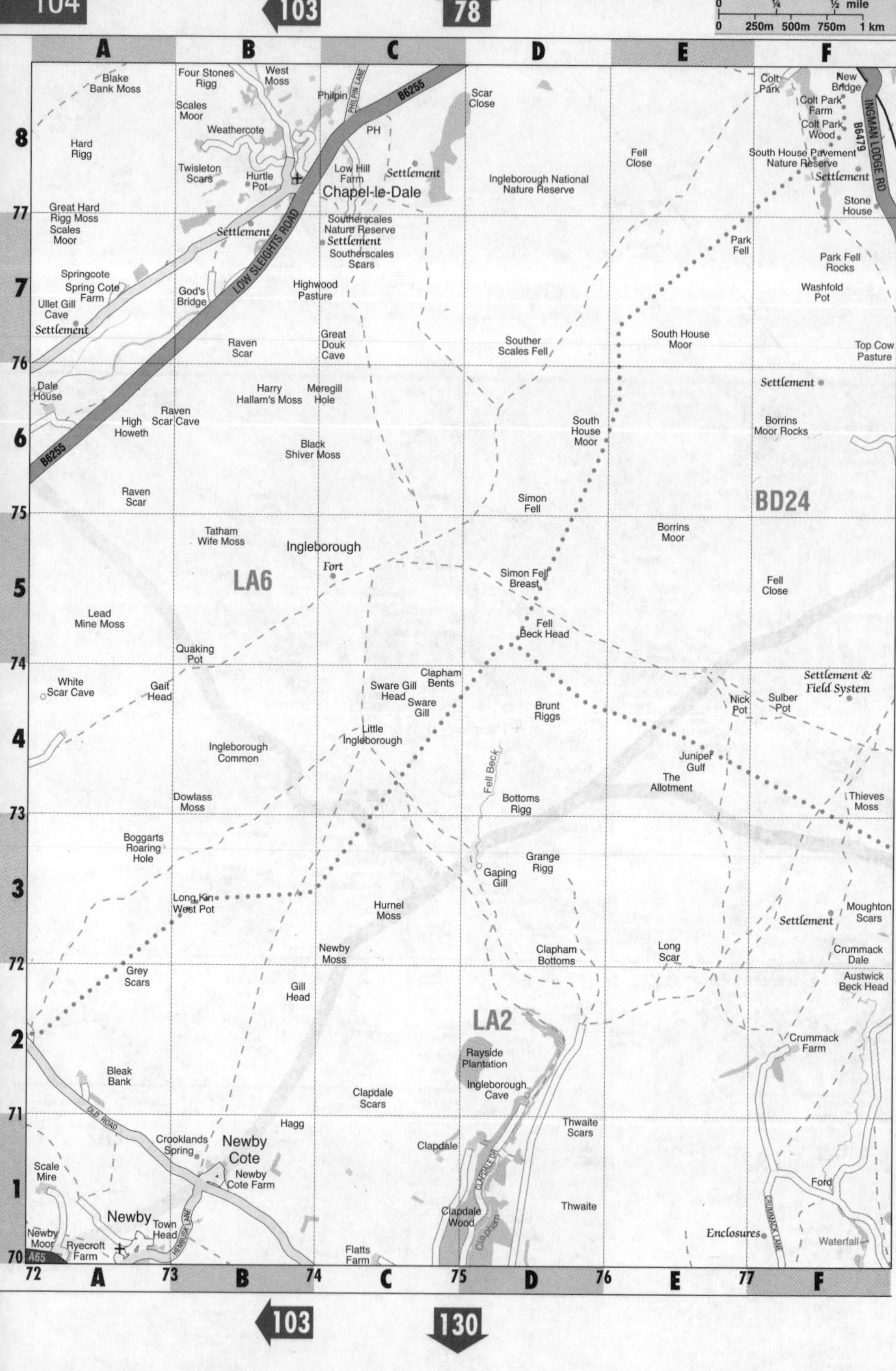
Scale: 1⅓ inches to 1 mile
0 ¼ ½ mile
0 250m 500m 750m 1 km
Blake Bank Moss
Four Stones Rigg
West Moss
Scales Moor
Philpin
PHILPIN LANE
B6255
Scar Close
Colt Park
New Bridge
Colt Park Farm
Colt Park Wood
INGMAN LODGE RD
B6479
Hard Rigg
Weathercote
PH
Twisleton Scars
Hurtle Pot
Low Hill Farm
Settlement
Chapel-le-Dale
Ingleborough National Nature Reserve
Fell Close
South House Pavement Nature Reserve
Settlement
Stone House
Great Hard Rigg Moss
Scales Moor
Settlement
LOW SLEIGHTS ROAD
Southerscales Nature Reserve
Settlement
Southerscales Scars
Park Fell
Park Fell Rocks
Springcote
Spring Cote Farm
Ullet Gill Cave
Settlement
God's Bridge
Highwood Pasture
Washfold Pot
Raven Scar
Great Douk Cave
Souther Scales Fell
South House Moor
Top Cow Pasture
Dale House
Harry Hallam's Moss
Meregill Hole
Settlement
High Howeth
Raven Scar Cave
South House Moor
Borrins Moor Rocks
Black Shiver Moss
B6255
Raven Scar
Simon Fell
BD24
Tatham Wife Moss
Ingleborough
Borrins Moor
Fort
LA6
Simon Fell Breast
Fell Close
Lead Mine Moss
Fell Beck Head
Quaking Pot
White Scar Cave
Gait Head
Clapham Bents
Swaregill Head
Swarе Gill
Brunt Riggs
Settlement & Field System
Nick Pot
Sulber Pot
Little Ingleborough
Ingleborough Common
Fell Beck
Juniper Gulf
The Allotment
Dowlass Moss
Bottoms Rigg
Thieves Moss
Boggarts Roaring Hole
Grange Rigg
Gaping Gill
Long Kin West Pot
Hurnel Moss
Moughton Scars
Settlement
Newby Moss
Clapham Bottoms
Long Scar
Crummack Dale
Grey Scars
Gill Head
Austwick Beck Head
LA2
Crummack Farm
Rayside Plantation
Bleak Bank
Ingleborough Cave
Clapdale Scars
OLD ROAD
Hagg
Thwaite Scars
Crooklands Spring
Newby Cote
Clapdale
CLAPDALE DR
Scale Mire
Newby Cote Farm
Ford
Newby
Town Head
HENBUSK LANE
Clapdale Wood
Clapham
Thwaite
Enclosures
CRUMMACK LANE
Waterfall
Newby Moor
Ryecroft Farm
A65
Flatts Farm

103
130

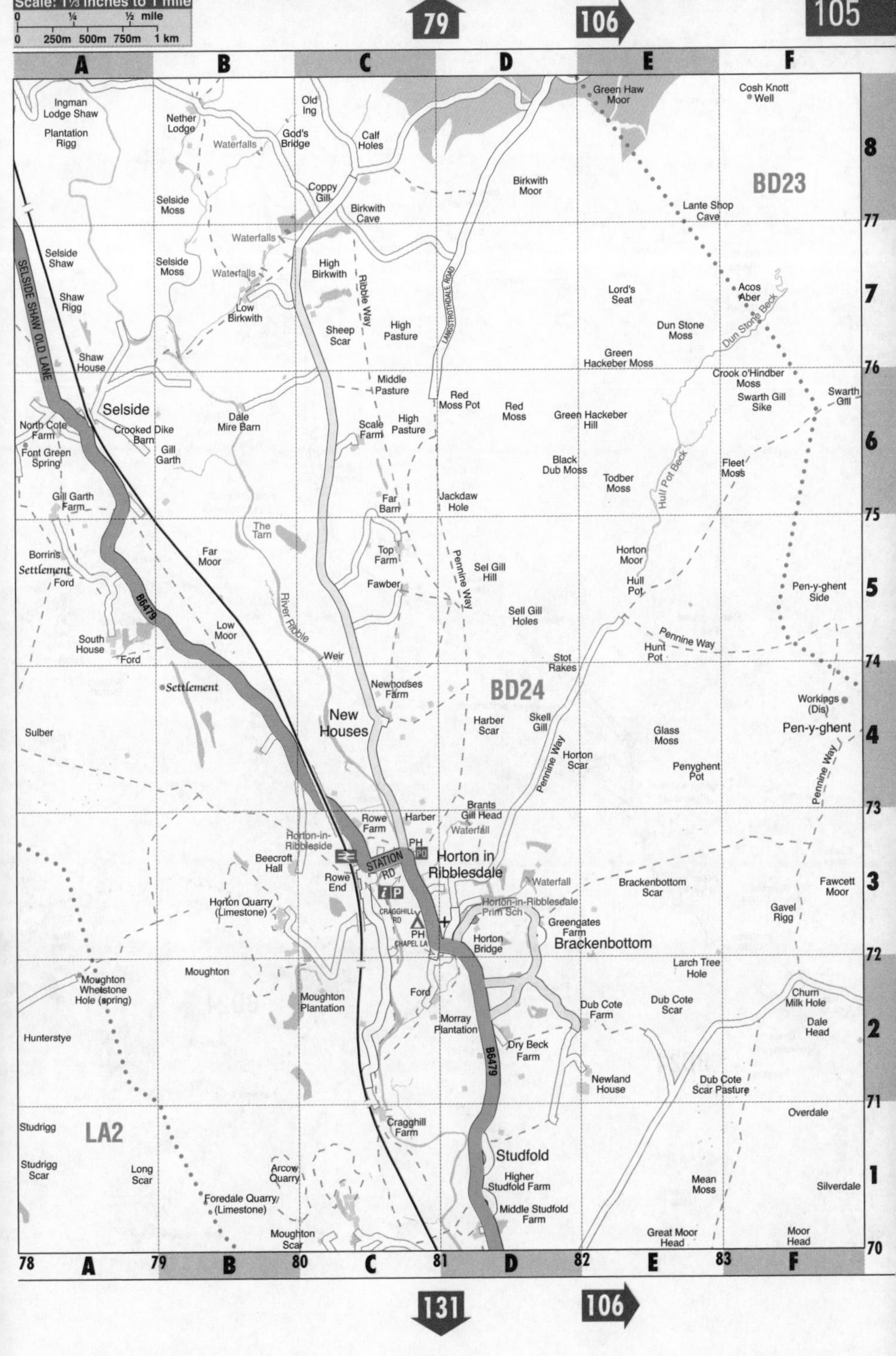
Scale: 1⅓ inches to 1 mile
0 ¼ ½ mile
0 250m 500m 750m 1 km
79
106
A B C D E F
Ingman Lodge Shaw
Plantation Rigg
Nether Lodge
Waterfalls
Old Ing
God's Bridge
Calf Holes
Green Haw Moor
Cosh Knott Well
Coppy Gill
Birkwith Cave
Birkwith Moor
BD23
Lante Shop Cave
Selside Moss
Waterfalls
Selside Shaw
Selside Moss
Waterfalls
High Birkwith
Ribble Way
LANGSTROTHDALE ROAD
Lord's Seat
Acos Aber
SELSIDE SHAW OLD LANE
Shaw Rigg
Low Birkwith
Sheep Scar
High Pasture
Dun Stone Moss
Dun Stone Beck
Shaw House
Green Hackeber Moss
Crook o'Hindber Moss
Middle Pasture
Red Moss Pot
Red Moss
Selside
Swarth Gill Sike
Swarth Gill
North Cote Farm
Crooked Dike Barn
Dale Mire Barn
Scale Farm
High Pasture
Green Hackeber Hill
Font Green Spring
Gill Garth
Black Dub Moss
Hull Pot Beck
Fleet Moss
Todber Moss
Gill Garth Farm
Far Barn
Jackdaw Hole
The Tarn
Borrins
Settlement
Far Moor
Top Farm
Horton Moor
Ford
Sel Gill Hill
Pennine Way
Hull Pot
Pen-y-ghent Side
B6479
Fawber
River Ribble
Sell Gill Holes
Low Moor
South House
Pennine Way
Hunt Pot
Weir
Stot Rakes
Ford
Settlement
Newhouses Farm
BD24
Workings (Dis)
New Houses
Harber Scar
Skell Gill
Sulber
Pen-y-ghent
Glass Moss
Horton Scar
Pennine Way
Penyghent Pot
Pennine Way
Brants Gill Head
Rowe Farm
Harber
Horton-in-Ribbleside
Waterfall
PH
PO
Beecroft Hall
STATION RD
Horton in Ribblesdale
Rowe End
Waterfall
Brackenbottom Scar
Fawcett Moor
Horton Quarry (Limestone)
CRAGGHILL RD
Horton-in-Ribblesdale Prim Sch
Gavel Rigg
PH
CHAPEL LA
Greengates Farm
Horton Bridge
Brackenbottom
Moughton
Moughton Whetstone Hole (spring)
Larch Tree Hole
Moughton Plantation
Ford
Churn Milk Hole
Dub Cote Farm
Dub Cote Scar
Dale Head
Morray Plantation
Hunterstye
Dry Beck Farm
B6479
Newland House
Dub Cote Scar Pasture
Overdale
Studrigg
LA2
Cragghill Farm
Studfold
Studrigg Scar
Long Scar
Arcow Quarry
Higher Studfold Farm
Mean Moss
Silverdale
Foredale Quarry (Limestone)
Middle Studfold Farm
Moughton Scar
Great Moor Head
Moor Head
8 77 7 76 6 75 5 74 4 73 3 72 2 71 1 70
78 79 80 81 82 83
131
106

105
80

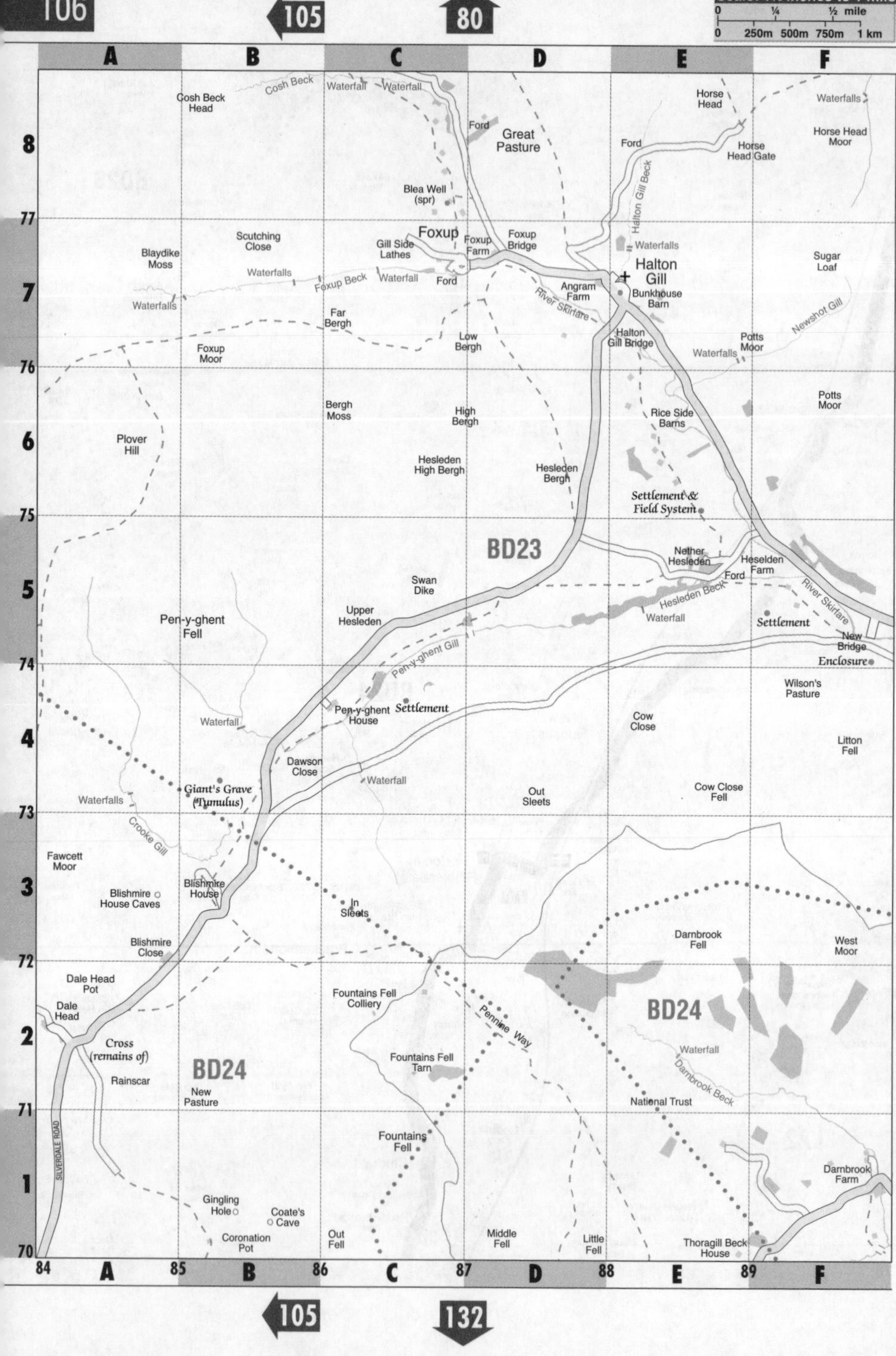
Scale: 1⅓ inches to 1 mile
0 ¼ ½ mile
0 250m 500m 750m 1 km
A B C D E F
8
77
7
76
6
75
5
74
4
73
3
72
2
71
1
70
84 85 86 87 88 89
Cosh Beck
Waterfall
Waterfall
Cosh Beck Head
Horse Head
Waterfalls
Ford
Great Pasture
Horse Head Moor
Ford
Horse Head Gate
Halton Gill Beck
Blea Well (spr)
Foxup
Scutching Close
Gill Side Lathes
Foxup Farm
Foxup Bridge
Waterfalls
Blaydike Moss
Waterfalls
Foxup Beck
Waterfall
Ford
Halton Gill
Sugar Loaf
Angram Farm
River Skirfare
Bunkhouse Barn
Waterfalls
Newshot Gill
Far Bergh
Low Bergh
Halton Gill Bridge
Waterfalls
Potts Moor
Foxup Moor
Potts Moor
Bergh Moss
High Bergh
Rice Side Barns
Plover Hill
Hesleden High Bergh
Hesleden Bergh
Settlement & Field System
BD23
Nether Hesleden
Heselden Farm
Ford
Swan Dike
Hesleden Beck
River Skirfare
Pen-y-ghent Fell
Upper Hesleden
Waterfall
Settlement
New Bridge
Enclosure
Pen-y-ghent Gill
Wilson's Pasture
Pen-y-ghent House
Settlement
Waterfall
Cow Close
Litton Fell
Dawson Close
Waterfall
Giant's Grave (Tumulus)
Waterfalls
Out Sleets
Cow Close Fell
Crooke Gill
Fawcett Moor
Blishmire House
Blishmire House Caves
In Sleets
Darnbrook Fell
West Moor
Blishmire Close
Dale Head Pot
Fountains Fell Colliery
BD24
Dale Head
Pennine Way
Cross (remains of)
Fountains Fell Tarn
Waterfall
Rainscar
BD24
Darnbrook Beck
New Pasture
National Trust
SILVERDALE ROAD
Fountains Fell
Darnbrook Farm
Gingling Hole
Coate's Cave
Coronation Pot
Out Fell
Middle Fell
Little Fell
Thoragill Beck House

105
132

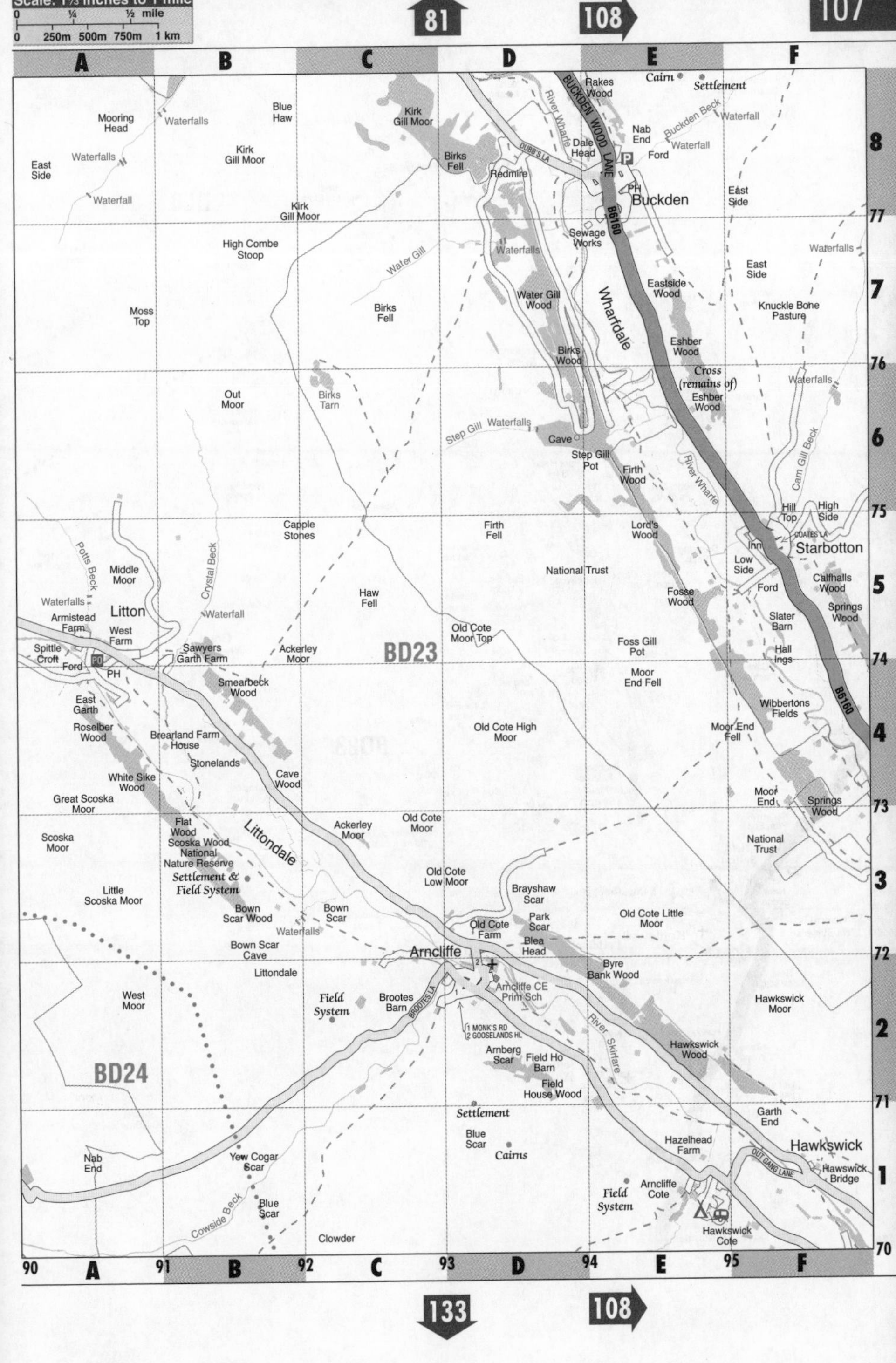
Scale: 1⅓ inches to 1 mile
81
108
Litton
Buckden
Starbotton
Arncliffe
Hawkswick
Wharfdale
Littondale
BD23
BD24
River Wharfe
River Skirfare
Kirk Gill Moor
Birks Fell
Old Cote Moor
Hawkswick Moor
Scoska Wood National Nature Reserve
133
108

107
82

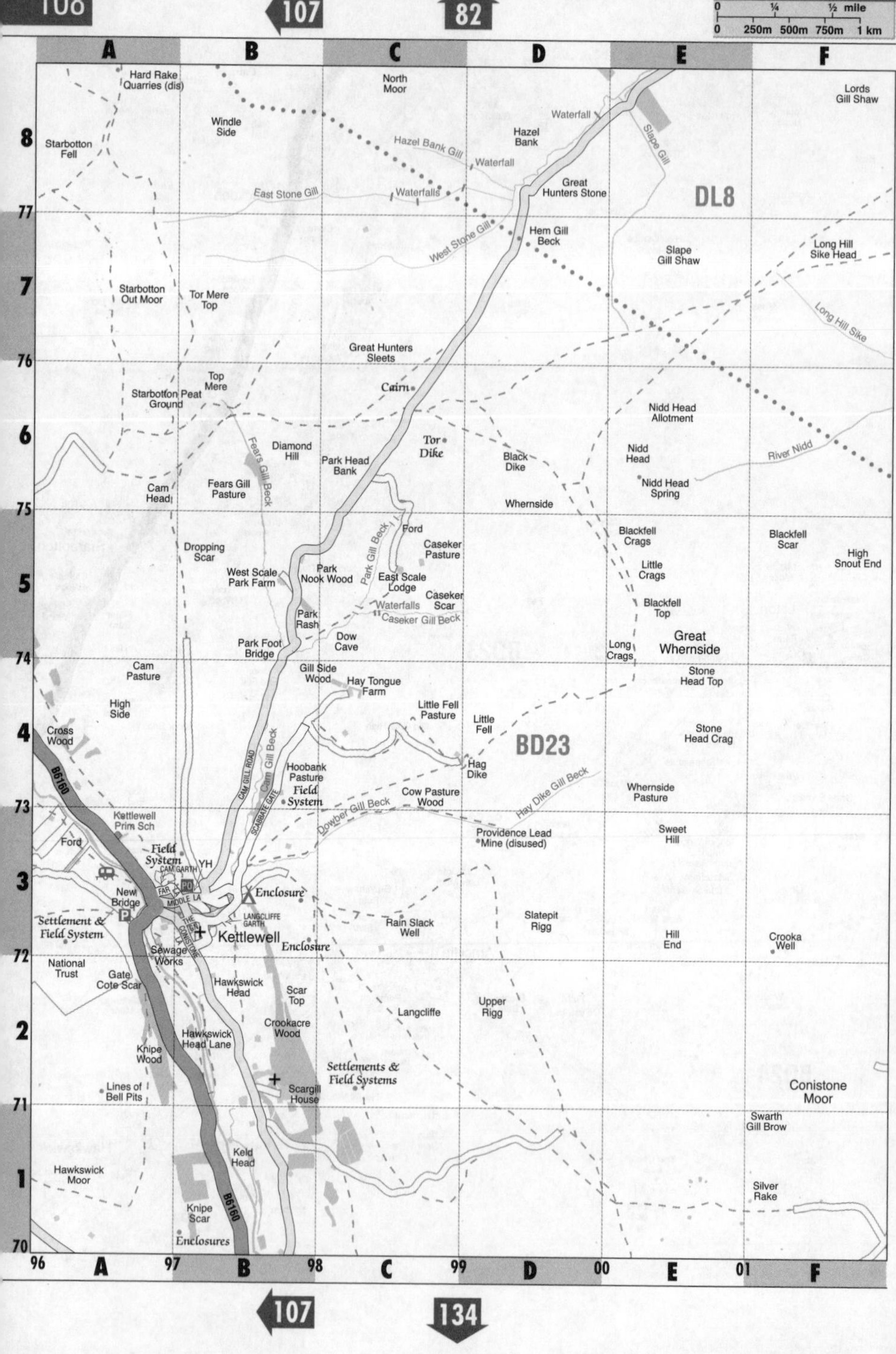
Scale: 1⅓ inches to 1 mile
0 ¼ ½ mile
0 250m 500m 750m 1 km
Hard Rake Quarries (dis)
North Moor
Lords Gill Shaw
Windle Side
Waterfall
Hazel Bank
Slape Gill
Starbotton Fell
Hazel Bank Gill
Waterfall
East Stone Gill
Waterfalls
Great Hunters Stone
DL8
Hem Gill Beck
West Stone Gill
Slape Gill Shaw
Long Hill Sike Head
Starbotton Out Moor
Tor Mere Top
Long Hill Sike
Great Hunters Sleets
Top Mere
Starbotton Peat Ground
Cairn
Nidd Head Allotment
Diamond Hill
Park Head Bank
Tor Dike
Black Dike
Nidd Head
River Nidd
Cam Head
Fears Gill Pasture
Fears Gill Beck
Nidd Head Spring
Whernside
Ford
Blackfell Crags
Blackfell Scar
Dropping Scar
Caseker Pasture
High Snout End
West Scale Park Farm
Park Nook Wood
Park Gill Beck
East Scale Lodge
Little Crags
Caseker Scar
Waterfalls
Caseker Gill Beck
Blackfell Top
Park Rash
Dow Cave
Park Foot Bridge
Long Crags
Great Whernside
Cam Pasture
Gill Side Wood
Hay Tongue Farm
Stone Head Top
High Side
Little Fell Pasture
Little Fell
Cross Wood
BD23
Stone Head Crag
B6160
Hag Dike
Hoobank Pasture
Field System
Cam Gill Road
Cam Gill Beck
Scabbate Gate
Cow Pasture Wood
Hay Dike Gill Beck
Whernside Pasture
Dowber Gill Beck
Kettlewell Prim Sch
Ford
Providence Lead Mine (disused)
Sweet Hill
Field System
Cam Garth
YH
Far
PO
New Bridge
Middle La
Enclosure
Langcliffe Garth
Settlement & Field System
The Lane
Conistone
Kettlewell
Rain Slack Well
Slatepit Rigg
Hill End
Crooka Well
Enclosure
Sewage Works
National Trust
Gate Cote Scar
Hawkswick Head
Scar Top
Upper Rigg
Langcliffe
Crookacre Wood
Hawkswick Head Lane
Knipe Wood
Settlements & Field Systems
Lines of Bell Pits
Scargill House
Conistone Moor
Swarth Gill Brow
Keld Head
Hawkswick Moor
Silver Rake
Knipe Scar
B6160
Enclosures
A B C D E F
96 97 98 99 00 01
70 71 72 73 74 75 76 77
1 2 3 4 5 6 7 8

107
134

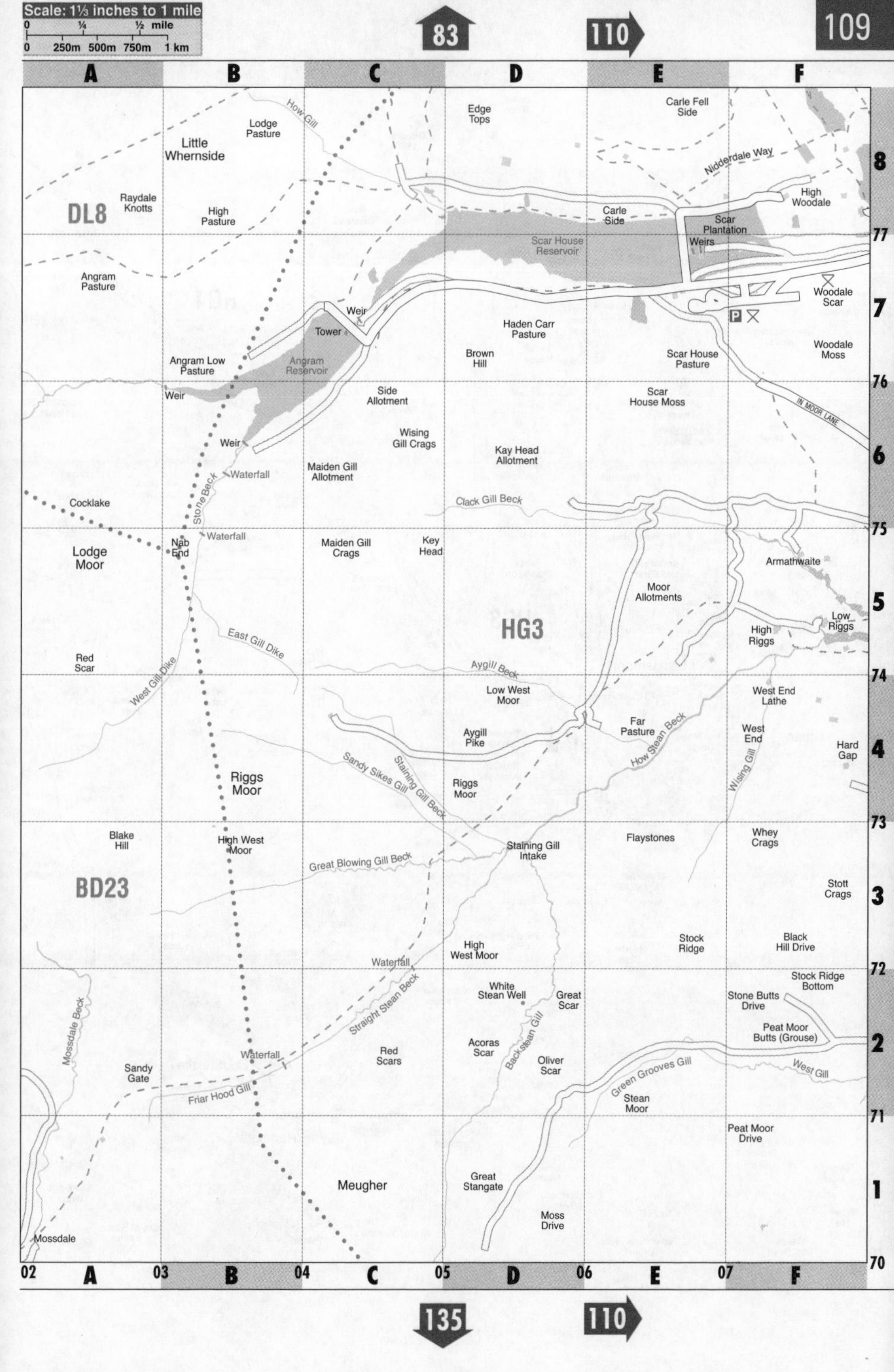

A   B   C   D   E   F

8

Edge
Tops

Carle Fell
Side

Nidderdale Way

Little
Whernside

Lodge
Pasture

How Gill

High
Woodale

DL8

Raydale
Knotts

High
Pasture

Carle
Side

Scar
Plantation

77

Scar House
Reservoir

Weirs

Angram
Pasture

Woodale
Scar

7

Weir

Tower

Haden Carr
Pasture

P

Woodale
Moss

Angram Low
Pasture

Angram
Reservoir

Brown
Hill

Scar House
Pasture

76

Weir

Side
Allotment

Scar
House Moss

IN MOOR LANE

6

Weir

Wising
Gill Crags

Kay Head
Allotment

Maiden Gill
Allotment

Waterfall

Clack Gill Beck

Stone Beck

75

Cocklake

Waterfall

Maiden Gill
Crags

Key
Head

Moor
Allotments

Armathwaite

Lodge
Moor

Nab
End

HG3

High
Riggs

Low
Riggs

5

Red
Scar

East Gill Dike

West Gill Dike

Aygill Beck

West End
Lathe

74

Low West
Moor

Far
Pasture

West
End

Hard
Gap

4

Riggs
Moor

Sandy Sikes Gill Beck

Staining Gill Beck

Aygill
Pike

Riggs
Moor

How Steam Beck

Wising Gill

Blake
Hill

High West
Moor

Staining Gill
Intake

Flaystones

Whey
Crags

73

BD23

Great Blowing Gill Beck

Stott
Crags

3

High
West Moor

Stock
Ridge

Black
Hill Drive

72

Waterfall

White
Stean Well

Great
Scar

Stone Butts
Drive

Stock Ridge
Bottom

Mossdale Beck

Straight Stean Beck

Acoras
Scar

Blackstean Gill

Peat Moor
Butts (Grouse)

2

Sandy
Gate

Waterfall

Red
Scars

Oliver
Scar

Green Grooves Gill

West Gill

Friar Hood Gill

Stean
Moor

Peat Moor
Drive

71

Meugher

Great
Stangate

Moss
Drive

1

Mossdale

70

A   02   B   03   04   C   05   D   06   E   07   F

109
84

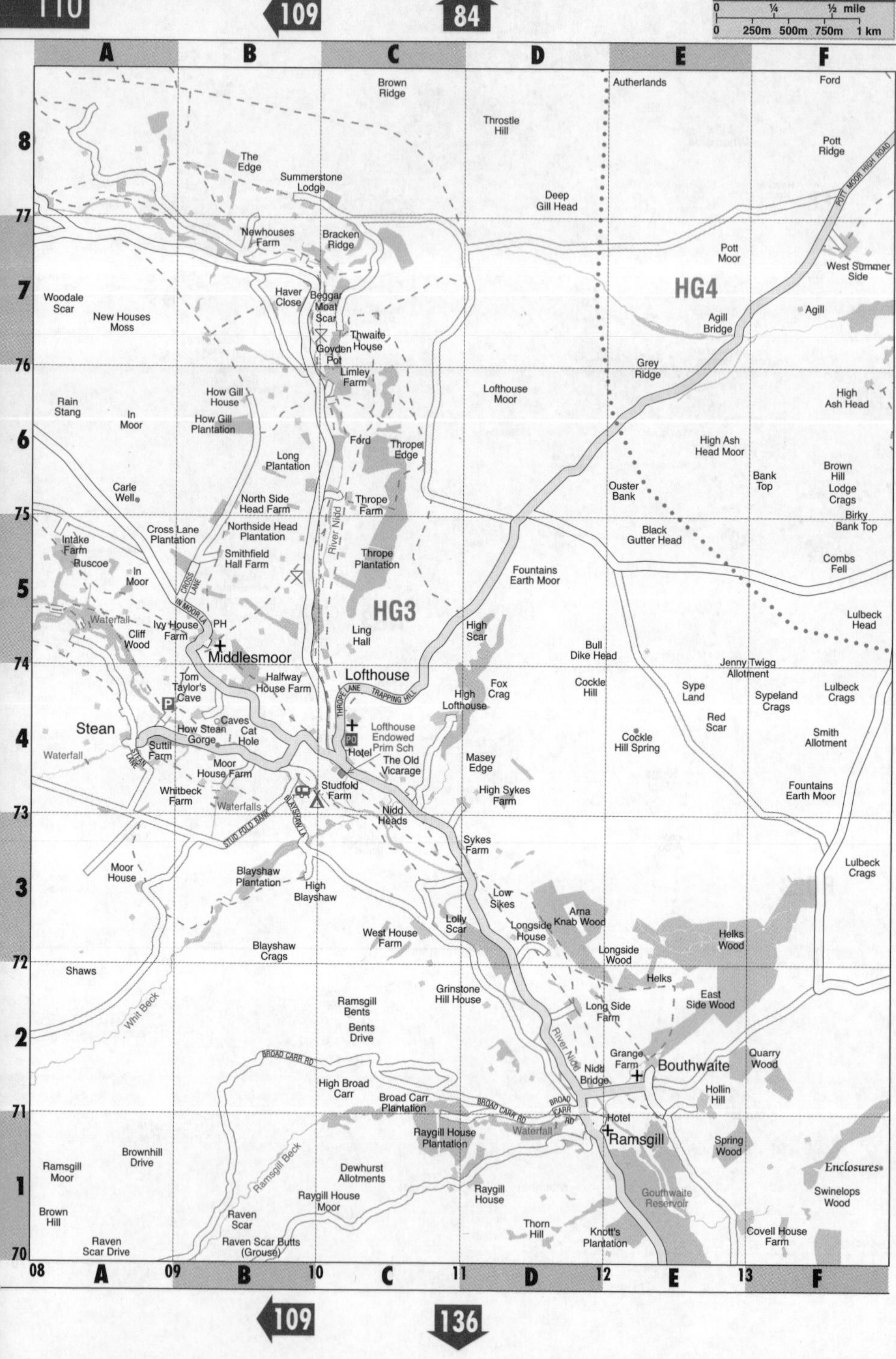
Scale: 1⅓ inches to 1 mile
0 ¼ ½ mile
0 250m 500m 750m 1 km
A B C D E F
8 77 7 76 6 75 5 74 4 73 3 72 2 71 1 70
08 09 10 11 12 13
Brown Ridge
Autherlands
Ford
Throstle Hill
Pott Ridge
The Edge
Summerstone Lodge
Deep Gill Head
POTT MOOR HIGH ROAD
Newhouses Farm
Bracken Ridge
Pott Moor
West Summer Side
HG4
Woodale Scar
Haver Close
Beggar Moat Scar
New Houses Moss
Agill
Agill Bridge
Thwaite House
Goyden Pot
Grey Ridge
Limley Farm
Rain Stang
How Gill House
Lofthouse Moor
High Ash Head
In Moor
How Gill Plantation
Ford
Thrope Edge
High Ash Head Moor
Long Plantation
Brown Hill Lodge Crags
Bank Top
Carle Well
North Side Head Farm
Thrope Farm
Ouster Bank
Birky Bank Top
Cross Lane Plantation
Northside Head Plantation
River Nidd
Black Gutter Head
Intake Farm
Thrope Plantation
Smithfield Hall Farm
Combs Fell
Ruscoe
In Moor
Fountains Earth Moor
CROSS LANE
IN MOOR LA
HG3
Waterfall
Ivy House Farm
PH
High Scar
Lulbeck Head
Cliff Wood
Ling Hall
Bull Dike Head
Middlesmoor
Jenny Twigg Allotment
Tom Taylor's Cave
Halfway House Farm
Lofthouse
THROPE LANE
TRAPPING HILL
Fox Crag
High Lofthouse
Cockle Hill
Sype Land
Sypeland Crags
Lulbeck Crags
Caves
Stean
How Stean Gorge
Cat Hole
Lofthouse Endowed Prim Sch
PO
Hotel
Red Scar
Smith Allotment
Cockle Hill Spring
Waterfall
Suttil Farm
STEAN LANE
Moor House Farm
The Old Vicarage
Masey Edge
Whitbeck Farm
Studfold Farm
High Sykes Farm
Fountains Earth Moor
Waterfalls
BLAYSHAW LA
STUD FOLD BANK
Nidd Heads
Sykes Farm
Moor House
Lulbeck Crags
Blayshaw Plantation
High Blayshaw
Low Sikes
Arna Knab Wood
Lolly Scar
West House Farm
Longside House
Helks Wood
Blayshaw Crags
Longside Wood
Shaws
Helks
Grinstone Hill House
Ramsgill Bents
Long Side Farm
East Side Wood
Whit Beck
Bents Drive
River Nidd
BROAD CARR RD
Grange Farm
Bouthwaite
Quarry Wood
Nidd Bridge
High Broad Carr
Broad Carr Plantation
BROAD CARR RD
BROAD CARR RD
Hollin Hill
Hotel
Waterfall
Raygill House Plantation
Ramsgill
Brownhill Drive
Ramsgill Beck
Spring Wood
Ramsgill Moor
Dewhurst Allotments
Enclosures
Raygill House
Gouthwaite Reservoir
Swinelops Wood
Raygill House Moor
Brown Hill
Raven Scar
Thorn Hill
Raven Scar Drive
Raven Scar Butts (Grouse)
Knott's Plantation
Covell House Farm

109
136

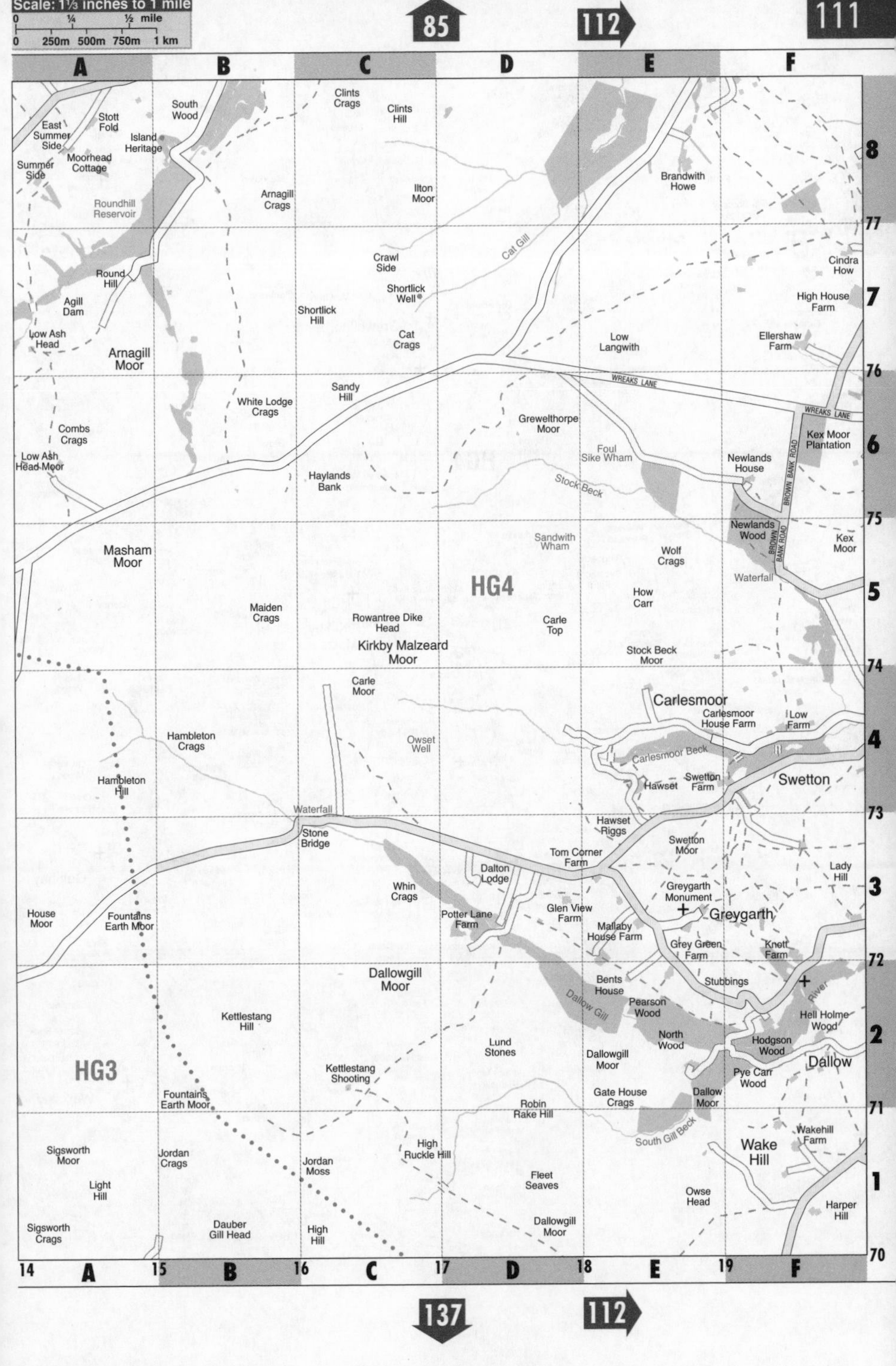
Scale: 1⅓ inches to 1 mile
0 ¼ ½ mile
0 250m 500m 750m 1 km
85
112
A B C D E F
South Wood
Clints Crags
Clints Hill
East Summer Side
Stott Fold
Island Heritage
Summer Side
Moorhead Cottage
Roundhill Reservoir
Arnagill Crags
Ilton Moor
Brandwith Howe
Cat Gill
Round Hill
Crawl Side
Shortlick Well
Cindra How
Agill Dam
Shortlick Hill
High House Farm
Low Ash Head
Cat Crags
Low Langwith
Ellershaw Farm
Arnagill Moor
Sandy Hill
WREAKS LANE
White Lodge Crags
Grewelthorpe Moor
Kex Moor Plantation
Combs Crags
Foul Sike Wham
Newlands House
BROWN BANK ROAD
Low Ash Head Moor
Haylands Bank
Stock Beck
Newlands Wood
Kex Moor
Masham Moor
Sandwith Wham
Wolf Crags
HG4
Waterfall
How Carr
Maiden Crags
Rowantree Dike Head
Carle Top
Kirkby Malzeard Moor
Stock Beck Moor
Carle Moor
Carlesmoor
Carlesmoor House Farm
Low Farm
Hambleton Crags
Owset Well
Carlesmoor Beck
Hambleton Hill
Hawset
Swetton Farm
Swetton
Waterfall
Stone Bridge
Hawset Riggs
Swetton Moor
Tom Corner Farm
Dalton Lodge
Lady Hill
Whin Crags
Greygarth Monument
Greygarth
House Moor
Fountains Earth Moor
Potter Lane Farm
Glen View Farm
Mallaby House Farm
Grey Green Farm
Knott Farm
Dallowgill Moor
Bents House
Stubbings
Dallow Gill
Pearson Wood
River
Kettlestang Hill
Hell Holme Wood
North Wood
Lund Stones
Hodgson Wood
Dallowgill Moor
HG3
Kettlestang Shooting
Dallow
Pye Carr Wood
Fountains Earth Moor
Gate House Crags
Dallow Moor
Robin Rake Hill
South Gill Beck
Wakehill Farm
Sigsworth Moor
Jordan Crags
High Ruckle Hill
Wake Hill
Jordan Moss
Fleet Seaves
Light Hill
Owse Head
Harper Hill
Sigsworth Crags
Dauber Gill Head
High Hill
Dallowgill Moor
8 77 7 76 6 75 5 74 4 73 3 72 2 71 1 70
14 15 16 17 18 19
137
112

111
86
Scale: 1⅓ inches to 1 mile

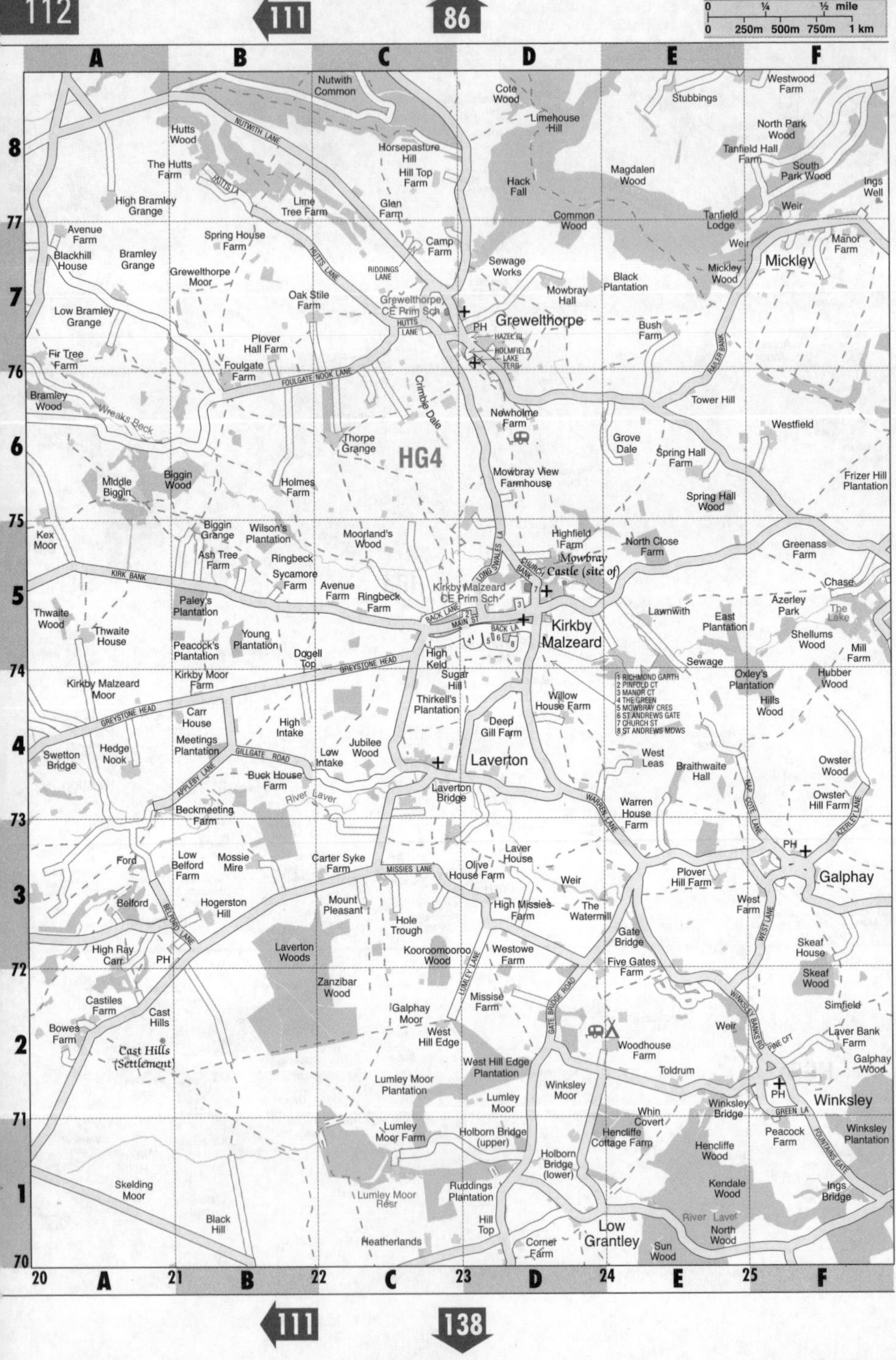
Nutwith Common
Cote Wood
Stubbings
Westwood Farm
Hutts Wood
Limehouse Hill
North Park Wood
Horsepasture Hill
Hill Top Farm
Tanfield Hall Farm
The Hutts Farm
Magdalen Wood
South Park Wood
Hack Fall
Ings Well
High Bramley Grange
Lime Tree Farm
Glen Farm
Weir
Common Wood
Tanfield Lodge
Avenue Farm
Spring House Farm
Camp Farm
Manor Farm
Blackhill House
Bramley Grange
Weir
Mickley
Sewage Works
Mickley Wood
Grewelthorpe Moor
Black Plantation
Oak Stile Farm
Mowbray Hall
Grewelthorpe CE Prim Sch
Grewelthorpe
Low Bramley Grange
Bush Farm
Plover Hall Farm
Fir Tree Farm
Foulgate Farm
Tower Hill
Bramley Wood
Crimble Dale
Newholme Farm
Westfield
Thorpe Grange
Grove Dale
Spring Hall Farm
HG4
Middle Biggin
Biggin Wood
Mowbray View Farmhouse
Frizer Hill Plantation
Holmes Farm
Spring Hall Wood
Kex Moor
Biggin Grange
Wilson's Plantation
Moorland's Wood
Highfield Farm
North Close Farm
Greenass Farm
Ash Tree Farm
Ringbeck
Mowbray Castle (site of)
Sycamore Farm
Chase
Avenue Farm
Ringbeck Farm
Kirkby Malzeard CE Prim Sch
Thwaite Wood
Paley's Plantation
Lawnwith
Azerley Park
East Plantation
Thwaite House
Kirkby Malzeard
Young Plantation
Shellums Wood
Peacock's Plantation
Dogell Top
High Keld
Mill Farm
Sewage
Kirkby Malzeard Moor
Kirkby Moor Farm
Sugar Hill
1 RICHMOND GARTH
2 PINFOLD CT
3 MANOR CT
4 THE GREEN
5 MOWBRAY CRES
6 ST ANDREWS GATE
7 CHURCH ST
8 ST ANDREWS MDWS
Oxley's Plantation
Hubber Wood
Thirkell's Plantation
Willow House Farm
Hills Wood
Carr House
High Intake
Deep Gill Farm
Swetton Bridge
Hedge Nook
Meetings Plantation
Low Intake
Jubilee Wood
Laverton
West Leas
Braithwaite Hall
Owster Wood
Buck House Farm
Laverton Bridge
Owster Hill Farm
Warren House Farm
Beckmeeting Farm
River Laver
Laver House
PH
Ford
Low Belford Farm
Mossie Mire
Carter Syke Farm
Olive House Farm
Weir
Plover Hill Farm
Galphay
Belford
Hogerston Hill
Mount Pleasant
High Missies Farm
The Watermill
West Farm
Hole Trough
Gate Bridge
Skeaf House
High Ray Carr
PH
Laverton Woods
Kooroomooroo Wood
Westowe Farm
Five Gates Farm
Skeaf Wood
Castiles Farm
Zanzibar Wood
Missies Farm
Simfield
Cast Hills
Galphay Moor
Weir
Laver Bank Farm
Bowes Farm
West Hill Edge
Woodhouse Farm
Cast Hills (Settlement)
West Hill Edge Plantation
Toldrum
Galphay Wood
Lumley Moor Plantation
Winksley Moor
Lumley Moor
PH
Winksley
Winksley Bridge
Whin Covert
Lumley Moor Farm
Holborn Bridge (upper)
Hencliffe Cottage Farm
Peacock Farm
Winksley Plantation
Hencliffe Wood
Holborn Bridge (lower)
Skelding Moor
Kendale Wood
Ruddings Plantation
Ings Bridge
Lumley Moor Resr
River Laver
Black Hill
Hill Top
Low Grantley
North Wood
Heatherlands
Corner Farm
Sun Wood
NUTWITH LANE
HUTTS LA
HUTTS LANE
RIDDINGS LANE
HUTTS LANE
PH
HAZEL GL
HOLMFIELD
LAKE TERR
FOULGATE NOOK LANE
RAILER BANK
Wreaks Beck
LONG SWALES LA
CHURCH BANK
KIRK BANK
BACK LANE
MAIN ST
BACK LA
GREYSTONE HEAD
GREYSTONE HEAD
GILLGATE ROAD
APPLEBY LANE
WARREN LANE
NAP COTE LANE
AZERLEY LANE
MISSIES LANE
BELFORD LANE
LUMLEY LANE
GATE BRIDGE ROAD
WEST LANE
WINKSLEY BANKS RD
FINE CFT
GREEN LA
FOUNTAINS GATE
A B C D E F
8 77 7 76 6 75 5 74 4 73 3 72 2 71 1 70
20 21 22 23 24 25

111
138

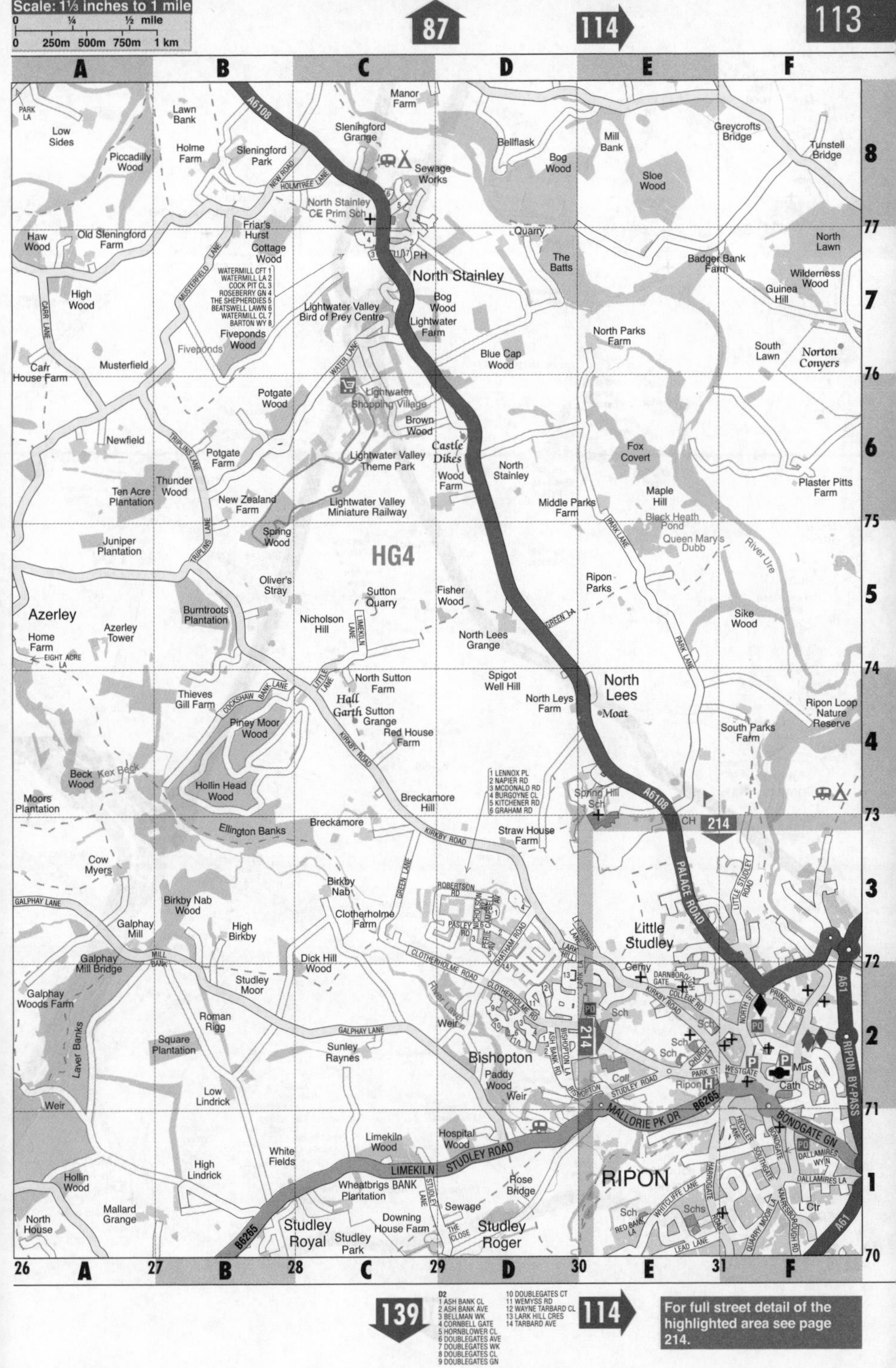

Scale: 1⅓ inches to 1 mile
0 ¼ ½ mile
0 250m 500m 750m 1 km
87
114
113
A B C D E F
8 77 7 76 6 75 5 74 4 73 3 72 2 71 1 70
26 27 28 29 30 31
PARK LA
Low Sides
Lawn Bank
Manor Farm
Sleningford Grange
Piccadilly Wood
Holme Farm
Sleningford Park
Sewage Works
Bellflask
Mill Bank
Greycrofts Bridge
Tunstell Bridge
Bog Wood
Sloe Wood
A6108
NEW ROAD
HOLMTREE LANE
North Stainley CE Prim Sch
Haw Wood
Old Sleningford Farm
Friar's Hurst
Cottage Wood
Quarry
The Batts
North Lawn
Badger Bank Farm
Wilderness Wood
Guinea Hill
PH
North Stainley
MUSTERFIELD LANE
WATERMILL CFT 1
WATERMILL LA 2
COCK PIT CL 3
ROSEBERRY GN 4
THE SHEPHERDIES 5
BEATSWELL LAWN 6
WATERMILL CL 7
BARTON WY 8
CARR LANE
High Wood
Bog Wood
Lightwater Valley Bird of Prey Centre
Lightwater Farm
Fiveponds Wood
Fiveponds
North Parks Farm
South Lawn
Norton Conyers
Carr House Farm
Musterfield
WATER LANE
Blue Cap Wood
Potgate Wood
Lightwater Shopping Village
Brown Wood
Castle Dikes
Newfield
TRIPLINS LANE
Potgate Farm
Lightwater Valley Theme Park
North Stainley
Fox Covert
Plaster Pitts Farm
Ten Acre Plantation
Thunder Wood
Wood Farm
New Zealand Farm
Lightwater Valley Miniature Railway
Maple Hill
Middle Parks Farm
Black Heath Pond
Queen Mary's Dubb
PARK LANE
River Ure
Spring Wood
Juniper Plantation
HG4
Oliver's Stray
Ripon Parks
Azerley
Azerley Tower
Burntroots Plantation
Sutton Quarry
Fisher Wood
GREEN LA
Nicholson Hill
LIMEKILN LANE
Sike Wood
Home Farm
EIGHT ACRE LA
North Lees Grange
Spigot Well Hill
North Lees
North Sutton Farm
North Leys Farm
Moat
Thieves Gill Farm
COCKSHAW BANK LANE
LITTLE LANE
Hall Garth
Sutton Grange
Ripon Loop Nature Reserve
Piney Moor Wood
Red House Farm
South Parks Farm
KIRKBY ROAD
1 LENNOX PL
2 NAPIER RD
3 MCDONALD RD
4 BURGOYNE CL
5 KITCHENER RD
6 GRAHAM RD
Beck Wood
Kex Beck
Hollin Head Wood
Spring Hill Sch
Breckamore Hill
Moors Plantation
Breckamore
CH
214
Ellington Banks
Straw House Farm
Cow Myers
GREEN LANE
PALACE ROAD
LITTLE STUDLEY ROAD
Birkby Nab
ROBERTSON RD
GALPHAY LANE
Birkby Nab Wood
Clotherholme Farm
PASLEY RD
CHATHAM ROAD
Galphay Mill
High Birkby
Little Studley
Galphay Mill Bridge
MILL BANK
Dick Hill Wood
CLOTHERHOLME ROAD
LARK HILL
Cemy
DARNBOROUGH GATE
COLLEGE RD
KIRKBY ROAD
PRINCESS RD
NORTH ST
Galphay Woods Farm
Studley Moor
River Laver
Weir
Sch
PO
Roman Rigg
GALPHAY LANE
Laver Banks
Square Plantation
Sunley Raynes
Bishopton
ASH BANK RD
BISHOPTON LA
CHURCH LA
WESTGATE
Mus
Cath
A61
RIPON BY-PASS
Paddy Wood
Coll
STUDLEY ROAD
PARK ST
Ripon
Low Lindrick
Weir
MALLORIE PK DR
B6265
Weir
BONDGATE GN
White Fields
Limekiln Wood
Hospital Wood
HECKLER LANE
SOUTHGATE
BONDGATE
DALLAMIRES WYN
DALLAMIRES LA
Hollin Wood
High Lindrick
LIMEKILN
STUDLEY ROAD
Rose Bridge
RIPON
HARROGATE ROAD
WHITCLIFFE LANE
Wheatbrigs BANK Plantation
STUDLEY LANE
Sewage
QUARRY MOOR LA
KNARESBOROUGH RD
L Ctr
North House
Mallard Grange
Studley Royal
Studley Park
Downing House Farm
THE CLOSE
Studley Roger
Sch
Schs
RED BANK LA
LEAD LANE
D2
1 ASH BANK CL
2 ASH BANK AVE
3 BELLMAN WK
4 CORNBELL GATE
5 HORNBLOWER CL
6 DOUBLEGATES AVE
7 DOUBLEGATES WK
8 DOUBLEGATES CL
9 DOUBLEGATES GN
10 DOUBLEGATES CT
11 WEMYSS RD
12 WAYNE TARBARD CL
13 LARK HILL CRES
14 TARBARD AVE
139
114
For full street detail of the highlighted area see page 214.

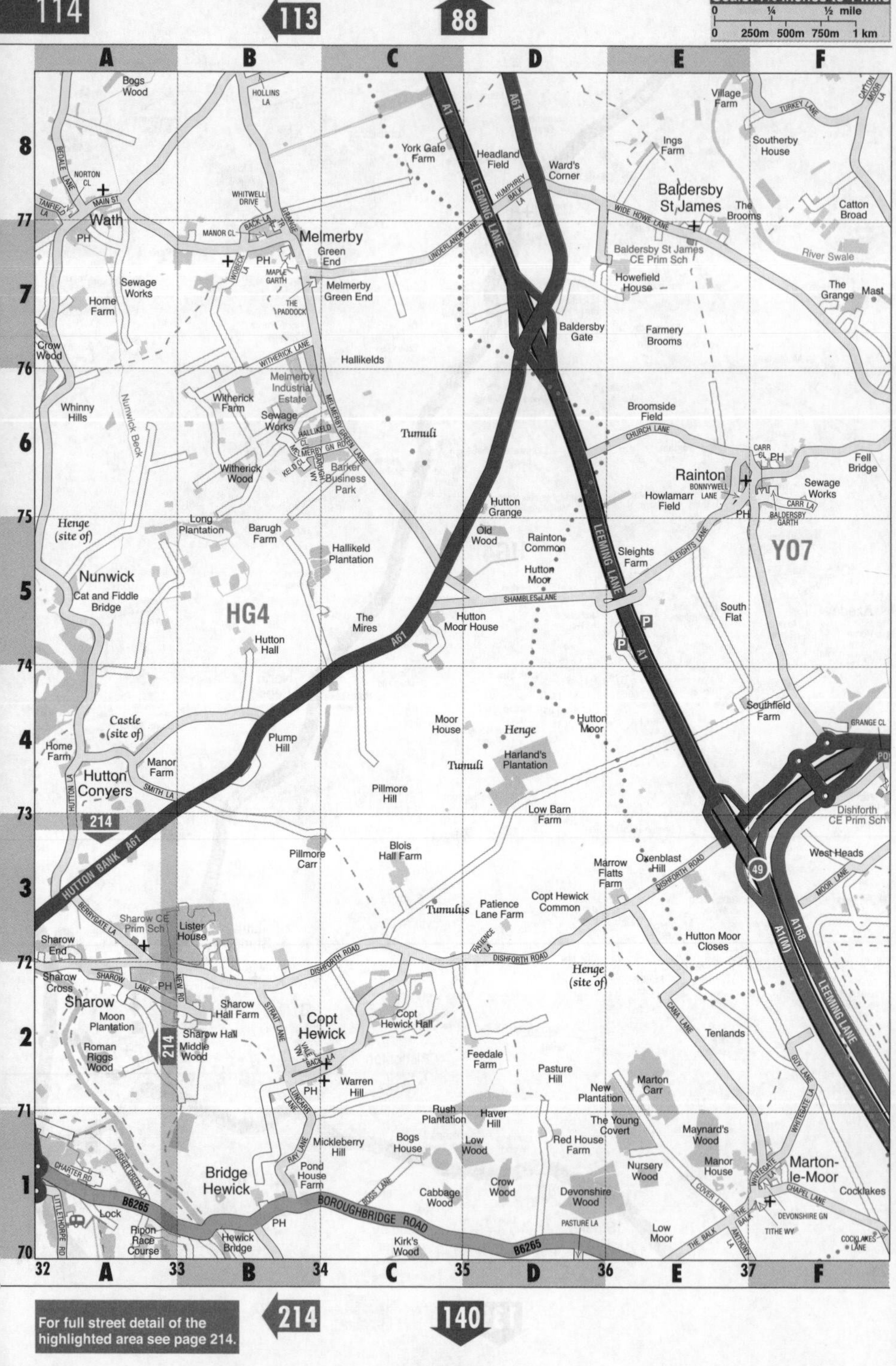

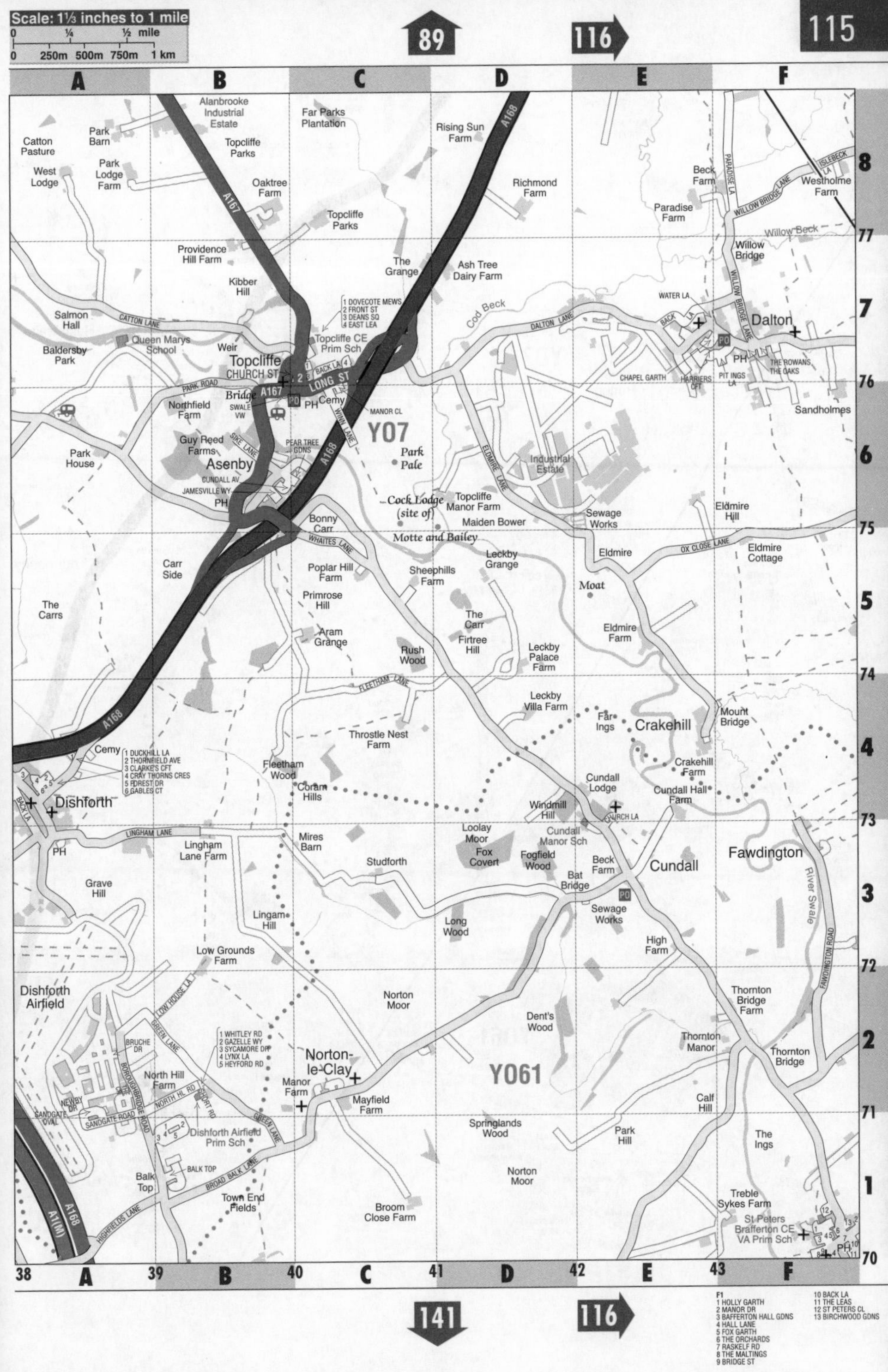

Scale: 1⅓ inches to 1 mile
0 ¼ ½ mile
0 250m 500m 750m 1 km
89
116
Alanbrooke Industrial Estate
Far Parks Plantation
Rising Sun Farm
Catton Pasture
Park Barn
Topcliffe Parks
Park Lodge Farm
West Lodge
Oaktree Farm
Richmond Farm
Beck Farm
Paradise Farm
Westholme Farm
Topcliffe Parks
Willow Bridge
Providence Hill Farm
The Grange
Ash Tree Dairy Farm
Kibber Hill
Salmon Hall
1 DOVECOTE MEWS
2 FRONT ST
3 DEANS SQ
4 EAST LEA
Cod Beck
Dalton
Queen Marys School
Topcliffe CE Prim Sch
Baldersby Park
Weir
Topcliffe
CHURCH ST
LONG ST
Northfield Farm
Cemy
MANOR CL
Y07
Sandholmes
Park House
Guy Reed Farms
Asenby
Park Pale
Industrial Estate
Cock Lodge (site of)
Topcliffe Manor Farm
Maiden Bower
Sewage Works
Eldmire Hill
Bonny Carr
Motte and Bailey
Eldmire
Eldmire Cottage
Carr Side
Poplar Hill Farm
Sheephills Farm
Leckby Grange
Moat
The Carrs
Primrose Hill
The Carr
Aram Grange
Rush Wood
Firtree Hill
Eldmire Farm
Leckby Palace Farm
Leckby Villa Farm
Far Ings
Crakehill
Mount Bridge
Throstle Nest Farm
Cemy
1 DUCKHILL LA
2 THORNFIELD AVE
3 CLARKE'S CFT
4 CRAY THORNS CRES
5 FOREST DR
6 GABLES CT
Fleetham Wood
Crakehill Farm
Cundall Lodge
Coram Hills
Cundall Hall Farm
Dishforth
Windmill Hill
Looloy Moor Fox Covert
Cundall Manor Sch
Mires Barn
Lingham Lane Farm
Fogfield Wood
Fawdington
Beck Farm
Studforth
Cundall
Bat Bridge
Grave Hill
Sewage Works
Lingam Hill
Long Wood
High Farm
Low Grounds Farm
Thornton Bridge Farm
Dishforth Airfield
Norton Moor
Dent's Wood
1 WHITLEY RD
2 GAZELLE WY
3 SYCAMORE DR
4 LYNX LA
5 HEYFORD RD
Thornton Manor
Thornton Bridge
Norton-le-Clay
North Hill Farm
Y061
Manor Farm
Mayfield Farm
Calf Hill
Dishforth Airfield Prim Sch
Springlands Wood
Park Hill
The Ings
Balk Top
Norton Moor
Town End Fields
Broom Close Farm
Treble Sykes Farm
St Peters Brafferton CE VA Prim Sch
River Swale
A167
A168
A1(M)
141
116
F1
1 HOLLY GARTH
2 MANOR DR
3 BAFFERTON HALL GDNS
4 HALL LANE
5 FOX GARTH
6 THE ORCHARDS
7 RASKELF RD
8 THE MALTINGS
9 BRIDGE ST
10 BACK LA
11 THE LEAS
12 ST PETERS CL
13 BIRCHWOOD GDNS

115
90

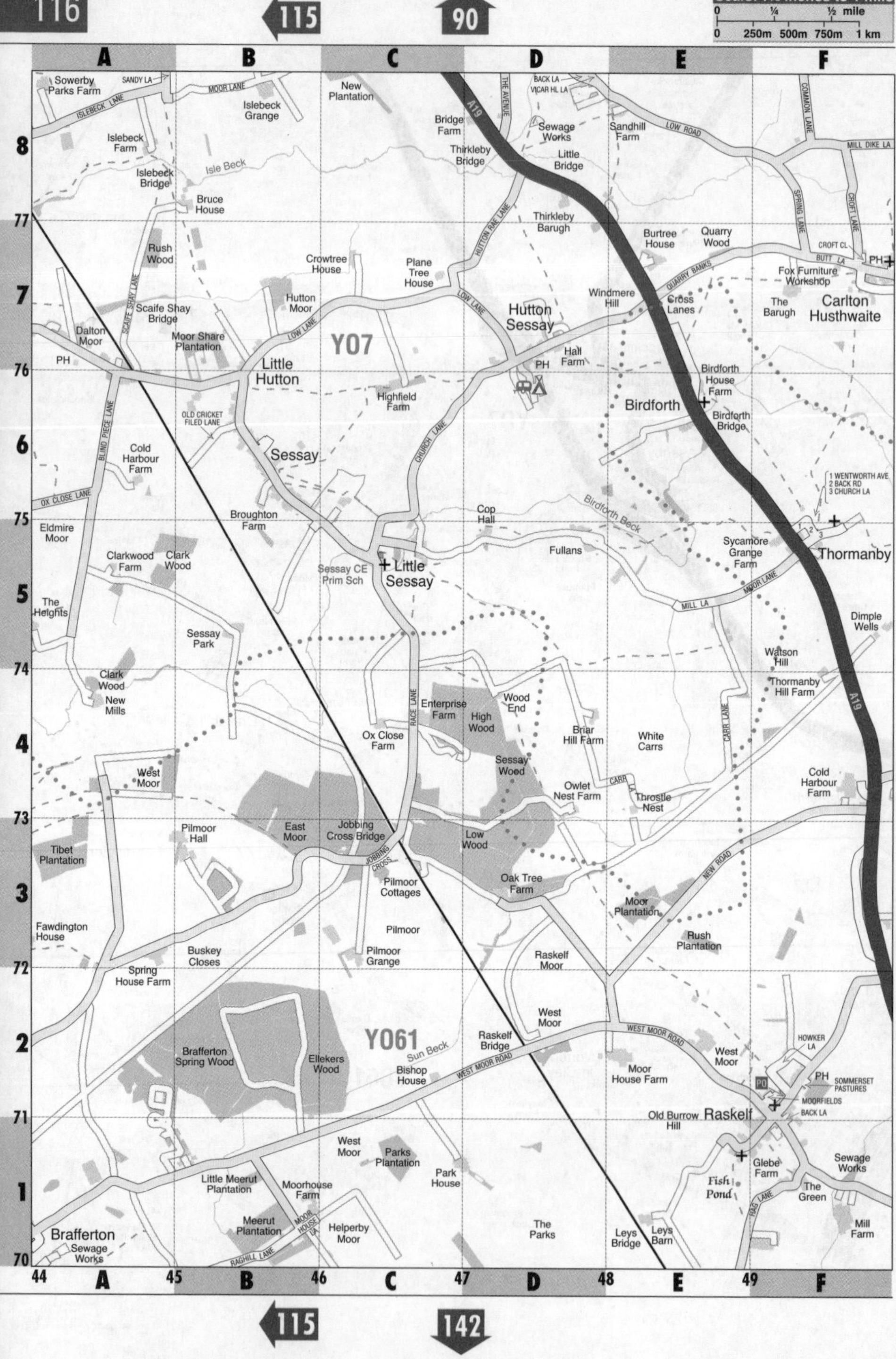
Scale: 1⅓ inches to 1 mile
0 ¼ ½ mile
0 250m 500m 750m 1 km
A B C D E F
8
77
7
76
6
75
5
74
4
73
3
72
2
71
1
70
44 45 46 47 48 49
Sowerby Parks Farm
SANDY LA
MOOR LANE
ISLEBECK LANE
Islebeck Grange
Islebeck Farm
Islebeck Bridge
Isle Beck
Bruce House
Rush Wood
SCAIFE SHAY LANE
Scaife Shay Bridge
Moor Share Plantation
Dalton Moor
PH
Little Hutton
LOW LANE
Hutton Moor
Crowtree House
New Plantation
Bridge Farm
THE AVENUE
A19
Thirkleby Bridge
BACK LA
VICAR HL LA
Sewage Works
Little Bridge
Sandhill Farm
LOW ROAD
COMMON LANE
MILL DIKE LA
SPRING LANE
CROFT LANE
CROFT CL
BUTT LA
PH
Fox Furniture Workshop
Thirkleby Barugh
HUTTON RAE LANE
Plane Tree House
Burtree House
Quarry Wood
QUARRY BANKS
Windmere Hill
Cross Lanes
The Barugh
Carlton Husthwaite
Hutton Sessay
Y07
Hall Farm
PH
Highfield Farm
OLD CRICKET FILED LANE
Birdforth House Farm
Birdforth
Birdforth Bridge
BLIND PIECE LANE
Cold Harbour Farm
Sessay
CHURCH LANE
OX CLOSE LANE
1 WENTWORTH AVE
2 BACK RD
3 CHURCH LA
Eldmire Moor
Broughton Farm
Cop Hall
Birdforth Beck
Thormanby
Sycamore Grange Farm
Fullans
Clarkwood Farm
Clark Wood
Sessay CE Prim Sch
Little Sessay
MOOR LANE
MILL LA
The Heights
Sessay Park
Dimple Wells
Watson Hill
Thormanby Hill Farm
Clark Wood
New Mills
RACE LANE
Enterprise Farm
High Wood
Wood End
Ox Close Farm
Briar Hill Farm
White Carrs
CARR LANE
West Moor
Sessay Wood
Owlet Nest Farm
CARR LA
Throstle Nest
Cold Harbour Farm
Pilmoor Hall
East Moor
Jobbing Cross Bridge
Low Wood
Tibet Plantation
JOBBING CROSS
NEW ROAD
Oak Tree Farm
Pilmoor Cottages
Moor Plantation
Fawdington House
Pilmoor
Rush Plantation
Buskey Closes
Pilmoor Grange
Raskelf Moor
Spring House Farm
West Moor
WEST MOOR ROAD
Y061
Sun Beck
Raskelf Bridge
HOWKER LA
Brafferton Spring Wood
Ellekers Wood
Bishop House
WEST MOOR ROAD
West Moor
Moor House Farm
PO
PH
SOMMERSET PASTURES
MOORFIELDS
BACK LA
Old Burrow Hill
Raskelf
West Moor
Parks Plantation
Glebe Farm
Sewage Works
Little Meerut Plantation
Park House
Fish Pond
The Green
Moorhouse Farm
HAG LANE
Meerut Plantation
MOOR HOUSE LA
Helperby Moor
The Parks
Leys Bridge
Leys Barn
Mill Farm
Brafferton
Sewage Works
RAGHILL LANE

115
142

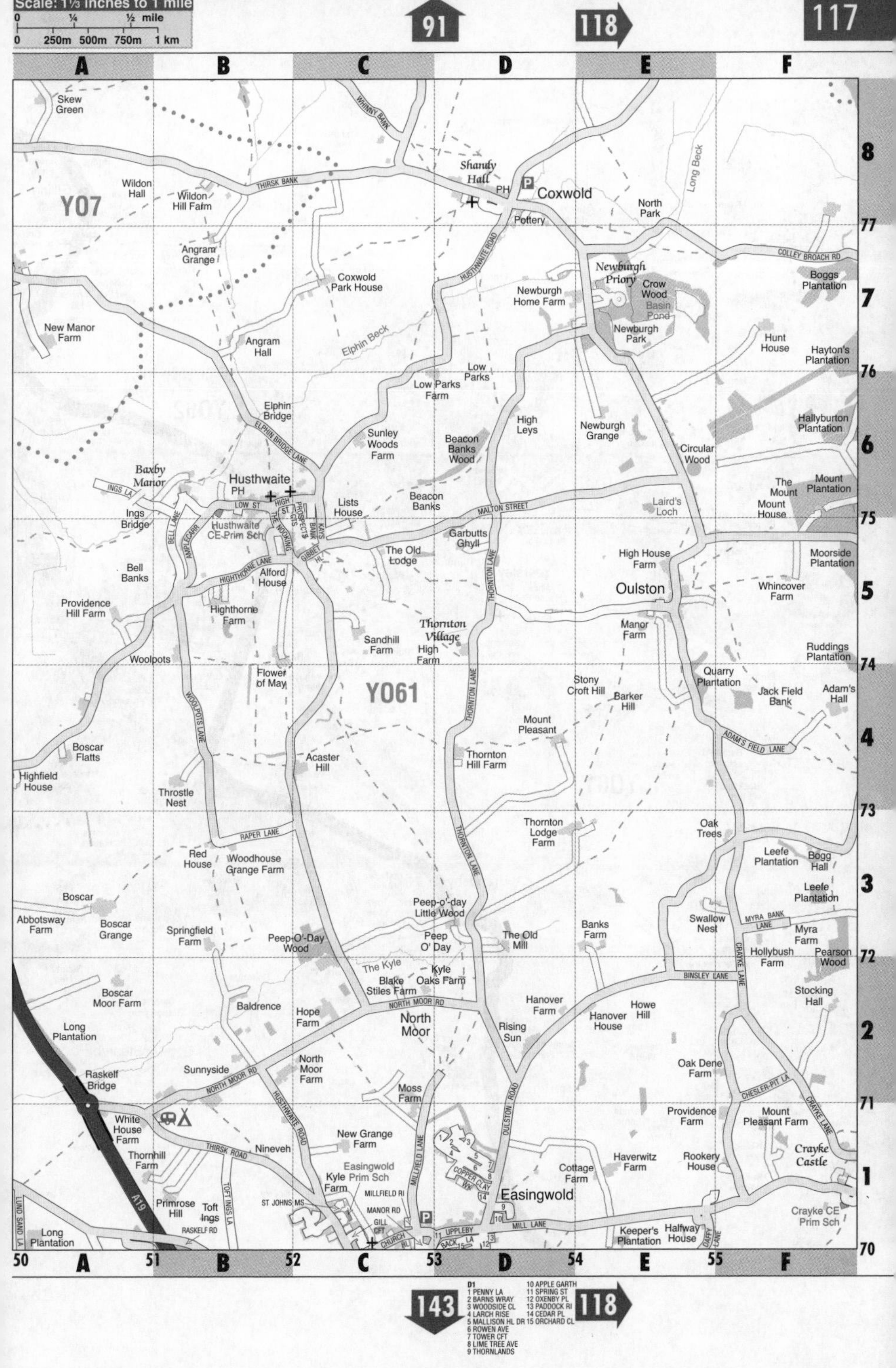
Scale: 1⅓ inches to 1 mile
0 ¼ ½ mile
0 250m 500m 750m 1 km
91
118
A B C D E F
8 77 7 76 6 75 5 74 4 73 3 72 2 71 1 70
50 51 52 53 54 55
Skew Green
Wildon Hall
Wildon Hill Farm
THIRSK BANK
WHINNY BANK
Shandy Hall
PH
Coxwold
Pottery
North Park
Long Beck
COLLEY BROACH RD
YO7
Angram Grange
Coxwold Park House
HUSTHWAITE ROAD
Newburgh Priory
Crow Wood
Basin Pond
Newburgh Home Farm
Newburgh Park
Boggs Plantation
New Manor Farm
Angram Hall
Elphin Beck
Low Parks
Low Parks Farm
Hunt House
Hayton's Plantation
Elphin Bridge
ELPHIN BRIDGE LANE
Sunley Woods Farm
Beacon Banks Wood
High Leys
Newburgh Grange
Circular Wood
Hallyburton Plantation
Baxby Manor
INGS LA
Ings Bridge
Husthwaite
PH
LOW ST
HIGH ST
THE NOOKING
PROSPECT CTS
KAYS BANK
GIBBET HL
Lists House
Beacon Banks
MALTON STREET
Laird's Loch
The Mount
Mount House
Mount Plantation
Husthwaite CE Prim Sch
BELL LANE
AMPLECARR
Garbutts Ghyll
The Old Lodge
High House Farm
Moorside Plantation
Bell Banks
HIGHTHORNE LANE
Alford House
THORNTON LANE
Oulston
Whincover Farm
Providence Hill Farm
Highthorne Farm
Thornton Village
Manor Farm
Sandhill Farm
High Farm
Ruddings Plantation
Woolpots
Flower of May
YO61
Stony Croft Hill
Barker Hill
Quarry Plantation
Jack Field Bank
Adam's Hall
WOOLPOTS LANE
Mount Pleasant
ADAM'S FIELD LANE
Boscar Flatts
Acaster Hill
Thornton Hill Farm
Highfield House
Throstle Nest
RAPER LANE
Thornton Lodge Farm
Oak Trees
Red House
Woodhouse Grange Farm
Leefe Plantation
Bogg Hall
Leefe Plantation
Boscar
Peep-o'-day Little Wood
Swallow Nest
MYRA BANK LANE
Abbotsway Farm
Boscar Grange
Springfield Farm
Peep-O'-Day Wood
Peep O' Day
The Old Mill
Banks Farm
Myra Farm
Hollybush Farm
Pearson Wood
CRAYKE LANE
The Kyle
Blake Stiles Farm
Kyle Oaks Farm
BINSLEY LANE
Stocking Hall
Boscar Moor Farm
Baldrence
NORTH MOOR RD
Hope Farm
North Moor
Hanover Farm
Hanover House
Howe Hill
Long Plantation
Rising Sun
Sunnyside
North Moor Farm
Raskelf Bridge
NORTH MOOR RD
Oak Dene Farm
CHESLER-PIT LA
Moss Farm
OULSTON ROAD
White House Farm
THIRSK ROAD
Nineveh
New Grange Farm
Providence Farm
Mount Pleasant Farm
Thornhill Farm
MILLFIELD LANE
COPPER CLAY WK
Easingwold Prim Sch
Haverwitz Farm
Rookery House
Cottage Farm
Crayke Castle
A19
TOFT INGS LA
Kyle Farm
MILLFIELD RI
Easingwold
LUND SAND LA
Primrose Hill
Toft Ings
ST JOHNS MS
MANOR RD
GILL CFT
UPPLEBY
MILL LANE
Crayke CE Prim Sch
RASKELF RD
CHURCH HL
BACK LA
Keeper's Plantation
Halfway House
DAFFY LANE
Long Plantation
D1
1 PENNY LA
2 BARNS WRAY
3 WOODSIDE CL
4 LARCH RISE
5 MALLISON HL DR
6 ROWEN AVE
7 TOWER CFT
8 LIME TREE AVE
9 THORNLANDS
10 APPLE GARTH
11 SPRING ST
12 OXENBY PL
13 PADDOCK RI
14 CEDAR PL
15 ORCHARD CL
143
118

117 92
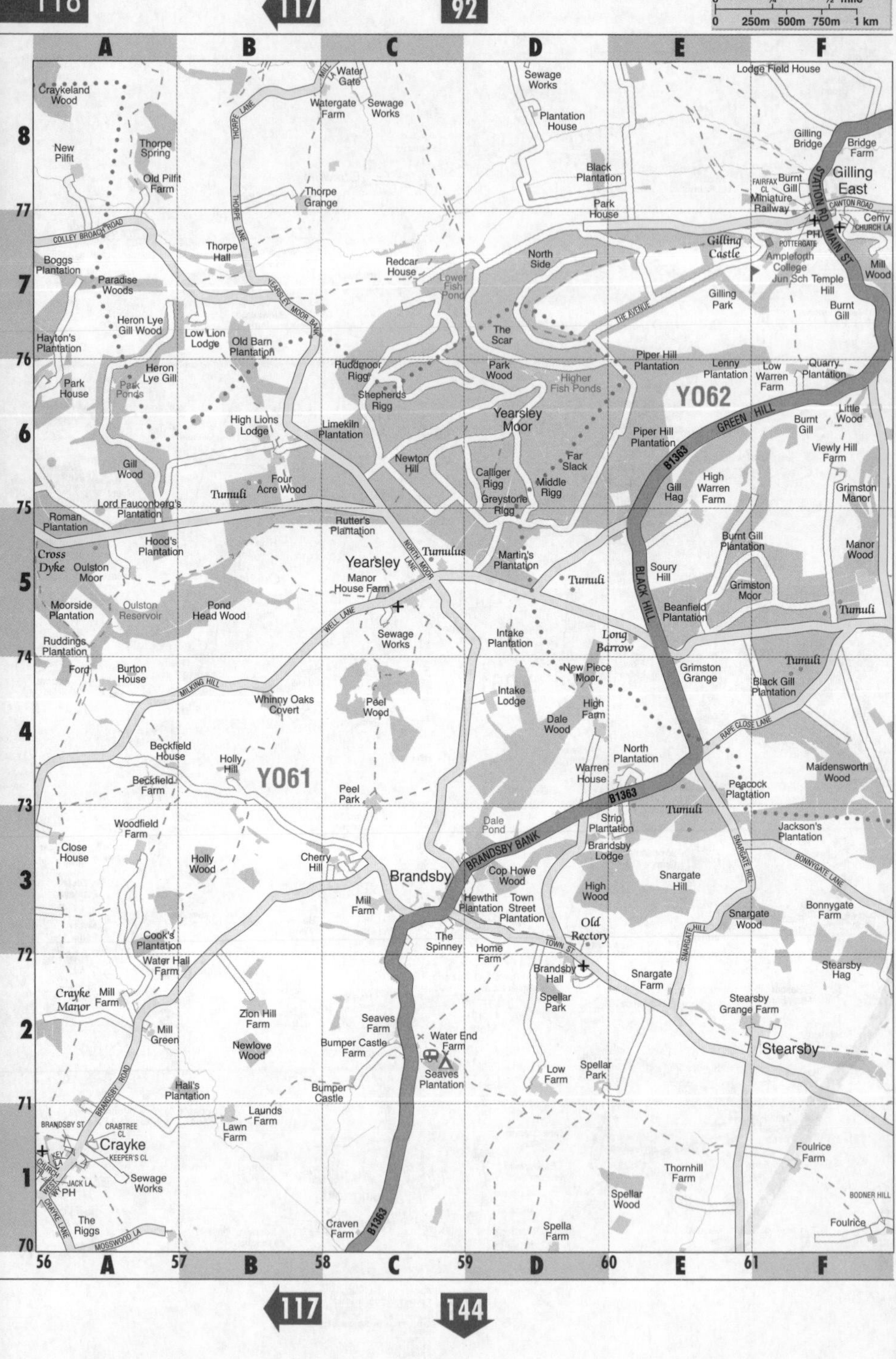
Scale: 1⅓ inches to 1 mile
Crayke
Brandsby
Yearsley
Stearsby
Gilling East
Yearsley Moor
YO61
YO62
Gilling Castle
Ampleforth College Jun Sch
Crayke Manor
Grimston Manor
Oulston Reservoir
B1363
BRANDSBY BANK
GREEN HILL
BLACK HILL
Tumuli
Long Barrow
Old Rectory
Cross Dyke
117 144

Scale: 1⅓ inches to 1 mile

93 120

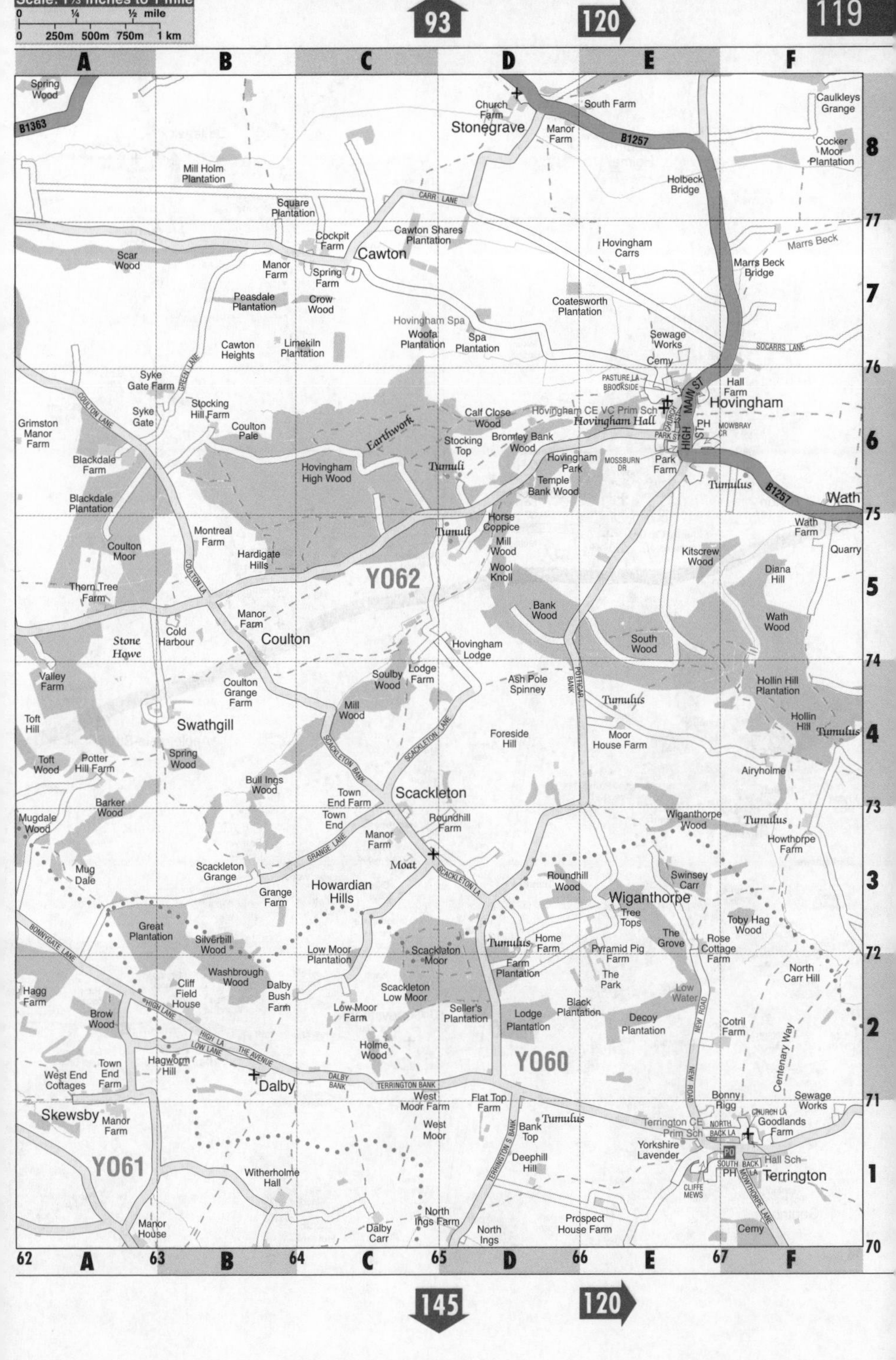

Spring Wood
B1363
Church Farm
Stonegrave
Manor Farm
South Farm
B1257
Caulkleys Grange
Cocker Moor Plantation
Mill Holm Plantation
Square Plantation
CARR LANE
Holbeck Bridge
Cockpit Farm
Cawton Shares Plantation
Cawton
Hovingham Carrs
Marrs Beck
Marrs Beck Bridge
Scar Wood
Manor Farm
Spring Farm
Peasdale Plantation
Crow Wood
Coatesworth Plantation
Hovingham Spa
Cawton Heights
Limekiln Plantation
Woofa Plantation
Spa Plantation
Sewage Works
SOCARRS LANE
Cemy
PASTURE LA
BROOKSIDE
Hall Farm
Hovingham
Syke Gate Farm
GREEN LANE
COULTON LANE
Syke Gate
Stocking Hill Farm
Calf Close Wood
Hovingham CE VC Prim Sch
Hovingham Hall
HIGH MAIN ST
CHURCH ST
PH
MOWBRAY CR
PARK ST
Grimston Manor Farm
Coulton Pale
Earthwork
Stocking Top
Bromley Bank Wood
Blackdale Farm
Hovingham High Wood
Tumuli
Hovingham Park
MOSSBURN DR
Park Farm
Temple Bank Wood
Tumulus
Blackdale Plantation
Wath
Horse Coppice
Wath Farm
Montreal Farm
Tumuli
Coulton Moor
Mill Wood
Kitscrew Wood
Quarry
Hardigate Hills
Wool Knoll
Diana Hill
COULTON LA
YO62
Thorn Tree Farm
Bank Wood
Wath Wood
Manor Farm
Cold Harbour
Coulton
South Wood
Stone Howe
Hovingham Lodge
Valley Farm
Coulton Grange Farm
Soulby Wood
Lodge Farm
Ash Pole Spinney
POTTICAR BANK
Tumulus
Hollin Hill Plantation
Mill Wood
Toft Hill
Swathgill
SCACKLETON BANK
SCACKLETON LANE
Foreside Hill
Moor House Farm
Hollin Hill
Tumulus
Spring Wood
Toft Wood
Potter Hill Farm
Airyholme
Bull Ings Wood
Town End Farm
Scackleton
Barker Wood
Town End
Roundhill Farm
Wiganthorpe Wood
Tumulus
Mugdale Wood
Manor Farm
Howthorpe Farm
GRANGE LANE
Mug Dale
Scackleton Grange
Moat
SCACKLETON LA
Roundhill Wood
Swinsey Carr
Howardian Hills
Grange Farm
Wiganthorpe
Tree Tops
Toby Hag Wood
BONNYGATE LANE
Great Plantation
Silverbill Wood
Low Moor Plantation
Scackleton Moor
Tumulus
Home Farm
Pyramid Pig Farm
The Grove
Rose Cottage Farm
Farm Plantation
The Park
North Carr Hill
Hagg Farm
Washbrough Wood
Cliff Field House
Dalby Bush Farm
Scackleton Low Moor
Low Water
Seller's Plantation
Black Plantation
HIGH LANE
Brow Wood
Low Moor Farm
Lodge Plantation
Decoy Plantation
NEW ROAD
Cotril Farm
Centenary Way
HIGH LA
LOW LANE
THE AVENUE
Holme Wood
Hagworm Hill
YO60
Town End Farm
West End Cottages
Dalby
DALBY BANK
TERRINGTON BANK
West Moor Farm
Flat Top Farm
Bonny Rigg
Sewage Works
Skewsby
Manor Farm
West Moor
Tumulus
Bank Top
Terrington CE Prim Sch
NORTH BACK LA
CHURCH LA
Goodlands Farm
Yorkshire Lavender
PO
Hall Sch
YO61
Witherholme Hall
TERRINGTON'S BANK
Deephill Hill
SOUTH BACK LA
PH
Terrington
CLIFFE MEWS
MOWTHORPE LANE
North Ings Farm
Prospect House Farm
Cemy
Manor House
Dalby Carr
North Ings
A B C D E F
62 63 64 65 66 67
77 76 75 74 73 72 71 70
8 7 6 5 4 3 2 1

145 120

119
94

Scale: 1⅓ inches to 1 mile

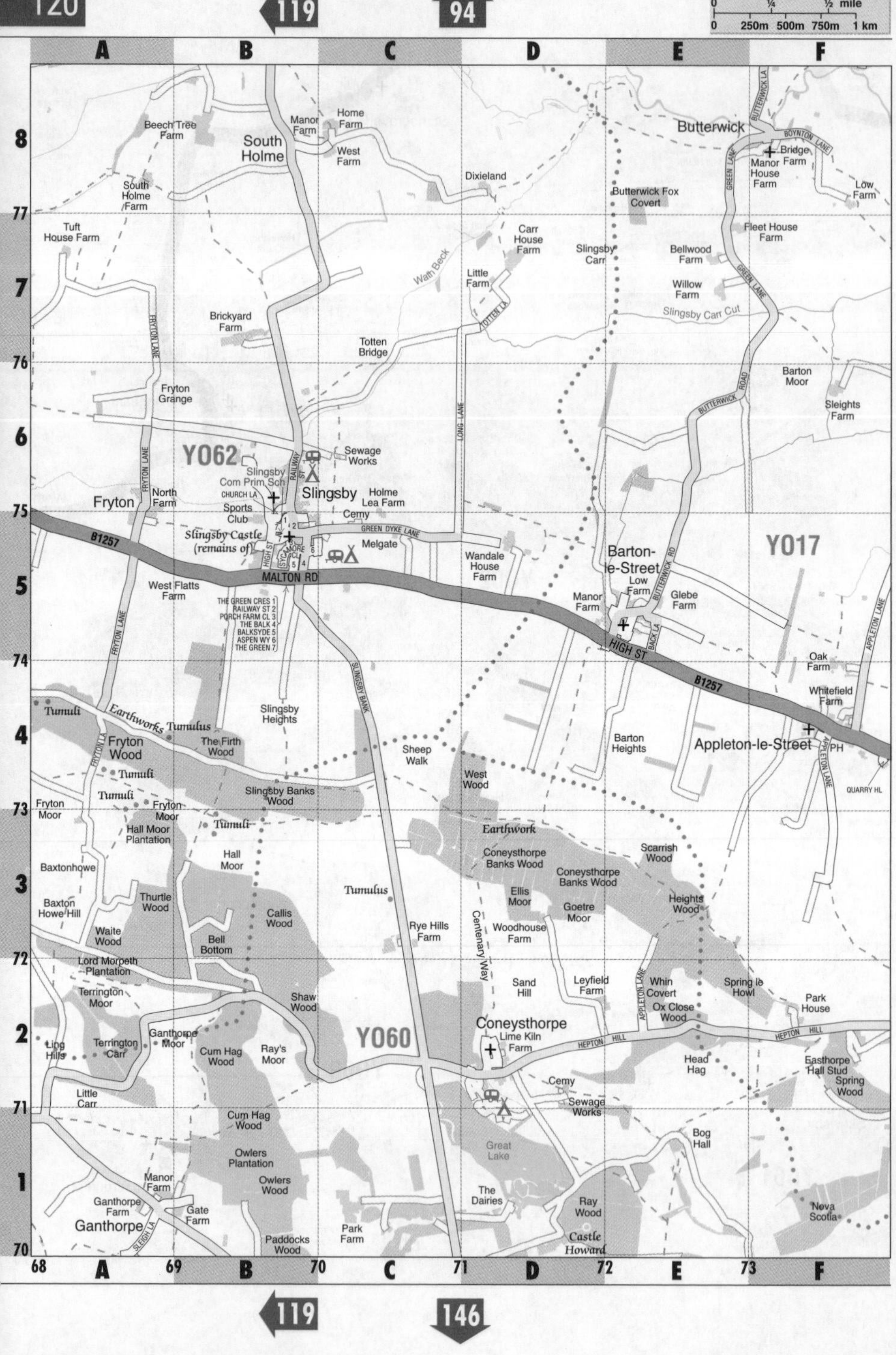
Scale: 1⅓ inches to 1 mile
0 ¼ ½ mile
0 250m 500m 750m 1 km
A B C D E F
South Holme
Beech Tree Farm
Manor Farm
Home Farm
West Farm
Dixieland
Butterwick
Bridge Farm
Manor House Farm
Low Farm
Butterwick Fox Covert
South Holme Farm
Tuft House Farm
Carr House Farm
Slingsby Carr
Fleet House Farm
Bellwood Farm
Willow Farm
Wath Beck
Little Farm
Slingsby Carr Cut
Brickyard Farm
Totten Bridge
Barton Moor
Sleights Farm
Fryton Grange
YO62
Sewage Works
Slingsby Com Prim Sch
Slingsby
Holme Lea Farm
Fryton
North Farm
Sports Club
Cemy
Slingsby Castle (remains of)
Melgate
Wandale House Farm
Barton-le-Street
YO17
B1257
MALTON RD
West Flatts Farm
Low Farm
Manor Farm
Glebe Farm
THE GREEN CRES 1
RAILWAY ST 2
PORCH FARM CL 3
THE BALK 4
BALKSYDE 5
ASPEN WY 6
THE GREEN 7
HIGH ST
Oak Farm
Whitefield Farm
Tumuli
Earthworks
Tumulus
Fryton Wood
The Firth Wood
Slingsby Heights
Sheep Walk
West Wood
Barton Heights
Appleton-le-Street
PH
QUARRY HL
Slingsby Banks Wood
Fryton Moor
Hall Moor Plantation
Earthwork
Scarrish Wood
Coneysthorpe Banks Wood
Baxtonhowe
Hall Moor
Ellis Moor
Goetre Moor
Heights Wood
Baxton Howe Hill
Thurtle Wood
Callis Wood
Rye Hills Farm
Woodhouse Farm
Waite Wood
Bell Bottom
Centenary Way
Lord Morpeth Plantation
Sand Hill
Leyfield Farm
Whin Covert
Spring le Howl
Park House
Terrington Moor
Shaw Wood
Ox Close Wood
Coneysthorpe
Ling Hills
Terrington Carr
Ganthorpe Moor
Cum Hag Wood
Ray's Moor
YO60
Lime Kiln Farm
HEPTON HILL
Head Hag
Easthorpe Hall Stud
Spring Wood
Little Carr
Cemy
Sewage Works
Bog Hall
Owlers Plantation
Great Lake
Manor Farm
Owlers Wood
Ganthorpe Farm
Gate Farm
Ganthorpe
The Dairies
Ray Wood
Castle Howard
Nova Scotia
Park Farm
Paddocks Wood
FRYTON LANE
FRYTON LA
SLEIGHT LA
SLINGSBY BANK
LONG LANE
TOTTEN LA
GREEN DYKE LANE
CHURCH LA
RAILWAY ST
BACK LA
BUTTERWICK RD
BUTTERWICK ROAD
GREEN LANE
BUTTERWICK LA
BOYNTON LANE
APPLETON LANE
8 77 7 76 6 75 5 74 4 73 3 72 2 71 1 70
68 69 70 71 72 73

119
146

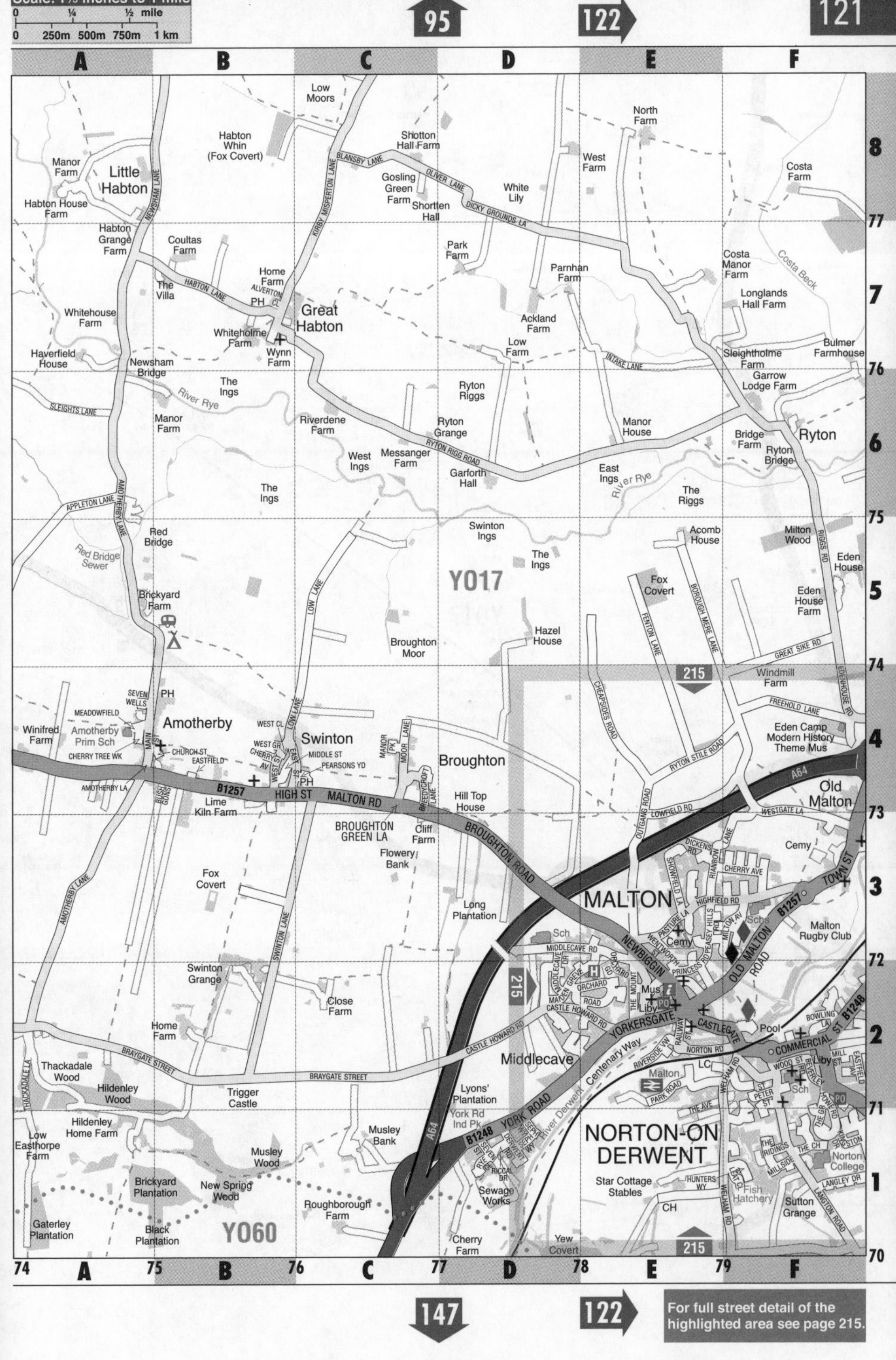

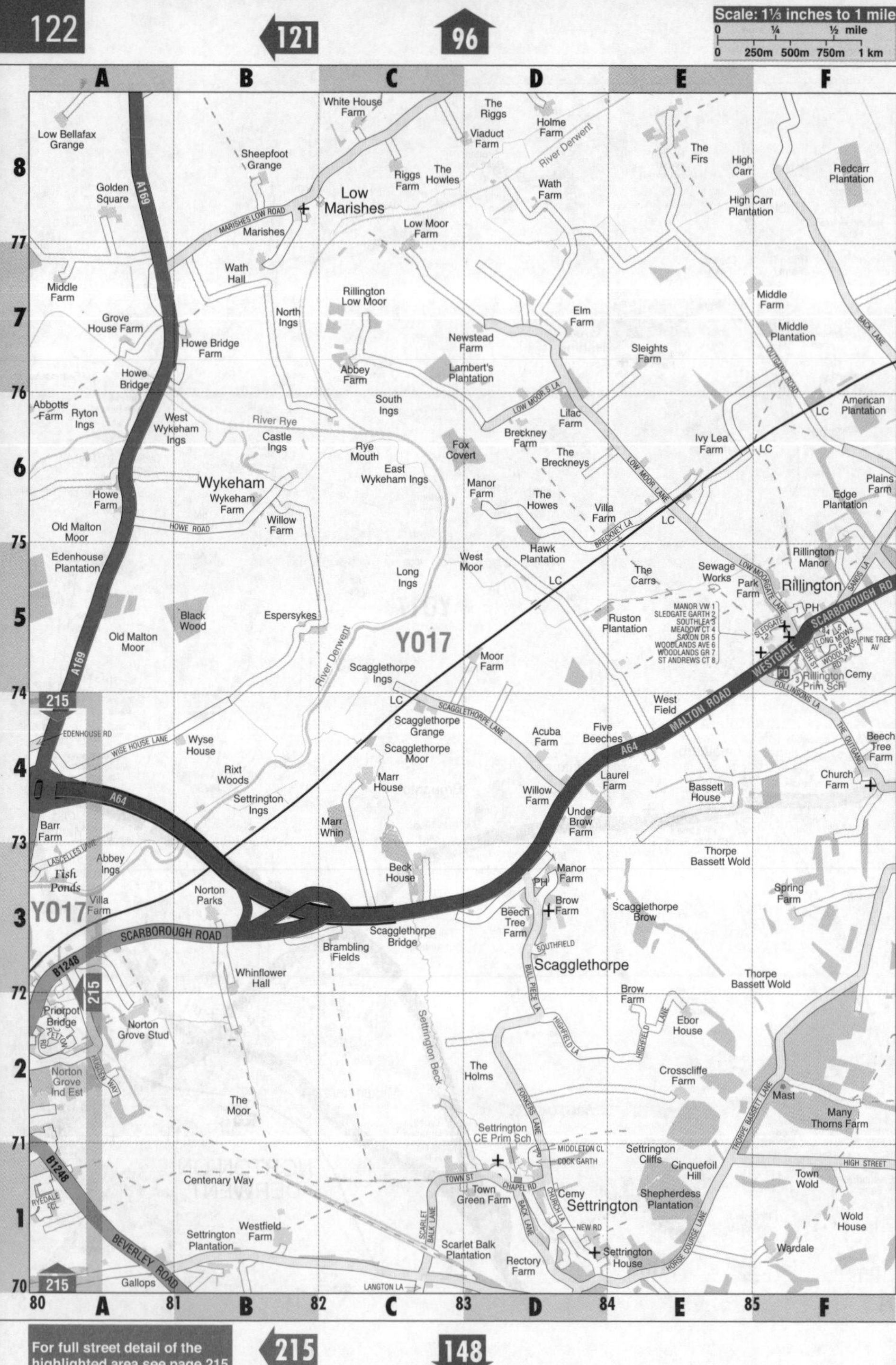

Scale: 1⅓ inches to 1 mile

| 0 | ¼ | ½ | mile |
| 0 | 250m 500m 750m | 1 km |

8

Low Bellafax Grange

Golden Square

White House Farm

Sheepfoot Grange

The Riggs

Viaduct Farm

Holme Farm

River Derwent

The Firs

High Carr

Redcarr Plantation

77

Marishes

Low Marishes

Riggs Farm

The Howles

Wath Farm

High Carr Plantation

7

Middle Farm

Grove House Farm

Wath Hall

North Ings

Rillington Low Moor

Newstead Farm

Elm Farm

Sleights Farm

Middle Farm

Middle Plantation

Howe Bridge Farm

Abbey Farm

Lambert's Plantation

Low Moor La.

76

Abbotts Farm

Ryton Ings

River Rye

West Wykeham Ings

Castle Ings

South Ings

Breckney Farm

Lilac Farm

The Breckneys

Ivy Lea Farm

LC

LC

American Plantation

6

Howe Farm

Wykeham

Wykeham Farm

Willow Farm

Rye Mouth

East Wykeham Ings

Fox Covert

Manor Farm

The Howes

Villa Farm

Breckney La.

LC

Edge Plantation

Plains Farm

75

Old Malton Moor

HOWE ROAD

Hawk Plantation

LC

Rillington Manor

Low Costa Lane

Edenhouse Plantation

Black Wood

Espersykes

Long Ings

West Moor

The Carrs

Sewage Works

Park Farm

Rillington

PH

Scarborough Rd

5

Y017

Scagglethorpe Ings

River Derwent

Moor Farm

Ruston Plantation

MANOR VW 1
SLEDGATE GARTH 2
SOUTHLEA 3
MEADOW CT 4
SAXON DR 5
WOODLANDS AV 6
WOODLANDS GR 7
ST ANDREWS CT 8

Westgate

PO

Rillington Cemy

Pine Tree Av

Rillington 'Prim Sch

74

215

A169

EDENHOUSE RD

WISE HOUSE LANE

LC

Scagglethorpe Lane

Scagglethorpe Grange

Acuba Farm

Five Beeches

West Field

Malton Road

A64

Beech Tree Farm

4

A64

Wyse House

Rixt Woods

Settrington Ings

Marr House

Scagglethorpe Moor

Willow Farm

Laurel Farm

Under Brow Farm

Bassett House

Church Farm

73

Barr Farm

LASCELLES LANE

Abbey Ings

Marr Whin

Beck House

PH

Manor Farm

Brow Farm

Scagglethorpe Brow

Thorpe Bassett Wold

Spring Farm

Fish Ponds

Villa Farm

Norton Parks

Scagglethorpe Bridge

Beech Tree Farm

SOUTHFIELD

3

Y017

SCARBOROUGH ROAD

Brambling Fields

Scagglethorpe

Brow Farm

Thorpe Bassett Wold

B1248

215

Whinflower Hall

Settrington Beck

BILL FIELD LA

Ebor House

72

Priorpot Bridge

Norton Grove Stud

The Moor

HAYFIELD LA

Crossdiffe Farm

Mast

Many Thorns Farm

2

Norton Grove Ind Est

The Holms

GROVES LANE

LINGFIELD LANE

71

B1248

RYEDALE

Centenary Way

Westfield Farm

Settrington CE Prim Sch

TOWN ST

MIDDLETON CL

DOCK GARTH

CHAPEL RD

Settrington Cliffs

Cinquefoil Hill

Shepherdess Plantation

THORPE BASSETT LANE

Settrington

High Street

Town Wold

1

BEVERLEY ROAD

Settrington Plantation

Westfield Farm

Town Green Farm

SCARLET BALK LANE

Scarlet Balk Plantation

Cemy

BACK LANE

NEW RD

NORTH COURSE LANE

Wardale

Wold House

70

215

Gallops

LANGTON LA

Rectory Farm

Settrington House

80   A   81   B   82   C   83   D   84   E   85   F

For full street detail of the highlighted area see page 215.

Scale: 1⅓ inches to 1 mile

97
124

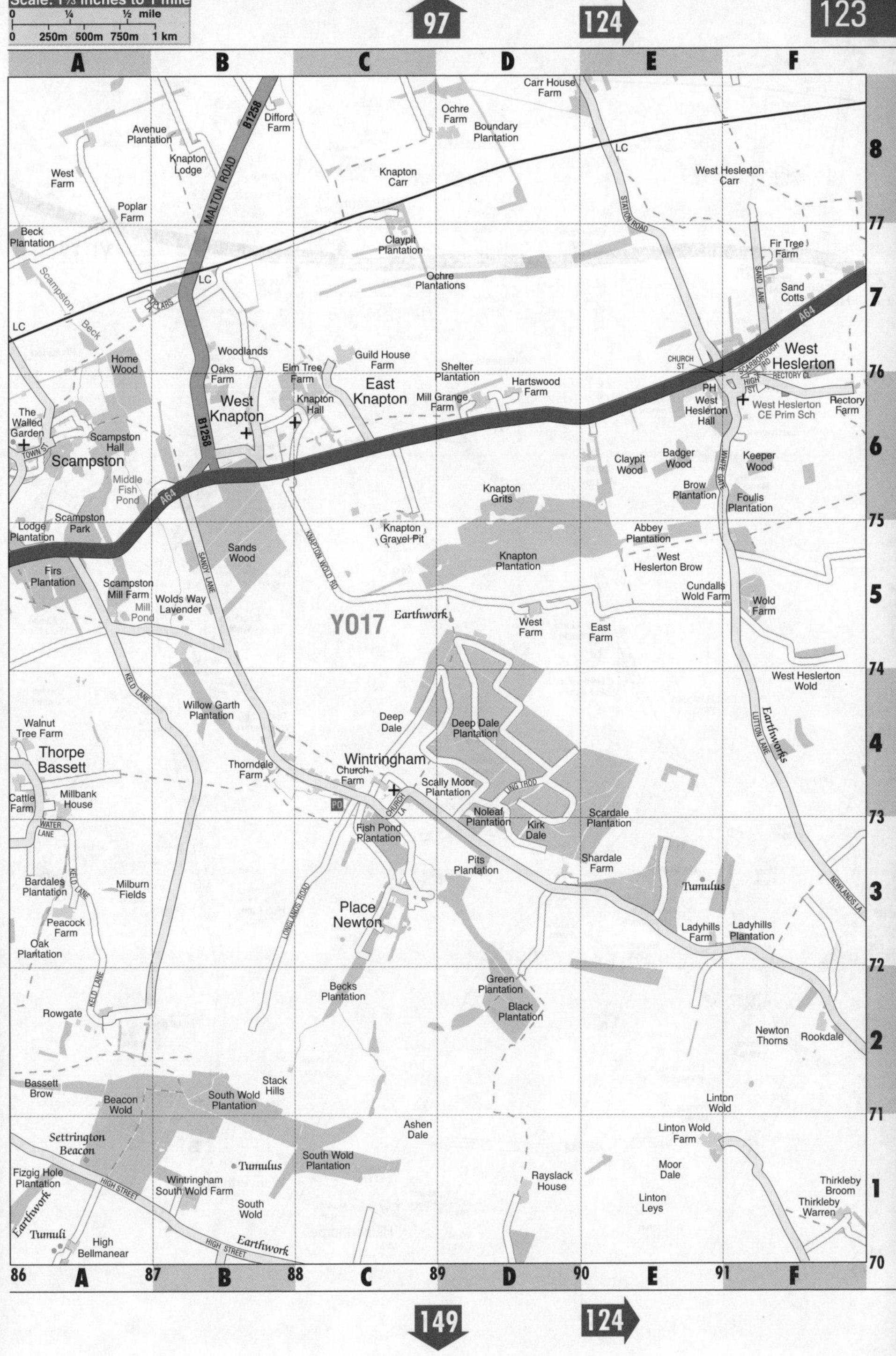
Carr House Farm
Ochre Farm
Boundary Plantation
Difford Farm
Avenue Plantation
Knapton Lodge
West Farm
Poplar Farm
Knapton Carr
West Heslerton Carr
Beck Plantation
Claypit Plantation
Fir Tree Farm
Ochre Plantations
Sand Cotts
Scampston Beck
Home Wood
Woodlands
Guild House Farm
Oaks Farm
Elm Tree Farm
East Knapton
Shelter Plantation
Hartswood Farm
West Heslerton
West Knapton
Knapton Hall
Mill Grange Farm
West Heslerton Hall
West Heslerton CE Prim Sch
Rectory Farm
The Walled Garden
Scampston Hall
Scampston
Middle Fish Pond
Claypit Wood
Badger Wood
Keeper Wood
Knapton Grits
Brow Plantation
Foulis Plantation
Lodge Plantation
Scampston Park
Knapton Gravel Pit
Abbey Plantation
Sands Wood
Knapton Plantation
West Heslerton Brow
Firs Plantation
Scampston Mill Farm
Wolds Way Lavender
Mill Pond
Cundalls Wold Farm
Wold Farm
YO17
Earthwork
West Farm
East Farm
West Heslerton Wold
Walnut Tree Farm
Willow Garth Plantation
Deep Dale
Deep Dale Plantation
Thorpe Bassett
Wintringham
Thorndale Farm
Church Farm
Cattle Farm
Millbank House
Scally Moor Plantation
PO
Noleaf Plantation
Kirk Dale
Scardale Plantation
Fish Pond Plantation
Bardales Plantation
Pits Plantation
Shardale Farm
Milburn Fields
Tumulus
Place Newton
Peacock Farm
Ladyhills Farm
Ladyhills Plantation
Oak Plantation
Becks Plantation
Green Plantation
Black Plantation
Rowgate
Newton Thorns
Rookdale
Bassett Brow
Stack Hills
Beacon Wold
South Wold Plantation
Linton Wold
Ashen Dale
Settrington Beacon
Linton Wold Farm
South Wold Plantation
Tumulus
Fizgig Hole Plantation
Wintringham South Wold Farm
Rayslack House
Moor Dale
Thirkleby Broom
South Wold
Linton Leys
Thirkleby Warren
Earthwork
Tumuli
High Bellmanear
Earthwork
Earthworks
MALTON ROAD
B1258
STATION ROAD
SAND LANE
A64
SCARBOROUGH RD
CHURCH ST
HIGH ST
RECTORY CL
PH
LC
TOWN ST
SANDY LANE
KNAPTON WOLD RD
WHITE GATE
LUTTON LANE
KELD LANE
WATER LANE
LING TROD
CHURCH LA
LONGLANDS ROAD
NEWLANDS LA
HIGH STREET
A B C D E F
86 87 88 89 90 91
70 71 72 73 74 75 76 77
1 2 3 4 5 6 7 8

149
124

123
98

Scale: 1⅓ inches to 1 mile

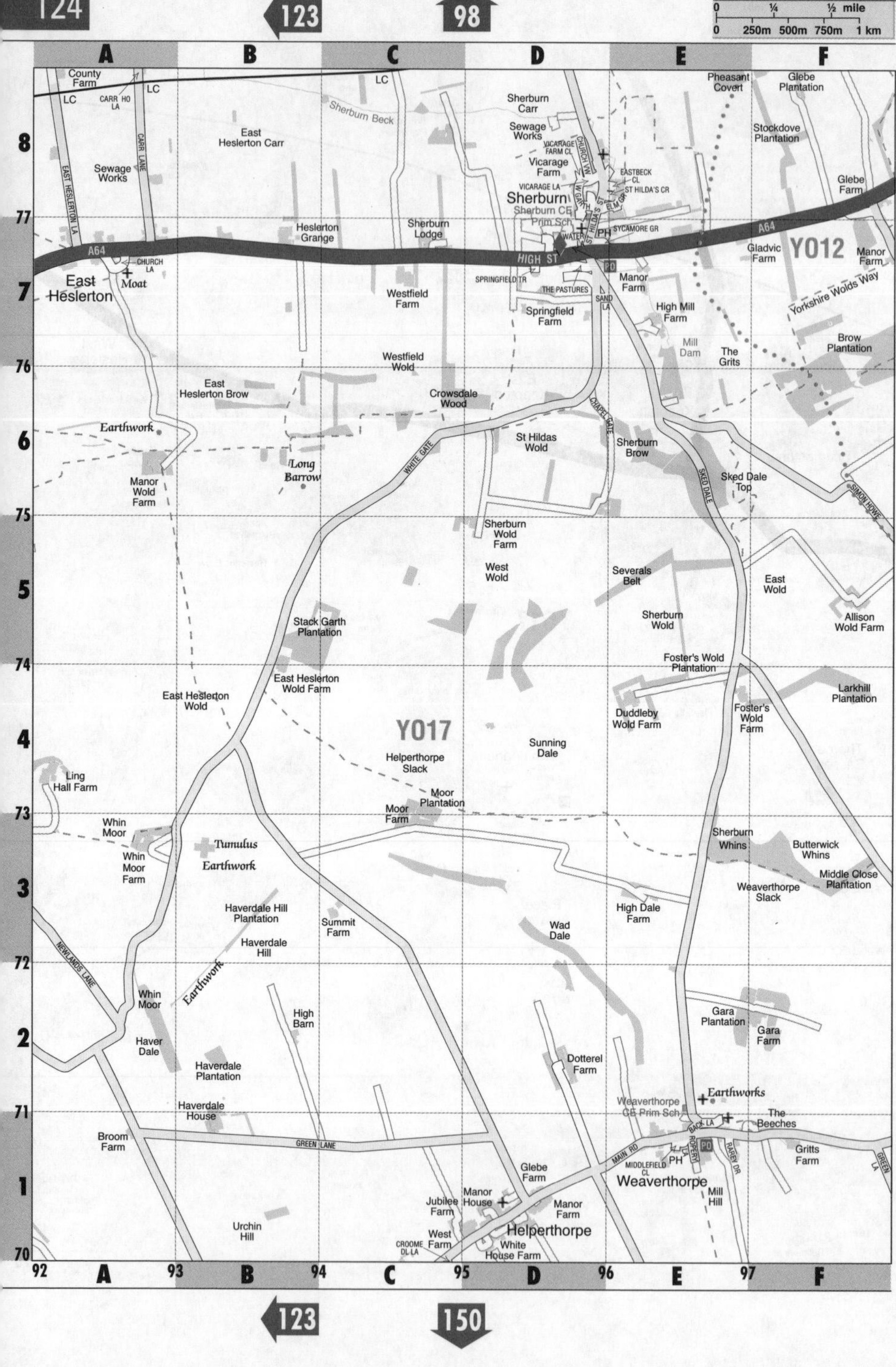
County Farm
East Heslerton Carr
Sherburn Beck
Sherburn Carr
Sewage Works
Vicarage Farm
Sherburn
Sherburn CE Prim Sch
Pheasant Covert
Glebe Plantation
Stockdove Plantation
Glebe Farm
Heslerton Grange
Sherburn Lodge
A64
HIGH ST
YO12
Gladvic Farm
Manor Farm
East Heslerton
Moat
Westfield Farm
Springfield Farm
High Mill Farm
Yorkshire Wolds Way
Westfield Wold
Mill Dam
The Grits
Brow Plantation
East Heslerton Brow
Crowsdale Wood
Earthwork
St Hildas Wold
Sherburn Brow
Long Barrow
Manor Wold Farm
Sked Dale Top
Sherburn Wold Farm
West Wold
Severals Belt
East Wold
Stack Garth Plantation
Sherburn Wold
Allison Wold Farm
East Heslerton Wold Farm
Foster's Wold Plantation
East Heslerton Wold
Larkhill Plantation
YO17
Dudleby Wold Farm
Foster's Wold Farm
Sunning Dale
Helperthorpe Slack
Ling Hall Farm
Moor Plantation
Moor Farm
Whin Moor
Whin Moor Farm
Tumulus
Earthwork
Sherburn Whins
Butterwick Whins
Middle Close Plantation
Weaverthorpe Slack
Haverdale Hill Plantation
Summit Farm
High Dale Farm
Wad Dale
Haverdale Hill
Whin Moor
High Barn
Gara Plantation
Gara Farm
Haver Dale
Haverdale Plantation
Dotterel Farm
Earthworks
Weaverthorpe CE Prim Sch
Haverdale House
The Beeches
Broom Farm
GREEN LANE
Gritts Farm
Glebe Farm
Weaverthorpe
Mill Hill
Jubilee Farm
Manor House
Manor Farm
Urchin Hill
West Farm
Helperthorpe
White House Farm
A B C D E F
8 77 7 76 6 75 5 74 4 73 3 72 2 71 1 70
92 93 94 95 96 97

123
150

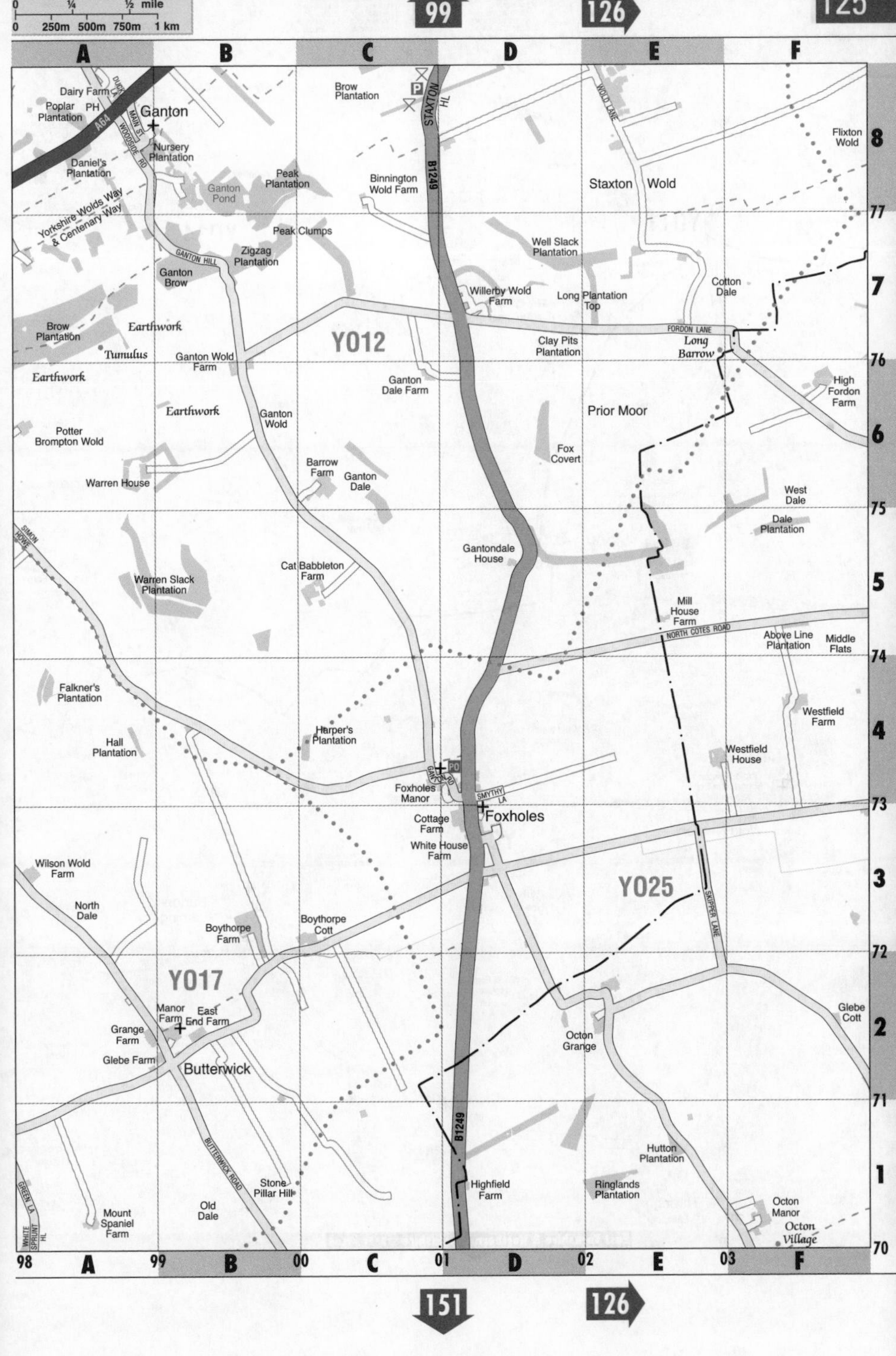

Scale: 1⅓ inches to 1 mile
0 ¼ ½ mile
0 250m 500m 750m 1 km
99
126
125
A
B
C
D
E
F
Dairy Farm
Poplar Plantation
PH
Ganton
A64
MAIN ST
WOODSIDE RD
Nursery Plantation
Daniel's Plantation
Ganton Pond
Peak Plantation
Yorkshire Wolds Way & Centenary Way
Peak Clumps
GANTON HILL
Zigzag Plantation
Ganton Brow
Brow Plantation
Earthwork
Tumulus
Earthwork
Ganton Wold Farm
Earthwork
Ganton Wold
Potter Brompton Wold
Warren House
SIMON HOWE
Warren Slack Plantation
Falkner's Plantation
Hall Plantation
Wilson Wold Farm
North Dale
Boythorpe Farm
Y017
Manor Farm
East End Farm
Grange Farm
Glebe Farm
Butterwick
BUTTERWICK ROAD
Stone Pillar Hill
Old Dale
Mount Spaniel Farm
GREEN LA
WHITE SPRUNT HL
Brow Plantation
STAXTON HL
B1249
Binnington Wold Farm
Willerby Wold Farm
Y012
Ganton Dale Farm
Barrow Farm
Ganton Dale
Cat Babbleton Farm
Gantondale House
Harper's Plantation
Foxholes Manor
GARTON RD
PO
SMYTHY LA
Foxholes
Cottage Farm
White House Farm
Boythorpe Cott
B1249
Highfield Farm
WOLD LANE
Staxton Wold
Well Slack Plantation
Long Plantation Top
Clay Pits Plantation
FORDON LANE
Long Barrow
Prior Moor
Fox Covert
Cotton Dale
Flixton Wold
High Fordon Farm
West Dale
Dale Plantation
Mill House Farm
NORTH COTES ROAD
Above Line Plantation
Middle Flats
Westfield Farm
Westfield House
Y025
SKIPPER LANE
Octon Grange
Glebe Cott
Hutton Plantation
Ringlands Plantation
Octon Manor
Octon Village
8
77
7
76
6
75
5
74
4
73
3
72
2
71
1
70
98
99
00
01
02
03
151
126

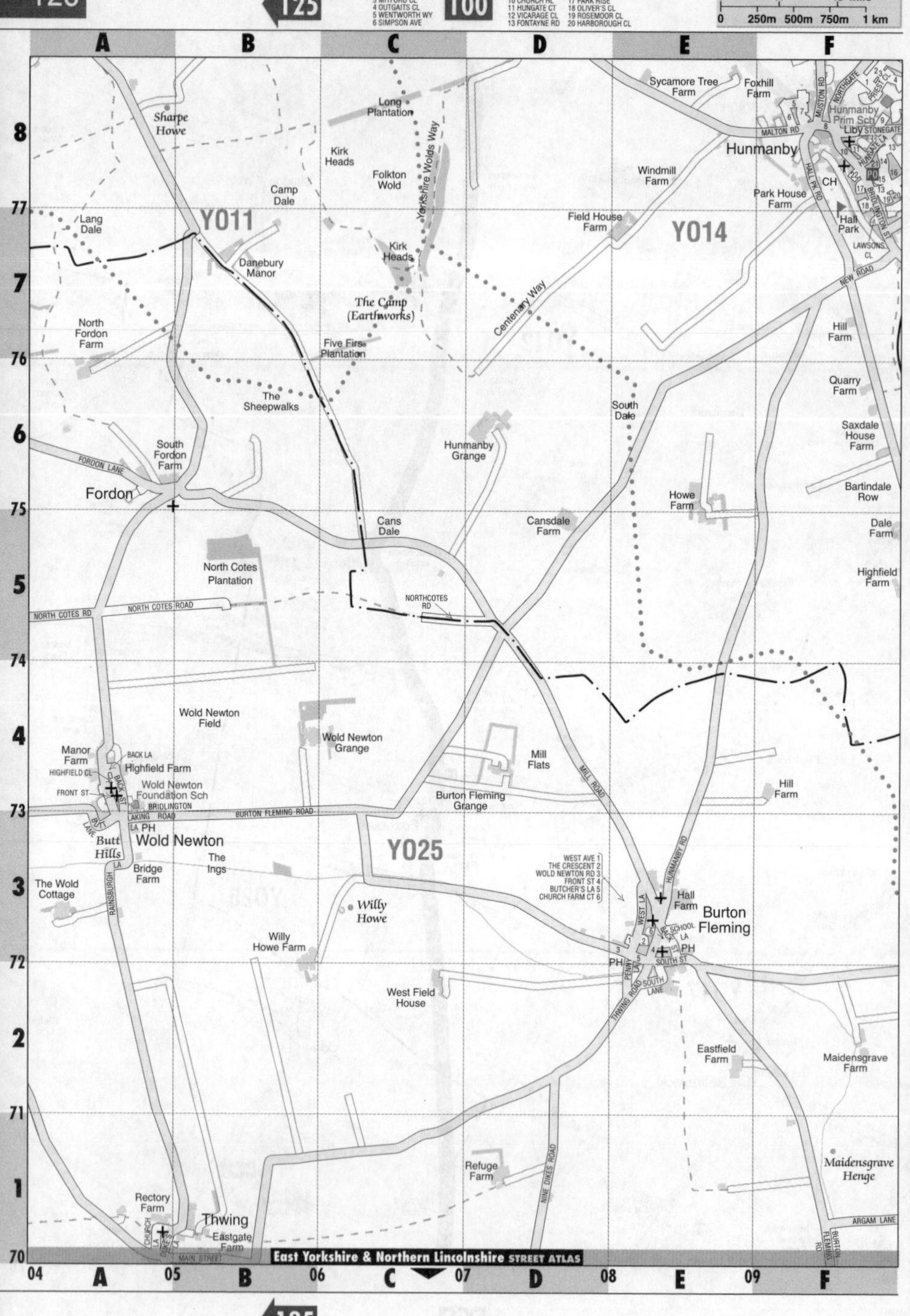

F6
1 OWSTON RD
2 MITFORD RD
3 MITFORD CL
4 OUTGAITS CL
5 WENTWORTH WY
6 SIMPSON AVE

7 HIGH CFT
8 CASTLE HIL
9 BOWLING GN LA
10 CHURCH HIL
11 HUNGATE CT
12 VICARAGE CL
13 FONTAYNE RD

14 BARDNEY RD
15 ROWEDALE CL
16 AMBREY CL
17 PARK RISE
18 OLIVER'S CL
19 ROSEMOOR CL
20 HARBOROUGH CL

21 EASTFIELD
22 GARTON LA

Scale: 1⅓ inches to 1 mile

YO11

YO14

YO25

East Yorkshire & Northern Lincolnshire STREET ATLAS

A8
1 WRANGHAM DR
2 LENNOX CL
3 BURLYN RD
4 CHERRY RD
5 HAWKE GARTH
6 MANOR GDNS
7 CECIL RD
8 HOWES RD
9 WATSON CL
10 HAMERTON RD
11 HAMERTON CL
12 GRIMSTON RD
13 STRICKLAND RD
14 PERCY RD
15 HAVERCROFT RD
16 COWLINGS CL

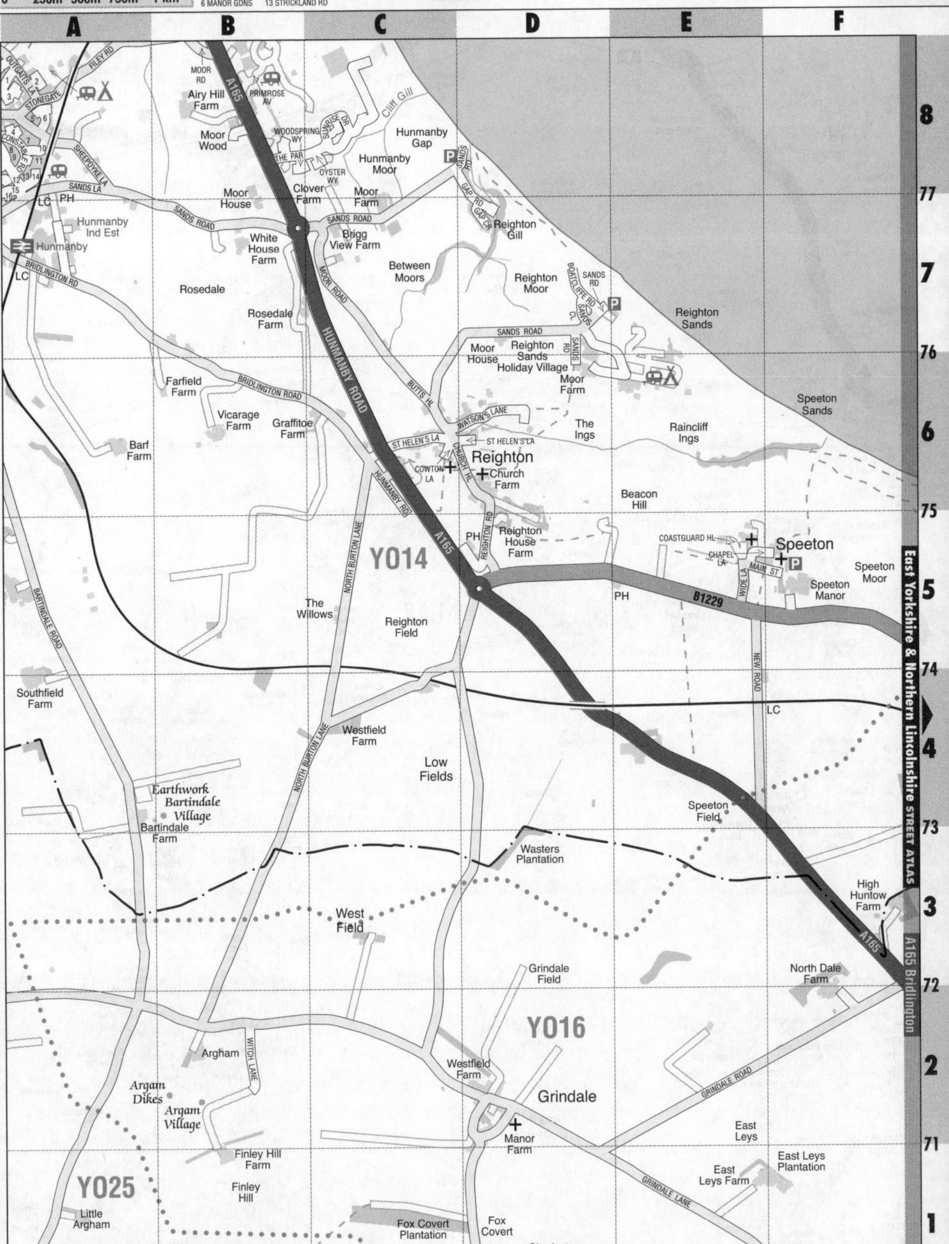

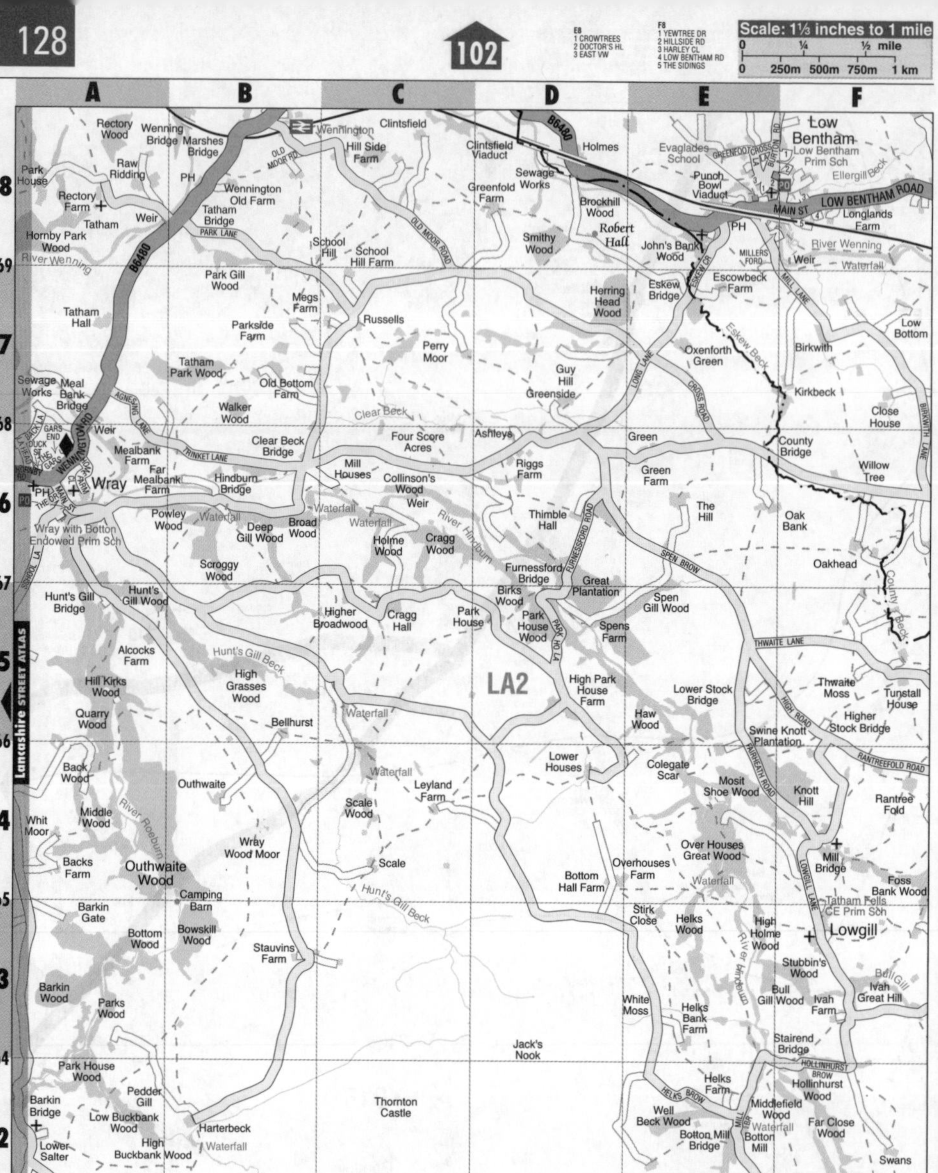

102

Scale: 1⅓ inches to 1 mile

E8
1 CROWTREES
2 DOCTOR'S HL
3 EAST VW

F8
1 YEWTREE DR
2 HILLSIDE RD
3 HARLEY CL
4 LOW BENTHAM RD
5 THE SIDINGS

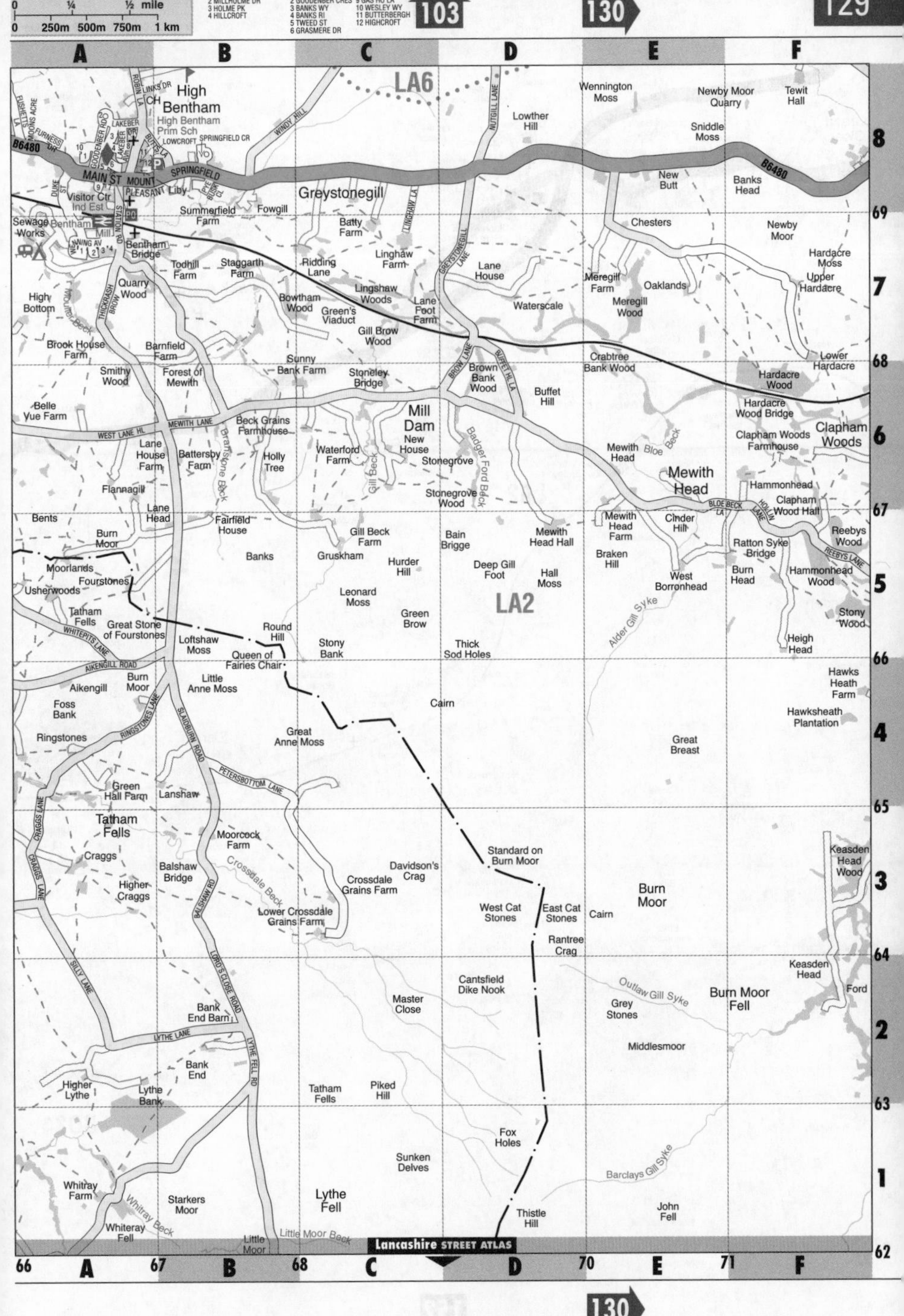

Scale: 1½ inches to 1 mile

0   ¼   ½ mile

0   250m 500m 750m 1 km

A7
1 MAYFIELD RD
2 MILLHOLME DR
3 HOLME PK
4 HILLCROFT

A8
1 WESLEY CL
2 GOODENBER CRES
3 BANKS WY
4 BANKS RI
5 TWEED ST
6 GRASMERE DR

7 KING ST
8 LAKEBER CL
9 GAS HO LA
10 WESLEY WY
11 BUTTERBERGH
12 HIGHCROFT

103

130

129

A · B · C · D · E · F

LA6

High Bentham
High Bentham Prim Sch
LOWCROFT
SPRINGFIELD CR

B6480

Wennington Moss
Newby Moor Quarry
Tewit Hall

Sniddle Moss

New Butt
Banks Head

B6480

8

Visitor Ctr & Ind Est
MAIN ST
MOUNT PLEASANT
Lily
SPRINGFIELD

Greystonegill

Lowther Hill

Newby Moor

69

Sewage Works
Bentham Bridge

Summerfield Farm
Fowgill

Batty Farm

Chesters

Hardacre Moss
Upper Hardacre

7

High Bottom

Quarry Wood
Todhill Farm
Staggarth Farm
Ridding Lane

Linghaw Farm
Lingshaw Woods
Lane House

Meregil Farm
Oaklands

Lower Hardacre

Brook House Farm
Barnfield Farm
Forest of Mewith

Bowtham Wood
Green's Viaduct
Lane Foot Farm
Gill Brow Wood

Waterscale

Meregill Wood

68

Smithy Wood
Sunny Bank Farm
Stoneley Bridge

Brown Bank Wood

Crabtree Bank Wood

Hardacre Wood

Belle Vue Farm

WEST LANE HL
MEWITH LANE

Beck Grains Farmhouse

Mill Dam
New House

Buffet Hill

Mewith Head

Clapham Woods Farmhouse

Hardacre Wood Bridge

Clapham Woods

6

Lane House Farm
Battersby Farm
Holly Tree
Waterford Farm
Stonegrove

Stonegrove Wood

Mewith Head

Hammonhead
Clapham Wood Hall

67

Flannagill

Fairfield House

Gill Beck Farm
Gruskham

Bain Brigge
Hurder Hill

Mewith Head Hall

Mewith Head Farm
Cinder Hill
Braken Hill

Ratton Syke Bridge
Burn Head

Reebys Wood

Bents

Burn Moor

Banks

Leonard Moss

Deep Gill Foot

Hall Moss

West Borronhead

Hammonhead Wood

5

Moorlands
Fourstones
Usherwoods

Great Stone of Fourstones

Round Hill

Green Brow

LA2

Stony Wood

Tatham Fells

Loftshaw Moss
Queen of Fairies Chair

Stony Bank

Thick Sod Holes

Heigh Head

66

Aikengill
Burn Moor

Little Anne Moss

Alder Gill Syke

Hawks Heath Farm

Foss Bank

Great Anne Moss

Cairn

Great Breast

Hawksheath Plantation

4

Ringstones

65

Green Hall Farm
Lanshaw

PETERSBOTTOM LANE

Davidson's Crag

Standard on Burn Moor

Keasden Head Wood

Tatham Falls
Craggs

Moorcock Farm

Crossdale Grains Farm

West Cat Stones

Burn Moor

3

Higher Craggs
Balshaw Bridge

Crossdale Beck

Lower Crossdale Grains Farm

East Cat Stones
Rantree Crag

Cairn

Keasden Head
Ford

64

Bank End Barn

Master Close

Cantsfield Dike Nook

Outlaw Gill Syke

Burn Moor Fell

LYTHE LANE

Bank End

Grey Stones

2

Higher Lythe
Lythe Bank

Tatham Fells
Piked Hill

Middlesmoor

Whitray Farm
Starkers Moor

Lythe Fell

Sunken Delves

Fox Holes

Barclays Gill Syke

1

Whiteray Fell
Little Moor

Little Moor Beck

Thistle Hill

John Fell

62

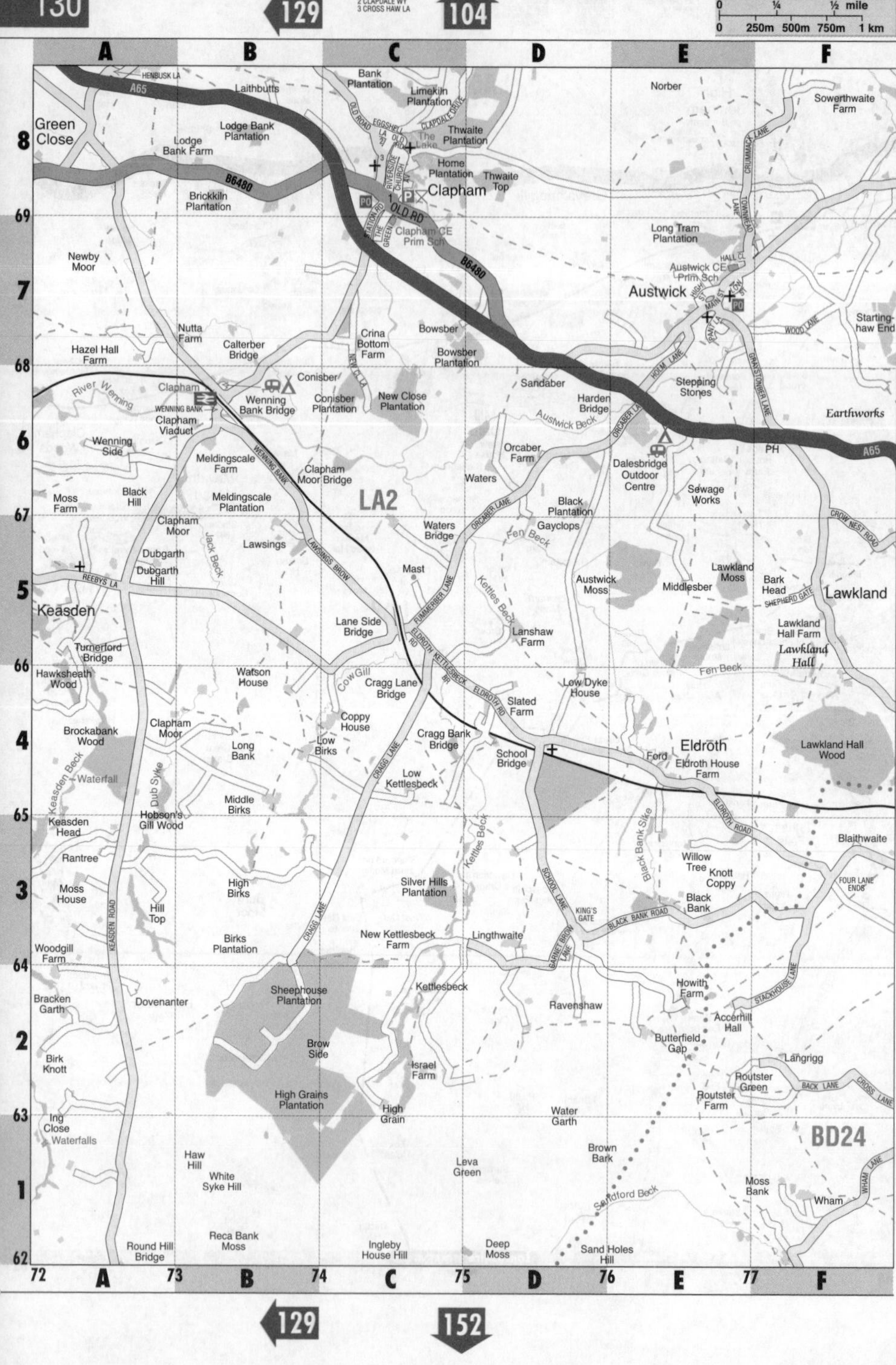

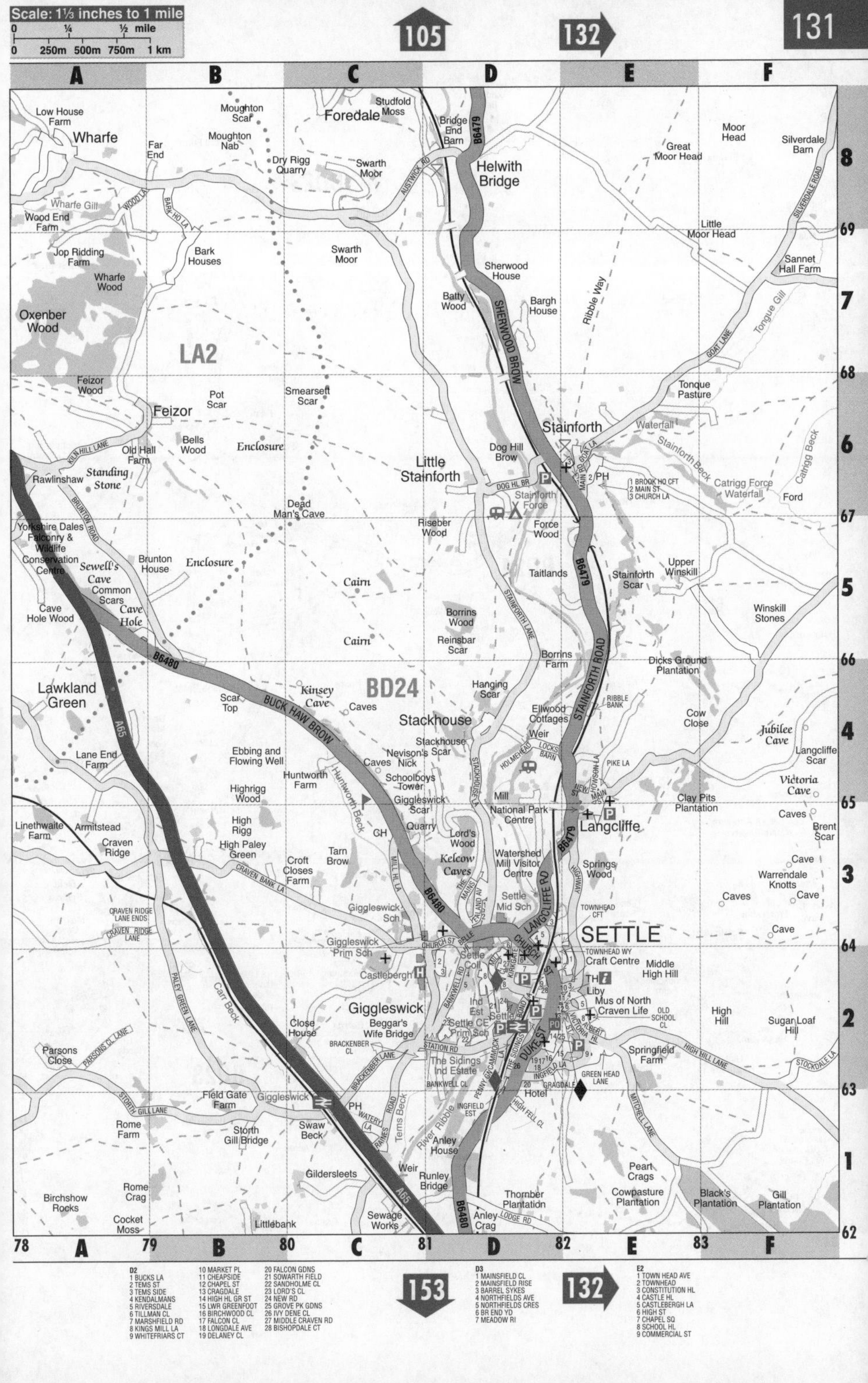
Scale: 1⅓ inches to 1 mile
0 ¼ ½ mile
0 250m 500m 750m 1 km
105
132
A B C D E F
Low House Farm
Wharfe
Moughton Scar
Moughton Nab
Far End
Foredale
Studfold Moss
Bridge End Barn
Helwith Bridge
Dry Rigg Quarry
Swarth Moor
Great Moor Head
Moor Head
Silverdale Barn
Wharfe Gill
Wood End Farm
Jop Ridding Farm
Wharfe Wood
Bark Houses
Swarth Moor
Sherwood House
Little Moor Head
Sannet Hall Farm
Oxenber Wood
Batty Wood
Bargh House
Ribble Way
Tongue Gill
LA2
SHERWOOD BROW
GOAT LANE
Feizor Wood
Pot Scar
Smearsett Scar
Tonque Pasture
Feizor
Bells Wood
Enclosure
Stainforth
Waterfall
Stainforth Beck
Catrigg Beck
Old Hall Farm
Dog Hill Brow
Little Stainforth
Rawlinshaw
Standing Stone
Stainforth Force
Catrigg Force Waterfall
Ford
1 BROOK HO CFT
2 MAIN ST
3 CHURCH LA
Dead Man's Cave
Riseber Wood
Force Wood
Yorkshire Dales Falconry & Wildlife Conservation Centre
Sewell's Cave
Brunton House
Enclosure
Taitlands
Upper Winskill
Common Scars
Cairn
Stainforth Scar
Cave Hole Wood
Cave Hole
Borrins Wood
Winskill Stones
Cairn
Reinsbar Scar
B6480
Borrins Farm
Dicks Ground Plantation
Lawkland Green
Kinsey Cave
BD24
Hanging Scar
STAINFORTH ROAD
Scar Top
Caves
Ellwood Cottages
RIBBLE BANK
Cow Close
BUCK HAW BROW
Stackhouse
Weir
Jubilee Cave
Lane End Farm
Ebbing and Flowing Well
Stackhouse Scar
Langcliffe Scar
A65
Nevison's Nick
Caves
Huntworth Farm
Schoolboys Tower
Victoria Cave
Highrigg Wood
Mill
Clay Pits Plantation
Giggleswick Scar
National Park Centre
Langcliffe
Caves
Brent Scar
Linethwaite Farm
Armitstead
High Rigg
Quarry
GH
Lord's Wood
Craven Ridge
High Paley Green
Tarn Brow
Kelcow Caves
Watershed Mill Visitor Centre
Springs Wood
Cave
Warrendale Knotts
Croft Closes Farm
CRAVEN BANK LA
Cave
Caves
Settle Mid Sch
CRAVEN RIDGE LANE ENDS
Giggleswick Sch
LANGCLIFFE RD
TOWNHEAD CFT
SETTLE
Cave
Giggleswick Prim Sch
Settle Coll
TOWNHEAD WY
Craft Centre
Middle High Hill
Castleberg
TH
Liby
Giggleswick
Ind Est
Mus of North Craven Life
OLD SCHOOL CL
High Hill
Sugar Loaf Hill
Beggar's Wife Bridge
Settle CE Prim Sch
Close House
Carr Beck
PALEY GREEN LANE
Settle
BRACKENBER CL
STATION RD
DUKE ST
Springfield Farm
HIGH HILL LANE
Parsons Close
PARSONS CL LANE
The Sidings Ind Estate
STOCKDALE LA
BANKWELL CL
GREEN HEAD LANE
Hotel
Field Gate Farm
Giggleswick
PH
Tems Beck
INGFIELD EST
HIGH FELL CL
STORTH GILL LANE
Rome Farm
Storth Gill Bridge
Swaw Beck
River Ribble
MITCHELL LANE
Anley House
Peart Crags
Gildersleets
Weir
Runley Bridge
Cowpasture Plantation
Black's Plantation
Gill Plantation
Birchshow Rocks
Rome Crag
Thornber Plantation
Sewage Works
Anley Crag
LODGE RD
Cocket Moss
Littlebank
8 69 7 68 6 67 5 66 4 65 3 64 2 63 1 62
78 79 80 81 82 83
D2
1 BUCKS LA
2 TEMS ST
3 TEMS SIDE
4 KENDALMANS
5 RIVERSDALE
6 TILLMAN CL
7 MARSHFIELD RD
8 KINGS MILL LA
9 WHITEFRIARS CT
10 MARKET PL
11 CHEAPSIDE
12 CHAPEL ST
13 CRAGDALE
14 HIGH HL GR ST
15 LWR GREENFOOT
16 BIRCHWOOD CL
17 FALCON CL
18 LONGDALE AVE
19 DELANEY CL
20 FALCON GDNS
21 SOWARTH FIELD
22 SANDHOLME CL
23 LORD'S CL
24 NEW RD
25 GROVE PK GDNS
26 IVY DENE CL
27 MIDDLE CRAVEN RD
28 BISHOPDALE CT
153
D3
1 MAINSFIELD CL
2 MAINSFIELD RISE
3 BARREL SYKES
4 NORTHFIELDS AVE
5 NORTHFIELDS CRES
6 BR END YD
7 MEADOW RI
132
E2
1 TOWN HEAD AVE
2 TOWNHEAD
3 CONSTITUTION HL
4 CASTLE HL
5 CASTLEBERGH LA
6 HIGH ST
7 CHAPEL SQ
8 SCHOOL HL
9 COMMERCIAL ST

131
106

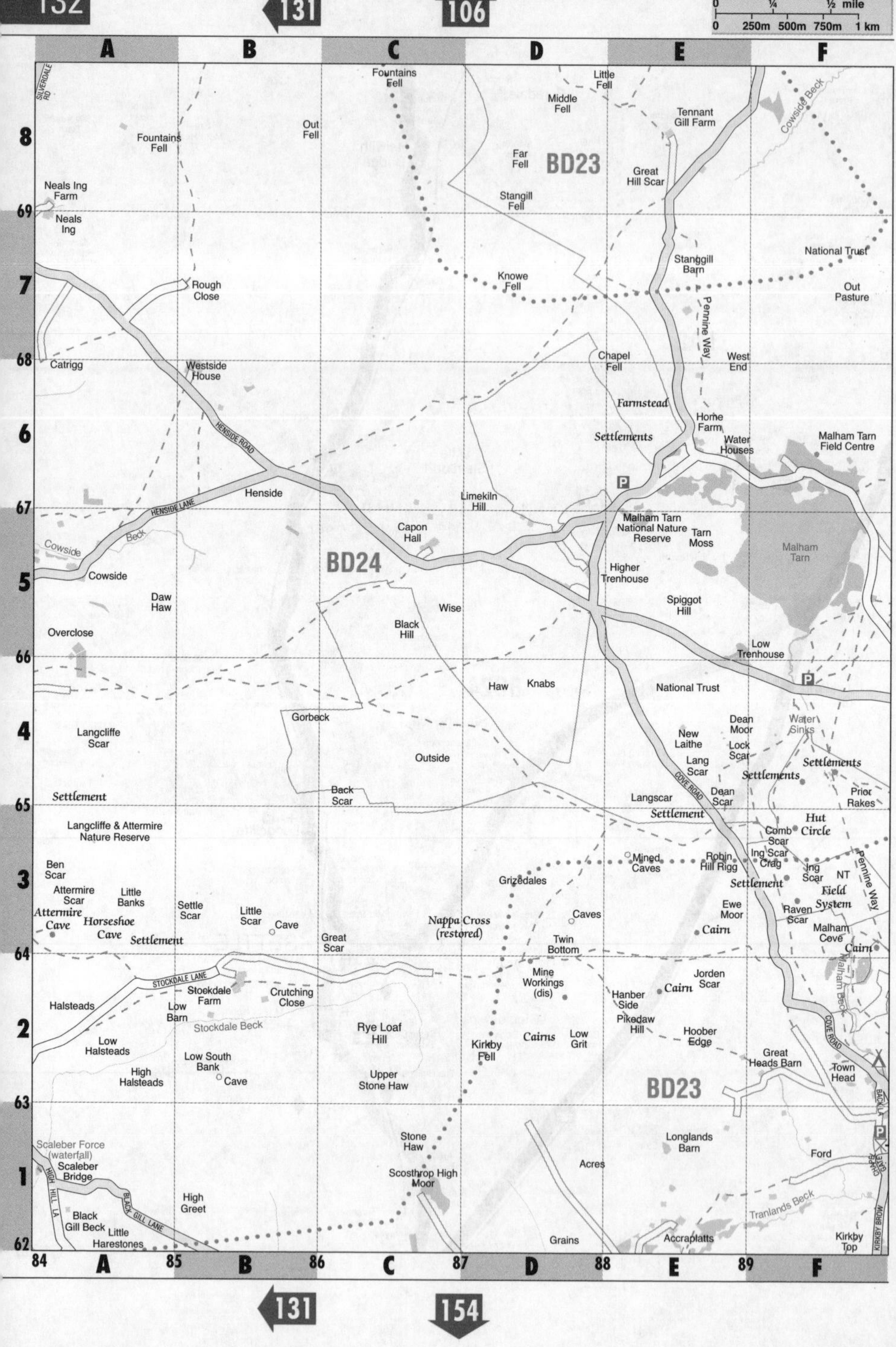
Scale: 1⅓ inches to 1 mile
0 ¼ ½ mile
0 250m 500m 750m 1 km
A B C D E F
Fountains Fell
Little Fell
Middle Fell
Tennant Gill Farm
Cowside Beck
Out Fell
Fountains Fell
Far Fell
BD23
Great Hill Scar
Neals Ing Farm
Neals Ing
Stangill Fell
National Trust
Stanggill Barn
Knowe Fell
Rough Close
Out Pasture
Pennine Way
Catrigg
Westside House
Chapel Fell
West End
Farmstead
Home Farm
Settlements
Water Houses
Malham Tarn Field Centre
HENSIDE ROAD
Henside
HENSIDE LANE
Limekiln Hill
Malham Tarn National Nature Reserve
Tarn Moss
Capon Hall
Cowside
Beck
BD24
Malham Tarn
Cowside
Higher Trenhouse
Daw Haw
Wise
Spiggot Hill
Black Hill
Overclose
Low Trenhouse
Haw
Knabs
National Trust
Gorbeck
Dean Moor
Water Sinks
Langcliffe Scar
New Laithe
Lock Scar
Outside
Lang Scar
Settlements
Settlements
COVE ROAD
Back Scar
Dean Scar
Settlement
Langscar
Prior Rakes
Settlement
Hut Circle
Langcliffe & Attermire Nature Reserve
Comb Scar
Mined Caves
Robin Hill Rigg
Ing Scar Crag
Ben Scar
Ing Scar
NT
Grizedales
Settlement
Attermire Scar
Little Banks
Field System
Settle Scar
Ewe Moor
Raven Scar
Attermire Cave
Little Scar
Cave
Nappa Cross (restored)
Caves
Horseshoe Cave
Cairn
Malham Cove
Settlement
Great Scar
Twin Bottom
Cairn
STOCKDALE LANE
Mine Workings (dis)
Jorden Scar
Stockdale Farm
Crutching Close
Cairn
Halsteads
Low Barn
Hanber Side
Malham Beck
Stockdale Beck
Pikedaw Hill
Rye Loaf Hill
Cairns
Low Grit
Hoober Edge
Low Halsteads
Kirkby Fell
COVE ROAD
Low South Bank
Great Heads Barn
Town Head
High Halsteads
Cave
Upper Stone Haw
BD23
BACK LA
Scaleber Force (waterfall)
Stone Haw
Longlands Barn
Scaleber Bridge
Ford
Scosthrop High Moor
Acres
HIGH HILL LA
BLACK GILL LANE
High Greet
Tranlands Beck
Black Gill Beck
Little Harestones
Grains
Accraplatts
Kirkby Top
KIRKBY BROW
SILVERDALE RD
8
69
7
68
6
67
5
66
4
65
3
64
2
63
1
62
84
85
86
87
88
89
A B C D E F

131
154

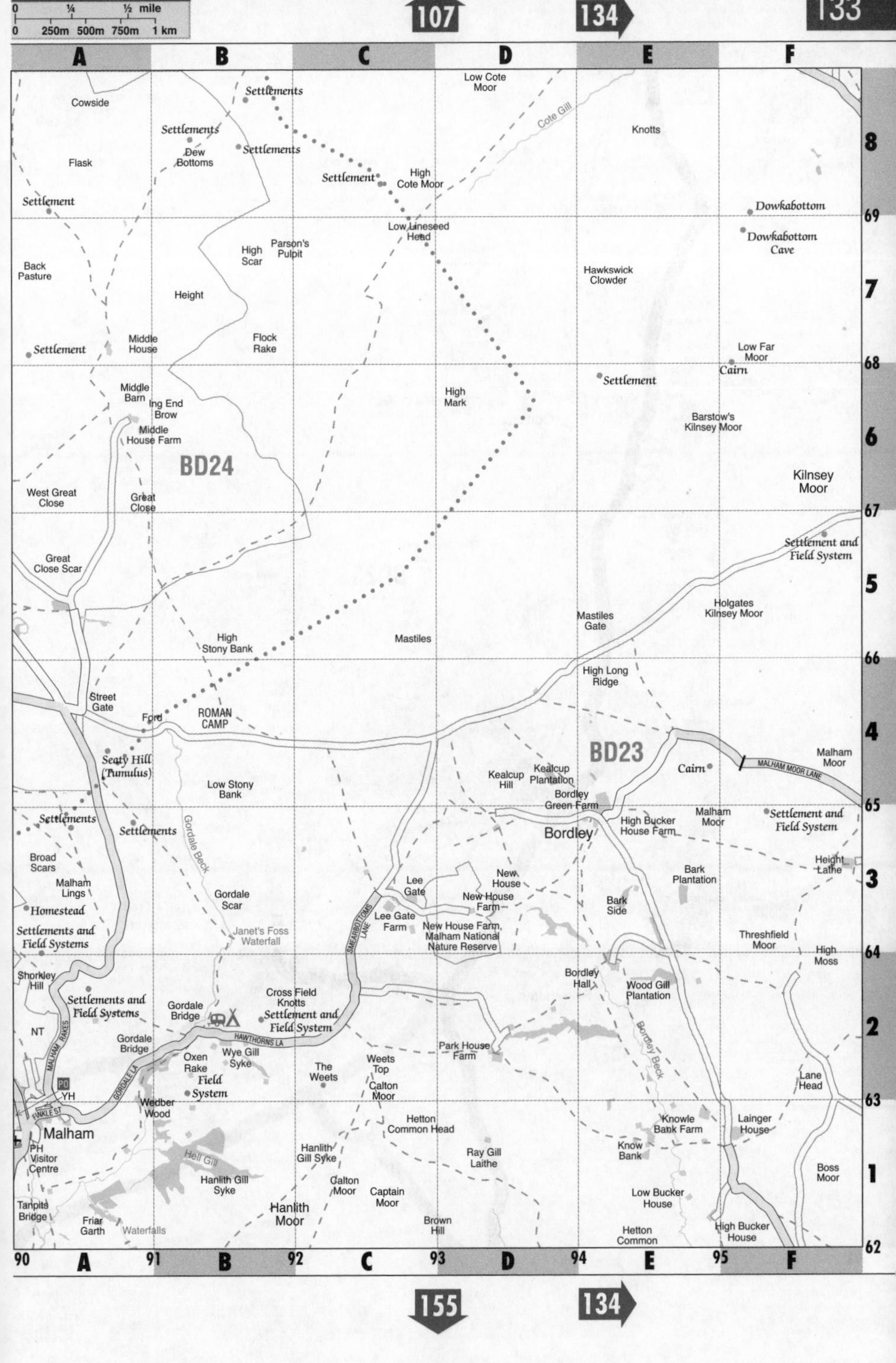

Scale: 1½ inches to 1 mile
0   ¼   ½ mile
0   250m 500m 750m   1 km

A   B   C   D   E   F

Cowside

Settlements

Low Cote
Moor

Cote Gill

Knotts

Settlements
Dew
Bottoms
Settlements

Flask

Settlement

High
Cote Moor

Dowkabottom

Settlement

Low Lineseed
Head

Dowkabottom
Cave

8

69

High
Scar

Parson's
Pulpit

Back
Pasture

Hawkswick
Clowder

7

Height

68

Settlement

Middle
House

Flock
Rake

High
Mark

Settlement

Low Far
Moor
Cairn

Middle
Barn

Ing End
Brow

Middle
House Farm

BD24

Barstow's
Kilnsey Moor

6

West Great
Close

Great
Close

Kilnsey
Moor

67

Great
Close Scar

High
Stony Bank

Mastiles

Mastiles
Gate

Holgates
Kilnsey Moor

Settlement and
Field System

5

66

Street
Gate

Ford

ROMAN
CAMP

High Long
Ridge

4

Seaty Hill
(Tumulus)

Low Stony
Bank

BD23

Kealcup
Hill

Kealcup
Plantation

Bordley
Green Farm

Cairn

MALHAM MOOR LANE

Malham
Moor

Malham
Moor

65

Settlement and
Field System

Settlements

Settlements

Gordale Beck

Bordley

High Bucker
House Farm

Height
Lathe

3

Broad
Scars

Malham
Lings

Gordale
Scar

Lee
Gate

New
House

New House
Farm

Bark
Plantation

Homestead

Janet's Foss
Waterfall

SMEARBOTTOMS LANE

Lee Gate
Farm

New House Farm,
Malham National
Nature Reserve

Bark
Side

Threshfield
Moor

64

Settlements and
Field Systems

High
Moss

Shorkley
Hill

Bordley
Hall

Wood Gill
Plantation

NT

Settlements and
Field Systems

Gordale
Bridge

Cross Field
Knotts
Settlement and
Field System

Bordley Beck

2

Gordale
Bridge

HAWTHORNS LA.

MALHAM RAKES

GORDALE LA.

Oxen
Rake
Field
System

Wye Gill
Syke

The
Weets

Park House
Farm

Lane
Head

PO
YH

Wedber
Wood

Weets
Top
Calton
Moor

Knowle
Bank Farm

Lainger
House

63

WINKLE ST.

Hetton
Common Head

Malham

PH
Visitor
Centre

Hanlith
Gill Syke

Ray Gill
Laithe

Know
Bank

Low Bucker
House

Boss
Moor

1

Tarnlith
Bridge

Hell Gill

Hanlith Gill
Syke

Calton
Moor

Captain
Moor

Friar
Garth

Waterfalls

Hanlith
Moor

Brown
Hill

Hetton
Common

High Bucker
House

62

A   B   C   D   E   F
90   91   92   93   94   95

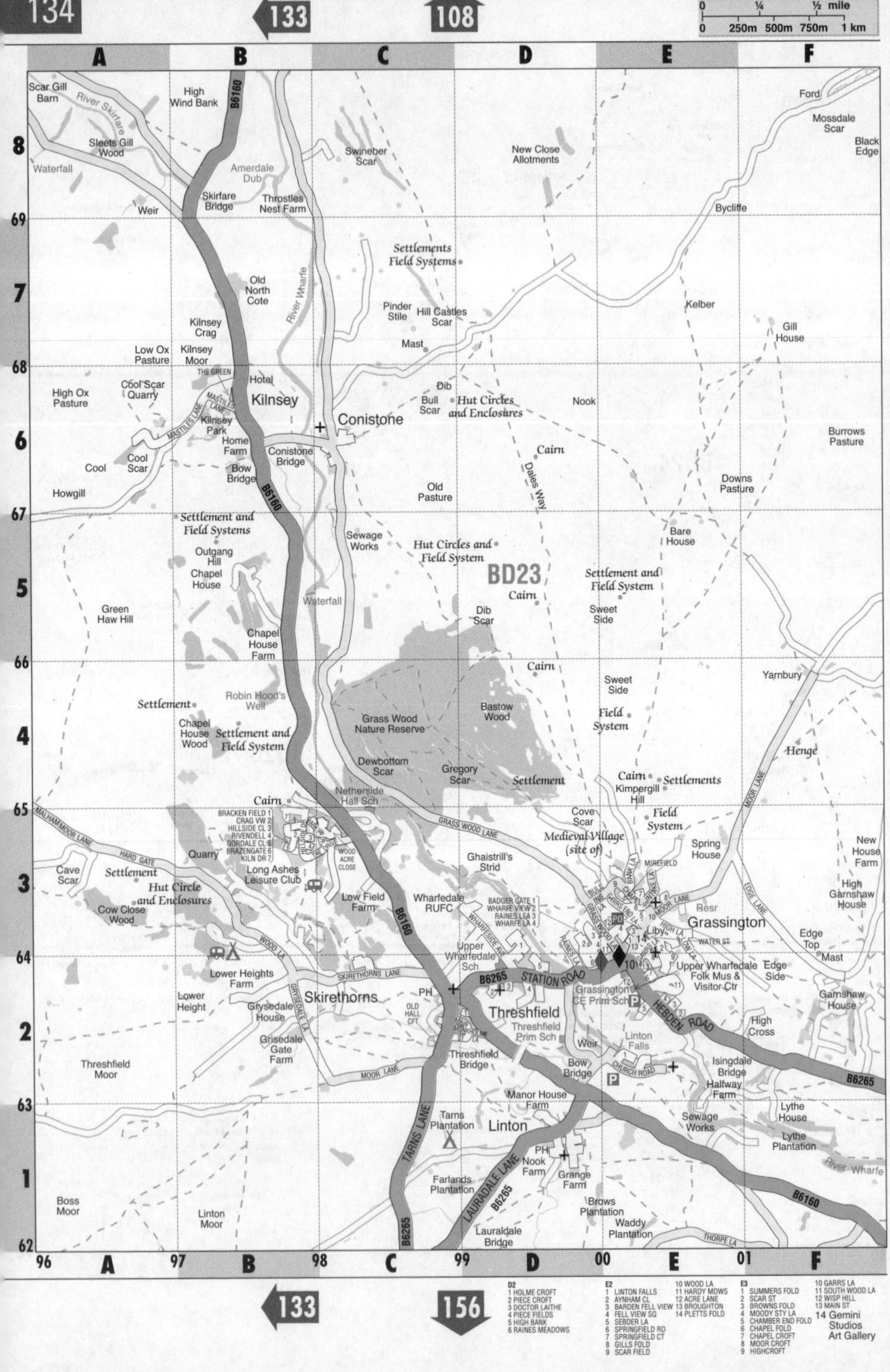

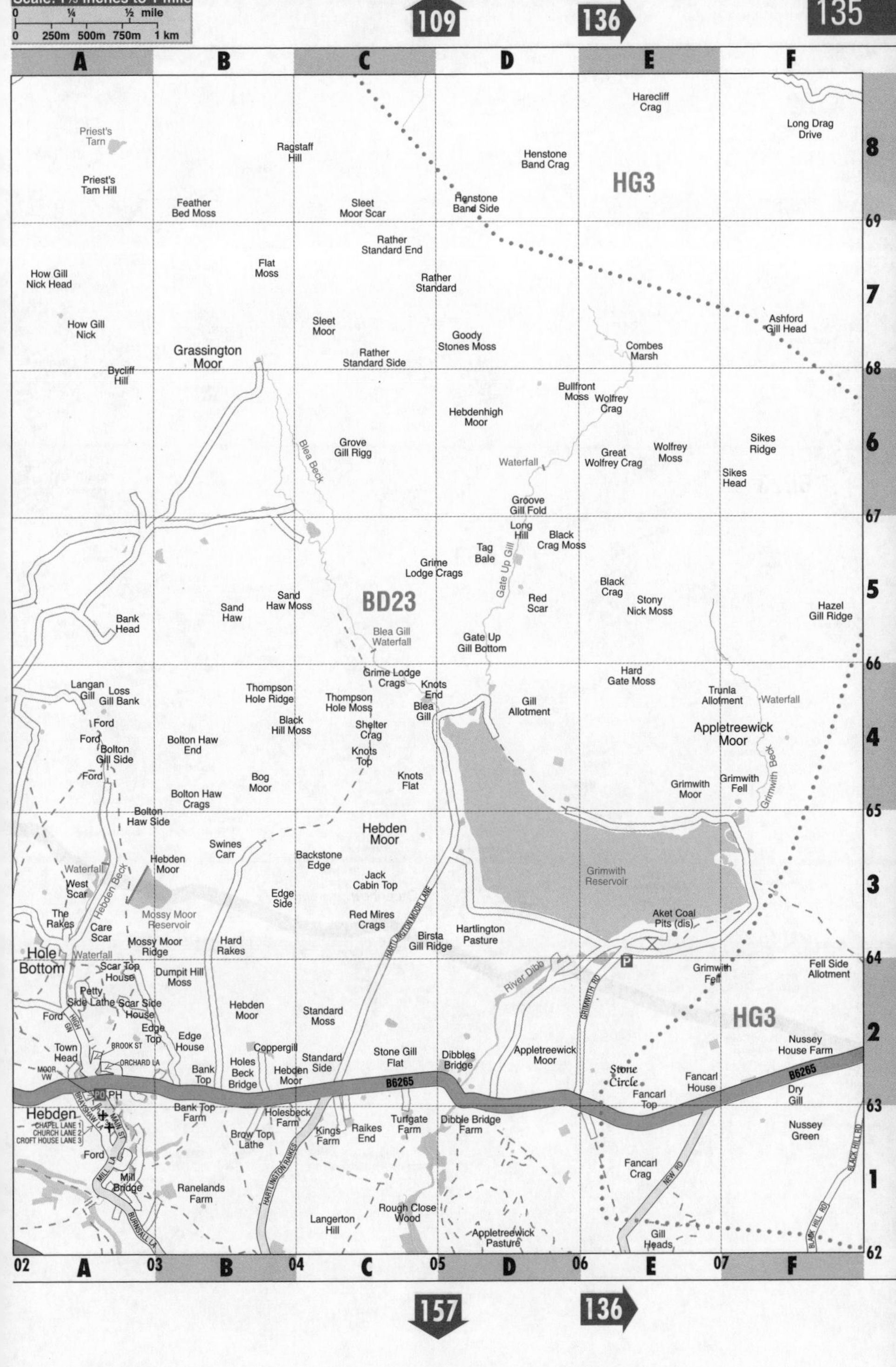

A B C D E F

Priest's Tarn
Priest's Tarn Hill
Ragstaff Hill
Harecliff Crag
Long Drag Drive
8

Feather Bed Moss
Sleet Moor Scar
Henstone Band Crag
Henstone Band Side
HG3
69

How Gill Nick Head
Flat Moss
Rather Standard End
7

How Gill Nick
Sleet Moor
Rather Standard
Goody Stones Moss
Combes Marsh
Ashford Gill Head

Bycliff Hill
Grassington Moor
Rather Standard Side
68

Grove Gill Rigg
Hebdenhigh Moor
Bullfront Moss
Wolfrey Crag
Sikes Ridge
6

Waterfall
Great Wolfrey Crag
Wolfrey Moss
Sikes Head

Blea Beck
Groove Gill Fold
67

Long Hill
Black Crag Moss
Tag Bale
Grime Lodge Crags
Gate Up Gill
BD23
Red Scar
Black Crag
Stony Nick Moss
Hazel Gill Ridge
5

Blea Gill Waterfall
Gate Up Gill Bottom
66

Grime Lodge Crags
Knots End
Hard Gate Moss
Trunla Allotment
Waterfall

Langan Gill
Loss Gill Bank
Thompson Hole Ridge
Thompson Hole Moss
Shelter Crag
Blea Gill
Gill Allotment
Appletreewick Moor

Ford
Black Hill Moss
Knots Top
Grimwith Beck
4

Ford
Bolton Gill Side
Bolton Haw End
Bog Moor
Knots Flat
Grimwith Moor
Grimwith Fell

Ford
Bolton Haw Crags

Bolton Haw Side
Hebden Moor
65

Waterfall
Swines Carr
Backstone Edge
Grimwith Reservoir

West Scar
Hebden Moor
Jack Cabin Top
Aket Coal Pits (dis)
3

The Rakes
Care Scar
Mossy Moor Reservoir
Edge Side
Red Mires Crags
Birsta Gill Ridge
Hartlington Pasture

Hole Bottom
Waterfall
Mossy Moor Ridge
Hard Rakes
Dumpit Hill Moss
Grimwith Fell
Fell Side Allotment
64

Scar Top House
Hebden Moor
Standard Moss
River Dibb
P
HG3

Petty Side Lathe Scar Side House
Edge House
Standard Side
Appletreewick Moor
Stone Circle
Fancarl House
Nussey House Farm
2

MOOR VW
Edge Top
Bank Top
Coppergill
Hebden Moor
Stone Gill Flat
Dibbles Bridge
Fancarl Top
B6265
Dry Gill

Town Head
BROOK ST
ORCHARD LA
Holes Beck Bridge
B6265

Hebden
CHAPEL LANE 1
CHURCH LANE 2
CROFT HOUSE LANE 3
Bank Top Farm
Holesbeck Farm
Kings Farm
Raikes End
Turfgate Farm
Dibble Bridge Farm
Fancarl Crag
Nussey Green
63

Ford
Brow Top Lathe

Mill Bridge
Ranelands Farm
Langerton Hill
Rough Close Wood
Appletreewick Pasture
Gill Heads
1

BINDLE LA
62

A 02 B 03 C 04 D 05 E 06 07 F

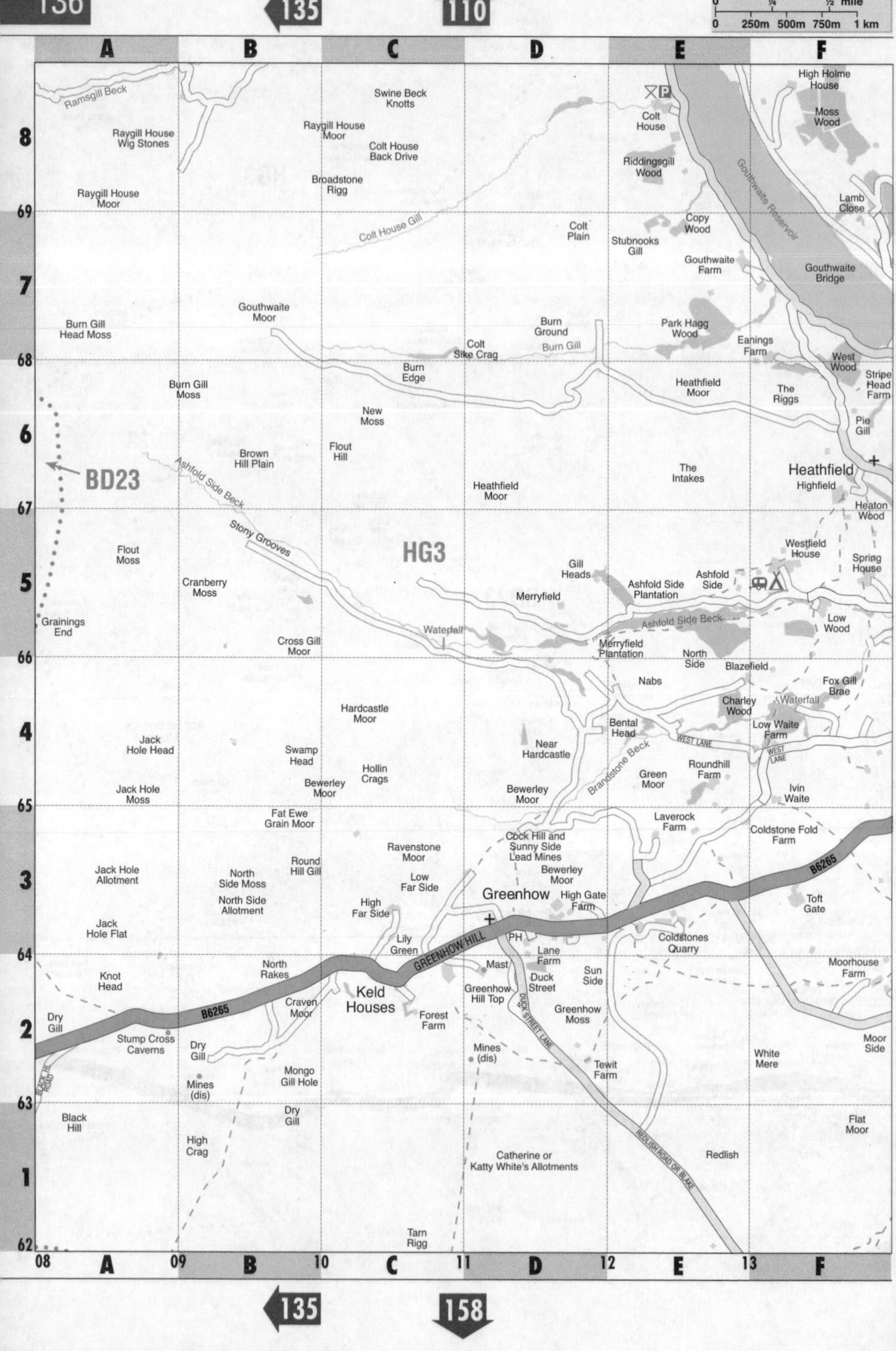
135
110
Scale: 1⅓ inches to 1 mile
0 ¼ ½ mile
0 250m 500m 750m 1 km
A B C D E F
Ramsgill Beck
Swine Beck Knotts
Raygill House Moor
Raygill House Wig Stones
Colt House Back Drive
Broadstone Rigg
Raygill House Moor
Colt House Gill
Colt House
Riddingsgill Wood
Gouthwaite Reservoir
High Holme House
Moss Wood
Lamb Close
Colt Plain
Stubnooks Gill
Copy Wood
Gouthwaite Farm
Gouthwaite Bridge
Gouthwaite Moor
Burn Gill Head Moss
Burn Ground
Burn Gill
Colt Sike Crag
Park Hagg Wood
Eanings Farm
West Wood
Burn Edge
Burn Gill Moss
Heathfield Moor
The Riggs
Stripe Head Farm
New Moss
Pie Gill
Brown Hill Plain
Flout Hill
Ashfold Side Beck
BD23
The Intakes
Heathfield
Highfield
Heathfield Moor
Heaton Wood
Stony Grooves
Flout Moss
HG3
Westfield House
Spring House
Gill Heads
Ashfold Side Plantation
Ashfold Side
Cranberry Moss
Merryfield
Low Wood
Grainings End
Waterfall
Ashfold Side Beck
Cross Gill Moor
Merryfield Plantation
North Side
Blazefield
Nabs
Fox Gill Brae
Hardcastle Moor
Charley Wood
Waterfall
Bental Head
Low Waite Farm
Jack Hole Head
West Lane
West Lane
Swamp Head
Near Hardcastle
Hollin Crags
Brandstone Beck
Roundhill Farm
Green Moor
Jack Hole Moss
Bewerley Moor
Bewerley Moor
Ivin Waite
Fat Ewe Grain Moor
Laverock Farm
Coldstone Fold Farm
Ravenstone Moor
Cock Hill and Sunny Side Lead Mines
Jack Hole Allotment
Round Hill Gill
North Side Moss
Low Far Side
Bewerley Moor
B6265
North Side Allotment
High Far Side
Greenhow
High Gate Farm
Toft Gate
Jack Hole Flat
Lily Green
Greenhow Hill
PH
Coldstones Quarry
Lane Farm
Knot Head
North Rakes
Mast
Moorhouse Farm
Sun Side
Keld Houses
Duck Street
Craven Moor
Greenhow Hill Top
Dry Gill
B6265
Forest Farm
Greenhow Moss
Duck Street Lane
Stump Cross Caverns
Moor Side
Dry Gill
Mines (dis)
Black Hill Road
White Mere
Mongo Gill Hole
Tewit Farm
Mines (dis)
Black Hill
Dry Gill
Flat Moor
High Crag
Redlish Road or Blake
Redlish
Catherine or Katty White's Allotments
Tarn Rigg
8 69 7 68 6 67 5 66 4 65 3 64 2 63 1 62
08 09 10 11 12 13
135
158

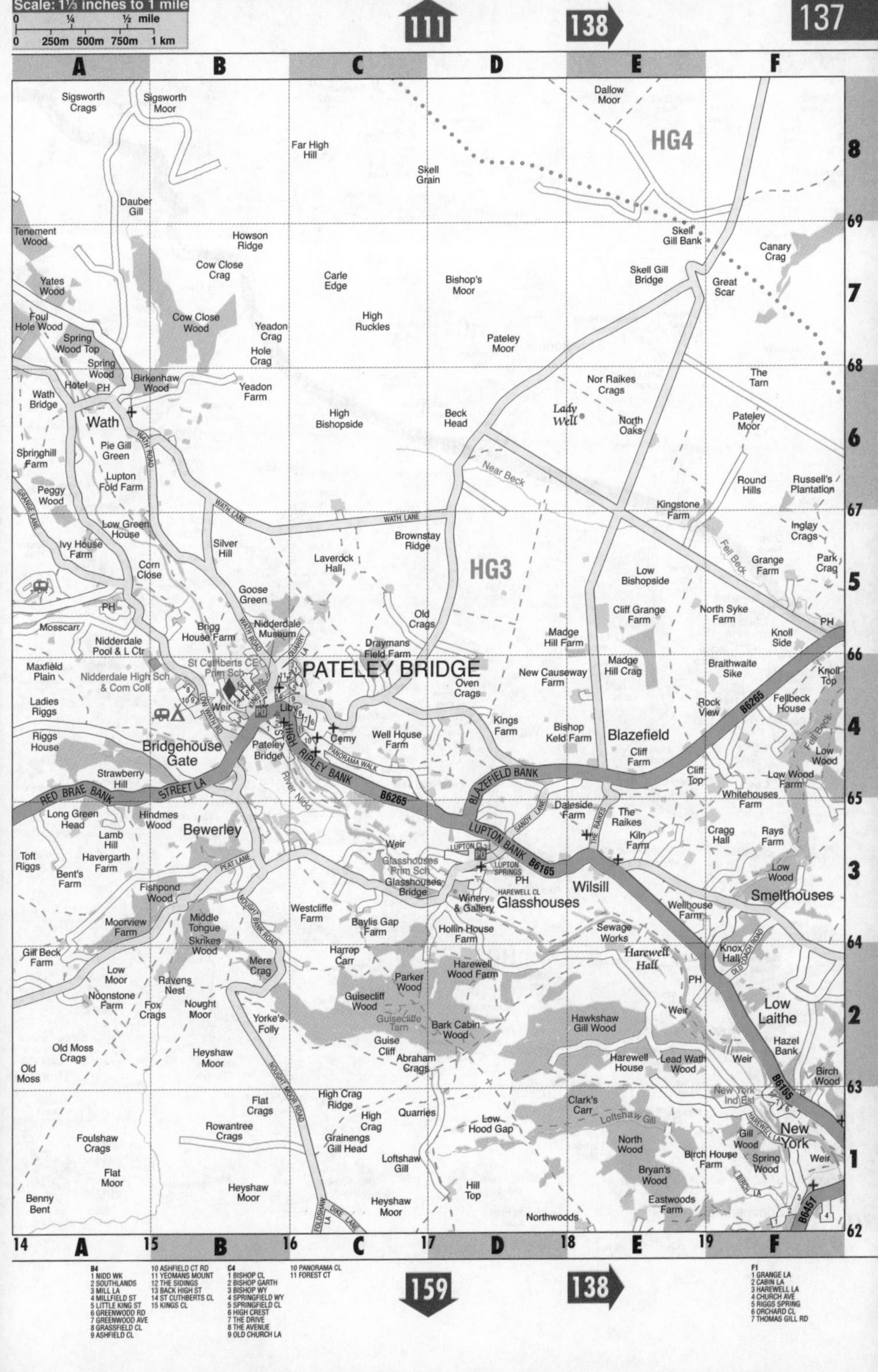

137
112

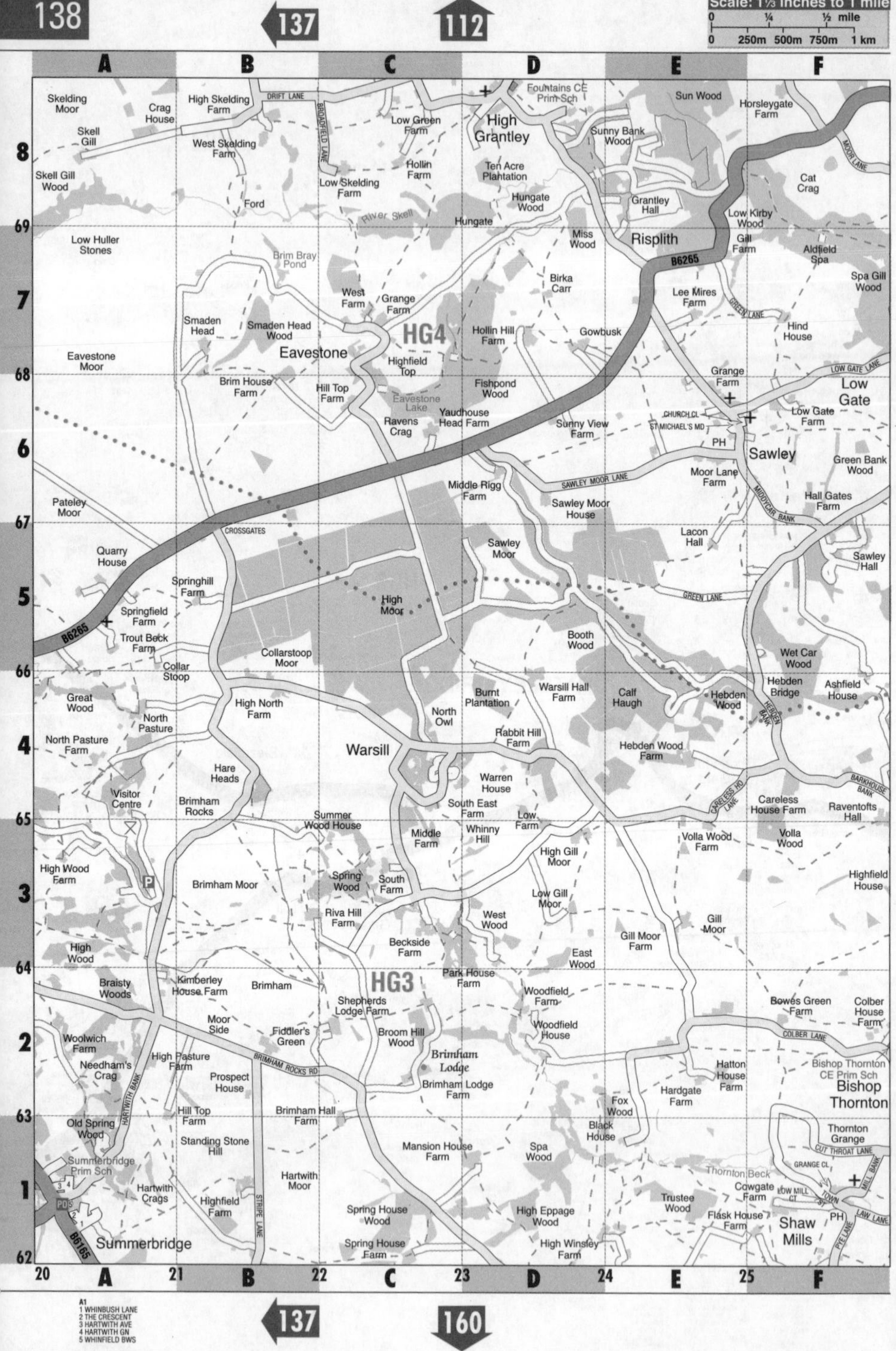
Scale: 1⅓ inches to 1 mile
0 ¼ ½ mile
0 250m 500m 750m 1 km
Skelding Moor
Crag House
High Skelding Farm
DRIFT LANE
BROADFIELD LANE
Low Green Farm
High Grantley
Fountains CE Prim Sch
Sun Wood
Horsleygate Farm
Skell Gill
West Skelding Farm
Hollin Farm
Ten Acre Plantation
Sunny Bank Wood
MOOR LANE
Skell Gill Wood
Low Skelding Farm
Ford
River Skell
Hungate Wood
Grantley Hall
Cat Crag
Hungate
Low Kirby Wood
Miss Wood
Risplith
Gill Farm
Aldfield Spa
Low Huller Stones
Brim Bray Pond
B6265
Birka Carr
Spa Gill Wood
West Farm
Grange Farm
Lee Mires Farm
GREEN LANE
Smaden Head
Smaden Head Wood
HG4
Hollin Hill Farm
Gowbusk
Hind House
Eavestone Moor
Eavestone
Highfield Top
Grange Farm
LOW GATE LANE
Low Gate
Brim House Farm
Hill Top Farm
Fishpond Wood
Eavestone Lake
Yaudhouse Head Farm
CHURCH CL
ST MICHAEL'S MD
Low Gate Farm
Ravens Crag
Sunny View Farm
PH
Sawley
Moor Lane Farm
Green Bank Wood
SAWLEY MOOR LANE
Middle Rigg Farm
MIDDYCAR BANK
Pateley Moor
Sawley Moor House
Hall Gates Farm
CROSSGATES
Lacon Hall
Quarry House
Sawley Moor
Sawley Hall
Springhill Farm
GREEN LANE
High Moor
Springfield Farm
B6265
Trout Beck Farm
Booth Wood
Collarstoop Moor
Wet Car Wood
Collar Stoop
Burnt Plantation
Warsill Hall Farm
Calf Haugh
Hebden Bridge
Hebden Wood
Ashfield House
Great Wood
High North Farm
HEBDEN BANK
North Pasture
North Owl
Rabbit Hill Farm
North Pasture Farm
Warsill
Hebden Wood Farm
Hare Heads
Warren House
BARKHOUSE BANK
Visitor Centre
Brimham Rocks
South East Farm
CARELESS HO LANE
Careless House Farm
Raventofts Hall
Summer Wood House
Low Farm
Middle Farm
Whinny Hill
Volla Wood Farm
Volla Wood
High Wood Farm
High Gill Moor
Highfield House
Brimham Moor
Spring Wood
South Farm
P
Low Gill Moor
Riva Hill Farm
West Wood
Gill Moor
Gill Moor Farm
High Wood
Beckside Farm
East Wood
Braisty Woods
Kimberley House Farm
Brimham
HG3
Park House Farm
Woodfield Farm
Bowes Green Farm
Colber House Farm
Shepherds Lodge Farm
Moor Side
Fiddler's Green
Broom Hill Wood
Woodfield House
COLBER LANE
Woolwich Farm
Needham's Crag
High Pasture Farm
BRIMHAM ROCKS RD
Brimham Lodge
Bishop Thornton CE Prim Sch
Prospect House
Brimham Lodge Farm
Hatton House Farm
Bishop Thornton
HARTWITH BANK
Hardgate Farm
Hill Top Farm
Brimham Hall Farm
Fox Wood
Old Spring Wood
Black House
Thornton Grange
Standing Stone Hill
Mansion House Farm
Spa Wood
CUT THROAT LANE
Summerbridge Prim Sch
GRANGE CL
MILL BANK
Thornton Beck
Hartwith Moor
Hartwith Crags
Cowgate Farm
LOW MILL CT
TOWN ST
Highfield Farm
Trustee Wood
STRIPE LANE
Spring House Wood
High Eppage Wood
Flask House Farm
PH
LAW LANE
Shaw Mills
PYE LANE
B6165
Summerbridge
Spring House Farm
High Winsley Farm
PO
A B C D E F
20 21 22 23 24 25
8 69 7 68 6 67 5 66 4 65 3 64 2 63 1 62

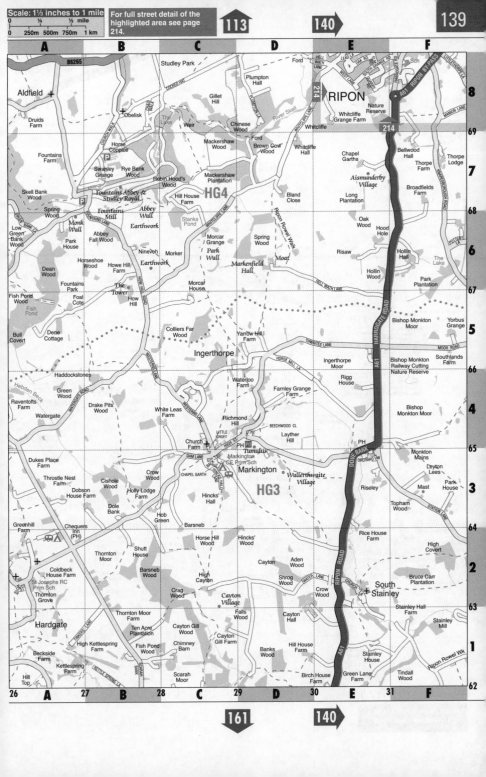

Map of area around Ripon, showing places like Aldfield, Fountains Abbey & Studley Royal, Markington, South Stainley, Ingerthorpe, etc.

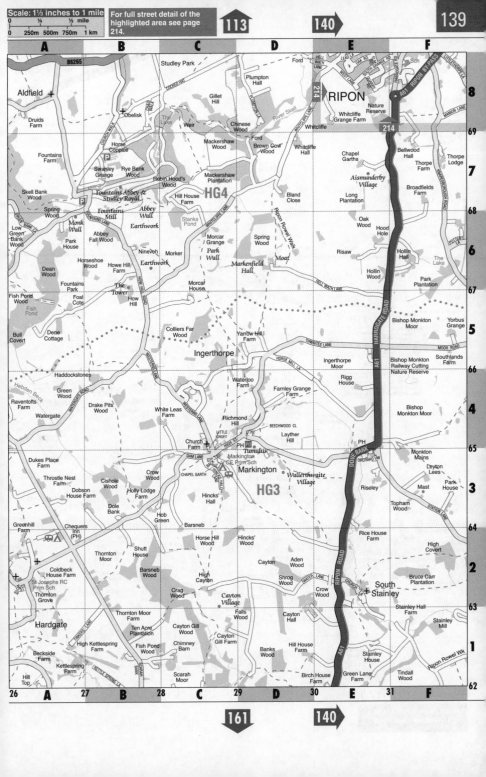

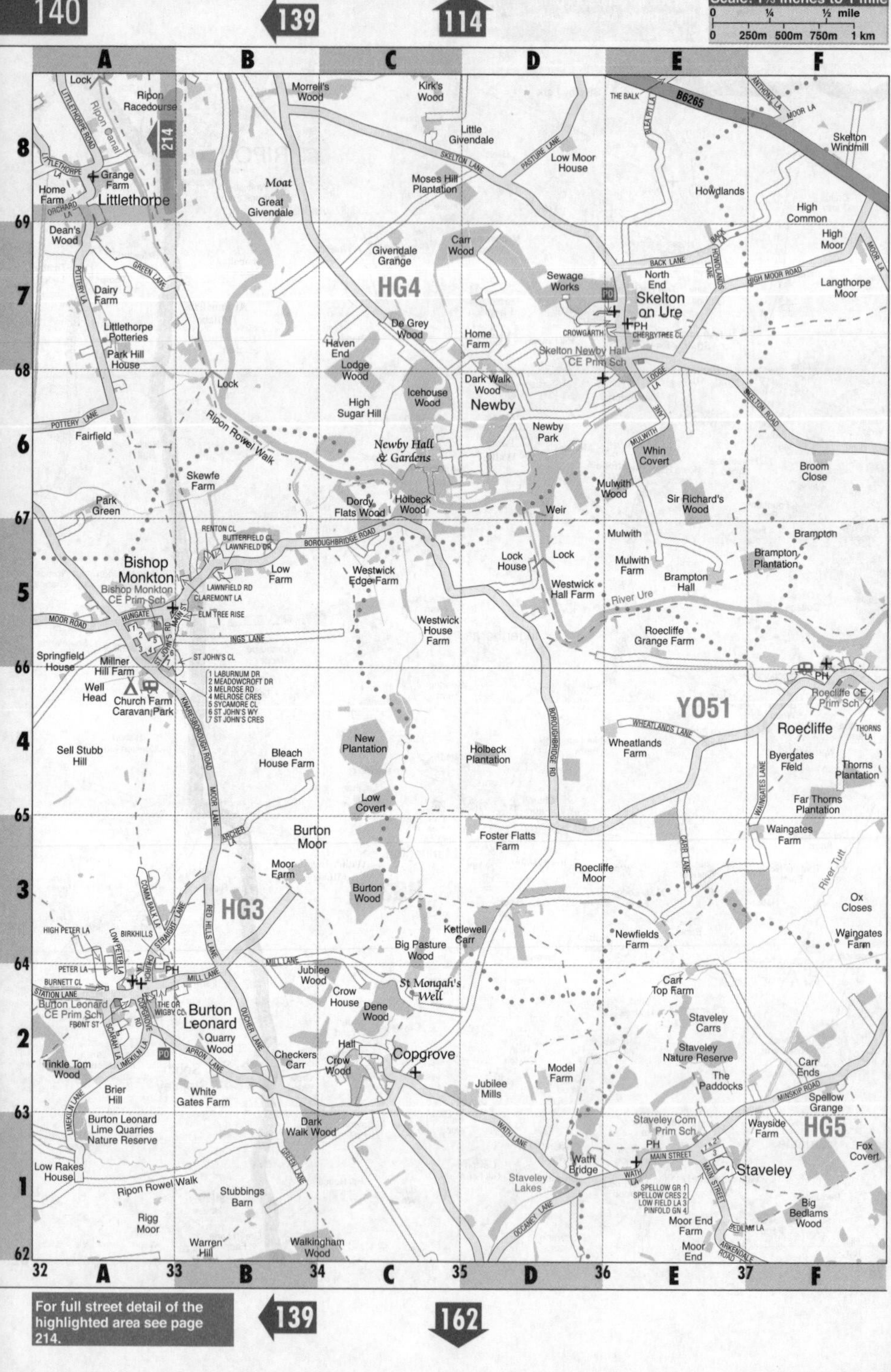

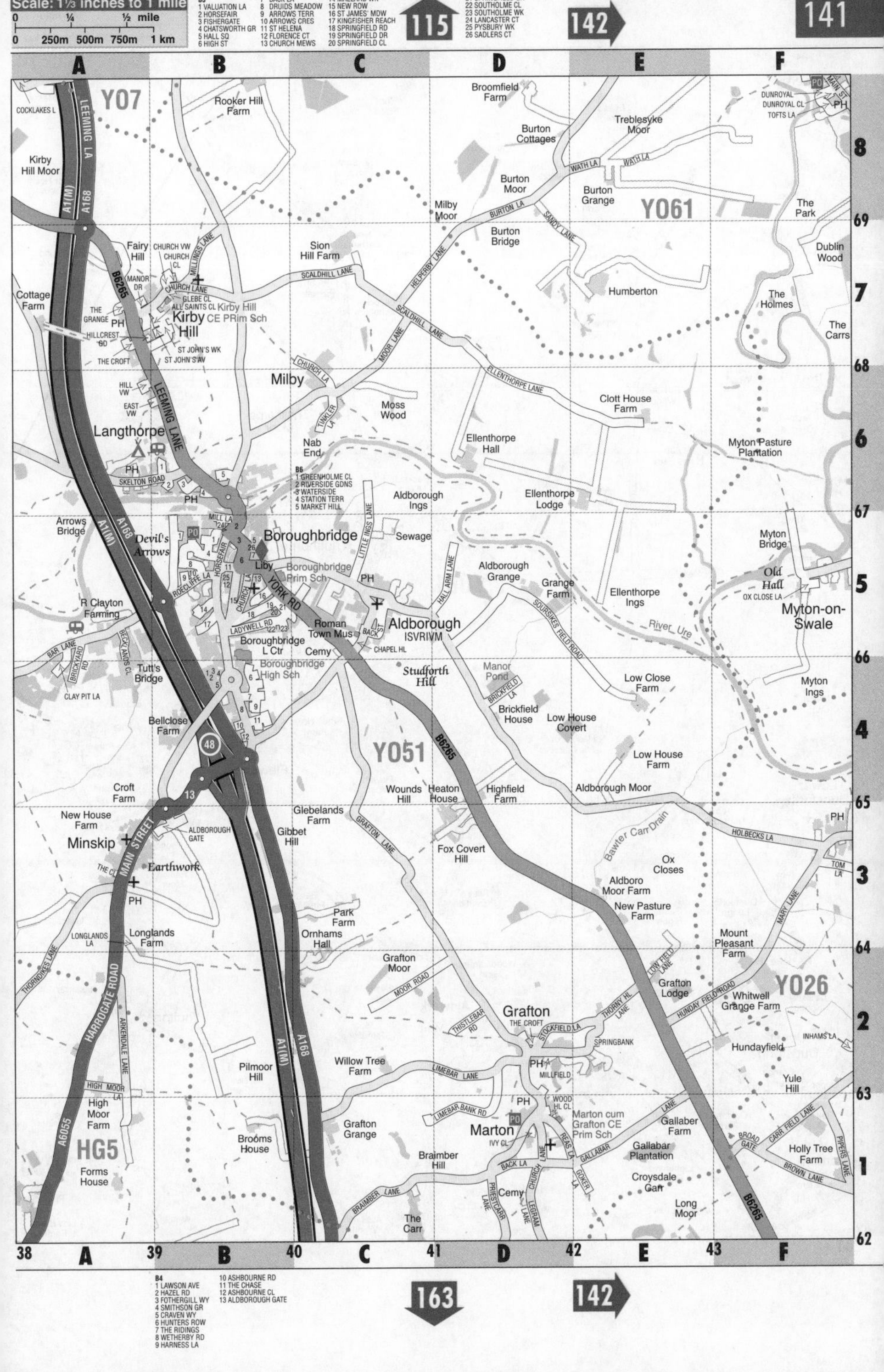
Scale: 1⅓ inches to 1 mile
0 ¼ ½ mile
0 250m 500m 750m 1 km
B5
1 VALUATION LA
2 HORSEFAIR
3 FISHERGATE
4 CHATSWORTH GR
5 HALL SQ
6 HIGH ST
7 BACK LA
8 DRUIDS MEADOW
9 ARROWS TERR
10 ARROWS CRES
11 ST HELENA
12 FLORENCE CT
13 CHURCH MEWS
14 MALLARD WK
15 NEW ROW
16 ST JAMES' MDW
17 KINGFISHER REACH
18 SPRINGFIELD RD
19 SPRINGFIELD DR
20 SPRINGFIELD CL
21 SPRINGFIELD GR
22 SOUTHOLME CL
23 SOUTHOLME WK
24 LANCASTER CT
25 PYSBURY WK
26 SADLERS CT
115
142
A B C D E F
YO7
COCKLAKES L
LEEMING LA
Rooker Hill Farm
Broomfield Farm
Burton Cottages
Treblesyke Moor
DUNROYAL
DUNROYAL CL
TOFTS LA
MAIN ST
PH
PO
Kirby Hill Moor
A1(M)
A168
WATH LA
Burton Moor
Burton Grange
YO61
Milby Moor
BURTON LA
SANDY LANE
The Park
Fairy Hill
CHURCH VW
CHURCH CL
MILLINGS LANE
Sion Hill Farm
Burton Bridge
Dublin Wood
B6265
MANOR DR
GLEBE CL
CHURCH LANE
ALL SAINTS CL
SCALDHILL LANE
HELPERBY LANE
Humberton
Cottage Farm
THE GRANGE
Kirby Hill
Kirby Hill CE PRim Sch
The Holmes
HILLCREST GD
ST JOHN'S WK
ST JOHN'S AV
THE CROFT
The Carrs
MOOR LANE
CHURCH LA
Milby
ELLENTHORPE LANE
HILL VW
EAST VW
LEEMING LANE
Moss Wood
TINKLER LA
Clott House Farm
Langthorpe
Nab End
Ellenthorpe Hall
Myton Pasture Plantation
SKELTON ROAD
B6
1 GREENHOLME CL
2 RIVERSIDE GDNS
3 WATERSIDE
4 STATION TERR
5 MARKET HILL
Aldborough Ings
Ellenthorpe Lodge
Arrows Bridge
MILL LA
Boroughbridge
LITTLE INGS LANE
Sewage
Myton Bridge
Devil's Arrows
HORSEFAIR
Liby
Boroughbridge Prim Sch
HALL ARM LANE
Aldborough Grange
Grange Farm
Old Hall
ROECLIFFE LA
CHURCH LA
YORK RD
Ellenthorpe Ings
OX CLOSE LA
R Clayton Farming
Myton-on-Swale
LADYWELL RD
Roman Town Mus
Aldborough
ISVRIVM
BACK ST
SOURSIKES FIELD ROAD
River Ure
BAR LANE
BRICKYARD RD
BECKLANDS CL
Boroughbridge L Ctr
Cemy
CHAPEL HL
Tutt's Bridge
Boroughbridge High Sch
Studforth Hill
Manor Pond
BRICKFIELD LA
Low Close Farm
Myton Ings
CLAY PIT LA
Brickfield House
Low House Covert
Bellclose Farm
48
B6265
YO51
Low House Farm
Croft Farm
13
Wounds Hill
Heaton House
Highfield Farm
Aldborough Moor
New House Farm
Glebelands Farm
PH
MAIN STREET
ALDBOROUGH GATE
Gibbet Hill
GRAFTON LANE
Bawter Carr Drain
HOLBECKS LA
Minskip
Fox Covert Hill
THE CL
Earthwork
Ox Closes
TOM LA
Aldboro Moor Farm
New Pasture Farm
MARY LANE
Park Farm
LONGLANDS LA
Longlands Farm
Ornhams Hall
Mount Pleasant Farm
THORNDIKES LANE
HARROGATE ROAD
Grafton Moor
MOOR ROAD
LOW FIELD LANE
Grafton Lodge
YO26
ARKENDALE LANE
HUNDAY FIELD ROAD
Whitwell Grange Farm
Grafton
THE CROFT
THISTLEBAR RD
STOCKFIELD LA
THORNY HL LANE
SPRINGBANK
INHAMS LA
Hundayfield
Willow Tree Farm
Pilmoor Hill
LIMEBAR LANE
MILLFIELD
HIGH MOOR LA
Yule Hill
WOOD HL CL
High Moor Farm
LIMEBAR BANK RD
Marton cum Grafton CE Prim Sch
Gallaber Farm
Grafton Grange
Marton
IVY CL
REAS LA
BROAD GATE
CARR FIELD LANE
PIPERS LANE
A6055
HG5
Brooms House
Braimber Hill
BACK LA
CHURCH LANE
GALLABAR LANE
Gallabar Plantation
Holly Tree Farm
Forms House
Croysdale Carr
BROWN LANE
BRAIMBER LANE
PRIESTCARR LANE
Cemy
GOKER LA
LEGRAM LANE
The Carr
Long Moor
B6265
8 69 7 68 6 67 5 66 4 65 3 64 2 63 1 62
38 39 40 41 42 43
B4
1 LAWSON AVE
2 HAZEL RD
3 FOTHERGILL WY
4 SMITHSON GR
5 CRAVEN WY
6 HUNTERS ROW
7 THE RIDINGS
8 WETHERBY RD
9 HARNESS LA
10 ASHBOURNE RD
11 THE CHASE
12 ASHBOURNE CL
13 ALDBOROUGH GATE
163
142

141
116

Scale: 1⅓ inches to 1 mile

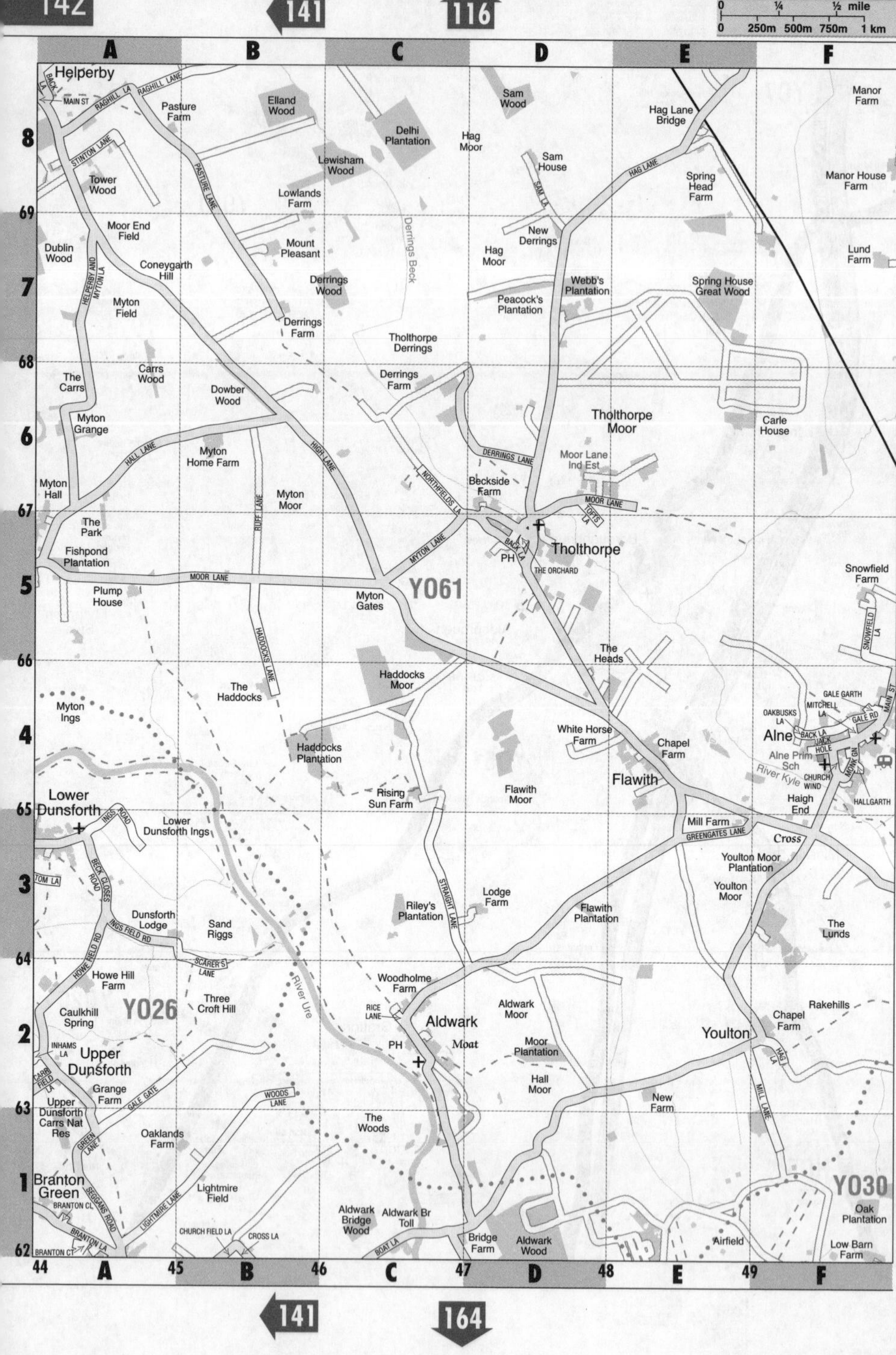
Helperby
Pasture Farm
Elland Wood
Delhi Plantation
Sam Wood
Hag Moor
Lewisham Wood
Hag Lane Bridge
Manor Farm
Tower Wood
Lowlands Farm
Sam House
Spring Head Farm
Manor House Farm
Moor End Field
Mount Pleasant
New Derrings
Dublin Wood
Coneygarth Hill
Derrings Wood
Hag Moor
Lund Farm
Webb's Plantation
Spring House Great Wood
Myton Field
Peacock's Plantation
Derrings Farm
Tholthorpe Derrings
Derrings Beck
The Carrs
Carrs Wood
Derrings Farm
Dowber Wood
Myton Grange
Tholthorpe Moor
Carle House
Myton Home Farm
Moor Lane Ind Est
Myton Hall
Myton Moor
Beckside Farm
The Park
Tholthorpe
Fishpond Plantation
PH
THE ORCHARD
Snowfield Farm
Plump House
Myton Gates
YO61
The Heads
The Haddocks
Haddocks Moor
Myton Ings
White Horse Farm
Chapel Farm
Alne
Haddocks Plantation
Alne Prim Sch
River Kyle
Flawith
Lower Dunsforth
Rising Sun Farm
Flawith Moor
Haigh End
Lower Dunsforth Ings
Mill Farm
Cross
Youlton Moor Plantation
Youlton Moor
Riley's Plantation
Lodge Farm
Flawith Plantation
Dunsforth Lodge
Sand Riggs
The Lunds
Howe Hill Farm
Woodholme Farm
YO26
Three Croft Hill
Aldwark Moor
Rakehills
Caulkhill Spring
Aldwark
Chapel Farm
River Ure
Moat
Youlton
Upper Dunsforth
PH
Moor Plantation
Grange Farm
Hall Moor
New Farm
Upper Dunsforth Carrs Nat Res
The Woods
Oaklands Farm
Branton Green
Lightmire Field
YO30
Oak Plantation
Aldwark Bridge Wood
Aldwark Br Toll
Bridge Farm
Aldwark Wood
Airfield
Low Barn Farm

141
164

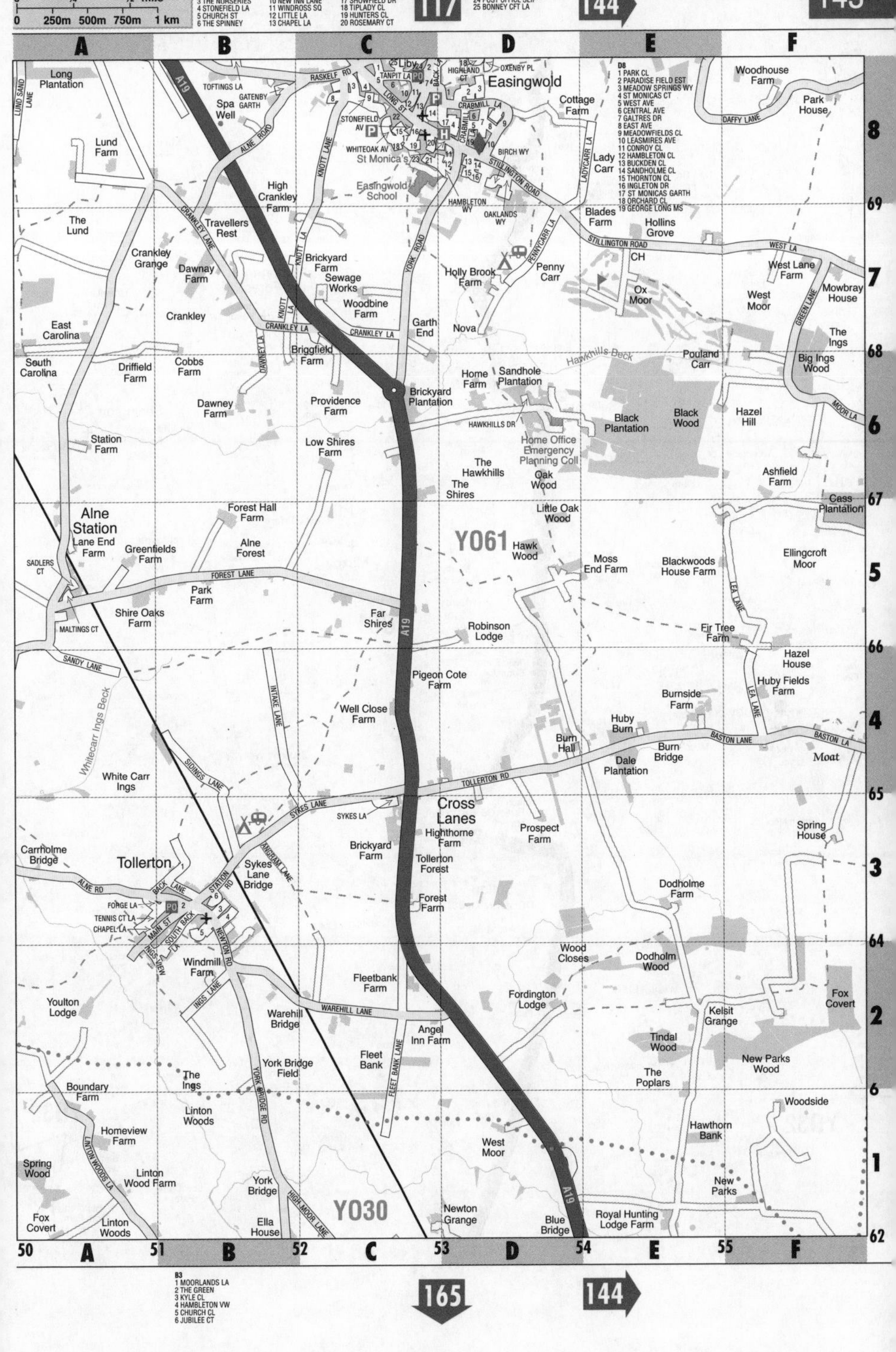

Scale: 1⅓ inches to 1 mile
0 ¼ ½ mile
0 250m 500m 750m 1 km
C8
1 THE OLD ORCHARD
2 SPRING ST
3 THE NURSERIES
4 STONEFIELD LA
5 CHURCH ST
6 THE SPINNEY
7 MARKET PL
8 DROVERS CT
9 STONEFIELD GARTH
10 NEW INN LANE
11 WINDROSS SQ
12 LITTLE LA
13 CHAPEL LA
14 CROFT CL
15 CATHERINE LOVE DR
16 CHASE GARTH RD
17 SHOWFIELD DR
18 TIPLADY CL
19 HUNTERS CL
20 ROSEMARY CT
21 HAMBLETON GARTH
22 WILKINSONS CT
23 GATE GRAINS LA
24 POST OFFICE SLIP
25 BONNEY CFT LA
117
144
D8
1 PARK CL
2 PARADISE FIELD EST
3 MEADOW SPRINGS WY
4 ST MONICAS CT
5 WEST AVE
6 CENTRAL AVE
7 GALTRES DR
8 EAST AVE
9 MEADOWFIELDS CL
10 LEASMIRES AVE
11 CONROY CL
12 HAMBLETON CL
13 BUCKDEN CL
14 SANDHOLME CL
15 THORNTON CL
16 INGLETON DR
17 ST MONICAS GARTH
18 ORCHARD CL
19 GEORGE LONG MS
A B C D E F
Long Plantation
LUND SAND LANE
Lund Farm
The Lund
East Carolina
South Carolina
Driffield Farm
Cobbs Farm
Dawney Farm
Station Farm
Alne Station
Lane End Farm
SADLERS CT
MALTINGS CT
SANDY LANE
Whitecarr Ings Beck
White Carr Ings
Carrholme Bridge
Tollerton
ALNE RD
FORGE LA
TENNIS CT LA
CHAPEL LA
MAIN ST
SOUTH BACK LA
INGS VIEW
BACK LANE
STATION RD
NEWTON RD
Windmill Farm
INGS LANE
Youlton Lodge
Boundary Farm
Homeview Farm
Spring Wood
Linton Wood Farm
LINTON WOODS LA
Fox Covert
Linton Woods
TOFTINGS LA
GATENBY GARTH
Spa Well
ALNE ROAD
A19
CRANKLEY LANE
Travellers Rest
Crankley Grange
Dawnay Farm
Crankley
High Crankley Farm
KNOTT LANE
KNOTT LA
Brickyard Farm
Sewage Works
Woodbine Farm
CRANKLEY LA
DAWNEY LA
Briggfield Farm
Providence Farm
Low Shires Farm
Forest Hall Farm
Alne Forest
Greenfields Farm
FOREST LANE
Park Farm
Shire Oaks Farm
Far Shires
INTAKE LANE
SIDINGS LANE
Well Close Farm
SYKES LANE
SYKES LA
LANGRAM LANE
Sykes Lane Bridge
Brickyard Farm
WAREHILL LANE
Warehill Bridge
Fleetbank Farm
Fleet Bank
FLEET BANK LANE
The Ings
York Bridge Field
YORK BRIDGE RD
Linton Woods
York Bridge
HIGH MOOR LANE
Ella House
YO30
RASKELF RD
Liby
TANPIT LA
PO
LONG ST
BACK LA
STONEFIELD AV
WHITEOAK AV
St Monica's
Easingwold School
HIGHLAND CT
OXENBY PL
Easingwold
CRABMILL LA
CRABMILL LA
BIRCH WY
STILLINGTON ROAD
HAMBLETON WY
OAKLANDS WY
YORK ROAD
PENNYCARR LA
Holly Brook Farm
Penny Carr
Garth End
Nova
Home Farm
Sandhole Plantation
Brickyard Plantation
HAWKHILLS DR
Home Office Emergency Planning Coll
The Hawkhills
The Shires
Oak Wood
Little Oak Wood
YO61
Hawk Wood
Robinson Lodge
Pigeon Cote Farm
TOLLERTON RD
Cross Lanes
Highthorne Farm
Tollerton Forest
Forest Farm
Prospect Farm
Angel Inn Farm
Fordington Lodge
West Moor
Newton Grange
Blue Bridge
Cottage Farm
LADYCARR LA
Lady Carr
Blades Farm
Hollins Grove
STILLINGTON ROAD
CH
Ox Moor
Hawkhills Beck
Black Plantation
Black Wood
Pouland Carr
Moss End Farm
Blackwoods House Farm
Burn Hall
Huby Burn
Burnside Farm
Burn Bridge
Dale Plantation
BASTON LANE
BASTON LA
Moat
Dodholme Farm
Wood Closes
Dodholm Wood
Kelsit Grange
Tindal Wood
The Poplars
Hawthorn Bank
New Parks
Royal Hunting Lodge Farm
Woodhouse Farm
Park House
DAFFY LANE
WEST LA
West Lane Farm
West Moor
Mowbray House
GREEN LANE
The Ings
Big Ings Wood
MOOR LA
Hazel Hill
Ashfield Farm
Cass Plantation
Ellingcroft Moor
LEA LANE
Fir Tree Farm
Hazel House
Huby Fields Farm
LEA LANE
Spring House
Fox Covert
New Parks Wood
Woodside
8 69 7 68 6 67 5 66 4 65 3 64 2 63 1 62
50 51 52 53 54 55
B3
1 MOORLANDS LA
2 THE GREEN
3 KYLE CL
4 HAMBLETON VW
5 CHURCH CL
6 JUBILEE CT
165
144

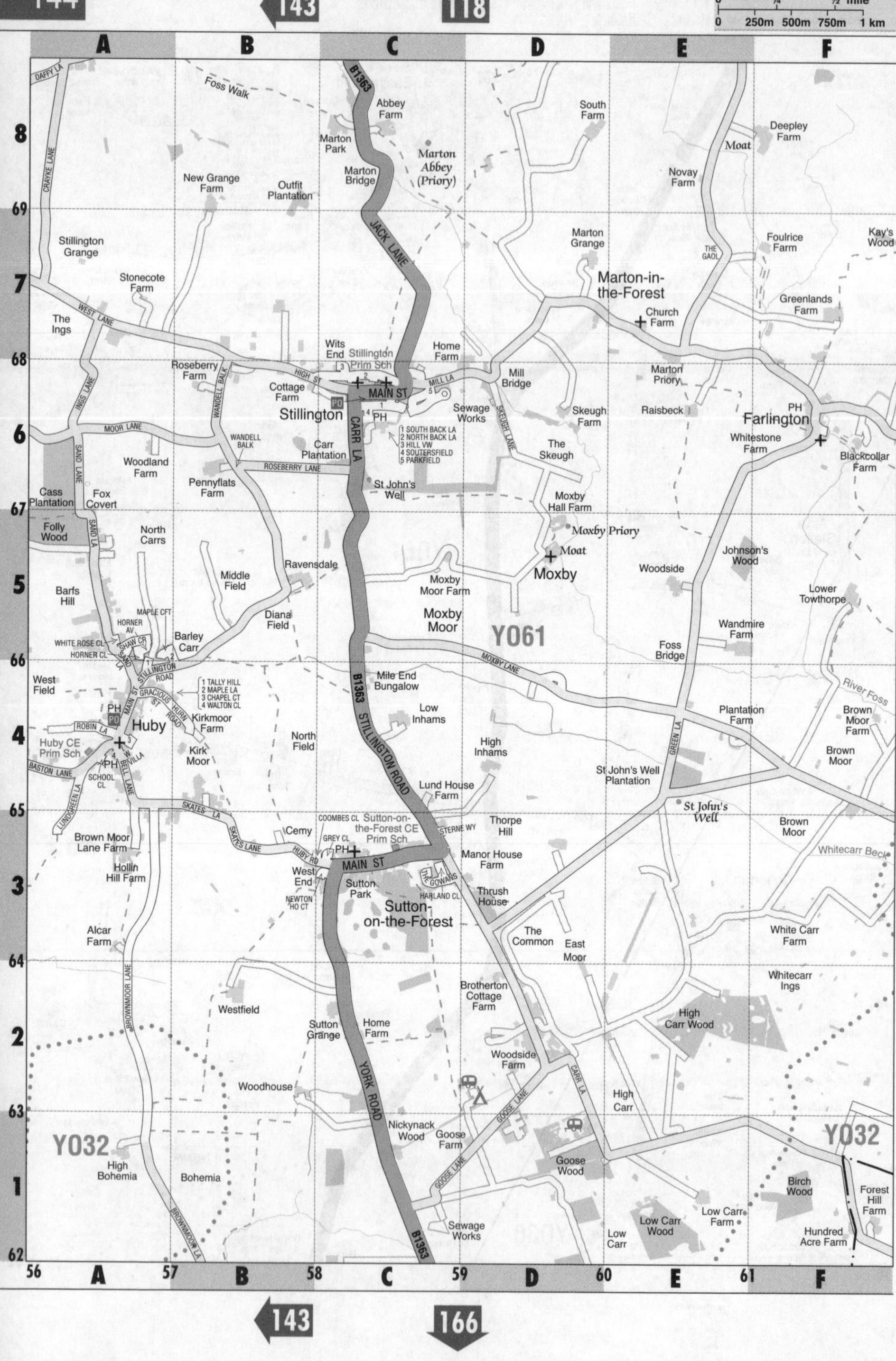
Stillington
Huby
Sutton-on-the-Forest
Marton-in-the-Forest
Farlington
Moxby
Moxby Moor
YO61
YO32
Marton Abbey (Priory)
Moxby Priory
St John's Well
Abbey Farm
Marton Park
Marton Bridge
New Grange Farm
Outfit Plantation
Stillington Grange
Stonecote Farm
The Ings
South Farm
Deepley Farm
Moat
Novay Farm
Marton Grange
Foulrice Farm
Kay's Wood
Greenlands Farm
Church Farm
Roseberry Farm
Wits End
Stillington Prim Sch
Home Farm
Mill Bridge
Marton Priory
Raisbeck
Whitestone Farm
Blackcollar Farm
Cottage Farm
Sewage Works
Skeugh Farm
The Skeugh
Woodland Farm
Pennyflats Farm
Carr Plantation
Cass Plantation
Fox Covert
Folly Wood
North Carrs
Moxby Hall Farm
Johnson's Wood
Woodside
Ravensdale
Middle Field
Moxby Moor Farm
Barfs Hill
Diana Field
Lower Towthorpe
Wandmire Farm
Barley Carr
Foss Bridge
West Field
Mile End Bungalow
Low Inhams
Plantation Farm
Brown Moor Farm
Kirkmoor Farm
Huby CE Prim Sch
North Field
Kirk Moor
High Inhams
Brown Moor
St John's Well Plantation
Lund House Farm
Brown Moor Lane Farm
Cemy
Sutton-on-the-Forest CE Prim Sch
Thorpe Hill
Manor House Farm
Whitecarr Beck
Hollin Hill Farm
West End
Sutton Park
Thrush House
Alcar Farm
The Common
East Moor
White Carr Farm
Whitecarr Ings
Brotherton Cottage Farm
Westfield
High Carr Wood
Sutton Grange
Home Farm
Woodside Farm
Woodhouse
High Carr
Nickynack Wood
Goose Farm
Goose Wood
High Bohemia
Bohemia
Birch Wood
Forest Hill Farm
Low Carr Wood
Low Carr Farm
Low Carr
Hundred Acre Farm
Sewage Works
River Foss
Foss Walk
JACK LANE
B1363
CARR LA
STILLINGTON ROAD
YORK ROAD
HIGH ST
MAIN ST
MILL LA
SKEUGH LANE
WANDELL BALK
ROSEBERRY LANE
MOXBY LANE
GREEN LA
CRAYKE LANE
DAFFY LA
WEST LANE
INGS LANE
MOOR LANE
SAND LANE
SKATES LANE
HUBY RD
BROWNMOOR LANE
GOOSE LANE
BASTON LANE
LUNDGREEN LA
BELL LANE
ROBIN LA
SCHOOL CL
STILLINGTON ROAD
1 SOUTH BACK LA
2 NORTH BACK LA
3 HILL VW
4 SOUTERSFIELD
5 PARKFIELD
1 TALLY HILL
2 MAPLE LA
3 CHAPEL CT
4 WALTON CL
HORNER AV
MAPLE CFT
WHITE ROSE CL
HORNER CL
SHAW CR
COOMBES CL
GREY CL
NEWTON HO CT
STERNE WY
THE GOWANS
HARLAND CL
THE GAOL
A B C D E F
56 57 58 59 60 61
62 63 64 65 66 67 68 69
1 2 3 4 5 6 7 8

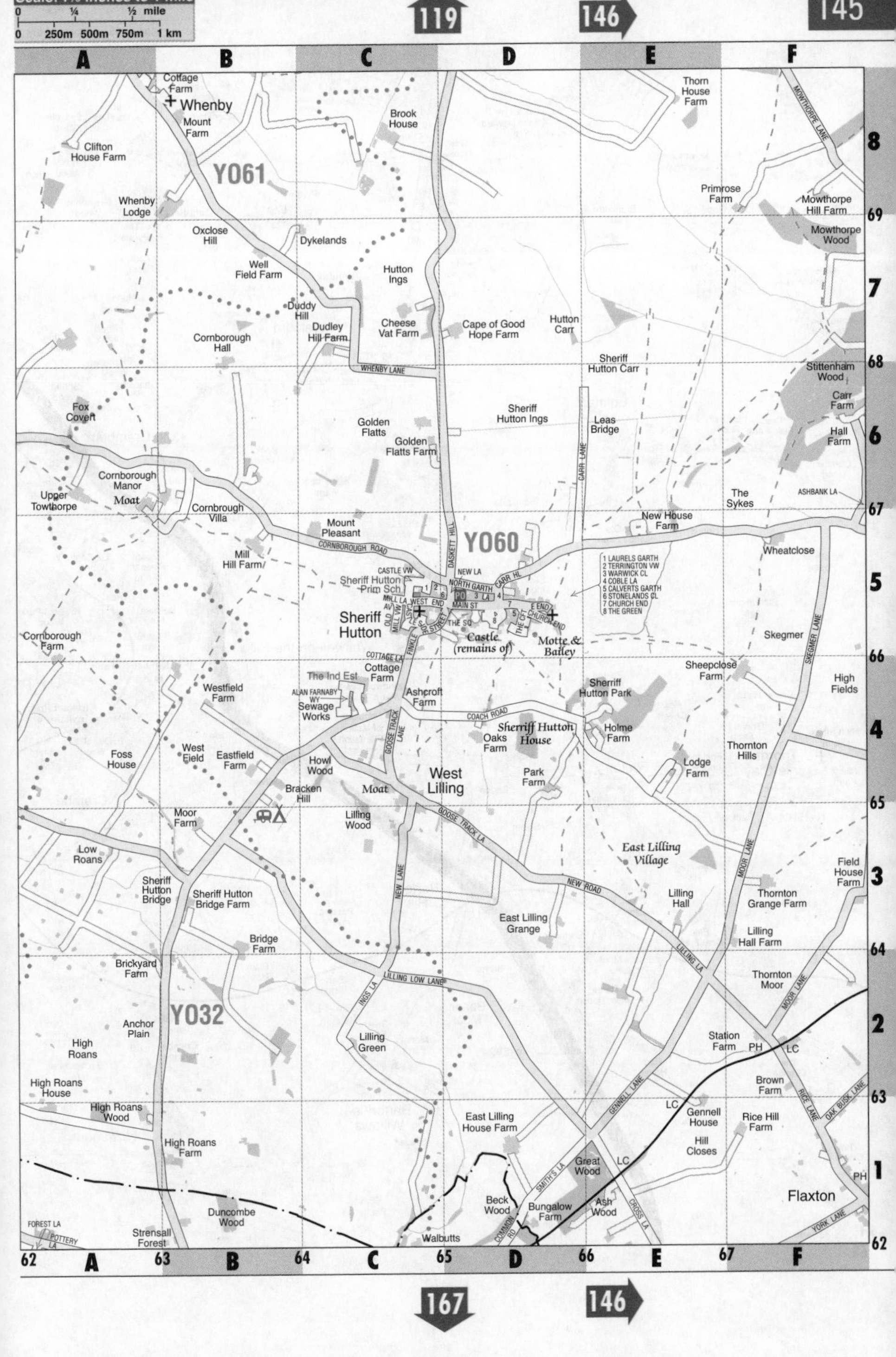
Scale: 1⅓ inches to 1 mile
119
146
Whenby
Cottage Farm
Mount Farm
Clifton House Farm
YO61
Whenby Lodge
Oxclose Hill
Dykelands
Well Field Farm
Brook House
Hutton Ings
Duddy Hill
Dudley Hill Farm
Cheese Vat Farm
Cape of Good Hope Farm
Hutton Carr
Cornborough Hall
Thorn House Farm
Primrose Farm
Mowthorpe Hill Farm
Mowthorpe Wood
MOWTHORPE LANE
Sheriff Hutton Carr
Stittenham Wood
Carr Farm
Hall Farm
WHENBY LANE
Fox Covert
Golden Flatts
Golden Flatts Farm
Sheriff Hutton Ings
Leas Bridge
CARR LANE
Cornborough Manor
Moat
Upper Towthorpe
Cornbrough Villa
The Sykes
ASHBANK LA
New House Farm
Mount Pleasant
DASKETT HILL
YO60
Wheatclose
CORNBOROUGH ROAD
Mill Hill Farm
1 LAURELS GARTH
2 TERRINGTON VW
3 WARWICK CL
4 COBLE LA
5 CALVERTS GARTH
6 STONELANDS CL
7 CHURCH END
8 THE GREEN
Sheriff Hutton Prim Sch
Sheriff Hutton
Castle (remains of)
Motte & Bailey
Skegmer
Cornborough Farm
COTTAGE LA
Cottage Farm
The Ind Est
Sheepclose Farm
High Fields
Westfield Farm
Sewage Works
Ashcroft Farm
Sherriff Hutton Park
SKEGMER LANE
COACH ROAD
Sheriff Hutton House
Holme Farm
Foss House
West Field
Eastfield Farm
Howl Wood
Oaks Farm
Thornton Hills
West Lilling
Lodge Farm
Park Farm
Bracken Hill
Moat
Moor Farm
Lilling Wood
GOOSE TRACK LA
Low Roans
East Lilling Village
MOOR LANE
Field House Farm
Sheriff Hutton Bridge
Sheriff Hutton Bridge Farm
NEW ROAD
Lilling Hall
Thornton Grange Farm
NEW LANE
East Lilling Grange
Bridge Farm
Lilling Hall Farm
Brickyard Farm
LILLING LOW LANE
LILLING LA
Thornton Moor
YO32
Anchor Plain
Lilling Green
High Roans
Station Farm
PH
LC
High Roans House
Brown Farm
High Roans Wood
East Lilling House Farm
Gennell House
Rice Hill Farm
High Roans Farm
Hill Closes
Great Wood
LC
Duncombe Wood
Beck Wood
Bungalow Farm
Ash Wood
Flaxton
FOREST LA
POTTERY LA
Strensall Forest
Walbutts
YORK LANE
OAK BUSK LANE
RICE LANE
GENNELL LANE
SMITH'S LA
CROSS LA
COMMON RD
INGS LA
GOOSE TRACK LANE
FINKLE
A B C D E F
62 63 64 65 66 67
1 2 3 4 5 6 7 8
62 63 64 65 66 67 68 69
167
146

145
120

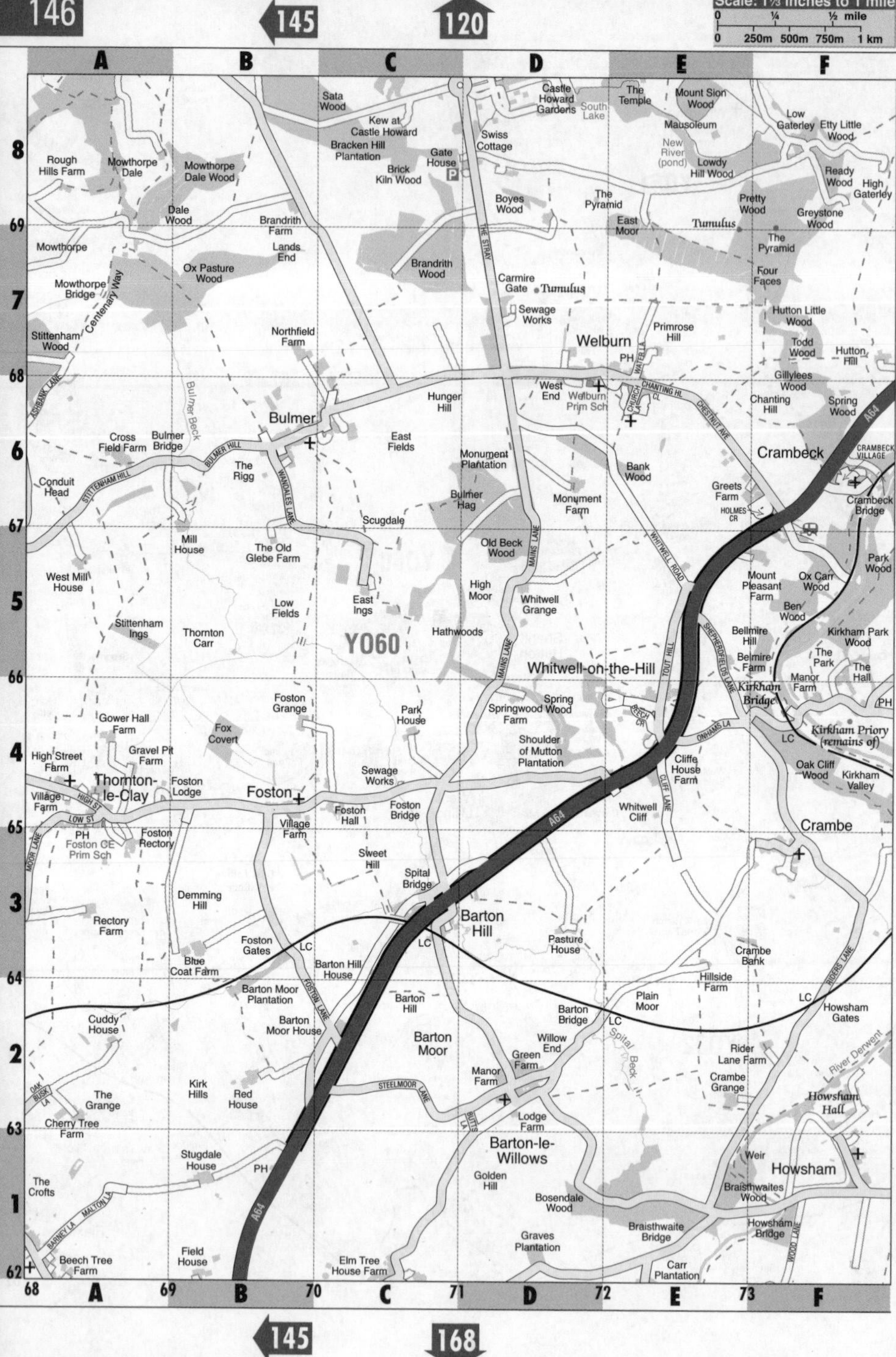
Scale: 1⅓ inches to 1 mile
0 ¼ ½ mile
0 250m 500m 750m 1 km
A
B
C
D
E
F
8
69
7
68
6
67
5
66
4
65
3
64
2
63
1
62
68
69
70
71
72
73
Sata Wood
Kew at Castle Howard
Bracken Hill Plantation
Brick Kiln Wood
Gate House
Swiss Cottage
Castle Howard Gardens
South Lake
The Temple
Mount Sion Wood
Mausoleum
New River (pond)
Lowdy Hill Wood
Low Gaterley
Etty Little Wood
Ready Wood
High Gaterley
Rough Hills Farm
Mowthorpe Dale
Mowthorpe Dale Wood
Dale Wood
Boyes Wood
The Pyramid
East Moor
Pretty Wood
Greystone Wood
Tumulus
The Pyramid
Four Faces
Mowthorpe
Brandrith Farm
Lands End
Ox Pasture Wood
Brandrith Wood
THE STRAY
Mowthorpe Bridge
Centenary Way
Carmire Gate
Tumulus
Sewage Works
Stittenham Wood
Northfield Farm
Primrose Hill
Welburn
Hutton Little Wood
Todd Wood
Hutton Hill
PH
WATER LA
ASHBANK LANE
Bulmer Beck
West End
Welburn Prim Sch
CHURCH LA
CHANTING HL
CL
CHESTNUT AVE
Gillylees Wood
Chanting Hill
Spring Wood
Hunger Hill
Bulmer
Cross Field Farm
Bulmer Bridge
BULMER HILL
East Fields
Monument Plantation
Crambeck
CRAMBECK VILLAGE
A64
Conduit Head
STITTENHAM HILL
The Rigg
WANDALES LANE
Bank Wood
Greets Farm
HOLMES CR
Crambeck Bridge
Bulmer Hag
Monument Farm
Scugdale
Mill House
The Old Glebe Farm
Old Beck Wood
MAINS LANE
WHITWELL ROAD
West Mill House
High Moor
Whitwell Grange
Mount Pleasant Farm
Ox Carr Wood
Park Wood
Low Fields
East Ings
Ben Wood
Stittenham Ings
Thornton Carr
Hathwoods
Y060
MAINS LANE
TOUT HILL
SHEPHERDFIELDS LANE
Bellmire Hill
Belmire Farm
Kirkham Park Wood
The Park
The Hall
Manor Farm
Whitwell-on-the-Hill
Kirkham Bridge
BEECH CR
PH
Foston Grange
Park House
Springwood Farm
Spring Wood
Gower Hall Farm
Fox Covert
Shoulder of Mutton Plantation
ONHAMS LA
Kirkham Priory (remains of)
LC
High Street Farm
Gravel Pit Farm
Cliffe House Farm
Oak Cliff Wood
Kirkham Valley
Thornton-le-Clay
Foston Lodge
Foston
Sewage Works
CLIFF LANE
Village Farm
HIGH ST
Foston Hall
Foston Bridge
Whitwell Cliff
LOW ST
Village Farm
Crambe
PH
Foston CE Prim Sch
Foston Rectory
MOOR LANE
Sweet Hill
Spital Bridge
Demming Hill
Barton Hill
Rectory Farm
Foston Gates
LC
LC
Pasture House
Barton Hill House
Crambe Bank
Blue Coat Farm
Hillside Farm
Barton Moor Plantation
FOSTON LANE
Barton Hill
Plain Moor
RIDERS LANE
LC
Howsham Gates
Cuddy House
Barton Moor House
Barton Bridge
LC
Barton Moor
Willow End
Spital Beck
River Derwent
Rider Lane Farm
Green Farm
Manor Farm
OAK BUSK LA
STEELMOOR LANE
Kirk Hills
Red House
Crambe Grange
The Grange
BUTTS LA
Howsham Hall
Lodge Farm
Cherry Tree Farm
Barton-le-Willows
Stugdale House
PH
Weir
Howsham
The Crofts
Golden Hill
Braisthwaites Wood
MALTON LA
BARNEY LA
Bosendale Wood
Braisthwaite Bridge
Howsham Bridge
WOOD LANE
Graves Plantation
Field House
Beech Tree Farm
Elm Tree House Farm
Carr Plantation

145
168

121
148
215

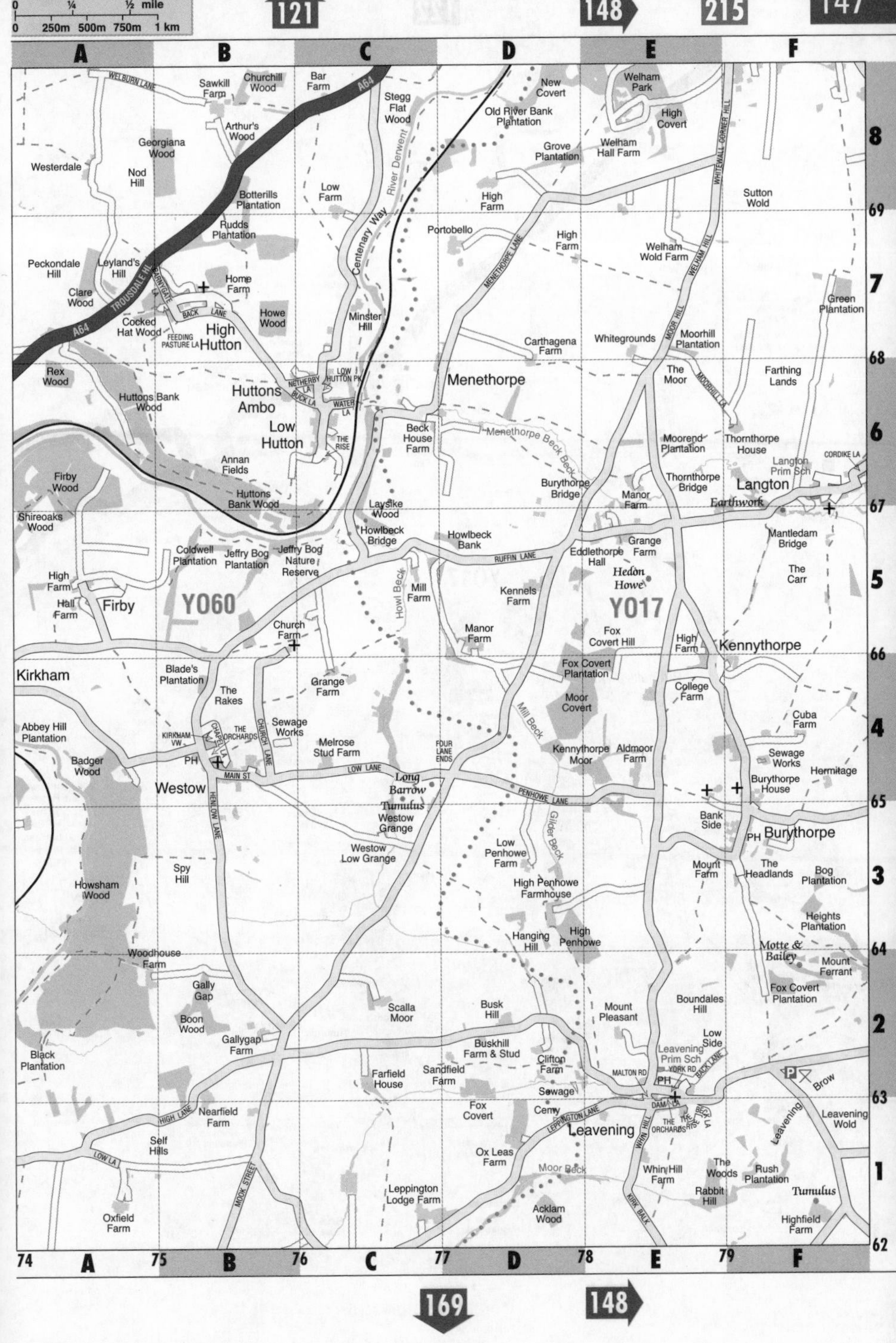
Scale: 1⅓ inches to 1 mile
0
¼
½ mile
0
250m
500m
750m
1 km
A
B
C
D
E
F
Welburn Lane
Sawkill Farm
Churchill Wood
Bar Farm
A64
Stegg Flat Wood
New Covert
Old River Bank Plantation
Welham Park
High Covert
Whitewall Corner Hill
Arthur's Wood
Georgiana Wood
Westerdale
Nod Hill
Grove Plantation
Welham Hall Farm
8
Botterills Plantation
Low Farm
River Derwent
High Farm
Sutton Wold
69
Rudds Plantation
Centenary Way
Portobello
Menethorpe Lane
High Farm
Welham Hill
Welham Wold Farm
Peckondale Hill
Leyland's Hill
Trousdale Hl
Barnygate La
Home Farm
Clare Wood
7
Back Lane
Howe Wood
Minster Hill
Moor Hill
Green Plantation
Cocked Hat Wood
High Hutton
Feeding Pasture La
Carthagena Farm
Whitegrounds
Moorhill Plantation
Rex Wood
Netherby La
Low Hutton Pk
Menethorpe
The Moor
Farthing Lands
68
Huttons Bank Wood
Huttons Ambo
Buck La
Water La
Moorhill La
Low Hutton
The Rise
Beck House Farm
Menethorpe Beck
Moorend Plantation
Thornthorpe House
6
Annan Fields
Beck
Langton Prim Sch
Cordike La
Firby Wood
Burythorpe Bridge
Thornthorpe Bridge
Langton
Huttons Bank Wood
Manor Farm
Earthwork
Shireoaks Wood
Layske Wood
67
Howlbeck Bridge
Howlbeck Bank
Grange Farm
Mantledam Bridge
Coldwell Plantation
Jeffry Bog Plantation
Jeffry Bog Nature Reserve
Ruffin Lane
Eddlethorpe Hall
Hedon Howe
High Farm
Howl Beck
Mill Farm
The Carr
5
Y060
Kennels Farm
Y017
Hall Farm
Firby
Church Farm
Fox Covert Hill
Manor Farm
High Farm
Kennythorpe
Kirkham
Blade's Plantation
66
Fox Covert Plantation
College Farm
The Rakes
Grange Farm
Moor Covert
Mill Beck
Cuba Farm
Abbey Hill Plantation
Kirkham Vw
Chapel La
The Orchards
Church Lane
Sewage Works
4
Melrose Stud Farm
Four Lane Ends
Kennythorpe Moor
Aldmoor Farm
Sewage Works
Badger Wood
PH
Low Lane
Main St
Long Barrow
Hermitage
Burythorpe House
Westow
Penhowe Lane
Tumulus
65
Westow Grange
Bank Side
Henlow Lane
Gilder Beck
PH
Burythorpe
Westow Low Grange
Low Penhowe Farm
Mount Farm
The Headlands
Bog Plantation
Spy Hill
3
Howsham Wood
High Penhowe Farmhouse
Heights Plantation
Hanging Hill
High Penhowe
Motte & Bailey
Mount Ferrant
64
Woodhouse Farm
Gally Gap
Fox Covert Plantation
Boundales Hill
Scalla Moor
Busk Hill
Mount Pleasant
2
Boon Wood
Gallygap Farm
Low Side
Buskhill Farm & Stud
Leavening Prim Sch
Black Plantation
Clifton Farm
Malton Rd
York Rd
Back Lane
Brow
Farfield House
Sandfield Farm
PH
63
Sewage
High Lane
Nearfield Farm
Fox Covert
Cemy
Dam La
The Orchards
The Rise
Beck La
Leavening Wold
Leppington Lane
Leavening
Self Hills
Whin Hill
Low La
Ox Leas Farm
Moor Beck
Leavening
The Woods
Rush Plantation
1
Whin Hill Farm
Mook Street
Leppington Lodge Farm
Kirk Balk
Rabbit Hill
Tumulus
Oxfield Farm
Acklam Wood
Highfield Farm
62
74
A
75
B
76
C
77
D
78
E
79
F

169
148

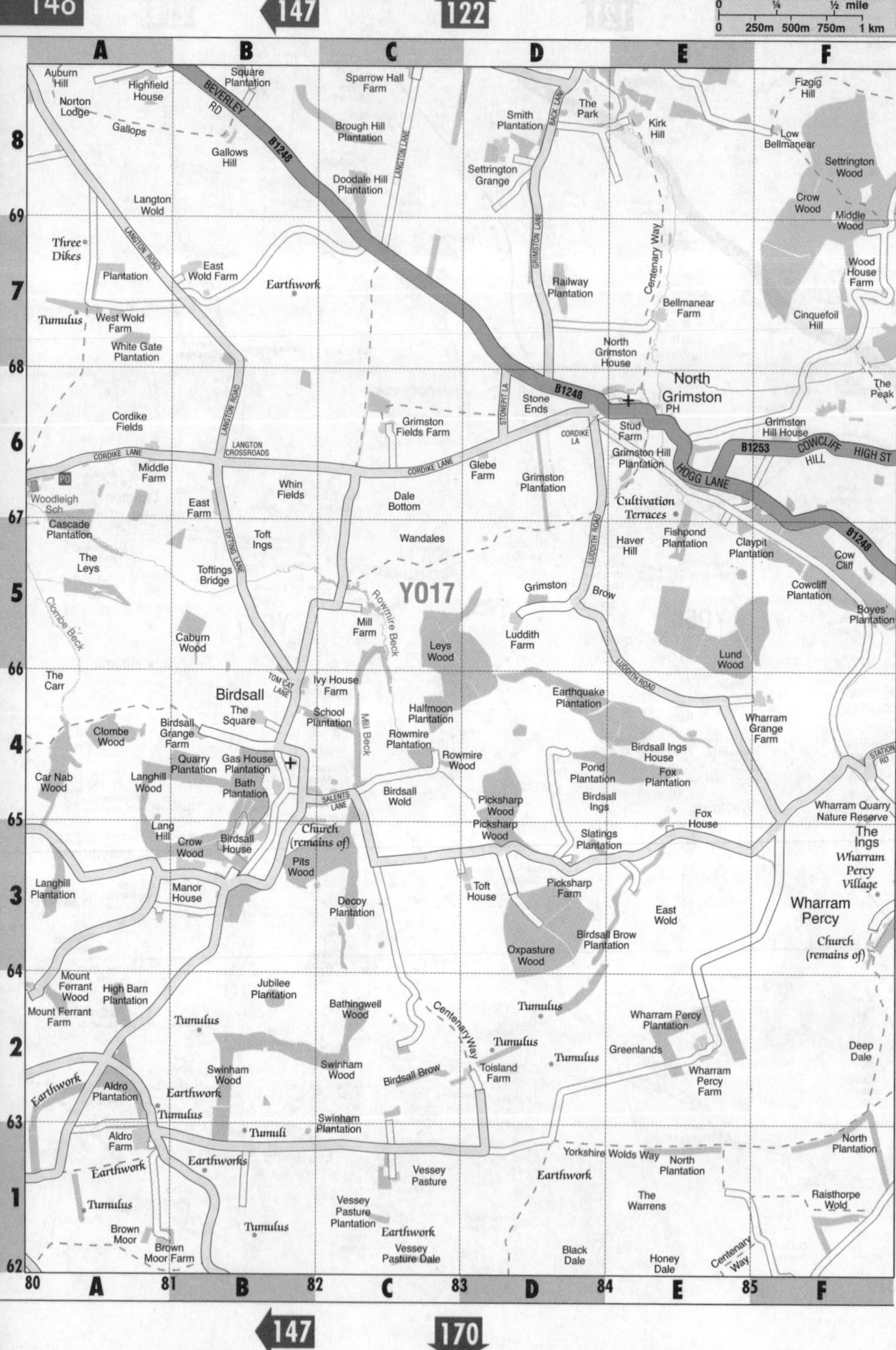

147

122

Scale: 1⅓ inches to 1 mile

0   ¼   ½ mile

0   250m   500m   750m   1 km

Row 8
Auburn Hill
Norton Lodge
Highfield House
Square Plantation
BEVERLEY RD
Sparrow Hall Farm
Smith Plantation
The Park
Kirk Hill
Fizigg Hill
Low Bellmanear
Settrington Wood
Gallops
Gallows Hill
Brough Hill Plantation
B1248
Doodale Hill Plantation
Settrington Grange
Crow Wood
Middle Wood

Row 69
Langton Wold
LANGTON LANE
Railway Plantation
Centenary Way
Wood House Farm

Row 7
Three Dikes
Plantation
East Wold Farm
Earthwork
Bellmanear Farm
Cinquefoil Hill
Tumulus
West Wold Farm
White Gate Plantation
North Grimston House
LANGTON ROAD

Row 68
Cordike Fields
STONEPIT LA
Stone Ends
B1248
North Grimston
PH
The Peak
Grimston Fields Farm
Glebe Farm
CORDIKE LA
Stud Farm
Grimston Hill House
Grimston Hill Plantation
Grimston Plantation
HOGG LANE
B1253
COWCLIFF HILL
HIGH ST

Row 6
Cordike Lane
CORDIKE LANE
Langton Crossroads
Middle Farm
Whin Fields
Dale Bottom
Cultivation Terraces
Haver Hill
Fishpond Plantation
Claypit Plantation
Cow Cliff
B1248

Row 67
Woodleigh Sch
PO
East Farm
Toft Ings
Wandales
Grimston
Brow
Cowcliff Plantation
Boyes' Plantation
Cascade Plantation
TATEPITS LANE
Toftings Bridge

Row 5
The Leys
Clombe Beck
Caburn Wood
Mill Farm
Rowmire Beck
YO17
Leys Wood
Luddith Farm
LUDDITH ROAD
Lund Wood

Row 66
The Carr
Ivy House Farm
School Plantation
Halfmoon Plantation
Earthquake Plantation
Birdsall Ings House
Wharram Grange Farm
TOM CAT LANE
Birdsall
The Square
Clombe Wood
Birdsall Grange Farm
Quarry Plantation
Gas House Plantation
Rowmire Plantation
Rowmire Wood
Pond Plantation
Fox Plantation
Birdsall Ings
STATION RD
Wharram Quarry Nature Reserve

Row 4
Car Nab Wood
Langhill Wood
Bath Plantation
Mill Beck
SALENTS LANE
Birdsall Wold
Pickshary Wood
Birdsall Ings
Fox House
The Ings
Wharram Percy Village

Row 65
Lang Hill
Crow Wood
Birdsall House
Church (remains of)
Pits Wood
Pickshary Wood
Slatings Plantation
Wharram Percy
Langhill Plantation
Manor House
Decoy Plantation
Toft House
Pickshary Farm
East Wold
Church (remains of)

Row 64
Mount Ferrant Wood
High Barn Plantation
Jubilee Plantation
Bathingwell Wood
Oxpasture Wood
Birdsall Brow Plantation
Wharram Percy Plantation
Greenlands
Deep Dale
Mount Ferrant Farm

Row 2
Earthwork
Aldro Plantation
Tumulus
Swinham Wood
Swinham Wood
Birdsall Brow
Centenary Way
Tumulus
Tumulus
Tumulus
Toisland Farm
Wharram Percy Farm

Row 63
Aldro Farm
Tumulus
Swinham Plantation
North Plantation

Row 1
Earthwork
Earthworks
Vessey Pasture
Yorkshire Wolds Way
North Plantation
Earthwork
The Warrens
Raisthorpe Wold
Tumulus
Vessey Pasture Plantation
Earthwork
Black Dale
Honey Dale
Centenary Way

Row 62
Brown Moor
Brown Moor Farm
Tumuli
Vessey Pasture Dale

Columns: A 80   B 81   C 82   D 83   E 84   F 85

147

170

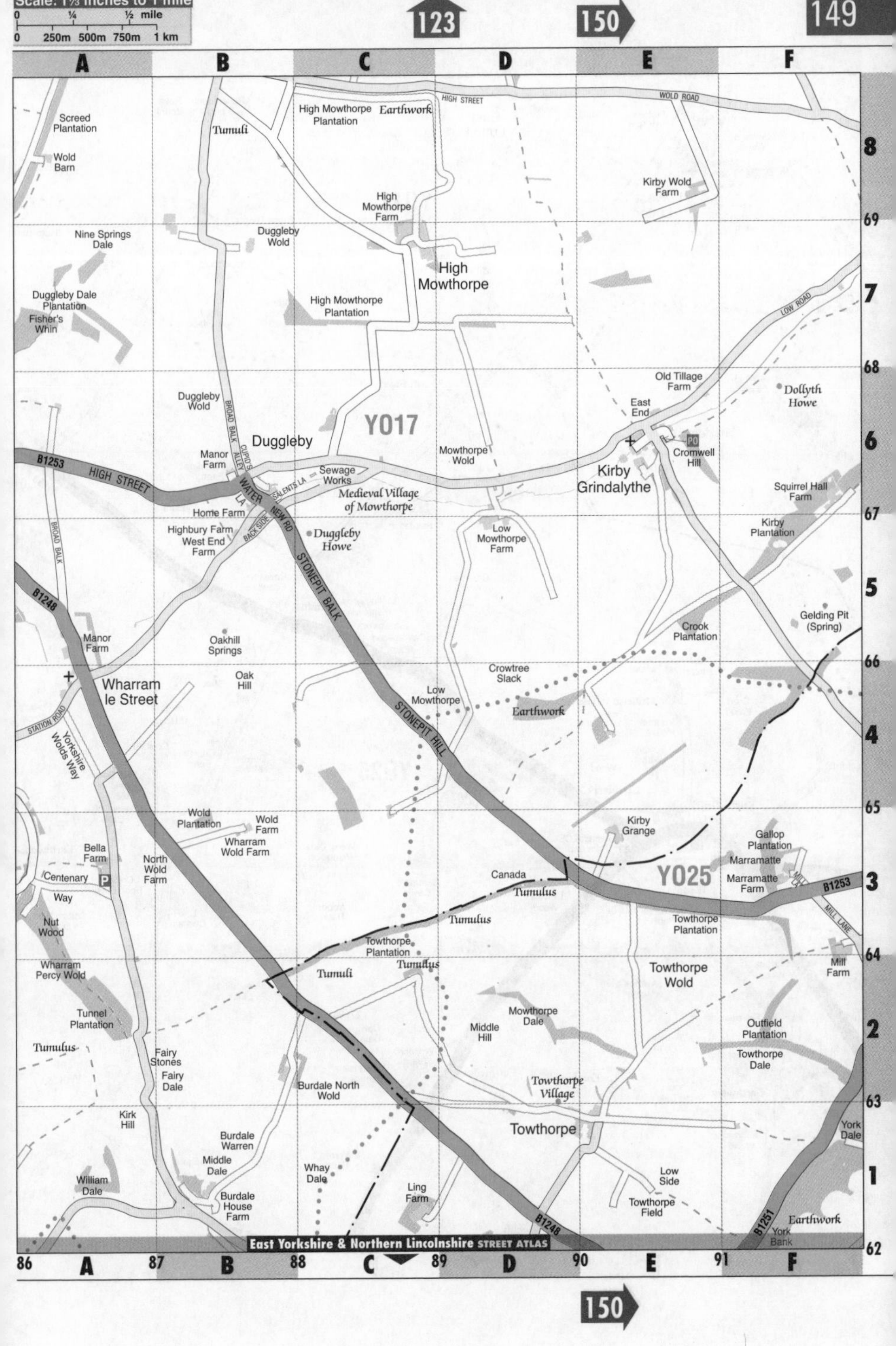
Scale: 1⅓ inches to 1 mile
0 ¼ ½ mile
0 250m 500m 750m 1 km
123
150
A B C D E F
Screed Plantation
Wold Barn
Tumuli
High Mowthorpe Plantation
Earthwork
HIGH STREET
WOLD ROAD
High Mowthorpe Farm
Kirby Wold Farm
Nine Springs Dale
Duggleby Wold
High Mowthorpe
Duggleby Dale Plantation
Fisher's Whin
High Mowthorpe Plantation
LOW ROAD
Old Tillage Farm
Dollyth Howe
East End
YO17
Duggleby
Manor Farm
Mowthorpe Wold
Cromwell Hill
Kirby Grindalythe
B1253
HIGH STREET
WATER LA
Sewage Works
SALENTS LA
Medieval Village of Mowthorpe
Squirrel Hall Farm
Home Farm
Highbury Farm
West End Farm
BACK SIDE
NEW RD
Duggleby Howe
Low Mowthorpe Farm
Kirby Plantation
BROAD BALK
B1248
STONEPIT BALK
Gelding Pit (Spring)
Crook Plantation
Manor Farm
Oakhill Springs
Oak Hill
Wharram le Street
Crowtree Slack
Low Mowthorpe
Earthwork
STATION ROAD
Yorkshire Wolds Way
STONEPIT HILL
Wold Plantation
Wold Farm
Wharram Wold Farm
Kirby Grange
Gallop Plantation
Bella Farm
North Wold Farm
Marramatte
Centenary Way
Canada
YO25
Marramatte Farm
Tumulus
B1253
MILL LANE
Tumulus
Towthorpe Plantation
Nut Wood
Towthorpe Plantation
Tumuli
Tumulus
Towthorpe Wold
Mill Farm
Wharram Percy Wold
Mowthorpe Dale
Middle Hill
Outfield Plantation
Tunnel Plantation
Tumulus
Towthorpe Dale
Fairy Stones
Fairy Dale
Burdale North Wold
Towthorpe Village
Kirk Hill
Towthorpe
York Dale
Burdale Warren
Middle Dale
Whay Dale
Low Side
William Dale
Ling Farm
Burdale House Farm
Towthorpe Field
B1251
Earthwork
York Bank
B1248
East Yorkshire & Northern Lincolnshire STREET ATLAS
8
69
7
68
6
67
5
66
4
65
3
64
2
63
1
62
86 87 88 89 90 91

150

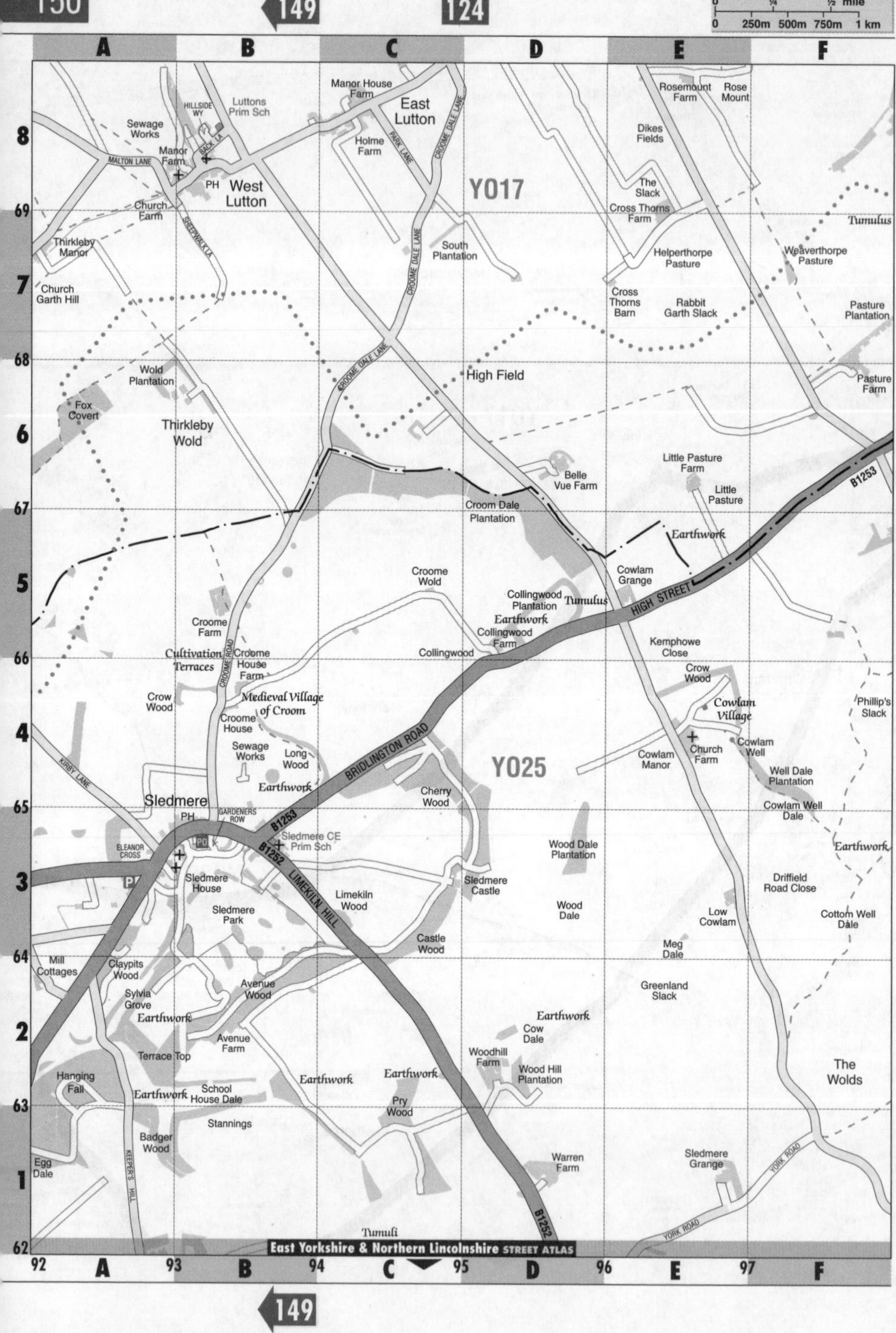

150

149

124

Scale: 1⅓ inches to 1 mile
0   ¼   ½ mile
0 250m 500m 750m 1 km

A **B** **C** **D** **E** **F**

8

HILLSIDE WY

Luttons Prim Sch

Manor House Farm

East Lutton

Rosemount Farm

Rose Mount

Sewage Works

MALTON LANE

Manor Farm

Holme Farm

Dikes Fields

69

PH

West Lutton

YO17

The Slack

Tumulus

Church Farm

GREENACRE LA

Cross Thorns Farm

Thirkleby Manor

South Plantation

Helperthorpe Pasture

Weaverthorpe Pasture

7

Church Garth Hill

CROOME DALE LANE

Cross Thorns Barn

Rabbit Garth Slack

Pasture Plantation

68

Wold Plantation

High Field

Pasture Farm

6

Fox Covert

Thirkleby Wold

Little Pasture Farm

Little Pasture

B1253

67

Croom Dale Plantation

Belle Vue Farm

Earthwork

5

Croome Wold

Collingwood Plantation

Tumulus

Cowlam Grange

HIGH STREET

Croome Farm

CROOME ROAD

Earthwork

Collingwood Farm

Kemphowe Close

Crow Wood

66

Cultivation Terraces

Croome House Farm

Collingwood

Cowlam Village

Phillip's Slack

Crow Wood

Croome Village

Cowlam Manor

Church Farm

Cowlam Well

4

HURST LANE

Medieval Village of Croom

Sewage Works

Long Wood

BRIDLINGTON ROAD

YO25

Well Dale Plantation

Cowlam Well Dale

Earthwork

Sledmere

Earthwork

Cherry Wood

Earthwork

65

PH

GARDENERS ROW

B1253

Wood Dale Plantation

Driffield Road Close

ELEANOR CROSS

PO

Sledmere CE Prim Sch

B1252

Limekiln Wood

Cottom Well Dale

3

P

Sledmere House

LIMEKILN HILL

Sledmere Castle

Wood Dale

Low Cowlam

Sledmere Park

Castle Wood

Meg Dale

64

Mill Cottages

Claypits Wood

Avenue Wood

Greenland Slack

Sylvia Grove

Earthwork

The Wolds

2

Avenue Farm

Earthwork

Earthwork

Earthwork

Cow Dale

Terrace Top

Woodhill Farm

Hanging Fall

School House Dale

Earthwork

Pry Wood

Wood Hill Plantation

63

KEEPERS HILL

Badger Wood

Stannings

Warren Farm

Sledmere Grange

YORK ROAD

1

Egg Dale

B1252

Tumuli

62

East Yorkshire & Northern Lincolnshire STREET ATLAS

A 93 **B** 94 **C** 95 **D** 96 **E** 97 **F**

92

YORK ROAD

149

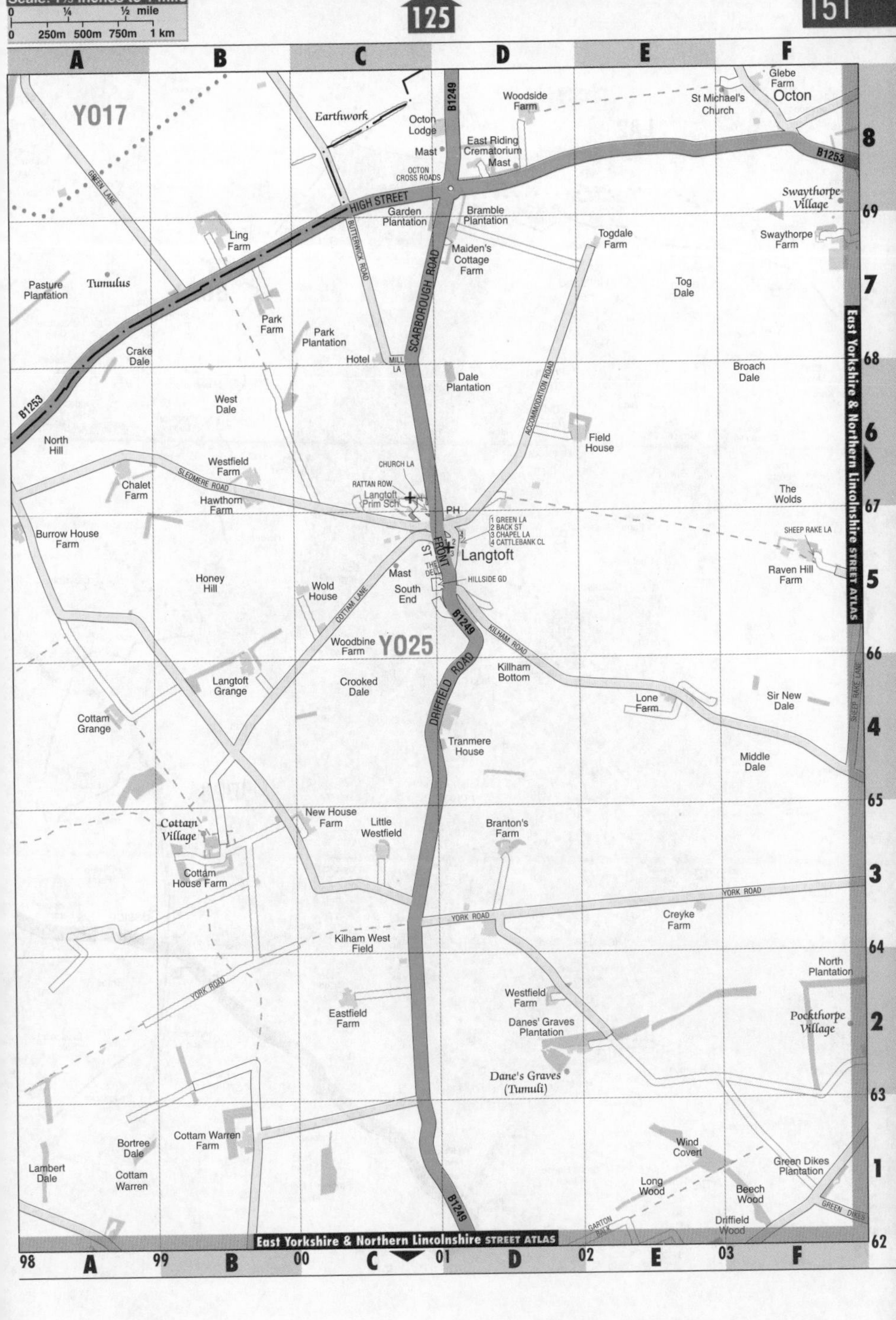

Scale: 1½ inches to 1 mile

0   ¼   ½ mile
0   250m 500m 750m 1 km

A   B   C   D   E   F

YO17

Earthwork

Octon Lodge

Woodside Farm

St Michael's Church

Glebe Farm
Octon

B1249

8

East Riding Crematorium Mast

Mast

B1253

OCTON CROSS ROADS

Swaythorpe Village

69

HIGH STREET

Garden Plantation

Bramble Plantation

Swaythorpe Farm

Ling Farm

BUTTERWICK ROAD

Maiden's Cottage Farm

Togdale Farm

7

Pasture Plantation

Tumulus

SCARBOROUGH ROAD

Tog Dale

Park Farm

Park Plantation

Hotel

Dale Plantation

ACCOMMODATION ROAD

68

B1253

Crake Dale

MILL LA

Broach Dale

North Hill

West Dale

Dale Plantation

Field House

6

Westfield Farm

SLEDMERE ROAD

CHURCH LA

The Wolds

Chalet Farm

RATTAN ROW

Langtoft Prim Sch

PH

SHEEP RAKE LA

67

Hawthorn Farm

1 GREEN LA
2 BACK ST
3 CHAPEL LA
4 CATTLEBANK CL

Raven Hill Farm

Burrow House Farm

COTTAM LANE

Langtoft

Honey Hill

Wold House

THE DELL

Mast

5

ST

South End

HILLSIDE GD

Woodbine Farm

YO25

KILHAM ROAD

66

Langtoft Grange

Crooked Dale

DRIFFIELD ROAD

Killham Bottom

Sir New Dale

Cottam Grange

Lone Farm

4

Tranmere House

Middle Dale

65

New House Farm

Little Westfield

Branton's Farm

Cottam Village

3

Cottam House Farm

YORK ROAD

Creyke Farm

YORK ROAD

Kilham West Field

64

YORK ROAD

Westfield Farm

North Plantation

Eastfield Farm

Danes' Graves Plantation

Pockthorpe Village

2

Dane's Graves (Tumuli)

63

Wind Covert

Green Dikes Plantation

Lambert Dale

Bortree Dale

Cottam Warren Farm

Long Wood

Beech Wood

GREEN DIKES

1

Cottam Warren

B1248

GARTON

Driffield Wood

62

98   A   99   B   00   C   01   D   02   E   03   F

Scale: 1½ inches to 1 mile

0   ¼   ½ mile
0   250m 500m 750m 1 km

A   **B**   **C**   **D**   **E**   **F**

Clapham Common
Round Hill
Frere Dike
Bents Hill
Foster's Craggs
Mill Stone
Knottend Well
Bowland Knotts
Crutchenber Fell
Old Moss
Cat Knot Well
Pike Side
The Height
Swire Clough Head
Green Pike
Higher Clough Farm
Lower Clough
New House
Holme House Wood
Nan Brow
Eak Hill
Ten Acre Hill
Black House

LA2

Austwick Common
Brown Bank
Top of The Clough
Hanging Stone
Green Knots
Knotteranum
Hell Hole
Birch Clough Rigg
Crutchenber Fell Gate
Gisburn Forest
Dalehead Farm
Coat Rakes Bridge
Cocklick End
Hasgill Wood
Hasgill
Rushton Hill
Laverick Hill
Hammerton Mere
Lower Barn
Brook House Green

Halstead Fell

BB7

White Swan Moss
Lawkland Fell
Rock Cat Knott
Great Hill
Fair Hill Copy
Sheep Hill
Old Moss
How Hill
Halsteads Farm
Old Ing
White Hill House
Hindley Head Clough
Hesbert Hall
Gisburn Forest
Ford
Park Wood
Bridge House Wood
Stephen Park
Causeway
Cocklet Hill
Four Lanes Ends
Wellhouse Farm

Black Hill
Resting Stone
Fair Hill Fell
Fair Hill
Dob Dale
Whelp Stone Crag
Herd Hill
Bottom Heights
Hindley Head
Tennel Hill Quarry
Quarry
Black Hill
Higher Sandy Sike
Skirden Hall Plantation
Moss End
High Head
Brock Thorn
Well House
Marl Barn
Stephen Moor Lodge

Gisburn Forest

BD23

Hesbert Hall Heights
Heath Farm
Holden Moor
Brayshaw
Long Gill Brook
Owlshaw
Whelpstone Lodge
Longtons Farm
The Plantation
Skirden Hall
Hartleys Farm
Higher Ghylls
Ghylls
Little Beck

Tosside
Skirden PH
B6478
Dam Head
Trees
Melling Dab
Tosside Fold
Sedgwicks Farm
Cracoe Hill Farm
Snape House Farm
Olivers Farm
Beck House Farm
Bent House

Giggleswick Common
Foxholes Crag
Big Hill
Rathmell Common
Gisburn Common
Badger Moss
Badger Hill
Bullhurst Pike
Bull Hurst
Black Hill
Cross Hills
Winterscale Bank Farm
Low Folds
Scouter Crag
Scouter End
Ragged Hall

BD24

Old Oliver Lane

Lancashire STREET ATLAS

Lancashire Street Atlas

72 **A** 73 **B** 74 **C** **D** 76 **E** 77 **F**

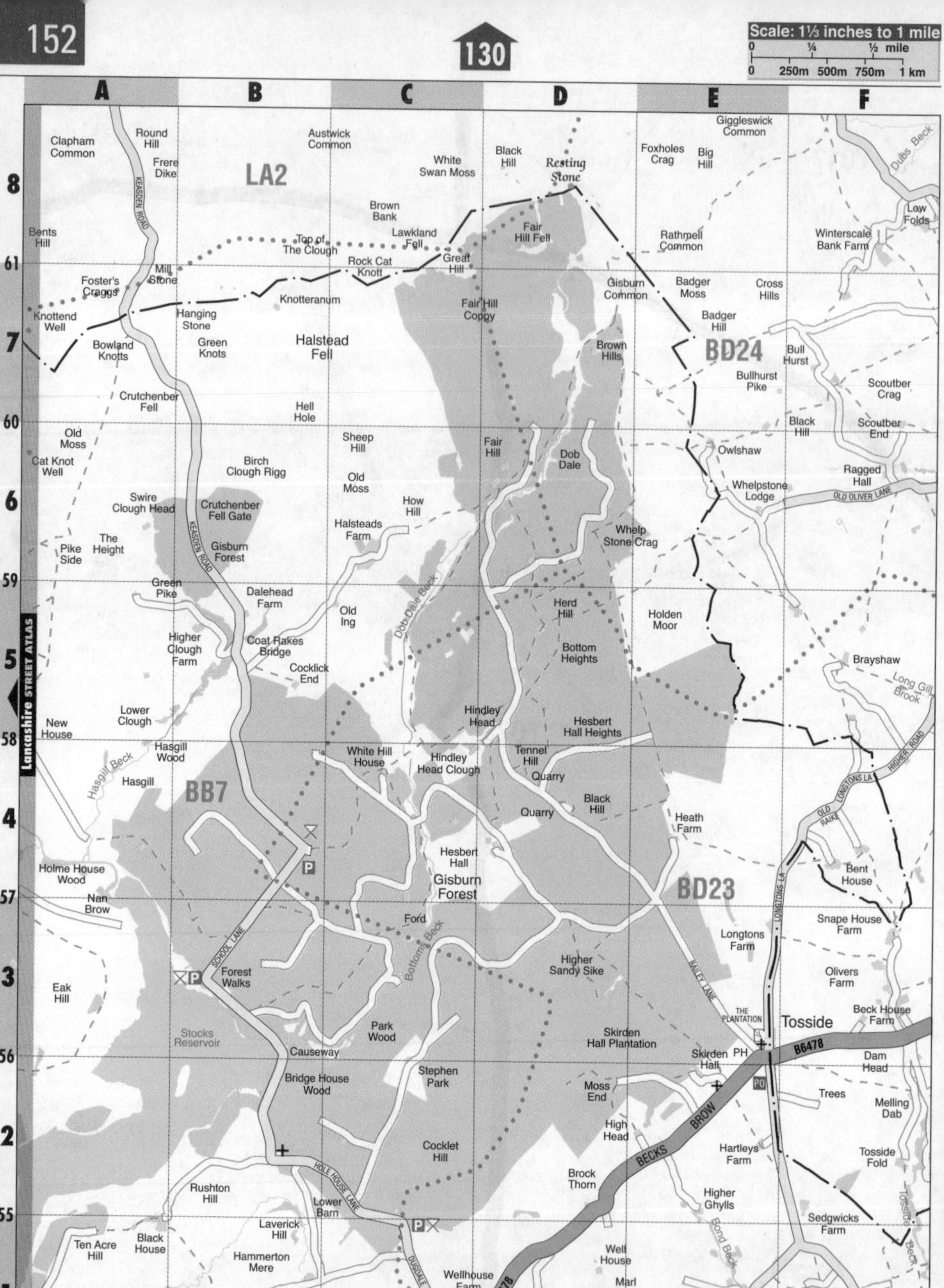

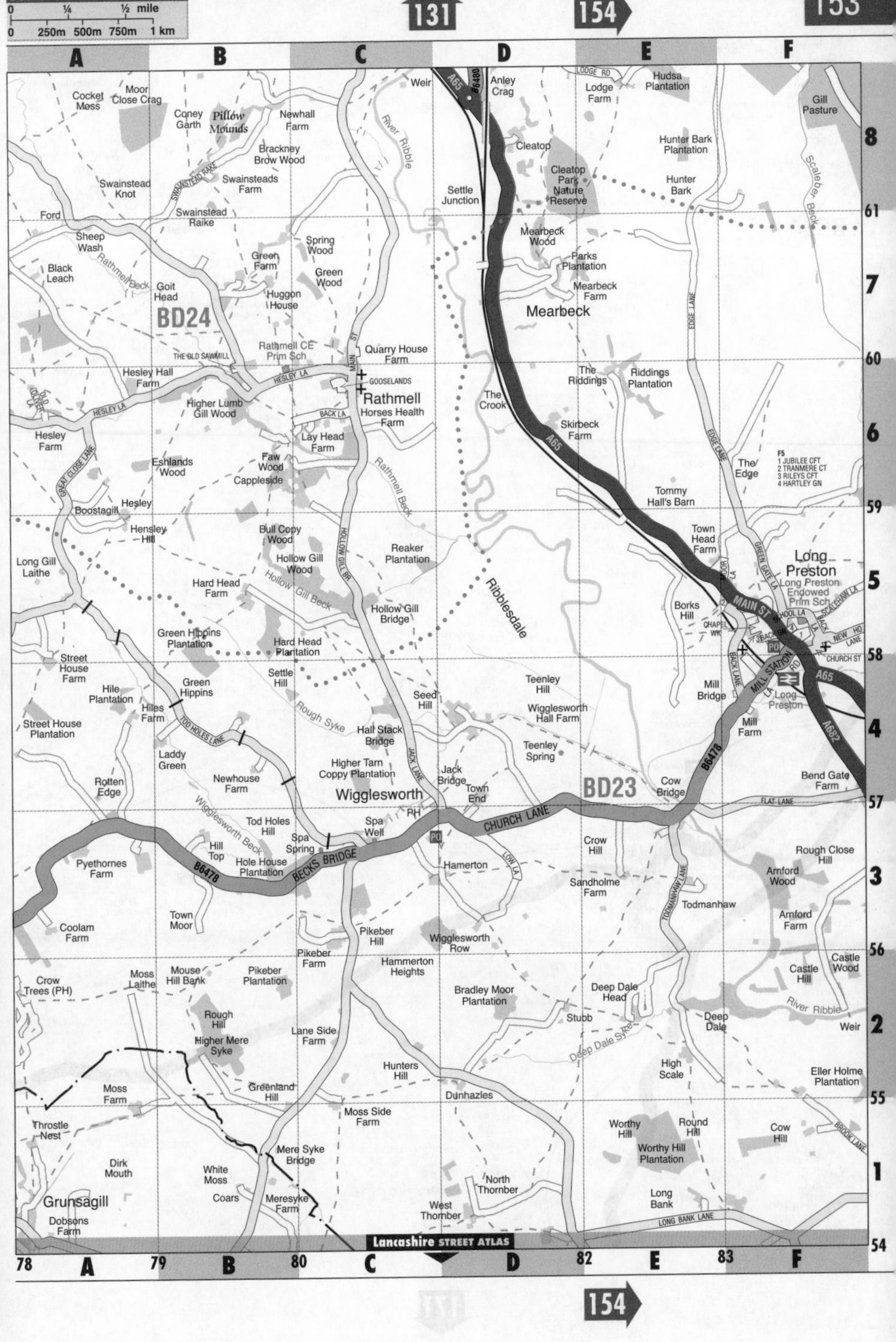
Scale: 1⅓ inches to 1 mile
0 ¼ ½ mile
0 250m 500m 750m 1 km
131
154
A B C D E F
Cocket Moss
Moor Close Crag
Coney Garth
Pillow Mounds
Newhall Farm
Weir
Anley Crag
Lodge Farm
Hudsa Plantation
Gill Pasture
River Ribble
Brackney Brow Wood
Cleatop
Hunter Bark Plantation
Swainstead Knot
Swainsteads Farm
Cleatop Park Nature Reserve
Settle Junction
Hunter Bark
Scaleber Beck
Ford
Swainstead Raike
Sheep Wash
Spring Wood
Mearbeck Wood
Black Leach
Rathmell Beck
Green Farm
Green Wood
Parks Plantation
Goit Head
Huggon House
Mearbeck Farm
BD24
Mearbeck
Rathmell CE Prim Sch
THE OLD SAWMILL
Quarry House Farm
GOOSELANDS
Rathmell
Horses Health Farm
BACK LA
HESLEY LA
Hesley Hall Farm
Higher Lumb Gill Wood
The Riddings
Riddings Plantation
The Crook
Skirbeck Farm
Hesley Farm
Lay Head Farm
A65
EDGE LANE
The Edge
F5
1 JUBILEE CFT
2 TRANMERE CT
3 RILEYS CFT
4 HARTLEY GN
Eshlands Wood
Faw Wood
Cappleside
GREAT CLOSE LANE
Tommy Hall's Barn
Boostagill
Hesley
Hensley Hill
Bull Copy Wood
HOLLOW GILL BR
Reaker Plantation
Town Head Farm
Long Preston
Long Preston Endowed Prim Sch
Long Gill Laithe
Hollow Gill Wood
Hard Head Farm
Hollow Gill Beck
Hollow Gill Bridge
Ribblesdale
Borks Hill
MAIN ST
SCHOOL LA
CHAPEL WK
BACK GN
NEW HO LANE
CHURCH ST
Green Hippins Plantation
Hard Head Plantation
Street House Farm
Settle Hill
Teenley Hill
Mill Bridge
BACK LANE
MILL STATION RD
Long Preston
Hile Plantation
Green Hippins
Seed Hill
Rough Syke
Wigglesworth Hall Farm
Hiles Farm
Street House Plantation
TOD HOLES LANE
Hall Stack Bridge
Mill Farm
A682
Teenley Spring
Laddy Green
Higher Tarn Coppy Plantation
JACK LANE
Jack Bridge
BD23
Cow Bridge
Bend Gate Farm
Rotten Edge
Newhouse Farm
Wigglesworth
Town End
FLAT LANE
B6478
Wigglesworth Beck
Tod Holes Hill
Spa Well
PH
CHURCH LANE
Crow Hill
Rough Close Hill
Hill Top
Spa Spring
PO
Pyethornes Farm
Hole House Plantation
BECKS BRIDGE
Hamerton
LOW LA
Sandholme Farm
Arnford Wood
TODMANHAW LANE
Todmanhaw
Town Moor
Coolam Farm
Pikeber Hill
Wigglesworth Row
Arnford Farm
Pikeber Farm
Hammerton Heights
Castle Wood
Castle Hill
Moss Laithe
Mouse Hill Bank
Pikeber Plantation
Crow Trees (PH)
Bradley Moor Plantation
Deep Dale Head
River Ribble
Stubb
Deep Dale
Weir
Rough Hill
Lane Side Farm
Higher Mere Syke
Deep Dale Syke
High Scale
Hunters Hill
Eller Holme Plantation
Moss Farm
Greenland Hill
Dunhazles
Moss Side Farm
Throstle Nest
Worthy Hill
Round Hill
Cow Hill
BROOK LANE
Mere Syke Bridge
Worthy Hill Plantation
Dirk Mouth
White Moss
North Thornber
Coars
Long Bank
Grunsagill
Meresyke Farm
West Thornber
Dobsons Farm
LONG BANK LANE
Lancashire STREET ATLAS
8 61 7 60 6 59 5 58 4 57 3 56 2 55 1 54
78 79 80 82 83
154

153
132

Scale: 1⅓ inches to 1 mile

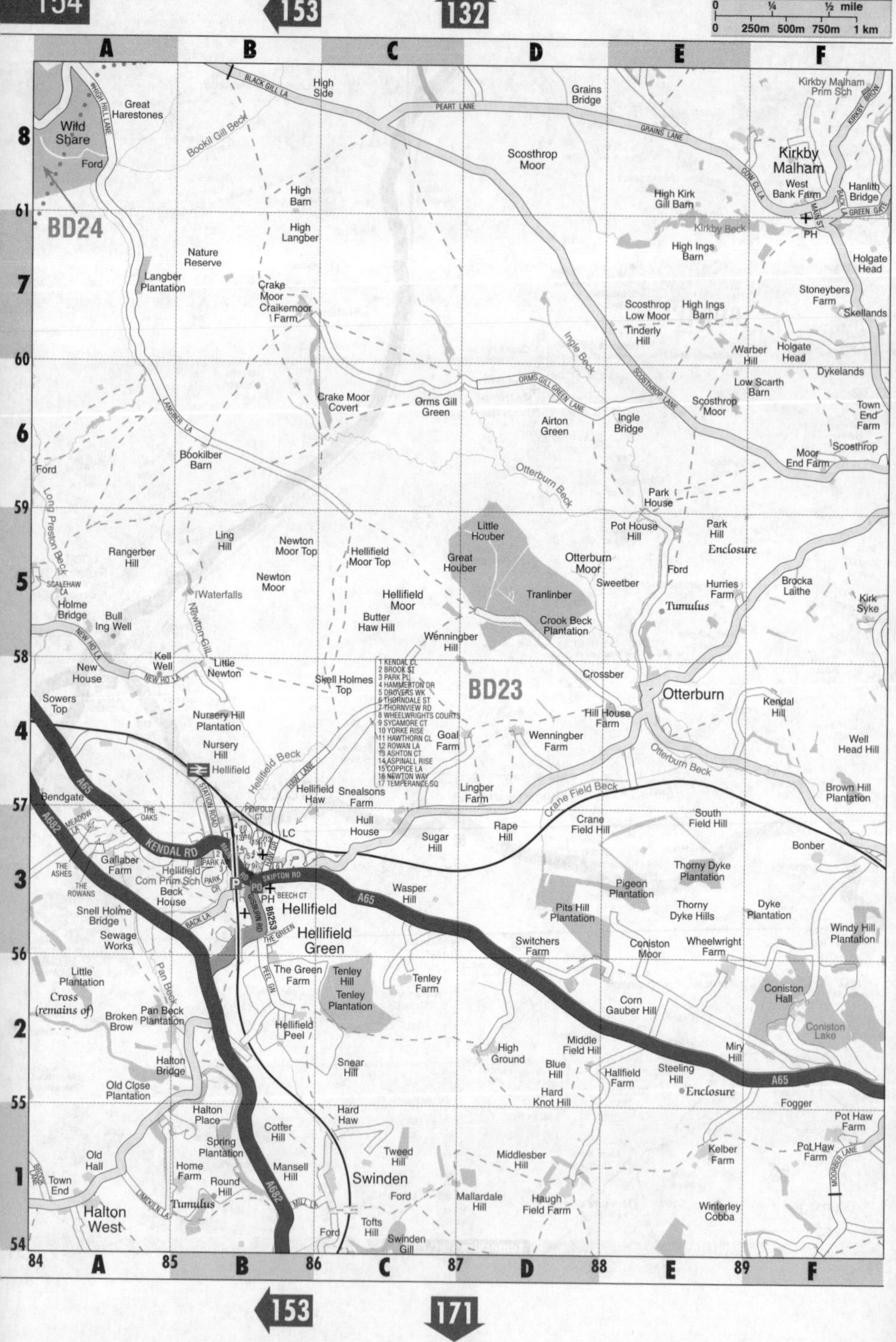
Wild Share
Great Harestones
Ford
BD24
High Side
Grains Bridge
Kirkby Malham Prim Sch
Kirkby Malham
West Bank Farm
Hanlith Bridge
Scosthrop Moor
High Barn
High Langber
High Kirk Gill Barn
Kirkby Beck
High Ings Barn
Holgate Head
Nature Reserve
Langber Plantation
Crake Moor
Craikemoor Farm
Scosthrop Low Moor
High Ings Barn
Stoneybers Farm
Skellands
Tinderly Hill
Warber Hill
Holgate Head
Dykelands
Low Scarth Barn
Crake Moor Covert
Orms Gill Green
Airton Green
Ingle Bridge
Scosthrop Moor
Town End Farm
Scosthrop
Moor End Farm
Bookilber Barn
Ford
Park House
Little Houber
Pot House Hill
Park Hill
Enclosure
Ling Hill
Newton Moor Top
Hellifield Moor Top
Rangerber Hill
Great Houber
Otterburn Moor
Newton Moor
Hellifield Moor
Tranlinber
Sweetber
Ford
Hurries Farm
Brocka Laithe
Kirk Syke
Holme Bridge
Bull Ing Well
Waterfalls
Butter Haw Hill
Crook Beck Plantation
Tumulus
Wenningber Hill
Kell Well
Little Newton
New House
Skell Holmes Top
BD23
Crossber
Otterburn
Sowers Top
Nursery Hill Plantation
Hill House Farm
Kendal Hill
Nursery Hill
Goal Farm
Wenningber Farm
Well Head Hill
Hellifield
Bendgate
Hellifield Haw
Snealsons Farm
Lingber Farm
Brown Hill Plantation
Crane Field Hill
South Field Hill
Hull House
Rape Hill
Sugar Hill
Bonber
Gallaber Farm
Thorny Dyke Plantation
Com Prim Sch
Wasper Hill
Pigeon Plantation
Beck House
Hellifield
Pits Hill Plantation
Thorny Dyke Hills
Dyke Plantation
Snell Holme Bridge
Hellifield Green
Sewage Works
Switchers Farm
Coniston Moor
Wheelwright Farm
Windy Hill Plantation
Little Plantation
The Green Farm
Tenley Hill
Tenley Farm
Coniston Hall
Cross (remains of)
Tenley Plantation
Corn Gauber Hill
Broken Brow
Pan Beck Plantation
Coniston Lake
Hellifield Peel
Middle Field Hill
Miry Hill
High Ground
Halton Bridge
Snear Hill
Blue Hill
Hallfield Farm
Steeling Hill
Old Close Plantation
Hard Knot Hill
Enclosure
Fogger
Halton Place
Hard Haw
Pot Haw Farm
Cotter Hill
Spring Plantation
Tweed Hill
Kelber Farm
Pot Haw Farm
Old Hall
Middlesber Hill
Home Farm
Mansell Hill
Swinden
Town End
Round Hill
Ford
Mallardale Hill
Haugh Field Farm
Winterley Cobba
Tumulus
Halton West
Tofts Hill
Ford
Swinden Gill
1 KENDAL CL
2 BROOK ST
3 PARK PL
4 HAMMERTON DR
5 DROVERS WK
6 THORNDALE ST
7 THORNVIEW RD
8 WHEELWRIGHTS COURTS
9 SYCAMORE CT
10 YORKE RISE
11 HAWTHORN CL
12 ROWAN LA
13 ASHTON CT
14 ASPINALL RISE
15 COPPICE LA
16 NEWTON WAY
17 TEMPERANCE SQ
A65
A682
B6253
KENDAL RD
SKIPTON RD
STATION ROAD
GISBURN RD
BLACK GILL LA
PEART LANE
GRAINS LANE
SCOSTHROP LANE
ORMS GILL GREEN LANE
LANGBER LA
HIGH HILL LANE
NEW HO LA
HAW LANE
MOORBER LANE
MILL LA
LIMEKILN LA
Bookil Gill Beck
Ingle Beck
Otterburn Beck
Hellifield Beck
Newton Gill
Long Preston Beck
Crane Field Beck
Pan Beck

153
171

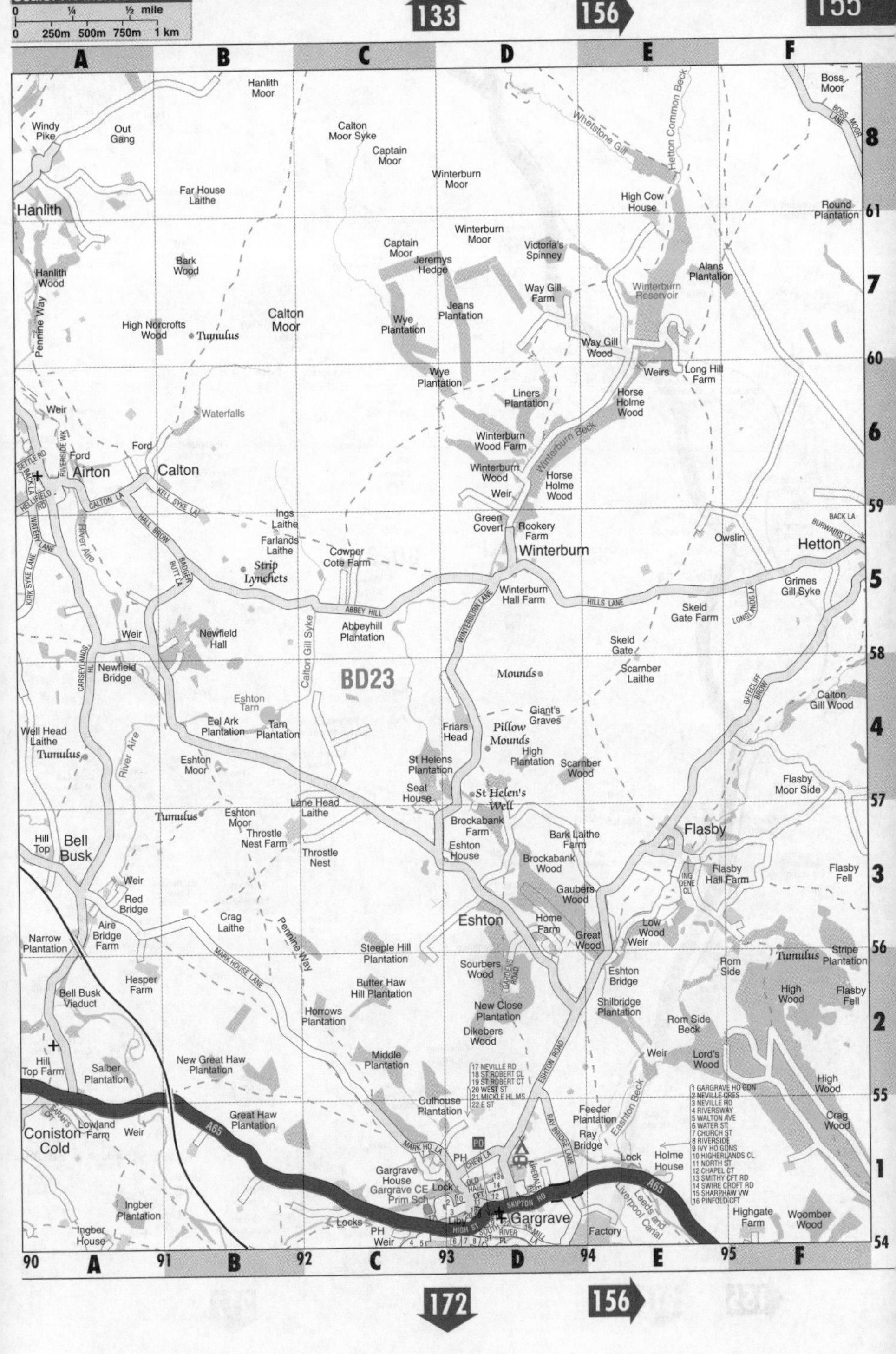
Scale: 1⅓ inches to 1 mile
0 ¼ ½ mile
0 250m 500m 750m 1 km
133
156
A
B
C
D
E
F
Hanlith Moor
Windy Pike
Out Gang
Calton Moor Syke
Captain Moor
Whetstone Gill
Hetton Common Beck
Boss Moor
BOSS MOOR LANE
8
Winterburn Moor
Far House Laithe
Hanlith
High Cow House
Round Plantation
61
Captain Moor
Winterburn Moor
Victoria's Spinney
Jeremys Hedge
Bark Wood
Hanlith Wood
Alans Plantation
Way Gill Farm
Winterburn Reservoir
7
Pennine Way
Jeans Plantation
Calton Moor
Wye Plantation
High Norcrofts Wood
Tumulus
Way Gill Wood
Weirs
Long Hill Farm
60
Wye Plantation
Liners Plantation
Horse Holme Wood
Weir
Waterfalls
Winterburn Beck
Winterburn Wood Farm
6
RIVERSIDE WK
SETTLE RD
Ford
Ford
Airton
Calton
Winterburn Wood
Horse Holme Wood
BACK LA
HELLIFIELD RD
CALTON LA
KELL SYKE LA
Weir
59
WATERY LANE
HALL BROW
Ings Laithe
Green Covert
Rookery Farm
BACK LA
Owslin
BURWAINS LA
River Aire
Farlands Laithe
Winterburn
Hetton
KIRK SYKE LANE
BADGER BUTT LA
Cowper Cote Farm
Strip Lynchets
Winterburn Hall Farm
Grimes Gill Syke
5
ABBEY HILL
WINTERBURN LANE
HILLS LANE
LONGLANDS LA
Skeld Gate Farm
Abbeyhill Plantation
Weir
Newfield Hall
Skeld Gate
58
CARSEYLANDS HL
Newfield Bridge
Calton Gill Syke
BD23
Mounds
Scarnber Laithe
GATECLIFF BROW
Eshton Tarn
Calton Gill Wood
Eel Ark Plantation
Tarn Plantation
Giant's Graves
Well Head Laithe
Friars Head
Pillow Mounds
4
Tumulus
River Aire
Eshton Moor
St Helens Plantation
High Plantation
Scarnber Wood
Flasby Moor Side
Seat House
St Helen's Well
57
Lane Head Laithe
Tumulus
Eshton Moor
Brockabank Farm
Hill Top
Bell Busk
Throstle Nest Farm
Bark Laithe Farm
Flasby
Eshton House
Throstle Nest
Brockabank Wood
Flasby Hall Farm
Flasby Fell
ING DENE CL
3
Weir
Gaubers Wood
Red Bridge
Crag Laithe
Pennine Way
Eshton
Home Farm
Low Wood
Weir
Aire Bridge Farm
Great Wood
Narrow Plantation
Tumulus
Stripe Plantation
56
MARK HOUSE LANE
Steeple Hill Plantation
Rom Side
Sourbers Wood
GARDENS ROAD
Eshton Bridge
Hesper Farm
Butter Haw Hill Plantation
High Wood
Flasby Fell
Bell Busk Viaduct
Horrows Plantation
New Close Plantation
Shilbridge Plantation
Rom Side Beck
2
Dikebers Wood
Hill Top Farm
Salber Plantation
New Great Haw Plantation
Middle Plantation
Weir
Lord's Wood
High Wood
ESHTON ROAD
17 NEVILLE RD
18 ST ROBERT CL
19 ST ROBERT CT
20 WEST ST
21 MICKLE HL MS
22 E ST
1 GARGRAVE HO GDN
2 NEVILLE CRES
3 NEVILLE RD
4 RIVERSWAY
5 WALTON AVE
6 WATER ST
7 CHURCH ST
8 RIVERSIDE
9 IVY HO GDNS
10 HIGHERLANDS CL
11 NORTH ST
12 CHAPEL CT
13 SMITHY CFT RD
14 SWIRE CROFT RD
15 SHARPHAW VW
16 PINFOLD CFT
55
A65
Great Haw Plantation
Culhouse Plantation
Eshton Beck
Feeder Plantation
Crag Wood
Lowland Farm
Coniston Cold
Weir
MARK HO LA
PO
RAY BRIDGE LANE
Ray Bridge
PH
CHEW LA
Lock
Holme House
1
Gargrave House
Gargrave CE Prim Sch
OLD HALL CFT
Lock
A65
Leeds and Liverpool Canal
Ingber Plantation
SKIPTON RD
Gargrave
Highgate Farm
Woomber Wood
Locks
Ingber House
PH
Weir
Liby
HIGH ST
SOUTH ST
RIVER PL
MILL LA
Factory
54
90
91
92
93
94
95
A
B
C
D
E
F
172
156

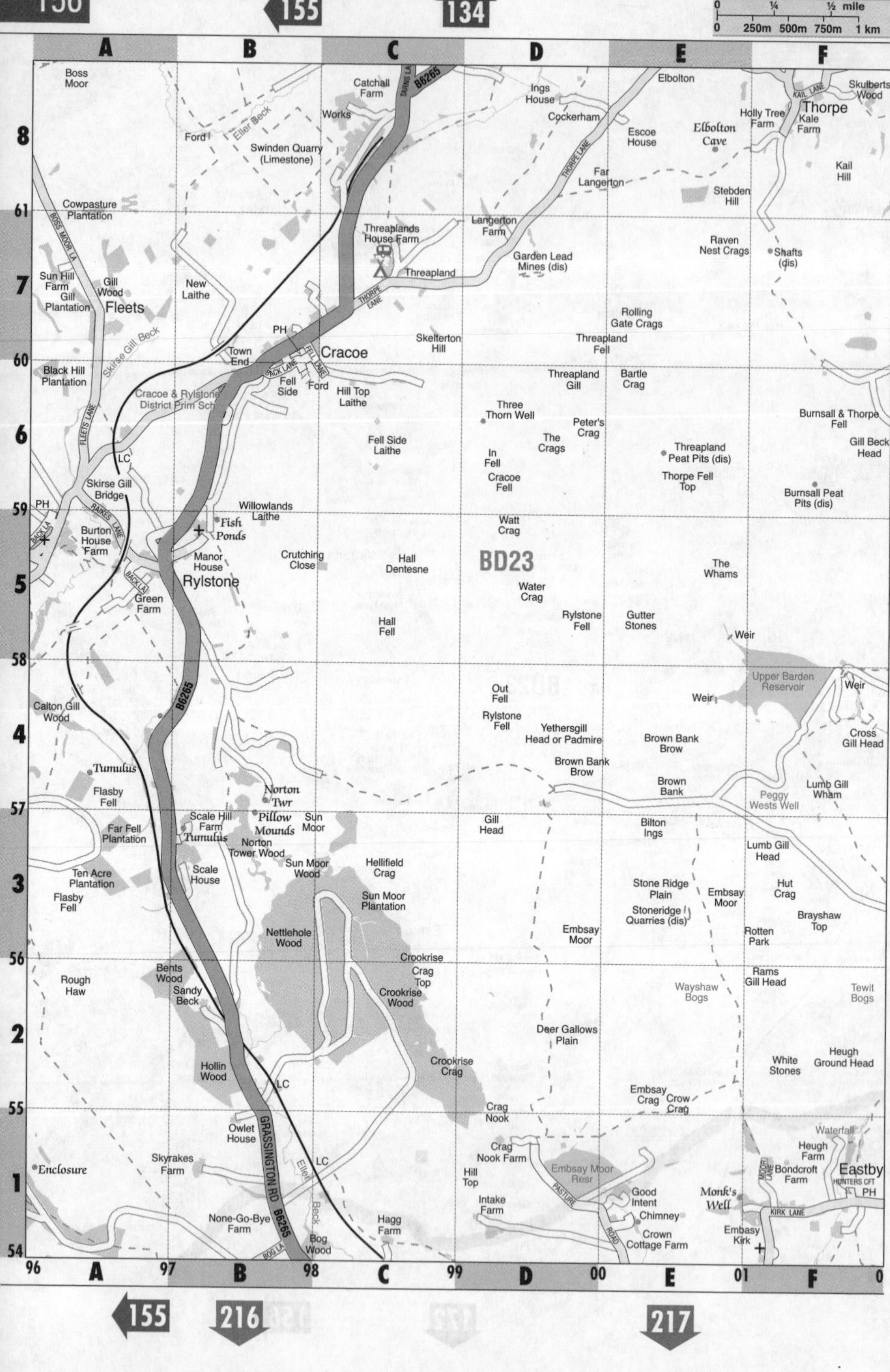
155
134
Scale: 1⅓ inches to 1 mile
BD23
Cracoe
Rylstone
Fleets
Thorpe
Eastby
B6265
GRASSINGTON RD
Boss Moor
Catchall Farm
Works
Swinden Quarry (Limestone)
Ford
Eller Beck
Ings House
Cockerham
Elbolton
Escoe House
Elbolton Cave
Holly Tree Farm
Kale Farm
Skulberts Wood
Kail Hill
Far Langerton
Stebden Hill
Cowpasture Plantation
Threaplands House Farm
Langerton Farm
Garden Lead Mines (dis)
Raven Nest Crags
Shafts (dis)
Threapland
Sun Hill Farm
Gill Wood
Gill Plantation
New Laithe
Rolling Gate Crags
Skelterton Hill
Threapland Fell
Town End
Black Hill Plantation
Skirse Gill Beck
Fell Side
Hill Top Laithe
Threapland Gill
Bartle Crag
Cracoe & Rylstone District Prim Sch
Three Thorn Well
Peter's Crag
Burnsall & Thorpe Fell
Fell Side Laithe
The Crags
Threapland Peat Pits (dis)
Gill Beck Head
In Fell
Cracoe Fell
Thorpe Fell Top
Burnsall Peat Pits (dis)
Skirse Gill Bridge
Willowlands Laithe
Watt Crag
Burton House Farm
Fish Ponds
Manor House
Crutching Close
Hall Dentesne
The Whams
Green Farm
Water Crag
Rylstone Fell
Gutter Stones
Hall Fell
Weir
Upper Barden Reservoir
Calton Gill Wood
Out Fell
Yethersgill Head or Padmire
Brown Bank Brow
Cross Gill Head
Tumulus
Norton Twr
Brown Bank
Lumb Gill Wham
Peggy Wests Well
Flasby Fell
Scale Hill Farm
Pillow Mounds
Sun Moor
Gill Head
Bilton Ings
Far Fell Plantation
Norton Tower Wood
Sun Moor Wood
Lumb Gill Head
Hellifield Crag
Ten Acre Plantation
Scale House
Stone Ridge Plain
Embsay Moor
Hut Crag
Sun Moor Plantation
Stoneridge Quarries (dis)
Brayshaw Top
Nettlehole Wood
Rotten Park
Crookrise Crag Top
Rams Gill Head
Bents Wood
Rough Haw
Sandy Beck
Crookrise Wood
Wayshaw Bogs
Tewit Bogs
Deer Gallows Plain
Hollin Wood
Crookrise Crag
White Stones
Heugh Ground Head
Embsay Crag
Crow Crag
Crag Nook
Owlet House
Waterfall
Heugh Farm
Crag Nook Farm
Skyrakes Farm
Enclosure
Embsay Moor Resr
Bondcroft Farm
Hunters Cft
Hill Top
Good Intent
Monk's Well
Intake Farm
Chimney
Kirk Lane
None-Go-Bye Farm
Hagg Farm
Crown Cottage Farm
Embsay Kirk
Bog Wood
Bog La
Pasture Road
Moor Lane
Tarns La
Kail Lane
Thorpe Lane
Boss Moor La
Fleets Lane
Raikes Lane
Back La
Back Lane
Fell Lane
LC
PH
155
216
217

135
158

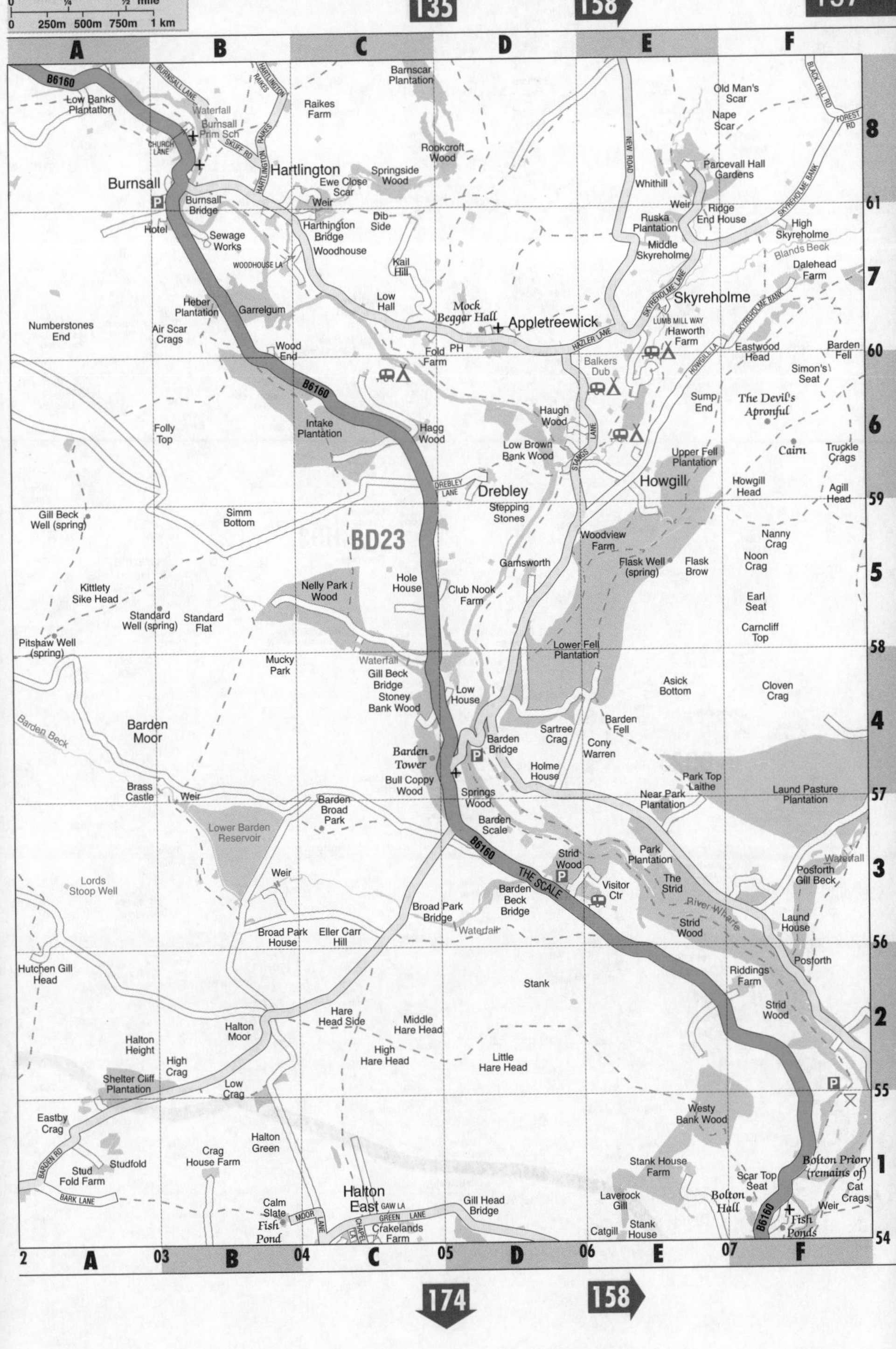
Scale: 1⅓ inches to 1 mile
0 ¼ ½ mile
0 250m 500m 750m 1 km
A
B
C
D
E
F
8
61
7
60
6
59
5
58
4
57
3
56
2
55
1
54
2
03
04
05
06
07
B6160
Low Banks Plantation
BURNSALL LANE
HARTLINGTON RAIKES
Waterfall
Burnsall Prim Sch
CHURCH LANE
SKUFF RD
HARTLINGTON RAIKES
Burnsall
Hartlington
Burnsall Bridge
Hotel
Sewage Works
WOODHOUSE LA
Raikes Farm
Barnscar Plantation
Rookcroft Wood
Springside Wood
Ewe Close Scar
Weir
Harthington Bridge
Woodhouse
Dib Side
Kail Hill
Low Hall
Mock Beggar Hall
Appletreewick
Fold Farm
PH
Heber Plantation
Garrelgum
Air Scar Crags
Numberstones End
Wood End
B6160
Intake Plantation
Hagg Wood
Folly Top
NEW ROAD
Whithill
Old Man's Scar
Nape Scar
Parcevall Hall Gardens
BLACK HILL RD
FOREST RD
SKYREHOLME BANK
Ruska Plantation
Weir
Ridge End House
High Skyreholme
Blands Beck
Middle Skyreholme
Dalehead Farm
Skyreholme
SKYREHOLME LANE
LUMB MILL WAY
Haworth Farm
HAZLER LANE
SKYREHOLME BANK
HOWGILL LA
Eastwood Head
Barden Fell
Balkers Dub
Simon's Seat
Haugh Wood
Sump End
The Devil's Apronful
Low Brown Bank Wood
STANGS LANE
Upper Fell Plantation
Cairn
Truckle Crags
Howgill
Howgill Head
Agill Head
DREBLEY LANE
Drebley
Stepping Stones
BD23
Gill Beck Well (spring)
Simm Bottom
Woodview Farm
Nanny Crag
Flask Well (spring)
Flask Brow
Noon Crag
Garnsworth
Nelly Park Wood
Hole House
Club Nook Farm
Kittlety Sike Head
Standard Well (spring)
Standard Flat
Earl Seat
Carncliff Top
Pitshaw Well (spring)
Lower Fell Plantation
Mucky Park
Waterfall
Gill Beck Bridge
Stoney Bank Wood
Low House
Asick Bottom
Cloven Crag
Barden Beck
Barden Moor
Barden Fell
Sartree Crag
Barden Bridge
Cony Warren
Barden Tower
Bull Coppy Wood
Holme House
Springs Wood
Park Top Laithe
Brass Castle
Weir
Barden Broad Park
Near Park Plantation
Laund Pasture Plantation
Lower Barden Reservoir
Barden Scale
B6160
THE SCALE
Strid Wood
Park Plantation
Waterfall
Posforth Gill Beck
Lords Stoop Well
Weir
Barden Beck Bridge
Visitor Ctr
The Strid
River Wharfe
Broad Park Bridge
Laund House
Broad Park House
Eller Carr Hill
Waterfall
Strid Wood
Hutchen Gill Head
Posforth
Riddings Farm
Stank
Hare Head Side
Middle Hare Head
Strid Wood
Halton Moor
Halton Height
High Crag
High Hare Head
Little Hare Head
Shelter Cliff Plantation
Low Crag
Eastby Crag
Westy Bank Wood
BARDEN RD
Halton Green
Crag House Farm
Studfold
Stud Fold Farm
Stank House Farm
Bolton Priory (remains of)
Scar Top Seat
Cat Crags
BARK LANE
Calm Slate
Halton East
GAW LA
Gill Head Bridge
Laverock Gill
Bolton Hall
Weir
Fish Pond
MOOR LANE
CHAPEL LA
GREEN LANE
Crakelands Farm
Catgill
Stank House
B6160
Fish Ponds

174
158

157
136

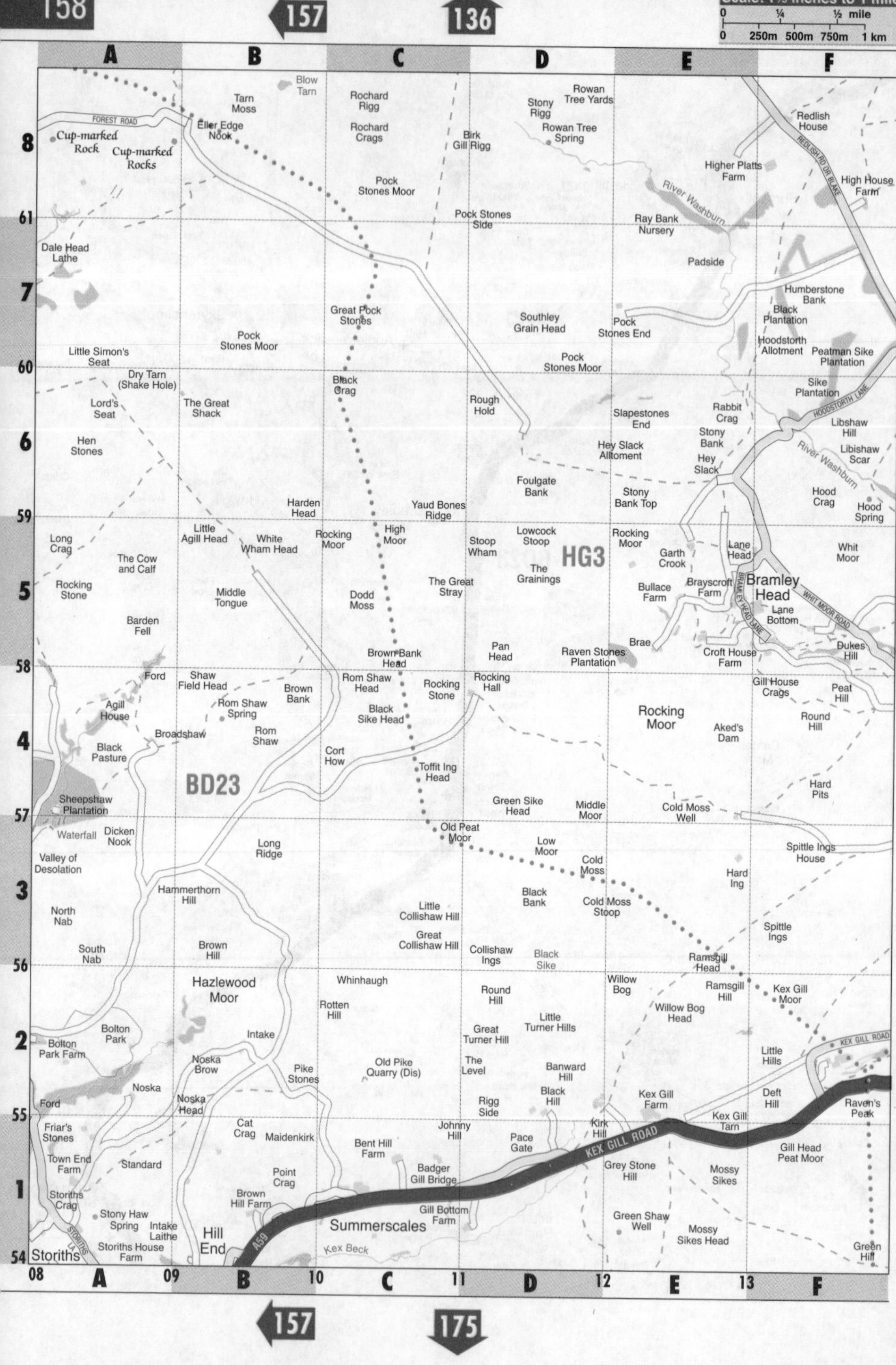
Scale: 1⅓ inches to 1 mile
0 ¼ ½ mile
0 250m 500m 750m 1 km
A B C D E F
8 61 7 60 6 59 5 58 4 57 3 56 2 55 1 54
08 09 10 11 12 13
Blow Tarn
Tarn Moss
Rochard Rigg
Rochard Crags
Stony Rigg
Rowan Tree Yards
Rowan Tree Spring
Redlish House
FOREST ROAD
Eller Edge Nook
Cup-marked Rock
Cup-marked Rocks
Birk Gill Rigg
Higher Platts Farm
REDLISH RD OR BLAKE
High House Farm
Pock Stones Moor
River Washburn
Pock Stones Side
Ray Bank Nursery
Dale Head Lathe
Padside
Humberstone Bank
Great Pock Stones
Southley Grain Head
Pock Stones End
Black Plantation
Hoodstorth Allotment
Peatman Sike Plantation
Little Simon's Seat
Dry Tarn (Shake Hole)
Black Crag
Sike Plantation
Lord's Seat
The Great Shack
Rough Hold
Slapestones End
Rabbit Crag
HOODSTORTH LANE
Libshaw Hill
Hen Stones
Stony Bank
Hey Slack Allotment
Libishaw Scar
Hey Slack
Foulgate Bank
Stony Bank Top
Hood Crag
Hood Spring
Harden Head
Yaud Bones Ridge
Little Agill Head
White Wham Head
Rocking Moor
High Moor
Lowcock Stoop
Stoop Wham
HG3
Garth Crook
Lane Head
Whit Moor
Long Crag
The Cow and Calf
The Grainings
The Great Stray
Bullace Farm
Brayscroft Farm
Bramley Head
BRAMLEY HEAD LANE
WHIT MOOR ROAD
Rocking Stone
Middle Tongue
Dodd Moss
Lane Bottom
Barden Fell
Brae
Pan Head
Brown Bank Head
Raven Stones Plantation
Croft House Farm
Dukes Hill
Ford
Shaw Field Head
Rom Shaw Head
Rocking Stone
Rocking Hall
Gill House Crags
Peat Hill
Brown Bank
Agill House
Rom Shaw Spring
Black Sike Head
Round Hill
Rocking Moor
Aked's Dam
Broadshaw
Rom Shaw
Black Pasture
Cort How
Toffit Ing Head
BD23
Hard Pits
Sheepshaw Plantation
Green Sike Head
Middle Moor
Cold Moss Well
Waterfall
Dicken Nook
Old Peat Moor
Long Ridge
Low Moor
Spittle Ings House
Valley of Desolation
Cold Moss
Hard Ing
Hammerthorn Hill
Black Bank
Cold Moss Stoop
North Nab
Little Collishaw Hill
Great Collishaw Hill
Spittle Ings
South Nab
Brown Hill
Collishaw Ings
Black Sike
Ramsgill Head
Hazlewood Moor
Whinhaugh
Willow Bog
Ramsgill Hill
Kex Gill Moor
Rotten Hill
Round Hill
Willow Bog Head
Bolton Park
Intake
Great Turner Hill
Little Turner Hills
KEX GILL ROAD
Bolton Park Farm
Little Hills
Noska Brow
Old Pike Quarry (Dis)
The Level
Banward Hill
Pike Stones
Noska
Black Hill
Kex Gill Farm
Deft Hill
Raven's Peak
Ford
Noska Head
Rigg Side
Friar's Stones
Cat Crag
Maidenkirk
Johnny Hill
Pace Gate
Kirk Hill
Kex Gill Tarn
Bent Hill Farm
KEX GILL ROAD
Gill Head Peat Moor
Town End Farm
Standard
Grey Stone Hill
Point Crag
Badger Gill Bridge
Mossy Sikes
Storiths Crag
Brown Hill Farm
Gill Bottom Farm
Stony Haw Spring
Intake Laithe
Summerscales
A59
Green Shaw Well
Mossy Sikes Head
STORITHS LA
Storiths House Farm
Hill End
Kex Beck
Green Hill
Storiths

157
175

137
160

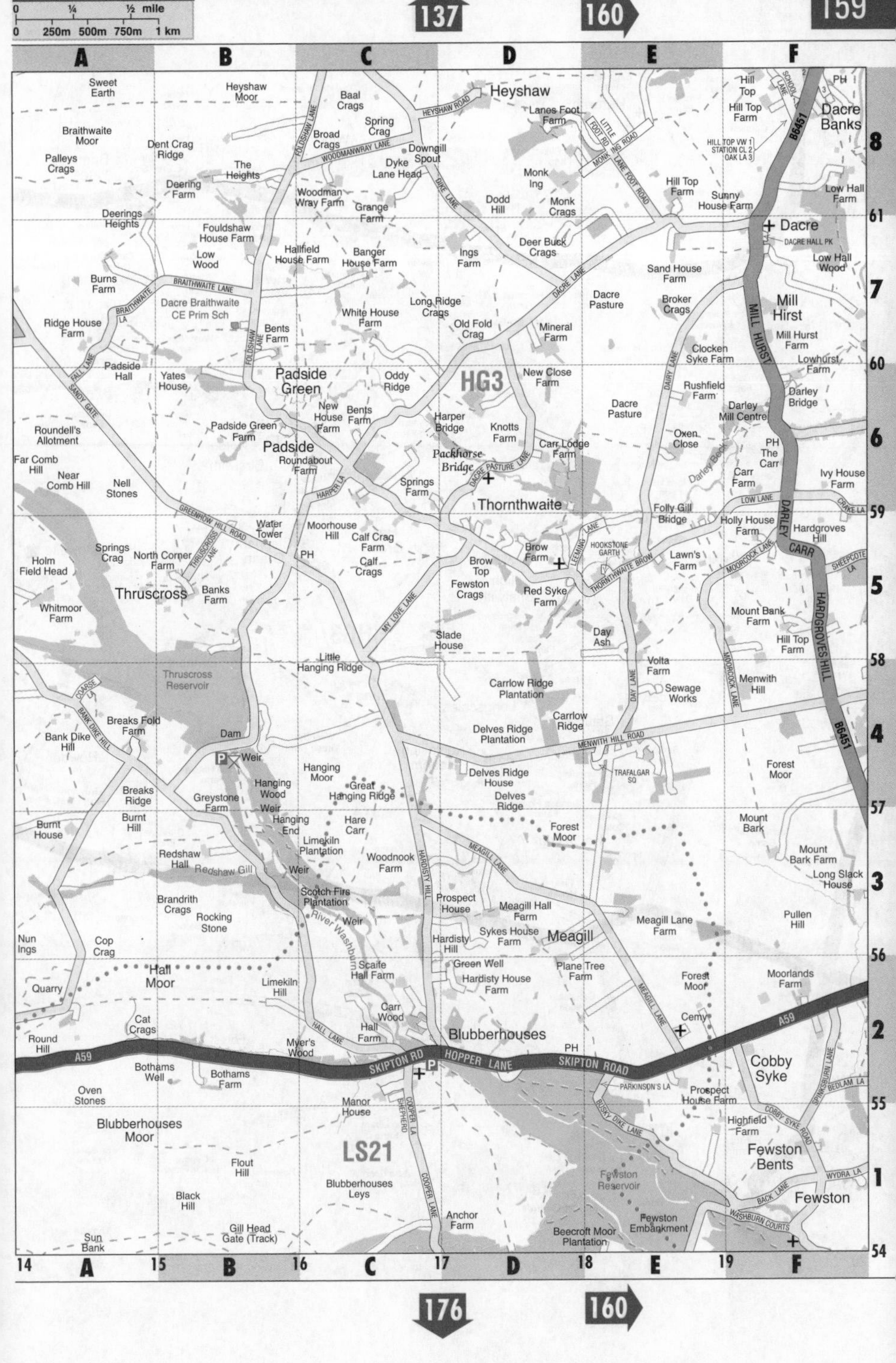
Scale: 1⅓ inches to 1 mile
0 ¼ ½ mile
0 250m 500m 750m 1 km
A
B
C
D
E
F
8
61
7
60
6
59
5
58
4
57
3
56
2
55
1
54
14
15
16
17
18
19
Sweet Earth
Heyshaw Moor
Baal Crags
Heyshaw
Hill Top
Hill Top Farm
Dacre Banks
PH
Braithwaite Moor
Spring Crag
Lanes Foot Farm
Broad Crags
Dent Crag Ridge
Palleys Crags
Downgill Spout
HILL TOP VW 1
STATION CL 2
OAK LA 3
B6451
The Heights
Dyke Lane Head
Monk Ing
Deering Farm
Woodman Wray Farm
Hill Top Farm
Sunny House Farm
Low Hall Farm
Deerings Heights
Grange Farm
Dodd Hill
Monk Crags
Dacre
DACRE HALL PK
Fouldshaw House Farm
Deer Buck Crags
Low Hall Wood
Hallfield House Farm
Banger House Farm
Ings Farm
Low Wood
Sand House Farm
Burns Farm
BRAITHWAITE LANE
Dacre Braithwaite CE Prim Sch
Long Ridge Crags
Dacre Pasture
Broker Crags
Mill Hirst
Ridge House Farm
White House Farm
Bents Farm
Old Fold Crag
Mineral Farm
Mill Hurst Farm
MILL HURST
Clocken Syke Farm
Lowhurst Farm
Padside Hall
Yates House
Padside Green
Oddy Ridge
HG3
New Close Farm
New House Farm
Bents Farm
Rushfield Farm
Darley Mill Centre
Darley Bridge
Dacre Pasture
Roundell's Allotment
Padside Green Farm
Harper Bridge
Knotts Farm
Carr Lodge Farm
Oxen Close
Padside
Roundabout Farm
Packhorse Bridge
PH
The Carr
Far Comb Hill
Near Comb Hill
Ivy House Farm
Nell Stones
Springs Farm
Thornthwaite
Carr Farm
Darley Beck
Folly Gill Bridge
LOW LANE
CRAKE LA
Water Tower
Moorhouse Hill
Calf Crag Farm
Holly House Farm
Hardgroves Hill
Springs Crag
North Corner Farm
Brow Farm
HOOKSTONE GARTH
Lawn's Farm
SHEEPCOTE LA
Holm Field Head
PH
Calf Crags
Brow Top
Fewston Crags
THORNTHWAITE BROW
Thruscross
Banks Farm
Red Syke Farm
Mount Bank Farm
Whitmoor Farm
Slade House
Day Ash
Hill Top Farm
HARDGROVES HILL
Little Hanging Ridge
Volta Farm
Menwith Hill
Thruscross Reservoir
Carrlow Ridge Plantation
Sewage Works
Breaks Fold Farm
Carrlow Ridge
Bank Dike Hill
Dam
Delves Ridge Plantation
MENWITH HILL ROAD
Weir
Hanging Moor
Delves Ridge House
TRAFALGAR SQ
Forest Moor
Breaks Ridge
Hanging Wood
Great Hanging Ridge
Delves Ridge
Greystone Farm
Weir
Burnt House
Burnt Hill
Hanging End
Hare Carr
Forest Moor
Mount Bark
Limekiln Plantation
Redshaw Hall
Redshaw Gill
Woodnook Farm
Mount Bark Farm
Weir
Long Slack House
Brandrith Crags
Scotch Firs Plantation
Prospect House
Meagill Hall Farm
Meagill Lane Farm
Pullen Hill
Rocking Stone
River Washburn
Weir
Sykes House Farm
Meagill
Nun Ings
Cop Crag
Hardisty Hill
Scaife Hall Farm
Green Well
Plane Tree Farm
Moorlands Farm
Hall Moor
Hardisty House Farm
Forest Moor
Quarry
Limekiln Hill
Cat Crags
Carr Wood
Cemy
A59
Round Hill
Hall Farm
Blubberhouses
Myer's Wood
PH
Cobby Syke
A59
SKIPTON RD
HOPPER LANE
SKIPTON ROAD
Bothams Well
Bothams Farm
PARKINSON'S LA
Prospect House Farm
Oven Stones
Manor House
Highfield Farm
Blubberhouses Moor
LS21
Fewston Bents
Flout Hill
Blubberhouses Leys
Fewston Reservoir
WYDRA LA
Black Hill
Anchor Farm
Fewston
Fewston Embankment
Sun Bank
Gill Head Gate (Track)
Beecroft Moor Plantation

176
160

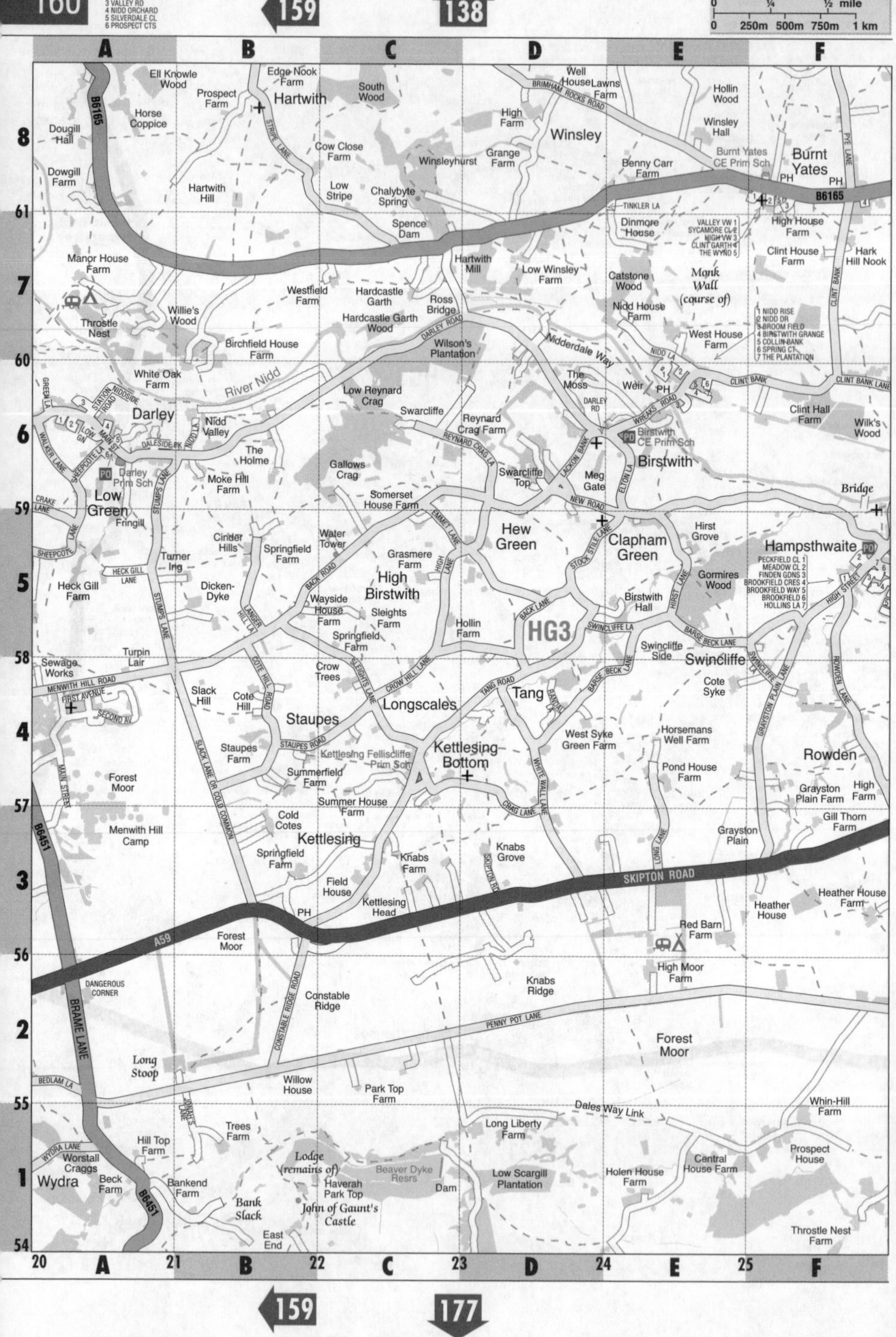

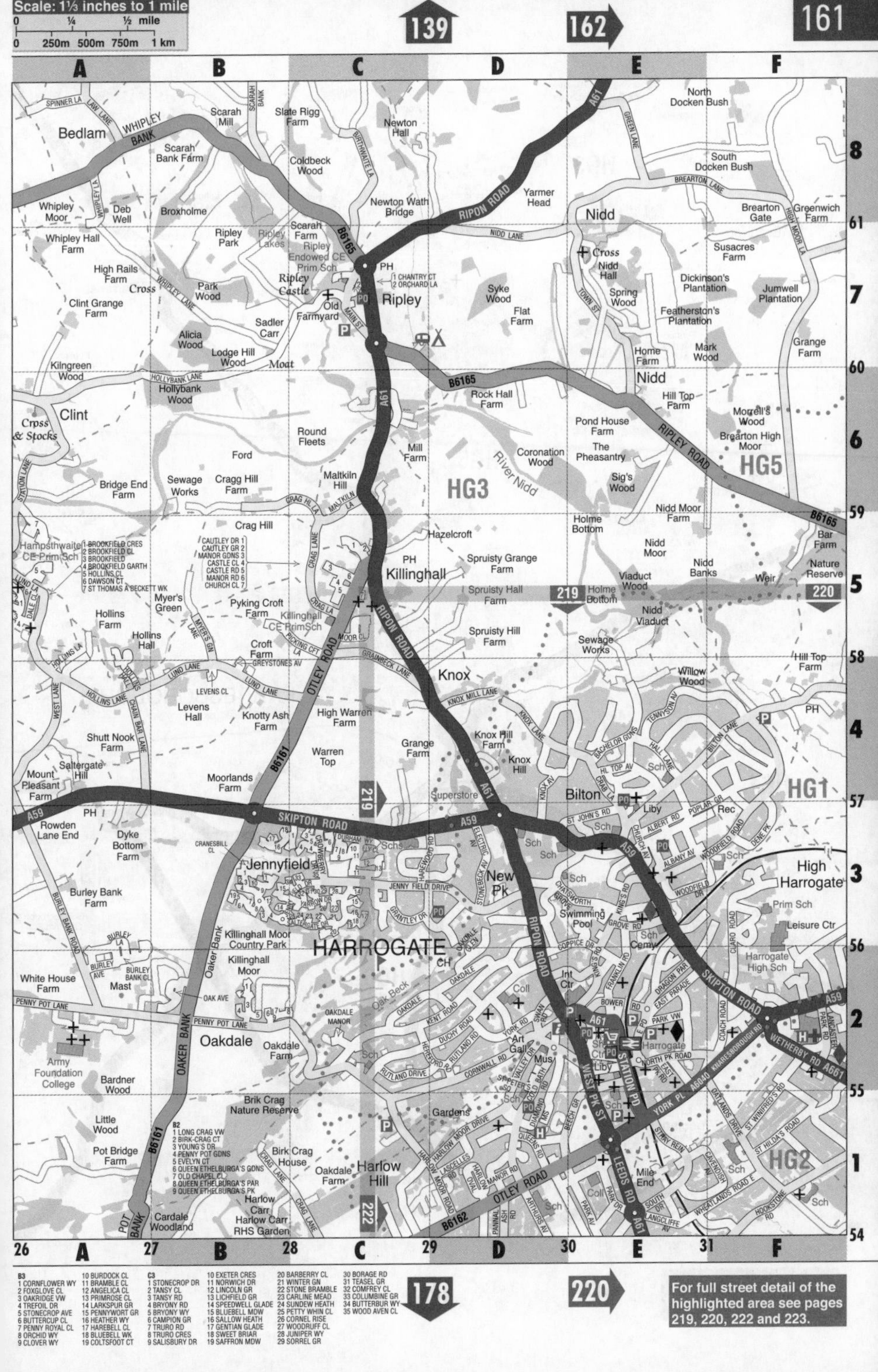
Scale: 1⅓ inches to 1 mile
0 ¼ ½ mile
0 250m 500m 750m 1 km
139
162
A B C D E F
Bedlam
WHIPLEY BANK
Scarah Mill
Slate Rigg Farm
Newton Hall
North Docken Bush
Scarah Bank Farm
Coldbeck Wood
South Docken Bush
BREARTON LANE
Whipley Moor
Deb Well
Broxholme
Newton Wath Bridge
RIPON ROAD
Yarmer Head
Nidd
Brearton Gate
Greenwich Farm
Whipley Hall Farm
Ripley Park
Ripley Lakes
Scarah Farm
Ripley Endowed CE Prim Sch
NIDD LANE
Cross
Nidd Hall
Susacres Farm
High Rails Farm
Cross
Ripley Castle
1 CHANTRY CT
2 ORCHARD LA
Ripley
Syke Wood
Spring Wood
Dickinson's Plantation
Jumwell Plantation
Clint Grange Farm
Park Wood
Old Farmyard
Flat Farm
Featherston's Plantation
Sadler Carr
Alicia Wood
Lodge Hill Wood
Moat
Home Farm
Mark Wood
Grange Farm
Kilngreen Wood
HOLLYBANK LANE
B6165
Nidd
Hollybank Wood
Rock Hall Farm
Hill Top Farm
Clint
Cross & Stocks
Round Fleets
Pond House Farm
Morrell's Wood
Ford
Mill Farm
Coronation Wood
The Pheasantry
Brearton High Moor
RIPLEY ROAD
River Nidd
HG5
Bridge End Farm
Sewage Works
Cragg Hill Farm
Maltkiln Hill
HG3
Sig's Wood
CRAG HL LA
MALTKILN LA
Nidd Moor Farm
Crag Hill
Holme Bottom
B6165
Hampsthwaite CE Prim Sch
1 BROOKFIELD CRES
2 BROOKFIELD CL
3 BROOKFIELD
4 BROOKFIELD GARTH
5 HOLLINS CL
6 DAWSON CT
7 ST THOMAS A BECKETT WK
CAUTLEY DR 1
CAUTLEY GR 2
MANOR GDNS 3
CASTLE CL 4
CASTLE RD 5
MANOR RD 6
CHURCH CL 7
Hazelcroft
Killinghall
Spruisty Grange Farm
Nidd Moor
Nidd Banks
Bar Farm
Weir
Nature Reserve
Viaduct Wood
Spruisty Hall Farm
219
Holme Bottom
220
Myer's Green
Pyking Croft Farm
Killinghall CE Prim Sch
Nidd Viaduct
Hollins Farm
Hollins Hall
MOOR CL
PICKING CFT LA
Spruisty Hill Farm
Sewage Works
Croft Farm
GREYSTONES AV
GRAINBECK LANE
Hill Top Farm
HOLLINS LA
LUND LANE
Knox
Willow Wood
LEVENS CL
KNOX MILL LANE
TENNYSON AV
HOLLINS LANE
CHAIN BAR LANE
Levens Hall
Knotty Ash Farm
OTLEY ROAD
High Warren Farm
KNOX LANE
Shutt Nook Farm
Warren Top
Grange Farm
Knox Hill Farm
Knox Hill
BACHELOR GDNS
HALL LANE
BILTON LANE
HG1
Saltergate Hill
Moorlands Farm
B6161
Mount Pleasant Farm
Superstore
Bilton
Liby
Rec
SKIPTON ROAD
A59
ST JOHN'S RD
ALBERT RD
POPLAR GR
Rowden Lane End
Dyke Bottom Farm
CRANESBILL CL
Jennyfield
ELECTRIC AV
Schs
Sch
ALBANY AV
WOODFIELD ROAD
DENE PK
High Harrogate
JENNY FIELD DRIVE
New Pk
CHATSWORTH GROVE
Swimming Pool
Burley Bank Farm
GRANTLEY DR
SALTERGATE DR
Prim Sch
Leisure Ctr
Killinghall Moor Country Park
OAKDALE GLEN
GROVE RD
Cemy
HARROGATE
BURLEY LA
BURLEY AVE
BURLEY BANK CL
Mast
Killinghall Moor
CH
COPPICE DR
Harrogate High Sch
Int Ctr
DRAGON PAR
EAST PARADE
White House Farm
OAK AVE
Oak Beck
OAKDALE
Coll
BOWER RD
PENNY POT LANE
Oakdale
OAKDALE MANOR
KENT ROAD
DUCHY ROAD
YORK RD
SWAN RD
PARK VW
Oakdale Farm
Oakdale Farm
RUTLAND RD
Art Gall
Mus
STATION PD
Harrogate
NORTH PK ROAD
KNARESBOROUGH RD
WETHERBY RD
A661
Army Foundation College
Bardner Wood
RUTLAND DRIVE
CORNWALL RD
VALLEY DR
WEST PK ST
YORK PL
A6040
Brik Crag Nature Reserve
Gardens
OATLANDS DRIVE
ST WINIFRED'S RD
B2
1 LONG CRAG VW
2 BIRK-CRAG CT
3 YOUNG'S DR
4 PENNY POT GDNS
5 EVELYN CT
6 QUEEN ETHELBURGA'S GDNS
7 OLD CHAPEL CL
8 QUEEN ETHELBURGA'S PAR
9 QUEEN ETHELBURGA'S PAR
HARLOW MOOR DRIVE
QUEENS RD
BEECH GR
STRAY REIN
CAVENDISH AV
ST HILDA'S ROAD
Little Wood
Pot Bridge Farm
Birk Crag House
CRAG LANE
LEEDS RD
Mile End
Sch
HG2
Oakdale Farm
Harlow Hill
LASCELLES RD
HARLOW OVAL
MANOR RD
OTLEY ROAD
Coll
PARK DR
SOUTH DR
WHEATLANDS ROAD E
Harlow Carr
Harlow Carr RHS Garden
222
HOOKSTONE RD
Cardale Woodland
POT BANK
B6162
PANNAL ASH RD
ARTHURS AV
PARK AV
LANGCLIFFE AV
A61
8 61 7 60 6 59 5 58 4 57 3 56 2 55 1 54
26 A 27 B 28 C 29 D 30 E 31 F
B3
1 CORNFLOWER WY
2 FOXGLOVE CL
3 OAKRIDGE VW
4 TREFOIL DR
5 STONECROP AVE
6 BUTTERCUP CL
7 PENNY ROYAL CL
8 ORCHID WY
9 CLOVER WY
10 BURDOCK CL
11 BRAMBLE CL
12 ANGELICA CL
13 PRIMROSE CL
14 LARKSPUR GR
15 PENNYWORT GR
16 HEATHER WY
17 HAREBELL CL
18 BLUEBELL WK
19 COLTSFOOT CT
C3
1 STONECROP DR
2 TANSY CL
3 TANSY RD
4 BRYONY RD
5 BRYONY WY
6 CAMPION GR
7 TRURO RD
8 TRURO CRES
9 SALISBURY DR
10 EXETER CRES
11 NORWICH DR
12 LINCOLN GR
13 LICHFIELD GR
14 SPEEDWELL GLADE
15 BLUEBELL MDW
16 SALLOW HEATH
17 GENTIAN GLADE
18 SWEET BRIAR
19 SAFFRON MDW
20 BARBERRY CL
21 WINTER GN
22 STONE BRAMBLE
23 CARLINE MEAD
24 SUNDEW HEATH
25 PETTY WHIN CL
26 CORNEL RISE
27 WOODRUFF CL
28 JUNIPER WY
29 SORREL GR
30 BORAGE RD
31 TEASEL GR
32 COMFREY CL
33 COLUMBINE GR
34 BUTTERBUR WY
35 WOOD AVEN CL
178
220
For full street detail of the highlighted area see pages 219, 220, 222 and 223.

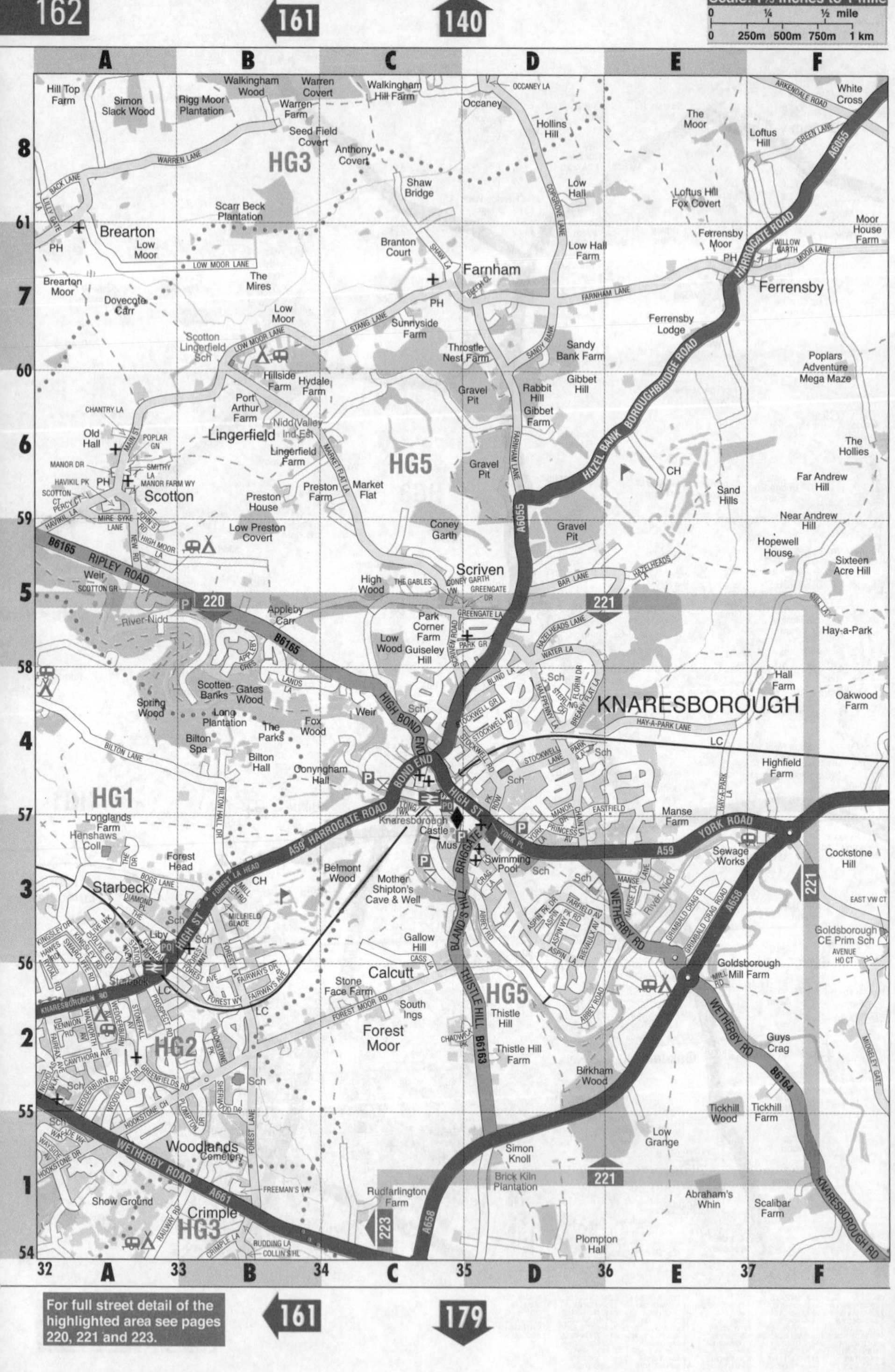

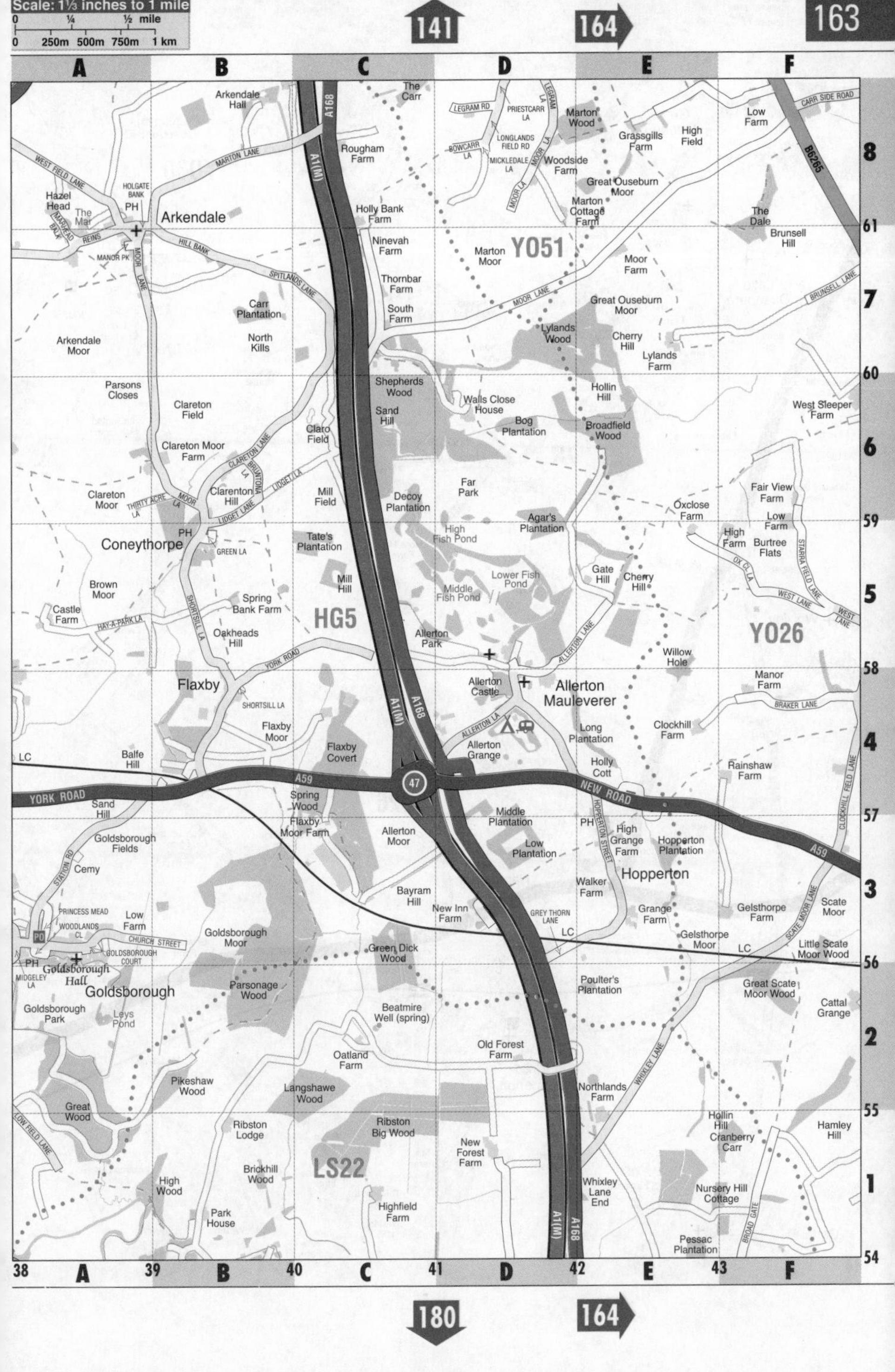
Scale: 1⅓ inches to 1 mile
0 ¼ ½ mile
0 250m 500m 750m 1 km
141
164
Arkendale Hall
Rougham Farm
The Carr
Marton Wood
Grassgills Farm
High Field
Low Farm
Woodside Farm
Great Ouseburn Moor
Hazel Head
Arkendale
Holly Bank Farm
Marton Cottage Farm
The Dale
Brunsell Hill
Ninevah Farm
Marton Moor
YO51
Moor Farm
Thornbar Farm
South Farm
Carr Plantation
Great Ouseburn Moor
Arkendale Moor
North Kills
Lylands Wood
Cherry Hill
Lylands Farm
Parsons Closes
Shepherds Wood
Hollin Hill
Clareton Field
Sand Hill
Walls Close House
Bog Plantation
West Sleeper Farm
Claro Field
Broadfield Wood
Clareton Moor Farm
Far Park
Fair View Farm
Clareton Moor
Clareton Hill
Mill Field
Decoy Plantation
Oxclose Farm
Low Farm
Agar's Plantation
Coneythorpe
Tate's Plantation
High Fish Pond
High Farm
Burtree Flats
Brown Moor
Mill Hill
Lower Fish Pond
Gate Hill
Cherry Hill
Castle Farm
Spring Bank Farm
Middle Fish Pond
HG5
YO26
Oakheads Hill
Allerton Park
Willow Hole
Flaxby
Allerton Castle
Allerton Mauleverer
Manor Farm
Flaxby Moor
Long Plantation
Clockhill Farm
Balfe Hill
Flaxby Covert
Allerton Grange
Holly Cott
Rainshaw Farm
YORK ROAD
Sand Hill
Spring Wood
Flaxby Moor Farm
Middle Plantation
High Grange Farm
Hopperton Plantation
Goldsborough Fields
Allerton Moor
Low Plantation
Cemy
Bayram Hill
Walker Farm
Hopperton
Low Farm
New Inn Farm
Grange Farm
Gelsthorpe Farm
Scate Moor
Goldsborough Moor
Gelsthorpe Moor
Little Scate Moor Wood
Green Dick Wood
Goldsborough Hall
Goldsborough
Parsonage Wood
Poulter's Plantation
Great Scate Moor Wood
Goldsborough Park
Leys Pond
Beatmire Well (spring)
Cattal Grange
Oatland Farm
Old Forest Farm
Pikeshaw Wood
Langshawe Wood
Northlands Farm
Great Wood
Ribston Lodge
Ribston Big Wood
Hollin Hill
Cranberry Carr
Hamley Hill
New Forest Farm
LS22
Brickhill Wood
High Wood
Whixley Lane End
Nursery Hill Cottage
Highfield Farm
Park House
Pessac Plantation
A B C D E F
8 7 6 5 4 3 2 1
61 60 59 58 57 56 55 54
38 39 40 41 42 43
180
164

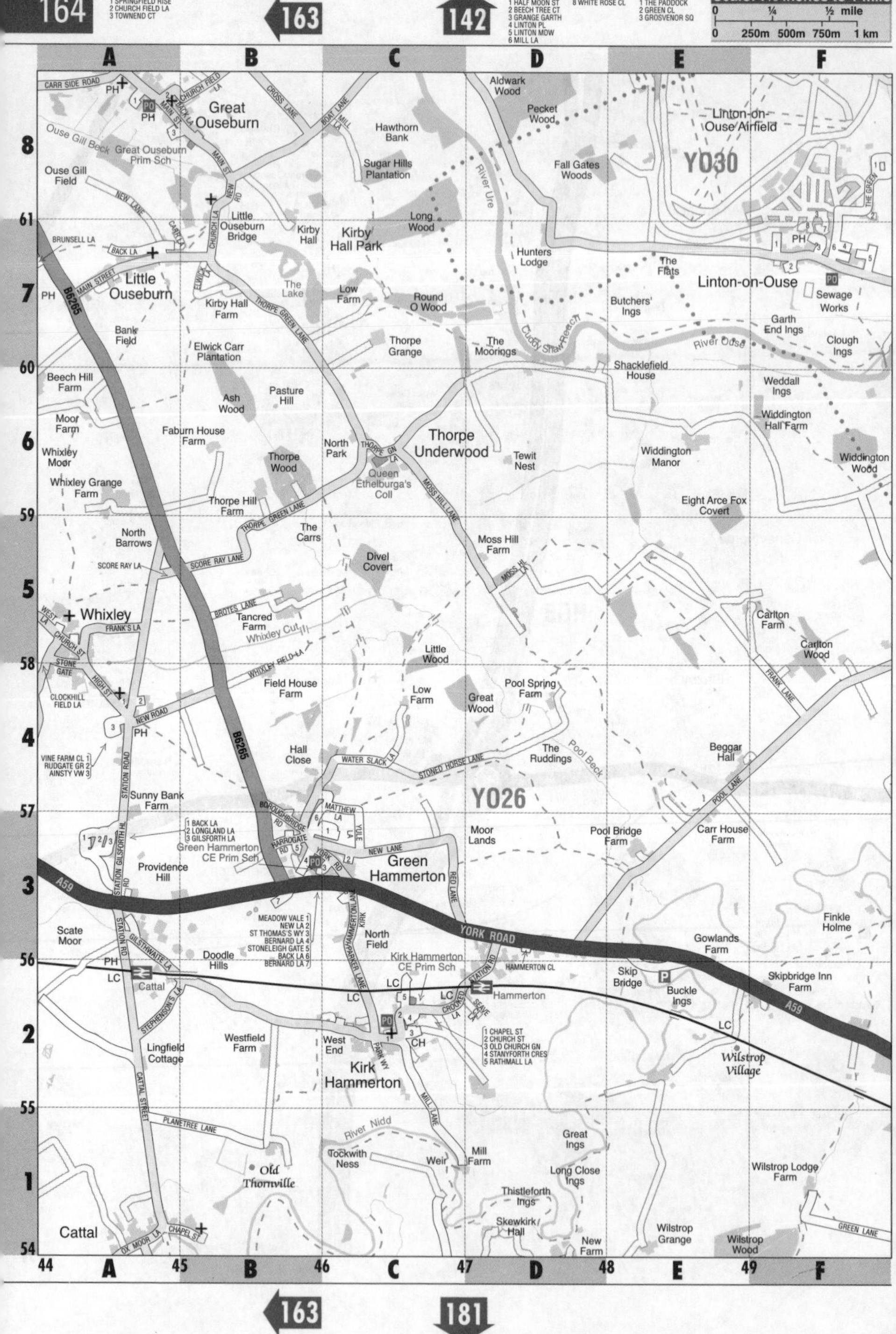

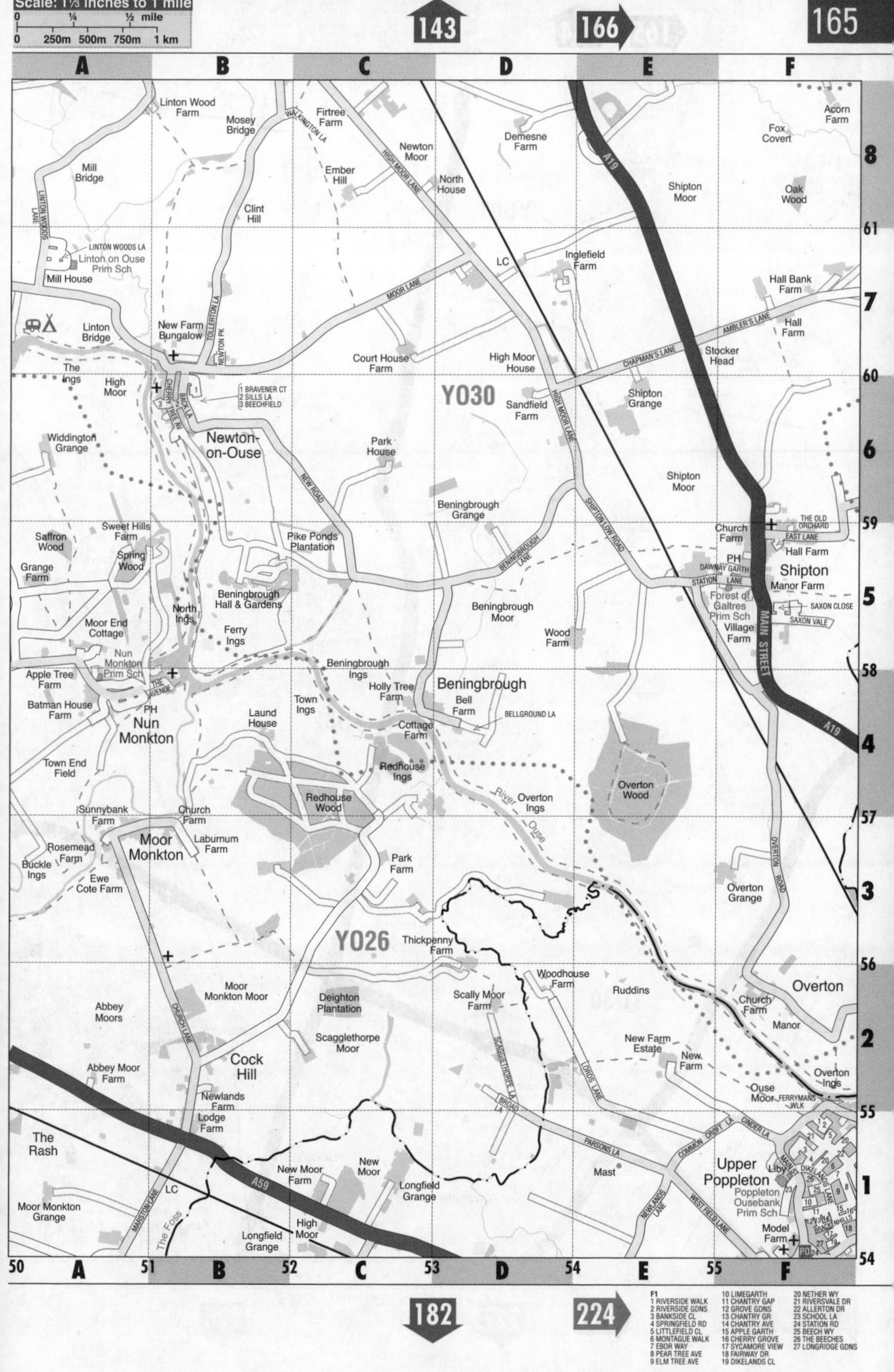

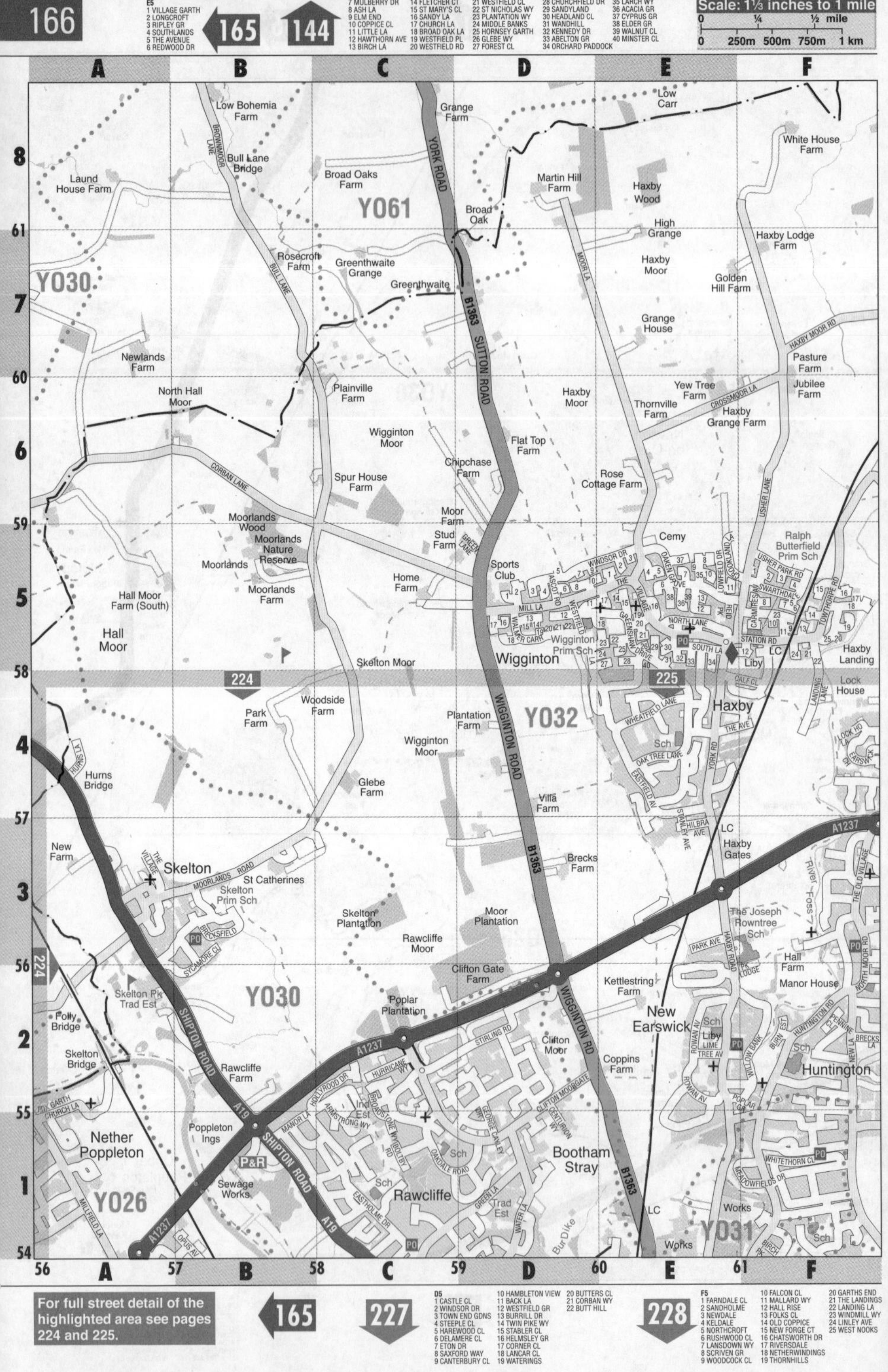

166

Scale: 1½ inches to 1 mile

0   ¼   ½ mile
0 250m 500m 750m 1 km

165   144

YO61

YO30

YO32

YO26

YO30

YO31

For full street detail of the highlighted area see pages 224 and 225.

165   227   228

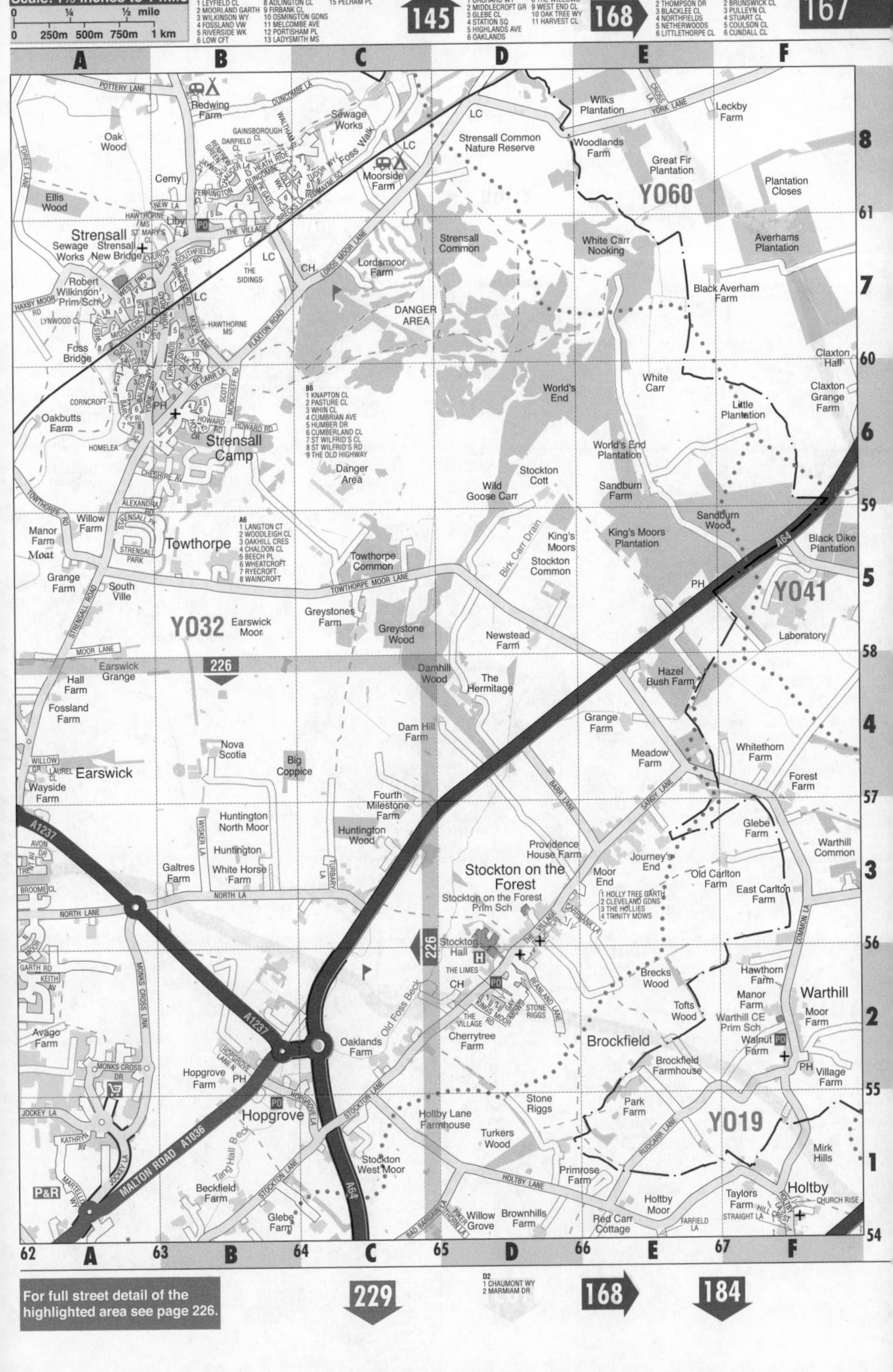

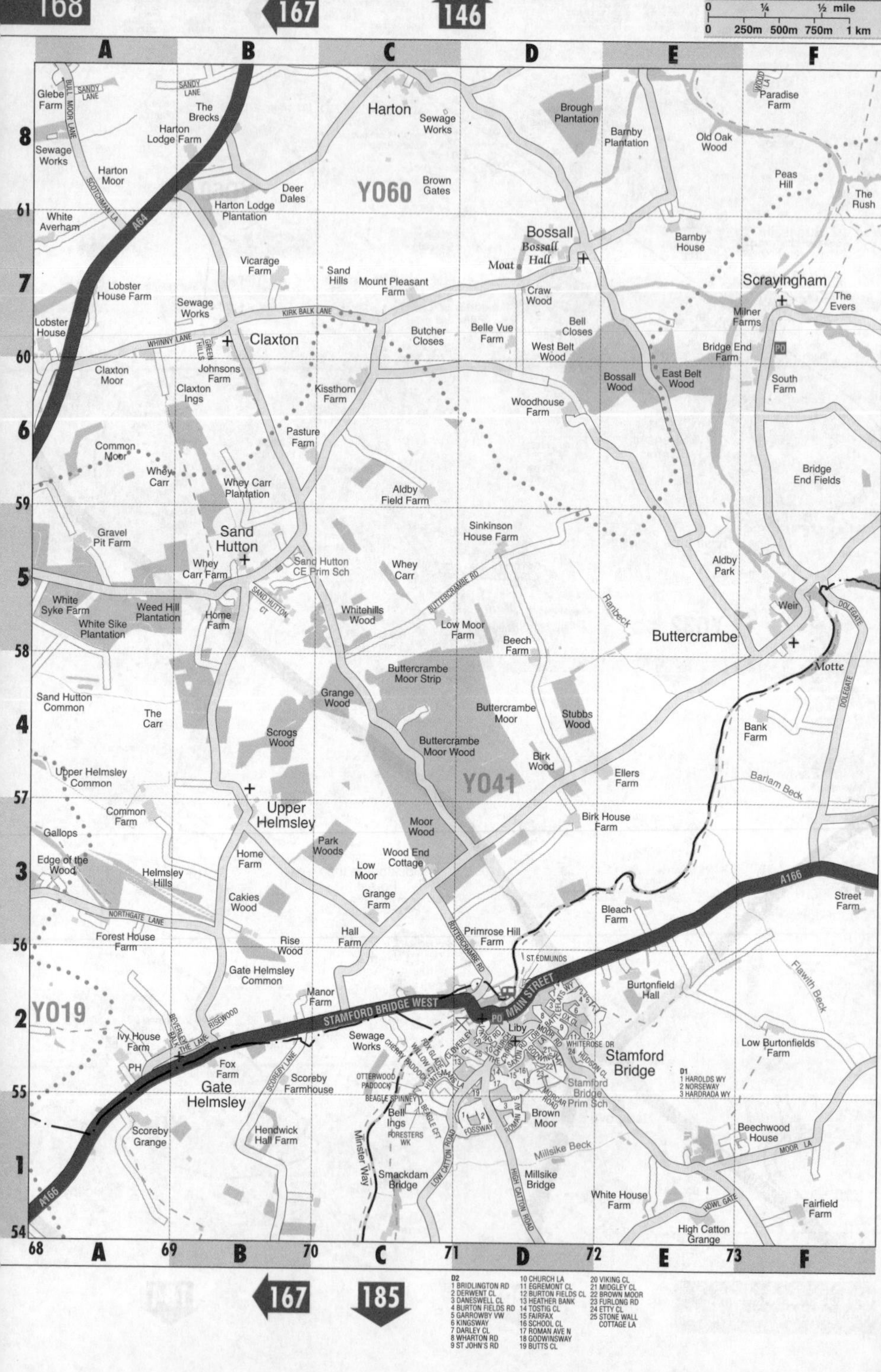

Scale: 1½ inches to 1 mile

Y060

Y041

Y019

Y0 41

D2
1 BRIDLINGTON RD
2 DERWENT CL
3 DANESWELL CL
4 BURTON FIELDS CL
5 GARROWBY VW
6 KINGSWAY
7 DARLEY CL
8 WHARTON RD
9 ST JOHN'S RD

10 CHURCH LA
11 EGREMONT CL
12 BURTON FIELDS CL
13 HEATHER BANK
14 TOSTIG CL
15 FAIRFAX
16 SCHOOL CL
17 ROMAN AVE N
18 GODWINSWAY
19 BUTTS CL

20 VIKING CL
21 MIDGLEY CL
22 BROWN MOOR
23 FURLONG RD
24 ETTY CL
25 STONE WALL
   COTTAGE LA

D1
1 HAROLDS WY
2 NORSEWAY
3 HARORADA WY

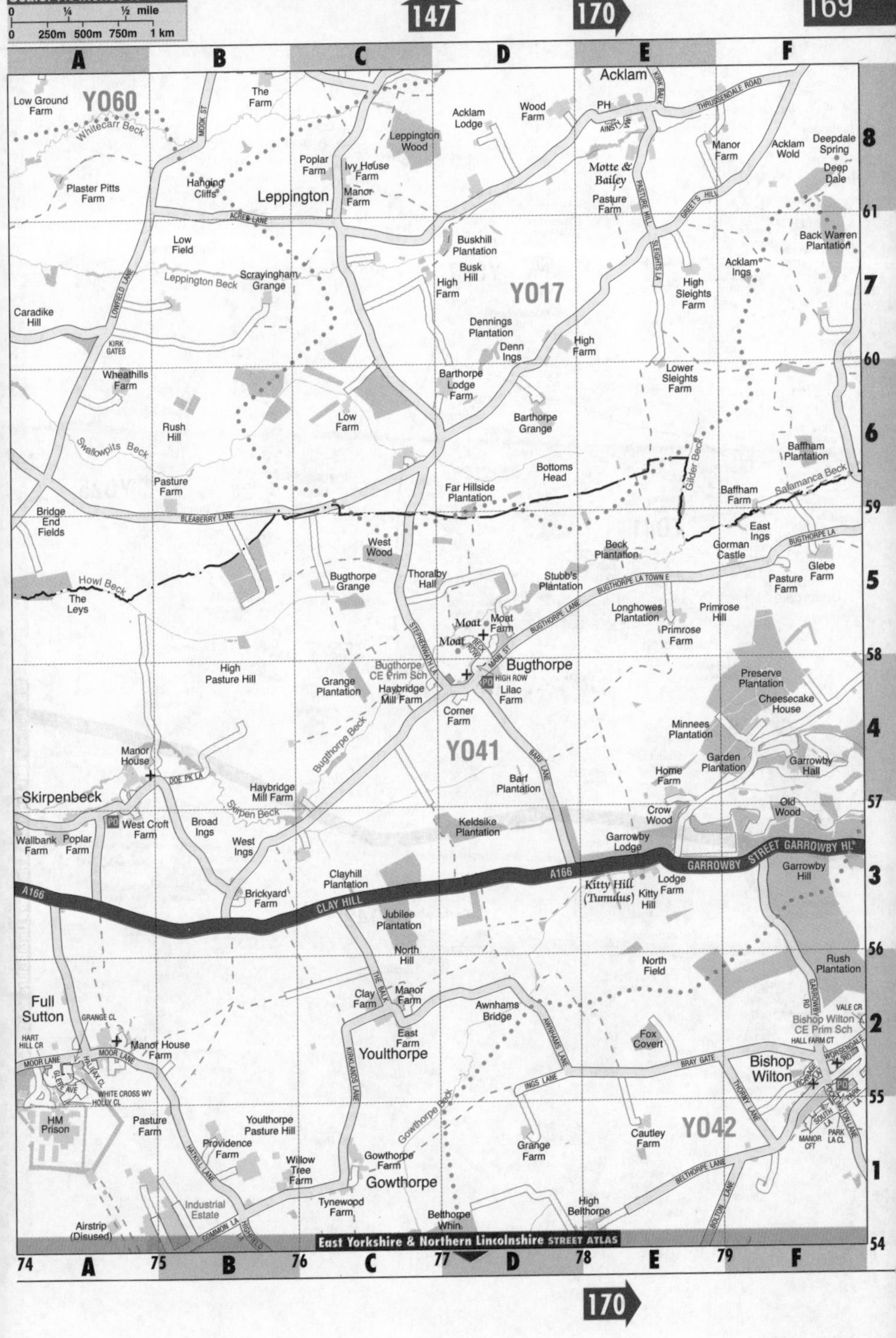
Scale: 1⅓ inches to 1 mile
147
170
Acklam
YO60
Leppington
YO17
Bugthorpe
YO41
Skirpenbeck
Full Sutton
Youlthorpe
Gowthorpe
Bishop Wilton
YO42
HM Prison
A166
CLAY HILL
GARROWBY STREET GARROWBY HILL
East Yorkshire & Northern Lincolnshire STREET ATLAS
170

169
148

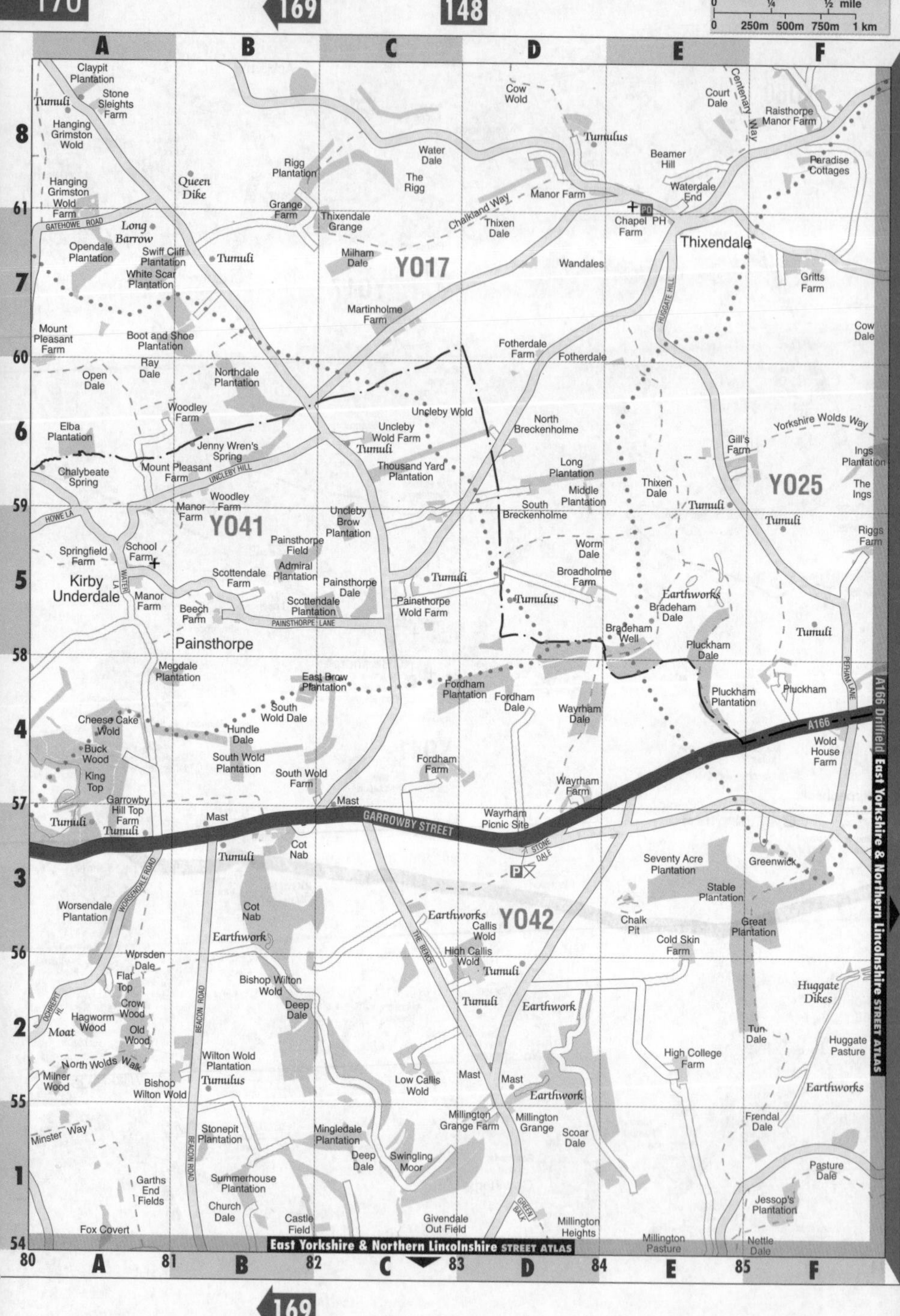
Scale: 1⅓ inches to 1 mile
0 ¼ ½ mile
0 250m 500m 750m 1 km
A B C D E F
Claypit Plantation
Stone Sleights Farm
Tumuli
Hanging Grimston Wold
Hanging Grimston Wold Farm
Queen Dike
Rigg Plantation
Grange Farm
Thixendale Grange
Water Dale
The Rigg
Cow Wold
Tumulus
Manor Farm
Chalkland Way
Thixen Dale
Court Dale
Centenary Way
Raisthorpe Manor Farm
Beamer Hill
Paradise Cottages
Waterdale End
Chapel Farm
PO
PH
Thixendale
GATEHOWE ROAD
Long Barrow
Opendale Plantation
Swift Cliff Plantation
White Scar Plantation
Milham Dale
YO17
Wandales
HUGGATE HILL
Gritts Farm
Martinholme Farm
Mount Pleasant Farm
Boot and Shoe Plantation
Ray Dale
Open Dale
Northdale Plantation
Fotherdale Farm
Fotherdale
Cow Dale
Woodley Farm
Uncleby Wold
North Breckenholme
Elba Plantation
Jenny Wren's Spring
Uncleby Wold Farm
Yorkshire Wolds Way
Gill's Farm
Ings Plantation
Chalybeate Spring
Mount Pleasant Farm
UNCLEBY HILL
Thousand Yard Plantation
Long Plantation
Middle Plantation
Thixen Dale
YO25
The Ings
HOWE LA
Woodley Farm
Manor Farm
YO41
Uncleby Brow Plantation
South Breckenholme
Riggs Farm
Springfield Farm
School Farm
Painsthorpe Field
Admiral Plantation
Worm Dale
Kirby Underdale
WATER LA
Scottendale Farm
Painsthorpe Dale
Broadholme Farm
Manor Farm
Beech Farm
Scottendale Plantation
Painsthorpe Wold Farm
Tumulus
Earthworks
Bradeham Dale
PAINSTHORPE LANE
Bradeham Well
Pluckham Dale
PEPHAM LANE
Painsthorpe
Megdale Plantation
East Brow Plantation
Fordham Plantation
Fordham Dale
Pluckham Plantation
Pluckham
South Wold Dale
Wayrham Dale
A166 Driffield
Cheese Cake Wold
Hundle Dale
A166
Buck Wood
Wold House Farm
South Wold Plantation
Fordham Farm
King Top
South Wold Farm
Wayrham Farm
Garrowby Hill Top Farm
Mast
Wayrham Picnic Site
GARROWBY STREET
STONE DALE
Cot Nab
Seventy Acre Plantation
Greenwick
Stable Plantation
Worsendale Plantation
WORSENDALE ROAD
Cot Nab
Earthworks
Callis Wold
YO42
Chalk Pit
Great Plantation
Earthwork
THE BEHOE
Cold Skin Farm
Worsden Dale
High Callis Wold
Flat Top
Bishop Wilton Wold
Huggate Dikes
Crow Wood
Deep Dale
Earthwork
Hagworm Wood
Moat
Old Wood
BEACON ROAD
Tun Dale
Huggate Pasture
North Wolds Walk
Wilton Wold Plantation
High College Farm
Milner Wood
Bishop Wilton Wold
Tumulus
Low Callis Wold
Mast
Earthwork
Earthworks
Minster Way
Stonepit Plantation
Mingledale Plantation
Millington Grange Farm
Millington Grange
Scoar Dale
Frendal Dale
Deep Dale
Swingling Moor
Pasture Dale
Garths End Fields
Summerhouse Plantation
Jessop's Plantation
Church Dale
GREEN BALK
Fox Covert
Castle Field
Givendale Out Field
Millington Heights
Millington Pasture
Nettle Dale
East Yorkshire & Northern Lincolnshire STREET ATLAS
8 61 7 60 6 59 5 58 4 57 3 56 2 55 1 54
80 81 82 83 84 85

169

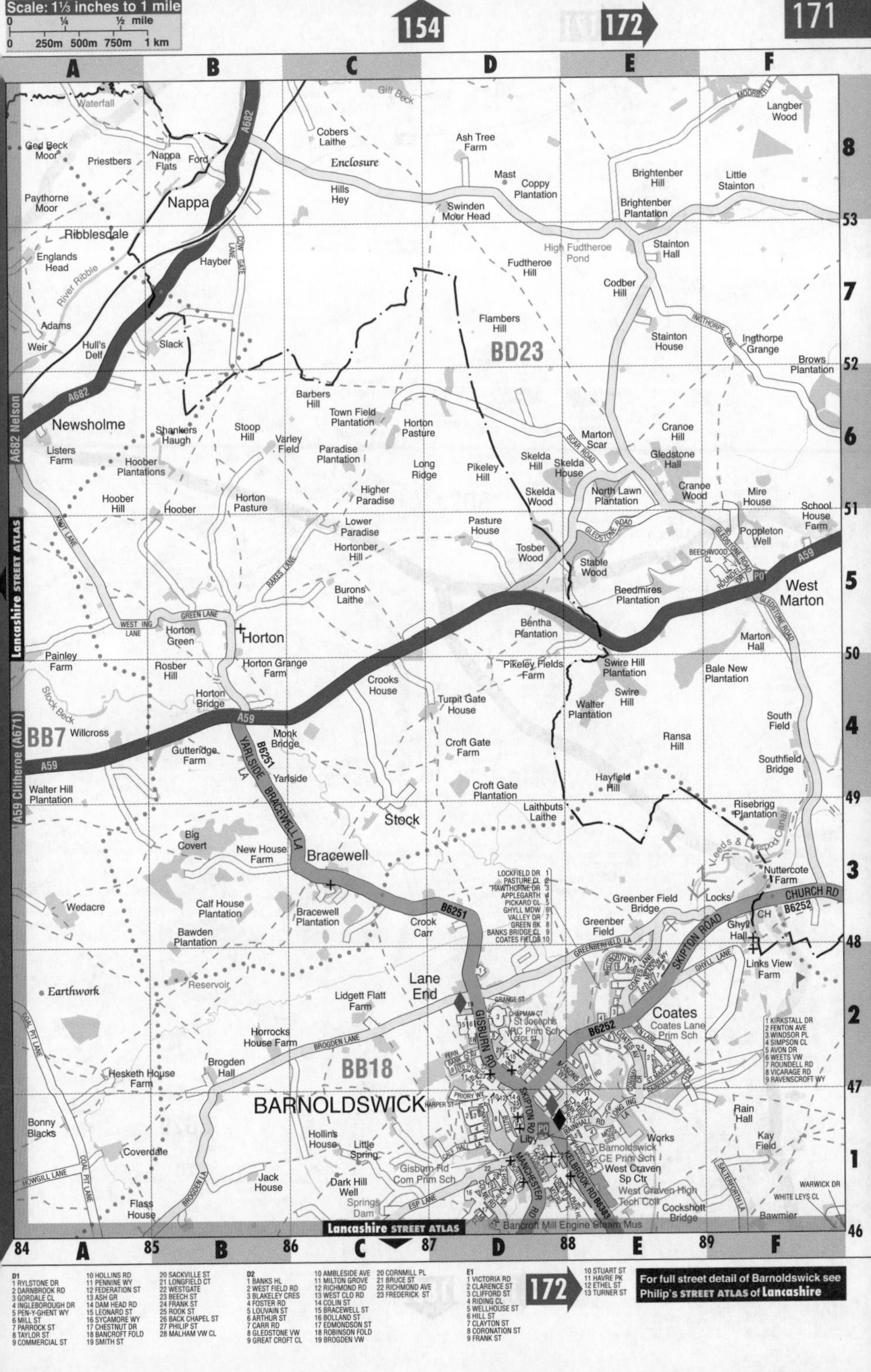

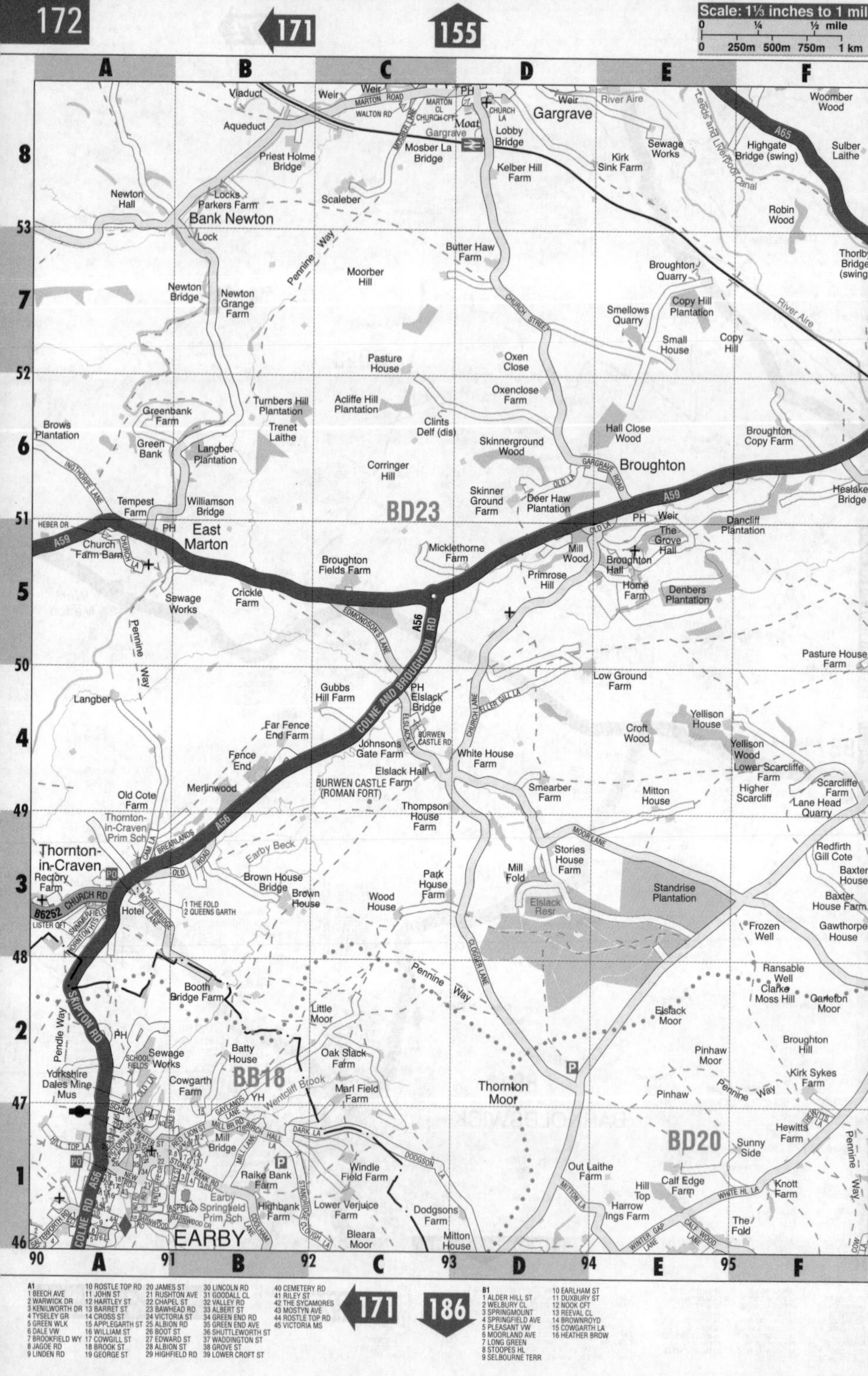

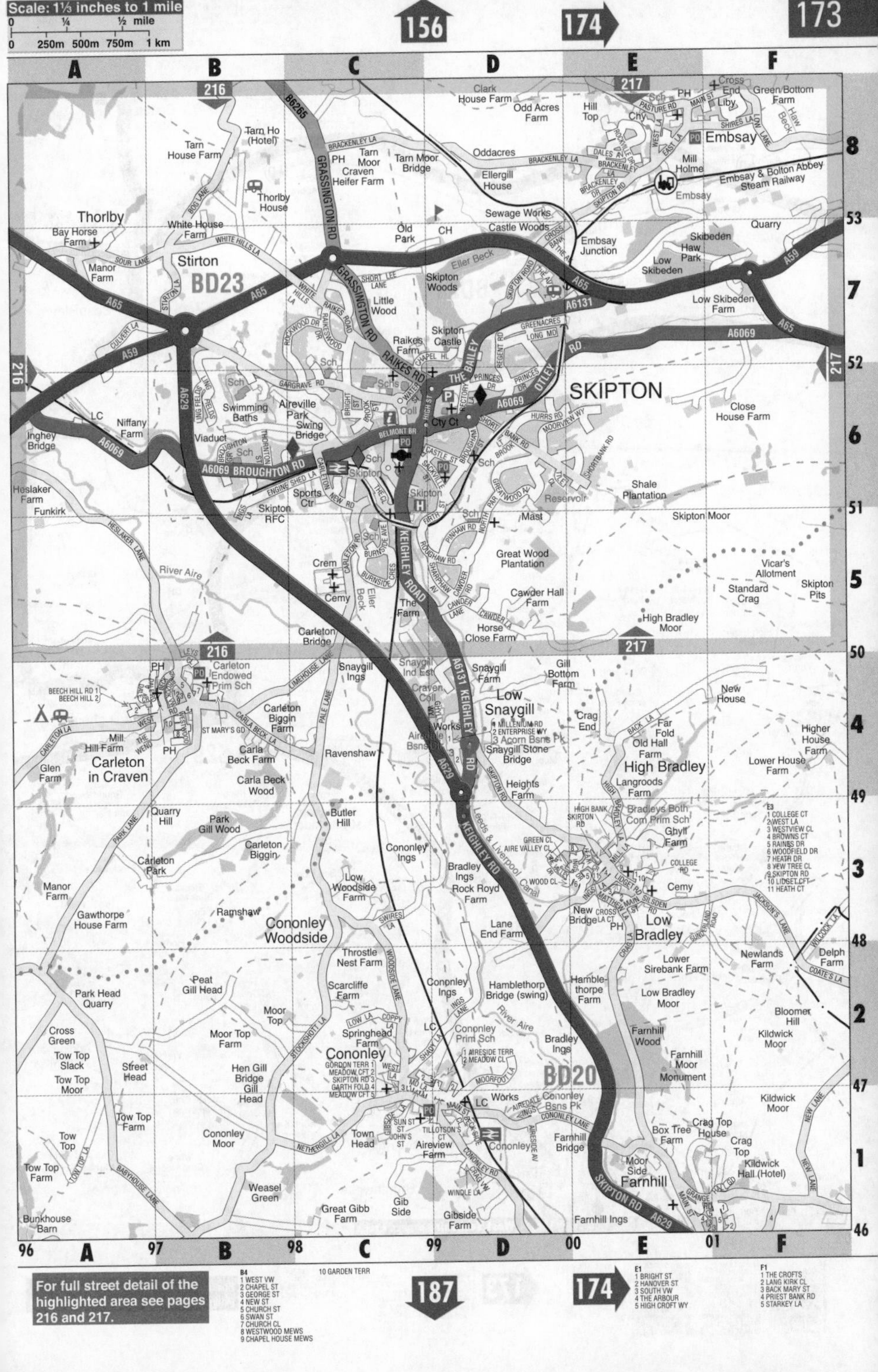

Scale: 1⅓ inches to 1 mile
0 ¼ ½ mile
0 250m 500m 750m 1 km
156
174
173
A B C D E F
216
217
Clark House Farm
Odd Acres Farm
Hill Top
Cross End
Green Bottom Farm
Haw Beck
Embsay
Liby
PASTURE RD
MAIN ST
SHIRES LA
LOW LANE
WEST LA
EAST LA
Tarn Ho (Hotel)
Tarn House Farm
B6265
BRACKENLEY LA
Tarn Moor
Craven Heifer Farm
Tarn Moor Bridge
Oddacres
Ellergill House
Mill Holme
Embsay & Bolton Abbey Steam Railway
GRASSINGTON RD
Thorlby House
Thorlby
Bay Horse Farm
White House Farm
BOG LANE
WHITE HILLS LA
SOUR LANE
Old Park
CH
Sewage Works
Castle Woods
Embsay Junction
Skibeden
Haw Park
Low Skibeden
Quarry
Manor Farm
Stirton
BD23
A65
SHORT LEE LANE
Eller Beck
Skipton Woods
Little Wood
SKIPTON ROAD
Low Skibeden Farm
A6131
GREENACRES
LONG MD
A6069
A59
CULVERT LA
Raikes Farm
Skipton Castle
CHAPEL HL
RAIKES RD
THE BAILEY
OTLEY RD
SKIPTON
GARGRAVE RD
Sch
Swimming Baths
Aireville Park
Swing Bridge
Coll
Cty Ct
HIGH ST
PRINCES DR
HURRS RD
MOORVIEW WY
Close House Farm
LC
Niffany Farm
Inghey Bridge
Viaduct
BELMONT BR
A6069 BROUGHTON RD
CASTLE ST
BANK RD
Heslaker Farm
Funkirk
ENGINE SHED LA
Sports Ctr
Skipton
Skipton RFC
SHORTBANK RD
Shale Plantation
Reservoir
Mast
Skipton Moor
HESLAKER LANE
River Aire
KEIGHLEY ROAD
Great Wood Plantation
Crem
Cemy
Eller Beck
The Farm
Cawder Hall Farm
Vicar's Allotment
Standard Crag
Skipton Pits
High Bradley Moor
Carleton Bridge
Horse Close Farm
Carleton Endowed Prim Sch
Snaygill Ings
Snaygill Ind Est
Craven Coll
Snaygill Farm
Gill Bottom Farm
Low Snaygill
New House
Carleton Biggin Farm
Works
1 MILLENIUM RD
2 ENTERPRISE WY
3 Acorn Bsns Pk
Crag End
Far Fold
Old Hall Farm
Higher House Farm
Mill Hill Farm
ST MARY'S GD
CARLA BECK LA
Carla Beck Farm
Ravenshaw
Snaygill Stone Bridge
High Bradley
Lower House Farm
Glen Farm
Carleton in Craven
Carla Beck Wood
A6131 KEIGHLEY RD
A629
Heights Farm
Langroods Farm
Quarry Hill
Park Gill Wood
Butler Hill
Bradleys Both Com Prim Sch
Ghyll Farm
Carleton Biggin
Cononley Ings
Leeds & Liverpool Canal
Carleton Park
Manor Farm
Low Woodside Farm
Bradley Ings
Rock Royd Farm
Cemy
Gawthorpe House Farm
Ramshaw
Lane End Farm
New Bridge
Low Bradley
Cononley Woodside
Throstle Nest Farm
Newlands Farm
Delph Farm
Lower Sirebank Farm
Peat Gill Head
Scarcliffe Farm
Cononley Ings
Hamblethorp Bridge (swing)
Hamblethorpe Farm
Low Bradley Moor
Park Head Quarry
Moor Top
River Aire
Bloomer Hill
Kildwick Moor
Cross Green
Moor Top Farm
Springhead Farm
Cononley Prim Sch
Farnhill Wood
Tow Top Slack
Tow Top Moor
Street Head
Hen Gill Bridge
Gill Head
Cononley
Bradley Ings
Farnhill Moor
Monument
BD20
Works
Cononley Bsns Pk
LC
Kildwick Moor
Tow Top Farm
Town Head
Aireview Farm
Cononley
Box Tree Farm
Crag Top House
Crag Top
Farnhill Bridge
Tow Top
Cononley Moor
Moor Side
Farnhill
Kildwick Hall (Hotel)
Weasel Green
Gib Side
Great Gibb Farm
Gibside Farm
Farnhill Ings
SKIPTON RD
Bunkhouse Barn
96 97 98 99 00 01
53 52 51 50 49 48 47 46
8 7 6 5 4 3 2 1
E3
1 COLLEGE CT
2 WEST LA
3 WESTVIEW CL
4 BROWNS CT
5 RAINES DR
6 WOODFIELD DR
7 HEATH DR
8 YEW TREE CL
9 SKIPTON RD
10 LIDGET CFT
11 HEATH CT
C1
GORDON TERR 1
MEADOW CFT 2
SKIPTON RD 3
GARTH FOLD 4
MEADOW CFT 5
For full street detail of the highlighted area see pages 216 and 217.
187
174
B4
1 WEST VW
2 CHAPEL ST
3 GEORGE ST
4 NEW ST
5 CHURCH ST
6 SWAN ST
7 CHURCH CL
8 WESTWOOD MEWS
9 CHAPEL HOUSE MEWS
10 GARDEN TERR
E1
1 BRIGHT ST
2 HANOVER ST
3 SOUTH VW
4 THE ARBOUR
5 HIGH CROFT WY
F1
1 THE CROFTS
2 LANG KIRK CL
3 BACK MARY ST
4 PRIEST BANK RD
5 STARKEY LA

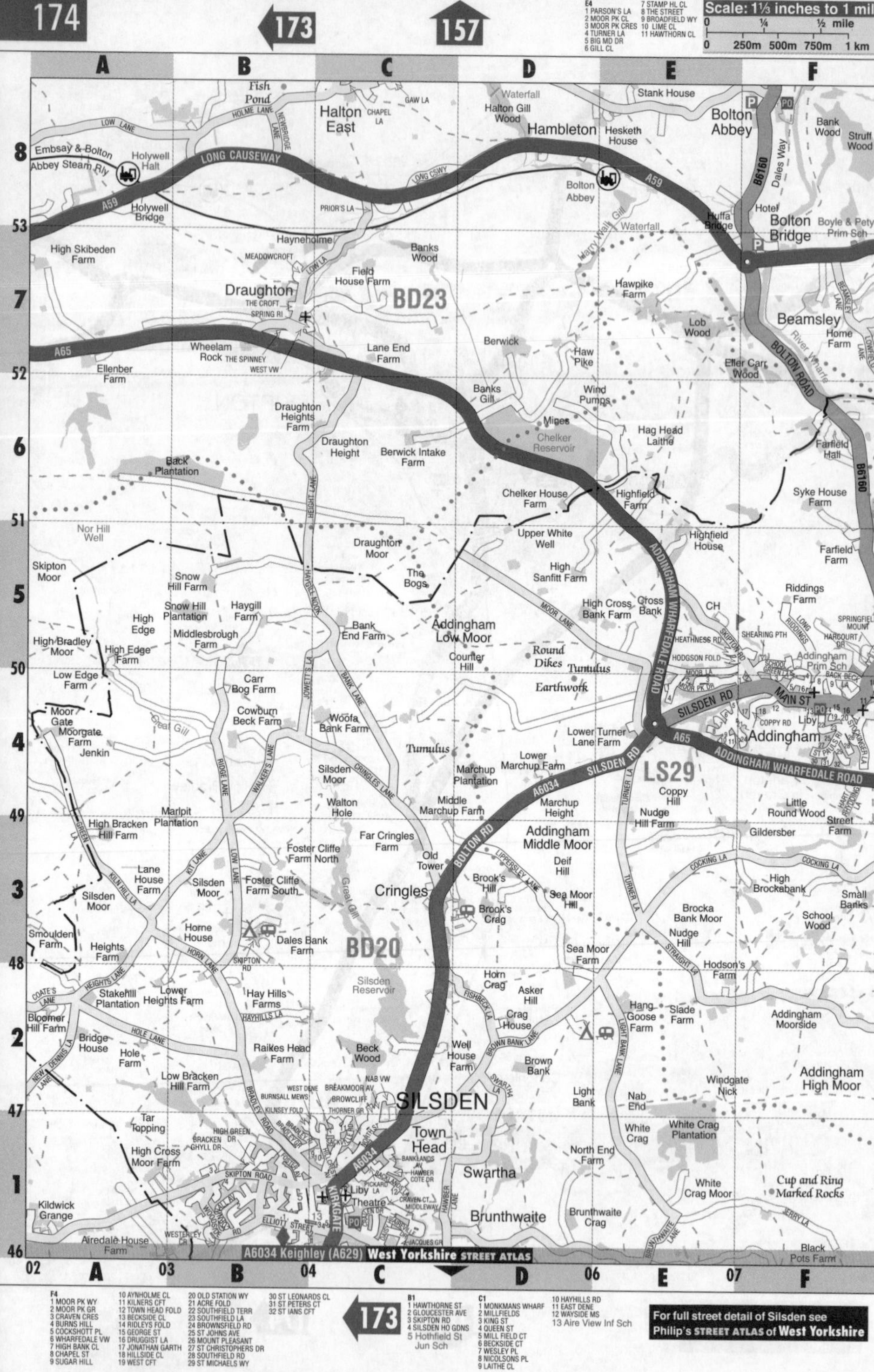

173
157
E4
1 PARSON'S LA
2 MOOR PK CL
3 MOOR PK CRES
4 TURNER LA
5 BIG MD DR
6 GILL CL
7 STAMP HL CL
8 THE STREET
9 BROADFIELD WY
10 LIME CL
11 HAWTHORN CL
Scale: 1⅓ inches to 1 mile
0 ¼ ½ mile
0 250m 500m 750m 1 km
A B C D E F
8 53 7 52 6 51 5 50 4 49 3 48 2 47 1 46
02 03 04 05 06 07
Fish Pond
Halton East
CHAPEL LA
GAW LA
Waterfall
Halton Gill Wood
Hambleton
Hesketh House
Stank House
Bolton Abbey
Bank Wood
Struff Wood
LOW LANE
HOLME LANE
NEWBRIDGE LANE
Embsay & Bolton Abbey Steam Rly
Holywell Halt
LONG CAUSEWAY
LONG CSWY
A59
B6160
Dales Way
Holywell Bridge
PRIOR'S LA
Bolton Abbey
Hayneholme
Waterfall
Hotel
Huffa Bridge
Bolton Bridge
Boyle & Petyt Prim Sch
High Skibeden Farm
MEADOWCROFT
LOW LA
Banks Wood
Field House Farm
Hawpike Farm
Draughton
THE CROFT
SPRING RI
BD23
Lob Wood
Beamsley
BEAMSLEY LANE
Home Farm
A65
Wheelam Rock
THE SPINNEY
WEST VW
Lane End Farm
Berwick
Haw Pike
Eller Carr Wood
BOLTON ROAD
River Wharfe
Ellenber Farm
Banks Gill
Wind Pumps
Draughton Heights Farm
Mines
Chelker Reservoir
Hag Head Laithe
Farfield Hall
Draughton Height
Berwick Intake Farm
Back Plantation
Chelker House Farm
Highfield Farm
Syke House Farm
HEIGHT LANE
Nor Hill Well
Draughton Moor
Upper White Well
Highfield House
Farfield Farm
Skipton Moor
High Sanfitt Farm
ADDINGHAM WHARFEDALE ROAD
The Bogs
HAYGILL NOOK
Snow Hill Farm
Riddings Farm
Snow Hill Plantation
Haygill Farm
MOOR LANE
High Cross Bank Farm
Cross Bank
CH
High Edge
Middlesbrough Farm
Bank End Farm
Addingham Low Moor
HEATHNESS RD
SKIPTON RD
SHEARING PTH
LONG RIDDINGS
SPRINGFIELD MOUNT
HARCOURT DR
High Bradley Moor
High Edge Farm
Counter Hill
Round Dikes
Tumulus
HODGSON FOLD
Addingham Prim Sch
Low Edge Farm
Carr Bog Farm
Earthwork
MOOR LA
MOOR PK DR
SCHOOL GREEN
BACK BECK LA
JOWETT'S LA
BANK LANE
SILSDEN RD
MAIN ST
Moor Gate
Cowburn Beck Farm
Great Gill
Woofa Bank Farm
Lower Turner Lane Farm
COPPY RD
Liby
Moorgate Farm
Jenkin
Addingham
ST PAUL'S RI
STOCKINGER LA
Tumulus
Lower Marchup Farm
SILSDEN RD
LS29
ADDINGHAM WHARFEDALE ROAD
RIDGE LANE
WALKER'S LANE
Silsden Moor
CRINGLES LANE
Marchup Plantation
A6034
Coppy Hill
TURNER LA
Walton Hole
Middle Marchup Farm
Marchup Height
Nudge Hill Farm
Little Round Wood
Street Farm
Marlpit Plantation
High Bracken Hill Farm
GREEN
Far Cringles Farm
BOLTON RD
Addingham Middle Moor
Gildersber
KIT LANE
LOW LANE
Foster Cliffe Farm North
Old Tower
LIPPERSLEY LANE
Deif Hill
COCKING LA
COCKING LA
Lane House Farm
KILN HILL LA
Silsden Moor
Foster Cliffe Farm South
Cringles
Brook's Hill
Sea Moor Hill
High Brockabank
Small Banks
Silsden Moor
Great Gill
Brook's Crag
Brocka Bank Moor
School Wood
Smoulden Farm
Horne House
Dales Bank Farm
Nudge Hill
Heights Farm
HORN LANE
SKIPTON RD
BD20
Sea Moor Farm
STRAIGHT LA
Hodson's Farm
HEIGHTS LANE
COATE'S LANE
Silsden Reservoir
Horn Crag
Stakehill Plantation
Lower Heights Farm
Hay Hills Farms
Asker Hill
LIGHT BANK LANE
Bloomer Hill Farm
HAYHILLS LA
FISHBECK LA
Crag House
Hang Goose Farm
Slade Farm
Addingham Moorside
HOLE LANE
Bridge House
Raikes Head Farm
Beck Wood
BROWN BANK LANE
Well House Farm
NEW DENNIS LANE
Hole Farm
Brown Bank
SWARTHA LA
Windgate Nick
Addingham High Moor
Low Bracken Hill Farm
NAB VW
BREAKMOOR AV
WEST DENE
BURNSALL MEWS
BROWCLIFF
KILNSEY FOLD
THORNER GR
SILSDEN
Light Bank
Nab End
BRADLEY ROAD
BRADLEY DR
Tar Topping
Town Head
White Crag
White Crag Plantation
HIGH GREEN DR
BRACKEN GHYLL DR
BANKLANDS AV
HAWBER COTE DR
North End Farm
High Cross Moor Farm
SKIPTON ROAD
Swartha
A6034
KIRKGATE
BACK LA
PICKARD LA
HAWBER LANE
White Crag Moor
Cup and Ring Marked Rocks
Liby
Theatre
CRAVEN CT
MIDDLEWAY
Kildwick Grange
WOODSIDE RD
ELLIOTT STREET
Bunthwaite Crag
Brunthwaite
BRUNTHWAITE LANE
JERRY LA
WESTERLEY CR
Airedale House Farm
JACQUES GR
Black Pots Farm
A6034 Keighley (A629)
West Yorkshire STREET ATLAS
F4
1 MOOR PK WY
2 MOOR PK GR
3 CRAVEN CRES
4 BURNS HILL
5 COCKSHOTT PL
6 WHARFEDALE VW
7 HIGH BANK CL
8 CHAPEL ST
9 SUGAR HILL
10 AYNHOLME CL
11 KILNERS CFT
12 TOWN HEAD FOLD
13 BECKSIDE CL
14 RIDLEYS FOLD
15 GEORGE ST
16 DRUGGIST LA
17 JONATHAN GARTH
18 HILLSIDE CL
19 WEST CFT
20 OLD STATION WY
21 ACRE FOLD
22 SOUTHFIELD TERR
23 SOUTHFIELD LA
24 BROWNSFIELD RD
25 ST JOHNS AVE
26 MOUNT PLEASANT
27 ST CHRISTOPHERS DR
28 SOUTHFIELD RD
29 ST MICHAELS WY
30 ST LEONARDS CL
31 ST PETERS CT
32 ST IANS CFT
173
B1
1 HAWTHORNE ST
2 GLOUCESTER AVE
3 SKIPTON RD
4 SILSDEN HO GDNS
5 Hothfield St Jun Sch
C1
1 MONKMANS WHARF
2 MILLFIELDS
3 KING ST
4 QUEEN ST
5 MILL FIELD CT
6 BECKSIDE CT
7 WESLEY PL
8 NICOLSONS PL
9 LAITHE CL
10 HAYHILLS RD
11 EAST DENE
12 WAYSIDE MS
13 Aire View Inf Sch
For full street detail of Silsden see Philip's STREET ATLAS of West Yorkshire

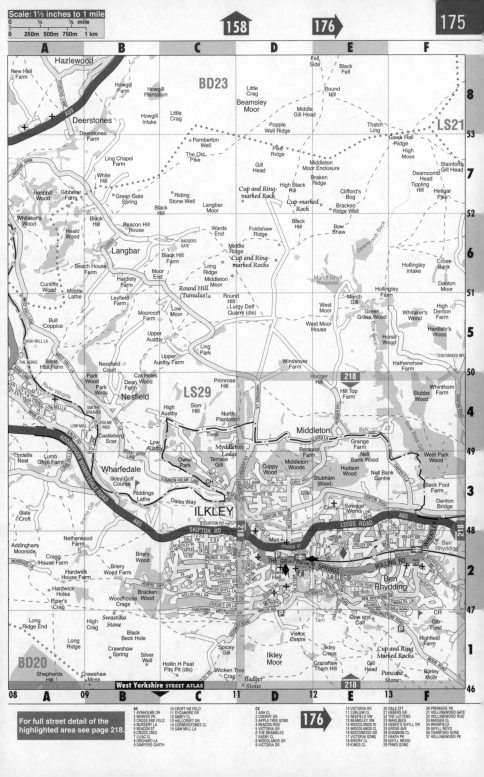

A   B   C   D   E   F

Hazlewood

New Hall Farm

BD23

Fell Side   Black Fell

Little Crag

Beamsley Moor

Howgill Farm

Howgill Plantation

Round Hill

Middle Gill Head

Thatch Ling

8

Deerstones

Howgill Intake

Little Crag

Popple Well Ridge

LS21

Deerstones Farm

Pemberton Well

Gawk Hall Ridge   High Moss

53

Ling Chapel Farm

The Old Pike

Pike Ridge

Gill Head

Stainforth Gill Head

Dearncomb Head Tippling Hill

7

White Hill

Middleton Moor Enclosure

Heligar Pike

Resphill Wood

Gibbeter Farm

Green Gate Spring

Riding Stone Well

Langbar Moor

Cup and Ring-marked Rock

High Black Hill

Braken Ridge

Clifford's Bog

Cup-marked Rock

Bracken Ridge Well

52

Whitaker's Wood

Heald Wood

Black Hill

Beacon Hill House

Wards End

Foldshaw Ridge

Black Hill

Bow Shaw

Cross Bank

6

Langbar

Black Hill Farm

Middle Ridge

Cup and Ring-marked Rocks

Hollingley Intake

Denton Moor

Beach House Farm

Moor End

Long Ridge Middleton Moor

March Ghyll Reservoir

Hollingley Farm

51

Cunliffe Wood

Hardisty Farm

Round Hill (Tumulus)

Round Hill

West Moor

March Gill

High Denton Farm

Middle Lathe

Leyfield Farm

Low Moor

Lurgy Delf Quarry (dis)

West Moor House

Green Grass Wood

Whitaker's Wood

Hardisty's Wood

5

Bull Coppice

Moorcroft Farm

Ling Park

Horse Wood

Hathenshaw Farm

Upper Austby

Windsover Farm

Nessfield Court

Upper Austby Farm

Hunger Hill

218

Hill Top Farm

Whinthorn Farm

50

West Hall Farm

Park Wood Park Wells

Cat Holes Dean Wood Farm

LS29

Primrose Hill

Stubbs Wood

Throstle Nest

Nesfield

High Austby

Sion Hill

North Plantation

Middleton

Grange Farm

West Park Wood

49

Lumb Ghyll Farm

Smithy Greaves

Holme Ings

Castleberg Scar

Low Austby

Tivoli

Mydleton Lodge Terrace Gill

Pontona Farm

Nell Bank Wood

Hudson Wood

Nell Bank Centre

Beck Foot Farm

3

Gate Croft

Wharfedale

Owler Park

Coppy Wood

Middleton Woods

Stubham Wood

Lido

Denton Bridge

Ilkley Golf Course

Riddings Lathe

Dales Way

CH

Gill Bank Wd

Curly Hill

Rupert Rd

Cemy

Sewage Works

A65

Denton

48

Addingham Moorside

Netherwood Farm

ILKLEY

Stourton Rd

SKIPTON RD

218

Mus

LEEDS ROAD

Ben Rhydding

2

Cragg House Farm

Briery Wood

The Grid

Town Hall

Springs

Coronation

BOLLING RD

Hardwick House Farm

Hardwick Holes

Woodhouse Crags

Bracken Wood

Parish Ghyll

Queen's Dr

WESTWOOD DR

Ben Rhydding

CH

47

Piper's Crag

Swastika Stone

High Crag

Black Beck Hole

WELLS RD

The Tarn

Cow and Call

Gib Field

1

Long Ridge End

Long Ridge

Crawshaw Spring

Silver Well

Spicey Gill

Hollin H Peat Pits Pit (dis)

Ilkley Moor

Ikley Crags

Crawshaw Thorn Hill

Gill Head

Cup and Ring Marked Rocks

Pancake Stone

Highfield Farm

Burley Moor

BD20

Shepherds Hill

Crawshaw Moss

Wicken Tree Crag

Badger Stone

218

West Yorkshire STREET ATLAS

08   A   09   B   10   C   11   D   12   E   13   F   **46**

For full street detail of the highlighted area see page 218.

A4
1 AYNHOLME DR
2 WHARFE PK
3 CROSS END FOLD
4 NURSERY LA
5 BEACON ST
6 CROSS CRES
7 LILAC CL
8 ORCHARD LA
9 SAWYERS GARTH

10 CROFT HO FOLD
11 SYCAMORE DR
12 ABBEY CL
13 HALLCROFT DR
14 CORNERSTONES CL
15 SAW MILL LA

C2
1 ASH CL
2 CHERRY GR
3 APPLE TREE GDNS
4 BEACON RISE
5 VICTORIA GR
6 THE BRAMBLES
7 EASBY CL
8 WOODLANDS GR
9 VICTORIA DR

10 VICTORIA RD
11 CURLEW CL
12 NESFIELD VW
13 BEAMSLEY VW
14 WOODLANDS RI
15 WOODLANDS CL
16 BEECHWOOD GR
17 VICTORIA GDNS
18 BRIERY CL
19 KINGS CL

20 DALE CFT
21 HEBERS GR
22 THE LUTYENS
23 WARLBECK
24 HEBER'S GHYLL DR
25 GROVE AVE
26 SHANNON CL
27 HEATH PK
28 GHYLL WOOD
29 PINES GDNS

30 PREMIERE PK
31 HOLLINGWOOD GATE
32 HOLLINGWOOD RISE
33 BADGER CL
34 WHINFIELD
35 SHELL ROYD
36 CRANFORD GDNS
37 HOLLINGWOOD PK

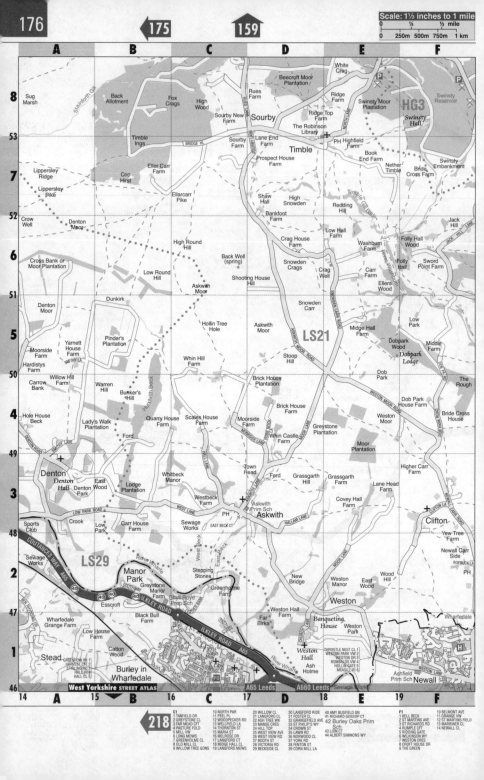

176

175

159

Scale: 1⅓ inches to 1 mile

0   ¼   ½   mile
0   250m 500m 750m   1 km

A   B   C   D   E   F

8

White Crag

Beecroft Moor Plantation

Sug Marsh

Back Allotment

Fox Crags

High Wood

Rues Farm

Ridge Farm

Swinsty Moor Plantation

Swinsty Reservoir

HG3

Swinsty Hall

Ridge Top Farm

Sourby New Farm

Sourby

53

Timble Ings

Sourby Farm

Lane End Farm

The Robinson Library

PH Highfield Farm

BRIDGE HILL

Eller Carr Farm

Timble

Book End Farm

Prospect House Farm

Nether Timble

Bride Cross Farm

Swinsty Embankment

7

Lippersley Ridge

Cop Hirst

Ellarcarr Pike

Lippersley Pike

Shaw Hall

High Snowden

Redding Hill

Timble Gill Beck

Jack Hill

JACK HILL LANE

52

Crow Well

Denton Moor

Bankfoot Farm

Crag House Farm

Low Hall Farm

Washburn Farm

Folly Hall Wood

High Round Hill

Back Well (spring)

Snowden Crags

Crag Well

Carr Farm

Folly Hall

Sword Point Farm

6

Cross Bank or Moor Plantation

Low Round Hill

Shooting House Hill

Askwith Moor

Ellers Wood

51

Denton Moor

Dunkirk

Snowden Carr

Midge Hall Farm

Low Park

Dobpark Wood

Middle Farm

5

Moorside Farm

Yarnett House Farm

Pinder's Plantation

Hollin Tree Hole

Askwith Moor

LS21

SNOWDEN CARR ROAD

MOOR ROAD

Dobpark Lodge

The Rough

SMITHY LA

Hardistys Farm

Whin Hill Farm

Stoop Hill

Dob Park

Dob Park House Farm

Bride Cross House

50

Carrow Bank

Willow Hill Farm

Warren Hill

Bunker's Hill

Brick House Plantation

Weston Moor

WESTON MOOR ROAD

DOB PARK RD

Huddith Beck

4

Hole House Beck

Lady's Walk Plantation

Quarry House Farm

Scales House Farm

Moorside Farm

Brick House Farm

Whin Castle Farm

Greystone Plantation

Weston Moor

SMITHY LANE

Ford

Ford

MOORSIDE LANE

MOOR LANE

Moor Plantation

DENTON ROAD

49

Denton

Denton Hall

East Wood

Lodge Plantation

Whitbeck Manor

Westbeck Farm

Town Head

Ford

Grassgarth Hill

Grassgarth Farm

Higher Carr Farm

Clifton

3

Denton Park

Denton Park

HALL LANE

WEST LANE

Askwith Prim Sch

Covey Hall Farm

Lane Head Farm

CLIFTON LANE

NELL CARR ROAD

48

Sports Club

Crook

Low Park

Carr House Farm

Sewage Works

PH

Askwith

EAST BECK CT

HALLAM LANE

Yew Tree Farm

Newall Carr Side

ROEBUCK LA

Low Park Road

LOW PARK ROAD

COUTANCES WAY

A65

PH

2

LS29

Manor Park

Greystone Manor Farm

River Wharfe

Stepping Stones

Greenholme Farm

Ghyll Royd Prep Sch

West Beck

East Beck

New Bridge

Weston Manor

East Wood

Wood Hill

Weston Park

A65

SOUTHWAY

ILKLEY ROAD

LEEDS ROAD

Far Birka

Weston Hall Farm

MOOR LANE

Banqueting House

Wharfedale

47

Esscroft

Black Bull Farm

ILKLEY ROAD

A65

Weston Hall

Ash Holme

Weston Park

WESTON LANE

H

Wharfedale Grange Farm

Low House Farm

Catton Wood

River Wharfe

Ashfield Prim Sch

Newall

1

Stead

GREENHOW DR 1 HARVEST DR 2 STIRLINGRD 3 HALL RI 4 HALL CL 5

Burley in Wharfedale

A65 Leeds

A660 Leeds

Sewage Works

46

West Yorkshire STREET ATLAS

14   A   15   B   16   C   17   D   18   E   19   F

C1
1 TANFIELD DR
2 GREYSTONE CL
3 FAR MEAD CFT
4 PASTURE FOLD
5 MILL VW
6 LONG MDWS
7 GREENHOLME CL
8 OLD MILL CL
9 WILLOW TREE GDNS

10 NORTH PAR
11 PEEL PL
12 WOODPECKER RD
13 WELLFIELD LA
14 THORNTON ST
15 MARIA ST
16 MELROSE DR
17 LANGFORD CT
18 MIDGE HALL CL
19 LANGFORD MEWS

20 WILLOW CL
21 LANGFORD CL
22 ASH TREE WK
23 MANSE CRES
24 HILL TOP
25 WEST VIEW AVE
26 WEST VIEW RD
27 BOOTH ST
28 VICTORIA RD
29 BECKSIDE GL

30 LANGFORD RIDE
31 FOSTER CL
32 GRANGEFIELD AVE
33 ST PHILIP'S WY
34 CROWN ST
35 LAWN RD
36 NORWOOD CL
37 YORK RD
38 FENTON ST
39 CORN MILL LA

40 AMY BUSFIELD GN
41 RICHARD GOSSOP CT
42 Burley Oaks Prim Sch
43 LION CT
44 ALBERT SIMMONS WY

F1
1 KELL BECK
2 ST MARTINS AVE
3 ST RICHARDS RD
4 RUMPLE CFT
5 RIDDING GATE
6 WILKINSON WY
7 WESTON CRES
8 CROFT HOUSE DR
9 THE GREEN

10 BELMONT AVE
11 GRANGE VW
12 ST MARTINS FIELD
13 MARRINER CL
14 NEWALL CL

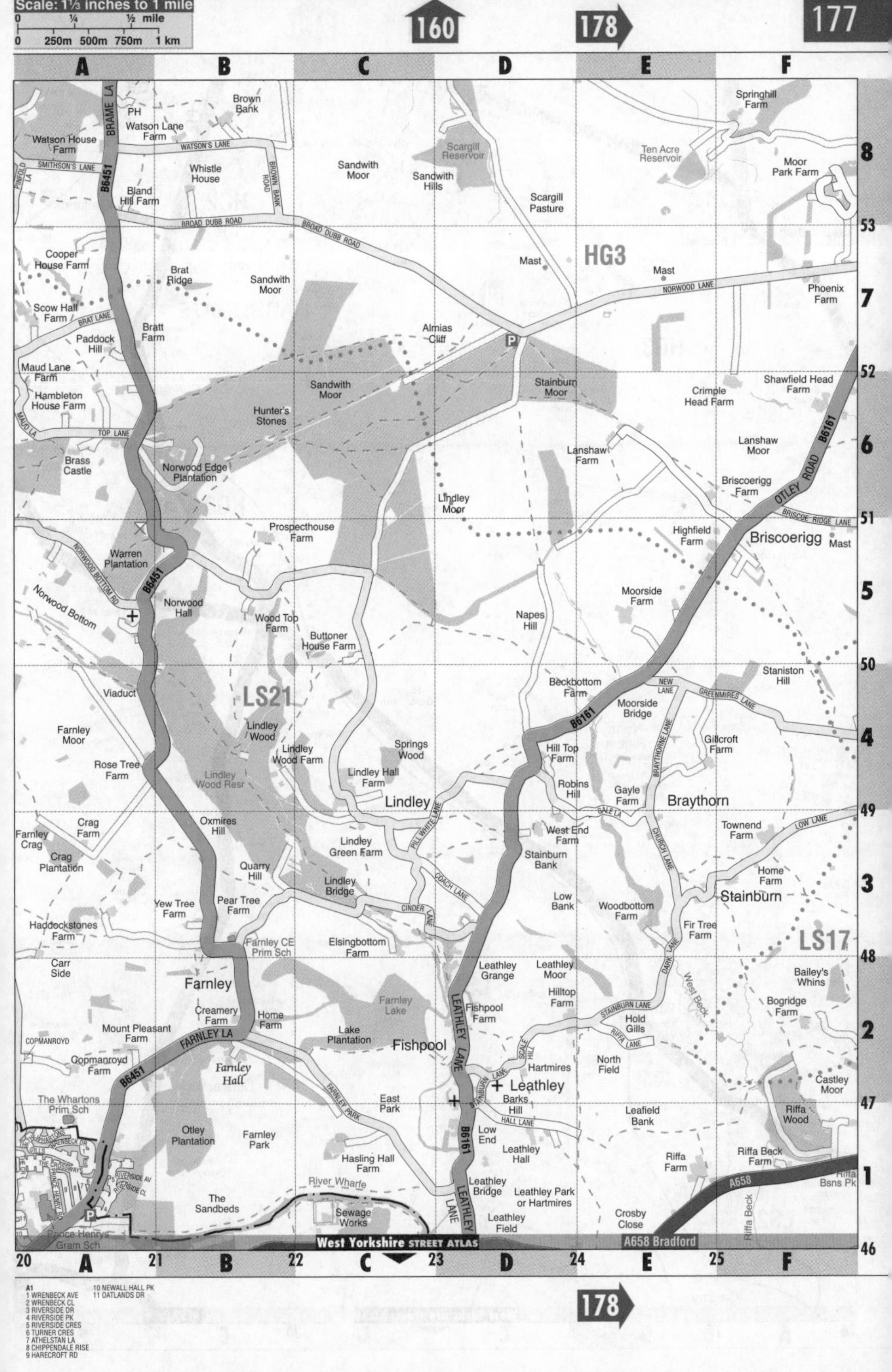

Scale: 1⅓ inches to 1 mile
0 ¼ ½ mile
0 250m 500m 750m 1 km
160
178
177
A B C D E F
8
53
7
52
6
51
5
50
4
49
3
48
2
47
1
46
20 21 22 23 24 25
Springhill Farm
Brown Bank
PH
Watson Lane Farm
Watson House Farm
WATSON'S LANE
SMITHSON'S LANE
PINFOLD LA
BRAME LA
B6451
Whistle House
BROWN BANK ROAD
Sandwith Moor
Scargill Reservoir
Sandwith Hills
Ten Acre Reservoir
Moor Park Farm
Bland Hill Farm
Scargill Pasture
BROAD DUBB ROAD
Cooper House Farm
HG3
Mast
Mast
Brat Ridge
Sandwith Moor
NORWOOD LANE
Phoenix Farm
Scow Hall Farm
BRAT LANE
Bratt Farm
Almias Cliff
P
Paddock Hill
Maud Lane Farm
Sandwith Moor
Stainburn Moor
Crimple Head Farm
Shawfield Head Farm
Hambleton House Farm
MAUD LA
TOP LANE
Hunter's Stones
Lanshaw Farm
Lanshaw Moor
B6161
Brass Castle
Norwood Edge Plantation
OTLEY ROAD
Lindley Moor
Briscoerigg Farm
BRISCOE RIDGE LANE
Prospecthouse Farm
Highfield Farm
Briscoerigg
Mast
NORWOOD BOTTOM RD
Warren Plantation
Norwood Bottom
Norwood Hall
Moorside Farm
Wood Top Farm
Napes Hill
Buttoner House Farm
Staniston Hill
Viaduct
LS21
Beckbottom Farm
NEW LANE
GREENMIRES LANE
Moorside Bridge
Lindley Wood
Farnley Moor
Lindley Wood Farm
Springs Wood
Hill Top Farm
BRAYTHORNE LANE
Gillcroft Farm
Rose Tree Farm
Lindley Wood Resr
Lindley Hall Farm
Robins Hill
Gayle Farm
Braythorn
Lindley
PILL WHITE LANE
GALE LA
Crag Farm
Farnley Crag
Oxmires Hill
West End Farm
CHURCH LANE
Townend Farm
LOW LANE
Crag Plantation
Lindley Green Farm
Stainburn Bank
Quarry Hill
Lindley Bridge
COACH LANE
Home Farm
Stainburn
Yew Tree Farm
Pear Tree Farm
CINDER LANE
Low Bank
Woodbottom Farm
Haddockstones Farm
Farnley CE Prim Sch
Elsingbottom Farm
Fir Tree Farm
LS17
DARK LANE
Carr Side
Leathley Grange
Leathley Moor
Bailey's Whins
Farnley
Farnley Lake
West Beck
Hilltop Farm
Bogridge Farm
Creamery Farm
Fishpool Farm
STAINBURN LANE
Hold Gills
Mount Pleasant Farm
Home Farm
Lake Plantation
RIFFA LANE
COPMANROYD
FARNLEY LA
Fishpool
LEATHLEY LANE
SCALE HILL
Copmanroyd Farm
Farnley Hall
North Field
Hartmires
STAINBURN LANE
Leathley
Castley Moor
The Whartons Prim Sch
East Park
FARNLEY PARK
Barks Hill
HALL LANE
Leafield Bank
Riffa Wood
Otley Plantation
Farnley Park
Low End
Leathley Hall
Hasling Hall Farm
Riffa Farm
Riffa Beck Farm
River Wharfe
Leathley Bridge
Leathley Park or Hartmires
A658
Riffa Bsns Pk
The Sandbeds
RIVERSIDE AV
RIVERSIDE CL
Sewage Works
Crosby Close
Riffa Beck
Leathley Field
Prince Henry's Gram Sch
West Yorkshire STREET ATLAS
A658 Bradford
A1
1 WRENBECK AVE
2 WRENBECK CL
3 RIVERSIDE DR
4 RIVERSIDE PK
5 RIVERSIDE CRES
6 TURNER CRES
7 ATHELSTAN LA
8 CHIPPENDALE RISE
9 HARECROFT RD
10 NEWALL HALL PK
11 OATLANDS DR
178

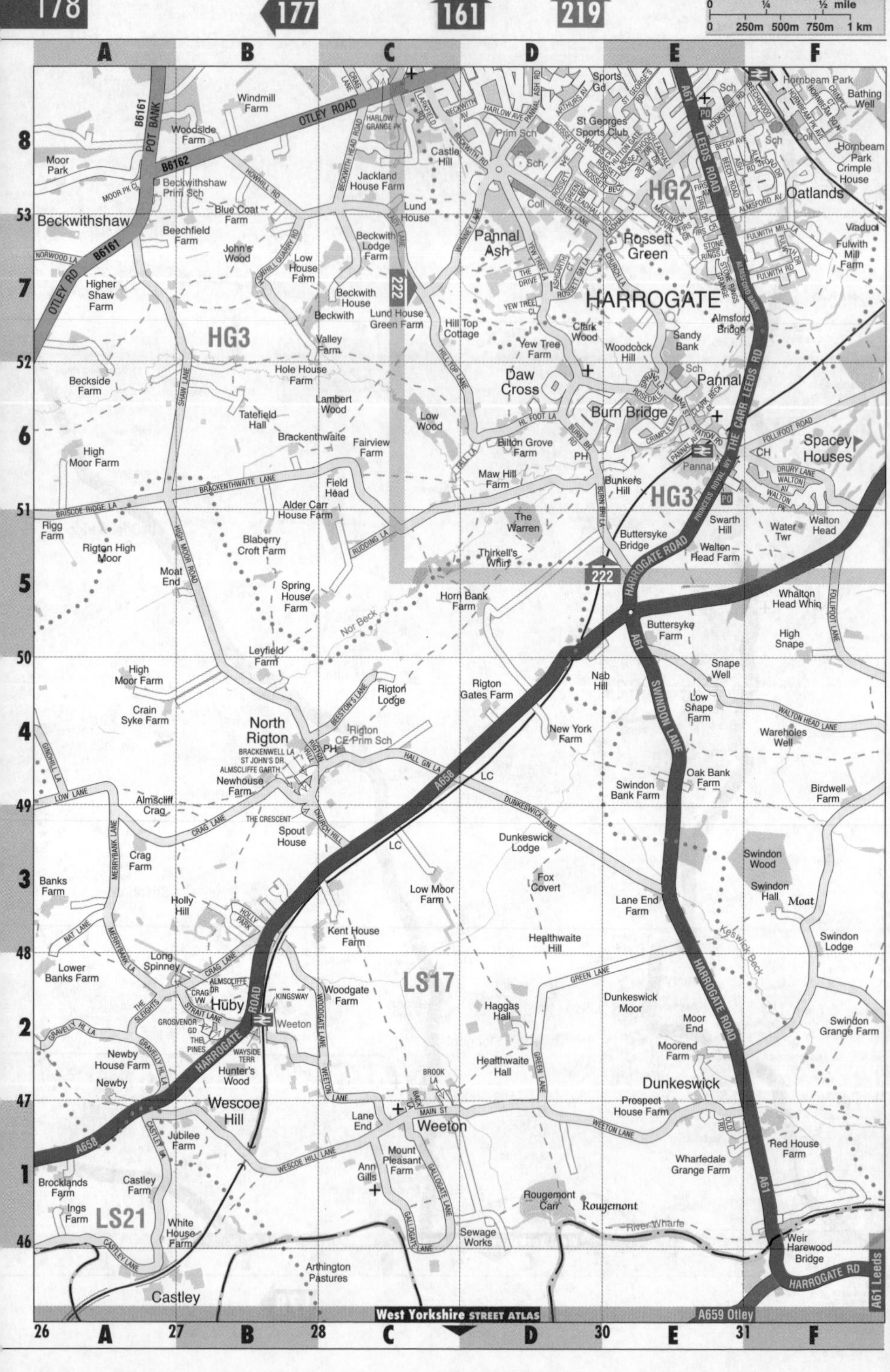
177
161
219
Scale: 1⅓ inches to 1 mile
HARROGATE
Beckwithshaw
Pannal Ash
Rossett Green
Daw Cross
Burn Bridge
Pannal
Spacey Houses
Oatlands
North Rigton
Huby
Weeton
Wescoe Hill
Castley
Dunkeswick
HG2
HG3
LS17
LS21
OTLEY ROAD
HARROGATE ROAD
LEEDS ROAD
SWINDON LANE
A61
A658
B6161
B6162
River Wharfe
Nor Beck
Almscliff Crag
Rigton High Moor
Swindon Wood
Rougemont Carr
Harewood Bridge
A61 Leeds
A659 Otley
West Yorkshire STREET ATLAS

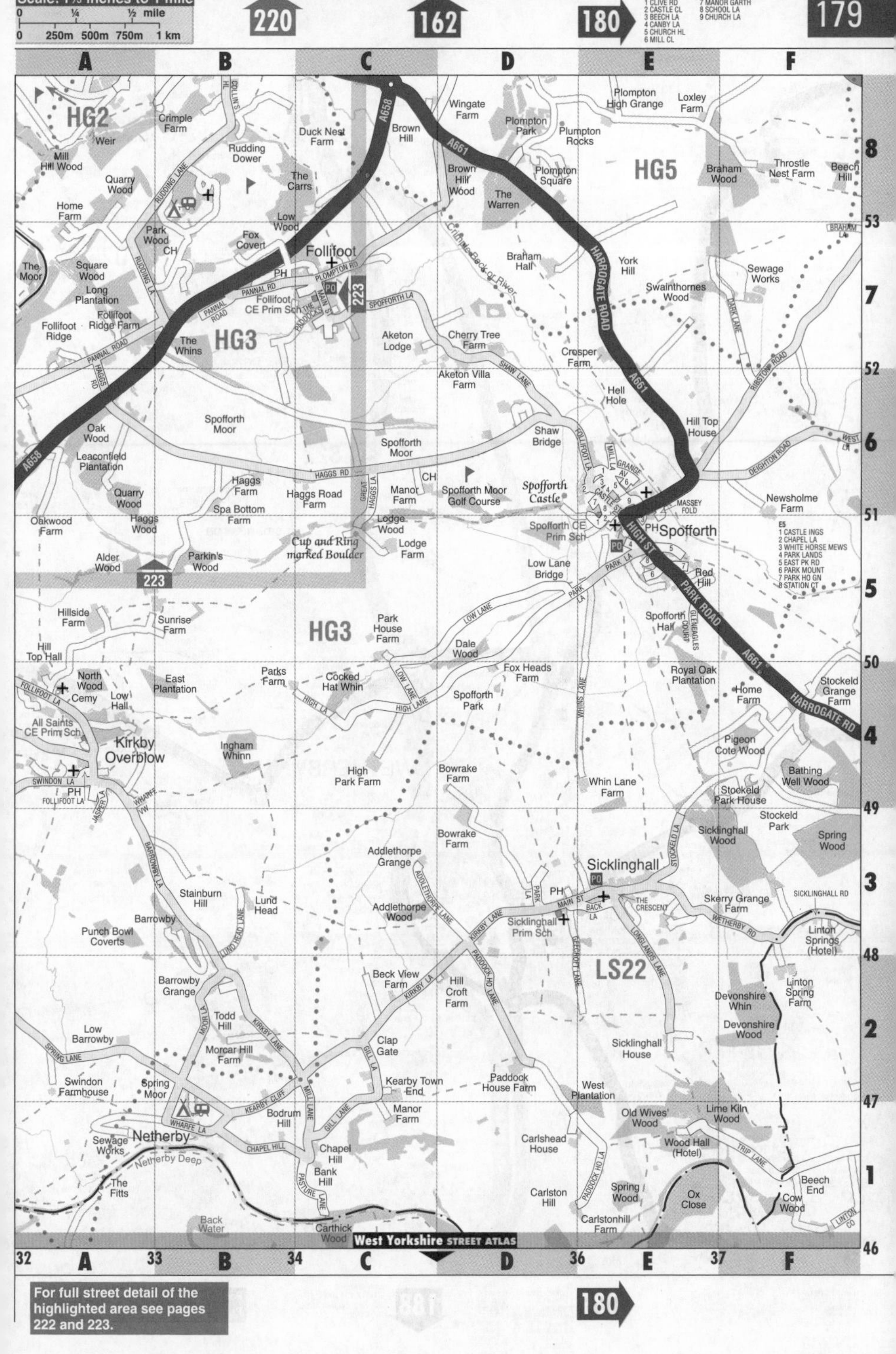

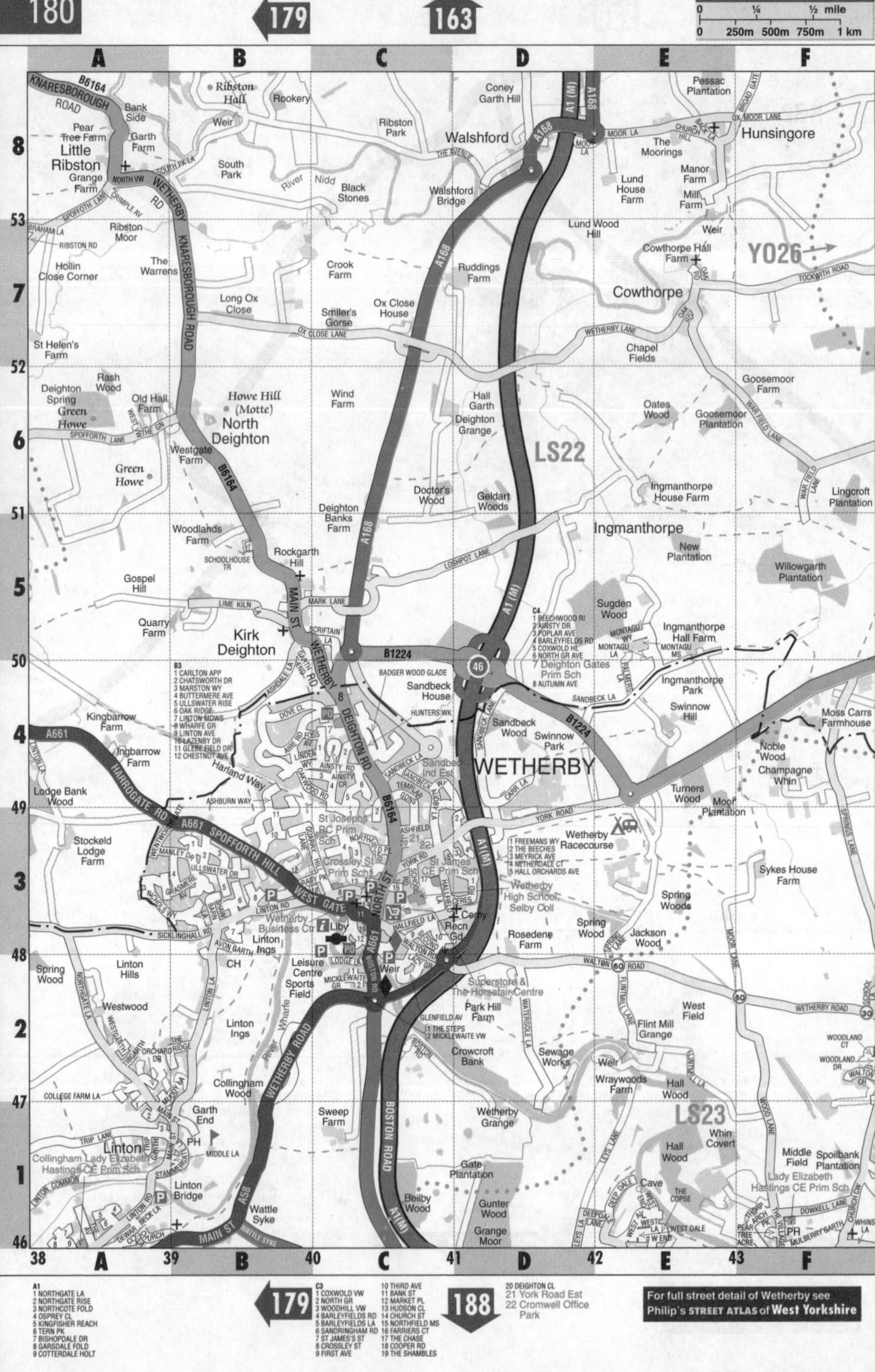
179
163
Scale: 1⅓ inches to 1 mile
0 ¼ ½ mile
0 250m 500m 750m 1 km
A B C D E F
Knaresborough Road
B6164
Bank Side
Ribston Hall
Rookery
Coney Garth Hill
A1(M)
A168
Pessac Plantation
Broad Gate
Ox Moor Lane
Hunsingore
Pear Tree Farm
Garth Farm
Little Ribston
Weir
Ribston Park
Walshford
Moor La
Church Hill
The Moorings
South Pk La
South Park
The Avenue
Grange Farm
North Vw
Wetherby Rd
River Nidd
Black Stones
Walshford Bridge
Lund House Farm
Manor Farm
Mill Farm
Spofforth Lane
Crimple Av
Braham La
Ribston Moor
Ribston Rd
Lund Wood Hill
Weir
Cowthorpe Hall Farm
YO26
Hollin Close Corner
The Warrens
Crook Farm
Ruddings Farm
Oak Rd
Tockwith Road
Cowthorpe
Knaresborough Road
Long Ox Close
Smiler's Gorse
Ox Close House
Ox Close Lane
Wetherby Lane
St Helen's Farm
Chapel Fields
Deighton Spring
Rash Wood
Green Howe
Old Hall Farm
West Vw
The Gn
Spofforth Lane
Howe Hill (Motte)
North Deighton
Wind Farm
Hall Garth
Deighton Grange
Oates Wood
Goosemoor Farm
Goosemoor Plantation
War Field Lane
LS22
Westgate Farm
Green Howe
Doctor's Wood
Geldart Woods
Ingmanthorpe House Farm
Lingcroft Plantation
Deighton Banks Farm
Woodlands Farm
Ingmanthorpe
New Plantation
Schoolhouse Tr
Rockgarth Hill
Loshpot Lane
Willowgarth Plantation
Gospel Hill
Main St
Mark Lane
Lime Kiln La
Sugden Wood
Quarry Farm
Kirk Deighton
Scriftain La
Montagu Wy
Montagu La
Montagu Ms
Ingmanthorpe Hall Farm
B1224
Deighton Gates Prim Sch
Palmers La
Ashdale La
Garth End
Wetherby Rd
Badger Wood Glade
Sandbeck House
46
Sandbeck La
Ingmanthorpe Park
Swinnow Hill
Dove Cl
Deighton Rd
Hunters Wk
Sandbeck Wood
Swinnow Park
Moss Carrs Farmhouse
Kingbarrow Farm
A661
Ingbarrow Farm
Aire Rd
Foss Av
Linden Wy
Ainsty Rd
Ainsty Cr
Sandbeck Ind Est
WETHERBY
Noble Wood
Champagne Whin
Linton La
Harland Way
Oakwood Rd
Sandbeck Way
Templar Gdns
Audby La
Carr La
Turners Wood
Moor Plantation
Lodge Bank Wood
Ashburn Way
York Road
Harrogate Rd
Spofforth Hill
St Josephs RC Prim Sch
Ashfield
Wetherby Racecourse
Wentworth Gate
Stockeld Lodge Farm
Manley Dr
Quarry Hill Lane
York Rd
St James CE Prim Sch
Ullswater Dr
Crossley St Prim Sch
Raby Pk
School
Wetherby High School, Selby Coll
Sykes House Farm
Grasmere
Shaw Barn
West Gate
North St
Nichols Wy
Linton Rd
Hallfield La
Ceres Rd
Cemy
Spring Woods
Wetherby Business Ctr
Liby
Recn Gd
Spring Wood
Jackson Wood
Sicklinghall Rd
Avon Garth
Linton Ings
Rosedene Farm
Spring Lane
Moor Lane
Lodge La
Walton Rd
Lacy Gr
Walton Road
Spring Wood
Linton Hills
CH
Leisure Centre Sports Field
Weir
Micklewaite Gr
Boston Rd
Superstore & The Horsefair Centre
Flintmill Lane
Northgate La
Westwood
Glenfield Av
Park Hill Farm
Watersole La
West Field
Wetherby Road
School
Westgate
Linton Ings
River Wharfe
Wetherby Road
Boston Rd
Flint Mill Grange
Woodland Ct
Woodland Dr
Orchard Dr
The Ridge
Crowcroft Bank
Sewage Works
Weir
Wraywoods Farm
Hall Wood
Collingham Wood
College Farm La
Garth End
Sweep Farm
Boston Road
Wetherby Grange
LS23
Whin Covert
Wood Lane
Trip Lane
Linton
PH
Middle La
Hall Wood
Middle Field
Spoilbank Plantation
Collingham Lady Elizabeth Hastings CE Prim Sch
Stammergate
Gate Plantation
Leys Lane
Cave
Lady Elizabeth Hastings CE Prim Sch
Linton Common
Linton Bridge
Deep Dale
The Copse
Dowkell Lane
Wattle Syke
Beilby Wood
Gunter Wood
Deepdale Lane
West End
West Dale
Thorp Arch Pk
The Village
Whins La
Mulberry Garth
Church Cswy
Dewar Cl
Beck La
Church
Main St
Wattle Syke
Grange Moor
Leys La
Pear Tree Acre
PH
B3
1 CARLTON APP
2 CHATSWORTH DR
3 MARSTON WY
4 BUTTERMERE AVE
5 ULLSWATER RISE
6 OAK RIDGE
7 LINTON MDWS
8 WHARFE GR
9 LINTON AVE
10 LAZENBY DR
11 GLEBE FIELD DR
12 CHESTNUT AVE
C4
1 BEECHWOOD RI
2 AINSTY DR
3 POPLAR AVE
4 BARLEYFIELDS RD
5 COXWOLD HL
6 NORTH GR AVE
7 Deighton Gates Prim Sch
8 AUTUMN AVE
1 FREEMANS WY
2 THE BEECHES
3 MEYRICK AVE
4 NETHERDALE CT
5 HALL ORCHARDS AVE
1 THE STEPS
2 MICKLEWAITE VW
38 39 40 41 42 43
8 53 7 52 6 51 5 50 4 49 3 48 2 47 1 46
A1
1 NORTHGATE LA
2 NORTHGATE RISE
3 NORTHCOTE FOLD
4 OSPREY CL
5 KINGFISHER REACH
6 TERN PK
7 BISHOPDALE DR
8 GARSDALE FOLD
9 COTTERDALE HOLT
179
C3
1 COXWOLD VW
2 NORTH GR
3 WOODHILL VW
4 BARLEYFIELDS RD
5 BARLEYFIELDS LA
6 SANDRINGHAM RD
7 ST JAMES'S ST
8 CROSSLEY ST
9 FIRST AVE
10 THIRD AVE
11 BANK ST
12 MARKET PL
13 HUDSON CL
14 CHURCH ST
15 NORTHFIELD MS
16 FARRIERS CT
17 THE CHASE
18 COOPER RD
19 THE SHAMBLES
188
20 DEIGHTON CL
21 York Road Est
22 Cromwell Office Park
For full street detail of Wetherby see Philip's STREET ATLAS of West Yorkshire

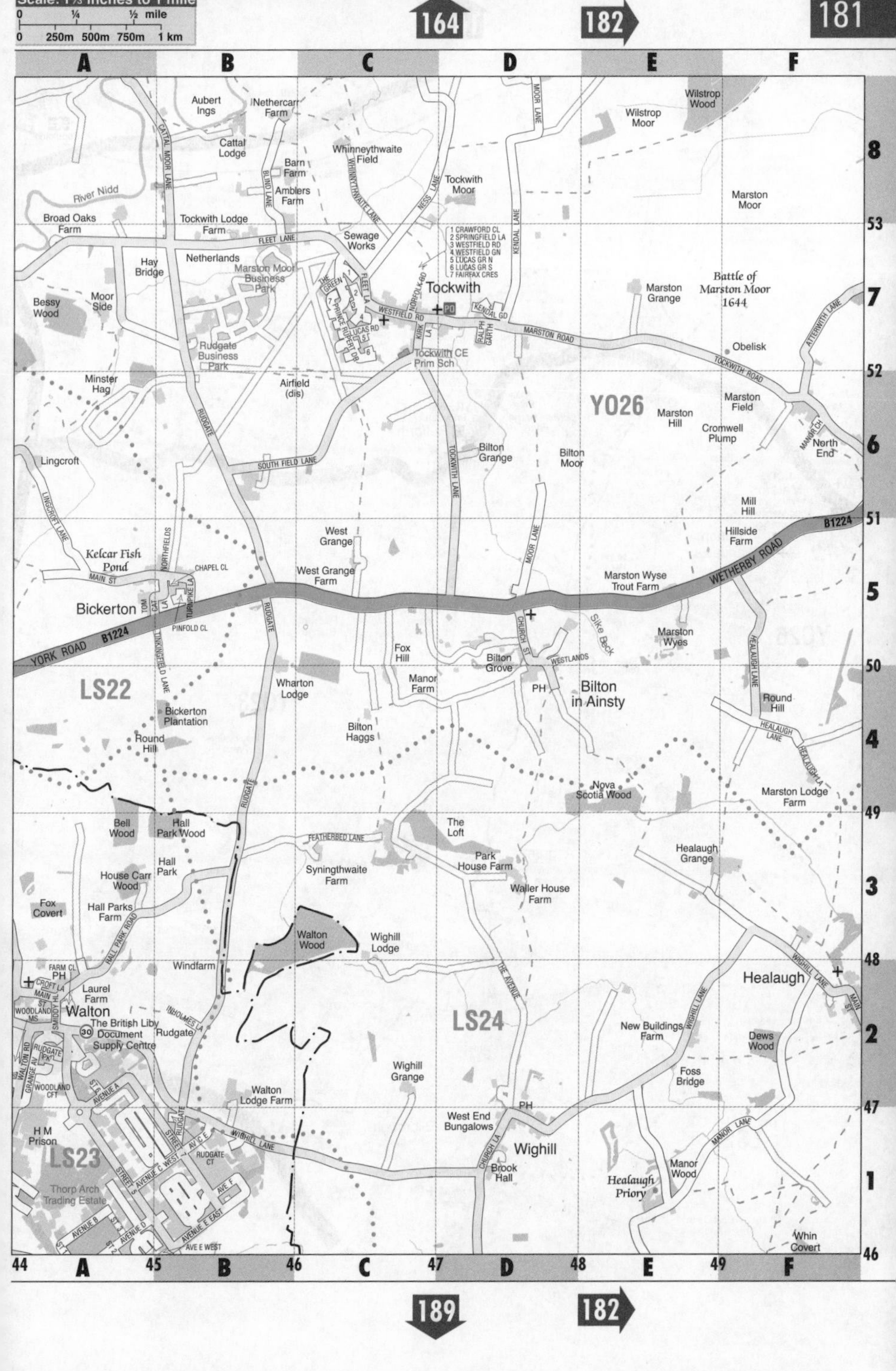
Scale: 1⅓ inches to 1 mile
164
182
189
Tockwith
Bickerton
Bilton in Ainsty
Walton
Wighill
Healaugh
YO26
LS22
LS24
LS23
Battle of Marston Moor 1644
Marston Moor
Wilstrop Wood
Wilstrop Moor
Tockwith Moor
Aubert Ings
Nethercarr Farm
Cattal Lodge
Whinneythwaite Field
Barn Farm
Amblers Farm
River Nidd
Broad Oaks Farm
Tockwith Lodge Farm
Sewage Works
Hay Bridge
Netherlands
Marston Moor Business Park
Bessy Wood
Moor Side
Rudgate Business Park
Minster Hag
Airfield (dis)
Tockwith CE Prim Sch
Marston Grange
Obelisk
Marston Field
Marston Hill
Cromwell Plump
North End
Bilton Grange
Bilton Moor
Lingcroft
Mill Hill
Hillside Farm
West Grange
Kelcar Fish Pond
West Grange Farm
Marston Wyse Trout Farm
Marston Wyes
Fox Hill
Bilton Grove
Manor Farm
Wharton Lodge
Bickerton Plantation
Round Hill
Bilton Haggs
Nova Scotia Wood
Marston Lodge Farm
Bell Wood
Hall Park Wood
The Loft
Park House Farm
Healaugh Grange
Hall Park
House Carr Wood
Syningthwaite Farm
Waller House Farm
Fox Covert
Hall Parks Farm
Walton Wood
Wighill Lodge
Windfarm
Laurel Farm
The British Liby Document Supply Centre
Rudgate
New Buildings Farm
Dews Wood
Wighill Grange
Foss Bridge
Walton Lodge Farm
West End Bungalows
H M Prison
Thorp Arch Trading Estate
Brook Hall
Healaugh Priory
Manor Wood
Whin Covert
1 CRAWFORD CL
2 SPRINGFIELD LA
3 WESTFIELD RD
4 WESTFIELD GN
5 LUCAS GR N
6 LUCAS GR S
7 FAIRFAX CRES
CATTAL MOOR LANE
BLIND LANE
WHINNYTHWAITE LANE
NESS LANE
MOOR LANE
KENDAL LANE
FLEET LANE
NORFOLK GD
WESTFIELD RD
KIRK LA
KENDAL GD
RALPH GARTH
MARSTON ROAD
TOCKWITH ROAD
ATTERWITH LANE
MANOR CH
THE GREEN
PRINCE RUPERT DR
LUCAS RD
SOUTH FIELD LANE
RUDGATE
TOCKWITH LANE
LINGCROFT LANE
NORTHFIELDS
CHAPEL CL
MAIN ST
TURNPIKE LA
TOM LA
PINFOLD CL
YORK ROAD
B1224
WETHERBY ROAD
CHURCH ST
WESTLANDS
Sike Beck
LINKFIELD LANE
HEALAUGH LANE
FEATHERBED LANE
HALL PARK ROAD
THE AVENUE
WIGHILL LANE
INHOLMES LA
FARM CL
CROFT LA
WOODLAND MS
SMIDDY HILL
WALTON RD
GRANGE AV
RUDGATE PK
WOODLAND CFT
AVENUE A
AVENUE B
AVENUE C WEST
AVENUE D
AVENUE E EAST
AVE E WEST
AVE F
RUDGATE CT
CHURCH LA
MANOR LANE
PH
PO

181
165

Scale: 1⅓ inches to 1 mile

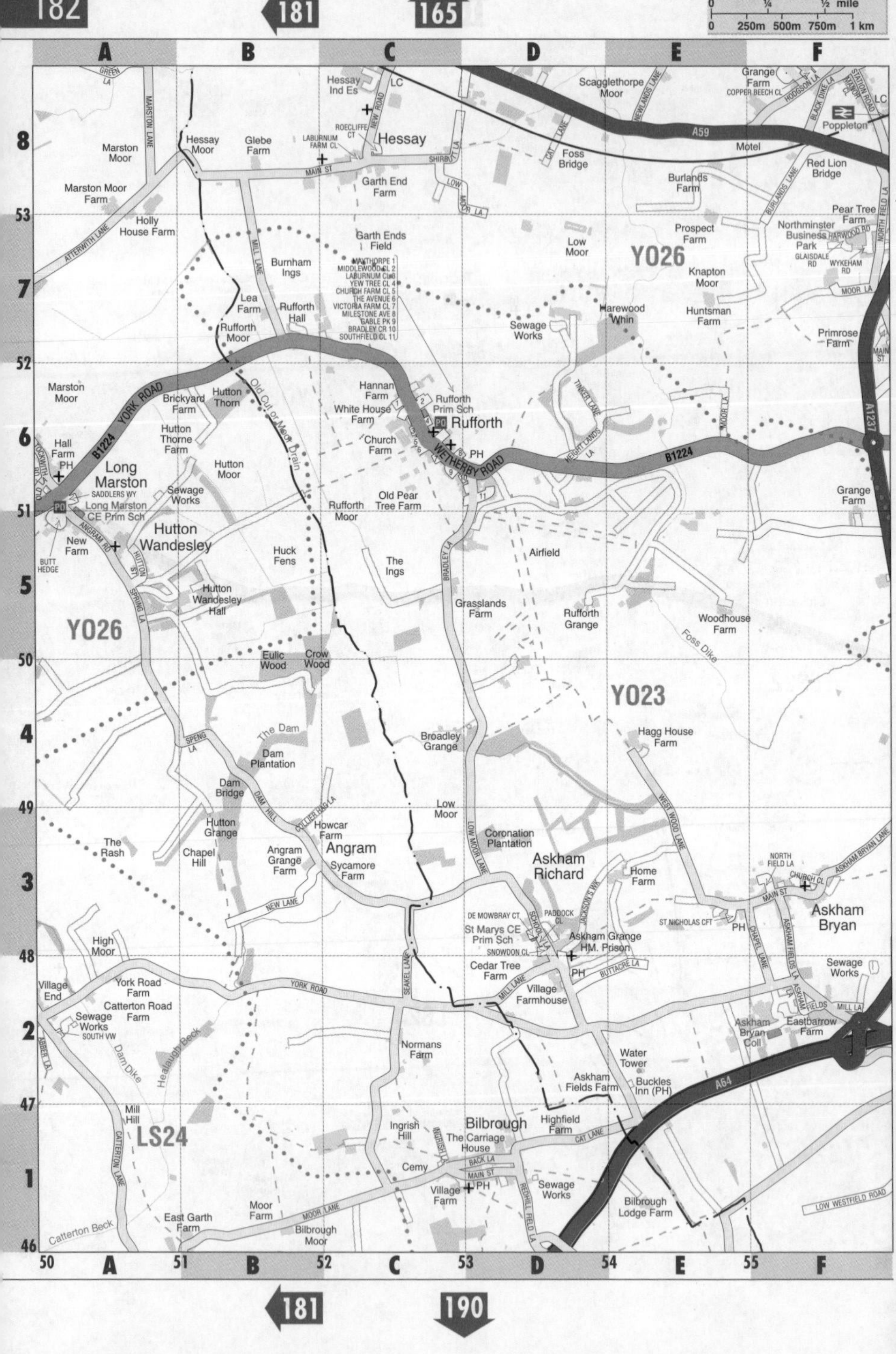
Hessay
Rufforth
Long Marston
Hutton Wandesley
Angram
Askham Richard
Askham Bryan
Bilbrough
Poppleton
YO26
YO23
LS24
A59
B1224
A1237
A64
York Road
Wetherby Road
Marston Moor
Hessay Moor
Glebe Farm
Garth End Farm
Garth Ends Field
Burnham Ings
Lea Farm
Rufforth Hall
Rufforth Moor
Scagglethorpe Moor
Foss Bridge
Burlands Farm
Prospect Farm
Knapton Moor
Huntsman Farm
Harewood Whin
Low Moor
Sewage Works
Airfield
Rufforth Grange
Grasslands Farm
Woodhouse Farm
Hagg House Farm
Broadley Grange
Coronation Plantation
Askham Grange HM. Prison
Water Tower
Buckles Inn (PH)
Askham Fields Farm
Highfield Farm
Bilbrough Lodge Farm
The Carriage House
Normans Farm
Moor Farm
East Garth Farm
Bilbrough Moor
Catterton Beck
Healaugh Beck
Dam Dike
Mill Hill
High Moor
Village End
York Road Farm
Catterton Road Farm
The Rash
Chapel Hill
Hutton Grange
Dam Bridge
Dam Plantation
Eulic Wood
Crow Wood
Huck Fens
The Ings
Old Pear Tree Farm
Church Farm
White House Farm
Hannah Farm
Rufforth Prim Sch
Brickyard Farm
Hutton Thorn
Hutton Thorne Farm
Hutton Moor
Hutton Wandesley Hall
Long Marston CE Prim Sch
New Farm
Hall Farm
Holly House Farm
Marston Moor Farm
Northminster Business Park
Pear Tree Farm
Red Lion Bridge
Primrose Farm
Grange Farm
Motel
St Marys CE Prim Sch
Cedar Tree Farm
Village Farmhouse
Home Farm
Askham Bryan Coll
Eastbarrow Farm
Howcar Farm
Angram Grange Farm
Sycamore Farm
Ingrish Hill
Cemy
Village Farm
Old Cut or Moor Drain
Foss Dike
Low Westfield Road

181
190

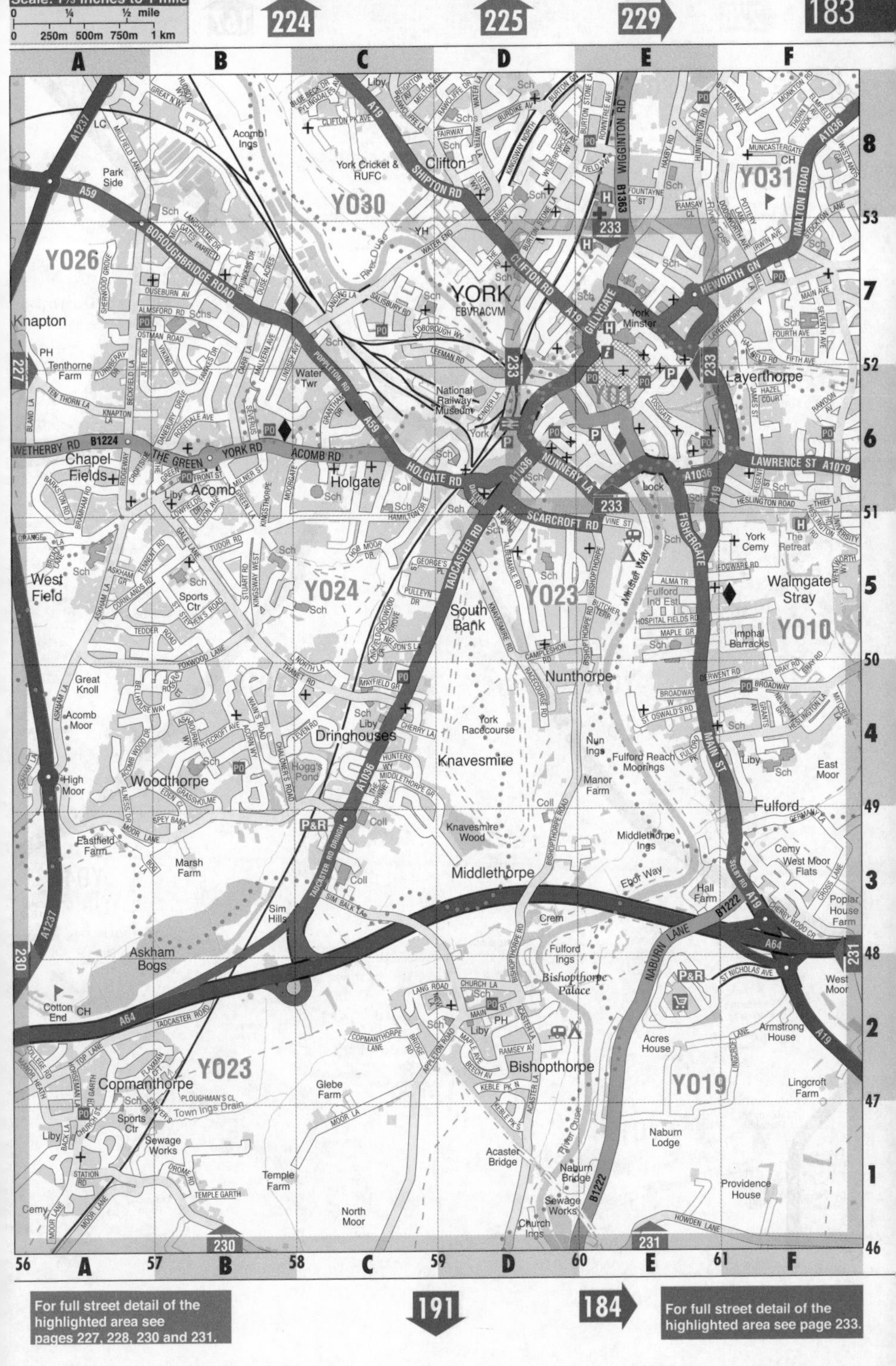

Scale: 1⅓ inches to 1 mile
0 ¼ ½ mile
0 250m 500m 750m 1 km
224
225
229
183
A B C D E F
YORK
EBVRACVM
YO30
YO26
YO31
YO1
YO24
YO23
YO10
YO19
Clifton
York Cricket & RUFC
Acomb Ings
Park Side
Knapton
Tenthorne Farm
Chapel Fields
Acomb
Holgate
Water Twr
National Railway Museum
York Minster
Layerthorpe
West Field
Sports Ctr
South Bank
Walmgate Stray
Fulford Ind Est
Imphal Barracks
Nunthorpe
York Cemy
The Retreat
Great Knoll
Acomb Moor
Dringhouses
York Racecourse
Knavesmire
Hogg's Pond
Woodthorpe
High Moor
Eastfield Farm
Marsh Farm
Knavesmire Wood
Middlethorpe
Nun Ings
Fulford Reach Moorings
Manor Farm
Middlethorpe Ings
Ebor Way
Fulford
East Moor
West Moor Flats
Poplar House Farm
Hall Farm
Sim Hills
Askham Bogs
Crem
Fulford Ings
Bishopthorpe Palace
Cotton End
Copmanthorpe
Sports Ctr
Sewage Works
Bishopthorpe
Glebe Farm
Acres House
Armstrong House
West Moor
Lingcroft Farm
Naburn Lodge
Acaster Bridge
Naburn Bridge
Temple Farm
North Moor
Church Ings
Providence House
Town Ings Drain
River Ouse
River Foss
WETHERBY RD
BOROUGHBRIDGE ROAD
SHIPTON RD
CLIFTON RD
WIGGINTON RD
HEWORTH GN
MALTON ROAD
GILLYGATE
POPPLETON RD
YORK RD
ACOMB RD
HOLGATE RD
NUNNERY LA
LAWRENCE ST
HESLINGTON ROAD
SCARCROFT RD
TADCASTER RD
FISHERGATE
MAIN ST
NABURN LANE
TADCASTER ROAD
HOWDEN LANE
A1237
A59
A19
A1036
A1079
A64
B1224
B1363
B1222
227
230
231
233
56 57 58 59 60 61
46 47 48 49 50 51 52 53
1 2 3 4 5 6 7 8
191
184
For full street detail of the highlighted area see pages 227, 228, 230 and 231.
For full street detail of the highlighted area see page 233.

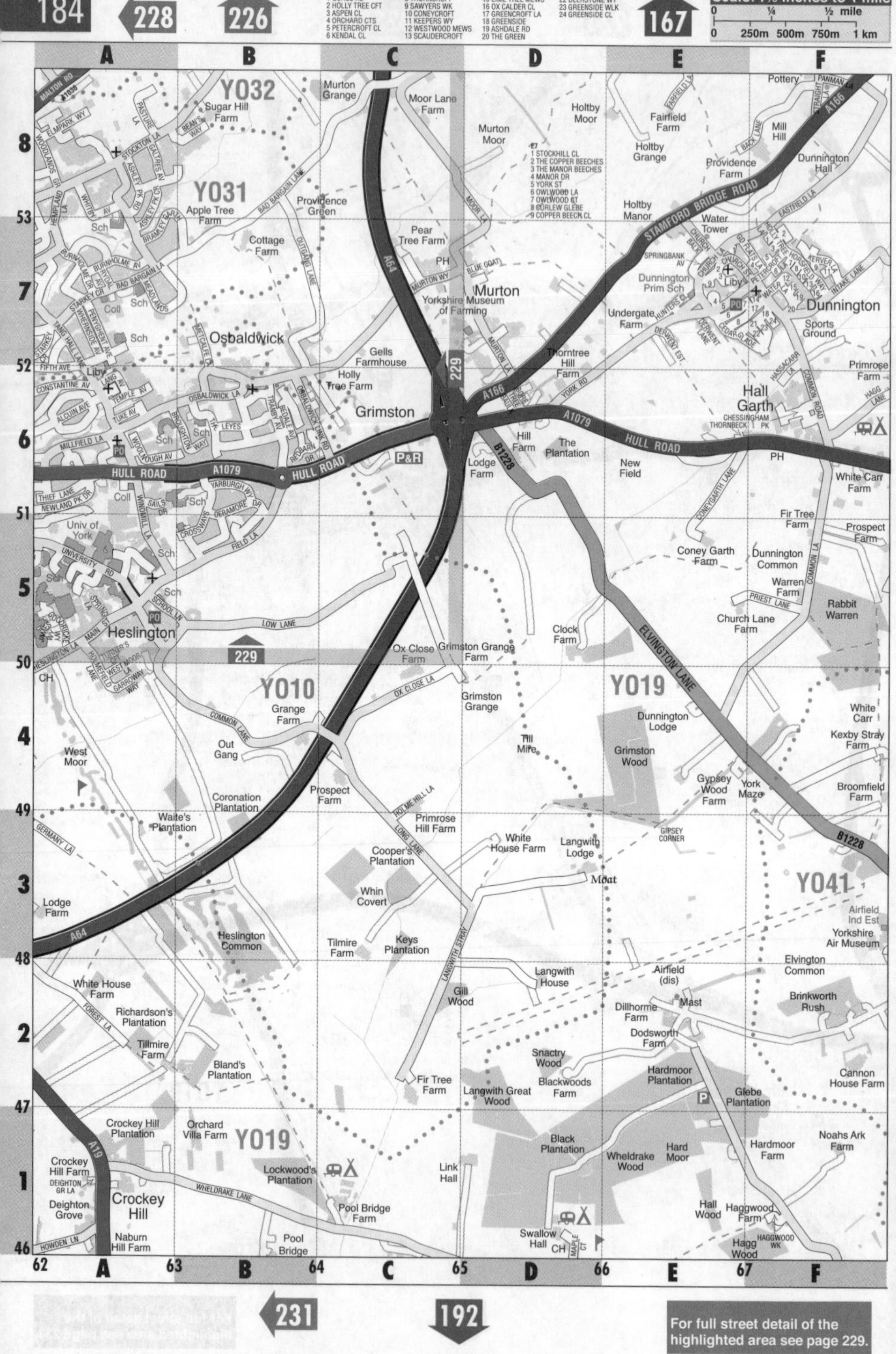

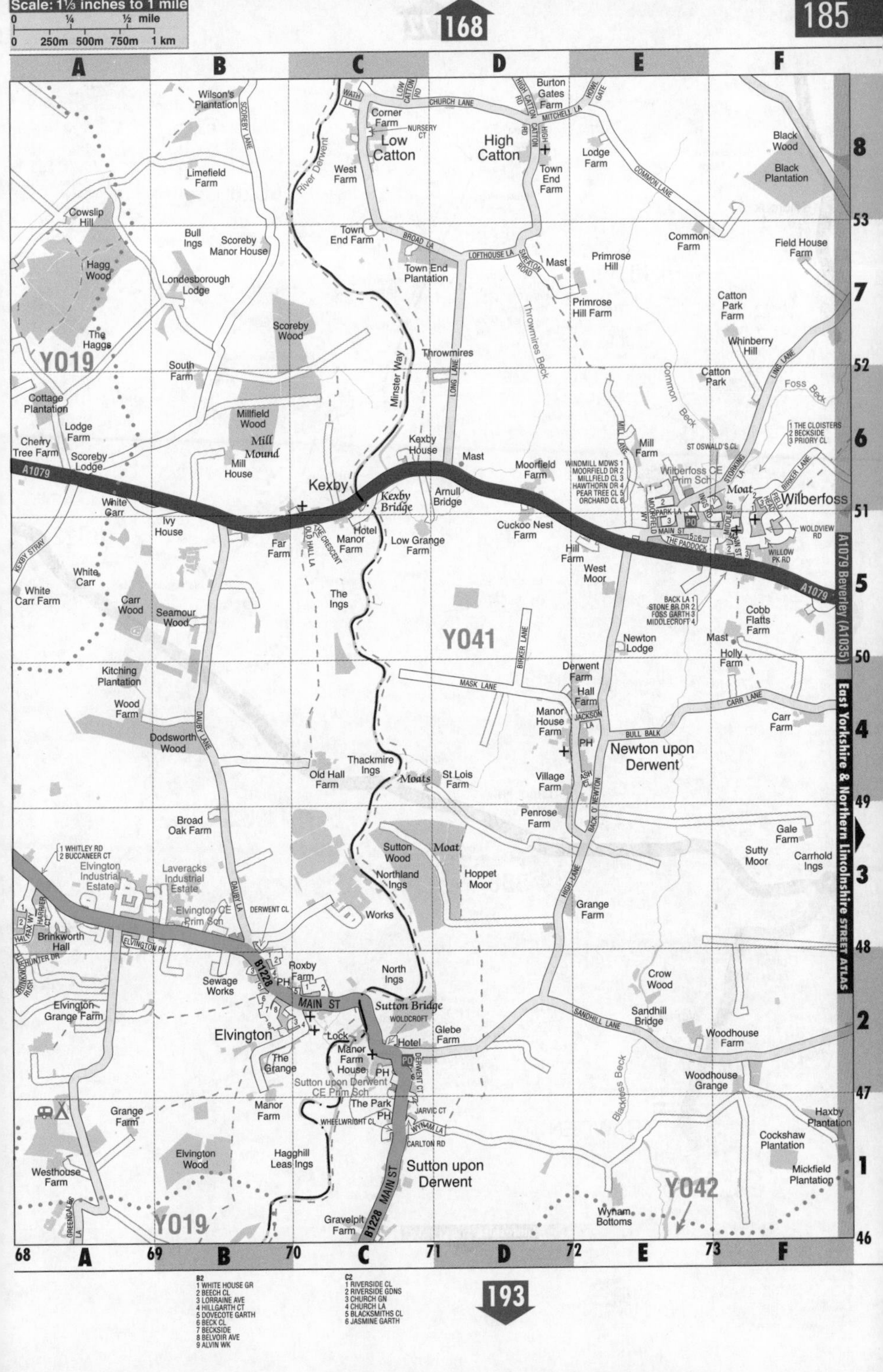

B2
1 WHITE HOUSE GR
2 BEECH CL
3 LORRAINE AVE
4 HILLGARTH CT
5 DOVECOTE GARTH
6 BECK CL
7 BECKSIDE
8 BELVOIR AVE
9 ALVIN WK

C2
1 RIVERSIDE CL
2 RIVERSIDE GDNS
3 CHURCH GN
4 CHURCH LA
5 BLACKSMITHS CL
6 JASMINE GARTH

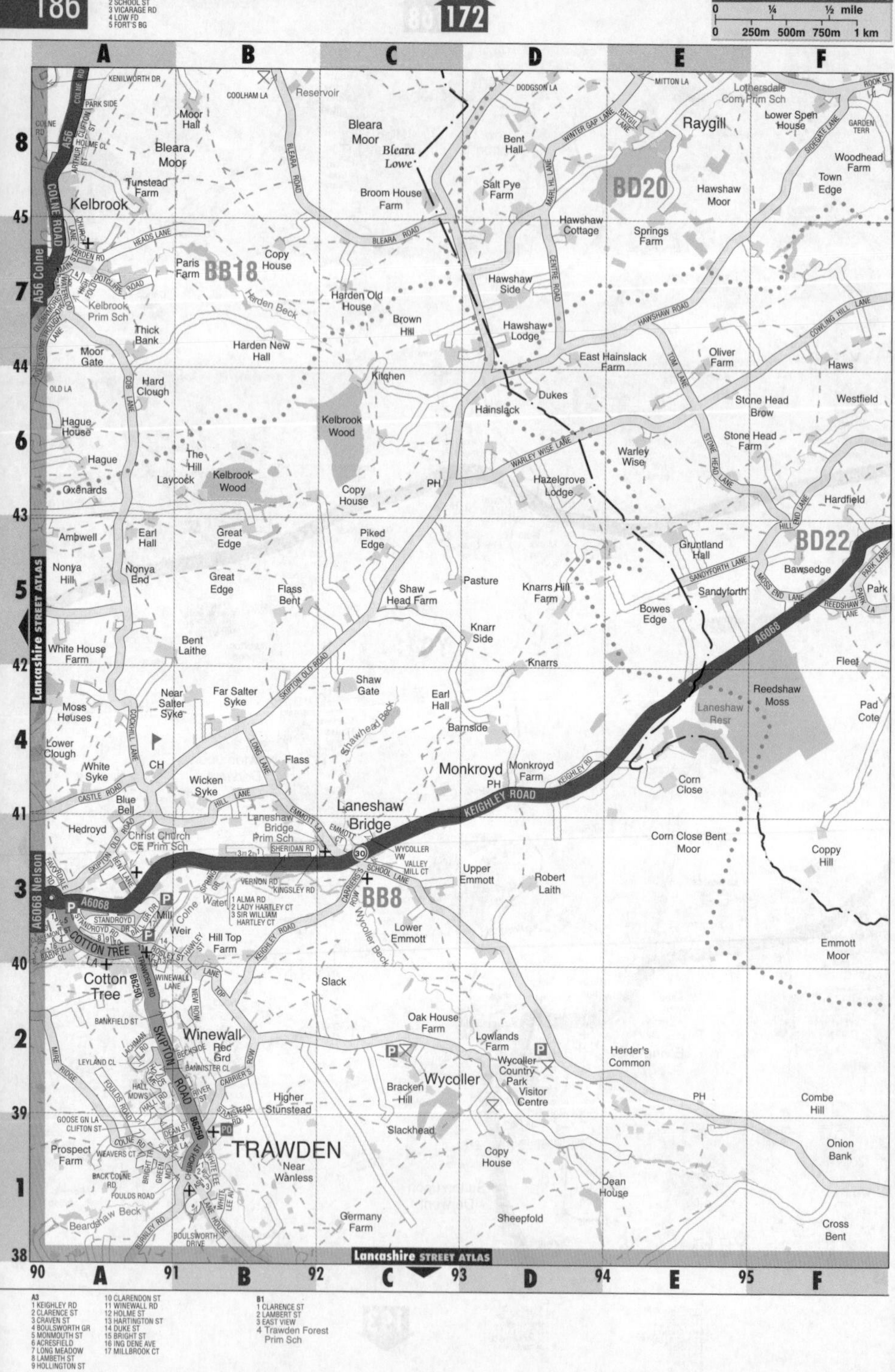

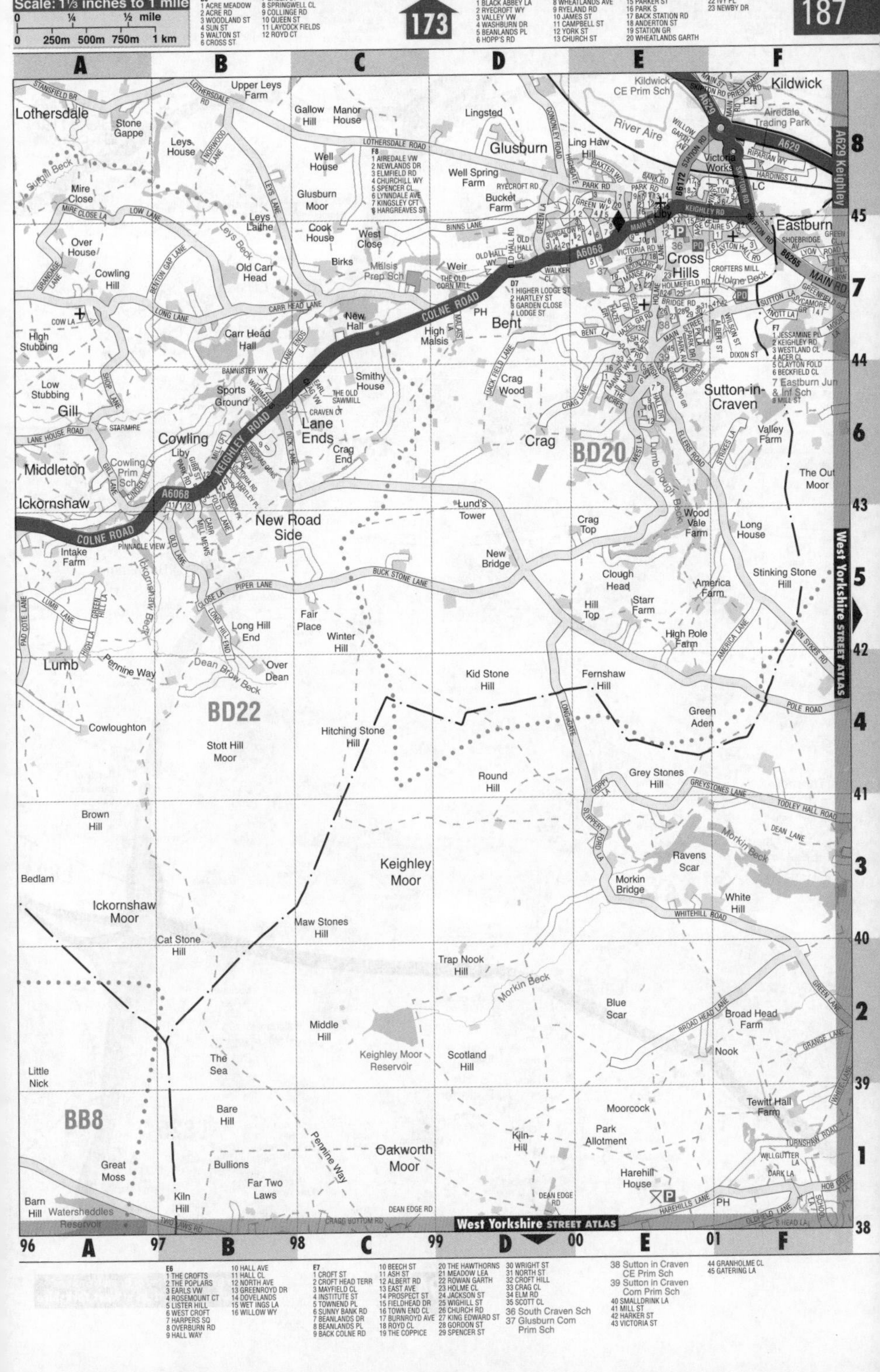

Scale: 1⅓ inches to 1 mile
0 ¼ ½ mile
0 250m 500m 750m 1 km
B6
1 ACRE MEADOW
2 ACRE RD
3 WOODLAND ST
4 SUN ST
5 WALTON ST
6 CROSS ST
7 GREEN ST
8 SPRINGWELL CL
9 COLLINGE RD
10 QUEEN ST
11 LAYCOCK FIELDS
12 ROYD CT
173
E8
1 BLACK ABBEY LA
2 RYECROFT WY
3 VALLEY VW
4 WASHBURN DR
5 BEANLANDS PL
6 HOPP'S RD
7 WHEATLANDS LA
8 WHEATLANDS AVE
9 RYELAND RD
10 JAMES ST
11 CAMPBELL ST
12 YORK ST
13 CHURCH ST
14 NORTH ST
15 PARKER ST
16 PARK S
17 BACK STATION RD
18 ANDERTON ST
19 STATION GR
20 WHEATLANDS GARTH
21 THOMAS ST
22 IVY PL
23 NEWBY DR
187
A B C D E F
Lothersdale
Stone Gappe
Upper Leys Farm
Leys House
Gallow Hill
Manor House
Lingsted
Kildwick CE Prim Sch
Kildwick
Airedale Trading Park
River Aire
A629
A629 Keighley
Glusburn
Ling Haw Hill
Well House
Well Spring Farm
Bucket Farm
Victoria Works
F8
1 AIREDALE VW
2 NEWLANDS DR
3 ELMFIELD RD
4 CHURCHILL WY
5 SPENCER CL
6 LYNNDALE AVE
7 KINGSLEY CFT
8 HARGREAVES ST
LOTHERSDALE ROAD
Mire Close
Sugill Beck
Glusburn Moor
Leys Laithe
Cook House
West Close
Eastburn
Over House
Cowling Hill
Old Carr Head
Birks
Malsis Prep Sch
Weir
Cross Hills
CROFTERS MILL
Holme Beck
MAIN RD
B6265
B6172
A6068
KEIGHLEY RD
High Stubbing
Carr Head Hall
New Hall
COLNE ROAD
High Malsis
PH
Bent
D7
1 HIGHER LODGE ST
2 HARTLEY ST
3 GARDEN CLOSE
4 LODGE ST
F7
1 JESSAMINE PL
2 KEIGHLEY RD
3 WESTLAND CL
4 ACER CL
5 CLAYTON FOLD
6 BECKFIELD CL
7 Eastburn Jun & Inf Sch
8 MILL ST
Low Stubbing
Gill
Sports Ground
Smithy House
Crag Wood
Sutton-in-Craven
Cowling
Cowling Prim Sch
Lane Ends
Crag End
Crag
BD20
Valley Farm
Middleton
Ickornshaw
KEIGHLEY ROAD
Lund's Tower
The Out Moor
Intake Farm
New Road Side
Crag Top
Wood Vale Farm
Long House
New Bridge
Clough Head
Stinking Stone Hill
BUCK STONE LANE
PIPER LANE
Fair Place
Hill Top
Starr Farm
America Farm
Long Hill End
Winter Hill
High Pole Farm
Lumb
Pennine Way
Over Dean
Dean Brow Beck
Kid Stone Hill
Fernshaw Hill
POLE ROAD
BD22
Green Aden
Cowloughton
Stott Hill Moor
Hitching Stone Hill
Round Hill
Grey Stones Hill
GREYSTONES LANE
TODLEY HALL ROAD
Brown Hill
DEAN LANE
Morkin Beck
Ravens Scar
Keighley Moor
Bedlam
Morkin Bridge
White Hill
WHITEHILL ROAD
Ickornshaw Moor
Maw Stones Hill
Cat Stone Hill
Trap Nook Hill
Blue Scar
Broad Head Farm
Middle Hill
Keighley Moor Reservoir
Scotland Hill
Nook
The Sea
Little Nick
BB8
Bare Hill
Moorcock
Tewitt Hall Farm
Kiln Hill
Park Allotment
Oakworth Moor
Great Moss
Bullions
Far Two Laws
Harehill House
Barn Hill
Watersheddles Reservoir
Kiln Hill
DEAN EDGE RD
CRAGG BOTTOM RD
West Yorkshire STREET ATLAS
96 A 97 B 98 C 99 D 00 E 01 F
38 39 40 41 42 43 44 45
8 7 6 5 4 3 2 1
E6
1 THE CROFTS
2 THE POPLARS
3 EARLS VW
4 ROSEMOUNT CT
5 LISTER HILL
6 WEST CROFT
7 HARPERS SQ
8 OVERBURN RD
9 HALL WAY
10 HALL AVE
11 HALL CL
12 NORTH AVE
13 GREENROYD DR
14 DOVELANDS
15 WET INGS LA
16 WILLOW WY
E7
1 CROFT ST
2 CROFT HEAD TERR
3 MAYFIELD CL
4 INSTITUTE ST
5 TOWNEND PL
6 SUNNY BANK RD
7 BEANLANDS DR
8 BEANLANDS PL
9 BACK COLNE RD
10 BEECH ST
11 ASH ST
12 ALBERT RD
13 EAST AVE
14 PROSPECT ST
15 FIELDHEAD DR
16 TOWN END CL
17 BURNROYD AVE
18 ROYD CL
19 THE COPPICE
20 THE HAWTHORNS
21 MEADOW LEA
22 ROWAN GARTH
23 HOLME CL
24 JACKSON ST
25 WIGHILL ST
26 CHURCH RD
27 KING EDWARD ST
28 GORDON ST
29 SPENCER ST
30 WRIGHT ST
31 NORTH ST
32 CROFT HILL
33 CRAG CL
34 ELM RD
35 SCOTT CL
36 South Craven Sch
37 Glusburn Com Prim Sch
38 Sutton in Craven CE Prim Sch
39 Sutton in Craven Com Prim Sch
40 SMALLDRINK LA
41 MILL ST
42 HARKER ST
43 VICTORIA ST
44 GRANHOLME CL
45 GATERING LA

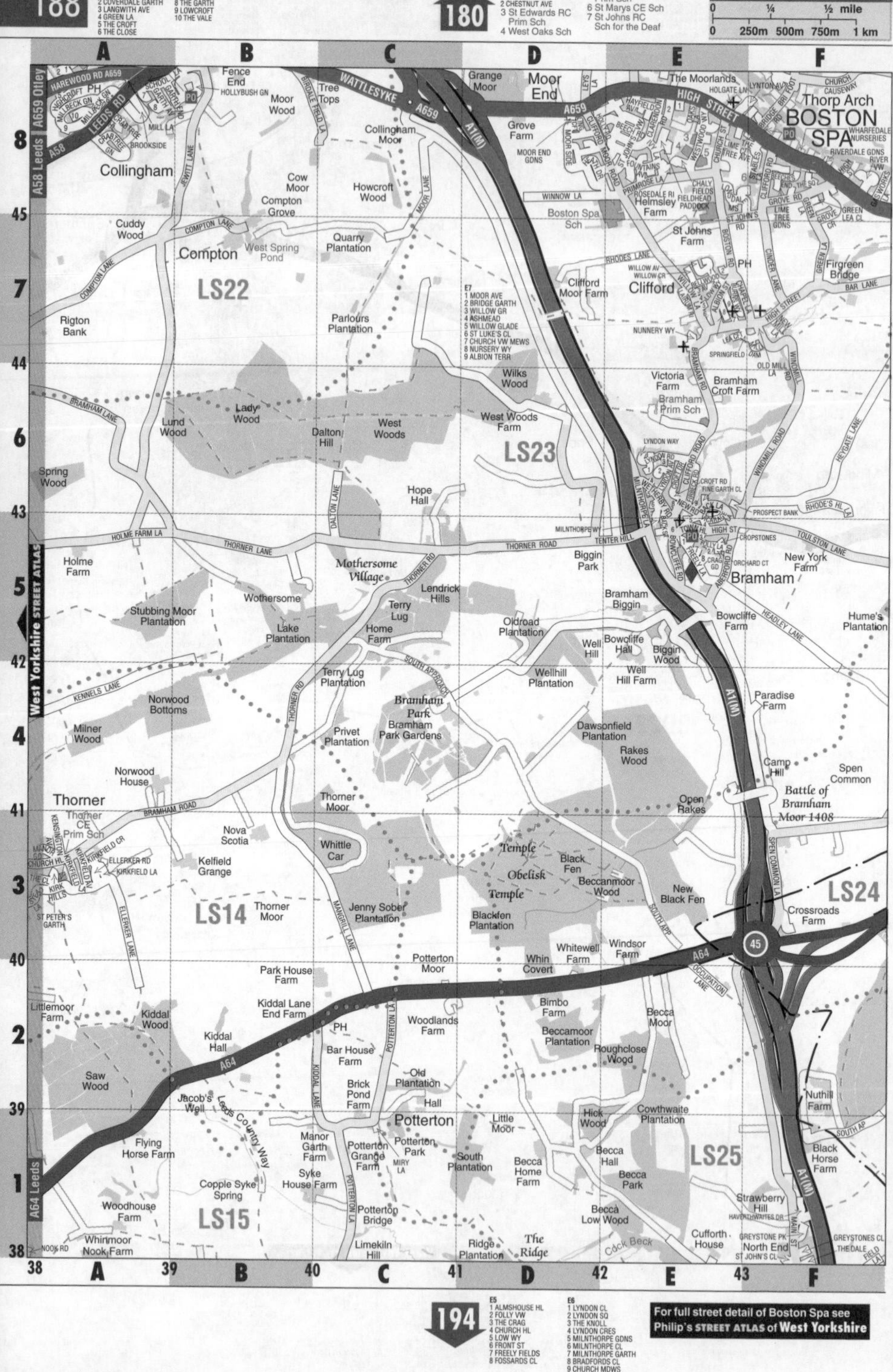

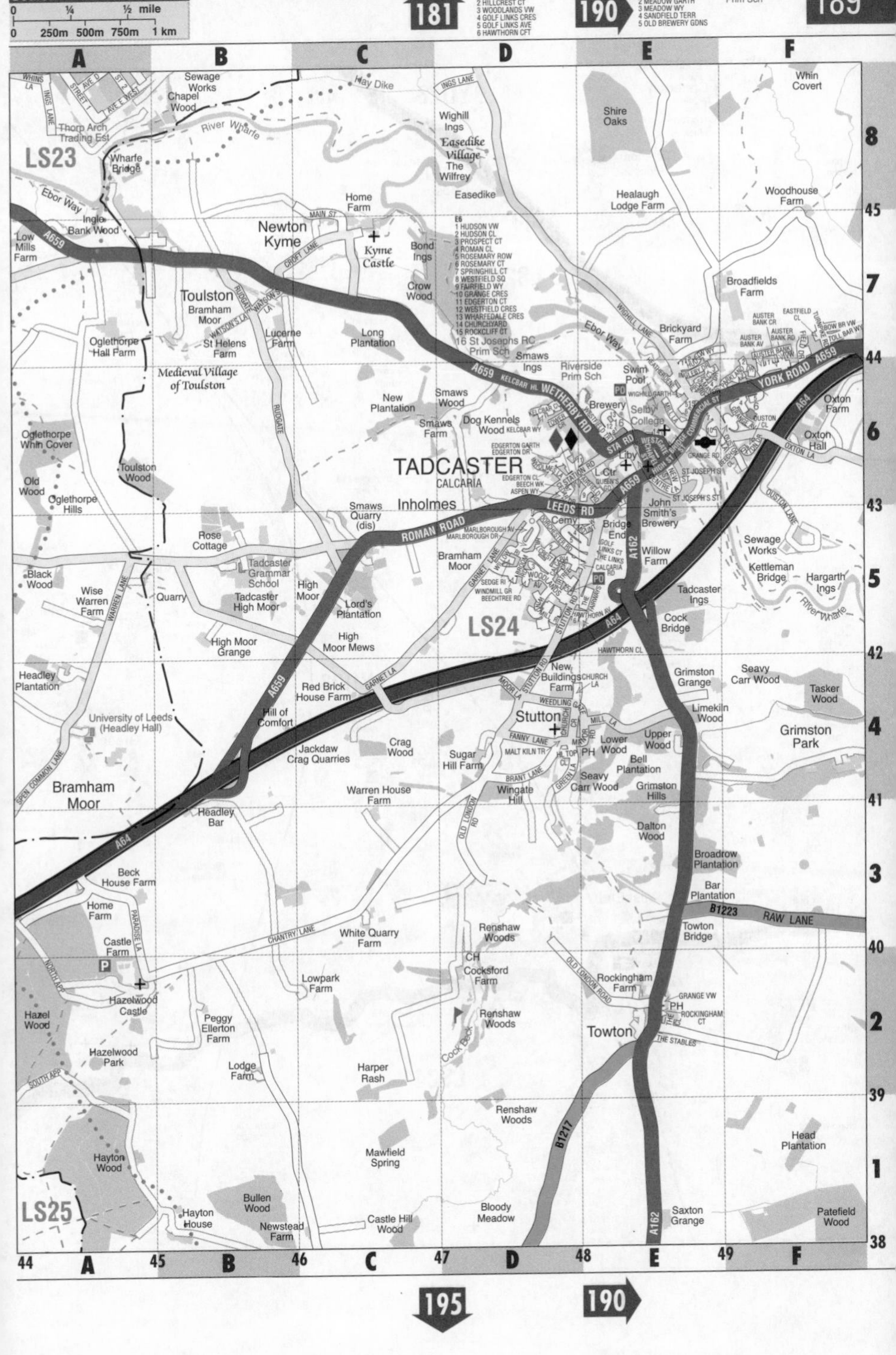

Scale: 1⅓ inches to 1 mile
0 ¼ ½ mile
0 250m 500m 750m 1 km
181
D5
1 GARNET LA
2 HILLCREST CT
3 WOODLANDS VW
4 GOLF LINKS CRES
5 GOLF LINKS AVE
6 HAWTHORN CFT
190
F6
1 THE SQUARE
2 MEADOW GARTH
3 MEADOW WY
4 SANDFIELD TERR
5 OLD BREWERY GDNS
6 Tadcaster East Prim Sch
189
A
B
C
D
E
F
8
45
7
44
6
43
5
42
4
41
3
40
2
39
1
38
Sewage Works
Chapel Wood
Thorp Arch Trading Est
Hay Dike
River Wharfe
INGS LANE
Wighill Ings
Easedike Village
The Wilfrey
Easedike
Shire Oaks
Whin Covert
LS23
Wharfe Bridge
Ebor Way
Ingle Bank Wood
Low Mills Farm
A659
Newton Kyme
MAIN ST
CROFT LANE
Home Farm
Kyme Castle
Bond Ings
Crow Wood
Healaugh Lodge Farm
Woodhouse Farm
E6
1 HUDSON VW
2 HUDSON CL
3 PROSPECT CT
4 ROMAN CL
5 ROSEMARY ROW
6 ROSEMARY CT
7 SPRINGHILL CT
8 WESTFIELD SQ
9 FAIRFIELD WY
10 GRANGE CRES
11 EDGERTON CT
12 WESTFIELD CRES
13 WHARFEDALE CRES
14 CHURCHYARD
15 ROCKCLIFF CT
16 St Josephs RC Prim Sch
Toulston
Bramham Moor
St Helens Farm
Lucerne Farm
Long Plantation
RUDGATE
Broadfields Farm
Brickyard Farm
WIGHILL LANE
Oglethorpe Hall Farm
Medieval Village of Toulston
Smaws Ings
Riverside Prim Sch
Swim Pool
YORK ROAD
A64
Oxton Farm
Oxton Hall
OXTON LA
New Plantation
Smaws Wood
Smaws Farm
Dog Kennels Wood
KELCBAR HL
WETHERBY RD
Brewery
Selby College
Oglethorpe Whin Cover
Toulston Wood
TADCASTER
CALCARIA
STA RD
WESTGATE
HIGH ST
BRIDGE ST
COMMERCIAL ST
GRANGE RD
ST JOSEPH'S ST
Old Wood
Oglethorpe Hills
Inholmes
Smaws Quarry (dis)
LEEDS RD
ROMAN ROAD
Cemy
Bridge End
John Smith's Brewery
DUSTON LANE
Sewage Works
Rose Cottage
Tadcaster Grammar School
MARLBOROUGH AV
MARLBOROUGH DR
Bramham Moor
Willow Farm
A162
Kettleman Bridge
Hargarth Ings
River Wharfe
Black Wood
Wise Warren Farm
WARREN LANE
Quarry
Tadcaster High Moor
High Moor
Lord's Plantation
GARNET LANE
SEDGE RI
WINDMILL GR
BEECHTREE RD
WOODLANDS
STUTTON RD
HAWTHORN AV
Tadcaster Ings
Cock Bridge
LS24
High Moor Grange
High Moor Mews
HAWTHORN CL
Headley Plantation
Red Brick House Farm
GARNET LA
MOOR LA
STUTTON RD
New Buildings Farm
CHURCH LA
Grimston Grange
Seavy Carr Wood
Tasker Wood
University of Leeds (Headley Hall)
Hill of Comfort
Stutton
WEEDLING GATE
MILL LA
Limekiln Wood
Grimston Park
Jackdaw Crag Quarries
Crag Wood
FANNY LANE
MALT KILN TR
Sugar Hill Farm
Lower Wood
Upper Wood
PH
Bell Plantation
SPEN COMMON LANE
Bramham Moor
Warren House Farm
BRANT LANE
Wingate Hill
GREEN LA
Seavy Carr Wood
Grimston Hills
Headley Bar
OLD LONDON RD
Dalton Wood
Broadrow Plantation
Beck House Farm
Bar Plantation
B1223
RAW LANE
Home Farm
PARADISE LA
CHANTRY LANE
White Quarry Farm
Renshaw Woods
Towton Bridge
Castle Farm
P
NORTH APP
CH
Cocksford Farm
OLD LONDON ROAD
Rockingham Farm
Hazel Wood
Hazelwood Castle
Lowpark Farm
Peggy Ellerton Farm
Renshaw Woods
GRANGE VW
PH
ROCKINGHAM CT
Towton
THE STABLES
Cock Beck
Hazelwood Park
Lodge Farm
Harper Rash
SOUTH APP
Renshaw Woods
B1217
Head Plantation
Hayton Wood
Mawfield Spring
LS25
Bullen Wood
Hayton House
Newstead Farm
Castle Hill Wood
Bloody Meadow
Saxton Grange
Patefield Wood
44
A
45
B
46
C
47
D
48
E
49
F
195
190

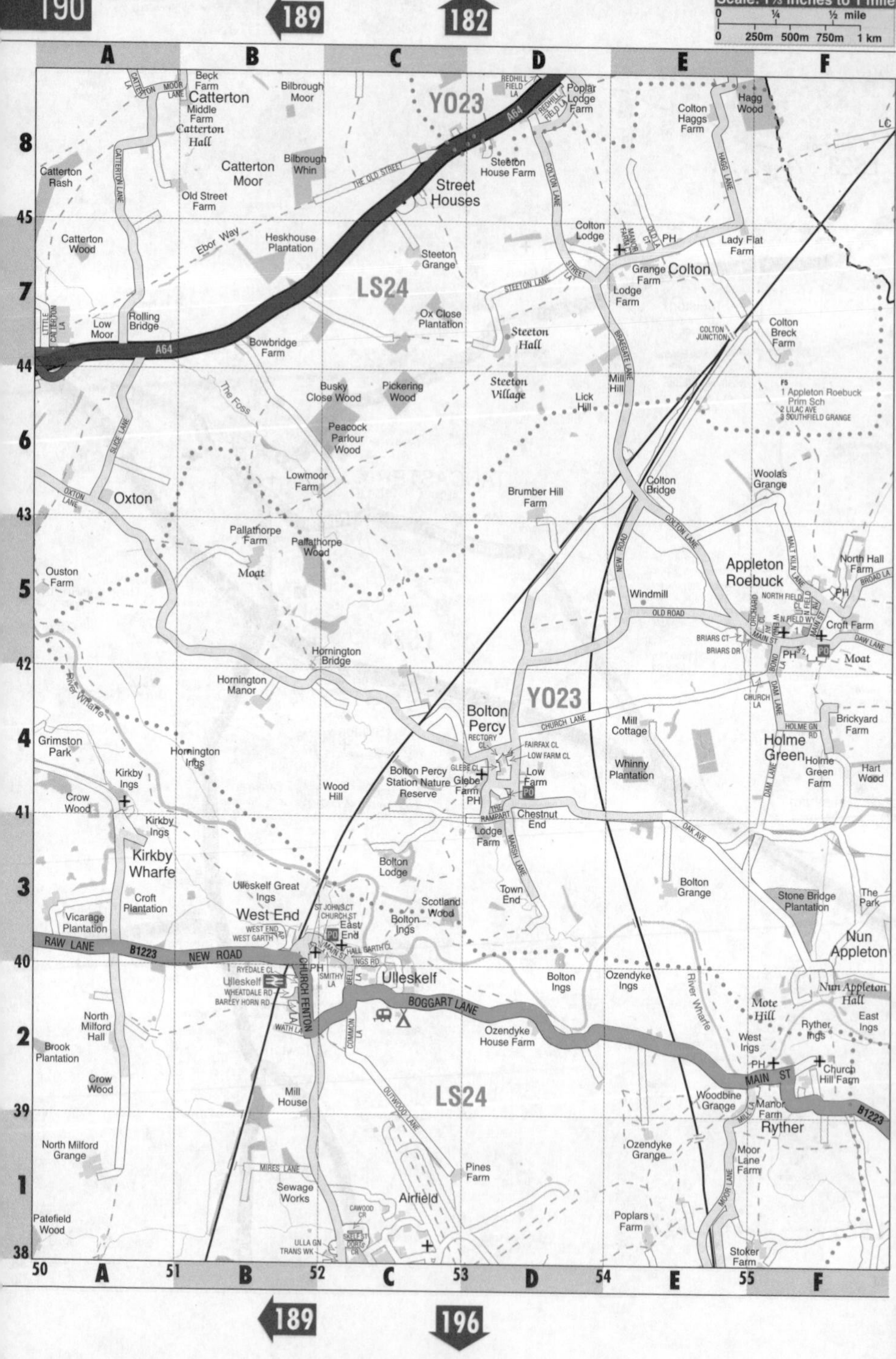

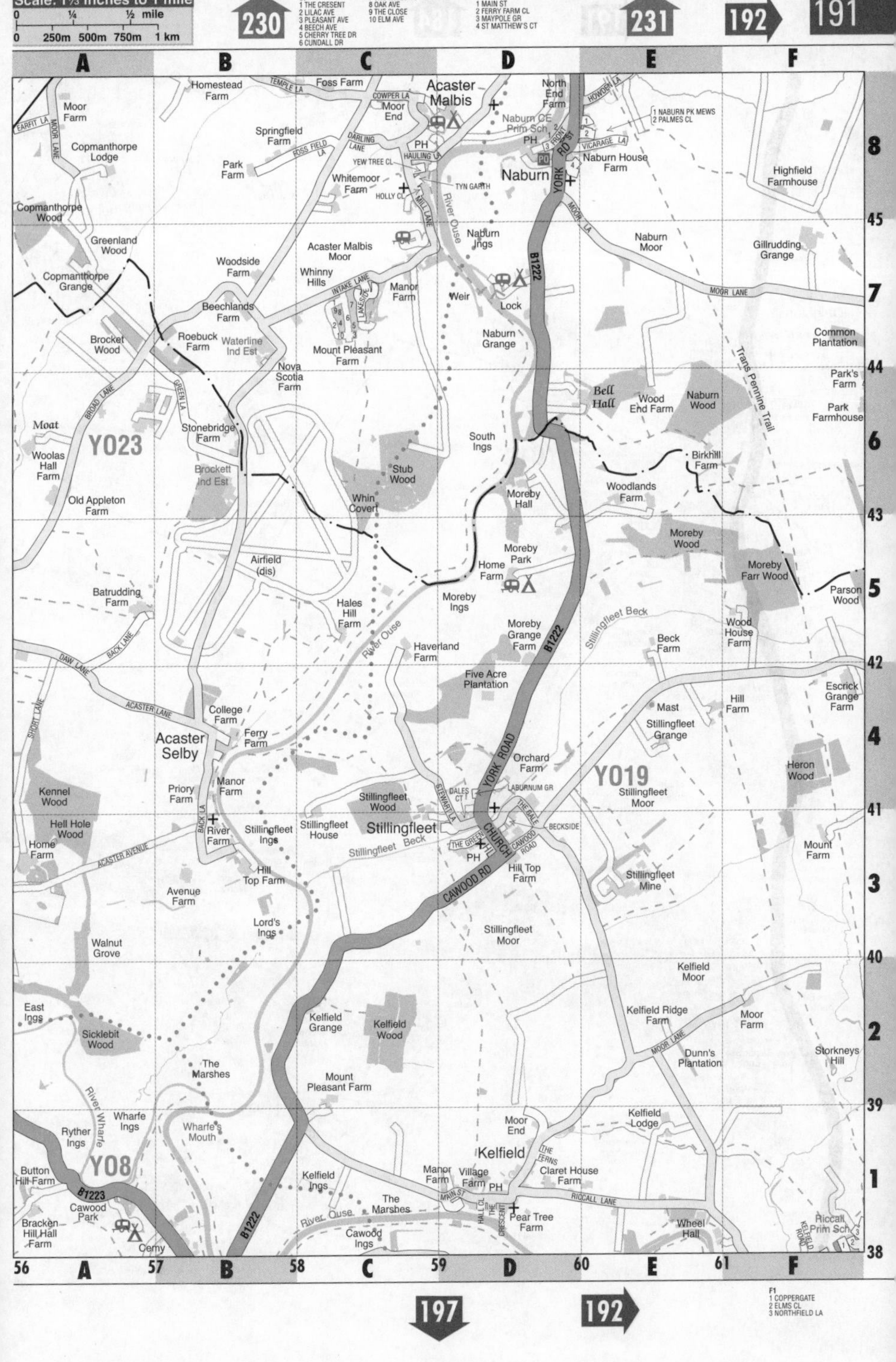
Scale: 1⅓ inches to 1 mile
0 ¼ ½ mile
0 250m 500m 750m 1 km
230
C7
1 THE CRESENT
2 LILAC AVE
3 PLEASANT AVE
4 BEECH AVE
5 CHERRY TREE DR
6 CUNDALL DR
7 THE WILLOWS
8 OAK AVE
9 THE CLOSE
10 ELM AVE
D8
1 MAIN ST
2 FERRY FARM CL
3 MAYPOLE GR
4 ST MATTHEW'S CT
231
192
A B C D E F
Homestead Farm
Foss Farm
Acaster Malbis
North End Farm
Moor Farm
Moor End
Naburn CE Prim Sch
1 NABURN PK MEWS
2 PALMES CL
Springfield Farm
Copmanthorpe Lodge
Park Farm
Naburn
Naburn House Farm
Whitemoor Farm
Highfield Farmhouse
Copmanthorpe Wood
River Ouse
Greenland Wood
Acaster Malbis Moor
Naburn Ings
Naburn Moor
Gillrudding Grange
Woodside Farm
Whinny Hills
Copmanthorpe Grange
Manor Farm
Weir
Lock
Beechlands Farm
Brocket Wood
Roebuck Farm
Waterline Ind Est
Mount Pleasant Farm
Naburn Grange
Common Plantation
Nova Scotia Farm
Trans Pennine Trail
Park's Farm
Bell Hall
Wood End Farm
Naburn Wood
Park Farmhouse
Moat
Stonebridge Farm
YO23
South Ings
Woolas Hall Farm
Brockett Ind Est
Stub Wood
Birkhill Farm
Moreby Hall
Woodlands Farm
Whin Covert
Old Appleton Farm
Moreby Wood
Airfield (dis)
Moreby Park
Home Farm
Moreby Farr Wood
Batrudding Farm
Hales Hill Farm
Moreby Ings
Parson Wood
Stillingfleet Beck
Moreby Grange Farm
Wood House Farm
Beck Farm
Haverland Farm
Five Acre Plantation
Escrick Grange Farm
Mast
Hill Farm
College Farm
Stillingfleet Grange
Acaster Selby
Ferry Farm
Orchard Farm
Heron Wood
YO19
Kennel Wood
Manor Farm
Priory Farm
Stillingfleet Wood
Stillingfleet Moor
Hell Hole Wood
River Farm
Stillingfleet Ings
Stillingfleet House
Stillingfleet
Home Farm
PH
Mount Farm
Hill Top Farm
Stillingfleet Mine
Avenue Farm
Lord's Ings
Stillingfleet Moor
Walnut Grove
Kelfield Moor
East Ings
Kelfield Grange
Kelfield Wood
Kelfield Ridge Farm
Moor Farm
Sicklebit Wood
The Marshes
Dunn's Plantation
Storkneys Hill
Mount Pleasant Farm
River Wharfe
Wharfe Ings
Kelfield Lodge
Moor End
Ryther Ings
Wharfe's Mouth
Kelfield
YO8
Button Hill Farm
Kelfield Ings
Manor Farm
Village Farm
Claret House Farm
Cawood Park
The Marshes
River Ouse
Pear Tree Farm
Wheel Hall
Riccall Prim Sch
Bracken Hill Hall Farm
Cemy
Cawood Ings
B1222
B1223
YORK ROAD
CAWOOD RD
MOOR LANE
RICCALL LANE
ACASTER LANE
DAW LANE
BACK LANE
ACASTER AVENUE
BROAD LANE
56 57 58 59 60 61
45 44 43 42 41 40 39 38
8 7 6 5 4 3 2 1
197
192
F1
1 COPPERGATE
2 ELMS CL
3 NORTHFIELD LA

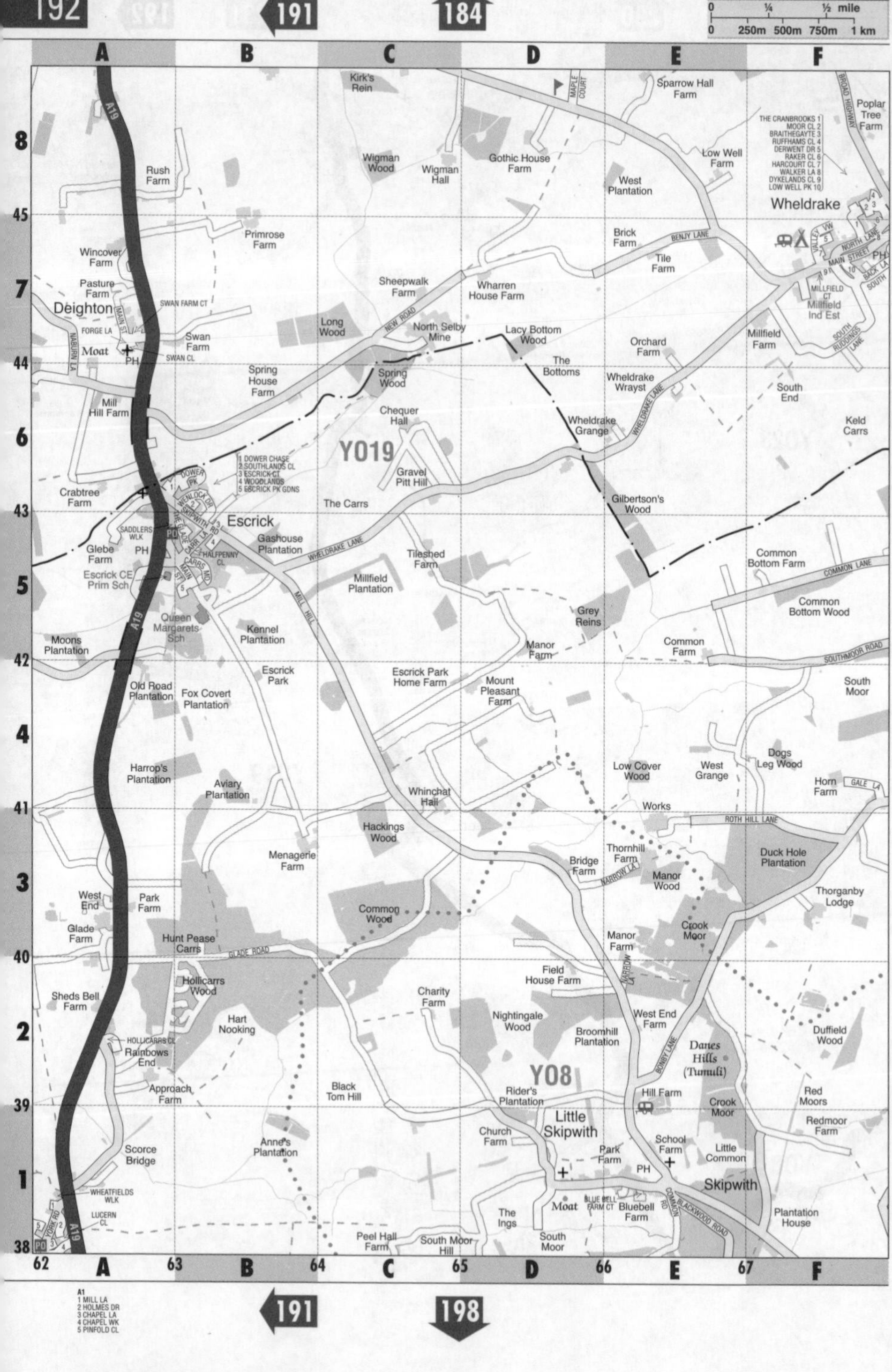

Scale: 1⅓ inches to 1 mile

0 ¼ ½ mile

0 250m 500m 750m 1 km

A B C D E F

Cheesecake Farm
Mount Pleasant
Gravelpit Plantation
Mayfield Grange Farm
Four Beck Ends
Eller Carr
The Carr
Town's Ings
Wheldrake CE Prim Sch
Sutton Rush
Storwood Carr
Hagg Bridge Farm
Hagg Bridge
Rossmoor Grange
Rossmoor Farm
The Grange
Frogs Nest Farm
Westfield Farm
Sutton Farm
Y041
South Wood
Broomhill Plantation
The Carr
Wheldrake
1 DALTON HL
2 KITTY GARTH
3 ST HELEN'S RISE
4 CHURCH CL
5 THE PADDOCKS
Storwood Grange
Rossmoor Lodge
Oakland Farm
Park Wood
Grove Farm
Storwood
White House Farm
Old Course of the River Derwent
Wheldrake Ings Nature Reserve
Suss Carrs
Farm Wood
Quakers' Wood
Eastroad Plantation
Moat
Mattie Brown Wood
West Farm
Stackyard Plantation
Thicket Priory
Park House Farm
Woodside Lodge Farm
Storwood Ings
The Rush
Ross Moor
South Wood
The Whin
Y019
Home Farm
North Hills
Crinklety Wood
Whincover Wood
Ball Hall Farm
Boundary Farm
Langrickgate Field
North Moor
Cottingwith Lock
Cemy
Forest Farm
Acre Farm
Willow Tree Farm
North Moor
Thornums Wood
East Cottingwith
Grange Farm
South Acre Farm
East End
East Cottingwith Common
South Moor
Glebe Farm
Thorganby Ings
Red Cap Farm
North Ross Farm
South Ross Farm
New Moor
Thorganby
Y042
Thorganby Hall Wood
Mill House
Pond Farm
East Cottingwith Ings
Spring House
Ings View Farm
Whitegate Bridge
Yew Tree Farm
Gale Farm
Fox Covert
Ellerton Common
Sike Bridge
New Lands
Woodfield Farm
East Lodge
Blue Slates Farm
Scruton Wood
Ruddings Wood
Priory Farm
Lofty Farm
East Grange Farm
South View Farm
North Grange
Far Woods
Priory Farm
Ellerton
Hall Farm
Ellerton Ings
Short Acre Farm
Aughton Ruddings
Lawns House Farm
South Grange
North Duffield Lodge
Aughton
Aughton Ruddings Grange
Red Moors
Great Wood
Lodge Farm
Stud Farm
Wentsford House Farm
Glebe Farm
Y08
Aughton Plantation
Longlane Plantation
Aughton Ings
York House Farm
Park Farm
North Duffield Carrs
Aughton Common
Autherthaws Farm
CH

68 A 69 B 70 C 71 D 72 E 73 F

East Yorkshire & Northern Lincolnshire STREET ATLAS

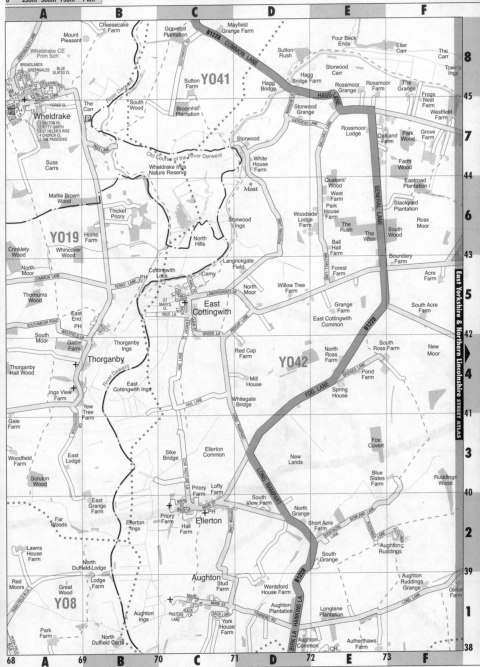

Scale: 1½ inches to 1 mile

0   ¼   ½ mile
0   250m 500m 750m 1 km

West Yorkshire STREET ATLAS

Labels (grid references)

LS15

Stockhield Lane
Stockhield Grange Farm
Rakehill Farm
Rake Hill
Springfield Farm
Hall Tower Hill
Wendel Av
Barwick in Elmet
Barwick In Elmet CE Prim Sch
PH
Welfare Av
Richmondfield Garth
Limekiln Hill
The Mount
Gascoigne Ct
Richmondfield Dr
Richmondfield Av
Barwick Bank
Highfield Farm
Highfield La
Honesty Farm
Lower Barnbow Farm
Upper Barnbow Farm
Barnbow Carr
Throstle Nest Farm
Moat
PH

Cherry Strip
1 MAYPOLE MEWS
2 CHURCH FARM VW
3 POTTERTON CL
4 ELMWOOD CT
5 SCHOOLGATE
6 CROFTWAY
7 THE COPPICE
8 GASCOIGNE VW
9 THE CLOSE
10 RICHMONDFIELD CROSS
11 RICHMONDFIELD WY
12 RICHMONDFIELD CRES
13 RICHMONDFIELD LO CL
14 RICHMONDFIELD GR
15 RICHMONDFIELD GR
16 PEAR TREE GDNS
17 THE SYCAMORES

Ridge Plantation
Ass Bridge
Moat
Leyfield Farm
Cattle Lane
Barwick Lodge Plantation
Willowgarth Plantation
Hungerhills Plantation
Old Wood
Home Farm
Aberford Park
Aberford CE Prim Sch
Aberford
Chantryhill Plantation
Folly Corner
St John's
Hayton Wood Vw
Becca Banks
Finfold Rd
Green Hill
A1 (M)
PH
Waterbeck Ms
SCHOOL LA
Cooper Wood
Hicklam House
Hangings Plantation
B1217
Dawson's Wood
Hook Moor
Parlington
Parlington Hollins
Bathingwell Plantation
Fox Covert
Parlington Park
Park House Farm
Aberford Road
Beech Plantation
Ridge Road Farm
M1
48/44
A1 (M)

Barnbow Wood
Carr Beck
Shippen Plantation
Barnbow Common Sports Ground
Willow Park Farm
Stank House
Lazencroft Farm
Shippen House Farm
Brown Moor
LC
Crawshaw Wood
Nanny Goat La
Barrowby Lane
White House Farm
Fushion Ct
St Benedicts RC Prim Sch
Beech House
Helios 47 Ind Est
Hawk's Nest Wood
Business Pk
New Hold Ind Est
Woodbridge Av
Cedar Ridge
Moule Rise
A656
LS25
47
Aberford Rd

M1 Wakefield (A650)
M1
Barrowby Carr
Carr Wood
Barrowby Hall
Clearview Farm
Moorhouse Farm
Bradbury Grange
Warren House Farm
Swillington Common Farm

A63 Leeds (A64)
Selby Road
Swillington Common
Hollinthorpe
Syke House Farm
Smeaton House Farm
Brecks Lane
Brecks Farm
Brecks Wood
LS26
Swillington
Whitecliffe
Swillington Prim Sch
Goody Cross Lane
Little Preston
Goody Cross
A642 Wakefield
A642
PO
CHURCH
PH

Wakefield Road A642
PH
Lilydchurch La
Strawberry Fields Prim Sch
Garforth Com Coll
Cemy
East Garforth Prim Sch
East Garforth
Turton Grange Lane
Three Acre Plantation
Sturton Grange
Garforth Squash & RL Ctr
Nineland Prim Sch
Stub Wood
Green Lane Prim Sch
West Garforth
Rookery Grange Gdn
Scholars Gate
Kippax Lane End
Hotel
Selby Road
A63
GARFORTH
Kippax North Prim Sch
B6137 Leeds Road
Sparrow Hall Farm
Valley Farm
Moorgate Rd
Roach Grange Farm
Long Meadow Gate
Milestone Farm
Peckfield House Farm
A63
Limekiln Farm
Sandgate La
Peckfield Bar
Peckfield Common
Warrenhouse Plantation
Ridge Road
Ledston Luck
Sycamore Av
Owlett Hall Farm
Townclose Hills
Townclose Wood
Little Preston
Kippax Ash Tree Prim Sch
Kippax Prim Sch
Greenfields Prim Sch
High St
B6137
Kippax
Sandgate Ter
Lime-Tree La
Sandgate Ri
Keble Garth
Church St
Ling Close Wood
Sheepcote Wood
A656
Sheepcote Farm
St Helen's Well
Well House Farm
St Helen's Dr
Sunningdale Av
Hallfield Terr
Churchill Av
St Mary's Wk
Mickelfield
Old Micklefield
Roman Ridge Bridge
Phoenix Avenue
Spoil Heap
Warren Farm
Quarry
Pit La

Index

A1
1 WHITECLIFFE DR
2 LOWTHER DR
3 LOWTHER CRES
4 CHURCH CL
5 SMEATON GR
6 THE PLEASANCE
7 SPRINGWELL AV
8 WOODLAND CRES
9 THE CREST
10 SPRINGWELL RD
11 SPRINGWELL AVE
12 THE DRIVE
13 SCOTT CL
14 ST MARY'S AVE
15 PRIMROSE HL DR
16 PRIMROSE HL GR

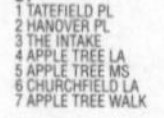

D1
1 TATERFIELD PL
2 HANOVER PL
3 THE INTAKE
4 APPLE TREE LA
5 APPLE TREE MS
6 CHURCHFIELD LA
7 APPLE TREE WALK

For full street detail of Garforth see Philip's STREET ATLAS of **West Yorkshire**

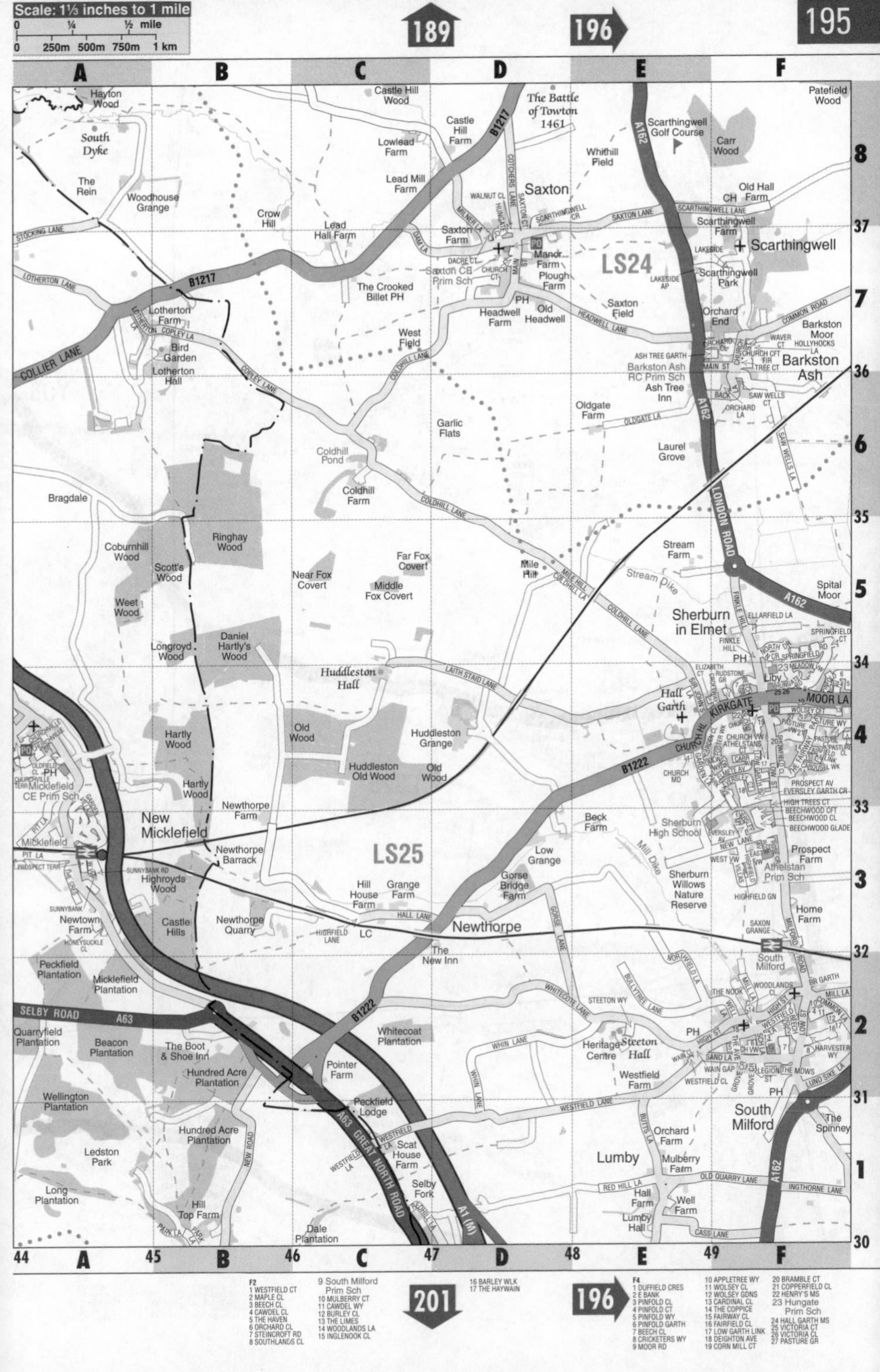
Scale: 1⅓ inches to 1 mile
0 ¼ ½ mile
0 250m 500m 750m 1 km
189
196
A B C D E F
Hayton Wood
South Dyke
The Rein
Woodhouse Grange
Castle Hill Wood
Castle Hill Farm
Lowlead Farm
Lead Mill Farm
The Battle of Towton 1461
Whitehill Field
Scarthingwell Golf Course
Carr Wood
Patefield Wood
Saxton
Old Hall Farm
Scarthingwell
Crow Hill
Lead Hall Farm
Saxton Farm
Manor Farm
Plough Farm
Saxton CE Prim Sch
LS24
Scarthingwell Park
STOCKING LANE
LOTHERTON LANE
B1217
The Crooked Billet PH
Headwell Farm
Old Headwell
Saxton Field
Orchard End
Barkston Moor
COMMON ROAD
Lotherton Farm
Bird Garden
Lotherton Hall
COLLIER LANE
COPLEY LANE
West Field
COLDHILL LANE
Barkston Ash RC Prim Sch
Barkston Ash
Ash Tree Inn
Oldgate Farm
OLDGATE LA
Garlic Flats
Laurel Grove
Coldhill Pond
Coldhill Farm
Bragdale
Ringhay Wood
Coburnhill Wood
Scott's Wood
Weet Wood
Near Fox Covert
Far Fox Covert
Middle Fox Covert
Mile Hill
MILE HILL
Stream Farm
Stream Dike
LONDON ROAD
A162
Spital Moor
Sherburn in Elmet
Daniel Hartly's Wood
Longroyd Wood
Huddleston Hall
LAITH STAID LANE
Hall Garth
KIRKGATE
MOOR LA
Old Wood
Huddleston Grange
Huddleston Old Wood
Old Wood
Hartly Wood
Micklefield CE Prim Sch
New Micklefield
Newthorpe Farm
B1222
CHURCH HL
Beck Farm
Sherburn High School
Prospect Farm
Athelstan Prim Sch
Newthorpe Barrack
LS25
Low Grange
Micklefield
PIT LA
PROSPECT TERR
SUNNYBANK RD
Highroyds Wood
Hill House Farm
Grange Farm
Gorse Bridge Farm
Sherburn Willows Nature Reserve
Mill Dike
Newtown Farm
Castle Hills
Newthorpe Quarry
HALL LANE
LC
Newthorpe
GORSE LANE
Home Farm
South Milford
Peckfield Plantation
Micklefield Plantation
The New Inn
WHITECOTE LANE
SELBY ROAD
A63
Quarryfield Plantation
Beacon Plantation
The Boot & Shoe Inn
Whitecoat Plantation
Heritage Centre
Steeton Hall
WHIN LANE
Hundred Acre Plantation
Pointer Farm
Westfield Farm
Wellington Plantation
Peckfield Lodge
WESTFIELD LANE
South Milford
The Spinney
Hundred Acre Plantation
Ledston Park
Scat House Farm
A63 GREAT NORTH ROAD
Orchard Farm
Lumby
Mulberry Farm
OLD QUARRY LANE
Long Plantation
Hill Top Farm
Selby Fork
A1 (M)
RED HILL LA
Hall Farm
Well Farm
Lumby Hall
CASS LANE
Dale Plantation
8 37 7 36 6 35 5 34 4 33 3 32 2 31 1 30
44 45 46 47 48 49
201
196
F2
1 WESTFIELD CT
2 MAPLE CL
3 BEECH CL
4 CAWDEL CL
5 THE HAVEN
6 ORCHARD CL
7 STEINCROFT RD
8 SOUTHLANDS CL
9 South Milford Prim Sch
10 MULBERRY CT
11 CAWDEL WY
12 BURLEY CL
13 THE LIMES
14 WOODLANDS LA
15 INGLENOOK CL
16 BARLEY WLK
17 THE HAYWAIN
F4
1 DUFFIELD CRES
2 E BANK
3 PINFOLD CL
4 PINFOLD CT
5 PINFOLD WY
6 PINFOLD GARTH
7 BEECH CL
8 CRICKETERS WY
9 MOOR RD
10 APPLETREE WY
11 WOLSEY CL
12 WOLSEY GDNS
13 CARDINAL CL
14 THE COPPICE
15 FAIRWAY CL
16 FAIRFIELD CL
17 LOW GARTH LINK
18 DEIGHTON AVE
19 CORN MILL CT
20 BRAMBLE CT
21 COPPERFIELD CL
22 HENRY'S MS
23 Hungate Prim Sch
24 HALL GARTH MS
25 VICTORIA CT
26 VICTORIA CL
27 PASTURE GR

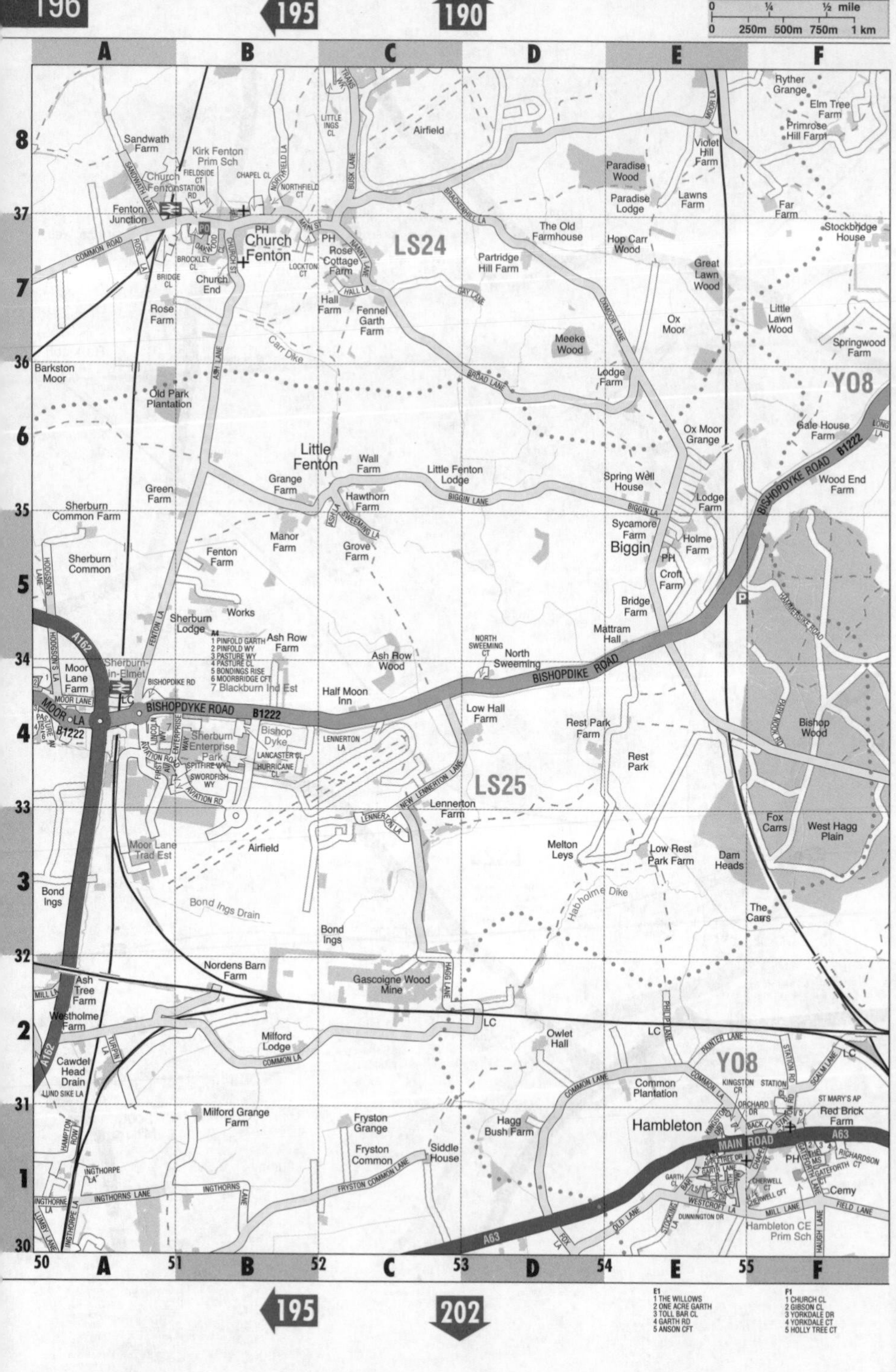

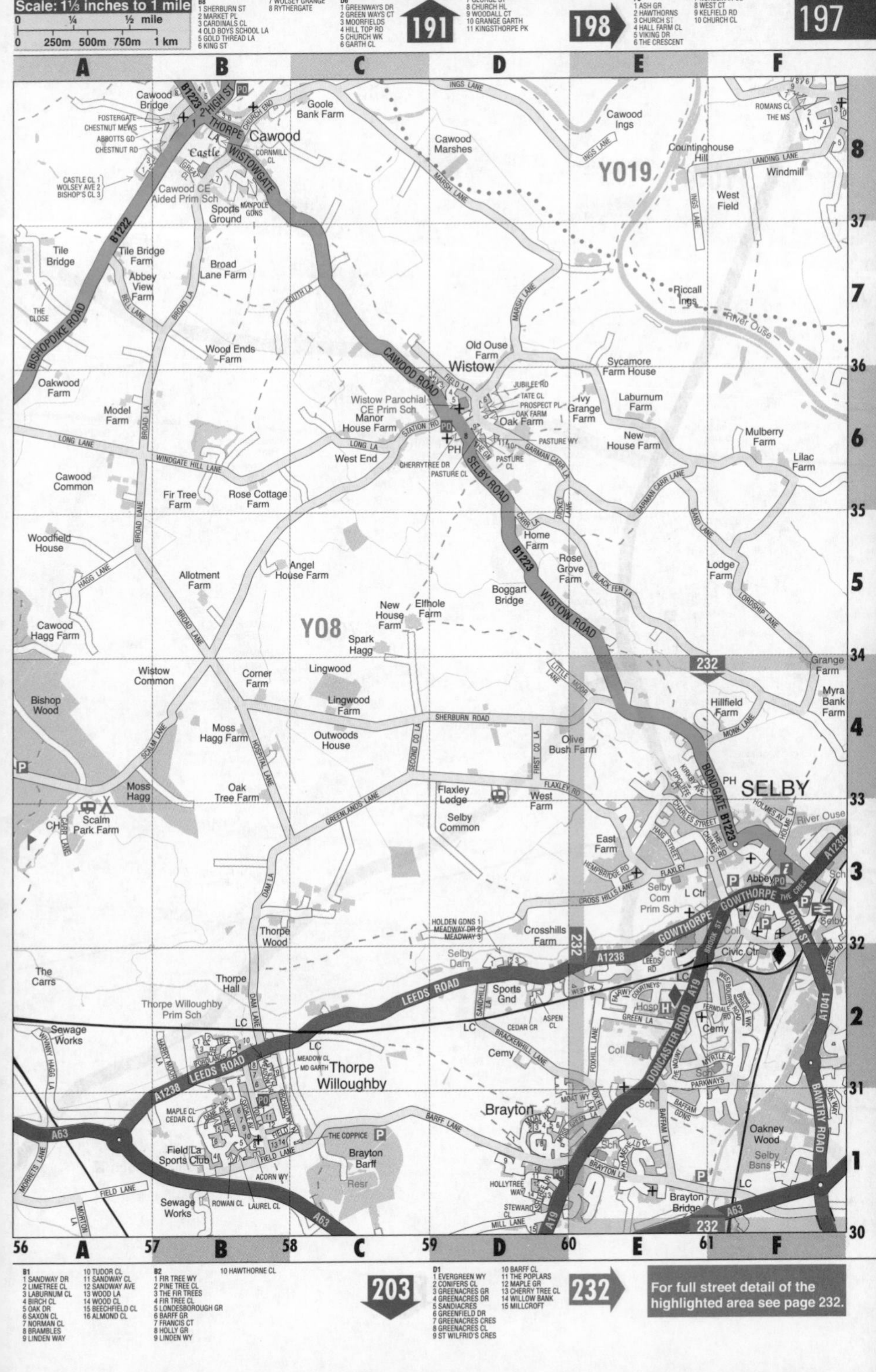
Scale: 1⅓ inches to 1 mile
0 ¼ ½ mile
0 250m 500m 750m 1 km
B8
1 SHERBURN ST
2 MARKET PL
3 CARDINALS CL
4 OLD BOYS SCHOOL LA
5 GOLD THREAD LA
6 KING ST
7 WOLSEY GRANGE
8 RYTHERGATE
D6
1 GREENWAYS DR
2 GREEN WAYS CT
3 MOORFIELDS
4 HILL TOP RD
5 CHURCH WK
6 GARTH CL
7 GEORGE ST
8 CHURCH HL
9 WOODALL CT
10 GRANGE GARTH
11 KINGSTHORPE PK
191
198
F8
1 ASH GR
2 HAWTHORNS
3 CHURCH ST
4 HALL FARM CL
5 VIKING DR
6 THE CRESCENT
7 NORSEMAN CL
8 WEST CT
9 KELFIELD RD
10 CHURCH CL
Cawood
Cawood Bridge
Castle
Cawood CE Aided Prim Sch
Sports Ground
Goole Bank Farm
Cawood Marshes
Cawood Ings
YO19
Countinghouse Hill
Windmill
West Field
Riccall Ings
River Ouse
Tile Bridge
Tile Bridge Farm
Abbey View Farm
Broad Lane Farm
Wood Ends Farm
Oakwood Farm
Model Farm
Old Ouse Farm
Wistow
Wistow Parochial CE Prim Sch
Manor House Farm
West End
Sycamore Farm House
Laburnum Farm
Ivy Grange Farm
Oak Farm
New House Farm
Mulberry Farm
Lilac Farm
Cawood Common
Fir Tree Farm
Rose Cottage Farm
Home Farm
Rose Grove Farm
Woodfield House
Allotment Farm
Angel House Farm
Lodge Farm
Cawood Hagg Farm
YO8
New House Farm
Elfhole Farm
Spark Hagg
Boggart Bridge
Wistow Common
Bishop Wood
Corner Farm
Lingwood
Lingwood Farm
Grange Farm
Myra Bank Farm
Hillfield Farm
Moss Hagg Farm
Outwoods House
Olive Bush Farm
Moss Hagg
Oak Tree Farm
Flaxley Lodge
Selby Common
West Farm
SELBY
Scalm Park Farm
East Farm
Selby Com Prim Sch
Abbey
Thorpe Wood
Crosshills Farm
The Carrs
Thorpe Hall
Selby Dam
Sports Gnd
Civic Ctr
Thorpe Willoughby Prim Sch
Sewage Works
Thorpe Willoughby
Cemy
Hosp
Brayton
Oakney Wood
Selby Bsns Pk
Field La Sports Club
Brayton Barff
Resr
Brayton Bridge
Sewage Works
CAWOOD ROAD
SELBY ROAD
WISTOW ROAD
LEEDS ROAD
DONCASTER ROAD
BAWTRY ROAD
BISHOPDIKE ROAD
GOWTHORPE
BONDGATE
SHERBURN ROAD
232
56 57 58 59 60 61
30 31 32 33 34 35 36 37
B1
1 SANDWAY DR
2 LIMETREE CL
3 LABURNUM CL
4 BIRCH CL
5 OAK DR
6 SAXON CL
7 NORMAN CL
8 BRAMBLES
9 LINDEN WAY
10 TUDOR CL
11 SANDWAY CL
12 SANDWAY AVE
13 WOOD LA
14 WOOD CL
15 BEECHFIELD CL
16 ALMOND CL
B2
1 FIR TREE WY
2 PINE TREE CL
3 THE FIR TREES
4 FIR TREE CL
5 LONDESBOROUGH GR
6 BARFF GR
7 FRANCIS CT
8 HOLLY GR
9 LINDEN WY
10 HAWTHORNE CL
203
D1
1 EVERGREEN WY
2 CONIFERS CL
3 GREENACRES GR
4 GREENACRES DR
5 SANDIACRES
6 GREENFIELD DR
7 GREENACRES CRES
8 GREENACRES CL
9 ST WILFRID'S CRES
10 BARFF CL
11 THE POPLARS
12 MAPLE GR
13 CHERRY TREE CL
14 WILLOW BANK
15 MILLCROFT
232
For full street detail of the highlighted area see page 232.

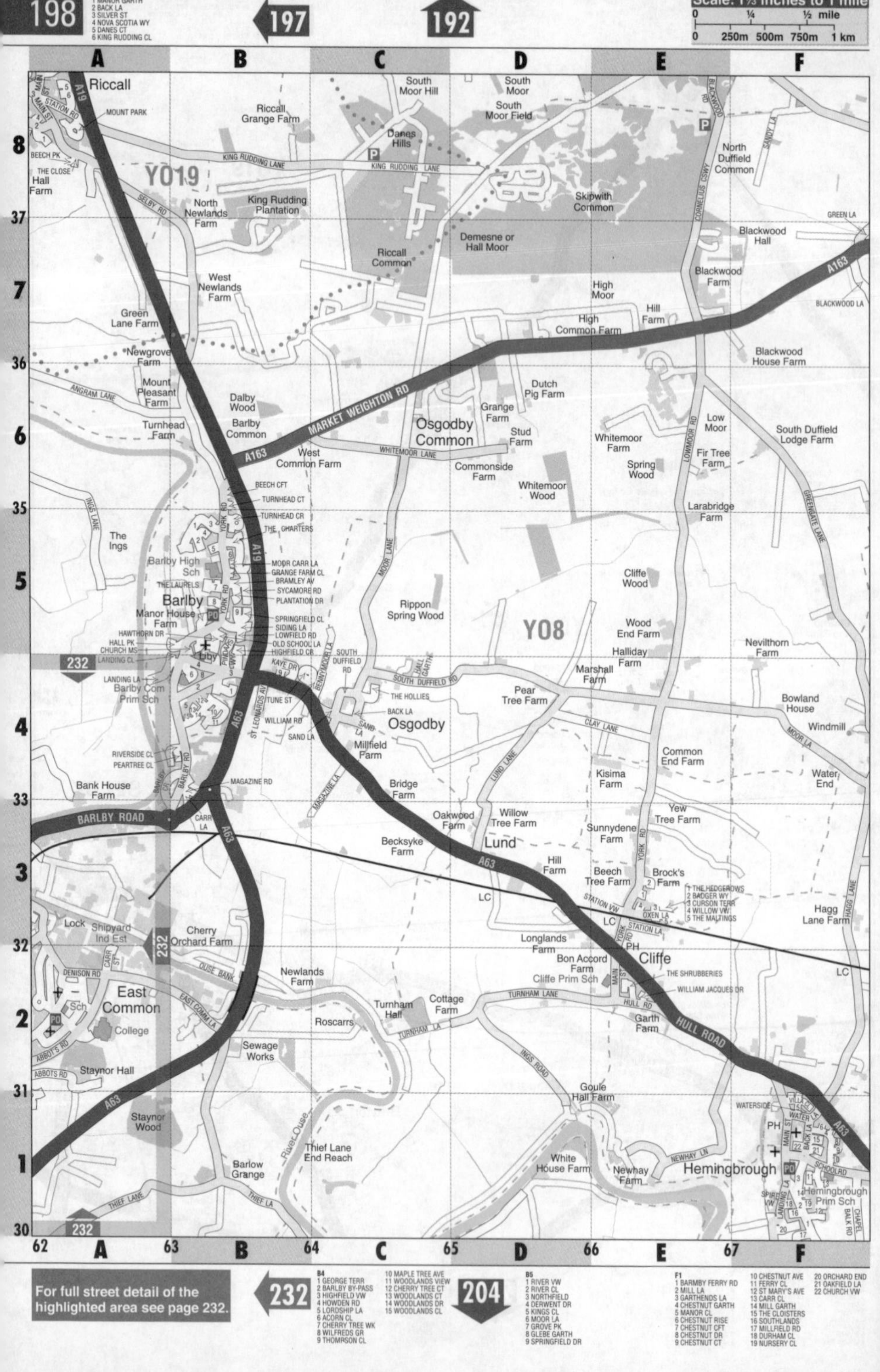
198
A8
1 MANOR GARTH
2 BACK LA
3 SILVER ST
4 NOVA SCOTIA WY
5 DANES CT
6 KING RUDDING CL
7 BECKWITH HALL DR
197
192
Scale: 1⅓ inches to 1 mile
0 ¼ ½ mile
0 250m 500m 750m 1 km
A B C D E F
8 37 7 36 6 35 5 4 33 3 32 2 31 1 30
62 63 64 65 66 67
Riccall
MOUNT PARK
STATION RD
MAIN ST
BEECH PK
THE CLOSE
Hall Farm
A19
Riccall Grange Farm
South Moor Hill
South Moor
South Moor Field
Danes Hills
KING RUDDING LANE
YO19
North Newlands Farm
King Rudding Plantation
SELBY RD
Riccall Common
Demesne or Hall Moor
Skipwith Common
North Duffield Common
BLACKWOOD RD
CORNELIUS CSWY
SANDY LA
GREEN LA
Blackwood Hall
Blackwood Farm
A163
BLACKWOOD LA
West Newlands Farm
Green Lane Farm
High Moor
High Common Farm
Hill Farm
Newgrove Farm
Mount Pleasant Farm
ANGRAM LANE
Blackwood House Farm
Dutch Pig Farm
MARKET WEIGHTON RD
Dalby Wood
Barlby Common
Turnhead Farm
Grange Farm
Osgodby Common
Stud Farm
West Common Farm
WHITEMOOR LANE
Commonside Farm
Whitemoor Farm
Low Moor
LOWMOOR RD
South Duffield Lodge Farm
Spring Wood
Fir Tree Farm
Whitemoor Wood
BEECH CFT
TURNHEAD CT
TURNHEAD CR
THE CHARTERS
INGS LANE
The Ings
Larabridge Farm
GREENGATE LANE
MOOR LANE
Barlby High Sch
MOOR CARR LA
GRANGE FARM CL
BRAMLEY AV
SYCAMORE RD
PLANTATION DR
THE LAURELS
Barlby
Manor House Farm
Rippon Spring Wood
YO8
Cliffe Wood
Wood End Farm
SPRINGFIELD CL
SIDING LA
LOWFIELD RD
OLD SCHOOL LA
HIGHFIELD CR
HAWTHORN DR
HALL PK
CHURCH MS
LANDING CL
232
Halliday Farm
Nevilthorn Farm
LANDING LA
Barlby Com Prim Sch
KAYE DR
SOUTH DUFFIELD RD
HALL GARTH
Marshall Farm
THE HOLLIES
BACK LA
Pear Tree Farm
Bowland House
TUNE ST
WILLIAM RD
SAND LA
Osgodby
CLAY LANE
Windmill
MOOR LA
ST LEONARDS AV
Millfield Farm
LUND LANE
Common End Farm
RIVERSIDE CL
PEARTREE CL
BARLBY RD
Kisima Farm
Water End
Bank House Farm
MAGAZINE RD
Bridge Farm
MAGAZINE LA
BARLBY ROAD
CARR LA
A63
Oakwood Farm
Willow Tree Farm
Yew Tree Farm
Sunnydene Farm
YORK RD
Becksyke Farm
Lund
Hill Farm
Beech Tree Farm
Brock's Farm
HAGG LANE
1 THE HEDGEROWS
2 BADGER WY
3 CURSON TERR
4 WILLOW VW
5 THE MALTINGS
LC
STATION VW
OXEN LA
Hagg Lane Farm
STATION LA
Lock
Shipyard Ind Est
Cherry Orchard Farm
Longlands Farm
Bon Accord Farm
PH
Cliffe
CARR ST
DENISON RD
OUSE BANK
Newlands Farm
Cliffe Prim Sch
THE SHRUBBERIES
WILLIAM JACQUES DR
East Common
EAST COMM LA
Sch
TURNHAM LANE
HULL RD
Turnham Hall
Cottage Farm
Garth Farm
College
ABBOT'S RD
Roscarrs
TURNHAM LA
HULL ROAD
Sewage Works
INGS ROAD
ABBOTS RD
Staynor Hall
Goule Hall Farm
WATERSIDE
WATER LA
MAIN ST
BACK LA
Staynor Wood
River Ouse
Thief Lane End Reach
White House Farm
NEWHAY LN
Barlow Grange
Newhay Farm
Hemingbrough
SCHOOL RD
SPIRE VW
LANDING LA
Hemingbrough Prim Sch
THIEF LANE
THIEF LA
BALK RD
CHAPEL
For full street detail of the highlighted area see page 232.
232
B4
1 GEORGE TERR
2 BARLBY BY-PASS
3 HIGHFIELD VW
4 HOWDEN RD
5 LORDSHIP LA
6 ACORN CL
7 CHERRY TREE WK
8 WILFREDS GR
9 THOMPSON CL
10 MAPLE TREE AVE
11 WOODLANDS VIEW
12 CHERRY TREE CT
13 WOODLANDS CT
14 WOODLANDS DR
15 WOODLANDS CL
204
B5
1 RIVER VW
2 RIVER CL
3 NORTHFIELD
4 DERWENT DR
5 KINGS CL
6 MOOR LA
7 GROVE PK
8 GLEBE GARTH
9 SPRINGFIELD DR
F1
1 BARMBY FERRY RD
2 MILL LA
3 GARTHENDS LA
4 CHESTNUT GARTH
5 MANOR CL
6 CHESTNUT RISE
7 CHESTNUT CFT
8 CHESTNUT DR
9 CHESTNUT CT
10 CHESTNUT AVE
11 FERRY CL
12 ST MARY'S AVE
13 CARR CL
14 MILL GARTH
15 THE CLOISTERS
16 SOUTHLANDS
17 MILLFIELD RD
18 DURHAM CL
19 NURSERY CL
20 ORCHARD END
21 OAKFIELD LA
22 CHURCH VW

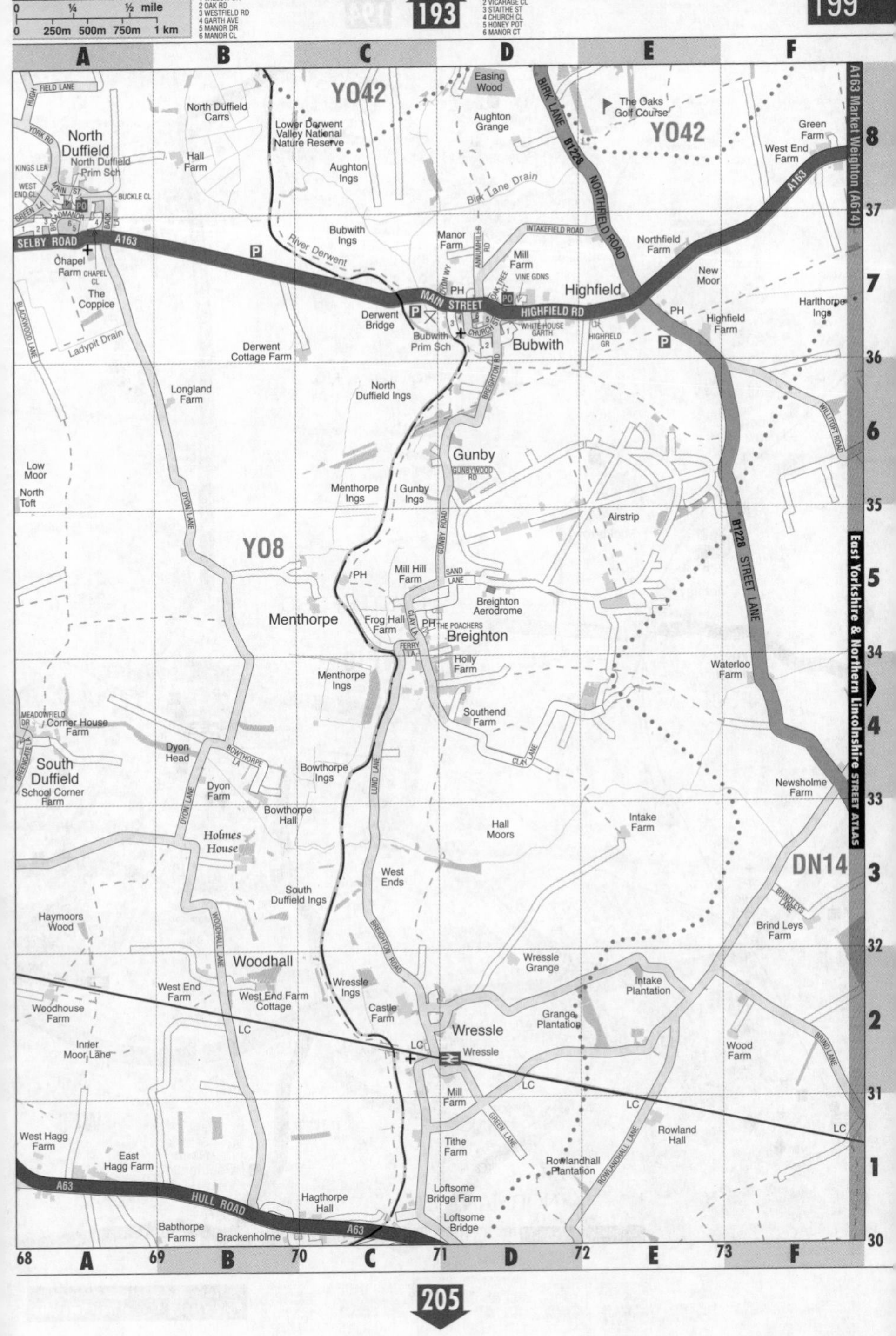

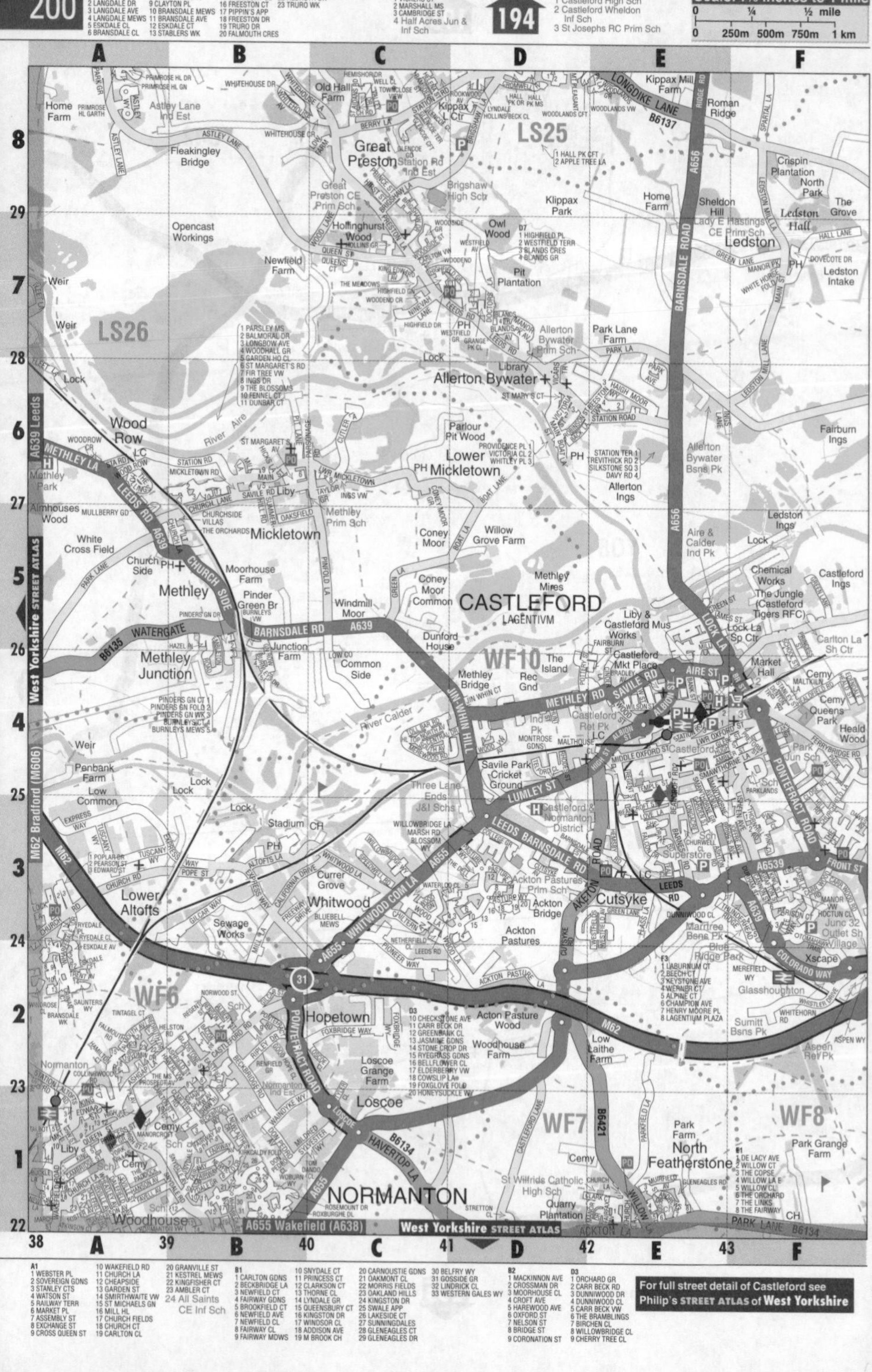

Scale: 1½ inches to 1 mile
0   ¼   ½   mile
0   250m   500m   750m   1 km

194

A2
1 STUART GR
2 LANGDALE DR
3 LANGDALE AV
4 LANGDALE MEWS
5 ESKDALE CL
6 BRANSDALE CL

7 ARMSTRONG CL
8 CLAYTON MEWS
9 CLAYTON PL
10 BRANSDALE MEWS
11 BRANSDALE AVE
12 ESKDALE CT
13 STABLERS WK

14 BROOME CL
15 SALISBURY CL
16 FREESTON CT
17 POPPIN S APP
18 FREESTON DR
19 TRURO DR
20 FALMOUTH CRES

21 POLPERRO CL
22 REDRUTH DR
23 TRURO WK

E4
1 VICKERS ST
2 MARSHALL MS
3 CAMBRIDGE ST
4 Half Acres Jun &
  Inf Sch

F4
1 Castleford High Sch
2 Castleford Wheldon
  Inf Sch
3 St Josephs RC Prim Sch

A1
1 WEBSTER PL
2 SOVEREIGN GDNS
3 STANLEY CTS
4 WATSON ST
5 RAILWAY TERR
6 MARKET PL
7 ASSEMBLY ST
8 EXCHANGE ST
9 CROSS QUEEN ST

10 WAKEFIELD RD
11 CHURCH LA
12 CHEAPSIDE
13 GARDEN ST
14 SMITHYWAITE VW
15 ST MICHAELS CL
16 MILL AL
17 CHURCH FIELDS
18 CHURCH CT
19 CARLTON CL

20 GRANVILLE CL
21 KESTREL MEWS
22 KINGFISHER CT
23 AMBLER CT
24 All Saints
   CE Inf Sch

B1
1 CARLTON GDNS
2 BECKBRIDGE LA
3 NEWFIELD CT
4 FAIRWAY GDNS
5 BROOKFIELD CT
6 NEWFIELD AVE
7 NEWFIELD CL
8 FAIRWAY CL
9 FAIRWAY MDWS

10 SNYDALE CT
11 PRINCESS CT
12 CLAWSON CT
13 THORNE CL
14 LYNDALE GR
15 QUEENSBERRY CT
16 KINGSTON DR
17 WINDSOR CL
18 ADDISON AVE
19 M BROOK CH

20 CARMOUSTIE GDNS
21 OAKMONT CL
22 MORRIS FIELDS
23 OAKLAND HILLS
24 KINGSTON DR
25 SWALE APP
26 LAKESIDE CT
27 SUNNINGDALE CT
28 GLENEAGLES CT
29 GLENEAGLES DR

30 BELFRY WY
31 GOSSIDE CT
32 LINDRICK CL
33 WESTERN GALES WY

B2
1 MACKINNON AVE
2 CROSSMAN DR
3 MOORHOUSE CL
4 CROFT AVE
5 HAREWOOD AVE
6 OXFORD ST
7 NELSON ST
8 BRIDGE ST
9 CORONATION ST

D3
1 ORCHARD GR
2 CARR BECK RD
3 DUNNWOOD DR
4 DUNNWOOD CL
5 CARR BECK VW
6 THE BRAMBLINGS
7 BIRCHEN CL
8 WILLOWBRIDGE CL
9 CHERRY TREE CL

For full street detail of Castleford see
Philip's STREET ATLAS of West Yorkshire

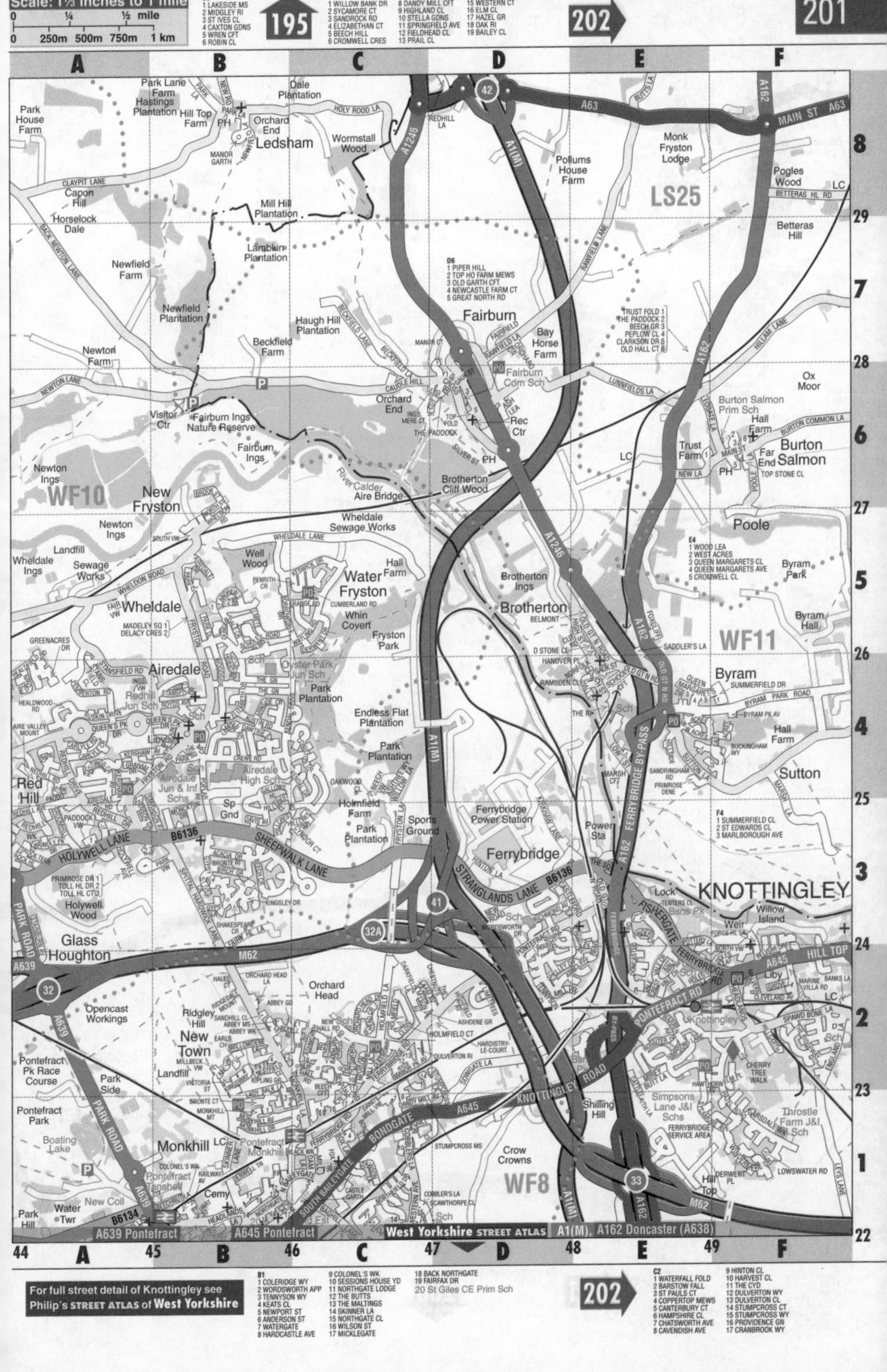

201
Scale: 1⅓ inches to 1 mile
0 ¼ ½ mile
0 250m 500m 750m 1 km
195
202
B2
1 LAKESIDE MS
2 MIDGLEY RI
3 ST IVES CL
4 CAXTON GDNS
5 WREN CFT
6 ROBIN CL
C1
1 WILLOW BANK DR
2 SYCAMORE CT
3 SANDROCK RD
4 ELIZABETHAN CT
5 BEECH HILL
6 CROMWELL CRES
7 WATER LA
8 DANDY MILL CFT
9 HIGHLAND CL
10 STELLA GDNS
11 SPRINGFIELD AVE
12 FIELDHEAD CL
13 PRAIL CL
14 EASTFIELD DR
15 WESTERN CT
16 ELM CL
17 HAZEL GR
18 OAK RI
19 BAILEY CL
A B C D E F
Park House Farm
Park Lane Farm
Hastings Plantation
Hill Top Farm
Dale Plantation
Orchard End
Ledsham
Wormstall Wood
Monk Fryston Lodge
Pogles Wood
Pollums House Farm
LS25
Capon Hill
Horselock Dale
Mill Hill Plantation
Lambkin Plantation
Betteras Hill
Newfield Farm
Newfield Plantation
Haugh Hill Plantation
D6
1 PIPER HILL
2 TOP HO FARM MEWS
3 OLD GARTH CT
4 NEWCASTLE FARM CT
5 GREAT NORTH RD
Fairburn
Bay Horse Farm
TRUST FOLD 1
THE PADDOCK 2
BEECH GR 3
PEPLOW CL 4
CLARKSON DR 5
OLD HALL CT 6
Newton Farm
Beckfield Farm
Fairburn Com Sch
Ox Moor
Orchard End
Burton Salmon Prim Sch
Hall Farm
Visitor Ctr
Fairburn Ings Nature Reserve
Rec Ctr
Trust Farm
Burton Salmon
Far End
Fairburn Ings
Newton Ings
WF10
New Fryston
Aire Bridge
Brotherton Cliff Wood
Wheldale Sewage Works
Poole
Newton Ings
Landfill
Wheldale Ings
Sewage Works
Well Wood
Water Fryston
Hall Farm
E4
1 WOOD LEA
2 WEST ACRES
3 QUEEN MARGARETS CL
4 QUEEN MARGARETS AVE
5 CROMWELL CL
Byram Park
Wheldale
Whin Covert
Fryston Park
Brotherton Ings
Brotherton
Byram Hall
WF11
Airedale
Redhill Jun Sch
Oyster Park Jun Sch
Park Plantation
Byram
Endless Flat Plantation
Hall Farm
Red Hill
Airedale High Sch
Airedale Jun & Inf Schs
Sp Gnd
Park Plantation
Sutton
Holmfield Farm
Sports Ground
Park Plantation
Ferrybridge Power Station
Power Sta
F4
1 SUMMERFIELD CL
2 ST EDWARDS CL
3 MARLBOROUGH AVE
Ferrybridge
KNOTTINGLEY
Holywell Wood
Willow Island
Glass Houghton
Orchard Head
Opencast Workings
Ridgley Hill
New Town
Knottingley
Pontefract Pk Race Course
Landfill
Park Side
Cherry Tree Walk
Pontefract Park
Simpsons Lane J&I Schs
Throstle Farm J&I Sch
Boating Lake
Monkhill
Pontefract Monkhill
Crow Crowns
Shilling Hill
Pontefract Tanshelf
Cemy
WF8
Hill Top
Park Hill
Water Twr
New Coll
A639 Pontefract
A645 Pontefract
West Yorkshire STREET ATLAS
A1(M), A162 Doncaster (A638)
44 45 46 47 48 49
A1(M) A1246 A63 A162 M62 B6136 A645 A639 B6134
For full street detail of Knottingley see Philip's STREET ATLAS of West Yorkshire
B1
1 COLERIDGE WY
2 WORDSWORTH APP
3 TENNYSON WY
4 KEATS CL
5 NEWPORT ST
6 ANDERSON ST
7 WATERGATE
8 HARDCASTLE AVE
9 COLONEL'S WK
10 SESSIONS HOUSE YD
11 NORTHGATE LODGE
12 THE BUTTS
13 THE MALTINGS
14 SKINNER LA
15 NORTHGATE CL
16 WILSON ST
17 MICKLEGATE
18 BACK NORTHGATE
19 FAIRFAX DR
20 St Giles CE Prim Sch
202
C2
1 WATERFALL FOLD
2 BARSTOW FALL
3 ST PAULS CT
4 COPPERTOP MEWS
5 CANTERBURY CT
6 HAMPSHIRE CL
7 CHATSWORTH AVE
8 CAVENDISH AVE
9 HINTON CL
10 HARVEST CL
11 THE CYD
12 DULVERTON WY
13 DULVERTON CL
14 STUMPCROSS CT
15 STUMPCROSS WY
16 PROVIDENCE GN
17 CRANBROOK WY

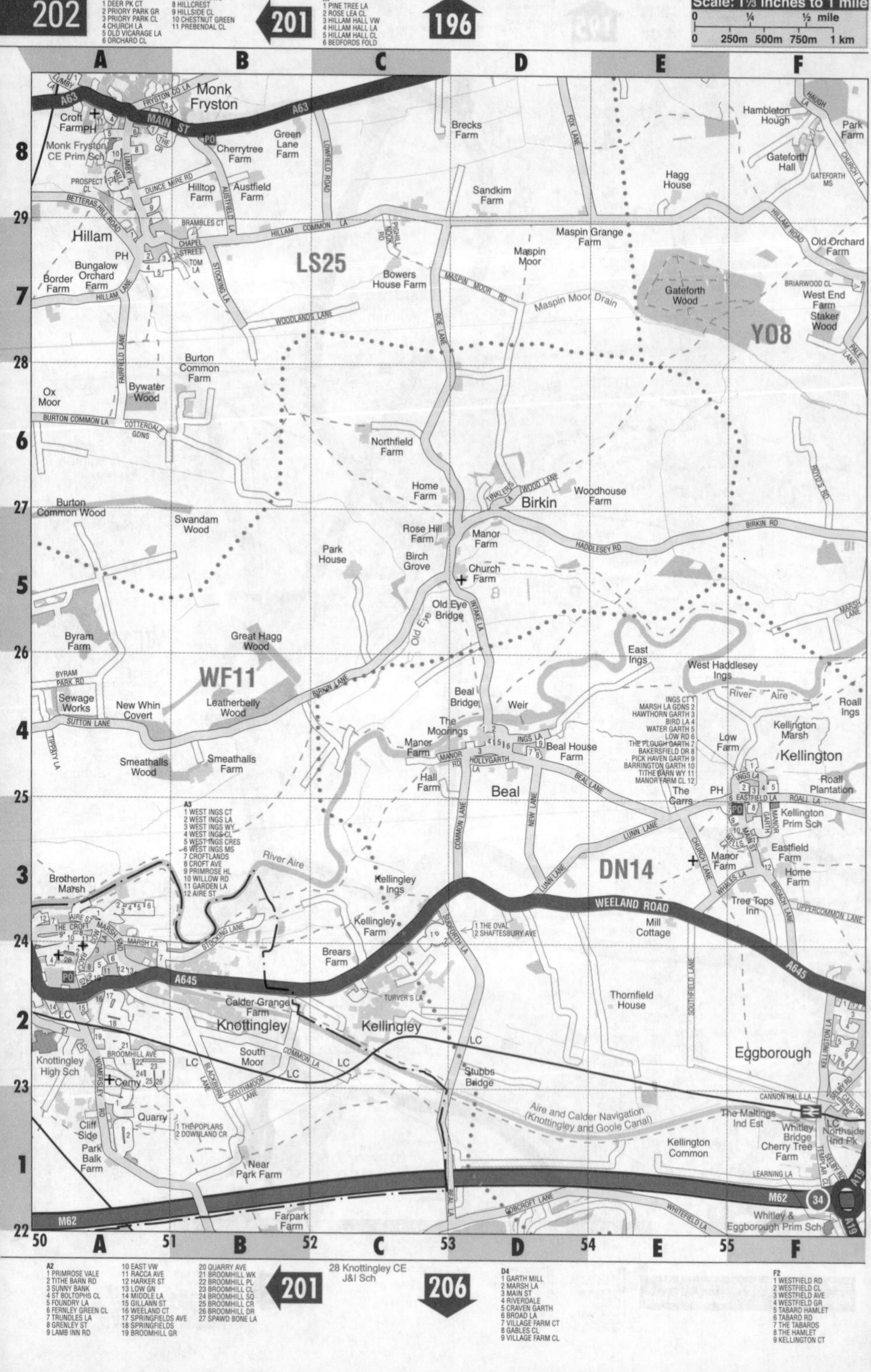
202
A8
1 DEER PK CT
2 PRIORY PARK GR
3 PRIORY PARK CL
4 CHURCH LA
5 OLD VICARAGE LA
6 ORCHARD CL
7 THE MEADOWS
8 HILLCREST
9 HILLSIDE CL
10 CHESTNUT GREEN
11 PREBENDAL CL
201
A7
1 PINE TREE LA
2 ROSE LEA CL
3 HILLAM HALL VW
4 HILLAM HALL LA
5 HILLAM HALL CL
6 BEDFORDS FOLD
196
Scale: 1⅓ inches to 1 mile
0 ¼ ½ mile
0 250m 500m 750m 1 km
A B C D E F
Monk Fryston
Croft Farm
Monk Fryston CE Prim Sch
Green Lane Farm
Cherrytree Farm
Brecks Farm
Hambleton Hough
Park Farm
Gateforth Hall
Hagg House
Hilltop Farm
Austfield Farm
Sandkim Farm
Hillam
Bungalow Orchard Farm
Border Farm
LS25
Bowers House Farm
Maspin Grange Farm
Maspin Moor
Maspin Moor Drain
Old Orchard Farm
Gateforth Wood
West End Farm
Staker Wood
YO8
Burton Common Farm
Bywater Wood
Ox Moor
Northfield Farm
Home Farm
Birkin
Woodhouse Farm
Burton Common Wood
Swandam Wood
Rose Hill Farm
Manor Farm
Park House
Birch Grove
Church Farm
Old Eye Bridge
Byram Farm
Great Hagg Wood
WF11
East Ings
West Haddlesey Ings
River Aire
Roall Ings
Sewage Works
New Whin Covert
Leatherbelly Wood
Beal Bridge
Weir
The Moorings
Manor Farm
Beal House Farm
Low Farm
Kellington Marsh
Kellington
Smeathalls Wood
Smeathalls Farm
Hall Farm
Beal
The Carrs
Roall Plantation
Kellington Prim Sch
A3
1 WEST INGS CT
2 WEST INGS LA
3 WEST INGS WY
4 WEST INGS CL
5 WEST INGS CRES
6 WEST INGS MS
7 CROFTLANDS
8 CROFT AVE
9 PRIMROSE HL
10 WILLOW RD
11 GARDEN LA
12 AIRE ST
INGS CT 1
MARSH LA GDNS 2
HAWTHORN GARTH 3
BIRD LA 4
WATER GARTH 5
LOW RD 6
THE PLOUGH GARTH 7
BAKERSFIELD DR 8
PICK HAVEN GARTH 9
BARRINGTON GARTH 10
TITHE BARN WY 11
MANOR FARM CL 12
Brotherton Marsh
Kellingley Ings
DN14
Manor Farm
Eastfield Farm
Home Farm
WEELAND ROAD
Tree Tops Inn
Kellingley Farm
Mill Cottage
1 THE OVAL
2 SHAFTESBURY AVE
Brears Farm
Thornfield House
Calder Grange Farm
Knottingley
Kellingley
South Moor
Stubbs Bridge
Eggborough
Knottingley High Sch
Cemy
Quarry
1 THE POPLARS
2 DOWNLAND CR
Aire and Calder Navigation (Knottingley and Goole Canal)
The Maltings Ind Est
Whitley Bridge
Northside Ind Pk
Cliff Side
Park Balk Farm
Kellington Common
Cherry Tree Farm
Near Park Farm
M62
34
Farpark Farm
Whitley & Eggborough Prim Sch
A63
A645
A19
A2
1 PRIMROSE VALE
2 TITHE BARN RD
3 SUNNY BANK
4 ST BOLTOPHS CL
5 FOUNDRY LA
6 FERNLEY GREEN CL
7 TRUNDLES LA
8 GRENLEY ST
9 LAMB INN RD
10 EAST VW
11 RACCA AVE
12 HARKER ST
13 LOW GN
14 MIDDLE LA
15 GILLANN ST
16 WEELAND CT
17 SPRINGFIELDS AVE
18 SPRINGFIELDS
19 BROOMHILL GR
20 QUARRY AVE
21 BROOMHILL WK
22 BROOMHILL PL
23 BROOMHILL CL
24 BROOMHILL SQ
25 BROOMHILL CR
26 BROOMHILL DR
27 SPAWD BONE LA
201
28 Knottingley CE J&I Sch
206
D4
1 GARTH MILL
2 MARSH LA
3 MAIN ST
4 RIVERDALE
5 CRAVEN GARTH
6 BROAD LA
7 VILLAGE FARM CT
8 GABLES CL
9 VILLAGE FARM CL
F2
1 WESTFIELD RD
2 WESTFIELD CL
3 WESTFIELD AVE
4 WESTFIELD GR
5 TABARD HAMLET
6 TABARD RD
7 THE TABARDS
8 THE HAMLET
9 KELLINGTON CT

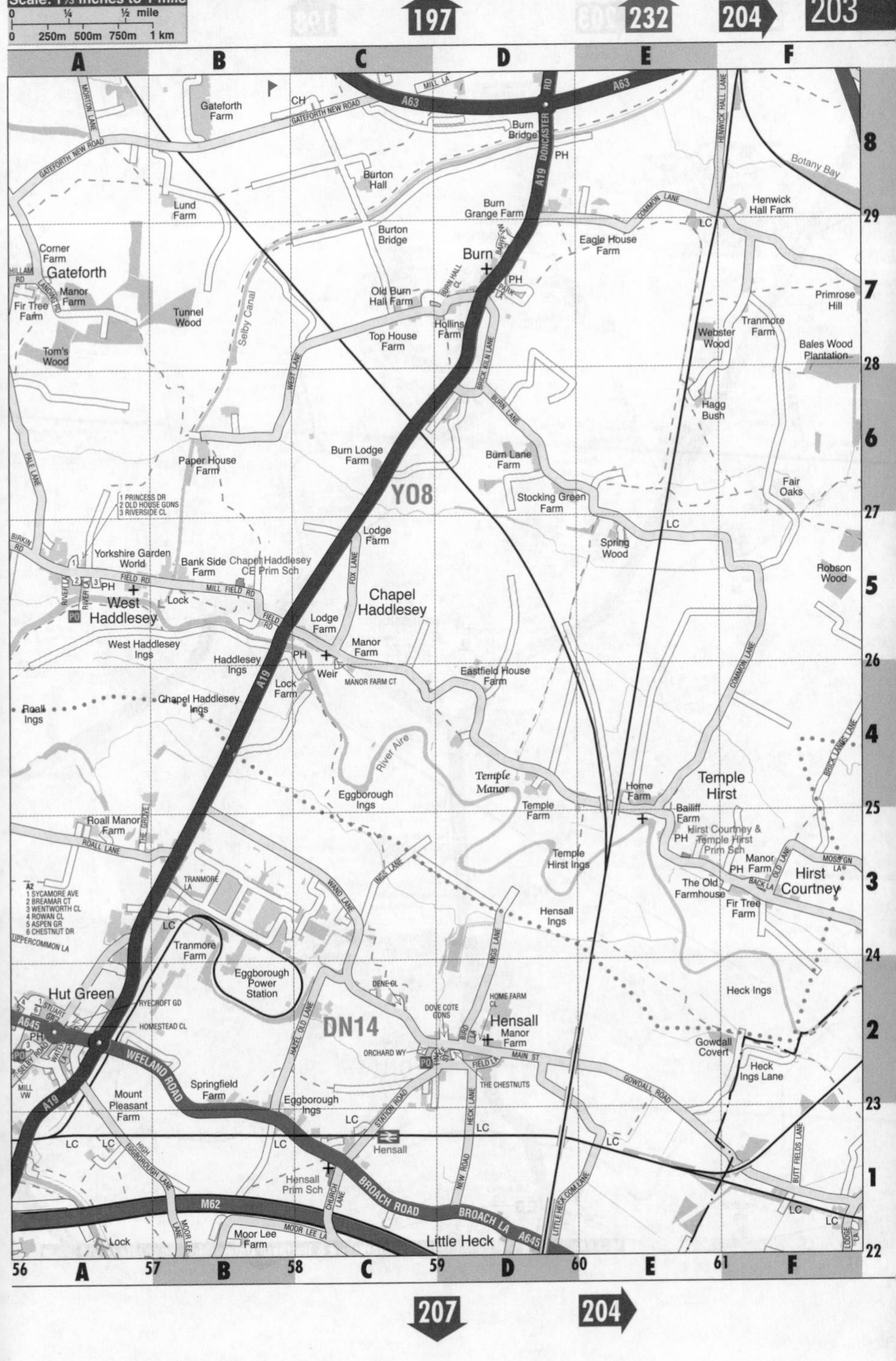

Scale: 1⅓ inches to 1 mile
0 ¼ ½ mile
0 250m 500m 750m 1 km
197
232
204
A B C D E F
8
29
7
28
6
27
5
26
4
25
3
24
2
23
1
22
56 57 58 59 60 61
Gateforth Farm
CH
Gateforth
Corner Farm
Manor Farm
Fir Tree Farm
Tom's Wood
Tunnel Wood
Lund Farm
Burton Hall
Burton Bridge
Burn Bridge
Burn Grange Farm
Burn
Old Burn Hall Farm
Top House Farm
Hollins Farm
Eagle House Farm
Henwick Hall Farm
Botany Bay
Primrose Hill
Tranmore Farm
Webster Wood
Bales Wood Plantation
Hagg Bush
Selby Canal
Paper House Farm
Burn Lodge Farm
Burn Lane Farm
Stocking Green Farm
Fair Oaks
YO8
Spring Wood
Robson Wood
Yorkshire Garden World
Bank Side Farm
Chapel Haddlesey CE Prim Sch
Lodge Farm
Chapel Haddlesey
West Haddlesey
Lock
West Haddlesey Ings
Haddlesey Ings
Manor Farm
Weir
Lock Farm
Eastfield House Farm
Roall Ings
Chapel Haddlesey Ings
River Aire
Temple Manor
Eggborough Ings
Temple Farm
Home Farm
Temple Hirst
Bailiff Farm
Hirst Courtney & Temple Hirst Prim Sch
Temple Hirst Ings
Manor Farm
Hirst Courtney
The Old Farmhouse
Fir Tree Farm
Roall Manor Farm
Hensall Ings
Tranmore Farm
Eggborough Power Station
Hut Green
DN14
Hensall
Manor Farm
Heck Ings
Gowdall Covert
Heck Ings Lane
Mount Pleasant Farm
Springfield Farm
Eggborough Ings
Hensall
Hensall Prim Sch
Moor Lee Farm
Little Heck
Lock
A2
1 SYCAMORE AVE
2 BREAMAR CT
3 WENTWORTH CL
4 ROWAN CL
5 ASPEN GR
6 CHESTNUT DR
1 PRINCESS DR
2 OLD HOUSE GDNS
3 RIVERSIDE CL
A63
A19
A645
M62
GATEFORTH NEW ROAD
MORTON LANE
HILLAM RD
LANDING RD
PALE LANE
BIRKIN RD
FIELD RD
MILL FIELD RD
WEST LANE
DONCASTER RD
MILL LA
COMMON LANE
HENWICK HALL LANE
BRICK KILN LANE
BURN LANE
FOX LANE
MANOR FARM CT
ROALL LANE
THE GROVE
TRANMORE LA
UPPERCOMMON LA
WAND LANE
INGS LANE
HAZEL OLD LANE
DENE CL
DOVE COTE GDNS
HOME FARM CL
ORCHARD WY
FIELD LA
MAIN ST
THE CHESTNUTS
GOWDALL ROAD
HECK LANE
NEW ROAD
STATION ROAD
CHURCH LANE
BROACH ROAD
BROACH LA
WEELAND ROAD
HIGH EGGBOROUGH LANE
MOOR LEE LANE
MOOR LEE LA
LITTLE HECK COM LANE
BUTT FIELDS LANE
BRICK LANDS LANE
MOSS GN LA
OLD LANE
BACK LA
RYECROFT GD
HOMESTEAD CL
STUART GR
SELBY ROAD
MILL VW
LODGE LA
PH
PO
LC

207
204

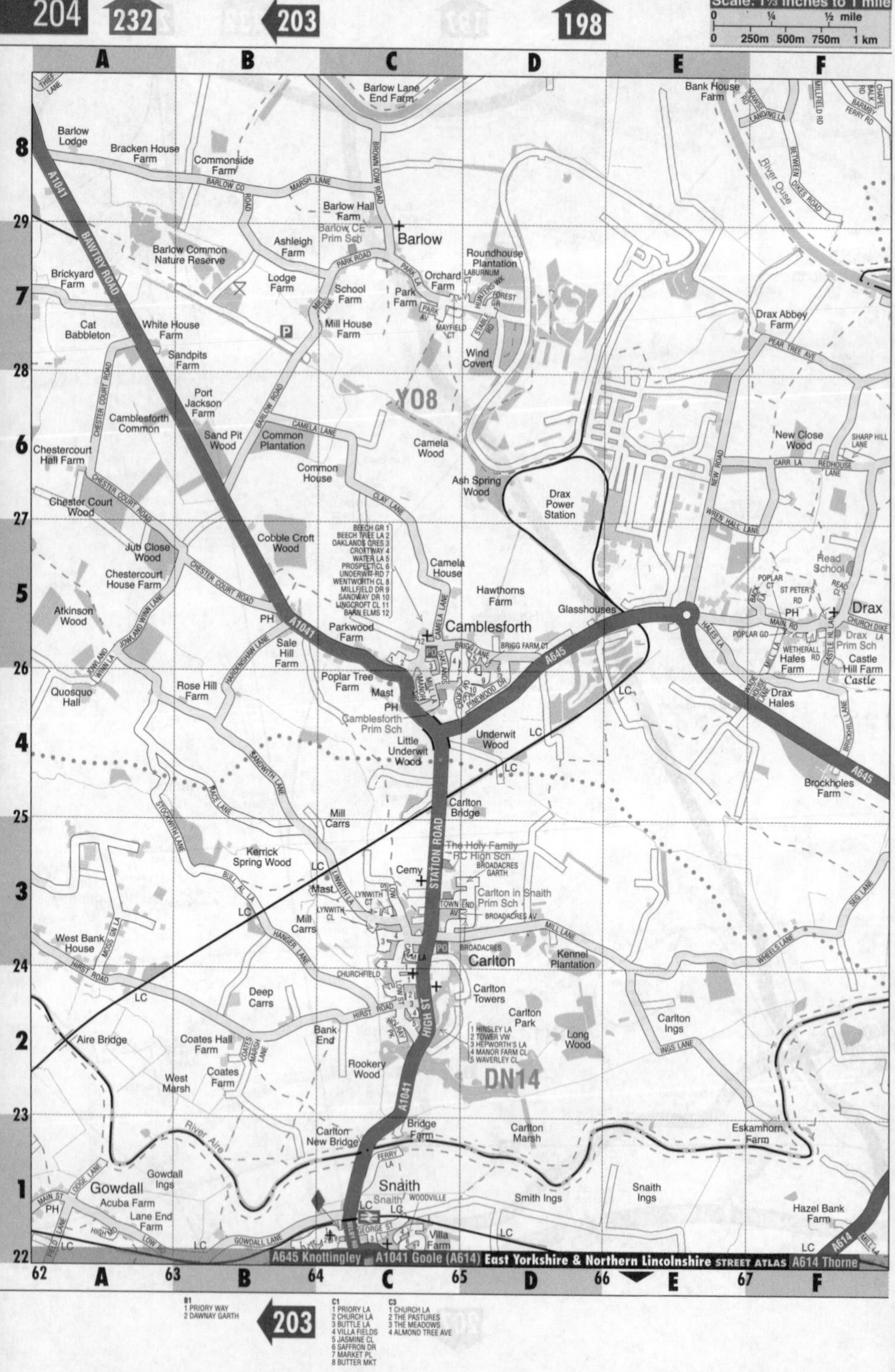

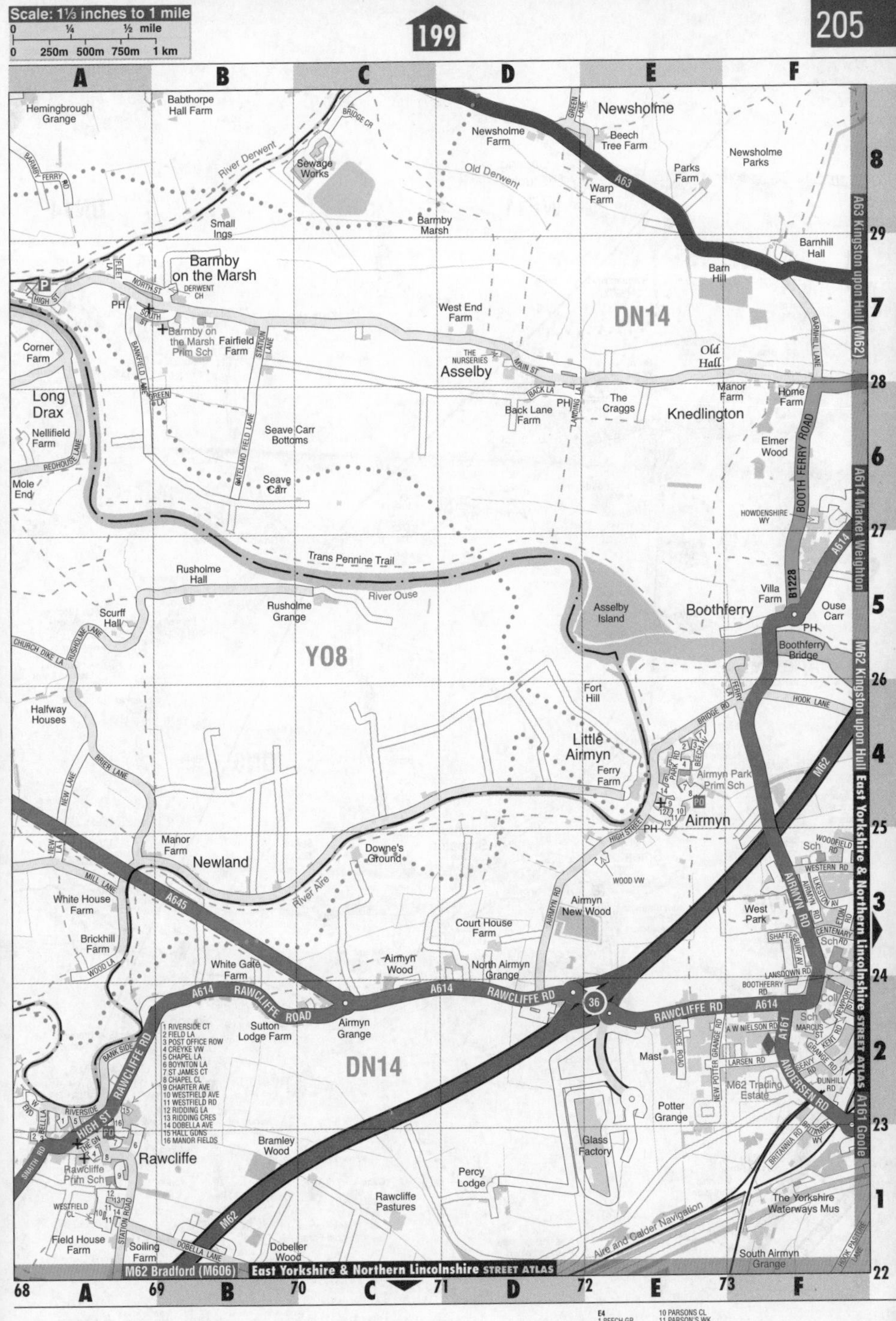

Hemingbrough Grange

Babthorpe Hall Farm

BRIDGE CR

GREEN LA

Newsholme

Newsholme Farm

Beech Tree Farm

A63

Parks Farm

Newsholme Parks

River Derwent

Sewage Works

Small Ings

Barmby Marsh

Old Derwent

Warp Farm

Barnhill Hall

Barmby on the Marsh

DERWENT CH

West End Farm

DN14

Barn Hill

Corner Farm

Barmby on the Marsh Prim Sch

Fairfield Farm

THE NURSERIES

Asselby

DN14

Old Hall

Manor Farm

Home Farm

Long Drax

Nellifield Farm

Back Lane Farm

PH

The Craggs

Knedlington

Elmer Wood

Mole End

Seave Carr Bottoms

Seave Carr

Trans Pennine Trail

Villa Farm

B1228

Ouse Carr

Rusholme Hall

River Ouse

Asselby Island

Boothferry

PH.

Scurff Hall

Rusholme Grange

YO8

Fort Hill

Boothferry Bridge

Halfway Houses

Little Airmyn

Ferry Farm

Airmyn Park Prim Sch

Hook Lane

M62

Manor Farm

Newland

Downe's Ground

Airmyn

PH

WOODFIELD

Sch

WESTERN RD

White House Farm

A645

River Aire

WOOD VW

Airmyn New Wood

West Park

Sch

Brickhill Farm

Court House Farm

North Airmyn Grange

LANSDOWN RD

BOOTHFERRY RD

Sch

ST MARCUS

White Gate Farm

Airmyn Wood

RAWCLIFFE ROAD

A614

RAWCLIFFE RD

A614

RAWCLIFFE RD

A614

A W NEILSON RD

36

LARSEN RD

M62 Trading Estate

1 RIVERSIDE CT
2 FIELD LA
3 POST OFFICE ROW
4 CREYKE VW
5 CHAPEL LA
6 BOYNTON LA
7 ST JAMES CT
8 CHAPEL CL
9 CHARTER AVE
10 WESTFIELD AVE
11 WESTFIELD RD
12 RIDDING LA
13 RIDDING CRES
14 DOBELLA AVE
15 HALL GDNS
16 MANOR FIELDS

Sutton Lodge Farm

Airmyn Grange

DN14

Bramley Wood

Mast

DUNHILL RD

Potter Grange

RIVERSIDE

HIGH ST

Rawcliffe

Rawcliffe Prim Sch

WESTFIELD CL

Rawcliffe Pastures

Percy Lodge

Glass Factory

The Yorkshire Waterways Mus

Field House Farm

Soiling Farm

Dobellar Wood

M62

A63 Kingston upon Hull (M62)

A614 Market Weighton

BOOTH FERRY ROAD

M62 Kingston upon Hull

East Yorkshire & Northern Lincolnshire STREET ATLAS

A161 Goole

E4
1 BEECH GR
2 CHESTNUT AVE
3 BEECH AVE
4 PERCY DR
5 HALL CL
6 PARK CL
7 COURTS CL
8 WOODLAND WY
9 ST DAVID'S VW
10 PARSONS CL
11 PARSON'S WK
12 CHURCH VW
13 THE CROSSINGS
14 THE PADDOCK

Scale: 1⅓ inches to 1 mile
0   ¼   ½   mile
0   250m 500m 750m 1 km

WF11

DN14

WHITEFIELD BUNGALOWS
WHITEFIELD LANE
CATCHCART CT
WHITLEY THORPE LA

8

21

7

Cridling Stubbs
PH
Spring Lodge
LC
LC
COPCROFT LANE
WRIGHTS LA
STUBBS LANE

Wake Wood
Beech House Farm
Scrombeck Farm
Rows Wood
Wormersley Quarry

20

Stapleton Park Farm
Bank Wood
Quarry (dis)
BANK WOOD ROAD
NEWROAD END
NORTHFIELD CL

Kelseycroft Wood
Grange Farm
Bell Lands Wood
Whitley Thorpe
Fulham House
FULHAM LANE
BOOTLANE

6

19

Stapleton Park
Fishpond Wood
Kingsland Wood
Sewage Works
Wormersley CE Prim Sch
Womersley Common
Low Farm
PARK LA
STATION RD
HIGHFIELD LA
LC

Ricketcroft Wood
Hodgsoncroft Wood
Clipsall Wood
Grove Wood
Saulcroft Wood

5

18

Castle Hill Wood
Castle Farm
Quarry (dis)
Nutwood End
Belt Plantation
The Rookery
WORMERSLEY PARK GDNS
Wormesley Park
Womersley Beck
HIGHFIELD LANE
Stocking Green Farm
Brown Ings Wood
Ox Stocking Wood
Dawland House Farm
Birdspring Wood

Sod Wall Plantation
JACKSON'S LA

DN6

4

17

Brockadale Nature Reserve
Brockadale Plantation
Smeaton Leys
LEYS LANE
LEYS LANE
Long Crag
SMEATSLEY LANE
CHURCHILL LA
CHURCHFIELD LANE
Smeaton Bridge
Grove Bridge
Little Grove Farm
Birka Wood
Stubbs Common Farm
COMMON LA

Smeaton Crags Quarry
River Went

WF8

Kirk Smeaton
PH
Little Smeaton
The Grove
MOUNT PLEASANT
Stubbs Bridge
Wells Farm
Home Farm
LC
Walden Stubbs
Manor Farm

3

16

Kirk Smeaton CE Prim Sch
PINFOLD CROSS
MANOR
Little Bottom Plantation
Willow Bridge
Sewage Works
STUBBS ROAD
NORTON AND KIRK SMEATON
WILLOWGARTH ROAD
LC
Tanpit Bridge
Sewage Works
LC

Middle Field
COAL PIT LA
MIDDLECROFT LANE
LONG LANE
Highfield Farm
WESTFIELD LANE
CLIFF HILL RD
Norton Priory
BARNSDALE VW
BACK LANE
LINKWAY
Norton
PASTURE GDNS
Bradley's Spring
NORTON CO LA

2

15

Sewage Works
Hotel
Barnsdale Bar Service Area
Windhill Plantation Quarry
Fox Covert
FOX COVERT RD
WHITLEY RD
GREENGATE LANE
Windmill
WINDMILL RD
STYGATE LA
Norton Inf & Jun Schs
PH THE CLOSE
East End Villas
Norton Ings
PINFOLD LA

A630 Pontefract
A1 Knottingley
A1
Shaft
Glebe Farm
Shaft
Barnsdale
Barnsdale Wood
Campsmount Sch
Cemy
Campsmount Home Farm
CHURCH FIELD LANE
Askern & Campsall Sports Ctr
P

1

14

West Yorkshire STREET ATLAS

South Moor
Works

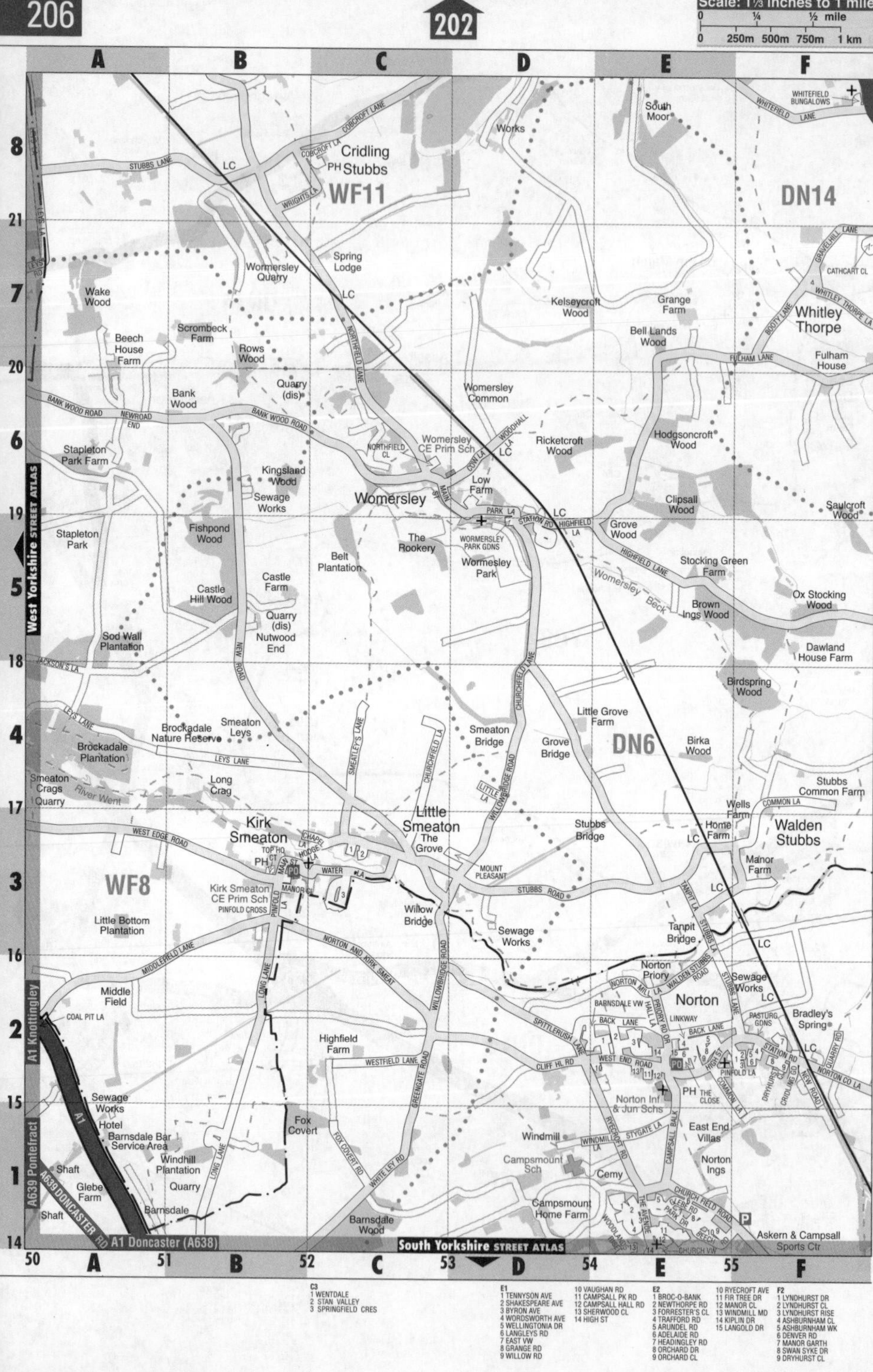

C3
1 WENTDALE
2 STAN VALLEY
3 SPRINGFIELD CRES

E1
1 TENNYSON AVE
2 SHAKESPEARE AVE
3 BYRON AVE
4 WORDSWORTH AVE
5 WELLINGTONIA DR
6 LANGLEYS RD
7 EAST VW
8 GRANGE RD
9 WILLOW RD
10 VAUGHAN RD
11 CAMPSALL PK RD
12 CAMPSALL HALL RD
13 SHERWOOD CL
14 HIGH ST

E2
1 BROC-O-BANK
2 NEWTHORPE RD
3 FORRESTER'S CL
4 TRAFFORD RD
5 ARUNDEL RD
6 ADELAIDE RD
7 HEADINGLEY RD
8 ORCHARD DR
9 ORCHARD CL
10 RYECROFT AVE
11 FIR TREE DR
12 MANOR CL
13 WINDMILL MD
14 KIPLIN DR
15 LANGOLD DR

F2
1 LYNDHURST DR
2 LYNDHURST CL
3 LYNDHURST RISE
4 ASHBURNHAM CL
5 ASHBURNHAM WK
6 DENVER RD
7 MANOR GARTH
8 SWAN SYKE DR
9 DRYHURST CL

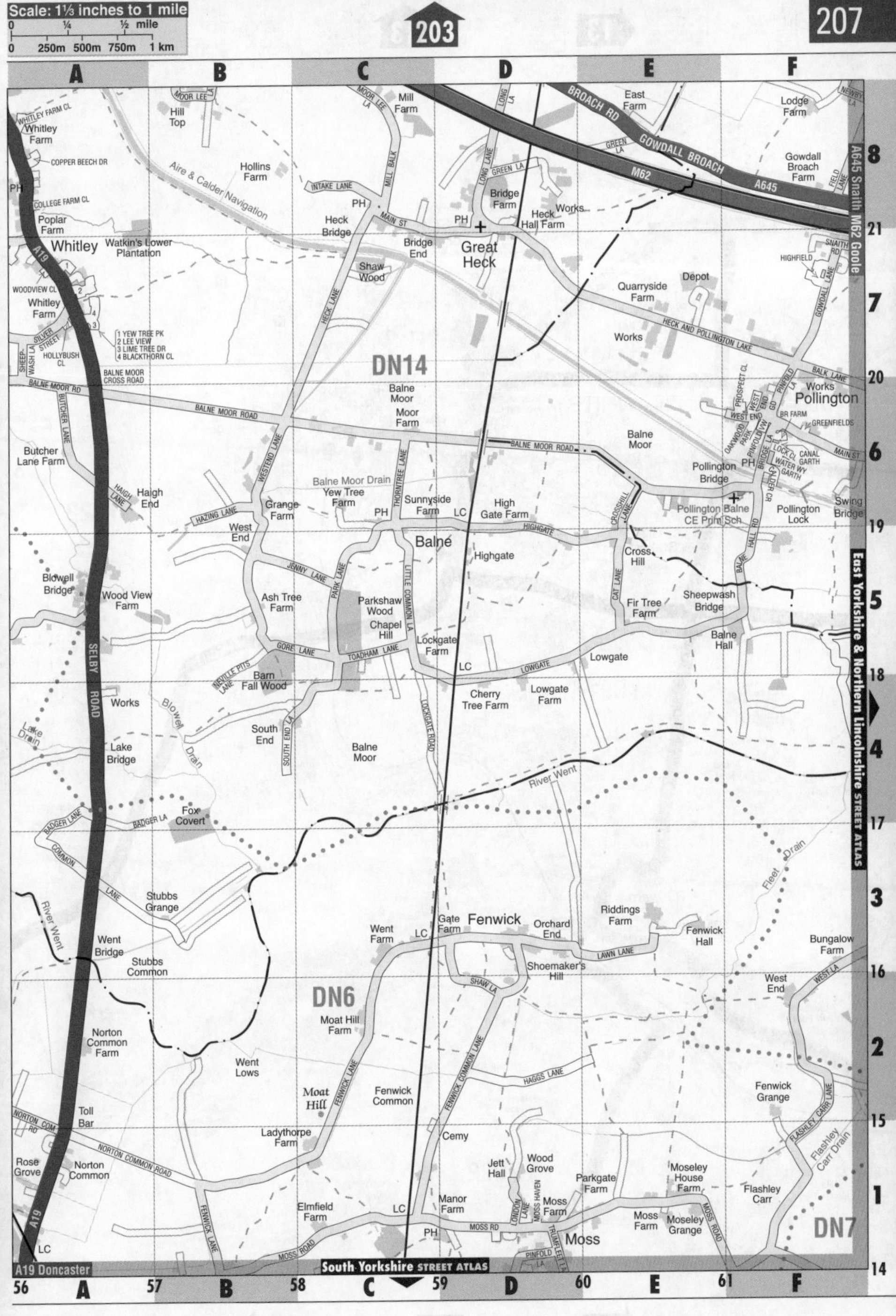

Scale: 1⅓ inches to 1 mile
203
DN14
DN6
DN7
Whitley
Great Heck
Balne
Pollington
Fenwick
Moss
Heck Bridge
Hollins Farm
Aire & Calder Navigation
Watkin's Lower Plantation
Balne Moor
Moor Farm
Balne Moor Road
Balne Moor Drain
High Gate Farm
Highgate
Parkshaw Wood
Chapel Hill
Lockgate Farm
Lowgate
Cherry Tree Farm
Lowgate Farm
Barn Fall Wood
South End
Blowell Bridge
Wood View Farm
Ash Tree Farm
Lake Bridge
River Went
Fox Covert
Stubbs Grange
Went Bridge
Stubbs Common
Norton Common Farm
Went Lows
Moat Hill
Moat Hill Farm
Fenwick Common
Toll Bar
Ladythorpe Farm
Rose Grove
Norton Common
Elmfield Farm
Manor Farm
Jett Hall
Wood Grove
Parkgate Farm
Moss Farm
Moseley House Farm
Moseley Grange
Flashley Carr
Fenwick Grange
Fenwick Hall
Riddings Farm
Orchard End
Shoemaker's Hill
Bungalow Farm
West End
Sheepwash Bridge
Fir Tree Farm
Cross Hill
Balne Hall
Pollington Bridge
Pollington Balne CE Prim Sch
Pollington Lock
Swing Bridge
Quarryside Farm
Depot
Works
East Farm
Lodge Farm
Gowdall Broach Farm
M62
A645
A19
Selby Road
A645 Snaith M62 Goole
A19 Doncaster
South Yorkshire STREET ATLAS
East Yorkshire & Northern Lincolnshire STREET ATLAS

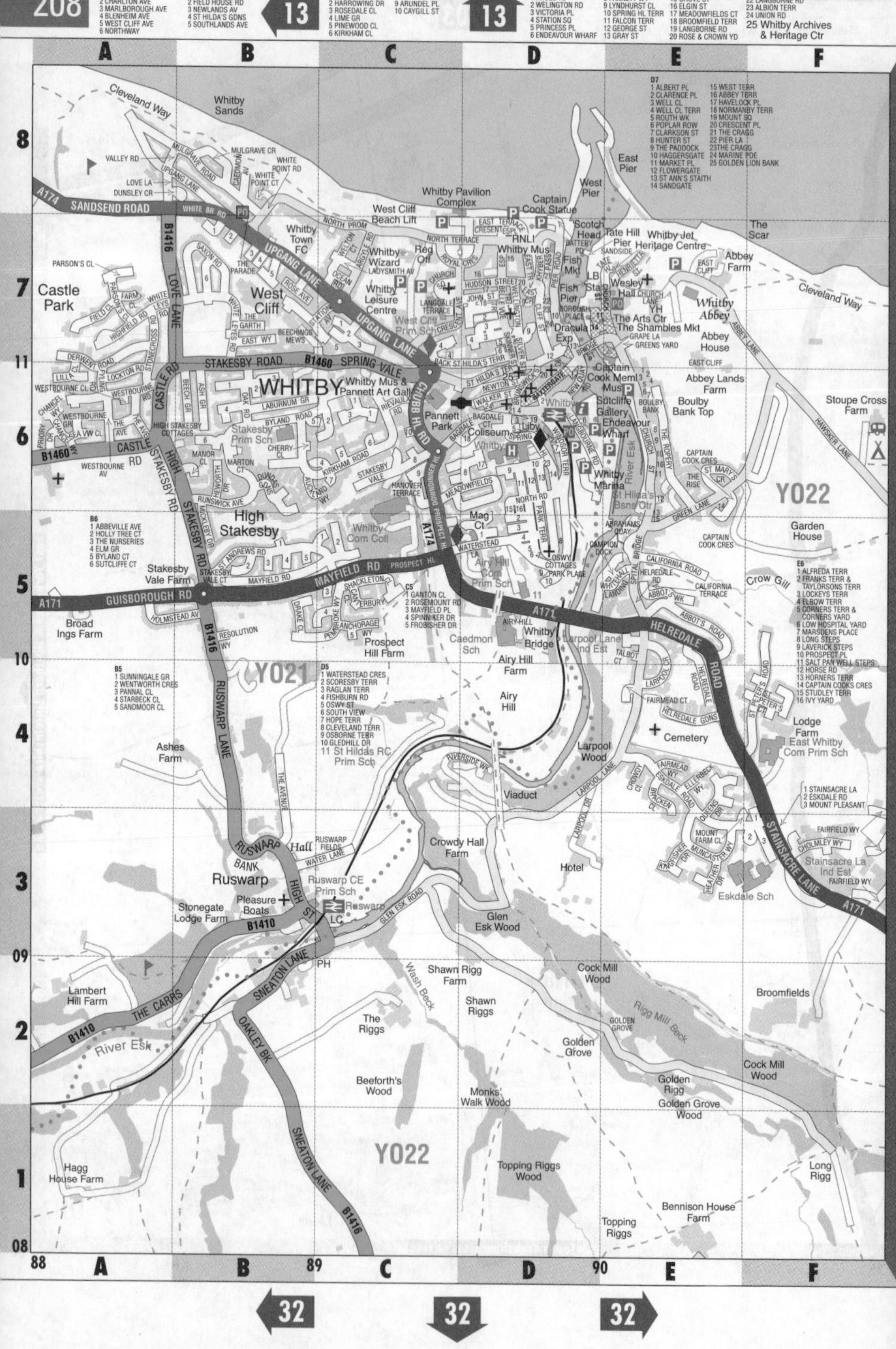
B7
1 WHITE POINT AVE
2 CHARLTON AVE
3 MARLBOROUGH AVE
4 BLENHEIM AVE
5 WEST CLIFF AVE
6 NORTHWAY
C7
1 WESTLANDS AVE
2 FIELD HOUSE RD
3 NEWLANDS AV
4 ST HILDA'S GDNS
5 SOUTHLANDS AVE
13
C6
1 FOUNTAINS CL
2 HARROWING DR
3 ROSEDALE CL
4 LIME GR
5 PINEWOOD CL
6 KIRKHAM CL
7 AUCKLAND WY
8 SOUTHEND GDNS
9 ARUNDEL PL
10 CAYGILL ST
13
D6
1 ANGEL YD
2 WELINGTON RD
3 VICTORIA PL
4 STATION SQ
5 PRINCESS PL
6 ENDEAVOUR WHARF
7 WINDSOR CRES
8 PANNETT WY
9 LYNDHURST CL
10 SPRING HL TERR
11 FALCON TERR
12 GEORGE ST
13 GRAY ST
14 ALBION PL
15 GROVE ST
16 ELGIN ST
17 MEADOWFIELDS CT
18 BROOMFIELD TERR
19 LANGBORNE RD
20 ROSE & CROWN YD
21 VICTORIA SQ
22 LANGBORNE RD
23 ALBION TERR
24 UNION RD
25 Whitby Archives & Heritage Ctr
A
B
C
D
E
F
D7
1 ALBERT PL
2 CLARENCE PL
3 WELL CL
4 WELL CL TERR
5 ROUTH WK
6 POPLAR ROW
7 CLARKSON ST
8 HUNTER ST
9 THE PADDOCK
10 HAGGERSGATE
11 MARKET PL
12 FLOWERGATE
13 ST ANN'S STAITH
14 SANDGATE
15 WEST TERR
16 ABBEY TERR
17 HAVELOCK PL
18 NORMANBY TERR
19 MOUNT SQ
20 CRESCENT PL
21 THE CRAGG
22 PIER LA
23 THE CRAGG
24 MARINE PDE
25 GOLDEN LION BANK
Cleveland Way
Whitby Sands
East Pier
West Pier
Whitby Pavilion Complex
Captain Cook Statue
West Cliff Beach Lift
Whitby Town FC
Whitby Wizard
Reg Off
Whitby Leisure Centre
West Cliff Prim Sch
RNLI
Whitby Mus
Scotch Head
Tate Hill Pier
Whitby Jet Heritage Centre
The Scar
Fish Mkt
Fish Pier
Wesley Hall
YH
Whitby Abbey
Abbey Farm
The Arts Ctr
The Shambles Mkt
Dracula Exp
Abbey House
Castle Park
West Cliff
WHITBY
Whitby Mus & Pannett Art Gall
Pannett Park
Coliseum
Captain Cook Meml Mus
Sutcliffe Gallery
Endeavour Wharf
Abbey Lands Farm
Boulby Bank Top
Stoupe Cross Farm
Stakesby Prim Sch
Whitby Marina
St Hilda's Bsns Ctr
YO22
Garden House
High Stakesby
Whitby Com Coll
Mag Ct
Airy Hill Com Prim Sch
B6
1 ABBEVILLE AVE
2 HOLLY TREE CT
3 THE NURSERIES
4 ELM GR
5 BYLAND CT
6 SUTCLIFFE CT
Stakesby Vale Farm
Crow Gill
C5
1 GANTON CL
2 ROSEMOUNT RD
3 MAYFIELD PL
4 SPINNIKER DR
5 FROBISHER DR
E6
1 ALFREDA TERR
2 FRANKS TERR & TAYLORSONS TERR
3 LOCKEYS TERR
4 ELBOW TERR
5 CORNERS TERR & CORNERS YARD
6 LOW HOSPITAL YARD
7 MARSDENS PLACE
8 LONG STEPS
9 LAVERICK STEPS
10 PROSPECT PL
11 SALT PAN WELL STEPS
12 HORSE RD
13 HORNERS TERR
14 CAPTAIN COOKS CRES
15 STUDLEY TERR
16 IVY YARD
Broad Ings Farm
Caedmon Sch
Whitby Bridge
Larpool Lane Ind Est
Prospect Hill Farm
Airy Hill Farm
Airy Hill
YO21
B5
1 SUNNINGALE GR
2 WENTWORTH CRES
3 PANNAL CL
4 STARBECK CL
5 SANDMOOR CL
D5
1 WATERSTEAD CRES
2 SCORESBY TERR
3 RAGLAN TERR
4 FISHBURN RD
5 OSWY ST
6 SOUTH VIEW
7 HOPE TERR
8 CLEVELAND TERR
9 OSBORNE TERR
10 GLEDHILL DR
11 St Hildas RC Prim Sch
Cemetery
Lodge Farm
East Whitby Com Prim Sch
Ashes Farm
Larpool Wood
Viaduct
1 STAINSACRE LA
2 ESKDALE RD
3 MOUNT PLEASANT
Ruswarp Hall
Crowdy Hall Farm
Hotel
Stainsacre La Ind Est
Ruswarp
Ruswarp CE Prim Sch
Stonegate Lodge Farm
Pleasure Boats
Eskdale Sch
Glen Esk Wood
Lambert Hill Farm
Shawn Rigg Farm
Cock Mill Wood
Broomfields
Shawn Riggs
The Riggs
Golden Grove
River Esk
Beeforth's Wood
Monks' Walk Wood
Golden Rigg
Golden Grove Wood
Cock Mill Wood
YO22
Hagg House Farm
Topping Riggs Wood
Long Rigg
Bennison House Farm
Topping Riggs
88
89
90
32
32
32

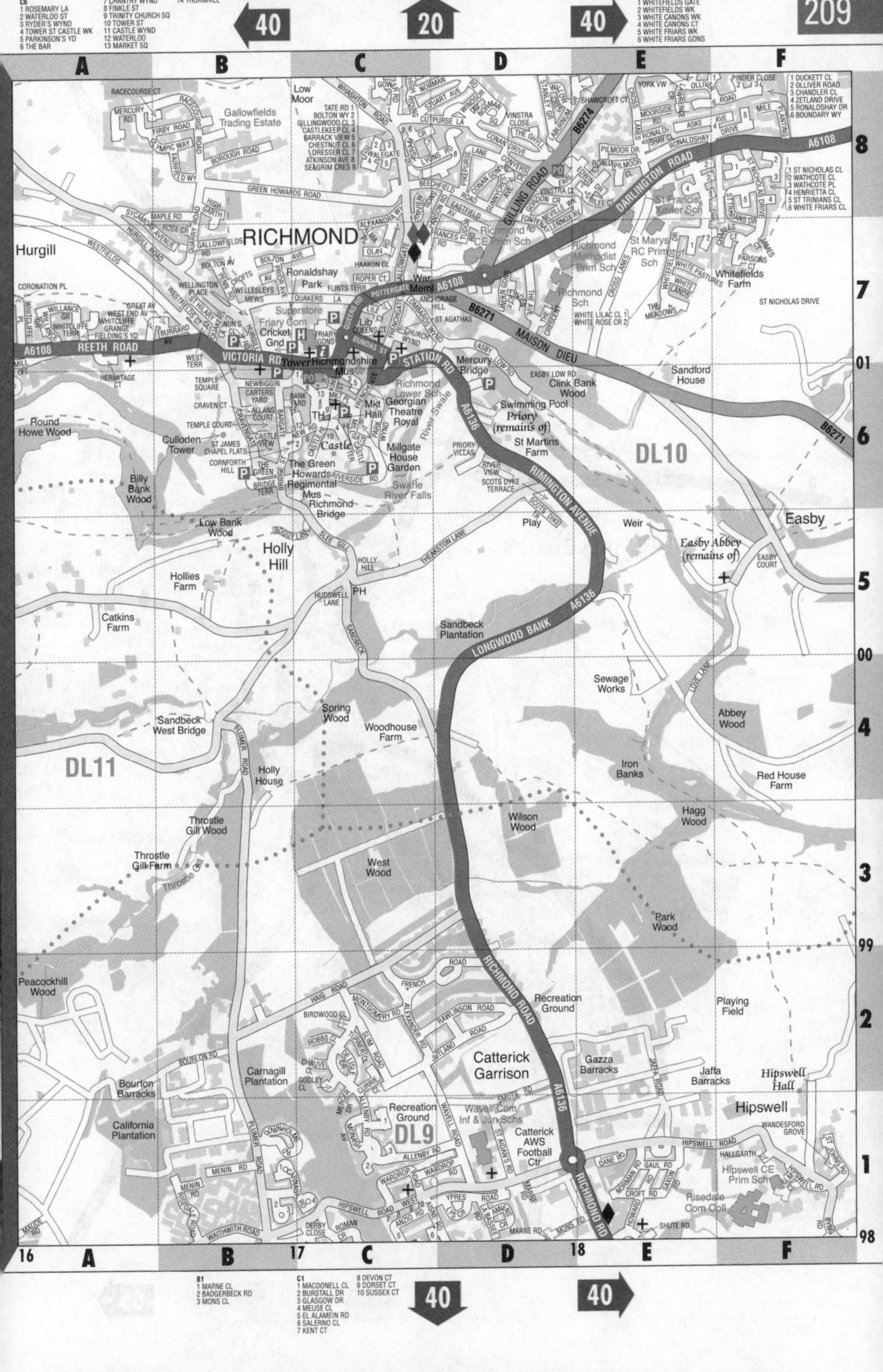

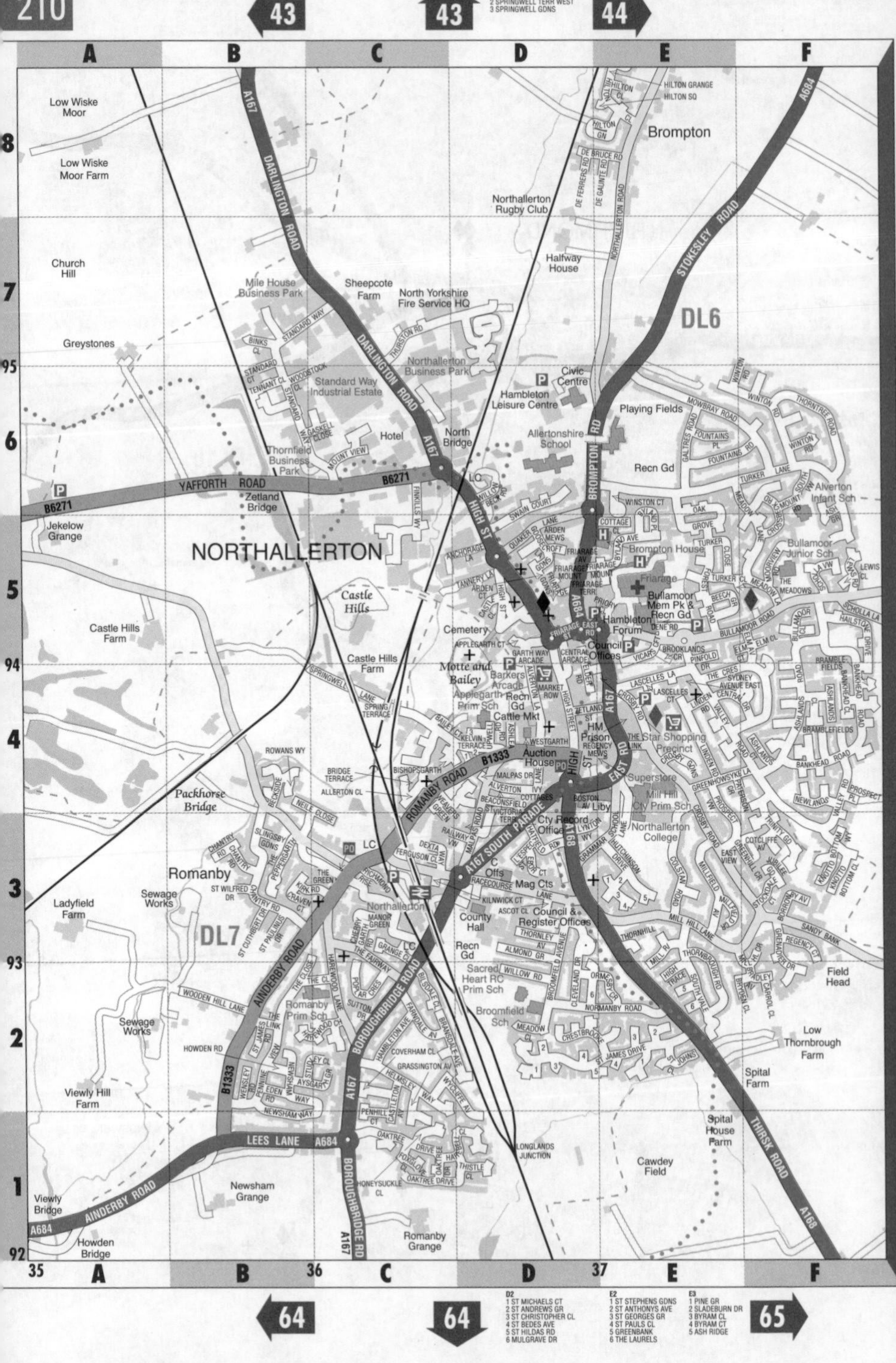

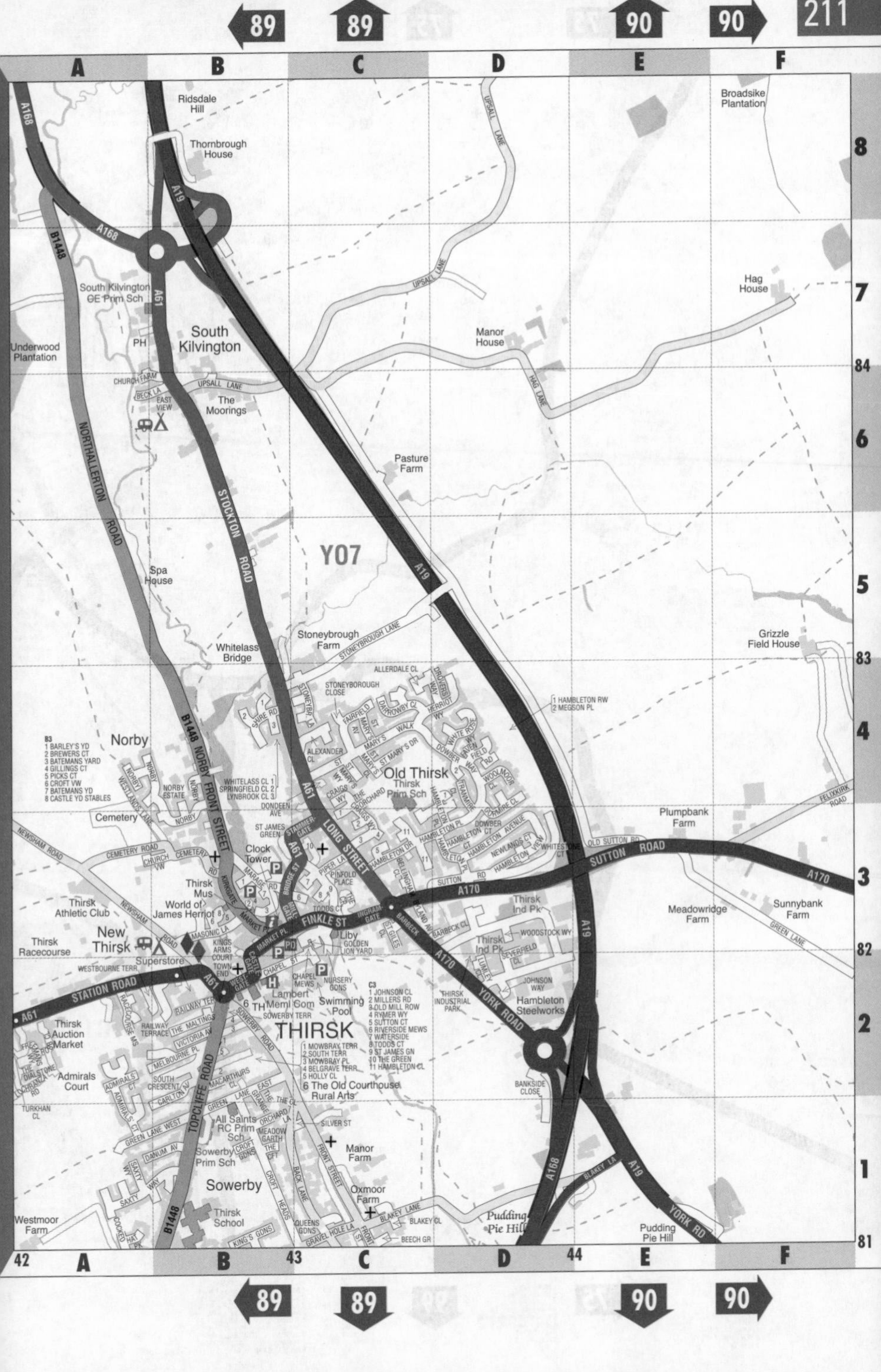

89 89 90 90

A B C D E F

8

7

84

6

5

83

4

3

82

2

1

81

Broadsike Plantation

Ridsdale Hill

Thornbrough House

A168
A19
B1448

South Kilvington CE Prim Sch
Underwood Plantation
South Kilvington
PH
CHURCH LA
EAST VIEW
UPSALL LANE
The Moorings

Hag House

Manor House

NORTHALLERTON ROAD
STOCKTON ROAD
A61
A19

YO7

Pasture Farm

Spa House

Grizzle Field House

Whitelass Bridge

Stoneybrough Farm

Stoneyborough Close
ALLERDALE CL

STONEYBOROUGH LANE

1 HAMBLETON RW
2 MEGSON PL

B1448 NORBY FRONT STREET
Norby

ALEXANDER

WHITELASS CL 1
SPRINGFIELD CL 2
LYNBROOK CL 3

Old Thirsk
Thirsk Prim Sch

FELIXKIRK

Plumbbank Farm

Cemetery

DONDSEN AVE

ST JAMES GREEN

LONG STREET
A61

SUTTON

A170
SUTTON ROAD
OLD SUTTON RD
A170

Meadowridge Farm

Sunnybank Farm
GREEN LANE

B3
1 BARLEY'S YD
2 BREWERS CT
3 BATEMANS YARD
4 GILLINGS CT
5 PICKS CT
6 CROFT VW
7 BATEMANS YD
8 CASTLE YD STABLES

NORBY ESTATE
CEMETERY ROAD
CHURCH
CEMETERY

Clock Tower
Thirsk Mus
World of James Herriot
P

MARKET PL
FINKLE ST

Thirsk Ind Pk

Thirsk Ind Est
WOODSTOCK WY
SEFIELD

Thirsk Athletic Club

Thirsk Racecourse

New Thirsk
Superstore

MASONIC LA
KINGS ARMS COURT
CHAPEL ST
P
P

CHAPEL MEWS
NURSERY CLOSE
Liby
GOLDEN LION YARD

BARRACK

CHANWICK CL

A170

YORK ROAD
A19

THIRSK INDUSTRIAL PARK
JOHNSON WY

Hambleton Steelworks

Thirsk Auction Market

Admirals Court
ADMIRALS CL

WESTBOURNE TERR
STATION ROAD
A61
RAILWAY TERR

TH
Lambert Meml Com
SOWERBY TERR
Swimming Pool

C3
1 JOHNSON CL
2 MILLERS RD
3 OLD MILL ROW
4 RYMER WY
5 SUTTON CT
6 RIVERSIDE MEWS
7 WATERSIDE
8 TODDS CT
9 ST JAMES GN
10 THE GREEN
11 HAMBLETON CL

TURKHAN CL

VICTORIA PL
MELBOURNE PL
SOUTH CRESCENT
CARLTON

MACARTHURS
EAST

THIRSK
1 MOWBRAY TERR
2 SOUTH TERR
3 MOWBRAY PL
4 BELGRAVE TERR
5 HOLLY CL
6 The Old Courthouse Rural Arts

All Saints RC Prim Sch

Sowerby Prim Sch

GREEN LANE WEST
TOPCLIFFE ROAD
DANUM RD
SALTX
B1448

Thirsk School

Sowerby

SILVER ST

Manor Farm

Oxmoor Farm

QUEENS
KING'S RD
HOLE LA
BLAKEY CL
BEECH GR

MANEY LANE

Pudding Pie Hill

BANKSIDE CLOSE
A168
BLAKEY LA
YORK RD
A19

Pudding Pie Hill

Westmoor Farm

42 A B 43 C D 44 E F 81

89 89 90 90

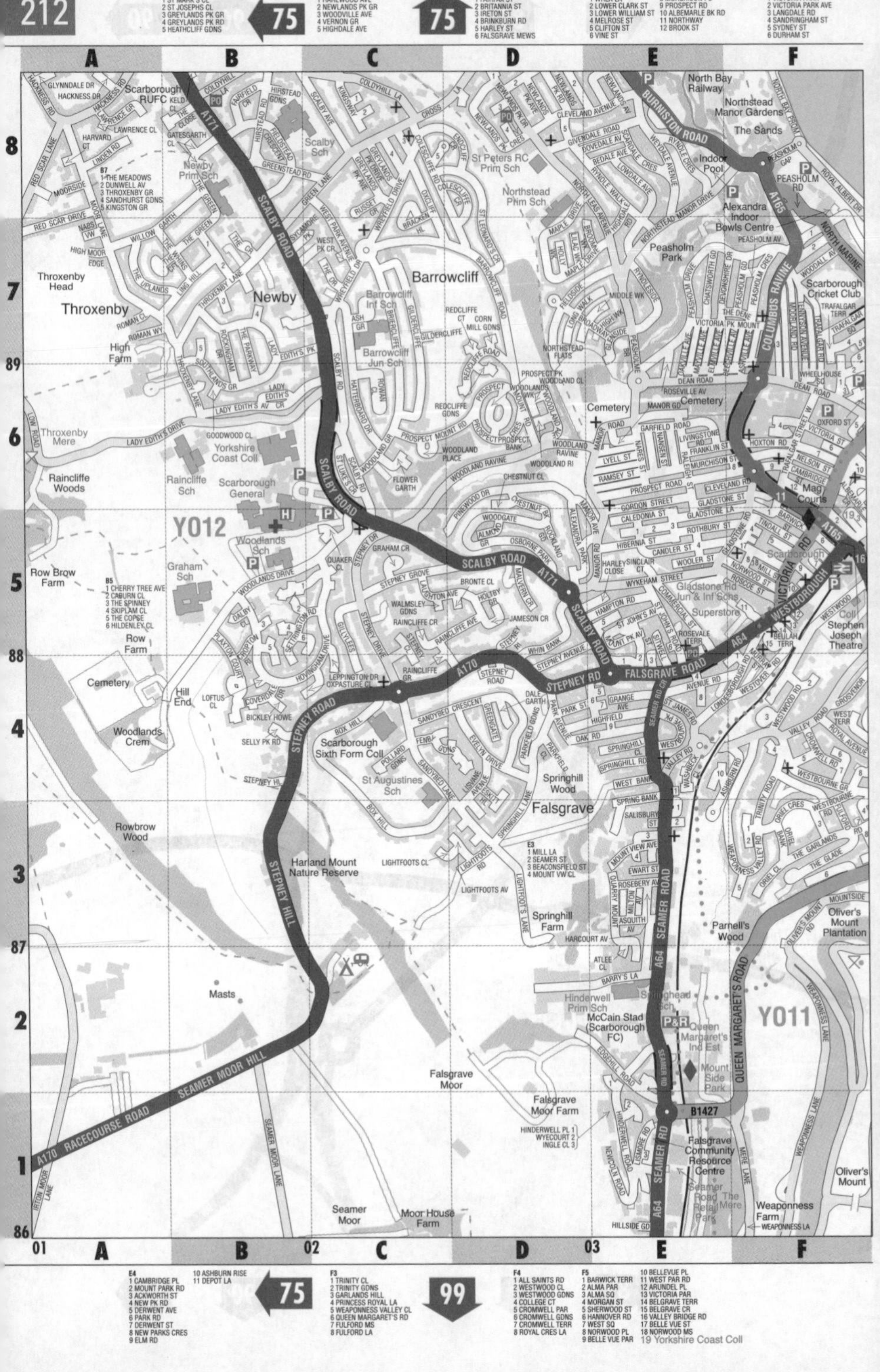

75
C8
1 ST MARK'S CL
2 ST JOSEPHS CL
3 GREYLANDS PK GR
4 GREYLANDS PK RD
5 HEATHCLIFF GDNS
D8
1 HAREWOOD AVE
2 NEWLANDS PK GR
3 WOODVILLE AVE
4 VERNON GR
5 HIGHDALE AVE
75
E5
1 FAIRFAX ST
2 BRITANNIA ST
3 IRETON ST
4 BRINKBURN RD
5 HARLEY ST
6 FALSGRAVE MEWS
F6
1 WREA LA
2 LOWER CLARK ST
3 LOWER WILLIAM ST
4 MELROSE ST
5 CLIFTON ST
6 VINE ST
7 FRANKLIN ST
8 MURCHISON PL
9 PROSPECT RD
10 ALBEMARLE BK RD
11 NORTHWAY
12 BROOK ST
F7
1 VICTORIA PARK
2 VICTORIA PARK AVE
3 LANGDALE RD
4 SANDRINGHAM ST
5 SYDNEY ST
6 DURHAM ST
A
B
C
D
E
F
8
7
89
6
5
88
4
3
87
2
1
86
01
02
03
Scarborough RUFC
Newby Prim Sch
Scalby Sch
St Peters RC Prim Sch
Northstead Prim Sch
North Bay Railway
Northstead Manor Gardens
The Sands
Indoor Pool
Alexandra Indoor Bowls Centre
Peasholm Park
Scarborough Cricket Club
Throxenby Head
Throxenby
Newby
Barrowcliff
Barrowcliff Inf Sch
Barrowcliff Jun Sch
High Farm
Throxenby Mere
Yorkshire Coast Coll
Raincliffe Woods
Raincliffe Sch
Scarborough General
YO12
Woodlands Sch
Graham Sch
Row Brow Farm
Row Farm
Cemetery
Hill End
Woodlands Crem
Cemetery
Mag Courts
Gladstone Rd Jun & Inf Schs
Superstore
Coll
Stephen Joseph Theatre
Scarborough Sixth Form Coll
St Augustines Sch
Springhill Wood
Falsgrave
Rowbrow Wood
Harland Mount Nature Reserve
Springhill Farm
Masts
Hinderwell Prim Sch
McCain Stad (Scarborough FC)
Queen Margaret's Ind Est
Mount Side Park
Parnell's Wood
Oliver's Mount Plantation
YO11
Falsgrave Moor
Falsgrave Moor Farm
Falsgrave Community Resource Centre
Seamer Road Retail Park
The Mere
Weaponness Farm
Oliver's Mount
Seamer Moor
Moor House Farm
SCALBY ROAD
STEPNEY ROAD
STEPNEY HILL
SEAMER MOOR HILL
RACECOURSE ROAD
A170
A171
A64
A165
B1427
SEAMER ROAD
FALSGRAVE ROAD
WESTBOROUGH
BURNISTON ROAD
COLUMBUS RAVINE
QUEEN MARGARET'S ROAD
HINDERWELL PL 1
WYECOURT 2
INGLE CL 3
E3
1 MILL LA
2 SEAMER ST
3 BEACONSFIELD ST
4 MOUNT VW CL
B7
1 THE MEADOWS
2 DUNWELL AV
3 THROXENBY GR
4 SANDHURST GDNS
5 KINGSTON GR
B5
1 CHERRY TREE AVE
2 CABURN CL
3 THE SPINNEY
4 SKIPLAM CL
5 THE COPSE
6 HILDENLEY CL
E4
1 CAMBRIDGE PL
2 MOUNT PARK RD
3 ACKWORTH ST
4 NEW PK RD
5 DERWENT AVE
6 PARK RD
7 DERWENT ST
8 NEW PARKS CRES
9 ELM RD
10 ASHBURN RISE
11 DEPOT LA
75
F3
1 TRINITY CL
2 TRINITY GDNS
3 GARLANDS HILL
4 PRINCESS ROYAL LA
5 WEAPONNESS VALLEY CL
6 QUEEN MARGARET'S RD
7 FULFORD MS
8 FULFORD LA
99
F4
1 ALL SAINTS RD
2 WESTWOOD CL
3 WESTWOOD GDNS
4 COLLEGE CT
5 CROMWELL PAR
6 CROMWELL GDNS
7 CROMWELL TERR
8 ROYAL CRES LA
F5
1 BARWICK TERR
2 ALMA PAR
3 ALMA SQ
4 MORGAN ST
5 SHERWOOD ST
6 HANNOVER RD
7 WEST SQ
8 NORWOOD PL
9 BELLE VUE PAR
10 BELLEVUE PL
11 WEST PAR RD
12 ARUNDEL PL
13 VICTORIA PAR
14 BELGRAVE TERR
15 BELGRAVE CR
16 VALLEY BRIDGE RD
17 BELLE VUE ST
18 NORWOOD MS
19 Yorkshire Coast Coll

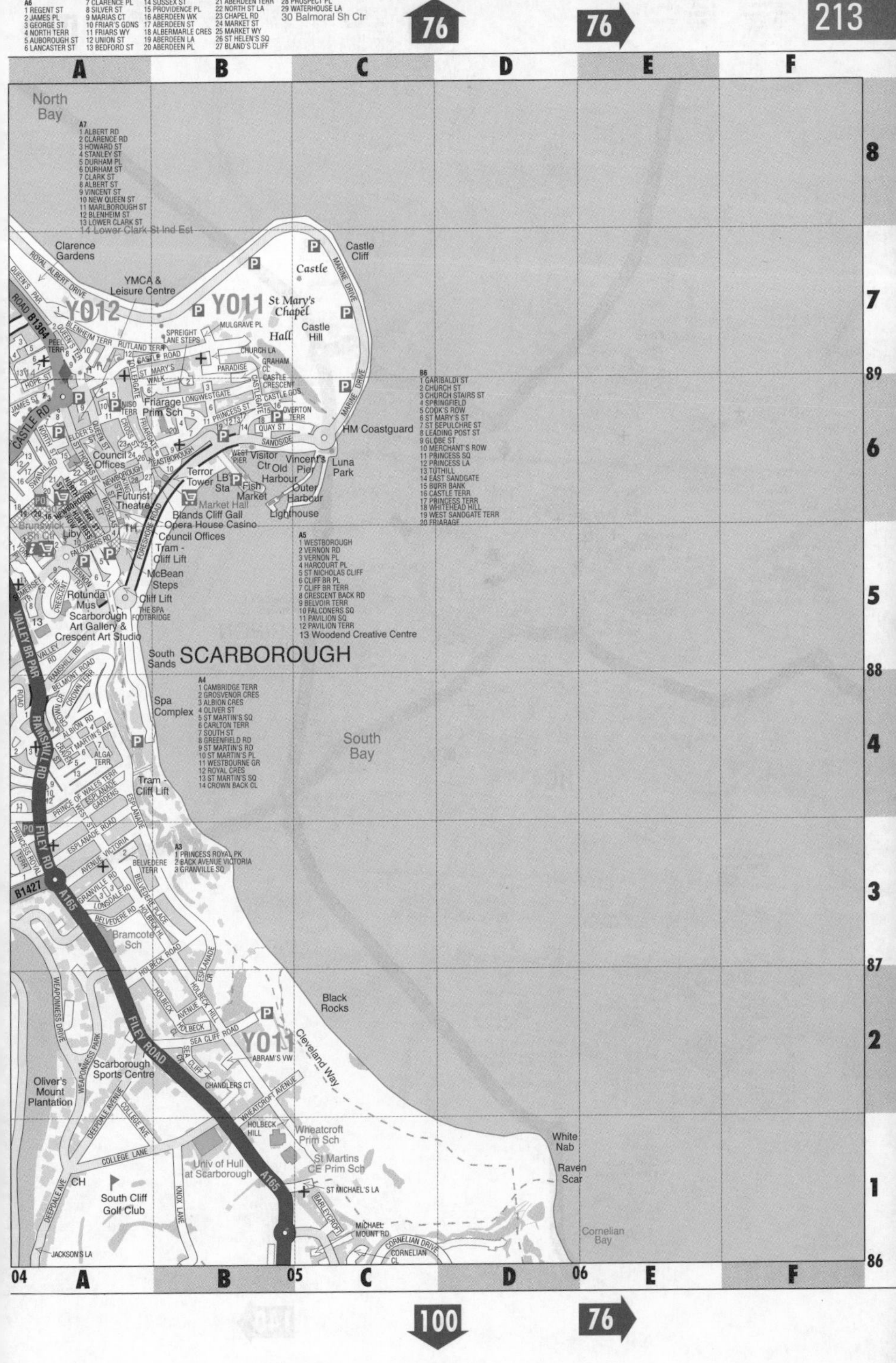

SCARBOROUGH

North Bay

South Bay

A6
1 REGENT ST
2 JAMES PL
3 GEORGE ST
4 NORTH TERR
5 AUBOROUGH ST
6 LANCASTER ST

A7
1 ALBERT RD
2 CLARENCE RD
3 HOWARD ST
4 STANLEY ST
5 DURHAM PL
6 DURHAM ST
7 CLARK ST
8 ALBERT ST
9 VINCENT ST
10 NEW QUEEN ST
11 MARLBOROUGH ST
12 BLENHEIM ST
13 LOWER CLARK ST
14 Lower Clark St Ind Est

7 CLARENCE PL
8 SILVER ST
9 MARIAS CT
10 FRIAR'S GDNS
11 FRIARS WY
12 UNION ST
13 BEDFORD ST

14 SUSSEX ST
15 PROVIDENCE PL
16 ABERDEEN WK
17 ABERDEEN ST
18 ALBERMARLE CRES
19 ABERDEEN LA
20 ABERDEEN PL

21 ABERDEEN TERR
22 NORTH ST LA
23 CHAPEL RD
24 MARKET ST
25 MARKET WY
26 ST HELEN'S SQ
27 BLAND'S CLIFF

28 PROSPECT PL
29 WATERHOUSE LA
30 Balmoral Sh Ctr

A5
1 WESTBOROUGH
2 VERNON RD
3 VERNON PL
4 HARCOURT PL
5 ST NICHOLAS CLIFF
6 CLIFF BR PL
7 CLIFF BR TERR
8 CRESCENT BACK RD
9 BELVOIR TERR
10 FALCONERS SQ
11 PAVILION SQ
12 PAVILION TERR
13 Woodend Creative Centre

A4
1 CAMBRIDGE TERR
2 GROSVENOR CRES
3 ALBION CRES
4 OLIVER ST
5 ST MARTIN'S SQ
6 CARLTON TERR
7 SOUTH ST
8 GREENFIELD RD
9 ST MARTIN'S RD
10 ST MARTIN'S PL
11 WESTBOURNE GR
12 ROYAL CRES
13 ST MARTIN'S SQ
14 CROWN BACK CL

A3
1 PRINCESS ROYAL PK
2 BACK AVENUE VICTORIA
3 GRANVILLE SQ

B6
1 GARIBALDI ST
2 CHURCH ST
3 CHURCH STAIRS ST
4 SPRINGFIELD
5 COOK'S ROW
6 ST MARY'S ST
7 ST SEPULCHRE ST
8 LEADING POST ST
9 GLOBE ST
10 MERCHANT'S ROW
11 PRINCESS SQ
12 PRINCESS LA
13 TUTHILL
14 EAST SANDGATE
15 BURR BANK
16 CASTLE TERR
17 PRINCESS TERR
18 WHITEHEAD HILL
19 WEST SANDGATE TERR
20 FRIARAGE

Castle
Castle Cliff
Castle Hill
St Mary's Chapel
Clarence Gardens
YMCA & Leisure Centre
HM Coastguard
Vincent's Pier
Luna Park
Visitor Ctr
Old Harbour
Fish Market
Outer Harbour
Lighthouse
Blands Cliff Gall
Opera House Casino
Council Offices
Tram - Cliff Lift
McBean Steps
Cliff Lift
THE SPA FOOTBRIDGE
Rotunda Mus
Scarborough Art Gallery & Crescent Art Studio
South Sands
Spa Complex
Tram - Cliff Lift
Belvedere Terr
Bramcote Sch
Black Rocks
Cleveland Way
Scarborough Sports Centre
Oliver's Mount Plantation
Holbeck Hill
Wheatcroft Prim Sch
St Martins CE Prim Sch
Univ of Hull at Scarborough
South Cliff Golf Club
White Nab
Raven Scar
Cornelian Bay
JACKSON'S LA

YO12
YO11

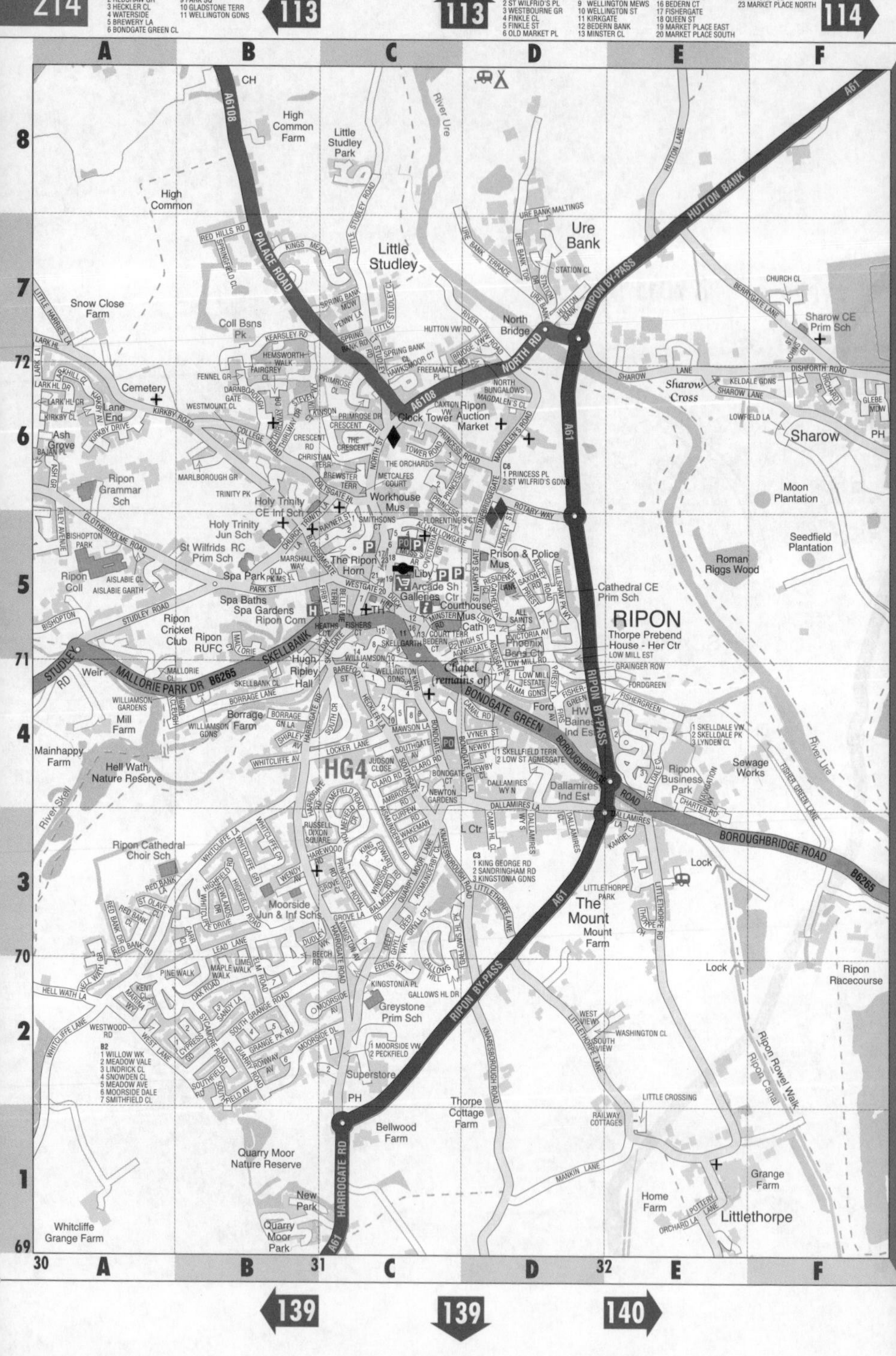

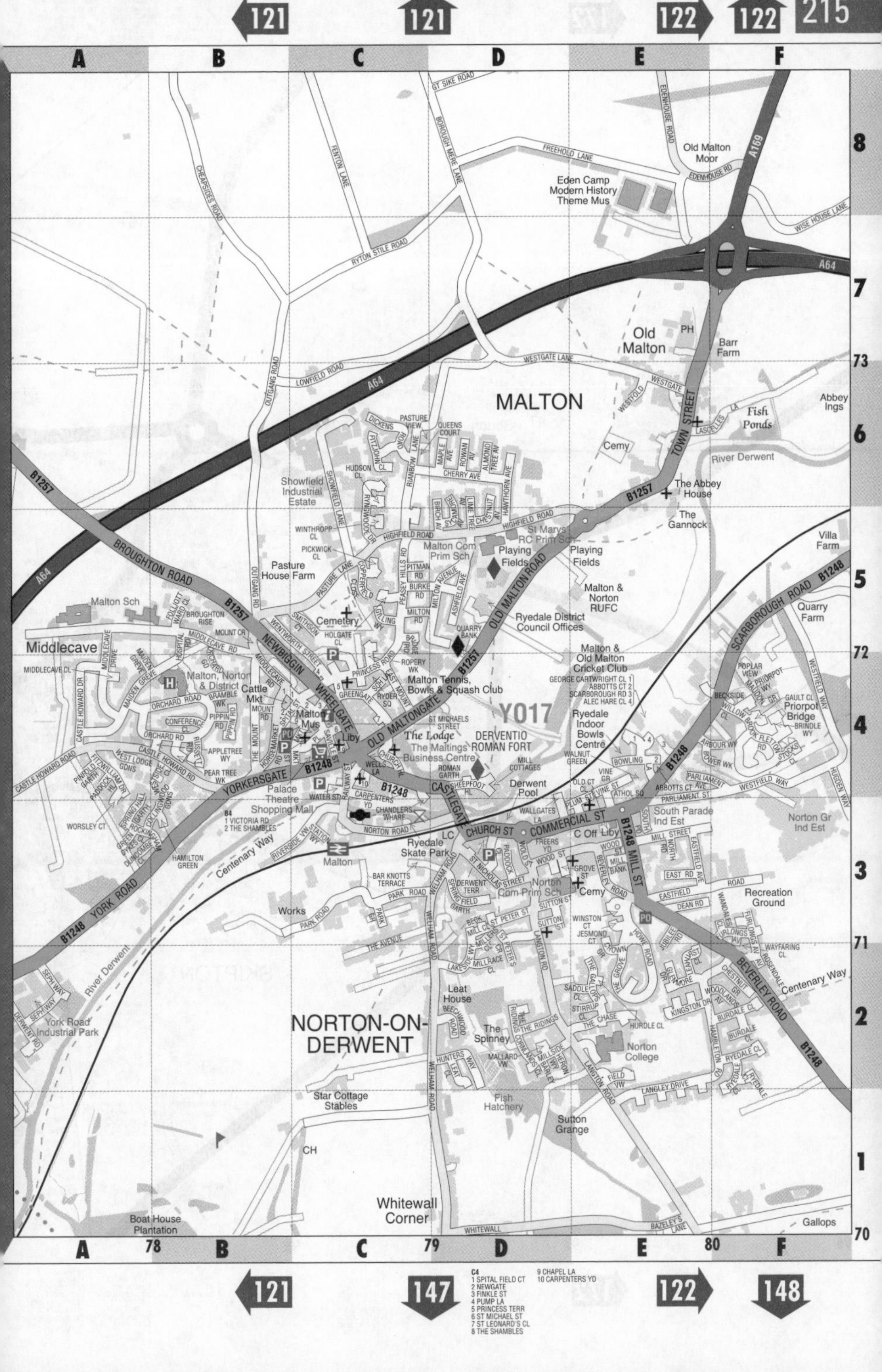
121
121
122
122
A
B
C
D
E
F
8
7
73
6
5
72
4
3
71
2
1
70
78
79
80
GT SIKE ROAD
EDENHOUSE ROAD
Old Malton Moor
A169
FREEHOLD LANE
EDENHOUSE RD
Eden Camp Modern History Theme Mus
FENTON LANE
BOROUGH MERE LANE
CHEAPSIDES ROAD
WISE HOUSE LANE
RYTON STILE ROAD
A64
Old Malton
PH
Barr Farm
WESTGATE LANE
OUTGANG ROAD
LOWFIELD ROAD
WESTGATE
WESTFOLD
TOWN STREET
MALTON
Abbey Ings
LASCELLES LA
Fish Ponds
Cemy
River Derwent
DICKENS
PASTURE VIEW
QUEENS COURT
FITZJOHN CL
MAPLE AVE
ROWAN AV
ALMOND TREE AV
HUDSON CL
RIANBOW LANE
CHERRY AVE
HAWTHORN AVE
Showfield Industrial Estate
SHOWFIELD LANE
RYNGWOOD DR
BIRCH AV
LIME TREE AV
CHESTNUT AV
B1257
The Abbey House
The Gannock
HIGHFIELD ROAD
St Marys RC Prim Sch
Playing Fields
WINTHROPP CL
PICKWICK CL
Malton Com Prim Sch
Villa Farm
BROUGHTON ROAD
Pasture House Farm
PASTURE LANE
PEASEY HILLS RD
PITMAN RD
BURKE RD
MILTON AVENUE
ASHFIELD AVE
OLD MALTON ROAD
Malton & Norton RUFC
SCARBOROUGH ROAD
B1248
Quarry Farm
Malton Sch
BROUGHTON RISE
MOUNT CR
SMITHSON CT
Cemetery
MILTON RD
QUARRY BANK
Ryedale District Council Offices
Middlecave
MIDDLECAVE RD
WENTWORTH STREET
HOLGATE CL
Malton & Old Malton Cricket Club
MIDDLECAVE CL
MIDDLECAVE DRIVE
MAIDEN GROVE
NEWBIGGIN
PRINCESS ROAD
ROPERY WK
GEORGE CARTWRIGHT CL 1
ABBOTTS CT 2
SCARBOROUGH RD 3
ALEC HARE CL 4
POPLAR VIEW
PRIORPOT WAY
WESTFIELD WAY
Malton, Norton & District
Cattle Mkt
ORCHARD ROAD
BRAMBLE WK
WHEELGATE
GREENGATE
RYDER SQ
EAST MOUNT
Malton Tennis, Bowls & Squash Club
Y017
Ryedale Indoor Bowls Centre
BECKSIDE
WILLOW BROOK CL
GAULT CL
Priorpot Bridge
BRINDLE WY
CASTLE HOWARD DR
CONFERENCE CL
PIPPIN RD
MOUNT RD
Malton Mus
Liby
OLD MALTONGATE
ST MICHAELS STREET
The Lodge
DERVENTIO ROMAN FORT
The Maltings Business Centre
ARBOUR WY
FLETTON RD
STOCKS CL
BOWER WK
ORCHARD RD
APPLETREE WY
CASTLE HOWARD RD
WEST LODGE GDNS
FITZWILLIAM DR
PINFOLD GARTH
PADDOCK
PEAR TREE WK
YORKERSGATE
B1248
WELLS LA
CHURCH HL
ROMAN GARTH
SHEEPFOOT HL
MILL COTTAGES
WALNUT GREEN
BOWLING
PARLIAMENT AVE
ABBOTTS CT
PARLIAMENT ST
HUGDEN WAY
Palace Theatre Shopping Mall
WATER ST
CARPENTERS YD
CASTLEGATE
Derwent Pool
OLD CT CL
VINE GR
VINE ST
ATHOL SQ
B4
1 VICTORIA RD
2 THE SHAMBLES
CHANDLERS WHARF
WALLGATES LA
PLUM ST
South Parade Ind Est
Norton Gr Ind Est
WORSLEY CT
SPRING HALL
ROCKINGHAM
DUNCOMBE CT
HAMILTON GREEN
Centenary Way
RIVERSIDE VW
STATION WAY
NORTON ROAD
Malton
LC
CHURCH ST
COMMERCIAL ST
FREERS YD
C Off
B1248 MILL ST
WOOD ST
MILL STREET
NORTH RD
EASTFIELD AVE
Ryedale Skate Park
ST NICHOLAS STREET
PADDOCK
WOLD ST
GROVE ST
MILL BANK
EAST RD
BEVERLEY ROAD
BAR KNOTTS TERRACE
PARK ROAD
DERWENT TERR
SPRING FIELD GARTH
Norton Com Prim Sch
Cemy
EASTFIELD
DEAN RD
Recreation Ground
YORK ROAD
Works
PARK RD
SUTTON ST
WINSTON CT
JESMOND CT
HOWE ROAD
JUBILEE RD
WANDALES
FURLONGS AV
THE AVENUE
ST PETER ST
MILLERS LA
MILLRACE CL
WELHAM ROAD
LANGTON RD
WAYFARING CL
BEVERLEY ROAD
Centenary Way
ROSENDALE
SEPH WAY
River Derwent
LAKESIDE WAY
THE GROVE
GLENMORE DR
CHESTNUT AV
Leat House
SADDLE CL
STIRRUP CL
WOODLANDS GR
KINGSTON DR
York Road Industrial Park
NORTON-ON-DERWENT
BEECHWOOD
The Spinney
THE RIDINGS
THE CHASE
HURDLE CL
BURDALE CL
Norton College
HAMBLETON RD
RYEDALE CL
HUNTERS WAY
MALLARD VW
HERON WY
BARLEY
FIELD VW
LANGLEY DRIVE
Star Cottage Stables
Fish Hatchery
Sutton Grange
CH
Whitewall Corner
WHITEWALL
BAZELEY'S LANE
Gallops
Boat House Plantation
121
147
122
148
C4
1 SPITAL FIELD CT
2 NEWGATE
3 FINKLE ST
4 PUMP LA
5 PRINCESS TERR
6 ST MICHAEL ST
7 ST LEONARD'S CL
8 THE SHAMBLES
9 CHAPEL LA
10 CARPENTERS YD

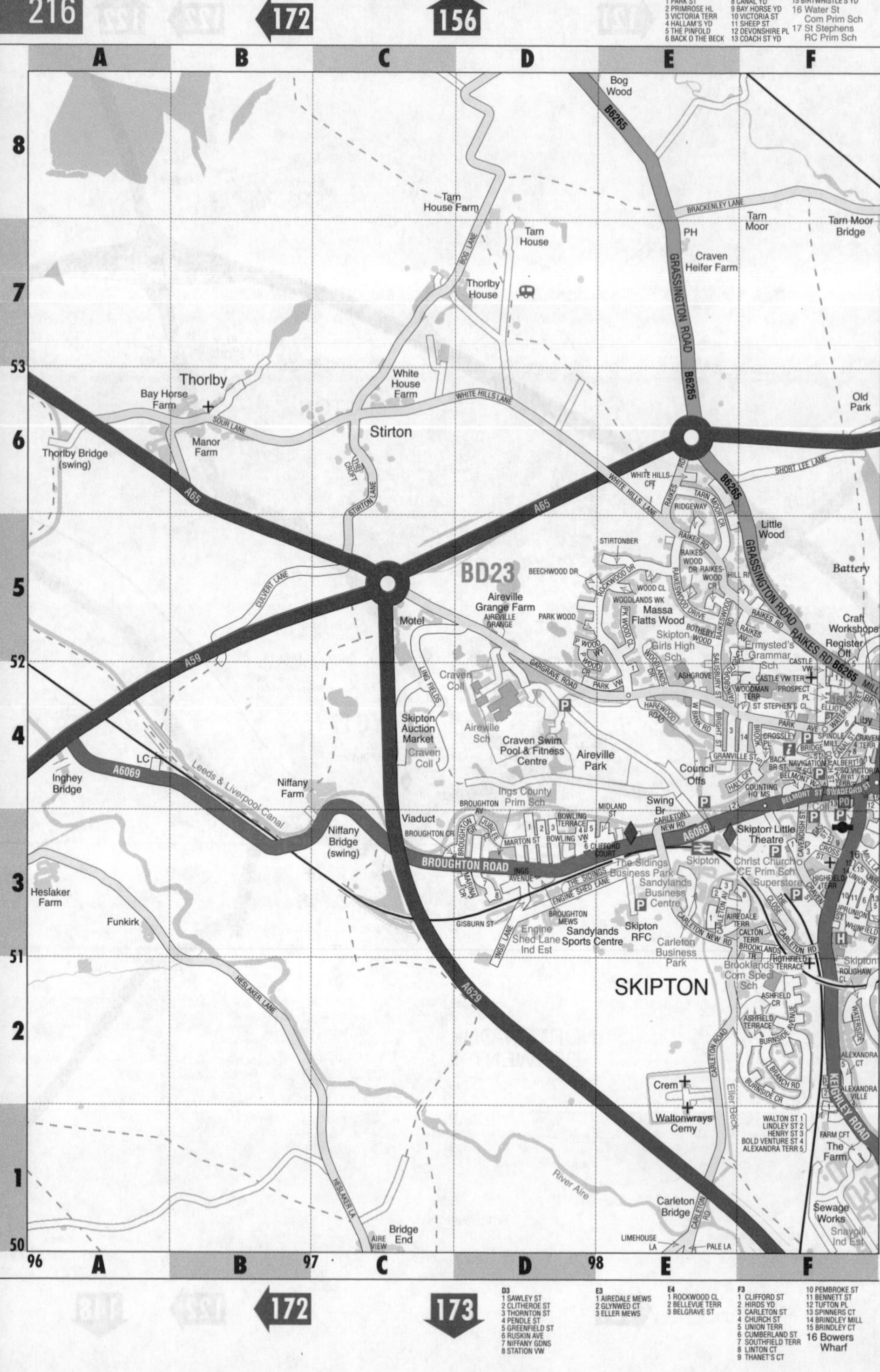

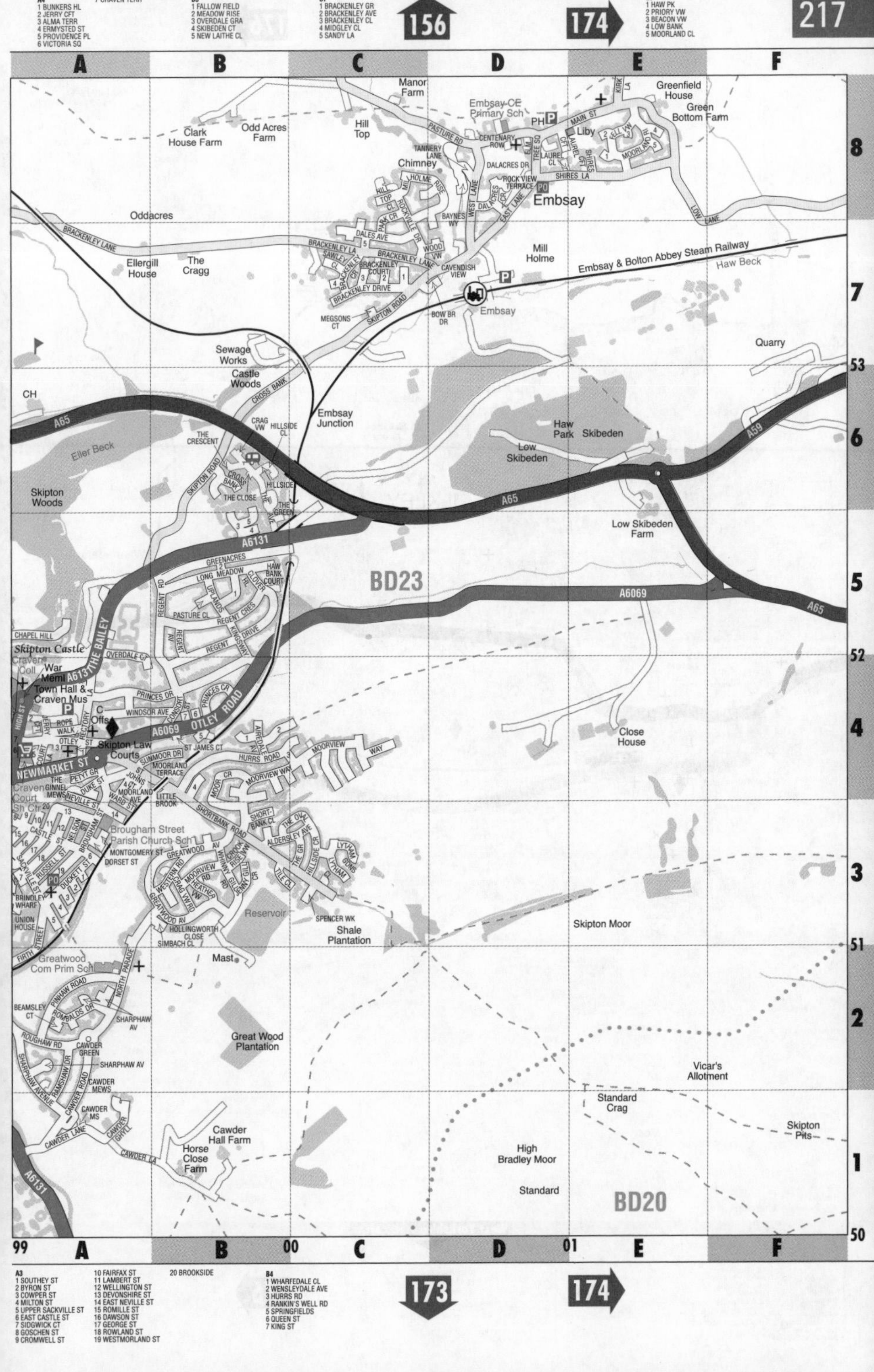
A4
1 BUNKERS HL
2 JERRY CFT
3 ALMA TERR
4 ERMYSTED ST
5 PROVIDENCE PL
6 VICTORIA SQ
7 CRAVEN TERR
B5
1 FALLOW FIELD
2 MEADOW RISE
3 OVERDALE GRA
4 SKIBEDEN CT
5 NEW LAITHE CL
C7
1 BRACKENLEY GR
2 BRACKENLEY AVE
3 BRACKENLEY CL
4 MIDGLEY CL
5 SANDY LA
156
174
E8
1 HAW PK
2 PRIORY VW
3 BEACON VW
4 LOW BANK
5 MOORLAND CL
A
B
C
D
E
F
8
7
53
6
5
52
4
3
51
2
1
50
Manor Farm
Greenfield House
Green Bottom Farm
Embsay CE Primary Sch
Hill Top
Clark House Farm
Odd Acres Farm
PASTURE RD
CENTENARY ROW
TANNERY LANE
MAIN ST
KIRK LA
Liby
Chimney
DALACRES DR
ROCK VIEW TERRACE
SHIRES LA
MOORLAND RI
Embsay
HOLME RISE
ROCKVILLE DR
WEST LANE
EAST LANE
BAYNES WY
LOW LANE
Oddacres
BRACKENLEY LANE
DALES AVE
BRACKENLEY LA
SAWLEY CR
BRACKENLEY COURT
BRACKENLEY DRIVE
CAVENDISH VIEW
Mill Holme
Embsay & Bolton Abbey Steam Railway
Haw Beck
Ellergill House
The Cragg
MEGSONS CT
SKIPTON ROAD
BOW BR DR
Embsay
Quarry
Sewage Works
Castle Woods
CROSS BANK
CH
Embsay Junction
A65
Eller Beck
CRAG VW
HILLSIDE CL
THE CRESCENT
Haw Park
Skibeden
Low Skibeden
A59
Skipton Woods
THE CLOSE
HILLSIDE
THE GREEN
A65
Low Skibeden Farm
A6131
GREENACRES
LONG MEADOW
HAW BANK COURT
BD23
REGENT RD
UPLANDS
CLOVER HL
PASTURE CL
REGENT CRES
KINGSWAY
REGENT DRIVE
A6069
A65
CHAPEL HILL
Skipton Castle
Craven Coll
THE BAILEY
OVERDALE GR
War Meml
Town Hall & Craven Mus
PRINCES DR
PRINCES CR
WINDSOR AVE
C Offs
OTLEY ROAD
ROPE WALK
Skipton Law Courts
ST JAMES CT
AIREDALE AV
HURRS ROAD
MOORVIEW WAY
Close House
NEWMARKET ST
SUMMOOR DR
MOORLAND TERRACE
PETYT GR
THE GINNEL MEWS
DUKE ST
Craven Court Sh Ctr
NEVILLE ST
LITTLE BROOK
MOOR CR
SHORTBANK ROAD
SHORT-BANK CL
ALDERSLEY AVE
HILLSIDE CR
LYTHAM GDNS
NELSON ST
BROUGHAM ST
Brougham Street Parish Church Sch
MONTGOMERY ST
DORSET ST
GREATWOOD AV
WESTERN RD
MOORVIEW
HEATHER VW
CROOK RISE
TILE CL
RUSSELL ST
SACKVILLE ST
BRINDLEY WHARF
UNION HOUSE
Reservoir
SPENCER WK
Shale Plantation
Skipton Moor
HOLLINGWORTH CLOSE
SIMBACH CL
FIRTH STREET
Greatwood Com Prim Sch
Mast
NORTH PARADE
PINHAW ROAD
BEAMSLEY CT
ROMBALDS DR
SHARPHAW AV
ROUGHAW RD
CAWDER GREEN
Great Wood Plantation
Vicar's Allotment
SHARPHAW AVENUE
RAMSHAW DR
CAWDER ROAD
CAWDER MEWS
CAWDER MS
Standard Crag
CAWDER LANE
CAWDER GHYLL
Cawder Hall Farm
CAWDER LA
Horse Close Farm
High Bradley Moor
Skipton Pits
Standard
BD20
A6131
99
00
01
A3
1 SOUTHEY ST
2 BYRON ST
3 COWPER ST
4 MILTON ST
5 UPPER SACKVILLE ST
6 EAST CASTLE ST
7 SIDGWICK CT
8 GOSCHEN ST
9 CROMWELL ST
10 FAIRFAX ST
11 LAMBERT ST
12 WELLINGTON ST
13 DEVONSHIRE ST
14 EAST NEVILLE ST
15 ROMILLE ST
16 DAWSON ST
17 GEORGE ST
18 ROWLAND ST
19 WESTMORLAND ST
20 BROOKSIDE
B4
1 WHARFEDALE CL
2 WENSLEYDALE AVE
3 HURRS RD
4 RANKIN'S WELL RD
5 SPRINGFIELDS
6 QUEEN ST
7 KING ST
173
174

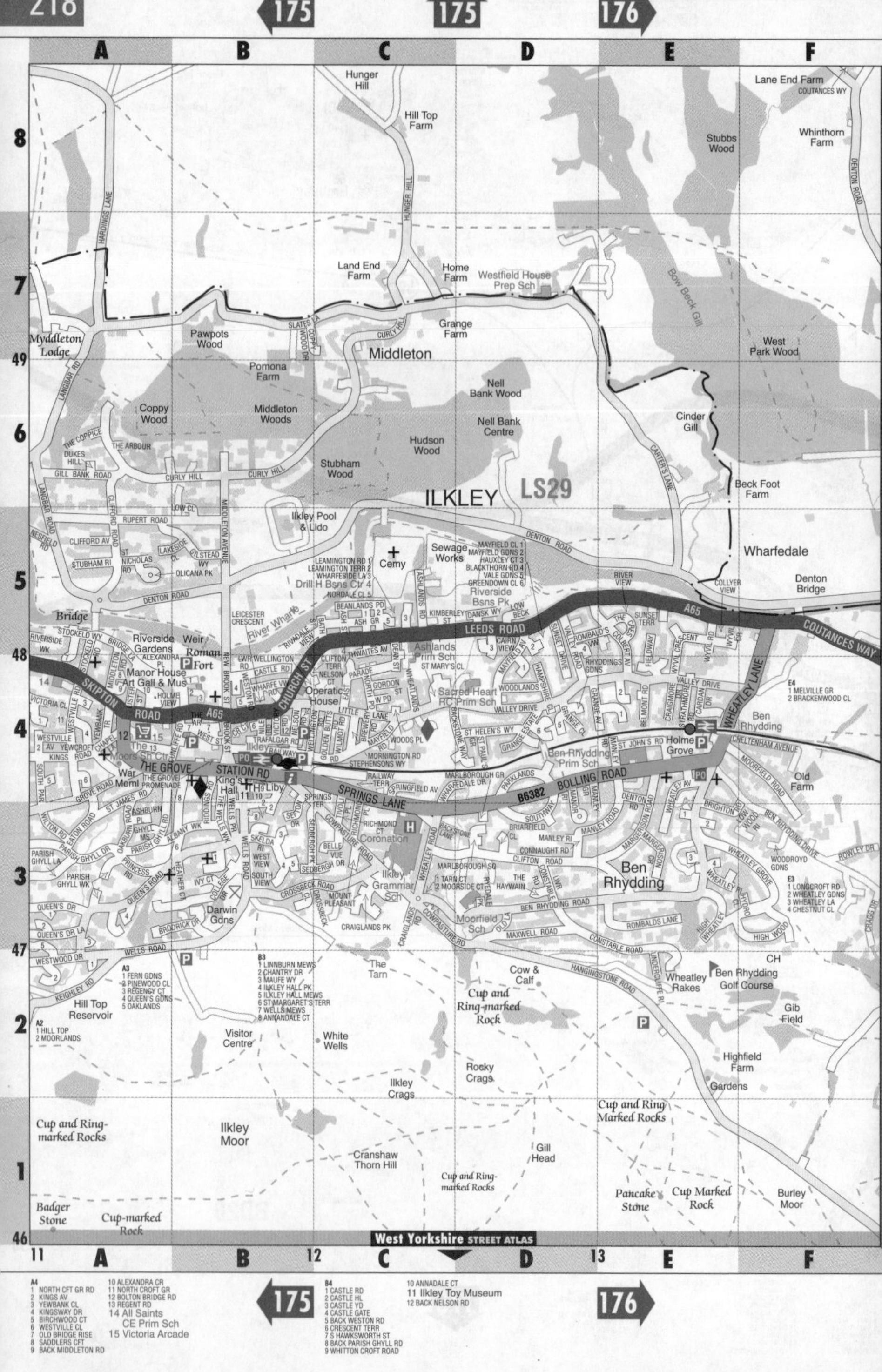

ILKLEY

LS29

Wharfedale

Middleton

Ben Rhydding

Ilkley Moor

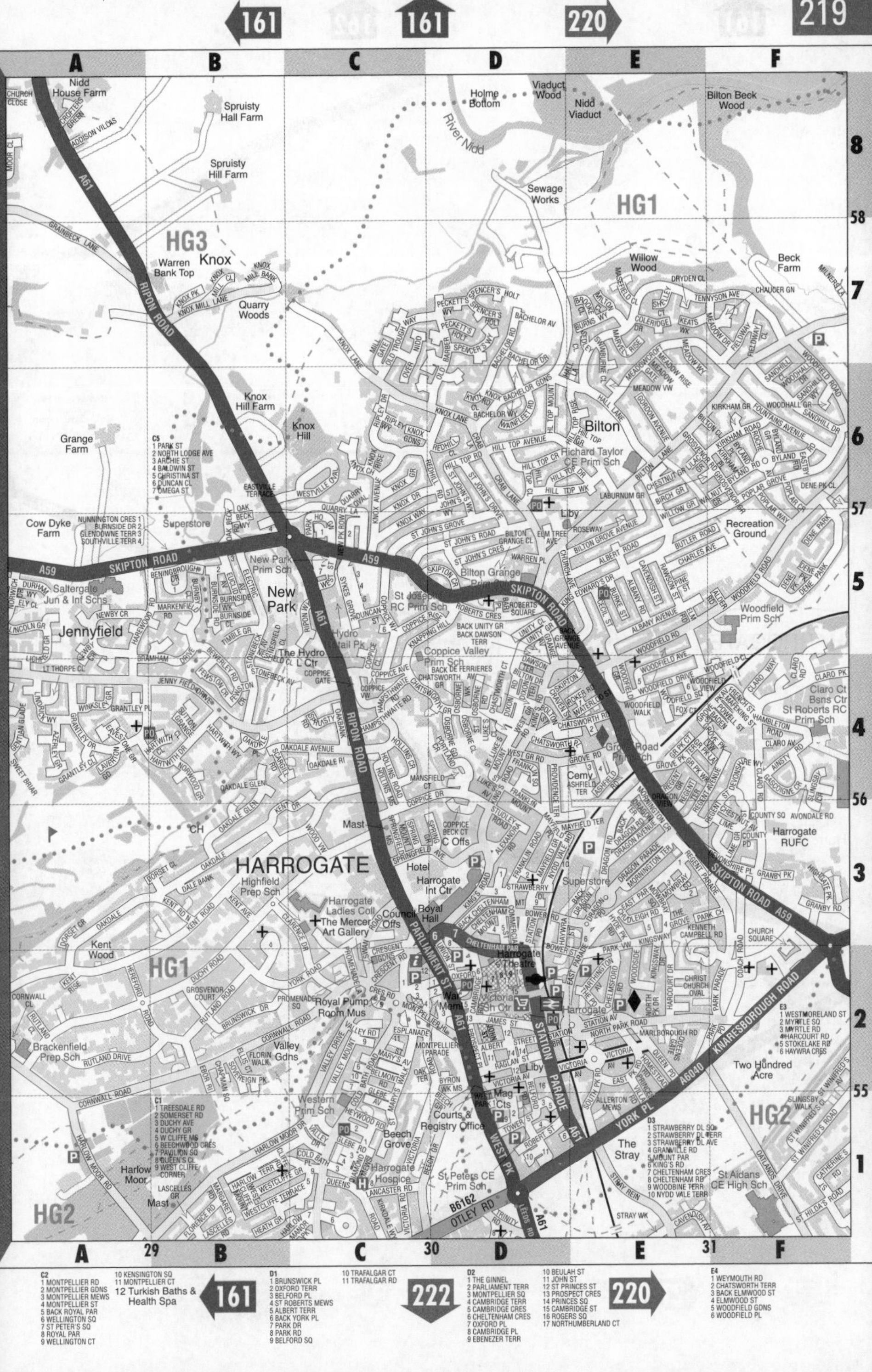

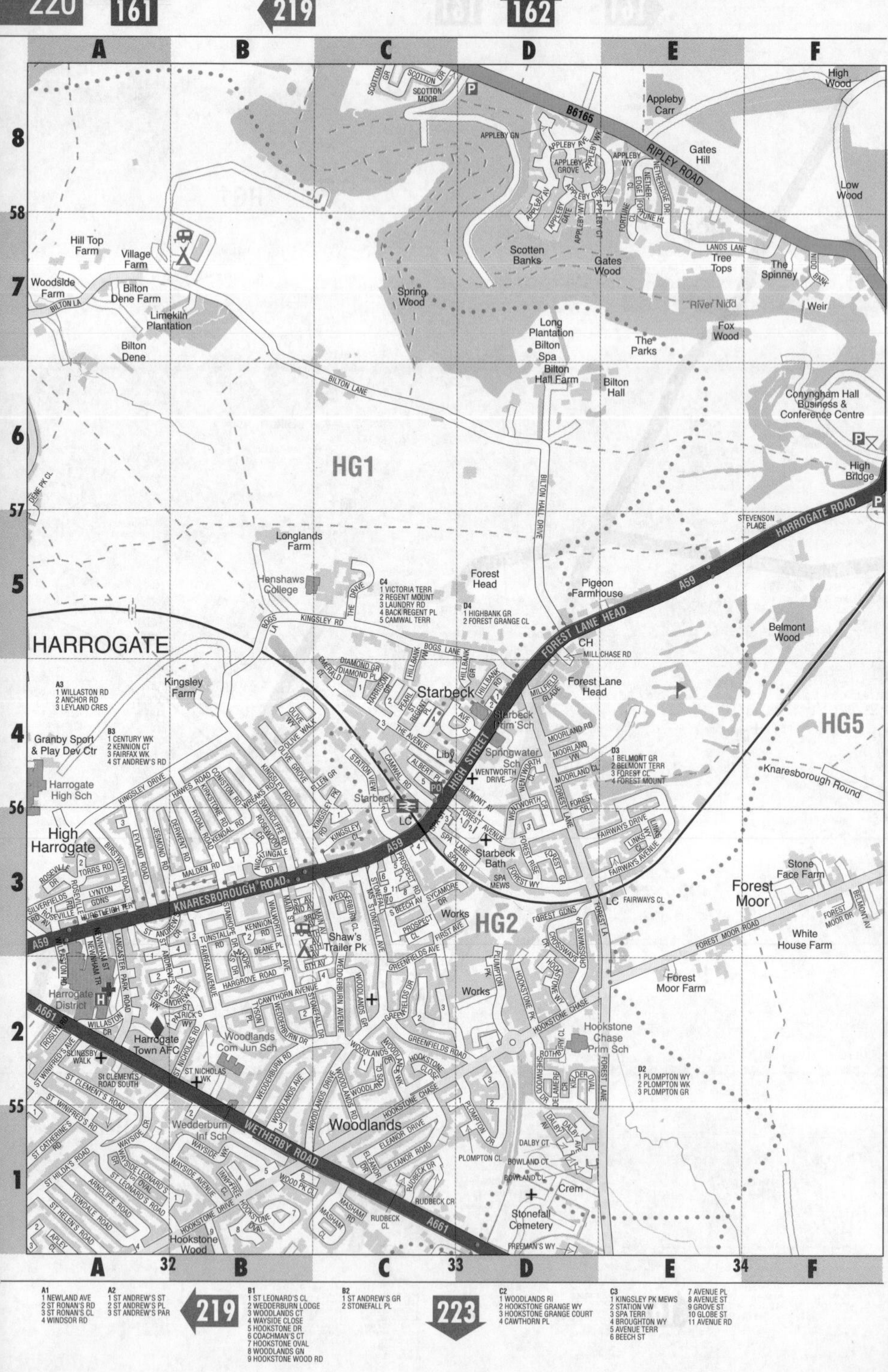
161
219
162
HARROGATE
HG1
HG2
HG5
Starbeck
High Harrogate
Woodlands
Forest Moor
Appleby Carr
Gates Hill
High Wood
Low Wood
Hill Top Farm
Village Farm
Woodside Farm
Bilton Dene Farm
Limekiln Plantation
Bilton Dene
Scotten Banks
Gates Wood
Tree Tops
The Spinney
Spring Wood
River Nidd
Weir
Long Plantation
Bilton Spa
Bilton Hall Farm
Bilton Hall
The Parks
Fox Wood
Conyngham Hall Business & Conference Centre
High Bridge
Longlands Farm
Henshaws College
Forest Head
Pigeon Farmhouse
Belmont Wood
Forest Lane Head
Kingsley Farm
Granby Sport & Play Dev Ctr
Harrogate High Sch
Starbeck Prim Sch
Springwater Sch
Starbeck Bath
Knaresborough Round
Stone Face Farm
White House Farm
Forest Moor Farm
Shaw's Trailer Pk
Works
Harrogate District
Harrogate Town AFC
Woodlands Com Jun Sch
Hookstone Chase Prim Sch
Wedderburn Inf Sch
Hookstone Wood
Stonefall Cemetery
Crem
B6165
RIPLEY ROAD
HARROGATE ROAD
A59
FOREST LANE HEAD
HIGH STREET
KNARESBOROUGH ROAD
WETHERBY ROAD
A661
BILTON LANE
BILTON HALL DRIVE
KINGSLEY RD
BOGS LANE
FOREST LANE
FOREST MOOR ROAD
C4
1 VICTORIA TERR
2 REGENT MOUNT
3 LAUNDRY RD
4 BACK REGENT PL
5 CAMWAL TERR
D4
1 HIGHBANK GR
2 FOREST GRANGE CL
A3
1 WILLASTON RD
2 ANCHOR RD
3 LEYLAND CRES
B3
1 CENTURY WK
2 KENNION CT
3 FAIRFAX WK
4 ST ANDREW'S RD
D3
1 BELMONT GR
2 BELMONT TERR
3 FOREST CL
4 FOREST MOUNT
D2
1 PLOMPTON WY
2 PLOMPTON WK
3 PLOMPTON GR
A
B
C
D
E
F
32
33
34
55
56
57
58
1
2
3
4
5
6
7
8
A1
1 NEWLAND AVE
2 ST RONAN'S RD
3 ST RONAN'S CL
4 WINDSOR RD
A2
1 ST ANDREW'S ST
2 ST ANDREW'S PL
3 ST ANDREW'S PAR
B1
1 ST LEONARD'S CL
2 WEDDERBURN LODGE
3 WOODLANDS CT
4 WAYSIDE CLOSE
5 HOOKSTONE DR
6 COACHMAN'S CT
7 HOOKSTONE OVAL
8 WOODLANDS GN
9 HOOKSTONE WOOD RD
B2
1 ST ANDREW'S GR
2 STONEFALL PL
223
C2
1 WOODLANDS RI
2 HOOKSTONE GRANGE WY
3 HOOKSTONE GRANGE COURT
4 CAWTHORN PL
C3
1 KINGSLEY PK MEWS
2 STATION VW
3 SPA TERR
4 BROUGHTON WY
5 AVENUE TERR
6 BEECH ST
7 AVENUE PL
8 AVENUE ST
9 GROVE ST
10 GLOBE ST
11 AVENUE RD

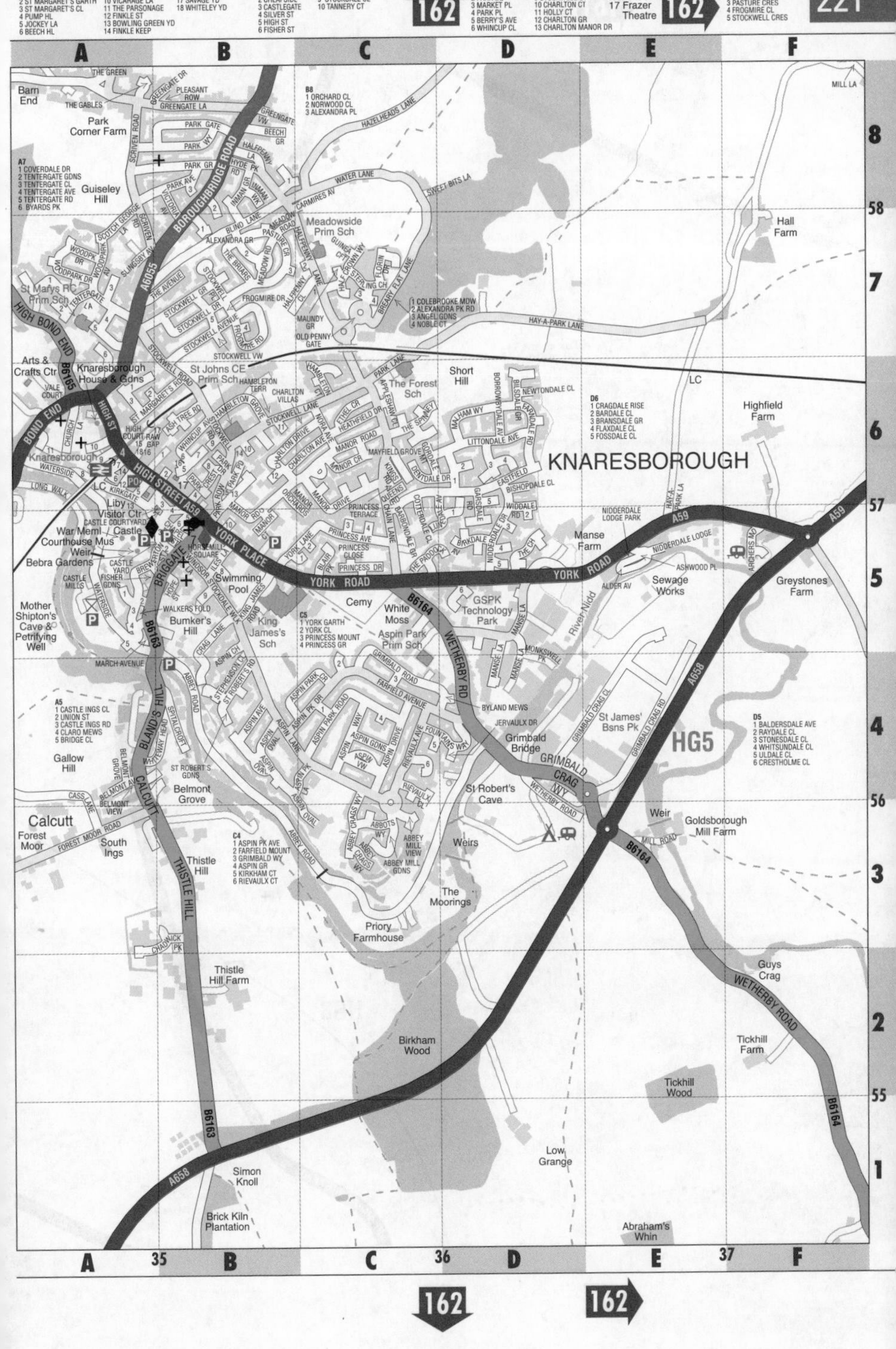
A6
1 ST MARGARET'S GDNS
2 ST MARGARET'S GARTH
3 ST MARGARET'S CL
4 PUMP HL
5 JOCKEY LA
6 BEECH HL
7 WATER BAG BANK
9 STATION RD
10 VICARAGE LA
11 THE PARSONAGE
12 FINKLE ST
13 BOWLING GREEN YD
14 FINKLE KEEP
15 PROSPECT TERR
16 WEST VIEW TERR
17 SAVAGE YD
18 WHITELEY YD
B5
1 WELLINGTON ST
2 CHEAPSIDE
3 CASTLEGATE
4 SILVER ST
5 HIGH ST
6 FISHER ST
7 GRACIOUS ST
8 ORCHARD CT
9 STOCKDALE CL
10 TANNERY CT
162
B6
1 COMMERCIAL YD
2 PARK SQ
3 MARKET PL
4 PARK PL
5 BERRY'S AVE
6 WHINCUP CL
7 WHINCUP GR
8 PARK CL
9 STOCKWELL CT
10 CHARLTON CT
11 HOLLY CT
12 CHARLTON GR
13 CHARLTON MANOR DR
14 PARK TERR
15 MANOR GDNS
16 BERRYS CT
17 Frazer Theatre
162
B7
1 NORWOOD CT
2 HAWTHORN AVE
3 PASTURE CRES
4 FROGMIRE CL
5 STOCKWELL CRES
A
B
C
D
E
F
B8
1 ORCHARD CL
2 NORWOOD CL
3 ALEXANDRA PL
A7
1 COVERDALE DR
2 TENTERGATE GDNS
3 TENTERGATE CL
4 TENTERGATE AVE
5 TENTERGATE RD
6 BYARDS PK
Barn End
Park Corner Farm
Guiseley Hill
St Marys RC Prim Sch
Meadowside Prim Sch
Hall Farm
MILL LA
HAZELHEADS LANE
WATER LANE
SWEET BITS LA
CARMIRES AV
BOROUGHBRIDGE ROAD
A6055
HIGH BOND END
BOND END
B6165
HIGH ST
HIGH STREET A59
YORK PLACE
YORK ROAD
A59
1 COLEBROOKE MDW
2 ALEXANDRA PK RD
3 ANGEL GDNS
4 NOBLE CT
HAY-A-PARK LANE
BREARY FLAT LANE
STOCKWELL AVENUE
STOCKWELL ROAD
Arts & Crafts Ctr
Knaresborough House & Gdns
St Johns CE Prim Sch
The Forest Sch
Short Hill
LC
D6
1 CRAGDALE RISE
2 BARDALE CL
3 BRANSDALE GR
4 FLAXDALE CL
5 FOSSDALE CL
Highfield Farm
KNARESBOROUGH
Knaresborough
Liby
Visitor Ctr
War Meml
Castle
Courthouse Mus
Weir
Bebra Gardens
Swimming Pool
NIDDERDALE LODGE PARK
Manse Farm
Sewage Works
Greystones Farm
Mother Shipton's Cave & Petrifying Well
Bumker's Hill
King James's Sch
Cemy
White Moss
C5
1 YORK GARTH
2 YORK CL
3 PRINCESS MOUNT
4 PRINCESS GR
Aspin Park Prim Sch
GSPK Technology Park
River Nidd
WETHERBY RD
B6164
B6163
MARCH AVENUE
A5
1 CASTLE INGS CL
2 UNION ST
3 CASTLE INGS RD
4 CLARO MEWS
5 BRIDGE CL
Gallow Hill
BLAND'S HILL
CALCUTT
Belmont Grove
St James' Bsns Pk
HG5
A658
D5
1 BALDERSDALE AVE
2 RAYDALE CL
3 STONESDALE CL
4 WHITSUNDALE CL
5 ULDALE CL
6 CRESTHOLME CL
Grimbald Bridge
GRIMBALD CRAG WY
St Robert's Cave
Calcutt
Forest Moor
South Ings
Thistle Hill
THISTLE HILL
C4
1 ASPIN PK AVE
2 FARFIELD MEWS
3 GRIMBALD WY
4 ASPIN GR
5 KIRKHAM CT
6 RIEVAULX CT
Weirs
Weir
Goldsborough Mill Farm
MILL ROAD
The Moorings
Priory Farmhouse
Thistle Hill Farm
Guys Crag
WETHERBY ROAD
Birkham Wood
Tickhill Farm
Tickhill Wood
Low Grange
Simon Knoll
Brick Kiln Plantation
Abraham's Whin
8
7
6
5
4
3
2
1
58
57
56
55
35
36
37
162
162

161
219

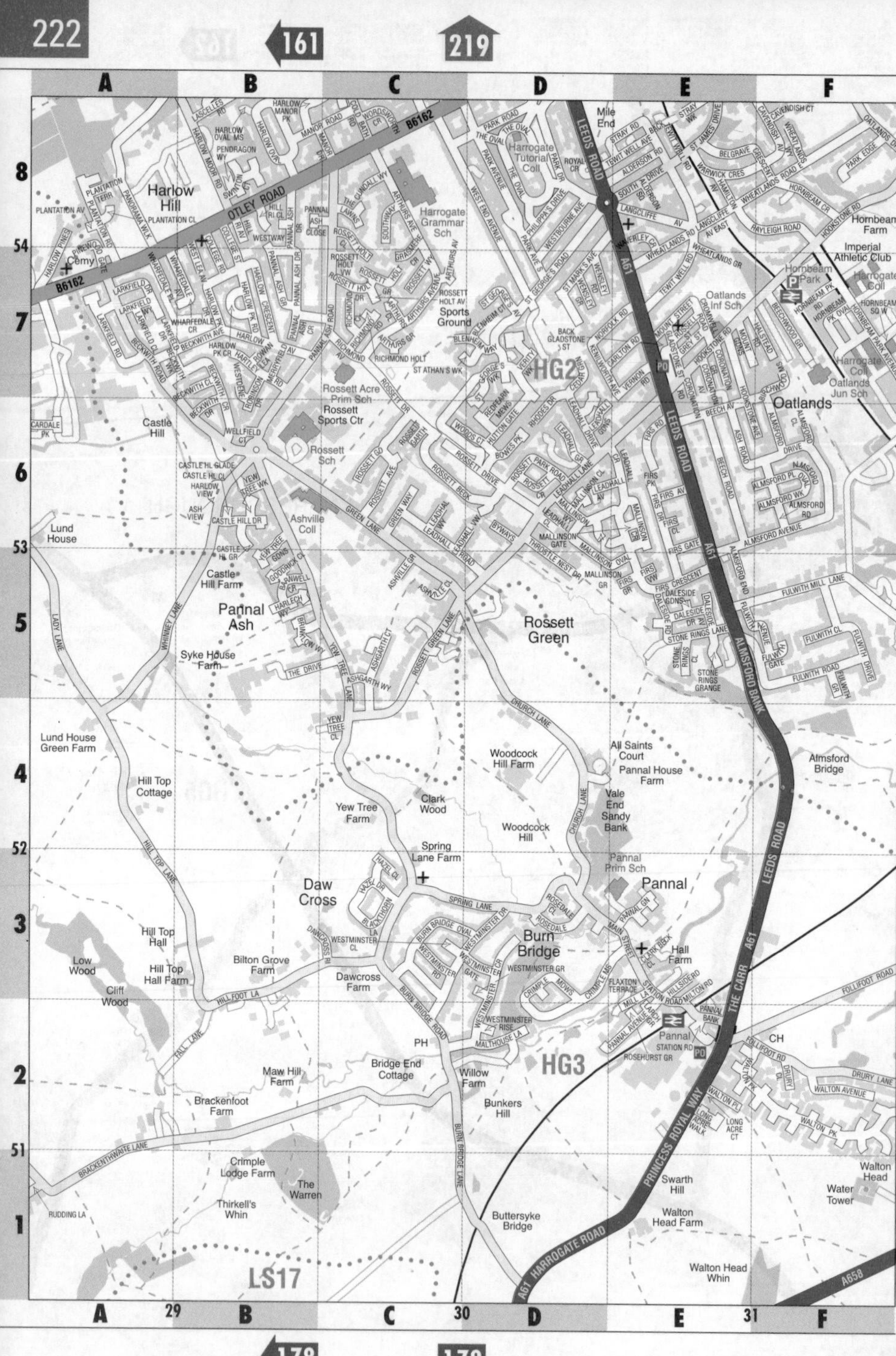
A
B
C
D
E
F
8
54
7
6
53
5
4
52
3
2
51
1
29
30
31
Harlow Hill
OTLEY ROAD
B6162
Cemy
Harrogate Grammar Sch
Harrogate Tutorial Coll
Mile End
LEEDS ROAD
A61
Hornbeam Farm
Imperial Athletic Club
Hornbeam Park
Harrogate Coll
Oatlands Inf Sch
Sports Ground
HG2
Oatlands
Harrogate Coll
Oatlands Jun Sch
Rossett Acre Prim Sch
Rossett Sports Ctr
Rossett Sch
Castle Hill
Ashville Coll
Lund House
Castle Hill Farm
Pannal Ash
Rossett Green
Syke House Farm
ALMSFORD BANK
STONE RINGS GRANGE
Lund House Green Farm
Woodcock Hill Farm
All Saints Court
Pannal House Farm
Almsford Bridge
Hill Top Cottage
Yew Tree Farm
Clark Wood
Vale End Sandy Bank
Woodcock Hill
Spring Lane Farm
Pannal Prim Sch
Pannal
Daw Cross
Hill Top Hall
Low Wood
Cliff Wood
Bilton Grove Farm
Hill Top Hall Farm
Dawcross Farm
Burn Bridge
Hall Farm
THE CARR
Pannal
PH
CH
Bridge End Cottage
HG3
Maw Hill Farm
Willow Farm
Brackenfoot Farm
Bunkers Hill
PRINCESS ROYAL WAY
BRACKENTHWAITE LANE
Crimple Lodge Farm
The Warren
Swarth Hill
Walton Head
Water Tower
Thirkell's Whin
Walton Head Farm
Buttersyke Bridge
HARROGATE ROAD
RUDDING LA
LS17
Walton Head Whin
A658
HILL TOP LANE
LADY LANE
WHINNEY LANE
CHURCH LANE
BURN BRIDGE LANE
BURN BRIDGE ROAD
SPRING LANE
FOLLIFOOT ROAD
DRURY LANE
WALTON AVENUE
FULWITH MILL LANE
ALMSFORD AVENUE
GREEN LANE
ROSSETT GREEN LANE
YEW TREE LANE

178
178

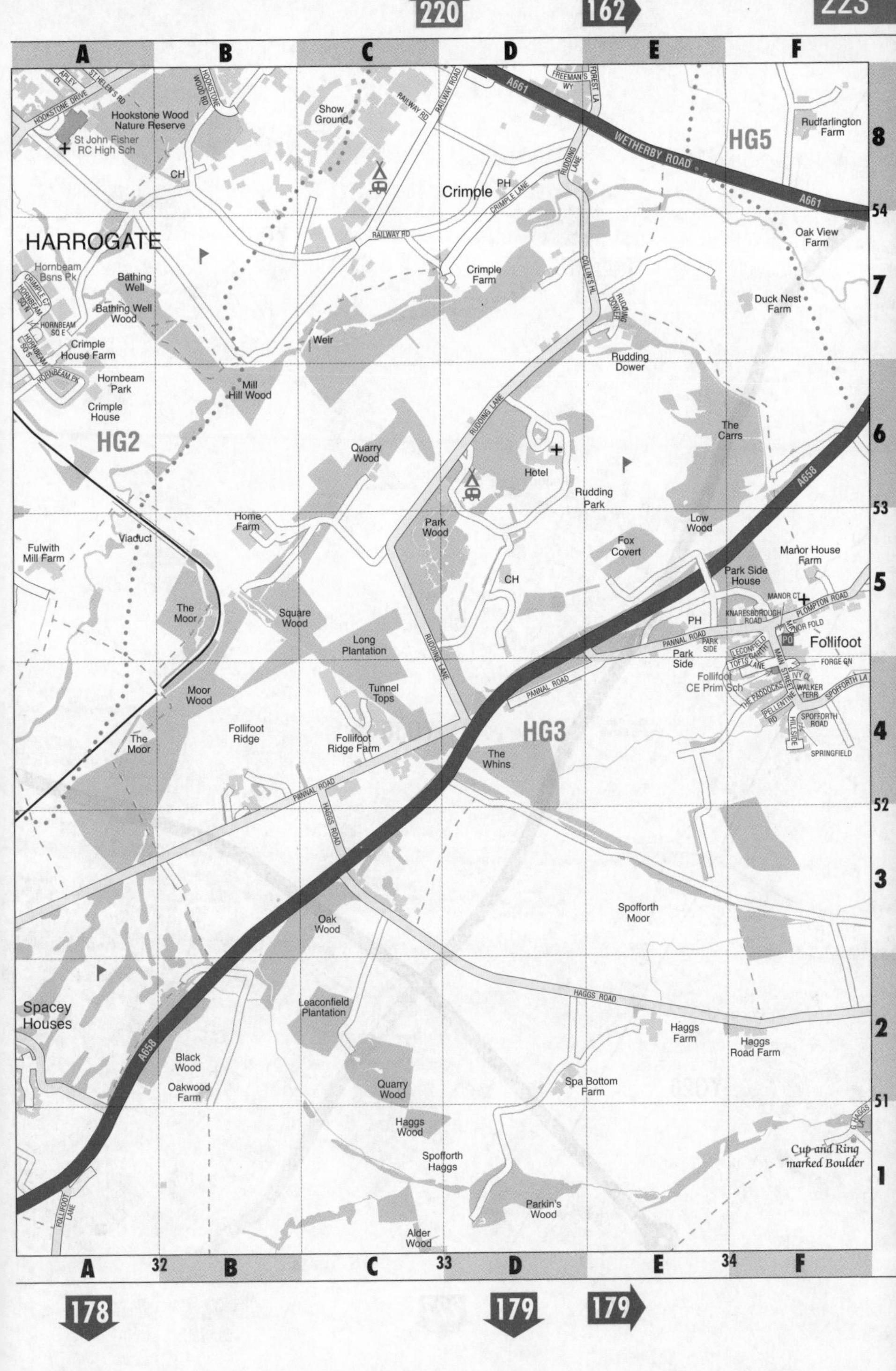

A **B** **C** **D** **E** **F**

8

Hookstone Wood
Nature Reserve

St John Fisher
RC High Sch

CH

Show Ground

Railway Rd

Crimple

PH

Crimple Lane

WETHERBY ROAD

A661

Freeman's Wy

Forst La

HG5

Rudfarlington
Farm

54

HARROGATE

Hornbeam
Bsns Pk

Bathing
Well

Bathing Well
Wood

Crimple
House Farm

Railway Rd

Crimple
Farm

Oak View
Farm

Duck Nest
Farm

7

Weir

Hornbeam
Park

Mill
Hill Wood

Rudding
Dower

Crimple
House

HG2

Quarry
Wood

Hotel

Rudding
Lane

Rudding
Park

The
Carrs

A658

6

53

Fulwith
Mill Farm

Viaduct

Home
Farm

Park
Wood

CH

Fox
Covert

Low
Wood

Manor House
Farm

Park Side
House

MANOR CL

Plompton Road

PO

Follifoot

5

The
Moor

Square
Wood

Long
Plantation

Knaresborough
Road

PH

Pannal Road

Park
Side

Park
Side

Follifoot
CE Prim Sch

Forge Gn

Spofforth La

Moor
Wood

Tunnel
Tops

Rudding Lane

Pannal Road

HG3

The Whins

Walker
Terr

Spofforth
Road

The
Moor

Follifoot
Ridge

Follifoot
Ridge Farm

Springfield

4

52

Pannal Road

Haggs Road

3

Oak
Wood

Spofforth
Moor

Spacey
Houses

A658

Leaconfield
Plantation

Haggs Road

Haggs
Farm

Haggs
Road Farm

2

Black
Wood

Quarry
Wood

Spa Bottom
Farm

51

Oakwood
Farm

Haggs
Wood

Cup and Ring
marked Boulder

Spofforth
Haggs

Parkin's
Wood

1

Follifoot Lane

Alder
Wood

A 32 **B** **C** 33 **D** **E** 34 **F**

◄ 165
166

A B C D E F

8

Hall Moor

Wide Open Farm

CH

Woodside Farm

SKELTON LANE

Park Farm

MOOR LANE

YO32

Wigginton Moor

7

A19

Hurns Bridge

Skelton Moor

Nova Scotia Plantation

57

6

New Farm

Hall

Skelton

MOORLANDS LANE

St Catherines

Skelton Moor

MOOR LANE

B5
1 THE GREEN
2 THE MEADOWS
3 ORCHARD VIEW
4 THE WHEELHOUSE
5 THE DELL
6 ARTHUR PLACE

THE VILLAGE

Skelton Prim Sch

Skelton Plantation

5

PH

CHURCH LANE

ST GILES ROAD

1 RATCLIFFE CT
2 GREGORY CL
3 ST CATHERINES CL

Rawcliffe Moor

56

CH

STRIPE LANE

1 THE ROWMANS
2 THE BEECHES

YO30

E3
1 CAITHNESS CL
2 CONWAY CL
3 HATFIELD CL
4 OSBOURNE DR
5 GREENWICH CL
6 SOMERSET CL
7 HIGHGROVE CL
8 LONGWOOD LINK
9 WINSCAR GR
10 BROADSTONE WY
11 MITCHELL WY

Rawcliffe Moor Farm

4

Folly Bridge

Skelton Park Trading Estate

Hotel

SHIPTON ROAD

Poplar Plantation

1 LANGSETT GR
2 RINGSTONE RD
3 BLAKELEY GR
4 ROSEBERRY DR

A1237

Clifton Moor Sh Ctr

3

Overton Ings

River Ouse

Skelton Bridge

CHURCH LANE

Moat

RAWCLIFFE LANDING

Rawcliffe Farm

Tom Cobleighs Riverside Farm

BLENHEIM CT

MARLBOROUGH CL

A19

A1237

SHIPTON ROAD

E2
1 CONINGHAM AVE
2 MANOR PK GR
3 ELMA GR
4 BARTON CL
5 RAWCLIFFE CL
6 CHESHIRE CL
7 DEANHEAD GR
8 SWINTON CL

Clifton Moor Retail Park

Rawcliffe Village

Rawcliffe Ind Est

STIRLING RD

Pioneer Bsns Pk

Lakeside County Prim Sch

55

Poppleton Hall Gd

Manor Farm

Nether Poppleton

YO26

HAREWOOD CL 1
KENSINGTON RD 2

2

ORCHARD RD

Hotel

WESTMINSTER PLACE

Poppleton Ings

Rawcliffe Ings

Sewage Works

P&R

Rawcliffe Inf Sch

Rawcliffe

STAINDALE CL

DALE DIKE GR

HAVERAH COURT

1

A1231

A19

54

56 A B 57 C D 58 E F

E1
1 CONISTON CL
2 WASDALE CL
3 GARBURN GR
4 SCAFELL CL
5 LOWESWATER RD
6 FYLINGDALES AVE

F1
1 EMBLETON DR
2 COLEDALE CL
3 LEIGHTON CFT
4 BARMBY CL
5 GRASMERE GR
6 BARDEN CT
7 SOUTHOLME DR
8 MILTON CARR
9 FEWSTON DR

10 REIGHTON DR
F2
1 MOREHALL CL
2 WHARNSCLIFFE DR
3 RYBURN CL

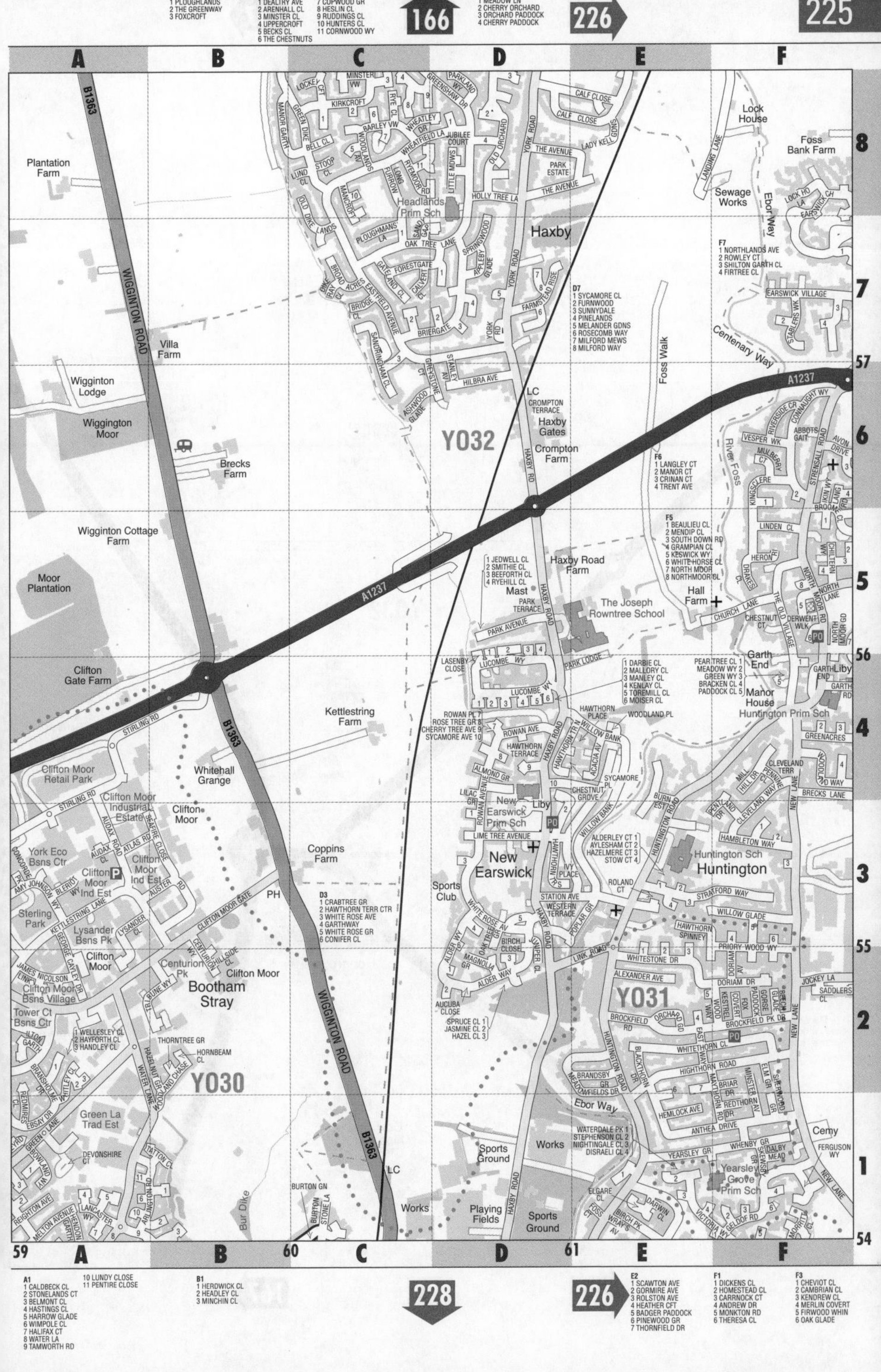
C7
1 PLOUGHLANDS
2 THE GREENWAY
3 FOXCROFT
C8
1 DEALTRY AVE
2 ARENHALL CL
3 MINSTER CL
4 UPPERCROFT
5 BECKS CL
6 THE CHESTNUTS
7 COPWOOD GR
8 HESLIN CL
9 RUDDINGS CL
10 HUNTERS CL
11 CORNWOOD WY
166
D8
1 MEADOW LN
2 CHERRY ORCHARD
3 ORCHARD PADDOCK
4 CHERRY PADDOCK
226
A
B
C
D
E
F
8
7
57
6
5
56
4
3
55
2
1
54
59
60
61
Plantation Farm
Villa Farm
Wigginton Lodge
Wiggington Moor
Brecks Farm
Wigginton Cottage Farm
Moor Plantation
Clifton Gate Farm
Kettlestring Farm
Whitehall Grange
Clifton Moor
Clifton Moor Retail Park
Clifton Moor Industrial Estate
York Eco Bsns Ctr
Clifton Moor Ind Est
Sterling Park
Lysander Bsns Pk
Centurion Pk
Bootham Stray
Clifton Moor Bsns Village
Tower Ct Bsns Ctr
Green La Trad Est
Coppins Farm
Y030
Y032
Y031
WIGGINTON ROAD
B1363
A1237
Haxby
Headlands Prim Sch
YORK ROAD
HAXBY ROAD
Haxby Gates
Crompton Farm
CROMPTON TERRACE
Haxby Road Farm
The Joseph Rowntree School
New Earswick
New Earswick Prim Sch
Sports Club
Huntington
Huntington Sch
Huntington Prim Sch
Lock House
Foss Bank Farm
Sewage Works
Ebor Way
Centenary Way
Foss Walk
River Foss
Hall Farm
Garth End
Manor House
Earswick Village
Works
Sports Ground
Playing Fields
Yearsley Grove Prim Sch
Cemy
Bur Dike
D7
1 SYCAMORE CL
2 FURNWOOD
3 SUNNYDALE
4 PINELANDS
5 MELANDER GDNS
6 ROSECOMB WAY
7 MILFORD MEWS
8 MILFORD WAY
F7
1 NORTHLANDS AVE
2 ROWLEY CT
3 SHILTON GARTH CL
4 FIRTREE CL
F6
1 LANGLEY CT
2 MANOR CT
3 CRINAN CT
4 TRENT AVE
F5
1 BEAULIEU CL
2 MENDIP CL
3 SOUTH DOWN RD
4 GRAMPIAN CL
5 KESWICK WY
6 WHITE HORSE CL
7 NORTH MOOR
8 NORTHMOOR CL
1 JEDWELL CL
2 SMITHIE CL
3 BEEFORTH CL
4 RYEHILL CL
1 DARBIE CL
2 MALLORY CL
3 MANLEY CL
4 KENLAY CL
5 TOREMILL CL
6 MOISER CL
ROWAN PL 7
ROSE TREE GR 8
CHERRY TREE AVE 9
SYCAMORE AVE 10
PEAR TREE CL 1
MEADOW WY 2
GREEN WY 3
BRACKEN CL 4
PADDOCK CL 5
ALDERLEY CT 1
AYLESHAM CT 2
HAZELMERE CT 3
STOW CT 4
D3
1 CRABTREE GR
2 HAWTHORN TERR CTR
3 WHITE ROSE AVE
4 GARTHWAY
5 WHITE ROSE GR
6 CONIFER CL
SPRUCE CL 1
JASMINE CL 2
HAZEL CL 3
1 WELLESLEY CL
2 HAYFORTH CL
3 HANDLEY CL
WATERDALE PK 1
STEPHENSON CL 2
NIGHTINGALE CL 3
DISRAELI CL 4
228
226
A1
1 CALDBECK CL
2 STONELANDS CT
3 BELMONT CL
4 HASTINGS CL
5 HARROW GLADE
6 WIMPOLE CL
7 HALIFAX CT
8 WATER LA
9 TAMWORTH RD
10 LUNDY CLOSE
11 PENTIRE CLOSE
B1
1 HERDWICK CL
2 HEADLEY CL
3 MINCHIN CL
E2
1 SCAWTON AVE
2 GORMIRE AVE
3 ROLSTON AVE
4 HEATHER CFT
5 BADGER PADDOCK
6 PINEWOOD GR
7 THORNFIELD DR
F1
1 DICKENS CL
2 HOMESTEAD CL
3 CARRNOCK CT
4 ANDREW DR
5 MONKTON RD
6 THERESA CL
F3
1 CHEVIOT CL
2 CAMBRIAN CL
3 KENDREW CL
4 MERLIN COVERT
5 FIRWOOD WHIN
6 OAK GLADE

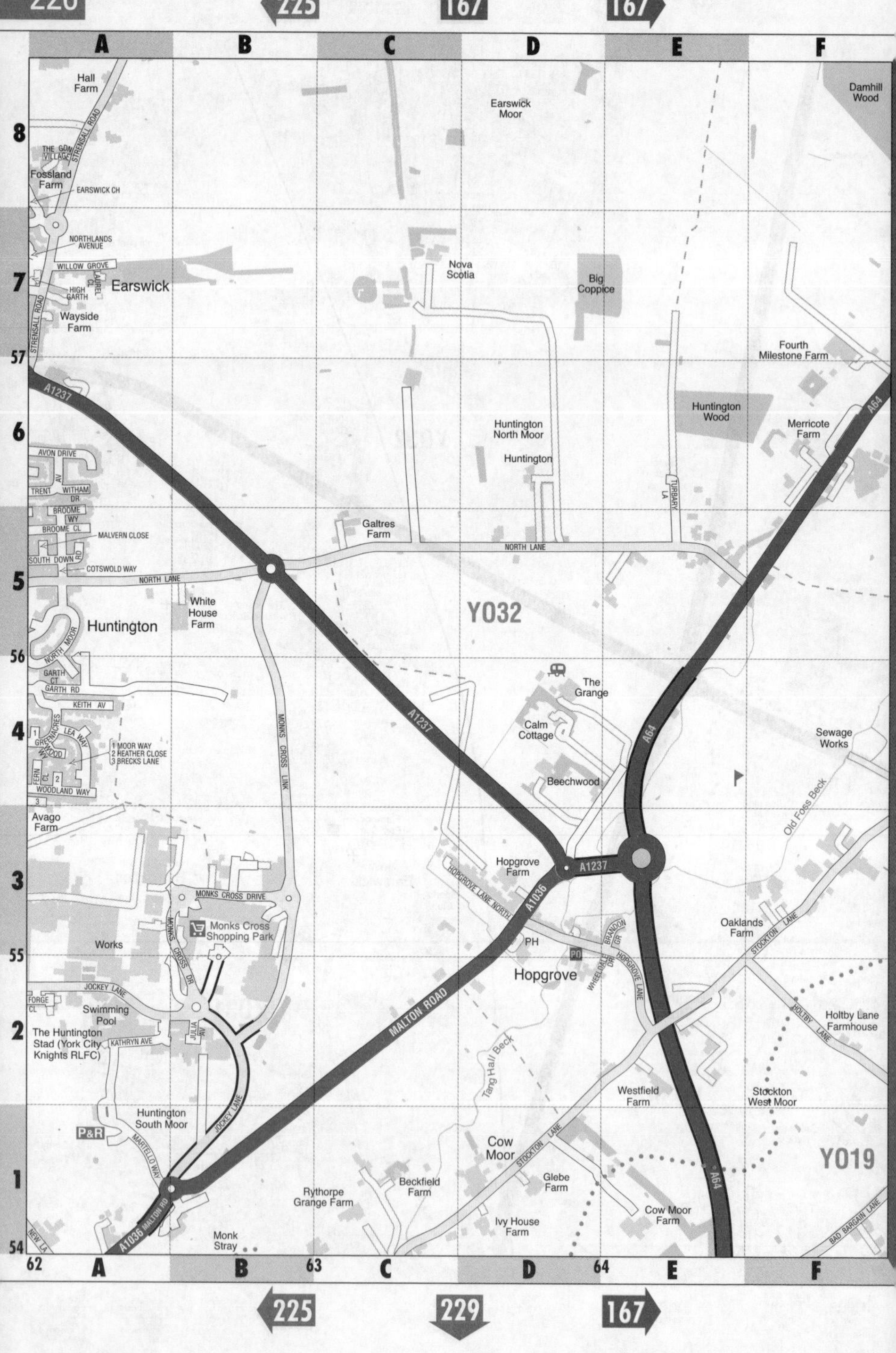
A
B
C
D
E
F
Hall Farm
STRENSALL ROAD
THE GDN VILLAGE
Fossland Farm
EARSWICK CH
NORTHLANDS AVENUE
WILLOW GROVE
LAUREL CL
HIGH GARTH
Earswick
Wayside Farm
STRENSALL ROAD
Earswick Moor
Nova Scotia
Big Coppice
Damhill Wood
Fourth Milestone Farm
Huntington Wood
Merricote Farm
A64
A1237
AVON DRIVE
TRENT AV
WITHAM DR
BROOME WY
BROOME CL
MALVERN CLOSE
SOUTH DOWN RD
COTSWOLD WAY
NORTH LANE
Huntington North Moor
Huntington
TURBARY LA
Galtres Farm
NORTH LANE
White House Farm
Huntington
NORTH MOOR
YO32
GARTH CT
GARTH RD
KEITH AV
GREENACRES
LEA WAY
WYCOD
FERN CL
1 MOOR WAY
2 HEATHER CLOSE
3 BRECKS LANE
WOODLAND WAY
MONKS CROSS LINK
A1237
The Grange
Calm Cottage
Beechwood
A64
Sewage Works
Old Foss Beck
Avago Farm
MONKS CROSS DRIVE
Monks Cross Shopping Park
Works
MONKS CROSS DR
Hopgrove Farm
HOPGROVE LANE NORTH
A1237
A1036
PH
PO
BRANDON GR
WHEELDALE DR
HOPGROVE LANE
Hopgrove
Oaklands Farm
STOCKTON LANE
JOCKEY LANE
FORGE CL
Swimming Pool
The Huntington Stad (York City Knights RLFC)
KATHRYN AVE
JULIA AV
MALTON ROAD
Tang Hall Beck
HOLTBY LANE
Holtby Lane Farmhouse
Westfield Farm
Stockton West Moor
Huntington South Moor
P&R
MARTELLO WAY
JOCKEY LANE
Cow Moor
STOCKTON LANE
Glebe Farm
YO19
A64
Rythorpe Grange Farm
Beckfield Farm
Ivy House Farm
Cow Moor Farm
MALTON RD
A1036
NEW LA
Monk Stray
BAD BARGAIN LANE
8
7
57
6
5
56
4
3
55
2
1
54
62
63
64

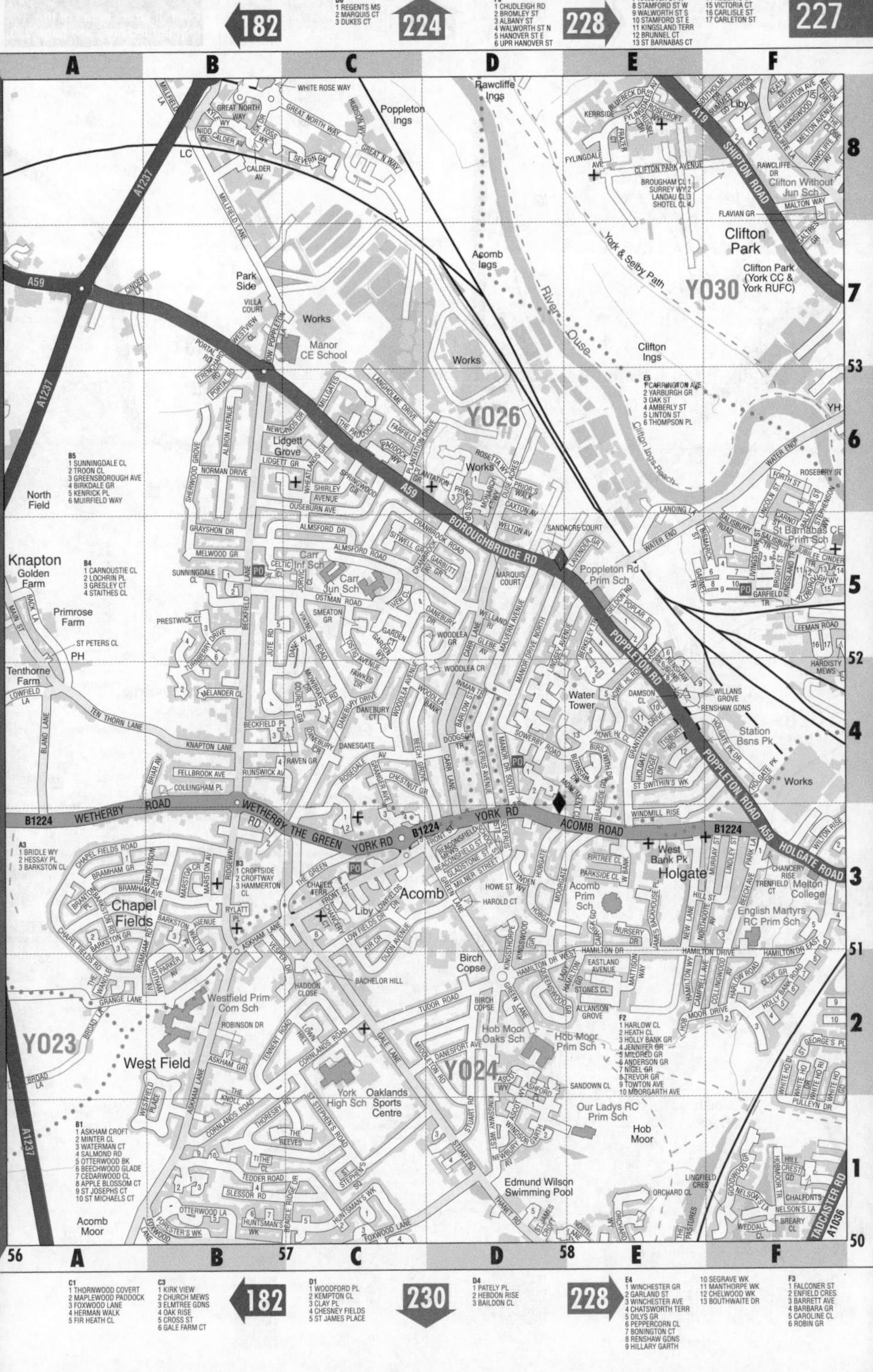
182
D6
1 REGENTS MS
2 MARQUIS CT
3 DUKES CT
224
F5
1 CHUDLEIGH RD
2 BROMLEY ST
3 ALBANY ST
4 WALWORTH ST N
5 HANOVER ST E
6 UPR HANOVER ST
228
7 HANOVER ST W
8 STAMFORD ST W
9 WALWORTH ST S
10 STAMFORD ST E
11 KINGSLAND TERR
12 BRUNNEL CT
13 ST BARNABAS CT
14 REGENTS CT
15 VICTORIA CT
16 CARLISLE ST
17 CARLETON ST
A
B
C
D
E
F
8
7
53
6
5
52
4
3
51
2
1
50
56
57
58
Rawcliffe Ings
Poppleton Ings
WHITE ROSE WAY
GREAT NORTH WAY
GREAT N WAY
SEVERN GN
CALDER AV
NIDD CL
MILLFIELD LA
MILLFIELD LANE
LC
A1237
A59
Park Side
VILLA COURT
Works
Manor CE School
Acomb Ings
River Ouse
York & Selby Path
Clifton Ings
Clifton Ings Reach
Clifton Park
Clifton Park (York CC & York RUFC)
Clifton Without Jun Sch
YO30
SHIPTON ROAD
A19
CLIFTON PARK AVENUE
FYLINGDALE AVE
KERRSIDE
BLUEBECK DR
ROSECROFT
BROUGHAM CL 1
SURREY WY 2
LANDAU CL 3
SHOTEL CL 4
RAWCLIFFE DR
MALTON WAY
FLAVIAN GR
MELTON AVENUE
LAWNSWOOD DR
REIGHTON AVE
RAWCLIFFE LA
Liby
E5
1 CARRINGTON AVE
2 YARBURGH GR
3 OAK ST
4 AMBERLY ST
5 LINTON ST
6 THOMPSON PL
YH
YO26
Lidgett Grove
B5
1 SUNNINGDALE CL
2 TROON CL
3 GREENSBOROUGH AVE
4 BIRKDALE GR
5 KENRICK PL
6 MUIRFIELD WAY
North Field
Knapton
Golden Farm
B4
1 CARNOUSTIE CL
2 LOCHRIN PL
3 GRESLEY CT
4 STAITHES CL
Primrose Farm
PH
Tenthorne Farm
ST PETERS CL
BACK LA
MAIN ST
LOWFIELD LA
BLAND LANE
TEN THORN LANE
KNAPTON LANE
BOROUGHBRIDGE RD
WATER END
LANDING LA
SALISBURY ROAD
St Barnabas CE Prim Sch
LEEMAN ROAD
HARDISTY MEWS
Poppleton Rd Prim Sch
POPPLETON RD
POPPLETON ROAD
Water Tower
WILLANS GROVE
RENSHAW GDNS
Station Bsns Pk
Works
Carr Inf Sch
Carr Jun Sch
MARQUIS COURT
SANDACRE COURT
BECKFIELD LANE
ALBION AVENUE
NORMAN DRIVE
SHERWOOD GROVE
GRAYSHON DR
MELWOOD GR
OUSEBURN AVE
ALMSFORD DR
ALMSFORD ROAD
OSTMAN ROAD
JUTE RD
DANEBURY DRIVE
DANESGATE
RAVEN GR
RUNSWICK AV
FELLBROOK AVE
COLLINGHAM PL
B1224
WETHERBY ROAD
THE GREEN
YORK RD
ACOMB ROAD
HOLGATE ROAD
A3
1 BRIDLE WY
2 HESSAY PL
3 BARKSTON CL
B3
1 CROFTSIDE
2 CROFTWAY
3 HAMMERTON CL
Chapel Fields
Acomb
Liby
West Bank Pk
Holgate
Acomb Prim Sch
Melton College
English Martyrs RC Prim Sch
CHANCERY RISE
TRENFIELD CT
HAMILTON DRIVE
HAMILTON DR EAST
Birch Copse
BACHELOR HILL
HADDON CLOSE
Westfield Prim Com Sch
ROBINSON DR
YO23
West Field
GRANGE LANE
BROAD LA
TUDOR ROAD
GALE LANE
Hob Moor Oaks Sch
Hob Moor Prim Sch
F2
1 HARLOW CL
2 HEATH CL
3 HOLLY BANK GR
4 JENNIFER GR
5 MILDRED GR
6 ANDERSON GR
7 NIGEL GR
8 TREVOR GR
9 TOWTON AVE
10 MOORGARTH AVE
YO24
York High Sch
Oaklands Sports Centre
SANDOWN CL
Our Ladys RC Prim Sch
Hob Moor
B1
1 ASKHAM CROFT
2 MINTER CL
3 WATERMAN CT
4 SALMOND RD
5 OTTERWOOD BK
6 BEECHWOOD GLADE
7 CEDARWOOD CL
8 APPLE BLOSSOM CT
9 ST JOSEPHS CT
10 ST MICHAELS CT
Acomb Moor
Edmund Wilson Swimming Pool
LINGFIELD CRES
ORCHARD CL
THE PASTURES
TADCASTER RD
A1036
CHALFONTS
NELSON'S LA
BREARY CL
WEDDALL CL
FOXWOOD LANE
HUNTSMAN'S WK
OTTERWOOD LA
SLESSOR RD
TEDDER ROAD
CORNLANDS ROAD
ASKHAM LANE
THORESBY RD
STUART RD
KINGSWAY WEST
THANET RD
C1
1 THORNWOOD COVERT
2 MAPLEWOOD PADDOCK
3 FOXWOOD LANE
4 HERMAN WALK
5 FIR HEATH CL
C3
1 KIRK VIEW
2 CHURCH MEWS
3 ELMTREE GDNS
4 OAK RISE
5 CROSS ST
6 GALE FARM CT
182
D1
1 WOODFORD PL
2 KEMPTON CL
3 CLAY PL
4 CHESNEY FIELDS
5 ST JAMES PLACE
230
D4
1 PATELY PL
2 HEBDON RISE
3 BAILDON CL
228
E4
1 WINCHESTER GR
2 GARLAND ST
3 WINCHESTER AVE
4 CHATSWORTH TERR
5 DILYS GR
6 PEPPERCORN CL
7 BONINGTON CT
8 RENSHAW GDNS
9 HILLARY GARTH
10 SEGRAVE WK
11 MANTHORPE WK
12 CHELWOOD WK
13 BOUTHWAITE DR
F3
1 FALCONER ST
2 ENFIELD CRES
3 BARRETT AVE
4 BARBARA GR
5 CAROLINE CL
6 ROBIN GR

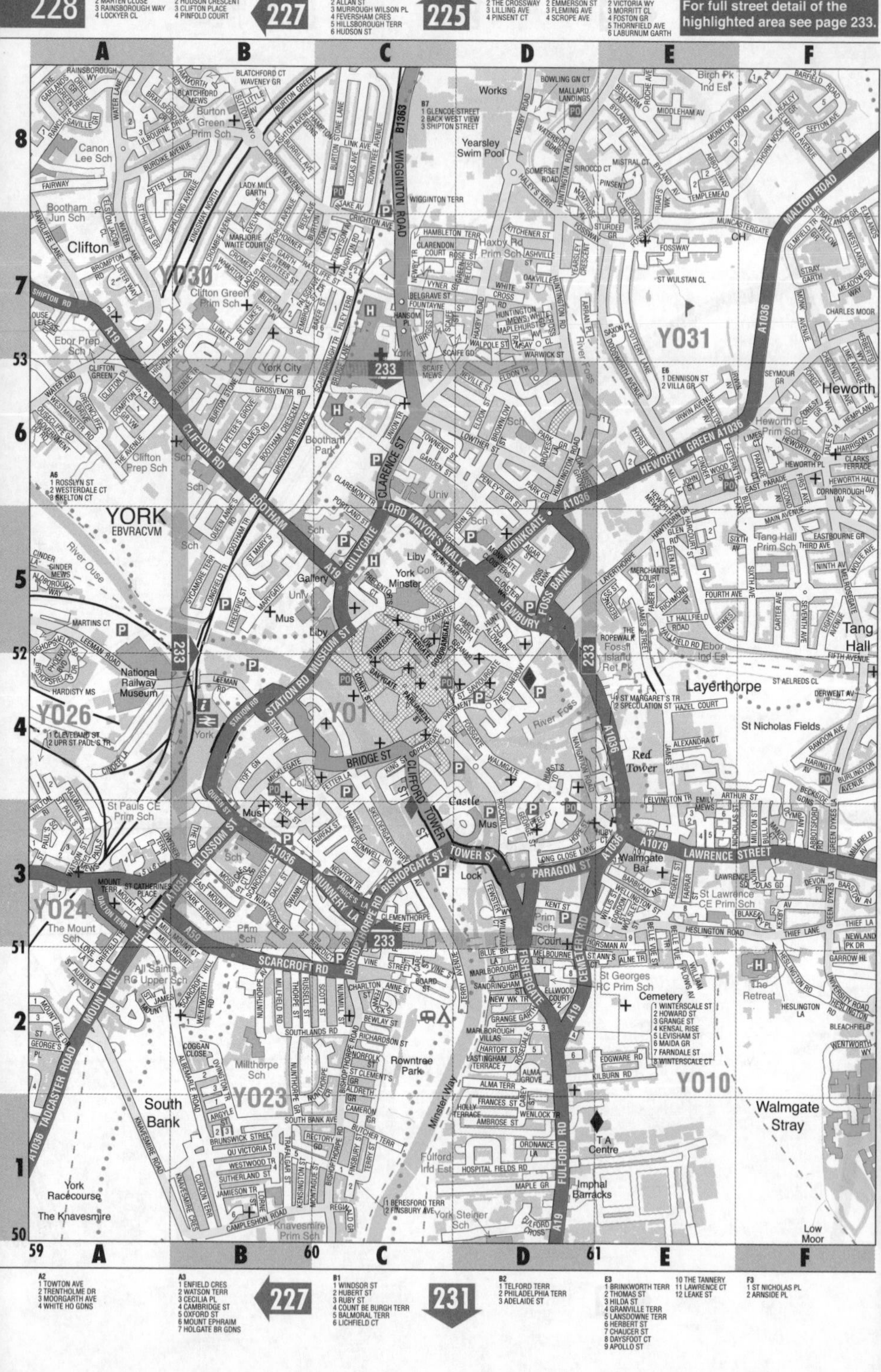
A8
1 LINDEN GROVE
2 MARTEN CLOSE
3 RAINSBOROUGH WAY
4 LOCKYER CL
A7
1 BELCOMBE WAY
2 HUDSON CRESCENT
3 CLIFTON PLACE
4 PINFOLD COURT
227
C7
1 UPR NEWBOROUGH ST
2 ALLAN ST
3 MURROUGH WILSON PL
4 FEVERSHAM CRES
5 HILLSBOROUGH TERR
6 HUDSON ST
225
E8
1 KIRKHAM AVE
2 THE CROSSWAY
3 LILLING AVE
4 PINSENT CT
E5
1 HAWTHORN ST
2 EMMERSON ST
3 FLEMING AVE
4 SCROPE AVE
F8
1 ALBERT CL
2 VICTORIA WY
3 MORRITT CL
4 FOSTON GR
5 THORNFIELD AVE
6 LABURNUM GARTH
For full street detail of the highlighted area see page 233.
A B C D E F
YORK
EBVRACVM
Clifton
Heworth
Tang Hall
Layerthorpe
South Bank
York Racecourse
The Knavesmire
Walmgate Stray
York Minster
National Railway Museum
Bootham Park
Rowntree Park
YO30
YO31
YO26
YO1
YO24
YO23
YO10
River Ouse
River Foss
B7
1 GLENCOE STREET
2 BACK WEST VIEW
3 SHIPTON STREET
A6
1 ROSSLYN ST
2 WESTERDALE CT
3 SKELTON CT
E6
1 DENNISON ST
2 VILLA GR
E4
1 ST MARGARET'S TR
2 SPECULATION ST
A4
1 CLEVELAND ST
2 UPR ST PAUL'S TR
E2
1 WINTERSCALE ST
2 HOWARD ST
3 GRANGE ST
4 KENSAL RISE
5 LEVISHAM ST
6 MAIDA GR
7 FARNDALE ST
8 WINTERSCALE CT
C1
1 BERESFORD TERR
2 FINSBURY AVE
A2
1 TOWTON AVE
2 TRENTHOLME DR
3 MOORGARTH AVE
4 WHITE HO GDNS
A3
1 ENFIELD CRES
2 WATSON TERR
3 CECILIA PL
4 CAMBRIDGE ST
5 OXFORD ST
6 MOUNT EPHRAIM
7 HOLGATE BR GDNS
227
B1
1 WINDSOR ST
2 HUBERT ST
3 RUBY ST
4 COUNT DE BURGH TERR
5 BALMORAL TERR
6 LICHFIELD CT
231
B2
1 TELFORD TERR
2 PHILADELPHIA TERR
3 ADELAIDE ST
E3
1 BRINKWORTH TERR
2 THOMAS ST
3 HILDA ST
4 GRANVILLE TERR
5 LANSDOWNE TERR
6 HERBERT ST
7 CHAUCER ST
8 DAYSFOOT CT
9 APOLLO ST
10 THE TANNERY
11 LAWRENCE CT
12 LEAKE ST
F3
1 ST NICHOLAS PL
2 ARNSIDE PL

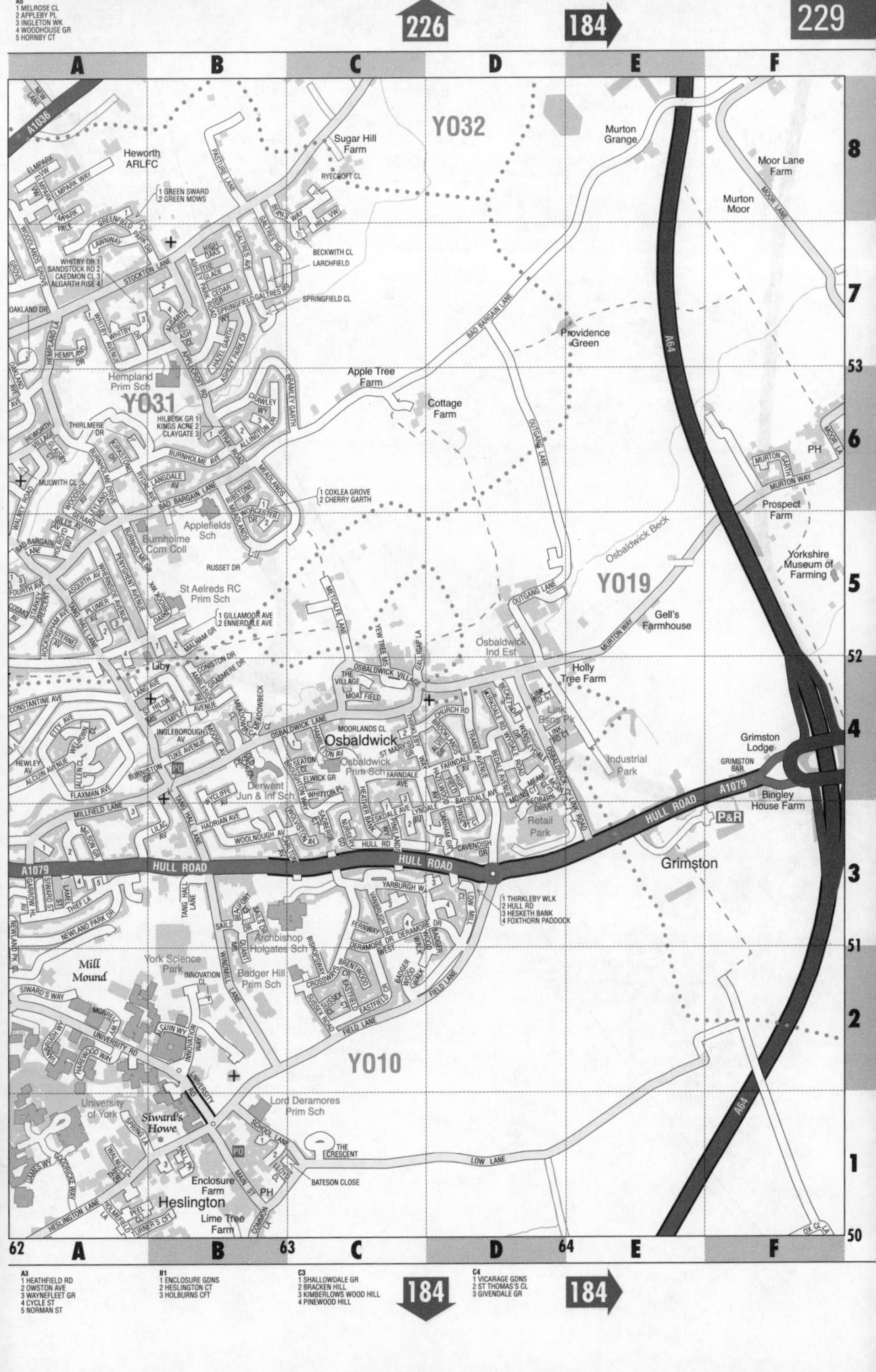
A5
1 MELROSE CL
2 APPLEBY PL
3 INGLETON WK
4 WOODHOUSE GR
5 HORNBY CT
226
184
A
B
C
D
E
F
YO32
YO31
YO19
YO10
Heworth ARLFC
Sugar Hill Farm
Murton Grange
Moor Lane Farm
Murton Moor
1 GREEN SWARD
2 GREEN MDWS
RYECROFT CL
BECKWITH CL
LARCHFIELD
SPRINGFIELD CL
WHITBY DR 1
SANDSTOCK RD 2
CAEDMON CL 3
ALGARTH RISE 4
STOCKTON LANE
BAD BARGAIN LANE
Providence Green
Apple Tree Farm
Cottage Farm
Hempland Prim Sch
HILBESK GR 1
KINGS ACRE 2
CLAYGATE 3
OUTGANG LANE
MURTON WAY
PH
1 COXLEA GROVE
2 CHERRY GARTH
Prospect Farm
Applefields Sch
Burnholme Com Coll
RUSSET DR
Osbaldwick Beck
Yorkshire Museum of Farming
St Aelreds RC Prim Sch
1 GILLAMOOR AVE
2 ENNERDALE AVE
Gell's Farmhouse
Osbaldwick Ind Est
Holly Tree Farm
OSBALDWICK VILLAGE
Osbaldwick
Osbaldwick Prim Sch
Link Bsns Pk
Industrial Park
Grimston Lodge
GRIMSTON BAR
Derwent Jun & Inf Sch
Bingley House Farm
Retail Park
HULL ROAD
A1079
P&R
Grimston
A64
1 THIRKLEBY WLK
2 HULL RD
3 HESKETH BANK
4 FOXTHORN PADDOCK
Mill Mound
York Science Park
Archbishop Holgates Sch
Badger Hill Prim Sch
UNIVERSITY RD
University of York
Siward's Howe
Lord Deramores Prim Sch
THE CRESCENT
LOW LANE
BATESON CLOSE
Enclosure Farm
Heslington
Lime Tree Farm
A3
1 HEATHFIELD RD
2 OWSTON AVE
3 WAYNEFLEET GR
4 CYCLE ST
5 NORMAN ST
B1
1 ENCLOSURE GDNS
2 HESLINGTON CT
3 HOLBURNS CFT
C3
1 SHALLOWDALE GR
2 BRACKEN HILL
3 KIMBERLOWS WOOD HILL
4 PINEWOOD HILL
C4
1 VICARAGE GDNS
2 ST THOMAS'S CL
3 GIVENDALE GR
184
184

182
227

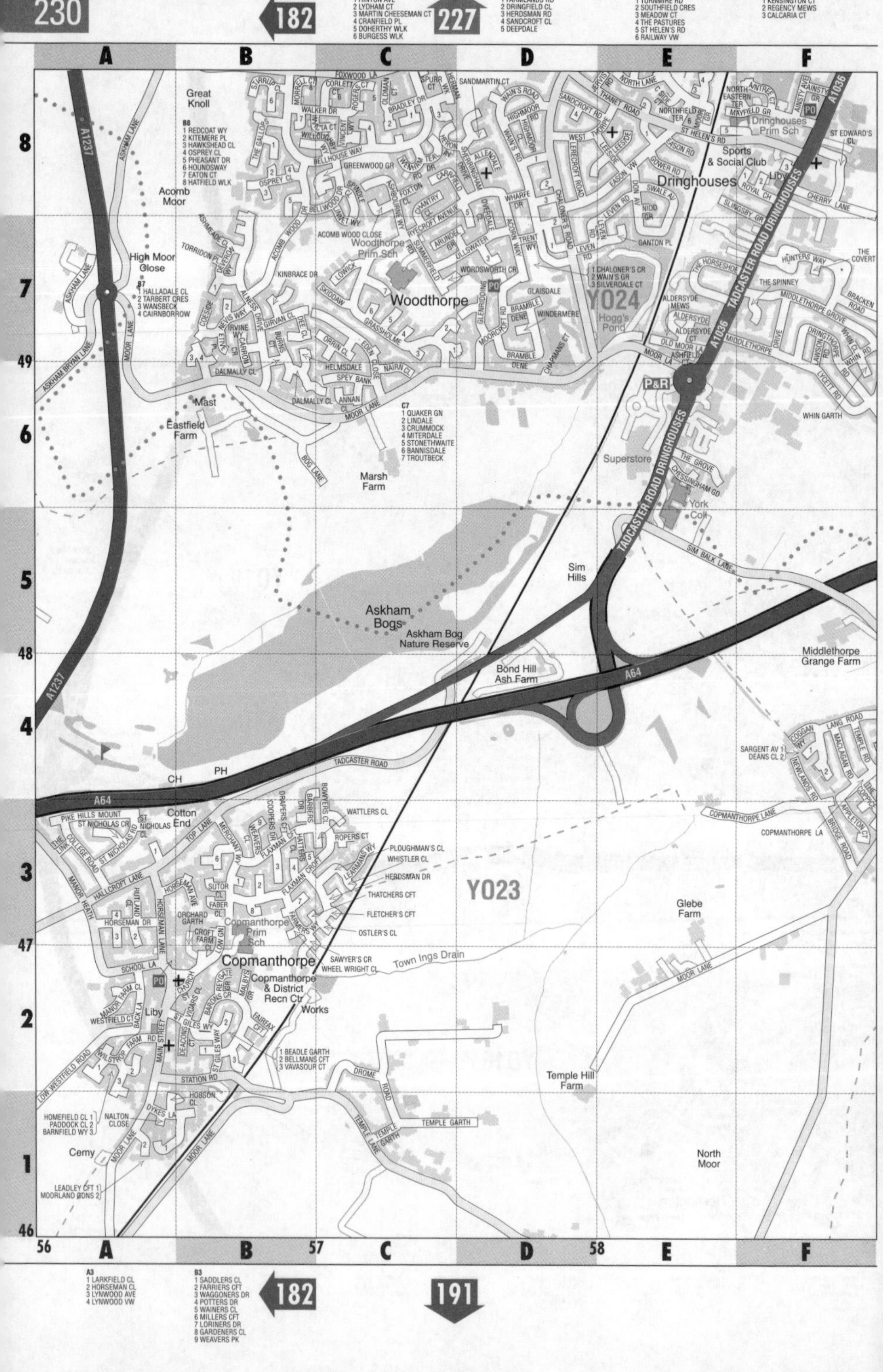
C8
1 HINTON AVE
2 LYDHAM CT
3 MARTIN CHEESEMAN CT
4 CRANFIELD PL
5 DOHERTHY WLK
6 BURGESS WLK
D8
1 FARMLANDS RD
2 DRINGFIELD CL
3 HERDSMAN RD
4 SANDCROFT CL
5 DEEPDALE
E8
1 TURNMIRE RD
2 SOUTHFIELD CRES
3 MEADOW CT
4 THE PASTURES
5 ST HELEN'S RD
6 RAILWAY VW
F8
1 KENSINGTON CT
2 REGENCY MEWS
3 CALCARIA CT
A
B
C
D
E
F
8
7
49
6
5
48
4
3
47
2
1
46
56
57
58
Great Knoll
B8
1 REDCOAT WY
2 KITEMERE PL
3 HAWKSHEAD CL
4 OSPREY CL
5 PHEASANT DR
6 HOUNDSWAY
7 EATON CT
8 HATFIELD WLK
Acomb Moor
High Moor Close
B7
1 HALLADALE CL
2 TARBERT CRES
3 WANSBECK
4 CAIRNBORROW
A1237
ASKHAM LANE
ASKHAM BRYAN LANE
MOOR LANE
FOXWOOD LA
WALKER DR
WILLOUGHBY WY
BELLHOUSE WAY
GREENWOOD GR
ACOMB WOOD DR
ACOMB WOOD CLOSE
Woodthorpe Prim Sch
Woodthorpe
KINBRACE DR
SKIDDAW
GRASSHOLME
HELMSDALE
SPEY BANK
DALMALLY CL
MOOR LANE
C7
1 QUAKER GN
2 LINDALE
3 CRUMMOCK
4 MITERDALE
5 STONETHWAITE
6 BANNISDALE
7 TROUTBECK
SANDMARTIN CT
WAIN'S ROAD
HIGHMOOR RD
WHARFE DR
ACORN WAY
WORDSWORTH CR
GLAISDALE
WINDERMERE
BRAMBLE DENE
CHAPMANS CT
NORTH LANE
THANET ROAD
WEST THORPE
LERECROFT ROAD
CHALONER'S ROAD
LEVEN RD
ST HELEN'S RD
EASON RD
SWALE AV
NIDD GR
GANTON PL
1 CHALONER'S CR
2 WAIN'S GR
3 SILVERDALE CT
YO24
Hogg's Pond
MOOR LA
Dringhouses
Sports & Social Club
Dringhouses Prim Sch
MAYFIELD GR
ST EDWARD'S CL
Liby
CHERRY LANE
SLINGSBY GR
ROYAL CH
A1036
TADCASTER ROAD DRINGHOUSES
HUNTERS WAY
THE COVERT
THE HORSESHOE
THE SPINNEY
MIDDLETHORPE GROVE
BRACKEN ROAD
ALDERSYDE MEWS
ALDERSYDE CT
OLD MOOR LA
ASHFIELD
MIDDLETHORPE DRIVE
DRINGTHORPE RD
LYCETT RD
WHIN GARTH
P&R
Mast
Eastfield Farm
BOG LANE
Marsh Farm
Superstore
THE GROVE
CHESSINGHAM GD
York Coll
SIM BALK LANE
Sim Hills
Askham Bogs
Askham Bog Nature Reserve
Bond Hill Ash Farm
A64
Middlethorpe Grange Farm
TADCASTER ROAD
CH
PH
Cotton End
PIKE HILLS MOUNT
ST NICHOLAS CR
COLLEGE ROAD
TOP LANE
MERCHANT WY
WATTLERS CL
ROPERS CT
PLOUGHMAN'S CL
WHISTLER CL
HERDSMAN DR
THATCHERS CFT
FLETCHER'S CFT
OSTLER'S CL
SAWYER'S CR
WHEEL WRIGHT CL
HALLCROFT LANE
MANOR HEATH
RUTLAND CL
HORSEMAN AVE
HORSEMAN DR
HORSEMAN LANE
ORCHARD GARTH
CROFT FARM CL
Copmanthorpe Prim Sch
Copmanthorpe
SCHOOL LA
Copmanthorpe & District Recn Ctr
Town Ings Drain
YO23
Works
MANOR FARM CL
WESTFIELD CT
BACK LA
Liby
MAIN STREET
WILSTROP FARM RD
LOW WESTFIELD ROAD
STATION RD
ST GILES WAY
FAIRFAX CFT
1 BEADLE GARTH
2 BELLMANS CFT
3 VAVASOUR CT
DROME ROAD
TEMPLE GARTH
TEMPLE LANE
HOBSON CL
DYKES LA
HOMEFIELD CL 1
PADDOCK CL 2
BARNFIELD WY 3
NALTON CLOSE
Cemy
MOOR LANE
LEADLEY CFT 1
MOORLAND GDNS 2
Glebe Farm
MOOR LANE
Temple Hill Farm
North Moor
SARGENT AV 1
DEANS CL 2
LANG ROAD
COGGAN WY
MACLAGAN RD
TEMPLE RD
NEWLANDS RD
COPMANTHORPE LANE
COPMANTHORPE LA
APPLETON CT
BRIDGE ROAD
A3
1 LARKFIELD CL
2 HORSEMAN CL
3 LYNWOOD AVE
4 LYNWOOD VW
B3
1 SADDLERS CL
2 FARRIERS CFT
3 WAGGONERS DR
4 POTTERS DR
5 WAINERS CL
6 MILLERS CFT
7 LORINERS DR
8 GARDENERS CL
9 WEAVERS PK

182
191

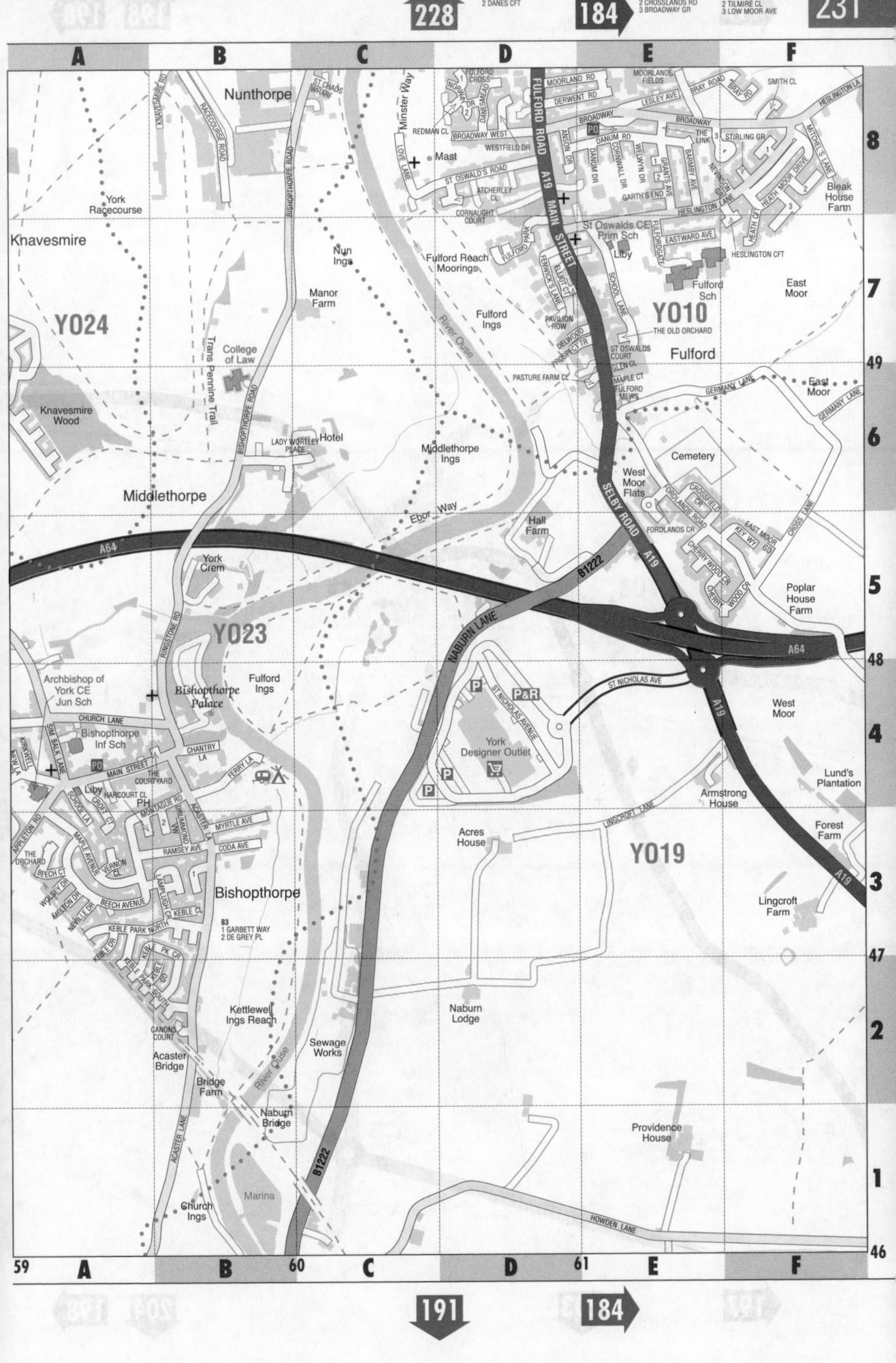
Nunthorpe
York Racecourse
Knavesmire
YO24
Knavesmire Wood
Middlethorpe
College of Law
Trans Pennine Trail
BISHOPTHORPE ROAD
LADY WORTLEY PLACE
Hotel
Manor Farm
Nun Ings
Minster Way
Mast
Fulford Reach Moorings
Fulford Ings
River Ouse
Middlethorpe Ings
Ebor Way
FULFORD ROAD
A19 MAIN STREET
St Oswalds CE Prim Sch
Liby
YO10
Fulford
Fulford Sch
East Moor
Bleak House Farm
THE OLD ORCHARD
PASTURE FARM CL
GERMANY LANE
Cemetery
West Moor Flats
SELBY ROAD
Hall Farm
A64
York Crem
YO23
B1222
NABURN LANE
Poplar House Farm
ST NICHOLAS AVE
P&R
York Designer Outlet
West Moor
Archbishop of York CE Jun Sch
Bishopthorpe Palace
Fulford Ings
Bishopthorpe Inf Sch
CHURCH LANE
MAIN STREET
PO
PH
Bishopthorpe
B3
1 GARBETT WAY
2 DE GREY PL
Acres House
LINGCROFT LANE
YO19
Armstrong House
Lund's Plantation
Forest Farm
Lingcroft Farm
Kettlewell Ings Reach
Sewage Works
Naburn Lodge
Acaster Bridge
Bridge Farm
Naburn Bridge
ACASTER LANE
Marina
Church Ings
Providence House
HOWDEN LANE
A
B
C
D
E
F
8
7
49
6
5
48
4
3
47
2
1
46
59
60
61

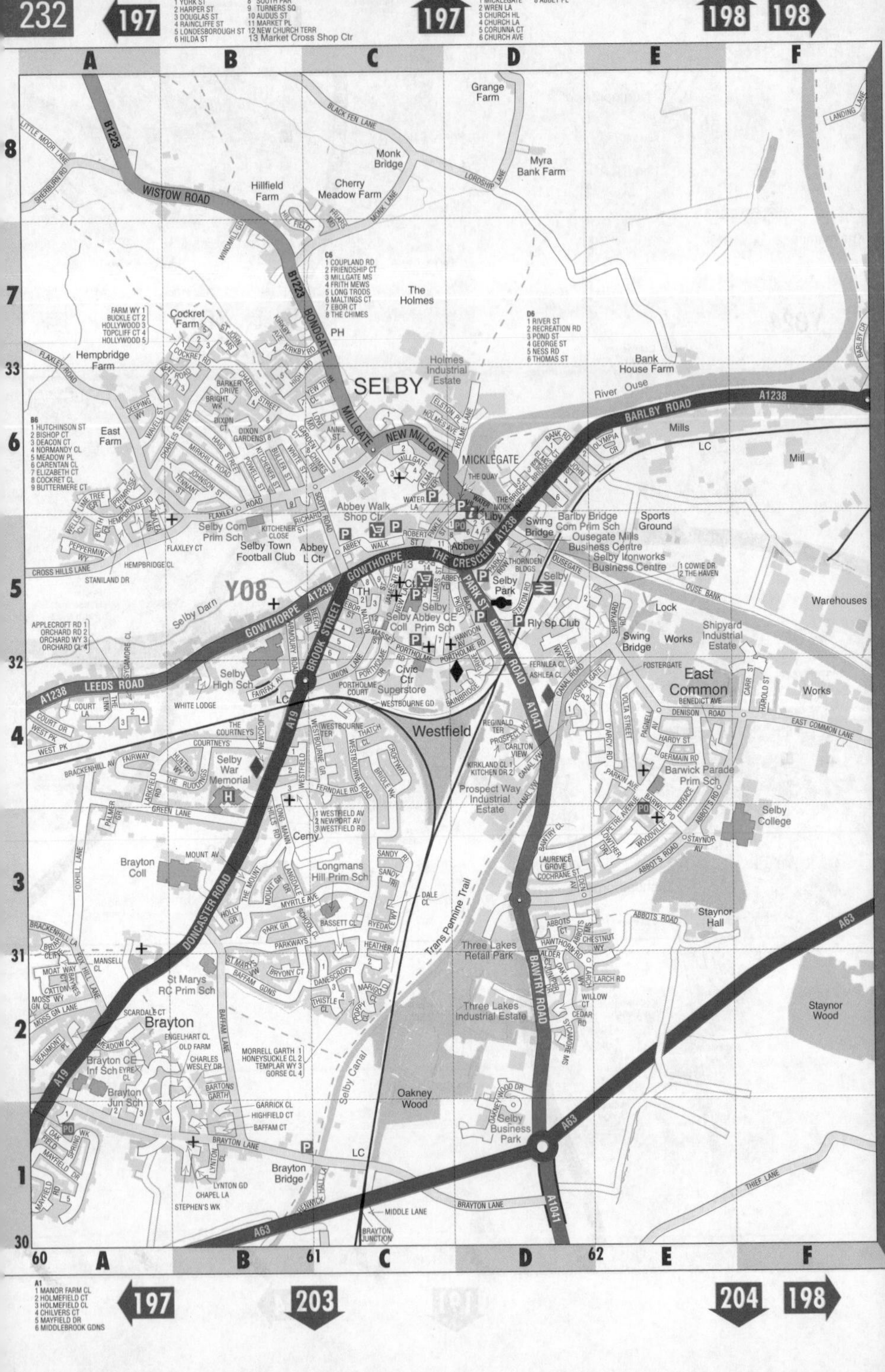
197
C5
1 YORK ST
2 HARPER ST
3 DOUGLAS ST
4 RAINCLIFFE ST
5 LONDESBOROUGH ST
6 HILDA ST
7 PORTHOLME CRES
8 SOUTH PAR
9 TURNERS SQ
10 AUDUS ST
11 MARKET PL
12 NEW CHURCH TERR
13 Market Cross Shop Ctr
14 MARKET LA
197
D5
1 MICKLEGATE
2 WREN LA
3 CHURCH HL
4 CHURCH LA
5 CORUNNA CT
6 CHURCH AVE
7 GANT WK
8 ABBEY PL
198
198
A
B
C
D
E
F
8
7
33
6
5
32
4
3
31
2
1
30
Grange Farm
BLACK FEN LANE
LITTLE MOOR LANE
SHERBURN RD
B1223
WISTOW ROAD
Monk Bridge
Cherry Meadow Farm
Hillfield Farm
Myra Bank Farm
LORDSHIP LANE
MONK LANE
LANDING LANE
WINDMILL GD
HILL FIELD
C6
1 COUPLAND RD
2 FRIENDSHIP CT
3 MILLGATE MS
4 FRITH MEWS
5 LONG TRODS
6 MALTINGS CT
7 EBOR CT
8 THE CHIMES
The Holmes
D6
1 RIVER ST
2 RECREATION RD
3 POND ST
4 GEORGE ST
5 NESS RD
6 THOMAS ST
FARM WY 1
BUCKLE CT 2
HOLLYWOOD 3
TOPCLIFF CT 4
HOLLYWOOD 5
Cockret Farm
B1223 BONDGATE
PH
Hempbridge Farm
FLAXLEY ROAD
COCKRET RD
KIRKBY RD
Holmes Industrial Estate
Bank House Farm
SELBY
River Ouse
A1238
BARLBY ROAD
BARLBY CR
B6
1 HUTCHINSON ST
2 BISHOP CT
3 DEACON CT
4 NORMANDY CL
5 MEADOW PL
6 CARENTAN CL
7 ELIZABETH CT
8 COCKRET CL
9 BUTTERMERE CT
East Farm
DEEPING WY
WAVELL ST
CHARLES STREET
BARKER DRIVE
BRIGHT WK
DIXON CT
DIXON GARDENS
MIRKHILL ROAD
HAIG STREET
KITCHENER ST
BULLER ST
WHITE ST
MILLGATE
NEW MILLGATE
ELSTON PL
HOLMES AVE
HOLME LANE
MICKLEGATE
Mills
LC
Mill
OLYMPIA CR
BANK RD
THE QUAY
WATER LA
THE NOOK
Abbey Walk Shop Ctr
Liby
Swing Bridge
Barlby Bridge Com Prim Sch
Sports Ground
Ousegate Mills Business Centre
Selby Ironworks Business Centre
PRIMROSE
HEMPBRIDGE RD
LIME TREE GR
FLAXLEY ROAD
Selby Com Prim Sch
KITCHENER CLOSE
RICHARD ST
SCOTT ROAD
ABBEY WALK
ROBERT ST
Abbey
THE CRESCENT A1238
Selby Town Football Club
Abbey L Ctr
PEPPERMINT WY
FLAXLEY CT
HEMPBRIDGE CL
CROSS HILLS LANE
STANILAND DR
GOWTHORPE
OUSEGATE
1 COWIE DR
2 THE HAVEN
OUSE BANK
Warehouses
Y08
Selby Darn
Selby Abbey CE Prim Sch
Selby Coll
TH
Selby Park
Selby
Lock
PARK ST
BAWTRY ROAD
STATION RD
Rly Sp Club
SHIPYARD
Swing Bridge
Works
Shipyard Industrial Estate
APPLECROFT RD 1
ORCHARD RD 2
ORCHARD WY 3
ORCHARD CL 4
SYCAMORE CL
GOWTHORPE A1238
ARMOURY ROAD
BROOK STREET
MASSEY ST
PORTHOLME RD
HAWDON AV
FERNLEA CL
ASHLEA CL
FOSTERGATE
East Common
BENEDICT AVE
DENISON ROAD
EAST COMMON LANE
CARR ST
HAROLD ST
Works
A1238 LEEDS ROAD
Selby High Sch
Civic Ctr
Superstore
PORTHOLME COURT
WESTBOURNE GD
UNION LANE
FAIRFAX AV
LC
BAINBRIDGE
CANAL ROAD
FOSTER GATE
VOLTA STREET
COURT LA
THE LINK
WHITE LODGE
COURT DR
WEST PK
WEST PK
THE COURTNEYS
NEWCROFT
COURTNEYS
WESTBOURNE THATCH CL
Westfield
REGINALD TER
PROSPECT WY
CARLTON VIEW
A1041
D'ARCY RD
PAGNELL AV
HARDY ST
GERMAIN RD
BRACKENHILL AV
FAIRWAY
HUNTERS WY
THE RUDDINGS
LARKFIELD RD
Selby War Memorial
H
A19
WESTFIELD
WESTBOURNE GR
WESTBOURNE ROAD
CROFTWAY
BRIDLE WK
FERNDALE RD
KIRKLAND CL 1
KITCHEN DR 2
Prospect Way Industrial Estate
CANAL VW
PARKIN AV
Barwick Parade Prim Sch
BARWIC PD
TERRACE
ABBOT'S RD
Selby College
PALMER GR
GREEN LANE
LONG MANN HILLS RD
1 WESTFIELD AV
2 NEWPORT AV
3 WESTFIELD RD
Cemy
PETRE AVENUE
LOWTHER DR
WOODVILLE
STAYNOR AV
BAWTRY CL
FOXHILL LANE
Brayton Coll
MOUNT AV
THE MOUNT
MOUNT GR
LANGDALE
Longmans Hill Prim Sch
SANDY RI
SANDY RI
LAURENCE GROVE
COCHRANE ST
EDEN AV
ABBOTS ROAD
DOUGLAS ROAD
DONCASTER ROAD
HOLLY GR
MYRTLE AVE
PARK GR
SCHOOL CL
BASSETT CL
RYEDALE WY
DALE CL
Trans Pennine Trail
ABBOTS ROAD
Staynor Hall
BRACKENHILL LA
PARKWAYS
HEATHER CL
Three Lakes Retail Park
ABBOTS CT
ABBOTS MS
CHESTNUT WY
HAWTHORN RD
ALDER CL
JUNIPER
OAK WY
LARCH RD
LARCH RD
A63
MANSELL CL
ST MARYS VW
BRYONY CT
BAFFAM GDNS
DANESCROFT
MARIGOLD
THISTLE CL
POPPY CL
MOAT WAY
FOX HILL LANE
St Marys RC Prim Sch
Three Lakes Industrial Estate
WILLOW CT
CEDAR RD
SYCAMORE MS
Staynor Wood
MOSS WY
MOSS GN LANE
SCARDALE CT
Brayton
ENGELHART CL
OLD FARM
BAFFAM LANE
MORRELL GARTH 1
HONEYSUCKLE CL 2
TEMPLAR WY 3
GORSE CL 4
Selby Canal
BEAUMONT PL
MEADOW CT
Brayton CE Inf Sch
EYRE CL
CHARLES WESLEY DR
BARTONS GARTH
A19
Brayton Jun Sch
GARRICK CL
HIGHFIELD CT
BAFFAM CT
Oakney Wood
OAKNEY WOOD DR
Selby Business Park
A63
SPRING WK
OAK FIELD
MAYFIELD DR
BRAYTON LANE
LYNTON CL
LYNTON GD
CHAPEL LA
STEPHEN'S WK
P
LC
Brayton Bridge
RENWICK HALL LA
MIDDLE LANE
BRAYTON LANE
THIEF LANE
A1041
A63
MAYFIELD RD
BRAYTON JUNCTION
60
A
B
61
C
D
62
E
F
A1
1 MANOR FARM CL
2 HOLMEFIELD CT
3 HOLMEFIELD CL
4 CHILVERS CT
5 MAYFIELD DR
6 MIDDLEBROOK GDNS
197
203
204
198

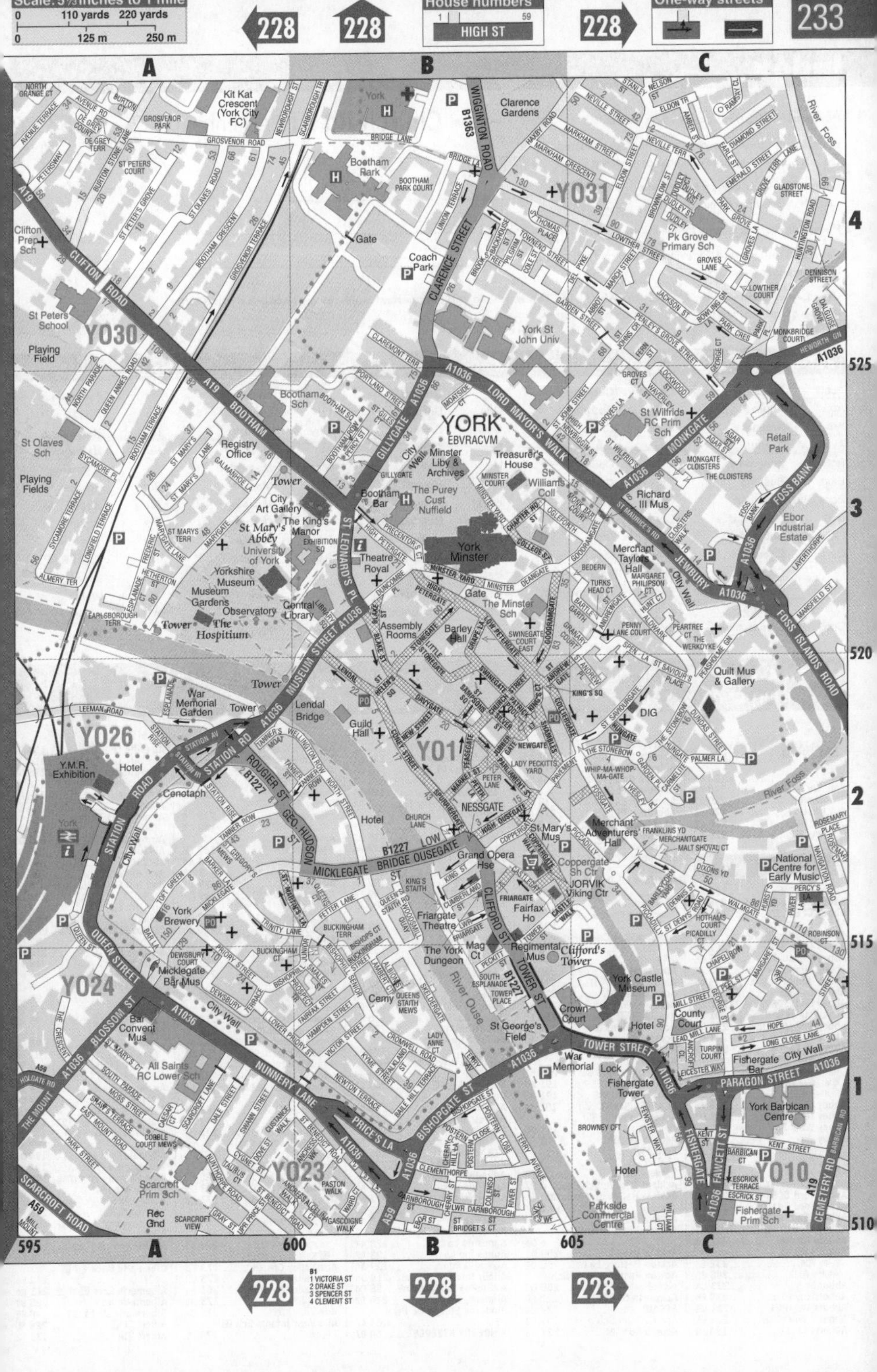
Scale: 5⅓ inches to 1 mile
0
110 yards
220 yards
125 m
250 m
228
228
House numbers
1
59
HIGH ST
228
One-way streets
A
B
C
4
3
2
1
525
520
515
510
595
600
605
YORK
EBVRACVM
YO31
YO30
YO26
YO24
YO23
YO1
YO10
Kit Kat Crescent (York City FC)
Clarence Gardens
River Foss
Bootham Park
Gate
Coach Park
York St John Univ
St Peters School
Playing Field
Playing Fields
St Olaves Sch
Clifton Prep Sch
Bootham Sch
Registry Office
City Wall
Minster Liby & Archives
Treasurer's House
St Williams Coll
Richard III Mus
Retail Park
Ebor Industrial Estate
St Wilfrids RC Prim Sch
Pk Grove Primary Sch
Tower
City Art Gallery
St Mary's Abbey
University of York
The King's Manor
Bootham Bar
The Purey Cust Nuffield
York Minster
Theatre Royal
Yorkshire Museum
Museum Gardens
Observatory
Central Library
The Hospitium
Assembly Rooms
Barley Hall
The Minster Sch
Merchant Taylors Hall
Quilt Mus & Gallery
War Memorial Garden
Lendal Bridge
Guild Hall
DIG
Y.M.R. Exhibition
Hotel
Cenotaph
NESSGATE
St Mary's Mus
Merchant Adventurers' Hall
Grand Opera Hse
Coppergate Sh Ctr
JORVIK Viking Ctr
National Centre for Early Music
York Brewery
Friargate Theatre
Fairfax Ho
The York Dungeon
Mag Ct
Regimental Mus
Clifford's Tower
York Castle Museum
Crown Court
Micklegate Bar Mus
Bar Convent Mus
All Saints RC Lower Sch
Cemy
River Ouse
St George's Field
County Court
War Memorial
Lock
Fishergate Tower
Fishergate Bar
York Barbican Centre
Scarcroft Prim Sch
Rec Gnd
Parkside Commercial Centre
Fishergate Prim Sch
CLIFTON
BOOTHAM
GILLYGATE
LORD MAYOR'S WALK
MONKGATE
FOSS BANK
JEWBURY
FOSS ISLANDS ROAD
ST LEONARD'S PL
MUSEUM STREET
STATION ROAD
ROUGIER ST
MICKLEGATE
BRIDGE
OUSEGATE
CLIFFORD ST
TOWER ST
TOWER STREET
PARAGON STREET
FISHERGATE
BISHOPGATE ST
NUNNERY LANE
BLOSSOM ST
QUEEN STREET
THE MOUNT
SCARCROFT ROAD
CEMETERY RD
CLARENCE STREET
WIGGINTON ROAD
A19
A1036
A59
B1227
B1363
228
B1
1 VICTORIA ST
2 DRAKE ST
3 SPENCER ST
4 CLEMENT ST
228
228

Index

Place name May be abbreviated on the map
Location number Present when a number indicates the place's position in a crowded area of mapping
Locality, town or village Shown when more than one place has the same name
Postcode district District for the indexed place
Page and grid square Page number and grid reference for the standard mapping

Church Rd [6] Beckenham BR2..........**53** C6

Cities, towns and villages are listed in CAPITAL LETTERS
Places of interest are highlighted in blue with a star★
Public and commercial buildings are highlighted in magenta

Abbreviations used in the index

Abbr.	Meaning	Abbr.	Meaning	Abbr.	Meaning	Abbr.	Meaning	Abbr.	Meaning
Acad	Academy	Comm	Common	Gd	Ground	L	Leisure	Prom	Promenade
App	Approach	Cott	Cottage	Gdn	Garden	La	Lane	Rd	Road
Arc	Arcade	Cres	Crescent	Gn	Green	Liby	Library	Recn	Recreation
Ave	Avenue	Cswy	Causeway	Gr	Grove	Mdw	Meadow	Ret	Retail
Bglw	Bungalow	Ct	Court	H	Hall	Meml	Memorial	Sh	Shopping
Bldg	Building	Ctr	Centre	Ho	House	Mkt	Market	Sq	Square
Bsns, Bus	Business	Ctry	Country	Hospl	Hospital	Mus	Museum	St	Street
Bvd	Boulevard	Cty	County	HQ	Headquarters	Orch	Orchard	Sta	Station
Cath	Cathedral	Dr	Drive	Hts	Heights	Pal	Palace	Terr	Terrace
Cir	Circus	Dro	Drove	Ind	Industrial	Par	Parade	TH	Town Hall
Cl	Close	Ed	Education	Inst	Institute	Pas	Passage	Univ	University
Cnr	Corner	Emb	Embankment	Int	International	Pk	Park	Wk, Wlk	Walk
Coll	College	Est	Estate	Intc	Interchange	Pl	Place	Wr	Water
Com	Community	Ex	Exhibition	Junc	Junction	Prec	Precinct	Yd	Yard

Index of towns, villages, streets, hospitals, industrial estates, railway stations, schools, shopping centres, universities and places of interest

1st–Alb

1st Ave HG2 .... 220 B3
2nd Ave HG2 .... 220 B3
3rd Ave HG2 .... 220 B3
4th Ave HG2 .... 220 B3
5th Ave HG2 .... 220 C3
6th Ave HG2 .... 220 B2

A

Abber La LS24 .... 182 A2
Abbeville Ave [1] YO21 .... 208 B6
Abbey Cl [12] LS29 .... 175 A4
Abbey Crags Way HG5 .... 221 C3
Abbeyfield Dr [10] TS16 .... 5 D5
Abbey Gdns WF8 .... 201 B2
Abbey Hill BD23 .... 155 C5
Abbey Infants Sch DL3 .... 3 B5
Abbey Junior Sch DL3 .... 3 B5
Abbey La YO22 .... 208 E7
Abbey L Ctr YO8 .... 232 C5
Abbey Mews WF8 .... 201 B2
Abbey Mill Gdns HG5 .... 221 C3
Abbey Mill View HG5 .... 221 C3
Abbey Pl [9] YO8 .... 232 D5
Abbey Rd
Darlington DL3 .... 3 B5
Knaresborough HG5 .... 221 B3
Sadberge DL2 .... 4 C7
Abbey St YO30 .... 228 A7
Abbey Terr [16] YO21 .... 208 D7
Abbey Walk Sh Ctr YO8 .... 232 C6
Abbey Wlk
Pontefract WF8 .... 201 B2
Selby YO8 .... 232 C5
Abbey Yd YO8 .... 232 C5
Abbots Ct YO8 .... 232 D3
Abbotsford Ct [7] TS17 .... 5 F5
Abbotsford Rd YO10 .... 228 F3
Abbots Gait YO32 .... 225 F6
Abbot's Garth YO12 .... 99 D6
Abbots Rd YO8 .... 232 E3
Abbot's Rd
Selby YO8 .... 232 E3
Whitby YO22 .... 208 E5
Abbot St YO31 .... 233 C4
Abbotsway YO31 .... 228 E8
Abbots Way HG5 .... 221 C3
Abbot's Wlk YO22 .... 208 E5
Abbotts Cl LS25 .... 194 F8
Abbotts Ct YO17 .... 215 E4
Abbotts Gdns YO8 .... 197 A8
Abbotts Mews YO8 .... 232 D3
Abelton Gr [33] YO32 .... 166 E5
Aberbran Ct [41] TS17 .... 5 F4
Aberdeen La [19] YO11 .... 213 A6
Aberdeen Pl [20] YO11 .... 213 A6
Aberdeen Rd DL1 .... 3 E8
Aberdeen St [17] YO11 .... 213 A6
Aberdeen Terr [21] YO11 .... 213 A6
Aberdeen Wlk [16] YO11 .... 213 A6
ABERFORD 194 F7
Aberford CE Prim Sch LS25 .... 194 F8
Aberford Rd
Barwick in Elmet & Scholes LS15 .... 194 C8
Bramham cum Oglethorpe LS23 .... 188 E5
Garforth LS25 .... 194 D4
Abrahams Quay YO22 .... 208 E5
Abram's View YO11 .... 213 B2
Acacia Ave YO32 .... 225 E4
Acacia Dr WF10 .... 201 B3
Acacia Gr [36] YO32 .... 166 E5
Academy Gdns DL2 .... 1 D8
Acaster Ave YO23 .... 191 A3
Acaster Dr LS25 .... 194 D3
Acaster La
Acaster Malbis YO23 .... 231 B1
Acaster Selby YO23 .... 191 A4
ACASTER MALBIS 191 D8
ACASTER SELBY 191 B4
Accommodation Rd YO25 .... 151 D6
Acer Cl [4] BD20 .... 187 F7
ACKLAM
169 E8
Middlesborough 6 E8
Acklam Grange Sch TS5 .... 6 D7
Acklam Hall Sixth Form Ctr TS5 .... 6 E7
Acklam Rd TS17 .... 6 C8
Acklam Whin Prim Sch TS5 .... 6 D6
Ackton La WF7 .... 200 D1
Ackton Pasture La WF7 .... 200 D2
Ackton Pastures Prim Sch WF10 .... 200 D3
Ackworth St [3] YO12 .... 212 E4
ACOMB 227 C3
Acomb Prim Sch YO24 .... 227 E3
Acomb Rd YO24 .... 227 D3
Acomb Wood Cl YO24 .... 230 C7
Acomb Wood Dr YO24 .... 230 B7
Acorn Bsns Pk BD23 .... 173 D4
Acorn Cl
[6] Barlby YO8 .... 198 B4
Middleton St George DL2 .... 4 D4
Acorn Way
Gateforth YO8 .... 197 B1
York YO24 .... 230 D7
Acre Fold [21] LS29 .... 174 F4
Acre La [12] BD23 .... 134 E2
Acre Mdw [1] BD22 .... 187 B6
Acre Rd [2] BD22 .... 187 B6
Acres Cl [24] YO62 .... 92 F6
Acresfield [6] BB8 .... 186 A3
Acres La
Brompton YO13 .... 98 C4
Helmsley YO62 .... 93 A6
Scrayingham YO41 .... 169 B8
Acres The
Addingham LS29 .... 175 A5
Glusburn BD20 .... 187 E6
Stokesley TS9 .... 26 C8
Adam's Field La YO61 .... 117 F4
Adcott Rd TS5 .... 6 E7
ADDINGHAM 174 F5
Addingham Prim Sch LS29 .... 174 F5
Addingham Wharfedale Rd LS29 .... 174 E4
Addison Ave [18] WF6 .... 200 B1
Addison Rd TS9 .... 8 A1
Addison Villas HG3 .... 219 A8
Addlethorpe La LS22 .... 179 C3
Adelaide Rd
Middlesbrough TS7 .... 7 B6
[6] Norton DN6 .... 206 E2
Adelaide St [3] YO23 .... 228 B2
Adlington Cl [8] YO32 .... 167 A7
Admirals Ct YO7 .... 211 A2
Admirals' Ct YO7 .... 211 A2
Agar St YO31 .... 233 C3
AGGLETHORPE 60 A1
Agnesgate HG4 .... 214 D5
Agnesing La LA2 .... 128 A7
Agnes Ing La LA2 .... 128 A7
Aikengill Rd LA2 .... 129 A4
Ailcey Rd HG4 .... 214 D5
AINDERBY QUERNHOW 88 C4
Ainderby Rd DL7 .... 210 B2
Ainderby Steepe CE Prim Sch DL7 .... 64 A7
AINDERBY STEEPLE 64 B7
Ainsford Way TS7 .... 7 D8
Ainstable Rd TS7 .... 7 D8
Ainsty Ave YO24 .... 230 F8
Ainsty Dr [2] LS22 .... 180 C4
Ainsty Gr YO24 .... 230 F8
Ainsty Rd
Harrogate HG1 .... 219 F4
Wetherby LS22 .... 180 C4
Ainsty View
Acklam YO17 .... 169 E8
Whixley YO26 .... 164 A4
Ainsworth Way TS7 .... 7 D8
AINTHORPE 29 C6
Ainthorpe La YO21 .... 29 C7
Aintree Ct
[9] Darlington DL1 .... 3 F6
York YO24 .... 230 F8
Aire & Calder Ind Pk WF10 .... 200 E5
Aire Cres BD20 .... 187 E7
AIREDALE 201 B4
Airedale Ave
Gargrave BD23 .... 155 D1
Skipton BD23 .... 217 B4
Airedale Bsns Ctr BD23 .... 173 D4
Airedale Dr WF10 .... 201 B5
Airedale High Sch WF10 .... 201 B4
Airedale Ings BD20 .... 173 D1
Airedale Junior & Infants Sch WF10 .... 201 B4
Airedale Mews [1] BD23 .... 216 E3
Airedale Rd
Castleford WF10 .... 201 A4
Scotton DL9 .... 40 D4
Airedale Terr BD23 .... 216 E3
Airedale Trading Pk BD20 .... 187 F8
Airedale View [1] BD20 .... 187 F8
Aire Rd LS22 .... 180 B4
Aireside Ave BD20 .... 173 D1
Aireside Terr BD20 .... 173 D2
Aire St
Castleford WF10 .... 200 E4
Glusburn BD20 .... 187 F7
Knottingley WF11 .... 202 A3
[12] Knottingley WF11 .... 202 A3
Aire Valley Cl BD20 .... 173 D3
Aire Valley Dr BD20 .... 173 D3
Aire Valley Mount WF10 .... 201 A4
AIRE VIEW 173 D1
Aire View BD23 .... 216 C1
Aire View Infants Sch [13] BD20 .... 174 C1
Aireville Dr BD20 .... 174 C1
Aireville Grange BD23 .... 216 D5
Aireville Sch BD23 .... 216 D4
Aireyholme La TS9 .... 8 B2
Airfield Ind Est YO41 .... 184 F3
AIRMYN 205 E4
Airmyn Park Prim Sch DN14 .... 205 E4
Airmyn Rd DN14 .... 205 D3
AIRTON 155 A6
AIRY HILL 208 D4
Airy Hill YO21 .... 208 D5
Airy Hill Com Prim Sch YO21 .... 208 D5
Airy Hill La TS12 .... 9 D8
AISKEW 63 A3
Aiskew Leeming Bar CE Prim Sch DL7 .... 63 C4
Aislabie Cl HG4 .... 214 A5
Aislabie Garth HG4 .... 214 A5
AISLABY
Egglescliffe 5 C3
Pickering 95 D8
Whitby 31 F7
Aislaby Carr La YO18 .... 95 C7
Aislaby La
Aislaby YO18 .... 95 C6
Aislaby YO21 .... 32 A8
Aislaby Rd TS16 .... 5 D4
Aismunderby Cl HG4 .... 214 C3
Aismunderby Rd HG4 .... 214 C4
Aisne Rd DL9 .... 209 C1
Aketon Rd WF10 .... 200 D3
Alanbrooke Ind Est YO7 .... 115 B8
Alanbrooke Prim Sch YO7 .... 89 A1
Alandale Cres LS25 .... 194 B3
Alandale Rd LS25 .... 194 B4
Alan Farnaby Way YO60 .... 145 C4
Albany Ave HG1 .... 219 E5
Albany Rd
Harrogate HG1 .... 219 E5
Middlesbrough TS7 .... 7 B6
Albany St [3] YO26 .... 227 F5
Albany Wlk LS29 .... 218 A3
Albatross Way DL1 .... 3 E5
Albemarle Back Rd [10] YO11 .... 212 F6
Albemarle Cres [18] YO11 .... 213 A6
Albemarle Rd YO23 .... 228 B2
Albermarle Dr [3] DL9 .... 40 F5
Albert Cl [1] YO32 .... 228 F8
Albert Hill BD24 .... 131 E2

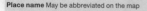

Albert Pl
Harrogate HG1 .... 220 C4
1 Whitby YO21 .... 208 D7
Albert Rd
Eaglescliffe TS16 .... 5 E5
12 Glusburn BD20 .... 187 E7
Harrogate HG1 .... 219 E5
1 Scarborough YO12 .... 213 A7
Albert Simmons Way St 44
LS29 .... 176 C1
Albert Sq BD23 .... 216 F4
Albert St
Darlington DL1 .... 3 D6
33 Earby BB18 .... 172 A1
Glusburn BD20 .... 187 F7
Harrogate HG1 .... 219 D2
Normanton South WF6 .... 200 B2
8 Scarborough YO12 .... 213 A7
York YO10 .... 233 C1
Albert Terr
5 Harrogate HG1 .... 219 D1
Skipton BD23 .... 216 F4
Albion Ave YO26 .... 227 B6
Albion Cres 3 YO11 .... 213 A4
Albion Pl 14 YO21 .... 208 D6
Albion Rd
25 Earby BB18 .... 172 A1
Scarborough YO11 .... 213 A4
Albion St
Boosbeck TS12 .... 9 E7
Boston Spa LS23 .... 188 E7
Castleford WF10 .... 200 E4
28 Earby BB18 .... 172 A1
York YO1 .... 233 B1
Albion Terr
9 Boston Spa LS23 .... 188 E7
23 Whitby YO21 .... 208 D6
Alcelina Ct YO23 .... 233 B1
Alcuin Ave YO10 .... 229 A4
Alcuin Way YO10 .... 229 B2
ALDBOROUGH 141 C5
Aldborough Gate 13
YO51 .... 141 B4
Aldborough Roman Town & Mus* YO51 .... 141 C5
Aldborough Way YO26 .... 227 F5
ALDBROUGH ST JOHN 2 A2
Aldenham Rd TS14 .... 8 E5
Alder Ave HG5 .... 221 E5
Alder Carr La YO18 .... 49 E2
Alder Cl YO8 .... 232 D2
Alder Ct 25 YO18 .... 95 F6
Alder Hill St 1 BB18 .... 172 B1
Alderley Ct YO32 .... 225 E3
Alderman Best Rd DL1 .... 4 A4
Alderman Leach Dr 13 DL2 .... 3 A7
Alderman Leach Prim Sch
DL2 .... 3 A7
Alder Rd HG1 .... 219 F5
Aldersley Ave BD23 .... 217 B3
Alderson Cres YO12 .... 99 E7
Alderson Rd HG2 .... 222 E8
Alderson Sq HG2 .... 222 E8
Alders Rd YO18 .... 49 C4
Aldersyde YO24 .... 230 E7
Aldersyde Ct YO24 .... 230 E7
Aldersyde Mews YO24 .... 230 E7
Alder Way YO32 .... 225 D2
ALDFIELD 139 A8
Aldreth Gr YO23 .... 228 C2
Aldridge Rd TS3 .... 7 B8
ALDWARK 142 C2
Aldwark YO1 .... 233 C3
Aldwych Cl TS6 .... 7 E8
Alec Hare Cl YO17 .... 215 E4
Alexander Ave
6 East Ayton/West Ayton YO13 .... 99 B8
York YO31 .... 225 E2
Alexander Cl YO7 .... 211 C4
Alexander Rd DL9 .... 209 C2
Alexandra Cres 10 LS29 .... 218 A4
Alexandra Ct
Skipton BD23 .... 216 F2
York YO10 .... 228 E4
Alexandra Gr HG5 .... 221 B7
Alexandra Park Rd HG5 .... 221 C7
Alexandra Pk YO12 .... 212 D5
Alexandra Pl
Ilkley LS29 .... 218 A4
3 Knaresborough HG5 .... 221 B8
Alexandra Rd
Harrogate HG1 .... 219 D3
Strensall YO32 .... 167 A6
Alexandra Terr BD23 .... 216 F2
Alexandra Ville BD23 .... 216 F2
Alexandra Way DL10 .... 209 C7
Alexandria Dr DL2 .... 4 D4
Alfreda Terr 1 YO22 .... 208 E6
Algarth Rd YO31 .... 229 B7
Algarth Rise YO31 .... 229 B7
Alga Terr YO11 .... 213 A4
Allans Ct DL10 .... 209 B6
Allanson Gr YO24 .... 227 E2
Allan St
Darlington DL1 .... 3 D6
2 York YO30 .... 228 C7
Allenby Rd
20 Helmsley YO62 .... 92 F6
Hipswell DL9 .... 209 C1
Allen Cl YO10 .... 229 A4
Allendale YO24 .... 230 D8
Allendale Rd TS7 .... 7 D8
Allen Gr TS9 .... 26 B7
Allensway TS17 .... 6 C7
Allens West Sta TS16 .... 5 D5
Allerdale Cl YO7 .... 211 C4
ALLERSTON 97 C5
Allerston La YO18 .... 97 C4
Allerston Way 5 TS14 .... 8 F7
Allerton Balk TS15 .... 5 D2
ALLERTON BYWATER 200 D6
Allerton Bywater Bsns Pk
WF10 .... 200 E6
Allerton Bywater Prim Sch
WF10 .... 200 D7
Allerton Castle* HG5 .... 163 D4
Allerton Cl DL7 .... 210 C4
Allerton Dr 22 YO26 .... 165 F1
Allerton La HG5 .... 163 D4
ALLERTON MAULEVERER 163 E4
Allerton Mews HG1 .... 219 E1
Allertonshire Sch DL6 .... 210 D6
Allerton Wath Rd YO7 .... 65 D4
Allhallowgate HG4 .... 214 C5
Alliance Ind Est DL1 .... 3 E6
Allington Dr YO31 .... 229 B6
Allington Way
Darlington DL1 .... 3 F5
Great Burdon DL1 .... 4 A5
Allison Ave TS17 .... 6 B4
Allison St TS14 .... 8 E6
Alloway Gr TS8 .... 6 F5
All Saints CE Infants Sch
WF6 .... 200 A1
All Saints CE Junior & Infants Sch WF7 .... 200 E1
All Saints CE Prim Sch 12
LS29 .... 218 A4
All Saints CE Sch
Ingleby Barwick TS17 .... 6 A4
Kirkby Overblow HG3 .... 179 A4
All Saints Cl YO51 .... 141 B7
All Saints RC Lower Sch
YO23 .... 233 A1
All Saints RC Prim Sch
YO7 .... 211 B2
All Saints RC Upper School
YO29 .... 228 B2
All Saints Rd 1 YO12 .... 212 F4
All Saints Sq HG4 .... 214 D5
Alma Gdns HG4 .... 214 D4
Alma Gr YO10 .... 228 D2
Alma Par 2 YO11 .... 212 F5
Alma Pl DL10 .... 209 C7
Alma Rd BB8 .... 186 B3
Alma Sq 3 YO11 .... 212 F5
Alma Terr
Selby YO8 .... 232 C6
3 Skipton BD23 .... 217 A4
York YO10 .... 228 D2
Alma Way 2 YO18 .... 96 A6
Almery Terr YO30 .... 233 A3
Almond Cl
7 Filey YO14 .... 101 B4
Hambleton YO8 .... 197 B1
Almond Ct 4 TS4 .... 6 F8
Almond Gr
11 Filey YO14 .... 101 B4
Northallerton DL7 .... 210 D3
Scarborough YO12 .... 212 D5
York YO32 .... 225 D4
Almond Tree Ave
4 Carlton DN14 .... 204 C3
Malton YO17 .... 215 D6
Almscliffe Dr LS17 .... 178 B2
Almscliffe Garth LS17 .... 178 B4
Almsford Ave HG2 .... 222 E6
Almsford Bank HG2 .... 222 E5
Almsford Cl HG2 .... 222 F6
Almsford Dr
Harrogate HG2 .... 222 F6
York YO26 .... 227 C5
Almsford End HG2 .... 222 E6
Almsford Oval HG2 .... 222 F6
Almsford Pl HG2 .... 222 E6
Almsford Rd
Harrogate HG2 .... 222 F6
York YO26 .... 227 C5
Almsford Wlk HG2 .... 222 F6
Almshouse Hill 1 LS23 .... 188 E5
ALNE 142 F4
Alne Prim Sch YO61 .... 142 F4
Alne Rd
Easingwold YO61 .... 143 B8
Tollerton YO61 .... 143 A3
Alness Dr YO24 .... 230 B7
ALNE STATION 143 A5
Alne Terr YO10 .... 228 E2
Alpine Ct 5 WF10 .... 200 F3
Altofts La WF10 .... 200 B3
Altofts Rd WF6 .... 200 A1
Alum House La TS9 .... 26 B2
Alverton Cl YO17 .... 121 B7
Alverton Dr DL3 .... 3 B8
Alverton Infants Sch DL6 .... 210 F6
Alverton La DL7 .... 210 D4
Alvin Wlk 9 YO41 .... 185 B2
Alvis Gr YO10 .... 229 D4
Alwyne Dr YO30 .... 224 E1
Alwyne Gr YO30 .... 224 E1
Alwyn Rd DL3 .... 3 D8
Amber Ct YO31 .... 233 C4
Amberly St 4 YO26 .... 227 E5
Amber St YO31 .... 233 C4
Amble Cl YO62 .... 70 B2
Ambler Ct 23 WF6 .... 200 A1
Ambler's La YO30 .... 165 F7
Ambler St WF10 .... 200 E4
Ambleside Ave
10 Barnoldswick BB18 .... 171 D2
York YO10 .... 229 B4
Ambleside Gr TS5 .... 6 E8
Ambleside Wlk DL1 .... 3 D4
Ambrey Cl 16 YO14 .... 126 F8
Ambrose Rd HG4 .... 214 C4
Ambrose St YO10 .... 228 D1
America La BD20 .... 187 F4
Amesbury Cres TS8 .... 6 F5
Amiens Cres DL9 .... 209 D1
AMOTHERBY 121 B4
Amotherby La YO17 .... 121 A6
Amotherby Prim Sch
YO17 .... 121 A4
Amplecarr YO61 .... 117 B5
AMPLEFORTH 92 C1
Ampleforth Coll YO62 .... 92 D1
Ampleforth Coll Junior Sch
YO62 .... 118 F7
Amy Busfield Gn 40
LS29 .... 176 C1
Amy Johnson Way YO30 .... 225 A3
Anchorage Hill DL10 .... 209 D7
Anchorage La DL7 .... 210 C5
Anchorage Way YO21 .... 208 C5
Anchorite La 7 YO18 .... 95 F7
Anchor Rd 2 HG1 .... 220 A3
Ancress Wlk YO23 .... 233 A1
Ancroft Sq YO1 .... 233 C1
Anderson Gr 6 YO24 .... 227 F2
Anderson St 6 WF8 .... 201 B1
Anderton St 18 BD20 .... 187 E8
Andrew Dr 4 YO32 .... 225 F1
Andrew La YO18 .... 71 B4
Anfield Ct 8 DL1 .... 3 F6
Angel Ct 8 TS9 .... 26 C7
Angel Gdns HG5 .... 221 C7
Angelica Cl 12 HG3 .... 161 B3
Angel Yd 1 YO21 .... 208 D6
ANGRAM
Keld 35 E6
York 182 C3
Angram Cl YO30 .... 224 F1
Angram La
Barlby with Osgodby YO8 .... 198 A6
Muker DL11 .... 35 E6
Tollerton YO61 .... 143 B3
Angram Rd YO26 .... 182 A5
Angrove Cl TS9 .... 7 F1
Angrove Dr TS9 .... 7 F1
Annan Cl YO24 .... 230 C6
Annandale Ct 8 LS29 .... 218 B2
Annandale Gr 1 YO13 .... 75 D5
Annas Garth DL8 .... 60 F4
Anne St YO23 .... 228 C2
Annie St YO8 .... 232 C6
Annumhills Rd YO8 .... 199 D7
Anserdale La YO62 .... 70 E5
Anson Croft 5 YO8 .... 196 E1
Anson Dr YO10 .... 231 D8
Anteforth View DL10 .... 20 E3
Anthea Dr YO31 .... 225 E1
Anthony La HG4 .... 114 E1
Anvil Sq 3 DL11 .... 38 B6
Anvil Way DL7 .... 22 C2
Anzio Rd DL9 .... 209 C1
Apedale Rd
Castle Bolton with East & West Bolton DL8 .... 37 F1
Redmire DL8 .... 59 C8
Apley Cl HG2 .... 220 A1
Apollo St 9 YO10 .... 228 E3
APPERSETT 56 C5
Apple Blossom Ct 8
YO24 .... 227 B1
Appleby Ave HG5 .... 220 D8
Appleby Cres HG5 .... 220 D8
Appleby Ct HG5 .... 220 D8
Appleby Gate HG5 .... 220 D7
Appleby Glade YO32 .... 225 D7
Appleby Gn HG5 .... 220 D8
Appleby Gr HG5 .... 220 D8
Appleby La
Aldbrough DL11 .... 1 F1
Kirkby Malzeard HG4 .... 112 B4
Appleby Pl 2 YO31 .... 229 A5
Appleby Way HG5 .... 220 D7
Appleby Wlk HG5 .... 220 D8
Applecroft Rd
Selby YO8 .... 232 A4
York YO31 .... 229 B7
Applefields Sch YO31 .... 229 B5
Applegarth
Barnoldswick BB18 .... 171 E2
Coulby Newham TS8 .... 7 A4
Apple Garth
10 Easingwold YO61 .... 117 D1
15 Poppleton YO26 .... 165 F1
Applegarth Ct DL7 .... 210 D5
Applegarth Prim Sch
DL7 .... 210 D4
Applegarth St 15 BB18 .... 172 A1
Appleshaw Cl HG5 .... 221 C6
Appleton Cl 13 TS14 .... 8 F7
Appleton Ct YO23 .... 230 F3
Appleton La
Appleton-le-Street with Easthorpe YO17 .... 120 F4
Coneysthorpe YO60 .... 120 E2
APPLETON-LE-MOORS 70 F2
APPLETON-LE-STREET 120 F4
Appleton Rd YO23 .... 231 A3
APPLETON ROEBUCK 190 F5
Appleton Roebuck Prim Sch
1 YO23 .... 190 F5
APPLETON WISKE 24 B3
Appleton Wiske Prim Sch
DL6 .... 24 B3
Appletree Dr YO8 .... 196 E1
Appletree Gdns 2 TS7 .... 7 D8
Apple Tree Gdns 2
LS29 .... 175 C2
Apple Tree La
Great Preston LS25 .... 200 D8
4 Kippax LS25 .... 194 D1
Apple Tree Mews 5
LS25 .... 194 D1
Appletree Way
Malton YO17 .... 215 B4
10 Sherburn in Elmet LS25 .... 195 F4
APPLETREEWICK 157 D7
Appletreewick Stone Circ*
BD23 .... 135 E2
Apple Tree Wlk 7 LS25 .... 194 D1
Appley Cl TS16 .... 5 E7
Apron La HG3 .... 140 B2
Apsley Way 6 TS17 .... 5 F5
Arbour The
4 Glusburn BD20 .... 173 E1
Ilkley LS29 .... 218 A6
Arbour Way YO17 .... 215 E4
Arcade Sh Ctr* HG4 .... 214 C5
Arcade The LS29 .... 218 B4
Archaeology Store*
YO62 .... 92 F6
Archbishop Holgates Sch
YO10 .... 229 B3
Archbishop of York CE Jun Sch YO23 .... 231 A4
ARCHDEACON NEWTON 2 F7
Archer La HG3 .... 140 B3
Archer Rd DL2 .... 4 D3
Archers Green The DL10 .... 41 C7
Archers Mdw HG5 .... 221 F5
Archie St 3 HG1 .... 219 C5
Archway La 13 YO18 .... 96 D5
Arden Ct DL7 .... 210 D5
Arden La YO62 .... 92 B8
Arden Mews DL7 .... 210 D5
Arena View 12 DL10 .... 41 D5
Arenhall Cl 2 YO32 .... 225 C8
Arennig Ct 43 TS17 .... 5 F4
Argam Dikes* YO25 .... 127 B2
Argam La YO25 .... 126 F1
Argill DL8 .... 60 F5
Argyle Rd YO21 .... 208 C7
Argyle St YO23 .... 228 B1
ARKENDALE 163 B8
Arkendale La HG5 .... 141 A2
Arkendale Rd HG5 .... 162 F8
Arkengarthdale CE Prim Sch
DL11 .... 17 D1
Arkengarthdale Rd DL11 .... 38 B7
Arkle Cres DL1 .... 3 C3
Arlington Rd
Middlesbrough TS5 .... 6 F8
York YO30 .... 225 A1
Armoury Rd YO8 .... 232 B5
Armstrong Cl 7 WF6 .... 200 A2
Armstrong Way YO32 .... 224 E3
Army Foundation Coll
HG3 .... 161 A2
ARNCLIFFE 107 D2
Arncliffe CE Prim Sch
BD23 .... 107 D2
Arncliffe Dr WF11 .... 201 D2
Arncliffe Gr DL3 .... 2 F5
Arncliffe Rd HG2 .... 220 A1
Arndale Way 8 YO14 .... 101 B4
Arnold Rd DL1 .... 3 E6
Arnside Cres WF10 .... 201 B4
Arnside Pl 2 YO10 .... 228 F3
Arran Cl 1 TS17 .... 6 B6
Arran Ct LS25 .... 194 C3
Arran Dr LS25 .... 194 C3
Arran Pl YO31 .... 228 D7
ARRATHORNE 62 A8
Arrows Cres 10 YO51 .... 141 B5
Arrows Terr 9 YO51 .... 141 B5
Arthington Ave HG1 .... 219 E2
Arthur Pl 6 YO30 .... 224 B5
Arthurs Ave HG2 .... 222 C7
Arthurs Cl HG2 .... 222 C7
Arthurs Gr HG2 .... 222 C7
Arthur St
6 Barnoldswick BB18 .... 171 D2
Earby BB18 .... 186 A8
Great Ayton TS9 .... 8 A2
York YO10 .... 228 E4
Arts Ctr The* YO22 .... 208 E7
Arundel Ct 1 TS17 .... 5 F5
Arundel Gr YO24 .... 230 C7
Arundel Pl
12 Scarborough YO11 .... 212 F5
9 Whitby YO21 .... 208 C6
Arundel Rd 5 DN6 .... 206 E2
Ascot Ave 6 DL9 .... 40 F4
Ascot Cl DL6 .... 210 D3
Ascot Rd
Kippax LS25 .... 194 C1
Wigginton YO32 .... 166 D5
Ascot Way YO24 .... 227 D1
Ascough Wynd DL8 .... 63 D3
ASENBY 115 B6
Ash Bank Ave 2 HG4 .... 113 D2
Ash Bank Cl 1 HG4 .... 113 D2
Ashbank La
Firby DL8 .... 62 F1
Sheriff Hutton YO60 .... 145 F6
Ash Bank Rd HG4 .... 113 D2
Ashbourne Cl 12 YO51 .... 141 B4
Ashbourne Rd 10 YO51 .... 141 B4
Ashbourne Way YO24 .... 230 C8
Ashbrook Ct DL10 .... 20 E3
Ashburnham Cl 4 DN6 .... 206 F2
Ashburnham Wlk 5
DN6 .... 206 F2
Ashburn Pl LS29 .... 218 A3
Ashburn Rise 10 YO11 .... 212 E4
Ashburn Way LS22 .... 180 B4
Ash Cl
1 Ilkley LS29 .... 175 C2
Newton on Derwent YO41 .... 185 E4
York YO31 .... 229 B7
Ash Croft 7 DL10 .... 41 D5
Ashdale Cl DL2 .... 4 E4
Ashdale La LS22 .... 180 B4
Ashdale Rd
19 Dunnington YO19 .... 184 F7
Helmsley YO62 .... 92 F6
Ashdene Gr WF8 .... 201 D2
Ashdowne Cl DL8 .... 62 E5
Ashdowne Ct DL8 .... 62 E5
Ashdown Rise YO13 .... 75 C8
Ashes The
Barton DL10 .... 21 C7
Hellifield BD23 .... 154 A3
Ashfield LS22 .... 180 C3
Ashfield Ave YO17 .... 215 D5
Ashfield Cl
9 Constable Burton DL8 .... 61 C5
9 Pateley Bridge HG3 .... 137 B4
Ashfield Court Rd 10
HG3 .... 137 B4
Ashfield Cres BD23 .... 216 F2
Ashfield Ct YO24 .... 230 E7
Ashfield Prim Sch LS21 .... 176 F1
Ashfield Rd
Danby YO21 .... 29 B6
Harrogate HG1 .... 219 E4
6 Pickering YO18 .... 96 A6
Ashfield St WF6 .... 200 A2
Ashfield Terr
Harrogate HG1 .... 219 E4
Skipton BD23 .... 216 F2
Ashford Ave TS5 .... 6 D8
Ashford Pl YO24 .... 227 D2
Ashgap La WF6 .... 200 A2
Ashgarth Ct HG2 .... 222 C5
Ashgarth Way HG2 .... 222 C5
Ash Gn TS8 .... 7 A4
Ash Gr
13 Barnoldswick BB18 .... 171 D1
Danby YO21 .... 29 A6
12 Filey YO14 .... 101 B4
Glusburn BD20 .... 187 E7
Ilkley LS29 .... 218 C5
7 Kirkbymoorside YO62 .... 70 B1
1 Kirklevington TS15 .... 24 E8
Northallerton DL6 .... 210 F5
1 Riccall YO19 .... 197 F8
Ripon HG4 .... 214 A6
Scarborough YO12 .... 212 C7
Whitby YO21 .... 208 B6
Ashgrove BD23 .... 216 E4
Ashgrove Cres LS25 .... 194 D2
Ash Hill TS8 .... 7 B5
Ash La
Church Fenton LS24 .... 196 B6
Garforth LS25 .... 194 D4
8 Haxby YO32 .... 166 E5
Little Fenton LS25 .... 196 C5
Ashlands Cl DL6 .... 210 F4
Ashlands Ct DL6 .... 210 F4
Ashlands Dr DL7 .... 63 C5
Ashlands Prim Sch LS29 .... 218 C5
Ashlands Rd
Ilkley LS29 .... 218 C5
Northallerton DL6 .... 210 F4
Ash Lea
Danby YO21 .... 29 A6
Fairburn WF11 .... 201 D6
Ashlea Cl YO8 .... 232 D4
Ashlea Rd DL7 .... 210 D4
Ashley Ct 2 YO14 .... 101 B3
Ashley Park Cres YO31 .... 229 B6
Ashley Park Rd YO31 .... 229 B7
Ashmead 4 LS23 .... 188 E7
Ashmeade Cl YO24 .... 230 B8
Ash Rd
13 Filey YO14 .... 101 B4
Guisborough TS14 .... 8 F7
Harrogate HG2 .... 222 E6
Ash Ridge 5 DL6 .... 210 E3
Ashridge Cl 4 TS17 .... 6 B5
Ash St
11 Glusburn BD20 .... 187 E7
Ilkley LS29 .... 218 C5
Trawden BB8 .... 186 B1
York YO26 .... 227 E4
Ashton Ave YO30 .... 228 B8
Ashton Ct BD23 .... 154 B3
Ashton Rd WF10 .... 200 E3
Ash Tree Cl DL8 .... 62 F2
Ashtree Dr YO8 .... 197 D1
Ash Tree Garth LS24 .... 195 E7
Ash Tree Rd
8 Bedale DL8 .... 63 A2
Knaresborough HG5 .... 221 B6
Ashtree Way WF11 .... 201 C4
Ash Tree Wlk 22 LS29 .... 176 C1
Ash View HG2 .... 222 B6
Ashville Ave
Eaglescliffe TS16 .... 5 E6
Scarborough YO12 .... 212 F6
Ashville Cl HG2 .... 222 C5
Ashville Coll HG2 .... 222 B6
Ashville Dr 9 DL2 .... 2 E8
Ashville Gr HG2 .... 222 C5
Ashville St YO31 .... 228 D7
Ashwood Cl 5 YO62 .... 92 F7
Ashwood Dr TS9 .... 26 C8
Ashwood Glade YO32 .... 225 C6
Ashwood Pl HG5 .... 221 E5
Ashworth Rd WF8 .... 201 C2

Askam Ave WF8 201 C2
Aske Ave DL10 209 E8
Aske Hall★ DL10 20 D2
Askern & Campsall Sports Ctr DN6 206 F1
Askew Dale TS14 8 D6
Askew Rigg La YO18 71 A5
Askham Bog Nature Reserve★ TO23 230 C5
ASKHAM BRYAN 182 F3
Askham Bryan Coll YO23 182 F2
Askham Bryan Coll (Bedale Ctr) DL8 63 A2
Askham Bryan Coll (Guisborough Ctr) 17 TS14 8 F7
Askham Bryan Coll (Pickering Ctr) YO18 95 F8
Askham Bryan La YO23 230 A6
Askham Croft 1 YO24 227 B1
Askham Fields La YO23 182 F2
Askham Gr YO24 227 B2
Askham La
Askham Bryan YO24 230 A8
Woodthorpe YO23 230 A7
York YO24 227 B1
ASKHAM RICHARD 182 D3
ASKRIGG 57 F6
Askrigg Prim Sch DL8 57 E5
ASKWITH 176 D3
Askwith La LS21 176 D3
Askwith Moor Rd LS21 176 D5
Askwith Prim Sch LS21 176 D3
Aspen Cl
3 Dunnington YO19 184 F7
Pickering YO18 95 F7
Selby YO8 197 D2
Aspen Gr BB18 172 B1
Aspen La BB18 172 A1
Aspen Pk WF10 200 F2
Aspen Way
Slingsby YO62 120 B5
Tadcaster LS24 189 D6
Aspinall Rise 13 BD23 154 B3
Aspin Ave HG5 221 B4
Aspin Chase HG5 221 B4
Aspin Dr HG5 221 C4
Aspin Gdns HG5 221 C4
Aspin Gr 4 HG5 221 C4
Aspin La HG5 221 C3
Aspin Oval HG5 221 B4
Aspin Park Ave 1 HG5 221 C4
Aspin Park Cres HG5 221 B4
Aspin Park Dr HG5 221 B4
Aspin Park La HG5 221 C4
Aspin Park Prim Sch HG5 221 C5
Aspin Park Rd HG5 221 C4
Aspin View HG5 221 C4
Aspin Way HG5 221 C4
Asquith Ave
Scarborough YO12 212 E3
York YO31 229 A5
ASSELBY 205 D7
Assembly St 7 WF6 200 A1
Astbury TS8 7 C4
Asterley Dr TS5 6 D8
Astley Ave LS26 194 A1
Astley La
Great & Little Preston LS26 200 B8
Swillington LS26 194 A1
Astley Lane Ind Est LS26 200 B8
Astley Way LS26 200 A8
Atcherley Cl YO10 231 D8
Athelstan La 7 LS21 177 A1
Athelstan Prim Sch LS25 195 F3
Athelstans Ct LS25 195 F4
Athol Sq YO17 215 E4
Atkinson Ave DL10 209 D8
Atkinson Ct WF6 200 A1
Atkinson La WF8 201 C1
Atlas Rd YO30 225 A3
Atlas Wynd TS16 5 E3
Atlee Cl YO12 212 E2
Attermire Cave★ BD24 132 A3
Atterwith La YO26 182 A7
Auborough St 5 YO11 213 A6
Auckland Ave DL3 3 B6
Auckland Oval 2 DL3 3 B7
Auckland St TS14 8 F7
Auckland Way 7 YO21 208 C6
Aucuba Cl YO32 225 D2
Audax Cl YO30 225 A3
Audax Rd YO30 225 A3
Audby La LS22 180 C4
Audus St 10 YO8 232 C5
AUGHTON 193 C1
Augusta Cl DL1 3 F7
Aumit La YO62 92 E1
Aunums Cl 7 YO18 96 D5
Auster Bank Ave LS24 189 F7
Auster Bank Cres LS24 189 F7
Auster Bank Rd LS24 189 F7
Auster Bank View LS24 189 F7
Auster Rd YO30 225 B3
Austfield La LS25 202 B8
Austin Dr DL9 41 A5
Austin Rd WF10 201 B4
AUSTWICK 130 E7
Austwick CE Prim Sch LA2 130 E7
Austwick Rd BD24 131 C8
Autumn Ave 8 LS22 8 C4
Avalon Ct TS8 6 F5
Ava Rd DL9 40 C4
Avens Way TS17 6 A5
Avenue A LS23 181 A2
Avenue B LS23 181 A1
Avenue Bank HG4 86 C4
Avenue C E LS23 181 B1
Avenue Cl HG2 220 D4
Avenue C W LS23 181 A1
Avenue D LS23 181 A1
Avenue E E LS23 181 B1
Avenue E W LS23 189 A8
Avenue F LS23 181 B1
Avenue G LS23 181 B1
Avenue House Ct HG5 162 F3
Avenue Pl
Guisborough TS14 8 F7
7 Harrogate HG2 220 C3
Avenue Prim Sch The TS7 7 D6
Avenue Rd
11 Harrogate HG2 220 C3
Scarborough YO12 212 E4
York YO30 233 A4
Avenue St 8 HG2 220 C3
Avenue Terr
5 Harrogate HG2 220 C3
York YO30 233 A4
Avenue The
Campsall DN6 206 E1
Collingham LS22 180 A1
Dalby-cum-Skewsby YO60 119 B2
Eaglescliffe TS16 5 E6
26 Filey YO14 101 B3
Gilling East YO62 118 E7
Great Ribston with Walshford LS22 180 C8
Guisborough TS14 8 D6
Harrogate HG1 220 C4
5 Haxby YO32 166 E5
Haxby YO32 225 D8
Knaresborough HG5 221 A7
Masham HG4 86 C3
Middlesbrough TS5 6 F8
Norton YO17 215 C2
Nun Monkton YO26 165 A4
Nunnington YO62 93 E1
8 Pateley Bridge HG3 137 C4
Richmond DL10 209 D7
Rufforth YO23 182 C6
Skipton BD23 217 B6
Skutterskelfe TS15 25 E6
1 Sleights YO22 32 A6
Snape with Thorp DL8 87 A7
South Milford LS25 195 F2
Stainton Dale YO13 54 A8
Stokesley TS9 26 C7
Thirkleby High & Low with Osgodby YO7 116 D8
West Hauxwell DL8 61 C8
Whitby YO21 208 B4
Wighill LS24 181 D2
York YO30 228 A6
Avenue Victoria YO11 213 A3
Aviation Rd LS25 196 A4
Aviator Ct YO30 224 F3
Aviemore Ct 10 DL1 3 F6
Aviemore Rd TS8 6 F5
Avocet Cres 11 YO12 99 F6
Avocet Sh Ctr 8 YO12 99 E6
Avondale Rd HG1 219 F4
Avon Dr
Barnoldswick BB18 171 E2
Guisborough TS14 8 E6
York YO32 225 F6
Avon Garth LS22 180 B3
Avon Rd 8 DL2 22 D8
Avro Cl TS18 5 F7
Awnhams La YO42 169 D2
Axminster Rd TS8 6 F5
Axton Cl TS17 6 A6
Aylesham Ct YO32 225 E3
Aylton Dr TS5 6 E6
Aynham Cl 2 BD23 134 E2
Aynholme Cl 10 LS29 174 F4
Aynholme Dr 1 LS29 175 A4
Ayresome Way 1 DL1 3 F6
AYSGARTH 58 E3
Aysgarth Falls★ DL8 58 F3
Aysgarth Gr DL7 210 B2
Aysgarth Rd DL1 3 D4
Aysgarth Sch DL8 62 A4
Ayton Castle★ YO13 99 A8
Ayton Ct TS14 8 E7
Ayton Rd YO12 99 C7
Azalea Mews YO8 232 A5
AZERLEY 113 A5
Azerley Gr HG3 219 A4
Azerley La HG4 112 F3

B

Babyhouse La BD20 173 A1
Bachelor Ave HG1 219 D7
Bachelor Dr HG1 219 D7
Bachelor Gdns HG1 219 D6
Bachelor Hill YO24 227 C2
Bachelor Rd HG1 219 D6
Bachelor Way HG1 219 D6
Back Avenue Victoria 2 YO11 213 A3
Back Beck La LS29 174 F4
Back Bridge St BD23 216 F4
Back Chatsworth Gr HG1 219 D4
Back Cheltenham Mount HG1 219 D3
Back Colne Rd
9 Glusburn BD20 187 E7
Back Colne Rd *continued*
Trawden BB8 186 A2
Back Dawson Terr HG1 219 D5
Back Dragon Par HG1 219 E3
Back Dragon Rd HG1 219 E3
Back Elmwood St 3 HG1 219 E4
Back Gate LA6 103 D3
Back Gladstone St HG2 222 D7
Back Gn BD23 153 F5
Back Grange Ave HG1 219 D5
Back High St 13 HG3 137 B4
Backhouse St YO31 233 B4
Back La
Acaster Selby YO23 191 B3
Airton BD23 155 A6
Aiskew DL7 63 C5
Alne YO61 142 F4
Ampleforth YO62 92 C1
Appleton-le-Moors YO62 70 F2
Appleton Roebuck YO23 191 A5
Asselby DN14 205 D6
Bagby YO7 90 B3
Barkston Ash LS24 195 F6
Barlby with Osgodby YO8 198 C4
Barton DL10 21 C7
Barton-le-Street YO17 120 E5
1 Bedale DL8 63 A3
Bilbrough YO23 182 D1
Birstwith HG3 160 D5
Bolton-on-Swale DL10 41 E5
7 Boroughbridge YO51 141 B5
Borrowby YO7 65 E4
Bradleys Both BD20 173 E4
10 Brafferton YO61 115 F1
Bramham LS23 188 E6
Brearton HG3 162 A8
Burley in Warfedale LS29 176 C1
Carthorpe DL8 87 E7
Cold Kirby YO7 91 C8
Copmanthorpe YO23 230 A2
Copt Hewick HG4 114 B2
Cottingwith YO42 193 C5
Crakehall DL8 62 E4
Crathorne TS15 24 F6
Dalton YO7 115 E7
Dishforth YO7 115 A4
Drax YO8 204 F5
Eaglescliffe TS16 5 E4
Easingwold YO61 117 D1
East Tanfield DL8 87 D2
Ebberston & Yedingham YO13 97 D5
Ellerton YO42 193 C1
Fewston HG3 159 F1
Giggleswick BD24 130 F2
Great & Little Broughton TS9 26 E5
Great Ouseburn YO26 164 A8
Great Preston WF10 200 D6
Gristlthorp YO14 100 E5
Guisborough TS9 8 A4
Hambleton YO8 196 F1
Harome YO62 93 C5
Hawsker-cum-Stainsacre YO22 32 F5
11 Haxby YO32 166 D5
Hellifield BD23 154 B3
Hemingbrough YO8 198 F1
Hetton BD23 155 F5
Hirst Courtney YO8 203 F3
Holtby YO19 184 E8
Hunsingore LS22 180 E8
Hutton-le-Hole YO62 70 C4
Huttons Ambo YO60 147 B7
Kirby Wiske YO7 88 E7
Kirkby Malham BD23 154 F8
Kirkby Malzeard HG4 112 C5
Leavening YO17 147 E2
Lockton YO18 72 E4
Longnewton TS21 4 F8
Long Preston BD23 153 F5
Low Coniscliffe & Merrybent DL2 2 E4
Low Worsall TS15 24 C7
Luttons YO17 150 B8
Malham BD23 132 F2
Markington with Wallerthwaite HG3 139 C3
Marton cum Grafton YO51 141 D1
Marton YO62 94 F5
Melmerby HG4 114 B7
8 Middleham DL8 60 E2
Morton-on-Swale DL7 64 A6
Moulton DL10 21 E3
Newby Wiske DL7 64 D3
Newholm-cum-Dunsley YO21 13 A1
Newton-on-Ouse YO30 165 B6
North Cowton DL7 22 B3
North Duffield YO8 199 A7
Norton DN6 206 E2
Osmotherley DL6 45 B4
Raskelf YO61 116 F2
Rathmell BD24 153 C6
Reeth, Fremington & Healaugh DL11 38 B6
2 Riccall YO19 198 A8
Rookwith HG4 86 A8
Scorton DL10 41 E6
Settrington YO17 148 D8
Sicklinghall LS22 179 E3
Sinnington YO62 95 A8
Skelton HG4 140 E7
Sutton-under-Whitestonecliffe YO7 90 E5
Thirkleby High & Low with Osgodby YO7 116 D8
Back La *continued*
Thirsk YO7 211 B1
Tholthorpe YO61 142 D5
Thormanby YO61 116 F6
Thornton Steward DL8 61 C2
Topcliffe YO7 115 C7
Trawden BB8 186 A1
Tunstall DL10 41 B3
Tunstall LA6 102 A4
Weaverthorpe YO17 124 E1
Weeton LS17 178 C2
Wennington LA2 102 C2
Westerdale YO21 28 E5
West Tanfield HG4 87 A1
West Witton DL8 59 C4
Whixley YO26 164 A3
Whorlton DL6 45 D8
Wilberfoss YO41 185 F5
Wold Newton YO25 126 A4
Wombleton YO62 93 E7
Wray-with-Botton LA2 128 A6
York YO26 227 A5
Back Lane S
Middleton YO18 95 E8
Wheldrake YO19 192 F7
Back Mary St 3 BD20 173 F1
Back Middleton Rd 9 LS29 218 A4
Back Nelson Rd 12 LS29 218 B4
Back Newton La WF10 201 A7
Back Nook 1 DL8 58 F1
Back Northgate 18 WF8 201 B1
Back of Parks Rd YO62 70 C2
Back of the Beck 6 BD23 216 F4
Back O' Newton YO41 185 E3
Back Parish Ghyll Rd 8 LS29 218 B4
Back Park St YO8 232 D5
Back Rd
Birstwith HG3 160 B5
Thormanby YO61 116 F5
Back Regent Pl 4 HG1 220 C4
Back Royal Par 5 HG1 219 C2
Back Sea View YO14 101 C1
Back Side YO17 149 B5
Backside La YO62 93 E6
Back St
Boroughbridge YO51 141 C5
Bramham LS23 188 E6
Burton Fleming YO25 126 E3
Langtoft YO25 151 D5
10 Middleham DL8 60 E2
Wold Newton YO25 126 A4
Back Station Rd 17 BD20 187 E8
Backstone La LS29 218 C3
Backstone Way LS29 218 C4
Back Street Hilda's Terr YO21 208 D7
Back Syke DL8 57 D5
Back Tewit Well Rd HG2 222 E8
Back Weston Rd 5 LS29 218 B4
Back West View 2 YO30 228 B7
Back York Pl 6 HG1 219 D1
Bacon Ave WF6 200 B2
Bad Bargain La YO31 229 A5
Baden St HG1 219 F4
Bader Ave TS17 6 B6
Bader Prim Sch TS17 6 B6
Badgerbeck Rd 2 DL9 209 B1
Badger Butt La BD23 155 B5
Badger Cl 33 LS29 175 C2
Badger Gate BD23 134 D3
Badger Hill Dr 14 DL8 63 B3
Badger Hill Prim Sch YO10 229 B2
Badger La DN6 207 A3
Badger Paddock 5 YO31 225 E2
Badgers Gate LS29 175 C6
Badger Way YO8 198 E3
Badger Wood Glade LS22 180 C4
Badger Wood Wlk YO10 229 D3
Badminton Ct 18 DL1 3 F6
Baek Chapel St 26 BB18 171 D1
Baffam Ct YO8 232 B1
Baffam Gdns YO8 232 B2
Baffam La YO8 232 B2
BAGBY 90 C3
Bagby La YO7 90 B2
Bagdale YO21 208 C6
Bagdale Ct YO21 208 D6
Baghill La WF8 201 C1
Baildon Ave LS25 194 D2
Baildon Cl 3 YO26 227 D4
Baile Hill Terr YO1 233 B1
Bailey Ct
Northallerton DL7 210 C4
28 Walkerville DL9 41 A5
Bailey La BD23 152 E3
Bailey St BB18 172 B1
Bailey The BD23 217 A4
BAINBRIDGE 57 D5
Bainbridge CE Prim Sch DL8 57 D5
Bainbridge Dr YO8 232 C4
Bajan Pl HG4 214 A6
Bakersfield Dr DN14 202 F3
Baker St
Appleton Wiske DL6 24 A3
York YO30 228 C7
Bakewell Mews 6 DL2 3 A7
Bala Cl 2 TS17 5 F4
BALDERSBY 88 D1
Baldersby Garth
Baldersby YO7 88 D1
Rainton YO7 114 F6
BALDERSBY ST JAMES 114 E8
Baldersby St James CE Prim Sch YO7 114 E7
Baldersdale Ave 1 HG5 221 D5
Baldoon Sands TS5 6 D6
Baldwin St 4 HG1 219 C5
Balfour St YO26 227 F5
Balfour Terr TS5 6 D8
Balfour Way YO32 167 A6
Baliol Croft TS21 5 A7
Balk La DN14 207 F7
Balksyde YO62 120 B5
Balk The
Bishop Wilton YO41 169 C2
Marton-le-Moor HG4 114 E1
Slingsby YO62 120 B5
Balk Top YO7 115 B1
Ball Grove Dr BB8 186 A3
Ballhall La YO42 193 E6
Ballowfield Nature Reserve★ DL8 58 C4
Balmer Hill DL2 1 C8
Balmoral Ave TS17 6 C8
Balmoral Dr LS26 200 B6
Balmoral Rd
Barmpton DL1 3 E8
Lingdale TS12 9 F6
Middlesbrough TS3 7 C8
Ripon HG4 214 C3
Balmoral Sh Ctr YO11 213 A6
Balmoral Terr 5 YO23 228 B1
BALNE 207 C5
Balne Hall Rd DN14 207 F5
Balne Moor Rd DN14 207 B6
Balshaw Rd LA2 129 B3
Baltimore Way DL1 3 D7
Bamburgh Ct TS17 5 F5
Banbury Rd WF8 201 C2
Bancroft Fold 18 BB18 171 D1
Bancroft Mill Engine Steam Mus★ BB18 171 D1
Bands La DL8 56 C4
Bank Bottom LA6 103 D3
Bank Cl 2 YO22 32 A6
Bank Dike Hill HG3 159 A4
Bankfield La DN14 205 A7
Bankfield St BB8 186 A2
Bank Hall Cl LA6 103 D4
Bankhead Cl DL6 210 F4
Bankhead Rd DL6 210 F4
Bank House La LA6 103 B5
Bank La
Egton YO21 30 E5
Faceby TS9 25 F1
Grassington BD23 134 E3
Great & Little Broughton TS9 26 F3
Silsden BD20 174 C4
Banklands Ave BD20 174 C1
Banklands La BD20 174 C1
BANK NEWTON 172 B8
Bank Rd
Glusburn BD20 187 E8
Selby YO8 232 D6
Banks Bridge Cl BB18 171 E2
Banksfields Ct TS6 7 F8
Banks Hill 1 BB18 171 D2
Bank Side
2 Eastfield YO11 100 A7
Rawcliffe DN14 205 A2
Bankside Cl
3 Poppleton YO26 165 F1
Thirsk YO7 211 D2
Banks La
Knottingley WF11 201 F2
Scorton DL10 41 E7
Banks Rd
Brompton DL6 44 A2
Darlington DL1 3 E6
Banks Rise 4 LA2 129 A8
Bank St
Barnoldswick BB18 171 D1
Castleford WF10 200 E4
11 Wetherby LS22 180 C3
Banks Way 3 LA2 129 A8
Bank The DL10 41 D4
Bank Top LA6 103 D3
Bank Top La 4 TS13 12 A7
Bankwell Cl BD24 131 D2
Bankwell Rd BD24 131 D2
Bank Wood Rd WF8 206 A6
Bank Yd DL10 209 C6
Bannisdale 6 YO24 230 C7
Bannister Cl BB8 186 B2
Bannister Wlk BD22 187 B6
Barbara Gr 4 YO24 227 F3
Barbeck YO7 211 C3
Barbeck Cl YO7 211 D3
Barberry TS8 7 B4
Barberry Cl
Ingleby TS17 6 B5
20 Killinghall HG3 161 B3
Barbers Dr YO23 230 B4
Barbican Ct YO10 233 C1
Barbican Mews YO10 228 E3
Barbican Rd YO10 233 C1
Barbondale Gr HG5 221 C5
Barbondale Rd LA6 77 A7
Bar Convent Mus★ YO24 233 A1
Bardale Cl 2 HG5 221 D6
BARDEN 61 A8
Barden Ct 6 YO30 224 F1
Barden Fell View 3 BD23 134 E2
Barden La DL8 40 B1
Barden Moor Rd DL1 3 E4
Barden Pl 9 YO14 101 A3

- Barden Rd BD23 157 A1
- Barden Twr★ BD23 157 C4
- Bardney Rd 14 YO14 126 F8
- Bardsley Cl TS16 5 E7
- Barefoot St HG4 214 C4
- Barf Bank DL8 61 A2
- Barff Cl 10 YO8 197 D1
- Barff Gr 6 YO8 197 B2
- Barff La YO8 197 C1
- Barff View YO8 203 D7
- Barfield Rd YO31 228 F8
- Barf La YO41 169 D4
- Bargate DL10 209 B6
- Barker Bsns Pk HG4 114 C6
- Barker Dr YO8 232 B6
- Barker La YO1 233 A2
- Barkers Arc DL6 210 D4
- Barker's La
  - Newholm-cum-Dunsley YO21 13 A1
  - Snainton YO13 98 A4
- Barkery The TS8 7 B3
- Barkhouse Bank HG3 138 F4
- Bark House La LA2 131 B8
- Barkhouse Wood La WF11 202 D6
- Bark La
  - Addingham LS29 175 A5
  - Embsay with Eastby BD23 157 A1
- Bar Knotts Terr YO17 215 C3
- BARKSTON ASH 195 F7
- Barkston Ash Cath Prim Sch LS24 195 E7
- Barkston Ave YO26 227 B3
- Barkston Cl 3 YO26 227 A3
- Barkston Gr YO26 227 A3
- Barkston Rd YO26 227 A3
- Bar La
  - Bramham cum Oglethorpe LS23 188 F7
  - Garforth LS25 194 D4
  - Hambleton YO8 196 E1
  - Knaresborough HG5 162 D5
  - Roecliffe YO51 141 A5
  - York YO1 233 A2
- BARLBY 198 B5
- Barlby Bridge Com Prim Sch YO8 232 D6
- Barlby By-pass 2 YO8 198 B4
- Barlby Com Prim Sch YO8 198 B4
- Barlby Cres YO8 232 F7
- Barlby High Sch YO8 198 B5
- Barlby Rd YO8 232 E6
- Barley Cl YO17 215 D2
- Barleycorn Yd YO1 233 C2
- Barleycroft YO11 213 C1
- Barleyfields La 5 LS22 180 C3
- Barley Fields Prim Sch TS17 6 A4
- Barleyfields Rd 4 LS22 180 C3
- Barley Hall★ YO1 233 B3
- Barleyhill Rd LS25 194 B4
- Barley Horn Rd LS24 190 B2
- Barley Rise YO32 167 A6
- Barley's Yd 1 YO7 211 B3
- Barley View YO32 225 C8
- Barley Wlk 16 LS25 195 F2
- BARLOW 204 C7
- Barlow CE Prim Sch YO8 204 C7
- Barlow Cl TS14 8 F6
- Barlow Comm Nature Reserve★ YO8 204 B7
- Barlow Comm Rd YO8 204 B8
- Barlow Rd YO8 204 B6
- Barlow St YO26 227 D4
- Barmby Ave YO10 231 E8
- Barmby Cl 4 YO30 224 F1
- Barmby Ferry Rd 1 YO8 198 F1
- BARMBY ON THE MARSH 205 B7
- Barmby on the Marsh Prim Sch DN14 205 B7
- Barmoor Cl YO13 75 D6
- Barmoor Gn YO13 75 D6
- Barmoor La YO13 75 C6
- Barmpton La DL1 3 F7
- Barnaby Pl TS14 8 E7
- Barnard La YO13 98 C4
- Barnard's Rd YO22 31 A4
- Barnbow La LS15 194 A6
- Barn Elms YO8 204 C5
- Barnes Rd
  - Castleford WF10 200 E3
  - Darlington DL3 3 A6
- Barney La YO60 146 A1
- Barn Field Cl BB8 186 A3
- Barnfield Way YO23 230 A2
- Barnhill La DN14 205 F7
- Barningham Rd DL11 18 G7
- BARNOLDSWICK
  - Earby 171 D1
  - Ingleton 103 A2
- Barnoldswick CE Prim Sch BB18 171 D1
- Barnoldswick La LA6 103 A2
- Barnsdale Est WF10 200 D3
- Barnsdale Rd
  - Ledston WF10 200 E7
  - Mickletown LS26 200 B5
- Barnsdale View DN6 206 E2
- Barns Wray 2 YO61 117 D1
- Barnwell Cres HG2 222 B5
- Barnwood Cres BB18 172 B1
- Barnwood Rd BB18 172 A1
- Barnygate La YO60 147 A7
- Barons Cres YO23 230 B2
- Bar Pl HG1 219 D5
- Barracks Bank DL10 21 A2
- Barrack View DL10 209 C8
- Barrel Sykes 3 BD24 131 D3
- Barret St 18 BB18 172 A1
- Barrett Ave 3 YO24 227 F3
- Barrett Rd DL3 3 A5
- Barrington Garth DN14 202 F3
- Barr La YO32 167 D4
- Barrowby La
  - Austhorpe LS15 194 A4
  - Kirkby Overblow HG3 179 A3
- BARROWCLIFF 212 D7
- Barrowcliff Infant Sch YO12 212 C7
- Barrowcliff Junior Sch YO12 212 C7
- Barrowcliff Rd YO12 212 D7
- Barry Bank YO21 11 F1
- Barry's La YO12 212 E2
- Barse Beck La HG3 160 D5
- Bar St YO11 213 A6
- Barstow Ave YO10 228 F3
- Barstow Fall 2 WF8 201 C2
- Bar The 6 DL10 209 C6
- Bartindale Rd YO14 127 A5
- Bartle Garth YO1 233 C3
- BARTON 21 D7
- Barton CE Prim Sch DL10 21 D7
- BARTON HILL 146 D3
- BARTON-LE-STREET 120 E5
- BARTON-LE-WILLOWS 146 D1
- Barton Quarry Ind Est DL10 20 B6
- Bartons Garth YO8 232 B2
- Barton St DL1 3 E6
- Barton Way HG4 113 C8
- Barugh La
  - Barugh (Great & Little) YO17 95 B2
  - Normanby YO62 94 F4
- Barugh Way HG4 114 B6
- Barwick Cl 9 ts17 6 A5
- Barwick Fields 8 TS17 6 A5
- BARWICK IN ELMET 194 B8
- Barwick in Elmet CE Sch LS15 194 C8
- Barwick La
  - Ingleby Barwick TS17 5 F5
  - Ingleby TS17 6 A4
- Barwick Parade Prim Sch YO8 232 E4
- Barwick Rd LS25 194 C5
- Barwick St YO12 212 F5
- Barwick Terr 1 YO12 212 F5
- Barwick View 10 TS17 6 A5
- Barwick Way TS17 6 A4
- Barwic Parade YO8 232 E4
- Bassett Cl YO8 232 C3
- Bassleton La TS17 6 A6
- Baston La YO61 143 E4
- Batemans Yd 3 YO7 211 B3
- Bates Ave DL3 3 B7
- Bateson Cl YO10 229 C1
- Bath St LS29 218 C5
- Battalion Ct DL9 41 A4
- BATTERSBY 27 D6
- Battersby Ave TS9 27 C7
- Battersby Sta TS9 27 C6
- Battery Par YO21 208 D7
- Battleflats Way YO41 168 D2
- Battle of Bramham Moor (site of)★ LS24 188 F4
- Battle of Marston Moor (site of)★ YO26 181 F7
- Battle of the Standard 1138 (site of)★ DL6 43 E4
- Battle of Towton (site of)★ LS24 195 D8
- Battling Hills La YO18 49 B5
- Bawhead Rd 23 BB18 172 A1
- Bawtry Cl YO8 232 D3
- Bawtry Rd YO8 232 D3
- Baxby Manor★ YO61 117 B6
- Baxby Terr 2 DL2 22 D8
- Baxtergate YO21 208 D6
- Baxter Wood BD20 187 E8
- Baxton's Sprunt 1 YO62 92 F7
- Bay Bolton Ave DL8 59 F3
- Bay Cres YO14 101 B2
- Baydale Rd DL3 3 A4
- Bay Horse Yd 9 BD23 216 F4
- Baynes Ct YO8 232 A2
- Baynes Way BD23 217 D8
- Baysdale Ave YO10 229 D3
- Baysdale Cl 3 TS14 8 F6
- Baysdale Rd TS17 6 B7
- Bazeley's La YO17 215 E1
- Beach Rd The YO14 101 B3
- Beach The YO14 101 B3
- Beacon Bank YO62 92 D1
- Beacon Brow Rd YO13 75 A7
- Beacon Grange Pk DL2 4 C7
- Beacon Hill DL1 4 B7
- Beacon Park First Ave 10 YO18 95 F7
- Beacon Park Second Ave 9 YO18 95 F7
- Beacon Rd
  - Millington YO42 170 B1
  - Seamer YO12 99 D7
- Beacon Rise 4 LS29 175 C2
- Beaconsfield Mews YO24 227 D3
- Beaconsfield St
  - Northallerton DL7 210 D4
  - 3 Scarborough YO12 212 E3
  - York YO24 227 D3
- Beacons La 18 TS17 5 F4
- Beacon St 5 LS29 175 A4
- Beacon View 3 BD23 217 E8
- Beacon Way YO22 32 D6
- BEADLAM 93 C7
- Beadlam Ave TS7 7 D6
- Beadle Garth YO23 230 B2
- Beadnell Cl 3 TS17 6 B5
- Beagle Croft YO41 168 C1
- Beagle Ridge Dr YO24 227 C1
- Beagle Spinney YO41 168 C1
- BEAL 202 D4
- Beale Cl TS17 6 B5
- Beal La
  - Beal DN14 202 D4
  - Cridling Stubbs WF11 202 C1
- BEAMSLEY 174 F7
- Beamsley Ct BD23 217 A2
- Beamsley La BD23 174 F7
- Beamsley View 13 LS29 175 C2
- Beancroft Rd WF10 200 E3
- Beancroft St WF10 200 E3
- Beanland La YO32 167 D2
- Beanlands Dr 7 BD20 187 E7
- Beanlands Par LS29 218 C5
- Beanlands Pl 8 BD20 187 E7
- Bean Sheaf La YO17 96 A3
- Bean's Way YO31 229 B8
- Beatswell Lawn HG4 113 C8
- Beaufighter Cl DL10 41 F6
- Beaufort Cl
  - Guisborough TS14 8 F5
  - York YO10 229 B3
- Beaulieu Cl 1 YO32 225 F5
- Beaumont Hill DL1 3 D8
- Beaumont Hill Sch & Tech Coll DL1 3 E7
- Beaumont Pl YO8 232 A2
- Beaverdyke YO30 224 F1
- Bebra Gdns★ HG5 221 A5
- Becca La LS25 194 F8
- Beckbridge La 2 WF6 200 B1
- Beckbridge Rd WF6 200 B2
- Beckbridge Way WF6 200 B1
- Beck Cl 6 YO41 185 B2
- Beckclose La DL8 87 F6
- Beck Closes Rd YO26 142 A3
- Beckdale Rd YO62 92 E7
- BECKERMONDS 80 D3
- Beckett Cl 8 YO62 93 D7
- Beckett Dr YO10 229 D4
- Beckfield Cl 6 BD20 187 F7
- Beckfield La
  - Fairburn WF11 201 C7
  - York YO26 227 B5
- Beckfield Pl YO26 227 B4
- Beckfields Ave TS17 6 A4
- Beck Hole 9 YO11 100 B6
- Beck Hole Rd YO22 31 C1
- Beck Holme YO22 32 B6
- Beck Isle Mus★ YO18 95 F7
- Beck La
  - Cloughton YO13 54 C1
  - Collingham LS22 180 A1
  - Farndale East YO62 48 F2
  - Leavening YO17 147 E1
  - Lebberston YO11 100 D5
  - South Kilvington YO7 211 B6
  - Wheldrake YO19 193 A8
- Becklands Cl YO51 141 A5
- Becklands La YO51 141 A4
- Beck Mdw LS15 194 C7
- Beck Mill Cl YO17 215 D3
- Beck Row YO41 169 D5
- Becks Brow BD23 153 C3
- Becks Cl 5 YO32 225 C8
- Beckside
  - Aberford LS25 194 F7
  - Catterick DL10 41 E4
  - 7 Elvington YO41 185 B2
  - Malton YO17 215 F4
  - Northallerton DL7 210 B4
  - 4 Staithes TS13 13 K2
  - Stillingfleet YO19 191 D3
  - Trawden Forest BB8 186 B2
  - Wilberfoss YO41 185 F6
- Beck Side BD23 173 B4
- Beckside Cl
  - 13 Addingham LS29 174 F4
  - 29 Burley in Warfedale LS29 176 C1
- Beck Side Cl BD20 173 D1
- Beckside Ct 6 BD20 174 C1
- Beckside Gdns YO10 228 F4
- Beckwith Ave HG2 222 B7
- Beckwith Cl
  - Harrogate HG2 222 A6
  - Heworth YO31 229 C7
- Beckwith Cres HG2 222 B7
- Beckwith Dr HG2 222 B6
- Beckwith Hall Dr 7 YO19 198 A8
- Beckwith Head Rd HG3 178 C8
- Beckwith Rd HG2 222 A7
- BECKWITHSHAW 178 A7
- Beckwithshaw Prim Sch HG3 178 A8
- Beckwith Wlk HG2 222 A7
- BEDALE 63 B2
- Bedale Ave
  - Scarborough YO12 212 E8
  - York YO10 229 D4
- Bedale CE Prim Sch DL8 63 A2
- Bedale High Sch DL8 63 A2
- Bedale La HG4 114 A8
- Bedale L Ctr DL8 63 A2
- Bedale Mus★ DL8 63 A3
- Bedale Rd
  - Aiskew DL7 63 C4
  - Hunton DL8 61 E7
  - Scotton DL9 40 F2
  - Well DL8 87 A4
- Bedale Sta DL8 63 A3
- Bedburn Dr DL3 2 F5
- Bede Ave YO30 228 B7
- Bedern YO1 233 C3
- Bedern Bank 13 HG4 214 C5
- Bedern Ct 16 HG4 214 C5
- Bedford Rd TS7 7 D6
- Bedfords Fold 6 LS25 202 A7
- Bedford St 13 YO11 213 A6
- BEDLAM 161 A8
- Bedlam Hill YO7 65 E4
- Bedlam La
  - Fewston HG3 159 F2
  - Staveley HG5 140 E1
- Bedlington's La YO22 33 C4
- Beech Ave
  - 3 Airmyn DN14 205 E4
  - Bishopthorpe YO23 231 A3
  - 1 Earby BB18 172 A1
  - Harrogate HG2 222 E6
  - 4 Naburn YO23 191 C7
  - 4 Topcliffe YO7 89 B1
  - York YO24 227 F3
- Beech Cl
  - Baldersby YO7 88 D1
  - 6 Eastfield YO11 100 A7
  - 2 Elvington YO41 185 B2
  - Farnham HG5 162 D7
  - Great Ayton TS9 7 F1
  - Hunton DL9 40 E2
  - Scruton DL7 63 E7
  - 7 Sherburn in Elmet LS25 195 F4
  - Snape with Thorp DL8 87 A7
  - 3 South Milford LS25 195 F2
  - Tadcaster LS24 189 F6
- Beech Cres
  - Castleford WF10 201 B3
  - Whitwell-on-the-Hill YO60 146 E4
- Beech Croft
  - Barlby with Osgodby YO8 198 B6
  - Pontefract WF8 201 C2
- Beechcroft Cl TS12 9 F6
- Beech Ct
  - Bishopthorpe YO23 231 A3
  - 2 Castleford WF10 200 F3
  - Hellifield BD23 154 B3
- Beech Dr
  - 6 Kirkbymoorside YO62 70 B1
  - 12 Scalby YO13 75 D5
  - South Milford LS25 195 F2
- Beecher Stowe Dr 39 DL9 41 A5
- Beeches End LS23 188 F8
- Beeches The
  - Middleton St George DL2 4 D4
  - Skelton YO30 224 C4
  - 11 Stokesley TS9 26 C7
  - 26 Upper Poppleton YO26 165 F1
  - Wetherby LS22 180 D4
- Beechfield
  - Coulby Newham TS8 7 A5
  - Hawsker-cum-Stainsacre YO22 33 A6
  - Newby Wiske DL7 64 F2
  - Newton-on-Ouse YO30 165 B6
- Beechfield Cl 15 YO8 197 B1
- Beechfield Rd DL10 209 C8
- Beech Glade YO31 225 F2
- Beech Gr
  - 1 Airmyn DN14 205 E4
  - Burton Salmon LS25 201 F6
  - Camblesforth YO8 204 C5
  - Harrogate HG2 219 C1
  - Knaresborough HG5 221 B8
  - Maltby TS8 6 C4
  - Northallerton DL6 210 E5
  - Selby YO8 232 C5
  - Sherburn in Elmet LS25 195 F4
  - Sowerby YO7 211 C1
  - Whitby YO21 208 B6
  - York YO26 227 C4
- Beech Hill
  - Carleton BD23 173 A4
  - 6 Knaresborough HG5 221 A6
  - 5 Pontefract WF8 201 C1
- Beech Hill Rd BD23 173 A4
- Beechings Mews YO21 208 B7
- Beech La
  - 8 East Ayton/West Ayton YO13 99 A7
  - 3 Spofforth HG3 179 E6
- Beechnut La WF8 201 B1
- Beech Pk YO19 198 A8
- Beech Pl 5 YO32 167 A6
- Beech Rd
  - Boston Spa LS23 188 E8
  - Campsall DN6 206 E1
  - Darlington DL1 3 F7
  - Harrogate HG2 222 E6
  - Ripon HG4 214 B3
- Beech Rise DL1 3 F7
- Beech St
  - 23 Barnoldswick BB18 171 D1
  - 10 Glusburn BD20 187 E7
  - 6 Harrogate HG2 220 C3
- Beech Tree Ct 2 YO30 164 F7
- Beech Tree La YO8 204 C5
- Beechtree Rd LS24 189 D5
- Beech View
  - Aberford LS25 194 E8
  - Ferrybridge WF11 201 C4
- Beechville Ave YO12 212 F6
- Beech Way 25 YO26 165 F1
- Beech Wlk
  - 5 Eastfield YO11 100 A7
  - Tadcaster LS24 189 D6
- Beechwood Ave 2 TS9 26 C8
- Beechwood Cl
  - 14 Bedale DL8 63 A2
  - Markington with Wallerthwaite HG3 139 D4
  - Sherburn in Elmet LS25 195 F3
  - West Marton BD23 171 F5
- Beechwood Cres 6 HG2 219 C1
- Beechwood Croft LS25 195 F3
- Beechwood Dr BD23 216 D5
- Beechwood Glade
  - Sherburn in Elmet LS25 195 F3
  - 6 York YO24 227 B1
- Beechwood Gr
  - Harrogate HG2 222 F7
  - 16 Ilkley LS29 175 C2
- Beechwood Rd YO17 215 D2
- Beechwood Rise 1 LS22 180 C4
- Beeforth Cl YO32 225 D5
- Beeston's La LS17 178 C4
- Beeston Way WF10 200 E6
- Beggarmans Rd DL8 80 C8
- Belbrough Cl 3 TS15 25 C4
- Belbrough La TS15 25 C4
- Belcombe Way 1 YO30 228 A7
- Belford La HG4 112 A3
- Belford Pl 3 HG1 219 D1
- Belford Rd HG1 219 D2
- Belford Sq 9 HG1 219 D1
- Belfry Way 30 WF6 200 B1
- Belgrave Cres
  - Harrogate HG2 222 E8
  - 15 Scarborough YO11 212 F5
- Belgrave St
  - 3 Skipton BD23 216 E4
  - York YO31 228 C7
- Belgrave Terr
  - 3 Hurworth-on-Tees DL2 22 D8
  - 14 Scarborough YO11 212 F5
  - Thirsk YO7 211 B2
- Bellaby Pk 7 YO62 93 D7
- Bellburn La DL3 3 B7
- BELL BUSK 155 A3
- Bell Cl
  - Haxby YO32 225 C8
  - 5 Seamer YO12 99 D6
- Belle Hill BD24 131 D3
- Bell End Gn YO18 49 D3
- BELLERBY 60 D7
- Bellerby Camp DL8 60 B7
- Bellerbyhurn Rd YO17 95 F2
- Bellerby Rd DL8 60 D6
- Belle Vue LS29 218 C3
- Belle Vue Cres 33 YO14 101 B3
- Belle Vue Par 9 YO11 212 F5
- Belle Vue Pl 10 YO11 212 F5
- Belle Vue St
  - 34 Filey YO14 101 B3
  - Scarborough YO12 212 F5
  - York YO10 228 E3
- Bellevue Terr
  - Ripon HG4 214 C5
  - 2 Skipton BD23 216 E4
- Belle Vue Terr
  - Whitby YO21 208 D7
  - York YO10 228 E3
- Bellfarm Ave YO31 228 E8
- Bellflower Cl 16 WF10 200 D3
- Bellground La YO30 165 D4
- Bell Hall★ YO19 191 E6
- Bell Horse Gate LA6 103 D4
- Bellhouse La YO21 29 C7
- Bellhouse Way YO24 230 B8
- Bellingham Cl YO7 211 C3
- Bell La
  - Cawood YO8 197 A7
  - Huby YO61 144 A4
  - Husthwaite YO61 117 B5
  - Rawcliffe DN14 205 A2
  - Ulleskelf LS24 190 C2
- Bellmans Croft YO23 230 B2
- Bellman Wlk 3 HG4 113 D2
- Bell's Ct 15 YO62 92 F6
- Bellwood Ave
  - Boston Spa LS23 188 E7
  - Lockwood TS12 9 E7
- Bellwood Dr YO24 230 B8
- Belmangate 2 TS14 8 F6
- Belmont WF11 201 D5
- Belmont Ave
  - Harrogate HG2 220 D4
  - 10 Otley LS21 176 F1
- Belmont Cl 3 YO30 225 A1
- Belmont Gr
  - Calcutt HG5 221 A4
  - 1 Harrogate HG2 220 D3
- Belmont Prim Sch 7 TS14 8 F6
- Belmont Rd
  - Harrogate HG2 219 C2
  - Ilkley LS29 218 E4
  - Scarborough YO11 213 A4
- Belmont St BD23 216 F4
- Belmont Terr 2 HG2 220 D3
- Belmont View HG5 221 A4
- Belmont Wharf BD23 216 F4
- Belthorpe La YO42 169 E1
- Belton Park Dr 7 DL9 40 E4
- Belvedere Pl YO11 213 A3
- Belvedere Rd YO11 213 A3
- Belvedere Terr YO11 213 A3
- Belvoir Ave 8 YO41 185 B2

- Belvoir Dr WF11 201 F2
- Belvoir Terr 9 YO11 213 A5
- Bence The YO42 170 C3
- Benedict Ave YO8 232 E4
- BENINGBROUGH 165 D4
- Beningbrough Dr HG3 219 B5
- Beningbrough Hall & Gdns* YO30 165 B5
- Beningbrough La YO30 165 D5
- Benjy La YO19 192 E7
- Benkhill Dr 16 DL8 63 A2
- Ben La BB18 171 E2
- Bennett St 11 BD23 216 F3
- Bennions Way 5 DL10 41 E4
- Bennison La YO21 13 A1
- Bennymoor La YO8 198 C4
- BEN RHYDDING 218 E3
- Ben Rhydding Dr LS29 218 F3
- Ben Rhydding Prim Sch LS29 218 E4
- Ben Rhydding Rd LS29 218 D3
- Ben Rhydding Sta LS29 218 F4
- Bensham Rd DL1 3 D8
- Benson La WF6 200 B2
- BENT 187 D7
- Bentham Moor Rd LA6 103 A2
- Bentham Rd LA6 103 B3
- Bentham Sta LA2 129 A7
- Bentinck Ave TS5 6 F8
- Bent La
  - Colne BB8 186 A3
  - Sutton BD20 187 E7
- Bentley Wynd TS16 5 D3
- Benton Gap La BD22 187 B7
- Bent Rigg La YO13 54 B7
- Bents La YO18 71 A5
- Beresford Cl 6 DL8 63 B2
- Beresford Terr YO23 228 C1
- Berghill La YO7 66 A7
- Berkeley Terr YO26 227 E5
- Berkley Dr TS14 8 F5
- Bernard La YO26 164 B3
- Bernica Gr TS17 6 A4
- Berry Bank DL2 1 A6
- Berrygate La HG4 214 E7
- Berry La LS26 200 C8
- Berry's Ave 5 HG5 221 B6
- Berrys Ct 16 HG5 221 B6
- Berwick Rd
  - Archdeacon Newton DL3 3 A7
  - 18 Scotton DL9 40 E4
- Bestmire La DL6 65 A4
- Betteras Hill Rd LS25 202 A8
- Betton Farm Visitor Ctr* YO13 99 C8
- Betton Rise YO13 99 B8
- Between Dikes Rd YO8 204 F8
- Beulah St 10 HG1 219 D2
- Beulah Terr YO11 212 F5
- Beverley Balk YO41 168 B2
- Beverley Cl 12 YO11 100 B6
- Beverley Gate YO12 99 D1
- Beverley Rd
  - 11 Eastfield YO11 100 B6
  - Middlesbrough TS7 7 D6
  - Norton YO17 215 E3
- Beverley Rise LS29 175 C2
- Beverley Sch TS4 6 F8
- BEWERLEY 137 B3
- Bewerley Rd HG1 219 B5
- Bewlay St YO23 228 C2
- Bewley Gr TS5 6 E7
- Bexhill Cl WF8 201 C1
- Bexley Dr TS6 7 E8
- BICKERTON 181 A5
- Bickerton Way LS21 176 F1
- Bickley Gate YO13 73 F6
- Bickley Howe YO12 212 B4
- Bickley Way TS8 7 A5
- Bielby Cl
  - 8 Bedale DL8 63 B3
  - 33 Scalby YO12 75 D5
- BIGGIN 196 E5
- Biggin La LS25 196 C6
- Big Meadow Dr 5 LS29 174 E4
- Big Sheep & Little Cow Farm* DL8 63 B3
- BILBROUGH 182 D1
- Bilsdale Cl
  - Northallerton DL7 210 C2
  - York YO30 224 E2
- Bilsdale Gr HG5 221 D6
- Bilsdale Midcable Chopgate CE Prim Sch TS9 46 F6
- BILTON 219 E6
- Bilton Cl HG1 219 E6
- Bilton Dr HG1 219 D4
- Bilton Grange Cl HG1 219 D5
- Bilton Grange Prim Sch HG1 219 D5
- Bilton Grove Ave HG1 219 E5
- Bilton Hall Dr HG1 220 D6
- BILTON IN AINSTY 181 E4
- Bilton La HG1 219 E6
- Binks Cl DL6 210 B7
- Binnington Carr La YO12 99 B1
- Binns La BD20 187 D7
- Binsley La YO61 117 E2
- BINSOE 86 F2
- Binsoe La HG4 86 F3
- Birch Ave
  - Malton YO17 215 D6
  - Sleights YO22 32 A6
- Birch Cl
  - 8 Filey YO14 101 B3
- Birch Cl *continued*
  - 9 Hunton DL9 40 F2
  - 2 Kirklevington TS15 24 E8
  - 4 Thorpe Willoughby YO8 197 B1
  - York YO32 225 D3
- Birch Copse YO24 227 D2
- Birch Cres 10 YO22 32 A6
- Birch Dr
  - 2 Faceby TS9 25 F1
  - Kippax LS25 194 D2
- Birchen Cl 7 WF10 200 D3
- Birches The TS8 7 A5
- Birchfield Dr TS16 5 D5
- Birch Gr
  - Castleford WF10 201 B3
  - Harrogate HG1 219 E6
  - Kippax LS25 194 D1
  - Sleights YO22 32 A6
- Birch Hall La BB18 172 B1
- Birch La
  - 13 Haxby YO32 166 E5
  - New York HG3 137 F1
- Birch Park Ind Est YO31 228 E8
- Birch Pk YO31 225 E1
- Birch Rd DL1 3 D8
- Birch View 8 YO18 96 A6
- Birch Way YO61 143 D8
- Birchwood Cl 16 BD24 131 D2
- Birchwood Ct 5 LS29 218 A4
- Birchwood Gdns 13 YO61 115 F1
- Birchwood Mews HG2 222 F7
- Birchwood Rd TS7 7 C6
- Birdale Field La LS22 188 B8
- BIRDFORTH 116 E6
- Birdforth Way 1 YO62 92 C1
- Bird Gdn* LS25 195 B7
- Bird La
  - Hensall DN14 203 D2
  - Kellington DN14 202 F4
- Bird Ridding La DL8 60 B1
- BIRDSALL 148 B4
- Birds of Prey & Conservation Ctr* YO7 88 F7
- Birdwood Cl DL9 209 C2
- Birk Brow Rd TS12 9 D5
- BIRKBY 23 B1
- Birkby La DL7 23 B1
- Birk-crag Ct 2 HG3 161 B2
- Birk Crag Nature Reserve* HG3 161 B1
- Birkdale Ave HG5 221 D5
- Birkdale Gr 4 YO26 227 B5
- Birkdale Rd 9 TS18 5 D8
- Birker La
  - Newton on Derwent YO41 185 D4
  - Wilberfoss YO41 185 F6
- Birkett La CA17 14 B7
- Birk Field Bank YO21 28 F6
- Birk Head La YO18 70 F4
- Birkhills HG3 140 A3
- BIRKIN 202 D6
- Birkin La WF11 202 B4
- Birkin Rd YO8 202 F5
- Birk La YO8 199 D8
- Birklands 1 YO62 93 D7
- Birkwith La LA2 128 F7
- BIRSTWITH 160 E6
- Birstwith CE Prim Sch HG3 160 E6
- Birstwith Dr YO26 227 E4
- Birstwith Grange HG3 160 E6
- Birstwith Rd HG1 220 A3
- Birthwaite La HG3 161 C8
- Birtley Ave TS5 6 E7
- Bishop Cl 1 HG3 137 C4
- Bishop Ct 2 YO8 232 B6
- Bishopdale Cl HG5 221 D6
- Bishopdale Ct 28 BD24 131 D2
- Bishopdale Dr 7 LS22 180 A1
- Bishopdike Rd
  - Cawood YO8 197 A6
  - Sherburn in Elmet LS25 196 A4
- Bishop Garth 2 HG3 137 C4
- Bishopgate St YO23 233 B1
- Bishophill Jun YO1 233 A1
- Bishophill Senior YO1 233 B1
- BISHOP MONKTON 140 A5
- Bishop Monkton CE Prim Sch HG3 140 A5
- Bishop Monkton Railway Cutting Nature Reserve* HG3 139 F5
- Bishop's Cl YO8 197 A8
- Bishops Ct YO1 233 B1
- Bishopsfields Dr YO26 228 A5
- Bishopsgarth DL7 210 C4
- Bishopsway YO10 229 C3
- Bishops Way DL10 41 D5
- BISHOP THORNTON 138 F2
- Bishop Thornton CE Prim Sch HG3 139 F2
- BISHOPTHORPE 231 B3
- Bishopthorpe Infant Sch YO23 231 A4
- Bishopthorpe Palace* YO23 231 B4
- Bishopthorpe Rd YO23 231 B5
- BISHOPTON 113 D2
- Bishopton HG4 214 A5
- Bishopton La
  - Great Burdon DL1 4 A7
  - Ripon HG4 113 D2
- Bishopton Pk HG4 214 A5
- Bishop Way 3 HG3 137 C4
- BISHOP WILTON 169 F2
- Bishop Wilton CE Prim Sch YO42 169 F2
- Bisley Ct 13 DL1 3 F6
- Bismarck St YO26 227 E5
- Bitterdale La YO62 70 A3
- Black Abbey La 1 BD20 187 E8
- Black Bank Rd LA2 130 E3
- BLACK BANKS 3 D2
- Blackbird Way 8 YO12 99 F6
- Black Bull Wynd TS16 5 C3
- Blackburn Ind Est 7 LS25 196 A4
- Blackburn La WF11 202 B2
- Black Diamond Way 3 TS16 5 D5
- Black Dike La YO26 182 F8
- Blackett Rd DL1 3 E6
- Black Fen La YO8 232 C8
- Black Gill La
  - Airton BD23 154 B8
  - Settle BD24 132 A1
- Black Hill YO62 118 E5
- Black Hill Rd HG3 157 F8
- Black Horse La TS15 25 C3
- Blacklee Cl 3 YO32 167 B8
- Blackmore Cl TS14 8 F5
- Black Sheep Brewery Visitor Ctr* HG4 86 C4
- Black Sike La YO13 98 B4
- Blacksmith Bank DL8 62 E5
- Blacksmith Ct DL7 22 C2
- Blacksmith Hill YO22 53 A7
- Blacksmiths Cl 5 YO41 185 C2
- Blackthorn TS8 7 B4
- Blackthorn Cl DN14 207 A7
- Blackthorn Dr YO31 225 E2
- Blackthorn La HG3 222 C3
- Blackthorn Rd LS29 218 D5
- BLACKWELL 3 B4
- Blackwell DL3 3 B3
- Blackwell La DL3 3 B4
- Black Wlk WF8 201 B1
- Blackwood La YO8 198 F7
- Blackwood Rd YO8 198 E8
- BLADES 37 B5
- Blair Ave TS17 5 F4
- Blair Pk HG5 221 C5
- Blake Ct YO19 193 A8
- Blake Gate HG3 136 E1
- Blakeley Cres 3 BB18 171 D2
- Blakeley Gr YO30 224 F3
- Blakeney Pl YO10 228 F3
- Blake St YO1 233 B3
- Blakey Bank YO62 49 A5
- Blakey Cl YO7 211 C1
- Blakey La YO7 211 C1
- Blakey Rd YO62 70 B6
- Blandford Rd DL9 40 E3
- Bland La YO26 227 A4
- Blands Ave WF10 200 D7
- Bland's Cliff 27 YO11 213 A6
- Blandscliff Gall* YO11 213 B6
- Blands Cres 3 WF10 200 D7
- Blands Gr 4 WF10 200 D7
- Bland's Hill HG5 221 A4
- Blands Terr WF10 200 D7
- Blansby La YO17 121 C8
- Blansby Park La YO18 96 A8
- Blatchford YO30 228 B8
- Blatchford Mews YO30 228 B8
- Blawath Rd YO18 51 A2
- Blayshaw La HG3 110 B4
- BLAZEFIELD 137 E4
- Blazefield Bank HG3 137 D3
- Bleaberry La YO41 169 B5
- Bleachfield YO10 228 F2
- Blea Moor Rd LA6 78 E2
- Blean La DL8 57 D3
- Blea Pit La HG4 140 E8
- Bleara Rd BB18 186 B8
- Blenheim Ave 4 YO21 208 B7
- Blenheim Cl DL10 41 F6
- Blenheim Ct
  - Harrogate HG2 222 D7
  - Rawcliffe YO30 224 D3
- Blenheim St 12 YO12 213 A7
- Blenheim Terr YO12 213 A7
- Blenheim Way HG2 222 C7
- Bleriot Way YO30 225 A3
- Blewhouse La DL8 61 E3
- Blind La
  - Aiskew DL8 63 B3
  - Barton DL10 21 D7
  - Burton in Lonsdale LA6 102 F3
  - Guisborough TS14 8 C6
  - Hurworth DL2 22 E8
  - Knaresborough HG5 221 B7
  - Scorton DL10 42 B8
  - Tockwith YO26 181 B8
- Blind Piece La YO7 116 A6
- Bloe Beck La LA2 129 E6
- Bloody Beck Hill YO13 54 A7
- Blorenge Ct 22 TS17 5 F4
- Blossomgate HG4 214 B5
- Blossom St YO24 233 A1
- Blossoms The LS26 200 B6
- Blossom Way WF10 200 D3
- BLUBBERHOUSES 159 D2
- Blue Bank YO22 32 A4
- Blue Barn La TS15 25 C6
- Bluebeck Dr YO30 227 E8
- Blue Bell Farm Ct YO8 192 E1
- Blue Bell Gr TS5 6 F6
- Bluebell Mdw 15 HG3 161 B3
- Bluebell Mews WF10 200 C3
- Bluebell Wlk 18 HG3 161 B3
- Blue Bridge La YO10 228 D2
- Blue Coat YO19 184 D7
- Blue Nile Way 25 DL9 41 A5
- Blue Ridge Pk WF10 200 E3
- Blue Slates Cl YO19 193 A8
- Blyth Cl YO8 232 A5
- Board St YO23 228 C2
- Boar La TS17 6 B5
- Boatcliffe Rd YO14 127 D7
- Boathouse La DL2 2 E4
- Boat La
  - Barforth DL11 1 C7
  - Great Ouseburn YO26 164 C8
  - Kirby Hall YO26 142 C1
  - Mickletown LS26 200 D5
- Bob La YO7 65 E3
- Bodmin Dr WF6 200 A2
- Bodner Hill YO61 118 F1
- Boeing Way TS18 5 F7
- Boggart La LS24 190 C2
- Boggy La DL10 209 B5
- Bog Hall YO21 208 D5
- Boghole Bank DL6 45 B3
- Boghouse La TS13 10 F3
- Bog La
  - Askham Bryan YO24 230 B6
  - Barwick in Elmet & Scholes LS15 194 A7
  - Stirton with Thorlby BD23 216 D7
- Bogs La
  - Bridge Hewick HG4 114 C1
  - Harrogate HG1 220 C5
- Bolckow St TS14 8 F7
- Boldron Cl 8 TS18 5 D8
- Bold Venture St BD23 216 F2
- Bolland St 16 BB18 171 D2
- Bolling Rd LS29 218 D4
- BOLTBY 66 F1
- Boltby Rd YO30 224 F2
- BOLTON ABBEY 174 E8
- Bolton Abbey Sta BD23 174 D8
- Bolton Ave DL10 209 B7
- BOLTON BRIDGE 174 F8
- Bolton Bridge Rd LS29 218 A4
- Bolton Castle* DL8 59 B6
- Bolton Cross DL10 41 F5
- Bolton Ct 14 DL8 60 D5
- Bolton Hall* BD23 157 F1
- Bolton La YO42 169 E1
- BOLTON-ON-SWALE 41 F6
- Bolton-on-Swale CE Prim Sch DL10 41 F6
- Bolton-on-Swale Lake Nature Reserve* DL10 41 F5
- BOLTON PERCY 190 D4
- Bolton Percy Station Nature Reserve* YO23 190 C4
- Bolton Priory (rems of)* BD23 157 F1
- Bolton Rd
  - Draughton BD23 174 F7
  - Ellerton DL10 41 E5
  - Silsden BD20 174 D3
- Bolton St HG1 219 D4
- Bolton Way
  - 13 Leyburn DL8 60 D5
  - Richmond DL10 209 C8
- Bonby La YO8 192 E2
- Bond End HG5 221 A6
- Bondgate
  - Darlington DL1 3 C5
  - Helmsley YO62 92 F6
  - Pontefract WF8 201 C1
  - Ripon HG4 214 C4
  - Selby YO8 232 B7
- Bondgate Ct HG4 214 C4
- Bondgate Gn HG4 214 D4
- Bondgate Green Cl 6 HG4 214 C4
- Bondgate Green La HG4 214 C4
- Bondings Rise 5 LS25 196 A4
- Bond La
  - Appleton Roebuck YO23 190 F5
  - Settle BD24 131 D2
- Bond St WF8 201 C1
- Bonington Ct 7 YO26 227 E4
- Bonney Croft La 25 YO61 143 C8
- Bonnygate La YO61 118 F3
- Bonny Gr TS8 7 C5
- Bonnygrove Way TS8 7 B5
- Bonnywell La YO7 114 E6
- Boonhill Rd YO62 69 F4
- BOOSBECK 9 E8
- Boosbeck Rd TS12 9 D8
- Bootham YO30 233 A3
- Bootham Bar* YO31 233 B3
- Bootham Cres YO30 233 A4
- Bootham Junior Sch YO30 228 A7
- Bootham Park Ct YO31 233 B4
- Bootham Park Hospl YO31 233 B4
- Bootham Row YO30 233 B3
- Bootham Sch YO30 233 A3
- Bootham Sq YO30 233 B3
- BOOTHAM STRAY 225 B2
- Bootham Terr YO30 233 A3
- Booth Bridge La BD23 172 A3
- BOOTHFERRY 205 E5
- Booth Ferry Rd DN14 205 F6
- Booth St 27 LS29 176 C1
- Boothwood Rd YO30 224 E2
- Boot St 26 BB18 172 A1
- Booty La DN14 206 F7
- BOOZE 17 F1
- Borage Rd 30 HG3 161 B3
- BORDLEY 133 D3
- Bore Tree Baulk YO19 184 D6
- Borogate 9 YO62 92 F6
- BOROUGHBRIDGE 141 C5
- Boroughbridge High Sch YO51 141 B5
- Boroughbridge L Ctr YO51 141 B5
- Boroughbridge Prim Sch YO51 141 B5
- Boroughbridge Rd
  - Bishop Monkton HG3 140 B5
  - Bridge Hewick HG4 114 B1
  - Dishforth YO7 115 A2
  - Knaresborough HG5 221 B7
  - Northallerton DL7 210 C1
  - North Otterington DL7 64 E6
  - Ripon HG4 214 E3
  - Scriven HG5 162 E6
  - Westwick YO51 140 D4
  - Whixley YO26 164 B4
  - York YO26 227 D5
- Borough Mere La YO17 215 D8
- Borough Rd
  - Darlington DL1 3 D5
  - Richmond DL10 208 D7
- Borrage Green La HG4 214 B4
- Borrage La HG4 214 B4
- BORROWBY
  - Northallerton 65 E4
  - Whitby 11 D6
- Borrowby Ave DL6 210 F3
- Borrowby Ct TS14 8 E7
- Borrowbydale Ave HG5 221 D6
- Borrowby La
  - Borrowby TS13 11 D7
  - Staithes TS13 13 J1
- Borrowdale Dr
  - Castleford WF10 201 B5
  - York YO30 224 F1
- Boscombe Gdns 2 TS8 6 F5
- BOSSALL 168 D7
- Boss Moor La BD23 155 F8
- Boston Ave DL6 210 D4
- Boston Dr TS7 7 B5
- Boston Rd
  - Clifford LS23 188 E7
  - Wetherby LS22 180 C2
- BOSTON SPA 188 F8
- Boston Spa Sch LS23 188 D8
- Botheby Wood BD23 216 E5
- Bottom House La YO22 33 B5
- Bottoms La YO22 33 B6
- BOTTON 29 B3
- Botton Rd LA2 128 E2
- Boulby Bank YO22 208 E6
- Bouldershaw La DL11 17 D1
- Boulsworth Dr BB8 186 B1
- Boulsworth Gr 4 BB8 186 A3
- Boundary Ave BD20 187 E7
- Boundary Way DL10 209 F8
- Bourlon Rd DL9 209 A2
- Bourn Ave DL1 3 E2
- Bournemouth Ave 2 TS3 7 C8
- Bournemouth Rd TS3 7 C8
- BOUTHWAITE 110 E2
- Bouthwaite Dr 13 YO26 227 E4
- Bow Bridge Dr BD23 217 D7
- Bowbridge La DL7 63 A8
- Bow Bridge La YO21 29 A7
- Bow Bridge View LS24 189 F7
- Bowcarr La YO26 163 D8
- Bowcliffe Rd LS23 188 E5
- Bowe Cres 8 DL8 63 B2
- Bowen Rd DL3 3 B7
- Bower Rd HG1 219 D3
- Bower St HG1 219 D2
- Bowers Wharf BD23 216 F3
- Bower Wlk YO17 215 E4
- Bowes Ave YO31 228 E5
- Bowes Ct DL1 3 D6
- Bowesfield Cres TS18 6 A8
- Bowesfield Ind Est TS18 6 A8
- Bowesfield La TS18 6 A7
- Bowes La YO14 100 F5
- Bowes Pk HG2 222 D6
- Bowland Cl HG2 220 D1
- Bowland Ct HG2 220 D1
- Bowland La YO42 193 E2
- Bowland View LA6 103 E3
- Bowland Way YO30 225 A1
- Bowling Green Ct YO31 228 D8
- Bowling Green La
  - 9 Hunmanby YO14 126 F8
  - Manfield DL2 2 B4
  - York YO31 233 C4
- Bowling Green Yd 13 HG5 221 A6
- Bowling La YO17 215 E4
- Bowling Terr BD23 216 D3
- Bowling View BD23 216 D3
- Bowman St DL3 3 D7
- Bowness Dr YO30 224 E1
- Bowood Cl 8 TS17 5 F5
- Bow St TS14 8 F7
- Bowthorpe La YO8 199 B4
- Bowyers Cl YO23 230 C4
- Box Hill YO12 212 C3
- Box La WF8 201 C1
- Boyle & Petyt Prim Sch BD23 174 F8
- Boyle The LS15 194 B8
- Boynton La
  - Barton-le-Street YO17 120 F8
  - Rawcliffe DN14 205 A1
- Boynton Rd DL7 22 E2
- Brabourn Gdns TS8 6 F5
- BRACEWELL 171 C3
- Bracewell La BD23 171 B4
- Bracewell St 15 BB18 171 D2
- Brackenber Cl BD24 131 C2

Brackenber La BD24 .... 131 C1
BRACKENBOTTOM 105 E3
Bracken Cl
Whitby YO22 ....208 E4
York YO32 ....225 F4
Bracken Cres TS14.........8 D6
Bracken Field BD23......134 B3
Brackenfield Prep Sch
HG1 ....219 A2
Bracken Ghyll Dr BD20...174 B1
Bracken Hill
Scarborough YO12.......212 C7
2 York YO10...........229 C3
Brackenhill Ave YO8 ....232 A4
Brackenhill La
Brayton YO8...........232 A3
Church Fenton LS24.........196 C8
Sleights YO22.............32 A5
Brackenhills YO26.........165 F1
Brackenley Ave 2 BD23. 217 C7
Brackenley Cl 3 BD23 .. 217 C7
Brackenley Cres BD23.... 217 C7
Brackenley Ct BD23....... 217 C7
Brackenley Dr BD23....... 217 C7
Brackenley Gr 1 BD23.. 217 C7
Brackenley La BD23..... 217 A7
Bracken Rd YO24 ....230 F7
Brackenthwaite La HG3 . 222 A1
Brackenwell La LS17.....178 B4
Brackenwood Cl 2 LS29 .218 E4
Brackit La YO61...........91 B2
Bracknell Rd TS17 ....6 C8
Bradfords Cl 8 LS23.....188 E6
Bradley Ave
Castleford WF10 ....200 E4
Northallerton DL6 ....210 F2
Bradley Cres YO23 ....182 D6
Bradley Dr YO24 ....230 C8
Bradley Gr BD20.........174 B1
Bradley La YO23 ....182 C5
Bradley Rd
Pickering YO18 ....71 F4
Silsden BD20..............174 B2
Bradley Rise BD20........174 B1
Bradleys Both Com Prim Sch
BD20 ....173 E3
Bradleys Terr 2 TS9 ....8 A2
Bradworth Cl 3 YO11....100 B7
Bradworth Dr 2 YO11 ...100 B7
Braeburn Infant Sch 14
YO11 ....100 A6
Braeburn Junior Sch 15
YO14 ....100 A6
Braegate La LS24 ....190 E7
Braemar Dr LS25 ....194 D4
Braeside 3 TS15 ....24 E8
Braeside Gdns YO24 .....227 E3
BRAFFERTON 116 A1
Brafferton Hall Gdn 3
YO61 ....115 F1
Braham La HG5............179 F7
BRAIDLEY..................83 B2
Brailsford Cres YO30.....228 A8
Braimber La YO51.........141 C1
Braithegayte YO19 ....192 F8
Braithwaite Hall★ DL8 ....84 D8
Braithwaite La
Dacre HG3...............159 A7
East Witton Town DL8 ....84 E8
Braker La YO26 ....163 F4
Bramall La 6 DL1 ....3 F6
Bramble Cl
13 Colburn DL9 ....41 A5
11 Killinghall HG3 ....161 B3
Bramble Ct 20 LS25 ......195 F4
Bramble Dene YO24........230 D7
Bramblefields DL6 ....210 F4
Brambles 8 YO8 ....197 B1
Brambles Ct LS25..........202 B7
Brambles The 6 LS29.....175 C2
Bramble Wlk YO17........215 B4
Brambling Fields La
YO17 ....122 C2
Bramblings The 6
WF10.......................200 D3
Bramcote Sch YO11 .....213 A3
Brame La HG3.............177 A8
Bramfield Way 6 TS17......6 D6
BRAMHAM..................188 F5
Bramham Ave YO26 ......227 A3
Bramham Dr HG3..........219 A4
Bramham Gr YO26 ....227 A3
Bramham La LS23 ....188 A6
Bramham Park Gdns★
LS23.......................188 C4
Bramham Prim Sch
LS23.......................188 E6
Bramham Rd
Boston Spa LS23 ....188 E7
Thorner LS14..............188 A3
York YO26 ....227 A2
Bramley Ave YO8 ....198 B5
Bramley Garth YO31 .....229 B6
Bramley Head La HG3....158 E5
Bramper La DL7 ....42 E1
Branch Rd BD23...........216 F2
Brandon Gr YO32 ....226 E3
BRANDSBY 118 C3
Brandsby Bank YO61 .....118 D3
Brandsby Gr YO31 ....225 E2
Brandsby Rd YO61 ....118 A1
Brandsby St YO61.........118 A1
Brankin Dr DL1 ....3 E4
Brankin Rd DL1..............3 D3
Branklyn Gdns TS17........6 A4
BRANKSOME 2 F6
Branksome Gr 1 TS18 .....5 E8
Branksome Sch DL3 ....3 A6
Bransdale TS14 ....8 D6
Bransdale Ave
Northallerton DL7 ....210 C2
11 Pontefract WF6 ....200 A2
Bransdale Cl 6 WF6.....200 A2
Bransdale Gr 3 HG5.....221 D6
Bransdale Mews 10 WF6 200 A2
Bransdale Rd YO62.........48 B1
Bransdale Wlk WF6 ....200 A2
Bransholme Dr YO30.....225 A2
Brant Bank La LS29 ....175 B3
Brantingham Dr 2 TS17 ...5 F5
Brant La LS24 ....189 D4
Branton Cl YO26 ....142 A1
Branton Ct YO26 ....142 A1
BRANTON GREEN.........142 A1
Branton La YO26...........142 A1
Branton Pl YO26 ....227 A3
Brass Castle La TS8 ....7 C3
Brat La LS21...............177 A7
Bravener Ct YO30 ....165 B6
BRAWBY...................94 F1
Brawby La YO17 ....94 E1
BRAWITH 26 A6
Bray Gate YO42 ....169 E2
Braygate Balk YO18 ....72 C5
Braygate La YO18 ....72 D5
Braygate St YO17 ....121 A2
Bray Rd YO10..............231 F8
Brayshaw La BD23 ....135 A2
BRAYTHORN 177 E4
Braythorne La LS21.......177 E4
BRAYTON 232 A2
Brayton CE Infant Sch
YO8 ....232 A2
Brayton Coll YO8 ....232 A3
Brayton Junc YO8..........232 C1
Brayton Junior Sch YO8. 232 A3
Brayton La YO8 ....232 B1
Brazengate BD23 ....134 B3
Breakmoor Ave BD20 .....174 C2
Breamar Ct 2 DN14 ......203 A2
Brearlands BD23...........172 A3
BREARTON.................162 A7
Brearton La HG3...........161 E8
Breary Cl YO24 ....227 F1
Breary Flat La HG5.......221 C7
Brechin Dr TS17 ....6 B6
Breckenbrough La DL10...41 A3
Breckenbrough Sch YO7 ..89 A6
Breckney La YO17.........122 D5
Breckon Hill YO62..........49 A1
Brecksfield YO30..........224 C5
Brecks La
Beadlam YO62 ....93 B8
Kippax LS25...............194 C2
Pockley YO62................93 B8
Strensall YO32 ....167 B7
Swillington LS26 ....194 B2
York YO32 ....225 F4
Brecon Cres TS17 ....5 F4
Breedycroft La YO17 .....121 C4
BREIGHTON 199 D5
Breighton Aerodrome★
YO8 ....199 D5
Breighton Rd
Bubwith YO8 ....199 D6
Wressle YO8 ....199 C3
Brendon Gr TS17..............6 A3
Brentwood DL8..............60 D5
Brentwood Cres YO10 ....229 C2
Brewers Ct YO7............211 B3
Brewerton St HG5 ....221 A5
Brewery La
5 Ripon HG4 ....214 C4
Skipton BD23...............216 F4
Brewery Rd LS29 ....218 C4
Brewster Terr HG4 ....214 C6
Briar Ave YO26.............227 B4
Briar Cl DL8..................59 C6
Briar Cliffe YO8............232 A3
Briardene Ave 9 YO12.....75 E5
Briar Dr YO31 ....225 F2
Briarfield Cl LS29.........218 D3
Briar Pk 5 YO62............93 D7
Briar Rd TS17................6 B7
Briars Ct YO23.............190 E5
Briars Dr YO23.............190 E5
Briars The HG5 ....221 B7
Briar Wlk DL3 ....3 B3
Briarwood Cl YO8........202 F7
Brickfield La YO51 ....141 D4
Brickhill La YO8 ....204 F4
Brickkiln La
Aldbrough DL11..............2 A3
Forcett & Carkin DL11.......20 C8
Brick Kiln La YO8 ....203 D6
Brick Lands La DN14......203 F4
Brickyard Rd YO51 ....141 A4
Bridge Beck La YO7........66 C7
Bridge Cl
Burniston YO13..............75 D7
Church Fenton LS24.......196 A7
3 Colburn DL9 ....41 A5
Haxby YO32 ....225 C7
5 Knaresborough HG5.... 221 A5
Newton-le-Willows DL8.....62 B4
Bridge Cres YO8...........205 C8
Bridge Ct YO8 ....232 D6
Bridge End DL6.............65 B5
Bridge End Yd 6 BD24.. 131 D3
Bridge Farm DN14 ....207 F6
Bridge Farm Cl 27 YO62....92 F6
Bridge Foot LS23 ....188 F8
Bridge Garth
2 Boston Spa LS23 ....188 E7
South Milford LS25 ....195 F2
Bridge Gn YO21............29 C7
BRIDGE HEWICK.........114 B1
Bridge Hill LS21 ....176 C7
Bridge Holm La YO22 .....33 C2
BRIDGEHOUSE GATE......137 B4
Bridge La
Ilkley LS29.................218 A5
Pollington DN14...........207 F6
York YO30 ....233 B4
Bridge Mews LA6 ....103 C4
Bridge Rd
Bishopthorpe YO23 ....230 F3
Boston Spa LS23 ....188 F8
Brompton-on-Swale DL10 ...41 B6
Glusburn BD20.............187 E7
Hurworth DL3 ....3 B3
Malton YO17 ....215 C5
Old Byland & Scawton YO7 ..91 F7
10 Stokesley TS9............26 C7
Bridges Ct YO8 ....232 D6
Bridges La YO42 ....193 E4
Bridge St
5 Bedale DL8.................63 A3
9 Brafferton YO61 ....115 F1
Castleford WF10 ....200 F4
Egglescliffe TS16..............5 D4
12 Helmsley YO62............92 F6
8 Normanton South WF6. 200 B2
16 Pickering YO18...........95 F7
Richmond DL10 ....209 B6
Skipton BD23...............216 F4
Tadcaster LS24 ....189 E6
Thirsk YO7 ....211 B3
Whitby YO22 ....208 D7
York YO1 ....233 B2
Bridge Terr
Northallerton DL7 ....210 C4
Richmond DL10 ....209 B6
Bridge View Rd HG4 ....214 C7
Bridle Way 1 YO26 ....227 A3
Bridle Wlk YO8 ....232 C4
Bridlington Rd
Hunmanby YO14 ....127 A7
Sledmere YO25 ....150 C4
1 Stamford Bridge YO41 . 168 D2
Wold Newton YO25 ....126 A4
Bridlington St YO14 ......126 F8
Briercliffe YO12...........212 C7
Briergate YO32 ....225 C7
Brier Hill YO21..............29 C7
Brier La YO8...............205 A4
Brierlands Cl LS25 ......194 D4
Brierlands La LS25.......194 E4
Brierley Rd YO12............99 E7
Briery Cl 18 LS29 ....175 C2
Brigantia Gdns 12 YO12 ....99 E6
Briggate HG5...............221 B5
Brigg Farm Ct YO8.......204 D5
Brigg La YO8 ....204 D5
Brigg Rd 55 YO14 ....101 B3
Brigg's Ave WF10 ....200 E3
Briggs St YO31............228 C7
BRIGGSWATH 32 B7
Brighton Rd LS29 ....218 E3
Bright St
18 Colne BB8..............186 A3
Darlington DL1................3 E5
1 Glusburn BD20..........173 E1
Skipton BD23...............216 E4
15 Trawden BB8 ....186 A3
York YO26 ....227 F5
Bright Terr BB8...........186 A1
Bright Wlk YO8 ....232 B6
Brigshaw Dr WF10 ....200 C8
Brigshaw High Sch
WF10.......................200 C8
Brigshaw La WF10 ....200 C8
Brimham Cl 2 TS17 ....6 B5
Brimham Rocks★ HG3 ...138 B4
Brimham Rocks Rd HG3. 138 B2
Brind La DN14.............199 F2
Brindle Park Dr WF10.... 201 A3
Brindle Way YO17.........215 F4
Brindley Ct 15 BD23 .....216 F3
Brindley Mill BD23.......216 F3
Brindleys La DN14 ....199 F3
Brindley Wharf BD23.....217 A3
Brinkburn Ave DL3..........3 B7
Brinkburn Dr 1 DL3 ....3 B6
Brinkburn Rd
Darlington DL3...............3 B6
4 Scarborough YO12 ....212 E5
Brinklow Way HG2 ....222 B5
Brinkworth Rush YO41 . 185 A2
Brinkworth Terr 1 YO10 .228 E3
Briscoe Ridge La HG3....177 F6
BRISCOERIGG..............177 F5
Briscoe Way TS8............6 E5
Britannia St 2 YO12 .....212 E5
Broach La
Heck DN14..................203 D1
Kellington DN14...........202 F3
Broach Rd
Heck DN14..................207 D8
Hensall DN14...............203 C1
Broadacres DN14 ....204 D3
Broad Acres YO32.........225 C7
Broadacres Ave DN14 ... 204 D3
Broadacres Garth DN14 . 204 D3
Broad Balk YO17 ....149 A5
Broad Balk La YO7........115 B1
Broad Carr Rd HG3 ....110 D2
Broad Cl
Askrigg DL8..................57 E6
Coulby Newham TS8 ....6 D5
Broad Dubb Rd HG3 .....177 C8
Broadfield La HG4 ....138 B8
Broadfield Way 9 LS29 ..174 E4
Broad Gate
Brompton YO13 ....98 B7
Hunsingore LS22..........180 F8
Marton cum Grafton YO26 ..141 F1
Broadgate Rd TS5...........6 E8
Broad Gate Rd YO21 ....28 E4
Broad Head La BD22 .....187 E2
Broad Highway YO19.....192 F8
Broad La
Appleton Roebuck YO23... 191 A6
6 Beal DN14 ....202 D4
Catton YO41...............185 C7
Cawood YO8................197 A6
Church Fenton LS25......196 D6
Rufforth YO23 ....227 A2
Upper Poppleton YO26 ... 165 D2
Wistow YO8 ....197 A5
Broadlands
2 Roundhill Village TS17 ....6 A5
Wheldrake YO19 ....193 A8
Broadlands Dr 5 YO13.....99 B8
Broadmanor YO8 ....199 A7
Broadmires La YO18 ....96 C5
Broad Oak La 18 YO32....166 E5
Broadrum La YO18 ....95 E6
Broadstone Way
10 Rawcliffe YO30.........224 E3
York YO30 ....224 E3
Broadway
Scarborough YO12.......212 D7
York YO10 ....231 E8
Broadway Gr 3 YO10 ....231 E8
Broadway The DL1..........3 E5
Broadway W YO10 ....231 D8
Broadwell Rd TS4...........7 A8
Brockadale Nature Reserve★
WF8.......................206 B4
Brockett Ind Est YO23....191 B6
BROCKFIELD 167 E2
Brockfield Park Dr YO31 .225 F2
Brockfield Rd YO31 ......225 E2
Brockholme La DL6........65 A4
Brocklesby Rd TS14..........8 F5
Brockley Cl LS24..........196 B7
Brockrigg Ct TS14 ....8 E7
Broc-o-Bank 1 DN6.......206 E2
Brodie Cl 9 TS17 ....5 F5
Brodrick Dr LS29 ....218 A3
Brogden La BB18 ....171 B1
Brogden View 19 BB18 ... 171 D2
Brokes La DL11 ....40 B6
Bromley La TS8..............7 B3
Bromley St 2 YO26 ......227 F5
BROMPTON..................43 F3
Brompton Ave 4 TS14 ......8 F7
BROMPTON-BY-SAWDON 98 C5
Brompton Carr La YO13...98 B4
Brompton Hall Sch YO13 ..98 C5
Brompton House Day Hospl
DL6.........................210 E5
Brompton Ings Rd YO13...98 D3
Brompton La DL6............43 E4
BROMPTON-ON-SWALE ..41 B7
Brompton-on-Swale Prim Sch DL10...........41 B7
Brompton Pk DL10.........41 B6
Brompton Prim Sch DL6 ..43 F3
Brompton Rd
Newton-le-Willows DL8.....62 B4
Northallerton DL6 ....210 D5
York YO30 ....228 A7
Brompton & Sawdon Prim Sch YO13 ....98 C5
Bronaber Cl 1 TS17 ....5 F4
Bronte Cl
Brompton on Swale DL10 ...41 C7
Scarborough YO12.........212 D5
Bronte Ct WF8.............201 B1
Bronte Dr 33 DL9 ....41 A5
Bronte Rise WF10..........201 B3
Brookacre 7 LA6..........103 D3
Brooke Cl
Harrogate HG1 ....219 E7
12 Kirkbymoorside YO62.....70 B1
BROOKFIELD...................6 E6
Brookfield HG3............160 F5
Brookfield Cl HG3 ....161 A5
Brookfield Cres HG3 .... 161 A5
Brookfield Ct 5 WF6 ....200 B1
Brookfield Garth HG3.... 161 A5
Brookfield Way
7 Earby BB18..............172 A1
Hampsthwaite HG3 ....160 F5
Brook House Croft BD24 .131 E6
Brook La
Danby YO21.................29 C6
Halton West BD23..........153 F1
Thornton Dale YO18.........96 D6
Weeton LS17 ....178 C2
Brookland 1 LA6..........102 F2
Brooklands
43 Filey YO14 ....101 B3
York YO10 ....229 D4
Brooklands Cl 44 YO14 ...101 B3
Brooklands Com Specl Sch
BD23......................216 F2
Brooklands Cres DL6......210 E5
Brooklands Terr BD23 ....216 F3
Brook Pk YO21..............32 A7
Brooksbank Rd TS7 ....7 D7
Brookside
Collingham LS22 ....188 A8
Hovingham YO62 ....119 E6
Skelton & Brotton TS12......9 D8
Skipton BD23...............217 A3
Sleights YO22...............32 B6
Spennithorne DL8 ....60 F4
Brookside Ave 1 DL8......63 B2
Brookside Cl 2 DL8 ......63 B2
Brook St
Castleford WF10 ....201 B6
18 Earby BB18..............172 A1
Hebden BD23...............135 A2
Hellifield BD23.............154 B3
Ilkley LS29.................218 B4
12 Scarborough YO12 .....212 F6
Selby YO8..................232 C4
Skipton BD23...............216 F4
York YO31 ....233 B4
Brook View BD23 ....173 B4
Brookwood Way TS16 ....5 E4
Broome Cl
14 Pontefract WF6 ....200 A2
York YO32 ....225 F5
Broome Way YO32 ....226 A5
Broom Field HG3 ....160 E6
Broomfield Ave DL7.......210 D2
Broomfield Sch DL7 ......210 D2
Broomfield Terr 18
YO21 ....208 D6
Broomhill WF10............201 A3
Broom Hill Ave 6 TS17 ....6 D5
Broomhill Cl 23 WF11 ....202 A2
Broomhill Cres 25 WF11. 202 A2
Broomhill Dr 26 WF11.. 202 A2
Broomhill Gr 19 WF11.... 202 A2
Broomhill Pl 22 WF11 ... 202 A2
Broomhill Sq 24 WF11... 202 A2
Broomhill Wlk 21 WF11 . 202 A2
Broom House La
Egton YO21 ....30 F4
Ugthorpe YO21 ....12 B2
Broom Rd LS24 ....189 D5
Broom Wlk YO12...........212 E7
Brootes La BD23.........107 C2
Brotes La YO26 ....164 B5
BROTHERTON 201 D5
Brotherton & Byram Com Prim Sch WF11..........201 E4
Brougham Cl
3 Egglescliffe TS17 ....5 F6
York YO30 ....227 F8
Brougham St
Darlington DL3...............3 C7
Skipton BD23.............217 A3
Brougham Street Parish Church Sch BD23.......217 A3
Brough Ave 5 DL9 ....41 A5
Brough Field Cl 4 TS17.....6 D6
Brough Hall★ DL10 ....41 B4
Brough Mdws 4 DL10 .....41 D5
Brough Rd 23 DL9 ....40 E4
BROUGHTON
Malton 121 D4
Skipton......................172 E6
Broughton Ave BD23 .... 216 D3
Broughton Cres BD23 ... 216 C3
Broughton Gr BD23 .... 216 D3
Broughton Green La
YO17 ....121 C4
Broughton Mews BD23.. 216 D3
Broughton Rd
Broughton YO17.............121 C3
11 East Ayton/West Ayton
YO13........................99 A7
Malton YO17 ....215 A5
Skipton BD23..............216 C3
Broughton Rise YO17 ....215 B5
Broughton Way
4 Harrogate HG2.........220 C3
York YO10 ....229 B4
Browcliff BD20 ....174 C2
Brow La LA2................129 D6
Brown Bank La BD20..... 174 D2
Brown Bank Rd
Kirkby Malzeard HG4.......111 F5
Norwood HG3 ....177 B8
Brown Cow Rd YO8 .....204 C8
Browney Croft YO10.......233 C1
Brown Howe Rd YO18 ......51 A1
Browning Cl 3 DL9.........40 E4
Brown La YO26 ....141 F1
Brownlow St YO31 ....233 C4
Brown Moor 22 YO41.... 168 D2
Brownmoor La
Huby YO61 ....144 A2
Sutton-on-the-Forest YO32 .166 B8
Brown Rigg Rd YO13......53 F5
Brownroyd 14 BB18 ....172 B1
Browns Ct 4 BD20 ....173 E3
Browns Fold 3 BD23 .....134 E3
Brown's Terr 4 TS13........11 F7
Brownswood Cotts YO21 ..31 A5
Browsfield Rd 24 LS29 ...174 F4
BROXA 74 C6
Broxa Hill YO13 ....74 C6
Broxa La YO13...............74 D5
Broxa Moor La YO13 ....74 C7
Bruce St 21 BB18 ....171 D2
Bruce Way 5 YO18 ....95 F6
Bruche Dr YO7.............115 A2
Brunel Ct 12 YO26 ....227 F5
Brunel Rd HG1 ....220 D5
Brunel Way DL1 ....3 D5
Brunsell La YO26..........163 F7
Brunswick Cl 2 YO32.....167 C8
Brunswick Dr HG1 ....219 B2
Brunswick Pl 1 HG1.......219 D1
Brunswick Sh Ctr YO11.. 213 A5
Brunswick St
Whitby YO21 ....208 D6
York YO23 ....228 B1

Brunt Acres Est DL8 . . . . .56 D5
Brunt Acres Rd DL8 . . . . .56 D4
BRUNTHWAITE 174 D1
Brunthwaite La BD20 . . . . .174 E1
Brunton Bank DL8 . . . . .59 A5
Brunton La HG5 . . . . .163 B6
Brunton Rd LA2 . . . . .131 A6
Bryan Cl 13 DL2 . . . . .3 E1
Bryden Cl DL6 . . . . .210 E2
Bry Hills YO12 . . . . .99 D6
Brymor Ice Cream Palour*
  HG4 . . . . .85 E7
Bryony Ct YO8 . . . . .232 B2
Bryony Rd 4 HG3 . . . . .161 B3
Bryony Way 5 HG3 . . . . .161 B3
BUBWITH 199 D7
Bubwith Prim Sch YO8 . . . .199 D7
Buccaneer Ct YO41 . . . . . . .185 A3
Buccleugh Cl TS14 . . . . .8 F5
BUCKDEN 107 E8
Buckden Cl 3 YO61 . . . . . . .143 D8
Buckden Wood La BD23 . . .107 D8
Buck Haw Brow BD24 . . . . .131 B4
Buckingham Ct YO41 . . . . . .233 A1
Buckingham Sq 7 YO62 . . . .92 F6
Buckingham St YO41 . . . . . .233 B1
Buckingham Terr YO11 . . . .233 B1
Buckingham Way WF11 . . . .201 F4
Buck La YO60 . . . . .147 B6
Buckle Cl YO8 . . . . .149 A8
Buckle Ct YO8 . . . . .232 B7
Buckle La WF6 . . . . .200 A1
Bucks La 1 BD24 . . . . .131 D2
Buck Stone La BD20 . . . . . .187 C5
Buess La DL1 . . . . .4 A7
Buffet Hill La LA2 . . . . .129 D7
BUGTHORPE 169 D4
Bugthorpe CE Prim Sch
  YO41 . . . . .169 D5
Bugthorpe La YO41 . . . . . . .169 D5
Bugthorpe Lane Town E
  YO41 . . . . .169 E5
Bull Alley La DN14 . . . . .204 B3
BULLAMOOR 44 B1
Bullamoor Cl DL6 . . . . .210 F5
Bullamoor Junior Sch
  DL6 . . . . .210 F5
Bullamoor Rd DL6 . . . . .210 F5
Bull Balk YO41 . . . . .185 E4
Buller St YO8 . . . . .232 B6
Bull Hill DL8 . . . . .61 E8
Bull Ing La BD23 . . . . .134 D3
Bull La
  Huby YO32 . . . . .166 B7
  York YO10 . . . . .228 F3
Bull Moor La YO60 . . . . .168 A8
Bullock La
  Newsham with Breckenbrough
    YO7 . . . . .89 A5
  Newsham YO7 . . . . .88 F8
Bull Piece La YO12 . . . . .122 D3
Bullytree La LS25 . . . . .195 E2
BULMER 146 B6
Bulmer Hill YO60 . . . . .146 B6
Bungalow Rd BD20 . . . . . . .187 D7
Bunkers Hill
  Aberford LS25 . . . . .194 F7
  1 Skipton BD23 . . . . .217 A4
Burdale Cl
  8 Eaglescliffe TS16 . . . . . . .5 D8
  Norton YO17 . . . . .215 F2
Burdike Ave YO30 . . . . .228 A8
Burdock Ct 16 HG3 . . . . . . .161 B3
Burdon Garth TS17 . . . . .6 D5
Burdon View 3 TS16 . . . . . . .5 D4
Burgate YO11 . . . . .95 F7
Burgess Wik YO4 . . . . .230 C8
Burghley Dr 1 TS17 . . . . .6 A5
Burgoyne Cl HG4 . . . . .113 D3
Burke St HG1 . . . . .219 E5
Burlands La YO26 . . . . .182 F7
Burley Ave HG3 . . . . .161 A2
Burley Bank Cl HG3 . . . . . . .161 A3
Burley Bank Rd HG3 . . . . . .161 A3
Burley Cl
  12 South Milford LS25 . . . .195 F2
  Thornton-le-Street YO7 . . . .65 B3
BURLEY IN
  WHARFEDALE 176 B1
Burley La HG3 . . . . .161 A3
Burley Oaks Prim Sch 13
  LS29 . . . . .176 C1
Burlington Ave YO10 . . . . . .228 F4
Burlyn Rd 3 YO14 . . . . .127 A8
Burma Rd DL3 . . . . .3 F2
BURN 203 D7
BURN BRIDGE 222 D2
Burn Bridge La HG3 . . . . . . .222 D2
Burn Bridge Oval HG3 . . . .222 D3
Burn Bridge Rd HG3 . . . . . .222 C3
Burnby Cl HG3. . . . . .219 B5
Burn Est YO32 . . . . .225 E4
BURNESTON 87 E7
Burneston Ct DL3 . . . . .2 F5
Burneston Hargill DL8 . . . . .87 F8
Burneston Prim Sch DL8 . .87 E8
Burnett Cl HG3 . . . . .140 A2
Burn Hall Cl YO8 . . . . .203 D7
Burnham Rd LS25 . . . . .194 C3
Burnholme Ave YO31 . . . . .229 B6
Burnholme Com Coll
  YO31 . . . . .229 A5
Burnholme Dr YO31 . . . . . .229 A6
Burnholme Gr YO31 . . . . . .229 A6

Carr La continued
Kilburn High & Low YO61 91 B3
Little Ouseburn YO26 164 A7
Long Drax YO8 204 F6
Muston YO14 100 F3
Newby & Scalby YO13 75 C5
Newton on Derwent YO41 185 F4
Rainton with Newby YO7 114 F6
Roecliffe YO51 140 E3
Sheriff Hutton YO60 145 E6
Stillington YO61 144 C6
Sutton-on-the-Forest YO61 144 D2
Thirlby YO7 90 F6
Thormanby YO61 116 E4
Wetherby LS22 180 D4
Wistow YO8 197 A3
York YO26 227 D5
Carr Leys La YO7 66 A5
Carr Mill Mews BD22 187 B5
Carrnock Ct 3 YO32 225 F1
Carrol Cl DL6 210 F2
Carroll Pl 2 DL2 22 C8
Carron Cres YO24 230 B7
Carr Rd 7 BB18 171 D2
Carrside 2 YO11 99 F6
Carr Side Rd YO26 163 F8
Carrs Mdw YO19 192 B5
Carr St YO8 232 F4
Carrs The YO21 208 A2
Carr The HG3 222 E2
Carr Wood Rd WF10 200 F3
Carseylands Hill BD23 155 A4
Carter Ave YO31 228 F5
Carter La 22 YO62 70 B1
Carter's La
Ilkley LS29 218 E6
Longnewton TS16 5 A4
Carters Yd DL10 209 B6
CARTHORPE 87 E6
Cartmell Terr DL3 3 C6
Cart Riggin YO7 66 A8
Cass House Rd TS8 6 E4
Cass La
Knaresborough HG5 221 A4
South Milford LS25 195 E1
Castelo Gr 1 YO18 96 A6
Castle Bank DL6 25 E1
Castlebergh Hospl BD24 131 C2
Castlebergh La 5 BD24 131 E2
CASTLE BOLTON 59 A6
Castle Cl
Cawood YO8 197 A8
1 Haxby YO32 166 D5
Killinghall HG3 161 C5
Middleton St George DL2 4 C3
Northallerton DL7 210 D5
2 Spofforth HG3 179 E6
1 Thornton Dale YO18 96 D5
Castle Cres YO11 213 B7
Castle Ctyd HG5 221 A5
Castle Dyke Wynd TS16 5 E3
Castle End DL8 59 B6
CASTLEFORD 200 E4
Castleford High Sch WF10 200 F4
Castleford La
Featherstone WF7 200 D1
Knottingley WF11 201 D3
Castleford Mus★ WF10 220 E4
Castleford & Normanton District Hospl WF10 200 D3
Castleford Rd WF6 200 B2
Castleford Redhill Junior Sch WF10 201 B4
Castleford Ret Pk WF10 200 E4
Castleford Sta WF10 200 E4
Castleford Three Lane Ends Prim Sch WF10 200 D4
Castle Garth
Pontefract WF8 201 C1
4 Thornton Dale YO18 96 D5
Castlegate
East Ayton/West Ayton YO13 99 A7
6 Helmsley YO62 92 F6
Kirkbymoorside YO62 70 B1
3 Knaresborough HG5 221 B5
Malton YO17 215 C4
19 Pickering YO18 95 F7
Scarborough YO11 213 B7
Thirsk YO7 211 B2
York YO1 233 B2
Castle Gate 4 LS29 218 B4
Castle Gdns YO11 213 B6
Castle Hill
8 Hunmanby YO14 126 F8
2 Ilkley LS29 218 B4
Richmond DL10 209 C6
4 Settle BD24 131 E2
Castle Hill Cl HG2 222 B6
Castle Hill Dr HG2 222 B6
Castle Hill Glade HG2 222 B6
Castle Hill Gr HG2 222 B6
Castle Hill La YO8 204 F5
Castle Howard★ YO60 120 D1
Castle Howard Dr YO17 215 A4
Castle Howard Rd YO17 215 A4
Castle Ings 1 HG3 179 E5
Castle Ings Cl 1 HG5 221 A5
Castle Ings Rd 3 HG5 221 A5
Castlekeep Cl DL10 209 C8
Castle La
Danby YO21 29 D6
10 East Ayton/West Ayton YO13 99 B8
Castle Mdws DL8 87 A7
Castle Mills HG5 221 A5
Castlemount Ave YO13 75 D6
Castle Rd
Colne BB8 186 A4
1 Ilkley LS29 218 B4
Killinghall HG3 161 C5
18 Pickering YO18 95 F7
Scarborough YO11 213 A6
Thornton Dale YO18 96 D5
Whitby YO21 208 A6
Castlereagh Cl TS21 5 A7
Castle Rise 1 YO13 99 A7
Castle Side YO60 145 C5
Castle St
Skipton BD23 217 A3
Spofforth HG3 179 E6
Castle Steads★ DL11 19 D6
Castle Steads (Fort)★ DL8 84 C8
Castle Terr
Richmond DL10 209 C6
16 Scarborough YO11 213 B6
CASTLETON 29 A6
Castleton Ave
Middlesbrough TS5 6 D8
Northallerton DL7 210 C1
Castleton Moor Sta YO21 29 A7
Castleton Prim Sch YO21 29 A7
Castleton Rd DL9 40 F4
Castle View
7 Newby & Scalby YO13 75 D5
Richmond DL10 209 B6
Sheriff Hutton YO60 145 C5
Castle View Terr BD23 216 F4
Castle Wlk YO1 233 C2
Castle Wynd 11 DL10 209 C6
CASTLEY 178 A1
Castle Yard Stables 8 YO7 211 B3
Castle Yd
3 Ilkley LS29 218 B4
Knaresborough HG5 221 A5
Castley La LS21 178 A1
Cat Bank DL11 39 C6
Cathcart Cl DN14 206 F7
Cathedral CE Prim Sch HG4 214 D5
Cathedral Cl HG4 214 D5
Catherine Love Dr 15 YO61 143 C8
Catherine St 2 TS12 9 F7
Cat La
Balne DN14 207 E5
Bilbrough YO23 182 D1
Cat Pottery The★ DL8 58 F1
CATTAL 164 A1
Cattal Moor La YO26 181 B8
Cattal St YO26 164 A2
Cattal Sta YO26 164 A2
CATTERICK 41 D5
Catterick AWS Football Ctr DL9 209 D1
CATTERICK BRIDGE 41 D6
Catterick Bridge★ DL10 41 C6
CATTERICK GARRISON 209 D2
Catterick La DL10 41 D3
Catterick Racecourse DL10 41 C5
Catterick Rd DL9 40 E4
CATTERTON 190 B8
Catterton La
Catterton LS24 190 A8
Healaugh LS24 182 A1
Cattle La LS25 194 F8
Cattlelaith La WF11 201 E2
CATTON 88 F1
Catton La YO7 115 A7
Catton Moor La YO7 114 F8
Catton Way YO8 232 A2
Caudle Hill WF11 201 C6
Causeway BD23 81 E3
Causeway The
Darlington DL1 3 E5
Lythe YO21 12 E3
Cautley Dr HG3 161 C5
Cautley Gr HG3 161 C5
Cavalry Ct 9 YO12 75 F5
Cavendish Ave
Harrogate HG2 219 E1
8 Pontefract WF8 201 C2
Cavendish Ct HG2 222 F8
Cavendish Gr YO10 229 D3
Cavendish Rd TS4 7 A8
Cavendish St
Barnoldswick BB18 171 D1
Harrogate HG1 219 E5
Skipton BD23 216 F3
Cavendish Terr 8 HG4 214 C4
Cavendish View BD23 217 D7
Caversham Rd TS4 7 A8
Cawcliff La YO18 97 A5
Cawdel Cl 4 LS25 195 F2
Cawdel Way 11 LS25 195 F2
Cawder Ghyll BD23 217 A1
Cawder Gn BD23 217 A2
Cawder La BD23 217 A1
Cawder Mews BD23 217 A1
Cawder Rd BD23 217 A1
CAWOOD 197 B8
Cawood CE Aided Prim Sch YO8 197 B8
Cawood Cres LS24 190 C1
Cawood Dr TS5 6 F7
Cawood Rd
Stillingfleet YO19 191 D3
Wistow YO8 197 C7
Cawthorn Ave HG2 220 B2
CAWTHORNE 71 D4
Cawthorne Cres YO14 101 A3
Cawthorne La YO18 71 D3
Cawthorn Pl 4 HG2 220 B3
CAWTON 119 C7
Cawton Rd YO62 118 F8
Caxton Ave YO26 227 D6
Caxton Cl 1 DL10 41 C7
Caxton Gdns 4 WF8 201 B2
Caxton View HG4 214 C6
Caxton Way YO11 99 F6
Caygill St 10 YO21 208 C6
Cayley Cl YO30 224 F1
Cayley La YO13 98 C5
Caymer Rd YO11 100 A7
CAYTON 100 C6
Cayton Low Rd YO11 99 F6
Cayton Low Road Ind Est YO11 100 A6
Cayton Prim Sch YO11 100 B6
Cecilia Pl 3 YO24 228 A3
Cecil Rd 7 YO14 127 A8
Cecil St
Barnoldswick BB18 171 D2
Harrogate HG1 219 E5
Cedar Cl
Hambleton YO8 197 B1
Ripon HG4 214 B3
Cedar Cres YO8 197 D2
Cedar Ct YO14 100 F5
Cedar Dr
Coulby Newham TS8 6 D4
Tadcaster LS24 189 D6
Cedar Glade YO19 184 E7
Cedar Gr
Barton DL10 21 C7
3 Filey YO14 101 B4
Middleton One Row DL2 4 D3
Sutton BD20 187 E7
York YO31 229 B7
Cedar Grange HG2 222 D7
Cedarhurst Dr TS12 9 F7
Cedar Mews 4 DL2 22 D8
Cedar Pl 14 YO61 117 D1
Cedar Rd
Darlington DL3 3 B6
Selby YO8 232 D2
Cedar Ridge LS25 194 E5
Cedar Vale 8 YO62 70 B1
Cedarwood 3 DL2 4 C4
Cedarwood Ave 1 TS9 26 C8
Cedarwood Cl 7 YO24 227 B1
Cedarwood Glade TS8 6 E4
Celtic Cl YO26 227 B5
Cemetery La DL3 3 A5
Cemetery Rd
40 Earby BB18 172 A1
Normanton South WF6 200 B1
Thirsk YO7 211 A3
York YO10 233 C1
Cennon Gr 15 TS17 5 F4
Centenary Row BD23 217 D8
Central Arc DL7 210 D5
Central Av 6 YO61 143 D8
Central Dr
Castleford WF10 200 C4
Northallerton DL6 210 E4
Central St TS16 5 E3
Central Way 6 TS9 8 A2
Centre La LS24 189 E6
Centrepoint Rd DL1 3 F6
Centre Rd BD20 186 D7
Centurian Cl 7 DL10 41 E4
Centurion Pk YO30 225 B2
Centurion Way
Clifton YO30 225 B3
Crossgates YO12 99 E6
Faverdale DL3 3 B8
Century Wlk 1 HG2 220 B3
Ceres Rd LS22 180 C3
Chacksfield Rd 16 DL10 41 E4
Chadderton Cl TS12 9 E8
Chadderton Dr 2 TS17 6 C7
Chadwell Ave 2 TS3 7 B8
Chadwick Pk HG5 221 B3
Chafer Wood Nature Reserve★ YO13 97 D6
Chain Bar La HG3 161 A4
Chain La HG5 221 C6
Chair Wlk HG4 139 B8
Chaldon Cl 4 YO32 167 A6
Chaldron Way TS16 5 D6
Chalfield Cl TS17 6 B4
Chalfonts YO24 227 F1
Chalford Oaks TS5 6 D8
Challacombe Cres TS17 6 A3
Challoner Rd TS15 5 D2
Chaloner Prim Sch 18 TS14 8 F7
Chaloner's Cres YO24 230 D7
Chaloner's Rd YO24 230 D8
Chaloner St 4 TS14 8 F6
Chaly Fields LS23 188 E8
Chamber End Fold 5 BD23 134 E3
Champion Ave 6 WF10 200 F3
Chancel Way YO21 208 A6
Chancery Ct YO24 227 C3
Chancery Rise
Stockton-on-Tees TS18 6 A6
York YO24 227 F3
Chandler Cl DL10 209 F8
Chandlers Ct YO11 213 B2
Chandlers Ridge Prim Sch TS7 7 D5
Chandlers Wharf YO17 215 C3
Chantilly Ave DL1 3 F7
Chanting Hill Cl YO60 146 E6
CHANTRY 59 D2
Chantry Ave 14 YO26 165 F1
Chantry Bank DL8 59 D3
Chantry Cl
1 Park End TS3 7 B8
York YO24 230 C8
Chantry Ct HG3 161 C7
Chantry Dr
East Ayton/West Ayton YO13 99 B8
2 Ilkley LS29 218 B3
Chantry Gap 11 YO26 165 F1
Chantry Garth DL8 59 D3
Chantry Gr 13 YO26 165 F1
Chantry La
Bishopthorpe YO23 231 B4
Scotton HG5 162 A6
Stutton with Hazlewood LS24 189 B3
Chantry Rd
9 East Ayton/West Ayton YO13 99 B8
Northallerton DL7 210 B3
Chantry Wynd 7 DL10 209 C6
Chapel Balk Rd YO8 198 F1
Chapel Cl
Bilton-in-Ainsty with Bickerton LS22 181 B5
Church Fenton LS24 196 B8
21 Helmsley YO62 92 F6
North Duffield YO8 199 A7
Rawcliffe DN14 205 A1
Chapel Cres DL7 63 C8
Chapel Croft 7 BD23 134 E3
Chapel Ct
Gargrave BD23 155 D1
Huby YO61 144 A4
CHAPEL FIELDS 227 B3
Chapel Fields Rd YO26 227 A3
Chapel Fold 6 BD23 134 E3
Chapel Garth
Dalton YO7 115 E7
Markington with Wallerthwaite HG3 139 C3
Thrintoft DL7 63 F7
Chapel Gate
Malham BD23 132 F1
Sherburn YO17 124 D6
CHAPEL HADDLESEY 203 C5
Chapel Haddlesey CE Prim Sch YO8 203 B5
Chapel Hill
Boroughbridge YO51 141 C5
Kearby with Netherby LS22 179 B1
Skipton BD23 217 A5
Chapel House Mews 9 BD23 173 B4
Chapel La
Askham Bryan YO23 182 F3
Barwick in Elmet LS15 194 C8
Boston Spa LS23 188 E7
Brayton YO8 232 B1
Brompton YO13 98 B7
5 Burton in Lonsdale LA6 102 F3
13 Easingwold YO61 143 C8
13 Eastfield YO11 100 B6
Finghall DL8 61 E4
Halton East BD23 174 C8
Harome YO62 93 C4
Hebden BD23 135 A2
Horton in Ribblesdale BD24 105 C3
Ilkley LS29 218 A4
Langtoft YO25 151 D5
Little Smeaton WF8 206 B3
9 Malton YO17 215 C4
Marton-le-Moor HG4 114 F1
Rawcliffe DN14 205 A2
Reighton YO14 127 E5
3 Riccall YO19 192 A1
3 Spofforth HG3 179 E5
3 Thornton Dale YO18 96 D5
Tollerton YO61 143 A3
Westow YO60 147 B4
CHAPEL-LE-DALE 104 C8
Chapel Mews YO7 211 C2
Chapel Rd
23 Scarborough YO11 213 A6
Settrington YO17 122 D1
Chapel Riggs 4 DL10 41 E4
Chapel Row YO10 233 C1
Chapel Sq 7 BD24 131 E2
Chapel St
8 Addingham LS29 174 F4
6 Beadlam YO62 93 D7
Carleton BD23 173 B4
Cattal YO26 164 A1
22 Earby BB18 172 A1
27 Filey YO14 101 B3
Grassington BD23 134 E3
Hambleton YO8 196 F1
Hillam LS25 202 B7
Kirk Hammerton YO26 164 C2
Knaresborough HG5 221 B5
Middleton St George DL2 4 C4
Nunnington YO62 93 E2
12 Settle BD24 131 D2
Tadcaster LS24 189 E6
Thirsk YO7 211 B2
Chapel Terr YO24 227 C3
Chapel Wlk
Long Preston BD23 153 F5
4 Riccall YO19 192 A1
Chapman Cl 1 YO32 167 C8
Chapman Ct BB18 171 D2
Chapman La 8 HG4 86 C3
Chapmans Ct YO24 230 D6
Chapman's La YO30 165 E7
Chapman Sq HG1 219 B2
Chapter House St YO1 233 B3
Charles Ave HG1 219 E5
Charles Ct DL10 209 F7
Charles Moor YO31 228 F7
Charles St YO8 232 B6
Charles Wesley Dr YO8 232 B2
Charlock TS8 7 B4
Charlton Ave
Knaresborough HG5 221 B6
2 Whitby YO21 208 B7
Charlton Ct 10 HG5 221 B6
Charlton Dr HG5 221 B6
Charlton Gr 12 HG5 221 B6
Charlton Manor Dr 13 HG5 221 B6
CHARLTONS 9 C6
Charlton St YO23 228 C2
Charlton Villas HG5 221 B6
Charnwood Dr TS7 7 D6
Charrington Ave TS17 6 A6
Charter Ave DN14 205 A1
Chartermark Way DL9 41 A4
Charter Rd HG4 214 E4
Charters The YO8 198 B5
Chartwell Cl TS17 6 B4
Chase Garth Rd 16 YO61 143 C8
Chase Side Ct YO24 230 E8
Chase The
11 Boroughbridge YO51 141 B4
Garforth LS25 194 D4
Hurworth-on-Tees DL2 3 E1
Knaresborough HG5 221 D5
Norton YO17 215 E2
17 Wetherby LS22 180 C3
Chastworth Ct HG1 219 D4
Chatham Rd HG4 113 D2
Chatsworth Ave 7 WF8 201 C2
Chatsworth Dr
16 Haxby YO32 166 F5
2 Wetherby LS22 180 B3
Chatsworth Gdns YO12 212 E7
Chatsworth Gr
4 Boroughbridge YO51 141 B5
Harrogate HG1 219 C4
Chatsworth Pl HG1 219 D4
Chatsworth Rd HG1 219 D4
Chatsworth Terr
2 Harrogate HG1 219 E4
4 York YO26 227 E4
Chaucer Gn HG1 219 F7
Chaucer La
Fadmoor YO62 69 F5
Strensall YO32 167 B8
Chaucer St 7 YO10 228 E3
Chaumont Way 1 YO32 167 D2
Chauvel Cl DL9 209 C2
Cheapside
2 Knaresborough HG5 221 B5
12 Normanton South WF6 200 A1
11 Settle BD24 131 D2
Cheapsides Rd YO17 215 B8
Checker La YO19 198 A7
Checkstone Ave 10 WF10 200 D2
Chedworth Ct 4 TS17 5 F6
Chelkar Way YO30 224 F1
Chelmsford Rd HG1 219 E2
Cheltenham Ave
Ilkley LS29 218 E4
Middlesbrough TS7 7 B5
Cheltenham Cres 6 HG1 219 D2
Cheltenham Ct DL2 4 C5
Cheltenham Mount HG1 219 D3
Cheltenham Par HG1 219 D3
Cheltenham Rd 8 HG1 219 D3
Chelwood Wlk 12 YO26 227 E4
Chepstow Cl 9 DL9 40 F4
Chepstow Ct 14 DL1 3 F6
Cherry Ave
Malton YO17 215 D6
Swinton YO17 121 B4
Cherry Cl YO21 208 B6
Cherry Garth YO31 229 B5
Cherry Garth Rd DL7 210 C3
Cherry Gr
7 Bedale DL8 63 B3
2 Ilkley LS29 175 C2
16 Poppleton YO26 165 F1
Cherry Hill La YO23 233 B1
Cherry La YO24 230 F8
Cherry Orch 2 YO32 225 D8
Cherry Paddock
4 Haxby YO32 225 D8
Kexby YO41 168 C2
Cherry Rd 4 YO14 127 A8
Cherry St YO23 233 B1
Cherry Tree Ave
Newton-on-Ouse YO30 165 B6
1 Scarborough YO12 212 B5
York YO32 225 D4
Cherrytree Cl HG4 140 E7
Cherry Tree Cl
13 Brayton YO8 197 D1
9 Castleford WF10 200 D3
Cherry Tree Ct
12 Barlby with Osgodby YO8 198 B4
Catterick DL10 41 E4
Salton YO62 94 D3
Cherrytree Dr YO8 197 D6
Cherry Tree Dr
Gristhorpe YO14 101 A4
5 Naburn YO23 191 C7
Cherry Tree Way 14 DL9 41 A5

Cherry Tree Wlk
Amotherby YO17 . . . 121 A4
7 Barlby YO8 . . . 198 B4
Knottingley WF11 . . . 201 F2
Cherrywood Ave 4 TS9 . . . 26 C8
Cherry Wood Cres YO19 . . 231 E5
Chervil Ct TS8 . . . 7 B4
Cherwell Croft YO8 . . . 196 F1
Cherwell Ct YO8 . . . 196 F1
Cheshire Ave YO32 . . . 167 A6
Cheshire Cl 6 YO32 . . . 224 E2
Cheshire Sq 5 YO7 . . . 89 B1
Chesler-Pit La YO61 . . . 117 F2
Chesney Fields 4 YO24 . 227 D1
Chessingham Gdns YO24 230 E6
Chessingham Pk YO19 . . 184 F6
Chester Court Rd YO8 . . 204 A6
Chester La DL6 . . . 65 D8
Chesterton Ave TS17 . . . 6 A6
Chestnut Ave
2 Airmyn DN14 . . . 205 E4
Harrogate HG1 . . . 219 F3
10 Hemingbrough YO8 . . . 198 F1
Malton YO17 . . . 215 D5
Thornton Dale YO18 . . . 96 D6
2 Topcliffe YO7 . . . 89 A1
Welburn YO60 . . . 146 E6
12 Wetherby LS22 . . . 180 B3
York YO31 . . . 228 F6
Chestnut Bank YO12 . . . 212 D6
Chestnut Cl
Bedale DL8 . . . 63 B3
3 Catterick DL10 . . . 41 D5
4 Ilkley LS29 . . . 218 E3
Richmond DL10 . . . 209 C8
Scarborough YO12 . . . 212 D6
Chestnut Cres
6 Catterick Garrison DL9 . . 40 F5
1 Catton YO7 . . . 89 A1
Hipswell DL9 . . . 40 F5
Chestnut Croft 7 YO8 . . . 198 F1
Chestnut Ct
9 Hemingbrough YO8 . . . 198 F1
York YO32 . . . 225 F5
Chestnut Dr
17 Barnoldswick BB18 . . . 171 D1
Firth Moor DL1 . . . 3 F4
8 Hemingbrough YO8 . . . 198 F1
Middlesbrough TS7 . . . 7 C6
Chestnut Garth 4 YO8 . . 198 F1
Chestnut Gn 10 LS25 . . . 202 A8
Chestnut Gr
Acomb YO26 . . . 227 C4
Harrogate HG1 . . . 219 E6
Huntington YO32 . . . 225 E4
Norton YO17 . . . 215 F2
Chestnut Mews YO8 . . . 197 A8
Chestnut Rd
Cawood YO8 . . . 197 A8
Eaglescliffe TS16 . . . 5 E6
Chestnut Rise 6 YO8 . . . 198 F1
Chestnuts The
6 Haxby YO32 . . . 225 C8
Hensall DN14 . . . 203 D2
Pontefract WF8 . . . 201 C2
Scarborough YO12 . . . 212 B7
Chestnut Way YO8 . . . 232 E3
Chevin Dr YO14 . . . 101 A3
Cheviot Cl 1 YO32 . . . 225 F3
Chew La
Gargrave BD23 . . . 155 D1
Seamer YO12 . . . 99 D6
Chichester Cl 18 YO13 . . . 75 D5
Chieftain Rd DL9 . . . 40 C4
Chiltern Ave WF10 . . . 200 C3
Chiltern Way YO32 . . . 225 F5
Chilvers Ct 4 YO8 . . . 232 A1
Chimes Rd YO8 . . . 232 C6
Chimes The 8 YO8 . . . 232 C6
China St DL3 . . . 3 D7
Chippendale Rise 8
LS21 . . . 177 A1
Chippenham Rd TS4 . . . 7 A7
Cholmley Way YO22 . . . 208 F3
CHOP GATE . . . 46 F6
Christ Church CE Prim Sch
Colne BB8 . . . 186 A3
Skipton BD23 . . . 216 F3
Christ Church Oval HG1 . . 219 E2
Christina St 5 HG1 . . . 219 C5
Christ's Hospl★ DL8 . . . 63 A1
Christ the King RC Prim Sch
TS17 . . . 6 C6
Christy Gate Rd YO21 . . . 28 E4
Chubb Hill Rd YO21 . . . 208 C6
Chudleigh Rd
Harrogate HG1 . . . 219 E3
1 York YO26 . . . 227 F5
Church Ave
Clapham LA2 . . . 130 C8
4 Dacre HG3 . . . 137 F1
Harrogate HG1 . . . 219 D5
6 Selby YO8 . . . 232 D5
Church Balk YO19 . . . 184 E7
Church Bank
Aysgarth DL8 . . . 58 F3
Hunton DL8 . . . 61 F7
Kirkby Malzeard HG4 . . . 112 D5
Church Cl
Askham Bryan YO23 . . . 182 F3
Bagby YO7 . . . 90 C3
4 Bubwith YO8 . . . 199 D7
Carleton BD23 . . . 173 B4
18 Filey YO14 . . . 101 B4
1 Hambleton YO8 . . . 196 F1
Church Cl *continued*
Killinghall HG3 . . . 219 A8
Kirby Hill YO51 . . . 141 B7
Middleton St George DL2 . . . 4 C3
Newby & Scalby YO13 . . . 75 C5
Redmire DL8 . . . 59 C5
10 Riccall YO19 . . . 197 F8
Sawley HG4 . . . 138 E6
Sharow HG4 . . . 214 F7
4 Swillington LS26 . . . 194 A1
5 Tollerton YO61 . . . 143 B3
Wheldrake YO19 . . . 193 A7
Church Cliff Dr 9 YO14 . . 101 B4
Church Cres
Stutton with Hazlewood
LS24 . . . 189 D4
Swillington LS26 . . . 194 A1
Church Croft
Barkston Ash LS24 . . . 195 F7
Gargrave BD23 . . . 172 C8
Church Cswy LS23 . . . 188 F8
Church Ct
18 Normanton South
WF6 . . . 200 A1
Saxton LS24 . . . 195 D7
Church Dike La YO8 . . . 204 F5
Church Dr
Great Ayton TS9 . . . 7 F1
Lockwood TS12 . . . 9 E7
Church End
Cawood YO8 . . . 197 B8
Sheriff Hutton YO60 . . . 145 D5
Church Farm YO7 . . . 211 A6
Church Farm Cl YO23 . . . 182 C6
Church Farm Ct YO25 . . . 126 E3
Church Farm View LS15 . 194 C8
CHURCH FENTON . . . 196 B7
Church Fenton La LS24 . . 190 B3
Church Fenton Sta LS24 . 196 A8
Churchfield DN14 . . . 204 C2
Churchfield Dr 28 YO32 . . 166 E5
Churchfield La
Castleford WF10 . . . 200 F3
6 Kippax LS25 . . . 194 D1
Little Smeaton WF8 . . . 206 C4
Church Field La 2 YO26 164 A8
Church Field Rd DN6 . . . 206 E1
Churchfields DL6 . . . 210 E4
Church Fields 17 WF6 . . . 200 A1
Church Garth DL6 . . . 23 C3
Church Gdns LS25 . . . 194 C3
Church Gn 3 YO41 . . . 185 C2
Church Hill
4 Bramham LS23 . . . 188 E5
Crayke YO61 . . . 118 A1
Easingwold YO61 . . . 117 C1
10 Hunmanby YO14 . . . 126 F8
Hunsingore LS22 . . . 180 E8
Malton YO17 . . . 215 C4
Newby & Scalby YO13 . . . 75 C5
North Rigton LS17 . . . 178 B3
Reighton YO14 . . . 127 C6
3 Selby YO8 . . . 232 D5
Sherburn in Elmet LS25 . . . 195 E4
5 Spofforth HG3 . . . 179 E6
Stillingfleet YO19 . . . 191 D3
Thorner LS14 . . . 188 A3
Thornton Dale YO18 . . . 96 D6
8 Wistow YO8 . . . 197 D6
CHURCH HOUSES . . . 48 F4
Churchill Cl 3 TS9 . . . 8 A2
Churchill Dr 41 DL9 . . . 41 A5
Churchill Way 4 BD20 . . . 187 F8
Church La
Allerston YO18 . . . 97 B5
Appleton Roebuck YO23 . . . 190 F4
Aysgarth DL8 . . . 58 F3
Bagby YO7 . . . 90 C3
Barton DL10 . . . 21 C8
Bishopthorpe YO23 . . . 231 A4
Bolton Percy YO23 . . . 190 D4
Boroughbridge YO51 . . . 141 B5
Brompton YO13 . . . 98 C5
Burnsall BD23 . . . 157 A8
Burton Leonard HG3 . . . 140 A2
1 Carlton DN14 . . . 204 C3
Catton YO41 . . . 185 D8
Cayton YO11 . . . 100 B6
Collingham LS22 . . . 180 A1
Cropton YO18 . . . 71 B4
Cundall with Leckby YO61 . . 115 E3
Dunnington YO19 . . . 184 E7
East Heslerton YO17 . . . 124 A7
Elslack BD23 . . . 172 D4
4 Elvington YO41 . . . 185 C2
Faceby TS9 . . . 25 F1
Fylingdales YO22 . . . 33 C4
Garforth LS25 . . . 194 C4
Gargrave BD23 . . . 172 D8
Gateforth YO8 . . . 202 F8
Gilling East YO62 . . . 118 F7
Guisborough TS7 . . . 7 E5
17 Haxby YO32 . . . 166 E5
Hebden BD23 . . . 135 A1
Hensall DN14 . . . 203 C1
Hutton Buscel YO13 . . . 98 F7
Ingleby Greenhow TS9 . . . 27 B5
Kelbrook & Sough BB18 . . . 186 A8
Kellington DN14 . . . 202 E3
Kirby Hall YO26 . . . 164 B7
Kirby Hill YO51 . . . 141 B7
Knaresborough HG5 . . . 221 A6
Langtoft YO25 . . . 151 C1
Low Worsall TS15 . . . 24 A8
Marton cum Grafton YO51 . 141 D1
Martons Both BD23 . . . 172 A5
Micklefield LS25 . . . 194 F4
Mickletown LS26 . . . 200 B5
Church La *continued*
Middlesbrough TS5 . . . 6 E7
Middleton St George DL2 . . . 4 C3
Middleton YO18 . . . 95 E8
Milby YO51 . . . 141 B7
4 Monk Fryston LS25 . . . 202 A8
Moor Monkton YO26 . . . 165 B2
Nether Poppleton YO26 . . . 224 B3
New Earswick YO32 . . . 225 F5
11 Normanton South WF6 . 200 A1
North Featherstone WF7 . . 200 E1
Pannal HG3 . . . 222 D4
Poppleton YO26 . . . 224 A3
Rainton YO7 . . . 114 E6
Redmire DL8 . . . 59 C5
Ripon HG4 . . . 214 B5
Sadberge DL2 . . . 4 C7
Scarborough YO11 . . . 213 B7
4 Selby YO8 . . . 232 D5
Sessay YO7 . . . 116 C6
Settrington YO17 . . . 122 D1
Sinnington YO62 . . . 71 A1
Skelton YO30 . . . 224 B5
Slingsby YO62 . . . 120 B6
2 Snaith DN14 . . . 204 C1
South Stainley with Cayton
HG3 . . . 139 E2
9 Spofforth HG3 . . . 179 E6
Stainburn LS21 . . . 177 E3
Stainforth BD24 . . . 131 E6
10 Stamford Bridge YO41 . 168 D2
Strensall YO32 . . . 167 A7
Stutton with Hazlewood
LS24 . . . 189 E4
Swillington LS26 . . . 194 A1
Terrington YO60 . . . 119 F1
Thormanby YO61 . . . 116 F5
Thornton Dale YO18 . . . 96 D6
Thwing YO25 . . . 126 A1
Tunstall LA6 . . . 102 B4
Welburn YO60 . . . 146 E6
Weston LS21 . . . 176 D1
Westow YO60 . . . 147 B4
Wheldrake YO19 . . . 193 A7
Whitby YO22 . . . 208 E7
Whorlton DL6 . . . 25 D1
Wigglesworth BD23 . . . 153 D3
Wighill LS24 . . . 181 D1
Wintringham YO17 . . . 123 C4
York YO1 . . . 233 B2
Church Lea DL7 . . . 64 B7
Church Mdw
Barton DL10 . . . 21 D8
Sherburn in Elmet LS25 . . . 195 E4
Church Mdws 9 LS23 . . . 188 E6
Church Mews
Barlby YO8 . . . 198 A5
13 Boroughbridge YO51 . . . 141 B5
Gainford DL2 . . . 1 A7
Sherburn in Elmet LS25 . . . 195 F4
2 York YO26 . . . 227 C3
Church Rd
26 Glusburn BD20 . . . 187 E7
Great Preston LS26 . . . 200 C8
Linton BD23 . . . 134 E2
Pontefract WF6 . . . 200 A3
Scotton DL9 . . . 40 E4
Stainton Dale YO13 . . . 54 A7
Stamford Bridge YO41 . . . 168 D2
Thornton in Craven BD23 . . 171 F3
York YO10 . . . 229 D4
Church Rise YO19 . . . 167 F1
Church Row
Hurworth-on-Tees DL2 . . . 3 E1
Melsonby DL10 . . . 20 F7
Church Side LS26 . . . 200 B5
Churchside Villas LS26 . . 200 B5
Church Sq
Harrogate HG1 . . . 219 F3
Whitby YO21 . . . 208 C7
Church St
Addingham LS29 . . . 175 A4
Amotherby YO17 . . . 121 B4
Asenby YO7 . . . 115 B7
Barkston Ash LS24 . . . 195 F7
Bellerby DL8 . . . 60 D7
Bilton-in-Ainsty with Bickerton
YO26 . . . 181 D5
Boston Spa LS23 . . . 188 E8
Broughton BD23 . . . 172 D7
Bubwith YO8 . . . 199 D7
Carleton BD23 . . . 173 B4
Church Fenton LS24 . . . 196 B7
Copmanthorpe YO23 . . . 230 B2
Danby YO21 . . . 29 B7
Dunnington YO19 . . . 184 E7
5 Easingwold YO61 . . . 143 C8
5 Filey YO14 . . . 101 B3
Gargrave BD23 . . . 155 D1
13 Glusburn BD20 . . . 187 E8
Goldsborough HG5 . . . 163 A3
Guisborough TS14 . . . 8 F7
5 Helmsley YO62 . . . 92 F6
Heslerton YO17 . . . 123 E7
Hovingham YO62 . . . 119 E6
Ilkley LS29 . . . 218 A4
Ingleton LA6 . . . 103 D4
Kirkby Malzeard HG4 . . . 112 D5
24 Kirkbymoorside YO62 . . . 70 B1
Kirk Hammerton YO26 . . . 164 C2
Knottingley WF11 . . . 201 E4
Long Preston BD23 . . . 153 F4
6 Masham HG4 . . . 86 C3
6 Middleham DL8 . . . 60 E2
Norton YO17 . . . 215 D3
Nunnington YO62 . . . 93 E2
3 Riccall YO19 . . . 197 F8
2 Scarborough YO11 . . . 213 B6
Church St *continued*
Settle BD24 . . . 131 D3
4 Skipton BD23 . . . 216 F3
5 Staithes TS13 . . . 13 K2
Trawden BB8 . . . 186 B1
Ulleskelf LS24 . . . 190 C3
Well DL8 . . . 87 A4
West Tanfield HG4 . . . 87 A1
14 Wetherby LS22 . . . 180 C3
Whitby YO22 . . . 208 E6
Whittington LA6 . . . 102 A7
Whixley YO26 . . . 164 A5
York YO1 . . . 233 B2
Church Stairs St 3
YO11 . . . 213 B6
Church View
12 Airmyn DN14 . . . 205 E4
3 Brompton DL6 . . . 43 F3
22 Hemingbrough YO8 . . . 198 F1
16 Hurworth DL2 . . . 3 E1
Kirby Hill YO51 . . . 141 B7
Ledston LS25 . . . 194 E1
Norton DN6 . . . 206 E1
Sherburn in Elmet LS25 . . . 195 F4
Sherburn YO17 . . . 124 D8
South Milford LS25 . . . 195 F2
Thirsk YO7 . . . 211 A3
Church View Mews 7
LS23 . . . 188 E7
Churchville LS25 . . . 195 A4
Churchville Ave LS25 . . . 194 F4
Churchville Dr LS25 . . . 195 A4
Churchville Terr LS25 . . . 195 A4
Church Wind
Alne YO61 . . . 142 F4
Burneston DL8 . . . 87 E7
Church Wlk
Lindrick with Studley Royal &
Fountains HG4 . . . 139 B7
1 Willerby YO12 . . . 99 D2
5 Wistow YO8 . . . 197 D6
Church Wynd DL10 . . . 209 C7
Churchyard 14 LS24 . . . 189 E6
Churwell Cl WF10 . . . 200 E3
Cinder Hill La BD22 . . . 187 A6
Cinder La
Castleford WF10 . . . 200 E4
Clifford LS23 . . . 188 F7
Lindley LS21 . . . 177 C3
Upper Poppleton YO26 . . . 227 A7
York YO26 . . . 227 F5
Cinder Mews YO26 . . . 228 A5
Citadilla Cl 5 DL10 . . . 41 C7
City Art Gallery★ YO30 . . . 233 B3
Clack La DL6 . . . 45 A4
Clapdale Dr LA2 . . . 130 C8
Clapdale Way 2 LA2 . . . 130 C8
Clapgate Bank DL11 . . . 39 D8
CLAPHAM . . . 130 C8
Clapham CE Prim Sch
LA2 . . . 130 C7
CLAPHAM GREEN . . . 160 E5
Clapham Old Rd LA6 . . . 103 E3
Clapham Sta LA2 . . . 130 A6
Clare Ave DL3 . . . 3 A5
Claremont 23 YO14 . . . 101 B3
Claremont Dr TS7 . . . 7 C5
Claremont La HG3 . . . 140 B5
Claremont St BB8 . . . 186 A3
Claremont Terr YO31 . . . 233 B4
Clarence Ave 47 YO14 . . . 101 B3
Clarence Dr
56 Filey YO14 . . . 101 B3
Harrogate HG1 . . . 219 B3
Clarence Pl
7 Scarborough YO11 . . . 213 A6
2 Whitby YO21 . . . 208 D7
Clarence Rd
Middlesbrough TS7 . . . 7 D5
2 Scarborough YO12 . . . 213 A7
Scorton DL10 . . . 41 F7
Clarence St
2 Barnoldswick BB18 . . . 171 E1
2 Colne BB8 . . . 186 A3
1 Trawden Forest BB8 . . . 186 B1
York YO31 . . . 233 B4
Clarendon Ct YO31 . . . 228 C7
Clarendon Rd
Boston Spa LS23 . . . 188 E8
Great Burdon DL1 . . . 3 F7
Thornaby TS17 . . . 6 B7
Clarendon St 10 BB8 . . . 186 A3
Clareton La HG5 . . . 163 B6
Clark Beck Cl HG3 . . . 222 E3
Clark Ct WF7 . . . 200 E1
Clarke's Croft YO7 . . . 115 A4
Clarkson Ct 12 WF6 . . . 200 B1
Clarkson Dr LS25 . . . 201 F6
Clarkson St 7 YO21 . . . 208 D7
Clarkson Way DL8 . . . 56 C4
Clark St 7 YO12 . . . 213 A7
Clarks Terr YO31 . . . 228 F6
Claro Ave HG1 . . . 219 F4
Claro Bsns Ctr . . . 219 F4
Claro Mews 4 HG5 . . . 221 A5
Claro Pk HG1 . . . 219 F4
Claro Rd
Harrogate HG1 . . . 219 F3
Ripon HG4 . . . 214 C4
Claro Way HG1 . . . 219 F4
Claude Ave TS5 . . . 6 E8
Claudius Gr YO12 . . . 99 E6
Claver Cl DL6 . . . 45 D8
Clavery Ley La YO62 . . . 67 E1
CLAXTON . . . 168 B7
Claxton Ave DL3 . . . 3 A6
Clay Bank TS9 . . . 27 A3
Claygate YO31 . . . 229 B6
Clay Hill YO41 . . . 169 C3
Clay La
Bubwith YO8 . . . 199 C5
Camblesforth YO8 . . . 204 C6
Cliffe YO8 . . . 198 D4
Claypit La
Carlton DN14 . . . 204 C3
Ledston WF10 . . . 201 A8
Clay Pit La YO51 . . . 141 A4
Clay Pl 3 YO24 . . . 227 D1
Clayton Fold 5 BD20 . . . 187 F7
Clayton Hall Rd BD20 . . . 187 F7
Clayton Mews 8 WF6 . . . 200 A2
Clayton Pl 9 WF6 . . . 200 A2
Clayton St 7 BB18 . . . 171 E1
CLEASBY . . . 2 F4
Cleasby La DL2 . . . 2 F1
Cleasby Way TS16 . . . 5 D6
Cleatop Park Nature
Reserve★ BD24 . . . 153 D8
Clementhorpe YO23 . . . 233 B1
Clement St 4 YO23 . . . 233 B1
Clevegate TS7 . . . 7 C5
Cleveland 1 TS16 . . . 5 D4
Cleveland Ave
Darlington DL3 . . . 3 C5
Knottingley WF11 . . . 201 F2
Scalby YO12 . . . 212 D8
Stokesley TS9 . . . 26 C8
Cleveland College of Art &
Design TS5 . . . 6 E8
Cleveland Dr
Middlesbrough TS7 . . . 7 B6
Northallerton DL7 . . . 210 D2
Cleveland Gdns YO32 . . . 167 D3
Cleveland Ind Est DL1 . . . 3 D6
Cleveland Rd
Boltby YO7 . . . 91 B8
Catterick Garrison DL9 . . . 40 F4
Scarborough YO12 . . . 212 E6
Scorton DL10 . . . 41 F7
Cleveland Rein YO7 . . . 66 A3
Cleveland St
Darlington DL1 . . . 3 D6
Great Ayton TS9 . . . 8 A2
Guisborough TS14 . . . 8 E6
York YO24 . . . 228 A4
Cleveland Terr
Darlington DL3 . . . 3 B5
8 Whitby YO21 . . . 208 D5
York YO32 . . . 225 F4
Cleveland Trad Est DL1 . . . 3 D6
Cleveland View 1 TS9 . . . 25 F1
Cleveland Way
1 Carlton Miniott YO7 . . . 89 C4
Helmsley YO62 . . . 92 E6
York YO32 . . . 225 F3
Cliff Bridge Pl 6 YO11 . . 213 A5
Cliff Bridge Terr 7
YO11 . . . 213 A5
Cliff Brow TS13 . . . 11 C7
Cliff Cres LS25 . . . 194 E1
Cliff Dr 24 DL8 . . . 60 D5
CLIFFE
198 E2
Darlington . . . 2 B6
Cliffe Mews YO60 . . . 119 E1
Cliffe Prim Sch YO8 . . . 198 E2
Cliffe Rd HG2 . . . 219 B1
Cliff Gate Rd DL11 . . . 35 E4
Cliff Hill Rd DN6 . . . 206 D2
Cliff La
Newholm-cum-Dunsley
YO21 . . . 13 B2
Snainton YO13 . . . 97 F5
Whitwell-on-the-Hill YO60 . . 146 E4
Wilton YO18 . . . 97 A5
Wrelton YO18 . . . 95 B8
CLIFFORD . . . 188 E7
Clifford Ave LS29 . . . 218 A5
Clifford Ct BD23 . . . 216 D3
Clifford Moor Rd LS23 . . 188 D8
Clifford Rd
Boston Spa LS23 . . . 188 F8
Ilkley LS29 . . . 218 A6
Clifford St
3 Barnoldswick BB18 . . . 171 E1
1 Skipton BD23 . . . 216 F3
York YO1 . . . 233 B2
Clifford's Terr 25 YO14 . . 101 B3
Clifford's Twr★ YO1 . . . 233 B1
Cliff Rd
Stainton Dale YO13 . . . 54 A8
Staithes TS13 . . . 13 K2
Cliff St YO21 . . . 208 D7
Cliff The YO22 . . . 32 B6
CLIFTON
228 A7
Ilkley . . . 176 F3
Clifton Ave TS18 . . . 5 E6
Clifton Dale YO30 . . . 228 A6
Clifton Gn YO30 . . . 228 A6
Clifton Green Prim Sch
YO30 . . . 228 B7
Clifton La LS21 . . . 176 F3
Clifton Moor Bsns Village
YO30 . . . 225 A2
Clifton Moorgate YO30 . . 225 B3
Clifton Moor Gate YO30 . 225 A2
Clifton Moor Ind Estate
YO30 . . . 225 A3
Clifton Moor Retail Pk
YO30 . . . 225 A4
Clifton Moor Sh Ctr
YO30 . . . 224 F3
Clifton Park Ave YO30 . . . 227 E8
Clifton Park (York CC & York
RUFC) YO30 . . . 227 F7

Clifton Pl 3 YO30 228 A7
Clifton Prep Sch YO30 233 A4
Clifton Rd
Darlington DL1 3 D4
Ilkley LS29 218 D3
York YO30 233 A4
Clifton St
Earby BB18 186 A8
5 Scarborough YO12 212 F6
Trawden Forest BB8 186 A1
Clifton Terr LS29 218 C4
Clifton Without Jun Sch YO30 227 F8
CLINT 161 A6
Clint Bank HG3 160 E6
Clint Bank La HG3 160 F6
Clint Garth HG3 160 F8
CLINTS 39 C7
Clipt La YO7 65 D2
Clitheroe St 2 BD23 216 D3
Clive Gr YO24 227 F2
Clive Rd 1 HG3 179 E6
Clockhill Field La YO26 163 F3
Clock Twr* HG4 214 C6
Clockwood Gdns TS16 5 E3
Cloggerby Rigg DL11 35 E5
Clogger La BD23 172 D3
Cloisters The
15 Hemingbrough YO8 198 F1
Wilberfoss YO41 185 F6
York YO31 233 C3
Cloisters Wlk YO31 233 C3
Close La BD22 187 B5
Close Rd WF10 200 F4
Close The
9 Acaster Malbis YO32 191 C7
Barwick in Elmet LS15 194 B7
Boroughbridge YO51 141 A3
Boston Spa LS23 188 E8
Cawood YO8 197 A7
6 Collingham LS22 188 A8
11 East Ayton/West Ayton YO13 99 B8
4 Fylingdales YO22 33 D4
Hunmanby Sands YO14 101 C1
Hutton Rudby TS15 25 C5
Kirkby Fleetham DL7 42 C1
Longnewton TS21 4 F7
Minskip YO51 141 A3
Neasham DL2 4 A1
Northallerton DL7 210 B2
Norton DN6 206 E2
Riccall YO19 198 A8
Scalby YO12 212 B8
Skipton BD23 216 F3
Studley Roger HG4 113 D1
Thirsk YO7 211 C1
Thorner LS14 188 A3
Thornton Dale YO18 96 D5
Towton LS24 189 E2
York YO30 227 F8
Clotherholme Rd HG4 214 A5
CLOUGH 55 A7
CLOUGHTON 54 C1
CLOUGHTON NEWLANDS 54 C2
Clover Hill BD23 217 B5
Cloverley Cl YO41 168 C2
Clover Way 9 HG3 161 B3
Clowbeck Ct DL3 3 B8
Clydach Gr 24 TS17 5 F4
Clyde Gr TS18 5 F8
Coach La
10 Hurworth-on-Tees DL2 3 E1
Lindley LS21 177 D3
Coachman's Ct 6 HG2 220 B1
Coach Rd
Harrogate HG1 219 F2
Sheriff Hutton YO60 145 D4
Sleights YO22 32 A6
Coach St BD23 216 F4
Coach Street Yd 13 BD23 216 F4
Coalmire La DL6 45 D7
Coal Pit La
Kirk Smeaton WF8 206 A2
Rimington BB7 171 A1
Coalpits La 10 DL2 3 A7
Coarse La HG3 159 A4
Coastal Rd YO13 75 D7
Coastguard Hill YO14 127 E5
Coate Cl TS8 6 E5
COATES 171 E2
Coates Ave BB18 171 E2
Coates Fields BB18 171 E2
Coates La
Barnoldswick BB18 171 E2
Kettlewell with Starbotton BD23 107 F5
Coate's La BD20 173 F2
Coates Lane Prim Sch BB18 171 E2
Coates Marsh La DN14 204 B2
Coatham Ave DL2 4 D3
Coatham La TS21 5 B7
Cobble Carr TS14 8 E6
Cobble Court Mews YO24 233 A1
Cobblers La WF8 201 C1
Cobbler's La WF8 201 C1
COBBY SYKE 159 F2
Cobby Syke Rd HG3 159 F1
Cobcroft La WF11 206 B8
Cobden St
Barnoldswick BB18 171 D1
Darlington DL1 3 E5
Thornaby TS17 6 B8
Cobham Way YO32 224 E3
Cob La BB18 186 A6
Coble La YO60 145 D5
Cobshaw La DL8 62 F6
Cochrane St YO8 232 D3
COCKAYNE 48 A5
Cockburn St 5 TS12 9 F7
Cocked Hat HG4 139 C8
Cocked Hat Pk YO7 211 A1
Cockerhill La YO62 93 E7
COCKERTON 3 B6
Cockerton CE Prim Sch DL3 3 A6
Cockerton Gn DL3 3 B6
Cock Garth YO17 122 D1
COCK HILL 165 B2
Cockhill La BB8 186 A4
Cocking La LS29 174 E3
Cock La
Gainford DL2 1 E8
Piercebridge DL2 2 A7
Cocklakes La YO7 114 F1
Cock Lodge (site of)* YO7 115 C6
Cockmoor Rd YO13 74 A1
Cock Pit Cl HG4 113 C7
Cockrah Rd YO13 74 F2
Cockret Cl 8 YO8 232 B6
Cockret Ct YO8 232 B7
Cockret Rd YO8 232 B7
Cockshaw Bank La HG4 113 B4
Cockshott Pl 5 LS29 174 F4
Coda Ave YO23 231 B3
Codlin Rd 1 TS15 25 C5
Coeside YO24 230 B7
Coggan Cl YO23 228 B2
Coggan Way YO23 230 F4
Colber La HG3 138 F2
Colbert Ave LS29 218 E5
COLBURN 41 A5
Colburn Com Prim Sch DL9 41 A5
Colburn Dr DL9 40 F5
Colburn La DL9 40 F6
Colburn Sidings DL9 40 F4
Cold Bath Pl HG2 219 C1
Cold Bath Rd HG2 222 C8
COLD COTES 103 F2
Cold Cotes Rd HG3 160 B4
Coldhill La LS25 195 C6
Coldie Hill 11 TS15 25 C5
COLD KIRBY 91 D7
Cold Kirby Rd YO7 91 C8
Coldstone La YO7 88 B2
Coldyhill La YO12 212 B8
Colebrooke Mdws HG5 221 C7
Coledale Cl 2 YO30 224 F1
Colenso St YO23 233 B1
Coleridge Dr HG1 219 E7
Coleridge Gdns DL1 3 D3
Coleridge Way 1 WF8 201 B1
Colescliffe Cres YO12 212 C8
Colescliffe Rd YO12 212 C8
Cole St YO31 233 B4
Colin St 14 BB18 171 D2
Coliseum* YO21 208 D6
College Ave YO11 213 A2
College Bsns Pk HG4 214 B7
College Ct
1 Low Bradley BD20 173 E3
4 Scarborough YO11 212 F4
College Dr LS29 218 B3
College Farm Cl DN14 207 A8
College Farm La LS22 180 A2
College Gdns DL1 3 B5
College Gr WF10 200 D3
College La
5 Masham HG4 86 C3
Scarborough YO11 213 A1
College of Law YO23 231 B7
College Rd
Bradleys Both BD20 173 E3
Copmanthorpe YO23 230 A3
Harrogate HG2 222 B8
Ripon HG4 214 B6
College St
Harrogate HG2 222 B8
York YO1 233 B3
Colley Broach Rd YO61 117 F7
Colliergate YO1 233 B2
Collier Hag La YO23 182 B3
Collier La
Lotherton cum Aberford LS25 195 A6
West Layton DL11 20 A8
Collin Ave TS4 6 F8
Collin Bank HG3 160 E6
Collinge Rd 9 BD22 187 B6
COLLINGHAM 188 A8
Collingham Dr TS7 7 D4
Collingham Lady Elizabeth Hastings CE Sch LS22 180 A1
Collingham Way 12 YO14 101 A3
Collingsway 4 DL2 3 A7
Collingwood Ave YO24 227 F2
Collingwood Gdns YO17 215 A3
Collingwood Rd WF6 200 A2
Collin's Hill HG3 223 D7
Collinsons La YO17 122 F5
Colliwath La DL8 60 F4
Collyer View LS29 218 E5
Colne & Broughton Rd BD23 172 C4
Colne Rd
Barnoldswick BB18 171 D1
Cowling BD22 187 A5
Earby BB18 172 A1
Kelbrook & Sough BB18 186 A8
Colne Rd *continued*
Sutton BD20 187 C7
Trawden Forest BB8 186 A1
Colonel's Wlk 9 WF8 201 B1
Colonley Bsns Pk BD20 173 D1
Colorado Way WF10 200 F2
Colstan Rd DL6 210 E3
COLSTERDALE 84 E4
COLTON 190 E7
Colton La YO23 190 E6
Coltsfoot Ct 19 HG3 161 B3
Coltsgate Hill HG4 214 B6
Columbine Gr 33 HG3 161 B3
Columbus Ravine YO12 212 F7
Columbus Way DL10 41 C7
Colville Cres 8 DL9 41 A5
Colville Rd 12 DL9 41 A5
Comercial St
9 Barnoldswick BB18 171 D1
Harrogate HG1 219 D3
Norton YO17 215 D3
Scarborough YO12 212 E5
Tadcaster LS24 189 E6
Comercial Yd 1 HG5 221 B6
Comets Garth 11 DL2 3 A7
Comfort La DL10 20 C5
Comfrey Cl 32 HG3 161 B3
Comfrey Manor TS8 7 B4
Commercial St 9 BD24 131 E2
Common Croft La YO26 165 E1
COMMONDALE 9 D1
Common La
Beal DN14 202 D3
Burn YO8 203 E7
Catton YO41 185 E8
Dunnington YO19 184 F5
Fangfoss YO41 169 B1
Knottingley WF11 202 B1
Norton DN6 206 E2
Sutton upon Derwent YO41 193 C8
Temple Hirst YO8 203 F4
Thorganby YO19 192 F5
Walden Stubbs DN6 206 F4
Warthill YO19 167 F2
York YO10 229 B1
Common Rd
Dunnington YO19 184 F7
Skipwith YO8 192 E1
Comon Balk La HG3 140 A3
Comondale Sta YO21 9 E1
Comon Holme La LS29 175 C3
Comon La
Carlton Husthwaite YO7 116 F8
Coverham with Agglethorpe DL8 60 A2
Glaisdale YO21 29 F1
Hambleton YO8 196 D2
Harome YO62 93 E5
Hartley CA17 14 A8
Scruton DL7 63 E7
South Milford LS25 195 F2
Ulleskelf LS24 190 C2
West Witton DL8 59 F2
Comon Rd
Barkston Ash LS24 195 F7
Church Fenton LS24 196 A7
Strensall YO60 145 D1
Compton La LS22 188 A7
Compton St YO30 228 A6
Conan Dr DL10 209 D8
Conan Gdns DL10 209 D8
Concorde Pk YO30 225 A3
Concorde Way TS18 5 F7
Coneycroft 10 YO19 184 F7
Coneygarth La
Dunnington YO19 184 E5
Tunstall LA6 102 A4
Coney Garth La YO7 89 B3
Coney Garth View HG5 162 C5
Coney Moor Gr LS26 200 C6
Coney St YO1 233 B2
CONEYSTHORPE 120 D2
CONEYTHORPE 163 A5
Conference Cl YO17 215 B4
Conifer Cl 6 YO32 225 D3
Conifers Cl 2 YO8 197 D1
Coningham Ave 1 YO30 224 E2
Conisclife Mews DL3 3 A4
Conisclife Rd DL3 3 A4
Coniston Ave BB18 171 D2
Coniston Cl 1 YO30 224 E1
CONISTON COLD 155 A1
Coniston Dr
Castleford WF10 201 C4
York YO10 229 B4
CONISTONE 134 C6
Conistone La BD23 108 B3
Coniston Gdns 6 YO12 99 F7
Coniston Gr TS5 6 E7
Coniston Rd HG1 220 B4
Coniston Way
3 Eastfield YO12 99 F7
Thirsk YO7 89 C4
Connaught Rd
Ilkley LS29 218 D3
Middlesbrough TS7 7 D6
Connaught Way YO32 225 F6
CONONLEY 173 C2
Cononley La BD20 173 D1
Cononley Prim Sch BD20 173 D2
Cononley Rd BD20 187 D8
Cononley Sta BD20 173 D1
CONONLEY WOODSIDE 173 C3
Conowl Cl 23 YO62 92 F6
Conroy Cl 11 YO61 143 D8
Consort St BD23 217 B4
CONSTABLE BURTON 61 C5
Constable Burton Hall Gdns* DL8 61 C6
Constable Rd
Hunmanby YO14 127 A8
Ilkley LS29 218 D3
Constable Ridge Rd HG3 160 B2
Constantine Ave
10 Colburn DL9 41 A5
York YO10 229 A4
Constantine Cres 11 YO12 99 E6
Constantine Gr 11 DL9 41 A5
Constitution Hill 3 BD24 131 E2
Conway Cl 2 YO30 224 E3
Conway Cres BB18 171 E1
Conway Gr 8 TS17 5 F4
Conyers Ave DL3 3 A6
Conyers Cl
Richmond DL10 209 D8
Yarm TS15 5 D2
Conyers Ings YO13 99 A7
Conyers La DL8 61 D6
Conyers Rd DL7 22 E2
Conyers Sch TS15 5 E2
Conygarth Way DL7 63 C5
Conyngham Hall HG5 220 F6
Cook Cl DL10 41 C7
Cookgate TS7 7 C5
Cooks Cl 2 DL6 45 A7
Cooks Gdns 3 YO13 75 D5
Cookson Way 34 DL9 41 A5
Cook's Row 5 YO11 213 B6
Coolham La BB18 186 B8
Coombe Dr DL1 3 F6
Coombes Cl YO61 144 C3
COOMBOOTS 75 B6
Coomboots Brow YO13 75 A6
Cooper Cl DL6 25 D2
Cooper La
Blubberhouses LS21 159 C1
Potto DL6 25 D2
Cooper Lane Shepherd LS21 159 C2
Cooper Rd
49 Filey YO14 101 B3
18 Wetherby LS22 180 C3
Coopers Dr YO23 230 B3
COPGROVE 140 C2
Copgrove La HG5 162 D8
Copgrove Rd HG3 140 A2
Cophill La YO7 66 A4
Copley La LS25 195 B7
Copmanroyd LS21 177 A2
COPMANTHORPE 230 B2
Copmanthorpe & District Recreation Ctr YO23 230 B2
Copmanthorpe La YO23 230 E3
Copmanthorpe Prim Sch YO23 230 B3
Copper Beech Cl
9 Dunnington YO19 184 E7
Upper Poppleton YO26 182 F8
Copper Beech Dr DN14 207 A8
Copper Beeches The 2 YO19 184 E7
Copperclay Wlk YO61 117 D1
Copperfield Cl
Malton YO17 215 C5
21 Sherburn in Elmet LS25 195 F4
Coppergate
1 Riccall YO19 191 F1
York YO1 233 B2
Coppergate Sh Ctr YO1 233 B2
Coppergate Wlk YO1 233 B2
Coppertop Mews 4 WF8 201 C2
Coppice Ave HG1 219 C4
Coppice Beck Ct HG1 219 D3
Coppice Cl
Harrogate HG1 219 C4
10 Haxby YO32 166 E5
Coppice Dr HG1 219 C3
Coppice Gate HG1 219 C4
Coppice La
14 Hellifield BD23 154 B3
Wrelton YO18 71 B1
Coppice Rise HG1 219 C5
Coppice The
Barwick in Elmet LS15 194 B7
Bishopthorpe YO23 230 F4
Brayton YO8 197 C1
Ilkley LS29 218 A6
Leeming DL7 63 F3
14 Sherburn in Elmet LS25 195 F4
19 Sutton BD20 187 E7
Coppice Valley Prim Sch HG1 219 C5
Coppice View HG1 219 C4
Coppice Way HG1 219 C5
Coppy La
Cononley BD20 173 C2
Sutton BD22 187 E4
Coppy Rd LS29 174 F4
Coppy Wood Dr LS29 218 B7
Copse Hill 1 YO14 101 A4
Copse The
Boston Spa LS23 180 E1
3 North Featherstone WF7 200 E1
5 Scarborough YO12 212 B5
Copsewood Wlk 5 TS9 26 C8
COPT HEWICK 114 C2
Copwood Gr 7 YO32 225 C8
Corban La YO32 166 B6
Corban Way 21 YO32 166 D5
Corber Hill 7 DL6 43 F3
Corbie Way YO18 96 A7
Corby Ave TS5 6 D8
Cordike La
Birdsall YO17 148 D6
Langton YO17 147 F6
Cordilleras La DL11 39 C8
Corlett Ct
Woodthorpe YO24 230 C8
York YO24 230 C8
Cormorant Cl 10 YO14 101 D4
Cornaught Ct YO10 231 D8
Cornbell Gate 4 HG4 113 D2
Cornborough Ave YO31 228 F6
Cornborough Rd YO60 145 C5
Cornelian Ave YO11 100 B8
Cornelian Cl YO11 213 C1
Cornelian Dr YO11 213 C1
Cornelius Cswy YO8 198 E8
Cornel Rise 26 HG3 161 B3
Corner Cl 17 YO32 166 D5
Corners Terr 5 YO22 208 E6
Cornerstones Cl LS29 175 A4
Corners Yd 5 YO22 208 E6
Cornfield Rd TS17 6 A8
Cornflower Way 1 HG3 161 B3
Cornforth Hill DL10 209 B6
Cornlands YO17 215 D2
Cornlands Rd YO24 227 B1
Cornmill Cl YO8 197 B8
Corn Mill Ct 19 LS25 195 F4
Corn Mill Gdns YO12 212 D7
Corn Mill La 39 LS29 176 D1
Cornmill Pl 20 BB18 171 D2
Cornmill Sh Ctr DL1 3 C5
Cornwall Ave
Darlington DL1 3 E6
Silsden BD20 174 B1
Cornwall Cl HG1 219 A2
Cornwall Dr YO10 231 E8
Cornwall Rd HG1 219 B2
Cornwood Way 11 YO32 225 C8
Coronation Ave
6 Colburn DL9 41 A5
Harrogate HG2 222 E7
1 Hinderwell TS13 11 F7
Coronation Gr HG2 222 E7
Coronation Hospl LS29 218 C3
Coronation Pl DL10 209 A7
Coronation Rd
Crakehall DL8 62 E5
Harrogate HG2 222 E7
Coronation St
8 Barnoldswick BB18 171 E1
Castleford WF6 200 B2
Corporation Rd DL3 3 C6
Corporation Road Prim Sch DL3 3 C6
Corpse Rd
North Otterington DL7 64 E5
Thornton-le-Moor DL6 65 A4
Corunna Ct 5 YO8 232 D5
Cosmo Ave YO31 229 A5
Costa La YO18 95 D6
Costa Way YO18 95 E7
Cotchers La LS24 195 D8
Cotcliffe Ave DL6 210 F3
Cotcliffe Bank DL6 65 E5
Cote Hill Rd HG3 160 B4
Cote La
Healey HG4 85 D5
Sproxton YO62 92 C4
Cotescue Bank DL8 60 C1
Cotherstone Cl TS16 5 C5
Cotswold Dr LS25 194 C3
Cotswold Way YO32 226 A5
Cottage Cl DL6 210 E5
Cottage La YO60 145 C4
Cottagers La DL2 2 C3
Cottam La YO25 151 C5
Cottee Way 16 DL9 41 A5
COTTERDALE 55 F8
Cotterdale Cl HG5 221 C6
Cotterdale Gdns LS25 202 A6
Cotterdale Holt 9 LS22 180 A1
Cottom La YO42 193 C2
COTTON TREE 186 A2
Cotton Tree La BB8 186 A3
Coulby Farm Way TS8 7 A5
Coulby La YO18 97 A6
Coulby Manor Way TS8 6 F6
COULBY NEWHAM 7 A5
Coulby Newham Sch TS8 7 A5
Coulson Cl 5 YO32 167 C8
Coulter Beck La LA6 102 D7
COULTON 119 B5
Coulton La YO62 119 A6
Count De Burgh Terr 4 YO23 228 B1
COUNTERSETT 57 C2
Counting House Mews BD23 216 F4
County Par HG1 219 F3
County Sq HG1 219 F3
Coupland Rd
Garforth LS25 194 C4
1 Selby YO8 232 C6
Courby Hill HG4 86 F2
Courcey Gr YO26 227 C4
Court Dr YO8 232 A4
Court Green Cl YO13 54 D1
Court La BD23 217 A4
Court Moor La YO62 70 A4
Courtneys
Selby YO8 232 B4
Wheldrake YO19 193 A8
Courtneys The YO8 232 B4

Courts Cl 7 DN14 205 E4
Court Terr HG4 214 C5
Court The 6 DL8 63 A2
Courtyard The
  Bishopthorpe YO23 231 B4
  11 Pontefract WF8 201 C2
Coutances Way LS29 218 F5
Cove Rd BD23 132 F2
Coverdale Dr
  1 Knaresborough HG5 221 A7
  Scarborough YO12 212 B4
Coverdale Garth 2 LS22 188 A8
Coverdale La TS13 12 A4
COVERHAM 60 C1
Coverham Abbey (rems of)* DL8 60 C1
Coverham Cl DL7 210 C2
Coverham La DL8 60 C1
Cover La
  Carlton Town DL8 83 E7
  Marton-le-Moor HG4 114 E1
Covert The
  Mount Pleasant TS8 7 B4
  9 Topcliffe YO7 89 B1
  York YO24 230 F7
COWAN BRIDGE 102 D7
Cowbar Bank 1 TS13 13 K2
Cowbar La TS13 13 J2
Cow & Calf Rocks* LS29 218 D2
Cowcliff Hill YO17 148 F6
Cow Cl La
  Kirkby Malham BD23 154 E8
  Lockwood TS12 10 B4
COWESBY 66 C4
Cowgarth La 15 BB18 172 B1
Cow Gate La BD23 171 B7
Cowgill St 17 BB18 172 A1
Cowhouse Bank YO62 68 F3
Cowie Dr YO8 232 D5
Cow La
  Cowling BD22 187 B6
  Knottingley WF11 202 A2
  Lothersdale BD20 172 F1
  Middleton Tyas DL10 21 E5
  Womersley DN6 206 D6
Cowland La YO7 88 D3
Cowley Cl TS16 5 E7
Cowley Rd TS5 6 E7
COWLING
  Bedale 62 D2
  Glusburn 187 B6
Cowling Hill La BD22 186 F7
Cowling La DL8 62 D3
Cowling Prim Sch BD22 187 A6
Cowling Rd DL8 62 D2
Cowlings Cl 16 YO14 127 A8
Cow Pasture La YO42 193 C3
Cowpasture Rd LS29 218 C3
Cowper La YO23 191 C8
Cowper St 3 BD23 217 A3
Cowslip La 18 WF10 200 D3
COWTHORPE 180 E7
Cowton Castle* DL7 22 D1
Cowton La YO14 127 C6
Cowton Way TS16 5 D6
Cow Wath Bank YO22 51 E8
Cow Wath Cl 30 YO12 75 D5
Coxlea Gr YO31 229 B6
Coxwain Cl YO14 101 B2
COXWOLD 117 D8
Coxwold Dr DL1 3 D4
Coxwold Hill 5 LS22 180 C4
Coxwold Pottery* YO61 117 D7
Coxwold View 1 LS22 180 C3
Crab La
  Harrogate HG1 219 D6
  Seamer YO12 99 E6
Crabmill La YO61 143 D8
Crabtree Cl YO61 118 A1
Crabtree Gn LS22 188 A8
Crabtree Gr 1 YO32 225 D3
Crabtree Hill LS22 188 A8
CRACKPOT 37 B3
CRACOE 156 C7
Cracoe & Rylstone District Prim Sch BD23 156 B6
Cradley Dr TS5 6 E6
Cradoc Gr 14 TS17 5 F4
CRAG 187 D6
Crag Bank YO21 28 B8
Crag Cl 33 BD20 187 E7
Cragdale 13 BD24 131 D2
Cragdale Rise 1 HG5 221 D6
Cragg Bottom Rd BD22 187 C1
Crag Gdns LS23 188 E5
Cragg Dr LS29 218 F3
Cragg Hill Rd BD24 105 C3
Cragg La LA2 130 C4
Craggs La
  Arrathorne DL10 41 A1
  Tatham LA2 129 A3
Cragg The 21 YO21 208 D7
Crag Hill La HG3 161 B6
Crag La
  Bradleys Both BD20 173 E2
  Felliscliffe HG3 160 D4
  Huby LS17 178 B2
  Killinghall HG3 161 B1
  Knaresborough HG5 221 B5
  North Rigton LS17 178 B3
  Pannal HG3 178 C8
  Sutton BD20 187 D6
Crag Side Rd DL8 57 B2
Crag The 3 LS23 188 E5
Crag View
  Cononley BD20 173 D1
  Skipton BD23 217 B6
  Threshfield BD23 134 B3
  Weeton LS17 178 B2
Crag View Rd BD23 217 B3
Craiglands Pk LS29 218 C3
Craiglands Rd LS29 218 C3
Craig Miller Pk DL3 2 F5
Craigmore Dr LS29 218 E4
Craig St DL3 3 C6
Craigs Way YO7 211 C4
Crakehall Prim Sch DL8 62 E4
CRAKEHILL 115 E4
Crake La HG3 159 F6
CRAMBE 146 F3
CRAMBECK 146 F6
Crambeck Village YO60 146 F6
Cranberry TS8 7 B5
Cranbrook Ave YO26 227 C5
Cranbrook Rd YO26 227 C5
Cranbrooks The YO19 192 F8
Cranbrook Way 17 WF8 201 C2
Cranesbill Cl HG3 161 B3
Cranfield Pl 4 YO24 230 C8
Cranford Gdns TS5 6 D8
Crank La DL7 63 B7
Crankley La YO61 143 B7
Cranwell Gr TS17 6 B6
CRATHORNE 25 A6
Craven Bank La BD24 131 B3
Craven Coll (Aireville Campus) BD23 216 D4
Craven Coll (High Street Campus) BD23 217 A4
Craven Coll (Snaygill Campus) BD23 173 D4
Craven Coll (The Academy of Hair) BD23 216 F4
Craven Coll (The Academy of Hair & Beauty) BD23 217 F4
Craven Coll (The Centre for Rural & Equine Studies) BD23 216 C4
Craven Coll (Tyro Training) BD23 216 F4
Craven Court Sh Ctr BD23 217 A4
Craven Cres 3 LS29 174 F4
Craven Ct
  Cowling BD22 187 C6
  Northallerton DL7 210 B3
  Richmond DL10 209 B6
  Silsden BD20 174 C1
Cravendale Rd 4 DL9 40 F5
Craven Dr BD20 174 C1
Craven Garth 5 DN14 202 D4
Cravengate DL10 209 B6
Craven Mus* BD23 217 A4
Craven Ridge La BD24 131 A2
Craven Ridge Lane Ends BD24 131 B3
Craven's Hill YO13 54 C3
Craven St
  3 Colne BB8 186 A3
  Harrogate HG1 219 D4
  Scarborough YO11 213 A4
  Skipton BD23 216 F3
Craven Swimming Pool BD23 216 D4
Craven Terr BD23 216 F4
Craven Way
  5 Boroughbridge YO51 141 B4
  Dent LA10 78 B8
Crawford Cl YO26 181 C7
Crawley Way YO31 229 B6
CRAY 81 E2
CRAYKE 118 A1
Crayke Castle* YO61 117 F1
Crayke CE Prim Sch YO61 117 F1
Crayke La YO61 117 F2
Crayke Manor* YO61 118 A2
Cray Thorns Cres YO7 115 A4
Crescent Ave YO21 208 C7
Crescent Back Rd 8 YO11 213 A5
Crescent Ct LS29 218 B4
Crescent Gdns HG1 219 C2
Crescent Hill 53 YO14 101 B3
Crescent Par HG4 214 C6
Crescent Pl 20 YO21 208 D7
Crescent Rd
  Harrogate HG1 219 C2
  Ripon HG4 214 B6
Crescent Terr 6 LS29 218 B4
Crescent The
  13 Bedale DL8 63 B3
  Burton Fleming YO25 126 E3
  Carlton TS9 26 A2
  Dishforth YO7 115 A2
  Eaglescliffe TS16 5 D4
  Filey YO14 101 B3
  Garforth LS25 194 D4
  17 Helmsley YO62 92 F6
  Ilkley LS29 218 E5
  1 Kelfield YO19 191 D1
  Kexby YO41 185 C5
  Kippax LS25 194 D1
  Micklefield LS25 195 A3
  Middlesbrough TS7 7 D6
  Middleton St George DL2 4 E4
  Monk Fryston LS25 202 A8
  Northallerton DL6 210 E4
  North Rigton LS17 178 B3
  Otley LS21 177 A1
  6 Riccall YO19 197 F8
  Richmond DL10 209 D7
Crescent The *continued*
  Ripon HG4 214 B6
  Scalby YO12 212 B7
  Scarborough YO11 213 A5
  Sicklinghall LS22 179 E3
  Skipton BD23 217 B6
  Stamford Bridge YO41 168 D2
  2 Summerbridge HG3 138 A1
  Thirsk YO7 211 C3
  Thornaby TS17 6 B8
  Thornton Dale YO18 96 D5
  York YO10 229 C1
  York YO24 233 A1
Crestbrooke DL7 210 D2
Crestholme Cl 6 HG5 221 D5
Crest The LS26 194 A1
Crewe Rd WF10 201 B4
Creyke View DN14 205 A1
Cribyn Cl 20 TS17 5 F4
Crichton Ave YO30 228 B8
Cricketers Cl LS25 194 D3
Cricketers Way 8 LS25 195 F4
Cricket La TS6 7 E8
Cridling Gdns DN6 206 F2
CRIDLING STUBBS 206 C8
CRIMPLE 223 D8
Crimple Ave LS22 180 A8
Crimple Ct HG2 223 A7
Crimple La HG3 223 D7
Crimple Mdws HG3 222 D3
Crinan Ct
  Pontefract WF6 200 A2
  3 York YO32 225 F6
Crindle Carr La DL7 65 B3
Cringle Moor Chase TS9 26 F4
CRINGLES 174 C3
Cringles La BD20 174 C4
Cringley La DL8 57 E5
CROCKEY HILL 184 A1
Crocus Ct 20 DL9 41 A5
Croft Ave
  8 Knottingley WF11 202 A3
  Middlesbrough TS5 6 D8
  4 Normanton South WF6 200 B2
  Otley LS21 176 F1
Croft Cl
  Carlton Husthwaite YO7 116 F7
  14 Easingwold YO61 143 C8
  Ingleton LA6 103 D3
Croft Ct YO23 231 A4
Croft Dr LS23 188 E6
Crofters Gn HG3 219 A8
Crofters Mill BD20 187 B7
Croft Farm Cl YO23 230 B3
Croft Gdns YO7 211 B1
Croft Heads YO7 211 B1
Croft Head Terr 2 BD20 187 E7
Croft Hill
  Carthorpe DL8 87 E6
  32 Glusburn BD20 187 E7
Croft Hills TS9 26 A7
Croft House Dr 8 LS21 176 F1
Croft House Fold 10 LS29 175 A4
Croft House La BD23 135 A1
Croft La
  Carlton Husthwaite YO7 116 F8
  Newton Kyme cum Toulston LS24 189 B7
  Snainton YO13 97 F5
  Walton LS23 181 A2
Croftlands 7 WF11 202 A3
Croft Motor Racing Circuit* DL2 22 C5
CROFT-ON-TEES 22 D8
Croft Prim Sch DL2 22 C8
Croft Rd
  Bramham cum Oglethorpe LS23 188 E6
  Camblesforth YO8 204 D4
  Catterick Garrison DL9 209 E1
  Eaglescliffe TS16 5 D4
  Hurworth DL2 3 B2
  Ingleton LA6 103 D3
Crofts Ave
  4 Pickering YO18 96 A6
  Richmond DL10 209 B7
Croftside 1 YO26 227 B3
Croft St 1 BD20 187 E7
Crofts The
  1 Glusburn BD20 173 F1
  1 Sutton BD20 187 E6
Croft The
  Beadlam YO62 93 D7
  Burton in Lonsdale LA6 102 F3
  Castleford WF10 200 F3
  5 Collingham LS22 188 A8
  Draughton BD23 174 B7
  1 Filey YO14 101 B3
  Grafton YO51 141 D2
  Knottingley WF11 202 A3
  Langthorpe YO51 141 A7
  Scalby YO12 212 B7
  Sheriff Hutton YO60 145 D5
  Stirton with Thorlby BD23 216 C6
  Thirsk YO7 211 B1
  West Tanfield DL8 87 B3
Croft View 6 YO7 211 B3
Croftway
  Barwick in Elmet LS15 194 C8
  Camblesforth YO8 204 C5
  Selby YO8 232 C4
  Sherburn in Elmet LS25 195 F4
  2 York YO26 227 B3
Crombie Ave YO30 228 B7
Cromer St YO30 228 B7
Crompton Terr YO32 225 D6
Cromwell Ave 22 YO14 101 B3
Cromwell Cl 5 WF11 201 E4
Cromwell Cres 6 WF8 201 C1
Cromwell Dr DL7 64 A6
Cromwell Gdns 6 YO11 212 F4
Cromwell Office Pk 22 LS22 180 C3
Cromwell Par 5 YO11 212 F4
Cromwell Rd
  Harrogate HG2 222 E7
  Scarborough YO11 212 F4
  York YO1 233 B1
Cromwell Rise LS25 200 D8
Cromwell St 9 BD23 217 A3
Cromwell Terr 7 YO11 212 F4
Crook Bank La DL11 38 F6
Crooked La YO26 164 C2
Crook La HG4 85 E5
Crookland La YO32 166 F5
Crook Rise View BD23 217 B3
Croome Dale La YO17 150 C6
Croome Rd YO25 150 B4
Croom Medieval Village* YO25 150 B4
Cropstones LS23 188 F5
CROPTON 71 B4
Cropton Brewery & Visitor Ctr* YO18 71 B3
Cropton La YO18 71 B2
Cropton Rise YO12 212 B4
Cropton Way TS8 7 B5
CROSBY COURT 65 B6
Crosby Gdns DL6 210 E4
Crosby Rd DL6 210 E4
Crosby St DL3 3 C7
Crosland Cl 22 YO62 92 F6
Cross Bank BD23 217 B6
Crossbeck Cl LS29 218 B3
Crossbeck Rd
  Ilkley LS29 218 B3
  Northallerton DL6 210 F5
Crossbeck Way TS7 7 D8
Crosscliff TS8 6 F5
Crossdale Rd YO18 72 E3
Cross End Fold 3 LS29 175 A4
Crossfield Cl 2 DL2 3 E1
Crossfield Cres YO19 231 E6
Crossfields TS8 7 A4
Cross Gate YO13 97 D5
Crossgate La 22 YO18 95 F6
CROSSGATES 99 E7
Crossgates HG3 138 B5
Cross Haw La 3 LA2 130 C8
Cross Head Bank DL8 60 D7
Cross Hill
  Fairburn WF11 201 D6
  Sutton-under-Whitestonecliffe YO7 90 D5
Crosshill La DN14 207 E6
CROSS HILLS 187 E7
Cross Hills La YO8 232 A5
Crossings The 13 DN14 205 E4
Cross La
  Bentham LA2 128 E8
  Brompton YO13 98 C5
  Burneston DL8 87 E8
  Burniston YO13 75 D7
  Farndale East YO62 48 E4
  Flaxton YO60 167 E8
  Fulford YO19 231 F5
  Giggleswick BD24 130 F2
  Great Ouseburn YO26 164 B8
  Little Ayton TS9 27 A8
  Pickhill with Roxby YO7 88 C6
  Scalby YO12 212 C8
  Sinnington YO62 95 A8
  Snainton YO13 97 F3
  Stonebeck Up HG3 110 B5
Crosslands Rd 2 YO10 231 E8
Cross Lane Ct BD20 173 E3
CROSS LANES 143 D3
Cross Lanes DL10 209 E7
Crossley Pl BD23 216 F4
Crossley St 8 LS22 180 C3
Crossley Street Prim Sch LS22 180 C3
Crossman Dr 2 WF6 200 B2
Crossmoor La YO32 166 E6
Cross Queen St 9 WF6 200 A1
Cross Rd LA2 128 E7
Cross Rein Bank DL7 23 A1
Cross Row
  Boosbeck TS12 9 E7
  Swillington LS15 194 A3
Cross St
  6 Cowling BD22 187 B6
  14 Earby BB18 172 A1
  Scarborough YO11 213 A6
  Skipton BD23 216 F3
  3 York YO24 227 C3
Cross The LS15 194 B8
Cross Top DL8 57 E7
Crossways YO10 229 C2
Crossways Cres HG2 220 D3
Crossways Dr HG2 220 D2
Crossways The LS21 177 A1
Crossway The
  Darlington DL1 3 E5
  2 York YO31 228 E8
Crosswell Pk 40 TS17 5 F4
Crowberry Dr HG3 161 B3
CROWDON 54 A4
Crowdy Cl YO22 208 E4
Crowfoot La DL6 43 D5
Crowgarth HG4 140 D7
Crow Hill La HG3 160 C4
Crown Close Back 14 YO11 213 A4
Crown Cres YO11 213 A4
Crow Nest Rd LA2 130 F6
Crown Gr YO17 215 E3
Crown Sq 26 YO62 70 B1
Crown St
  34 Burley in Warfedale LS29 176 C1
  Darlington DL1 3 C5
Crown Terr YO11 213 A4
Crowood Ave TS9 26 C8
Crowtrees 1 LA2 128 E8
Crummack La LA2 130 E8
Crummock 3 YO24 230 C7
CUBECK 57 F4
Cuddy Brown Cl 7 YO18 96 A6
Cuddy La DL6 45 B4
Culloden Twr* DL10 209 B6
Culvert La BD23 216 A4
Cumberland Cl 6 YO32 167 B6
Cumberland Gdns DL10 21 C4
Cumberland Rd 1 WF10 201 C5
Cumberland St
  6 Skipton BD23 216 F3
  York YO1 233 B2
Cumbernauld Rd TS17 6 C7
Cumboots Brow YO13 75 B6
Cumbrian Ave 4 YO32 167 B6
CUNDALL 115 E3
Cundall Ave YO7 115 B6
Cundall Cl 6 YO32 167 C8
Cundall Dr 6 YO32 191 C7
Cundall Manor Sch YO61 115 E3
Cundall Way HG2 222 C8
Cunliffe Rd LS29 218 B4
Cunningham Ave TS17 6 B6
Cunningham Rd 4 DL9 40 F4
Cupid's Alley YO17 149 B6
Curfew Rd HG4 214 C3
Curlew Cl
  11 Ilkley LS29 175 C2
  Leyburn DL8 60 E4
Curlew Cres 2 DL9 40 F2
Curlew Dr
  13 Crossgates YO12 99 E6
  3 Filey YO14 101 A3
Curlew Glebe 8 YO19 184 E7
Curly Hill LS29 218 C7
Currer La LS29 175 B6
Currie Cl DL9 209 C2
Curson Terr YO8 198 E3
Curtain La DL11 1 D5
Curtain The DL11 1 D4
Curteis Dr DL10 41 B6
Curzon Terr YO23 228 B1
Custance Wlk YO23 233 A1
Cutler La LS26 200 C6
Cutpurse La DL10 209 C8
Cut Rd WF11 201 D6
CUTSYKE 200 E3
Cutsyke Ave WF10 200 D3
Cutsyke Rd WF10 200 D2
Cut Throat La HG3 138 F1
Cycle St 4 YO10 229 A3
Cygnet Cl 7 YO14 101 A4
Cygnet Dr TS18 6 A7
Cygnet St YO23 233 A1
Cyndor Ct WF10 201 C3
Cypress Cl DL3 3 B4
Cypress Gdns HG4 214 B2
Cypress Rd TS7 7 C6
Cyprus Gr 37 YO32 166 E5

D

DACRE 159 F7
DACRE BANKS 159 F8
Dacre Braithwaite CE Prim Sch HG3 159 B7
Dacre Ct LS24 195 D7
Dacre Hall Pk HG3 159 F7
Dacre La HG3 159 D7
Dacre Pasture La HG3 159 D6
Daffy La YO61 117 E1
Dairy La HG3 159 E6
Daisy Cl DL9 41 A5
Daisy Hill BD20 174 C1
Dakyn Cl DL7 22 F2
Dalacres Cres BD23 217 D8
Dalacres Dr BD23 217 D8
DALBY 119 B2
Dalby Ave HG2 220 D1
Dalby Bank YO60 119 C2
Dalby Cl YO12 212 B5
Dalby Ct HG2 220 D1
Dalby Forest Dr YO18 96 E8
Dalby Mead YO32 225 F1
Dalby Way TS8 7 A5
Dale Ave YO13 75 C8
Dale Bank HG1 219 B3
Dale Cl
  Burniston YO13 75 C8
  Hampsthwaite HG3 161 A5
  7 Hurworth-on-Tees DL2 3 E1
  Selby YO8 232 C3
  Thornton Watlass HG4 86 D8
Dale Cres BD23 173 A4
Dale Croft 20 LS29 175 C2
Dale Dike Gr YO30 224 F2
Dale Edge 11 YO11 99 F7
Dale End
  Danby YO21 29 C7
  Kirkbymoorside YO62 70 B1
Dale End Rd YO62 70 A7
Dalefield Ave WF6 200 A1
Dalefield Rd WF6 200 A1
Dale Garth YO12 212 D4
Dale Gr DL8 60 D6

Dalehouse Bank TS13 ..... 13 J1
Dale Rd
Carleton BD23 .... 173 A4
Darlington DL3 .... 3 B5
Sadberge DL2 .... 4 C7
Dale Rise YO13 .... 75 C8
Dales Ave BD23 .... 217 C7
Dalesbridge Outdoor Ctr★
LA2 .... 130 E6
Dales Countryside Mus★
DL8 .... 56 D5
Dales Ct YO19 .... 191 D3
Daleside Ave HG2 .... 222 E5
Daleside Dr HG2 .... 222 E5
Daleside Gdns HG2 .... 222 E5
Daleside Pk HG3 .... 160 A6
Daleside Rd
Farndale East YO62 .... 48 C7
Farndale West YO62 .... 48 B6
Harrogate HG2 .... 222 E5
Rosedale East Side YO18 .... 49 C5
Rosedale West Side YO18 .... 49 C3
Dale's La YO31 .... 228 F6
Dales Park Rd TS8 .... 6 E5
Dales Sch The DL7 .... 64 A7
Dale St
Earby BB18 .... 172 B1
York YO23 .... 233 A1
Dale Stone Cl WF11 .... 201 D5
Dale The LS25 .... 188 F1
Dale View
6 Earby BB18 .... 172 A1
Ilkley LS29 .... 175 C2
Dale Way 2 DL8 .... 60 D5
Dalewood Wlk 3 TS9 .... 26 C8
Dalguise Gr YO31 .... 233 C4
Dallamires Cl HG4 .... 214 D3
Dallamires Ind Est HG4 .... 214 D4
Dallamires La HG4 .... 214 E3
Dallamires Way N HG4 .... 214 D4
Dallamires Way S HG4 .... 214 D3
Dallas Ct TS8 .... 6 F5
DALLOW 111 F2
Dalmally Cl YO24 .... 230 B6
DALTON
Newsham 19 D7
Topcliffe 115 F7
DALTON GATES 22 D4
Dalton Hill YO19 .... 193 A8
Dalton La
Dalton YO7 .... 115 D7
Wothersome LS23 .... 188 C5
DALTON-ON-TEES 22 E6
Dalton Terr YO24 .... 228 A3
Dam Bank YO8 .... 232 C6
Dame La DL8 .... 58 F1
Dam Head Rd 14 BB18 .... 171 D1
Dam Hill YO23 .... 182 B4
Dam La
Appleton Roebuck YO23 .... 190 F4
Markington with Wallerthwaite
HG3 .... 139 C3
Saxton with Scarthingwell
LS24 .... 195 C7
Selby YO8 .... 197 B3
Damson Cl YO26 .... 227 E4
DANBY 29 C7
Danby Castle★ YO21 .... 29 D6
Danby CE Sch YO21 .... 29 B6
Danby La DL7 .... 43 C5
Danby St 3 DL9 .... 40 F4
Danby Sta YO21 .... 29 C7
DANBY WISKE 43 C5
Dandy Mill Ave WF8 .... 201 C1
Dandy Mill Croft 8 WF8 .... 201 C1
Dandy Mill View WF8 .... 201 C1
Dane Ave
Thorpe Willoughby YO8 .... 197 B1
York YO26 .... 227 C5
Danebury Cres YO26 .... 227 C4
Danebury Ct YO26 .... 227 C4
Danebury Dr YO26 .... 227 C4
Danelaw Fields 1 DL6 .... 43 F3
Danelaw Rd 2 DL6 .... 43 F3
Dane Rd DL9 .... 209 E1
Danescroft YO8 .... 232 C2
Danes Croft 2 YO10 .... 231 D8
Danes Ct 5 YO19 .... 198 A8
Danes Dyke 34 YO12 .... 75 D5
Danesfort Ave YO24 .... 227 D2
Danesgate YO26 .... 227 C4
Dane's Graves (Tumuli)★
YO25 .... 151 D2
Danes Hills (Tumuli)★
YO8 .... 192 E2
Danesmead YO10 .... 231 D8
Danesmoor Cres DL3 .... 3 B5
Daneswell Cl 3 YO41 .... 168 D2
Dangerous Cnr HG3 .... 160 A2
Dansk Way LS29 .... 218 D5
Danum Ave YO7 .... 211 A1
Danum Dr YO10 .... 231 E8
Danum Rd YO10 .... 231 E8
Darbie Cl YO32 .... 225 D4
D'arcy Ct DL9 .... 40 F4
D'arcy Rd YO8 .... 232 E4
Darfield Cl YO32 .... 167 B8
Darkfield La WF8 .... 201 C2
Dark La
Brompton YO13 .... 98 C5
Earby BB18 .... 172 B1
Newsham DL11 .... 19 C8
Sinnington YO62 .... 71 A1
Spofforth with Stockeld
HG5 .... 179 F7
Stainburn LS21 .... 177 E2
Sutton BD22 .... 187 F1
DARLEY 160 A6
Darley Carr HG3 .... 159 F6
Darley Cl 7 YO41 .... 168 D2
Darley Mill Ctr★ HG3 .... 159 F6
Darley Prim Sch HG3 .... 160 A6
Darley Rd HG3 .... 160 D6
Darling La YO23 .... 191 C8
DARLINGTON 3 E6
Darlington Arts Ctr★ 2
DL3 .... 3 C5
Darlington Back La DL2 .... 4 E8
Darlington (Bank Top) Sta
DL1 .... 3 D4
Darlington Civic Theatre★
DL1 .... 3 D5
Darlington Coll DL1 .... 3 D6
Darlington Coll at Catterick
Garrison 28 DL9 .... 40 E4
Darlington Meml Hospl
DL3 .... 3 C6
Darlington Rd
Easby DL10 .... 20 F1
Longnewton TS21 .... 5 A7
Northallerton DL6 .... 210 C7
Richmond DL10 .... 209 E8
Sadberge DL2 .... 4 B7
Stockton-on-Tees TS18 .... 5 E8
Darlington Ret Pk DL1 .... 3 F5
Darlington Sta DL1 .... 3 D4
Darnborough Gate HG4 .... 214 B6
Darnborough St YO23 .... 233 B1
Darnbrook Rd 2 BB18 .... 171 D1
Darnbrook Wlk YO31 .... 229 B5
Darnholme La YO22 .... 51 D8
Darnton Dr TS4 .... 7 A7
Darrowby Cl YO7 .... 211 C4
Darrowby Dr DL3 .... 3 C6
Darwin Cl YO31 .... 225 E1
Darwin Dr 40 DL9 .... 41 A5
Daskett Hill YO60 .... 145 D5
Dauby La YO41 .... 185 B3
Davenport Rd TS15 .... 5 D2
David La YO18 .... 72 F5
Davis Ave WF10 .... 201 B3
Davison Rd DL1 .... 3 D7
Davison St TS12 .... 9 F7
Davygate YO1 .... 233 B2
Davy Rd WF10 .... 200 E6
DAW CROSS 222 B3
Dawcross Rise HG3 .... 222 B3
Dawes Ave WF10 .... 201 A3
Daw La YO23 .... 191 A5
Dawnay Cl 5 YO12 .... 99 F7
Dawnay Garth
Shipton YO30 .... 165 E5
2 Snaith DN14 .... 204 B1
Dawney La YO61 .... 143 B6
Dawson Ct HG3 .... 161 A5
Dawson's La HG4 .... 85 F4
Dawson St 16 BD23 .... 217 A3
Dawson Terr HG1 .... 219 D4
Dawtrie St WF10 .... 201 B4
Day La HG3 .... 159 E4
Daysfoot Ct 8 YO10 .... 228 E3
Deacon Ct 3 YO8 .... 232 B6
Deacons Ct YO23 .... 230 B2
Dealtry Ave 1 YO32 .... 225 C8
Dean Edge Rd BD22 .... 187 D1
Deane Pl HG2 .... 220 B3
Deangate YO1 .... 233 B3
Dean Hall Brow YO22 .... 32 C5
Deanhead Gr 7 YO30 .... 224 E2
Dean La BD22 .... 187 F3
Dean Rd
Norton YO17 .... 215 E3
Scarborough YO12 .... 212 E6
Deans Cl YO23 .... 230 F4
Deans Sq YO7 .... 115 C7
Dean St
Ilkley LS29 .... 218 C5
Trawden Forest BB8 .... 186 A1
De Bruce Rd DL6 .... 210 D8
Debruse Ave TS15 .... 5 D2
De Brus Pk TS8 .... 7 C4
De Brus Way TS14 .... 8 F7
De Burgh Ct DL9 .... 41 A5
Dee Cl YO24 .... 230 B7
DEEPDALE 80 F2
Deepdale
Guisborough TS14 .... 8 D6
7 Hutton Rudby TS15 .... 25 C5
5 York YO24 .... 230 D8
Deep Dale LS23 .... 180 E1
Deepdale Ave
Eastfield YO11 .... 100 A8
Middlesbrough TS4 .... 7 A8
Scarborough YO11 .... 213 A1
Deepdale La
Boston Spa LS23 .... 180 D1
Dent LA10 .... 77 F8
Deepdale Way 7 DL1 .... 3 F6
Deep Ghyll Croft HG4 .... 214 C3
Deep Ghyll Wlk HG4 .... 214 C3
Deeping Way YO8 .... 232 A6
Deer Hill Gr YO30 .... 224 F3
Deer Park Ct 1 LS25 .... 202 A8
DEERSTONES 175 B8
Deerstone Way 22 YO19 .... 184 F7
De Ferrers Rd DL6 .... 210 D8
De Ferrieres Ave HG1 .... 219 D4
De Gaunte Rd DL6 .... 210 E8
De Grey Ct YO30 .... 233 A4
De Grey Pl 2 YO23 .... 231 B3
DEIGHTON
192 A7
Brompton 44 A8
Deighton Ave 18 LS25 .... 195 F4
Deighton Cl LS22 .... 180 C3
Deighton Grove La YO19 .... 184 A1
Deighton La
Brompton DL6 .... 43 E5
Little Smeaton DL6 .... 23 E1
Deighton Rd
Coulby Newham TS4 .... 7 A7
Spofforth with Stockeld
HG3 .... 179 F6
Wetherby LS22 .... 180 C4
Deigton Gates Prim Sch 7
LS22 .... 180 C4
De Lacy Ave 1 WF7 .... 200 E1
Delacy Cres WF10 .... 201 B5
Delamere Cl 6 YO32 .... 166 D5
Delamere Cres HG2 .... 220 D1
Delamere Rd TS3 .... 7 B8
Delaney Cl 19 BD24 .... 131 D2
Delf La YO7 .... 66 A4
De Lisle Cres DL9 .... 209 C2
Dell The
Langtoft YO25 .... 151 C5
5 Skelton YO30 .... 224 B5
Del Pyke YO31 .... 233 C4
Delves La YO22 .... 30 F3
Delwood YO10 .... 231 D7
De Mowbray Ct YO23 .... 182 D3
Dene Cl DN14 .... 203 C2
Dene Gr DL3 .... 3 C6
Dene Mdw 1 YO13 .... 99 B8
Dene Park Cl HG1 .... 219 F6
Dene Pk HG1 .... 219 F5
Dene Rd DL6 .... 210 E5
Deneside Rd DL3 .... 3 B6
Denesway LS25 .... 194 D3
Dene The YO12 .... 212 E7
Denevale TS15 .... 5 E3
Denison Ave 8 YO12 .... 99 D6
Denison Rd YO8 .... 232 E4
Dennis La BD20 .... 174 A2
Dennison St YO31 .... 233 C4
Dennis St YO1 .... 233 C2
Dentdale Dr HG5 .... 221 C6
DENTON 176 A3
Denton Rd LS29 .... 218 A5
Denton Terr WF10 .... 200 F4
Denver Dr DL2 .... 4 D4
Denver Rd 6 DN6 .... 206 F2
Denwell Terr WF8 .... 201 B1
Depot La 11 YO12 .... 212 E4
Deramore Dr YO10 .... 229 C3
Deramore Drive W YO10 .... 229 C3
Derby Cl DL9 .... 209 C1
Derby Rd TS14 .... 8 E6
Derby The TS7 .... 7 B6
Derby Way 8 DL9 .... 40 F4
Dere St DL7 .... 63 D3
Dere Street Roman Rd★
DL11 .... 2 B2
Derrings La YO61 .... 142 D6
Derventio Roman Fort★
YO17 .... 215 D4
Derwent Ave
Garforth LS25 .... 194 C3
5 Scarborough YO12 .... 212 E4
York YO31 .... 228 F4
Derwent Chase DN14 .... 205 B7
Derwent Cl
East Cottingwith YO42 .... 193 C5
Elvington YO41 .... 185 B3
2 Stamford Bridge YO41 .... 168 D2
Derwent Ct YO41 .... 185 C2
Derwent Dr
4 Barlby YO8 .... 198 B5
Castleford WF10 .... 201 C5
Wheldrake YO19 .... 192 F7
Derwent Est YO19 .... 184 E7
Derwent Infant Sch
YO10 .... 229 B4
Derwent Junior Sch
YO10 .... 229 B4
Derwent La YO19 .... 184 E7
Derwent Pk YO19 .... 193 A8
Derwent Pl WF11 .... 201 F1
Derwent Pool & Fitness Ctr
YO17 .... 215 D4
Derwent Rd
Harrogate HG1 .... 220 B3
Huttons Ambo YO17 .... 215 A2
Whitby YO21 .... 208 A7
York YO10 .... 231 D8
Derwent St 7 YO12 .... 212 E4
Derwent Terr YO17 .... 215 D3
Derwent Wlk YO32 .... 225 F5
Desmond Rd DL2 .... 4 C3
Desmond Way DL3 .... 3 C6
Deveron Way YO24 .... 230 B7
Devil's Arrows Standing
Stones★ YO51 .... 141 B5
Devon Ct 8 DL9 .... 209 C1
Devon Pl YO10 .... 228 F3
Devonshire Ct YO30 .... 225 A1
Devonshire Dr YO12 .... 212 E7
Devonshire Gn HG4 .... 114 F1
Devonshire Pl
Harrogate HG1 .... 219 E3
12 Skipton BD23 .... 216 F4
Devonshire Rd DL1 .... 3 E6
Devonshire St 13 BD23 .... 217 A3
Devonshire Way HG1 .... 219 F4
Dewberry TS8 .... 7 B4
Dew La TS7 .... 7 D7
Dewsbury Ct YO1 .... 233 A1
Dewsbury Terr YO1 .... 233 A1
Dexta Way DL7 .... 210 C3
Dialstone The YO7 .... 211 A2
Diamond Ct TS18 .... 5 F7
Diamond Gr HG1 .... 220 C4
Diamond Pl HG1 .... 220 C4
Diamond Rd TS17 .... 6 B8
Diamond St YO31 .... 233 C4
Dibble Bridge Bank YO21 .... 28 F6
Dibdale Rd DL2 .... 4 A1
Dickens Cl 1 YO32 .... 225 F1
Dickens Dr 32 DL9 .... 41 A5
Dickens Rd YO17 .... 215 C6
Dickey La YO8 .... 197 D5
Dick La BD22 .... 187 B6
Dick Scot La DL11 .... 19 D7
Dicky Grounds La YO17 .... 121 D8
Didsbury Cl YO30 .... 224 E2
DIG★ YO1 .... 233 C2
Dijon Ave YO24 .... 227 C2
Dikehollin La DL8 .... 58 E2
Dike La HG3 .... 159 C8
Dikelands Cl 19 YO26 .... 165 F1
Dikelands La YO26 .... 165 F1
Dike Ray Cl YO32 .... 225 C7
Dikes La TS9 .... 8 C2
Diligence Way 2 TS16 .... 5 D5
Dilys Gr 5 YO26 .... 227 E4
Dimmingdale Rd TS12 .... 10 A3
Dinas Ct 12 TS17 .... 5 F4
Dinsdale Ave TS5 .... 6 E7
Dinsdale Cl 7 DL2 .... 4 C4
Dinsdale Cres DL1 .... 3 D5
Dinsdale Ct 6 DL2 .... 4 C4
Dinsdale Dr TS16 .... 5 E5
Dinsdale Sta DL2 .... 4 C4
Diomed Ct TS7 .... 7 B7
DISHFORTH 115 A4
Dishforth Airfield YO7 .... 115 A2
Dishforth Airfield Prim Sch
YO7 .... 115 B2
Dishforth CE Prim Sch
YO7 .... 114 F4
Dishforth Rd
Copt Hewick HG4 .... 114 B2
Sharow HG4 .... 214 F6
Disraeli Cl YO32 .... 225 E1
Dixon Ct YO8 .... 232 B6
Dixon Gdns YO8 .... 232 B6
Dixon Rd HG1 .... 219 D4
Dixons Bank TS8 .... 7 C5
Dixon St BD20 .... 187 F7
Dixons Yd YO1 .... 233 C2
Dixon Terr HG1 .... 219 D4
Dobella Ave DN14 .... 205 A1
Dob Park Rd LS21 .... 176 F4
Doctor Laithe 3 BD23 .... 134 D2
Doctor's Hill 2 LA2 .... 128 E8
Doctors La WF10 .... 200 D7
Doctor's La TS15 .... 25 C5
Dodder Carr Rd TS13 .... 10 F3
Dodford Rd TS8 .... 6 F5
Dodgson La
Lothersdale BD20 .... 186 D8
Thornton in Craven BB18 .... 172 C1
Dodgson Terr YO26 .... 227 D4
Dodmire Junior & Infant Sch
DL1 .... 3 E4
Dodsworth Ave YO31 .... 228 E7
Doe Park La YO41 .... 169 B4
Doe Pk YO30 .... 224 F2
Dog Hill DL8 .... 60 E3
Dog Hill Brow BD24 .... 131 D6
Dog Kennel La YO18 .... 96 E5
Doherty Wlk YO24 .... 230 C8
Dolegate YO41 .... 168 F4
Dolly La DL7 .... 64 C8
Dollyth Howe★ YO17 .... 149 F6
Dolphin Ctr The DL3 .... 3 C5
Dolphin Way YO14 .... 100 F5
Donald Smith Ct DL8 .... 61 C5
Don Ave YO24 .... 230 E8
Doncaster Rd
Brayton YO8 .... 232 B3
Knottingley WF11 .... 201 E2
North Elmsall WF8 .... 206 A1
Dondeen Ave YO7 .... 211 C4
Don Pedro Ave WF6 .... 200 B1
Don Pedro Cl WF6 .... 200 B1
Doran Cl 45 YO14 .... 101 B3
Dorchester Rd LS24 .... 189 D5
Doriam Ave YO31 .... 225 F2
Doriam Dr YO31 .... 225 F2
Dorkings The TS9 .... 26 E5
Dorset Cl HG1 .... 219 A3
Dorset Cres HG1 .... 219 A3
Dorset Ct 9 DL9 .... 209 C1
Dorset Rd TS14 .... 8 E5
Dorset St BD23 .... 217 A3
Dorts Cres LS24 .... 190 C1
Dotcliffe Rd BB18 .... 186 A7
Doublegates Ave 6
HG4 .... 113 D2
Doublegates Cl 8 HG4 .... 113 D2
Doublegates Ct 10 HG4 .... 113 D2
Doublegates Gn 9 HG4 .... 113 D2
Doublegates Wlk 7
HG4 .... 113 D2
Doubting Castle★ YO21 .... 10 D1
Douglas Cl TS18 .... 5 F7
Douglas St 3 YO8 .... 232 C5
Douky Bottom Cave★
BD23 .... 133 F7
Dove Bank HG3 .... 139 E3
Dove Cl LS22 .... 180 B4
Dovecot Cl YO14 .... 100 E4
Dovecote Dr WF10 .... 200 F7
Dovecote Garth 5 YO41 .... 185 B2
Dove Cote Gdns DN14 .... 203 D2
Dovecote Mews YO7 .... 115 C7
Dovedale Ave YO12 .... 212 D8
Dovelands 14 BD20 .... 187 E6
Dove St YO23 .... 233 A1
Dove Way YO62 .... 94 C8
Dovey Ct 7 TS17 .... 5 F4
Dowber Ct YO7 .... 211 D3
Dowber Way YO7 .... 211 D4
Dower Chase YO19 .... 192 A6
Dower Pk YO19 .... 192 B6
Dowkell La LS23 .... 180 F1
Downdale Rd YO13 .... 54 B4
Downdinner Hill YO21 .... 208 C6
DOWNHOLME 39 D4
Downholme Rd DL9 .... 209 B1
Downland Cres WF11 .... 202 A1
Downside Rd TS5 .... 6 D8
Dracula Experience★
YO21 .... 208 D7
Dragon Ave HG1 .... 219 E3
Dragon Par HG1 .... 219 E3
Dragon Rd HG1 .... 219 E3
Dragon Terr HG1 .... 219 E3
Dragon View HG1 .... 219 E4
Drake Cl YO21 .... 208 B5
Drakes Cl
38 Colburn DL9 .... 41 A5
York YO32 .... 225 F5
Drake St 2 YO23 .... 233 B1
Drapers Croft YO23 .... 230 B4
DRAUGHTON 174 B7
DRAX 204 F5
Drax Castle Earthworks★
YO8 .... 204 F4
Drax Prim Sch YO8 .... 204 F5
Dreaken Fold 4 YO13 .... 99 A7
DREBLEY 157 D6
Drebley La BD23 .... 157 D6
Dresser Cl DL10 .... 209 C8
Driffield Rd YO25 .... 151 C4
Driffield Terr YO24 .... 228 A2
Drift La HG4 .... 138 B8
Drill Hall Bsns Ctr LS29 .... 218 C5
Dringfield Cl 2 YO24 .... 230 D8
DRINGHOUSES 230 E8
Dringhouses Prim Sch
YO24 .... 230 F8
Dringhouses Sports Club
YO24 .... 230 F8
Dringthorpe Rd YO24 .... 230 F7
Drive The
Harrogate HG1 .... 220 C5
7 High & Low Bishopside
HG3 .... 137 C4
Kippax LS25 .... 194 D1
Middlesbrough TS17 .... 6 A6
Skipton BD23 .... 217 B5
12 Swillington LS26 .... 194 A1
Threshfield BD23 .... 134 B3
Drome Rd YO23 .... 230 C2
Drovers Ct 8 YO61 .... 143 C8
Drovers Way YO7 .... 211 D4
Drovers Wlk BD23 .... 154 B3
Druggist La 16 LS29 .... 174 F4
Druggon Rd DL9 .... 40 E3
Druids Mdw 8 YO51 .... 141 B5
Drummond View YO23 .... 231 B4
Drury Cl HG3 .... 222 F2
Drury La HG3 .... 222 F2
Drury St DL3 .... 3 C6
Dryden Cl HG1 .... 219 E7
Dryhurst Cl 9 DN6 .... 206 F2
Dubbing Garth La DL11 .... 37 B4
Dubb's La BD23 .... 81 C1
Duchy Ave
3 Harrogate HG2 .... 219 C1
11 Scalby YO13 .... 75 D5
Duchy Gr 4 HG2 .... 219 C1
Duchy Rd HG1 .... 219 B2
Duckett Cl DL10 .... 209 F8
Duckett St BD23 .... 217 A3
Duck Hill HG4 .... 214 C5
Duckhill La YO7 .... 115 A4
Duck La YO12 .... 125 A8
Duck St LA2 .... 128 A6
Duck Street La HG3 .... 136 D2
Dudley Ct YO31 .... 233 C4
Dudley Mews YO31 .... 233 C4
Dudley Rd DL1 .... 4 A5
Dudley St YO31 .... 233 C4
Dudley Wlk HG4 .... 214 B3
Duffield Cres 1 LS25 .... 195 F4
Dugdale La BD23 .... 152 C1
DUGGLEBY 149 B6
Duggleby Howe★ YO17 .... 149 C5
Dukes Ct 3 YO26 .... 227 D6
Dukes Hill LS29 .... 218 A6
Duke's La YO25 .... 126 A1
Duke St
6 Burton in Lonsdale
LA6 .... 102 F3
High Bentham LA2 .... 129 A8
Settle BD24 .... 131 D2
Skipton BD23 .... 217 A4
14 Trawden Forest BB8 .... 186 A3
Dukesway TS17 .... 6 B5
Dukes Wharf YO23 .... 233 B1
Dulverton Cl
2 High Leven TS17 .... 6 A3
13 Pontefract WF8 .... 201 C2
Dulverton Rise WF8 .... 201 C2
Dulverton Way
5 Guisborough TS14 .... 8 F6
12 Pontefract WF8 .... 201 C2
Dumb Tom's La LA6 .... 103 B1
Dumfries Sq 8 DL9 .... 40 E4
Duna Way 6 YO62 .... 70 C1
Dunbar Ct LS26 .... 200 B6
Duncan Cl 6 HG1 .... 219 C5
Duncan St HG1 .... 219 C5
Dunce Mire Rd LS25 .... 202 A8

Duncombe Cl
2 Eastfield YO12 99 F7
Malton YO17 215 A3
Duncombe Dr
24 Pickering YO18 95 F7
Strensall YO32 167 B8
Duncombe La YO32 167 B8
Duncombe Park National Nature Reserve* YO62 92 E6
Duncombe Pl YO1 233 B3
Dundas Gdns YO21 208 B6
Dundas St
Richmond DL10 209 C7
York YO1 233 C2
Dunderdale Cres WF10 201 B5
Dunelm Wlk DL1 3 E7
Dunholm Ave 1 TS3 7 D8
DUNKESWICK 178 E2
Dunkeswick La LS17 178 D4
Dunn Gr 3 YO11 100 A7
DUNNINGTON 184 F7
Dunnington Dr YO8 196 E1
Dunnington Prim Sch YO19 184 E7
Dunniwood Cl 4 WF10 200 D3
Dunniwood Dr 3 WF10 200 D3
Dunroyal YO61 141 F8
Dunroyal Cl YO61 141 F8
DUNSLEY 12 F2
Dunsley Cres YO21 208 A8
Dunsley La YO21 32 A8
Dunslow Ct YO11 99 F6
Dunslow Rd YO11 99 F6
Dunsmore Cl TS8 6 C4
Dunwell Ave 2 YO12 212 B7
Durham Cl 18 YO8 198 F1
Durham La TS16 5 D5
Durham Lane Ind Pk TS16 5 D6
Durham Lane Prim Sch 13 TS16 5 D5
Durham Pl 5 YO12 213 A7
Durham St
Castleford WF10 200 F3
6 Scarborough YO12 212 F7
Durham Tees Valley Airport DL2 4 F4
Durham Way HG3 219 A5
Durlston Dr YO32 167 A7
Duxbury St 11 BB18 172 B1
Dyke Hall La LA10 78 A8
Dykelands Cl YO19 192 F7
Dykes La YO23 230 A1
Dyon La YO8 199 B3
Dyon Rd YO8 199 D7
Dyon Way YO8 199 D7
Dyson La DL11 18 G7

E

Eagle Pk TS8 7 C5
EAGLESCLIFFE 5 E5
Eaglescliffe Sta TS16 5 E6
EARBY 172 B1
Earby Springfield Prim Sch BB18 172 B1
Earfit La YO23 191 A8
Earl Crag View BD22 187 C6
Earl Edwin Dr DL10 209 D8
Earle St YO31 233 C4
Earlham St 10 BB18 172 B1
Earlsborough Terr YO30 233 A3
Earls Chase WF8 201 B2
Earls Court Rd TS8 6 F5
Earlsdon Ave TS5 6 D7
Earls View 3 BD20 187 E6
Earlsway TS17 6 C5
EARSWICK 226 A7
Earswick Chase YO32 225 F7
Earswick Village YO32 225 F7
EASBY
Richmond 209 F5
Stokesley 27 B7
Easby Abbey (rems of)* DL10 209 E5
Easby Ave TS5 6 F8
Easby Cl
4 Bedale DL8 63 B2
7 Ilkley LS29 175 C2
Easby Ct DL10 209 F5
Easby Dr LS29 175 C2
Easby La
Easby TS9 27 A8
Great Ayton TS9 7 F1
Easby Low Rd DL10 209 D7
EASINGTON 11 A8
EASINGWOLD 143 D8
Easingwold Prim Sch YO61 117 C1
Easingwold Sch YO61 143 C8
Eason Rd YO24 230 E8
Eason View YO24 230 E8
Easson Rd DL3 3 C5
East Acres WF11 201 F4
EAST APPLETON 41 D2
East Ave
8 Easingwold YO61 143 D8
13 Glusburn BD20 187 E7
21 Scalby YO13 75 D5
EAST AYTON 99 B8
East Ayton Prim Sch YO13 99 A8
East Bank 2 LS25 195 F4
EAST BARNBY 12 C3
East Barnby La YO21 12 C3
Eastbeck Cl YO17 124 E8
East Beck Ct LS21 176 C3
Eastborough YO11 213 B6
EASTBOURNE 3 E4
Eastbourne Comp Sch DL1 3 E5
Eastbourne Gdns TS3 7 C8
Eastbourne Gr YO31 228 F5
Eastbourne Rd DL1 3 D5
Eastbourne Sports Complex DL1 3 E5
East Brow Rd YO18 72 C4
EASTBURN 187 F7
Eastburn Junior & Infant Sch BD20 187 F7
Eastbury Cl TS17 6 B4
EASTBY 156 F1
Eastby Rd HG1 219 F6
East Carr 18 YO11 100 B6
East Castle St 6 BD23 217 A3
East Cl DL2 4 C7
East Cliff YO22 208 E7
East Comm La YO8 232 F4
EAST COMMON 232 E4
EAST COTTINGWITH 193 C5
EAST COWTON 22 F2
East Cowton CE Prim Sch DL7 22 E1
East Cres 19 YO21 208 D7
East Dene 11 BD20 174 C1
East Down WF10 201 A4
East End YO60 145 D5
Eastern Terr YO31 228 E6
Easter Pk TS17 6 C5
EASTERSIDE 7 A7
Easterside La YO62 67 F4
Easterside Prim Sch TS4 7 A7
Easterside Rd TS4 7 A7
EASTFIELD 100 A7
Eastfield
Amotherby YO17 121 B4
Hunmanby YO14 126 F8
Knaresborough HG5 221 D6
Eastfield Ave
Haxby YO32 225 C7
Norton YO17 215 E3
Richmond DL10 209 D8
Eastfield Cl LS24 189 F7
Eastfield Cres YO10 229 C2
Eastfield Ct YO10 229 C2
Eastfield Dr 14 WF8 201 C1
Eastfield Gr WF6 200 B2
Eastfield La
Dunnington YO19 184 F8
Kellington DN14 202 F4
Spennithorne DL8 61 A3
Thoralby DL8 58 E2
Eastfield Rd
Norton YO17 215 E3
Pickering YO18 96 A6
Eastfields TS9 26 C7
EAST GARFORTH 194 E4
East Garforth Prim Sch LS25 194 D4
East Garforth Sta LS25 194 D3
Eastgate
16 Helmsley YO62 92 F6
Pickering YO18 96 A6
3 Seamer YO12 99 D6
East Gate YO13 98 D6
East Grange Cl DL7 63 E7
EAST HARLSEY 44 E6
EAST HAUXWELL 61 D8
EAST HESLERTON 124 A7
East Heslerton La YO17 124 A8
Eastholme Dr YO30 224 E1
Easthorpe Dr YO26 224 A1
East Ings La YO18 95 F4
EAST KNAPTON 123 C6
East La
Ampleforth YO62 92 D1
Castle Bolton with East & West Bolton DL8 59 B6
Embsay BD23 217 D7
Yafforth DL7 43 C1
Eastland Ave YO24 227 E2
EAST LAYTON 20 C8
East Lea YO7 115 C7
East Lea View 21 YO11 100 B6
EAST LUTTON 150 C8
EAST MARTON 172 B6
East Moor Gdns YO19 231 F5
East Mount YO17 215 C4
Eastmount Rd DL1 3 D6
East Mount Rd YO24 233 A1
EAST NESS 94 B1
East Neville St 11 BD23 217 A3
EAST NEWTON 93 C2
Easton La YO21 29 D6
Easton Way
Catterick DL10 41 D5
29 Walkerville DL9 41 A5
East Par
Harrogate HG1 219 E2
Ilkley LS29 218 C4
East Parade YO31 228 F6
East Park Rd
Harrogate HG1 219 E2
15 Scalby YO13 75 D5
3 Spofforth HG3 179 E5
Eastpoint Rd DL1 3 F6
East Rd
Melsonby DL10 20 F7
Northallerton DL6 210 E4
Norton YO17 215 E3
EAST ROUNTON 24 E2
EAST ROW 13 A3
East Sandgate 14 YO11 213 B6
East Side 5 TS15 25 D5
East St
Gargrave BD23 155 D1
Gayles DL11 19 E6
Swinton YO17 121 B4
East Terr YO21 208 D7
East Terrace Cres YO21 208 D7
East View
Barton DL10 21 D8
7 Campsall DN6 206 E1
Kippax LS25 194 D1
10 Knottingley WF11 202 A2
Langthorpe YO51 141 A6
3 Low Bentham LA2 128 E8
Middleton St George DL2 4 D3
Northallerton DL6 210 E3
Sherburn in Elmet LS25 195 F3
South Kilvington YO7 211 B6
3 Trawden BB8 186 B1
East View Ct HG5 162 F3
Eastville Terr HG1 219 B6
Eastward Ave YO10 231 E7
Eastway YO11 100 A7
East Way
Whitby YO21 208 B7
York YO31 225 E2
Eastway Cl 2 YO62 70 C1
East Whitby Com Prim Sch YO22 208 F4
EAST WITTON 61 A1
East Witton Rd DL8 60 E2
Eaton Ct 7 YO24 230 B8
Eaton Rd LS29 218 A3
EAVESTONE 138 B7
Eavestone Gr HG3 219 A4
EBBERSTON 97 E5
Ebberston Hall* YO13 97 D6
Ebenezer Terr 9 HG1 219 D2
Ebor Cl DL10 21 A1
Ebor Ct
Northallerton DL7 210 D3
7 Selby YO8 232 C6
Ebor Ind Est YO31 233 C3
Ebor Mount LS25 194 D1
Ebor Prep Sch YO30 228 A7
Ebor Rise HG1 219 B2
Ebor St
Selby YO8 232 C5
York YO23 233 B1
Ebor Way YO26 224 A2
Ebsay Dr YO30 225 A1
Eccles Cl YO30 224 D2
Echo Hill YO22 32 B7
Eddison Way 1 TS8 6 F5
Eden Ave YO8 232 D3
Eden Camp Modern History Theme Mus* YO17 215 E8
Eden Cl
2 Hurworth-on-Tees DL2 3 D1
1 Hutton Rudby TS15 25 C4
York YO24 230 C7
Eden Cres DL1 3 C4
Eden Crest DL2 1 D7
Edendale WF10 200 F4
Edenhouse Rd YO17 215 E8
Eden La DL2 1 D8
Eden Park Rd 2 TS15 25 C4
Eden Pk DL2 1 D7
Eden Rd DL7 210 B2
Edens Way HG4 214 C2
Edgecombe Dr DL3 3 A6
Edge Dell YO12 99 E8
Edgehill Rd YO12 212 E2
Edge La
Grassington BD23 134 F3
Long Preston BD23 153 E6
Edgemoor Rd
Darlington DL1 3 E3
2 Firth Moor DL1 3 E4
Edgerton Cl LS24 189 D6
Edgerton Ct 11 LS24 189 D6
Edgerton Dr LS24 189 D6
Edgerton Garth LS24 189 D6
Edgware Rd YO10 228 E2
Edinburgh Dr DL3 3 A4
Edmondson's La BD23 172 C5
Edmondson St 17 BB18 171 D2
Edmund Wilson Swimming Pool YO24 227 D1
Edston Dr 9 TS14 8 F7
Edward Kitching Terr 14 TS9 8 A2
Edward Pease Way DL3 3 A7
Edwards Street Ind Est DL1 3 D6
Edward St
27 Earby BB18 172 A1
Pontefract WF6 200 A3
EGGBOROUGH 202 F2
EGGLESCLIFFE 5 E4
Egglescliffe CE Sch TS16 5 E4
Egglescliffe Sch TS16 5 D4
Eggleston View DL3 3 A6
Eggshell La LA2 130 C8
Eglington Ave TS14 8 F6
Egremont Cl 11 YO41 168 D2
EGTON 31 B5
Egton Ave TS7 7 C5
EGTON BRIDGE 31 A4
Egton CE Prim Sch YO21 31 B5
Egton Cliff YO21 31 A4
Egton La YO21 30 F5
Egton Sta YO21 31 A4
Eight Acre La HG4 113 A5
Eighth Ave YO31 228 F5
El Alamein Rd 5 DL9 209 C1
Elbolton Cave* BD23 156 E8
Elbow Terr 4 YO22 208 E6
Elderberry View 17 WF10 200 D3
Elder Gr 38 YO32 166 E5
Elder Rd DL7 210 D4
Elder's St YO11 213 A6
Eldmire La YO7 115 D6
Eldon St YO31 233 C4
Eldon Terr YO31 233 C4
ELDROTH 130 E4
Eldroth Rd LA2 130 C5
Eldwick Cl YO30 224 F2
Eleanor Dr HG2 220 C1
Eleanor Rd HG2 220 C1
Electric Ave HG1 219 B5
Elgar Cl YO31 225 E1
Elgin Rd TS17 6 B6
Elgin St 16 YO21 208 D6
Elizabethan Ct 4 WF8 201 C1
Elizabeth Ct
7 Selby YO8 232 B6
Sherburn in Elmet LS25 195 E4
Elizabeth Dr WF10 201 B4
Elland Ct 12 DL1 3 F6
Ellarfield La LS25 195 F5
Ellen Gr HG1 220 C4
Ellenthorpe La YO51 141 D6
ELLERBECK 44 F3
Ellerbeck Ct TS9 26 D6
Ellerbeck Way
Great & Little Broughton TS9 26 D6
Middlesbrough TS7 7 D8
Whitby YO22 208 E4
ELLERBURN 96 E7
Ellerburn Bank Nature Reserve* YO18 72 F1
Ellerburn Rd YO18 96 F7
Ellerby Bank TS13 11 F4
Ellerby La TS13 11 F5
Ellerclose Rd 23 DL8 60 D5
Eller Gates YO21 30 C6
Eller Gill La BD23 172 D4
Ellerholme La DL11 38 F5
Ellerington Cl 5 LA6 103 D3
Ellerker La LS14 188 A3
Ellerker Rd LS14 188 A3
Eller Mews 3 BD23 216 E3
Ellers La DL8 59 A2
Ellers Rd BD20 187 E6
ELLERTON
193 C2
Catterick 41 F4
Ellerton Priory (rems of)* DL11 39 A4
Ellerton Rd TS18 5 D8
ELLINGSTRING 85 D6
Elliot Ct YO10 231 D7
Elliot St BD23 216 F4
Elliott St BD20 174 B1
Ellis Ct HG1 219 B2
Ellis Gdns 6 YO13 75 D5
Ellis La LS25 194 C5
Ellison Ave 32 YO12 75 D5
Ellwood Cotts BD24 131 D4
Ellwood Ct YO10 228 D2
Elma Gr 3 YO30 224 E2
Elm Ave
Kippax LS25 194 C2
Northallerton DL6 210 F5
Elm Avenue 10 YO32 191 C7
Elm Cl
Barnoldswick BB18 171 D1
10 Filey YO14 101 B4
Hipswell DL9 209 F1
Northallerton DL6 210 F5
Elm Ct DL6 210 E5
Elm Dr TS7 7 B6
Elm End 9 YO32 166 E5
Elmet Dr LS15 194 C8
Elmete Ave LS25 195 F4
Elmete Rd WF10 201 B5
Elmet Rd LS15 194 C7
Elmfield Ave YO31 228 F8
Elmfield Rd
3 Glusburn BD20 187 F8
Hurworth DL2 3 D1
Hurworth-on-Tees DL2 22 D8
Elmfield Terr YO31 228 F7
Elm Gn 7 YO62 92 F7
Elm Gr
Robin Hood's Bay YO22 33 D4
Sherburn YO17 124 D8
Thornaby TS17 6 B8
4 Whitby YO21 208 B6
York YO31 225 F2
Elmlands Gr YO31 228 F8
Elmpark Vale YO31 229 A8
Elmpark View YO31 229 A8
Elmpark Way YO31 229 A8
Elm Pl WF11 201 F2
Elm Rd
34 Glusburn BD20 187 E7
Guisborough TS14 8 F7
Harrogate HG1 219 E5
Ripon HG4 214 B2
9 Scarborough YO12 212 E4
3 Topcliffe YO7 89 B1
Elms Cl 2 YO19 191 F1
Elmslac Cl 1 YO62 92 F6
Elmslac Rd 3 YO62 92 F7
Elm St YO8 232 D6
Elms The YO32 167 D2
Elm Tree Ave
Harrogate HG1 219 D5
9 Poppleton YO26 165 F1
Elmtree Gdns 3 YO24 227 C3
Elm Tree Rise HG3 140 B5
Elm Tree Sq BD23 217 D8
Elm View YO18 96 A6
Elmville Ave YO12 212 E6
Elm Wlk 6 DL10 41 D5
Elmwood Ave LS15 194 B8
Elmwood Chase LS15 194 B8
Elmwood Cl 6 TS9 26 C8
Elmwood La LS15 194 B8
Elmwood Rd TS16 5 E6
Elmwood St 4 HG1 219 E4
Elphin Bridge La YO61 117 B6
Elslack La BD23 172 C4
Elston Cl YO30 228 A8
Elston Pl YO8 232 C6
Eltham Cres TS17 6 C6
ELTON 5 C8
Elton La HG3 160 E6
Elton Par DL3 3 B5
Elton Rd DL3 3 B5
ELVINGTON 185 B2
Elvington CE Prim Sch YO41 185 B3
Elvington Ind Est YO41 185 A3
Elvington La YO19 184 E5
Elvington Pk YO41 185 A3
Elvington Terr YO10 228 E4
Elwick Ave TS5 6 E7
Elwick Gr YO10 229 C4
Elwick La YO26 164 B7
Ely Cl HG3 219 A5
Embleton Dr 1 YO30 224 F1
Embleton Rd LS26 200 B4
EMBSAY 217 D8
Embsay & Bolton Abbey Steam Rly* BD23 217 E7
Embsay CE Prim Sch BD23 217 D8
Embsay Sta BD23 217 D7
Emerald Cl HG1 220 C4
Emerald St YO31 233 C4
Emerson Ave TS5 6 F8
Emerson Cl 2 DL6 25 D1
Emerson Rd DL2 3 E1
Emery Cl DL2 3 E1
Emgate 2 DL8 63 A3
Emily Mews YO10 228 E4
Emley Moor Rd DL1 3 E4
Emley View LS25 194 C2
Emmerson St 2 YO31 228 E5
Emmet La HG3 160 C5
Emmott Ct BB8 186 C3
Emmott La BB8 186 B4
Emsworth Dr TS16 5 D5
Enclosure Gdns 1 YO10 229 B1
Endcliff Cres YO12 212 D8
Endeavour Wharf 6 YO21 208 D6
Endfields Rd 1 YO10 231 E8
Endican La DL7 65 D3
Endsleigh Dr TS5 6 D8
Enfield Chase TS14 8 F5
Enfield Cl 4 DL9 40 E4
Enfield Cres 1 YO24 228 A3
Engelhart Cl YO8 232 A2
Engine Shed La BD23 216 D3
Engine Shed Lane Ind Est BD23 216 D3
England La WF11 201 F2
England Lane Junior & Infant Sch WF11 201 F2
English Martyrs RC Prim Sch YO24 227 F3
Ennerdale Ave YO31 229 B5
Enter La LA6 103 D3
ENTERPEN 25 C4
Enterpen TS15 25 C4
Enterprise Way
Bradleys Both BD20 173 D4
Pickering YO18 96 A6
Sherburn in Elmet LS25 196 B4
Whitby YO22 32 F8
EPPLEBY 1 E4
Eppleby Forcett CE Prim Sch DL11 1 D4
Epsom Ct 11 DL1 3 F6
Eridge Rd TS14 8 F6
Ermysted's Gram Sch BD23 216 F4
Ermysted St 4 BD23 217 A4
ERYHOLME 23 A7
Eryholme La DL2 22 F7
ESCRICK 192 B5
Escrick CE Prim Sch YO19 192 A5
Escrick Ct YO19 192 B5
Escrick Park Gdns YO19 192 B5
Escrick St YO10 233 C1
Escrick Terr YO10 233 C1
Esher Ave TS6 7 E8
Eshington La DL8 58 F2
ESHTON 155 D3
Eshton Rd BD23 155 D2
Eskdale Ave
Normanton WF6 200 A2
York YO10 229 C3
Eskdale Cl
5 Pontefract WF6 200 A2
Sleights YO22 32 A5
Eskdale Croft WF6 200 A2
Eskdale Ct 12 WF6 200 A2
Eskdale Rd YO22 208 F3
Eskdale Sch YO22 208 E3
Eskdaleside YO22 31 F5
Esk Dr YO26 227 B8
Eskew Cres LA2 128 E7
Eskew La LA2 128 E7
Eskitt Hill YO12 212 D4
Esk Rd DL1 3 D3

Esplanade
Harrogate HG2 219 C2
Scarborough YO11 213 A4
Whitby YO21 208 D7
York YO26 233 A2
Esplanade Cres YO11 213 B2
Esplanade Ct YO30 233 A3
Esplanade Gdns YO11 213 A4
Esplanade Rd YO11 213 A3
Esplande La BB18 171 C1
Estell La YO13 74 C5
Estill Cl 2 YO11 100 B6
Estoril Road S DL1 3 F4
Ethel Cres HG5 221 C6
Ethel St 12 BB18 171 E1
Etive Pl YO24 230 B7
Eton Dr 7 YO32 166 D5
Eton Rd TS5 6 E8
Ettersgill Cl TS16 5 D5
Ettersgill Dr DL3 3 A5
Ettington Ave TS3 7 B8
Etty Ave YO10 229 A4
Etty Cl 24 YO41 168 D2
Euclid Ave HG1 219 B5
Eva Ave YO30 224 D2
Evaglades Sch LA2 128 E8
Evelyn Cres YO30 228 B7
Evelyn Ct 5 HG3 161 B2
Evelyn Dr YO12 212 D4
Evergreen Way 1 YO8 197 D1
Evergreen Wlk 2 TS4 6 F8
Everingham Rd TS15 5 D2
EVERLEY 74 F4
Eversley Ave LS25 195 F3
Eversley Ct LS25 195 F4
Eversley Garth Cres LS25 195 F4
Eversley Mount LS25 195 F3
Evesham Rd TS3 7 B8
Evron Ctr YO14 101 B3
Ewart St YO12 212 E3
Ewden Cl 16 YO14 101 A3
Ewelands Hill YO7 90 C7
Ewe Leys La YO7 66 A5
Exchange St 8 WF6 200 A1
EXELBY 63 D1
Exelby Cl DL8 63 D1
Exelby La DL7 63 D3
Exeter Cres 10 HG3 161 B3
Exeter Dr DL1 3 F7
Exford Cl 8 TS17 6 A3
Exhibition Sq YO1 233 B3
Express Way WF6 200 A3
Eyre Cl
Brayton YO8 232 A2
Selby YO8 232 A2

F

Faber Cl YO23 230 B3
Faber St YO31 228 E5
FACEBY 25 F2
Faceby Rd TS9 26 A2
FADMOOR 69 F4
Fadmoor Bank YO62 69 E6
Fadmoor La YO62 69 F4
FAIRBURN 201 D7
Fairburn Com Sch WF11 201 D6
Fairburn Dr LS25 194 D3
Fairburn St WF10 200 E4
Fairfax 15 YO41 168 D2
Fairfax Ave
Harrogate HG2 220 B2
North Featherstone WF7 200 E1
Selby YO8 232 B4
Fairfax Cl
2 Ampleforth YO62 92 C1
Bolton Percy YO23 190 D4
Gilling East YO62 118 F8
Fairfax Cres YO26 181 C7
Fairfax Croft YO23 230 B2
Fairfax Dr 19 WF8 201 B1
Fairfax House* YO1 233 C2
Fairfax Rd DL2 4 D4
Fairfax St
1 Scarborough YO12 212 E5
10 Skipton BD23 217 A3
York YO1 233 B1
Fairfax Wlk 3 HG2 220 B3
Fairfield
Fairburn WF11 201 D7
Thirsk YO7 211 C4
Fairfield Ave TS7 7 D7
Fairfield Cl 16 LS25 195 F4
Fairfield Cres YO12 212 B8
Fairfield La LS25 202 A6
Fairfield Link LS25 195 F4
Fairfield Rd
Staithes TS13 13 K2
Stokesley TS9 26 B7
Tadcaster LS24 189 E6
Fairfields Dr YO30 224 B5
Fairfield St DL3 3 C6
Fairfield Way
Richmond DL10 209 B8
9 Tadcaster LS24 189 E6
Whitby YO22 208 F3
Fairgrey Cl HG4 214 B6
Fair Head La YO22 31 D4
Fairheath Rd LA2 128 E5
Fairholme La DL7 64 A4
Fairmead Ct YO22 208 E4
Fairmead Way YO22 208 E4
Fairview TS21 5 A7
Fair View WF10 201 A5
Fairview Gdns DL10 209 C8
Fairway
Normanton South WF6 200 B1
4 Scalby YO12 75 E5
Selby YO8 232 A4
York YO30 228 A8
Fairway App WF6 200 B1
Fairway Ave WF6 200 B1
Fairway Cl
8 Normanton South WF6 200 B1
15 Sherburn in Elmet LS25 195 F4
Fairway Dr
Normanton South WF6 200 B1
18 Poppleton YO26 165 F1
Fairway Gdns 4 WF6 200 B1
Fairway Mdws 9 WF6 200 B1
Fairways Ave HG2 220 E3
Fairways Cl HG2 220 E3
Fairways Dr HG2 220 D3
Fairways The LS24 189 E5
Fairway The
Darlington DL1 3 E5
Middlesbrough TS8 7 C5
Northallerton DL7 210 C3
8 North Featherstone WF7 200 E1
Sherburn in Elmet LS25 195 F4
Fairwood Pk TS8 7 C5
Fairy Hill La WF8 201 B3
Fairy La YO18 71 C3
Falcon Ave 7 YO12 99 E6
Falconberg Way TS15 5 D2
Falcon Cl
10 Haxby YO32 166 F5
1 Scotton DL9 40 F2
17 Settle BD24 131 D2
Falcon Dr WF10 200 E3
Falconers Rd YO11 213 A5
Falconers Sq 10 YO11 213 A5
Falconer St 1 YO24 227 F3
Falcon Gdns 20 BD24 131 D2
Falcon Terr 11 YO21 208 D6
Falcon Way TS14 8 D6
Falcon Wlk TS15 6 C2
Falkland Rd 2 DL9 40 F5
Falkland St YO1 233 B1
Falling Foss (Waterfall)* YO22 32 C2
Fall La
Pannal HG3 222 B2
Thornthwaite with Padside HG3 159 A6
Fallow Field 1 BD23 217 B5
Falmer Rd DL1 3 D4
Falmouth Ave WF6 200 A2
Falmouth Cres 20 WF6 200 A2
Falmouth Dr DL3 3 C8
Falmouth Rd WF6 200 A2
FALSGRAVE 212 D3
Falsgrave Cres YO30 228 B7
Falsgrave Mews 6 YO12 212 E5
Falsgrave Rd YO12 212 F5
Fanacurt Rd TS14 8 D6
Fancy Bank TS14 9 B6
Fane Gr TS5 6 E7
FANGDALE BECK 47 A1
Fanny La
Knayton YO7 65 F2
Stutton with Hazlewood LS24 189 D4
Farfield YO26 227 C6
Farfield Ave HG5 221 C4
Farfield La YO19 184 E8
Farfield Mount 2 HG5 221 C4
Farfields Cl TS21 4 F6
Far La
Hutton Buscel YO13 98 F8
Kettlewell with Starbotton BD23 108 A3
FARLINGTON 144 F6
Farmanby Cl 12 YO18 96 D5
Farmbank Rd TS7 7 E7
Farm Cl
Walton LS23 181 A2
Whitby YO21 208 A7
Farmcote Ct TS8 6 E5
Farm Croft BD23 216 F1
Far Mead Croft 3 LS29 176 C1
Farmers Way YO23 230 B3
Farm Garth TS9 8 A2
Farm La TS17 6 A5
Farmlands Rd 1 YO24 230 D8
Farmside Mews TS8 7 C4
Farmstead Rise YO32 225 D7
Farm Way YO8 232 B7
Farnborough Ct 10 DL2 4 C4
Farndale Ave
Northallerton DL7 210 C2
York YO10 229 D4
Farndale Cl 1 YO32 166 F5
Farndale Cres DL3 3 B6
Farndale Dr TS14 8 D6
Farndale Rd HG5 221 D6
Farndale St YO10 228 D2
FARNHAM 162 D7
Farnham La HG5 162 D7
FARNHILL 173 E1
FARNLEY 177 B2
Farnley CE Prim Sch LS21 177 B3
Farnley Hall* LS21 177 B2
Farnley La LS21 177 B2
Farnley Pk LS21 177 C2
Farrar St YO10 228 E3
Farriers Croft 2 YO23 230 B3
Farriers Ct 16 LS22 180 C3
Farrow House Sch 19 YO11 212 F5
Farside Garth YO13 75 D6
Farside Rd YO13 99 A7
Farthingale Way TS8 6 E4
Favell Ave WF6 200 A1
Faven Field Rd YO7 211 D4
FAVERDALE 3 B8
Faverdale DL3 3 B7
Faverdale Ind Est DL3 3 B7
Faverdale N DL3 3 B7
Faverdale Rd DL3 3 B7
Faverdale W DL3 3 B7
Faversham Cl TS8 6 F4
Favordale Rd BB8 186 A3
Fawcett Ave TS8 6 E4
Fawcett St YO10 233 C1
FAWDINGTON 115 F3
Fawdington Rd YO61 115 F2
Fawkes Dr YO26 227 C4
FEARBY 85 F4
Fearby Rd
Fearby HG4 85 F4
Masham HG4 86 A4
7 Stockton-on-Tees TS18 5 D8
Fearnhead TS8 7 C5
Feasegate YO1 233 B2
Featherbeck Cl 8 LA6 103 D3
Featherbed La
Bilton-in-Ainsty with Bickerton LS24 181 C3
Ellerbeck DL6 44 E4
Feather Bed La YO21 32 A7
Federation St 12 BB18 171 D1
Feeding Pasture La YO60 147 B7
FEETHAM 37 C5
Feetham Ave DL1 3 F7
FEIZOR 131 B6
Felbrigg La TS17 6 A4
Feldom La DL11 19 E1
FELIXKIRK 90 C7
Felixkirk Rd YO7 211 F4
Felixstowe Dr 10 DL9 40 E4
Fellbrook Ave YO26 227 B4
Fell La
Cracoe BD23 156 B7
Winton CA17 14 C8
Fell Rd LA6 77 A4
Fell View BD23 217 E8
Fell View Sq 4 BD23 134 E2
Fenby Ave DL1 3 E4
Fenby Gdns YO12 212 C4
Fence Dike La DL7 63 C7
Fennel Ct LS26 200 B6
Fennel Gr HG4 214 B6
Fenton Ave BB18 171 E2
Fenton Cl 10 YO11 100 B7
Fenton La
Malton YO17 215 C8
Sherburn in Elmet LS25 196 A5
Fenton St
Boosbeck TS12 9 D7
38 Burley in Warfedale LS29 176 C1
FENWICK 207 D3
Fenwick Cl 1 YO11 100 B6
Fenwick Common La DN6 207 D2
Fenwick La DN6 207 B1
Fenwick's La YO10 231 D7
Fenwick St YO23 228 C2
Ferguson Cl DL7 210 C3
Ferguson Way YO32 225 F1
Fern Bank Ave BB18 171 D2
Fern Cl YO32 226 A4
Ferndale Rd YO8 232 C4
Fern Gdns 1 LS29 218 A3
Fernie Rd TS14 8 F5
Fernlea Cl YO8 232 D4
Fernley Green Cl 6 WF11 202 A2
Fern St YO31 233 C4
Ferns The YO19 191 D1
Fernway YO10 229 C3
Fernwood TS8 7 A4
Fernwood Cl 9 DL6 43 F3
FERRENSBY 162 F7
FERRYBRIDGE 201 D3
Ferrybridge By-pass WF11 201 E3
Ferrybridge Infant Sch WF11 201 E3
Ferrybridge Rd
Castleford WF10 200 F4
Pontefract WF8 201 C1
Ferry Cl 11 YO8 198 F1
Ferry Farm Cl 2 YO19 191 D8
Ferry La
Bishopthorpe YO23 231 B4
Bubwith YO8 199 C5
Snaith & Cowick DN14 204 C1
Thorganby YO19 193 B5
Ferrymans Wlk YO26 165 F2
Fetter La YO1 233 B2
Feversham Cres 4 YO31 228 C7
Feversham Dr 16 YO62 70 B1
Feversham Rd YO62 92 F7
Fewster Way YO10 233 C1
FEWSTON 159 F1
FEWSTON BENTS 159 F1
Fewston Cl 11 YO14 101 A3
Fewston Cres HG1 219 B4
Fewston Dr 9 YO30 224 F1
Field Ave YO8 197 B1
Field Cl YO21 208 A7
Field Cl Rd 16 YO13 75 D5
Field Dr
1 Pickering YO18 95 F6
Field Dr *continued*
Tadcaster LS24 189 F7
Field Gr 7 DL9 40 E3
Field Head YO41 185 F6
Fieldhead Cl 12 WF8 201 C1
Fieldhead Dr
Barwick in Elmet LS15 194 C8
15 Glusburn BD20 187 E7
Fieldhead Paddock LS23 188 E8
Field House Rd 2 YO21 208 C7
Fielding's Yd DL10 209 A7
Field La
Aberford LS25 194 F8
Burniston YO13 75 D8
Gowdall DN14 207 F8
Hambleton YO8 196 F1
Hensall DN14 203 D2
Heslington YO10 229 C2
Newby & Scalby YO13 75 E5
Rawcliffe DN14 205 A1
Wistow YO8 197 C7
Field Lane Sports Club YO8 197 B1
Field Rd YO8 203 A5
Fieldside YO12 212 D7
Fieldside Ct LS24 196 B8
Fieldstead Cres YO12 212 B8
Field View
Norton YO17 215 E2
York YO31 228 C7
Fieldway
Harrogate HG1 219 F7
Ilkley LS29 218 E4
Fieldway Cl HG1 219 F7
Fifth Ave
24 Colburn DL9 41 A5
York YO31 228 F4
FILEY 101 C3
Filey Ave HG4 214 A6
Filey CE Infant Sch YO14 101 B3
Filey Cl 12 DL9 40 E4
Filey Dams Nature Reserve* YO14 101 A3
Filey Junior Sch YO14 101 B3
Filey Mus* YO14 101 B3
Filey Rd
Folkton YO11 100 A2
Hunmanby YO14 127 A8
Scarborough YO11 213 A2
Filey Sch YO14 101 A3
Filey Sta YO14 101 B3
Filey Terr YO30 228 C7
Finchley Ct TS5 6 E6
Finden Gdns HG3 160 F5
Fine Garth Cl LS23 188 E6
FINGHALL 61 D4
Finghall Sta DL8 61 E5
Finkills Way DL7 210 C6
Finkle Cl 4 HG4 214 C5
Finkle Hill LS25 195 F5
Finkle Keep 14 HG5 221 A6
Finkle St
Hensall DN14 203 D2
12 Knaresborough HG5 221 A6
Malham BD23 133 A1
3 Malton YO17 215 C4
8 Richmond DL10 209 C6
5 Ripon HG4 214 C5
Selby YO8 232 C5
Sheriff Hutton YO60 145 C5
Thirsk YO7 211 C3
Finsbury Ave YO23 228 C1
Finsbury St YO23 228 C1
Firbank Cl 9 YO32 167 A7
Firbeck Rd LS23 188 E6
Firbeck Wlk TS17 6 B6
FIRBY
Bedale 63 A1
Westow 147 A5
Firby La HG4 214 B5
Firby Rd
Bedale DL8 63 A2
Richmond DL10 209 B8
Fir Gr TS17 6 B8
Fir Heath Cl 5 YO24 227 C1
Firs Ave
Harrogate HG2 222 E6
Ripon HG4 214 D4
Firs Cl HG2 222 E6
Firs Cres HG2 222 E5
Firs Dr HG2 222 E6
Firs Gate HG2 222 E5
Firs Gr HG2 222 E5
Firs Pk HG2 222 E6
Firs Rd HG2 222 E6
First Ave
23 Colburn DL9 41 A5
Harrogate HG2 220 C3
Menwith with Darley HG3 160 A4
Sherburn in Elmet LS25 196 A4
9 Wetherby LS22 180 C3
York YO31 228 F6
First Common La YO8 197 D4
Firs View HG2 222 E5
Firthfields LS25 194 D4
Firthland Rd YO18 95 F7
FIRTH MOOR 3 F4
Firthmoor Cres DL1 3 E4
Firthmoor Prim Sch DL1 3 F4
Firth St BD23 217 A2
Firtree Ave TS6 7 E8
Firtree Cl
4 Earswick YO32 225 F7
York YO24 227 E3
Fir Tree Cl
Hilton TS15 6 C2
Thorpe Willoughby YO8 197 B2
Firtree Cres LS24 189 D5
Fir Tree Ct LS24 195 F7
Fir Tree Dr
Filey YO14 101 B4
11 Norton DN6 206 E2
Fir Tree La YO8 197 B2
Fir Trees The YO8 197 B2
Fir Tree View LS26 200 C6
Fir Tree Way YO8 197 B2
Firville Ave WF6 200 A1
Firwood Whin 5 YO31 225 F3
Fishbeck La BD20 174 D2
Fishbourne Gr 2 TS17 5 F6
Fishburn Rd 4 YO21 208 D5
Fishergate
3 Boroughbridge YO51 141 B5
Knottingley WF11 201 E3
17 Ripon HG4 214 C5
York YO10 233 C1
Fishergate Prim Sch YO10 233 C1
Fisher Gdns HG5 221 A5
Fishergreen HG4 214 D4
Fisher Green La HG4 214 F4
Fisher Row 14 HG4 86 C3
Fishers Ct HG4 214 C5
Fishers Garth 10 YO18 95 F6
Fisher St 6 HG5 221 B5
FISHPOOL 177 C2
Fitzalan Rd 18 DL8 63 A2
Fitzjohn Cl YO17 215 C6
Fitzwilliam Dr
Darlington DL1 3 D7
Malton YO17 215 A4
Five Hills La DL10 21 D5
Five Lane Ends HG4 86 D5
Flake La TS13 12 A3
Flamingo Land Theme Pk & Zoo* YO17 95 D2
FLASBY 155 E3
Flashley Carr La DN6 207 F1
Flask La DL8 87 C3
Flass La WF10 200 E3
Flat Cliffs YO14 101 C1
Flat La
Bolton-on-Swale DL10 41 E6
Hellifield BD23 153 F3
Flats Bank DL11 19 F6
Flats La
Barwick in Elmet LS15 194 B7
Thirkleby High & Low with Osgodby YO7 90 D1
West Witton DL8 59 D4
Flatts La
Eston & South Bank TS6 7 F7
Welburn YO62 94 A7
Wombleton YO62 93 F6
Flavian Gr YO30 227 F8
FLAWITH 142 E4
FLAXBY 163 B4
Flaxdale Cl 4 HG5 221 D6
Flaxley Ct YO8 232 B5
Flaxley Rd YO8 232 A7
Flaxman Ave YO10 229 A4
Flaxman Croft YO23 230 B3
Flaxmill Cl DL11 18 G7
FLAXTON 145 F1
Flaxton Rd YO32 167 B7
Flaxton Terr HG3 222 E3
Fleck Way TS17 6 B5
Fleet Bank La YO61 143 C1
Fleetham La
Cundall with Leckby YO7 115 C4
Kirkby Fleetham with Fencote DL7 63 C8
Fleet La
Barmby on the Marsh DN14 205 A7
Mickletown LS26 200 A6
Tockwith YO26 181 C7
FLEETS 156 A7
Fleets La BD23 156 A6
Fleming Ave 3 YO31 228 E5
Fletcher Ct 4 YO32 166 E5
Fletcher's Croft YO23 230 C3
Fletton Rd YO17 215 F4
Flintmill La LS23 180 E2
Flints Terr DL10 209 C7
FLIXTON 99 F2
Flixton Carr La YO11 99 F4
Flock Leys 24 YO13 75 D5
Flora Ave DL3 3 B5
Florence Ct 12 YO51 141 B5
Florence Gr YO30 224 D2
Florence Rd HG2 219 B1
Florentine's Ct HG4 214 C5
Florin Dr HG5 221 C7
Florin Wlk HG1 219 B2
Flotmanby La YO14 100 D2
Flow Edge DL8 57 F7
Flower Ct 19 YO11 100 B6
Flower Garth
40 Filey YO14 101 B3
Scarborough YO12 212 C6
Flowergate 12 YO21 208 D7
Flywheel St DL10 41 F7
Fog La YO42 193 E4
Fold La BD22 187 B6
Foldshaw La HG3 159 C8
Fold The
Filey YO14 101 B1
Thornton in Craven BD23 172 A3
Fold Wlk YO32 167 B8
Folks Cl 13 YO32 166 F5
FOLKTON 100 B2
FOLLIFOOT 223 F5

Follifoot CE Prim Sch HG3 223 F4
Follifoot Rd HG3 222 F3
Folliott Ward Cl YO17 215 B5
Folly La LS23 188 E5
Folly View 2 LS23 188 E5
Fontenay Rd DL10 209 D8
Fonteyn Ct TS8 6 F5
Forbes Ct 42 DL9 41 A5
Forbidden Cnr The* DL8 60 B1
FORCETT 1 D3
Forcett Cl
East Layton DL11 20 C8
Middlesbrough TS5 6 E7
Forcett Gdns DL11 1 D3
Forcett La DL10 20 D5
Ford Dike La DL2 1 D8
Fordgreen HG4 214 E4
Fordlands YO8 197 B2
Fordlands Cres YO19 231 E5
Fordlands Rd YO19 231 E6
FORDON 126 A6
Fordon La
Willerby YO12 125 E7
Wold Newton YO25 126 A6
Fordon Pl TS4 7 A8
Fordyce Rd TS8 6 E4
FOREDALE 131 C8
Fore La
Cowesby YO7 66 B4
West Tanfield DL8 87 D3
Whorlton TS9 25 F1
Foreshore Rd YO11 213 A5
FOREST 42 B7
Forest Ave HG2 220 D3
Forest Cl
3 Harrogate HG2 220 D3
27 Haxby YO32 166 E5
Forest Cres HG2 220 D4
Forest Ct 11 HG3 137 C4
Forest Dr
Colburn DL9 41 A5
Dishforth YO7 115 A4
Middlesbrough TS7 7 D7
Foresters Ct 5 YO12 75 F5
Foresters Wlk YO41 168 C1
Forester's Wlk YO24 227 B1
Forestgate YO32 225 C7
Forest Gdns HG2 220 D3
Forest Gr
Barlow YO8 204 D7
Harrogate HG2 220 D3
York YO31 228 F6
Forest Grange Cl 2 HG2 220 D4
Forest La
Alne YO61 143 B5
Fulford YO19 184 A2
Harrogate HG2 220 D3
Kirklevington TS15 24 D8
Strensall YO32 167 A8
Forest Lane Head HG2 220 D5
FOREST MOOR 220 F3
Forest Moor Dr HG5 220 F3
Forest Moor Rd HG5 220 E3
Forest Mount 4 HG2 220 D3
Forest of Galtres Prim Sch YO30 165 F5
Forest Rd
Appletreewick HG3 157 F8
Northallerton DL6 210 E5
Pickering YO18 96 A6
Forest Rise HG2 220 D3
Forest Sch The HG5 221 C6
Forest Way
Harrogate HG2 220 D3
York YO31 228 F6
Forge Cl
Huntington YO32 226 A2
Wheldrake YO19 193 A7
Forge Gn HG3 223 F4
Forge Hill La WF11 201 F3
Forge La
Deighton YO19 192 A7
Kirkby Fleetham with Fencote DL7 42 C1
Tollerton YO61 143 A3
Forge Valley Wood National Nature Reserve* YO12 75 A1
Forge Way DL1 3 D6
Forkers La YO17 122 D2
Forrester's Cl 3 DN6 206 E2
Forth St YO26 227 F6
Fort's Bldgs 5 BB18 186 A7
Fortune Cl HG5 220 E7
Fortune Hill HG5 220 E8
Fossards Cl 3 LS23 188 E5
Foss Ave LS22 180 B4
Foss Bank YO31 233 C3
Foss Ct YO31 225 E1
Fossdale Cl 5 HG5 221 D6
Fossel Island Retail Park YO31 228 E5
Fosse Way LS25 194 D3
Foss Field La YO23 191 B8
Foss Garth YO41 185 F5
Fossgate YO1 233 C2
Foss Islands Rd YO31 233 C3
Foss La YO22 32 C2
Fossland View 4 YO32 167 A7
Fossway
Stamford Bridge YO41 168 D1
York YO31 228 D7
Foss Way 30 DL9 41 A5
Foss Wlk YO26 227 B8
Foster Ave
Normanton South WF6 200 A1
Silsden BD20 174 B1
Foster Cl 31 LS29 176 C1
Fostergate YO8 197 A8
Foster Gate YO8 232 D4
Foster Rd 4 BB18 171 D2
Foster Wlk LS25 195 F4
FOSTON 146 B4
Foston CE Prim Sch YO60 146 A3
Foston Gr 4 YO31 228 F8
Foston La YO60 146 B2
Fothergill Way 3 YO51 141 B4
Fother Ingay Dr DL1 3 F8
Fothill La YO13 98 E6
Foulbridge La YO13 97 F3
Foulds Rd BB8 186 A1
Foulgate Nook La HG4 112 B6
FOUL GREEN 9 E1
Foundry La 5 WF11 202 A2
Fountains Abbey & Studley Royal* HG4 139 B7
Fountains Ave
Boston Spa LS23 188 E8
Harrogate HG1 219 F6
Ingleby TS17 6 B5
Fountains CE Prim Sch HG4 138 D8
Fountains Cl
1 Guisborough TS14 8 F6
1 Whitby YO21 208 C6
Fountains Ct YO7 90 E5
Fountains Dr TS5 6 E8
Fountains Gate HG4 112 F1
Fountains La HG4 139 B7
Fountains Mill* HG4 139 B7
Fountains Pl DL6 210 E6
Fountains Rd DL6 210 E6
Fountain St TS14 8 F6
Fountains View DL3 3 A6
Fountains Way
Knaresborough HG5 221 C4
Morton-on-Swale DL7 64 A7
Fountayne Rd 13 YO14 126 F8
Fountayne St YO31 228 C7
Fouracre Dr 11 YO22 32 A6
Four Lane Ends
Burythorpe YO16 147 D4
Lawkland BD24 130 F3
Four Lanes Ends BB7 152 C1
Four Riggs DL3 3 C5
Fourth Ave
26 Colburn DL9 41 A5
York YO31 228 E5
Foxberry Ave TS5 6 D6
Foxbridge Way WF6 200 C2
Fox Cl 6 DL2 22 D8
Foxcliff WF11 201 E5
Fox Covert YO31 225 F2
Fox Covert Cl 15 DL8 63 B3
Fox Covert Rd WF8 206 C1
Foxcroft 3 YO32 225 C7
Fox Ct HG1 219 E4
Foxdale Ave YO8 197 B1
Foxe Howe TS8 7 A6
Fox Furniture Workshop* YO7 116 F7
Fox Garth
5 Brafferton YO61 115 F1
Poppleton YO26 224 A3
Fox Glade YO41 168 C2
Foxglove Cl
2 Killinghall HG3 161 B3
Northallerton DL7 210 C1
Foxglove Covert Nature Reserve* DL9 40 B4
Foxglove Ct 19 DL9 41 A5
Foxglove Fold 19 WF10 200 D3
Foxhill La YO8 232 A3
Fox Hill La YO8 232 A3
FOXHOLES 125 D3
Foxholme La HG4 86 B3
Foxhunter Ave 7 DL9 40 F4
Fox La
Chapel Haddlesey YO8 203 C5
Hambleton LS25 202 D8
Thornton-le-Dale YO18 96 C3
Thorpe Willoughby YO8 197 B1
Fox Terr WF8 201 C1
Foxthorn Paddock YO10 229 D3
FOXTON 44 E3
Foxton Cl YO24 230 C8
Foxton La DL6 44 E2
FOXUP 106 C7
Foxwood La 3 YO24 227 C1
Frances Rd DL10 209 C7
Frances St YO10 228 D1
Francis Ct 7 YO8 197 B2
Francis Dr 27 DL9 41 A5
Frankfield Mews TS9 8 D1
Frank La YO26 164 F4
Franklin Mount HG1 219 D4
Franklin Rd HG1 219 D3
Franklin Sq HG1 219 D4
Franklin St 7 YO12 212 F6
Frank's La YO26 164 A5
Frank St 9 BB18 171 E1
Franks Terr 2 YO22 208 E6
Fraser Rd 8 TS18 5 E8
Frazer Ct YO30 227 E8
Frazer Theatre* HG5 221 B6
Frederick St 23 BB18 171 D2
Frederic St YO30 233 A3
Freebrough Rd TS12 10 A4
Freeholder's Wood & Riddings Field Nature Reserve* DL8 58 F3
Freehold La YO17 215 D8
Freely Fields 7 LS23 188 E5
Freely La LS23 188 E5
Freemans Way
Leeming DL7 63 C4
New Thirsk YO7 211 A2
Wetherby LS22 180 D3
Freeman's Way HG3 223 D8
Freemantle Pl HG4 214 C6
Freers Yd YO17 215 D3
Freeston Bsns & Enterprise Coll The WF6 200 A1
Freeston Ct 16 WF6 200 A2
Freeston Dr 18 WF6 200 A2
Freeway Dr WF10 200 B3
FREMINGTON 38 D6
Frenchgate DL10 209 C6
French Rd DL9 209 C2
French St HG1 219 F4
Friarage 20 YO11 213 B6
Friarage Ave DL6 210 D5
Friarage Gdns DL6 210 D5
Friarage Hospl DL6 210 E5
Friarage Mount DL6 210 D5
Friarage Prim Sch YO11 213 B6
Friarage St DL6 210 D5
Friarage Terr DL6 210 D5
Friargate
Scarborough YO11 213 A6
York YO1 233 B2
Friargate Theatre YO1 233 B2
Friars Cl YO19 184 D7
Friar's Gdns 10 YO11 213 A6
Friars Hill YO62 95 A8
Friars Mdw YO8 232 C8
Friars Pardon DL2 3 E1
Friar's Way 11 YO11 213 A6
Friar's Wlk YO31 228 E8
Friary Com Hospl DL10 209 B7
Friendship Ct 2 YO8 232 C6
Frith Mews 4 YO8 232 C6
Frobisher Dr
37 Colburn DL9 41 A5
5 Whitby YO21 208 C5
Frogmire Cl 4 HG5 221 B7
Frogmire Dr HG5 221 B7
Frogmire Rd HG5 221 B7
Front Nook 2 DL8 58 F1
Front St
Appleton Wiske DL6 24 B3
6 Bramham LS23 188 E5
Burton Fleming YO25 126 E3
Burton Leonard HG3 140 A2
Castleford WF10 200 F3
Grosmont YO22 31 C4
Langtoft YO25 151 C5
Lastingham YO62 70 E5
Naburn YO19 191 D8
Thirsk YO7 211 C1
Topcliffe YO7 115 C7
Wold Newton YO25 126 A4
York YO24 227 C3
Front The DL2 4 D3
Fryer Cres DL1 3 F7
Fryston Comm La LS25 202 A8
Fryston La WF11 201 C3
Fryston Rd WF10 201 B5
FRYTON 120 A6
Fryton La YO62 120 A7
Fryup Cres TS14 8 E5
Fulbeck Rd TS3 7 D8
FULFORD 231 E7
Fulford Cross YO10 228 D1
Fulfordgate YO10 231 E7
Fulford Ind Est YO10 228 C1
Fulford La 8 YO11 212 F3
Fulford Mews
7 Scarborough YO11 212 F3
York YO10 231 E6
Fulford Pk YO10 231 D7
Fulford Rd
Scarborough YO11 212 F3
York YO10 231 D8
Fulford Sch YO10 231 E7
Fulham La DN14 206 E7
Fuller-Good Rd 17 DL10 41 E4
Fullicar La DL6 43 F3
FULL SUTTON 169 A2
Fulmar Head TS14 8 D6
Fulthorpe Ave DL3 3 A5
Fulthorpe Gr DL3 3 A5
Fulwith Ave HG2 222 E5
Fulwith Cl HG2 222 F5
Fulwith Dr HG2 222 F5
Fulwith Gate HG2 222 F5
Fulwith Gr HG2 222 F5
Fulwith Mill La HG2 222 F5
Fulwith Rd HG2 222 F5
Fummerber La LA2 130 C5
Furlong Rd 23 YO41 168 D2
Furlongs Ave YO17 215 F3
Furnace La HG4 87 A1
Furness Dr
Bentham LA2 129 A8
York YO30 224 E1
Furnessford Rd LA2 128 D6
Furnwood 2 YO32 225 D7
Furrows The 16 YO11 100 B7
Fushetts La LA2 129 A8
Fusion Ct LS25 194 D4
Futurist Theatre* YO11 213 A6
Fylingdales Ave 6 YO30 224 E1
Fylingdales CE Prim Sch YO22 33 C4
Fyling Rd YO21 208 A6
FYLINGTHORPE 33 B3

G

Gable Pk YO23 182 C6
Gables Cl 8 DN14 202 D4
Gables Ct YO7 115 A4
Gables The
15 Hurworth-on-Tees DL2 3 E1
Knaresborough HG5 221 A8
Middlesbrough TS7 7 B6
Scriven HG5 162 C5
GAINFORD 1 D8
Gainford CE Prim Sch DL2 1 C7
Gainforth Wath Rd YO13 53 F5
Gainsborough Cl YO32 167 B8
Gainsborough Ct BD23 216 E4
Gaits DL8 56 C4
Gale Bank DL8 60 B3
Gale Farm Ct 6 YO24 227 C3
Gale Garth YO61 142 F4
Gale Gate YO26 142 A1
Gale La
Beadlam YO62 93 D6
Stainburn LS21 177 E3
Thorganby YO19 192 F4
York YO24 227 C2
Gale Rd YO61 142 F4
Gale The YO19 191 D4
Gallabar La YO51 141 E1
Galley Hill Prim Sch 3 TS14 8 D6
Galligap La YO10 229 C4
Gallogate La LS17 178 C1
Gallops The
Norton YO17 215 E2
York YO24 230 B8
Gallowfields Rd DL10 209 B7
Gallowfields Trad Est DL10 209 B8
Gallowgate DL10 209 C7
Gallowheads La YO18 95 A6
Gallows Hill
Castleford WF10 201 B4
Ripon HG4 214 C2
Gallows Hill Dr HG4 214 C2
Gallows Hill La YO13 98 D5
Gallows Hill Pk HG4 214 D2
Galmanhoe La YO30 233 A3
GALPHAY 112 F3
Galphay La HG4 113 A3
Galtres Ave YO31 229 B7
Galtres Dr 7 YO61 143 D8
Galtres Gr YO30 227 F7
Galtres Rd
Northallerton DL6 210 E6
York YO31 229 B7
GAMMERSGILL 83 C5
GANTHORPE 120 A1
GANTON 125 A8
Ganton Cl 1 YO21 208 C5
Ganton Hill YO12 125 B7
Ganton Pl YO24 230 E7
Ganton Rd YO25 125 C4
Gant Wlk 7 YO8 232 D5
Gaol The YO61 144 E7
Gap Cres YO14 127 D7
Gap Rd YO14 127 D8
Garbett Way 1 YO23 231 B3
Garburn Gr 3 YO30 224 E1
Garbutt Gr YO26 227 D5
Garbutt La 1 DL6 25 D1
Garbutts La TS15 25 B5
Garbutt Wood Nature Reserve* YO7 91 A6
Garden Cl
3 Glusburn BD20 187 D7
Sherburn in Elmet LS25 195 E4
Garden Ct
Selby YO8 232 B6
York YO26 227 C5
Gardeners Cl 8 YO23 230 B3
Gardeners Row YO25 150 B3
Garden Flats La YO19 184 E7
Garden House Cl LS26 200 B6
Garden La
11 Knottingley WF11 202 A3
Sherburn in Elmet LS25 195 E4
Garden Pl YO1 233 C2
Gardens Rd BD23 155 D2
Garden St
Castleford WF10 200 E3
13 Normanton South WF6 200 A1
York YO31 233 B4
Gardens The 15 YO14 101 B4
Garden Terr
10 Carleton in Craven BD23 173 B4
Lothersdale BD20 186 F8
Garden Village LS25 195 A3
Garden Village The YO32 226 A8
Garden Way
3 Pickering YO18 95 F6
York YO26 227 C5
Garfield Rd YO12 212 E6
Garfield Terr YO26 227 F5
GARFORTH 194 C4
Garforth Com Coll LS25 194 C3
Garforth Squash & L Ctr LS25 194 D3
Garforth Sta LS25 194 C4
GARGRAVE 155 D1
Gargrave CE Prim Sch BD23 155 C1
Gargrave House Gdn BD23 155 C1
Gargrave Rd
Broughton BD23 172 D6
Gargrave Rd *continued*
Skipton BD23 216 D4
Gargrave Sta BD23 172 C8
Garibaldi St 1 YO11 213 B6
Garlands Hill 3 YO11 212 F3
Garland St 2 YO26 227 E4
Garlands The
Scarborough YO11 212 F3
York YO30 228 A8
Garman Carr La YO8 197 D6
Garnet Brow La LA2 130 D2
Garnet La 1 LS24 189 D5
Garnet Rd TS17 6 B8
Garnet Terr YO26 227 E5
Garrick Cl YO8 232 B1
GARRISTON 61 B7
Garroway Way YO10 184 A4
Garrowby Hill YO41 169 F3
Garrowby Rd YO42 169 F2
Garrowby St YO41 169 E3
Garrowby View 5 YO41 168 D2
Garrow Hill YO10 228 F2
Garrow Hill Ave YO10 229 A3
Garrs End La BD23 134 E3
Garrs La 10 BD23 134 E3
Garsbeck Way TS7 7 D8
Garsdale Fold 8 LS22 180 A1
Garsdale Rd HG5 221 D6
Garsdale Sta LA10 55 A6
Gars End LA2 128 A6
Gars The LA2 128 A6
Garth Ave
Collingham LS22 188 A8
4 North Duffield YO8 199 A7
Garth Cl
11 Catterick DL10 41 D5
Hambleton YO8 196 E1
6 Wistow YO8 197 D6
Garth Ct YO32 226 A4
Garth Dr YO8 196 E1
Garth End
Collingham LS22 188 A8
Kirk Deighton LS22 180 B5
York YO32 225 F4
Garth End Rd YO13 99 A7
Garthends La 3 YO8 198 F1
Garth Fold BD20 173 C1
Garth La
Hambleton YO8 196 E1
Snainton YO13 98 A5
Garth Mdws 13 DL10 41 D5
Garth Mill 1 DN14 202 D4
Garthorne Ave DL3 3 A5
Garth Rd
4 Hambleton YO8 196 E1
York YO32 225 F4
Garths End 20 YO32 166 F5
Garth's End YO10 231 E8
Garthside DL10 41 F6
Garths La DL8 58 E3
Garth Terr YO30 228 B7
Garth The
8 Collingham LS22 188 A8
Mount Pleasant TS8 7 A4
Sinnington YO62 95 A8
4 Stokesley TS9 26 C7
Tunstall DL10 41 B2
Whitby YO21 208 B7
Garth View YO8 196 E1
Garthway 4 YO32 225 D3
Garth Way Arc DL7 210 D5
Garton La 22 YO14 126 F8
Gascoigne Ave LS15 194 B7
Gascoigne Cres HG1 219 F4
Gascoigne Ct LS15 194 B7
Gascoigne Rd LS15 194 B7
Gascoigne View LS15 194 B7
Gascoigne Wlk YO23 233 B1
Gascoigne Wood Mine LS25 196 C2
Gas House La 9 LA2 129 A8
Gaskell Cl DL6 210 C6
Gas St BD23 216 F3
Gas Works La LS23 188 F8
Gate Bridge Rd HG4 112 D2
Gatecliff Brow BD23 155 F4
GATEFORTH 203 A7
Gateforth Ct YO8 196 F1
Gateforth La YO8 196 F1
Gateforth Mews YO8 202 F8
Gateforth New Rd YO8 203 A8
Gate Grains La 23 YO61 143 C8
Gatehead La YO42 193 D7
GATE HELMSLEY 168 B2
Gatehowe Rd YO17 170 A7
Gate La
Borrowby YO7 65 E4
Low Coniscliffe & Merrybent DL2 2 E4
Gateland Cl YO32 225 C7
Gateland Field La DN14 205 B6
Gatela Rd YO13 53 D2
GATENBY 64 A2
Gatenby Garth YO61 143 B8
Gatering La 45 BD22 187 E7
Gatesgarth Cl YO12 212 B8
Gate Way YO21 29 B4
Gatherley Rd DL10 41 C7
Gatherley Road Ind Est DL10 41 C7
GAUBER 78 F1
Gauber Rd LA6 78 F1
Gaudy La DL8 56 C3
Gauk St WF11 201 D6
Gaul Rd DL9 209 E1
Gault Cl YO17 215 F4
Gaw La BD23 174 C8
Gawtersike La YO62 94 B8

Gay La LS24 196 C7
Gaylands La BB18 172 B1
GAYLE 56 D4
Gayle La DL8 56 C4
Gayle Moor Cl 9 TS17 6 A3
GAYLES 19 E6
Gay Mdws YO32 167 D2
Gayton Sands TS5 6 D6
Gazelle Way YO7 115 B1
Geecroft La LS22 179 D3
Geldof Rd YO32 225 F1
General La YO42 193 E6
Geneva Cres DL1 3 D4
Geneva La DL1 3 D4
Geneva Rd DL1 3 E5
Gennell La YO60 145 E1
Gentian Glade HG3 219 A4
George Cartwright Cl YO17 215 E4
George Cayley Dr YO30 225 A3
George Ct YO31 233 C3
George Hudson St YO1 233 B2
George Long Mews 19 YO61 143 D8
George Pindar Com Sports Coll YO11 100 A6
George St
15 Addingham LS29 174 F4
Carleton BD23 173 B4
19 Earby BB18 172 A1
3 Scarborough YO12 213 A6
4 Selby YO8 232 D6
17 Skipton BD23 217 A3
Snaith DN14 204 C1
12 Whitby YO21 208 D6
7 Wistow YO8 197 D6
York YO1 233 C1
George Terr 1 YO8 198 B4
Georgian Theatre Royal* DL10 209 C6
Gerard Ave YO31 229 A5
Germain Rd YO8 232 E4
Germany La YO10 231 E6
GERRICK 10 C3
Gerrick La TS12 10 C3
Ghyll Brow YO21 30 D4
Ghyll La BB18 171 E2
Ghyll Mdws BB18 171 E2
Ghyll Mews LS29 218 A3
Ghyll Royd Prep Sch LS29 176 B2
Ghyll The DL10 209 D8
Ghyll Way BD23 173 D4
Ghyll Wood 28 LS29 175 C2
Gibbet Hill YO61 117 C5
Gibb St BD22 187 B6
Gibside La BD20 173 C1
Gibson Cl 2 YO8 196 F1
Gibson La LS25 194 D1
GIGGLESWICK 131 C2
Giggleswick Prim Sch BD24 131 C3
Giggleswick Sch BD24 131 C3
Giggleswick Sta BD24 131 C1
Gilcar St WF6 200 B2
Gilcar Way WF10 200 B3
Gildercliffe YO12 212 C7
Giles Ave YO31 229 A5
GILL 187 A6
GILLAMOOR 70 A5
Gillamoor Ave YO31 229 B5
Gillamoor Bank YO62 70 A5
Gillamoor CE Prim Sch YO62 70 A4
Gillamoor Rd YO62 70 A2
Gillann St 15 WF11 202 A2
Gill Bank Rd LS29 218 A6
Gill Cl 6 LS29 174 E4
Gill Croft YO61 117 C1
Gillgate Rd HG4 112 B4
Gilling Castle* YO62 118 E7
Gilling Cres DL1 3 E4
GILLING EAST 118 F8
Gilling Rd
Aske DL10 20 E1
Richmond DL10 209 D7
Gillings Ct 4 YO7 211 B3
Gilling Way YO17 215 C5
GILLING WEST 20 E4
Gillingwood Cl DL10 209 C8
Gillingwood Rd YO30 224 F3
Gill La
Cowling BD22 187 A6
Kearby with Netherby LS22 179 C1
Nesfield with Langbar LS29 175 B4
Rosedale West Side YO18 49 E2
Gills Fold 8 BD23 134 E2
Gills The LS21 177 A1
Gillygate YO31 233 B3
Gillylees YO12 212 C5
Gilmonby Rd TS3 7 B8
Gilsforth Hill YO26 164 A3
Gilsforth La YO26 164 A3
Gilstead Way LS29 218 B5
Gilsthwaite La YO26 164 A3
Gilwern Ct 23 TS17 5 F4
Gindhill La LS17 178 A4
Ginnel Mews The BD23 217 A4
Ginnel The 1 HG1 219 D2
Gipsey Cnr YO19 184 E3
Girrick Cl 3 TS8 6 E5
GIRSBY 23 D7
Girton Wlk DL1 3 D7
Girvan Cl YO24 230 B7
Gisburn Rd
Barnoldswick BB18 171 D2
Gisburn Rd continued
Hellifield BD23 154 B3
Gisburn Road Com Prim Sch BB18 171 D1
Gisburn St
Barnoldswick BB18 171 D2
Skipton BD23 216 D3
Givendale Gr 3 YO10 229 C4
Givendale Rd YO12 212 D8
Glade Rd YO19 192 B2
Glade The
Escrick YO19 192 A6
Scarborough YO11 212 F3
York YO31 229 B7
Gladstone La YO12 212 E5
Gladstone Rd YO12 212 E5
Gladstone Road Infant Sch YO12 212 E5
Gladstone Road Junior Sch YO12 212 E5
Gladstone St
Acomb YO24 227 D3
Darlington DL3 3 C5
Harrogate HG2 222 E7
Normanton South WF6 200 B2
Scarborough YO12 212 E6
14 Skipton BD23 216 F4
York YO24 227 D3
York YO31 233 C4
Gladstone Terr 10 HG4 214 C4
Glaisby Ct YO31 229 A6
GLAISDALE 30 D4
Glaisdale YO24 230 D7
Glaisdale Ave TS5 6 F8
Glaisdale Ct DL3 3 B5
Glaisdale Hall La YO21 30 C4
Glaisdale Prim Sch YO21 30 D4
Glaisdale Rd
Eaglescliffe TS15 5 F3
Knapton YO26 182 F7
Glaisdale Sta YO21 30 E4
Glasgow Dr 3 DL9 209 C1
GLASS HOUGHTON 201 A3
Glasshoughton Infant Sch WF10 200 F4
Glasshoughton Sta WF10 200 F2
GLASSHOUSES 137 D4
Glasshouses Prim Sch HG3 137 D3
Glaves Cl YO13 99 B7
Glebe Ave
Full Sutton YO41 169 A2
Harrogate HG2 219 C2
York YO26 227 D5
Glebe Cl
15 Bedale DL8 63 A2
Bolton Percy YO23 190 D4
Kirby Hill YO51 141 B7
Manfield DL2 2 C4
3 Strensall YO32 167 B7
Glebe Ct DL10 21 A7
Glebe Field Dr 11 LS22 180 B3
Glebe Garth 8 YO8 198 B5
Glebe Gdns TS13 11 A8
Glebe La DL2 2 C4
Glebe Mdw HG4 214 F6
Glebe Rd
Campsall DN6 206 E1
Darlington DL1 3 D8
Harrogate HG2 219 C1
Stokesley TS9 26 C7
Glebe Sq DL7 63 C5
Glebe St WF10 200 E4
Glebe Way 26 YO32 166 E5
Gledhill Dr 10 YO21 208 D5
Gledstone Rd BD23 171 E5
Gledstone View 8 BB18 171 D2
Glen Ave YO31 228 E5
Glen Cl
Newby & Scalby YO13 75 C5
York YO10 231 E6
Glencoe Cl LS25 200 C8
Glencoe Croft LS25 200 C8
Glencoe Gdns LS25 200 C8
Glencoe St 1 YO30 228 B7
Glencoe Terr LS25 200 C8
Glendale
Guisborough TS14 8 D5
9 Hutton Rudby TS15 25 C5
Glendale Rd TS5 6 F8
Glendowne Terr HG1 219 B5
Gleneagles Ct
28 Castleford WF6 200 B1
Spofforth HG3 179 E5
Gleneagles Dr 29 WF6 200 B1
Gleneagles Rd
Darlington DL1 3 F8
Middlesbrough TS4 7 A8
North Featherstone WF7 200 E1
Glen Esk Rd YO22 208 C3
Glenfield Ave LS22 180 C2
Glenmore Dr YO17 215 E2
Glenn Cres TS7 7 B5
Glen Rd YO31 228 E5
Glenridding YO24 230 D7
Glenside YO12 212 E7
Globe St
10 Harrogate HG2 220 C3
9 Scarborough YO11 213 B6
Gloucester Ave 2 BD20 174 B1
GLUSBURN 187 D8
Glusburn Com Prim Sch 37 BD20 187 E7
Glyder Ct 6 TS17 5 F4
Glynndale Dr YO12 212 A8
Glynwed Ct 2 BD23 216 E3
GOATHLAND 51 E8
Goathland Gr TS14 8 E5
Goathland Prim Sch YO22 51 C8
Goathland Sta YO22 51 D8
Goat La BD24 131 F7
Goats Rd DL11 18 D2
Godfrey Way 12 DL10 41 E4
Godley Cl DL9 209 C2
Godwinsway 18 YO41 168 D2
Goker La YO51 141 E1
Golden Acres DL7 22 E2
Golden Butts Rd LS29 218 C4
Goldenfields YO13 75 C5
Golden Gr YO22 208 E2
Golden Lion Bank 25 YO21 208 D7
Golden Lion Yd YO7 211 C3
Goldhill La YO7 90 D6
GOLDSBOROUGH
Knareborough 163 A2
Whitby 12 D5
Goldsborough CE Prim Sch HG5 162 F3
Goldsborough Ct HG5 163 A3
Goldsborough La YO21 12 C4
Gold Thread La 5 YO8 197 B8
Golf Links Ave 5 LS24 189 D5
Golf Links Cres 4 LS24 189 D5
Golf Links Ct LS24 189 E5
GOLLINGLITH FOOT 85 B3
Goodall Cl 31 BB18 172 A1
Goodenber Cres 2 LA2 129 A8
Goodenber Rd LA2 129 A8
Good Hope Cl WF6 200 B2
Goodramgate YO1 233 B2
Goodrick Cl HG2 222 B5
Goodricke Way 5 YO10 229 A1
Goods Yd The YO8 232 D5
Goodwood Ave LS25 194 C1
Goodwood Cl
Sadberge DL2 4 B8
Scalby YO12 212 B6
Goodwood Gr YO24 227 F1
Goodwood Rd 3 DL9 40 E3
Goody Cross LS26 194 B1
Goody Cross La LS26 194 A1
Goosecroft Gdns DL6 210 D5
Goosecroft La
East Harlsey DL6 44 D6
Northallerton DL6 210 D5
Goose Green Cl 2 DL9 40 E3
Goose Green La BB8 186 A1
Goose La YO61 144 C1
Gooselands BD24 153 C6
Gooselands Hill BD23 107 D2
Goose Mire La YO12 99 C6
Goosepastures TS16 5 E3
Goose Track La YO60 145 C3
Gordale Cl
3 Barnoldswick BB18 171 D1
Skirethorns BD23 134 B3
Gordale La BD23 133 A2
Gordale Mount HG5 221 C6
Gordon Ave HG1 219 E6
Gordon Cres DL10 209 D8
Gordon St
28 Glusburn BD20 187 E7
Ilkley LS29 218 C4
Scarborough YO12 212 E5
York YO10 228 E3
Gordon Terr BD20 173 C1
Gore La DN14 207 B5
Gore Sands TS5 6 D6
Gorman Cl 9 TS17 5 F4
Gormire Ave 2 YO31 225 E2
Gormire Cl YO7 211 D3
Gorse Cl YO8 232 C2
Gorse Hill 1 YO19 184 F7
Gorse La LS25 195 D3
Gorse Paddock YO32 225 F2
Goschen St 8 BD23 217 A3
Goslipgate 9 YO18 95 F6
Gosside Gr 31 WF6 200 B1
Gough Rd DL9 40 D4
Gouldings Cl YO11 100 A7
GOULTON 25 E3
Goulton La TS9 25 E3
Gouthwaith Cl YO30 224 F2
Government House Rd YO30 228 A6
Gowans The YO61 144 C3
GOWDALL 204 A1
Gowdall Broach DN14 207 E8
Gowdall La
Pollington DN14 207 F7
Snaith & Cowick DN14 204 B1
Gowdall Rd DN14 203 E2
Gower Rd
Aske DL10 20 D1
Richmond DL10 209 C8
York YO24 230 E8
Gowland La YO13 54 B2
GOWTHORPE 169 C1
Gowthorpe YO8 232 C5
Gracious St
Huby YO61 144 A4
7 Knaresborough HG5 221 B5
GRAFTON 141 D2
Grafton Cl TS14 8 F6
Grafton La YO51 141 C3
Grafton St WF10 200 F3
Graham Cl YO11 213 B7
Graham Cres YO12 212 C5
Graham Dr WF10 201 A4
Graham Rd HG4 113 D3
Graham Sch YO12 212 B5
Grainary The* YO13 53 E3
Grainbeck La HG3 219 A7
Grainger Cl 6 TS16 5 D5
Grainger Row HG4 214 D5
Grainger St DL1 3 D4
Grains La BD23 154 E8
Grammar Sch La
Northallerton DL6 210 D3
Yarm TS15 5 E3
Grampian Cl 4 YO32 225 F5
Granary Ct
13 Pickering YO18 96 A6
York YO1 233 B3
Granby Pk HG1 219 F3
Granby Rd HG1 219 F3
Granby Sport & Play Development Ctr HG1 220 A4
Grandage La BD22 187 A7
Grand Opera House York* YO1 233 B2
GRANGE 57 D5
Grange Ave
Aiskew DL7 63 C4
Filey YO14 101 B3
Garforth LS25 194 C3
Harrogate HG1 219 D5
3 Hurworth-on-Tees DL2 3 D1
Ilkley LS29 218 D4
Scarborough YO12 212 E4
Spofforth HG3 179 E6
Tadcaster LS24 189 F6
Thorp Arch LS23 181 A2
3 Willerby YO12 99 D2
Grange Cl
10 Bedale DL8 63 A2
Bishop Thornton HG3 138 F1
Dishforth YO7 114 F4
Full Sutton YO41 169 A2
Ilkley LS29 218 D4
Lebberston YO11 100 D5
Northallerton DL7 210 C3
Skelton YO30 224 B5
Grange Close E DL7 63 E7
Grange Cres
Middlesbrough TS7 7 B5
10 Tadcaster LS24 189 E6
Grange Ct YO12 99 D7
Grange Dr TS9 26 C7
Grange Est LS29 218 D4
Grange Farm Cl YO8 198 B5
Grangefield Ave 32 LS29 176 C1
Grange Garth
3 Linton-on-Ouse YO30 164 F7
10 Wistow YO8 197 D6
York YO10 228 D2
Grange La
1 Dacre HG3 137 F1
Rufforth YO26 227 A2
Scackleton YO62 119 C3
Stonebeck Down HG3 137 A6
Sutton BD22 187 F2
Grangemoor Cl 5 DL1 3 E4
Grange Park Cl WF10 200 D7
Grange Park Rd HG4 214 B2
Granger Ave YO26 227 C4
Grange Rd
19 Bedale DL8 63 A2
Brompton-on-Swale DL10 41 B6
Burley in Warfedale LS29 176 C1
8 Campsall DN6 206 E1
Castleford WF10 201 B5
Colburn DL9 40 F5
Darlington DL1 3 C4
Farnhill BD20 173 E1
Tadcaster LS24 189 E6
Thornaby TS17 6 B8
Grangeside DL3 3 B4
Grange St YO10 228 D2
Grange Terr HG4 114 B8
Grange The
Kirby Hill YO51 141 A7
Leeming DL7 63 D4
Thirsk YO7 211 B2
Grange View
11 Otley LS21 176 F1
Towton LS24 189 E2
Granholme Cl 44 BD22 187 E7
Grant Cl DL6 45 B4
Grantham Dr YO26 227 E4
Grantley Cl HG3 219 A4
Grantley Dr HG3 219 A4
Grantley Pl HG3 219 A4
Grantly 3 DL3 3 B6
Grants Ave YO10 231 E8
Granville Rd
21 Filey YO14 101 B3
4 Harrogate HG1 219 D3
Scarborough YO11 213 A3
Granville Sq 3 YO11 213 A3
Granville St
20 Normanton South WF6 200 A1
Skipton BD23 216 E4
Granville Terr 4 YO10 228 E3
Grape La
Whitby YO22 208 E7
York YO1 233 B3
Grasmere Ave LS22 180 A3
Grasmere Cres HG2 222 C7
Grasmere Dr
6 High Bentham LA2 129 A8
York YO10 229 B4
Grasmere Gr 5 YO30 224 F1
Grass Croft TS21 5 A7
Grassfield Cl 8 HG3 137 B4
Grassgill La DL8 59 E3
Grassholme YO24 230 C7
Grassholme Way TS16 5 D5
GRASSINGTON 134 E3
Grassington Ave DL7 210 C2
Grassington CE Prim Sch BD23 134 E2
Grassington Rd
Middlesbrough TS4 7 A8
Skipton BD23 216 F5
Grass Wood La BD23 134 C3
Grass Wood Nature Reserve* BD23 134 C4
Gravelhill La DN14 206 F7
Gravel Hole La
Sowerby YO7 89 E3
Thirsk YO7 211 C1
Gravelly Hill La LS17 178 A2
Gray La YO62 70 D1
Grayshon Dr YO26 227 B5
Grays Rd YO62 69 F6
Gray St
13 Whitby YO21 208 D6
York YO23 233 A1
Graystonber La LA2 130 E7
Graystone Ct 12 YO18 96 A6
Grayston Plain La HG3 160 F4
Great Auk TS14 8 D6
Great Ave DL10 209 A7
GREAT AYTON 7 F2
Great Ayton Sta TS9 8 B1
GREAT BARUGH 95 A1
GREAT BROUGHTON 26 E5
GREAT BURDON 3 F8
GREAT BUSBY 26 C4
Great Cl YO8 197 B8
Great Close La BD24 153 A6
GREAT CRAKEHALL 62 E4
Great Croft Cl 9 BB18 171 D2
GREAT EDSTONE 94 C7
GREAT FENCOTE 63 C8
GREAT HABTON 121 C7
GREAT HECK 207 D7
GREAT LANGTON 42 D3
Great Moor Rd YO13 74 D2
Great North Rd
5 Fairburn WF11 201 D6
Ledsham LS25 195 C1
Micklefield LS25 194 F5
Great North Way YO26 227 B8
GREAT OUSEBURN 164 B8
Great Ouseburn Prim Sch YO26 164 B8
Great Pasture LS29 176 C1
GREAT PRESTON 200 C8
Great Preston CE Prim Sch LS26 200 C8
Great Sike Rd YO17 215 D8
GREAT SMEATON 23 C3
Great Smeaton Prim Sch DL6 23 C3
GREAT THIRKLEBY 90 D1
Greatwood Ave BD23 217 A3
Greatwood Cl BD23 217 B3
Greatwood Com Prim Sch BD23 217 A2
Greaves Smithy LS29 175 B4
Grebe Ave DL9 40 E2
Grebe Way YO18 95 F7
Greenacre Cl TS9 7 F1
Greenacres
Hunton DL8 61 E7
Morton-on-Swale DL7 64 A6
Skipton BD23 217 B5
Stainton & Thornton TS8 6 D5
York YO32 225 F4
Greenacres Cl 8 YO8 197 D1
Greenacres Cres 7 YO8 197 D1
Greenacres Dr
Airedale WF10 201 A4
4 Brayton YO8 197 D1
Greenacres Gr 3 YO8 197 D1
Green Ave LS25 194 C2
Green Balk
Great & Little Broughton TS9 26 F5
Millington YO42 170 D1
Greenbank 5 DL6 210 E2
Green Bank BB18 171 E2
Greenbank Cl 12 WF10 200 D3
Green Bank La HG4 139 A6
Greenbank Rd DL3 3 C6
Greenberfield La BB18 171 E2
Green Cl
Bradleys Both BD20 173 D3
2 Linton-on-Ouse YO30 164 F8
Middlesbrough TS7 7 D5
Steeton with Eastburn BD20 187 F7
York YO30 228 A8
Greencliffe Dr YO30 228 A6
GREEN CLOSE 130 A8
Green Cres The YO62 120 B5
Greencroft Ct 14 YO19 184 F7
Green Croft Gdns 24 YO11 100 B6
Greencroft La 17 YO19 184 F7
Green Dike YO32 225 C8
Green Dikes La YO25 151 F1
Greendown Cl LS29 218 D4
Green Dyke La YO62 120 C5
Green Dykes YO17 215 A3
Green Dykes La YO10 228 F3
Green End Ave 35 BB18 172 A1
Green End Rd 34 BB18 172 A1
Greenfield Ave LS25 194 D1
Greenfield Cl DL2 3 E1
Greenfield Dr
6 Brayton YO8 197 D1
Eaglescliffe TS16 5 D5

Greenfield Gdns BD20 187 F7
Greenfield Park Dr YO31 229 A7
Greenfield Rd 8 YO11 213 A4
Greenfields
 Pollington DN14 207 F6
 York YO31 228 D7
Greenfields Ave HG2 220 C2
Greenfields Dr HG2 220 C2
Greenfields Rd HG2 220 C2
Greenfield St 5 BD23 216 D3
Greenfinch Cl 1 YO12 99 E6
Greenfoot La LA2 128 E8
Greengales Ct YO19 193 A8
Greengales La YO19 193 A8
Greengate
 Malton YO17 215 C4
 Scarborough YO12 212 D4
Green Gate
 Exelby, Leeming & Newton DL7 63 D2
 Hawsker-cum-Stainsacre YO22 33 A6
 Kirkby Malham BD23 154 F8
 West Witton DL8 59 C3
Greengate Dr HG5 221 B8
Greengate La
 Cliffe YO8 198 F6
 Kirkby Fleetham with Fencote DL7 42 B1
 Knaresborough HG5 221 B8
Green Gate La
 Crakehall DL8 62 E5
 Kildale YO21 27 F8
 Long Preston BD23 153 F5
Greengate Rd WF8 206 C1
Greengates La YO61 142 E3
Greengate View HG5 221 B8
Green Haggs La HG3 223 F1
GREEN HAMMERTON 164 C3
Green Hammerton CE Prim Sch YO26 164 B3
Green Head La BD24 131 E2
GREEN HILL 194 F8
Green Hill YO62 118 E6
Greenhill Cres DL6 210 E3
Greenhill La YO7 66 B4
Green Hill La BD22 187 A5
Green Hills YO60 168 B7
Green Hills La DL7 64 B6
Greenholme Cl
 1 Boroughbridge YO51 141 B6
 7 Burley in Wharfedale LS29 176 C1
GREENHOW 136 D3
Green Howard's Dr 8 YO12 75 F5
Green Howards Rd
 Pickering YO18 96 A6
 Richmond DL10 209 B8
Green Howards Regimental Mus The* DL10 209 C6
Greenhow Hill HG3 136 C2
Greenhow Hill Rd HG3 159 B6
Greenhow Pk LS29 176 B1
Greenhowsyke La DL6 210 E4
Green Island YO12 99 D7
Green La
 Acomb YO24 227 D2
 Addingham LS29 174 F4
 Appleton Roebuck YO23 191 B6
 Barmby on the Marsh DN14 205 A6
 Barton-le-Street YO17 120 E8
 Bedale DL8 62 F3
 Boston Spa LS23 188 F7
 Bradleys Both BD20 174 A3
 Burton Leonard HG3 140 B2
 Burton-on-Yore DL8 86 D6
 Castleford WF10 200 E3
 Cawton YO62 119 B6
 Collingham LS22 188 A8
 Coneythorpe & Clareton HG5 163 B5
 Constable Burton DL8 61 A6
 Cottingwith YO42 193 C5
 Darlington DL1 3 D8
 Dishforth YO7 115 A2
 East Rounton DL6 24 F4
 Fadmoor YO62 69 E3
 Farndale West YO62 48 E1
 Ferrensby HG5 162 F8
 Flixton YO11 99 F1
 Garforth LS25 194 D4
 Glusburn BD20 187 D7
 Great Ouseburn YO26 142 A1
 Halton East BD23 157 C1
 Harome YO62 93 C6
 Harrogate HG2 222 C6
 Heck DN14 207 D8
 Horton BD23 171 B5
 Hudswell DL11 39 F5
 Hurgill DL10 40 B8
 Hutton Rudby TS15 25 B4
 Ilkley LS29 176 C2
 Ingleton LA6 103 E2
 Kippax LS25 194 C2
 Kirby Wiske YO7 88 F7
 Kirkby Overblow LS17 178 D2
 Kirklevington TS15 5 E2
 Langtoft YO25 151 D5
 Lebberston YO11 100 D5
 Ledston WF10 200 E7
 Little Ayton TS9 27 A8
 Littlethorpe HG4 140 A7
 Marrick DL11 38 E7
Green La *continued*
 Maunby YO7 64 D1
 Menwith with Darley HG3 160 A6
 Mickletown LS26 200 C5
 Middlesbrough TS5 6 E8
 Moor Monkton YO26 164 F1
 Newby TS7 7 C3
 North Cowton DL7 22 B2
 North Duffield YO8 198 F8
 North Lees HG4 113 D5
 Otley LS21 176 F1
 Rawcliffe YO30 225 A1
 Ripon HG4 113 C3
 Sawley HG4 138 E7
 Scalby YO12 212 C8
 Selby YO8 232 A3
 South Stainley with Cayton HG3 161 E8
 Stutton with Hazlewood LS24 189 D4
 Sutton BD22 187 F2
 Sutton-on-the-Forest YO61 144 E4
 Thirsk YO7 211 F3
 Weaverthorpe YO17 124 F1
 Welbury DL6 44 C8
 Wensley DL8 60 A4
 Whitby YO22 208 E5
 Whorlton DL6 45 F7
 Wigginton YO32 166 D5
 Winksley HG4 112 F2
 Wressle DN14 205 D8
Greenland La YO17 95 B3
Greenlands TS15 25 C6
Greenlands La YO8 197 C3
Greenlands Rd YO18 95 F6
Green Lane E YO7 211 B1
Green Lane Prim Sch
 Garforth LS25 194 D3
 Middlesbrough TS5 6 E8
Green Lane Trading Est YO30 225 A1
Green Lane Villas LS25 194 D4
Green Lane W YO7 211 A1
Green Lea Cl LS23 188 F8
Greenless La DL11 1 A2
Green Mdw BB8 186 A1
Green Mdws YO31 229 A7
Green Meadow Cl 11 LA6 103 D3
Greenmires La LS21 177 E4
Green Park Ave 15 YO11 100 B6
Green Park Rd 14 YO11 100 B6
Green Pastures DL8 62 C5
Green Row LS26 200 B5
Greenroyd Gr 13 BD20 187 E6
Greensborough Ave 3 YO26 227 B5
Greenshaw Dr YO32 225 C8
Greenside 18 YO19 184 F7
Greenside Cl 24 YO19 184 F7
Greenside Ct 9 DL2 3 E1
Greenside View TS12 9 D8
Greenside Wlk 23 YO19 184 F7
Green St
 Castleford WF10 200 E5
 7 Cowling BD22 187 B6
 Darlington DL1 3 D5
Greenstead Rd YO12 212 B8
Green Sward YO31 229 A8
Greens Yd YO22 208 E7
Green Sykes Rd BD22 187 F4
Green The
 Brompton DL6 43 F3
 Castleford WF10 201 B4
 1 Clapham LA2 130 C8
 Cleasby DL2 2 F4
 Conistone with Kilnsey BD23 134 B6
 20 Dunnington YO19 184 F7
 Garforth LS25 194 D3
 Hellifield BD23 154 B3
 High Coniscliffe DL2 2 C6
 Kettlewell with Starbotton BD23 108 B3
 Kirkby Malzeard HG4 112 D5
 8 Kirklevington TS15 24 E8
 Knaresborough HG5 221 A8
 Linton-on-Ouse YO30 164 F8
 Longnewton TS21 5 A7
 Middlesbrough TS17 6 D7
 Northallerton DL7 210 C3
 North Deighton LS22 180 A6
 9 Otley LS21 176 F1
 Rawcliffe DN14 205 A1
 Richmond DL10 209 B6
 Scalby YO12 212 B7
 Seamer TS9 6 F1
 6 Seamer YO12 99 D6
 Sheriff Hutton YO60 145 D5
 1 Skelton YO30 224 B5
 Skipton BD23 217 B6
 Slingsby YO62 120 B5
 Stillingfleet YO19 191 D3
 10 Thirsk YO7 211 C3
 Thornaby-on-Tees TS17 6 B7
 Tockwith YO26 181 C7
 2 Tollerton YO61 143 B3
 7 Topcliffe YO7 89 B1
 Wistow YO8 197 D6
 York YO26 227 C3
Green Village YO7 88 C5
Green Way
 Glusburn BD20 187 E8
 Harrogate HG2 222 C6
 Middlesbrough TS7 7 D5
 York YO32 225 F4
Green Ways Ct 2 YO8 197 D6
Greenways Dr 1 YO8 197 D6
Greenways The DL7 63 C8
Greenway The
 2 Haxby YO32 225 C7
 2 Middleton St George DL2 4 C4
Greenwich Cl 5 YO30 224 E3
Green Wlk 5 BB18 172 A1
Greenwood Ave 7 HG3 137 B4
Greenwood Gr YO24 230 C8
Greenwood Rd 6 HG3 137 B4
Greet's Hill YO17 169 E7
Gregory Cl YO30 224 C5
Grenadier Dr DL6 210 F3
Grendon Gdns 1 DL2 4 C4
Grenley St 8 WF11 202 A2
Grenville Rd TS17 6 B6
Gresham Cl DL1 3 D7
Gresley Ct 3 YO26 227 B4
Greta Ave DL10 209 D7
Greta Heath 2 LA6 102 F2
GREWELTHORPE 112 D7
Grewelthorpe CE Prim Sch HG4 112 C7
Grey Cl YO61 144 C3
GREYGARTH 111 F3
Greylands Park Ave YO12 212 C8
Greylands Park Dr YO12 212 C8
Greylands Park Gr 3 YO12 212 C8
Greylands Park Rd YO12 212 C8
Grey St HG2 222 E7
Greystoke Rd YO30 224 E1
Greystone Cl 2 LS29 176 C1
Greystone Ct YO32 225 C7
GREYSTONEGILL 129 C8
Greystonegill La LA2 129 D7
Greystone Head HG4 112 A4
Greystone La DL11 1 E4
Greystone Pk LS25 188 F1
Greystone Prim Sch HG4 214 C2
Greystones Ave HG3 161 B4
Greystones Cl LS25 188 F1
Greystones Dr 2 DL3 3 B6
Greystones La BD22 187 E4
Grey Thorn La HG5 163 D3
Grey Towers Dr TS7 7 D5
Grimbald Crag Cl HG5 221 D4
Grimbald Crag Rd HG5 221 E4
Grimbald Crag Way HG5 221 D4
Grimbald Rd HG5 221 C5
Grimbald Way 3 HG5 221 C4
GRIMSTON 229 E3
Grimston Bar YO19 229 F4
Grimston La YO17 148 D7
Grimston Rd 12 YO14 127 A8
Grimwith Garth YO30 224 F2
Grimwith Rd BD23 135 E2
GRINDALE 127 D2
Grindale Rd YO16 127 E2
Grinkle La TS13 10 F5
GRINTON 38 C5
Grinton Rd TS18 5 D8
Grisedale Cres TS16 5 E4
GRISTHORPE 100 E4
Gristhwaite La YO7 89 D1
GROSMONT 31 D3
Grosmont Gall* YO22 31 C4
Grosmont Sta YO22 31 C4
Grosvenor Cres 2 YO11 213 A4
Grosvenor Ct HG1 219 B2
Grosvenor Gdns LS17 178 B2
Grosvenor Gr HG1 219 F6
Grosvenor House YO30 233 A4
Grosvenor Pk YO30 233 A4
Grosvenor Pl TS14 8 E6
Grosvenor Rd
 Harrogate HG1 219 E6
 Scarborough YO11 212 F4
 York YO30 233 A4
Grosvenor Sq 3 YO30 164 F8
Grosvenor Terr YO30 233 A4
Grove Ave 25 LS29 175 C2
Grove Bank 4 TS15 24 E8
Grove Cl HG4 214 C3
Grove Cres
 Boston Spa LS23 188 F8
 South Milford LS25 195 F2
Grove Gdns 12 YO26 165 F1
Grove Hill Rd 4 YO14 101 B4
Grove La
 Knottingley WF11 201 F2
 Ripon HG4 214 C3
Grove Park Ave HG1 219 E4
Grove Park Ct HG1 219 E4
Grove Park Gdns 25 BD24 131 D2
Grove Park La HG1 219 E4
Grove Park Terr HG1 219 E4
Grove Park View HG1 219 E4
Grove Park Wlk HG1 219 E4
Grove Pk 7 YO8 198 B5
Grove Prom The LS29 218 A4
Grove Rd
 Boston Spa LS23 188 F8
 14 Filey YO14 101 B4
 Harrogate HG1 219 D4
 Ilkley LS29 218 A3
Grove Road Prim Sch HG1 219 E4
Groves Ct YO31 233 C3
Groves La YO31 233 C3
Grove Sq DL8 60 D5
Grove St
 38 Earby BB18 172 A1
 9 Harrogate HG2 220 C3
 Norton YO17 215 E3
 15 Whitby YO21 208 D6
Grove Terr 11 DL8 60 E2
Grove Terrace La YO31 233 C4
Grove The
 Eaglescliffe TS15 5 E2
 Guisborough TS14 8 D5
 Harrogate HG1 219 E3
 1 Hutton Rudby TS15 25 D5
 Ilkley LS29 218 A4
 Kellington DN14 203 A3
 Kippax LS25 194 D1
 Middlesbrough TS5 6 E6
 Normanton South WF6 200 A1
 Norton YO17 215 E2
 1 Seamer YO12 99 D6
 Skipton BD23 217 C3
 Swillington LS26 194 A1
 York YO24 230 E6
Grove View YO30 228 A6
Grundy Way 11 DL10 41 E4
GRUNSAGILL 153 A1
Grunton La DL2 2 C4
Grysedale La BD23 134 B2
GSPK Tech Pk HG5 221 D5
Guadaloupe Rd DL9 40 C4
Guards Ct 10 YO12 75 F5
Guildford Rd TS6 7 E8
Guinea Croft HG5 221 C7
GUISBOROUGH 8 D7
Guisborough Forest & Walkway Ctry Pk* TS14 8 C6
Guisborough Mus* TS14 8 F7
Guisborough Priory* TS14 8 F7
Guisborough Rd
 Aislaby YO21 31 F8
 Great Ayton TS9 7 F1
 Lockwood TS12 10 A5
 Middlesbrough TS7 7 D5
 6 Thornaby TS17 6 B8
 Whitby YO21 208 A5
Guisborough Swimming Pool TS14 8 E7
Guiseley Way TS16 5 D6
GUNBY 199 D6
Gunby Rd YO8 199 D5
Gunbywood Rd YO8 199 D6
Guncroft La YO62 69 D1
Guning La DL11 36 B4
Gunnergate La TS8 7 B5
GUNNERSIDE 36 F4
Gunnerside Methodist Prim Sch DL11 36 E5
Gurney Pease Prim Sch DL1 3 D6
Gurney St DL1 3 D6
Guy La HG4 114 F2
Gyll Hall La DL10 41 E1
Gypsy La
 Castleford WF10 201 B3
 Middlesbrough TS7 7 C6
Gypsy Lane Sta TS7 7 D6

H

Haakon Cl DL10 209 C7
Habton La YO17 121 B7
Habton Rd YO17 95 D1
HACKFORTH 62 E8
Hackforth & Hornby CE Prim Sch DL8 62 E8
Hackforth Rd 2 TS18 5 D8
HACKNESS 74 F5
Hackness CE Prim Sch YO13 74 E5
Hackness Dr YO12 212 A8
Hackness Rd YO12 212 A8
Haddlesey Rd WF11 202 D5
Haddocks La YO61 142 B4
Haddon Cl YO24 227 C2
Hadrian Ave YO10 229 B3
Hadrians Wlk YO12 99 E6
Hadrian Way TS17 5 F5
Haggersgate 10 YO21 208 D7
Haggitt Hill La DL6 24 E3
Hagg La
 Colton LS24 190 E8
 Cottingwith YO42 193 E8
 Cowesby YO7 66 C4
 Dunnington YO19 184 F6
 Hemingbrough YO8 198 F3
 South Milford YO8 196 C2
Hagg Rd YO62 69 F2
Hagg Side La YO13 97 D6
Haggs La DN6 207 D2
Haggs Rd HG3 223 C4
Haggwood Wlk YO19 184 F1
Hag La
 Cottingwith YO42 193 C4
 Raskelf YO61 142 E8
 South Kilvington YO7 211 D6
 Sproxton YO62 92 D4
 Youlton YO61 142 F2
Hague Ave 31 YO12 75 D5
Hagworm Hill* YO12 75 C2
Haigh La DN14 207 A6
Haigh Moor Way WF10 200 E6
Haig Rd DL9 209 C2
Haig St YO8 232 B6
Hailsham Ave TS17 6 B5
Hailstone Dr DL6 210 F5
Hales Ct WF8 201 B2
Hales La YO8 204 E5
Haley's Terr YO31 228 D8
Half Acres Junior & Infant Sch WF10 200 E4
Half Crown Way HG5 221 C7
Half Moon St 1 YO30 164 F7
Halfpenny Cl HG5 221 C7
Halfpenny La HG5 221 B7
Halifax Cl YO41 169 A2
Halifax Ct 7 YO30 225 A1
Halifax Way YO41 185 A3
Halladale Cl 1 YO24 230 B7
Hallam Cl 41 YO14 101 B3
Hallam La LS21 176 D3
Hallam's Yd 4 BD23 216 F4
Hallard Way 7 YO32 167 B7
Hall Arm La YO51 141 D5
Hall Ave 10 BD20 187 E6
Hall Brow BD23 155 A5
Hall Cl
 5 Airmyn DN14 205 E4
 Austwick LA2 130 E7
 Burley in Warfedale LS29 176 B1
 Cawood YO8 191 D1
 11 Glusburn BD20 187 E6
Hall Croft BD23 216 E4
Hallcroft Dr 13 LS29 175 A4
Hallcroft La YO23 230 A3
Hall Ct WF11 201 E4
Hall Dr
 Burley in Warfedale LS29 176 B1
 Glusburn BD20 187 E6
 Middlesbrough TS5 6 F7
Hall Farm Cl 4 YO19 197 F8
Hall Farm Ct YO42 169 F2
Hall Farm Pk LS25 194 F4
Hallfield Ave LS25 194 F4
Hallfield La
 Nawton YO62 69 C3
 Wetherby LS22 180 C3
Hallfield Rd YO31 228 E5
Hallfield Terr LS25 194 F4
HALL GARTH 184 F6
Hallgarth
 Alne YO61 142 F4
 Great & Little Broughton TS9 26 E5
 Hipswell DL9 209 F1
Hall Garth
 Osgodby YO8 198 C4
 25 Pickering YO18 95 F7
Hall Garth* LS25 195 E4
Hall Garth Cl LS24 190 C3
Hallgarth Ct DL11 18 C7
Hall Garth Mews 24 LS25 195 F4
Hall Garth Sch TS5 6 E7
Hall Gdns
 Ellerburn YO18 96 E7
 Farnhill BD20 173 F1
 Rawcliffe DN14 205 B2
Hall Green La LS17 178 C4
Hallikeld Cl HG4 114 B6
Hall Ings La YO62 70 E4
Hall La
 Askwith LS21 176 C4
 Bilton HG1 219 E6
 Blubberhouses LS21 159 C2
 4 Brafferton YO61 115 F1
 Caldwell DL11 1 C4
 Church Fenton LS24 196 C7
 Harome YO62 93 C4
 Harrogate HG1 219 E6
 Hawnby DL6 46 B1
 Huddleston with Newthorpe LS25 195 C3
 Leathley LS21 177 D1
 Ledston WF10 200 F7
 Myton-on-Swale YO61 142 A6
Hall Mdws BB8 186 A2
Hall Moor Cl 7 TS15 24 E8
Hall Orchards Ave LS22 180 D3
Hall Park Cl 23 YO13 75 D5
Hall Park Croft LS25 200 D8
Hall Park Gr 25 YO13 75 D5
Hall Park Mdws LS25 200 D8
Hall Park Orch LS25 200 D8
Hall Park Rd
 Hunmanby YO14 126 F8
 Walton LS23 181 A2
Hall Pasture 9 YO22 32 A6
Hall Pk
 Wistow YO8 198 A5
 York YO10 229 B1
Hall Rd
 Swillington LS26 194 A1
 Trawden Forest BB8 186 A2
Hall Rise
 Burley in Warfedale LS29 176 B1
 12 Haxby YO32 166 F5
Hall Sq 5 YO51 141 B5
Hall Tower Hill* LS15 194 B8
Hall View Gr DL3 3 A6
Hall Way 9 BD20 187 E6
Hallwith Rd DL8 61 A3
Halnaby Ave DL3 2 F5
Halstead Rd HG2 222 E7
HALTON EAST 174 C8
HALTON GILL 106 E7
HALTON WEST 154 A1
HAMBLETON
 Selby 196 F1
 Skipton 174 D8
Hambleton Ave
 Northallerton DL7 210 C2
 Thirsk YO7 211 D3
 York YO10 229 C4
Hambleton CE Prim Sch YO8 196 F1
Hambleton Cl
 12 Easingwold YO61 143 D8
 11 Thirsk YO7 211 C3

Hambleton Ct
Great Smeaton DL6 23 C3
Knaresborough HG5 221 C6
Old Thirsk YO7 211 D3
Hambleton Dr YO7 211 C3
Hambleton Forum★ DL6 210 E5
Hambleton Garth 21
YO61 143 C8
Hambleton Gate TS9 26 C7
Hambleton Gr HG5 221 B6
Hambleton La YO61 91 F2
Hambleton L Ctr DL6 210 D6
Hambleton Pl YO7 211 C3
Hambleton Rd
6 Catterick Garrison DL9 40 E3
Harrogate HG1 219 F4
Hawnby YO7 67 A3
Norton YO17 215 E2
Hambleton Row YO7 211 D4
Hambleton Terr
Knaresborough HG5 221 B6
York YO31 228 C7
Hambleton View
10 Haxby YO32 166 D5
Thirsk YO7 211 D3
4 Tollerton YO61 143 B3
Hambleton Way
Easingwold YO61 143 D8
York YO32 225 F3
Hamer Bank YO18 49 F4
Hamerton Cl 11 YO14 127 A8
Hamerton Rd 10 YO14 127 A8
Hamhall La DL7 63 D6
Hamilton Ave HG2 222 E8
Hamilton Cl YO13 75 C5
Hamilton Ct WF6 200 A2
Hamilton Dr
Darlington DL1 3 D8
York YO24 227 E2
Hamilton Drive E YO24 227 F2
Hamilton Drive W YO24 227 D2
Hamilton Gn YO17 215 B3
Hamilton Way YO24 227 E2
Hamlet The 8 DN14 202 F2
Hamley La YO62 70 F3
Hammer Rd HG4 85 B7
Hammersike Rd
Cawood LS25 196 F5
Wistow YO8 197 A4
Hammerton Cl
Green Hammerton YO26 164 D3
3 York YO26 227 B3
Hammerton Dr
Garforth LS25 194 D3
Hellifield BD23 154 B3
Hammertonlane Kirk
YO26 164 C3
Hammerton Sta YO26 164 D2
Hammond Dr DL1 3 C4
Hammond Rd YO13 54 A8
Hampden St YO1 233 B1
Hampden Way TS17 6 B6
Hampshire Cl
Ilkley LS29 218 D4
6 Pontefract WF8 201 C2
Hampson Gdns YO30 228 B8
HAMPSTHWAITE 160 F5
Hampsthwaite CE Prim Sch
HG3 161 A5
Hampsthwaite Rd HG1 219 C4
Hampton Gdns YO30 228 C8
Hampton Rd YO12 212 E5
Hampton Row LS25 196 A1
Hanbury Gdns LS25 194 C4
Hancow Rd
Hartoft YO18 50 A1
Rosedale East Side YO18 49 F3
Handale Cl TS14 9 A6
Handley Cl
Stockton-on-Tees TS18 5 F7
York YO30 225 A2
Hang Bank DL10 21 B8
Hanger La DN14 204 B3
Hanghow La DL8 84 C8
Hanging Stone La YO18 49 E4
Hangingstone Rd LS29 218 D2
Hankins La YO42 193 D1
HANLITH 155 A8
Hanover Pl
2 Kippax LS25 194 D1
Knottingley WF11 201 D4
Hanover Rd 6 YO11 212 F5
Hanover St 2 BD20 173 E1
Hanover Street E 5
YO26 227 F5
Hanover Street W 7
YO26 227 F5
Hanover Terr YO21 208 C6
Hansom Pl YO31 228 C7
Hanson Ave WF6 200 A1
Harborough Cl 20 YO14 126 F8
Harbour Rise 5 DL8 63 A2
Harbour View 7 DL8 63 A3
Harcourt Ave YO12 212 E3
Harcourt Cl
Bishopthorpe YO23 231 A4
Wheldrake YO19 192 F7
Harcourt Dr
Addingham LS29 174 F5
Harrogate HG1 219 E2
Harcourt Pl 4 YO11 213 A5
Harcourt Rd 4 HG1 219 E3
Harcourt St YO31 228 E5
Hardcastle Ave 8 WF8 201 B1
Harden Cl YO30 224 F2
Harden Rd BB18 186 A7
Hardenshaw La YO8 204 B4
HARDGATE 139 A1
Hard Gate BD23 134 A3
Hardgroves Hill HG3 159 F5
Hardigate Rd YO18 72 B7
Hardings La
Glusburn BD20 187 F8
Middleton LS29 218 A8
Harding's Yd YO17 95 E2
Hardistry-le-Court WF8 201 D2
Hardisty Hill HG3 159 C3
Hardisty Mews YO26 228 A4
Hardrada Way 3 YO41 168 D1
HARDRAW 56 C6
Hard Stiles DL11 39 B7
Hardy Mdws 11 BD23 134 E2
Hardy St YO8 232 E4
Harebell Cl
17 Harrogate HG3 161 B3
Northallerton DL7 210 C1
Harecroft Rd 9 LS21 177 A1
Haregill Bank HG4 85 E6
Harehills La BD22 187 E1
Haresfield Way TS17 6 A5
Harewell Cl HG3 137 D3
Harewell La 3 HG3 137 F1
Harewood Ave
5 Normanton South
WF6 200 B2
1 Scalby YO12 212 D8
Harewood Chase DL7 210 B2
Harewood Cl
Morton-on-Swale DL7 64 A6
Rawcliffe YO30 224 D2
5 Wigginton YO32 166 D5
Harewood Dr 4 YO14 101 A3
Harewood La DL7 210 C3
Harewood Prim Sch TS17 6 B8
Harewood Rd
Collingham LS22 188 A8
Harrogate HG3 219 A5
Ripon HG4 214 B3
Skipton BD23 216 E4
Harewood Way YO10 229 A2
Harford Rd YO11 100 B6
Hargill
Gilling with Hartforth &
Sedbury DL10 20 E4
Harmby DL8 60 E4
West Witton DL8 59 C3
Hargill Cl DL8 60 E4
Hargill La
Finghall DL8 61 E4
6 Leeming DL7 63 D4
Redmire DL8 59 C7
Hargill Rd DL8 61 A3
Hargreaves St 8 BD20 187 F8
Hargrove Rd HG2 220 B2
Harington Ave YO10 228 F4
Harker Hill DL8 56 C4
Harker St
42 Cross Hills BD20 187 E7
12 Knottingley WF11 202 A2
Harkness Cl DL7 63 C4
Harkness Dr DL7 63 C4
Harland Cl YO61 144 C3
Harland Mount Nature
Reserve★ YO12 212 B3
Harlech Ct 11 TS17 5 F4
Harlech Way HG2 222 B5
Harley Cl
3 Low Bentham LA2 128 F8
Scarborough YO12 212 E5
Harley Cres DL9 40 F4
Harley La 2 DL9 40 F4
Harley St 5 YO12 212 E5
Harlow Ave HG2 222 B7
Harlow Carr RHS Gdn★
HG3 161 B1
Harlow Cl 1 YO24 227 F2
Harlow Cres HG2 222 B7
Harlow Grange Pk HG3 178 C8
HARLOW HILL 222 A8
Harlow Manor Pk HG2 222 B8
Harlow Moor Dr HG2 219 B1
Harlow Moor Rd HG2 219 A1
Harlow Oval HG2 222 B8
Harlow Oval Mews HG2 222 B8
Harlow Park Cres HG2 222 B7
Harlow Park Dr HG2 222 B7
Harlow Park Rd HG2 222 B7
Harlow Pines HG3 222 A7
Harlow Rd YO24 227 F2
Harlow Terr HG2 219 B1
Harlow View HG2 222 B6
Harlsey Castle★ DL6 44 D5
Harlsey Cres TS18 5 E8
Harlsey Rd TS18 5 E8
HARMBY 60 E4
Harmby Rd 12 DL8 60 D5
Harness La 9 YO51 141 B4
Harold Ct YO24 227 D3
Harold St YO8 232 F4
Harolds Way 1 YO41 168 D1
HAROME 93 C4
Harome Heads La YO62 93 B6
Harome Heads Rd YO62 93 C6
Harper Gr BD20 187 E6
Harper La HG3 159 C6
Harpers Sq 7 BD20 187 E6
Harper St
Barnoldswick BB18 171 C1
2 Selby YO8 232 C5
Harpers Terr DL2 4 B5
Harper Terr 7 TS18 5 E8
Harr Gill DL8 58 A6
Harrier Ct YO41 185 A3
Harriers Croft YO7 115 E7
Harringay Cres 20 DL1 3 F6
Harris Dr 9 DL10 41 E4
Harrison Gr HG1 220 C4
Harrison St
Barnoldswick BB18 171 E1
York YO31 228 F6
Harris St DL1 3 E4
HARROGATE 219 D1
Harrogate Coll HG2 222 A7
Harrogate District Hospl
HG2 220 A2
Harrogate Gram Sch
HG2 222 C8
Harrogate High Sch
HG1 220 A4
Harrogate Hill Sch DL3 3 D7
Harrogate Hospice (BMI)
HG2 219 C1
Harrogate Int Ctr★ HG1 219 D3
Harrogate Ladies Coll
HG1 219 C3
Harrogate Rd
Bishop Monkton HG3 139 E5
Boroughbridge HG5 141 A2
Ferrensby HG5 162 E7
Green Hammerton YO26 164 B3
Kirkby Overblow HG3 222 D1
Knaresborough HG5 220 F5
Littlethorpe HG4 214 C1
Spofforth with Stockeld
LS22 180 A4
Weeton LS17 178 B2
Harrogate Sta HG1 219 D2
Harrogate Theatre★
HG1 219 D2
Harrogate Tutorial Coll
HG2 222 D8
Harrow Cliff La YO18 96 E4
HARROWGATE HILL 3 C8
HARROWGATE VILLAGE 3 E8
Harrow Glade 5 YO30 225 A1
Harrowing Dr 2 YO21 208 C6
Harrow Rd TS5 6 E8
Harry Moor La YO8 197 B2
Hartburn Village TS18 5 E8
HARTFORTH 20 D5
Hartforth La DL10 20 E4
Hart Hill Cres YO41 169 A2
Hartington St 13 BB8 186 A3
Hartington Way DL3 3 C7
HARTLEY 14 A7
Hartley Gn 4 BD23 153 F5
Hartley La CA17 14 A7
Hartley Pl BD22 187 B6
Hartley Rd HG2 222 B7
Hartley St
12 Earby BB18 172 A1
2 Glusburn BD20 187 D7
HARTLINGTON 157 C8
Hartlington Moor La
BD23 135 C3
Hartlington Raikes BD23 157 B8
Hartoft St YO10 228 D2
HARTON 168 C8
Hart Rhydding La LS29 174 F4
HARTWITH 160 B8
Hartwith Ave 3 HG3 138 A1
Hartwith Bank HG3 138 A1
Hartwith Cl HG3 219 A4
Hartwith Dr HG3 219 B4
Hartwith Gn 4 HG3 138 A1
Hartwith Way HG3 219 B4
Harvard Ct YO12 212 A8
Harvest Cl
10 Pontefract WF8 201 C2
11 Strensall YO32 167 B7
Harvest Croft LS29 176 B1
Harvester Way LS25 195 F2
Harvest Way YO11 100 B7
HARWOOD DALE 53 E2
Harwood Dale Rd YO13 54 A1
Harwood Rd YO26 182 F7
Hasguard Way 37 TS17 5 F4
Hassacarr La YO19 184 F6
Hastings Cl 4 YO30 225 A1
Hastings Cres WF10 201 A4
Hatcase La 23 YO18 95 F7
Hatfield Ave TS5 6 E8
Hatfield Cl 3 YO30 224 E3
Hatfield Rd DL7 210 D3
Hatfield Wlk YO24 230 B8
Hatkill La YO41 169 B1
Hatterall Ct 44 TS16 5 F4
Hatterboard Dr YO12 212 C6
Hatters Cl YO23 230 B3
Haugh La YO8 202 F8
Haughton Com Sch DL1 3 E7
HAUGHTON LE SKERNE 3 F6
Haughton Rd
Darlington DL1 3 D6
York YO30 228 C7
Hauling La YO23 191 C8
Hauxley Ct LS29 218 D5
Havelock Pl 17 YO21 208 D7
Havelock St TS17 6 B8
Haven The
Selby YO8 232 D5
5 South Milford LS25 195 F2
Haverah Ct YO30 224 F1
Havercroft Rd 15 YO14 127 A8
Havernook La HG4 86 A3
Havers Hill YO11 100 A6
Haverthwaites Dr LS25 188 F1
Havertop La WF6 200 C1
Havikil La HG5 162 A5
Havikil Pk HG5 162 A6
Havilland Rd TS17 6 B6
Havre Pk 11 BB18 171 E1
Haw Bank Ct BD23 217 B5
Hawber Cote Dr BD20 174 C1
Hawber La BD20 174 C1
Hawdon Ave YO8 232 D5
HAWES 56 D4
Hawes Prim Sch DL8 56 D4
Hawes Rd HG1 220 B4
Hawford Cl 1 TS17 6 B5
Haw Gr BD23 154 B3
Haw Hill View WF6 200 A2
Hawke Garth 5 YO14 127 A8
Hawkins Dr 36 DL9 41 A5
Hawkridge Cl TS17 6 A3
Hawkshead Cl 3 YO24 230 B8
Hawksmoor Ct HG4 214 C6
Hawkstone TS8 7 C4
Hawkstone Cl TS14 8 E6
Hawkswell La DL9 40 E1
HAWKSWICK 107 F1
Hawkswood 1 DL2 3 D1
Haw La BD23 154 B3
Hawley St BB8 186 B3
HAWNBY 67 E4
Haw Pk 1 BD23 217 E8
Hawse Rd YO8 204 E8
Hawshaw Rd BD22 186 E7
Hawsker Intake Rd YO22 32 F5
Hawsker La
Hawsker-cum-Stainsacre
YO22 13 F1
Whitby YO22 208 F6
Hawsker with Stainsacre CE
Prim Sch YO22 33 A7
Hawson Cl 9 YO11 100 B7
Hawthorn Ave
2 Knaresborough HG5 221 B7
Knottingley WF11 201 E2
Malton YO17 215 D5
Tadcaster LS24 189 D5
Hawthorn Cl
11 Addingham LS29 174 E4
Hellifield BD23 154 B3
25 Leyburn DL8 60 D5
3 Pickering YO18 96 A6
Stutton with Hazlewood
LS24 189 E5
Hawthorn Cres TS7 7 C6
Hawthorn Croft 6 LS24 189 D5
Hawthorn Dr
2 Topcliffe YO7 89 B1
Wilberfoss YO41 185 E5
Wistow YO8 198 A5
Hawthorne Ave
12 Haxby YO32 166 E5
10 Scotton DL9 40 F2
Hawthorne Cl
Burniston YO13 75 D7
10 Thorpe Willoughby YO8 197 B2
Hawthorne Dr
Barnoldswick BB18 171 E2
Guisborough TS14 8 E6
Hawthorne Gr YO31 228 E5
Hawthorne Mews YO32 167 B7
Hawthorne St 1 BD20 174 B1
Hawthorn Garth DN14 202 F4
Hawthorn Gr YO31 228 E5
Hawthorn La
9 Bedale DL8 63 B2
Pickering YO18 96 A6
Hawthorn Pl YO32 225 E4
Hawthorn Rd YO8 232 D3
Hawthorns 2 YO19 197 F8
Hawthorns La BD23 133 B2
Hawthorn Spinney YO31 225 E3
Hawthorn St 1 YO31 228 E5
Hawthorns The
20 Glusburn BD20 187 E7
10 Great Ayton TS9 8 A2
Hawthorn Terr YO32 225 D4
Hawthorn Terrace Ctr 2
YO32 225 D3
Hawthorn Terrace N
YO32 225 D4
Hawthorn Terrace S
YO32 225 D3
Hawthorn Way YO14 101 C1
Hawthorn Wlk 1 YO11 100 A7
HAXBY 225 D7
Haxby Moor Rd
Haxby YO32 166 F7
Towthorpe YO32 167 A7
Haxby Rd
Clifton YO31 225 D1
Middleton St George DL2 4 C5
New Earswick YO32 225 D6
York YO31 233 B4
Haxby Rd Prim Sch
YO31 228 D7
Hay-a-Park La HG5 221 D7
Hay Brow Cl YO13 75 C5
Hay Brow Cres YO13 75 C5
Hayfield Ave LS23 188 E8
Hayforth Cl YO30 225 A2
Haygate La YO18 95 F5
Haygill Nook BD20 174 B5
Hayhills La BD20 174 B2
Hayhills Rd 10 BD20 174 C1
Hay La YO13 75 C5
Hayton Wood View LS25 194 F8
Haywain The
Ilkley LS29 218 D3
17 South Milford LS25 195 F2
Haywra Cres 6 HG1 219 E3
Haywra St HG1 219 D3
Hazel Bank HG5 162 D6
Hazel Brow Farm★ DL11 37 C4
Hazel Cl
Pannal HG3 222 C3
York YO32 225 D2
Hazel Ct
11 Bedale DL8 63 B3
York YO10 228 E4
Hazel Dr HG3 222 C3
Hazel Garth YO31 229 B7
Hazel Gr
Middlesbrough TS7 7 C6
Pontefract WF8 201 C1
Sutton BD20 187 E7
Hazel Grove Rd BD20 187 E7
Hazelheads La HG5 221 C8
Hazel Hill YO12 75 A2
Hazelmere Ct YO32 225 E3
Hazelnut Gr YO30 225 B2
Hazel Old La DN14 203 C2
Hazel Rd
2 Boroughbridge YO51 141 B4
2 Filey YO14 101 A4
Knottingley WF11 201 F1
Hazel Rise LS26 200 B5
Hazelwood Ave
Garforth LS25 194 D3
York YO10 229 D4
Hazing La DN14 207 B6
Hazler La BD23 157 D7
HAZLEWOOD 175 A8
Headingley Cres 3 DL1 3 F6
Headingley Rd 7 DN6 206 E2
Headland Cl 30 YO32 166 E5
Headland La YO18 72 B4
Headlands La
Howgrave DL8 87 F2
Knottingley WF11 201 F2
Pontefract WF8 201 B1
Headlands Prim Sch
YO32 225 D8
Headlands Rd YO62 70 E2
Headlands The DL3 3 A5
Headley Cl 2 YO30 225 B1
Headley La LS23 188 F5
Head of Steam-Darlington
Railway Mus DL3 3 C6
Heads Bank DL8 58 F3
Heads La BB18 186 A7
Heads Rd
Newton YO18 51 B1
Pickering YO18 71 F8
Headwell La LS24 195 E7
HEALAUGH 37 F6
Healaugh La YO26 181 F4
Healaugh Pk TS15 5 E2
Healaugh Priory★ LS24 181 E1
Heald Brow BB18 171 D2
Healdfield Rd WF10 201 A4
Heald St WF10 200 F4
Healdwood Rd WF10 200 F4
HEALEY 85 E3
Healey Gr YO31 228 F8
Healthfield Prim Sch DL1 3 E5
Heath Cl 2 YO24 227 F2
Heathcliff Gdns 5 YO12 212 C8
Heath Cres BD20 173 E3
Heath Croft YO10 231 F7
Heath Ct 11 BD20 173 E3
Heath Dr
Boston Spa LS23 188 D8
7 Low Bradley BD20 173 E3
Heather Bank
13 Stamford Bridge
YO41 168 D2
York YO10 229 C4
Heather Brow 16 BB18 172 B1
Heather Cl
Selby YO8 232 C3
3 Whorlton DL6 25 D1
York YO32 226 A4
Heather Croft 4 YO31 225 E2
Heather Ct LS29 218 B3
Heatherdene LS24 189 E6
Heatherdene Rd 1 DL9 40 E4
Heather Dr YO22 208 E3
Heather View BD23 217 B3
Heather Way 16 HG3 161 B3
HEATHFIELD 136 F6
Heathfield Dr HG5 221 C6
Heathfield Pk DL2 4 C5
Heathfield Rd 1 YO10 229 A3
Heath Gr HG2 219 B1
Heath Moor Dr YO10 231 F8
Heathness Rd LS29 174 E5
Heath Pk 27 LS29 175 C2
Heath Ride YO32 167 B8
Heathrow TS17 6 C7
Heathrow Cl 13 DL2 4 C4
Heaths Ct HG4 214 C5
HEATHWAITE 45 E8
HEBDEN 135 A1
Hebden Bank HG4 138 F4
Hebden Rd BD23 134 E2
Hebdon Rise 2 YO26 227 D4
Heber Dr BD23 172 A5
Hebers Ghyll Dr 24 LS29 175 C2
Hebers Gr 21 LS29 175 C2
Hebron Ct TS9 26 B7
Hebron Rd TS9 26 B7
Heck Gill La HG3 160 A5
Heck La
Heck DN14 207 C7
Hensall DN14 203 D1
Heckler Cl 3 HG4 214 C4
Heckler La HG4 214 C4
Heck & Pollington Lake
DN14 207 E7
Heddon Gr TS17 6 A3
Hedgerows The YO8 198 E3

Hedley St TS14 .... 8 F7
Height La BD23 .... 174 C6
Height Lands La YO23 .... 182 D6
Heights La BD20 .... 174 A2
Helena St LS25 .... 200 C8
Helks Brow LA2 .... 128 E2
HELLIFIELD 154 B3
Hellifield Com Prim Sch
BD23 .... 154 B3
HELLIFIELD GREEN 154 B3
Hellifield Rd BD23 .... 155 A6
Hellifield Sta BD23 .... 154 B4
Hell Wath Gr HG4 .... 214 A2
Hell Wath La
Littlethorpe HG4 .... 214 A2
Markingfield Hall HG4 .... 139 E6
Hell Wath Nature Reserve★
HG4 .... 214 A4
HELM 57 D6
Helmsdale YO24 .... 230 C6
HELMSLEY 92 F7
Helmsley Castle★ YO62 .... 92 E6
Helmsley Dr TS14 .... 8 E7
Helmsley Gr 16 YO32 .... 166 D5
Helmsley Prim Sch YO62 .... 92 F7
Helmsley Rd TS9 .... 26 C7
Helmsley Walled Gdn★
YO62 .... 92 E6
Helmsley Way DL7 .... 210 C2
Hel'os 47 LS25 .... 194 D5
HELPERBY 142 A8
Helperby La YO51 .... 141 C7
Helperby & Myton La
YO61 .... 142 A7
HELPERTHORPE 124 D1
Helredale Gdns YO22 .... 208 E4
Helredale Rd YO22 .... 208 E4
Helston Rd WF6 .... 200 A2
Helwath Rd YO13 .... 53 D5
HELWITH BRIDGE 131 D8
Helwith Rd DL11 .... 38 E7
HEMINGBROUGH 198 F1
Hemingbrough Prim Sch
YO8 .... 198 F1
Hemingford Gdns TS15 .... 5 E2
Hemishor Dr LS26 .... 200 C8
HEMLINGTON 6 F4
Hemlington Hall Prim Sch
TS8 .... 6 E5
Hemlington Hall Rd TS8 .... 6 E5
Hemlington Lake & Recn Ctr
TS8 .... 6 E5
Hemlington Rd TS8 .... 6 E5
Hemlock Ave YO31 .... 225 E1
Hempbridge Cl YO8 .... 232 A5
Hempbridge Rd YO8 .... 232 A5
Hempland Ave YO31 .... 228 F6
Hempland Dr YO31 .... 229 A7
Hempland La YO31 .... 229 A7
Hempland Prim Sch
YO31 .... 229 B6
Hemsby Rd WF10 .... 200 E3
Hemsworth Wlk HG4 .... 214 B7
Henbusk La LA2 .... 130 A8
Hendon Garth YO30 .... 225 A1
Henlow La YO60 .... 147 B4
Henrhyd Cl 26 TS17 .... 5 F4
Henrietta Cl
Richmond DL10 .... 209 F8
3 Thornaby-on-Tees TS17 .... 6 B8
Henrietta St YO22 .... 208 E7
Henry Moore Pl WF10 .... 200 F3
Henry's Mews 22 LS25 .... 195 F4
Henry St BD23 .... 216 F1
HENSALL 203 D2
Hensall Prim Sch DN14 .... 203 C1
Hensall Sta DN14 .... 203 C1
Hensfield Gr DL3 .... 3 C7
Henshaws Coll HG1 .... 220 B5
Henside La BD24 .... 132 A5
Henside Rd BD24 .... 132 B6
Henson Gr WF10 .... 201 A4
Henson Rd DL1 .... 3 F5
Henwick Hall La YO8 .... 232 C1
Hepton Hill YO17 .... 120 F2
Hepworth's La DN14 .... 204 C2
Herbert St 6 YO10 .... 228 E3
Herberts Way YO31 .... 228 F7
Hercules St DL1 .... 3 E7
Herdborough Rd YO11 .... 100 A7
Herdsman Dr YO23 .... 230 C3
Herdsman Rd 3 YO24 .... 230 D8
Herdwick Cl 1 YO30 .... 225 B1
Hereford Rd HG1 .... 219 A2
Hergill La
Baldersby HG4 .... 88 C1
Kirkby Fleetham with Fencote
DL7 .... 63 C8
Herisson Cl 20 YO18 .... 95 F7
Herman Wlk YO24 .... 230 C8
Hermitage Ct DL10 .... 209 A7
Hermitage The★ HG4 .... 86 C8
Hermitage Way YO22 .... 32 A5
Heron Ave YO24 .... 230 C8
Heron Cl
1 Bedale DL8 .... 63 B3
11 Thornton Dale YO18 .... 96 D5
Heron Ct
6 Filey YO14 .... 101 A4
6 Hunton DL9 .... 40 F2
Heron Dr DL1 .... 3 E5
Herongate YO18 .... 95 F6
Heron Gate TS14 .... 8 D6
Heron La YO12 .... 99 E6
Heron Rise YO32 .... 225 F5
Heron Tree Cl DL8 .... 60 D7
Heron Way YO17 .... 215 D2
Herriot Dr DL9 .... 41 A5
Herriot Way YO7 .... 211 C4
Hertford Cl 4 YO11 .... 100 A7
Hertford Vale CE Prim Sch
YO12 .... 99 D2
Hesketh Ave TS4 .... 7 A7
Hesketh Bank YO10 .... 229 D3
Heslaker La BD23 .... 216 C1
Hesleden Ave TS5 .... 6 D6
Hesley La BD24 .... 153 A6
Heslin Cl 8 YO32 .... 225 C8
HESLINGTON 229 B1
Heslington Croft YO10 .... 231 F7
Heslington Ct 2 YO10 .... 229 B1
Heslington Gdns 2 TS14 .... 8 F7
Heslington La
Heslington YO10 .... 229 A1
York YO10 .... 228 F3
Heslington Rd YO10 .... 228 E3
HESSAY 182 C8
Hessay Ind Est YO26 .... 182 C8
Hessay Pl 2 YO26 .... 227 A3
Hetherton St YO30 .... 233 A3
HETTON 155 F5
Hetton Garth 18 DL8 .... 60 D5
HEW GREEN 160 D5
Hewitson Rd DL1 .... 3 E5
Hewitts La BD20 .... 172 F2
Hewley Ave YO10 .... 229 A4
Hewley Dr 9 YO13 .... 99 A7
HEWORTH 228 F6
Heworth YO31 .... 229 A6
Heworth CE Prim Sch
YO31 .... 228 F6
Heworth Dr YO21 .... 208 B6
Heworth Gn YO31 .... 233 C4
Heworth Hall Dr YO31 .... 228 F6
Heworth Mews YO31 .... 228 E6
Heworth Pl YO31 .... 228 F6
Heworth Rd YO31 .... 228 F6
Heworth Village YO31 .... 229 A6
Heyford Rd YO7 .... 115 B1
Heygate Bank YO18 .... 49 F3
Heygate La LS23 .... 188 F6
HEYSHAW 159 D8
Heyshaw Rd HG3 .... 159 C8
Heythrop Dr
Guisborough TS14 .... 8 F6
Middlesbrough TS5 .... 6 D7
Heywood Rd HG2 .... 219 C1
Hibernia St YO12 .... 212 E5
Hicks La LS26 .... 200 B6
Hickstead Ct 16 DL1 .... 3 F6
Hidcote Gdns TS17 .... 6 A4
High Back Side YO18 .... 95 E8
High Bank
Ampleforth YO62 .... 92 B2
Bradleys Both BD20 .... 173 E3
5 Threshfield BD23 .... 134 D2
High Bank Cl 7 LS29 .... 174 F4
Highbank Gr 1 HG2 .... 220 D4
High Barmer YO13 .... 75 B7
HIGH BENTHAM 129 B8
High Bentham Prim Sch
LA2 .... 129 B8
HIGH BIRSTWITH 160 D5
High Bond End HG5 .... 221 A7
HIGH BRADLEY 173 E4
High Bradley La BD20 .... 173 E4
Highbury Ave TS5 .... 6 F8
HIGH CATTON 185 D8
High Catton Rd YO41 .... 185 D8
High Church Wynd TS16 .... 5 D3
High Cleugh HG4 .... 214 A4
Highcliffe Ct YO30 .... 228 A6
Highcliffe Prim Sch TS14 .... 8 E5
High Cliff Rd TS14 .... 8 E4
HIGH CONISCLIFFE 2 C6
High Coniscliffe CE Sch
DL2 .... 2 C6
High Cragwell YO21 .... 31 F7
High Crest 6 HG3 .... 137 C4
Highcroft
Collingham LS22 .... 188 A8
9 Grassington BD23 .... 134 E3
12 High Bentham LA2 .... 129 A8
High Croft 7 YO14 .... 126 F8
High Croft Way 5 BD20 .... 173 E1
High Ct HG5 .... 221 A6
Highdale Ave 5 YO12 .... 212 D8
Highdale Rd YO12 .... 212 E7
High Eggborough La
DN14 .... 203 A1
HIGH ELLINGTON 85 F6
Higherlands Cl BD23 .... 155 D1
Higher Lodge St 1
BD20 .... 187 D7
Higher Rd BD23 .... 152 F4
High Fell Cl BD24 .... 131 D1
HIGHFIELD 199 E7
Highfield
Pollington DN14 .... 207 F7
Scarborough YO12 .... 212 E4
High Field YO10 .... 229 D4
Highfield Ave WF8 .... 201 D2
Highfield Cl YO25 .... 126 A4
Highfield Cres YO8 .... 198 B5
Highfield Ct YO8 .... 232 B1
Highfield Dr
Allerton Bywater WF10 .... 200 C7
Garforth LS25 .... 194 C3
Highfield Gn
Allerton Bywater WF10 .... 200 C7
Sherburn in Elmet LS25 .... 195 F3
Highfield Gr
Great Preston WF10 .... 200 C7
Highfield Gr *continued*
Highfield YO8 .... 199 E7
Highfield La
Barwick in Elmet & Scholes
LS15 .... 194 B7
Fangfoss YO41 .... 169 B1
Gillamoor YO62 .... 69 F5
Huddleston with Newthorpe
LS25 .... 195 C3
Nawton YO62 .... 69 C2
Scagglethorpe YO17 .... 122 E2
Womersley DN6 .... 206 D5
Highfield Pl 1 WF10 .... 200 D7
Highfield Prep Sch HG1 .... 219 B3
Highfield Rd
Aberford LS25 .... 194 F8
29 Earby BB18 .... 172 A1
Highfield YO8 .... 199 D7
Malton YO17 .... 215 C5
Ripon HG4 .... 214 B3
Whitby YO21 .... 208 A7
Highfields La YO7 .... 115 A1
Highfield Terr BD23 .... 216 F3
Highfield View 3 YO8 .... 198 B4
Highfield Villas LS25 .... 195 F3
High Fold BB18 .... 186 A7
High Garth
Earswick YO32 .... 226 A7
Eastfield YO11 .... 100 A7
Richmond DL10 .... 209 B8
Highgate
Balne DN14 .... 207 D6
Glusburn BD20 .... 187 D8
Highgate Pk HG1 .... 219 F3
High Gill Rd TS7 .... 7 D6
High Gn
Catterick DL10 .... 41 D4
Hebden BD23 .... 135 A2
HIGH GRANTLEY 138 D8
High Green Dr BD20 .... 174 B1
Highgrove Cl 7 YO30 .... 224 E3
HIGH HARROGATE 220 A3
HIGH HAWSKER 33 B6
High Hill Grove St 14
BD24 .... 131 D2
High Hill La BD24 .... 131 E2
HIGH HUTTON 147 B7
HIGH KILBURN 91 B2
High La
Beadlam YO62 .... 93 C8
Birstwith HG3 .... 160 C5
Cowling BD22 .... 187 A4
Cropton YO18 .... 71 C4
Dalby-cum-Skewsby YO60 .... 119 A2
Dalton DL11 .... 19 D7
Fylingdales YO22 .... 33 C5
Gillamoor YO62 .... 70 A6
Grassington BD23 .... 134 E3
Grinton DL11 .... 37 D4
Hawes DL8 .... 56 F4
Howsham YO60 .... 147 B1
Kirby Sigston DL6 .... 44 E1
Leake DL6 .... 65 E6
Maltby TS8 .... 6 C4
Muston YO14 .... 100 F1
Myton-on-Swale YO61 .... 142 B6
Newsham DL11 .... 18 G7
Reeth, Fremington & Healaugh
DL11 .... 37 F5
Spofforth with Stockeld
HG3 .... 179 C4
Sutton upon Derwent
YO41 .... 185 D3
Thirlby YO7 .... 90 D6
Thornton Watlass DL8 .... 62 C2
West Scrafton DL8 .... 83 F6
West Witton DL8 .... 59 D2
Highland Cl 9 WF8 .... 201 C1
Highlands Ave 5 YO32 .... 167 B7
Highlands Cl YO14 .... 101 B1
High Leir La YO7 .... 67 D1
HIGH LEVEN 6 A3
HIGH MARISHES 96 B1
High Market Pl 27 YO62 .... 70 B1
High Mdw
Gowdall DN14 .... 204 A1
Selby YO8 .... 232 B6
Highmead Wlk 3 TS3 .... 7 B8
High Mill Dr 1 YO12 .... 75 E5
High Mill La LS29 .... 175 A5
Highmoor Cl YO24 .... 230 D8
High Moor Edge YO12 .... 212 A7
High Moor La
Boroughbridge HG5 .... 141 A2
Brearton HG3 .... 161 F8
Newton-on-Ouse YO30 .... 165 C8
Scotton HG5 .... 162 A5
Highmoor Rd YO24 .... 230 D8
High Moor Rd
North Rigton HG3 .... 178 A5
Skelton YO51 .... 140 F7
High Moor Way 11 YO11 .... 100 A6
HIGH MOWTHORPE 149 D7
High Newbiggin St YO31 .... 233 B3
High Oaks YO31 .... 229 B7
High Ousegate YO1 .... 233 B2
High Peak TS14 .... 8 F5
High Petergate YO1 .... 233 B3
High Peter La HG3 .... 140 A3
High Rd LA2 .... 128 F5
High Riding
Aske DL10 .... 20 D1
Richmond DL10 .... 209 C8
High Rifts TS8 .... 6 E5
High Riggs La YO18 .... 96 C3
High Row
Bugthorpe YO41 .... 169 D4
Caldwell DL11 .... 1 C4
High Row *continued*
Darlington DL1 .... 3 C5
Gainford DL2 .... 1 C7
Melsonby DL10 .... 20 F7
HIGH SHAW 56 D7
High Skellgate 7 HG4 .... 214 C5
High St
Airmyn DN14 .... 205 E3
Ampleforth YO62 .... 92 C3
Aske DL10 .... 20 E2
Austwick LA2 .... 130 E7
Barmby on the Marsh
DN14 .... 205 A7
Barnby YO21 .... 12 C4
Barton-le-Street YO17 .... 120 E5
Beadlam YO62 .... 93 D7
Boosbeck TS12 .... 9 D8
6 Boroughbridge YO51 .... 141 B5
Boston Spa LS23 .... 188 E8
Bramham LS23 .... 188 E5
Buckton/Bempton YO13 .... 97 D6
Burniston YO13 .... 75 C8
Burton in Lonsdale LA6 .... 102 F3
Carlton DN14 .... 204 C2
Castleford WF10 .... 200 E4
Catterick DL10 .... 41 D5
Cawood YO8 .... 197 B8
Cottam YO25 .... 150 E5
Cropton YO18 .... 71 B4
Danby YO21 .... 29 A6
Eaglescliffe TS15 .... 5 D4
13 Eastfield YO11 .... 100 A6
Gargrave BD23 .... 155 D1
Glaisdale YO21 .... 30 D4
Glusburn BD20 .... 187 E6
Great Ayton TS9 .... 7 F1
Great Broughton TS9 .... 26 E4
Hampsthwaite HG3 .... 160 F5
Harrogate HG2 .... 220 C4
4 Helmsley YO62 .... 92 F6
Heslerton YO17 .... 123 F6
Hinderwell TS13 .... 11 F7
Hovingham YO62 .... 119 E6
Husthwaite YO61 .... 117 B6
Ingleton LA6 .... 103 D4
Kippax LS25 .... 194 D1
Kirby Grindalythe YO17 .... 149 D8
5 Knaresborough HG5 .... 221 B5
Knottingley WF11 .... 201 E5
Langtoft YO25 .... 151 C8
Lastingham YO62 .... 70 E5
9 Leyburn DL8 .... 60 D5
Lingdale TS12 .... 9 F7
Lockwood TS12 .... 10 A5
Markington with Wallerthwaite
HG3 .... 139 C4
Mickleby TS13 .... 12 A4
Middlesbrough TS7 .... 7 C8
Newton Mulgrave TS13 .... 11 E4
Normanton South WF6 .... 200 A1
Northallerton DL7 .... 210 D6
14 Norton DN6 .... 206 E1
Old Byland & Scawton YO62 .... 92 A4
Oldstead YO7 .... 91 E5
Pateley Bridge HG3 .... 137 B4
Rawcliffe DN14 .... 205 A1
Rillington YO17 .... 122 F5
Scalby YO13 .... 75 D5
6 Settle BD24 .... 131 E2
Settrington YO17 .... 122 F1
Sherburn YO17 .... 124 D7
Skipton BD23 .... 217 A4
Slingsby YO62 .... 120 B5
Snainton YO13 .... 98 A5
Snaith DN14 .... 204 B1
South Milford LS25 .... 195 E2
Spofforth HG3 .... 179 E5
3 Staithes TS13 .... 13 K2
Stillington YO61 .... 144 B6
Stokesley TS9 .... 26 C7
Swinton YO17 .... 121 B4
Tadcaster LS24 .... 189 E6
Thornton Dale YO18 .... 96 E6
Thornton-le-Clay YO60 .... 146 A4
Wharram YO17 .... 149 A6
Whitby YO21 .... 208 B3
Whixley YO26 .... 164 A4
Whorlton DL6 .... 45 D8
Wombleton YO62 .... 93 E7
Wrelton YO18 .... 71 C1
HIGH STAKESBY 208 B5
High Stakesby Rd YO21 .... 208 A6
High Stell DL2 .... 4 C4
High Street Agnesgate
HG4 .... 214 C5
Highthorne La YO61 .... 117 B5
Highthorn Rd YO31 .... 225 E2
High Town Bank Rd YO7 .... 91 C5
High Trace DL6 .... 210 E2
High Trees Ct LS25 .... 195 F4
High View HG3 .... 160 F8
Highway BD24 .... 131 E3
High Wheatley LS29 .... 218 E3
High Wlk YO12 .... 212 E7
High Wood LS29 .... 218 F3
HIGH WORSALL 24 A8
Hilbeck Gr YO31 .... 229 B6
Hilbra Ave YO32 .... 225 D6
Hilda St
6 Selby YO8 .... 232 C5
3 York YO10 .... 228 E3
Hildenley Cl 6 YO12 .... 212 B5
Hilderthorpe TS7 .... 7 C6
Hildewell 3 TS13 .... 11 F7
Hildyard Cl TS9 .... 26 C8
HILLAM 202 A7
Hillam Comm La LS25 .... 202 B7
Hillam Hall La 4 LS25 .... 202 A7
Hillam Hall View 3
LS25 .... 202 A7
Hillam House Cl 5 LS25 .... 202 A7
Hillam La
Burton Salmon LS25 .... 201 F7
Hillam LS25 .... 202 A7
Hillam Rd YO8 .... 202 F8
Hillary Garth 9 YO26 .... 227 E4
Hill Bank HG5 .... 163 B7
Hillbank Gr HG1 .... 220 D4
Hillbank Rd HG1 .... 220 D4
Hillbank View HG1 .... 220 C4
Hill Cl DL11 .... 38 B6
Hillcrest
8 Monk Fryston LS25 .... 202 A8
Tadcaster LS24 .... 189 D5
Hill Crest YO19 .... 167 F1
Hillcrest Ave
Newby & Scalby YO12 .... 75 E5
Poppleton YO26 .... 224 A2
Silsden BD20 .... 174 C1
Hillcrest Cl WF10 .... 201 B3
Hillcrest Ct 2 LS24 .... 189 D5
Hillcrest Dr
Castleford WF10 .... 201 B3
Loftus TS13 .... 10 D8
Hillcrest Gdns YO51 .... 141 A7
Hill Crest Gdns YO24 .... 227 F1
Hillcrest Gr 2 YO12 .... 75 E5
Hillcrest Mount WF10 .... 201 B3
Hillcroft 4 LA2 .... 129 A7
Hill End La BD22 .... 186 F5
Hill Field YO8 .... 232 B8
Hill Foot La HG3 .... 222 B2
Hillgarth WF11 .... 201 F2
Hillgarth Ct 4 YO41 .... 185 B2
Hillhouse La DL2 .... 4 C7
Hill House La DL2 .... 4 C8
Hillingdon Rd TS4 .... 7 B8
Hill La BB8 .... 186 B4
Hillocks La TS12 .... 10 A5
Hill Rd WF10 .... 200 F3
Hill Rise
Middleton St George DL2 .... 4 D3
Skipton BD23 .... 216 E5
Hill Rise Ave HG2 .... 222 B8
Hill Rise Cl HG2 .... 222 B8
Hillsborough Terr 5
YO30 .... 228 C7
Hillshaw Parkway HG4 .... 214 D5
Hillside
Byram WF11 .... 201 E4
Follifoot HG3 .... 223 F4
3 Ingleby Arncliffe DL6 .... 45 A7
Skipton BD23 .... 217 B6
Hill Side DL2 .... 3 A3
Hillside Cl
18 Addingham LS29 .... 174 F4
Bootham Stray YO30 .... 225 B2
9 Monk Fryston LS25 .... 202 A8
Skipton BD23 .... 217 B6
Threshfield BD23 .... 134 B3
Hillside Cres BD23 .... 217 C3
Hillside Dr BD23 .... 134 B3
Hillside Gdns
Langtoft YO25 .... 151 D5
Scarborough YO12 .... 212 E1
Hillside Rd
2 Low Bentham LA2 .... 128 F8
Pannal HG3 .... 222 E3
Hillside Way YO17 .... 150 B8
Hills La BD23 .... 155 E5
Hill St
6 Barnoldswick BB18 .... 171 E1
York YO24 .... 227 E3
Hill The DL8 .... 56 D4
Hill Top
24 Burley in Warfedale
LS29 .... 176 C1
Castleford WF10 .... 200 C4
Ilkley LS29 .... 218 A2
Knottingley WF11 .... 201 F2
Hill Top Ave HG1 .... 219 D6
Hill Top Cl
Embsay BD23 .... 217 C8
Harrogate HG1 .... 219 D6
Stutton with Hazlewood
LS24 .... 189 D4
Hilltop Cres DL9 .... 40 E4
Hill Top Cres HG1 .... 219 D6
Hill Top Ct DL7 .... 22 C3
Hill Top Dr HG1 .... 219 D6
Hill Top Gr HG1 .... 219 E6
Hill Top La
Earby BB18 .... 172 A1
Pannal HG3 .... 222 A4
Hill Top Mount HG1 .... 219 D6
Hill Top Rd
Harrogate HG1 .... 219 D6
4 Wistow YO8 .... 197 D6
Hill Top Rise HG1 .... 219 E6
Hill Top View HG3 .... 159 F8
Hill Top Wlk HG1 .... 219 D6
Hill View
Langthorpe YO51 .... 141 A6
Stillington YO61 .... 144 C6
York YO31 .... 229 C7
Hillway 7 TS17 .... 6 A5
HILTON 6 C2
Hilton Cl DL6 .... 210 E8
Hilton Gn DL6 .... 210 D8
Hilton Grange DL6 .... 210 E8
Hilton La 7 HG5 .... 221 A6
Hilton Rd TS9 .... 6 F1
Hilton Sq DL6 .... 210 E8
Hincks Hall La HG3 .... 139 C3
HINDERWELL 11 F7
Hinderwell Ind Pk TS13 .... 11 F7

Hinderwell La
Hinderwell TS13 11 E8
Staithes TS13 13 K1
Hinderwell Pl YO12 212 E2
Hinderwell Prim Sch YO12 212 D2
Hinderwell Rd YO12 212 E1
Hindle Dr 39 YO14 101 B3
Hinsley La DN14 204 C2
Hinton Ave 1 YO24 230 C8
Hinton Cl 9 WF8 201 C2
Hinton La WF11 201 D3
HIPSWELL 209 F1
Hipswell CE Prim Sch DL9 209 F1
Hipswell Rd DL9 209 E1
Hipswell Road W DL9 209 C1
Hird Ave 22 DL8 63 A2
Hird Rd TS15 5 D2
Hirds Yd 2 BD23 216 F3
HIRST COURTNEY 203 F3
Hirst Courtney & Temple Hirst Prim Sch YO8 203 E3
Hirstead Gdns YO12 212 B8
Hirstead Rd YO12 212 B8
Hirst La HG3 160 E5
Hirst Rd DN14 204 A3
Hirst St WF10 200 C8
Hobart Rd WF10 201 B5
Hobb Nook La LS21 176 D4
Hobbs Cl DL9 209 C2
Hob Cote La BD22 187 F1
Hobgate YO24 227 D3
Hob Moor Dr YO24 227 E2
Hob Moor Oaks Sch YO26 227 D2
Hob Moor Prim Sch YO24 227 E2
Hobmoor Terr YO24 227 F1
Hobson Cl YO23 230 B1
Hoctun Cl WF10 200 F3
Hodge La WF8 206 B3
Hodgson Fold LS29 174 E5
Hodgson Hill YO13 54 B4
Hodgson La YO26 182 F8
Hodgson's La LS25 196 A5
Hogg La YO17 148 E6
Holbeck Ave
Middlesbrough TS5 6 E6
Scarborough YO11 213 B2
Holbeck Cl YO11 213 B2
Holbeck Hill YO11 213 B1
Holbeck Rd YO11 213 A2
Holbeck's La YO26 141 F3
Holburns Croft 3 YO10 229 B1
Holden Gdns YO8 197 D2
Holderness Dr
7 Darlington DL2 3 A7
4 Faverdale DL2 3 B7
HOLE BOTTOM 135 A3
Hole House La BB7 152 B2
Hole La BD20 174 A2
Holes La WF11 201 E2
HOLGATE 227 F3
Holgate DL6 45 E8
Holgate Bank HG5 163 A8
Holgate Bridge Gdn 7 YO24 228 A3
Holgate Cl YO17 215 C5
Holgate La LS23 188 E8
Holgate Lodge Dr YO26 227 E4
Holgate Rd YO24 233 A1
Holl Gate DL8 59 E3
Hollicarrs Cl YO19 192 A2
Hollies The
Barlby with Osgodby YO8 198 C4
Stockton on the Forest YO19 167 D3
Hollin Gate LS21 176 E1
Hollings The LS26 200 A6
Hollington St 9 BB8 186 A3
Hollingwood Gate 31 LS29 175 C2
Hollingwood Pk 37 LS29 175 C2
Hollingwood Rise 32 LS29 175 C2
Hollingworth Cl BD23 217 B3
Hollin Hall Dr LS29 175 C2
Hollinhurst Brow LA2 128 F2
Hollin La LA2 129 F6
Hollins DL8 60 B3
Hollins Beck Cl LS25 200 D8
Hollins Cl HG3 161 A5
Hollins Cres HG1 219 C4
Hollins Gr WF10 200 C7
Hollins Hall HG3 161 A4
Hollins La
Firby DL8 63 B1
Hampsthwaite HG3 160 F5
Melmerby HG4 114 B8
Middleton Quernhow HG4 88 C1
Rosedale East Side YO18 49 D4
Hollins Mews HG1 219 C4
Hollins Rd
10 Barnoldswick BB18 171 D1
Harrogate HG1 219 C4
HOLLINTHORPE 194 A2
Hollin Top La YO21 29 C7
Hollis Cres YO32 167 B6
Hollow Gill Brow BD24 153 C5
Hollow Moor La DL8 62 E7
Holly Bank Gr 3 YO24 227 F2
Hollybank La HG3 161 B6
Holly Bank Rd YO24 227 F2
Hollybush Ave TS17 6 B5
Hollybush Cl DN14 207 A7
Hollybush Gn LS22 188 B8
Holly Cl
Acaster Malbis YO23 191 C8
Firth Moor DL1 3 F4
Full Sutton YO41 169 A2
Thirsk YO7 211 B2
Wrelton YO18 71 C1
Holly Ct 11 HG5 221 B6
Holly Garth 1 YO61 115 F1
Holly Garth Cl TS9 7 F1
Hollygarth La DN14 202 D4
Holly Gr
Selby YO8 232 B3
8 Thorpe Willoughby YO8 197 B2
HOLLY HILL 209 B5
Holly Hill DL10 209 C5
Holly Hill Cl TS7 7 D7
Hollyhocks La LS24 195 F7
Hollyhurst Ave 1 TS4 6 F8
Hollyhurst Rd DL3 3 C6
Holly Pk LS17 178 B3
Holly Rd
10 Bedale DL8 63 B3
Boston Spa LS23 188 D8
Hollyrood Rd YO30 224 E3
Holly Terr YO10 228 D1
Holly Tree Croft 2 YO19 184 F7
Holly Tree Ct
5 Hambleton YO8 196 F1
2 Whitby YO21 208 B6
Holly Tree Garth YO32 167 E3
Holly Tree La
Dunnington YO19 184 F7
Haxby YO32 225 D8
Hollytree Way YO8 197 D1
Hollywalk Ave TS6 7 E8
Holly Wlk YO12 212 D7
Hollywood YO8 232 B7
HOLME 88 D5
Holmebeck La HG4 88 B1
Holme Cl
Earby BB18 186 A8
23 Sutton BD20 187 E7
Holme Cres BB8 186 A2
Holme Croft 1 BD23 134 D2
Holme Farm La LS23 188 A5
Holmefield Cl 3 YO8 232 A1
Holmefield Cres HG4 214 C3
Holmefield Ct 2 YO8 232 A1
Holmefield La YO10 229 A1
Holmefield Rd
Glusburn BD20 187 E7
Ripon HG4 214 C3
Holmefields Rd TS6 7 E8
HOLME GREEN 190 F4
Holme Green Rd YO23 190 F4
Holmehead BD24 131 D4
Holme Hill 2 YO11 100 A6
Holme Hill La YO10 184 C4
Holme Ings LS29 175 B4
Holme La
Glusburn BD20 187 E7
Halton East BD23 174 B8
Newbiggin DL8 58 E1
Rudby TS9 25 E7
Selby YO8 232 D6
Holmemead TS9 26 E5
Holme Pk 3 LA2 129 A7
Holmes Ave YO8 232 C6
Holmes Cres YO60 146 E6
Holmes Dr 2 YO19 192 A1
Holmes Ind Est YO8 232 D6
Holme St 12 BB8 186 A3
Holme The TS9 26 E4
Holme View LS29 218 A4
Holmfield HG4 112 D7
Holmfield Cl WF8 201 C2
Holmfield Ct WF8 201 D2
Holmfield La WF8 201 C2
Holm Hill YO13 54 C2
Holm La LA2 130 E6
Holmstead Ave YO21 208 A5
Holmtree La HG4 113 B8
Holmwood Ave TS5 6 F8
Holmwood Sch TS4 7 A7
Holnicote Cl 3 TS17 6 A3
Holray Pk DN14 204 C2
Holroyd Ave YO31 229 A5
HOLTBY 167 F1
Holtby Gr YO12 212 D5
Holtby La
Holtby YO19 167 D1
Stockton on the Forest YO19 226 F2
Holy Family RC High Sch The DN14 204 C3
Holy Family RC Prim Sch 1 DL3 3 B6
Holy Family & St Michaels RC Prim Sch WF8 201 D1
Holyrood Ave DL3 3 A5
Holyrood Cl TS17 6 B8
Holy Rood La LS25 201 C8
Holystone Dr TS17 6 A4
Holy Trinity CE Infant Sch HG4 214 B6
Holy Trinity Junior Sch HG4 214 B5
Holywell Ave WF10 201 A3
Holywell Gn TS16 5 E5
Holywell Halt BD23 174 A8
Holywell La
Castleford WF10 201 A3
North Cowton DL7 22 C2
Home Farm Cl
Hensall DN14 203 D2
Wray-with-Botton LA2 128 A6
Homefield Cl YO23 230 A2
Homelea YO32 167 A6
Home Office Emergency Planning Coll YO61 143 D6
Homestead Cl
Eggborough DN14 203 A2
2 York YO32 225 F1
Homestead Garth 1 TS17 6 D6
Homestead Rd HG1 219 E2
Honey Pot 5 YO8 199 D7
Honeypot La
Darlington DL3 3 C7
8 Faverdale DL2 3 B7
Honey Pot Rd 2 DL10 41 C6
Honeysuckle Cl
New Micklefield LS25 195 A3
Romanby DL7 210 C1
Selby YO8 232 C2
Honeysuckle Way 20 WF10 200 D3
Honister Gr TS5 6 D7
Honoldu Ct 29 TS17 5 F4
Hood La YO13 54 D2
Hoodstorth La HG3 158 F6
Hookstone Ave HG2 222 E7
Hookstone Chase HG2 220 D2
Hookstone Chase Prim Sch HG2 220 D2
Hookstone Cl HG2 220 C2
Hookstone Dr HG2 223 A8
Hookstone Garth HG3 159 E5
Hookstone Grange Ct 3 HG2 220 C2
Hookstone Grange Way 2 HG2 220 C2
Hookstone Oval 7 HG2 220 B1
Hookstone Pk HG2 220 D2
Hookstone Rd HG2 222 E7
Hookstone Way HG2 220 D2
Hookstone Wood Nature Reserve★ HG2 223 A3
Hookstone Wood Rd 9 HG2 220 B1
Hope St
30 Filey YO14 101 B3
Knaresborough HG5 221 B5
Scarborough YO12 213 A6
York YO10 233 C1
Hope Terr 7 YO21 208 D5
HOPETOWN 200 C2
Hopetown La DL3 3 C6
HOPGROVE 226 D2
Hopgrove Lane N YO32 226 C3
Hopgrove Lane S YO32 226 E3
Hopper Hill Rd YO11 99 F6
Hopper La LS21 159 C2
HOPPERTON 163 E3
Hopperton St HG5 163 E4
Hopps's Rd 6 BD20 187 E8
Horcum Ct 4 TS8 6 E5
Hornbeam HG2 223 A7
Hornbeam Cl YO30 225 B2
Hornbeam Cres HG2 222 F8
Hornbeam Park Ave HG2 222 F7
Hornbeam Park Oval HG2 222 F7
Hornbeam Park Rd HG2 222 F7
Hornbeam Park Sta HG2 222 F7
Hornbeam Pk HG2 222 F7
Hornbeam Pk HG2 223 A6
Hornbeam Square N HG2 223 A7
Hornbeam Square S HG2 223 A7
Hornbeam Square W HG2 222 F7
Hornblower Cl 5 HG4 113 D2
HORNBY
Bedale 62 B8
Croft-on-Tees 23 E4
Hornby Castle★ DL8 62 C8
Hornby Cl 1 DL2 3 E1
Hornby Rd
Appleton Wiske DL6 24 A3
Roeburndale LA2 128 A2
Wray-with-Botton LA2 128 A6
Horndale Rd 5 YO14 101 B4
Horner Ave YO61 144 A5
Horner Cl YO61 144 A5
Horne Rd DL9 40 F4
Horner St YO30 228 B7
Horners Terr 13 YO22 208 E6
Horn La BD20 174 B3
Hornsea Rd TS8 6 E5
Hornsey Garth 25 YO32 166 E5
Horse Course La YO17 122 E1
Horsefair 2 YO51 141 B5
Horsefair Sh Ctr LS23 180 C3
HORSEHOUSE 83 C4
Horseman Ave YO23 230 A3
Horseman Cl 2 YO23 230 A3
Horseman Dr YO23 230 A3
Horseman La YO23 230 A3
Horsemarket Rd YO17 215 B4
Horse Mill La HG3 139 D5
Horsemill Sq HG5 221 B5
Horse Rd 12 YO22 208 E6
Horseshoe Cave★ BD24 132 A3
Horseshoe Cl DL9 40 F4
Horseshoe The YO24 230 E7
Horseway Gn YO18 49 D4
Horsfield Way YO19 184 F7
Horsman Ave YO10 233 C1
HORTON 171 B5
HORTON IN RIBBLESDALE 105 C3
Horton-in-Ribblesdale Prim Sch BD24 105 D3
Horton-in-Ribbleside Sta BD24 105 C3
Hospital Fields Rd YO10 228 D1
Hospital La YO8 197 B4
Hospital Rd YO17 215 B4
Hospitium The★ YO1 233 A3
Hostess La YO18 72 E4
Hotham Ave YO26 227 B2
Hothams Ct YO1 233 C2
Hothfield Street Junior Sch 5 BD20 174 C1
Hothfield Terr BD23 216 F3
Houghton Ave WF11 201 D2
Houghton Banks 3 TS17 6 D6
HOULSYKE 29 F6
Houndgate DL1 3 C5
Houndsway 6 YO24 230 B8
HOVINGHAM 119 F6
Hovingham CE VC Prim Sch YO62 119 E6
Hovingham Dr
6 Guisborough TS14 8 F7
Scarborough YO12 212 B4
Hovingham Hall★ YO62 119 E6
Howard Ct DL10 41 F7
Howard Dr YO30 224 E2
Howard Link YO30 224 D2
Howard Rd
Catterick Garrison DL9 209 E1
Towthorpe YO32 167 B6
Howard St
3 Scarborough YO12 213 A7
York YO10 228 D2
Howden Dike TS15 5 E2
Howden La YO19 231 E1
Howden Rd
4 Barlby YO8 198 B4
Romanby DL7 210 B2
Silsden BD20 174 C1
Howdenshire Way DN14 205 F6
Howlands La HG4 140 E7
HOWE 88 E3
Howe Ave DL10 41 E4
Howe Bank YO21 29 B7
Howe End YO62 70 B1
Howe Field Rd YO26 142 A2
Howe Hill Bank TS8 7 B2
Howe Hill Cl YO26 227 E4
Howe Hill La DL10 41 C6
Howe Hill Rd YO26 227 E4
Howe La YO41 170 A5
Howe Rd
Malton YO17 122 A6
Norton YO17 215 E3
Howes Rd 8 YO14 127 A8
Howe St YO24 227 D3
Howgate DL8 57 F6
HOWGILL 157 E6
Howgill La
Barden BD23 157 E6
Rimington BB7 171 A1
Howhill Quarry Rd HG3 178 B7
Howhill Rd HG3 178 B8
How Hill Rd HG4 139 B6
Howker La YO61 116 F2
Howlbeck Rd TS14 8 E7
Howldale La
Appleton-le-Moors YO62 70 F4
3 Beadlam YO62 93 D7
Howl Gate YO41 185 E8
Howlgate La YO21 13 A1
HOWSHAM 146 F1
Howsham Hall★ YO60 146 F2
Howson La BD24 131 E4
How Stean Gorge★ HG3 110 B4
Hoxton Rd YO12 212 F6
Hoylake Rd TS4 6 F8
Hoylake Way TS16 5 E4
Hubback Sq 5 DL2 3 A7
HUBBERHOLME 81 C1
Hubert St 2 YO23 228 B1
HUBY
Harrogate 178 B2
Stillington 144 A4
Huby CE Prim Sch YO61 144 A4
Huby Ct
3 Guisborough TS14 8 F7
York YO10 228 E3
Huby Rd YO61 144 B3
Hudgin La
Lockton YO18 72 E4
Wykeham YO13 98 D4
Hudson Cl
Malton YO17 215 C6
Stamford Bridge YO41 168 D2
2 Tadcaster LS24 189 E6
13 Wetherby LS22 180 C3
Hudson Cres 2 YO30 228 A7
Hudson St
Whitby YO21 208 D7
6 York YO30 228 C7
Hudson View 1 LS24 189 E6
Hudson Way
Clifton Park YO26 227 C8
Tadcaster LS24 189 E6
HUDSWELL 40 A7
Hudswell La DL10 209 C5
Hugden Cl YO18 96 A6
Hugden Way YO17 215 F4
Huggate Dikes★ YO42 170 F2
Huggate Hill YO17 170 E7
Hugh Field La YO8 199 A8
Hugh Field North La YO8 193 A1
Hugh St WF10 200 E4
Hull Rd
Cliffe YO8 198 E2
Hemingbrough YO8 199 B1
Hull Rd *continued*
Osbaldwick YO10 229 D3
York YO10 229 B3
Humber Dr 5 YO32 167 B6
Humber Rd TS17 6 B7
HUMMERSKNOTT 3 A5
Hummersknott Ave DL3 3 A5
Hummersknott Sch & Language Coll DL3 3 A4
Humphrey Balk La YO7 114 D8
Humphrey Hill DL8 58 D1
Hundale Rd 5 TS15 25 C5
Hunday Field Rd YO51 141 E2
Hundens Day Hospl DL1 3 E5
Hundens La DL1 3 D6
Hungate
Bishop Monkton HG3 140 A5
Brompton YO13 98 C5
Pickering YO18 95 F6
York YO1 233 C2
Hungate Cl LS24 195 D8
Hungate Ct 11 YO14 126 F8
Hungate La YO14 126 F8
Hungate Prim Sch 23 LS25 195 F4
Hungate Rd LS25 195 F4
Hunger Hill LS29 218 C7
Hungerhill La YO62 93 F6
HUNMANBY 126 F8
Hunmanby Ind Est YO14 127 A1
Hunmanby Prim Sch YO14 126 F8
Hunmanby Rd
Burton Fleming YO25 126 E3
Reighton YO14 127 C6
Hunmanby St YO14 100 F2
Hunmanby Sta YO14 127 A7
HUNSINGORE 180 F8
Hunt Ct YO31 233 C3
Hunter Dr YO41 185 A2
Hunters Cl
Dunnington YO19 184 E7
19 Easingwold YO61 143 C8
10 Haxby YO32 225 C8
4 Hurworth-on-Tees DL2 3 D1
Osgodby YO11 100 B7
Hunters Croft BD23 156 F1
Hunters Gn
Eaglescliffe TS16 5 D5
Low Dinsdale DL2 4 C3
Hunters Ride DL6 24 B3
Hunters Row 6 YO51 141 B4
Hunter St 8 YO21 208 D7
Hunters Way
Norton YO17 215 D2
Selby YO8 232 B4
York YO24 230 F7
Hunters Wlk
Barlow YO8 204 D7
Kirk Deighton LS22 180 C4
Hunters Wood Way 21 YO19 184 F7
Hunt House Rd YO22 51 B6
HUNTINGTON 225 E3
Huntington Mews YO31 228 D7
Huntington Prim Sch YO32 225 F4
Huntington Rd YO31 233 C4
Huntington Sch YO32 225 E3
Huntington Stadium (York City Knights RLFC) The YO32 226 A2
HUNTON 61 E7
Hunton & Arrathorne Com Prim Sch DL8 61 F7
Hunton Rd DL9 40 E1
Huntriss Row YO11 213 A6
Huntsmans La YO41 168 C2
Huntsman's Wlk YO24 227 B1
Hunt St WF10 200 D4
Hurdle Cl YO17 215 E2
HURGILL 209 A7
Hurgill Rd DL10 209 A7
Hurn Rd YO61 144 A4
Hurns La YO30 224 A7
Hurrell La YO18 96 E5
Hurricane Cl LS25 196 B4
Hurricane Way YO30 224 E3
Hurrs Rd 3 BD23 217 B4
Hurstleigh Terr HG1 220 A3
Hurst's Yd YO1 233 C2
Hurworth Comp Sch DL2 22 D8
Hurworth House Sch DL2 3 E1
HURWORTH-ON-TEES 3 E1
HURWORTH PLACE 3 D1
Hurworth Prim Sch DL2 3 E1
Hurworth Rd
Hurworth DL2 3 F1
Hurworth-on-Tees DL2 22 D8
Neasham DL2 4 A1
Hussars Ct 6 YO12 75 F5
Husthwaite CE Prim Sch YO61 117 B5
Husthwaite Rd
Coxwold YO61 117 D7
Easingwold YO61 117 B2
Hutchinson Dr DL6 210 E3
Hutchinson St 1 YO8 232 B6
HUT GREEN 203 A2
Hutton Ave DL1 3 E7
Hutton Bank
3 Hutton Rudby TS15 25 D5
Ripon HG4 214 D7
HUTTON BONVILLE 43 C7
HUTTON BUSCEL 98 E7

Hutton Cl YO26 224 A2
HUTTON CONYERS 114 A4
Hutton Cross Rd YO13 98 E8
HUTTON GATE 8 D6
Hutton Gate HG2 222 D6
HUTTON HANG 61 D3
Hutton La
Guisborough TS14 8 E5
Hutton Conyers HG4 114 A4
Sharow HG4 214 E8
HUTTON-LE-HOLE 70 C5
HUTTON MULGRAVE 12 D1
Hutton Rae La YO7 116 D7
HUTTON RUDBY 25 C5
Hutton Rudby Prim Sch TS15 25 C5
HUTTONS AMBO 147 B6
HUTTONS SESSAY 116 D7
Hutton's Mon* DL11 39 C6
Hutton St YO26 182 A5
Hutton View Rd HG4 214 C7
HUTTON VILLAGE 8 E4
Hutton Village Rd TS14 8 D5
HUTTON WANDESLEY 182 A5
Hutts La HG4 112 C7
HW Baines Ind Est HG4 214 D4
Hyde Park Rd
Harrogate HG1 219 E3
Knaresborough HG5 221 B8
Hydro Cl LS29 218 F3
Hydro L Ctr The HG2 219 C5
Hydro Ret Pk 219 C5
Hyrst Gr YO31 228 E6

I

I'Anson Cl DL8 60 D6
I'Anson Rd DL10 209 D7
Ian St TS17 6 B8
Ibbetson Cl 16 HG4 86 C3
Iburndale La YO22 32 A6
ICKORNSHAW 187 A6
Iddison Dr DL8 63 A2
Ikin Way YO32 225 F6
ILKLEY 218 B4
Ilkley Gr TS14 8 E5
Ilkley Gram Sch LS29 218 C3
Ilkley Hall Mews 5 LS29 218 B3
Ilkley Hall Pk 4 LS29 218 B3
Ilkley Pool & Lido LS29 218 B5
Ilkley Rd
Addingham LS29 175 A4
Ilkley LS29 176 C1
Ilkley Sta LS29 218 B4
Ilkley Toy Mus* 9 LS29 218 B4
ILTON 85 E1
Ilton Bank HG4 85 E1
Ilton Garth YO30 225 A2
Imperial Ave TS17 6 B8
Ind Est The YO60 145 C4
Ingdale Howl YO62 92 C7
Ingdale La YO7 66 C3
Ing Dene Ave 16 BB8 186 A3
Ing Dene Cl BD23 155 E3
INGERTHORPE 139 C5
Ingfield Est BD24 131 D1
Ingfield La BD24 131 D2
Ingham Cl YO22 32 A6
Ingleborough Ave YO10 229 B4
Ingleborough Cave* LA2 104 D2
Ingleborough Dr 4 BB18 171 D1
Ingleborough National Nature Reserve* LA6 104 D8
Ingleborough Park Cl 3 LA6 103 D3
Ingleborough Park Dr 2 LA6 103 D3
INGLEBY ARNCLIFFE 45 B8
Ingleby Arncliffe CE Prim Sch DL6 45 A8
Ingleby Ave TS9 27 B6
INGLEBY BARWICK 6 B4
INGLEBY CROSS 45 A7
Ingleby Dr LS24 189 E6
INGLEBY GREENHOW 27 C5
Ingleby Greenhow CE Prim Sch TS9 27 C5
Ingleby Manor* TS9 27 C4
Ingleby Mill Prim Sch TS17 6 A3
Ingleby Rd
Great Broughton TS9 26 E5
Great & Little Broughton TS9 27 A5
Ingleby Way TS17 6 B5
Ingle Cl YO12 212 E1
Inglenook Cl 18 LS25 195 F2
Ingles The 10 LA6 103 D3
INGLETON 103 D3
Ingleton Dr 16 YO61 143 D8
Ingleton Ind Est LA6 103 D3
Ingleton Mid Sch LA6 103 D3
Ingleton Prim Sch LA6 103 D3
Ingleton Wlk 3 YO31 229 A5
Ingman Lodge Rd BD24 78 F1
INGMANTHORPE 180 E5
Ingramgate YO7 211 C3
Ingrish La YO23 182 C1
Ings Ave BD23 216 D3
Ings Cl
6 Pickering YO18 95 F6
5 Willerby YO12 99 D2
Ings Com Cty Sch BD23 216 D3
Ings Ct DN14 202 F4
Ings Dr
Low Bradley BD20 173 E3
Mickletown LS26 200 C6
Ings Field Rd YO26 142 A3
Ingsgarth YO18 95 F6
Ings La
Ainderby Quernhow YO7 88 D4
Beal DN14 202 D4
Bishop Monkton HG3 140 B5
Bishop Wilton YO42 169 D2
Bradleys Both BD20 173 E3
Brompton YO13 98 C4
Carlton DN14 204 E2
Cawood YO19 197 D8
Cononley BD20 173 D2
Cottingwith YO42 193 C5
Crakehall DL8 62 F5
Ebberston & Yedingham YO13 97 E4
Great Preston WF10 200 E6
Harome YO62 93 D4
Hensall DN14 203 D2
Husthwaite YO61 117 A6
Hutton Buscel YO13 99 A3
Kellington DN14 202 F4
21 Kirkbymoorside YO62 70 B1
Kirkbymoorside YO62 94 B7
Lastingham YO62 70 F5
Lillings Ambo YO32 145 C2
Nether Poppleton YO26 224 B1
Pickering YO18 95 E4
Riccall YO19 197 E8
Roundhill Village TS15 5 D2
Skipton BD23 216 D2
Snape with Thorp DL8 87 B7
Stillington YO61 144 A6
Thorganby YO19 193 B5
Thorp Arch LS23 189 A8
Tollerton YO61 143 B2
Welburn YO62 94 A5
Wheldrake YO19 193 B7
Wighill LS24 189 D8
4 Willerby YO12 99 D2
Wistow YO8 198 A6
Ings Mere Ct WF11 201 C6
Ings Rd
Cliffe YO8 198 D2
Dunsforths YO26 142 A3
Thorganby YO19 193 B4
Ulleskelf LS24 190 C3
West Ayton YO13 99 B6
Wilberfoss YO41 185 E6
Ings Terr YO22 31 C4
Ings View
2 Bedale DL8 63 B3
Castleford WF10 201 A4
Mickletown LS26 200 C6
Tollerton YO61 143 A2
York YO30 224 D2
Ingthorne La LS25 195 F1
Ingthorns La LS25 195 F1
Ingthorpe La
Martons Both BD23 171 E7
Monk Fryston LS25 196 A1
Inhams La YO26 141 F2
INHOLMES 189 C6
Inholmes La
Tadcaster LS24 189 D6
Walton LS23 181 B2
Inman Gr HG5 221 B8
Inman Terr YO26 227 D4
Inman Wlk HG5 221 B8
In Moor La HG3 109 F6
Innisfree Cl HG2 220 B1
Innovation Cl YO10 229 B2
Innovation Way YO10 229 B2
Institute St 4 BD20 187 E7
Intake Ave YO30 228 C8
Intakefield Rd YO8 199 D7
Intake La
Acaster Malbis YO23 191 C7
Beal WF11 202 D5
Dunnington YO19 184 F7
Grassington BD23 134 E3
Habton YO17 121 E7
Heck DN14 207 C8
Tollerton YO61 143 B4
West Haddlesey YO8 202 F6
Intake The
3 Kippax LS25 194 D1
Osgodby YO11 100 B7
Invicta Ct YO24 230 B8
IREBY 102 F6
Ireby Rd LA6 102 F3
Ireton St 3 YO12 212 E5
Iron Row LS29 176 C1
IRTON 99 D6
Irton Moor La YO12 212 A1
Irvine Way YO24 230 B7
Irwin Ave YO31 228 E6
Isabella Rd LS25 194 D5
Island Heritage* HG4 111 B8
Islebeck La YO7 115 F8
IVELET 36 D5
Iver Cl YO26 227 C5
Ivy Bank Ct 4 YO13 75 D5
Ivy Cl
Follifoot HG3 223 F4
Marton YO51 141 D1
Ivy Cotts DL7 210 D4
Ivy Cres DL8 62 B4
Ivy Ct LS29 218 B3
Ivy Dene Cl 26 BD24 131 D2
Ivy House Cl 6 YO11 100 B6
Ivy House Gdns BD23 155 D1
Ivy La LS23 188 E8
Ivy Pl
22 Cross Hills BD20 187 E8
York YO32 225 D3
Ivy Yd 16 YO22 208 E6

J

Jack Field La BD20 187 D6
Jack Hill La LS21 176 F6
Jack Hole YO61 142 F4
Jack La
Crayke YO61 118 A1
Stillington YO61 144 C7
Wigglesworth BD23 153 C4
Jackson Cl YO11 100 B6
Jackson Dr TS9 26 C8
Jackson La YO41 185 E4
Jackson's La
Bradleys Both BD20 173 F3
Eastfield YO11 100 A8
Kirk Smeaton WF8 206 A4
Scarborough YO11 213 A1
Jackson St
24 Glusburn BD20 187 E7
York YO31 233 C4
Jackson's Wlk YO23 182 D3
Jacobi Cl YO30 228 A7
Jacques Gr BD20 174 C1
Jaffa Rd DL9 209 E2
Jagger La DL10 20 E6
Jagoe Rd 8 BB18 172 A1
James Backhouse Pl YO24 227 E3
James Cl LS25 194 D4
James Cook Univ Hospl The TS4 7 B8
James Ct DL10 209 F7
James La DL10 41 A2
James Nicolson Link YO30 225 A2
Jameson Cres YO12 212 D5
James Pl 2 YO12 213 A6
James St
Castleford WF10 200 E5
20 Earby BB18 172 A1
10 Glusburn BD20 187 E8
Harrogate HG1 219 D2
Scarborough YO12 213 A6
Selby YO8 232 C5
York YO10 228 E4
Jamesville Way YO7 115 B6
James Way YO10 229 A1
Jamieson Terr YO23 228 B1
Janesway LS25 194 C1
Janet's Foss* BD23 133 B2
Jasmine Cl
5 Snaith DN14 204 C1
York YO32 225 D2
Jasmine Fields 1 TS15 24 F8
Jasmine Garth 6 YO41 185 C2
Jasmine Gdns 13 WF10 200 D3
Jasper La HG3 179 A3
Jay Ave TS17 6 B4
Jaywick Cl YO32 167 B8
Jedburgh Dr DL3 2 F7
Jedwell Cl YO32 225 D5
Jeffry Bog Nature Reserve* YO60 147 C5
Jenkins Fold LA6 103 D3
Jennifer Gr 4 YO24 227 F2
JENNYFIELD 219 A5
Jenny Field Dr HG3 219 B4
Jenny Frisk Rd TS12 9 E6
Jenny Gill Cres BD23 217 B3
Jenny La DN14 207 B5
Jerry Carr Bank YO62 92 B1
Jerry Croft 2 BD23 217 A4
Jerry La BD20 174 F1
Jersey Ct YO12 99 C7
Jervaulx Abbey* HG4 85 D8
Jervaulx Dr HG5 221 D4
Jervaulx Rd DL7 64 A6
Jervis Ct YO41 185 C1
Jervis Rd YO24 230 E8
Jesmond Ct YO17 215 E3
Jesmond Gr 5 TS18 5 E8
Jesmond Rd
Darlington DL1 3 F7
Harrogate HG1 220 A3
Jessamine Pl 1 BD20 187 F7
Jewbury YO31 233 C3
Jewitt La LS22 188 B8
Jin Whin Ct WF10 200 D4
Jin-Whin Hill WF10 200 C4
Jobbing Cross YO61 116 C3
Jockey La
Huntington YO32 225 F2
5 Knaresborough HG5 221 A6
Joffre Ave WF10 200 F3
John Breckon Rd YO21 28 D5
John Dixon La DL1 3 D5
John Fowler Way 14 DL2 3 A7
John of Gaunt's Castle* HG3 160 B1
John Smiths Brewery* LS24 189 E6
Johnson Cl
Brompton on Swale DL10 41 C7
1 Thirsk YO7 211 C3
Johnson St YO8 232 B6
Johnson Way YO7 211 D2
John St
Darlington DL1 3 D6
11 Earby BB18 172 A1
35 Filey YO14 101 B3
Great Ayton TS9 8 A2
11 Harrogate HG1 219 D2
John St *continued*
Selby YO8 232 D6
Whitby YO21 208 D7
York YO31 228 E6
Jolby La
Cleasby DL10 2 E1
Croft-on-Tees DL2 22 B8
Newton Morrell DL2 21 F8
Jonah's La HG3 160 B1
Jonathan Garth 17 LS29 174 F4
Jorvik Cl YO26 227 C5
JORVIK Viking Ctr* YO1 233 C2
Joseph Rowntree Sch The YO32 225 E5
Jowett's La BD20 174 B4
Jowland Winn La YO8 204 A4
Jubber Gate YO1 233 B2
Jubilee Bank TS7 7 C8
Jubilee Cave* BD24 131 F4
Jubilee Cl BD23 216 D3
Jubilee Croft 1 BD23 153 F5
Jubilee Ct
Richmond DL10 209 E8
6 Tollerton YO61 143 B3
Wigginton YO32 225 D8
Jubilee Gdns DL6 210 F3
Jubilee Rd
Norton YO17 215 E3
Wistow YO8 197 D6
Jubilee Terr YO26 227 F5
Judson Cl HG4 214 C4
Julia Ave YO32 226 B2
JUNCTION 187 F8
Junction 32 Sh Village* WF10 200 F3
Junction Farm Prim Sch TS16 5 D5
Jungle (Castleford Tigers RFC) The WF10 200 F5
Juniper Cl YO32 225 D3
Juniper Dr YO8 232 D2
Juniper Gr TS21 5 C8
Juniper Way 28 HG3 161 B3
Jura Dr DL1 3 E8
Jute Rd YO26 227 B5
Jutland Rd DL9 209 C2

K

Kader Ave TS5 6 D7
Kader Prim Sch TS5 6 E7
Kail La BD23 156 F8
Kangel Cl HG4 214 E3
Kareen Ave 3 YO12 99 E6
Kathryn Ave YO32 226 A2
Kaye Dr YO8 198 B4
Kay House La TS15 24 D5
Kays Bank YO61 117 C5
Kearby Cliff LS22 179 B1
Kearsley Cl TS16 5 E7
Kearsley Rd HG4 214 B7
Kearton DL11 37 D6
KEASDEN 130 A5
Keasden Rd LA2 130 A3
Keats Cl
4 Pontefract WF8 201 B1
York YO30 227 F8
Keats Wlk HG1 219 E7
Keble Cl YO23 231 B3
Keble Dr YO23 231 A2
Keble Garth LS25 194 E1
Keble Gdns YO23 231 B2
Keble Park Cres YO23 231 A2
Keble Park N YO23 231 A3
Keble Park S YO23 231 A2
Keeper's Cl YO61 118 A1
Keepers Gate 18 YO18 95 F6
Keeper's Hill YO25 150 A1
Keepers Way 11 YO19 184 F7
Keighley Rd
Bradleys Both BD23 173 D3
1 Colne BB8 186 A3
Cowling BD22 187 B6
2 Glusburn BD20 187 F7
Ilkley LS29 218 A2
Laneshaw Bridge BB8 186 D3
Skipton BD23 216 F2
Trawden Forest BB8 186 B3
Keilder Rise TS8 6 F5
Keith Ave YO32 226 A4
Keith Rd TS4 6 F8
KELBROOK 186 A8
Kelbrook Prim Sch BB18 186 A7
Kelbrook Rd BB18 171 D1
Kelcbar Cl LS24 189 D6
Kelcbar Hill LS24 189 D6
Kelcbar Way LS24 189 D6
Kelcow Caves* BD24 131 D3
KELD 35 E8
Keldale 4 YO32 166 F5
Keldale Gdns HG4 214 F6
Keld Cl
Melmerby HG4 114 B6
Pickering YO18 95 E7
Scalby YO12 212 B8
Keldgate Rd YO18 72 A3
Keldhead YO18 95 E8
Keld Head Orch 1 YO62 70 B1
Keld Head Rd YO62 70 A1
Keldheads La DL8 59 F5
KELDHOLME 70 D1
KELD HOUSES 136 C2
Keld La
Hutton-le-Hole YO62 70 C5
Newton YO18 72 A5
Thorpe Bassett YO17 123 A3
Keld Runnels Rd YO13 75 A4
KELFIELD 191 D1
Kelfield Rd 9 YO19 197 F8
Kellaw Rd DL1 3 F5
Kell Bank HG4 85 E3
Kell Bank CE Prim Sch HG4 85 E3
Kell Beck 1 LS21 176 F1
KELLINGLEY 202 C2
KELLINGTON 202 F4
Kellington Ct 9 DN14 202 F2
Kellington La DN14 202 F2
Kellington Prim Sch DN14 202 F3
Kell Syke La BD23 155 A6
Kelvin Terr DL7 210 D4
Kemmel Cl DL9 40 E2
Kempton Cl 2 YO24 227 D1
Kempton Ct 15 DL1 3 F6
Kendal Cl
6 Dunnington YO19 184 F7
Hellifield BD23 154 B3
Kendal Dr WF10 201 B4
Kendal Gdns YO26 181 D7
Kendal La YO26 181 D7
Kendalmans 4 BD24 131 D2
Kendal Rd
Harrogate HG1 220 B3
Long Preston BD23 154 A3
Kendrew Cl
11 Bedale DL8 63 A2
3 York YO32 225 F3
Kenilworth Ave HG2 222 D7
Kenilworth Dr 3 BB18 172 A1
Kenlay Cl YO32 225 D4
Kennedy Dr 32 YO32 166 E5
Kennels La LS14 188 A4
Kenneth Campbell Rd HG1 219 E2
Kennet La LS25 194 D3
Kennion Ct 2 HG2 220 B3
Kennion Rd HG2 220 B3
KENNYTHORPE 147 F5
Kenrick Pl 5 YO26 227 B5
Kensal Rise YO10 228 D2
Kensington Ave
Eston & South Bank TS6 7 E8
Thorner LS14 188 A3
Kensington Ct 1 YO24 230 F8
Kensington Gdns DL1 3 E5
Kensington Rd YO30 224 D2
Kensington Sq 10 HG2 219 C2
Kensington St YO23 228 B1
Kent Ave HG1 219 B3
Kent Cl HG4 214 A2
Kent Ct 7 DL9 209 C1
Kent Dr HG1 219 B3
Kentmere Dr YO30 224 F1
Kenton Cl 4 TS18 5 E8
Kent Rd
Guisborough TS14 8 E5
Harrogate HG1 219 B3
Selby YO8 232 A6
Kent Rise HG1 219 A2
Kent Road N HG1 219 B3
Kent St YO10 233 C1
KEPWICK 66 C6
Kerrside YO30 227 E8
Kershaw Ave WF10 201 A4
Kerver La YO19 184 F7
Kesteven Rd TS4 7 A7
Kestrel Dr 7 DL9 40 F2
Kestrel Mews 21 WF6 200 A1
Kestrel View 2 YO12 99 E6
Kestrel Wood Way YO31 225 F2
Keswick Dr WF10 201 C5
Keswick Gr
4 Darlington DL1 3 D4
Middlesbrough TS5 6 D7
Keswick Way 5 YO32 225 F5
Kettle End DL10 21 C7
KETTLENESS 12 D6
Kettlesbeck Brow LA2 130 C5
KETTLESING 160 C3
KETTLESING BOTTOM 160 D4
Kettlesing Felliscliffe Prim Sch HG3 160 C4
Kettle Spring La HG3 139 B1
Kettlestring La YO30 225 A3
KETTLEWELL 108 B3
Kettlewell La DL8 57 A5
Kettlewell Prim Sch BD23 108 A3
Kew at Castle Howard* YO60 146 C8
KEXBY 185 C6
Kexby Ave YO10 228 F3
Kexby Stray YO41 185 A5
Kex Gill Rd HG3 158 F2
KEY GREEN 31 A3
Key La YO61 118 A1
Keys Beck Rd YO18 71 F8
Keystone Ave 3 WF10 200 F3
Key Way YO19 231 F5
Khyber Pass YO21 208 D7
Kiddal La LS15 188 C2
Kidstones Bank DL8 81 E3
Kielder Dr DL1 3 E7
Kielder Oval HG2 220 D2
KILBURN 91 B2
Kilburn Rd YO10 228 D2
KILDALE 27 E8
Kildale Sta YO21 27 E8
Kildare Garth 5 YO62 70 C1
KILDWICK 187 F8
Kildwick CE Prim Sch BD20 187 F8
Kilgram La HG4 85 E8

Kilham Rd YO25 151 D5
KILLERBY 100 C5
Killerby Dr 2 DL10 41 E4
Killerby La YO11 100 C5
KILLINGHALL 161 C5
Killinghall CE Prim Sch HG3 161 C5
Killin Rd DL1 3 E7
Kilmarnock Rd DL1 3 E8
Kiln Dr BD23 134 B3
Kilners Croft 11 LS29 174 F4
Kiln Hill La
- Lawkland LA2 131 A6
- Silsden BD20 174 A3
Kiln La LA2 128 A6
KILNSEY 134 B6
Kilnsey Fold BD20 174 A1
Kilnsey Pk* BD23 134 B6
Kilnwick Ct DL7 210 D3
Kilton Ct DL11 2 A2
Kilton La TS12 9 F7
KILTON THORPE 10 B8
Kilton Thorpe La TS12 10 B8
Kimberley St LS29 218 C5
Kimberlows Wood Hill 3 YO10 229 C3
Kinbrace Dr YO24 230 B7
King Edward Ave WF10 200 C7
King Edward Rd HG4 214 C3
King Edward's Dr HG1 219 D5
King Edward St
- 27 Glusburn BD20 187 E7
- Normanton South WF6 200 A1
Kingfisher Cl 7 YO12 99 F6
Kingfisher Ct
- 22 Castleford WF10 200 A1
- 3 Scotton DL9 40 F2
Kingfisher Dr
- 3 Bedale DL8 63 B3
- Guisborough TS14 8 D6
- 14 Pickering YO18 95 F6
- Whitby YO22 208 E3
Kingfisher La LS25 194 F8
Kingfisher Reach
- 17 Boroughbridge YO51 141 B5
- 5 Collingham LS22 180 A1
King Garth 3 DL8 58 F1
King George Rd 1 HG4 214 C3
King Hill YO14 101 A2
King James Rd HG5 221 B5
King James's Sch HG5 221 B5
King Rudding Cl 6 YO19 198 A8
King Rudding La YO19 198 B8
Kings Acad The TS8 7 A5
Kings Acre YO31 229 B6
Kings Arms Ct YO7 211 B3
Kings Ave 2 LS29 218 A4
Kings Cl
- 5 Barlby YO8 198 B5
- 19 Ilkley LS29 175 C2
- 15 Pateley Bridge HG3 137 B4
King's Cl 9 DL10 41 D5
Kingsclere YO32 225 F6
Kings Ct YO1 233 B2
King's Gate LA2 130 D3
King's Gdns YO7 211 B1
Kings Keld Bank DL8 86 F8
Kings La YO13 97 D5
Kingsland Terr 11 YO26 227 F5
Kings Lea YO8 199 A8
Kingsley Ave WF11 201 D3
Kingsley Cl HG1 220 C3
Kingsley Croft 7 BD20 187 F8
Kingsley Dr
- Castleford WF10 201 B3
- Harrogate HG1 220 A4
- 2 Middleham DL8 60 E2
Kingsley Park Mews 1 HG1 220 C3
Kingsley Park Rd HG1 220 C3
Kingsley Rd
- Harrogate HG1 220 B5
- Trawden Forest BB8 186 B3
Kings Manor Sch TS5 6 E7
Kings Mdws YO7 89 E3
Kings Mead HG4 214 B7
Kings Mill La 8 BD24 131 D2
Kings Moor Rd YO32 167 D2
Kings Rd
- Ilkley LS29 218 A4
- Knaresborough HG5 221 C6
King's Rd 6 HG1 219 D3
King's Sq YO1 233 C2
King's St 7 BD23 217 B4
King's Staith YO1 233 B2
King St
- Castleford WF10 200 F3
- 6 Cawood YO8 197 B8
- 7 High Bentham LA2 129 A8
- Muston YO14 100 F2
- Normanton South WF6 200 A1
- Pateley Bridge HG3 137 B4
- Richmond DL10 209 C6
- Ripon HG4 214 C4
- Scarborough YO11 213 A6
- 3 Silsden BD20 174 C1
- York YO1 233 B2
Kingsthorpe YO24 227 D2
Kingsthorpe Pk 11 YO8 197 D6
Kingston Ave HG4 214 C3
Kingston Cres YO8 196 E2
Kingston Dr
- 24 Castleford WF6 200 B1
- Hambleton YO8 196 E1
- 16 Normanton WF6 200 B1
- Norton YO17 215 E2
Kingston Garth 2 YO22 33 C3
Kingston Gr 5 YO12 212 B7
Kingstonia Gdns 3 HG4 214 C3
Kingstonia Pl HG4 214 C2
Kingsway
- Garforth LS25 194 B3
- Harrogate HG1 219 E3
- Pontefract WF8 201 B2
- Scalby YO12 212 C8
- Skipton BD23 217 B5
- 6 Stamford Bridge YO41 168 D2
- Weeton LS17 178 B2
Kingsway Dr
- Harrogate HG1 219 E2
- 4 Ilkley LS29 218 A4
Kingsway Garth LS25 194 B3
Kingsway N YO30 228 B7
Kingsway W YO24 227 D1
Kingswood Gr YO24 227 D3
Kinloss Cl TS17 6 C7
Kinsey Cave* BD24 131 C4
Kintyre Dr TS17 6 B6
KIPLIN 42 B4
Kiplin Dr 14 DN6 206 E2
Kipling Dr 35 DL9 41 A5
Kipling Gr WF8 201 B2
Kiplin Hall* DL10 42 B4
KIPPAX 194 E1
Kippax Ash Tree Prim Sch LS25 194 D1
Kippax Greenfield Prim Sch LS25 194 D1
Kippax L Ctr LS25 200 D8
Kippax North Prim Sch LS25 194 C2
KIRBY GRINDALYTHE 149 E6
KIRBY HILL
- Boroughbridge 141 B7
- Moulton 20 A5
Kirby Hill CE Prim Sch YO51 141 B7
KIRBY KNOWLE 66 C2
Kirby La
- Ebberston & Yedingham YO17 97 E1
- Sledmere YO25 150 A4
KIRBY MISPERTON 95 D2
Kirby Misperton La YO17 121 C7
Kirby Misperton Rd YO17 95 F2
KIRBY SIGSTON 44 D1
KIRBY UNDERDALE 170 A5
KIRBY WISKE 88 F8
Kir Cres YO24 227 C3
Kirk Balk YO17 169 E8
Kirk Balk La YO60 168 B7
Kirk Bank
- Conistone with Kilnsey BD23 134 B4
- Kirkby Malzeard HG4 112 A5
Kirkbank La CA17 14 A8
KIRKBRIDGE 62 F5
KIRKBY 26 D5
Kirkby Ave
- Ripon HG4 214 A6
- Selby YO8 232 B7
Kirkby Brow
- Kirkby Malham BD23 154 F8
- Malham BD23 132 F1
Kirkby Cl HG4 214 A6
Kirkby Dr HG4 214 A6
KIRKBY FLEETHAM 42 D1
Kirkby Fleetham CE Prim Sch DL7 42 C1
Kirkby & Great Broughton CE Prim Sch TS9 26 E5
Kirkby La
- Gillamoor YO62 70 A3
- Kearby with Netherby HG3 179 B2
- Kirkby Fleetham with Fencote DL7 42 C2
- Kirkby TS9 26 D6
- Sicklinghall LS22 179 D3
KIRKBY MALHAM 154 F8
Kirkby Malham Prim Sch BD23 154 F8
KIRKBY MALZEARD 112 D5
Kirkby Malzeard CE Prim Sch HG4 112 D5
KIRKBY MILLS 94 C8
Kirkby Mills Ind Est YO62 94 C8
KIRKBYMOORSIDE 70 B1
Kirkbymoorside Prim Sch YO62 70 A1
KIRKBY OVERBLOW 179 A4
Kirkby Rd
- North Stainley with Sleningford HG4 113 C4
- Ripon HG4 214 A6
- Selby YO8 232 B7
KIRKBY WHARFE 190 A3
Kirkcaldy Fold WF6 200 B1
Kirkcroft YO32 225 C8
Kirkdale La YO62 93 F8
Kirkdale Rd YO10 229 D4
Kirkdale Way HG2 219 C1
KIRK DEIGHTON 180 B5
Kirk Fenton Prim Sch LS24 196 B8
Kirkfield Ave LS14 188 A3
Kirkfield Cres LS14 188 A3
Kirkfield La LS14 188 A3
Kirkfield Rd DL3 3 D8
Kirkgate
- Knaresborough HG5 221 A6
- 7 Middleham DL8 60 E2
- 12 Ripon HG4 214 C5
- Settle BD24 131 D2
- Sherburn in Elmet LS25 195 E4
Kirkgate *continued*
- Silsden BD20 174 C1
- Thirsk YO7 211 B3
Kirk Gate
- Brompton YO13 98 C7
- Silpho YO13 74 E6
Kirkgate La YO62 70 F4
KIRKHAM 147 A4
Kirkham Ave 1 YO31 228 E8
Kirkham Bridge* YO60 146 F4
Kirkham Cl 6 YO21 208 C6
Kirkham Ct 5 HG5 221 C4
Kirkham Gr HG1 219 F6
KIRK HAMMERTON 164 C2
Kirk Hammerton CE Prim Sch YO26 164 C2
Kirk Hammerton La YO26 164 C3
Kirkham Pl HG1 219 F6
Kirkham Priory (rems of)* YO60 146 F4
Kirkham Rd
- Harrogate HG1 219 F6
- Middlesbrough TS7 7 D6
- Whitby YO21 208 C6
Kirkham View YO60 147 B4
Kirkhaw La WF11 201 D4
Kirk Hills LS14 188 A3
Kirk Ings La YO7 66 B7
Kirk La
- Embsay with Eastby BD23 217 E8
- Tockwith YO26 181 C7
Kirkland Cl YO8 232 D4
Kirklands YO32 167 B6
Kirklands La YO41 169 C2
Kirkleavington Hall Dr TS15 5 E1
KIRKLEVINGTON 24 F8
Kirklevington Prim Sch TS15 24 F8
KIRKLINGTON 88 A4
Kirk Rd
- Eaglescliffe TS15 5 F2
- Northallerton DL7 210 B3
KIRK SMEATON 206 B3
Kirk Smeaton CE Prim Sch WF8 206 B3
Kirkstall Dr BB18 171 E2
Kirkstone Dr YO31 229 A6
Kirkstone Rd HG1 220 B4
Kirk Syke La BD23 155 A5
Kirk View 1 YO26 227 C3
Kirkwell YO23 231 A4
Kitchen Dr YO8 232 D4
Kitchener Cl YO8 232 B5
Kitchener Rd
- Ripon HG4 113 D3
- Scotton DL9 40 E4
Kitchener St
- Selby YO8 232 B6
- York YO31 228 D7
Kitemere Pl 2 YO24 230 B8
Kit Kat Crescent (York City FC) YO31 228 B7
Kit La BD20 174 B3
Kitter La YO21 31 C8
Kitty Garth YO19 193 A7
Kitty Hill (Tumulus)* YO41 169 E3
Knapping Hill HG1 219 C5
KNAPTON 227 A5
Knapton Cl 1 YO32 167 B6
Knapton La YO26 227 B4
Knapton Wold Rd YO17 123 C5
KNARESBOROUGH 221 A6
Knaresborough Ave TS7 7 B5
Knaresborough Castle* HG5 221 A5
Knaresborough House & Gdns* HG5 221 A6
Knaresborough Mus* HG5 221 A5
Knaresborough Rd
- Bishop Monkton HG3 140 B4
- Follifoot HG3 223 F5
- Harrogate HG1 219 F2
- Little Ribston LS22 180 A8
- Ripon HG4 214 C3
Knaresborough Sta HG5 221 A6
Knaresborough Swimming Pool HG5 221 B5
KNAVESMIRE 231 A7
Knavesmire Cl YO62 93 C5
Knavesmire Cres YO23 228 B1
Knavesmire Prim Sch YO23 228 B1
Knavesmire Rd
- Nunthorpe YO23 231 B8
- York YO23 228 A1
KNAYTON 65 F2
Knayton CE Prim Sch YO7 65 E3
KNEDLINGTON 205 E6
Kneeton Cl DL10 21 C5
Kneeton La DL10 21 C5
Knightsway LS25 194 B3
Knipe Point Dr 8 YO11 100 B8
Knolls Cl 11 YO11 100 B7
Knolls La YO62 67 F5
Knoll The
- 3 Bramham LS23 188 E6
- York YO24 227 B2
Knot La BB7 171 A5
KNOTTINGLEY 201 F3
Knottingley High Sch WF11 202 A2
Knottingley Rd WF8 201 D1
Knottingley Sta WF11 201 F2
Knottingley Vale Junior & Infant Sch WF11 201 E2
Knott La
- Easingwold YO61 143 C8
- Steeton with Eastburn BD20 187 F7
Knotto Bottom Cl DL6 210 F3
Knotto Bottom Way DL6 210 F3
Knott Rd YO18 49 D5
Knotts La BD23 152 E1
Knowle La
- Ilton-cum-Pott HG4 85 D1
- Kirby Knowle YO7 66 C2
Knowles Cl 5 TS15 24 E8
KNOX 219 B7
Knox Ave HG1 219 C5
Knox Chase HG1 219 C6
Knox Cl HG1 219 D6
Knox Dr HG1 219 C6
Knox Gdns HG1 219 C6
Knox Gr HG1 219 C6
Knox La
- Harrogate HG1 219 D6
- Scarborough YO11 213 B1
Knox Mill Bank HG3 219 B7
Knox Mill Cl HG3 219 B7
Knox Mill La HG3 219 B7
Knox Pk HG3 219 B7
Knox Rd HG1 219 D6
Knox Rise HG1 219 C6
Knox Way HG1 219 C5
Kyle Cl 3 YO61 143 B3
Kyle Way YO26 227 B8
Kyme Castle* LS24 189 C7
Kyme St YO1 233 B1

L

La Bassee Rd DL9 209 D1
Laburnum Ave
- Fylingdales YO22 33 C4
- Thornaby TS17 6 B7
Laburnum Cl
- Rufforth YO23 182 C6
- 3 Thorpe Willoughby YO8 197 B1
Laburnum Ct
- Barlow YO8 204 D7
- 1 Castleford WF10 200 F3
Laburnum Dr HG3 140 A5
Laburnum Farm Cl YO26 182 C8
Laburnum Garth 6 YO31 228 F8
Laburnum Gr
- Harrogate HG1 219 E6
- Richmond DL10 209 D8
- Stillingfleet YO19 191 D4
- Whitby YO21 208 B6
Laburnum Rd TS7 7 D8
Lacey Ave YO12 99 D7
Lachman Rd BB8 186 A2
Lack La YO62 93 C2
Lackon Bank HG3 160 D6
Lacy Gr LS22 180 C2
Ladgate La TS5 6 F6
Lady Anne Ct YO1 233 B1
Lady Balk La WF8 201 B1
Ladycarr La YO61 143 E8
Lady East Hastings CE Prim Sch WF10 200 F7
Lady Edith's Ave YO12 212 B6
Lady Edith's Cres YO12 212 B6
Lady Edith's Dr YO12 212 A6
Lady Edith's Pk YO12 212 B7
Lady Elizabeth Hastings CE Prim Sch LS23 180 F1
Lady Grace's Ride YO12 212 A3
Lady Hamilton Gdns YO24 227 E2
Lady Hartley Ct BB8 186 B3
Lady Hullocks Ct 12 TS9 26 C7
Lady Kell Gdns YO32 225 E8
Lady La HG3 222 A5
Lady Lumleys Sch YO18 95 F7
Lady Mill Garth YO30 228 B8
Lady Peckitts Yd YO1 233 B2
Lady Rd YO30 228 B7
Ladysmith Ave YO21 208 C7
Ladysmith Mews 13 YO32 167 A7
Ladysmith Rd DL9 40 C4
Ladywell La YO51 141 C5
Ladywell Rd YO51 141 B5
Lady Wortley Pl YO23 231 B6
Lagentium Plaza
- 8 Castleford WF10 200 F3
- 9 Castleford WF10 200 F3
Lairs Cres YO13 98 A5
Lairs La YO13 98 A5
Lairum Rise LS23 188 E7
Laithe Cl 9 BD20 174 C1
Laith Staid La LS25 195 D4
Lakeber Ave LA2 129 A8
Lakeber Dr LA2 129 A8
Lakeber St 8 LA2 129 A8
Lakeside
- Acaster Malbis YO23 191 C7
- Darlington DL1 3 C4
- Hunmanby Sands YO14 101 B1
- Scarthingwell LS24 195 F7
Lakeside App LS24 195 E7
Lakeside Cl LS29 218 A5
Lakeside County Prim Sch YO30 224 F2
Lakeside Ct 26 WF6 200 B1
Lakeside Gr 1 YO32 167 B8
Lakeside Mdws 1 WF8 201 B2
Lakeside Way YO17 215 D2
Lake Terr HG4 112 D7
Lake View WF8 201 B2
Laking La YO25 126 A3
Lambert Ct YO1 233 B1
Lambert Meml Hospl YO7 211 B2
Lambert St
- 11 Skipton BD23 217 A3
- 2 Trawden BB8 186 B1
Lambeth St 8 BB8 186 A3
Lambfield Way 8 TS17 6 A6
Lamb Inn Rd 9 WF11 202 A2
Lamb La TS17 6 A4
Lambourne Dr TS7 7 C6
Lambs La 12 YO18 95 F7
Lamb's La TS9 27 B4
Lamel St YO10 229 A3
Lamplugh Cres YO23 231 B3
Lanacar La DL8 56 A4
Lancar Cl 18 YO32 166 D5
Lancaster Cl
- 9 Scalby YO13 75 D5
- Sherburn in Elmet LS25 196 B4
Lancaster Ct 24 YO51 141 B5
Lancaster Park Rd HG2 220 A3
Lancaster Rd
- Harrogate HG2 219 C1
- North Cowton DL7 22 C2
Lancaster St 6 YO11 213 A6
Lancaster Way
- Middlesbrough TS17 6 B6
- 17 Scalby YO13 75 D5
- York YO30 225 A1
Lancers Ct 4 YO12 75 F5
Landalewood Rd YO30 224 F2
Landau Cl YO30 227 F8
Landing La
- Asselby DN14 205 D6
- Barlby with Osgodby YO8 232 F8
- 22 Haxby YO32 166 F5
- Hemingbrough YO8 204 F8
- Riccall YO19 197 F8
- York YO26 227 E6
Landing Rd YO8 203 A7
Landings The 21 YO32 166 F5
Lands La HG5 220 E7
LANE END 171 C2
LANE ENDS 187 C6
Lane Ends La BD22 187 B7
Lane Foot Rd HG3 159 E8
Lanehead La DL11 18 H8
Lane House La BB8 186 B1
Lanehouse Rd TS17 6 B8
Lane House Rd BD22 187 A6
LANESHAW BRIDGE 186 C4
Laneshaw Bridge Prim Sch BB8 186 B3
Lane The
- Gate Helmsley YO41 168 B2
- Mickleby TS13 12 A4
Lang Ave YO10 229 A4
LANGBAR 175 B6
Langbar Rd LS29 218 A6
LANGBAURGH 7 F2
Langbaurgh Cl TS9 8 A2
Langbaurgh Rd TS15 25 C4
Langber End La LA6 103 D1
Langber La BD23 154 A8
Langborne Rd 19 YO21 208 D6
Langbourne Rd YO21 208 D6
Langburn La YO21 29 A7
Langburn's Bank YO21 29 A7
LANGCLIFFE 131 E3
Langcliffe & Attermire Nature Reserve* BD24 132 A3
Langcliffe Ave HG2 222 E8
Langcliffe Avenue E HG2 222 E8
Langcliffe Garth BD23 108 B3
Langcliffe Rd BD24 131 D3
Langdale TS14 8 D6
Langdale Ave
- 3 Pontefract WF6 200 A2
- York YO31 229 B6
Langdale Dr 2 WF6 200 A2
Langdale Gr YO8 232 B3
Langdale Mews 4 WF6 200 A2
Langdale Rd 3 YO12 212 F7
Langdale Terr YO21 208 C7
Langdon Way TS16 5 D5
Langer Hill La HG3 160 B5
Langford Cl 21 LS29 176 C1
Langford Ct 17 LS29 176 C1
Langford La LS29 176 C1
Langford Mews 19 LS29 176 C1
Langford Rd LS29 176 C1
Langford Ride 30 LS29 176 C1
Lang Gate YO13 74 E4
Langholm Cres DL3 3 C5
Langholme Dr YO26 227 C6
Langhorne Dr 2 DL11 38 B6
Lang Kirk Cl 2 BD20 173 F1
Langley Ave TS17 6 B8
Langley Ct 1 YO32 225 F6
Langley Dr YO17 215 E1
Langleys Rd 6 DN6 206 E1
Langold Dr 15 DN6 206 E2
Lang Rd
- Bishopthorpe YO23 230 F4
- York YO32 225 F6
Langrickgate La YO42 193 C5
Langsett Ave 7 YO14 101 A3
Langsett Gr YO30 224 F3
Langstrothdale Rd BD24 105 D7
LANGTHORNE 62 F6

LANGTHORPE 141 A6
LANGTHWAITE 17 E1
Langthwaite La DL8 59 C3
LANGTOFT 151 D5
Langtoft Prim Sch YO25 151 C5
LANGTON 147 F6
Langton Crossroads YO17 148 B6
Langton Ct 1 YO32 167 A6
Langton La YO17 148 C8
Langton Prim Sch YO17 147 F5
Langton Rd
Langton YO17 148 A7
Norton YO17 215 E2
Langwith Ave LS22 188 A8
Langwith Stray YO10 184 C2
Lansdowne Rd TS15 5 E3
Lansdowne Terr 5 YO10 228 E3
Lansdown Way 7 YO32 166 F5
Lanshaw Bank BD23 175 A7
Lanshaw Croft YO30 224 F1
Lantsbury Dr TS13 10 D8
Larch Ct DL1 3 F4
Larchfield YO31 229 C7
Larchfield Com TS8 6 F4
Larchfield Sports Ctr DL3 3 C5
Larchfield St DL3 3 C5
Larch Gr
1 Filey YO14 101 B4
Pannal HG3 222 E2
Larch Rd
Guisborough TS14 8 E7
Selby YO8 232 E2
6 Topcliffe YO7 89 A1
Larch Rise 4 YO61 117 D1
Larch Way
35 Haxby YO32 166 E5
Selby YO8 232 D2
Larkfield Cl
1 Copmanthorpe YO23 230 A3
Harrogate HG2 222 A7
Larkfield Dr HG2 222 A7
Larkfield Rd
Harrogate HG2 222 A7
Selby YO8 232 A4
Larkfield Way HG2 222 A7
Lark Hill HG4 214 A7
Larkhill Cl HG4 214 A6
Lark Hill Cres 13 HG4 113 D2
Lark Hill Dr HG4 214 A6
Lark La HG4 214 A6
Larkspur Gr 14 HG3 161 B3
Larkspur Rd TS7 7 A6
Larpool Cres YO22 208 E4
Larpool Dr YO22 208 D3
Larpool La YO22 208 D4
Larpool Lane Ind Est YO22 208 D5
Lartington Way TS16 5 D5
Larun Beat The TS15 5 E2
Lascelles Ct DL6 210 E4
Lascelles Gr HG2 219 B1
Lascelles La
Malton YO17 215 E6
Northallerton DL6 210 E4
Lascelles Rd HG2 222 B8
Lasenby Cl YO32 225 D5
LASTINGHAM 70 F5
Lastingham Terr YO10 228 D2
Latimer La TS14 8 E6
Latimer Rd DL1 3 E7
Lauderdale Dr TS14 8 F6
Laughton Ave YO12 212 C5
Laundry La LA6 103 D3
Laundry Rd
4 Filey YO14 101 B3
3 Harrogate HG1 220 C4
Lauradale La BD23 134 D1
Laurel Ave TS4 7 A8
Laurel Cl
Burniston YO13 75 D8
Earswick YO32 226 A7
Embsay BD23 217 D8
Gateforth YO8 197 B1
Laurel Croft BD23 217 D8
Laurels Garth YO60 145 C5
Laurels The
Barlby YO8 198 B5
6 Northallerton DL6 210 E2
Laurence Gr YO8 232 D3
Laurence Jackson Sch TS14 8 F7
Lavender Ct 21 DL9 41 A5
Lavender Gr YO26 227 E5
Laveracks Ind Est YO41 185 B3
Laverick Terr 9 YO22 208 E6
LAVERTON 112 D4
Laverton Gdns HG3 219 A4
LAWKLAND 130 F5
LAWKLAND GREEN 131 A4
Law La HG3 138 F1
Lawn Ave LS29 176 C1
Lawnfield Dr HG3 140 B5
Lawnfield Rd HG3 140 B5
Lawn La DN6 207 E3
Lawn Rd 33 LS29 176 C1
Lawns Rd YO21 29 E6
Lawns The HG2 222 C8
Lawnswood Dr YO30 227 F8
Lawnway YO31 229 A7
Lawrence Cl YO12 212 A8
Lawrence Cres DL10 209 E8
Lawrence Ct 11 YO10 228 E3
Lawrence Gr YO12 212 A8
Lawrence Sq YO10 228 F3
Lawrence St YO10 228 E3
Lawsings Brow LA2 130 B5
Lawson Ave 1 YO51 141 B4
Lawson Rd YO24 230 F7
Lawsons Cl YO14 126 F7
Lawson's Ct DL2 2 C6
Laycock Fields 11 BD22 187 B6
LAYERTHORPE 228 E4
Layerthorpe YO31 233 C3
Layfield Prim Sch TS15 5 D2
Lazenby Dr 10 LS22 180 B3
Lea Croft LS23 188 E7
Leadhall Ave HG2 222 D6
Leadhall Cl HG2 222 D6
Leadhall Cres HG2 222 E6
Leadhall Dr HG2 222 D7
Leadhall Gdns HG2 222 D6
Leadhall Gr HG2 222 D6
Leadhall La HG2 222 D6
Leadhall Rd HG2 222 C6
Leadhall View HG2 222 C5
Leadhall Way HG2 222 C6
Leading Post St 8 YO11 213 B6
Lead La
Brompton DL6 43 F3
Nether Silton YO7 66 B7
Ripon HG4 214 B3
Westerdale YO21 28 E4
Leadley Croft YO23 230 A1
Lead Mill La YO1 233 C1
Leafield Rd DL1 3 D4
Leahope Ct TS17 6 C6
Leahurst Cl YO17 215 E2
LEAKE 65 F5
Leake La YO7 65 F6
Leake St
Castleford WF10 200 F4
12 York YO10 228 E3
Lea La YO61 143 F4
LEALHOLM 30 B6
Lealholm Cres TS3 7 C8
Lealholm La YO21 30 B5
Lealholm Prim Sch YO21 30 C6
LEALHOLM SIDE 30 D7
Lealholm Sta YO21 30 B6
Leamington Rd LS29 218 C5
Leamington Terr LS29 218 C5
Learmans Way YO23 230 C3
Learning La DN14 202 F1
Lease Rigg La YO22 31 A3
Leases La DL10 41 E2
Leases Rd DL7 63 C5
Leas Head Rd YO22 32 B2
Leas La YO18 95 F5
Leasmires Ave 10 YO61 143 D8
Leas The
11 Brafferton YO61 115 F1
Darlington DL1 3 D8
8 Eastfield YO11 99 F7
Leat Cl YO17 215 D2
Leather Bank LS29 176 C1
LEATHLEY 177 D2
Leathley La LS21 177 D1
LEAVENING 147 E1
Leavening Prim Sch YO17 147 E2
Lea Way YO32 226 A4
Leazon Hill 5 TS17 6 D6
LEBBERSTON 100 D5
Le Cateau Prim Sch DL9 40 F4
Le Cateau Rd DL9 40 E4
LECK 102 E7
Leck CE Prim Sch LA6 102 E7
Leconfield DL3 3 B5
Leconfield Garth HG3 223 F5
Ledbury Way TS14 8 E6
Ledgate La LS25 201 E6
LEDSHAM 201 B8
LEDSTON 200 F7
Ledston Ave LS25 194 D3
Ledston Hall* WF10 200 F8
LEDSTON LUCK 194 F1
Ledston Mill La WF10 200 F8
Leech La DL10 41 E4
Lee Ct DN14 207 A7
Leeds Barnsdale Rd WF10 200 D3
Leeds La LS15 194 A3
Leeds Rd
Allerton Bywater WF10 200 D7
Barwick in Elmet & Scholes LS15 194 A7
Castleford WF10 200 E3
Collingham LS22 188 A8
Great Preston WF10 200 C7
Harrogate HG2 219 D1
Ilkley LS29 218 D5
Kippax LS25 194 C2
Mickletown LS26 200 A6
Pannal HG3 222 F3
Selby YO8 232 A4
Tadcaster LS24 189 D5
Leeman Rd YO26 233 A2
LEEMING 63 D4
LEEMING BAR 63 C5
Leeming Bar Ind Est DL7 63 C5
Leeming Bar Sta DL7 63 C5
Leeming La
Brough with St Giles DL10 41 D5
Burneston DL8 87 F8
4 Burton in Lonsdale LA6 102 F3
Catterick DL10 41 E4
Kirklington-cum-Upsland YO7 88 A6
Langthorpe YO51 141 B6
Leeming DL7 63 C4
Melmerby YO7 114 D8
Theakston DL7 63 E1
Leeming La *continued*
Thornthwaite with Padside HG3 159 D5
Leeming & Londonderry Com Prim Sch DL7 63 D4
Leeming (RAF) Cty Prim Sch DL7 63 F3
Leeside YO24 230 E8
Lees La DL7 210 B1
Lee View DN14 207 A7
Lee Way WF10 200 F3
Legion Ave DL3 3 B8
Legion St LS25 195 F2
Legram La YO26 163 D8
Legram Rd YO26 163 D8
Leicester Cres LS29 218 B5
Leicester Way
Aislaby TS16 5 D4
York YO1 233 C1
LEIGHTON 85 C2
Leighton Cl YO12 99 E6
Leighton Croft 3 YO30 224 F1
Leighton Rd 6 TS18 5 D8
Leith Rd DL3 3 A5
Lendal YO1 233 B2
Lendales La YO17 95 E3
Lennerton La LS25 196 C3
Lennox Ave DL10 209 D7
Lennox Cl 2 YO14 127 A8
Lennox Pl HG4 113 D3
Leonard St 15 BB18 171 D1
LEPPINGTON 169 C8
Leppington Dr YO12 212 C4
Leppington La YO60 147 D1
Lerecroft Rd YO24 230 D8
Lesley Ave YO10 231 E8
L'Espec St DL7 210 D3
Leven Bank Rd TS15 5 F2
Leven Cl TS16 5 D4
Leven Ct TS9 8 A1
Levendale 6 TS15 25 C5
Levendale Prim Sch TS15 5 F3
Leven Rd
Eaglescliffe TS15 5 E3
Stokesley TS9 26 B7
York YO24 230 D7
Levens Cl HG3 161 B4
Levenside
Great Ayton TS9 7 F1
4 Hutton Rudby TS15 25 D5
Stokesley TS9 26 C7
Leven Wynd 9 TS9 26 C7
Levick Cres TS5 6 D8
Levington Ct 3 TS15 24 F8
Levington Mews 4 TS15 24 F8
LEVISHAM 72 D5
Levisham St YO10 228 D2
Levisham Sta YO18 72 B5
Lewes Rd DL1 3 D4
Lewis Cl
1 Croft-on-Tees DL2 22 C8
Northallerton DL6 210 F5
Lewis Rd DL6 210 F5
Lexden Ave TS5 6 D8
LEYBURN 60 D5
Leyburn Bsns Pk DL8 60 D5
Leyburn Gr 1 TS18 5 D8
Leyburn Old Glebe Field Nature Reserve* DL8 60 B4
Leyburn Pl 8 YO14 101 A3
Leyburn Prim Sch DL8 60 D5
Leyburn Rd
Askrigg DL8 57 F6
Darlington DL1 3 D7
Hunton DL8 61 E7
Masham HG4 86 B4
Middleham DL8 60 E3
Scotton DL9 40 C4
Leyburn Sta DL8 60 D5
Leyes The YO10 229 C4
Leyfield Cl 1 YO32 167 A7
Leyland Cl BB8 186 A2
Leyland Cres 3 HG1 220 A3
Leyland Rd
Harrogate HG1 220 A3
York YO31 229 A5
Leys La
Boston Spa LS23 188 D8
Darrington WF11 206 A8
Glusburn BD20 187 B8
Knottingley WF11 201 F1
Little Smeaton WF8 206 B4
Leys Rd WF11 206 A7
LEYSTHORPE 93 B1
Leysthorpe La YO62 93 B2
Liardet Rd 19 DL10 41 E4
Libanus Ct 16 TS17 5 F4
Library Sq YO1 233 B3
Lichfield Ct 6 YO23 228 B1
Lichfield Gr HG3 219 A4
Lickley St HG4 214 D5
Lidget Croft 10 BD20 173 E3
Lidget La HG5 163 B5
Lidget Rd BD20 173 E3
Lidgett Gr YO26 227 B6
Lidgett La LS25 194 C3
Lidice Rd DN14 205 E2
Lidsty Hill YO62 70 E5
Light Bank La BD20 174 E2
Lightfoots Ave YO12 212 D3
Lightfoots Cl YO12 212 C3
Lightfoot's La YO12 212 D3
Lightfoots Rd YO12 212 D3
Light La DL8 59 E5
Lightmire La YO26 142 A1
Lightwater Sh Village HG4 113 C6
Lightwater Valley Bird of Prey Ctr* HG4 113 C7
Lightwater Valley Miniature Rly* HG4 113 C6
Lightwater Valley Theme Pk* HG4 113 C6
Lilac Ave
2 Appleton Roebuck YO23 190 F5
Thornaby TS17 6 B7
York YO10 229 B3
Lilac Cl 7 LS29 175 A4
Lilac Gr
Harrogate HG1 219 E6
New Earswick YO32 225 D4
Lilac Rd TS7 7 D7
Lilac Wlk YO12 212 D7
Lilbourne Dr YO30 228 A8
Lile Cl DL10 209 C7
Lilla Cl YO21 208 A6
Lilling Ave 3 YO31 228 E8
Lilling La YO60 145 E3
Lilling Low La YO32 145 C2
Lilly Gate La HG3 162 A8
Limber Hill YO21 30 E4
Lime Ave YO31 228 F7
Limebar Bank Rd YO51 141 D1
Limebar La YO51 141 C2
Lime Chase 10 YO62 70 B1
Lime Cl 10 LS29 174 E4
Limegarth 10 YO26 165 F1
Lime Gr
Harrogate HG1 219 F3
4 Whitby YO21 208 C6
Limehouse La BD23 216 E1
Limekiln Bank HG4 113 C1
Limekiln Hill YO25 150 B3
Limekiln La
Burton Leonard HG3 140 A1
8 Eastfield YO11 100 B6
East Layton DL11 1 B1
Halton West BD23 154 A1
North Stainley with Sleningford HG4 113 C5
Snape with Thorp HG4 86 D5
Lime Kiln La LS22 180 B5
Limekiln Rd YO7 65 F5
Lime La DL8 87 F2
Lime Rd
Eaglescliffe TS16 5 E6
Guisborough TS14 8 E7
Sinnington YO62 94 D8
Limes Ct YO31 228 F6
Lime St HG1 219 F3
Limes The
Burniston YO13 75 C8
Helmsley YO62 92 F6
13 South Milford LS25 195 F2
Stockton on the Forest YO32 167 D2
Limestone Gr YO13 75 C8
Limestone La YO13 75 A5
Limestone Rd YO13 75 B7
Limestone Way YO13 75 C8
Lime Tree Ave
Boston Spa LS23 188 E8
8 Easingwold YO61 117 D1
Malton YO17 215 D6
York YO32 225 D3
Limetree Cl 2 YO8 197 B1
Lime-Tree Cres LS25 194 E1
Lime Tree Dr DN14 207 A7
Lime Tree Gdns LS23 188 E8
Lime Tree Gr YO8 232 A6
Lime Tree Mews 15 YO19 184 F7
Limetrees WF8 201 D2
Lime Wlk HG4 214 B2
Limpsey Gate La YO18 72 D6
Limpton Gate TS15 5 E2
Linacre Way DL1 3 D7
Lincoln Gr HG3 219 A5
Lincoln Pl 1 TS17 6 B8
Lincoln Rd 30 BB18 172 A1
Lincoln St YO26 227 F5
Lincoln Way LS25 196 A4
Lindale 2 YO24 230 C7
Linden Ave
Darlington DL3 3 B5
Great Ayton TS9 7 F1
Linden Cl
Great Ayton TS9 7 F2
4 Hutton Rudby TS15 25 C4
Richmond DL10 209 D7
Sleights YO21 32 B7
York YO32 225 F5
Linden Cres
Great Ayton TS9 7 F1
5 Hutton Rudby TS15 25 C4
Middlesbrough TS7 7 B6
Linden Dr
Hurworth DL2 3 D1
1 Hurworth-on-Tees DL2 22 D8
Linden Gdns DL10 209 D7
Linden Gr
Great Ayton TS9 7 F1
Thornaby TS17 6 B8
1 York YO30 228 A8
Linden Rd
9 Earby BB18 172 A1
Great Ayton TS9 7 F1
Northallerton DL6 210 E4
Scalby YO12 212 A8
Linden Way
9 Thorpe Willoughby YO8 197 B1
Wetherby LS22 180 B4
Lindhead Prim Sch YO13 75 C8
Lindhead Rd YO13 75 B8
Lindisfarne Ave 4 TS17 6 B8
Lindisfarne Rd TS3 7 C8
LINDLEY 177 C4
Lindley Rd YO30 224 F1
Lindley St
Skipton BD23 216 F2
York YO24 227 F3
Lindley Wood Gr YO30 224 E3
Lindon Rd DL10 20 F1
Lindrick Cl
32 Castleford WF6 200 B1
3 Ripon HG4 214 B2
Lindrick Way HG3 219 A4
Lindsay Rd LS25 194 C3
Lindsey Ave YO26 227 D4
Linen Way 10 DL6 43 F3
Lingcrag Gdns BD22 187 B6
Ling Croft LS23 188 D8
Lingcroft Cl YO8 204 D4
Lingcroft La
Naburn YO19 231 E3
Tockwith LS22 181 A6
LINGDALE 9 F7
Lingdale Prim Sch TS12 9 F7
Lingdale Rd
Lockwood TS12 9 E7
Thornaby TS17 6 C7
LINGERFIELD 162 B6
LINGFIELD 3 F5
Lingfield Ash TS8 7 A5
Lingfield Cl
Great Burdon DL1 3 F5
10 Hipswell DL9 40 F4
Lingfield Cres YO24 227 F1
Lingfield Prim Sch TS7 7 B5
Lingfield Rd TS15 5 F3
Ling Fields BD23 216 C4
Lingfield Way DL1 4 A5
Ling Gill National Nature Reserve* BD24 79 C1
Lingham La YO7 115 A3
Linghaw La LA2 129 C7
Ling Hill YO12 212 B7
Lingholm Cres 9 YO11 99 F7
Lingholm La YO11 100 D4
Ling La YO41 185 F6
Lingrow Cl 3 TS13 12 A7
Ling Trod YO17 123 D4
Link Ave YO30 228 C8
Link Bsns Pk YO10 229 D4
Linkfoot La YO62 93 A6
Link Rd YO32 225 E2
Link Road Ct YO10 229 D4
Links Cl HG2 220 E3
Links Dr LA2 129 A8
Links Prim Sch The TS16 5 E5
Links The
7 North Featherstone WF7 200 E1
Tadcaster LS24 189 E5
Links Way HG2 220 E3
Link The
Copmanthorpe YO23 230 A3
Middlesbrough TS3 7 C8
Northallerton DL7 210 B2
Selby YO8 232 A4
York YO10 231 E8
Linkway DN6 206 E2
Link Wlk 5 YO11 100 A6
Linley Ave 24 YO32 166 F5
Linnburn Mews 1 LS29 218 B3
Linnet Way YO24 230 C8
LINTON
Grassington 134 D1
Wetherby 180 A1
Linton Ave 9 LS22 180 B3
Linton Cl
Cloughton YO13 54 D1
19 Filey YO14 101 B3
Linton Com LS22 179 F1
Linton Ct 8 BD23 216 F3
Linton Falls 1 BD23 134 E2
Linton La LS22 180 B2
Linton Mdw 5 YO30 164 F7
Linton Mdws 7 LS22 180 B3
LINTON-ON-OUSE 164 E7
Linton on Ouse Prim Sch YO30 165 A7
Linton Pl 4 YO30 164 F7
Linton Rd
Collingham LS22 180 A1
Poppleton YO26 224 A1
Wetherby LS22 180 B3
Linton Rise 17 DL9 40 E4
Linton St 5 YO26 227 E5
Linton Woods YO30 165 A7
Linton Woods La YO30 165 A8
Linwith La DN14 204 C3
Linwood Ave TS9 26 C8
Lion Ct 43 LS29 176 C1
Lippersley La LS29 174 D3
Lisheen Ave WF10 200 F4
Lismore Pl YO12 212 E1
Lismore Rd YO12 212 E1
Lister Croft BD23 172 A3
Lister Hill 5 BD20 187 E6
Lister St LS29 218 A4
Lister Way YO30 228 A7
Lisvane Ave YO12 212 D4
Litley Bank YO7 66 B5
LITTLE AIRMYN 205 E4
Little Ave YO30 228 B8
LITTLE AYTON 8 B1
Little Ayton La
Great Ayton TS9 8 A1
27 Roundhill Village TS17 5 F4
LITTLE BARUGH 95 C2

Little Beck Bank YO22 32 C4
Littlebeck Dr DL1 3 E7
Little Beck La YO22 32 B3
Little Beck Wood Nature Reserve★ YO22 32 B3
Littleboy Dr TS17 6 C8
Little Brook BD23 217 B4
Little Catterton La LS24 190 A7
Little Church La LS26 200 B5
Little Common La DN14 207 C5
LITTLE CRAKEHALL 62 D5
Little Croft HG3 139 C4
Little Crossing HG4 214 E2
Littledale YO18 95 F7
LITTLE FENCOTE 63 C8
LITTLE FENTON 196 B6
Littlefield Cl 5 YO26 165 F1
Little Field La YO18 72 C5
Little Garth YO26 224 A2
LITTLE HABTON 121 A8
Little Hallfield Rd YO31 228 E5
Little Harries La HG4 214 A7
LITTLE HECK 203 D1
Little Heck Common La DN14 203 D1
Little Hoppers Adventure World★ YO11 99 F6
LITTLE HUTTON 116 B7
Little Hutton La DL11 1 A4
Little Ings Cl LS24 196 C8
Little Ings La YO51 141 C5
Little King St 5 HG3 137 B4
Little La
Brompton DL6 44 A3
12 Easingwold YO61 143 C8
Ellerton YO42 193 C1
11 Haxby YO32 166 E5
Ilkley LS29 218 C4
Little Smeaton WF8 206 D4
North Stainley with Sleningford HG4 113 C4
Little Mdws YO32 225 D8
Little Moor Cl YO13 54 C1
Little Moor La YO8 232 A8
LITTLE OUSEBURN 164 A7
Little Pasture 3 TS17 6 D5
LITTLE PRESTON 194 B1
LITTLE RIBSTON 180 A8
LITTLE SESSAY 116 C5
Little Shambles YO1 233 B2
Littleside DL8 83 E7
LITTLE SKIPWITH 192 D1
LITTLE SMEATON
206 C3
North Cowton 23 C2
LITTLE STAINFORTH 131 D6
Little Stonegate YO1 233 B3
LITTLE STUDLEY 214 C7
Little Studley Cl HG4 214 C7
Little Studley Pk HG4 214 C8
Little Studley Rd HG4 214 C7
LITTLETHORPE 214 F1
Littlethorpe Cl
Harrogate HG3 219 A4
6 Strensall YO32 167 B8
Littlethorpe La HG4 214 D2
Littlethorpe Pk HG4 214 E3
Littlethorpe Potteries★ HG4 140 A7
Littlethorpe Rd HG4 214 E3
Little Westfield YO25 151 C3
Little Wood St YO17 215 E3
LITTON 107 A5
Littondale Ave HG5 221 D6
LIVERTON 10 D6
Liverton La TS13 10 D6
Liverton Mill Bank TS12 10 B6
LIVERTON MINES 10 C8
Liverton Rd TS13 10 D7
Livingstone Rd YO12 212 E6
Livingstone St YO26 227 F5
Lloyd Cl YO10 229 B1
Lob La YO41 168 D2
Lochranza Rd YO7 211 A2
Lochrin Pl 2 YO26 227 B4
Lock Cl DN14 207 F6
Locker La HG4 214 C4
Lockey Croft YO32 225 C8
Lockeys Terr 3 YO22 208 E6
Lockfield Dr BB18 171 E2
Lockgate Rd DN14 207 C4
Lockheed Cl TS18 5 F7
Lock House La YO32 225 F8
Lock La
Castleford WF10 200 E5
Lower Altofts WF6 200 A3
Lock Lane Sports Ctr WF10 200 F5
Locks Barn BD24 131 D4
LOCKTON 72 D4
Lockton Cres TS17 6 A6
Lockton Ct LS24 196 B7
Lockton La YO18 72 E4
Lockton Rd YO21 208 A6
Lock Walk DL10 41 E4
Lockwood Chase YO13 54 D1
Lockwood Prim Sch TS12 9 D7
Lockwood St YO31 233 C3
Lockyer Cl 4 YO30 228 A8
Locomotion Ct 5 TS16 5 D5
Locomotion La 7 DL3 3 B7
Loders Gn 5 YO11 99 F6
Lodge Cl 7 YO11 100 B6
Lodge Gdns YO14 100 E4
LODGE GREEN 36 F5
Lodge La
5 Brompton DL6 43 F3
Danby YO21 29 D7
Lodge La *continued*
Gowdall DN14 203 F1
Newby with Mulwith HG4 140 E6
Wennington LA2 102 B1
Wetherby LS22 180 C2
Lodge Rd
Hutton-le-Hole YO62 70 C5
Lythe YO21 12 E3
Settle BD24 153 E8
Lodge St 4 BD20 187 D7
Lodore Gr TS5 6 D7
LOFTHOUSE 110 C4
Lofthouse Endowed Prim Sch HG3 110 B4
Lofthouse La YO41 185 D7
Loftus Cl YO12 212 B4
Lombards Wynd DL10 209 C7
Londesborough Gr 5 YO8 197 B2
Londesborough Pk 10 YO12 99 D6
Londesborough Rd YO12 212 E4
Londesborough St 5 YO8 232 C5
LONDONDERRY 63 E2
London La DN6 207 D1
Longacre WF10 200 E3
Long Acre Ct HG3 222 E2
Long Acre Wlk HG3 222 E2
Long Ashes L & Beauty Club BD23 134 B3
Long Band DL8 58 A8
Long Bank DL11 19 C6
Long Bank La BD23 153 E1
Longbank Rd TS7 7 D7
Longber La LA6 102 D4
Longbow Ave LS26 200 B6
Long Cl La YO10 233 C1
Long Crag View 1 HG3 161 B2
Longcroft 2 YO32 166 E5
Longcroft Rd 1 LS29 218 E3
Long Cswy
Arkengarthdale DL11 16 C6
Halton East BD23 174 B8
Thirkleby High & Low with Osgodby YO7 90 D1
Long Cswy Rd
Danby YO21 29 E3
Hutton Buscel YO13 99 A4
Longdale Ave 18 BD24 131 D2
Longdike La
Kippax LS25 200 E8
Thornton Steward HG4 61 E1
LONG DRAX 205 A6
Longfield Comp Sch DL3 3 C8
Longfield Ct 21 BB18 171 D1
Longfield Rd DL3 3 C7
Longfield Terr YO30 233 A3
Long Furrow YO32 225 C8
Long Gate BD22 187 D4
Long Gn 7 BB18 172 B1
Long Heads La LS25 195 F1
Long Hill End BD22 187 B5
Long Ing La BB18 171 E1
Long La
Barwick in Elmet LS15 194 C7
Borrowby YO7 65 E5
Brompton DL6 44 A6
Catton YO41 185 D6
Cawood YO8 197 A6
Cowling BD22 187 B7
East Ayton YO13 99 B7
Ellerton YO42 193 F1
Farndale East YO62 48 F4
Felliscliffe HG3 160 E3
Gayles DL11 19 E6
Heck DN14 207 D8
Heslington YO10 184 C3
Kirk Smeaton WF8 206 B1
Laneshaw Bridge BB8 186 B4
Lockwood TS12 10 B5
Normanby YO62 95 A4
Picton TS15 24 E6
Seamer YO12 99 E6
Slingsby YO62 120 D6
Tatham LA2 128 E7
Well DL8 87 C4
Longland La YO26 164 A3
Longlands Field Rd YO26 163 D8
Longlands La
Boroughbridge YO51 141 A3
Danby YO21 29 B6
Hetton BD23 155 F5
Sicklinghall LS22 179 E3
Thornton-le-Dale YO18 96 E5
Longlands Rd YO17 123 B3
LONG LEASE 33 A7
Long Level LA6 102 C8
Long Mann Hills Rd YO8 232 B4
Longmans Hill Sch YO8 232 C3
LONG MARSTON 182 A6
Long Marston CE Prim Sch YO26 182 A6
Long Mdw
7 Colne BB8 186 A3
Skipton BD23 217 B5
Long Mdws
Garforth LS25 194 C3
6 Ilkley LS29 176 C1
Rillington YO17 122 F5
Long Meadow Gate LS25 194 C2
LONGNEWTON 5 A7
Long Newton La TS21 5 A6
LONG PRESTON 153 F5
Long Preston Endowed Prim Sch BD23 153 F5
Long Preston Sta BD23 153 F4
Long Rampart YO42 193 D3
Long Riddings LS29 174 F5
Long Ridge Dr YO26 224 A1
Longridge Gdns 27 YO26 165 F1
Long Ridge La YO26 224 A1
LONGSCALES 160 C4
Long St
Asenby YO7 115 B6
Easingwold YO61 143 C8
Thirsk YO7 211 C3
Topcliffe YO7 115 C6
Long Stoop Standing Stone★ HG3 160 A2
Long Stps 8 YO22 208 E6
Long Swales La HG4 112 D5
Longtons La BD23 152 F4
Long Trods 5 YO8 232 C6
Longwestgate YO11 213 B6
Long Wlk
Knaresborough HG5 221 A6
Scarborough YO12 212 D7
Longwood Bank DL10 209 D5
Longwood Link 8 YO30 224 E3
Longwood Rd YO30 224 F3
Lonsdale Mdws LS23 188 E8
Lonsdale Pl 12 YO13 99 B8
Lonsdale Rd YO11 213 A3
Loos Rd DL9 40 F3
Loraine Cres DL1 3 C4
Lord Ave TS17 6 B5
Lord Deramores Prim Sch YO10 229 C1
Lord Mayor's Wlk YO31 233 B3
Lord's Cl 23 BD24 131 D2
Lord's Close Rd LA2 129 B3
Lordship La
5 Barlby YO8 198 A4
Wistow YO8 232 D8
Lords La
Ainderby Mires with Holtby DL8 41 F1
Hackforth DL8 62 E8
Upper Poppleton YO26 165 E2
Lord's La DL8 63 C2
Lords Moor La YO32 167 C7
Loriners Dr 7 YO23 230 B3
Loring Rd YO13 54 A7
Lorne St YO23 228 B1
Lorraine Ave 3 YO41 185 B2
LOSCOE 200 C1
Loscoe Cl WF6 200 C2
Loshpot La LS22 180 C5
LOTHERSDALE 187 A8
Lothersdale Com Prim Sch BD20 186 F8
Lothersdale Rd BD20 187 B8
Lotherton La LS25 195 A7
Lotherton Way LS25 194 C4
Louisa St DL1 3 D5
Lousy Hill La YO22 32 C3
Louvain St 5 BB18 171 D2
Love La
Brawby YO17 94 F1
Castleford WF10 200 E3
Easby DL10 209 E4
8 Leyburn DL8 60 D5
Nunthorpe YO10 231 C8
Whitby YO21 208 A7
York YO24 228 A2
Lovers' La DL7 64 F2
Low Bank
4 Embsay BD23 217 E8
Over Silton DL6 66 A8
Low Beck LS29 218 D5
LOW BENTHAM 128 F8
Low Bentham Prim Sch LA2 128 F8
Low Bentham Rd LA2 128 F8
LOW BRADLEY 173 E3
LOW CATTON 185 C8
Low Catton Rd YO41 185 C8
Low Cl LS29 218 A5
Low Comm LS26 200 C4
LOW CONISCLIFFE 2 F4
Lowcroft
9 Collingham LS22 188 A8
High Bentham LA2 129 B8
Low Croft 6 YO32 167 A7
Lowcross Ave TS14 8 E5
Lowcross Dr TS9 26 E5
LOW DALBY 72 F2
Lowdale Ave YO12 212 E8
Lowdale Ct 4 YO22 32 A6
Low Demesne LA6 103 D3
Low Demesne Cl 4 LA6 103 D3
LOW DINSDALE 4 C1
LOW ELLINGTON 86 A6
LOWER ALTOFTS 200 A3
Lower Clark St
2 Scarborough YO12 212 F6
13 Scarborough YO12 213 A7
Lower Clark Street Ind Est 14 YO12 213 A7
Lower Constable Rd LS29 218 D3
Lower Croft St 39 BB18 172 A1
Lower Darnborough St YO23 233 B1
Lower Derwent Valley Nat Nature Reserve★ YO42 199 C8
LOWER DUNSFORTH 142 A4
Lower Flat Cliffs YO14 101 C1
Lower Friargate YO1 233 B2
Lower Greenfoot 15 BD24 131 D2
LOWER MICKLETOWN 200 D6
Lower Mickletown LS26 200 C6
Lower Oxford St WF10 200 E4
Lower Priory St YO1 233 A1
Lower Station Rd 3 WF6 200 A1
Lower Union St BD23 216 F3
Lower Wellington Rd LS29 218 B4
LOWER WESTHOUSE 103 B4
Lower William St 3 YO12 212 F6
Lower York Ct HG1 220 D6
Loweswater Rd 5 YO30 224 E1
Low Farm LS26 200 C8
Low Farm Cl
Bolton Percy YO23 190 D4
Thornton TS8 6 D4
Lowfield
3 Eastfield YO11 100 A6
Hawes DL8 56 C4
Lowfield Dr YO32 166 E5
Lowfield La
Beamsley BD23 174 F7
Kirkby Fleetham with Fencote DL7 42 D2
Rufforth YO26 227 A4
Scrayingham YO41 169 A7
Sharow HG4 214 F6
Snape with Thorp DL8 87 A7
Low Field La
Cold Kirby YO7 91 D7
Goldsborough HG5 163 A1
Marton cum Grafton YO51 141 E2
Staveley HG5 140 E1
Lowfield Rd
Barlby with Osgodby YO8 198 B5
Hillam LS25 202 C8
Malton YO17 215 C6
Lowfields 2 YO12 99 D2
Lowfields Ave
Ingleby Barwick TS17 6 A5
Roundhill Village TS17 6 D5
Low Fields Dr YO24 227 C3
Lowfields La YO7 88 C6
Low Fold 4 BB18 186 A7
LOW GARTH 29 F4
Low Garth YO22 32 A6
Low Garth Link 17 LS25 195 F4
Low Garth Rd LS25 195 F4
LOW GATE 138 F6
Lowgate DN14 207 D5
Low Gate DL8 57 F5
Low Gate La HG4 138 F7
LOW GATHERLEY 21 D1
LOWGILL 128 F3
Lowgill La LA2 128 F4
Low Gn
Catterick DL10 41 D4
Copmanthorpe YO23 230 B2
13 Knottingley WF11 202 A2
Menwith with Darley HG3 160 A6
LOW GRANTLEY 112 E1
LOW GREEN 160 A6
LOW HAWSKER 33 A6
Low Holland WF11 201 C6
Low Hospital Yd 6 YO22 208 E6
Low House La
Carlton Miniott YO7 89 C2
Dishforth YO7 115 B2
LOW HUTTON 147 C6
Low Hutton Pk YO60 147 C6
Lowick YO24 230 C7
Lowkber La LA6 103 E2
Low La
Askrigg DL8 58 B4
Carperby-cum-Thoresby DL8 58 F4
Cononley BD20 173 C2
Cowling BD22 187 A8
Cropton YO18 71 B4
Dalby-cum-Skewsby YO60 119 B2
Dalton DL11 19 D7
Embsay with Eastby BD23 217 E8
Grassington BD23 134 E3
Grinton DL11 37 E5
Heslington YO10 229 D1
Howsham YO60 147 A1
Hutton-Sessay YO7 116 B7
Leck LA6 102 D7
Leyburn DL8 60 C4
Lythe YO21 12 D3
Maltby TS17 6 B3
Menwith with Darley HG3 159 F6
Mickleby TS13 12 A3
Middlesbrough TS5 6 E6
Muker DL11 36 C4
Newsham DL11 18 H7
Reeth, Fremington & Healaugh DL11 37 F5
Silsden BD20 174 B3
Spofforth with Stockeld HG3 179 C4
Stainburn LS21 177 F3
Sutton-under-Whitestonecliffe YO7 90 E6
Swinton YO17 121 C4
Thirkleby High & Low with Osgodby YO7 90 C1
Westow YO60 147 C4
West Rounton DL6 24 D3
Wigglesworth BD23 153 D3
LOW LAITHE 137 F2
Lowlands Dr DL7 63 C5
LOW MARISHES 122 C8
Low Mdw YO8 232 C6
LOW MILL 48 E2
Low Mill LS29 175 A4
Low Mill Cl YO10 229 D3
Low Mill Ct HG3 138 F1
Low Mill Est HG4 214 E5
Low Mill La LS29 175 A4
Low Mill Rd HG4 214 D4
Low Moor Ave 3 YO10 231 F8
Low Moorgate La YO17 122 F5
Low Moor La
Askham Richard YO23 182 D3
Brearton HG5 162 B7
East Harlsey DL6 44 C7
Fearby HG4 85 F3
Hessay YO26 182 C8
Rillington YO17 122 E6
Lowmoor Rd YO8 198 E6
Low Moor Rd YO18 71 F5
Low Moor South La YO17 122 D6
LOWNA 70 A6
Lowna Rd YO62 70 B5
Lown Hill YO24 227 C2
Lownorth Rd YO13 53 C2
Low Ousegate YO1 233 B2
Low Park Rd LS29 176 A3
Low Petergate YO1 233 B3
Low Peter La HG3 140 A3
Low Poppleton La YO26 227 B7
Low Rd
Gainford DL2 1 C7
Gowdall DN14 204 A1
Irton YO12 75 B3
Kellington DN14 202 F4
Kirby Grindalythe YO17 149 F7
Newby & Scalby YO12 212 A6
Thirkleby High & Low with Osgodby YO7 116 E8
LOW ROW 37 C4
Low Row DL11 37 E5
Low Skellgate HG4 214 C5
Low Sleights Rd LA6 104 B7
LOW SNAYGILL 173 D4
Low St
Aiskew DL7 63 C6
Austwick LA2 130 E7
Burton in Lonsdale LA6 102 F3
Carlton DN14 204 C2
Husthwaite YO61 117 B6
Kirkby Fleetham with Fencote DL7 41 F2
Knottingley WF11 201 E4
Lastingham YO62 70 E5
Nunnington YO62 93 E2
Oswaldkirk YO62 92 F3
Ripon HG4 214 D5
22 Scalby YO13 75 D5
Sherburn in Elmet LS25 195 F4
Thornton-le-Clay YO60 146 A4
Low Stanghow Rd TS12 9 F6
Low Street Agnesgate HG4 214 D4
Lowswater Rd WF11 201 F1
Lowther Cres 3 LS26 194 A1
Lowther Ct YO31 233 C4
Lowther Dr
Garforth LS25 194 C3
Selby YO8 232 E3
2 Swillington LS26 194 A1
Lowther St YO31 233 C4
Lowther Terr YO24 228 A3
Low Thorpe DL8 85 D8
LOW TOWN 5 B1
Low Town Bank Rd YO7 91 B4
Low Tun Way YO62 69 A2
Low Wath Rd HG3 137 B4
Low Way 5 LS23 188 E5
Low Well Pk YO19 192 F7
Low Westfield Rd YO23 230 A1
LOW WHITA 37 D5
Low Wood La
Glaisdale YO21 30 C6
Leyburn DL8 60 C4
Low Wood Rise LS29 218 F3
LOW WORSALL 24 A8
Loxley Cl YO30 224 F2
Loy La TS13 10 F8
Loyne Pk LA6 102 A7
Lucas Ave YO30 228 C8
Lucas Grove N YO26 181 C7
Lucas Grove S YO26 181 C7
Lucas Rd YO26 181 C7
Luccombe Cl 7 TS17 6 A3
Lucerne Cl YO19 192 A1
Lucerne Dr TS14 8 E6
Lucia La TS14 8 E6
Lucky La YO7 89 E8
Lucombe Way YO32 225 D4
Luddith Rd YO17 148 D5
Ludlow Ave LS25 194 D4
Lufton Cl 4 TS17 5 F5
Lullingstone Cres TS17 5 F6
Lulsgate TS17 6 C7
LUMB 187 A4
Lumb Gill La LS29 175 A3
Lumb La
Cowling BD22 187 A5
Topcliffe YO7 89 B1
Lumb Mill Way BD23 157 E7
LUMBY 195 E1
Lumby Hill LS25 202 A8
Lumby La
Monk Fryston LS25 202 A8
South Milford LS25 196 A1
Lumley Cl YO7 211 D2
Lumley La
Azerley HG4 112 D2
Kirkby Fleetham with Fencote DL7 42 B1

Lumley Rd YO30 228 B7
Lumley St WF10 200 D3
Luna Pk* YO11 213 C6
Luncarr La HG4 114 B2
LUND 198 D3
Lund Cl YO32 225 C8
Lundgreen La YO61 144 A3
Lund Head La HG3 179 B2
Lund La
Bubwith YO8 199 C4
Cliffe YO8 198 D4
Hampsthwaite HG3 161 A5
Lund Rd YO62 70 B7
Lund Sand La
Easingwold YO61 143 A8
Raskelf YO61 117 A1
Lund Sike La LS25 195 F2
Lund's Twr* BD20 187 D6
Lundy Cl 10 YO30 225 A1
Lunebeck Wlk TS17 6 C6
Lunedale Ave
Knaresborough HG5 221 C5
Middlesbrough TS5 6 E8
Lunedale Rd DL3 3 A6
Lunnfields La WF11 201 E6
Lunn La DN14 202 D3
Lupton Bank HG3 137 D3
Lupton Cl HG3 137 D3
Lupton Springs HG3 137 D3
Lutton La YO17 123 F4
Luttons Prim Sch YO17 150 B8
Lutyens The 22 LS29 175 C2
Lycett Rd YO24 230 F6
Lych Gate 14 DL2 3 E1
Lydford Rd 18 DL10 41 E4
Lydham Ct 2 YO24 230 C8
Lyell St YO12 212 E6
Lynbrook Cl YO7 211 B4
Lyndale
Guisborough TS14 8 D5
Kippax LS25 200 D8
Lyndale Ave YO10 229 C3
Lyndale Gr 14 WF6 200 B1
Lynden Cl HG4 214 E4
Lynden Way YO24 227 D3
Lyndhurst Cl
2 Norton DN6 206 F2
9 Whitby YO21 208 D6
Lyndhurst Dr 1 DN6 206 F2
Lyndhurst Rise 3 DN6 206 F2
Lyndon Ave
Bramham LS23 188 E6
Garforth LS25 194 C4
Lyndon Cl 1 LS23 188 E6
Lyndon Cres 4 LS23 188 E6
Lyndon Rd LS23 188 E6
Lyndon Sq 2 LS23 188 E6
Lyndon Way LS23 188 E6
Lynmouth Cl 2 TS8 6 E5
Lynndale Ave 6 BD20 187 F8
Lynton Ave LS23 188 E8
Lynton Cl YO8 232 B1
Lynton Gdns
Brayton YO8 232 B1
Darlington DL1 3 E5
Harrogate HG1 220 A3
Lynton Way DL6 210 D3
Lynwith Cl DN14 204 C3
Lynwith Ct DN14 204 C3
Lynwith Dr DN14 204 C3
Lynwood Ave 3 YO23 230 A3
Lynwood Cl YO32 167 A7
Lynwood View 4 YO23 230 A3
Lynx La YO7 115 B1
Lyonette Rd DL1 3 E7
Lyon Rd BD20 187 F7
Lyons Rd DL10 209 C8
Lysander Bsns Pk YO30 225 A3
Lysander Cl YO30 225 A3
Lys Cres DL9 209 D1
Lytham Cl BD23 217 C3
Lytham Gdns BD23 217 C3
Lytham Rd DL1 3 D8
LYTHE 12 E4
Lythe Bank
Lythe YO21 12 F4
Sutton with Howgrave DL8 87 F2
Lythe CE Prim Sch YO21 12 E3
Lythe Fell Rd LA2 129 B2
Lythe La LA2 129 A2

M

Mcan Cl YO10 229 D4
MacArthurs Cl YO7 211 B2
McBean Steps* YO11 213 A5
McCain Stad (Scarborough FC) YO11 212 E2
McDonald Rd HG4 113 D3
MacDonell Cl 1 DL9 209 C1
MacKeridge La YO62 48 F4
Mackie Dr TS14 8 F7
MacKinnon Ave 1 WF6 200 B2
MacLagan Rd YO23 230 F4
McMullen Rd DL1 3 E6
Madeley Sq WF10 201 B5
Mafeking St HG1 219 F4
Magazine La YO8 198 C4
Magazine Rd YO8 198 B4
Magdalen's Cl HG4 214 D6
Magdalen's Rd HG4 214 D6
Magister Rd TS17 6 B7
Magnolia Gr YO32 225 D2
Magpie Garth YO12 99 E6
Maida Gr YO10 228 D2
Maiden Bower (Motte & Bailey)* YO7 115 D5
Maiden Castle* DL11 38 A5
Maiden Greve YO17 215 A4
Maidensgrave Henge* YO25 126 F1
Maidstone Dr TS7 7 C6
Main Ave
Woodlands HG2 220 C3
York YO31 228 F5
Main Rd
Drax YO8 204 F5
Gainford DL2 1 D7
Hambleton YO8 196 E1
Hellifield BD23 154 B3
Stainforth BD24 131 E6
Steeton with Eastburn BD20 187 F7
Weaverthorpe YO17 124 E1
Mainsfield Cl 1 BD24 131 D3
Mainsfield Rise 2 BD24 131 D3
Mains La YO60 146 D5
Main St
Aberford LS25 194 F8
Addingham LS29 174 F4
Allerston YO18 97 B5
Alne YO61 142 F4
Amotherby YO17 121 A4
Appleton Roebuck YO23 190 F5
Askham Bryan YO23 182 F3
Askrigg DL8 57 E6
Asselby DN14 205 D7
Austwick LA2 130 E7
Aysgarth DL8 58 E3
Barkston Ash LS24 195 E7
Barwick in Elmet LS15 194 B8
3 Beal DN14 202 D4
Bentham LA2 128 E8
Bilbrough YO23 182 C1
Bilton-in-Ainsty with Bickerton LS22 181 A5
Bishop Monkton HG3 140 B5
Bishopthorpe YO23 231 A4
Boroughbridge YO51 141 A3
Brafferton YO61 141 F8
Bubwith YO8 199 C7
Bugthorpe YO41 169 D4
Burley in Warfedale LS29 176 C1
Burton Salmon LS25 201 F6
Church Fenton LS24 196 B7
Cliffe YO8 198 E2
Cononley BD20 173 D1
Copmanthorpe YO23 230 A2
Cottingwith YO42 193 C5
Darley HG3 160 A6
Deighton YO19 192 A7
Earby BB18 186 A7
East Ayton/West Ayton YO13 99 A7
Eastfield YO11 100 B6
Ebberston & Yedingham YO13 97 D5
Ellerton YO42 193 C1
Elvington YO41 185 C2
Embsay BD23 217 E8
Escrick YO19 192 B5
Farnhill BD20 173 E1
Folkton YO11 100 A2
Follifoot HG3 223 F5
Ganton YO12 125 A8
Garforth LS25 194 C3
Gillamoor YO62 70 A4
Gilling East YO62 118 F7
Glusburn BD20 187 E7
Gowdall DN14 204 A1
13 Grassington BD23 134 E3
Great Ouseburn YO26 164 B8
Great Preston WF10 200 D6
Gristlthorp YO14 100 E4
Harome YO62 93 C5
Healaugh LS24 181 F2
Hebden BD23 135 A1
Heck DN14 207 C8
Helperby YO61 142 A8
Hemingbrough YO8 198 F1
Hensall DN14 203 D2
Heslington YO10 229 B1
Hessay YO26 182 B8
High Bentham LA2 129 A8
Hovingham YO62 119 E6
Huby YO61 144 A4
Ingleton LA6 103 D3
Irton YO12 99 C6
Kelfield YO19 191 D1
Kellington DN14 202 F3
Kirkby Malham BD23 154 F8
Kirkby Malzeard HG4 112 C5
Kirk Deighton LS22 180 B5
Kirk Smeaton WF8 206 B3
Knapton YO26 227 A5
Langcliffe BD24 131 E4
Ledston WF10 200 F7
Linton LS22 180 A1
Little Ouseburn YO26 164 A7
Long Preston BD23 153 F5
Low Bradley BD20 173 E3
Menwith with Darley HG3 160 A4
Mickletown LS26 200 B6
Middleton YO18 95 E8
Monk Fryston LS25 201 F8
Monk Fryston LS25 202 A8
1 Naburn YO19 191 D8
Newton Kyme cum Toulston LS24 189 C7
North Duffield YO8 199 A8
Nunthorpe YO10 231 D8
Pannal HG3 222 D3
Main St *continued*
Pollington DN14 207 F6
Poppleton YO26 165 F1
Rathmell BD24 153 C6
Reighton YO14 127 E5
Riccall YO19 198 A8
Ryther cum Ossendyke LS24 190 E2
Saxton with Scarthingwell LS24 195 D7
Scholes LS15 194 A7
Scotton HG5 162 A6
Seamer YO12 99 D6
Sheriff Hutton YO60 145 D5
Shipton YO30 165 F5
Sicklinghall LS22 179 D3
Sinnington YO62 95 A8
Stainforth BD24 131 E6
Stamford Bridge YO41 168 D2
Staveley HG5 140 E1
Stillington YO61 144 C6
Sutton-on-the-Forest YO61 144 C3
Threshfield BD23 134 C2
Thwing YO25 126 B1
Tollerton YO61 143 A3
Ulleskelf LS24 190 C3
Walton LS23 181 A2
Wath HG4 114 A8
Weeton LS17 178 C1
Westow YO60 147 B4
West Tanfield HG4 87 A1
Wheldrake YO19 192 F7
Whittington LA6 102 A7
Wilberfoss YO41 185 E5
Wombleton YO62 93 E6
Womersley DN6 206 C6
Woodlands HG2 220 B3
Wray-with-Botton LA2 128 A6
Mains The BD24 131 D3
Maison Dieu DL10 209 D7
Major St DL3 3 C6
Malais La BD20 187 D7
Malbys Gr YO23 230 B2
Malden Rd HG1 220 B3
MALHAM 133 A1
Malham Gr YO31 229 B5
Malham Moor La BD23 133 F4
Malham Rakes BD23 133 A2
Malham Tarn Field Ctr* BD24 132 F6
Malham Tarn National Nature Reserve* BD24 132 E5
Malham View Cl 28 BB18 171 D1
Malham Way HG5 221 D6
Malim Rd DL1 3 F5
Mallard Cl
8 Filey YO14 101 A4
12 Pickering YO18 95 F6
15 Ripon HG4 214 C5
Mallard Landings YO31 228 D8
Mallard Rd 4 DL9 40 F2
Mallard View YO17 215 D2
Mallard Way
4 Eastfield YO12 99 F6
11 Haxby YO32 166 F5
Mallard Wlk 14 YO51 141 B5
Mallinson Cl HG2 222 D6
Mallinson Cres HG2 222 E6
Mallinson Gate HG2 222 E6
Mallinson Gr HG2 222 D6
Mallinson Oval HG2 222 D6
Mallinson Way HG2 222 D6
Mallison Hill Dr 5 YO61 117 D1
Mallorie Cl HG4 214 A5
Mallorie Ct HG4 214 B5
Mallorie Park Dr HG4 214 A4
Mallory Cl YO32 225 D4
Mallory Ct 17 DL1 3 F6
Mallowdale TS7 7 C5
Malltraeth Sands TS17 6 D6
Malpas Dr DL7 210 D4
Malpas Rd
Brompton YO13 98 C4
Northallerton DL7 210 D3
Malsis Prep Sch BD20 187 C7
MALTBY 6 C4
Maltby Pl 2 TS17 6 B8
Maltby Rd TS8 6 D4
Malt Dubs Cl LA6 103 D3
Malthouse Cl WF10 200 E4
Malthouse La HG3 222 D2
Maltings Bsns Ctr The YO17 215 C3
Maltings Ct
Alne YO61 143 A5
6 Selby YO8 232 C6
Maltings Ind Est The DN14 202 F1
Maltings The
8 Brafferton YO61 115 F1
Cliffe YO8 198 E3
13 Pontefract WF8 201 B1
Thirsk YO7 211 B2
Maltkiln La
Castleford WF10 200 F4
Killinghall HG3 161 C6
Malt Kiln La YO23 190 F5
Malt Kiln Terr LS24 189 D4
Maltings The LA6 102 A7
MALTON 215 C4
Malton Ave YO31 228 E6
Malton Com Prim Sch YO17 215 D5
Malton Gate YO18 96 D5
Malton La
Allerston YO18 97 B4
Malton La *continued*
Flaxton YO60 146 A1
Kirby Grindalythe YO17 150 A8
Malton Mus* YO17 215 C4
Malton & Norton District Hospl YO17 215 B4
Malton Rd
Hunmanby YO14 126 F8
Huntington YO32 226 A1
Leavening YO17 147 E2
Pickering YO18 95 F6
Rillington YO17 122 E4
Scampston YO17 123 B7
Slingsby YO62 120 B5
Swinton YO17 121 C4
York YO31 228 F7
Malton Sch YO17 215 A5
Malton St YO61 117 D6
Malton Sta YO17 215 C3
Malton Way YO30 227 F8
Malt Shoval Ct YO1 233 C2
Malvern Ave YO26 227 D5
Malvern Cl
Huntington YO32 226 A5
8 Hurworth-on-Tees DL2 3 E1
Stokesley TS9 26 C7
Malvern Cres
Darlington DL3 2 F7
Scarborough YO12 212 D5
Malvern Dr
Middlesbrough TS5 6 E6
Stokesley TS9 26 C7
Malvern Rd WF11 201 F2
Manchester Rd BB18 171 D1
Mancroft YO32 225 C8
Mandale Mill Prim Sch TS17 6 B8
Mandale Rd TS5 6 D8
MANFIELD 2 B4
Manfield CE Prim Sch DL2 2 B4
Mangrill La LS14 188 C3
Manham Hill YO11 99 F7
Mankin La HG4 214 D1
Manley Cl YO32 225 D4
Manley Dr LS22 180 A3
Manley Gr LS29 218 D4
Manley Rd LS29 218 E4
Manley Rise LS29 218 D3
Manor Ave YO12 212 D6
Manor Beeches The 3 YO19 184 E7
Manor CE Sch YO26 227 C7
Manor Chase YO26 181 F6
Manor Cl
Burton in Lonsdale LA6 102 F3
5 Hemingbrough YO8 198 F1
Ingleton LA6 103 D3
13 Kirkbymoorside YO62 70 B1
Kirk Smeaton WF8 206 B3
Low Worsall TS15 24 B8
6 North Duffield YO8 199 A7
12 Norton DN6 206 E2
5 Stokesley TS9 26 C7
Topcliffe YO7 115 C6
Upper Poppleton YO26 182 F8
Wath HG4 114 B7
Whitby YO21 208 B6
Manor Cres HG5 221 C6
Manorcroft WF6 200 A1
Manor Croft YO42 169 F1
Manor Ct
6 Bubwith YO8 199 D7
Fairburn WF11 201 D7
Follifoot HG3 223 F5
Kirkby Malzeard HG4 112 D5
Knaresborough HG5 221 B5
York YO10 228 F3
2 York YO32 225 F6
Manor Dr
2 Brafferton YO61 115 F1
Camblesforth YO8 204 C4
4 Dunnington YO19 184 E7
Harrogate HG2 222 C8
Hilton TS15 6 C2
Kirby Hill YO51 141 A7
Knaresborough HG5 221 C6
5 North Duffield YO8 199 A7
North Featherstone WF7 200 E1
Pickering YO18 95 E7
Scotton HG5 162 A6
Manor Drive N YO26 227 D4
Manor Drive S YO26 227 D4
Manor Farm LA6 102 A7
Manor Farm Cl
1 Brayton YO8 232 A1
Carlton DN14 204 C2
Copmanthorpe YO23 230 A2
Kellington DN14 202 F3
Manor Farm Ct
Chapel Haddlesey YO8 203 C4
Colton LS24 190 E7
Manor Farm Way
Coulby Newham TS8 6 F5
Scotton HG5 162 A6
Manorfields 11 DL2 3 E1
Manor Fields DN14 205 B2
Manor Fold HG3 223 F5
Manor Garth
Haxby YO32 225 B8
Kellington DN14 202 F3
12 Kirklevington TS15 24 E8
Ledsham LS25 201 B8
7 Norton DN6 206 F2
1 Riccall YO19 198 A8
7 Spofforth HG3 179 E6
Manor Garth Rd LS25 194 E1
Manor Gdns
6 Hunmanby YO14 127 A8
Manor Gdns *continued*
Killinghall HG3 161 C5
Kirkbymoorside YO62 70 B1
15 Knaresborough HG5 221 B6
Scarborough YO12 212 E6
Thorner LS14 188 A3
Manor Gn
Northallerton DL7 210 C3
Patrick Brompton DL8 62 C6
Manor Gr
Colburn DL9 40 F5
Great Broughton TS9 26 E5
Manor Heath YO23 230 A3
Manor House Art Gall & Mus* LS29 218 B4
Manor La
Healaugh LS24 181 E1
Rawcliffe YO30 224 D2
Manor Orchards HG5 221 B6
MANOR PARK 176 B2
Manor Park Ave
Great Preston WF10 200 D7
Pontefract WF8 201 C2
Manor Park Cl YO30 224 E2
Manor Park Gr 2 YO30 224 E2
Manor Park Rd YO30 224 E2
Manor Pk
Arkendale HG5 163 A7
Cowling BD22 187 B6
Ledston WF10 200 F7
Swinton YO17 121 C4
Manor Rd
Beal DN14 202 C4
Darlington DL3 3 C4
Easingwold YO61 117 C1
Fylingdales YO22 33 C4
Harrogate HG2 222 B8
Hurworth-on-Tees DL2 3 D1
Killinghall HG3 161 C5
Knaresborough HG5 221 B6
Scarborough YO12 212 E5
Stutton with Hazlewood LS24 189 D4
Manor Rise LS29 218 D4
Manor Vale La 23 YO62 70 B1
Manor View
Castleford WF10 200 F3
Oswaldkirk YO62 93 A1
Rillington YO17 122 F5
Manor View Rd YO11 100 D5
Manor Way
Glusburn BD20 187 E6
York YO30 224 E2
Manor Wood TS8 6 F6
Manse Cres 23 LS29 176 C1
Manse La HG5 221 D4
Mansell Cl YO8 232 A2
Manse Rd LS29 176 C1
Manse Way BD20 187 E7
Mansfield Ave TS17 6 B8
Mansfield Ct HG1 219 C4
Mansfield Rd LS29 176 B1
Mansfield St YO31 233 C3
Manston Ct 14 DL2 4 C4
Manston La LS15 194 A5
Manton Ave TS5 6 D8
Maple Ave
Bishopthorpe YO23 231 A3
Malton YO17 215 D6
Maple Cl
5 Colburn DL9 40 F5
Hambleton YO8 197 B1
2 South Milford LS25 195 F2
Maple Croft YO61 144 A5
Maple Ct
Wheldrake YO19 192 D8
York YO10 231 E6
Maple Dr YO12 212 D7
Maple Garth HG4 114 B7
Maple Gr
12 Brayton YO8 197 D1
7 Linton-on-Ouse YO30 164 F7
York YO10 228 D1
Maplehurst Ave YO31 228 D7
Maple La YO61 144 A5
Maple Rd DL10 209 A8
Maple Tree Ave 10 YO8 198 B4
Maple Wlk HG4 214 B2
Maplewood Paddock 2 YO24 227 C1
Marage Rd YO7 211 B3
Marazion Dr DL3 3 C8
March Ave HG5 221 A4
Marchlyn Cres TS17 5 F4
March St
Normanton South WF6 200 A1
York YO31 233 C4
Marderby La YO7 90 C7
Maresfield Rd DL9 40 E3
Margaret Philipson Ct YO1 233 C3
Margaret Rd HG2 219 B1
Margaret St YO10 233 C1
Margerison Cres LS29 218 E3
Margerison Rd LS29 218 E3
Margrove Heritage Ctr* TS12 9 D6
MARGROVE PARK 9 D6
Marhead Balk HG5 163 A7
Marias Ct 9 YO11 213 A6
Maria St 15 LS29 176 C1
Marigold Cl YO8 232 C2
Marina Cres BD23 216 D3
Marina Rd DL3 3 D8
Marina Way HG4 214 A2
Marine Dr YO11 213 C7
Marine Espl YO13 54 A8
Marine Par 24 YO21 208 D7

Mariner's Terr 16 YO14 ... 101 B3
Marine Villa Rd WF11 ... 201 F2
Marion Ave TS16 ... 5 D4
Marishes La
Allerston YO17 ... 97 A2
Thornton-le-Dale YO17 ... 96 E1
Marishes Low Rd YO17 ... 122 B8
Marjorie Waite Ct YO30 ... 228 B7
Markenfield Hall* HG4 ... 139 D6
Markenfield Rd HG3 ... 219 B5
Market Cross Sh Ctr 13
YO8 ... 232 C5
Market Flat La HG5 ... 162 C6
Market Hall YO11 ... 213 B6
Market Hill 5 YO51 ... 141 B6
Market La 14 YO8 ... 232 C5
Market Pl
Askrigg DL8 ... 57 E5
4 Bedale DL8 ... 63 A3
2 Cawood YO8 ... 197 B8
7 Easingwold YO61 ... 143 C8
Hawes DL8 ... 56 C4
10 Helmsley YO62 ... 92 F6
25 Kirkbymoorside YO62 ... 70 B1
3 Knaresborough HG5 ... 221 B6
Malton YO17 ... 215 C4
9 Masham HG4 ... 86 C3
9 Middleham DL8 ... 60 E2
6 Normanton South WF6 ... 200 A1
Pickering YO18 ... 95 F7
Richmond DL10 ... 209 C6
11 Selby YO8 ... 232 C5
10 Settle BD24 ... 131 D2
7 Snaith DN14 ... 204 C1
Thirsk YO7 ... 211 B3
12 Wetherby LS22 ... 180 C3
11 Whitby YO22 ... 208 D7
Market Place E 19 HG4 ... 214 C5
Market Place N 23 HG4 ... 214 C5
Market Place S 20 HG4 ... 214 C5
Market Place W 21 HG4 ... 214 C5
Market Row DL7 ... 210 D4
Market Sq 13 DL10 ... 209 C6
Market St
Malton YO17 ... 215 C4
Normanton South WF6 ... 200 A1
24 Scarborough YO11 ... 213 A6
York YO1 ... 233 B2
Market Way 25 YO11 ... 213 A6
Market Weighton Rd
YO8 ... 198 B6
Markham Cres YO31 ... 233 B4
Markham St YO31 ... 233 B4
Mark House La BD23 ... 155 C1
MARKINGTON ... 139 D3
Markington CE Prim Sch
HG3 ... 139 C3
Mark La
Fylingdales YO22 ... 33 C3
Kirk Deighton LS22 ... 180 B5
Marlborough Ave
3 Byram WF11 ... 201 F4
Tadcaster LS24 ... 189 D5
3 Whitby YO21 ... 208 B7
Marlborough Cl YO30 ... 224 D3
Marlborough Dr
Darlington DL1 ... 3 C4
Tadcaster LS24 ... 189 D5
Marlborough Gr
Ilkley LS29 ... 218 D3
Ripon HG4 ... 214 B6
York YO10 ... 228 D2
Marlborough Rd HG1 ... 219 E2
Marlborough Sq LS29 ... 218 C3
Marlborough St 11 YO12 ... 213 A7
Marlborough Villas
YO10 ... 228 D2
Marl Hill La BD20 ... 186 D8
Marmiam Dr 2 YO32 ... 167 D2
Marmion Ct HG4 ... 87 A1
Marmion Twr* HG4 ... 87 A1
Marne Cl 1 DL9 ... 209 B1
Marne Rd DL9 ... 209 D1
Marquis Ct 2 YO26 ... 227 D6
MARRICK ... 38 F5
Marrick Priory Outdoor Ctr*
DL11 ... 38 E4
Marrick Rd TS18 ... 5 D8
Marridales DL8 ... 56 D4
Marriforth La HG4 ... 61 F2
Marriner Cl 13 LS21 ... 176 F1
Marr The YO14 ... 100 F5
Marrtree Bsns Pk WF10 ... 200 E3
Marsdens Pl 7 YO22 ... 208 E6
Marsden Wlk DL3 ... 3 C8
MARSETT ... 57 A1
Marsett La DL8 ... 57 B2
Marshall Dr YO18 ... 96 A7
Marshall Mews 2 WF10 ... 200 E4
Marshall Way HG4 ... 214 C5
Marsh Croft WF11 ... 201 E4
Marsh End WF11 ... 202 A3
Marshfield Rd 7 BD24 ... 131 D2
Marsh La
Asselby DN14 ... 205 D7
Barlow YO8 ... 204 B8
2 Beal DN14 ... 202 D4
Bolton Percy YO23 ... 190 D3
Byram cum Sutton WF11 ... 201 F4
Cawood YO8 ... 197 D8
Ingleby Greenhow TS9 ... 27 B5
Knottingley WF11 ... 202 A2
West Haddlesey YO8 ... 202 F5
Marsh Lane Gdns DN14 ... 202 F4
Marsh Rd WF10 ... 200 D3
MARSKE ... 39 C7
Mars La TS13 ... 11 A4
Marston Ave YO26 ... 227 B3
Marston Bsns Pk YO26 ... 181 B7
Marston Cres YO26 ... 227 B3
Marston La
Long Marston YO26 ... 182 A8
Moor Monkton YO26 ... 165 A1
Marston Moor Rd 4 DL1 ... 3 F4
Marston Rd YO26 ... 181 D7
Marston Way 3 LS22 ... 180 B3
Martello Way YO32 ... 226 A1
Marten Cl 2 YO30 ... 228 A8
Martin Cheeseman Ct 3
YO24 ... 230 C8
Martindale Rd DL1 ... 3 D7
Martinet Ct TS17 ... 6 A7
Martinet Rd TS17 ... 6 B7
Martinhoe Cl 4 TS17 ... 6 A3
Martins Ct YO26 ... 228 A5
MARTON
Boroughbridge ... 141 D1
Middlesbrough ... 7 B7
Pickering ... 94 F6
Marton Abbey (Priory)*
YO61 ... 144 C8
Marton Ave TS4 ... 7 B8
Marton Cl BD23 ... 172 C8
Marton Ct YO21 ... 208 B6
Marton cum Grafton CE Prim
Sch YO51 ... 141 D1
Marton Gr 1 TS3 ... 7 C8
MARTON-IN-THE-
FOREST ... 144 E7
Marton La
Arkendale HG5 ... 163 B8
Wrelton YO18 ... 95 C7
MARTON-LE-MOOR ... 114 F1
Marton Manor Prim Sch
TS7 ... 7 B6
Marton Moor Rd TS7 ... 7 D5
Marton Rd
Coulby Newham TS4 ... 7 A7
Gargrave BD23 ... 172 C8
Marton YO62 ... 94 F6
Sinnington YO62 ... 95 A7
Martonside Way TS4 ... 7 A8
Marton St BD23 ... 216 D3
Marton Sta TS7 ... 7 C7
Marvell Rise HG1 ... 219 E7
Marwood CE VC Infant Sch
TS9 ... 7 F1
Marwood Dr TS9 ... 7 F1
Marygate
Barton DL10 ... 21 D7
York YO30 ... 233 A3
Marygate La YO30 ... 233 A3
Marykirk Rd TS17 ... 6 B6
Mary La YO26 ... 141 F3
Masefield Cl HG1 ... 219 E7
MASHAM ... 86 B3
Masham Bank HG4 ... 85 D8
Masham CE Prim Sch
HG4 ... 86 C3
Masham Cl HG2 ... 220 C1
Masham La DL8 ... 87 A4
Masham Rd
Firby DL8 ... 62 F1
Harrogate HG2 ... 220 C1
Snape with Thorp DL8 ... 86 E8
Mask La YO41 ... 185 D4
MASONGILL ... 103 A6
Masongill Fell La LA6 ... 103 A6
Masonic La YO7 ... 211 B3
Masons Way BB18 ... 171 D2
Maspin Moor Rd LS25 ... 202 C7
Massa Flatts Wood BD23 ... 216 E5
Massey St YO8 ... 232 C5
Master Rd TS17 ... 6 B7
Master's Gate YO18 ... 49 D4
Mastil Cl DL8 ... 62 D5
Mastiles La BD23 ... 134 A6
Mastil La DL8 ... 62 D5
Matfen Ave TS7 ... 7 D6
Matthew La
Bradleys Both BD20 ... 173 E3
Green Hammerton YO26 ... 164 C4
Mattison Way YO24 ... 227 E2
Maude Rd DL9 ... 209 A1
Maud La LS21 ... 177 A6
Maudon Ave YO18 ... 96 A6
Maudon Gr YO17 ... 215 F4
Maufe Way 3 LS29 ... 218 B3
MAUNBY ... 64 D1
Maunby La YO7 ... 64 D1
Maundy Gr HG5 ... 221 C7
Mawson Gr DL6 ... 65 B5
Mawson La HG4 ... 214 C4
Maxim Cl 5 DL9 ... 40 E4
Maxwell Rd LS29 ... 218 D3
Mayfair Ave TS6 ... 7 E8
Mayfair Rd DL1 ... 3 D8
Mayfield DL7 ... 64 F2
Mayfield Ave
Ilkley LS29 ... 218 D4
7 Scalby YO12 ... 75 E5
Mayfield Cl
3 Glusburn BD20 ... 187 E7
Ilkley LS29 ... 218 D4
Mayfield Cres TS16 ... 5 D5
Mayfield Ct YO8 ... 204 C7
Mayfield Dr
5 Brayton YO8 ... 232 A1
4 Seamer YO12 ... 99 D6
Mayfield Gdns LS29 ... 218 D5
Mayfield Gr
Harrogate HG1 ... 219 D3
Knaresborough HG5 ... 221 C6
York YO24 ... 230 E8
Mayfield Pl
Harrogate HG1 ... 219 D3
Mayfield Pl *continued*
3 Whitby YO21 ... 208 C5
Mayfield Rd
Brayton YO8 ... 232 A1
1 High Bentham LA2 ... 129 A7
Ilkley LS29 ... 218 C4
Middlesbrough TS7 ... 7 D6
Whitby YO21 ... 208 B5
Mayfield Terr HG1 ... 219 D3
Mayfly Ct 26 YO18 ... 95 F6
Maypole Gdns YO8 ... 197 B8
Maypole Gr 3 YO19 ... 191 D8
Maypole Mews LS15 ... 194 B8
Maythorn Rd YO31 ... 225 E2
Maythorpe YO23 ... 182 C6
Mayville Ave YO12 ... 212 E6
Mead Cres TS17 ... 6 C8
Meadlands YO31 ... 229 B6
Meadow Ave 5 HG4 ... 214 B2
Meadowbank Rd TS7 ... 7 D7
Meadowbeck Cl YO10 ... 229 B4
Meadow Brook Chase 19
WF6 ... 200 B1
Meadow Cl
Cononley BD20 ... 173 D2
7 Eastfield YO11 ... 100 A6
Hampsthwaite HG3 ... 160 F5
Northallerton DL7 ... 210 D2
Thorpe Willoughby YO8 ... 197 C2
Meadowcroft
Draughton BD23 ... 174 B7
Harrogate HG1 ... 219 E6
Meadow Croft
Brayton YO8 ... 232 A2
Colonley BD20 ... 173 C2
Meadowcroft Dr HG3 ... 140 A5
Meadow Ct
Rillington YO17 ... 122 F5
Scruton DL7 ... 63 E7
6 Willerby YO12 ... 99 D2
3 York YO24 ... 230 E8
Meadow Dale Ct TS12 ... 9 F7
Meadow Dr
7 East Ayton/West Ayton
YO13 ... 99 B8
Harrogate HG1 ... 219 E7
Scruton DL7 ... 63 E7
Thorpe Willoughby YO8 ... 197 B2
Meadowfield
Amotherby YO17 ... 121 A4
9 Bedale DL8 ... 63 B3
1 Bubwith YO8 ... 199 D7
Lythe YO21 ... 13 A3
8 Stokesley TS9 ... 26 C8
Meadowfield Dr
Eaglescliffe TS16 ... 5 D5
South Duffield YO8 ... 199 A4
Meadowfield Rd
9 Colburn DL9 ... 41 A5
Darlington DL3 ... 3 A7
Meadowfields YO21 ... 208 C6
Meadowfields Cl 9
YO61 ... 143 D8
Meadowfields Ct 17
YO21 ... 208 D6
Meadowfields Dr YO31 ... 225 D2
Meadow Garth
2 Tadcaster LS24 ... 189 F6
Thirsk YO7 ... 211 B1
Thorpe Willoughby YO8 ... 197 C2
Meadow Gate HG1 ... 219 E6
Meadow Gr 20 DL8 ... 63 A2
Meadowings The TS15 ... 5 D2
Meadow La
Cononley BD20 ... 173 C2
2 Darley HG3 ... 160 A6
8 Eastfield YO11 ... 100 A6
1 Haxby YO32 ... 225 D8
Hellifield BD23 ... 154 A3
Northallerton DL6 ... 210 E6
Snape DL8 ... 87 A7
Meadowlands Cl 2 TS13 ... 11 A8
Meadow Lea 21 BD20 ... 187 E7
Meadow Pl 5 YO8 ... 232 B6
Meadow Rd
Garforth LS25 ... 194 D4
Knaresborough HG5 ... 221 B7
2 Pickering YO18 ... 95 F7
Meadow Rise
Harrogate HG1 ... 219 E7
7 Settle BD24 ... 131 D3
2 Skipton BD23 ... 217 B5
Meadowside Prim Sch
HG5 ... 221 C7
Meadow Springs Way 3
YO61 ... 143 D8
Meadows The
3 Carlton DN14 ... 204 C3
Castleford LS25 ... 200 C7
Coulby Newham TS8 ... 7 B5
Hambleton YO8 ... 196 F1
8 Middleton St George DL2 ... 4 C4
7 Monk Fryston LS25 ... 202 A8
Northallerton DL6 ... 210 E5
Riccall YO19 ... 197 F8
Richmond DL10 ... 209 E7
Scalby YO12 ... 212 B7
2 Skelton YO30 ... 224 B5
South Milford LS25 ... 195 F2
Meadow Vale
Green Hammerton YO26 ... 164 C3
2 Ripon HG4 ... 214 B2
Meadow View
Barwick in Elmet & Scholes
LS15 ... 194 B8
Gristhorpe YO14 ... 100 E4
Harrogate HG1 ... 219 E6
Sherburn in Elmet LS25 ... 195 F4
Meadow Way
Barnoldswick BB18 ... 171 E2
Harrogate HG1 ... 219 E7
Heworth YO31 ... 228 F7
Huntington YO32 ... 225 F4
3 Tadcaster LS24 ... 189 F6
Meads La YO12 ... 99 E5
Meads The 3 YO11 ... 99 F6
Mead The DL1 ... 3 E5
Meadway YO8 ... 197 D2
Meadway Dr YO8 ... 197 D2
MEAGILL ... 159 D3
Meagill La LS21 ... 159 E2
Meagill Rise LS21 ... 176 E1
Meam Cl YO10 ... 229 D4
Meanee Rd 11 DL9 ... 40 F2
MEARBECK ... 153 D7
Medbourne Gdns TS5 ... 6 E7
Megson Pl YO7 ... 211 C4
Megsons Ct BD23 ... 217 C7
Melander Cl YO26 ... 227 B4
Melander Gdns 5 YO32 ... 225 D7
Melbourne Dr YO7 ... 90 E5
Melbourne Pl YO7 ... 211 B2
Melbourne St YO10 ... 228 D2
Melcombe Ave 11 YO32 ... 167 A7
Meldyke La TS8 ... 6 D5
Mellersh Rd 15 DL10 ... 41 E4
Melling (St Wilfrid) CE Prim
Sch LA6 ... 102 A2
Melltown's Gn YO7 ... 88 C6
MELMERBY
Carlton ... 83 F8
Ripon ... 114 C7
Melmerby Green La HG4 ... 114 C6
Melmerby Green Rd
HG4 ... 114 B6
Melmerby Ind Est HG4 ... 114 B6
Melrose Cl 1 YO31 ... 229 A5
Melrose Cres
Bishop Monkton HG3 ... 140 A5
Guisborough TS14 ... 9 A6
Melrose Dr 16 LS29 ... 176 C1
Melrosegate YO31 ... 228 F5
Melrose Rd HG3 ... 140 A5
Melrose St 4 YO12 ... 212 F6
MELSONBY ... 21 A7
Melsonby Methodist Prim
Sch DL10 ... 20 F7
Melton Ave YO30 ... 227 F8
Melton Coll YO24 ... 227 F3
Melton Dr
Bishopthorpe YO23 ... 231 A3
York YO30 ... 227 F8
Melville Gr 1 LS29 ... 218 E4
Melville Terr 52 YO14 ... 101 B3
Melwood Gr YO26 ... 227 B5
Memorial Dr TS7 ... 7 B6
Mendip Cl 2 YO32 ... 225 F5
MENETHORPE ... 147 D6
Menethorpe La YO17 ... 147 D7
Menin Rd DL9 ... 209 B1
MENTHORPE ... 199 C5
Menwith Hill Rd HG3 ... 159 D4
Mercer Art Gall The*
HG2 ... 219 C3
Mercer Dr DL9 ... 209 C1
Merchant Adventurers' Hall*
YO1 ... 233 C2
Merchantgate YO1 ... 233 C2
Merchants Ct YO31 ... 228 E5
Merchant's Row 10 YO11 ... 213 B6
Merchant Way YO23 ... 230 B3
Mercury Pk DL7 ... 63 C5
Mercury Rd DL10 ... 209 A8
Merefield Way WF10 ... 200 E2
Mere La YO11 ... 212 F1
Mere View Gdns YO12 ... 99 F8
Merewood Rd WF10 ... 200 C4
Merioneth Cl 5 TS17 ... 5 F4
Merlin Covert 4 YO31 ... 225 F3
Merlinwood BD23 ... 172 B4
Merrington Ave TS17 ... 6 D6
Merrybank La LS17 ... 178 A3
MERRYBENT ... 2 E5
Merrybent Dr DL2 ... 2 F5
Merry Dale YO11 ... 100 A7
Merryfield HG2 ... 222 B7
Messines Rd DL9 ... 40 E3
Metcalfe La YO19 ... 229 C5
Metcalfes Ct HG4 ... 214 C6
Metes La YO12 ... 99 E5
METHLEY ... 200 B5
METHLEY JUNCTION ... 200 A4
Methley La LS26 ... 200 A6
Methley Park Hospl
LS26 ... 200 A6
Methley Prim Sch LS26 ... 200 B6
Methley Rd WF10 ... 200 D4
Meuse Cl 4 DL9 ... 209 C1
Mewburn Rd DL3 ... 3 C8
MEWITH HEAD ... 129 E6
Mewith La LA2 ... 129 B6
Mews The WF6 ... 200 A2
Meynell Rd DL3 ... 3 C7
Meyrick Ave LS22 ... 180 D4
Michael Mount Rd YO11 ... 213 C1
Michael Syddall CE Prim Sch
DL10 ... 41 E5
Micklebury La HG4 ... 86 A3
MICKLEBY ... 12 A4
Mickleby Dr YO21 ... 208 B6
Mickleby La TS13 ... 11 F4
Mickledale La YO26 ... 163 D8
MICKLEFIELD ... 194 F4
Micklefield CE Prim Sch
LS25 ... 195 A4
Micklefield Sta LS25 ... 195 A3
Micklegate
17 Pontefract WF8 ... 201 B1
1 Selby YO8 ... 232 D5
York YO1 ... 233 A2
Micklegate Bar Mus*
YO24 ... 233 A1
Mickle Hill Mews BD23 ... 155 D1
Micklethwaite View
LS22 ... 180 C2
MICKLETOWN ... 200 B5
Mickletown Rd LS26 ... 200 B6
Micklewaite Gr LS22 ... 180 C2
MICKLEY ... 112 F7
Middle Bank Rd TS7 ... 7 D7
Middle Banks 24 YO32 ... 166 E5
Middlebrook Gdns YO8 ... 232 A2
MIDDLECAVE ... 215 A5
Middlecave Cl YO17 ... 215 A4
Middlecave Dr YO17 ... 215 A4
Middlecave Rd YO17 ... 215 B4
Middle Craven Rd 27
BD24 ... 131 D2
Middlecroft YO41 ... 185 F5
Middlecroft Dr YO32 ... 167 A7
Middlecroft Gr 2 YO32 ... 167 B7
Middlefield Cl
19 Osgodby YO11 ... 100 B7
Weaverthorpe YO17 ... 124 E1
Middlefield La
Kirk Smeaton WF8 ... 206 A2
Melmerby DL8 ... 84 A8
MIDDLEHAM ... 60 E2
Middleham Ave YO31 ... 228 E8
Middleham Castle* DL8 ... 60 E2
Middleham CE Prim Sch
DL8 ... 60 E2
Middleham La DL8 ... 60 E4
Middle Head Rd YO18 ... 71 E8
Middle La
Brayton YO8 ... 232 C1
Brompton YO13 ... 98 C7
Collingham LS22 ... 180 B1
Hutton Buscel YO13 ... 74 E1
Kettlewell with Starbotton
BD23 ... 108 A3
14 Knottingley WF11 ... 202 A2
Snainton YO13 ... 97 F4
Middle Moor La DL11 ... 39 F5
Middle Oxford St WF10 ... 200 E4
Middle Rd TS17 ... 6 A5
Middlesbrough Rd TS7 ... 7 E6
MIDDLESMOOR ... 110 B5
Middle St
Gayles DL11 ... 19 E6
Swinton YO17 ... 121 B4
Wilberfoss YO41 ... 185 F5
MIDDLETHORPE ... 231 B6
Middlethorpe Dr YO24 ... 230 E7
Middlethorpe Gr YO24 ... 230 F7
MIDDLETON
Glusburn ... 187 A6
Ilkley ... 218 C7
Pickering ... 95 E8
Middleton Ave
Ilkley LS29 ... 218 B6
Thornaby TS17 ... 6 B6
Middleton Carr La YO18 ... 95 D7
Middleton Cl
Egglescliffe TS16 ... 5 C5
Settrington YO17 ... 122 D1
Middleton La
Middleton St George DL2 ... 4 C3
Middleton YO18 ... 95 E8
MIDDLETON ONE ROW ... 4 D3
MIDDLETON-ON-LEVEN ... 25 D8
MIDDLETON QUERNHOW ... 88 B1
Middleton Rd
Hutton Rudby TS15 ... 25 D6
Ilkley LS29 ... 218 A4
Pickering YO18 ... 95 E7
Sadberge DL2 ... 4 C7
York YO24 ... 227 C2
MIDDLETON ST GEORGE ... 4 B4
Middleton St George Hospl
(Private) DL2 ... 4 E4
MIDDLETON TYAS ... 21 D5
Middleton Tyas La DL10 ... 21 B4
Middleton Tyas Prim Sch
DL10 ... 21 C5
Middleway BD20 ... 174 C1
Middle Wlk YO12 ... 212 E7
Middlewood Cl
3 Fylingdales YO22 ... 33 C3
Rufforth YO23 ... 182 C6
Middlewood Cres 5
YO22 ... 33 C3
Middlewood Garth 4
YO22 ... 33 C3
Middlewood La YO22 ... 33 C3
Middycar Bank HG4 ... 138 F6
Midge Hall Cl 18 LS29 ... 176 C1
Midgeley Gate HG5 ... 162 F2
Midgeley La HG5 ... 163 A3
Midgley Cl
4 Embsay BD23 ... 217 C7
21 Stamford Bridge YO41 ... 168 D2
Midgley Rd LS29 ... 176 C1
Midgley Rise 2 WF8 ... 201 B2
Midhope Way 15 YO14 ... 101 A3
Midland St BD23 ... 216 E3
Midway Ave YO26 ... 224 A1
Mightens' Bank DL8 ... 60 D4
Milbank Rd DL3 ... 3 B5
Milburn La YO7 ... 89 D3
MILBY ... 141 B6

Mildred Gr 5 YO24 227 F2
Mildred Sylvester Way WF6 200 B1
Mile Hill Coldhill La LS25 195 E5
Mile House Bsns Pk DL6 210 B7
Mile Planting DL10 209 F8
Milestone Ave YO23 182 C6
Milford Mews 7 YO32 225 D7
Milford Rd LS25 195 F3
Milford Way 8 YO32 225 D7
Milking Hill YO61 118 B4
Mill Balk DN14 207 C8
Mill Bank
Bishop Thornton HG3 138 F1
Fylingdales YO22 33 D2
Lindrick with Studley Royal & Fountains HG4 113 A3
Norton YO17 215 E3
Millbank Ct YO7 89 D4
Millbank La TS17 6 B7
Mill Bank Rd YO18 72 D5
Millbeck Gn LS22 188 A8
Millbeck View WF8 201 B2
Mill Bridge BD23 216 F4
Millbrook Ct 17 BB8 186 A3
Mill Brow LA2 128 E2
Mill Brow Rd BB18 172 B1
Mill Chase Rd HG2 220 D5
Mill Cl
Monk Fryston LS25 202 A8
Ravensworth DL11 19 F6
Settle BD24 131 D2
6 Spofforth HG3 179 E6
Mill Close La DL8 62 D6
Mill Cotts YO17 215 D4
Millcroft 15 YO8 197 D1
Mill Croft
Cowling BD22 187 B6
Richmond DL10 209 A7
MILL DAM 129 C6
Mill Dam LS23 188 F7
Mill Dam La WF8 201 C1
Mill Dike La YO7 116 F8
Millenium Rd BD20 173 D4
Millers Cl YO17 215 D2
Millers Croft 6 YO23 230 B3
Millers Ford LA2 128 E8
Millers La TS12 9 F6
Millers Rd 2 YO7 211 C3
Millfield YO51 141 D2
Millfield Ave
Northallerton DL6 210 E3
York YO10 228 F3
Millfield Cl
Eaglescliffe TS16 5 D4
1 Leeming DL7 63 D4
Pickering YO18 95 F6
Wilberfoss YO41 185 E5
Millfield Cres DL6 210 E3
Millfield Ct YO19 192 F7
Mill Field Ct 5 BD20 174 C1
Millfield Dr YO8 204 D4
Millfield Gdns YO26 224 A2
Millfield Glade HG2 220 D4
Millfield Ind Est YO19 192 F7
Millfield La
Easingwold YO61 117 C1
Nether Poppleton YO26 227 B8
Poppleton YO26 224 A2
York YO10 229 A3
Mill Field La YO61 91 B1
Millfield Rd
17 Hemingbrough YO8 198 F1
Hemingbrough YO8 204 F8
York YO23 228 B2
Mill Field Rd YO8 203 B5
Millfield Rise YO61 117 C1
Millfields 2 BD20 174 C1
Millfield St 4 HG3 137 B4
Mill Flats La DL8 60 F3
Mill Garth 14 YO8 198 F1
Millgarth Ct 7 LS22 188 A8
Millgate
10 Masham HG4 86 C3
Richmond DL10 209 C6
Selby YO8 232 C6
Thirsk YO7 211 B3
Mill Gate
Gilling with Hartforth & Sedbury DL10 20 E3
Harrogate HG1 219 C7
Knayton with Brawith YO7 65 E2
Millgate House Gdn* DL10 209 C6
Millgate Mews 3 YO8 232 C6
Millgates YO26 227 C6
Mill Green Way The YO22 51 D8
Mill Hill
Escrick YO19 192 B5
16 Normanton South WF6 200 A1
Mill Hill Cl 8 DL6 43 F3
Mill Hill Cres DL6 210 E3
Mill Hill Cty Prim Sch DL6 210 E4
Mill Hill Dr YO32 225 F4
Mill Hill La
Giggleswick BD24 131 C3
Northallerton DL6 210 E3
MILL HIRST 159 F7
Millholme Dr 2 LA2 129 A7
Millholme Rise BD23 217 C8
Mill House YO7 65 D1
Mill Hurst HG3 159 F7
Millings La YO51 141 B7
Mill La
Acaster Malbis YO23 191 C8
Ampleforth YO62 118 C8
Askham Richard YO23 182 D2
Askrigg DL8 57 E6
Aysgarth DL8 58 E3
Barlow YO8 204 B7
Bellerby DL8 60 E8
Bentham LA2 128 F7
3 Bewerley HG3 137 B4
Boroughbridge YO51 141 B5
Brayton YO8 203 C8
Buckton/Bempton YO13 97 D5
Burniston YO13 75 C8
Burton Leonard HG3 140 B2
Carlton DN14 204 D3
Castleford WF10 200 E5
Cayton YO11 100 C6
Constable Burton DL8 61 C5
Darlington DL1 3 F6
Drax YO8 204 F5
Earby BB18 172 B1
Easingwold YO61 117 D1
3 East Ayton/West Ayton YO13 99 A7
Eskdaleside cum Ugglebarnby YO22 32 B6
Exelby, Leeming & Newton DL7 63 D3
Faceby TS9 25 F2
Farndale East YO62 48 E4
Gargrave BD23 155 D1
Great Ouseburn YO26 164 C8
Hambleton YO8 196 F1
Haxby YO32 166 D5
Hebden BD23 135 A1
2 Hemingbrough YO8 198 F1
Hessay YO23 182 B7
High Coniscliffe DL2 2 C6
Kearby with Netherby LS22 179 C2
Kirk Hammerton YO26 164 C2
Knaresborough HG5 221 F8
Langtoft YO25 151 C7
Leyburn DL8 60 E4
6 Linton-on-Ouse YO30 164 F7
Longnewton DL2 4 F6
Long Preston BD23 153 F4
Low Bradley BD20 173 E3
Low Hawsker YO22 33 A6
Mickletown LS26 200 B6
Middleton St George DL2 4 D5
Muston YO14 101 A2
Nether Burrow LA6 102 B6
Newland YO8 205 A3
Northallerton DL7 210 C3
Pannal HG3 222 E2
Pickering YO18 95 F6
Pontefract WF8 201 C2
Rawcliffe DN14 204 F1
Redmire DL8 59 C5
1 Riccall YO19 192 A1
Ryther cum Ossendyke LS24 190 E1
1 Scarborough YO12 212 E3
Scruton DL7 63 E5
Sherburn in Elmet LS25 195 F2
Skipton BD23 216 F3
Sledmere YO25 149 F3
Snape with Thorp DL8 87 B7
South Milford LS25 195 F2
Spofforth with Stockeld HG3 179 E6
Stillington YO61 144 C6
Stutton with Hazlewood LS24 189 E4
Swinden BD23 154 B1
Thirkleby High & Low with Osgodby YO7 90 D2
Thormanby YO61 116 E5
Thrintoft DL7 63 F8
Whitwood WF10 200 B2
Wilberfoss YO41 185 E6
York YO31 228 E6
Youlton YO61 142 F2
Mill Lane Ave YO60 145 C5
Mill Mount YO24 228 A3
Mill Mount Ct YO24 228 A3
Millrace Cl YO17 215 D2
Mill Race The 4 DL2 22 C8
Mill Rd
Burton Fleming YO25 126 D4
Gillamoor YO62 70 A5
Goldsborough HG5 221 F3
Mill Riggs TS9 26 D7
Mill Rise DL6 210 E2
Mill Row BD20 187 F7
Millside YO17 215 D2
Mill St
6 Barnoldswick BB18 171 D1
8 Eastburn BD20 187 F7
41 Glusburn BD20 187 F7
Guisborough TS14 8 F6
Harome YO62 93 C4
Malton YO17 215 E3
Scarborough YO12 212 F5
York YO1 233 C1
Millthorpe Sch YO23 228 B2
Mill View
5 Burley in Warfedale LS29 176 C1
Hut Green DN14 203 A2
Knottingley WF11 201 D2
Millway YO62 92 C1
Mill Wynd TS16 5 E3
Milner La LS24 195 D8
Milner Rd DL1 3 D4
Milners La HG1 219 F7
Milner St YO24 227 D3
Milnthorpe Cl 6 LS23 188 E6
Milnthorpe Garth 7 LS23 188 E6
Milnthorpe Gdns 5 LS23 188 E6
Milnthorpe La LS23 188 E6
Milnthorpe Way LS23 188 D5
Milson Gr YO10 229 A3
Milton Ave
Malton YO17 215 D5
Scarborough YO12 212 E3
Milton Carr 8 YO30 224 F1
Milton Cl HG1 219 E7
Milton Gr 11 BB18 171 D2
Milton Rd
Malton YO17 215 C5
Pannal HG3 222 E3
Milton St
Darlington DL1 3 E5
4 Skipton BD23 217 A3
York YO10 228 F3
Minchin Cl 3 YO30 225 B1
Miniskip Cl 12 TS14 8 F7
Minors Cres DL3 3 A7
MINSKIP 141 A3
Minskip Rd HG5 140 F2
Minster Ave YO31 225 F2
Minster Cl
3 Haxby YO32 225 C8
23 Ripon HG4 214 C5
40 Wigginton YO32 166 E5
York YO1 233 B3
Minster Ct YO1 233 B3
Minsterley Dr TS5 6 D7
Minster Rd HG4 214 C5
Minster Sch The YO1 233 B3
Minster View YO32 225 C8
Minster Wlk 12 DL2 3 E1
Minster Yd YO1 233 B3
Minter Cl 2 YO24 227 B1
Mire Bank La DL8 56 F4
Mire Close La BD22 187 A8
Mire Ridge BB8 186 A2
Mires La
Carthorpe DL8 87 D6
Ulleskelf LS24 190 B1
Mire Syke La HG5 162 A5
Mirey Butt La WF11 201 E2
Mirkhill Rd YO8 232 B6
Miry La LS15 188 C1
Missies La HG4 112 C3
Mistral Ct YO31 228 E8
Mitchell Ave TS17 6 B7
Mitchell Gr 43 DL9 41 A5
Mitchell La
Alne YO61 142 F4
Catton YO41 185 D8
Settle BD24 131 E1
Mitchell Way 11 YO30 224 E3
Mitchel's La YO10 231 F8
Miterdale 4 YO24 230 C7
Mitford Cl 3 YO14 126 F8
Mitford Rd 2 YO14 126 F8
Mitford St 24 YO14 101 B3
Mitton La BD20 172 D1
MLS Bsns Centres YO30 225 A2
Moat Field YO10 229 C4
Moatside Ct YO31 233 B3
Moat Way YO8 232 A2
Mock Beggar Hall* BD23 157 D7
Moins Ct YO10 229 D4
Moiser Cl YO32 225 D4
Mole End 15 YO18 95 F6
Monarch Way YO26 227 D6
Monash Ave DL9 209 C1
Monckton Dr WF10 201 B3
Monk Ave YO31 228 F7
Monk Bar Ct YO1 233 B3
Monkbridge Ct YO31 233 C4
Monket House Bank YO62 48 C4
MONK FRYSTON 202 B8
Monk Fryston CE Prim Sch LS25 202 A8
Monk Gardens La YO62 93 A7
Monkgate YO31 233 C3
Monkgate Cloisters YO31 233 C3
Monk Gn YO61 142 F4
MONKHILL 201 B1
Monkhill Ave WF8 201 B1
Monkhill Dr WF8 201 B1
Monkhill La WF8 201 B2
Monkhill Mount WF8 201 B1
Monkholme La BD23 134 C2
Monk Ing Rd HG3 159 E8
Monk La YO8 232 C7
Monkmans Wharfe 1 BD20 174 C1
Monk Park Farm* YO7 90 D4
MONKROYD 186 D4
Monkroyd Ave BB18 171 D1
Monks Cross Dr YO32 226 A3
Monks Cross Link YO32 226 B4
Monks Cross Sh Pk YO32 226 B3
Monk's Rd BD23 107 D2
Monkswell Pk HG5 221 D5
Monkton Rd 5 YO31 225 F1
Monkton Rise 7 TS14 8 F7
Monmouth Dr TS16 5 E5
Monmouth St 5 BB8 186 A3
Mons Cl 3 DL9 209 B1
Mons Rd DL9 40 F4
Montage Studio Gall* YO21 29 A7
Montague Cres LS25 194 D4
Montague Rd YO23 231 A3
Montague St YO23 228 C1
Montague Wlk 6 YO26 165 F1
Montagu La LS22 180 E5
Montagu Mews LS22 180 E5
Montagu's Harrier TS14 8 D6
Montagu Way LS22 180 E5
Montgomery Rd DL9 209 C2
Montgomery St BD23 217 A3
Montpellier Ct 11 HG2 219 C2
Montpellier Gdns 2 HG1 219 C2
Montpellier Hill HG2 219 C2
Montpellier Mews 3 HG1 219 C2
Montpellier Par HG1 219 C2
Montpellier Rd 1 HG1 219 C2
Montpellier Sq 3 HG1 219 D2
Montpellier St 4 HG1 219 C2
Montrose Ave YO31 228 D8
Montrose Gdns WF10 200 D4
Monument Cl YO24 227 E3
Moody Sty La 4 BD23 134 E3
Mook St YO60 169 B8
Moons Acre LA2 129 A8
Moor Ave 1 LS23 188 E7
Moorber La BD23 171 F8
Moorberries TS15 6 C2
Moorbridge Croft 6 LS25 196 A4
Moor Carr La
Barlby with Osgodby YO8 198 B5
Barlby YO8 198 B5
Moor Cl
Killinghall HG3 219 A8
10 Kirklevington TS15 24 E8
Lockwood TS12 10 A5
Wheldrake YO19 192 F8
Moorcock La HG3 159 F5
Moor Cres BD23 217 B4
Moor Croft 8 BD23 134 E3
Moorcroft Rd YO24 230 D7
Moore Ave YO10 229 B4
MOOR END 188 D8
Moor End Gdns LS23 188 D8
Moor End La
Crakehall DL8 62 C3
Sowerby YO7 90 A2
Moor End Rd YO13 53 F2
Moorfield Cl 6 DL1 3 E4
Moorfield Dr YO41 185 E6
Moorfield Rd LS29 218 F4
Moorfields
Raskelf YO61 116 F2
3 Wistow YO8 197 D6
Moorfield Sch LS29 218 C3
Moorfields La YO62 93 E5
Moorfield Way YO41 185 E6
Moorfoot La BD20 173 D2
Moorgarth LA6 103 D2
Moorgarth Ave 10 YO24 227 F2
Moorgate YO24 227 D3
Moorgate Dr LS25 194 D1
Moorgate Rd LS25 194 D2
Moor Gn TS7 7 D5
Moor Gr YO24 230 E8
Moor Hill YO17 147 E7
Moorhill La YO17 147 E6
Moorhills DL8 56 C4
Moorhouse Cl 3 WF6 200 B2
Moorhouse La YO7 89 E8
Moor House La YO61 116 B1
Moor La
Addingham LS29 174 D5
Aislaby YO21 31 F7
Aldfield HG4 138 F8
Arkendale HG5 162 F7
Arrathorne DL10 41 A2
Askwith LS21 176 D4
Bagby YO7 90 C4
6 Barlby YO8 198 B5
Bilbrough LS24 182 B1
Bilton-in-Ainsty with Bickerton YO26 181 D5
Bishopthorpe YO23 230 E2
Borrowby TS13 11 C6
Brawby YO17 94 F2
Brompton YO13 74 B1
Broughton YO17 121 C4
Burton Leonard HG3 140 B4
Carthorpe DL8 87 D4
Catterton LS24 190 A8
Cleasby DL2 2 F2
Cliffe YO8 198 F4
Cloughton YO13 54 C1
Collingham LS23 188 C8
Coneythorpe & Clareton HG5 163 B6
Copmanthorpe YO23 230 A1
Cropton YO18 71 B6
Crosby DL6 65 C5
Dalton DL11 19 C6
Dalton YO7 116 B8
Dishforth YO7 114 F3
Earswick YO32 226 C8
East Ayton/West Ayton YO13 99 B8
Eastfield YO11 100 A6
East Layton DL11 20 B8
Elslack BD23 172 D3
Embsay with Eastby BD23 156 F1
Full Sutton YO41 168 F1
Grassington BD23 134 E3
Great Ouseburn YO26 163 D7
Great Ribston with Walshford LS22 180 E8
Halton East BD23 157 B1
Moor La *continued*
Haxby YO32 166 D7
Hunton DL8 61 E8
Hutton-le-Hole YO62 70 C5
Kearby with Netherby HG3 179 B2
Kelfield YO19 191 E2
Kirby Hill HG4 140 F8
Knapton YO26 182 E6
Long Preston BD23 153 F5
Milby YO51 141 C7
Murton YO19 229 F8
Myton-on-Swale YO61 142 B5
Naburn YO19 191 D8
Nether Silton DL6 66 C8
Newsham DL11 19 A7
Newsham with Breckenbrough YO7 65 A1
Newton-on-Ouse YO30 165 C7
Rufforth YO26 182 E6
Ryther cum Ossendyke LS24 196 E8
Scalby YO12 212 A8
Settrington YO17 122 C1
Sherburn in Elmet LS25 195 F4
Skelton YO30 224 D6
Snape with Thorp DL8 86 E6
Steeton with Eastburn BD20 187 F7
Stillington YO61 143 F6
Strensall YO32 167 B7
Stutton with Hazlewood LS24 189 D4
Thirkleby High & Low with Osgodby YO7 90 C1
Thirsk YO7 89 D5
Tholthorpe YO61 142 D6
Thormanby YO61 116 E5
Thornton-le-Clay YO60 145 F2
Thornton Steward HG4 61 E2
Thorp Arch LS23 180 E3
Threshfield BD23 134 B2
Welburn YO62 94 A5
Weston LS21 176 E2
West Tanfield HG4 87 B2
Wilstrop YO26 181 D8
Yafforth DL7 43 B2
York YO24 230 C6
Moorland Ave
6 Earby BB18 172 B1
Skipton BD23 217 A4
Moorland Cl
5 Embsay BD23 217 E8
Harrogate HG2 220 D4
Moorland Garth 2 YO32 167 A7
Moorland Gdns
Copmanthorpe YO23 230 A1
York YO23 230 A1
Moorland Rd
Harrogate HG2 220 D4
Scarborough YO12 212 F7
York YO10 231 D8
Moorland Rise BD23 217 E8
Moorlands
Ilkley LS29 218 A2
Skelton YO32 166 B5
Moorlands Cl YO10 229 C4
Moorlands Fields YO10 231 E8
Moorlands La
Skelton YO30 224 C6
1 Tollerton YO61 143 B3
Moorlands Nature Reserve* YO32 166 B5
Moorlands Pk YO21 29 A6
Moorland Terr BD23 217 B4
Moorland View HG2 220 D4
Moor Lane Ind Est YO61 142 D6
Moor Lane Trad Est LS25 196 A3
Moor Lee La
Eggborough DN14 207 B8
Heck DN14 203 B1
MOOR MONKTON 165 A3
Moor Park Cl
2 Addingham LS29 174 E4
Pannal HG3 178 A8
Moor Park Cres 3 LS29 174 E4
Moor Park Dr LS29 174 E4
Moor Park Gr 2 LS29 174 F4
Moor Park Way 1 LS29 174 F4
Moor Pk TS7 7 D5
Moor Rd
Askrigg DL8 57 E6
Bishop Monkton HG3 139 F5
Filey YO14 101 B1
Hunmanby YO14 127 B7
Ilkley LS29 218 F1
Knayton with Brawith YO7 65 F3
Leyburn DL8 60 C5
Marton cum Grafton YO51 141 C2
Melsonby DL10 20 F6
Muston YO14 101 A2
9 Sherburn in Elmet LS25 195 F4
Stamford Bridge YO41 168 D2
Wykeham YO13 74 B4
Moors Ctr The* YO21 29 D7
MOORSHOLM 10 B5
Moorsholm La TS12 10 C6
Moorside
Melling-with-Wrayton LA6 102 A2
Scalby YO12 212 A8
Moor Side LS23 188 D8
Moorside Ave HG4 214 B2
Moorside Cl LA6 102 A2
Moorside Ct LS29 218 C3
Moorside Dale 6 HG4 214 B2
Moorside Junior & Infant Schs HG4 214 B3

Moorside La
  Addingham LS29 175 A2
  Askwith LS21 176 C4
Moorside Rd DL10 209 E8
Moorside View HG4 214 C2
Moors Shop Ctr The LS29 218 A4
Moor View
  Hebden BD23 135 A2
  [2] Hinderwell TS13 11 F7
Moorview Rd
  Northallerton DL6 210 F5
  Skipton BD23 217 B3
Moorview Way BD23 217 B4
Moor Way YO32 226 A4
Morcar Rd YO41 168 D1
Morehall Cl YO30 224 F2
Morgan Dr TS14 8 E6
Morgan St [4] YO12 212 F5
Morlais Ct [28] TS17 5 F4
Morley Dr [10] YO13 99 A7
Morley Gate DL11 37 E5
Mornington Cres HG1 219 E4
Mornington Rd LS29 218 C4
Mornington Terr HG1 219 E3
Morpeth Ave
  Coulby Newham TS4 7 A7
  Darlington DL1 3 E7
Morpeth Gate DL8 58 F1
Morrell Ct
  Woodthorpe YO24 230 B8
  York YO24 230 B8
Morrell Garth YO8 232 C2
Morrell Way YO10 229 A2
Morrets La YO8 197 A1
Morris Fields [22] WF6 200 B1
Morrison Rd TS14 8 F7
Morritt Cl [3] YO31 228 F8
Morton Carr La TS7 7 E6
Morton La YO8 203 A8
MORTON-ON-SWALE 64 A6
Morton Rd DL1 4 A5
Mosber La BD23 172 C8
MOSS 207 D1
Moss Arc HG4 214 C5
Mossburn Dr YO62 119 E6
Mossdale Gr TS14 8 D6
Moss End La BD22 186 F5
Moss Green Cl YO8 232 A2
Moss Green La
  Brayton YO8 232 A2
  Hirst Courtney YO8 203 F3
Moss Haven DN6 207 D1
Moss Hill La YO26 164 D5
Mossra La HG4 85 F4
Moss Rd DN6 207 B1
Moss Side BB18 171 E1
Moss St YO23 233 A1
Moss Way TS18 5 F7
Mosswood Cres TS5 6 D7
Mosswood La YO61 118 A1
Mossy La DL8 56 C4
Mostyn Ave [43] BB18 172 A1
Mother Shipton's Cave & Petryfying Well* HG5 221 A5
Moule Rise LS25 194 E5
MOULTON 21 D3
Moulton Hall* DL10 21 D2
Moulton La DL7 22 C3
Mounstrall La DL7 43 C1
Mount Ave YO8 232 B3
Mount Bank DL6 45 A5
Mount Cres YO17 215 B5
Mount Dr DL8 60 D5
Mount Ephraim [6] YO24 228 A3
Mount Farm Cl YO22 208 E3
Mount Gdns HG2 222 E7
Mount Gr YO8 232 B3
Mount Grace Priory* DL6 45 B5
Mount Leven Rd TS15 5 F3
Mount Par
  [5] Harrogate HG1 219 D3
  York YO24 228 A3
Mount Park Ave YO12 212 E5
Mount Park Rd [2] YO12 212 E4
Mount Pk YO19 198 A8
MOUNT PLEASANT 7 B5
Mount Pleasant
  [26] Addingham LS29 174 F4
  High Bentham LA2 129 A8
  Ilkley LS29 218 C3
  Kippax LS25 200 D8
  Little Smeaton WF8 206 D3
  Newby & Scalby YO13 75 C5
  Whitby YO22 208 F3
Mount Pleasant Cl [9] DL2 4 C4
Mount Pleasant E [2] YO22 33 D4
Mount Pleasant Grange TS18 6 A8
Mount Pleasant N [1] YO22 33 D4
Mount Pleasant Prim Sch DL3 3 A7
Mount Pleasant S [3] YO22 33 D4
Mount Pleasant Way TS9 26 D6
Mount Rd
  Malton YO17 215 B4
  Northallerton DL6 210 F6
Mount Sch The YO24 228 A3
Mountside YO11 212 F3
Mount Side Pk YO11 212 E2
Mount St HG2 222 E7
Mount Terr YO24 228 A3
MOUNT THE 214 D3
Mount The
  Barwick in Elmet & Scholes LS15 194 B7
  Castleford WF10 201 B4
  Malton YO17 215 B4
  Middlesbrough TS6 7 E8
  Selby YO8 232 B3
  [8] Thornton Dale YO18 96 D5
  York YO24 233 A1
Mount Vale YO24 228 A2
Mount Vale Dr YO24 228 A2
Mount View
  Muston YO14 101 A2
  Northallerton DL6 210 C6
Mount View Ave YO12 212 E3
Mount View Cl [4] YO12 212 E3
Mount View Rd [3] YO11 100 B6
Mouseman Visitor Ctr* YO61 91 B2
Mowbray Castle (site of)* HG4 112 D5
Mowbray Cres
  [17] Bedale DL8 63 A2
  Hovingham YO62 119 E6
  Kirkby Malzeard HG4 112 D5
Mowbray Dr
  [4] Hurworth-on-Tees DL2 3 E1
  York YO26 227 C4
Mowbray Pl YO7 211 B2
Mowbray Rd
  [5] Catterick DL10 41 D5
  Northallerton DL6 210 E6
Mowbray Sch DL8 63 A2
Mowbray Sq HG1 219 E3
Mowbray Terr
  Thirsk YO7 211 B2
  West Tanfield HG4 87 A2
MOWDEN 3 A6
Mowden Infant Sch DL3 3 A6
Mowthorpe La YO60 145 F8
Mowthorpe Medieval Village* YO17 149 C6
Mowthorp Rd YO12 75 A3
MOXBY 144 D5
Moxby La YO61 144 D5
Moxby Priory* YO61 144 D5
Muddy La LS22 180 A1
Muff La TS8 7 A3
Muirfield TS7 7 D5
Muirfield Ave WF7 200 E1
Muirfield Rd TS16 5 E5
Muirfield Way [6] YO26 227 B5
MUKER 36 A5
Mulberry Ct
  [10] South Milford LS25 195 F2
  York YO32 225 F6
Mulberry Dr [7] YO32 166 E5
Mulberry Garth LS23 188 F8
Mulgrave Castle* YO21 12 E2
Mulgrave Cres YO21 208 B8
Mulgrave Dr [6] DL7 210 D2
Mulgrave Pl YO11 213 B7
Mulgrave Rd YO21 208 A8
Mulgrave View YO22 32 F7
Mullberry Gdns LS26 200 A5
Mulwith Cl YO31 229 A6
Mulwith La HG4 140 E6
Muncastergate YO31 228 E7
Muncaster Way YO22 208 E3
Murchison Pl [8] YO12 212 F6
Murchison St YO12 212 E6
Murrayfield Way [5] DL1 3 F6
Murray St
  [31] Filey YO14 101 B3
  Scarborough YO12 212 F5
  York YO24 227 F3
Murray Wlk DL3 3 A5
Murrough Wilson Pl [3] YO31 228 C7
MURTON 184 D7
Murton Bank YO62 67 E3
Murton Garth YO19 229 F6
Murton La YO19 184 D7
Murton Way YO19 229 E5
MUSCOATES 94 A3
Muscoates La YO62 93 F3
Museum of North Craven Life* BD24 131 E2
Museum of Victorian Science* YO22 208 D7
Museum St YO1 233 B2
Musham Bank Rd YO12 99 F7
Music in Miniature* YO22 33 D3
Musterfield La HG4 113 B7
MUSTON 100 F2
Muston Rd
  Filey YO14 101 A3
  Hunmanby YO14 126 F8
Mutton Scalp Rd TS12 9 E7
Myer's Green La HG3 161 B5
Myers La DL7 64 A8
My Love La HG3 159 C5
Myra Bank La YO61 117 F3
Myron Rd TS17 5 F5
Myrtle Ave
  Bishopthorpe YO23 231 B3
  Selby YO8 232 B3
Myrtle Gdns DL1 3 D8
Myrtle Rd
  Eaglescliffe TS16 5 E6
  [3] Harrogate HG1 219 E3
Myrtle Sq [2] HG1 219 E3
Myson Ave WF8 201 C2
Myton La YO61 142 C5
MYTON-ON-SWALE 141 F5
Myton Park Prim Sch TS17 5 F4
Myton Rd TS17 6 A4

N

Nabs View YO12 212 A7
NABURN 191 D8
Naburn CE Prim Sch YO19 191 D8
Naburn La
  Deighton YO19 192 A7
  Fulford YO19 231 D4
Naburn Park Mews YO19 191 E8
Nab View BD20 174 C2
Nairn Cl YO24 230 C6
Nairnhead Cl
  [1] Coulby Newham TS8 6 E5
  [5] Stainton TS8 6 E5
Nalton Cl YO23 230 A1
Nalton St YO8 232 C5
Nanny Goat La
  Barwick in Elmet & Scholes LS25 194 B4
  Hunton DL8 61 F8
Nanny La LS24 196 C7
Nansen St YO12 212 E6
Nap Cote La HG4 112 E4
Napier Cres YO12 99 D7
Napier Rd HG4 113 D3
NAPPA 171 B8
Nares St YO12 212 E6
Narrowfield [8] YO22 32 A6
Narrow La
  Cottingwith YO42 193 D7
  Skipwith YO8 192 E3
National Ctr for Early Music* YO1 233 C2
National Rly Mus* YO26 228 A4
Nat La LS17 178 A3
Nattrass Wlk [7] DL8 63 B2
Navigation Rd YO1 233 C2
Navigation Sq BD23 216 F4
Navigation Way HG4 214 E4
Navigator Ct TS18 6 D8
NAWTON 93 E7
Nawton Com Prim Sch YO62 93 D7
Nawton Rd YO62 93 E7
NEASHAM 4 A1
Neasham Ct TS9 26 C8
Neasham Hill DL2 4 B1
Neasham Rd
  Darlington DL1 3 D4
  Low Dinsdale DL2 4 B3
Needham Garth DL8 58 E4
Neile Cl DL7 210 B4
Nell Bank Ctr* LS29 218 D6
Nelson Ct LS29 218 C4
Nelson Rd LS29 218 B4
Nelson's La YO24 227 F1
Nelson St
  [7] Normanton South WF6 200 B2
  Scarborough YO12 212 F6
  Skipton BD23 217 A3
  York YO31 233 C4
NESFIELD 175 B4
Nesfield Cl
  [17] Eastfield YO11 100 B6
  Harrogate HG1 219 B5
Nesfield Rd LS29 218 A5
Nesfield View [12] LS29 175 C2
Nessgate YO1 233 B2
Ness La
  Pickhill with Roxby YO7 88 B6
  Tockwith YO26 181 C8
Ness Rd [5] YO8 232 D6
Nestfield Cl WF8 201 B2
Nestfield Ind Est DL1 3 D6
NETHER BURROW 102 B6
NETHERBY 179 B1
Netherby Cl [6] YO22 32 A6
Netherby La
  Huttons Ambo YO60 147 B6
  Sinnington YO62 71 A1
Netherdale Ct LS22 180 D4
Netheredge Cl HG5 220 E8
Netheredge Dr HG5 220 E8
Netherfield Cl WF10 200 C3
Nethergill La BD20 173 B1
NETHER POPPLETON 224 A2
Netherside Hall Sch BD23 134 C4
NETHER SILTON 66 B7
Nether Way [20] YO26 165 F1
Netherwindings [18] YO32 166 F5
Netherwoods [5] YO32 167 B8
Nettledale Cl [1] TS13 12 A7
Nettledale La YO13 97 F6
Nevern Cres TS17 5 F4
Neville Cl DL2 1 D8
Neville Cres BD23 155 D1
Neville Dr YO23 231 A3
Neville Gr LS26 194 A1
Neville Pits La DN14 207 B4
Neville Rd
  Darlington DL3 3 B5
  Gargrave BD23 155 D1
Neville Row DL8 87 D7
Neville St
  Normanton South WF6 200 A1
  Skipton BD23 217 A4
  York YO31 233 C4
Neville Terr YO31 233 C4
Neville Wlk
  [31] Kirkbymoorside YO62 70 B1
  Richmond DL10 209 D7
Nevinson Gr YO10 231 E8
Nevison Ave WF8 201 C2
Nevis Way YO24 230 B7
NEWALL 176 F1
Newall Ave LS21 176 F1
Newall Carr Rd LS21 176 F3
Newall Cl [14] LS21 176 F1
Newall Hall Pk [10] LS21 177 A1
NEWBIGGIN
  Askrigg 57 F6
  Filey 101 A5
  Thoralby 82 D8
Newbiggin
  Malton YO17 215 B5
  Richmond DL10 209 B6
Newbiggin Cl TS16 5 C5
Newborough YO11 213 A6
Newborough St YO30 233 A4
NEWBRIDGE 96 A8
Newbridge La BD23 174 B8
New Brook St LS29 218 B5
Newburgh Priory* YO61 117 E7
Newbury Ave YO24 227 D1
NEWBY
  Ingleton 104 A1
  Middlesbrough 7 A3
  Ripon 140 D6
  Scarborough 75 E5
Newby Cl HG4 214 D4
NEWBY COTE 104 B1
Newby Cres HG3 219 A4
Newby Dr
  [23] Cross Hills BD20 187 E8
  Dishforth YO7 115 A2
Newby Farm Cl [35] YO12 75 D5
Newby Farm Cres [36] YO12 75 D5
Newby Farm Rd YO12 75 D5
Newby Hall & Gdns* HG4 140 C6
Newby La DN14 207 F8
Newby Pk* HG4 140 D6
Newby Prim Sch YO12 212 B8
Newby St HG4 214 D4
Newby Terr YO31 228 C7
NEWBY WISKE 64 E2
Newcastle Farm Ct [4] WF11 201 D6
Newchase Ct YO11 99 F6
New Church Terr [12] YO8 232 C5
New Cl La LA2 130 C7
New Coll WF8 201 A1
Newcoln Rd YO12 212 E1
Newcroft YO8 232 B4
Newdale [3] YO32 166 F5
New Dales La BD20 173 D4
NEW EARSWICK 225 D3
New Earswick Prim Sch YO32 225 D4
New Earswick Sports Club YO32 225 D3
Newfield Ave [6] WF6 200 B1
Newfield Cl [7] WF6 200 B1
Newfield Cres
  Middlesbrough TS17 6 D7
  Normanton South WF6 200 B1
Newfield Ct [3] WF6 200 B1
Newfield La LS25 201 B8
New Forge Ct [15] YO32 166 F5
NEW FRYSTON 201 B6
Newgate
  [2] Malton YO17 215 C4
  York YO1 233 B2
Newgate Bank YO62 68 A4
Newgate Cl [36] TS17 5 F4
Newgate Ct YO1 233 B2
New Hall Rd WF8 201 C2
Newham Bridge Prim Sch TS5 6 F8
Newham Way TS8 7 B5
Newhay La YO8 198 E1
Newhold LS25 194 D4
New Hold Ind Est LS25 194 D4
NEWHOLM 13 A1
New House Farm Malham National Nature Reserve* BD23 133 D3
New House La BD23 153 F5
NEW HOUSES 105 C4
New Ings La YO18 96 E4
Newington Rd TS4 7 A8
New Inn La
  Carthorpe DL8 87 F6
  [10] Easingwold YO61 143 C8
Newkin DL8 57 D5
New La
  Aislaby YO18 95 D8
  Beal DN14 202 D3
  Bishopthorpe YO23 231 A4
  Burton Salmon WF11 201 E6
  Green Hammerton YO26 164 C3
  Hawes DL8 56 E4
  Holgate YO24 227 E3
  Huntington YO32 225 F1
  Kildwick BD20 173 F1
  Lillings Ambo YO60 145 C3
  Little Ouseburn YO26 164 A8
  Long Marston YO23 182 B3
  Neasham DL2 4 A1
  Newland YO8 205 A3
  Ravensworth DL11 20 A7
  Selby YO8 232 C5
  Sherburn in Elmet LS25 195 F3
  Sheriff Hutton YO60 145 D5
  Stainburn LS21 177 E4
  Strensall YO32 167 B8
  West Tanfield DL8 87 C2
New Laithe Cl [5] BD23 217 B5
Newlaithes Cres WF6 200 B1
NEWLAND 205 B3
Newland Ave [1] HG2 220 A1
Newland Park Cl YO10 229 A3
Newland Park Dr YO10 228 F3
Newlands DL6 210 F4
Newlands Ave
  Scarborough YO12 212 E8
  [3] Whitby YO21 208 C7
Newlands Ct YO7 211 D3
Newlands Dr
  [2] Glusburn BD20 187 F8
  Ripon HG4 214 B3
  York YO26 227 B6
Newlands La
  Burniston YO13 54 D1
  Upper Poppleton YO26 182 E8
  Wintringham YO17 123 F3
Newlands Park Ave YO12 212 D8
Newlands Park Cres YO12 212 D8
Newlands Park Dr YO12 212 D8
Newlands Park Gr [2] YO12 212 D8
Newlands Park Rd YO12 212 D8
Newlands Rd
  Bishopthorpe YO23 230 F4
  Boosbeck TS12 9 D8
  Darlington DL3 3 B6
Newlands Sch The TS4 6 F7
New Lennerton La LS25 196 C3
Newlyn Dr DL3 3 C8
Newmarket St BD23 217 A4
NEW MICKLEFIELD 195 A3
New Millgate YO8 232 C6
New Mill La LS23 188 F7
Newnham St HG2 220 A3
Newnham Terr HG2 220 A3
NEW PARK 219 B5
New Park Prim Sch HG1 219 C5
New Park Rd [4] YO12 212 E4
New Park Row HG1 219 C5
New Parks Cres [8] YO12 212 E4
Newport Ave YO8 232 B4
Newport Cl [42] TS17 5 F4
Newport St [5] WF8 201 B1
New Potter Grange Rd DN14 205 E2
New Quay Rd YO21 208 D6
New Queen St [10] YO12 213 A7
New Rd
  Allerston YO13 73 D6
  Allerton Mauleverer with Hopperton HG5 163 E4
  Appleton Roebuck YO23 190 E5
  Appletreewick BD23 157 E8
  Beningborough YO30 165 C6
  Birstwith HG3 160 D6
  Bramham LS23 188 E6
  Earby BB18 172 A1
  Fylingdales YO22 33 D4
  Glaisdale YO21 29 F3
  Guisborough TS14 8 F6
  Heck DN14 203 D1
  Hessay YO26 182 C8
  Hunmanby YO14 126 F7
  Kirby Grindalythe YO17 149 B6
  Kirby Hall YO26 164 B8
  Kirkbymoorside YO62 70 B1
  Knottingley WF11 201 D3
  Ledsham LS25 201 B8
  Lillings Ambo YO60 145 D3
  Long Drax YO8 204 E6
  Newsham DL11 18 J8
  North Stainley with Sleningford HG4 113 B8
  Norton DN6 206 F2
  Raskelf YO7 116 E3
  Reighton YO14 127 E5
  Richmond DL10 209 C6
  Rosedale East Side YO18 49 E3
  Scotton HG5 162 A5
  [24] Settle BD24 131 D2
  Settrington YO17 122 D1
  Spaunton YO62 70 E5
  Stapleton WF8 206 B5
  Terrington YO60 119 E2
  Thornton in Lonsdale LA6 103 B4
  Ulleskelf LS24 190 B3
  Westerdale YO21 28 F6
  Wheldrake YO19 192 C7
  Whixley YO26 164 A4
Newroad End WF8 206 A6
NEW ROAD SIDE 187 B5
NEW ROW 8 F1
New Row
  [15] Boroughbridge YO51 141 B5
  Eppleby DL11 1 D4
  Trawden Forest BB8 186 B2
Newsam Rd TS16 5 D5
NEWSHAM
  Barnard Castle 19 D8
  Thirsk 89 A8
Newsham Hill DL11 18 J8
Newsham La
  Barugh (Great & Little) YO17 95 A1
  Habton YO17 121 A8
Newsham Rd YO7 211 A3
Newsham Way DL7 210 B1
NEWSHOLME 205 E8
  Barnoldswick 171 A6
New St
  Carleton BD23 173 B4
  Kippax LS25 194 D1

New St *continued*
Langcliffe BD24 131 E4
Tadcaster LS24 189 E6
York YO1 233 B2
Newstead La HG4 85 C7
Newsteads 12 DL8 63 B3
New Sturton La LS25 194 D4
NEW THIRSK 211 A3
NEWTHORPE 195 D3
Newthorpe Rd 2 DN6 206 E2
Newton Cres 4 DL7 63 D4
Newtondale Cl HG5 221 D6
Newtondale Forest Dr
YO18 72 B6
Newtondale Halt YO18 51 D1
Newton Dr TS17 6 B6
Newton Gdns HG4 214 C4
Newton House Ct YO61 144 B3
NEWTON KYME 189 B7
Newton La
Archdeacon Newton DL2 2 F8
Ledsham WF10 201 A6
Newton Mulgrave TS13 11 F6
NEWTON-LE-WILLOWS 62 B4
NEWTON MORRELL 21 E8
NEWTON MULGRAVE 11 E6
NEWTON-ON-OUSE 165 B6
NEWTON-ON-RAWCLIFFE 72 A5
Newton Pk YO30 165 B7
Newton Rd
Great Ayton TS9 8 A2
Tollerton YO61 143 B3
Newton St YO21 208 D6
Newton Terr YO1 233 B1
NEWTON UNDER ROSEBERRY 8 B4
NEWTON UPON DERWENT 185 E4
Newton Way 15 BD23 154 B3
NEW TOWN 201 B2
New Walk Terr YO10 228 D2
New Way YO21 29 C4
NEW YORK 137 F1
New York Ind Est HG3 137 F1
Nicholas Gdns YO10 228 F3
Nicholas St YO10 228 F3
Nicholson Ave HG4 113 D3
Nichols Way LS22 180 A3
Nickey Nackey La YO8 197 B8
Nicklaus Dr TS16 5 E5
Nickstream La DL3 3 A7
Nicolsons Pl 8 BD20 174 C1
NIDD 161 E6
Nidd Bank HG5 220 F7
Nidd Cl YO26 227 B8
Nidd Dr HG3 160 E6
Nidderdale Dr HG5 221 D5
Nidderdale High Sch & Com Coll HG3 137 B4
Nidderdale Lodge HG5 221 E5
Nidderdale Lodge Pk
HG5 221 E5
Nidderdale Mus* HG3 137 B4
Nidderdale Pool & L Ctr
HG3 137 A5
Nidd Gr YO24 230 E8
Nidd La
Birstwith HG3 160 E7
Darley HG3 160 B6
Ripley HG3 161 D7
Nidd Orch 4 HG3 160 A6
Nidd Rise HG3 160 E6
Niddside HG3 160 A6
Nidd Valley Ind Est HG5 162 B6
Nidd Viaduct* HG3 219 E8
Nidd Wlk 1 HG3 137 B4
Niffany Gdns 7 BD23 216 D3
Nigel Gr 7 YO24 227 F2
Nightingale Cl YO32 225 E1
Nightingale Dr HG1 220 B3
Nightingale La 9 YO12 99 F6
Nile Rd LS29 218 B4
Ninelands La LS25 194 D3
Ninelands Prim Sch
LS25 194 D3
Ninelands Spur LS25 194 C3
Ninevah La WF10 200 C7
Ninth Ave YO31 228 F5
Niso Terr YO11 213 A6
Noble Ct HG5 221 C7
Noel's Ct DL10 41 E5
Nolton Ct 35 TS17 5 F4
No Man's Moor La DL8 61 E3
Nook Croft 12 BB18 172 B1
Nookfield Cl YO22 33 C4
Nooking The YO61 117 B6
Nook Rd LS15 188 A1
Nook The
Selby YO8 232 D6
South Milford LS25 195 F2
Nora Ave HG5 221 C6
NORBY 211 A4
Norby YO7 211 B3
Norby Est YO7 211 B4
Norby Front St YO7 211 B4
Nordale Cl LS29 218 C5
Norfolk Cl WF11 201 E4
Norfolk Cres TS3 7 C8
Norfolk Gdns YO26 181 C7
Norfolk Rd HG2 222 D7
Norfolk St YO23 228 C2
NORMANBY 94 F4
Normanby Prim Sch TS6 7 F8
Normanby Rd
Middlesbrough TS7 7 D8
Northallerton DL7 210 D2
Normanby Terr 18 YO21 208 D7
Norman Cl
22 Pickering YO18 95 F7
7 Thorpe Willoughby YO8 197 B1
Norman Cres 11 YO14 101 B3
Norman Dr YO26 227 B6
Normandy Cl 4 YO8 232 B6
Norman Rd
Aske DL10 20 D1
Catterick Garrison DL9 209 E1
Richmond DL10 209 C8
Norman Sq DL10 209 D8
Norman St 5 YO10 229 A3
NORMANTON 200 C1
Normanton Com Prim Sch
WF6 200 B2
Normanton Ind Est WF6 200 B1
Normanton Junior Sch
WF6 200 A1
Normanton Sta WF6 200 A2
Norseman Cl 7 YO19 197 F8
Norseway 2 YO41 168 D1
NORTHALLERTON 210 C5
Northallerton Bsns Pk
DL6 210 C7
Northallerton Coll DL6 210 E4
Northallerton Rd
Brompton DL6 210 E7
Dalton-on-Tees DL2 22 E6
Leeming DL7 63 C4
Thirsk YO7 211 A6
5 Thornaby TS17 6 B7
Northallerton Rigg DL6 43 D4
Northallerton Sta DL7 210 C3
North App LS24 189 A2
North Ave
Castleford WF10 200 C4
12 Glusburn BD20 187 E6
North Back La
Stillington YO61 144 C6
Terrington YO60 119 E1
North Baileygate WF8 201 B1
North Bay Prom YO12 212 F8
North Bay Rly* YO12 212 E8
North Bglws HG4 214 D6
North Burton La YO14 127 B4
Northcarrs La YO61 144 A4
North Cliff Ave YO12 75 F5
North Cliff Ctry Pk*
YO14 101 C4
Northcliffe Gr 3 TS15 25 C5
Northcote Ave YO24 227 E3
Northcote Fold 3 LS22 180 A1
North Cotes Rd
Hunmanby YO25 126 C5
Wold Newton YO25 125 E5
NORTH COWTON 22 C3
North Cres LS25 195 F5
Northcroft 5 YO32 166 F5
Northcroft Gr 11 LS29 218 A4
North Croft Grove Rd 1
LS29 218 A4
NORTH DEIGHTON 180 B6
North Dr
Kippax LS25 194 D2
Sherburn in Elmet LS25 195 F5
NORTH DUFFIELD 199 A8
North Duffield Prim Sch
YO8 199 A8
North Eastern Terr YO24 230 E8
North End
Bedale DL8 63 A3
2 Hutton Rudby TS15 25 C5
Osmotherley DL6 45 B4
Northern Ryedale L Ctr
YO18 95 F7
NORTH FEATHERSTONE 200 E1
Northfield 3 YO8 198 B5
North Field Ave YO23 190 F5
Northfield Cl
Stokesley TS9 26 C7
Womersley DN6 206 C6
North Field Cl YO23 190 F5
Northfield Ct LS24 196 B8
Northfield Dr
Pontefract WF8 201 C1
Stokesley TS9 26 C8
Northfield La
Church Fenton LS24 196 B8
Pockley YO62 69 B2
3 Riccall YO19 191 F1
South Milford LS25 195 E2
Womersley DN6 206 C7
North Field La
Askham Bryan YO23 182 F3
Upper Poppleton YO26 182 F7
Northfield Mews 15
LS22 180 C2
Northfield Pl LS22 180 C3
Northfield Rd YO8 199 E8
Northfields
Bickerton LS22 181 B5
4 Hutton Rudby TS15 25 C5
4 Strensall YO32 167 B8
Northfields Ave 4 BD24 131 D3
Northfields Cres 5
BD24 131 D3
Northfields La YO61 142 C6
Northfield Terr YO24 230 E8
Northfield Way YO13 75 D6
North Field Way YO23 190 F5
North Garth La YO60 145 D5
Northgate
Darlington DL1 3 D5
Northgate *continued*
Guisborough TS14 8 F7
Hunmanby YO14 126 F8
Muston YO14 100 F1
Pontefract WF8 201 B1
Northgate Cl 15 WF8 201 B1
Northgate La
1 Linton LS22 180 A1
Warthill YO41 168 A3
Northgate Lodge 11
WF8 201 B1
Northgate Rise 2 LS22 180 A1
North Gr 2 LS22 180 C3
North Grange Ct YO30 233 A4
NORTH GRIMSTON 148 E6
North Grove Ave 6
LS22 180 C4
North Hill Rd YO7 115 B2
NORTH INGS 119 D1
NORTH KILVINGTON 89 E8
North La
Dringhouses YO24 230 E8
Eastfield YO11 100 B6
Gainford DL2 1 D8
Great Timble LS21 176 E8
Huntington YO32 225 F5
Hutton Hang DL8 61 C4
Wheldrake YO19 192 F7
Northlands Ave 1 YO32 225 F7
Northleach Dr TS8 6 F5
North Leas Ave YO12 212 D8
NORTH LEES 113 E4
North Lodge Ave 2 HG1 219 C5
North Marine Rd YO12 212 F7
Northminster Bsns Pk
YO26 182 F7
North Moor 7 YO32 225 F5
Northmoor Cl 8 YO32 225 F5
North Moor Gdns YO32 225 F5
North Moor La YO61 118 C5
North Moor Rd
Easingwold YO61 117 B2
York YO32 225 F5
Northolme Dr YO30 224 E1
NORTH OTTERINGTON 64 D4
North Parade
10 Burley in Warfedale
LS29 176 C1
Ilkley LS29 218 C4
Skipton BD23 217 A2
York YO30 233 A3
North Park Dr HG1 219 E2
North Park Rd HG1 219 E2
North Prom YO21 208 C7
North Rd
Darlington DL1 3 D7
Glusburn BD20 187 E7
Grosmont YO22 31 C4
Hackforth DL8 62 E8
3 Middleham DL8 60 E2
Norton YO17 215 E3
Ripon HG4 214 D6
Stokesley TS9 26 C7
Whitby YO21 208 D6
North Riding Rise DL7 65 B3
NORTH RIGTON 178 B5
North Road Ind Est DL3 3 C7
North Road Prim Sch DL1 3 D7
North Road Sta DL1 3 D6
North Side TS15 25 C5
Northside Ind Pk DN14 202 F1
North & South Cowton Prim Sch DL7 22 C3
North St
Addingham LS29 175 A4
Barmby on the Marsh
DN14 205 A7
Barnoldswick BB18 171 D1
Castleford WF10 201 B6
Folkton YO11 100 A2
Gargrave BD23 155 D1
31 Glusburn BD20 187 E7
Newby & Scalby YO13 75 C6
Ripon HG4 214 C6
Scarborough YO11 213 A6
Silsden BD20 174 C1
Wetherby LS22 180 C3
York YO1 233 B2
NORTH STAINLEY 113 D7
North Stainley CE Prim Sch
HG4 113 C8
Northstead Flats YO12 212 D7
Northstead Manor Dr
YO12 212 E7
Northstead Prim Sch
YO12 212 D8
North Street La 22 YO11 213 A6
North Sweeming Ct
LS25 196 D5
North Terr
Gainford DL2 1 D7
4 Scarborough YO11 213 A6
Whitby YO21 208 C7
Northumberland Ct 17
HG1 219 D2
Northumberland Rd TS17 6 B8
North View
Knottingley WF11 201 F2
Little Ribston LS22 180 A8
Northway
Pickering YO18 95 E7
11 Scarborough YO12 212 F6
6 Whitby YO21 208 B7
Northwell Gate LS21 176 F1
Northwold Rd YO11 100 A7
North Yorkshire Moors Rly*
YO18 95 F7
NORTON 206 E2
Norton Back La DL2 4 D8
Norton Cl HG4 114 A8
Norton Coll YO17 215 E2
Norton Comm La DN6 206 F2
Norton Comm Rd DN6 207 A1
Norton Com Prim Sch
YO17 215 E3
Norton Conyers* HG4 113 F7
Norton Cres DL2 4 C8
Norton Grove Ind Est
YO17 215 F4
Norton Junior & Infant Schs
DN6 206 E2
Norton & Kirk Smeat
WF8 206 C3
NORTON-LE-CLAY 115 C2
Norton Mill La DN6 206 E2
NORTON-ON-DERWENT 215 D3
Norton Priory DN6 206 E2
Norton Rd
Norton YO17 215 C3
Sadberge DL2 4 C7
Norton Twr* BD23 156 B4
Norway Dr YO10 231 D8
Norwich Cl YO13 75 D6
Norwich Dr HG3 219 A5
Norwood Ave LS29 176 C1
Norwood Bottom Rd
LS21 177 A5
Norwood Cl
36 Burley in Warfedale
LS29 176 C1
2 Knaresborough HG5 221 B8
Norwood Ct 1 HG5 221 B7
Norwood Gr HG3 219 B4
Norwood La
Glusburn BD20 187 B8
Pannal HG3 177 E7
Norwood Mews 18 YO12 212 F5
Norwood Pl 8 YO12 212 F5
Norwood St
Normanton WF6 200 B2
Scarborough YO12 212 F5
Nossill La DL8 59 C3
NOSTERFIELD 87 B3
Nosterfield Nature Reserve*
HG4 87 B2
Nosterfield Rd HG4 87 B2
Notagreen Rd DL11 39 F6
Nought Bank Rd HG3 137 B3
Nought Moor Rd HG3 137 B2
Nova Scotia Way 4
YO19 198 A8
NUN APPLETON 190 F3
Nuneaton Dr TS8 6 E5
Nunmill St YO23 228 C2
NUN MONKTON 165 A4
Nun Monkton Prim Sch
YO26 165 A5
Nunnery La
Darlington DL3 3 A5
York YO23 233 B1
Nunnery Way LS23 188 E7
NUNNINGTON 93 E2
Nunnington Cl TS17 6 B5
Nunnington Cres HG3 219 A5
Nunnington Hall* YO62 93 F2
Nunnington Studios*
YO62 93 E2
Nun's Cl DL10 209 B7
Nuns Green La YO21 29 E3
NUNTHORPE
231 C8
Middlesbrough 7 D5
Nunthorpe Ave YO23 228 B2
Nunthorpe Cres YO23 228 B1
Nunthorpe Gdns TS7 7 D5
Nunthorpe Gr YO23 228 B2
Nunthorpe Prim Sch TS7 7 E6
Nunthorpe Rd YO23 233 A1
Nunthorpe Sch TS7 7 E6
Nunthorpe Sta TS7 7 E6
NUNWICK 114 A5
Nurseries The
Asselby DN14 205 D7
3 Easingwold YO61 143 C8
East Ayton YO13 99 C8
10 Leyburn DL8 60 D5
3 Whitby YO21 208 B6
Nursery Cl 19 YO8 198 F1
Nursery Ct
Low Catton YO41 185 C8
Nether Poppleton YO26 224 A2
Nursery Dr YO24 227 E3
Nursery Gdns
Thirsk YO7 211 C3
York YO10 229 C3
Nursery La
4 Addingham LS29 175 A4
Merrybent DL2 2 E5
Nursery Rd YO26 224 A2
Nursery Way 8 LS23 188 E7
Nusery Gdn DL10 41 B4
Nutgill La
Bentham LA2 129 D8
Ingleton LA6 103 D1
Nutwith La HG4 112 B8
Nydd Vale Rd HG1 219 D3
Nydd Vale Terr 10 HG1 219 D3

O

Oak Ave
Appleton Roebuck YO23 190 E3
Garforth LS25 194 C4
Killinghall HG3 161 B2
Oakbank HG1 219 C4
Oak Beck Rd HG1 219 B5
Oak Beck Way HG1 219 B6
Oakburn Rd LS29 218 A3
Oak Busk La YO60 145 F1
Oakbusks La YO61 142 F4
Oak Cl
Filey YO14 101 B4
9 Kirkbymoorside YO62 70 B1
Oak Cres LS25 194 C4
OAKDALE 161 B2
Oakdale HG1 219 A3
Oakdale Ave HG1 219 B4
Oakdale Glen HG1 219 B3
Oakdale Manor HG1 161 B2
Oakdale Pl HG1 219 B4
Oakdale Rd YO30 224 F2
Oakdale Rise HG1 219 C4
Oak Dr
8 Acaster Malbis YO32 191 C7
Garforth LS25 194 C4
5 Thorpe Willoughby YO8 197 B1
3 Topcliffe YO7 89 A1
Oakenshaw Dr TS5 6 E7
Oaker Bank HG3 161 B2
Oak Farm YO8 197 D6
Oak Field YO8 232 A1
Oak Field Ave YO22 51 D8
Oakfield La 21 YO8 198 F1
Oakfields DL10 21 D4
Oak Glade 6 YO31 225 F3
Oak Gr
Harrowgate Village DL1 3 D8
Northallerton DL6 210 E6
Oak Hill TS8 7 B5
Oakhill Cres 3 YO32 167 A6
Oak La HG3 159 F8
Oakland Ave YO31 229 A7
Oakland Dr YO31 229 A7
Oakland Hills 23 WF6 200 B1
Oaklands
Camblesforth YO8 204 C5
9 Great Ayton TS9 8 A2
5 Ilkley LS29 218 A3
5 Pickering YO18 96 A6
5 Strensall YO32 167 B7
Oaklands Cres YO8 204 C5
Oaklands Rd TS6 7 F8
Oaklands Sports Ctr
YO24 227 C2
Oaklands The DL2 4 D3
Oaklands Way YO61 143 D8
Oakley Bank YO22 208 B2
Oakley Cl TS14 8 F5
Oakley Rd TS12 9 E7
Oakmont Cl 21 WF6 200 B1
Oakmoor Cl 7 DL1 3 E4
Oakney Wood Dr YO8 232 D1
Oak Rd
Eaglescliffe TS16 5 E6
Garforth LS25 194 C4
Guisborough TS14 8 F7
2 North Duffield YO8 199 A7
Ripon HG4 214 B2
Scarborough YO12 212 D4
Tockwith LS22 180 E7
Whitby YO21 208 B6
Oak Ridge 6 LS22 180 B3
Oakridge Prim Sch TS13 11 F7
Oakridge View 3 HG3 161 B3
Oak Rise 4 YO24 227 C3
Oaksfield LS26 200 B5
Oaks La LS23 188 E8
Oak St 3 YO26 227 E5
Oaks The
Coulby Newham TS8 6 E5
Dalton YO7 115 F7
Hellifield BD23 154 A3
7 Masham HG4 86 C3
Oak Tree DL2 4 E4
Oak Terr HG2 219 C2
OAK TREE 4 E4
Oaktree Ave DL9 40 E2
Oaktree Bank YO7 65 F3
Oak Tree Cl
2 Bedale DL8 63 A2
Strensall YO32 167 B7
Tees-side Airport DL2 4 E4
Oak Tree Ct
Bubwith YO8 199 D7
4 Wigginton YO32 225 D7
Oaktree Dr DL7 210 C1
Oak Tree Dr DL8 62 F2
Oaktree Gr 6 TS18 5 D8
Oak Tree Gr YO32 225 D3
Oaktree Hill DL6 43 D6
Oaktree Junc DL2 4 D4
Oak Tree La YO32 225 C7
Oak Tree Rd 7 DL8 63 A2
Oak Tree Way 10 YO32 167 B7
Oakville Ave YO12 212 E6
Oakville St YO31 228 D7
Oak Way YO8 232 D2
Oakwood Cl
Church Fenton LS24 196 B7
Ferrybridge WF11 201 C4
Oakwood Pk DN14 207 F6
Oakwood Rd LS22 180 B4
OATLANDS 222 F6
Oatlands Dr
Harrogate HG2 222 F8
11 Otley LS21 177 A1
Oatlands Gr 3 TS13 11 A8
Oatlands Infant Sch HG2 222 E7
Oatlands Junior Sch
HG2 222 F7
Occaney La HG3 162 D8
Occupation La LS24 188 E2

Occupation Rd TS6 7 F8
Ocean Rd YO21 208 C7
Ocean Terr YO14 100 F6
Ochrepit Hill YO42 170 A2
OCTON 151 F8
Oddie's La LA6 103 D5
Offerton Dr TS8 6 F5
Ogleforth YO1 233 B3
Okehampton Dr TS7 7 B6
Olav Rd DL10 209 C7
Old Barber HG1 219 D6
Old Boys Sch La [4] YO8 197 B8
Old Brewery Gdns [5] LS24 189 F6
Old Bridge Rise [7] LS29 218 A4
OLD BYLAND 91 F8
Old Chapel Cl [7] HG3 161 B2
Old Church Gn YO26 164 C2
Old Church La [9] HG3 137 C4
Old Coach Rd HG3 137 F2
Old Coastguard Sta★ YO22 33 D3
Old Coppice [14] YO32 166 F5
Old Corn Mill The BD20 187 D7
Old Court Cl
Malton YO17 215 D4
Norton-on-Derwent YO17 215 E3
Old Courthouse Rural Arts The★ YO7 211 B2
Old Cricket Field La YO7 116 B6
Old Dike Lands YO32 225 C8
Olde Mkt The TS16 5 D3
Old Farm Cl [5] YO18 95 F7
Old Farm Way YO8 232 B2
Old Farmyard★ HG3 161 C7
Old Favourites Wlk [8] DL2 3 A7
Oldfield Cl LS25 195 A4
Oldfield La
Collingham LS22 180 C1
Spaunton YO62 70 E4
Sutton BD22 187 F1
Old Garth Croft [3] WF11 201 D6
Oldgate La LS24 195 E6
Old Gayle La DL8 56 D4
Old Great North Rd WF11 201 E4
Old Hall Cl BD20 187 D7
Old Hall Croft BD23 155 D1
Old Hall Ct LS25 201 F6
Old Hall La
Gilling with Hartforth & Sedbury DL10 20 D3
Kexby YO41 185 C5
Old Hall Rd BD20 187 D7
Old Hall Way BD20 187 D7
Oldham Cl TS12 9 E8
Oldham St TS12 9 D7
Old Highway The [9] YO32 167 B6
Old Hospital Compound [25] DL9 40 E3
Old House Gdns YO8 203 A5
Old La
Addingham LS29 175 B3
Broughton BD23 172 D5
Cowling BD22 187 B5
Earby BB18 172 A2
Hambleton YO8 196 E1
Hirst Courtney YO8 203 F3
Horton in Ribblesdale BD24 105 A7
Ilkley LS29 218 D3
Kelbrook & Sough BB18 186 A6
Long Marston YO26 182 A6
Old Lane Ct LS24 190 E7
Old London Rd LS24 189 D3
OLD MALTON 215 E7
Old Maltongate YO17 215 C4
Old Malton Rd
Malton YO17 215 D5
[7] Willerby YO12 99 D2
Oldman Ct
Woodthorpe YO24 230 C8
York YO24 230 C8
Old Market Pl [6] HG4 214 C5
OLD MICKLEFIELD 194 F4
Old Mill Cl [8] LS29 176 C1
Old Mill La LS23 188 F7
Old Mill Row [3] YO7 211 C3
Old Mill View YO60 145 C5
Old Mill Wynd TS9 8 A1
Old Moor La YO24 230 E7
Old Moor Rd LA2 128 B8
Old Oliver La BD24 152 F6
Old Orchard YO32 225 D8
Old Orchard The
Fulford YO10 231 E7
Shipton YO30 165 F5
Old Orch The
[1] Easingwold YO61 143 C8
[14] Hutton Rudby TS15 25 C5
Old Park La YO21 31 D6
Old Park Mews HG4 214 B5
Old Penny Gate HG5 221 C7
Old Quarry La LS25 195 E1
Old Raike BD23 152 F4
Old Rd
Appleton Roebuck YO23 190 E5
Clapham LA2 130 C8
Garsdale LA10 55 A6
Kirkbymoorside YO62 70 B1
Kirkby Overblow LS17 178 E1
Thornton in Craven BD23 172 A3
Old St The LS24 190 C8
Old Sawmill The
Lane Ends BD22 187 C6
Rathmell BD24 153 B7
Old School Cl
Osbaldwick YO10 229 B4
Settle BD24 131 E2
West Witton DL8 59 D3
Old School La YO8 198 B5
Old Station Rd [4] YO62 92 C1
Old Station Way [20] LS29 174 F4
OLDSTEAD 91 C3
Oldstead Rd YO61 91 B3
Old Stone Trough La BB18 186 A6
Old Stubble The [6] TS13 13 K2
Old Sutton Rd YO7 211 E3
OLD THIRSK 211 C4
Old Trough Way HG1 219 C6
Old Vicarage La [5] LS25 202 A8
Old Village The YO32 225 F5
Old Wife's Way YO18 73 A8
Olicana Pk LS29 218 B5
Olive Gr HG1 220 B4
Oliver La YO17 121 C8
Oliver's Cl [18] YO14 126 F8
Oliver's Mount Rd YO11 212 F2
Oliver St [4] YO11 213 A4
Olive Way HG1 220 B4
Olive Wlk HG1 220 B4
Olliver La DL10 20 F1
Olliver Rd DL10 209 E8
Olympia Cres YO8 232 E6
Olympian Ct YO10 228 F4
Olympian Trad Est YO11 100 A6
Olympic Way DL10 209 B8
Omega St [7] HG1 219 C5
Onams La YO62 69 F4
One Acre Garth [2] YO8 196 E1
Onhams La YO60 146 E4
OPSA Bsns Ctr YO1 233 B2
Opus Ave YO26 224 C1
Oran La DL10 41 E4
Orcaber La LA2 130 E6
Orchard Cl
Appleton Roebuck YO23 190 F5
Barkston Ash LS24 195 E7
Dalton-on-Tees DL2 22 D7
[15] Easingwold YO61 117 D1
Eggborough DN14 202 F2
[1] Great Ayton TS9 8 A2
[6] Hartwith cum Winsley HG3 137 F1
[1] Knaresborough HG5 221 B8
[6] Monk Fryston LS25 202 A8
[9] Norton DN6 206 E2
Selby YO8 232 A4
Sharow HG4 214 F6
[6] South Milford LS25 195 F2
Wilberfoss YO41 185 E6
York YO24 227 E1
Orchard Cotts [4] YO19 184 F7
Orchard Ct
Bramham cum Oglethorpe LS23 188 F5
[8] Knaresborough HG5 221 B5
Orchard Dr
Fairburn WF11 201 D7
Hambleton YO8 196 F2
Linton LS22 180 A2
Orchard End [20] YO8 198 F1
Orchard Garth YO23 230 B2
Orchard Gdns
Malton YO17 215 B4
York YO31 225 E2
Orchard Gr
[4] Brompton DL6 43 F3
[1] Castleford WF10 200 D3
Orchard Head Cres WF8 201 C2
Orchard Head Dr WF8 201 C2
Orchard Head La WF8 201 B2
Orchard Head Prim Sch WF8 201 C2
Orchard La
[8] Addingham LS29 175 A4
Barkston Ash LS24 195 F6
Hebden BD23 135 A2
Ripley HG3 161 C7
Ripon HG4 214 E1
Thirsk YO7 211 B1
Orchard Mews [9] DL9 40 E3
Orchard Paddock
[34] Haxby YO32 166 E5
[3] Haxby YO32 225 D8
Orchard Rd
Malton YO17 215 B4
Selby YO8 232 A4
[3] Sleights YO22 32 A6
Upper Poppleton YO26 224 A1
Orchards The
[2] Beadlam YO62 93 D7
[3] Brafferton YO61 115 F1
Leavening YO17 147 E1
Mickletown LS26 200 B5
Ripon HG4 214 C6
Westow YO60 147 B4
Orchard The
[5] Ampleforth YO62 92 C1
Ampleforth YO62 92 C1
Bishopthorpe YO25 231 A3
Burniston YO13 75 D8
Burton Leonard HG3 140 A2
Heslington YO10 229 A1
[6] North Featherstone WF7 200 E1
[11] Pickering YO18 96 A6
[5] Roundhill Village TS17 6 D5
Sadberge DL2 4 C7
Scalby YO12 212 C7
Snainton YO13 98 A4
Thirsk YO7 211 C4
Tholthorpe YO61 142 D5
Orchard The *continued*
Wray LA2 128 A6
Orchard View
Markington with Wallerthwaite HG3 139 E3
[3] Skelton YO30 224 B5
Orchard Way
Hensall DN14 203 C2
Middlesbrough TS7 7 D8
Selby YO8 232 A4
[1] Strensall YO32 167 B7
Thorpe Willoughby YO8 197 B2
York YO24 227 E1
Orchid Ct [17] DL9 41 A5
Orchid Way [8] HG3 161 B3
Ordmerstones La YO18 96 C4
Ordnance La YO10 228 D1
Oriel Bank YO11 212 F3
Oriel Cl YO11 212 F3
Oriel Cres YO11 212 F3
Oriel Gr YO30 228 A8
ORMESBY 7 C8
Ormesby Bank TS7 7 D7
Ormesby Cres DL7 210 D2
Ormesby Prim Sch TS7 7 D8
Ormesby Rd TS3 7 C8
Orms Gill Green La BD23 154 D6
Orpington Rd TS3 7 C8
Orr Cres [10] YO7 89 B1
Orrin Cl YO24 230 C7
OSBALDWICK 229 C4
Osbaldwick Ind Est YO19 229 D5
Osbaldwick La YO10 229 B4
Osbaldwick Link Rd YO10 229 D4
Osbaldwick Prim Sch YO10 229 C4
Osbaldwick Village YO10 229 C4
Osborne Cl HG1 219 D4
Osborne Gdns HG1 219 D4
Osborne Pk YO12 212 D5
Osborne Rd HG1 219 D4
Osborne Terr [9] YO21 208 D5
Osborne Wlk HG1 219 D4
Osbourne Dr [4] YO30 224 E3
OSGODBY
Seamer 100 B7
Selby 198 C4
Osgodby Cl [9] YO11 100 B8
OSGODBY COMMON 198 C6
Osgodby Cres YO11 100 B7
Osgodby Gr [10] YO11 100 B8
Osgodby Hall Rd YO11 100 B7
Osgodby Hill YO11 100 B7
Osgodby La [12] YO11 100 B8
Osgodby Way [11] YO11 100 B8
Osgoodby Bank YO7 90 F3
Osmington Gdns [10] YO32 167 A7
OSMOTHERLEY 45 C4
Osmotherley Prim Sch DL6 45 B4
Osprey Cl
[4] Collingham LS22 180 A1
Guisborough TS14 8 D6
[5] Scotton DL9 40 F2
[4] York YO24 230 B8
Osprey Garth [4] YO12 99 E6
Ostler's Cl YO23 230 C3
Ostman Rd YO26 227 C5
Oswaldene DL6 45 B4
OSWALDKIRK 93 A1
Oswaldkirk Bank YO62 93 A1
Oswestry Gn TS4 7 A7
Oswin Gr DL10 20 E4
Oswy Cotts YO21 208 D5
Oswy St [5] YO21 208 D5
Otley Rd
Harrogate HG2 222 B8
Killinghall HG3 161 B4
Pannal HG3 178 A7
Skipton BD23 217 B4
Stainburn HG3 177 F6
Otley St BD23 217 A4
Otterbeck Way [16] DL8 63 B3
OTTERBURN 154 E4
Otter Dr [13] YO18 95 F6
Otter Way TS17 6 A5
Otterwood Bank [5] YO24 227 B1
Otterwood La YO24 227 B1
Otterwood Paddock YO41 168 C2
Oucher La HG3 140 B2
OUGHTERSHAW 80 C4
Oughtershaw Rd BD23 80 B6
OULSTON 117 E5
Oulston Rd YO61 117 D1
Our Ladys RC Prim Sch YO24 227 E1
Ouse Acres YO26 227 D6
Ouse Bank YO8 232 E5
Ouseburn Ave YO26 227 C6
Ousecliffe Gdns YO30 228 A6
Ousegate YO8 232 D5
Ousegate Mills Business Centre YO8 232 D5
Ouse Lea YO30 228 A7
Ouston Cl LS24 189 F6
Ouston La LS24 189 F6
Out Croft La YO18 95 C8
Outgaits Cl [4] YO14 126 F8
Outgaits La
Hunmanby YO14 127 A8
Muston YO14 100 F1
Outgang La
Osbaldwick YO19 229 D6
[21] Pickering YO18 95 F6
Thornton-le-Dale YO18 96 E6
Out Gang La BD23 107 F1
Outgang Rd
Malton YO17 215 B5
Pickering YO18 96 A6
Scampston YO17 122 F7
Outgang The YO17 122 F4
Outgate Cnr DL6 23 F4
OUTHGILL 34 A8
Outwood La LS24 190 C2
Oval The
Harrogate HG2 222 D8
Hurworth DL2 3 F1
Kellingley DN14 202 C3
Middlesbrough TS5 6 E6
Otley LS21 176 F1
[3] Scarborough YO11 100 B8
Skipton BD23 217 B3
Overburn Rd [8] BD20 187 E6
OVER BURROW 102 B7
Overdale YO11 100 A7
Overdale Cl YO24 230 D8
Overdale Com Prim Sch [7] YO11 100 A7
Overdale Ct BD23 217 A5
Overdale Grange [3] BD23 217 B5
Overdale Rd TS3 7 C8
Overgreen Cl YO13 75 D8
Overgreen La YO13 75 C8
Overgreen View YO13 75 D8
Over Nidd HG1 219 C6
Overscar La YO18 72 E3
OVER SILTON 66 B8
OVERTON 165 F2
Overton Rd YO30 165 F3
Overton Terr YO11 213 B6
OVERTOWN 102 C7
Ovington La DL11 1 A6
Ovington Terr YO23 228 B2
Owler Park Rd LS29 175 C3
Owlwood Ct [7] YO19 184 E7
Owlwood La [6] YO19 184 E7
Owmen Field La YO62 93 C5
Owston Ave [2] YO10 229 A3
Owston Rd [1] YO14 126 F8
Ox Calder Cl [16] YO19 184 F7
Ox Carr La YO32 167 B6
Ox Cl YO41 168 D2
Oxcliff YO12 212 C8
Oxclose La YO62 70 C4
Ox Close La
Eldmire with Crakehill YO7 115 E5
Grimston YO10 184 C4
Myton-on-Swale YO61 141 F5
North Deighton LS22 180 B7
Whixley YO26 163 F5
Oxcroft [23] YO62 70 B1
Oxenby Pl [12] YO61 117 D1
Oxen La YO8 198 E3
Oxford Dr LS25 194 D1
Oxford Pl [7] HG1 219 D2
Oxford St
Harrogate HG1 219 D2
[6] Normanton South WF6 200 B2
Scarborough YO12 212 F6
Skelton & Brotton TS12 9 D7
[5] York YO24 228 A3
Oxford Terr [2] HG1 219 D1
Oxmoor La LS24 196 D7
Ox Moor La
Cattal YO26 164 A1
Hunsingore LS22 180 E8
Oxpasture Cl YO12 212 C4
OXTON 190 A6
Oxton Dr LS24 189 F6
Oxton La LS24 189 F6
Oyster Park Infants Sch WF10 201 B5
Oyster Park Junior Sch WF10 201 B4
Oyster Way YO14 127 C8

P

Packhorse Bridge★
Dacre HG3 159 D6
Romanby DL7 210 B4
Padbury Ave [50] YO14 101 B3
Padbury Cl [48] YO14 101 B3
Pad Cote La BD22 187 A5
Paddock Cl
Askham Richard YO23 182 D3
Copmanthorpe YO23 230 A2
Helmsley YO62 92 F6
Huntington YO32 225 F4
Norton YO17 215 D3
[2] Pickering YO18 95 F6
Paddock Farm Water Gdns★ DL2 22 D4
Paddock Hill YO17 215 A4
Paddock House La LS22 179 E1
Paddock Rise [13] YO61 117 D1
Paddocks The
Follifoot HG3 223 F4
Wheldrake YO19 193 A7
Paddock The
[14] Airmyn DN14 205 E4
Appleton Wiske DL6 24 B3
Burton Salmon LS25 201 F6
Catterick DL10 41 D4
Fairburn WF11 201 D6
Knaresborough HG5 221 C5
Paddock The *continued*
Leeming DL8 63
[1] Linton-on-Ouse YO30 164 F8
Melmerby HG4 114 B7
Middleton St George DL2 4 C3
Newby Wiske DL7 64 E2
Normanton South WF6 200 A1
Stokesley TS9 26 C8
[9] Whitby YO21 208 D7
Wilberfoss YO41 185 E5
York YO26 227 C6
Paddock View WF10 201 A3
Paddock Way YO26 227 C6
PADSIDE 159 B6
PADSIDE GREEN 159 C6
Page La YO62 93 E6
Pagnell Ave YO8 232 E4
PAINSTHORPE 170 B5
Painsthorpe La YO41 170 B5
Painter La YO8 196 E2
Palace Rd HG4 214 B7
Palace Theatre Sh Mall YO17 215 C4
Pale La
Carleton BD23 216 E1
Gateforth YO8 202 F7
Paley Green La BD24 131 B2
Pallet Hill [10] DL10 41 D5
Palmer Gr YO8 232 A3
Palmer La YO1 233 C2
Palmers La LS22 180 E4
Palmes Cl YO19 191 E8
Palms Ct DL2 4 A5
Panman La YO19 184 F8
PANNAL 222 E3
PANNAL ASH 222 B5
Pannal Ash Cl HG2 222 C8
Pannal Ash Cres HG2 222 B7
Pannal Ash Dr HG2 222 B7
Pannal Ash Gr HG2 222 B7
Pannal Ash Rd HG2 222 B7
Pannal Ave HG3 222 E2
Pannal Bank HG3 222 E2
Pannal Cl [3] YO21 208 B5
Pannal Gn HG3 222 E3
Pannal Prim Sch HG3 222 E3
Pannal Rd HG3 223 B4
Pannal Sta HG3 222 E2
Pannett Art Gall★ YO21 208 C6
Pannett Way [8] YO21 208 D6
Pannierman La TS7 7 E2
Panorama Cl [10] HG3 137 C4
Panorama Dr LS29 175 C1
Panorama Walk HG2 222 A8
Panorama Wlk HG3 137 C4
Pant La LA2 130 E7
Parade Ct YO31 228 F6
Parade The
Harrogate HG1 219 E2
Hunmanby YO14 127 B8
Whitby YO21 208 B7
Paradise YO11 213 B7
Paradise Cotts YO17 170 F8
Paradise Field Est [2] YO61 143 D8
Paradise La
Dalton YO7 115 F8
Stutton with Hazlewood LS24 189 A3
Paradise Rd YO7 67 A2
Paradise Way [6] DL2 3 B7
Paragon St YO10 233 C1
Parcevall Hall Gdns★ BD23 157 E8
Parish Ghyll Dr LS29 218 A3
Parish Ghyll La LS29 218 A3
Parish Ghyll Rd LS29 218 A3
Parish Ghyll Wlk LS29 218 A3
Parison Ct WF10 200 F3
PARK 186 F5
Park Ave
Barlow YO8 204 C7
Castleford WF10 200 F4
Glusburn BD20 187 E7
Great Preston WF10 200 E6
Harrogate HG2 219 C1
Hellifield BD23 154 B3
Kippax LS25 194 E1
Knaresborough HG5 221 B8
New Earswick YO32 225 D5
Normanton South WF6 200 A1
Scarborough YO12 212 D4
Sherburn in Elmet LS25 195 E4
Skipton BD23 216 F4
Swillington LS26 194 A1
Thornaby TS17 6 B8
Park Avenue S HG2 222 D8
Park Bank YO21 29 E7
Park Chase
Harrogate HG1 219 E3
Hornby DL8 62 C8
Park Cl
[6] Airmyn DN14 205 E4
[1] Easingwold YO61 143 D8
[8] Knaresborough HG5 221 B6
Skelton YO30 224 B4
Park Cres
[6] Addingham LS29 175 A4
Castleford WF10 201 B4
Darlington DL1 3 D4
Embsay BD23 217 C7
Hellifield BD23 154 B3
York YO31 233 C4
Park Crest HG5 221 B6
Park Dale WF10 201 B5

Park Dr
Campsall DN6 206 E1
Glusburn BD20 187 E7
Harrogate HG2 222 D8
Knaresborough HG5 221 B6
13 Masham HG4 86 C3
Park Edge HG2 222 F8
PARK END 7 B8
Park End Prim Sch TS3 7 C8
Parker Ave YO26 227 B2
Parker Dr 21 DL8 63 A2
Parker La YO26 164 C3
Parkers Mount 20 YO62 70 B1
Parker St
Barnoldswick BB18 171 C2
15 Glusburn BD20 187 E8
Park Est YO32 225 D8
Parkfield YO61 144 C6
Parkfield Ave TS5 6 E8
Parkfield Cl YO12 212 D4
Parkfield Gdns YO12 212 D4
Parkfield La WF7 200 E1
Parkgate DL1 3 D5
Park Gate
Knaresborough HG5 221 B8
Strensall YO32 167 B8
Parkgate La DL10 41 B7
Park Gr
Knaresborough HG5 221 B8
Norton YO17 215 C3
Selby YO8 232 B3
Swillington LS26 200 A8
York YO31 233 C4
Park Grove Prim Sch
YO31 233 C4
Park Hill BB18 171 E1
Park House Gn
Harrogate HG1 219 C5
7 Spofforth HG3 179 E5
Park House La LA2 128 D5
Parkin Ave YO8 232 E4
Parkins Garth DL8 57 F6
Parkinson App LS25 194 C4
Parkinson's La LS21 159 E2
Parkinson's Yd 5 DL10 209 C6
Park Junior Sch WF10 200 F4
Park La
Balne DN14 207 C5
Barlow YO8 204 C7
Bishop Wilton YO42 169 F1
Borrowby YO7 65 E4
Buckden BD23 81 E2
Burn YO8 203 D7
Carleton BD23 173 A3
Cowling BD22 186 F5
Darlington DL1 3 D4
5 Easington TS13 11 A8
Glusburn BD20 187 E7
Great Preston WF10 200 E7
Guisborough TS14 8 E6
Kippax LS25 200 E8
Kirkbymoorside YO62 70 B1
Knaresborough HG5 221 C6
Ledsham LS25 201 B8
Luttons YO17 150 C8
Mickletown LS26 200 A5
5 Middleham DL8 60 E2
North Featherstone WF8 200 F1
North Stainley with Sleningford
HG4 113 E5
Spofforth with Stockeld
HG3 179 D5
Tatham LA2 128 B8
West Tanfield HG4 113 A8
Wilberfoss YO41 185 E5
Womersley DN6 206 D6
York YO24 227 F3
Parkland Dr
Darlington DL3 3 A6
Tadcaster LS24 189 F6
Parklands
Castleford WF10 200 F4
Ilkley LS29 218 D4
Park Lands 4 HG3 179 E5
Parklands The
1 Ingleby Arncliffe DL6 45 A7
Scruton DL7 63 D7
Parkland Way YO32 225 D8
Park Lane Cl YO42 169 F1
Park Lodge YO32 225 D4
Park Mount 6 HG3 179 E5
Park Nook Rd LS25 196 F4
Park Par
Harrogate HG1 219 F2
Knaresborough HG5 221 B6
Park Pl
Darlington DL1 3 D5
Hellifield BD23 154 B3
4 Knaresborough HG5 221 B6
York YO31 233 C4
Park Rd
Airmyn DN14 205 E4
Asenby YO7 115 B6
Barlow YO8 204 C7
Castleford WF10 201 A3
Cowling BD22 187 B6
Glusburn BD20 187 E8
8 Harrogate HG2 219 D1
Norton-on-Derwent YO17 215 C3
Pontefract WF8 201 A1
6 Scarborough YO12 212 E4
Spofforth HG3 179 E5
Park Rise 17 YO14 126 F8
Park Row
Knaresborough HG5 221 B5
Park Row *continued*
Selby YO8 232 D5
Parkshill Ct DL10 20 F7
Parkside DL1 3 C4
Park Side
Earby BB18 186 A8
Follifoot HG3 223 E5
Parkside Cl YO24 227 E3
Parkside Commercial Ctr
YO23 233 C1
Park Sq
2 Knaresborough HG5 221 B6
9 Ripon HG4 214 C4
Park St
16 Glusburn BD20 187 E8
1 Harrogate HG1 219 C5
Hovingham YO62 119 E6
Masham HG4 86 C3
Pickering YO18 95 F7
Ripon HG4 214 B5
Scarborough YO12 212 D4
Selby YO8 232 D5
1 Skipton BD23 216 F4
York YO24 233 A1
Parkstone Pl TS16 5 E4
Park Terr
14 Knaresborough HG5 221 B6
Whitby YO21 208 D6
York YO32 225 D5
Park The 14 YO13 75 D5
Park View
Castleford WF10 201 B3
Glaisdale YO21 30 D4
Harrogate HG1 219 E2
22 Leyburn DL8 60 D5
Middleton Tyas DL10 21 C4
Skipton BD23 216 D4
Swillington LS26 194 A1
Park View Dr BD23 134 B3
Park Way
Kirk Hammerton YO26 164 C2
Knaresborough HG5 221 B8
Parkways YO8 232 B3
Parkway The YO12 212 B7
Park Wood BD23 216 D5
Park Wood Cl BD23 216 E5
Park Wood Cres BD23 216 D5
Parkwood Dr 6 TS18 5 E8
Park Wood Way BD23 216 D5
Park Wynd DL10 209 C6
Parliament Ave YO17 215 E4
Parliament St
Harrogate HG1 219 C3
Norton YO17 215 E3
York YO1 233 B2
Parliament Terr 2 HG1 219 D2
PARLINGTON 194 E6
Parlington Ct LS15 194 C8
Parlington Dr LS25 194 E8
Parlington La LS25 194 E7
Parlington Mdw LS15 194 C7
Parlington Villas LS25 194 E8
Parracombe Cl 6 TS17 6 A3
Parrock St 7 BB18 171 D1
Parsley Mews LS26 200 B6
Parsonage Rd LS26 200 C6
Parsonage The 11 HG5 221 A6
Parson Back La DL6 25 B2
Parsons Cl 10 DN14 205 E4
Parson's Cl YO21 208 A7
Parsons Close La BD24 131 A2
Parsons Ct DL10 209 F7
Parsons La YO26 165 E1
Parson's La
1 Addingham LS29 174 E4
Hutton Rudby DL6 25 A2
Parson's Wlk 11 DN14 205 E4
Pasley Rd HG4 113 D3
Paston Wlk YO23 233 B1
Pasture Ave LS25 196 A4
Pasture Cl
Barnoldswick BB18 171 E2
4 Sherburn in Elmet LS25 196 A4
Skelton YO30 224 B5
Skipton BD23 217 B5
2 Strensall YO32 167 B6
Wistow YO8 197 D6
Pasture Cres
Filey YO14 101 A4
3 Knaresborough HG5 221 B7
Pasture Ct LS25 195 F4
Pasture Dr
Bedale DL8 63 A2
Castleford WF10 200 D3
Pasture Farm Cl YO10 231 D6
Pasture Field La YO22 32 C5
Pasture Fold 4 LS29 176 C1
Pasture Gdns DN6 206 F2
Pasture Gr 27 LS25 195 F4
Pasture Hill YO17 169 E8
Pasture La
Ellerton YO42 193 C1
Helperby YO61 142 B8
Heworth YO31 229 B8
Hovingham YO62 119 E6
Kearby with Netherby
LS22 179 C1
Malton YO17 215 C5
Marton-le-Moor HG4 140 D8
2 Seamer YO12 99 D6
Pasture Rd
Embsay with Eastby
BD23 217 C8
Lockton YO18 73 A5
Pastures Gn DL8 62 C5
Pastures The
2 Carlton DN14 204 C3
Coulby Newham TS8 7 B5
Pastures The *continued*
16 Eastfield YO11 100 B6
Sherburn YO17 124 D7
4 York YO24 230 E8
Pasture The 4 TS17 6 D5
Pasture View
Malton YO17 215 C6
Sherburn in Elmet LS25 195 F4
Pasture Way
Castleford WF10 200 D3
Sherburn in Elmet LS25 195 F4
Whitwood WF10 200 D3
Wistow YO8 197 D6
PATELEY BRIDGE 137 C4
Pateley Moor Cres DL2 3 E3
Pately Pl 1 YO26 227 D4
Paterson Cres DL6 210 E4
Pathways Sch WF10 201 B4
Patience La HG4 114 D3
PATRICK BROMPTON 62 C5
Patrick Pool YO1 233 B2
Patterdale Dr YO30 224 E1
Patterham La DL8 59 D4
Pavement YO1 233 B2
Paver La YO1 233 C2
Pavilion Row YO10 231 D7
Pavilion Sq
7 Harrogate HG2 219 C1
11 Scarborough YO11 213 A5
Pavilion Terr 12 YO11 213 A5
Peacocks Cl TS9 26 C8
Peacock's Cl DL7 63 E7
Peak Alum Works* YO13 53 F8
Peak Scar Rd YO62 67 C3
Pearl Rd TS17 6 B8
Pearl St HG1 220 C4
Pearson Garth YO13 99 A7
Pearson St WF6 200 A3
Pearsons Yd YO17 121 C4
Peart La BD23 154 C8
Pear Tree Acre LS23 180 F1
Pear Tree Ave
Long Drax YO8 204 F7
8 Poppleton YO26 165 F1
Pear Tree Cl
Skeeby DL10 20 F1
York YO32 225 F4
Peartree Ct YO1 233 C3
Pear Tree Gdns
Asenby YO7 115 C6
Barwick in Elmet LS15 194 D7
Pear Tree Wlk YO17 215 B4
Pease Ct
1 Eaglescliffe TS16 5 D5
Guisborough TS14 8 D5
4 Lingdale TS12 9 F7
Pease St
Darlington DL1 3 E5
6 Lingdale TS12 9 F7
Peasey Hills Rd YO17 215 C5
Peasholm Ave YO12 212 F7
Peasholm Cres YO12 212 F7
Peasholm Dr YO12 212 E7
Peasholme Bridge YO12 212 E7
Peasholme Gn YO1 233 C2
Peasholm Gap YO12 212 F8
Peasholm Gdns YO12 212 F7
Peasholm Rd YO12 212 F8
Peasland La YO7 66 B5
Peaslands La YO18 96 D5
Peat La HG3 137 B3
Peatmoor La DL8 58 E5
Peckett's Holt HG1 219 D7
Peckett's Way HG1 219 D7
Peckfield HG4 214 C2
Peckfield Cl HG3 160 F5
Peckitt St YO1 233 B1
Peel Cl YO10 229 A1
Peel Gn BD23 154 B2
Peel Pl 11 LS29 176 C1
Peel St
Thornaby TS17 6 B8
York YO1 233 C1
Peel Terr YO12 213 A7
Pefham La YO25 170 F4
Pegman Cl TS14 8 F7
Peirse Cl DL8 63 A2
Pelham Pl 15 YO32 167 A7
Pellentine Rd HG3 223 F4
Pemberton Cres TS4 7 A8
Pemberton Rd WF10 201 A4
Pembroke St
10 Skipton BD23 216 F3
York YO30 228 B7
Pembroke Way YO21 208 C5
Pembury Mews DL10 41 B6
Penberry Gdns 33 TS17 5 F4
Penders La TS15 5 E1
Penderyn Cres TS17 5 F4
Pendle St 4 BD23 216 D3
Pendleton Rd DL1 3 D7
Pendragon Castle* CA17 14 A1
Pendragon Way HG2 222 B8
Penfold Ct BD23 154 B3
Penhill Ct DL7 210 C1
Penhowe La YO17 147 D4
Penistone Rd TS3 7 C8
Penley's Grove St YO31 233 C4
Pennine Cl YO32 225 F4
Pennine View
Burneston DL8 87 E8
Northallerton DL7 210 B2
Pennine Way
11 Barnoldswick BB18 171 D1
Ingleby TS17 6 A4
Pennine Way BD20 172 E2
Penniston La YO13 97 C4
Penn La DL8 56 D4
Penn Rd DL10 209 B7
Pennycarr La YO61 143 D7
Penny Gn BD24 131 D1
Penny La
Burton Fleming YO25 126 E2
Darlington DL1 3 C4
1 Easingwold YO61 117 D1
Ripon HG4 214 C7
Penny La Ct YO1 233 C3
Pennyman Gn TS8 6 C4
Pennyman Prim Sch TS3 7 D8
Penny Pot Gdns 4 HG3 161 B2
Pennypot La TS18 5 E7
Penny Pot La HG3 160 D2
Penny Pot La or Rough Rd
HG3 161 A2
Penny Royal Cl 7 HG3 161 B3
Pennywort Gr 15 HG3 161 B3
Penrith Cres WF10 201 B5
Penrith Rd TS3 7 B8
Pentire Cl 11 YO30 225 A1
Pentland Dr YO32 225 E3
Penton Rd 20 YO11 100 B6
Penyghent Ave YO31 229 A5
Penyghent Way TS17 6 A3
Pen-y-Ghent Way 5
BB18 171 D1
Peplow Cl LS25 201 F6
Peppercorn Cl 6 YO26 227 E4
Peppergarth The DL7 210 B3
Peppermint Dr 15 DL9 41 A5
Peppermint Way YO8 232 A5
Per Ardua Way 6 DL10 41 E4
Percy Cross Rigg YO21 9 A1
Percy Ct HG5 162 A6
Percy Dr 4 DN14 205 E4
Percy Rd
Darlington DL3 3 C7
14 Hunmanby YO14 127 A8
Percy's La YO1 233 C2
Percy St YO31 233 B3
Peregrine Ct 2 TS14 8 D6
Perie Ave HG4 113 D3
Perry Ave TS17 6 B5
Petercroft Cl 5 YO19 184 F7
Petercroft La YO19 184 F7
Peter Hill Dr YO30 228 A8
Peterhouse Cl DL1 3 D7
Peter La
Burton Leonard HG3 140 A2
York YO1 233 B2
Petersbottom La LA2 129 B4
Petersway YO30 233 A4
Petre Ave YO8 232 E3
Petty Whin Cl 25 HG3 161 B3
Petyt Gr BD23 217 A4
Pew Tree Cl YO41 185 E6
Pheasant Dr 5 YO24 230 B8
Pheasantry The 14 YO12 99 E6
Philadelphia Terr 2
YO23 228 B2
Philip La YO8 196 E2
Philippa's Dr HG2 222 D8
Philip St 27 BB18 171 D1
Philpin La LA6 104 C8
Phlashetts La DL8 87 A4
Phoenix Ave LS25 194 F3
Phoenix Bsns Ctr HG4 214 D5
Phoenix Bvd YO26 228 A4
Phoenix Pk TS8 6 F6
Piave Rd DL9 40 D4
Picadilly Ct YO1 233 C2
Piccadilly YO1 233 C2
Pickard Cl BB18 171 E2
Pickard La BD20 174 C1
PICKERING 95 E6
Pickering Ave LS25 194 D4
Pickering Castle* YO18 95 F7
Pickering Com Junior Sch 26
YO18 95 F7
Pickering Infant Sch
YO18 96 A7
Pickeringmoor La YO7 64 C2
Pickering Rd
East Ayton/West Ayton
YO13 99 A7
Thornaby TS17 6 B8
Thornton-le-Dale YO18 96 C6
Pickering Sta YO18 95 F7
Pick Haven Garth DN14 202 F3
PICKHILL 88 C6
Pickhill CE Prim Sch YO7 88 C6
Picking Croft La HG3 161 B5
Picks Ct 5 YO7 211 B3
Pickwick Cl YO17 215 C5
PICTON 24 D6
Piece Croft 2 BD23 134 D2
Piece Fields 4 BD23 134 D2
PIERCEBRIDGE 2 A6
Piercy End YO62 70 B1
Pier La 22 YO21 208 D7
Pier Rd YO21 208 D7
Pierremont Rd DL3 3 B6
Piggy La DL2 1 C7
Pighill Nook Rd LS25 202 C7
Pike Hills Mount YO23 230 A3
Pike La BD24 131 E4
Pikepurse La DL10 209 D8
Pike Rd 8 YO18 95 F6
Piker Thorn La YO19 167 D1
Pilgrim St YO31 233 B4
Pill White La LS21 177 C3
Pilmoor Cl DL10 209 E8
Pilmoor Dr DL10 209 E8
Pindar L Ctr YO11 100 A6
Pindar Rd YO11 100 A6
Pindars Way YO8 198 B4
Pinder Cl DL10 209 F8
Pinders Cres WF11 201 E3
Pinders Green Ct LS26 200 B5
Pinders Green Dr LS26 200 B5
Pinders Green Fold LS26 200 B5
Pinders Green Wlk LS26 200 B4
Pine Cl
Castleford WF10 200 F3
Skipton BD23 216 E4
Pine Croft HG4 112 F2
Pine Gr 1 DL6 210 E3
Pine Hill TS8 7 B5
Pinelands 4 YO32 225 D7
Pinelands Way YO10 229 C3
Pine Rd
Guisborough TS14 8 E7
Middlesbrough TS7 7 D8
Pines Gdns 29 LS29 175 C2
Pine St HG1 219 E5
Pines The LS17 178 B2
Pine Tree Ave YO17 122 F5
Pine Tree Cl YO8 197 B2
Pinetree Gr DL2 4 C4
Pine Tree La 1 LS25 202 A7
Pine Wlk HG4 214 D2
Pinewood Ave YO14 101 B4
Pinewood Cl
5 Easington TS13 11 A8
3 Firth Moor DL1 3 E4
2 Ilkley LS29 218 A3
5 Whitby YO21 208 C6
Pinewood Dr
Camblesforth YO8 204 D4
Scarborough YO12 212 D5
Pinewood Gate HG2 222 A7
Pinewood Gr
13 Bedale DL8 63 A2
6 York YO31 225 E2
Pinewood Hill 4 YO10 229 C3
Pinewood Rd TS7 7 C6
Pinewood Wlk 7 TS9 26 C8
Pinfold Ave LS25 195 F4
Pinfold Cl
Bilton-in-Ainsty with Bickerton
LS22 181 B5
5 Riccall YO19 192 A1
3 Sherburn in Elmet LS25 195 F4
Pinfold Croft BD23 155 D1
Pinfold Ct
Kirkby Malzeard HG4 112 D5
4 Sherburn in Elmet LS25 195 F4
4 York YO30 228 A7
Pinfold Dr DL6 210 E5
Pinfold Garth
Malton YO17 215 A4
6 Sherburn in Elmet LS25 195 F4
Pinfold Gn HG5 140 E1
Pinfold Hill YO8 197 D6
Pinfold La
Kirk Smeaton WF8 206 B3
Mickletown LS26 200 C5
Moss DN6 207 D1
Norton DN6 206 E2
Norwood HG3 177 A8
Pollington DN14 207 F6
Pinfold Pl YO7 211 C3
Pinfold Rise LS25 194 F8
Pinfold The 5 BD23 216 F4
Pinfold View DN14 207 F6
Pinfold Way 5 LS25 195 F4
Pinhaw Rd BD23 217 A2
Pinnacle View BD22 187 A5
Pinsent Ct 4 YO31 228 E8
Pioneer Bsns Pk YO30 224 F3
Pioneer Ct DL1 4 A4
Pioneer Way WF10 200 C2
Piper Hill 1 WF11 201 D6
Piper Hill Cl DL10 21 D7
Piper La
Cowling BD22 187 B5
Thirsk YO7 211 C3
Piper Rd DL6 45 F6
Pipers Acre 4 YO18 95 F7
Pipers La YO26 141 F1
Pippin Rd YO17 215 B4
Pippin's App 17 WF6 200 A2
Pit Ings La YO7 115 F6
Pit La
Ledston Luck LS25 194 F1
Micklefield LS25 195 A4
Mickletown LS26 200 B6
Pitman Rd YO17 215 C5
Place Hill DL11 38 B6
PLACE NEWTON 123 C3
Planetree La
Kirkby Fleetham with Fencote
DL7 42 A1
Thornville YO26 164 A1
Plane Tree Way YO14 101 A4
Plantation Ave HG3 222 A8
Plantation Cl HG2 222 A8
Plantation Dr
Barlby with Osgodby
YO8 198 B5
York YO26 227 C6
Plantation Gr YO26 227 C6
Plantation Rd HG2 222 A8
Plantation Terr HG2 222 A8
Plantation The
Birstwith HG3 160 E6
Gisburn Forest BD23 152 E3
Plantation Way 23 YO32 166 E5
Plaxton Ct YO12 212 B5
Player Ct TS16 5 E5
Pleasance The 6 LS26 194 A1
Pleasant Row HG5 221 B8
Pleasant View 5 BB18 172 B1
Plews Way DL7 63 C5
Plompton Cl HG2 220 D1

Plompton Dr HG2 220 D2
Plompton Gr 3 HG2 220 D2
Plompton Rd HG3 223 F5
Plompton Way 1 HG2 220 D2
Plompton Wlk 2 HG2 220 D2
Plough Garth The DN14 202 F3
Ploughlands 1 YO32 225 C7
Ploughman's Cl YO23 230 C3
Ploughmans Ct 14 YO11 100 B7
Ploughmans' La YO32 225 C7
Plover Gdns 1 YO12 99 F6
Plumer Ave YO31 229 A5
Plumer Rd DL9 209 B1
Plumpton La HG4 139 D8
Plumpton Pk HG2 220 D3
Plumpton Rocks* HG5 179 D8
Plum St YO17 215 D3
Pluntrain Dale La YO18 96 B7
Poachers The YO8 199 C5
POCKLEY 69 B1
Pocklington La YO42 169 F2
Pockthorpe La YO25 151 F2
Pocock Pl DL10 41 E4
Polam Hall Sch DL1 3 C4
Polam La DL1 3 C4
Polam Rd DL1 3 C4
Pole Rd BD22 187 F4
Pollard Gdns YO12 212 C4
Pollard Rd YO31 53 F8
POLLINGTON 207 F6
Pollington Balne CE Prim Sch DN14 207 F6
Polperro Cl 21 WF6 200 A2
Pond Farm Cl TS13 11 F7
Pond Field Cl DL3 3 A4
Pondfields Dr LS25 194 D1
Pond St 3 YO8 232 D6
Pond View DL6 65 F7
Pontefract Monkhill Sta WF8 201 B1
Pontefract Park Racecourse* WF8 200 F2
Pontefract Rd
- Castleford WF10 200 F4
- Knottingley WF11 201 D2
- Normanton South WF6 200 B2
Pontefract Tanshelf Sta WF8 201 A1
Pool Ct 20 YO18 95 F6
POOLE 201 F5
Poole La LS25 201 F6
Pool La YO26 164 E4
Pope St WF6 200 B3
Poplar Ave
- Castleford WF10 201 B4
- 6 Hutton Rudby TS15 25 D5
- 4 Kirkbymoorside YO62 70 B1
- 3 Wetherby LS22 180 C4
Poplar Cres
- Harrogate HG1 219 F6
- Northallerton DL7 210 C2
Poplar Ct YO8 204 F5
Poplar Dr WF6 200 A3
Poplar Gdns YO8 204 F5
Poplar Gn HG5 162 A6
Poplar Gr
- Harrogate HG1 219 F6
- York YO32 225 E3
Poplar Pl TS14 8 E7
Poplar Row 6 YO21 208 D7
Poplars Adventure Mega Maze* HG5 162 F6
Poplars La YO17 123 A7
Poplar St YO26 227 E5
Poplars The
- 11 Brayton YO8 197 D1
- 2 Glusburn BD20 187 E6
- Knottingley WF11 202 A1
Poplar View YO17 215 F4
Poplar Way HG1 219 F6
Poppleton Hall Gdn YO26 224 A3
Poppleton Ousebank Prim Sch YO26 165 F1
Poppleton Rd YO26 227 E4
Poppleton Rd Prim Sch YO26 227 E5
Poppleton Sta YO26 182 F8
Poppy Cl YO8 232 C2
Poppy Ct DL9 41 A5
Porchester Cl 3 TS17 5 F5
Porch Farm Cl YO62 120 B5
Porch The DL10 21 D7
Pornic Ave YO13 75 D5
Porritt La YO12 99 D7
Portal Rd
- Knapton YO26 227 B7
- York YO26 227 B6
Portholme Cres 7 YO8 232 C5
Portholme Ct YO8 232 C4
Portholme Dr YO8 232 C4
Portholme Rd YO8 232 C5
Portisham Pl 12 YO32 167 A7
Portland Cres HG1 219 D4
Portland St YO31 233 B4
Portland Way DL7 63 C5
Portman Rise TS14 8 F5
PORT MULGRAVE 11 F8
Postern Cl YO23 233 B1
Postern La YO42 193 D6
Post Office Row DN14 205 A1
Post Office Slip 24 YO61 143 C8
Pot Bank HG3 178 A8
Potlands DL7 63 C4
Pott Bank HG4 85 A1
Potter Cl YO13 99 B8
Pottergate
- Gilling East YO62 118 F7
- 14 Helmsley YO62 92 F6
- Richmond DL10 209 C7
Potter Hill 11 YO18 95 F7
Potter La DL7 64 A5
Potters Dr 4 YO23 230 B3
Potter's Side La YO21 9 D1
POTTERTON 188 C1
Potterton Cl LS15 194 C8
Potterton La
- Barwick in Elmet LS15 194 C8
- Barwick in Elmet & Scholes LS15 188 C1
Pottery La
- Bishop Monkton HG4 140 A6
- Knottingley WF11 201 E3
- Littlethorpe HG4 214 E1
- Strensall YO32 145 A1
- Strensall YO32 167 A8
- York YO31 228 E7
Pottery St WF10 200 D4
Potticar Bank YO62 119 D4
Pott Moor High Rd HG4 110 F8
POTTO 25 D2
Pounteys Cl 4 DL2 4 C4
Powell St
- Harrogate HG1 219 F4
- Selby YO8 232 B6
Prail Cl 13 WF8 201 C1
Prebendal Cl 11 LS25 202 A8
Precentor's Ct YO31 233 B3
Preen Dr TS5 6 D8
Premiere Pk 30 LS29 175 C2
Premier Rd TS7 7 D7
Preseli Gr 31 TS17 5 F4
Preston Field Cross Rd YO13 74 E1
Preston Hall Mus* TS18 5 F6
Preston La
- Great Preston WF10 200 C7
- Preston-on-Tees TS18 5 E7
PRESTON-ON-TEES 5 F7
Preston-on-Tees Prim Sch TS16 5 E6
PRESTON-UNDER-SCAR 59 E6
Preston View LS26 194 A1
Preston Way TS9 26 C8
Prestwick Ct
- 15 Middleton St George DL2 4 C4
- Rufforth YO26 227 B5
Pretoria St WF10 200 F4
Price's La YO23 233 B1
Priest Bank Rd 4 BD20 173 F1
Priestcarr La YO26 163 D8
Priest Cl YO14 126 F8
Priest Gill Bank DL11 19 F5
Priest La
- Dunnington YO19 184 F5
- Ripon HG4 214 D4
Primrose Ave
- Hunmanby Sands YO14 101 B1
- Hunmanby YO14 127 B8
- Swillington LS26 194 A1
Primrose Cl
- Guisborough TS14 8 E6
- 13 Killinghall HG3 161 B3
- Ripon HG4 214 C6
Primrose Ct 18 DL9 41 A5
Primrose Dene WF11 201 E4
Primrose Dr
- Castleford WF10 201 D3
- Filey YO14 101 B1
- Ripon HG4 214 C6
Primrose Gr YO8 232 A6
Primrose Hill
- 9 Knottingley WF11 202 A3
- 2 Skipton BD23 216 F4
Primrose Hill Cl LS26 194 A1
Primrose Hill Dr
- Great & Little Preston LS26 200 A8
- 15 Swillington LS26 194 A1
Primrose Hill Garth LS26 200 A8
Primrose Hill Gdns LS26 194 A1
Primrose Hill Gn LS26 200 A8
Primrose Hill Gr 16 LS26 194 A1
Primrose La LS23 188 E8
Primrose Lane Prim Sch 5 LS23 188 E8
Primrose Vale 1 WF11 202 A2
PRIMROSE VALLEY 101 C1
Primrose Valley Rd YO14 101 B1
Prince Henry Rd LS21 177 A1
Prince Henrys Gram Sch LS21 177 A1
Prince of Wales Terr YO11 213 A4
Prince Rupert Dr YO26 181 C7
Princes Cres BD23 217 B4
Princes Dr BD23 217 A4
Princess Ave HG5 221 C5
Princess Cl
- Knaresborough HG5 221 C5
- Ripon HG4 214 C6
Princess Ct 11 WF6 200 B1
Princess Dr
- Knaresborough HG5 221 C5
- West Haddlesey YO8 203 A5
- York YO26 227 D6
Princess Gr 4 HG5 221 C5
Princess La 12 YO11 213 B6
Princess Mead HG5 163 A3
Princess Mount 3 HG5 221 C5
Princess Pl
- 1 Ripon HG4 214 C6
- 5 Whitby YO21 208 D6
Princes Sq
- 14 Harrogate HG1 219 D2
- Thornaby TS17 6 B6
Princess Rd
- Darlington DL3 3 D8
- Ilkley LS29 218 A3
- Malton YO17 215 C4
- Ripon HG4 214 C6
- Strensall YO32 167 B7
Princess Royal La 4 YO11 212 F3
Princess Royal Pk 1 YO11 213 A3
Princess Royal Rd HG4 214 C3
Princess Royal Terr YO11 213 A3
Princess Royal Way HG3 222 E1
Princess Sq 11 YO11 213 B6
Princess St
- Castleford WF10 200 F5
- Normanton South WF6 200 A1
- Scarborough YO11 213 B6
Princess Terr
- Knaresborough HG5 221 C6
- 17 Scarborough YO11 213 B6
Prince St WF10 200 C8
Princes Villa Rd HG1 219 E2
Prior Ave DL10 209 B7
Priorpot Way YO17 215 F4
Prior Pursglove Coll 16 TS14 8 F7
Prior's La BD23 174 C8
Prior's Wlk YO26 227 D6
Prior Wath Rd YO13 54 A5
Priorwood Gdns TS17 6 A4
Priory Cl
- Guisborough TS14 8 F7
- Northallerton DL6 210 E5
- Wilberfoss YO41 185 F6
Priory Dr YO21 208 A6
Priory La 1 DN14 204 C1
Priory Park Cl 3 LS25 202 A8
Priory Park Gr 2 LS25 202 B8
Priory Pk YO22 31 C4
Priory Pl YO11 100 B7
Priory Road or House DN6 206 E2
Priory St YO1 233 A1
Priory View 2 BD23 217 E8
Priory Villas DL10 209 D6
Priory Way
- Barnoldswick BB18 171 D1
- 4 Ingleby Arncliffe DL6 45 A7
- 1 Snaith DN14 204 B1
Priory Wood Way YO31 225 F2
Prison & Pol Mus* HG4 214 D5
Pritchett Rd TS3 7 C8
Promenade La HG1 219 C3
Promenade Sq HG1 219 C2
Prospect Ave
- Normanton South WF6 200 A2
- Sherburn in Elmet LS25 195 F4
Prospect Bank
- Bramham cum Oglethorpe LS23 188 F6
- Scarborough YO12 212 D6
Prospect Cl
- Camblesforth YO8 204 D5
- Harrogate HG2 220 C3
- Monk Fryston LS25 202 A8
- Pollington DN14 207 F6
Prospect Cotts 6 HG3 160 A6
Prospect Cres
- 13 Harrogate HG1 219 D2
- Scarborough YO12 212 D6
Prospect Ct 3 LS24 189 E6
Prospect Dr LS24 189 E6
Prospect Field 5 YO22 33 D4
Prospect Hill YO21 208 C5
Prospect Mount Rd YO12 212 C6
Prospect Pk YO12 212 D6
Prospect Pl
- Harrogate HG1 219 D2
- Northallerton DL6 210 F4
- 28 Scarborough YO11 213 A6
- Skipton BD23 216 F4
- Thornton-le-Dale YO18 96 D6
- 10 Whitby YO22 208 E6
- Wistow YO8 197 D6
Prospect Rd
- Harrogate HG2 220 C3
- 9 Scarborough YO12 212 F6
Prospects Cotts YO61 117 C6
Prospect St 14 BD20 187 E7
Prospect Terr
- Fulford YO10 231 D6
- 15 Knaresborough HG5 221 A6
- 1 Lingdale TS12 9 F7
- Micklefield LS25 195 A3
- York YO1 233 B1
Prospect View
- Appleton Wiske DL6 24 B3
- Northallerton DL6 210 E4
Prospect Way
- 5 Leeming DL7 63 D4
- Selby YO8 232 D4
Prospect Way Ind Est YO8 232 D4
Providence Gn 16 WF8 201 C2
Providence Pl
- 13 Filey YO14 101 B3
- Mickletown WR10 200 D6
- 15 Scarborough YO11 213 A6
- Skipton BD23 217 A4
Providence Terr HG1 219 D4
Pry Hills La
- Hartoft YO18 71 A8
- Rosedale East Side YO18 49 F2
Pudding Hill Rd DL11 1 B6
Pudding La YO13 97 F5
Pudding Pie Hill* YO7 211 D1
Pudsey Wlk 3 DL1 3 D4
Pudsley Wlk DL1 3 D4
Pulleyn Cl 3 YO32 167 C8
Pulleyn Dr YO24 227 F1
Pump Hill 4 HG5 221 A6
Pump La
- Kirklevington TS15 24 F8
- 4 Malton YO17 215 C4
Purey Cust Nuffield Hospl The YO31 233 B3
Pye Busk Cl LA2 129 B8
Pye La HG3 160 F8
Pysbury Wlk 25 YO51 141 B5

Q

Quaker Cl
- 1 Reeth, Fremington & Healaugh DL11 38 B6
- Scarborough YO12 212 C5
Quaker Gn 1 YO24 230 C7
Quaker La DL6 210 D5
Quakers La DL10 209 B7
Quaker's La DL6 44 D7
Quant Mews YO10 229 B3
Quarry Ave 20 WF11 202 A2
Quarry Bank YO17 215 D5
Quarry Banks YO7 116 E7
Quarry Dr TS8 6 E5
Quarry Gate YO13 74 C1
Quarry Hill YO17 120 F4
Quarry Hill La LS22 180 B3
Quarry Hills La 26 DL8 60 D5
Quarry La
- Harrogate HG1 219 C6
- Osmotherley DL6 45 C5
- Pateley Bridge HG3 137 C4
Quarry Moor La HG4 214 C3
Quarry Moor Nature Reserve* HG4 214 B1
Quarry Mount YO12 212 E3
Quarry Oval HG1 219 C6
Quarry Rd
- Eaglescliffe TS18 5 F7
- Norton DN6 206 F2
- Richmond DL10 209 B7
- Ripon HG4 214 B2
Quay St YO11 213 B6
Quay The YO8 232 D6
Queen Anne's Ct 3 DL8 63 A2
Queen Anne's Dr 4 DL8 63 A2
Queen Annes Rd YO30 233 A3
Queen Elizabeth Dr 10 YO13 75 D5
Queen Elizabeth's Sixth Form Coll 1 DL3 3 C5
Queen Elizabeth Way TS18 6 D6
Queen Ethelburga's Coll YO26 164 C6
Queen Ethelburga's Gdns 6 HG3 161 B2
Queen Ethelburga's Par 8 HG3 161 B2
Queen Ethelburga's Pk 9 HG3 161 B2
Queen Margarets Ave 4 WF11 201 E4
Queen Margarets Cl 3 WF11 201 E4
Queen Margaret's Dr WF11 201 E4
Queen Margaret's Ind Est YO11 212 E2
Queen Margaret's Rd 6 YO11 212 F3
Queen Margarets Sch YO19 192 A5
Queen Marys Sch YO7 115 A7
Queens Ave DL9 40 E3
Queensbury Ct 15 WF6 200 B1
Queens Cl DL10 41 E5
Queen's Cl 8 HG2 219 C1
Queens Ct
- Gainford DL2 1 D7
- Great Preston LS26 200 C7
- Malton YO17 215 D6
- Richmond DL10 209 C7
Queen's Ct YO1 233 B2
Queens Dr
- 9 Stokesley TS9 26 C8
- Whitby YO22 208 E3
Queen's Dr LS29 218 A3
Queen's Drive La LS29 218 A3
Queens Garth BD23 172 A3
Queens Gate HG1 219 E2
Queens Gdns YO7 211 C1
Queen's Gdns
- 4 Ilkley LS29 218 A3
- Tadcaster LS24 189 E6
Queen's Par YO12 213 A7
Queen's Park Dr WF10 201 A4
Queens Rd
- Knaresborough HG5 221 C6
- Richmond DL10 209 C7
Queen's Rd
- Harrogate HG2 219 C1
- Ilkley LS29 218 A3
Queen's St 6 BD23 217 B4
Queens Staith Mews YO1 233 B1
Queen's Staith Rd YO1 233 B2
Queen St
- 10 Cowling BD22 187 B6
- Great Preston LS26 200 C7
- Normanton South WF6 200 A1
- 18 Ripon HG4 214 C5
- Scarborough YO11 213 A6
- 4 Silsden BD20 174 C1
- Skelton & Brotton TS12 9 D7
- York YO24 233 A2
Queen's Terr
- 3 Filey YO14 101 B3
- Scarborough YO12 213 A7
Queensway WF8 201 C2
Queen's Way YO62 70 B1
Queenswood Gr YO24 227 D2
Queen Victoria St YO23 228 B1
Quentin Rd 19 DL9 40 E4
Quernmore Dr BB18 186 A7
Quilt Mus & Gall The* YO1 233 C2

R

Raby La DL7 22 E3
Raby Pk LS22 180 B3
Raby Terr DL3 3 C5
Racca Ave 11 WF11 202 A2
Racca Gn WF11 202 A2
Racecourse Ct DL10 209 A8
Racecourse La DL7 210 D3
Racecourse Mews YO7 211 A2
Racecourse Rd
- East Ayton/West Ayton YO13 99 B8
- Irton YO12 212 A1
- Richmond DL10 209 B8
- York YO23 231 B8
Race La
- Carlton DN14 204 B4
- Sessay YO61 116 C4
Rachel La DL11 20 B5
Raghill La YO61 142 A8
Raglan St HG1 219 D2
Raglan Terr 3 YO21 208 D5
Rag Robin Turn YO7 66 D6
Raikes Ave BD23 216 F5
Raikes La BD23 156 A6
Raikes' La YO22 32 E3
Raikes Rd BD23 216 F5
Raikes The HG3 137 E3
Raikeswood Cres BD23 216 E5
Raikeswood Dr BD23 216 E5
Raikeswood Rd BD23 216 E5
Railer Bank HG4 112 E6
Railway Ave WF8 201 B1
Railway Cotts HG4 214 D1
Railway Rd
- Follifoot HG3 223 C7
- Ilkley LS29 218 B4
Railway St
- 16 Leyburn DL8 60 D5
- Norton YO17 215 C3
- Slingsby YO62 120 B5
Railway Terr
- Hurworth-on-Tees DL2 22 D8
- Ilkley LS29 218 C4
- 5 Normanton South WF6 200 A1
- Thirsk YO7 211 B2
- York YO24 228 A4
Railway View
- Darlington DL1 3 D4
- Northallerton DL7 210 D3
- York YO24 230 E8
Raincliffe Ave
- 29 Filey YO14 101 B3
- Scarborough YO12 212 C5
Raincliffe Cres YO12 212 C5
Raincliffe Gr YO12 212 C4
Raincliffe Sch YO12 212 B6
Raincliffe St 4 YO8 232 C5
Raindale Rd YO18 71 F6
Raines Dr 5 BD20 173 E3
Raines La BD23 134 D3
Raines Lea BD23 134 D3
Raines Mdws 6 BD23 134 D2
Raines Rd BD24 131 C1
Rainford Cl 7 YO12 99 D6
Rainhall Cres BB18 171 E1
Rainhall Rd BB18 171 D1
Rainham Cl TS17 6 B4
Rainhill Way 5 DL2 3 B7
Rainsborough Way 3 YO30 228 A8
Rainsburgh La YO25 126 A3
RAINTON 114 E6
Raisdale Rd TS9 26 D1
Rakehill Rd LS15 194 B8
Rake La YO21 30 D6
Raker Cl YO19 192 F7
Rakes La BD23 171 B5
Rake The LA6 103 D4
Raleigh St YO12 212 E6
Ralph Butterfield Prim Sch YO32 166 F5
Ralph Garth YO26 181 D7
Rampart The YO23 190 D4
Ramsay Cl YO31 233 C4
Ramsden Cl WF11 201 D4
Ramsden St LS25 200 C8
Ramsey Ave YO23 231 B3
Ramsey Gdns 38 TS17 5 F4
Ramsey St YO12 212 E6
RAMSGILL 110 E1

Ramsgill DL1 3 E4
Ramshaw Dr BD23 217 A1
Ramshill Rd YO11 213 A4
Randal La HG3 160 D4
Range Rd DL9 40 A2
Rankin's Well Rd 4 BD23 217 B4
Rantreefold Rd LA2 128 F4
Rape Close La YO62 118 E4
Rape La YO62 93 B7
Raper La YO61 117 B3
Raper View LS25 194 F8
Rarber Top La LA6 103 D2
Rarey Dr YO17 124 E1
RASKELF 116 E2
Raskelf Rd
7 Brafferton YO61 115 F1
Easingwold YO61 117 B1
Ratcliffe Ct YO30 224 C5
Ratcliffe St YO30 228 B7
Rathmall La YO26 164 C2
RATHMELL 153 C6
Rathmell CE Prim Sch BD24 153 B7
Rattan Row YO25 151 C6
Ratten Row
Hunton DL8 61 E7
Seamer YO12 99 C5
Raven Cl 10 YO12 99 F6
Raven Gr YO26 227 C4
Raven Hall Rd YO13 53 F7
RAVENSCAR 54 A8
Ravens Cl Brow LA2 102 C1
Ravenscroft Way BB18 171 E2
Ravensdale Rd DL3 3 B4
RAVENSEAT 15 C2
Ravensthorpe Prep Sch DL3 3 B5
Ravensville 1 BD20 187 F7
RAVENSWORTH 20 A7
Ravensworth Castle* DL11 20 A6
Ravensworth CE Prim Sch DL11 20 A6
Ravine Hill 17 YO14 101 B4
Ravine Rd YO14 101 B4
Ravine Top 7 YO14 101 B3
RAW 33 B4
Raw Bank DL11 37 E8
RAWCLIFFE
Goole 205 A1
York 224 E2
Rawcliffe Ave YO30 227 F8
Rawcliffe Cl 5 YO30 224 E2
Rawcliffe Croft YO30 224 D2
Rawcliffe Dr YO30 227 F8
Rawcliffe Ind Est YO30 224 E3
Rawcliffe Infant Sch YO30 224 E1
Rawcliffe La YO30 224 F1
Rawcliffe Landing YO30 224 C3
Rawcliffe Prim Sch DN14 205 A1
Rawcliffe Village YO30 224 E3
Rawcliffe Way YO30 224 E2
Rawcliff Rd YO18 72 A5
Rawdon Ave YO10 228 F4
Rawfield La WF11 201 D7
Raw Gap HG5 221 A6
Raw La
Fylingdales YO22 33 B4
Kirkby Wharfe with North Milford LS24 190 A3
Towton LS24 189 F3
Rawlinson Rd DL9 209 D2
Raw Pasture Bank YO22 33 B5
Raw Pasture La YO22 33 C5
Rawson St HG1 219 E5
Ray Bridge La BD23 155 D1
RAYDALE 57 A1
Raydale Cl 2 HG5 221 D5
RAYGILL 186 E8
Raygill La BD20 186 E8
Ray La HG4 114 B1
Rayleigh Rd HG2 222 E8
Raylton Ave TS7 7 B5
Rayner St HG4 214 C5
Raynes Ct DL8 56 D5
Read Cl YO8 204 F5
Read Sch YO8 204 F5
Reas La YO51 141 D1
Reasty Hill YO13 53 E1
Reasty Rd YO13 53 D2
Recreation Rd
17 Pickering YO18 95 F6
2 Selby YO8 232 D6
Rectory Cl
Bolton Percy YO23 190 D4
Heslerton YO17 123 F6
Rectory Gdns YO23 228 B1
Rectory La
Guisborough TS14 8 E6
3 Hurworth-on-Tees DL2 22 C8
Longnewton TS21 5 A7
Skipton BD23 217 A4
Thornton-le-Dale YO18 96 E5
Red Bank Cl HG4 214 A3
Red Bank Dr HG4 214 A3
Red Bank La HG4 214 A3
Red Bank Rd HG4 214 A3
Redbarn Dr YO10 229 D4
Red Barnes Way DL1 3 E6
Red Brae Bank HG3 137 A3
Red Brow YO13 74 C5
Redcap La YO42 193 C5
Redcar Rd
Guisborough TS14 8 F7
Thornaby TS17 6 B7
Redcliff Cl 12 YO11 100 B7
Redcliffe Ct YO12 212 D7
Redcliffe Gdns YO12 212 C6
Redcliffe La YO11 100 D6
Redcliffe Rd YO12 212 D6
Redcoat Way 1 YO24 230 B8
Redeness St YO31 228 E5
Redfearn Mews HG2 222 D6
Red Gate DL8 57 C6
Redgrave Cl 4 YO31 228 E8
Red Hall La TS15 6 A1
Red Hall Prim Sch DL1 3 F6
RED HILL 201 A4
Redhill Ave WF10 201 A3
Redhill Cl HG1 219 D6
Redhill Dr WF10 201 A3
Redhill Field La YO23 182 D1
Redhill Infant Sch WF10 201 B4
Redhill Junior Sch WF10 201 B4
Redhill La LS25 201 D8
Red Hill La LS25 195 E1
Redhill Rd
Castleford WF10 201 A4
Harrogate HG1 219 C6
Red Hills La HG3 140 B3
Red Hills Rd HG4 214 B7
Redhill Wlk WF10 201 A3
Redhouse La YO8 204 F6
Red La
Green Hammerton YO26 164 C3
4 Masham HG4 86 C3
Red Lion St BB18 172 B1
Redlish Rd HG3 136 E1
Redman Cl YO10 231 C8
Redmayne Sq YO32 167 B8
REDMIRE 59 C6
Redmires Cl YO30 225 A2
Redmire Sta DL8 59 C6
Red Rose Cl 3 DL2 3 A7
Redruth Dr 22 WF6 200 A2
Red Scar Dr YO12 212 A7
Red Scar La
Newby & Scalby YO12 75 C4
Scalby YO12 212 A8
Redshaw Cl 1 HG4 214 C4
Redshaw Gr 2 HG4 214 C4
Redthorn Dr YO31 225 F1
Red Twr* YO1 228 E4
Red Way
Brompton DL6 43 F6
Danby YO21 29 E6
Farndale East YO62 48 E4
Nether Silton DL6 45 D1
Redwing Rising 1 TS14 8 D6
Redwood Cl DL1 3 F4
Redwood Dr 6 YO32 166 E5
Reebys La LA2 129 F5
Reedshaw La BD22 186 F5
REETH 38 B6
Reeth Com Prim Sch DL11 38 B6
Reeth Rd
Middlesbrough TS5 6 E8
Richmond DL10 209 A7
2 Stockton-on-Tees TS18 5 E8
Reeval Cl 13 BB18 172 B1
Reeves The YO24 227 C1
Regency Ave TS6 7 E8
Regency Ct
3 Ilkley LS29 218 A3
Northallerton DL6 210 F3
Regency Mews
Northallerton DL7 210 D4
2 York YO24 230 F8
Regency Pk TS17 6 B4
Regent Ave
Harrogate HG1 219 E3
Skipton BD23 217 B5
Regent Cres BD23 217 B5
Regent Dr BD23 217 B5
Regent Gr HG1 219 E4
Regent Mount 2 HG1 220 C4
Regent Par HG1 219 E3
Regent Pl HG1 220 C4
Regent Rd
Ilkley LS29 218 A4
Skipton BD23 217 B5
Regents Ct
Walkerville DL9 41 A4
14 York YO26 227 F5
Regents Mews 1 YO26 227 D6
Regent St
Castleford WF10 200 E4
Harrogate HG1 219 F3
Normanton WF6 200 B2
1 Scarborough YO12 213 A6
York YO10 228 E3
Regent Terr HG1 219 E3
Regimental Mus* YO1 233 B1
Reginald Gr YO23 228 C1
Reginald Terr YO8 232 D4
Reid Pk YO32 166 E5
Reid St Prim Sch DL3 3 C6
Reid Terr TS14 8 F6
REIGHTON 127 D6
Reighton Ave YO30 227 F8
Reighton Dr 10 YO30 224 F1
Rein Ct LS25 194 F8
Reins HG5 163 A7
Reivaulx Dr TS5 6 F8
Renfield Gr WF6 200 B2
Renshaw Gdns 8 YO26 227 E4
Renton Cl HG3 140 B5
Reservoir La 7 YO11 100 B8
Residence La HG4 214 D5
Resolution Way YO21 208 B5
Retreat Hospl The YO10 228 F2
Reygate Gr YO23 230 B2
Reynard Crag La HG3 160 C6
Reynolds St 15 YO14 101 B3
Rhobell View 3 TS17 5 F4
Rhodes Dr HG2 222 D6
Rhode's Hill La LS23 188 F6
Rhodes La LS23 188 D7
Rhodes St WF10 200 D4
Rhyddings Gdns LS29 218 D4
Rianbow La YO17 215 C6
Ribble Bank BD24 131 E4
Ribble Dr DL1 3 C3
Ribblehead Sta LA6 78 E1
Ribblehead Viaduct* LA6 78 D2
Ribstone Gr YO31 229 B6
Ribston Rd
Little Ribston LS22 180 A7
Spofforth with Stockeld HG3 179 F6
Riccal Dr
25 Helmsley YO62 92 F6
Huttons Ambo YO17 121 C1
RICCALL 198 A8
Riccall La YO19 191 D1
Riccall Prim Sch YO19 191 F1
Riccal Moor La YO62 93 E4
Rice Gate YO13 74 D8
Rice La
Aldwark YO61 142 C2
Flaxton YO60 145 F2
Richard Gossop Ct 41 LS29 176 C1
Richard III Mus* YO31 233 C3
Richardson Ct YO8 196 F1
Richardson Rd TS17 6 A7
Richardson St YO23 228 C2
Richard St YO8 232 B5
Richard Taylor CE Prim Sch HG1 219 E6
Richard Thorntons CE (VA) Prim Sch LA6 102 E3
RICHMOND 209 C7
Richmond Ave
22 Barnoldswick BB18 171 D2
Harrogate HG2 222 C7
Knottingley WF11 201 D3
Richmond Castle* DL10 209 C6
Richmond CE Prim Sch DL10 209 D7
Richmond Cl HG2 222 C7
Richmond Ct LS29 218 C3
Richmondfield Ave LS15 194 C7
Richmondfield Cl LS15 194 C7
Richmondfield Cres LS15 194 C7
Richmondfield Cross LS15 194 C7
Richmondfield Dr LS15 194 B7
Richmondfield Garth LS15 194 C8
Richmondfield Gr LS15 194 C7
Richmondfield La LS15 194 C7
Richmondfield Mount LS15 194 C7
Richmondfield Way LS15 194 C8
Richmond Garth HG4 112 C5
Richmond Gate DL8 58 C4
Richmond Holt HG2 222 C7
Richmond Lower Sch DL10 209 C6
Richmond Methodist Prim Sch DL10 209 E7
Richmond Pl LS29 218 C3
Richmond Rd
12 Barnoldswick BB18 171 D2
Barton DL10 21 E6
Brompton-on-Swale DL10 41 A6
Croft-on-Tees DL10 21 F6
Harrogate HG2 222 C7
Hipswell DL9 209 D1
Leyburn DL8 60 D5
Skeeby DL10 20 F1
Richmond Rise DL7 210 C3
Richmond Sch DL10 209 D7
Richmondshire Mus* DL10 209 C7
Richmond St YO31 228 E5
Richmond Swimming Pool DL10 209 D6
Richmond Way DL1 3 F4
Ridding Cres DN14 205 A1
Ridding Gate 5 LS21 176 F1
Ridding La DN14 205 A1
Riddings La HG4 112 C7
Riddings Rd LS29 218 B3
Riders La YO60 146 F2
Ridgedale Mount WF8 201 B2
Ridge Gn YO13 75 D5
Ridge La
Roxby TS13 11 A6
Silsden BD20 174 B4
Sleights YO21 32 B7
Staithes TS13 13 H1
Ridge Rd LS25 200 E8
Ridge The
Coulby Newham TS8 7 A4
Linton LS22 180 B2
Ridgeway
Coulby Newham TS8 7 D5
Darlington DL3 3 C8
10 Eastfield YO11 99 F7
Skipton BD23 216 E6
York YO26 227 B3
Ridgeway The WF11 201 F2
Ridgewood Cl DL1 3 F4
Riding Cl 4 BB18 171 E1
Ridings The
7 Boroughbridge YO51 141 B4
Norton YO17 215 D2
Ridley Ave TS5 6 E8
Ridleys Fold 14 LS29 174 F4
Ridsdale St DL1 3 D5
RIEVAULX 92 B8
Rievaulx Abbey* YO62 92 B8
Rievaulx Ave HG5 221 C4
Rievaulx Bank YO62 92 B8
Rievaulx Cl HG5 221 C4
Rievaulx Ct 6 HG5 221 C4
Rievaulx Dr DL7 64 A6
Rievaulx Rd YO21 208 C6
Rievaulx Terr & Temples* YO62 92 B7
Rievaulx Way TS14 8 F6
Riffa Bsns Pk LS21 176 F1
Riffa La LS21 177 E2
Rigg Bank HG4 85 E3
Riggs Rd YO17 121 F5
Riggs Spring 5 HG3 137 F1
Rigg The TS15 5 E2
Rigg View YO22 32 F7
Rigton CE Prim Sch LS17 178 C4
Rigton Hill LS17 178 B4
Rileys Croft 3 BD23 153 F5
Riley St 41 BB18 172 A1
RILLINGTON 122 F5
Rillington Prim Sch YO17 122 F5
Rimington Ave DL10 209 D6
Rimington Way YO11 100 B7
Ringing Keld Hill YO13 54 A3
Rings The TS17 5 F5
Ringstone Rd
Bishopthorpe YO23 231 B5
York YO30 224 F3
Ringstones La LA2 129 A4
Ringway LS25 194 B3
Ringway Gr 11 DL2 4 C4
Ringwood Rd DL9 40 F3
Riparian Way BD20 187 F8
RIPLEY 161 C7
Ripley Bank HG3 137 C4
Ripley Castle* HG3 161 C7
Ripley Cl
11 Kirkbymoorside YO62 70 B1
Normanton South WF6 200 B1
Ripley Dr
Harrogate HG1 219 C6
Normanton South WF6 200 B2
Ripley Endowed CE Prim Sch HG3 161 C7
Ripley Gr 3 YO32 166 E5
Ripley Rd
Knaresborough HG5 220 E8
Nidd HG3 161 E6
Scotton HG5 162 A5
Ripley's Rd YO13 54 B1
Ripley Way HG1 219 C6
RIPON 214 E5
Ripon Bsns Pk HG4 214 E4
Ripon By-pass HG4 214 C2
Ripon Cath* HG4 214 C5
Ripon Coll HG4 214 A5
Ripon Com Hospl HG4 214 B5
Ripon Courthouse Mus* HG4 214 C5
Ripon Dr DL1 3 D4
Ripon Gram Sch HG4 214 A6
Ripon Horn The* HG4 214 C5
Ripon L Ctr HG4 214 D3
Ripon Loop Nature Reserve* HG4 113 F4
Ripon Racecourse* HG4 214 F2
Ripon RC Choir Sch HG4 214 A3
Ripon Rd
Harrogate HG3 219 A7
Middlesbrough TS7 7 E6
Ripley HG3 161 D8
South Stainley with Cayton HG3 139 E2
Ripon Spa Baths HG4 214 B5
Ripon Way
Carlton Miniott YO7 89 C4
Harrogate HG1 219 C5
Riseber DL8 60 C5
Risedale Com Coll DL9 209 F1
Risedale Rd DL9 209 B1
Rise The
Huttons Ambo YO60 147 C6
Kippax LS25 194 D1
Knottingley WF11 201 E4
Leavening YO17 147 E1
Thornton Dale YO18 96 D5
Whitby YO22 208 E6
Risewood YO41 168 B2
Rishworth Gr YO30 224 F2
RISPLITH 138 E7
Rivadale View LS29 218 B5
Rivelin Way
10 Filey YO14 101 A3
York YO30 224 F2
Rivendell BD23 134 B3
Riverbank Trad Est DL1 3 D7
River Cl 2 YO8 198 B5
Riverdale 4 DN14 202 D4
Riverdale Gdns LS23 188 F8
Rivergarth DL1 3 F7
River La
Brompton-on-Swale DL10 41 B6
Kilburn High & Low YO61 91 B2
West Haddlesey YO8 203 A5
River Pl BD23 155 D1
River Rd YO61 91 C2
Riversdale
17 Haxby YO32 166 F5
5 Settle BD24 131 D2
Riversdene TS9 26 B7
Riverside
Clapham LA2 130 C8
Gargrave BD23 155 D1
Rawcliffe DN14 205 A2
28 Scalby YO12 75 D5
Riverside Ave LS21 177 A1
Riverside Bsns Pk LS29 218 D5
Riverside Cl
1 Elvington YO41 185 C2
Farnley LS21 177 A1
West Haddlesey YO8 203 A5
Riverside Cres
5 Otley LS21 177 A1
York YO32 225 F6
Riverside Ct DN14 205 A2
Riverside Dr 3 LS21 177 A1
Riverside Gdns
2 Boroughbridge YO51 141 B6
2 Elvington YO41 185 C2
2 Poppleton YO26 165 F1
Riverside Mews 6 YO7 211 C3
Riverside Pk 4 LS21 177 A1
Riverside Prim Sch LS24 189 E6
Riverside Rd DL10 209 C6
Riverside View YO17 215 B3
Riverside Way DL1 3 E7
Riverside Wlk
Airton BD23 155 A6
Ilkley LS29 218 A5
1 Poppleton YO26 165 F1
Ruswarp YO22 208 C4
5 Strensall YO32 167 A7
Riverslea TS9 26 B7
River St
1 Selby YO8 232 D6
Trawden BB8 186 B2
York YO23 233 B1
Riversvale Dr 21 YO26 165 F1
Riversway BD23 155 C1
River View
1 Barlby YO8 198 B5
Boston Spa LS23 188 F8
Ilkley LS29 218 E5
Richmond DL10 209 D6
Riverview Ind Est DL1 3 D6
River View Rd HG4 214 C7
RNLI Whitby Mus* YO21 208 D7
Roach Grange Ave LS25 194 D2
Roald Ct DL10 209 E8
Roall La DN14 202 F4
Robb Cl YO7 211 A2
Roberts Cres HG1 219 D5
Robertson Rd
Colburn DL9 40 F4
Ripon HG4 113 D3
Roberts Sq HG1 219 D5
Robert St
Harrogate HG1 219 D1
Selby YO8 232 C5
Robert Wilkinson Prim Sch YO32 167 A7
Robin Cl 6 WF8 201 B2
Robin Gr 6 YO24 227 F3
Robin Hood Cl YO21 29 A6
Robin Hood Rd YO13 53 F8
ROBIN HOOD'S BAY 33 D4
Robin Hood's Bay Mus* YO22 33 D4
Robin Hood's Bay Rd YO22 33 A3
Robin La
Bentham LA2 103 A1
High Bentham LA2 129 A8
Huby YO61 144 A4
Robinson Ct YO1 233 C2
Robinson Dr
Harrogate HG2 222 B6
York YO24 227 B2
Robinson Fold 18 BB18 171 D2
Robinson Rd 13 DL10 41 E4
Robinson St WF10 200 D6
Robson Ave TS17 6 B5
Roche Ave
Harrogate HG1 219 F6
York YO31 228 E8
Rockbourne Way 1 TS17 5 F6
Rockcliff Ct 15 LS24 189 E6
Rock Hill WF10 201 A3
Rockingham Ave YO31 229 A5
Rockingham Cl YO17 215 A3
Rockingham Ct LS24 189 E2
Rockingham Dr YO12 212 B7
Rockland Gdns YO12 212 D5
Rockley Grange Gdn LS25 194 B3
Rocks La YO13 75 D7
Rocks Lane Cl YO13 75 D7
Rock Terr WF10 201 A3
Rock View Terr BD23 217 D8
Rockville Dr BD23 217 C8
Rockwell Ave DL1 3 E7
Rockwood Cl 1 BD23 216 E4
Rockwood Dr BD23 216 E5
Rodney Terr 15 HG4 86 C3
Roebuck La LS21 176 F2
ROECLIFFE 140 F4
Roecliffe CE Prim Sch YO51 140 F4
Roecliffe Ct YO26 182 C8
Roecliffe La YO51 141 B5
Roedean Dr TS16 5 E4

Roe La LS25 .... 202 C7
Roger La TS8 .... 6 C4
Rogers Ct
Woodthorpe YO24 .... 230 C8
York YO24 .... 230 C8
Rogers Sq 16 HG1 ...... 219 D2
Roker Cl DL1 .... 3 F6
Roker Rd HG1 .... 219 E4
Roland Ct YO32 .... 225 E3
Rolston Ave 3 YO31 ..... 225 E2
Roman Avenue N 17
YO41 .... 168 D2
Roman Avenue S YO41 .. 168 D1
ROMANBY 210 B3
Romanby Prim Sch DL7 .. 210 B2
Romanby Rd DL7 .... 210 C3
Roman Cl
Newby & Scalby YO12 .... 212 A7
4 Tadcaster LS24 .... 189 E6
Roman Cres DL9 .... 209 C1
Roman Fort of Olicana★
LS29 .... 218 B4
Roman Garth YO17 ...... 215 D4
Roman Rd
Leeming DL7 .... 63 D4
Middlesbrough TS5 .... 6 E8
Tadcaster LS24 .... 189 C5
Romans Cl YO19 .... 197 F8
Roman Signal Sta★ YO21 .. 12 D6
Roman Way YO12 .... 212 A7
Romany Rd 11 TS9 .... 8 A2
Rombalds Dr BD23 .... 217 A2
Rombalds La LS29 .... 218 E3
Rombalds View LS21 ..... 176 E1
Rombald's View LS29 ... 218 D5
Romille St 15 BD23 ..... 217 A3
Ronaldshay Cl DL10 ..... 209 E8
Ronaldshay Dr DL10 ..... 209 E8
Ronway Ave HG4 .... 214 B2
Rookery Rd BB18 .... 171 E1
Rook St
25 Barnoldswick BB18 ... 171 D1
Lothersdale BD20 .... 186 F8
ROOKWITH 62 A1
Rookwood Ave LS25 ...... 200 C8
Rookwood Rd TS7 .... 7 D6
Roomer La HG4 .... 86 B1
Roper Ct DL10 .... 209 C7
Ropers Ct YO23 .... 230 C3
Ropery La YO17 .... 124 E1
Ropery The
15 Pickering YO18 .... 95 F7
Whitby YO22 .... 208 E6
Ropery Wlk YO17 .... 215 C4
Ropewalk The YO31 ...... 228 E5
Rope Wlk BD23 .... 217 A4
Ropner Gdns DL2 .... 4 C3
Rosamund Ave 21 YO18 ... 95 F7
Roscoe St YO12 .... 212 F5
Rose Ave
Sherburn in Elmet LS25 .... 195 F3
Whitby YO21 .... 208 B7
Roseberry Ave
Great Ayton TS9 .... 8 A2
Stokesley TS9 .... 26 D8
Roseberry Cres TS9 .... 8 A2
Roseberry Ct TS9 .... 26 D6
Roseberry Dr 8 TS9 .... 8 A2
Roseberry Gn HG4 .... 113 C7
Roseberry Gr YO30 .... 224 F3
Roseberry La
Guisborough TS9 .... 8 B3
Stillington YO61 .... 144 B6
Roseberry Mount TS14 ...... 8 E6
Roseberry Prim Sch TS9 ... 8 A2
Roseberry Rd TS9 .... 8 A2
Roseberry Topping★ TS9 ... 8 C3
Rosebery Ave YO12 ...... 212 E3
Rosebery St YO26 .... 227 F6
Rosecomb Way 6 YO32 . 225 D7
Rose Cres
Richmond DL10 .... 209 B7
Sherburn in Elmet LS25 .... 195 F3
Rosecroft Ave TS13 .... 10 D8
Rosecroft La TS13 .... 10 D8
Rosecroft Way YO30 ...... 227 E8
Rose & Crown Yd 20
YO21 .... 208 D6
Rose Ct LS25 .... 194 D4
Rosedale HG3 .... 222 D3
ROSEDALE ABBEY 49 E3
Rosedale Abbey Prim Sch
YO18 .... 49 E2
Rosedale Ave YO26 ...... 227 C4
Rosedale Chy Bank YO18 .. 49 E1
Rosedale Cl
Pannal HG3 .... 222 D3
3 Whitby YO21 .... 208 C6
Rosedale Cres
Darlington DL3 .... 3 A6
Guisborough TS14 .... 8 D6
Rosedale La
Hinderwell TS13 .... 11 F8
Staithes TS13 .... 13 L1
Rosedale Rd TS7 .... 7 D6
Rosedale Rise LS23 ...... 188 E8
Rosedale St YO10 .... 228 D2
Rosegarth Ct TS9 .... 26 E5
Rosehill TS9 .... 8 A1
Rose Hill Dr 13 TS9 .... 26 C7
Rosehill Sq 11 HG5 ...... 221 B5
Rose Hill Way TS9 .... 26 C7
Rosehurst Gr HG3 .... 222 E2
Rose La LS24 .... 196 A7
Roseland Dr TS7 .... 7 C7
Rose Lea Cl 2 LS25 ...... 202 A7
Rosemary Ct
20 Easingwold YO61 ..... 143 C8
Rosemary Ct *continued*
6 Tadcaster LS24 .... 189 E6
York YO1 .... 233 C2
Rosemary La 1 DL10 ... 209 C6
Rosemary Pl YO1 .... 233 C2
Rosemary Row 5 LS24 ... 189 E6
Rosemoor Cl
Coulby Newham TS8 .... 7 B5
19 Hunmanby YO14 .... 126 F8
Rosemount Ct 4 BD20 ... 187 E6
Rosemount Dr WF6 .... 200 C1
Rosemount Rd 2 YO21 ... 208 C5
Rosendale Ave YO17 ..... 215 F2
Rose St YO31 .... 228 C7
Rose Tree Gr YO32 ...... 225 D4
Rosetta Way YO26 .... 227 D6
Rosevale Terr YO12 ...... 212 E5
Roseville Ave
Harrogate HG1 .... 220 A3
Scarborough YO12 .... 212 E6
Roseville Dr HG1 .... 220 A3
Roseville Rd HG1 .... 220 A3
Roseway HG1 .... 219 E5
Rosewood Cres HG1 ..... 220 B3
Rosewood Prim Sch TS8 ... 7 A4
Roseworth TS9 .... 26 E5
Rosley St BB8 .... 186 B3
Roslyn Rd HG2 .... 220 A2
Rossett Acre Prim Sch
HG2 .... 222 C7
Rossett Ave HG2 .... 222 C6
Rossett Beck HG2 .... 222 C6
Rossett Cres HG2 .... 222 D6
Rossett Dr HG2 .... 222 C6
Rossett Garth HG2 .... 222 C6
Rossett Gdns HG2 .... 222 C6
ROSSETT GREEN 222 D5
Rossett Green La HG2 ... 222 C5
Rossett Holt Ave HG2 ... 222 C7
Rossett Holt Cl HG2 ..... 222 C8
Rossett Holt Dr HG2 ..... 222 C7
Rossett Holt Gr HG2 ..... 222 C7
Rossett Holt View HG2 .. 222 C7
Rossett Park Rd HG2 .... 222 D6
Rossett Sch HG2 .... 222 B6
Rossett Sports Ctr HG2 . 222 C6
Rossett Way HG2 .... 222 C7
Rossiter Dr WF11 .... 201 E2
Rosslyn Ct TS18 .... 5 F8
Rosslyn St 1 YO30 ...... 228 A6
Rossway DL1 .... 3 F8
Rostle Top Rd 10 BB18 .. 172 A1
Rotary Way
Faverdale DL3 .... 3 B8
Ripon HG4 .... 214 D6
Rothbury Cl HG2 .... 220 D2
Rothbury St YO12 .... 212 E5
Rothesay Gr TS7 .... 7 D6
Roth Hill La YO19 .... 192 E3
Rotunda Mus★ YO11 .... 213 A5
Roughaw Cl BD23 .... 216 F2
Roughaw Rd BD23 .... 217 A2
Roughley Bank DL7 .... 63 C5
Rough Rd HG3 .... 161 A2
Rougier St YO1 .... 233 A2
Roundell Dr BD23 .... 171 F5
Roundell Rd BB18 .... 171 E2
Roundhill Ave TS17 .... 5 F4
Roundhill Cl 5 DL2 .... 3 E1
Roundhill Junior Sch
WF11 .... 201 D3
Round Hill Link YO30 .... 224 F2
Roundhill Rd DL2 .... 3 E1
ROUNDHILL VILLAGE 5 F5
Roundhouse Rd DL3 .... 3 B8
Routh Wlk 5 YO21 ...... 208 D7
Rowan Ave
3 Filey YO14 .... 101 A4
Malton YO17 .... 215 D6
York YO32 .... 225 D4
Rowan Cl
Gateforth YO8 .... 197 B1
4 Hut Green DN14 .... 203 A2
Scarborough YO12 .... 212 C6
Rowan Ct
8 Catterick DL10 .... 41 D5
Leyburn DL8 .... 60 D5
Rowan Dr 5 TS9 .... 8 A2
Rowan Fields YO12 .... 99 E7
Rowan Garth 22 BD20 ... 187 E7
Rowan La
16 Hellifield BD23 .... 154 B3
Skirethorns BD23 .... 134 B3
Rowan Lea HG2 .... 222 B7
Rowan Pl YO32 .... 225 D4
Rowans The
Dalton YO7 .... 115 F7
Hellifield BD23 .... 154 A3
Rowans Way DL7 .... 210 B4
ROWDEN 160 F4
Rowden La HG3 .... 160 F5
Rowedale Cl 15 YO14 .... 126 F8
Rowen Ave 6 YO61 ...... 117 D1
Rowlandhall La DN14 .... 199 E1
Rowland Keld TS14 .... 8 E5
Rowland St 18 BD23 ..... 217 A3
Rowley Ct 2 YO32 .... 225 F7
Rowley Dr LS29 .... 218 F3
Rowmans The YO30 ...... 224 C4
Rowntree Ave YO30 ...... 228 C8
Roxburghe Dale WF7 ..... 200 C1
ROXBY 11 C7
Roxby Ave TS14 .... 8 E5
Roxby Gdns
4 Eastfield YO12 .... 99 F7
5 Thornton Dale YO18 ..... 96 D5
Roxby La
Roxby TS13 .... 11 C7
Roxby La *continued*
Staithes TS13 .... 13 J1
Roxby Rd YO18 .... 96 D5
Roxby Terr 6 YO18 .... 96 D5
Royal Albert Dr YO12 .... 212 F8
Royal Ave YO11 .... 212 F4
Royal Chase YO24 .... 230 F8
Royal Cres
Harrogate HG2 .... 222 D8
12 Scarborough YO11 .... 213 A4
Whitby YO21 .... 208 C7
Royal Cres La 8 YO11 ... 212 F4
Royal George Dr TS16 ...... 5 D5
Royal Hall★ HG1 .... 219 D3
Royal Par
Filey YO14 .... 101 B3
8 Harrogate HG1 .... 219 C2
Royal Pump Room Mus★
HG2 .... 219 C2
Royd Cl 18 BD20 .... 187 E7
Royd Ct 12 BD22 .... 187 B6
Royds Ave WF10 .... 201 B4
Royd's Rd YO8 .... 202 F6
Royd The TS15 .... 5 D2
Ruby St 3 YO23 .... 228 B1
Rudbeck Cl HG2 .... 220 C1
Rudbeck Cres HG2 .... 220 C1
Rudbeck Dr HG2 .... 220 C1
RUDBY 25 D5
Rudby Bank TS15 .... 25 D5
Rudby Lea TS15 .... 25 D6
Rudcarr La YO19 .... 167 E1
Rudda Rd YO13 .... 53 F6
Rudding Dower HG3 ...... 223 E7
Rudding La
Follifoot HG3 .... 223 C5
North Rigton HG3 .... 222 A1
Ruddings YO19 .... 193 A8
Ruddings Cl 9 YO32 ..... 225 C8
Ruddings La
Cowesby YO7 .... 66 C4
Crakehall DL8 .... 62 D4
Ellerton YO42 .... 193 E2
Ruddings Rd YO18 .... 72 B3
Ruddings The
Selby YO8 .... 232 A4
Wheldrake YO19 .... 193 A8
Rudgate
Bilton-in-Ainsty with Bickerton
YO26 .... 181 B6
Newton Kyme cum Toulston
LS24 .... 189 B6
Walton LS23 .... 181 B1
Rudgate Bsns Pk YO26 .. 180 B7
Rudgate Ct LS23 .... 181 B1
Rudgate Gr YO26 .... 164 A4
Rudgate Pk LS23 .... 181 A2
Rudstone Gr LS25 .... 195 F4
Ruebury La DL6 .... 45 B4
Rues La LS21 .... 176 C8
Ruffa La YO18 .... 96 A6
Ruffhams Cl YO19 .... 192 F8
Ruffin La YO17 .... 147 D5
Ruff La YO61 .... 142 B5
Rufford Cl TS14 .... 8 F5
RUFFORTH 182 C6
Rufforth Prim Sch YO23 . 182 C6
Rumford Way DL8 .... 60 D6
Rumple Croft 4 LS21 .... 176 F1
Runnymede TS7 .... 7 D5
Runs Bank DL8 .... 60 D8
Runswick Ave
Middlesbrough TS5 .... 6 E6
Whitby YO21 .... 208 B6
York YO26 .... 227 B4
RUNSWICK BAY 12 A7
Runswick La TS13 .... 11 F7
Rupert Rd LS29 .... 218 A5
Rushmere TS8 .... 7 B5
Rusholme La YO8 .... 205 A5
RUSHTON 98 D6
Rushton Ave 21 BB18 .... 172 A1
Rushwood Cl 6 YO32 .... 166 F5
Ruskin Ave
Middlesbrough TS5 .... 6 D7
6 Skipton BD23 .... 216 D3
Ruskin Cl DL2 .... 22 D7
Ruskin Dr WF10 .... 201 A4
Russell Dixon Sq HG4 .... 214 B3
Russell Dr YO30 .... 227 E8
Russell St
Harrogate HG2 .... 222 E7
Skipton BD23 .... 217 A3
York YO23 .... 228 B2
Russell Terr DL7 .... 63 D2
Russet Dr YO31 .... 229 B5
Russet Gr YO12 .... 212 C8
Russett Rd YO17 .... 215 B4
Ruston La YO13 .... 98 D7
RUSWARP 208 B3
Ruswarp Bank YO21 ...... 208 B3
Ruswarp CE Prim Sch
YO21 .... 208 B3
Ruswarp Fields YO22 .... 208 C3
Ruswarp La YO21 .... 208 B4
Ruswarp Pleasure Boats★
YO21 .... 208 B3
Ruswarp Sta YO22 ...... 208 C3
Rutland Cl
Copmanthorpe YO23 ..... 230 A3
Harrogate HG1 .... 219 A2
Rutland Dr HG1 .... 219 A2
Rutland Pl 4 YO62 .... 92 F7
Rutland Rd HG1 .... 219 B2
Rutland St 38 YO14 ...... 101 B3
Rutland Terr YO12 .... 213 A7
Rutmoor Rd YO18 .... 71 E8
Ryburn Cl YO30 .... 224 F2
Rycroft Rd 3 YO12 .... 75 E5
Rydal Ave
Middlesbrough TS5 .... 6 E8
York YO31 .... 229 A6
Rydal Cl 2 YO7 .... 89 C4
Rydal Cres 7 YO12 .... 99 F7
Rydal Rd
Darlington DL1 .... 3 E4
Harrogate HG1 .... 220 B3
Ryder Cres 3 YO62 .... 70 B1
Ryder Sq YO17 .... 215 C4
Ryder's Wynd 3 DL10 .. 209 C6
Rye Cl
Haxby YO32 .... 225 C8
Huttons Ambo YO17 ..... 121 C1
Ryecroft 7 YO32 .... 167 A6
Ryecroft Ave
10 Norton DN6 .... 206 E2
York YO24 .... 230 C7
Ryecroft Cl YO31 .... 229 C8
Ryecroft Gdns DN14 .... 203 A2
Ryecroft Rd
Glusburn BD20 .... 187 D8
Norton DN6 .... 206 E1
Ryecroft Way 2 BD20 ... 187 E8
Ryedale Cl
Helmsley YO62 .... 92 F7
Norton YO17 .... 215 F1
Pontefract WF6 .... 200 A3
Ulleskelf LS24 .... 190 B2
Ryedale Folk Mus★ YO62 .. 70 C5
Ryedale Pk LS29 .... 218 D3
Ryedale Pl WF6 .... 200 A3
Ryedale Pool YO18 .... 95 F6
Ryedale Sch YO62 .... 93 D7
Ryedale State Pk YO17 .. 215 C3
Ryedale View 2 YO62 ..... 70 B1
Ryedale Way YO8 .... 232 C3
Ryefield Cl 12 YO11 .... 99 F7
Ryefield Rd 1 YO11 ...... 100 A6
Ryegate 13 YO62 .... 92 F6
Ryegrass Gdns 15 WF10 . 200 D3
Ryehill Cl YO32 .... 225 D5
Rye Hill Way TS8 .... 7 B4
Ryelands Pk 1 TS13 ...... 11 A8
Ryeland St 9 BD20 ...... 187 E8
Ryemoor Rd YO32 .... 225 C8
Rylatt Pl YO26 .... 227 B3
RYLSTONE 156 B5
Rylstone Dr 1 BB18 .... 171 D1
Rymers Ct DL1 .... 3 E7
Rymer Way 4 YO7 .... 211 C3
Ryndle Cres YO12 .... 212 E8
Ryndleside YO12 .... 212 E7
Ryndle Wlk YO12 .... 212 E8
Ryngwoode Dr YO17 .... 215 C6
RYTHER 190 F1
Rythergate 8 YO8 .... 197 B8
RYTON 121 F6
Ryton Old La YO17 ...... 121 F5
Ryton Stile Rd YO17 ..... 215 C7

S

Sackville Rd BD20 ...... 174 C1
Sackville St
20 Barnoldswick BB18 ... 171 D1
Skipton BD23 .... 217 A3
Sacred Heart Prim Sch The
LS29 .... 218 D4
Sacred Heart RC Prim Sch
Ilkley LS29 .... 218 D4
Romanby DL7 .... 210 D2
SADBERGE 4 B8
Sadberge Ct YO10 .... 229 C3
Sadberge Rd DL2 .... 4 C5
Saddle Cl YO17 .... 215 D2
Saddlers Cl
1 Copmanthorpe YO23 ... 230 B3
Huntington YO32 .... 225 F2
Saddlers Croft 8 LS29 .. 218 A4
Saddlers La WF11 .... 201 E5
Saddler's La WF11 .... 201 E5
Saddlers Way YO26 ...... 182 A6
Saddlers Wlk YO19 ...... 192 A5
Sadler Dr TS7 .... 7 B6
Sadler Forster Way TS17 ... 6 B5
Sadlers Ct
Alne YO61 .... 143 A5
26 Boroughbridge YO51 .. 141 B5
Saffron Dr 6 DN14 ...... 204 C1
Saffron Mdw 19 HG3 ..... 161 B3
Sails Dr YO10 .... 229 B3
St Aelreds Cl YO31 ...... 228 F4
St Aelreds RC Prim Sch
YO31 .... 229 B5
St Agathas DL10 .... 209 C7
St Aidans CE High Sch
HG2 .... 219 F1
St Aidans Rd LS26 .... 200 C8
St Aidan's Rd DL9 .... 209 D1
St Alkelda's Rd 1 DL8 .... 60 E2
St Andrewgate YO1 ...... 233 B2
St Andrew Pl YO1 .... 233 C2
St Andrew's Ave HG2 ... 220 A3
St Andrew's Cres HG2 ... 220 A3
St Andrews Ct
Rillington YO17 .... 122 F5
Sadberge DL2 .... 4 C8
St Andrews Dr WF7 ...... 200 E1
St Andrews Gate HG4 ... 112 D5
St Andrews Gr 2 DL7 ... 210 D2
St Andrew's Gr 1 HG2 .. 220 B2
St Andrews Mdws HG4 .. 112 D5
St Andrew's Par 3 HG2 . 220 A2
St Andrew's Pl 2 HG2 .. 220 A2
St Andrews Rd YO21 ..... 208 B5
St Andrew's Rd
Castleford WF10 .... 201 B5
4 Harrogate HG2 .... 220 B3
St Andrew's St 1 HG2 ... 220 A2
St Andrew's Wlk HG2 ... 220 A2
St Ann Ct YO10 .... 228 E2
St Anne's Cres 3 DL10 ... 41 E4
St Annes Gdns DL2 .... 4 C3
St Ann's Ct YO10 .... 228 D2
St Ann's Staith 13 YO21 . 208 D7
St Anthonys Ave 2 DL7 . 210 E2
St Athan's Wlk HG2 ..... 222 C7
St Aubyn's Pl YO24 ...... 228 A2
St Augustines RC Prim Sch
Coulby Newham TS8 .... 7 B5
Darlington DL3 .... 3 C5
St Augustines Sch YO12 . 212 C4
St Barnabas CE Prim Sch
YO26 .... 227 F5
St Barnabas Ct 13 YO26 . 227 F5
St Bedes Ave 4 DL7 ..... 210 D2
St Bedes RC Prim Sch DL1 3 D8
St Benedict Rd YO23 .... 233 A1
St Benedicts RC Prim Sch
Ampleforth YO62 .... 92 C1
Garforth LS25 .... 194 C4
St Bernadettes RC Prim Sch
TS7 .... 7 D6
St Boltophs Cl 4 WF11 .. 202 A2
St Brides Ct 30 TS17 .... 5 F4
St Bridget's Ct YO23 ..... 233 B1
St Catherines Cl YO30 ... 224 C5
St Catherines Pl YO24 ... 228 A3
St Catherine's Rd HG2 ... 219 F1
St Chads Wharf YO23 ... 231 C8
St Christopher Cl 3
DL7 .... 210 D2
St Christophers Dr 27
LS29 .... 174 F4
St Clares Abbey DL3 .... 3 B5
St Clares RC Prim Sch TS5 . 6 D6
St Clement's Gr YO23 ... 228 C2
St Clement's Rd HG2 .... 220 A2
St Clements Road S HG2 220 A2
St Cuthbert Ave TS7 .... 7 C5
St Cuthbert Dr DL7 ...... 210 B3
St Cuthbert's Ave 4 DL9 .. 41 A5
St Cuthberts CE Prim Sch
HG3 .... 137 B4
St Cuthberts Cl 15 HG3 .. 137 B4
St Cuthbert's Gn DL10 .... 21 D8
St Cuthberts Wlk TS13 .... 10 D8
St Davids Gr 34 TS17 .... 5 F4
St Davids RC Tech Coll
TS5 .... 6 E7
St Davids Rd LS21 .... 176 F1
St David's View 9 DN14 . 205 E4
St Denys' Rd YO1 .... 233 C2
St Edmunds YO41 .... 168 D2
St Edmunds Cl 1 DL10 .... 41 C6
St Edwards Cl 2 WF11 ... 201 F4
St Edward's Cl YO24 .... 230 F8
St Edwards RC Prim Sch 3
LS23 .... 188 E8
St Edwin's Cl DL2 .... 2 C6
St Francis of Assisi CE Prim
TS17 .... 6 A5
St Francis Xavier Sch
DL10 .... 209 E8
St Gabriels RC Prim Sch
TS7 .... 7 D8
St George's Ave HG2 .... 222 D7
St Georges CE Prim Sch
DL2 .... 4 C4
St George's Gate DL2 ...... 4 B5
St Georges Gr 3 DL7 .... 210 E2
St George's Pl YO24 ..... 227 F2
St Georges RC Prim Sch
Eastfield YO11 .... 100 A7
York YO10 .... 228 D2
St George's Rd HG2 ..... 222 D7
St Georges Terr TS13 ...... 10 D8
St George's Wlk HG2 ... 222 D6
St Gerards RC Prim Sch
TS8 .... 6 F5
St Giles CE VA Prim Sch
WF8 .... 201 B1
St Giles Cl YO7 .... 211 C3
St Giles' Cl 1 DL9 .... 41 A5
St Giles Ct YO31 .... 233 B3
St Giles Rd YO30 .... 224 B5
St Giles Way YO23 ...... 230 A2
St Gregory's Cl DL8 .... 62 E4
St Gregory's Mews YO1 . 233 A2
St Heddas RC Prim Sch
YO21 .... 31 A4
St Helena 11 YO51 .... 141 B5
St Helens Cl DL7 .... 64 A7
St Helens Dr DL7 .... 64 A7
St Helen's Dr LS25 ...... 194 F4
St Helen's La
Borrowby YO7 .... 65 E4
Reighton YO14 .... 127 C6
St Helen's Rd
Harrogate HG2 .... 223 A8
5 York YO24 .... 230 E8
St Helen's Rise YO19 ... 193 A7
St Helen's Sq
26 Scarborough YO11 ... 213 A6
York YO1 .... 233 B2
St Helen's Way LS29 .... 218 D4
St Helens Wlk TS13 .... 10 D8
St Hilary Cl DL10 .... 209 B7
St Hildas Bsns Ctr YO22 . 208 E6

St Hildas CE Prim Sch YO62 92 C1
St Hilda's Cres YO17 124 E8
St Hildas Gdns 4 YO21 208 C7
St Hildas Mews YO10 229 B4
St Hildas RC Prim Sch 11 YO21 208 D5
St Hildas Rd 5 DL7 210 D2
St Hilda's Rd HG2 219 F1
St Hilda's St YO17 124 D7
St Hilda's Terr YO21 208 D6
St Hilda's Wlk 6 YO62 92 C1
St Ians Croft 32 LS29 174 F4
St Ives Cl 3 WF8 201 B2
St Ives Cres WF10 201 B3
St James' Bsns Pk HG5 221 E4
St James CE Prim Sch LS22 180 C3
St James Chapel Flats DL10 209 B6
St James Cl
Melsonby DL10 20 F7
York YO30 224 E3
St James Croft YO24 227 D1
St James Ct
Rawcliffe DN14 205 A1
Skipton BD23 217 B4
St James Dr DL7 210 D2
St James' Dr HG2 222 E8
St James Gn 9 YO7 211 C3
St James' Mdw 16 YO51 141 B5
St James Mount YO23 228 A2
St James Pl 5 YO24 227 D1
St James Rd
Northallerton DL7 210 B2
Scarborough YO12 212 E4
St James' Rd LS29 218 A3
St James's St 7 LS22 180 C3
St James Terr YO8 232 C5
St John Fisher RC High Sch HG2 223 A8
St John Mews YO8 232 B7
ST JOHN'S 194 F8
St Johns Ave 25 LS29 174 F4
St John's Ave
42 Filey YO14 101 B3
Milby YO51 141 B7
Scarborough YO12 212 E5
St Johns CE Junior Sch HG5 221 B6
St Johns CE Prim Sch DL1 3 E4
St Johns Cl
Northallerton DL7 210 E2
Sharow HG4 214 F7
St John's Cl
Aberford LS25 188 F1
Bishop Monkton HG3 140 B5
St John's Cres
Bishop Monkton HG3 140 A5
Harrogate HG1 219 D5
3 Leeming DL7 63 D4
York YO31 233 C4
St Johns Ct
Skipton BD23 217 A4
Ulleskelf LS24 190 C3
St John's Dr
Harrogate HG1 219 D6
North Rigton LS17 178 B4
St John's Garth
Aberford LS25 194 F8
Ingleby Arncliffe DL6 45 A8
St John's Gr HG1 219 C5
St Johns Mdws YO61 117 C1
St Johns Pk DL11 2 A1
St Johns RC Sch for the Deaf 7 LS23 188 E8
St Johns Rd DL9 209 F1
St John's Rd
Bishop Monkton HG3 140 A5
Clifford LS23 188 E7
Harrogate HG1 219 D5
Ilkley LS29 218 E4
2 Leeming DL7 63 D4
Scarborough YO12 212 E5
Scotton HG5 162 A6
9 Stamford Bridge YO41 168 D2
St John's St BD20 173 C1
St John St
Harrogate HG1 219 D2
York YO31 233 B3
St John's View LS23 188 E8
St John's Way
Bishop Monkton HG3 140 A5
Harrogate HG1 219 D6
St John's Wlk
Harrogate HG1 219 D6
Milby YO51 141 B7
St John the Baptist RC Prim Sch WF6 200 B1
St Joseph's Cl 2 YO12 212 C8
St Josephs Ct 9 YO24 227 B1
St Joseph's Ct LS25 194 C3
St Josephs RC Prim Sch
Barnoldswick BB18 171 D2
Bishop Thornton HG3 139 A2
Castleford WF10 200 F4
Harrogate HG1 219 C5
Loftus TS13 10 D8
27 Pickering YO18 95 F7
16 Tadcaster LS24 189 E6
Wetherby LS22 180 C3
St Joseph's St LS24 189 E6
St Lawrences CE Prim Sch YO10 228 E3
St Leonards Ave YO8 198 B4
St Leonards Cl 30 LS29 174 F4
St Leonard's Cl
1 Harrogate HG2 220 B1
7 Malton YO17 215 C4
St Leonard's Cres YO12 212 D8
St Leonard's Oval HG2 220 A1
St Leonard's Pl YO30 233 B3
St Leonards Rd TS14 8 E6
St Leonard's Rd HG2 220 A1
St Luke's Ave HG1 219 D4
St Lukes Cl DL7 22 C2
St Luke's Cl
6 Boston Spa LS23 188 E7
Harrogate HG1 219 D4
St Luke's Cres YO12 212 C6
St Luke's Gr YO30 228 B7
St Lukes Hospl TS4 7 A8
St Luke's Mount HG1 219 D4
St Margaret's Ave LS26 200 B6
St Margarets Cl DL2 4 C3
St Margaret's Cl 3 HG5 221 A6
St Margaret's Garth 2 HG5 221 A6
St Margaret's Gdns 1 HG5 221 A6
St Margaret's Rd
Knaresborough HG5 221 A6
Mickletown LS26 200 B6
St Margaret's Terr
6 Ilkley LS29 218 B3
York YO1 228 E4
St Mark's Ave HG2 222 D7
St Mark's Cl 1 YO12 212 C8
St Mark's Gr YO30 224 E2
St Martins Ave 2 LS21 176 F1
St Martin's Ave YO11 213 A4
St Martins CE Prim Sch YO11 213 C1
St Martins Cl
15 Catterick Garrison DL9 40 E4
Liverton Mines TS13 10 D8
St Martins Field 12 LS21 176 F1
St Martin's La YO1 233 A2
St Martin's Pl 10 YO11 213 A4
St Martin's Rd 9 YO11 213 A4
St Martin's Sq 5 YO11 213 A4
St Martins Way 11 TS15 24 E8
St Mary's YO30 233 A3
St Mary's Abbey* YO1 233 A3
St Mary's App YO8 196 F1
St Mary's Ave
Barnoldswick BB18 171 E2
Harrogate HG2 219 C2
12 Hemingbrough YO8 198 F1
14 Swillington LS26 194 A1
Thirsk YO7 211 C4
St Marys Cath TS8 7 B5
St Marys CE Prim Sch YO23 182 D3
St Marys CE Sch
6 Boston Spa LS23 188 E8
Longnewton TS21 5 A7
St Mary's Chapel* YO11 213 C7
St Marys Cl
Cottingwith YO42 193 C5
14 Stokesley TS9 26 C7
St Mary's Cl
Barton DL10 21 D7
15 Haxby YO32 166 E5
Ilkley LS29 218 C4
South Cowton DL7 22 E2
Strensall YO32 167 A7
Thirsk YO7 211 C4
St Marys Coll TS4 6 F7
St Mary's Cres YO22 208 E6
St Marys Ct YO7 90 C3
St Mary's Ct
Allerton Bywater LS26 200 D6
York YO23 233 A1
St Mary's Dr YO7 211 C4
St Mary's Gate HG4 214 D5
St Maurice's Gdns BD23 173 B4
St Mary's Gr YO10 229 C4
St Mary's La YO30 233 A3
St Mary's Mus* YO1 233 B2
St Marys RC Prim Sch
Knaresborough HG5 221 A7
Malton YO17 215 D5
Richmond DL10 209 E7
Selby YO8 232 B2
St Mary's St 6 YO11 213 B6
St Marys Terr YO30 233 A3
St Mary's Terr YO30 233 A3
St Marys View YO8 232 B2
St Mary's Way YO7 211 C4
St Mary's Wlk
Harrogate HG2 219 C1
Micklefield LS25 194 F4
Middlesbrough TS5 6 E8
Scarborough YO11 213 A7
Thirsk YO7 211 C4
St Matthew's Cl
20 Leyburn DL8 60 D5
4 Naburn YO19 191 D8
St Maurice's Rd YO31 233 C3
St Michaels Ct
1 Northallerton DL7 210 D2
10 West Field YO24 227 B1
St Michaels Gn 15 WF6 200 A1
St Michael's La YO11 213 C1
St Michael's Mead HG4 138 E6
St Michael St 6 YO17 215 C4
St Michaels Way 29 LS29 174 F4
St Monicas Ct 4 YO61 143 D8
St Monicas Garth 17 YO61 143 D8
St Monica's Hospl YO61 143 C8
St Nicholas Ave YO19 231 E4
St Nicholas CE Prim Sch HG4 87 A1
St Nicholas Cl
Copmanthorpe YO23 230 A3
Richmond DL10 209 F8
St Nicholas Cliff 5 YO11 213 A5
St Nicholas Cres YO23 230 A3
St Nicholas Croft YO23 182 E3
St Nicholas Dr DL10 209 F7
St Nicholas Fields* YO10 228 F4
St Nicholas Gdns TS15 5 F2
St Nicholas Pl 1 YO10 228 F3
St Nicholas Rd
Copmanthorpe YO23 230 A3
Harrogate HG2 220 B2
Ilkley LS29 218 A5
St Nicholas St
Norton YO17 215 D3
Scarborough YO11 213 A6
St Nicholas Way 22 YO32 166 E5
St Nicholas Wlk HG2 220 B2
St Olave's Cl HG4 214 A3
St Olave's Rd YO30 233 A4
St Olaves Sch YO30 233 A3
St Oswalds CE Prim Sch YO10 231 E7
St Oswalds Cl
14 Catterick Garrison DL9 40 E4
Sowerby YO7 89 F3
St Oswald's Cl
Catton YO41 185 F6
Oswaldkirk YO62 93 A1
St Oswalds Ct
6 Filey YO14 101 B3
York YO10 231 E7
St Oswalds Rd 13 DL9 40 E4
St Oswald's Rd YO10 231 D8
St Patricks RC Comp Sch TS17 6 C7
St Patricks RC Prim Sch TS17 6 B8
St Patrick's Way HG2 220 B2
St Paulinus Dr DL7 210 B3
St Paulinus RC Prim Sch TS14 8 D6
St Pauls CE Prim Sch YO24 228 A3
St Pauls Cl 4 DL7 210 E2
St Paul's Cl DL10 41 B6
St Pauls Ct 3 WF8 201 C2
St Paul's Dr DL10 41 B6
St Paul's Gr LS29 218 D4
St Pauls Mews YO24 228 A3
St Paul's Rd TS17 6 B8
St Pauls Rise LS29 174 F4
St Paul's Sq YO24 228 A3
St Paul's Terr
Darlington DL3 3 C7
York YO24 228 A4
St Peter & St Paul RC Prim Sch DL8 60 D5
St Peters Brafferton CE VA Prim Sch YO61 115 F1
St Peters CE Prim Sch HG2 219 D1
St Peters Cl
12 Brafferton YO61 115 F1
Rufforth YO26 227 A5
St Peter's Cl 2 DL9 41 A5
St Peter's Cres YO17 215 D3
St Peters Ct
31 Addingham LS29 174 F4
York YO30 233 A4
St Peter's Ct YO22 208 F4
St Peter's Garth LS14 188 A3
St Peter's Gr YO30 233 A4
St Peters RC Prim Sch YO12 212 D8
St Peter's Rd
Drax YO8 204 F5
Whitby YO22 208 F4
St Peters Sch YO30 233 A4
St Peter's Sq 7 HG2 219 C2
St Peter St YO17 215 D3
St Philip's Gr YO30 228 A8
St Philip's Way 33 LS29 176 C1
St Princes St 12 HG1 219 D2
St Richards Rd 3 LS21 176 F1
St Robert Cl BD23 155 D1
St Robert Ct BD23 155 D1
St Robert's Cave* HG5 221 D4
St Robert's Gdns HG5 221 B4
St Roberts Mews 4 HG1 219 D1
St Roberts RC Prim Sch HG1 219 F4
St Robert's Rd HG5 221 B4
St Ronan's Cl 3 HG2 220 A1
St Ronan's Rd 2 HG2 220 A1
St Sampsons Sq YO1 233 B2
St Saviourgate YO1 233 C2
St Saviour's Pl YO1 233 C2
St Sepulchre St 7 YO11 213 B6
St Stephen's Cl BD23 216 F4
St Stephens Com Prim Sch 16 BD23 216 F4
St Stephens Gdns 1 DL7 210 E2
St Stephens Mews YO30 225 A2
St Stephen's Rd YO24 227 C2
St Stephen's Sq YO24 227 C1
St Swithin's Wlk YO26 227 E4
St Teresas RC Prim Sch DL1 3 E4
St Therese of Lisieux RC Prim Sch TS17 6 A4
St Thomas A Beckett Wlk HG3 161 A5
St Thomas More RC Prim Sch TS4 7 A7
St Thomas' Pl YO31 233 B4
St Thomas's Cl 2 YO10 229 C4
St Thomas St YO11 213 A6
St Thomas's Way YO26 164 C3
St Trinians Cl DL10 209 F8
St Trinians Dr DL10 209 F8
St Wilfred Dr DL7 210 B3
St Wilfreds RC Prim Sch YO31 233 C3
St Wilfrid's Cl 7 YO32 167 B6
St Wilfrid's Cres 9 YO8 197 D1
St Wilfrid's Ct YO31 233 C3
St Wilfrid's Gdns HG4 214 C6
St Wilfrid's Pl 2 HG4 214 C5
St Wilfrids RC High Sch WF7 200 E1
St Wilfrids RC Prim Sch HG4 214 B5
St Wilfrid's Rd
1 Ripon HG4 214 C5
8 Strensall YO32 167 B6
St Williams Coll YO1 233 B3
St Winifred's Ave HG2 219 F1
St Winifred's Cl HG2 219 F1
St Winifred's Rd HG2 219 F1
St Wulstan Cl YO31 228 E7
Salents La
Birdsall YO17 148 C4
Duggleby YO17 149 B6
Salerno Cl 6 DL9 209 C1
Salisbury Cl 15 WF6 200 A2
Salisbury Dr 9 HG3 161 B3
Salisbury Rd YO26 227 F5
Salisbury St
Scarborough YO12 212 E3
Skipton BD23 216 E5
Salisbury Ter YO26 227 F5
Sallow Heath 16 HG3 161 B3
Salmond Rd 4 YO24 227 B1
Salmon La DL8 87 B6
Saltburn Rd TS17 6 B8
Salterforth La BB18 171 E1
Salterforth Rd BB18 172 A1
Saltergate Bank YO18 72 F8
Saltergate Com Junior & Infant Sch HG3 219 A5
Saltergate Dr HG3 161 B3
Saltergill La TS15 24 C8
Salter Rd YO11 99 F6
Salters Ave DL1 3 E6
Saltersgill Ave
Easterside TS4 7 A7
Middlesbrough TS4 6 F8
Saltersgill Cl 3 TS4 6 F8
Salters La DL1 3 F4
Salters Lane N DL1 3 D8
Salters Lane S DL1 3 E7
SALTON 94 D3
Salton La YO62 94 B1
Salt Pans Rd YO13 54 D2
Salt Pan Well Steps 11 YO22 208 E6
Salutation Rd DL3 3 A4
Samian Way DL3 3 C8
Sam La YO61 142 D8
Samuel Smith Old Brewery* LS24 189 E6
San Carlos Cl 1 DL9 40 E3
Sandacre Ct YO26 227 D5
Sandbeck DL10 209 C5
Sandbeck Ind Est LS22 180 C4
Sandbeck La LS22 180 D4
Sandbeck Way LS22 180 C4
Sandcroft Cl 4 YO24 230 D8
Sandcroft Rd YO24 230 D8
Sanderson Ave WF6 200 A1
Sanderson Ct YO26 227 B3
Sanderson Rd DL2 3 F1
Sanders Way DL10 41 E4
Sandfield La YO7 88 D4
Sandfield Terr 4 LS24 189 F6
Sandgate 14 YO22 208 D7
Sandgate Dr LS25 194 D1
Sandgate La LS25 194 E2
Sandgate Oval YO7 115 A2
Sandgate Rd YO7 115 A1
Sandgate Rise LS25 194 E1
Sandgate Terr LS25 194 E1
Sandhill Bank YO21 9 E1
Sandhill Cl
Harrogate HG1 219 F6
Pontefract WF8 201 B2
Sandhill Dr HG1 219 F6
Sandhill La
17 Bedale DL8 63 B3
Brayton YO8 197 D2
Sutton upon Derwent YO41 185 E2
Sandhill Rise WF8 201 B2
Sandhill Way HG1 219 F6
Sandholme 2 YO32 166 F5
Sandholme Cl
14 Easingwold YO61 143 D8
22 Settle BD24 131 D2
Sandholmes La YO7 89 E3
Sandhurst Gdns 4 YO12 212 B7
SANDHUTTON 89 A4
SAND HUTTON 168 B5
Sand Hutton CE Prim Sch YO41 168 B5
Sand Hutton Ct YO41 168 B5
Sandhutton La YO7 89 B4
Sandiacres 5 YO8 197 D1
Sand La
Barlby with Osgodby YO8 198 B4
Bubwith YO8 199 D5
Heslerton YO17 123 F7
Huby YO61 144 A5
Oldstead YO61 91 D3
Sherburn YO17 124 D7
South Milford LS25 195 F2
Stillington YO61 144 A6
Wistow YO8 197 E6
Sandmartin Ct YO24 230 D8
Sandmoor Cl 5 YO21 208 B5
Sandown Cl
Bagby YO7 90 B3
York YO24 227 E2
Sandpiper Cl
6 Eastfield YO12 99 E6
1 Filey YO14 101 A3
Sandpit La YO62 69 B1
Sandriggs DL3 3 B7
Sandringham Cl YO32 225 C7
Sandringham Rd
Byram cum Sutton WF11 201 E4
Lockwood TS12 9 F6
Middlesbrough TS3 7 B8
2 Ripon HG4 214 C3
6 Wetherby LS22 180 C3
Sandringham St
4 Scarborough YO12 212 F7
York YO10 228 D2
Sandrock Rd 3 WF8 201 C1
Sands Cl YO14 127 D7
SANDSEND 13 A3
Sandsend Rd
Newholm-cum-Dunsley YO21 13 A3
Whitby YO21 208 A8
Sandside
Scarborough YO11 213 B6
Whitby YO22 208 D7
Sands La
Hunmanby YO14 127 A8
Rillington YO17 122 F5
Sandsprunt La YO13 97 E6
Sands Rd YO14 127 B7
Sandstock Rd YO31 229 B7
Sandwath La LS24 196 A8
Sandway Ave 12 YO8 197 B1
Sandway Cl 11 YO8 197 B1
Sandway Dr
Camblesforth YO8 204 D4
1 Thorpe Willoughby YO8 197 B1
Sandwith La DN14 204 B4
Sandwood Pk TS14 8 D5
Sandy Bank
Farnham HG5 162 D7
Northallerton DL6 210 F3
Romanby DL6 65 A7
Sandybed Cres YO12 212 C4
Sandybed La
Scarborough YO12 212 C4
Wykeham YO13 98 F6
Sandy Flatts La TS5 6 F6
Sandyforth La BD22 186 E5
Sandy Gap YO32 225 C7
Sandy Gate HG3 159 A6
Sandy La
Alne YO61 143 A4
Dalton YO7 116 A8
5 Embsay BD23 217 C7
Harton YO60 168 B8
16 Haxby YO32 166 E5
High & Low Bishopside HG3 137 D3
Humberton YO61 141 D8
North Duffield YO8 198 F8
Ripon HG4 214 B2
Scampston YO17 123 B5
Stockton on the Forest YO32 167 E4
Sandyland 29 YO32 166 E5
Sandylands Bsns Ctr BD23 216 E3
Sandylands Sports Ctr BD23 216 F3
Sandy Leas La TS21 5 A8
Sandyridge YO26 224 A1
Sandy Rise YO8 232 C3
Sarah's Croft BD23 155 A1
Sargent Ave YO23 230 F4
SATRON 36 D4
Saunters Way WF6 200 A2
Savage Yd 17 HG5 221 A6
Savile Rd
Castleford WF10 200 E4
Mickletown LS26 200 B6
Saville Gr YO30 228 A8
Saville St YO17 215 C4
SAWDON 98 C7
SAWLEY 138 F6
Sawley Cl BD23 217 C7
Sawley Moor La HG4 138 D6
Sawley St 1 BD23 216 D3
Sawmill La YO62 92 F6
Saw Mill La 15 LS29 175 A4
Saw Wells Ct LS24 195 F6
Saw Wells La LS24 195 F6
Sawyer's Cres YO23 230 C2
Sawyers Garth 5 LS29 175 A4
Sawyers Wlk 9 YO19 184 F7
Saxford Way 8 YO32 166 D5
Saxon Cl
Shipton YO30 165 F5
6 Thorpe Willoughby YO8 197 B1
Saxon Dr YO17 122 F5
Saxonfield TS8 7 A6

Saxon Grange LS25 195 F3
Saxon Pl YO31 228 E7
Saxon Rd
- Catterick Garrison DL9 209 E1
- Ripon HG4 214 D5
- Stamford Bridge YO41 168 D2
- Whitby YO21 208 B7

Saxon Vale YO30 165 F5
SAXTON 195 D8
Saxton CE Prim Sch LS24 195 D7
Saxton Ct LS24 195 D8
Saxton La LS24 195 E8
Saxty Way YO7 211 A1
Scabbate Gate BD23 108 B3
SCACKLETON 119 C4
Scackleton Bank YO62 119 C4
Scackleton La YO62 119 C3
Scafell Cl 4 YO30 224 E1
Scaggiethorpe La YO26 165 D2
SCAGGLETHORPE 122 D3
Scagglethorpe La YO17 122 C4
Scaife Gdns YO31 228 C7
Scaife Mews YO31 228 C7
Scaife Shay La YO7 116 A7
Scaife St YO31 228 C7
SCALBY 75 D6
Scalby Ave YO12 212 C8
Scalby Beck Rd 27 YO13 75 D5
Scalby Mills Rd YO12 75 F5
Scalby Rd YO12 212 D5
Scalby Sch YO12 212 B8
Scaldhill La YO51 141 C7
Scalehaw La BD23 153 F5
Scale Hill LS21 177 D2
Scale The BD23 157 D3
SCALING 11 A4
SCALING DAM 11 A4
Scallow Bank La DL8 59 B6
Scalm La
- Hambleton YO8 196 F2
- Selby YO8 197 A4

SCAMPSTON 123 A6
Scampston Hall★ YO17 123 A6
Scampton Cl TS17 6 A6
Scarah Bank HG3 161 B8
Scarah La HG3 140 A2
Scarbeck Bank DL11 19 D7
SCARBOROUGH 213 B5
Scarborough Art Gall & Cres Art Studio★ YO11 213 A5
Scarborough Bsns Pk YO11 99 F6
Scarborough Castle★ YO11 213 C7
Scarborough General Hospl YO12 212 B6
Scarborough Indoor Pool★ YO12 212 E8
Scarborough Rd
- Gristhorpe YO14 101 A4
- Heslerton YO17 123 F6
- Langtoft YO25 151 C7
- Norton-on-Derwent YO17 122 A3
- Norton YO17 215 F4
- Seamer YO12 99 D6
- Stainton Dale YO13 53 F8

Scarborough Sixth Form Coll YO12 212 C4
Scarborough Sports Ctr YO11 213 A2
Scarborough Sta YO11 212 F5
Scarborough Terr YO30 233 B4
Scarcroft Hill YO24 228 B2
Scarcroft La YO23 233 A1
Scarcroft Prim Sch YO23 233 A1
Scarcroft Rd YO24 233 A1
Scarcroft View YO23 233 A1
Scardale Cres YO12 212 E8
Scardale Ct YO8 232 A2
Scarer's La YO26 142 B2
Scar Field 9 BD23 134 E2
Scargill Rd HG1 219 B4
Scar Hos DL11 35 F5
Scarhouse La DL11 17 E2
Scarlet Balk La YO17 122 C1
Scar Rd BD23 171 E6
Scar St 2 BD23 134 E2
Scarth Cl 3 TS12 9 F7
SCARTHINGWELL 195 F7
Scarthingwell Cres LS24 195 D8
Scarthingwell La LS24 195 E8
Scarth Nick
- Preston-under-Scar DL8 59 E6
- Whorlton DL6 45 D6

Scate Moor La YO26 163 F3
Scaudercroft 13 YO19 184 F7
Scawling End Rd YO61 91 C3
Scawthorpe Cl WF8 201 C1
SCAWTON 91 E6
Scawton Ave 1 YO31 225 E2
Scholars Gate
- Guisborough TS14 8 E5
- West Garforth LS25 194 C3

Scholars Pk DL3 3 B5
Scholes La BD22 187 F1
Scholes Park Ave 3 YO12 75 F5
Scholes Park Cliff 1 YO12 75 F5
Scholes Park Dr 2 YO12 75 F5
Scholes Park Rd YO12 75 E5
Scholes Rd WF10 201 B5
Scholla La DL6 210 F5
Scholla View DL6 210 F5
School Bank DL10 21 C4
School Cl
- Huby YO61 144 A4

School Cl *continued*
- Selby YO8 232 B3
- 16 Stamford Bridge YO41 168 D2

School Croft WF11 201 E4
School Fields BB18 172 A2
School Garth YO7 89 E3
Schoolgate LS15 194 C8
School Hill
- Bainbridge DL8 57 D5
- 8 Settle BD24 131 E2

School House Dr YO12 99 D6
Schoolhouse Terr LS22 180 B5
School La
- Addingham LS29 174 F5
- Askham Richard YO23 182 D3
- Bellerby DL8 60 D7
- Bishopthorpe YO23 231 A4
- Burton Fleming YO25 126 E3
- Collingham LS22 188 A8
- Copmanthorpe YO23 230 A2
- Dacre HG3 159 F8
- Earby BB18 172 A1
- Easington BB7 152 B3
- Eppleby DL11 1 D4
- Great Ayton TS9 8 A1
- Heslington YO10 229 B1
- Laneshaw Bridge BB8 186 C3
- Lawkland LA2 130 D3
- Lotherton cum Aberford LS25 194 F8
- Malton YO17 215 C4
- 4 Nawton YO62 93 D7
- Newton-le-Willows DL8 62 B4
- Osmotherley DL6 45 B4
- 23 Poppleton YO26 165 F1
- South Milford LS25 195 F2
- 8 Spofforth HG3 179 E6
- Thornton-le-Beans DL6 65 B5
- Walton LS23 180 F2
- Wray-with-Botton LA2 128 A6
- York YO10 231 E7

School Rd
- Hemingbrough YO8 198 F1
- Wetherby LS22 180 C3

School St
- Castleford WF10 200 F5
- 2 Earby BB18 186 A7
- York YO24 227 D3

Scoreby La
- Gate Helmsley YO41 168 B2
- Kexby YO41 168 B1
- Low Catton YO41 185 B8

Score Ray La YO26 164 A5
Scoresby Terr 2 YO21 208 D5
SCORTON 41 F7
Scoska Wood National Nature Reserve★ BD23 107 B3
Scosthrop La BD23 154 E6
Scotch Cnr
- Middleton Tyas DL10 21 B4
- Oldstead YO61 91 C4

Scotch George La HG5 221 A7
Scotchman La YO60 168 A8
Scot Gate DL8 59 D3
Scots Dike Terr DL10 209 D6
Scots Dyke Cl DL10 20 F7
Scott Cl
- Catterick DL10 41 E4
- 35 Glusburn BD20 187 E7
- 13 Swillington LS26 194 A1

Scott Hill DL8 57 D5
Scott Moncrieff Rd YO32 167 B6
SCOTTON
- Harrogate 162 A6
- Richmond 40 F2

Scotton Bank DL8 40 D2
Scotton Ct HG5 162 A6
Scotton Dr HG5 220 C8
Scotton Gdns 8 DL9 40 E3
Scotton Gr
- Knaresborough HG5 220 C8
- Scotton HG5 162 A5

Scotton Lingerfield Sch HG5 162 B7
Scotton Moor HG5 220 C8
Scotton Pk DL9 40 E3
Scotton Rd DL9 40 E3
Scott Rd YO8 232 C6
Scott St YO23 228 C2
Scraper La YO22 32 F7
SCRAYINGHAM 168 F7
Scriftain La LS22 180 C5
SCRIVEN 162 D5
Scriven Gr 8 YO32 166 F5
Scriven Rd HG5 221 A7
Scroggs La DL8 86 E7
Scrogs La DL8 59 B6
Scrope Ave 4 YO31 228 E5
SCRUTON 63 D7
Scugdale Rd DL6 45 E8
Scurragh House La DL10 21 C2
Scurragh La DL10 21 B2
Sea App YO14 100 F6
Sea Cliff Cres YO11 213 B2
Sea Cliff Rd YO11 213 B2
Seafield Ave 1 YO11 100 B7
Seafire Cl YO30 225 A3
Seagram Cres DL10 209 C8
Seakel La YO23 182 C2
Seal Bank BD23 81 D1
Sea Life & Marine Sanctuary★ YO12 75 F5
SEAMER
- Middlesbrough 6 F1
- Scarborough 99 E6

Seamer & Irton Prim Sch YO12 99 D6
Seamer Moor Hill YO12 212 B1
Seamer Moor La YO12 212 B1
Seamer Rd
- East Ayton YO13 99 B7
- Eastfield YO12 99 F8
- Hilton TS15 6 C2
- Maltby TS8 6 E3
- Scarborough YO12 212 E3
- Thornton TS8 6 D4

Seamer Road Cnr YO12 212 E4
Seamer Road Ret Pk YO12 212 E1
Seamer St 2 YO12 212 E3
Seamer Sta YO11 99 F6
Seaton Cl YO10 229 C4
Seaton Cres TS13 13 K2
Seaton Garth TS13 13 K2
Seave Close La YO26 164 D2
Seavegate 4 YO13 99 B8
Seavegate Cl 3 YO13 99 B8
SEAVE GREEN 47 A7
Sea View YO14 101 C1
Seaview Ave 5 YO12 75 E5
Sea View Cl
- 5 Scarborough YO11 100 B8
- Whitby YO21 208 A6

Sea View Cres YO11 100 B8
Sea View Dr 13 YO11 100 B8
Sea View Gdns 6 YO11 100 B8
Sea View Gr 4 YO11 100 B8
Second Ave
- Menwith with Darley HG3 160 A4
- Wetherby LS22 180 C3
- York YO31 228 F6

Second Comm La YO8 197 C4
Sedbergh Dr LS29 218 B3
Sedbergh Pk LS29 218 B3
Sedber La 5 BD23 134 E2
SEDBUSK 56 E6
Sedbusk La DL8 56 D6
Sedgefield Rd TS5 6 E6
Sedge Rise LS24 189 D5
Sedley Cl HG1 219 E7
Seed Hill LA6 103 D4
Sefton Ave YO31 228 F8
Sefton Dr LS29 218 B3
Sefton Way TS15 5 D2
Seggans Rd YO26 142 A1
Seg La YO8 204 F3
Segrave Rd DL9 40 E4
Segrave Wlk 10 YO26 227 E4
Selaby Ct DL2 1 C8
Selbourne Terr 9 BB18 172 B1
SELBY 232 C6
Selby Abbey★ YO8 232 D5
Selby Abbey CE Prim Sch YO8 232 C5
Selby Bsns Pk YO8 232 D1
Selby Coll YO8 232 F3
Selby Coll (1811 Ctr) YO8 232 C5
Selby Coll (Tadcaster Learning Ctr) LS24 189 E6
Selby Com Prim Sch YO8 232 B5
Selby Cres DL3 3 A7
Selby High Sch YO8 232 B4
Selby Ironworks Bsns Ctr YO8 232 D5
Selby Rd
- Eggborough DN14 202 F1
- Fulford YO19 231 E6
- Garforth LS15 194 A3
- Ledston LS25 195 A2
- Riccall YO19 198 A8
- Snaith DN14 204 C1
- Swillington LS15 194 A3
- Wistow YO8 197 D6
- Womersley DN14 207 A4

Selby Rly Sports Club YO8 232 D5
Selby Sta YO8 232 D5
Selby War Memorial Hospl YO8 232 B4
Seldon Rd YO26 227 E5
Self Gdns YO62 70 F3
Selley Park Dr YO12 212 B4
SELLY HILL 32 A8
Selly Park Rd YO12 212 B4
SELSIDE 105 A6
Selside Shaw BD24 105 A7
Selstone Cres 7 YO22 32 A6
Semer Water Nature Reserve★ DL8 57 B1
Senhouse Rd DL1 3 F5
Seph Way YO17 215 A2
Sergeant Bank HG4 86 B8
Serinity Hallow TS12 9 E8
SESSAY 116 B6
Sessay CE Prim Sch YO7 116 C5
Sessions House Yd 10 WF8 201 B1
Seton Cty Prim Sch TS13 13 K2
SETTLE 131 E3
Settle CE Prim Sch BD24 131 E2
Settle Coll BD24 131 D2
Settle Mid Sch BD24 131 D3
Settle Rd BD23 155 A6
Settle Sta BD24 131 D2
SETTRINGTON 122 D1
Settrington CE Prim Sch YO17 122 D1
Settrington Rd YO12 212 B5
Seven St YO17 121 C1
Seventh Ave YO31 228 F5
Seven Wells YO17 121 A4
Severfield Cl YO7 211 D2
Severn Dr
- Garforth LS25 194 D3
- Guisborough TS14 8 E6

Severn Gn YO26 227 C8
Severn Way DL1 3 D3
Severus Ave YO24 227 D4
Severus St YO24 227 D3
Sewell's Cave★ LA2 131 A5
SEXHOW 25 D4
Sexhow La TS9 25 F4
Seymour Cres TS16 5 D4
Seymour Gr
- Eaglescliffe TS16 5 D4
- York YO31 228 F6

Shackleton Cl YO21 208 C5
Shady La BD20 173 C2
Shaftesbury Ave DN14 202 C3
Shaker Stile Rd YO18 96 B7
Shakespeare Ave 2 DN6 206 E1
Shakespeare Cl 3 DL10 41 C7
Shakespeare Cres WF10 201 B3
Shallowdale Gr 1 YO10 229 C3
Shambles La HG4 114 D5
Shambles The 8 YO17 215 C4
Shandon Pk TS8 7 B5
Shandy Hall★ YO61 117 D8
Shannon Cl 26 LS29 175 C2
Shannon Lea DL2 4 D4
SHAROW 214 F6
Sharow CE Prim Sch HG4 214 F7
Sharow La HG4 214 E6
Sharpe Howe★ YO11 126 A8
Sharphaw Ave BD23 217 A2
Sharphaw View BD23 155 D1
Sharp Hill Cl 13 DL8 60 E2
Sharp Hill La YO8 204 F6
Shaw Ave WF6 200 B1
Shaw Barn La LS22 180 B3
Shaw Cl
- Garforth LS25 194 D3
- Normanton South WF6 200 B1

Shawclose La YO62 67 E4
Shaw Cres YO61 144 A5
Shawcroft Ct DL10 209 E8
Shaw Dr YO62 70 B1
Shaw La
- Farnham HG5 162 C7
- Fenwick DN6 207 D2
- North Rigton HG3 178 B6
- Spofforth with Stockeld HG3 179 D7

Shawl Terr 11 DL8 60 D5
SHAW MILLS 138 F1
Shaw Rise WF6 200 B1
Shaws La
- Barwick in Elmet & Scholes LS15 194 B7
- Hawes DL8 56 E4

Shaw's Terr YO24 233 A1
Shearing Path LS29 174 F5
Sheepcote La HG3 159 F5
Sheepdyke La YO14 127 A8
Sheepfoot Hill YO17 215 D4
Sheep Rake La YO25 151 F4
Sheep St 11 BD23 216 F4
Sheepwalk La
- Castleford WF10 201 B3
- Kirby Grindalythe YO17 150 B7

Sheepwash Bank YO7 66 D5
Sheepwash La DN14 207 A7
Sheldrake Cl 9 YO14 101 A4
Sheldrake Rd WF10 200 E3
Shelley Cl YO11 100 B6
Shelley Ct HG1 219 E7
Shelley Dr WF11 201 D2
Shelley Gr YO30 224 F1
Shelley Rd TS4 6 F8
Shelton Ave 2 YO13 99 B8
Shepherd Ct TS12 9 E7
Shepherdfields La YO60 146 E5
Shepherd Gate LA2 130 F5
Shepherd Hill DL6 45 D8
Shepherdies The HG4 113 C8
Shepherds Dr 13 YO11 100 B7
Sherbrooke Cl 18 YO62 70 B1
SHERBURN 124 D8
Sherburn CE Prim Sch YO17 124 D7
Sherburn Enterprise Pk LS25 196 B4
Sherburn High Sch LS25 195 F3
SHERBURN IN ELMET 195 E5
Sherburn in Elmet Sta LS25 196 A4
Sherburn Rd YO8 232 A8
Sherburn St 1 YO8 197 B8
Sherburn Willows Nature Reserve★ LS25 195 E3
Sheridan Rd BB8 186 B3
SHERIFF HUTTON 145 C5
Sheriff Hutton Castle (rems of)★ YO60 145 D5
Sheriff Hutton Prim Sch YO60 145 C5
Sherriff Hutton House★ YO60 145 D4
Sherringham Dr YO24 230 D8
Sherwood Brow BD24 131 D7
Sherwood Cl
- Hunton DL8 61 E7
- 13 Norton DN6 206 E1

Sherwood Dr HG2 220 D2
Sherwood Gr
- Huntington YO32 225 F1
- York YO26 227 B6

Sherwood Rd TS17 6 B6
Sherwood St 5 YO12 212 F5
Shetland Cl TS5 6 E6
Shilton Garth Cl 3 YO32 225 F7
SHIPTON 165 F5
Shipton Low Rd YO30 165 E5
Shipton Rd
- Clifton YO30 227 F8
- Rawcliffe YO30 224 D2
- York YO30 228 A7

Shipton St 3 YO30 228 B7
Shipyard Ind Est YO8 232 E5
Shipyard Rd YO8 232 E5
Shirbutt La YO26 182 C8
Shire Cl 18 YO11 100 B7
Shire Croft 17 YO11 100 B7
Shire Fold YO11 100 B6
Shire Garth DL6 24 B1
Shire Gr YO17 95 D2
Shire Rd YO7 211 B4
Shires Croft BD23 217 E8
Shires La BD23 217 D8
Shirley Ave
- Ripon HG4 214 B4
- York YO26 227 C6

Shoebridge Ave BD20 187 F7
Shop Hill YO22 33 B4
Shop La
- Cowling BD22 187 A6
- Danby YO21 29 B3
- Middleton YO18 95 D8

Shortacre La YO42 193 E2
Shortbank Cl BD23 217 B3
Shortbank Rd BD23 217 B3
Short Cl TS18 5 F7
Shorthorn La 1 DL2 3 A7
Short La
- Acaster Selby YO23 191 A4
- Farndale East YO62 48 F4
- West Haddlesey YO8 202 F6

Short Lee La BD23 216 F6
Short Rd YO7 115 B2
Shortsill La HG5 163 B5
Shotel Cl YO30 227 F8
Showfield Cl LS25 195 F4
Showfield Dr 17 YO61 143 C8
Showfield La YO17 215 C6
Shrubberies The YO8 198 E2
Shute Rd DL9 209 E1
Shutt La DL8 56 E6
Shuttleworth St 36 BB18 172 A1
Shuttocks Fold LS25 194 D2
SICKLINGHALL 179 E3
Sicklinghall Prim Sch LS22 179 D3
Sicklinghall Rd LS22 179 F3
Side Gate YO12 99 D1
Sidegate La BD20 186 F8
Sidgwick Ct 7 BD23 217 A3
Siding La YO8 198 B5
Sidings Ind Est The BD24 131 D2
Sidings La YO61 143 B4
Sidings The
- 12 Bridgehouse Gate HG3 137 B4
- 5 Low Bentham LA2 128 F8
- Settle BD24 131 D2
- Skipton BD23 216 E3
- Strensall YO32 167 B7

Sidmouth Cl TS8 7 D6
Sidmouth Sq 9 DL9 40 E4
Signals Ct 7 YO12 75 F5
Sigston Castle★ DL6 44 D2
Sike La YO7 115 B6
Silicar La HG4 88 B1
Silkstone Sq WF10 200 E6
Sills La YO30 165 B6
Silly La LA2 129 A2
SILPHO 74 E7
SILSDEN 174 C2
Silsden Rd
- Addingham LS29 174 D4
- Low Bradley BD20 173 E3

Silverdale Cl 5 HG3 160 A6
Silverdale Ct YO24 230 D7
Silverdale Rd BD24 131 F8
Silverfields Rd HG1 220 A3
Silver Garth DL10 21 C7
Silver Hill DL7 22 C2
Silverlink Bsns Pk DL1 3 D6
Silver Mdws DL10 21 D7
Silver St
- Askrigg DL8 57 E5
- Barton DL10 21 C7
- Fairburn WF11 201 D6
- Hackforth DL8 62 E8
- 4 Knaresborough HG5 221 B5
- Masham HG4 86 C3
- Reeth, Fremington & Healaugh DL11 38 B6
- 8 Riccall YO19 198 A8
- 3 Scarborough YO11 213 A6
- Thirsk YO7 211 C1
- Whitby YO21 208 D7
- Whitley DN14 207 A7
- York YO1 233 B2

Silverton Rd TS14 8 F5
Silverwood Ave 5 YO14 101 A3
Simbach Cl BD23 217 B3
Sim Balk La YO23 230 E5
Simon Howe
- Ganton YO12 125 A5
- Sherburn YO12 124 F6

SIMONSTONE 56 D6
Simpson Ave 6 YO14 126 F8

Simpson Cl BB18 171 E2
Simpsons La WF11 201 E2
Simpsons Lane Junior & Infant Sch WF11 201 E2
Sinclair Ct YO12 212 E5
SINDERBY 88 C4
Sinderby La YO7 88 B4
Sinks La DL8 62 C4
SINNINGTON 95 A8
Sinnington Cl TS14 8 F6
Sinnington Cliff Rd YO62 95 A8
Sinnington Prim Sch YO62 94 F8
Sinnington Rd TS17 6 B6
Sir Douglas Pk TS17 6 A7
Sir John's La LS25 195 E4
Sirocco Ct YO31 228 D8
Sir William Hartley Ct BB8 186 B3
Sissy Bank DL8 59 D6
Sitwell Gr YO26 227 C5
Sitwell St YO12 212 E5
Siwards Howe* YO10 229 B1
Siward St YO10 229 A3
Siward's Way YO10 229 A2
Sixth Ave YO31 228 E5
Skates La YO61 144 B3
Sked Dale YO17 124 E6
SKEEBY 21 A1
Skeeby Cl 3 TS18 5 D8
Skegmer La YO60 145 F4
Skelda Rise LS29 218 B3
Skeldergate YO1 233 B2
Skelder Rd YO21 31 E8
Skelf St LS24 190 C1
Skelgate La DL11 38 B6
Skellbank HG4 214 B4
Skellbank Cl HG4 214 B4
Skelldale Cl HG4 214 E4
Skelldale Pk HG4 214 E4
Skelldale View HG4 214 E4
Skellfield Terr HG4 214 D4
Skellgarth HG4 214 C5
Skellgill La DL8 57 C6
SKELTON 224 C6
Skelton Ct
10 Guisborough TS14 8 F7
3 York YO30 228 A6
Skelton Ellers TS14 9 A8
Skelton La
Givendale HG4 140 C8
Marske DL11 39 B7
Skelton YO32 224 D8
Skelton Newby Hall CE Prim Sch HG4 140 E7
SKELTON ON URE 140 E7
Skelton Park Trading Est YO30 225 B4
Skelton Prim Sch YO30 224 C5
Skelton Rd
Skelton YO51 140 E6
Thornaby TS17 6 B8
Skelton Windmill* YO51 140 F8
SKERNE PARK 3 C3
Skerne Park Prim Sch DL1 3 A3
Skerningham Ave 9 DL2 3 A7
Skeugh Head La DL11 35 E6
Skeugh La YO61 144 D6
SKEWSBY 119 A1
Skewsby Gr YO31 225 F1
Skibeden BD23 217 E6
Skibeden Ct 4 BD23 217 B5
Skiddaw YO24 230 C7
Skiddaw Ct TS7 7 C6
Skinner La 14 WF8 201 B1
Skinner St YO21 208 D7
Skiplam Cl 4 YO12 212 B5
Skiplam Rd YO62 69 D2
Skipper La YO25 125 E3
SKIPTON 216 F4
Skipton Castle* BD23 217 A5
Skipton Cres HG1 219 D5
Skipton Girls High Sch BD23 216 E5
Skipton Hospl BD23 216 E3
Skipton Little Theatre* BD23 216 F3
Skipton Old Rd BB8 186 A3
SKIPTON-ON-SWALE 88 E2
Skipton Rd
Addingham LS29 174 E5
Barnoldswick BB18 171 E2
Bradleys Both BD20 173 D4
Colne BB8 186 A2
Cononley BD20 173 C2
Earby BB18 172 A2
Embsay with Eastby BD23 217 C7
Farnhill BD20 187 E8
Felliscliffe HG3 160 E3
Fewston LS21 159 D2
Gargrave BD23 155 D1
Glusburn BD20 187 F8
Harrogate HG3 219 A5
Hellifield BD23 154 B3
Ilkley LS29 218 A4
Silsden BD20 174 B1
Silsden BD20 174 B3
Skipton BD23 217 B6
Skipton St HG1 219 D4
Skipton Sta BD23 216 E3
SKIPWITH 192 E1
Skipwith Comm* YO8 198 E8
Skipwith Rd YO19 192 B6
SKIRETHORNS 134 C2
SKIRPENBECK 169 A4
Skirt Bank YO7 66 C7
Skottowe Cres TS9 7 F2
Skottowe Dr TS9 7 F2
Skuff Rd BD23 157 B8
Skurkhill La YO62 92 E7
SKYREHOLME 157 E7
Skyreholme Bank BD23 157 F7
Skyreholme La BD23 157 E7
Slackgap La CA17 14 A8
Slack La HG3 160 B4
Sladeburn Dr 2 DL6 210 E3
Slaidburn Rd LA2 129 B4
SLAPEWATH 9 C6
Slate Hill YO21 29 D4
Slates La LS29 218 B7
Slayde The TS15 5 E2
Sledgate YO17 122 F5
Sledgate Garth YO17 122 F5
Sled Gates YO22 33 B3
Sled La DL10 41 F4
SLEDMERE 150 B4
Sledmere CE Prim Sch YO25 150 B3
Sledmere House* YO25 150 B3
Sledmere Rd YO25 151 B6
Slee Gill DL10 209 C5
Sleigh La YO60 120 A1
Sleightholme Dale Rd YO62 69 D5
Sleightholme Moor Rd DL11 16 D7
SLEIGHTS 32 A6
Sleights CE Prim Sch YO22 32 A6
Sleights Ct 15 TS14 8 F7
Sleights La
Acklam YO17 169 E7
Amotherby YO17 121 A6
Birstwith HG3 160 C4
Rainton with Newby YO7 114 E5
Sleights Rd YO62 69 D6
Sleights Sta YO22 32 A7
Sleights The LS17 178 A2
Slessor Rd
8 Catterick DL10 41 E4
York YO24 227 B1
Slice La LS24 190 A6
Slim Rd DL9 209 C2
SLINGSBY 120 C6
Slingsby Ave HG5 221 A7
Slingsby Bank YO62 120 C4
Slingsby Castle (rems of)* YO62 120 B5
Slingsby Com Prim Sch YO62 120 B5
Slingsby Cres HG1 219 F4
Slingsby Garth 19 YO62 70 B1
Slingsby Gdns DL7 210 B3
Slingsby Gr YO24 230 E8
Slingsby Wlk HG2 219 F1
Slip Inn Bank DL11 19 E6
Slippery Ford La BD22 187 E3
Slope La 8 YO12 99 D2
Smales' St YO1 233 B1
SMALL BANKS 174 F3
Smalldrink La 40 BD20 187 E7
Smary La YO19 184 D7
Smawthorne Ave WF10 200 E4
Smawthorne Gr WF10 200 E4
Smawthorne Henry Moore Prim Sch WF10 200 E3
Smawthorne La WF10 200 E4
Smay La YO22 33 D5
Smearbottoms La BD23 133 C3
Smeathorns Rd TS12 9 F4
Smeatley's La WF8 206 C4
Smeaton Gr
5 Swillington LS26 194 A1
York YO26 227 C5
Smeaton Rd YO41 185 D7
SMELTHOUSES 137 F3
Smiddyfields 5 YO22 32 A6
Smiddy Hill
19 Pickering YO18 95 F6
Walton LS23 181 A2
Smirthwaite View 14 WF6 200 A1
Smith Cl YO10 231 F8
Smithfield Cl 7 HG4 214 B2
Smithfield Rd DL1 3 D4
Smithgutter La DL10 21 C4
Smithie Cl YO32 225 D5
Smith La HG4 114 A4
Smith's La
Egton YO22 30 E3
Flaxton YO60 145 D1
Smithson Ave WF10 201 B3
Smithson Cl DL10 21 D2
Smithson Ct YO17 215 B5
Smithson Gr 4 YO51 141 B4
Smithsons Ct HG4 214 C5
Smithson's La HG3 177 A8
Smith St 19 BB18 171 D1
Smithy Croft Rd BD23 155 D1
Smithy Greaves LS29 175 B4
Smithy La
Denton LS29 176 A4
Scotton HG5 162 A6
Thornton in Lonsdale LA6 103 A4
Ulleskelf LS24 190 C2
Smuts Rd DL9 209 D1
Smythy La YO25 125 D4
SNAINTON 98 A5
Snainton CE Prim Sch YO13 98 A5
Snainton La YO13 97 F7
SNAITH 204 C1
Snaith Rd
Pollington DN14 207 F7
Rawcliffe DN14 205 A1
Snaith Sta DN14 204 C1
Snaizeholme Rd DL8 55 E1
SNAPE 87 A7
Snape Castle* DL8 87 A7
Snape Hill YO62 93 E7
Snape Prim Sch DL8 87 A7
Snargate Hill YO61 118 E3
SNEATON 32 D6
Sneaton La YO22 208 B1
SNEATONTHORPE 32 F5
Sneaton Thorpe La YO22 32 E5
Sneck Gate La TS8 7 B2
Sneck Yate Bank YO7 67 A2
Snipe Cl 5 YO14 101 A4
Snipe La
Hurworth DL2 3 C3
Loftus TS13 11 A6
Snowden Carr Rd LS21 176 E5
Snowden Cl 4 HG4 214 B2
Snowdon Cl YO23 182 D3
Snowdon Gr 4 TS17 5 F4
Snowfield Ind Est YO17 215 C6
Snowfield La YO61 142 F5
Snydale Ave WF6 200 B1
Snydale Cl WF6 200 B1
Snydale Ct 10 WF6 200 B1
Snydale Gr WF6 200 B1
Snydale Rd WF6 200 A1
Sober Hall Ave TS17 6 A4
Socarrs La YO62 119 F7
SOCKBURN 23 C6
Sockburn La DL2 23 B8
Somerset Cl
Hipswell DL9 40 D4
6 York YO30 224 E3
Somerset Rd
2 Harrogate HG2 219 C1
York YO31 228 D8
Somerset Terr YO11 213 A5
Somme Barracks DL9 40 F3
Sommerset Pastures YO61 116 F2
Sopwith Cl TS18 5 F8
Sorrel Gr 29 HG3 161 B3
Sorrell Gr TS14 8 D6
Sough La BB18 186 A8
SOURBY 176 D8
Sourby La LS21 176 D7
Sour La BD23 216 B6
Soursikes Field Rd YO51 141 D5
Soutersfield YO61 144 C6
South App
Aberford LS25 188 F1
Bramham cum Oglethorpe LS23 188 C5
Stutton with Hazlewood LS25 189 A2
South Ave
Castleford WF10 200 C4
20 Scalby YO13 75 D5
South Back La
Stillington YO61 144 C6
Terrington YO60 119 E1
Tollerton YO61 143 B2
South Baileygate WF8 201 C1
SOUTH BANK 228 A1
South Bank Ave YO23 228 B1
South Beech Ave HG2 220 C3
South Cliff Dr YO14 101 B1
South Craven Sch 36 BD20 187 E7
South Cres
Ripon HG4 214 C4
Thirsk YO7 211 B2
South Cres Ave 54 YO14 101 B3
South Cres Cl 51 YO14 101 B3
South Cres Rd YO14 101 B3
Southdean Dr TS8 6 F6
Southdene 48 YO14 101 B3
South Down Rd 3 YO32 225 F5
South Dr HG2 222 E8
SOUTH DUFFIELD 199 A4
South Duffield Rd YO8 198 C4
South End
Bedale DL8 63 A3
Burniston YO13 75 D7
Osmotherley DL6 45 B3
Southend Ave DL3 3 C4
South End Ave 6 DL8 63 A3
South End Cl YO13 75 D7
Southend Gdns 8 YO21 208 C6
South End La DN14 207 B4
Southerscales Nature Reserve* LA6 104 C7
South Esplanade YO1 233 B1
Southey St 1 BD23 217 A3
Southfield YO17 122 D3
Southfield Ave HG4 214 B2
Southfield Cl
6 Hurworth-on-Tees DL2 3 E1
Rufforth YO23 182 D6
Southfield Cres 2 YO24 230 E8
Southfield Grange 3 YO23 190 F5
Southfield La
23 Addingham LS29 174 F4
Kellington DN14 202 E2
South Field La YO26 181 B6
Southfield Rd
28 Addingham LS29 174 F4
Burley in Warfedale LS29 176 C1
Littlethorpe HG4 214 B2
Southfields Rd YO32 167 B7
Southfield Terr
22 Addingham LS29 174 F4
Southfield Terr *continued*
7 Skipton BD23 216 F3
Southgate
Eastfield YO12 99 E6
Pickering YO18 95 F7
Ripon HG4 214 C4
South Gate 18 YO62 92 F6
Southgate Ave HG4 214 C4
Southgate Cl 7 HG4 214 C4
South Grange Rd HG4 214 B2
South Hawksworth St 7 LS29 218 B4
SOUTH HOLME 120 B8
South House Pavement Nature Reserve* BD24 104 F8
South Ings La YO62 70 F3
SOUTH KILVINGTON 211 B7
South Kilvington CE Prim Sch YO7 211 A7
South La
Bishop Wilton YO42 169 F1
Burton Fleming YO25 126 E2
Cawood YO8 197 B7
Thornton Dale YO18 96 D6
Southlands
4 Haxby YO32 166 E5
19 Helmsley YO62 92 F6
16 Hemingbrough YO8 198 F1
2 High & Low Bishopside HG3 137 B4
Southlands Ave 5 YO21 208 C7
Southlands Cl
Escrick YO19 192 B6
8 South Milford LS25 195 F2
Southlands Gr YO12 212 B7
Southlands Rd YO23 228 B2
Southlea YO17 122 F5
SOUTH LOFTUS 10 E8
SOUTH MILFORD 195 F1
South Milford Prim Sch 9 LS25 195 F2
South Milford Sta LS25 195 F2
Southmoor La WF11 202 B1
South Moor La
Garriston DL8 61 A7
Sowerby YO7 89 F3
Southmoor Rd YO19 192 F5
Southolme Cl 22 YO51 141 B5
Southolme Dr 7 YO30 224 F1
Southolme Wlk 23 YO51 141 B5
SOUTH OTTERINGTON 64 F2
South Otterington CE Prim Sch DL7 64 F2
South Parade
Hurworth-on-Tees DL2 22 C8
Ilkley LS29 218 A4
Northallerton DL7 210 D3
Norton YO17 215 E3
8 Selby YO8 232 C5
York YO23 233 A1
South Parade Ind Est YO17 215 E3
South Park Ave TS6 7 E8
South Park La LS22 180 A8
South Park Rd HG1 219 E1
South Ridge LS25 194 D1
South Ruddings La YO19 192 F7
South Side TS15 25 C5
South St
Barmby on the Marsh DN14 205 A7
Burton Fleming YO25 126 E2
Scalby YO13 75 D5
7 Scarborough YO11 213 A4
SOUTH STAINLEY 139 E2
South Terr YO7 211 B2
South Town La TS13 10 E8
South Vale DL6 210 E2
South View
Burniston YO13 75 D7
Castleford WF10 201 B5
2 Egglescliffe TS16 5 D4
3 Glusburn BD20 173 E1
Healaugh LS24 182 A2
Hunton DL8 61 E7
Ilkley LS29 218 B3
19 Leyburn DL8 60 D5
Northallerton DL6 210 F6
Ripon HG4 214 D2
2 Rudby TS15 25 D5
6 Whitby YO21 208 D5
South View Terr BD20 174 B1
Southville Terr HG1 219 B5
Southway
Harrogate HG2 222 C8
Ilkley LS29 218 D3
Manor Park LS29 176 B2
Southwold 7 YO11 100 B7
Southwold Cl 5 YO11 100 B7
Southwold Rise 6 YO11 100 B7
Southwood TS8 7 B4
South Wood La 11 BD23 134 E3
Southwood Rd YO41 193 C8
Sovereign Gdns 2 WF6 200 A1
Sovereign Pk HG1 219 B2
Sowarth Field 21 BD24 131 D2
Sowarth Ind Est BD24 131 D2
SOWERBY 211 B1
Sowerby Cres TS9 26 B7
Sowerby Prim Sch YO7 211 B1
Sowerby Rd
Thirsk YO7 211 B2
York YO26 227 D4
Sowerby Terr YO7 211 B2
Sowerby Way TS16 5 D5
Sowgate La WF8 201 D2
SPACEY HOUSES 223 A2
Spa Complex* YO11 213 B4
Spa Gdns* HG4 214 B5
Spa La
Harrogate HG2 220 C3
Middleton YO18 95 B6
Spalding Ave YO30 228 B7
Spa Mews HG2 220 D3
Spa Pk* HG4 214 B5
Spa Rd
Gainford DL2 1 C7
Harrogate HG2 220 C3
Sparrow Hall Dr DL1 3 E8
Spartal La LS25 200 F8
Spa St HG2 220 C3
Spa Terr 3 HG2 220 C3
SPA THE 213 B4
Spa The YO11 213 A4
SPAUNTON 70 E4
Spaunton Bank YO62 70 E5
Spaunton La YO62 70 E4
Spawd Bone La
Knottingley WF11 201 F2
27 Knottingley WF11 202 A1
Speculation St YO1 228 E4
Speedwell Rd WF10 200 C3
SPEETON 127 F5
Speeton Ave TS5 6 F7
Spellow Cres HG5 140 E1
Spellow Gr HG5 140 E1
Spen Brow LA2 128 E6
Spence Ct 4 TS9 8 A2
Spenceley Pl DL11 2 A2
Spencer Cl 5 BD20 187 F8
Spencer's Holt HG1 219 D7
Spencer St
29 Glusburn BD20 187 E7
3 York YO23 233 B1
Spencer's Way HG1 219 D7
Spencer Wlk BD23 217 C3
Spen Comon La LS24 188 F3
Speng La YO23 182 B4
Spen La YO1 233 C3
SPENNITHORNE 60 F3
Spennithorne CE Prim Sch DL8 60 F4
Spey Bank YO24 230 C6
Spiker's Hill La YO13 74 F2
Spindle Cl YO24 230 C8
Spindle Mill BD23 216 F4
Spink La WF8 201 B1
Spinksburn La HG3 159 F1
Spinner La HG3 161 A8
Spinners Ct BD23 216 F4
Spinney The
Darlington DL3 3 B4
Draughton BD23 174 B7
6 Easingwold YO61 143 C8
Knaresborough HG5 221 C6
3 Scarborough YO12 212 B5
Tees-side Airport DL2 4 D4
York YO24 230 F7
Spinniker Dr 4 YO21 208 C5
Spire View 21 YO8 198 F1
Spital Bridge YO22 208 E5
Spitalcroft HG5 221 B4
Spital Farm Craft Ctr* YO12 99 E2
Spital Field Ct 1 YO17 215 C4
Spitalfields TS15 5 D2
Spital Rd YO12 99 E3
Spital St YO17 215 B4
Spital The TS15 5 D3
Spitfire Ct DL10 41 F6
Spitfire Way LS25 196 B4
Spitlands La HG5 163 B7
Spittal Hardwick La WF10 201 B3
Spittlerush La DN6 206 D2
SPOFFORTH 179 E5
Spofforth Castle* HG3 179 D6
Spofforth CE Prim Sch HG3 179 E5
Spofforth Hill LS22 180 B3
Spofforth La
Follifoot HG3 223 F4
North Deighton LS22 180 A6
Spofforth Rd HG3 223 F4
Spoffoth La LS22 180 A7
Spout La LA2 102 B2
Spreight Lane Steps YO11 213 B7
Springbank
Marton cum Grafton YO51 141 E2
Swillington LS25 194 B3
Spring Bank YO12 212 E3
Springbank Ave YO19 184 E7
Spring Bank Cl HG4 214 C7
Spring Bank Mdw HG4 214 C7
Spring Bank Rd HG4 214 C7
Spring Cl
Garforth LS25 194 D4
Middlesbrough TS18 6 B8
12 Sleights YO22 32 A6
Spring Ct HG3 160 E6
Springfield
Bentham LA2 129 B8
Clifford LS23 188 E7
Follifoot HG3 223 F4
4 Scarborough YO11 213 B6
Skeeby DL10 21 A1
Stokesley TS9 26 C7
Springfield Ave
4 Earby BB18 172 B1
Harrogate HG1 219 C3
Ilkley LS29 218 C4
11 Pontefract WF8 201 C1

Springfield Cl
Barlby with Osgodby YO8 198 B5
20 Boroughbridge YO51 141 B5
Heworth YO31 229 C7
1 Leyburn DL8 60 D5
5 Pateley Bridge HG3 137 C4
Ripon HG4 214 B7
Thirsk YO7 211 B4
Springfield Cres
Bentham LA2 129 B8
3 Kirk Smeaton WF8 206 C3
Springfield Ct
7 Grassington BD23 134 E2
Sherburn in Elmet LS25 195 F5
Springfield Dr
9 Barlby YO8 198 B5
19 Boroughbridge YO51 141 B5
Springfield Garth YO17 215 D3
Springfield Gdns 1 TS9 26 C7
Springfield Gr
21 Boroughbridge YO51 141 B5
Kirklevington TS15 5 F1
Springfield La
3 Kirkbymoorside YO62 70 C1
Tockwith YO26 181 C7
Springfield Mews HG1 219 C3
Springfield Mount LS29 174 F5
Springfield Pl LS25 194 B3
Springfield Prim Sch DL1 3 E7
Springfield Rd
18 Boroughbridge YO51 141 B5
Darlington DL1 3 E7
6 Grassington BD23 134 E2
4 Poppleton YO26 165 F1
Sherburn in Elmet LS25 195 F5
Springfield Rise 1 YO26 164 A8
Springfields
18 Knottingley WF11 202 A2
5 Skipton BD23 217 B4
Springfields Ave 17 WF11 202 A2
Springfield Terr YO17 124 D7
Springfield Way
4 Pateley Bridge HG3 137 C4
York YO31 229 B7
Spring Gdns 10 YO11 100 B6
Spring Gr
Harrogate HG1 219 C3
Laneshaw Bridge BB8 186 B3
Spring Hall Garth YO17 215 A3
Springhead Sch YO12 212 E2
Spring Hill
Stonegrave YO62 93 C1
Welbury DL6 24 B1
Whitby YO21 208 D6
Springhill Cl YO12 212 E4
Springhill Ct 7 LS24 189 E6
Springhill La YO12 212 D3
Springhill Rd YO12 212 E4
Spring Hill Sch HG4 113 E4
Spring Hill Terr 10 YO21 208 D6
Spring La
Birdforth YO7 116 F8
Kirkby Overblow HG3 179 A2
Long Marston YO26 182 A5
Pannal HG3 222 C3
Wetherby LS22 180 E3
York YO10 229 A1
Springmead Dr LS25 194 C3
Springmount 3 BB18 172 B1
Spring Mount HG1 219 C3
Spring Rise BD23 174 B7
Springs La
Ellerton-on-Swale DL10 41 F4
Ilkley LS29 218 C4
Walton LS23 180 F3
Whashton DL11 20 B4
Spring St 2 YO61 143 C8
Springs Terr LS29 218 B4
Springs The 4 DL8 60 E2
Spring Terr DL7 210 C4
Spring Vale YO21 208 C6
Springwater Sch HG2 220 D4
Spring Way TS18 5 F8
Springwell Ave 11 LS26 194 A1
Springwell Cl 8 BD22 187 B6
Springwell Gdns 3 DL7 210 D4
Springwell La DL7 210 B4
Springwell Rd 10 LS26 194 A1
Springwell Terrace E 1 DL7 210 D4
Springwell Terrace W 2 DL7 210 D4
Spring Wlk YO8 232 A1
Springwood YO32 225 D7
Springwood Gr YO26 227 C6
Spring Wood Rd TS14 8 F6
SPROXTON 92 F4
Spruce Cl YO32 225 D2
Spruce Gill Ave 4 DL8 63 B3
Spruce Gill Dr 5 DL8 63 B3
Spruisty Rd HG1 219 C4
Spurr Ct YO24 230 C8
Spurriergate YO1 233 B2
Square The
Boston Spa LS23 188 F8
Castleford WF10 201 B4
Ingleton LA6 103 D4
Kippax LS25 194 D1
Knottingley WF11 201 E3
Leeming DL7 63 F3
Sheriff Hutton YO60 145 D5
1 Tadcaster LS24 189 F6
Stabler Cl 15 YO32 166 D5
Stable Rd YO8 204 D7
Stablers Wlk
Earswick YO32 225 F7
13 Pontefract WF6 200 A2
Stables La LS23 188 F8
Stables The LS24 189 E2
STACKHOUSE 131 D4
Stackhouse La
Giggleswick BD24 131 D4
Lawkland BD24 130 F2
Stags Way DL10 41 F7
STAINBURN 177 F3
Stainburn Ave WF10 201 A3
Stainburn La LS21 177 E2
Staindale TS14 8 D6
Staindale Cl YO30 224 E2
Staindrop Dr TS5 6 E7
Staindrop Rd DL3 3 A6
Stained Glass Ctr★ YO11 100 C5
STAINFORTH 131 E6
Stainforth Gdns TS17 6 B5
Stainforth La BD24 131 D5
Stainforth Rd BD24 131 E4
STAINSACRE 32 F7
Stainsacre La
Hawsker-cum-Stainsacre YO22 32 F6
Whitby YO22 208 F3
Stainsacre Lane Ind Est YO22 208 F3
Stainsby Rd TS5 6 D8
Stainthorpe Row DL7 64 F2
STAINTON
Marrick 39 C3
Middlesbrough 6 D5
STAINTONDALE 54 B5
Staintondale Shire Horse Farm★ YO13 54 C5
Stainton Rd TS9 6 F1
Stainton Way
Coulby Newham TS8 7 A5
Stainton & Thornton TS8 6 E5
STAITHES 13 J2
Staithes Cl 4 YO26 227 B4
Staithes Gall★ TS13 13 K2
Staithes La TS13 13 K2
Staithe St 3 YO8 199 D7
Stake Rd DL8 57 C1
Stakesby Prim Sch YO21 208 B6
Stakesby Rd YO21 208 B6
Stakesby Vale YO21 208 C6
Stakesby Vale Ct YO21 208 B5
STALLING BUSK 81 B8
STAMFORD BRIDGE 168 E2
Stamford Bridge Prim Sch YO41 168 D2
Stamford Bridge Rd YO19 184 E7
Stamford Bridge W YO41 168 C2
Stamford Street E 10 YO26 227 F5
Stamford Street W 8 YO26 227 F5
Stammergate YO7 211 C3
Stammergate La LS22 180 A1
Stamp Hill Cl 7 LS29 174 E4
Standard Ct DL7 210 B6
Standard Way DL6 210 B6
Standard Way Ind Est DL6 210 C6
Standridge Clough La BB18 172 B1
Standroyd Dr BB8 186 A3
Standroyd Rd BB8 186 A3
Stanghow Rd TS12 9 F8
Stang La
Arkengarthdale DL11 17 E3
Farnham HG5 162 C7
Hope DL11 18 A8
Stangs La BD23 157 D6
Stang Top
Arkengarthdale DL11 17 F5
Hope DL11 18 A6
Stanhope Dr HG2 220 B2
Stanhope Gr TS5 6 E8
Stanhope Road N DL3 3 C5
Staniland Dr YO8 232 A5
Stanley Ave YO32 225 D7
Stanley Cl
4 Catterick Garrison DL9 40 E3
22 Eastfield YO11 100 B6
Stanley Gr
Aske DL10 20 D1
Great Ayton TS9 7 F1
Richmond DL10 209 D8
Stanley St
Castleford WF10 200 F4
4 Scarborough YO12 213 A7
York YO31 233 C4
Stansfield Brow BD20 187 A8
Stansfield Cl WF10 201 A4
Stansfield Dr WF10 201 B4
Stansfield Rd WF10 201 A4
Stanstead Way TS17 6 C7
Stansted Gr DL2 4 D4
Stan Valley 2 WF8 206 C3
STANWICK-ST-JOHN 1 E2
Stanyforth Cres YO26 164 C2
STAPE 71 F8
Stape Rd YO18 71 F7
STAPLETON 3 A2
Stapleton Bank DL2 3 A2
Stapleton Cl
3 Bedale DL8 63 B2
11 Seamer YO12 99 D6
Stapley La DL8 87 F4
STARBECK 220 C4
Starbeck Baths HG2 220 D3
Starbeck Cl 4 YO21 208 B5
Starbeck Prim Sch HG2 220 D4
Starbeck Sta HG2 220 C4
STARBOTTON 107 F5
Star Carr La YO12 99 E4
Starfits La
Fadmoor YO62 69 F3
Welburn YO62 94 A8
Stark Bank Rd HG4 85 C7
Starkey Cres YO31 229 A5
Starkey La 5 BD20 173 F1
Starmire BD22 187 A6
Starra Field La YO26 163 F5
Star Sh Prec DL6 210 E4
Station Ave
20 Filey YO14 101 B3
Harrogate HG1 219 E2
New Earswick YO32 225 D3
Whitby YO21 208 B7
York YO1 233 A2
Station Bridge HG1 219 D2
Station Bsns Pk YO26 227 F4
Station Cl
Dacre HG3 159 F8
6 East Ayton/West Ayton YO13 99 A7
Hambleton YO8 196 F2
Sharow HG4 214 D7
Station Ct 8 HG5 179 E5
Station Dr HG4 214 D7
Station Fields LS25 194 C4
Station Gr 19 BD20 187 F8
Station La
Barmby on the Marsh DN14 205 B7
Burton Leonard HG3 139 F3
Cliffe YO8 198 E3
Cloughton YO13 54 D1
Gristhorpe YO14 100 E4
Hampsthwaite HG3 161 A6
Morton-on-Swale DL7 64 A7
Shipton YO30 165 E5
Station Par HG1 219 D2
Station Plaza★ LS29 218 B3
Station Rd
Ampleforth YO62 92 C1
Beadlam YO62 93 D7
Brompton DL6 43 F4
Brompton-on-Swale DL10 41 B6
Burley in Warfedale LS29 176 C1
Carlton DN14 204 C3
Castleford WF10 200 E4
Cayton YO11 100 B5
Church Fenton LS24 196 B7
Clapham LA2 130 C7
Copmanthorpe YO23 230 B2
Danby YO21 29 A7
Eaglescliffe TS16 5 E6
Fylingdales YO22 33 C4
Gainford DL2 1 C8
Gilling East YO62 118 F8
Glusburn BD20 187 E8
Goldsborough HG5 163 A3
Great Ayton TS9 8 A1
Great Preston WF10 200 E6
Hambleton YO8 196 F1
Haxby YO32 166 F5
Hellifield BD23 154 B4
Helmsley YO62 92 F6
Hensall DN14 203 C1
Heslerton YO17 97 D1
High Bentham LA2 129 A8
Hinderwell TS13 11 F7
Horton in Ribblesdale BD24 105 C3
Ilkley LS29 218 B4
Kildale YO21 27 E8
Kippax LS25 200 C8
Kirk Hammerton YO26 164 D2
9 Knaresborough HG5 221 A6
Long Preston BD23 153 F4
Menwith with Darley HG3 160 A6
Mickletown LS26 200 A6
Middleton St George DL2 4 C5
Normanton WF6 200 A2
Norton DN6 206 F2
Nunnington YO62 93 E2
Pannal HG3 222 E2
24 Poppleton YO26 165 F1
Rawcliffe DN14 205 A1
Riccall YO19 198 A8
Richmond DL10 209 C7
Scalby YO13 75 D5
Scruton DL7 63 E6
Selby YO8 232 D5
Settle BD24 131 C2
Sleights YO22 32 A6
Snainton YO13 97 F4
South Otterington DL7 64 F2
Sowerby YO7 211 A2
Stainton Dale YO13 54 A8
Stokesley TS9 26 C7
Tadcaster LS24 189 D6
Thirsk YO7 89 D4
Threshfield BD23 134 D2
Tollerton YO61 143 B3
Wharram YO17 148 F4
Wharram YO17 149 A4
Whixley YO26 164 A3
Wistow YO8 197 C6
Womersley DN6 206 D5
Wood Row LS26 200 B6
York YO24 233 A2
Station Rise YO1 233 A2
Station Road Ind Est
Brompton DL6 43 F3
Great Preston LS25 200 C8
Station Sq
4 Strensall YO32 167 B7
4 Whitby YO21 208 D6
Station Terr
4 Boroughbridge YO51 141 B6
Great Preston WF10 200 E6
Station View
Cliffe YO8 198 D3
2 Harrogate HG2 220 C3
Seamer YO12 99 E7
8 Skipton BD23 216 D3
Station Way YO17 215 C3
STAUPES 160 C4
Staupes Rd HG3 160 B4
STAVELEY 140 F1
Staveley Com Prim Sch HG5 140 E1
Staveley Nature Reserve★ HG5 140 E2
STAXTON 99 E2
Staxton Carr La YO12 99 D3
Staxton Hill YO12 125 C8
Staynor Ave YO8 232 E3
STEAD 176 A1
Stead La LS14 188 A3
STEAN 110 A4
Stean La HG3 110 A4
STEARSBY 118 F2
Steelmoor La YO60 146 C2
Steeple Cl 4 YO32 166 D5
Steeton La LS24 190 D7
Steeton Way LS25 195 E2
Steincroft Rd 7 LS25 195 F2
Stella Gdns 10 WF8 201 C1
Stelling Rd DL11 38 E7
Stephen Bank DL11 18 H8
Stephen Joseph Theatre★ YO11 212 F5
Stephenson Cl
Knaresborough HG5 221 B4
York YO31 225 E1
Stephenson Rd 2 DL10 41 C7
Stephenson's La YO26 164 A2
Stephensons Way LS29 218 C4
Stephenson Way YO26 227 F5
Stephen's Wlk YO8 232 B1
Stephenwath La YO41 169 C5
Stepin Turn YO62 49 B1
Stepney Ave YO12 212 D4
Stepney Cl YO12 212 C5
Stepney Dr YO12 212 C5
Stepney Gr YO12 212 C5
Stepney Hill YO12 212 B4
Stepney Rd YO12 212 D4
Stepney Rise YO12 212 D5
Steps The LS22 180 C2
Sterling Chase HG5 221 C7
Sterling Pk YO30 225 A3
Sterne Ave YO31 229 A5
Sterne Way YO61 144 C3
Stevenson Pl HG5 220 F5
Steven Way HG4 214 B6
Steward Cl YO8 197 D1
Stewart La YO19 191 C4
STILLINGFLEET 191 C3
STILLINGTON 144 C6
Stillington Prim Sch YO61 144 C7
Stillington Rd
Easingwold YO61 143 D8
Huby YO61 144 A4
Stinton La
Boroughbridge YO51 141 C4
Helperby YO61 142 A8
Stirling Gr YO10 231 F8
Stirling Rd
Burley in Warfedale LS29 176 B1
York YO30 224 F3
Stirling Way TS17 6 B6
Stirrup Cl
Norton YO17 215 E2
York YO24 230 B8
STIRTON 216 C6
Stirtonber BD23 216 E5
Stirton La BD23 216 C5
Stittenham Hill YO60 146 A6
Stobarts La TS15 5 B1
STOCK 171 C3
Stockdale Cl 9 HG5 221 B5
Stockdale Ct DL6 210 F3
Stockdale La BD24 131 F2
Stockdale Wlk HG5 221 B5
Stockeld La LS22 179 E3
Stockeld Park House★ LS22 179 F4
Stockeld Rd LS29 218 A4
Stockeld Way LS29 218 A5
Stockfield La YO51 141 D2
Stockhill Cl 1 YO19 184 E7
Stockholm Cl 1 YO10 231 D8
Stockinger La LS29 174 F4
Stocking Hill TS9 25 E2
Stocking La
Hambleton YO8 196 E1
Hillam LS25 202 B7
Knottingley WF11 202 B2
Lotherton cum Aberford LS25 195 A7
Stockings La YO62 92 F2
Stocks Cl YO17 215 F4
Stockshill YO12 99 D6
Stockshott La BD20 173 C2
Stocks La 1 HG3 160 A6
Stock Stile La HG3 160 D5
Stockton Hall Hospl YO32 167 D3
Stockton La
Heworth YO32 226 D1
York YO31 229 A7
STOCKTON ON THE FOREST 167 D3
Stockton on the Forest Prim Sch YO32 167 D3
Stockton Rd
Darlington DL1 3 F7
Sadberge DL2 4 C7
South Kilvington YO7 211 B6
Stockwell Ave
Ingleby TS17 6 B5
Knaresborough HG5 221 B7
Stockwell Cres 5 HG5 221 B7
Stockwell Ct 9 HG5 221 B6
Stockwell Dr HG5 221 B7
Stockwell Gr HG5 221 B7
Stockwell La HG5 221 B6
Stockwell Pl HG5 221 B7
Stockwell Rd HG5 221 B6
Stockwell View HG5 221 B7
Stockwith La DN14 204 A4
Stokelake Rd 5 HG1 219 E3
STOKESLEY 26 D7
Stokesley Ind Pk TS9 26 D6
Stokesley L Ctr TS9 26 D7
Stokesley Prim Sch TS9 26 C7
Stokesley Rd
Brompton DL6 44 A3
Coulby Newham TS7 7 B7
Guisborough TS14 8 C6
Middlesbrough TS7 7 B6
Northallerton DL6 210 E7
Stokesley Sch TS9 26 D7
Stonebeck Ave HG1 219 B4
Stonebeck Gate La YO21 29 D4
Stonebow The
Thornton-le-Beans DL6 65 B5
York YO1 233 C2
Stone Bramble 22 HG3 161 B3
Stonebridge Cres 2 TS17 6 D6
Stone Bridge Dr YO41 185 F5
Stonebridgegate HG4 214 D5
Stonecrop Ave 5 HG3 161 B3
Stonecrop Dr 1 HG3 161 B3
Stone Crop Dr 14 WF10 200 D3
Stonecross Rd YO21 208 A6
Stone Ct 6 YO13 75 D5
Stone Dale YO42 170 D3
Stoned Horse La YO26 164 C4
Stonefall Ave HG2 220 C3
Stonefall Dr HG2 220 B2
Stonefall Mews HG2 220 C3
Stonefall Pl 2 HG2 220 B2
Stonefield Ave YO61 143 C8
Stonefield Garth 9 YO61 143 C8
Stonefield La 4 YO61 143 C8
Stone Garth 3 YO62 92 F6
STONEGATE 30 D8
Stonegate
Hunmanby YO14 126 F8
York YO1 233 B3
Stone Gate YO26 164 A4
STONEGRAVE 119 D8
Stonehaven Way DL1 3 F8
Stone Head La BD22 186 E6
STONE HOUSE 78 F8
Stonelands Cl YO60 145 D5
Stonelands Ct 2 YO30 225 A1
Stoneleigh Gate YO26 164 B3
Stone Man La DL11 19 C5
Stonepit Balk YO17 149 C5
Stonepit Hill YO17 149 C4
Stonepit La
Birdsall YO17 148 D6
Gristhorpe YO14 100 E5
Stone Quarry Rd YO13 75 C8
Stone Riggs YO32 167 D2
Stone Rings Cl HG2 222 E5
Stone Rings Grange HG2 222 E5
Stone Rings La HG2 222 E5
Stones Cl YO24 227 E2
Stonesdale Cl 3 HG5 221 D5
Stonesdale La DL11 35 E8
Stone Stoup Hill TS9 27 C5
Stonethwaite 5 YO24 230 C7
Stonewall Cottage La 25 YO41 168 D2
Stoney Bank Rd BB18 172 B1
Stoneyborough Cl YO7 211 C4
Stoneybrough La YO7 211 C4
Stoney Haggs Rd YO12 99 E7
Stony Cross YO62 93 E7
Stony Ct 5 YO13 75 D5
Stonygate Bank DL11 20 A5
Stony La
East Harlsey DL6 44 F5
8 Scalby YO13 75 D5
Stoop Cl YO32 225 C8
Stooperdale Ave DL3 3 B7
Stoopes Hill 8 BB18 172 B1
Storey Cl 26 YO62 92 F6
Storiths La BD23 175 A8
Storking La YO41 185 F6
Storr La YO13 74 E5
Storth Gill La BD24 131 A1
Stourton Rd LS29 175 C3
Stow Ct YO32 225 E3
Strafford Rd 14 DL10 41 E4
Straight La
Addingham LS29 174 E3
Aldwark YO61 142 C3

Straight La continued
Burton Leonard HG3 140 A3
Holtby YO19 184 F8
Middleham DL8 60 F2
Straights The DL8 58 C4
Strait La Copt Hewick HG4 114 B2
Danby YO21 29 C6
Hurworth DL2 3 F1
Stainton & Thornton TS8 6 D5
Weeton LS17 178 B2
Well DL8 87 A3
Straits La YO13 99 A3
STRANGHOW 9 F6
Stranglands La WF11 201 C3
Stratford Way YO32 225 E3
Strathmore Dr 9 TS15 24 E8
Strathmore Rd LS29 218 E4
Strawberrry Fileds Prim Sch LS25 194 C3
Strawberry Ct YO12 212 D4
Strawberry Dale HG1 219 D3
Strawberry Dale Ave 3 HG1 219 D3
Strawberry Dale Sq 1 HG1 219 D3
Strawberry Dale Terr 2 HG1 219 D3
Straw Gate DL2 3 A2
Strawgate Gr DL2 3 A3
Stray Garth YO31 228 F7
Straylands Gr YO31 228 F8
Stray Rd Harrogate HG2 222 D8
York YO31 229 B6
Stray Rein HG2 219 E1
Stray The Darlington DL1 3 E5
Henderskelfe YO60 146 D8
Longnewton TS21 5 A7
Stray Wlk HG2 222 E8
STREET 29 F3
Street 1 LS23 189 A8
Street 2 LS23 181 A1
Street 3 LS23 181 A1
Street 5 LS23 181 A1
Street 6 LS23 181 A2
Street 7 LS23 181 B1
Street 8 LS23 181 B1
Street Head La BD22 187 F1
STREET HOUSES 190 C8
Street La Bewerley HG3 137 B4
Bubwith DN14 199 F5
Colton LS24 190 D7
Glaisdale YO21 29 E3
Middleton YO18 95 E7
Pickhill with Roxby YO7 88 B6
STREETLAM 42 F5
Street The 8 LS29 174 E4
STRENSALL 167 A7
STRENSALL CAMP 167 B6
Strensall Comm Nature Reserve* YO60 167 D8
Strensall Dr 11 YO12 75 F5
Strensall Pk YO32 167 A5
Strensall Rd
Earswick YO32 226 A7
York YO32 225 F6
Stretton Cl WF7 200 D1
Strickland Rd 13 YO14 127 A8
Strikes La BD20 187 F6
Stripe La Hartwith cum Winsley HG3 160 B8
Skelton YO30 224 B5
Stripe The 6 TS9 26 C7
Stuart Ave DL10 209 C8
Stuart Cl
4 Scarborough YO11 100 B7
4 Strensall YO32 167 C8
Stuart Gr
Eggborough DN14 203 A2
1 Pontefract WF6 200 A2
9 Thorpe Willoughby YO8 197 B1
Stuart Rd YO24 227 D1
Stuart St
10 Barnoldswick BB18 171 E1
Pontefract WF8 201 B1
Stubbing La BD23 81 B1
Stubbing Nook La DL8 62 B2
Stubbs La
Cridling Stubbs WF11 206 A8
Norton DN6 206 E2
Stainton Dale YO13 53 F5
Stubbs Rd WF8 206 D3
Stubden Gr YO30 224 F2
Stubham Rise LS29 218 A5
Studdah Cl DL8 60 D7
STUDFOLD 105 D1
Stud Fold Bank HG3 110 B3
Studford Ring* YO62 92 C2
Studley Cl DL7 210 B2
Studley La HG4 113 C1
Studley Rd
Harrogate HG1 219 D3
Ripon HG4 214 A4
Studley Roger HG4 113 D1
STUDLEY ROGER 113 D1
STUDLEY ROYAL 113 C1
Studley Terr 15 YO22 208 E6
Stump Cross TS14 8 E6
Stump Cross Caverns* HG3 136 A2
Stumpcross Ct 14 WF8 201 C2
Stumpcross La WF8 201 C2
Stumpcross Mdws WF8 201 D1
Stumpcross Way 15 WF8 201 C2
Stumps La HG3 160 A5
Stunstead Rd BB8 186 B2
Sturdee Gr YO31 228 D7
Sturdy House La
Marske DL11 19 E2
Whashton DL11 20 A4
Sturton Grange La LS25 194 D4
Sturton La LS25 194 D4
Steville Cl 4 YO62 70 C1
STUTTON 189 D4
Stutton Rd LS24 189 D4
Stygate La DN6 206 E1
Sudforth La DN14 202 C3
SUFFIELD 75 A5
Suffield Hill YO13 75 A5
Sugar Hill 9 LS29 174 F4
Sugar Loaf Ct 13 TS17 5 F4
Sumitt Pk WF10 200 F2
SUMMERBRIDGE 138 A1
Summerbridge Prim Sch HG3 138 A1
Summerfield BD23 172 A3
Summerfield Cl 1 WF11 201 F4
Summerfield Dr WF11 201 F4
Summerfield La YO22 33 A7
Summerfield Rd YO24 230 C7
Summer Gdns YO30 227 F8
Summerhill Rd LS26 200 B6
Summer Hill Rd LS26 200 B6
SUMMERSCALES 158 C1
Summers Fold 1 BD23 134 E3
Sunderland Rd BD20 173 E3
Sundew Heath 24 HG3 161 B3
Sun Gdns TS17 6 A8
Sun La LS29 176 C1
Sunmoor Dr BD23 217 A4
Sunningdale LS25 194 F4
Sunningdale Cl
Knapton YO26 227 B5
1 York YO26 227 B5
Sunningdale Dr TS16 5 E5
Sunningdale Gr 1 YO21 208 B5
Sunningdales 27 WF6 200 B1
Sunnybank LS25 195 A3
Sunny Bank 3 WF11 202 A2
Sunnybank Rd LS25 195 A3
Sunny Bank Rd 6 BD20 187 E7
Sunnycrest Ave DL10 209 D8
Sunnydale 3 YO32 225 D7
Sunnyfield TS9 7 F1
Sunnyside TS8 7 D5
Sunnyside Prim Sch TS8 7 A6
Sunrise Dr YO14 127 C8
Sunset Dr LS29 218 D5
Sunset Terr LS29 218 E5
Sun St Cononley BD20 173 C1
4 Cowling BD22 187 B6
Thornaby TS17 6 A8
Sunstar Gr TS7 7 B6
Sur Gate
Harwood Dale YO13 53 F1
Suffield-cum-Everley YO13 74 F8
Surrey Way YO30 227 F8
Surtees St Darlington DL3 3 C6
York YO30 228 B7
Sussex Cl Bedale DL8 63 A2
York YO10 229 C2
Sussex Ct 10 DL9 209 C1
Sussex Rd YO10 229 C2
Sussex St Bedale DL8 63 A2
14 Scarborough YO11 213 A6
Sussex Way 14 YO32 167 A7
Sutcliffe Ct 6 YO21 208 B6
Sutcliffe Gall* YO21 208 D7
Sutherland Rd YO18 71 C6
Sutherland St YO23 228 B1
Sutor Cl YO23 230 B3
SUTTON 201 F4
Sutton Ave 7 DL9 41 A5
Sutton Bank YO7 91 A5
Sutton Bank Visitor Ctr* YO7 91 B6
Sutton Bridge* YO41 185 C2
Sutton Ct 5 YO7 211 C3
Sutton Dr DL7 210 C2
Sutton Grange Cl HG3 219 B4
SUTTON HOWGRAVE 87 F1
SUTTON-IN-CRAVEN 187 F6
Sutton in Craven CE Prim Sch 39 BD20 187 E7
Sutton in Craven Com Prim Sch 38 BD20 187 E7
Sutton La
Byram cum Sutton WF11 202 A4
Byram WF11 201 E4
Ellington High & Low HG4 86 A5
Fearby HG4 85 F4
Steeton with Eastburn BD20 187 F7
SUTTON-ON-THE-FOREST 144 C3
Sutton-on-the-Forest CE Prim Sch YO61 144 C3
Sutton Pk* YO61 144 C3
Sutton Rd Bagby YO7 211 E3
Wigginton YO32 166 D7
Sutton St YO17 215 D3
SUTTON-UNDER-WHITESTONECLIFFE 90 E5
SUTTON UPON DERWENT 185 C1
Sutton upon Derwent CE Prim Sch YO41 185 C2
Sutton Way
Middlesbrough TS4 6 F8
York YO30 228 B8
Swadford St BD23 216 F4
SWAINBY 45 E8
Swainby Abbey* DL8 88 B8
Swainby Ellers DL6 25 D1
Swainby La DL8 87 F7
Swainby & Potto Prim Sch DL6 45 D8
Swain Ct
Middleton St George DL2 4 D4
Northallerton DL6 210 D5
Swainsea Dr 3 YO18 95 F7
Swainsea La YO18 95 F8
Swainstead Raike BD24 153 B8
Swainston Cl TS5 6 E7
Swale App 25 WF6 200 B1
Swale Ave YO24 230 E8
SWALEDALE 37 C4
Swaledale Ave DL3 3 B6
Swaledale Mus* DL11 38 C6
Swaledale Rd 22 DL9 40 E4
Swalegate DL10 209 C8
Swale Gr DL1 3 C3
Swale Hall La DL11 38 B5
Swale La DL10 41 E5
Swale Pasture La DL10 41 E5
Swale View YO7 115 B6
Swallow Cl Firth Moor DL1 3 F4
Guisborough TS14 8 D6
Swan Cl YO19 192 A7
Swan Farm Ct YO19 192 A7
Swang Rd YO13 75 A6
Swan Hill Rd YO11 213 A6
Swanhills La YO13 98 F3
Swan La YO7 65 F2
Swanland Rd YO62 92 F7
Swann St YO23 233 A1
Swan Rd HG1 219 C2
Swan St BD23 173 B4
Swan Syke Dr 8 DN6 206 F2
Swarcliffe Rd HG1 220 B4
SWARTHA 174 D1
Swartha La BD20 174 D2
Swarthlands La YO13 75 D7
SWATHGILL 119 B4
Sweeming La LS25 196 C5
Sweetbecks Cl 12 YO11 100 A6
Sweet Bits La HG5 221 C8
Sweet Briar HG3 219 A4
SWETTON 111 F4
SWILLINGTON 194 A1
SWILLINGTON COMMON 194 A3
Swillington La LS26 194 A2
Swillington Prim Sch LS26 194 A1
Swinburn Ct 12 HG4 86 C3
Swinburne Cl HG1 219 E7
Swinburne Rd TS16 5 E6
Swinburn Rd 11 HG4 86 C3
SWINCLIFFE 160 E4
Swincliffe La HG3 160 D5
Swindale La TS12 9 F5
SWINDEN 154 C1
Swindon La HG3 178 E4
Swinegate YO1 233 B2
Swinegate Court E YO1 233 B3
Swineherd La YO62 70 C1
SWINITHWAITE 59 C4
Swinneybeck Bank HG4 85 E5
Swinsty Ct YO30 224 F1
SWINTON Malton 121 C4
Masham 86 B2
Swinton Cl 8 YO30 224 E2
Swinton Ct HG2 222 B8
Swinton La YO17 121 B3
Swinton Rd Masham HG4 86 C3
Swinton HG4 86 B2
Swinton Terr HG4 86 C3
Swires La BD20 173 C3
Swire Way DL10 20 F7
Swordfish Way LS25 196 B4
Sycamore Ave
4 Catton YO7 89 A1
19 Filey YO14 101 B4
1 Hut Green DN14 203 A2
Kippax LS25 194 C1
Knottingley WF11 201 E1
Malton YO17 215 D5
Richmond DL10 209 A8
York YO32 225 D4
Sycamore Cl
Bishop Monkton HG3 140 A5
Clint HG3 160 F8
1 Haxby YO32 225 D7
3 Hurworth-on-Tees DL2 3 E1
Selby YO8 232 A4
Skelton YO30 224 C5
Slingsby YO62 120 B5
Spennithorne DL8 60 F4
Sycamore Ct
2 Catterick DL10 41 D5
Hellifield BD23 154 B3
2 Pontefract WF8 201 C1
Sycamore Dr
11 Addingham LS29 175 A4
9 Bedale DL8 63 A2
Harrogate HG2 220 C3
Norton-le-Clay YO7 115 B1
Sycamore Gr
Sherburn YO17 124 E7
Steeton with Eastburn BD20 187 F7
Sycamore La DL7 63 D4
Sycamore Mews YO8 232 D2
Sycamore Pk YO12 212 B7
Sycamore Pl
New Earswick YO32 225 D4
York YO30 233 A3
Sycamore Rd Barlby with Osgodby YO8 198 B5
Ripon HG4 214 B2
Sycamores The
Barwick in Elmet LS15 194 B8
42 Earby BB18 172 A1
Sycamore Terr YO30 233 A3
Sycamore View 17 YO26 165 F1
Sycamore Way 16 BB18 171 D1
Sydall's Way 1 DL10 41 E4
Sydney Avenue E DL6 210 E4
Sydney St 5 YO12 212 F7
Sykehead La YO62 93 D6
Sykes Gr HG1 219 C5
Sykes La YO61 143 B3

T

Tabard Hamlet 5 DN14 202 F2
Tabard Rd 6 DN14 202 F2
Tabards The 7 DN14 202 F2
TADCASTER 189 D6
Tadcaster East Prim Sch 6 LS24 189 F6
Tadcaster Gram Sch LS24 189 B5
Tadcaster L Ctr LS24 189 E6
Tadcaster Rd
Copmanthorpe YO23 230 C4
York YO24 227 F1
Tadcaster Rd Dringhouses YO23 230 E5
Tadcaster Swimming Pool LS24 189 E6
Talbenny Gr 32 TS17 5 F4
Talbot Ct YO22 208 E5
Talbot St WF6 200 A1
Talisman Cl 9 TS16 5 D5
Tally Hill YO61 144 A4
Talybont Gr 19 TS17 5 F4
TAME BRIDGE 26 A7
Tameside TS9 26 C8
Tamworth Rd 9 YO30 225 A1
Tanfield Dr 1 LS29 176 C1
Tanfield La HG4 114 A8
TANG 160 D4
TANG HALL 228 F5
Tang Hall La YO31 229 A5
Tang Hall Prim Sch YO31 228 F5
Tang Rd HG3 160 D4
Tanner Row YO1 233 A2
Tanner's Moat YO1 233 A2
Tanner St YO1 233 B2
Tannery Ct 10 HG5 221 B5
Tannery La Embsay BD23 217 D8
Northallerton DL7 210 D5
Tannery The 10 YO10 228 E3
Tanpit La
Easingwold YO61 143 C8
Walden Stubbs DN6 206 E3
Tansy Cl 2 HG3 161 B3
Tansy Rd 3 HG3 161 B3
TANTON 7 C1
Tanton Cl TS9 7 A1
Tanton Rd TS9 7 B1
Tarbard Ave 14 HG4 113 D2
Tarbert Cres 2 YO24 230 B7
Tarell Ct 45 TS17 5 F4
Tarn Ct LS29 218 C3
Tarn Moor Cres BD23 216 E6
Tarns La BD23 134 C1
Tarr Steps TS17 6 A3
Tasmania Sq TS7 7 C6
Tate Cl YO8 197 D6
Tatefield Pl 1 LS25 194 D1
Tate Hill YO22 208 E7
Tate Rd DL10 209 C8
Tatham Fells CE Prim Sch LA2 128 F3
Tatton Cl YO30 225 A1
Taurus Ct YO23 233 A1
Taylor Gr LS26 200 C6
Taylor Hill YO18 71 F7
Taylor La LS15 194 A7
Taylorsons Terr 2 YO22 208 E6
Taylor St 8 BB18 171 D1
Tayport Cl DL1 3 D8
Teal Cl Castleford WF10 200 E3
2 Filey YO14 101 A3
Teal Dr YO24 230 C8
Teal La 6 YO18 95 F7
Teal Rd DL1 3 E5
Teapottery The* DL8 60 E5
Teasel Gr 31 HG3 161 B3
Tebay Cl
2 Eastbourne DL1 3 D4
Middlesbrough TS7 7 D8
Tedder Ave TS17 6 B6
Tedder Rd YO24 227 B1
Tedworth Cl TS14 8 F5
Tees Bank Ave TS18 5 E6
Tees Cottage Pumping Sta* DL2 2 F4
Teesdale Ave DL3 3 A4
Teesdale Rd DL9 40 E4
Teesdale Terr 27 DL9 40 E4
Teesgate TS17 6 C8
Tees Grange Ave DL3 3 A5
Tees-Side Airport Sta DL2 4 F4
Teesside High Sch TS16 5 E5
Teesside Ind Est TS17 6 C5
Tees View
Gainford DL2 1 D7
Hurworth DL2 3 C1
Hurworth-on-Tees DL2 22 C8
Teeswater Dr 12 DL2 3 A7
Teesway DL2 4 A1
Telford Cl WF10 200 D4
Telford Terr 1 YO24 228 B2
Temperance Sq BD23 154 B3
Templar Cl DN14 202 F1
Templar Gdns LS22 180 C4
Templar Way YO8 232 C2
Temple Ave YO10 229 B4
Temple Bank DL8 59 A3
Temple Ct DL10 209 B6
Temple Garth YO23 230 C1
TEMPLE HIRST 203 E4
Temple La
Burton cum Walden DL8 82 D3
Copmanthorpe YO23 230 C1
Templemead YO31 228 E8
Temple Rd YO23 230 F4
Temple Sq DL10 209 B6
Temple St WF10 200 E4
Tems Side 3 BD24 131 D2
Tems St 2 BD24 131 D2
Tennant St YO8 232 B6
Tennent Rd YO24 227 B2
Tennis Court La YO61 143 A3
Tennyson Ave
1 Campsall DN6 206 E1
Harrogate HG1 219 E7
Scarborough YO12 212 F7
York YO30 228 C7
Tennyson Cl WF8 201 D2
Tennyson Way 3 WF8 201 B1
Tenter Fields YO7 88 D1
Tentergate Ave 4 HG5 221 A7
Tentergate Cl 3 HG5 221 A7
Tentergate Gdns 2 HG5 221 A7
Tentergate La HG5 221 A7
Tentergate Rd 5 HG5 221 A7
Tenter Hill LS23 188 D5
Tenters Cl WF11 201 E3
Ten Thorn La YO26 227 A4
Tern Pk 6 LS22 180 A1
TERRINGTON 119 F1
Terrington Bank YO60 119 C2
Terrington CE Prim Sch YO60 119 E1
Terrington Cl YO32 167 B8
Terrington Hall Sch YO60 119 F1
Terrington South Bank YO60 119 D1
Terrington View YO60 145 C5
Terror Twr* YO11 213 B6
Terry Ave YO1 233 B1
Terry Dicken Ind Est TS9 26 D6
Terry St YO23 228 C1
Tetherings La YO13 98 F5
Tewit Well Ave HG2 222 D8
Tewit Well Rd HG2 222 E7
Thackadale La YO17 121 A1
Thackeray Gr TS5 6 E8
Thacking La LA6 103 D4
Thames Ave
Guisborough TS14 8 E6
Thornaby TS17 6 B7
Thanet Rd YO24 227 D1
Thanets Ct 9 BD23 216 F3
Thatch Cl YO8 232 C4
Thatchers Croft YO23 230 C3
THEAKSTON 87 E8
Theakston Hargill DL8 87 E8
Theakston La DL10 209 C5
Theresa Cl 6 YO31 225 F1
Thickrash Brow LA2 129 A7
Thiefgate La DL8 86 E3
Thiefhole La DL7 65 B3
Thief La Barlow YO8 232 F1
York YO10 228 F3
THIMBLEBY 45 A2
Third Ave
10 Wetherby LS22 180 C3
York YO31 228 F5
Thirkleby Walk 1 YO10 229 D3
Thirkleby Way YO10 229 C4
THIRLBY 90 E7
Thirlby Way 8 TS14 8 F7
Thirlmere Cl 3 YO7 89 C4
Thirlmere Dr YO31 229 A6
Thirlway Dr HG4 214 B6
THIRN 86 B8
THIRSK 211 C2
Thirsk Bank
Angram Grange YO7 117 B8
Thornton-le-Moor DL7 65 B3
Thirsk Bsns Pk YO7 211 B2
Thirsk Ind Pk YO7 211 D2
Thirsk Mus* YO7 211 B3
Thirsk Prim Sch YO7 211 C4
Thirsk Racecourse* YO7 211 A3
Thirsk Rd
Eaglescliffe TS15 5 E2
Easingwold YO61 117 B1
Kirkby TS9 26 C6
Romanby DL6 210 F1
Thirsk Sch YO7 211 B1
Thirsk Sta YO7 89 D4
Thirsk Swimming Pool YO7 211 C2
Thirty Acre La HG5 163 A6
Thirwall Dr TS17 6 A4
Thistlebar Rd YO51 141 D2
Thistle Cl
Northallerton DL7 210 D1
Selby YO8 232 C2
Thistle Hill HG5 221 B3
Thistle Rise TS8 6 F6
THIXENDALE 170 E7
THOLTHORPE 142 D5
Thomas Gill Rd 7 HG3 137 F1
Thomason Foss (Waterfall)* YO22 31 C1

Thomas St
21 Cross Hills BD20 187 E8
6 Selby YO8 232 D6
2 York YO10 228 E3
Thompson Cl
9 Barlby YO8 198 B4
29 Scalby YO12 75 D5
Thompson Dr 2 YO32 167 B8
Thompson Pl 6 YO26 227 E5
Thompson Street E DL1 3 D7
Thompson Street W DL3 3 C7
THORALBY 58 E1
Thoresby La DL8 59 B5
Thoresby Rd YO24 227 B1
THORGANBY 193 B4
THORGILL 49 C3
Thorington Gdns TS17 6 B4
THORLBY 216 B6
THORMANBY 116 F5
Thornaby CE Prim Sch TS17 6 B7
Thornaby Com Sch TS17 6 B7
THORNABY-ON-TEES 6 A7
Thornaby Rd TS17 6 B7
Thornaby Swimming Pool TS17 6 A8
Thornbeck YO19 184 E6
THORNBOROUGH 87 C2
Thornborough Cres 4 DL8 60 D5
Thornbrough Rd DL6 210 E3
Thornburgh Rd 6 YO11 99 F6
Thorncroft 8 YO19 184 F7
Thorndale St BD23 154 B3
Thornden Bldgs YO8 232 D5
Thorndikes La HG5 141 A2
Thorne Cl 13 WF6 200 B1
Thorner CE Prim Sch LS14 188 A3
Thorner Gr BD20 174 C2
Thorner La LS23 188 B5
Thorner Rd LS23 188 B4
Thornfield Ave
Dishforth YO7 115 A4
5 York YO31 228 F8
Thornfield Bsns Pk DL7 210 B6
Thornfield Dr 7 YO31 225 E2
Thornfield Gr TS5 6 E8
Thornfield Rd DL8 87 C3
Thornhill
6 Eastfield YO11 100 A6
Northallerton DL6 210 E3
14 Richmond DL10 209 C6
Thornhill Rd WF10 200 F3
Thornhills 19 YO32 166 F5
Thornlands 9 YO61 117 D1
Thornley Ave DL7 210 D3
Thorn Nook YO31 228 F8
THORNS 35 E7
Thorns La YO51 140 F4
THORNTHWAITE 159 D6
Thornthwaite Brow HG3 159 E5
THORNTON 6 E4
Thornton Cl
15 Easingwold YO61 143 D8
Stainton & Thornton TS8 6 D4
Thornton Dale CE Prim Sch YO18 96 C5
Thornton Hts BD23 172 A3
THORNTON-IN-CRAVEN 172 A3
Thornton-in-Craven Prim Sch BD23 172 A3
THORNTON IN LONSDALE 103 C4
Thornton La Dent LA10 78 A4
Marishes YO17 96 B1
Thornton in Lonsdale LA6 103 C4
Thornton-on-the-Hill YO61 117 D4
THORNTON-LE-BEANS 65 B5
THORNTON-LE-CLAY 146 A4
THORNTON-LE-DALE 96 D5
THORNTON-LE-MOOR 65 B3
THORNTON-LE-STREET 65 D1
Thornton Moor Cl YO30 224 F2
Thornton Rd
Coulby Newham TS8 6 D4
Pickering YO18 96 A6
Thornton Road Ind Est YO18 96 A5
THORNTON RUST 58 B4
Thornton St
14 Burley in Warfedale LS29 176 C1
Darlington DL3 3 C5
3 Skipton BD23 216 D3
THORNTON STEWARD 61 D1
Thornton Vale TS8 6 E4
THORNTON WATLASS 86 D8
Thornton Watlass CE Prim Sch HG4 86 D8
Thorn Tree Ave 6 YO14 101 B4
Thorntree Gdns DL2 4 C4
Thorntree Gr YO30 225 B2
Thorntree La DN14 207 C6
Thorntree Rd
Northallerton DL6 210 F6
Thornaby TS17 6 B7
Thornview Rd BD23 154 B3
Thorn Wath La YO62 48 E4
Thornwood Ave TS17 6 A5
Thornwood Covert 1 YO24 227 C1
Thorny Hill La YO51 141 E2
Thorny La YO42 169 F2
THORP ARCH 188 F8
Thorp Arch Pk LS23 180 F1
Thorp Arch Trad Est LS23 189 A8
THORPE 156 F8
Thorpe Bank 6 YO22 33 C3
THORPE BASSETT 123 A4
Thorpe Bassett La YO17 122 E1
Thorpe Chase HG4 214 E3
Thorpe Green Bank 1 YO22 33 C3
Thorpe Green La YO26 164 B7
Thorpe La
Ampleforth YO62 118 B8
Cawood YO8 197 B8
Cracoe BD23 156 C7
Fylingdales YO22 33 C4
Thorpe BD23 156 D8
Thorpe Prebend House - Heritage Ctr* HG4 214 C5
Thorpe Rd HG4 86 C2
Thorpe St YO23 228 B2
THORPE UNDERWOOD 164 C6
THORPE WILLOUGHBY 197 C2
Thorpe Willoughby Prim Sch YO8 197 B2
Thorp Perrow Arboretum & Falconry Ctr* DL8 87 A8
Threapland BD23 156 C7
Three Lakes Ind Est YO8 232 D2
Three Lakes Ret Pk YO8 232 D3
Three Lane Ends Junior & Infant Sch WF10 200 D4
Three Tuns Wynd 7 TS9 26 C7
THRESHFIELD 134 D2
Threshfield Prim Sch BD23 134 D2
THRINTOFT 64 A8
Thrintoft La DL7 64 A7
Thrintoft Moor La DL7 64 A8
Thrope La HG3 110 C4
Throstle Farm Junior & Infant Sch WF11 201 F1
Throstle Nest Cl LS21 176 E1
Throstle Nest Dr HG2 222 D6
THROXENBY 212 A7
Throxenby Gr 3 YO12 212 B7
Throxenby La YO12 212 B7
THRUSCROSS 159 A5
Thruscross La HG3 159 B5
Thrussendale Rd YO17 169 E8
Thunderhead Ridge WF10 200 F3
Thurland Castle* LA6 102 B3
Thurston Rd DL6 210 C7
THWAITE 35 F5
Thwaite Holme La DL8 57 F5
Thwaite La LA2 128 E5
Thwaites Ave LS29 218 C4
Thwaites La Markington with Wallerthwaite HG3 139 D5
Nether Silton YO7 66 C7
Thirkleby High & Low with Osgodby YO7 90 E1
Thweng Way TS14 8 E5
THWING 126 B1
Thwing Rd YO25 126 E2
Tibby Butts 26 YO13 75 D5
Tibgarth LS22 180 A2
Tickergate La DL7 63 A8
Tidkin La TS14 8 E6
Tile Cl BD23 217 B3
Tillman Cl 6 BD24 131 D2
Tillotson's Ct BD20 173 D1
Tilmire Cl 2 YO10 231 F8
TIMBLE 176 D7
Timble Gr HG1 219 B5
Timmys La DL2 3 F1
Tindall St YO12 212 F5
Tinker La YO23 182 D6
Tinkers' La HG3 139 A1
Tinkingfield La LS22 181 A5
Tinkler La Milby YO51 141 C6
Winsley HG3 160 E8
Tinkler's La WF11 202 D6
Tinley Garth YO62 70 B1
Tinley Gdns 14 YO62 70 B1
Tintagel Ct WF6 200 A2
Tiplady Cl 18 YO61 143 C8
Tippaty La WF11 202 A4
Tirril Way TS7 7 C5
Tithe Barn Fold LS15 194 B8
Tithe Barn Rd 2 WF11 202 A2
Tithe Barn Way DN14 202 F3
Tithe Cl YO24 227 B1
Tithe Way HG4 114 F1
Tivoli Pl LS29 218 C3
Toadham La DN14 207 C5
Toby Ct YO32 167 A7
TOCKWITH 181 D7
Tockwith CE Prim Sch YO26 181 C7
Tockwith La YO26 181 D6
Tockwith Rd
Long Marston YO26 181 F6
Tockwith LS22 180 F7
Toc La YO18 97 C5
Todd La DL7 63 B8
Todds Ct 8 YO7 211 C3
Tod Holes La BD23 153 B4
Todley Hall Rd BD22 187 F3
Todmanhaw La BD23 153 E3
Tofta Rd YO13 54 A5
Toft Gn YO1 233 A2
Tofting La YO17 148 B5
Toft Ings La YO61 143 B8
Tofts Cl TS15 24 B8
Tofts Fort The* DL11 1 E2
Tofts La
Danby YO21 29 B5
Follifoot HG3 223 F4
Humberton YO61 141 F8
Pickering YO18 95 F3
Tholthorpe YO61 142 D6
Welbury DL6 24 B1
Tofts Rd YO17 95 F3
Toll Bar Cl 3 YO8 196 E1
Toll Bar Rd WF10 200 C4
Toll Bar Way LS24 189 F7
Tollergate YO11 213 A7
TOLLERTON 143 A3
Tollerton La YO30 165 B7
Tollerton Rd YO61 143 D4
TOLLESBY 7 A6
Tollesby Bridge TS8 7 A6
Tollesby La TS7 7 B6
Tollesby Rd TS5 6 F8
Tollesby Specl Sch TS4 6 F8
Toll Hill Ct WF11 201 A3
Toll Hill Dr WF11 201 A3
Tomahawk Trail WF10 200 F3
Tom Cat La Bilton-in-Ainsty with Bickerton LS22 181 A5
Birdsall YO17 148 B4
Tom Dando Cl WF6 200 C1
Tomgill Bank DL8 58 E2
Tom Hall Ct 12 DL8 63 A2
Tom La
Cowling BD22 186 E7
Dunsforths YO26 141 F3
Hillam LS25 202 B7
Tomlinson Way LS25 195 E4
Tom Smith's Cross YO62 92 B4
Topcliff Ct YO8 232 B7
TOPCLIFFE 115 B7
Topcliffe CE Prim Sch YO7 115 C7
Topcliffe Rd Sowerby YO7 89 E3
Thirsk YO7 211 B1
Thornaby TS17 6 C7
Top Fold WF11 201 D6
Top House Ct WF8 206 B3
Top House Farm Mews 2 WF11 201 D6
Top La Colne BB8 186 B2
Copmanthorpe YO23 230 B3
Norwood LS21 177 A6
Top Stone Cl LS25 201 F6
Toremill Cl YO32 225 D4
Torrance Dr DL1 3 F8
Torridon Pl YO24 230 B7
Torrs Rd HG1 220 A3
TOSSIDE 152 F3
Tostig Ave YO26 227 C5
Tostig Cl 14 YO41 168 D2
Totten La YO62 120 D7
TOULSTON 189 B7
Toulston La LS23 188 F5
Tout Hill YO60 146 E5
Tower Cres LS24 189 D6
Tower Croft 7 YO61 117 D1
Tower Ct YO30 225 A2
Tower Grange DL3 3 B7
Tower Pl YO1 233 B1
Tower Rd
Darlington DL3 3 B6
Ripon HG4 214 C6
Towers Paddock WF10 201 A4
Tower St
Harrogate HG1 219 D1
10 Richmond DL10 209 C6
York YO1 233 B1
Tower Street Castle W 4 DL10 209 C6
Tower View DN14 204 C2
Townclose View LS25 200 C8
Town End YO7 211 B2
Town End Ave DN14 204 C3
Town End Cl
16 Glusburn BD20 187 E7
2 Kirklevington TS15 24 F8
9 Pickering YO18 96 A6
Townend Ct 3 YO26 164 A8
Town End Gdns 3 YO32 166 D5
Townend Pl 5 BD20 187 E7
Townend Rd YO42 193 D1
Townend St YO31 233 B4
Town Farm Cl 15 YO62 70 B1
Town Green Dr TS9 26 E5
TOWN HEAD 174 C1
Townhead 2 BD24 131 E2
Town Head Ave 1 BD24 131 E2
Townhead Croft BD24 131 E3
Town Head Fold 12 LS29 174 F4
Townhead La LA2 130 E8
Townhead Way BD24 131 E2
Town Head Way 14 BD24 131 D2
Town Hill LS23 188 E5
Town St
Bishop Thornton HG3 138 F1
Brandsby-cum-Stearsby YO61 118 D3
Malton YO17 215 E6
Nidd HG3 161 E7
Scampston YO17 123 A6
Settrington YO17 122 C1
Townville Infant Sch WF10 201 B4
Tow Scar Rd LA6 103 C5
TOWTHORPE Duggleby 149 D1
York 167 B5
Towthorpe Moor La YO32 167 C5
Towthorpe Rd YO32 166 F5
TOWTON 189 E2
Towton Ave 9 YO24 227 F2
Tow Top La BD20 173 A1
Trafalgar Ct 10 HG1 219 D1
Trafalgar Rd
11 Harrogate HG1 219 D1
Ilkley LS29 218 B4
Scarborough YO12 212 F7
Trafalgar Sq
Meagill LS21 159 E4
Scarborough YO12 212 F7
Trafalgar St YO23 228 B1
Trafalgar Street W YO12 212 F6
Trafalgar Terr YO12 212 F7
Trafford Ct 19 DL1 3 F6
Trafford Rd 4 DN6 206 E2
Train La 14 YO18 95 F7
Tranby Ave YO10 229 D4
Tranmere Ct 2 BD23 153 F5
Tranmire Cl YO7 211 D4
Tranmore La DN14 203 B3
Trans Wlk LS24 190 B1
Tranter Rd TS4 6 F8
Trapping Hill HG3 110 C4
Trattles Hill YO13 54 D2
Travellers Garth YO17 121 C1
TRAWDEN 186 B1
Trawden Forest Prim Sch 4 BB8 186 A1
Trawden Rd BB8 186 A3
Treasurer's House* YO1 233 B3
Trecastell 25 TS17 5 F4
Treesdale Rd 1 HG2 219 C1
Trefoil Cl TS14 8 D6
Trefoil Dr 4 HG3 161 B3
Trefoil Wood TS7 7 B7
Trencar La YO61 91 A2
Trenchard Ave TS17 6 B6
Trenchard Rd YO26 227 B6
Trenchard St 8 YO7 89 B1
Trenfield Ct YO24 227 F3
Trenholme Cl 7 TS17 6 D6
Trenholme La TS15 25 B3
Trent Ave
Garforth LS25 194 D3
Pontefract WF6 200 A2
4 York YO32 225 F6
Trentholme Dr 2 YO24 228 A2
Trent Way YO24 230 D7
Trevine Gdns TS17 5 F4
Trevino Ct TS16 5 E5
Trevithick Cl 7 TS16 5 D5
Trevithick Rd WF10 200 E6
Trevor Gr 8 YO24 227 F2
Triangle The TS14 8 D6
Tribune Way YO30 225 B2
Trimdon Ave TS5 6 D6
Trinity Church Sq 9 DL10 209 C6
Trinity Cl 1 YO11 212 F3
Trinity Gdns
Northallerton DL6 210 F3
2 Scarborough YO11 212 F3
Trinity La
Ripon HG4 214 B5
York YO1 233 A2
Trinity Mdws YO32 167 D3
Trinity Mews DL3 3 C5
Trinity Pk HG4 214 B6
Trinity Rd
Darlington DL3 3 C5
Harrogate HG2 219 D1
Scarborough YO11 212 F3
Trinket La LA2 128 B6
Trip Garth LS22 180 A1
Trip La
Collingham LS22 180 A1
Sicklinghall LS22 179 F1
Triplins La HG4 113 B6
Tristram Ave DL3 3 C7
Troon Cl 2 YO26 227 B5
Trousdale Hill YO60 147 A7
Troutbeck 7 YO24 230 C7
Troutbeck Cl 11 YO18 95 F6
Troutsdale Ave YO30 224 E2
Trumfleet La DN6 207 D1
Trundles La 7 WF11 202 A2
Truro Cres 8 HG3 161 B3
Truro Dr 19 WF6 200 A2
Truro Rd 7 HG3 161 B3
Truro Wlk 23 WF6 200 A2
Trust Fold LS25 201 E6
Tubwell Rd DL1 3 C5
Tucker Cl DL6 210 E5
Tudor Cl 10 YO8 197 B1
Tudor Ct 7 DL10 41 C7Tudor Rd
Richmond DL10 209 D7
York YO24 227 C2
Tudor Way YO32 167 C8
Tufton Pl BD23 216 F3
Tuke Ave YO10 229 B4
Tumbledown Cl 5 DL9 40 E3
Tune St YO8 198 B4
TUNSTALL Catterick 41 B2
Cowan Bridge 102 B4
Tunstall Rd
Catterick DL10 41 D4
Harrogate HG2 220 B3
Turbary La YO32 226 E6
Turbary Rd LA6 103 B7
Turfy Hill DL8 56 C4
Turker Cl DL6 210 E5
Turker La DL6 210 F6
Turkey La Baldersby YO7 88 D1
Catton YO7 114 F8
Turkhan Cl YO7 211 A2
Turkish Baths & Health Spa HG2 219 C2
Turks Head Ct YO1 233 C3
Turnberry Ave TS16 5 E4
Turnberry Dr YO26 227 B4
Turnberry Way TS8 7 C5
Turner Cl DL9 209 C2
Turner Cres 6 LS21 177 A1
Turner La 4 LS29 174 E4
Turner's Croft YO10 229 A1
Turners Sq 9 YO8 232 C5
Turner St 13 BB18 171 E1
Turnham La YO8 198 C2
Turnhead Cres YO8 198 B5
Turnhead Ct YO8 198 B6
Turnmire Rd 1 YO24 230 E8
Turnpike La LS22 181 B5
Turnpike Rd LS24 189 F7
Turnshaw Rd BD22 187 F1
Turpin Ct YO1 233 C1
Turpin La LS25 196 A2
Turton Rd TS15 5 D2
Turver's La WF11 202 C2
Tuscany Way WF6 200 A3
Tuthill 13 YO11 213 B6
Tutin Rd DL7 63 C5
Tweed Ave TS17 6 B7
Tweed St 5 LA2 129 A8
Twelve Acre Bank DL9 40 E1
Twine Wlk 7 LA6 102 F3
Twin Pike Way 14 YO32 166 D5
Twizzie Gill View 6 TS13 11 A8
Two Laws Rd BB8 187 B1
Tyler Cl WF6 200 C1
Tyne Cres DL1 3 D3
Tyn Garth YO19 191 D8
Typhoon Cl DL10 41 F6
Tyseley Gr 4 BB18 172 A1
Tyson Pl HG2 220 B2

U

UCKERBY 21 E1
UGGLEBARNBY 32 C6
UGTHORPE 11 F2
Uldale Cl 5 HG5 221 D5
Uldale Dr TS16 5 E4
Ulla Gn LS24 190 B1
ULLESKELF 190 C2
Ulleskelf Sta LS24 190 B2
Ullswater YO24 230 D7
Ullswater Ave TS5 6 E8
Ullswater Dr LS22 180 B3
Ullswater Rise 5 LS22 180 B3
Ulnaby La DL2 2 C7
ULSHAW 61 A2
Ulswater Ave 5 DL1 3 D4
Under Cliffe 17 YO18 95 F7
Undercliffe Rise LS29 218 E2
Undercroft 7 YO19 184 F7
Underlands 4 HG4 114 C7
Underwit Rd YO8 204 C4
Union House BD23 217 A3
Union La YO8 232 C4
Union Rd 24 YO21 208 D6
Union St
28 Filey YO14 101 B3
Harrogate HG1 219 D3
2 Knaresborough HG5 221 A5
12 Scarborough YO11 213 A6
Union Terr
5 Skipton BD23 216 F3
York YO31 233 B4
Unity Cl HG1 219 D5
Unity Gr HG1 219 D5
Unity St 1 BB18 186 A7
University of Hull (Scarborough Campus) YO12 213 B1
University of Leeds (Headley Hall) LS24 189 A4
University of York (King's Manor) YO30 233 A3
University of York (Main Campus) YO10 229 A1
University Rd YO10 228 F2
University of Hull @ Scarborough YO11 213 B1
Upgang La YO21 208 B7
Upgarth Cl 2 TS13 12 A7
Uplands BD23 217 B5
Uplands Ave 8 YO13 99 B8
Uplands Rd DL3 3 B5
Uplands The YO12 212 A7
Upper Carr La YO18 96 A4
Uppercommon La DN14 202 F3
Uppercroft 4 YO32 225 C8
UPPER DUNSFORTH 142 A2
Upper Dunsforth Carrs Nature Reserve* YO26 142 A1
Uppergate LA6 103 D4
Upper Green La TS18 6 A7
Upper Hanover St 6 YO26 227 F5
UPPER HELMSLEY 168 B3
Upper Newborough St 1 YO30 228 C7
UPPER POPPLETON 165 F1
Upper Price St YO23 233 A1
Upper Sackville St 5 BD23 217 A3
Upper St Paul's Terr YO24 228 A4
Upper Union St BD23 216 F3
Upper Wharfedale Folk Mus* BD23 134 E2

Upper Wharfedale Sch BD23 134 D2
Uppleby YO61 117 D1
UPSALL 66 B2
Upsall Dr DL3 3 C4
Upsall La
South Kilvington YO7 211 C7
Thornborough YO7 90 A8
Upsall YO7 66 B1
Upsall Rd YO7 66 B1
Upwell Rd DL7 210 D4
URE BANK 214 D7
Ure Bank HG4 214 D7
Ure Bank Maltings HG4 214 D8
Ure Bank Terr HG4 214 C7
Ure Bank Top HG4 214 D7
Uredale Glass* HG4 86 C3
URLAY NOOK 5 B5
Urlay Nook Rd TS16 5 C5
URRA 47 A8
Usher La YO32 166 F6
Usk Ct 21 TS17 5 F4

V

Vale Ave WF11 201 E2
Vale Cres
Bishop Wilton YO42 169 F2
Knottingley WF11 201 E2
Vale Crest WF11 201 E2
Vale Ct HG5 221 A6
Vale Gdns LS29 218 D4
Vale The
10 Collingham LS22 188 A8
Middlesbrough TS5 6 F8
Skelton YO30 224 B5
Vale View HG4 114 B2
Valient Way TS17 6 B6
Valley Bride Rd 16 YO11 213 F5
Valley Bridge Par YO11 213 A5
Valley Dr
Barnoldswick BB18 171 E2
Eaglescliffe TS15 5 E3
Great Preston LS26 200 C8
Harrogate HG2 219 C1
Ilkley LS29 218 D4
Valley Gdn TS16 5 D4
Valley Gdns* HG2 219 C2
Valley Mill Ct BB8 186 C3
Valley Mount HG2 219 C2
Valley Rd
Barnoldswick BB18 171 E1
3 Darley HG3 160 A6
32 Earby BB18 172 A1
Harrogate HG2 219 C2
Ilkley LS29 218 D5
Kippax LS25 194 C2
Northallerton DL6 210 F3
Scarborough YO12 212 E4
Whitby YO21 208 A8
Valley Ridge LS25 194 C2
Valley Street N DL1 3 D5
Valley View
3 Ampleforth YO62 92 C1
Clint HG3 160 F8
Danby YO21 29 C6
3 Glusburn BD20 187 E8
Wheldrake YO19 192 F7
Valuation La 1 YO51 141 B5
Vanbrugh Dr YO10 229 C3
Vanbrugh Way YO10 229 A2
Vane Ct TS21 4 F7
Vane Terr DL3 3 C5
Van Mildert Way TS18 5 F8
Vasey Cl 5 DL8 63 B2
Vaughan Rd 10 DN6 206 E1
Vavasour Ct YO23 230 B2
Vaynor Dr 17 TS17 5 F4
Venables Rd TS14 8 E7
Verity Wlk HG2 222 D7
Vernon Cl YO23 231 A3
Vernon Ct TS8 6 E5
Vernon Gr 4 YO12 212 D8
Vernon Pl 3 YO11 213 A5
Vernon Rd
Harrogate HG2 222 E7
2 Scarborough YO11 213 A5
Trawden Forest BB8 186 B3
York YO30 224 E2
Vesper Dr YO24 227 B3
Vesper Wlk YO32 225 F6
Vicarage Cl
2 Bubwith YO8 199 D7
12 Hunmanby YO14 126 F8
Seamer YO12 99 D6
Vicarage Farm Cl YO17 124 D8
Vicarage Gdns 1 YO10 229 C4
Vicarage La
Bishop Wilton YO42 169 F2
Bramham LS23 188 E5
10 Knaresborough HG5 221 A6
Naburn YO19 191 E8
Sherburn YO17 124 D8
Vicarage Rd
Barnoldswick BB18 171 E2
16 Catterick Garrison DL9 40 E4
Darlington DL1 3 D5
3 Kelbrook & Sough BB18 186 A7
Vicar Hill La YO7 116 D8
Vicars Cl YO23 230 B2
Vicars Croft DL6 210 E5
VICAR'S GREEN 39 F7
Vicar's La YO61 144 C6
Vicars Terr WF10 200 D6
Vickers Cl TS18 5 F7
Vickers Rd 2 DL9 40 E4
Vickers St 1 WF10 200 E4
Victoria Arc LS29 218 A4
Victoria Ave
10 Filey YO14 101 B3
Harrogate HG1 219 D2
Ilkley LS29 175 C2
Knaresborough HG5 221 B8
Ripon HG4 214 D5
Thirsk YO7 211 B2
Victoria Cave* BD24 131 F4
Victoria Cl
Great Preston WF10 200 E6
Ilkley LS29 218 A4
26 Sherburn in Elmet LS25 195 F4
Victoria Ct
25 Sherburn in Elmet LS25 195 F4
15 York YO26 227 F5
Victoria Dr 9 LS29 175 C2
Victoria Emb DL1 3 C4
Victoria Farm Cl YO23 182 C6
Victoria Gdns 17 LS29 175 C2
Victoria Gr 5 Ilkley LS29 175 C2
Ripon HG4 214 C5
Victoria Mews 45 BB18 172 A1
Victoria Par 13 YO11 212 F5
Victoria Park Ave 2 YO12 212 F7
Victoria Park Mount YO12 212 E7
Victoria Pk 1 YO12 212 F7
Victoria Pl 3 YO21 208 D6
Victoria Rd
1 Barnoldswick BB18 171 E1
28 Burley in Warfedale LS29 176 C1
Cowling BD22 187 B6
Darlington DL1 3 C5
Earby BB18 172 A1
Glusburn BD20 187 E7
Harrogate HG2 219 C1
10 Ilkley LS29 175 C2
1 Malton YO17 215 B4
Richmond DL10 209 B7
Scarborough YO11 212 F5
Thornaby TS17 6 B8
Victoria Sh Ctr HG1 219 D2
Victoria Sq Skipton BD23 216 F4
21 Whitby YO21 208 D6
Victoria St
24 Earby BB18 172 A1
43 Glusburn BD20 187 E7
Great Preston WF10 200 D6
Pontefract WF8 201 B2
Scarborough YO12 212 F6
Settle BD24 131 E2
10 Skipton BD23 216 F4
1 York YO23 233 B1
Victoria Terr
1 Harrogate HG1 220 C4
Northallerton DL7 210 D4
3 Skipton BD23 216 F4
Victoria Way 2 YO32 228 F8
Victoria Works Ind Est BD20 187 F8
Victor St YO1 233 B1
Victory Rd LS29 218 B4
Viewley Hill Ave TS8 6 F5
Viewley Hill Prim Sch TS8 6 F5
Viking Cl 20 YO41 168 D2
Viking Dr 5 YO19 197 F8
Viking Rd
Stamford Bridge YO41 168 D2
York YO26 227 C5
Vikings Ct 6 DL6 43 F3
Villa Cl YO8 198 F1
Villa Ct YO26 227 B7
Villa Fields 4 DN14 204 C1
Village Farm Cl 9 DN14 202 D4
Village Farm Ct 7 DN14 202 D4
Village Fold DL7 42 B1
Village Garth 1 YO32 166 E5
Village Paddock TS18 5 E8
Village Prim Sch TS17 6 B7
Village Rd TS15 24 B8
Village St YO30 224 E3
Village The
Boston Spa LS23 180 F1
Haxby YO32 166 E5
Skelton YO30 224 B5
Stockton on the Forest YO32 167 D2
Strensall YO32 167 B7
York YO10 229 C4
Village Wy DL7 42 B1
Villa Gr 2 YO31 228 E6
Villiers Ct 8 YO62 92 F6
Vimy Rd DL9 40 E3
Vincent St 9 YO12 213 A7
Vincent Way YO24 230 C8
Vine Cl TS14 8 F6
Vine Farm Cl YO26 164 A4
Vine Gdns YO8 199 D7
Vine Gr YO17 215 E4
Vine St Darlington DL3 3 B6
Norton YO17 215 E4
6 Scarborough YO12 212 F6
York YO23 228 C2
Vinstra Cl DL10 209 D8
Virginia Gdns TS5 6 E6
Vivars Way YO8 232 D5
Vivers Pl 1 YO62 70 C1
Vivis La YO18 95 F6
Volta St YO8 232 E4
Vulcan Way TS17 6 B6
Vyner St Ripon HG4 214 D4
York YO31 228 C7

W

Waddington St 37 BB18 172 A1
Wade House La YO8 204 F4
Waggoners Dr 3 YO23 230 B3
Wain Cl
15 Eastfield YO11 100 B7
South Milford LS25 195 E2
Waincroft 8 YO32 167 A6
Wainds Field 30 YO62 70 B1
Waindyke Way WF6 200 B1
Wainers Cl 5 YO23 230 B3
Wainfleet Rd HG1 219 D6
Wain Gap LS25 195 F2
Waingates La YO51 140 F4
Wainman's Cl BD22 187 B6
Wain's Gr YO24 230 D7
Wain's La YO12 99 D2
Wain's Rd YO24 230 D8
Wainstones Cl TS9 7 F1
Wainstones Dr TS9 7 F1
Waite La YO13 53 F2
WAITHWITH BANKS 40 B5
Waithwith Rd DL9 209 B1
Waitlands La DL11 20 A7
Wakefield Rd
Garforth LS25 194 B3
10 Normanton South WF6 200 A1
Swillington LS26 194 A2
WAKE HILL 111 F1
Wakeman Rd HG4 214 C3
Walburn Head DL11 39 D3
WALDEN STUBBS 206 F3
Walden Stubbs Rd DN6 206 E2
Wales St DL3 3 C7
Walker Cl BD20 187 D7
Walker Dr YO24 230 C8
Walker La
Menwith with Darley HG3 160 A6
Wheldrake YO19 192 F7
Walkers Fold HG5 221 B5
Walker's La BD20 174 B4
Walkers Row TS14 8 F7
Walker St YO21 208 D6
Walker Terr HG3 223 F4
WALKERVILLE 41 A4
Walkerville Ave 22 DL9 41 A5
Walkerville Ind Est DL9 41 B5
Walkington La YO30 165 B8
Walled Gdn The* YO17 123 A6
Wallgates La YO17 215 D4
Walmer Carr
Haxby YO32 166 D5
Wigginton YO32 166 D5
Walmgate YO1 233 C2
WALMGATE STRAY 228 F1
Walmsley Gdns YO12 212 C5
Walney Rd YO31 229 A5
Walnut Cl
39 Haxby YO32 166 E5
Saxton with Scarthingwell LS24 195 D8
38 Wigginton YO32 166 E5
York YO10 229 A1
Walnut Gn YO17 215 E3
Walnut Gr HG1 219 E6
Walpole St YO31 228 D7
WALSHFORD 180 D8
Waltham Cl YO32 167 B8
WALTON 181 A2
Walton Ave
Gargrave BD23 155 C1
Middlesbrough TS5 6 E8
Pannal HG3 222 F2
Walton Chase LS23 180 F2
Walton Cl YO61 144 A4
Walton Head La HG3 178 F4
Walton Pk HG3 222 E2
Walton Pl Pannal HG3 222 E2
York YO26 227 B3
Walton Rd
Gargrave BD23 172 C8
Walton LS23 181 A2
Wetherby LS22 180 E2
Walton St
5 Cowling BD22 187 B6
Skipton BD23 216 F1
Walworth Ave HG2 220 B3
Walworth Street N 4 YO26 227 F5
Walworth Street S 9 YO26 227 F5
Wandale La YO17 95 A2
Wandales Cl YO17 215 F3
Wandales Ct YO13 75 D8
Wandales Dr YO13 75 D8
Wandales La YO60 146 B6
Wandales Rd YO13 75 D8
Wandell Balk YO61 144 B6
Wandels La YO21 29 B6
Wandesford Gr DL9 209 F1
Wandhill 31 YO32 166 E5
Wand Hill TS12 9 E8
Wandhill Gdns TS12 9 E8
Wandhill La YO7 66 D1
Wand La DN14 203 C3
Wandle The YO26 227 A2
Wansbeck 3 YO24 230 B7
Wapping La YO62 94 C7
Warbler Cl 11 TS17 6 A5
Wardale Ave TS5 6 E6
Ward Ct YO23 233 B1
War Dike La YO13 54 B6
Wardrop Rd DL9 209 C1
Ward St BD23 217 A4
Wareham Rd YO11 99 F6
Warehill La YO61 143 C2
War Field La LS22 180 F6
WARLABY 64 D6
Warlbeck 23 LS29 175 C2
Warley Wise La BB8 186 D6
Warren Ave WF11 201 E2
Warren Cl DL1 3 F4
Warrener La DL10 20 C6
Warren La Bramham cum Oglethorpe LS24 189 A5
Brearton HG3 162 A8
Kirkby Malzeard HG4 112 D4
Warren Pl HG1 219 D5
WARSILL 138 C4
WARTHERMARSKE 86 A1
WARTHILL 167 F2
Warthill CE Prim Sch YO19 167 F2
Warth La LA6 103 C3
Warwick Cl YO60 145 D5
Warwick Cres HG2 222 E8
Warwick Dr 2 BB18 172 A1
Warwick Pl 2 YO62 92 F7
Warwick St YO31 228 D7
Wasdale Cl 2 YO30 224 E1
Washbeck Cl YO12 212 E4
Wash Beck La YO62 93 F6
Washbrook Dr DL3 3 C8
Washburn Cl 13 YO14 101 A3
Washburn Cotts LS21 159 F1
Washburn Courts HG3 159 F1
Washburn Dr 4 BD20 187 E8
WASHFOLD 18 D1
Washfold La DL8 60 B6
Washford Cl TS17 6 A3
Washington Ave DL2 4 D4
Washington Cl HG4 214 E2
WASS 91 F2
Wass Bank Rd YO61 91 F2
Wass Way TS16 5 D5
Waste La YO62 48 F2
Watchet Rd 11 DL9 40 E4
Water Avens Way TS18 6 A7
Water Bag Bank 8 HG5 221 A6
Waterdale Pk YO31 225 E1
Water End YO26 227 E5
Waterfall Fold 1 WF8 201 C2
Waterfalls Wlk* LA6 103 D6
WATER FRYSTON 201 C5
Water Gap YO18 97 B5
Water Garth DN14 202 F4
Watergate
Mickletown LS26 200 A5
7 Pontefract WF8 201 B1
Watergate Rd HG3 139 A4
Water Hill La YO8 232 D6
Waterhouse La 29 YO11 213 A6
Water Houses BD24 132 E6
Waterings 19 YO32 166 D5
Water La
Camblesforth YO8 204 D5
8 Clifton YO30 225 A1
Dalton YO7 115 E7
Dunnington YO19 184 F7
Eggborough DN14 203 A2
Exelby, Leeming & Newton DL7 63 D4
Hemingbrough YO8 198 F1
Huttons Ambo YO60 147 C6
Kirby Grindalythe YO17 149 B6
Kirby Underdale YO41 170 A5
Kirk Smeaton WF8 206 C3
Knaresborough HG5 221 C8
Loftus TS13 10 E8
North Stainley with Sleningford HG4 113 C6
7 Pontefract WF8 201 C1
Selby YO8 232 C6
Sherburn YO17 124 D7
South Stainley with Cayton HG3 139 D2
Thorpe Bassett YO17 123 A3
Welburn YO60 146 E7
Whitby YO21 208 B3
York YO30 228 A7
Waterline Ind Est YO23 191 B7
Waterloo Grosmont YO22 31 C4
12 Richmond DL10 209 C6
Waterloo Cl WF10 200 C3
Waterloo Rd BB18 186 A7
Waterloo St
Harrogate HG1 219 E4
2 Richmond DL10 209 C6
Waterman Ct 3 YO24 227 B1
Watermill Cl HG4 113 C7
Watermill Croft HG4 113 C7
Watermill La HG4 113 C7
Waters End DL2 1 D7
Watershed Mill Bsns Ctr BD24 131 D3
Watershed Mill Visitor Ctr* BD24 131 D3
Waterside
3 Boroughbridge YO51 141 B6
Hemingbrough YO8 198 F1
Knaresborough HG5 221 A5
4 Ripon HG4 214 C4
Skipton BD23 216 F2
7 Thirsk YO7 211 C3
Waterside Gdns YO31 228 D8
Waterside Mdws LS25 194 F8
Water Skellgate HG4 214 C5
Waters La DL10 20 E3
Water Slack La YO26 164 C4
Watersmeet Cl 5 TS17 6 A3
Watersole La LS22 180 D2
Water St Earby BB18 172 A1
Gargrave BD23 155 D1
Malton YO17 215 C4
Skipton BD23 216 F4
Waterstead Cres 1 YO21 208 D5
Waterstead La YO21 208 C5
Water Street Prim Sch 15 BD23 216 F4
Water Way Garth DN14 207 F6
Watery La Airton BD23 155 A5
Giggleswick BD24 131 C1
Snape with Thorp DL8 86 F7
WATH Hovingham 119 F6
Pateley Bridge 137 A6
Ripon 114 A7
Wathcote Cl DL10 209 F8
Wathcote Pl DL10 209 F8
Wathgill Camp DL11 39 C3
Wath La Catton YO41 185 C8
Copgrove HG3 140 D1
High & Low Bishopside HG3 137 B6
Humberton YO61 141 E8
Ulleskelf LS24 190 B2
Wath Rd HG3 137 B5
Watlass La DL8 86 E8
Watlass Moor La HG4 86 D7
Watling Cl DL11 19 E6
Watling Rd WF10 201 C5
Watson Cl 9 YO14 127 A8
Watson's Houses 7 BD23 216 F4
Watson's La Newton Kyme cum Toulston LS24 189 B7
Norwood HG3 177 B8
Reighton YO14 127 D6
Watson St
4 Normanton South WF6 200 A1
York YO24 228 A3
Watson Terr 2 YO24 228 A3
Wattlers Cl YO23 230 C3
Wattlesyke LS22 188 C8
Wattle Syke LS22 180 B1
Wavell Com Infant & Junior Schs DL9 209 D1
Wavell Rd DL9 209 D1
Wavell St YO8 232 A6
Waveney Gr YO30 228 B8
Waver Ct LS24 195 F7
Waver La DL6 43 F8
Waverley Cl DN14 204 C2
Waverley Cres HG2 222 E8
Waverley St YO31 233 C3
Waydale Cl YO62 70 A2
Wayfaring Cl YO17 215 F2
Waynefleet Gr 3 YO10 229 A3
Wayne Tarbard Cl 12 HG4 113 D2
Wayside Ave HG2 220 B1
Wayside Cl 4 HG2 220 B1
Wayside Cres HG2 220 A1
Wayside Gr HG2 220 A1
Wayside Mews 12 BD20 174 C1
Wayside Terr LS17 178 B2
Wayside The DL2 3 E1
Waytail Slack TS13 10 D7
Weaponness Dr YO11 213 A2
Weaponness La
Eastfield YO11 99 F8
Scarborough YO11 212 F1
Weaponness Pk YO11 213 A2
Weaponness Valley Cl 5 YO11 212 F3
Weaponness Valley Rd YO11 212 E3
Weardale TS14 8 D5
Weardale Rd 20 DL9 40 E4
Weary Bank TS15 25 B8
Weavers Cl YO23 230 C3
Weavers Ct
3 Stokesley TS9 26 C7
Trawden BB8 186 A1
Weavers Gn DL7 210 C3
Weavers Pk
9 Copmanthorpe YO23 230 B3
York YO23 230 B3
WEAVERTHORPE 124 E1
Weaverthorpe CE Prim Sch YO17 124 E2
Webster Pl 1 WF6 200 A1
Weddall Cl YO24 227 F1
Wedderburn Ave HG2 220 C2
Wedderburn Cl HG2 220 C3
Wedderburn Dr HG2 220 B2
Wedderburn Infant Sch HG2 220 B2
Wedderburn Lodge 2 HG2 220 B1
Wedderburn Rd HG2 220 B2
Weedling Gate LS24 189 D4
Weeland Ct 16 WF11 202 A2
Weeland Rd DN14 202 E3
WEETON 178 C1
Weeton La LS17 178 D1
Weeton Sta LS17 178 B2
Weets View BB18 171 E2
Welbeck Ave DL1 3 E7
Welborn Cl YO10 229 A4
Welborn Ct YO11 99 F2
Welbourn Dr 12 YO12 99 D6
WELBURN Pickering 94 A7
Westow 146 D7
Welburn Gr TS7 7 D7
Welburn Hall Sch YO62 94 A7
Welburn La YO60 147 A8

Welburn Prim Sch YO60. 146 D6
WELBURY 24 B1
Welbury Cl 2 BB18 172 B1
Welfare Ave LS15 194 C8
Welford Rd 36 YO14 101 B3
Welham Hill YO17 147 E7
Welham Rd YO17 215 D3
WELL 87 A4
Welland Dr LS25 194 D3
Welland Rise YO26 227 D5
Well Bank DL8 87 A4
Wellbrook Cl TS17 6 B4
Well Cl Great & Little Preston LS25 200 C8
3 Whitby YO21 208 D7
Well Cl Terr 4 YO21 208 D7
Wellesley Cl YO30 225 A2
Wellesleys Mews DL10 209 B7
Wellfield Ct HG2 222 B6
Wellfield La 13 LS29 176 C1
Wellhouse St 5 BB18 171 E1
Wellington Ct 9 HG2 219 C2
Wellington Gdns 11 HG4 214 C4
Wellingtonia Dr 5 DN6 206 E1
Wellington Mews 9 HG4 214 C5
Wellington Pl DL10 209 B7
Wellington Rd
Ilkley LS29 218 B4
2 Whitby YO21 208 D6
Wellington Row YO1 233 A2
Wellington Sq 6 HG2 219 C2
Wellington St
1 Knaresborough HG5 221 B5
10 Ripon HG4 214 C5
12 Skipton BD23 217 A3
York YO10 228 E3
Wellington Terr YO21 208 D7
Wellington Way 4 DL10 41 C7
Well La Kippax LS25 194 D1
Redmire DL8 59 C5
Seamer TS9 6 F2
Snape with Thorp DL8 87 A6
South Milford LS25 195 F2
Yearsley YO61 118 C5
Wells Cl YO8 232 A5
Wells Gn DL10 21 D7
Wells La Barton DL10 21 D7
Kellington DN14 202 E3
Malton YO17 215 C4
Wells Mews 7 LS29 218 B3
Wellspring Cl TS17 6 D7
Wells Prom LS29 218 B4
Wells Rd LS29 218 B3
Wells Wlk 13 YO18 95 F7
Wells Wlk The LS29 218 B4
Welton Ave YO26 227 D5
Welton Ct YO21 208 C7
Welwyn Dr YO10 231 E8
Wemyss Rd 11 HG4 113 D2
Wendel Ave LS15 194 B8
Wend The BD23 173 A4
Wendy Ave HG4 214 B3
Wenham Rd YO24 230 C8
Wenlock Dr YO19 192 B6
Wenlock Terr YO10 228 D1
Wenning Ave LA2 129 A7
Wenning Bank LA2 130 A6
WENNINGTON 102 B1
Wennington Hall Sch LA2 102 B1
Wennington Rd LA2 128 A6
Wennington Sta LA2 128 B8
WENSLEY 60 A4
WENSLEYDALE 57 A5
Wensleydale Ave 2 BD23 217 B4
Wensleydale Creamery★ DL8 56 C4
Wensleydale Dr YO10 229 D4
Wensleydale Gdns 3 TS17 6 C7
Wensleydale Pottery★ DL8 56 D4
Wensleydale Rd 21 DL9 40 E4
Wensleydale Rly★ DL8 60 B5
Wensleydale Sch The DL8 60 D5
Wensley Gr HG2 222 D7
Wensley Rd
Harrogate HG2 222 D7
15 Leyburn DL8 60 D5
Northallerton DL7 210 B2
Wentcliffe Dr BB18 172 A1
Wentdale 1 WF8 206 C3
Wentworth Ave YO61 116 F5
Wentworth Cl
Camblesforth YO8 204 D4
Harrogate HG2 220 D4
3 Kellington DN14 203 A2
Wentworth Cres
Harrogate HG2 220 D3
2 Whitby YO21 208 B5
Wentworth Dr HG2 220 D4
Wentworth Gate LS22 180 A3
Wentworth Rd YO24 228 B2
Wentworth St YO17 215 B5
Wentworth Way
Eaglescliffe TS16 5 E4
5 Hunmanby YO14 126 F8
York YO10 228 F2
Werkdyke The YO1 233 C3
Werner Ct 4 WF10 200 F3
WESCOE HILL 178 B1
Wescoe Hill La LS17 178 B1
Wesley Cl 1 LA2 129 A8
Wesley Pl
7 Silsden BD20 174 C1
York YO1 233 C2
Wesley Rd YO22 33 C4
Wesley Sq 2 TS13 13 K2
Wesley Way 10 LA2 129 A8
Wesson Cl 6 DL9 40 E4
Westacres 5 DL2 4 C4
West Acres 2 WF11 201 E4
West Acres Cl 7 YO13 99 A7
WEST APPLETON 41 C1
West Auckland Rd DL3 3 A7
West Ave
Boston Spa LS23 180 E1
Burton Fleming YO25 126 E3
5 Easingwold YO61 143 D8
Filey YO14 101 B3
19 Scalby YO13 75 D5
WEST AYTON 99 A7
West Bank
Scarborough YO12 212 E4
York YO24 227 E3
West Bank Rd BD23 216 E4
WEST BARNBY 12 C3
West Barnby La YO21 12 B3
Westbeck Gdns TS5 6 F8
West Beck Way TS8 7 B6
Westborough 1 YO11 213 A5
Westbourne Ave
Harrogate HG2 222 D8
Whitby YO21 208 A6
Westbourne Cl YO21 208 A6
Westbourne Cres LS25 194 B3
Westbourne Gdns YO8 232 C4
Westbourne Gr
8 Pickering YO18 95 F7
3 Ripon HG4 214 C5
11 Scarborough YO11 213 A4
Selby YO8 232 C4
Whitby YO21 208 A6
Westbourne Pk YO12 212 E4
Westbourne Rd
Scarborough YO11 212 F3
Selby YO8 232 C4
Whitby YO21 208 A6
Westbourne Terr
Selby YO8 232 C4
Thirsk YO7 211 A2
West Brow YO13 98 C5
WEST BURTON 58 F1
West Burton CE Prim Sch DL8 58 F1
Westbury St TS17 6 B8
West Cam Rd BD23 79 E6
West Cl
Carthorpe DL8 87 E6
Middleton Tyas DL10 21 C4
Normanton WF6 200 A1
Swinton YO17 121 B4
WEST CLIFF 208 B7
West Cliff Ave 5 YO21 208 B7
West Cliffe Cnr 9 HG2 219 C1
Westcliffe Gr HG2 219 B1
West Cliffe Mews 5 HG2 219 C1
Westcliffe Mount HG2 219 B1
Westcliffe Terr HG2 219 B1
West Cliff Prim Sch YO21 208 C7
West Close Rd 13 BB18 171 D2
West Craven High Tech Coll BB18 171 E1
West Craven Sports Ctr BB18 171 E1
West Croft
19 Addingham LS29 174 F4
6 Glusburn BD20 187 E6
Westcroft La YO8 196 E1
West Ct
Muston YO14 100 F2
8 Riccall YO19 197 F8
West Dale LS23 180 E1
Westdene HG2 222 B7
West Dene BD20 174 B2
West Dike Rd YO18 71 F5
West Edge Rd WF8 206 A3
West End
Boston Spa LS23 180 E1
Guisborough TS14 8 E6
Hurworth-on-Tees DL2 3 E1
Hutton Rudby TS15 25 C5
Kirkbymoorside YO62 70 B1
Muston YO14 100 F2
Osmotherley DL6 45 B4
Pollington DN14 207 F6
Rawcliffe DN14 205 A2
Sheriff Hutton YO60 145 C5
Stokesley TS9 26 C7
Strensall YO32 167 A7
West End App LS24 190 B3
West End Ave
Appleton Roebuck YO23 190 F5
Harrogate HG2 222 D8
Richmond DL10 209 A7
West End Cl
North Duffield YO8 199 A8
9 Strensall YO32 167 B7
West End Ct 5 YO11 100 B6
West End Gdns
Eaglescliffe TS16 5 D4
Pollington DN14 207 F6
Westend La DN14 207 B6
West End Rd DN6 206 E2
West End View 4 YO11 100 B6
West End Way TS18 5 F8
WESTERDALE 28 E4
Westerdale 4 YO18 95 F6
Westerdale Ct 2 YO30 228 A6
Westerley Cres BD20 174 B1
Western Ave WF8 201 C1
Western Ct 15 WF8 201 C1
Western Gales Way 33 WF6 200 B1
Western Prim Sch HG2 219 C1
Western Rd BD23 217 B3
Westerns La HG3 139 C4
Western Terr YO32 225 D3
Western Way 1 YO18 95 E7
WESTFIELD 232 C4
WEST FIELD 227 A2
Westfield YO8 232 B4
Westfield Ave
Castleford WF10 200 E2
3 Eggborough DN14 202 F2
Rawcliffe DN14 205 A1
6 Scalby YO12 75 E5
Selby YO8 232 B4
Westfield Cl
2 Eggborough DN14 202 F2
21 Haxby YO32 166 E5
Rawcliffe DN14 205 A1
South Milford LS25 195 E2
Westfield Cres 12 LS24 189 E6
Westfield Ct
Copmanthorpe YO23 230 A2
1 South Milford LS25 195 F2
Westfield Dr
Hurworth-on-Tees DL2 3 E1
York YO10 231 D8
Westfield Gn YO26 181 C7
Westfield Gr
Allerton Bywater WF10 200 D7
4 Eggborough DN14 202 F2
12 Haxby YO32 166 D5
Westfield La
Exelby, Leeming & Newton DL8 63 C2
Kippax LS25 194 C1
Ledsham LS25 195 C1
Lockton YO18 72 E4
Normanby YO62 94 F4
Norton WF8 206 C2
South Milford LS25 195 F2
Thirsk YO7 211 A3
Thoralby DL8 58 D1
Thorganby YO19 193 A5
Thornton-le-Dale YO18 96 C5
Wigginton YO32 166 D5
West Field La
Arkendale HG5 163 A8
East Witton Town DL8 60 F1
Upper Poppleton YO26 165 E1
Westfield Mews 32 YO62 70 B1
Westfield Pl
19 Haxby YO32 166 E5
York YO24 227 A1
Westfield Prim Com Sch YO24 227 B2
Westfield Rd
1 Eggborough DN14 202 F2
20 Haxby YO32 166 E5
3 North Duffield YO8 199 A7
Rawcliffe DN14 205 A1
Selby YO8 232 B4
2 Stokesley TS9 26 C7
Tockwith YO26 181 C7
West Field Rd 2 BB18 171 D2
Westfields
Castleford WF10 200 E3
Richmond DL10 209 A7
Scorton DL10 41 E7
West Fields YO62 70 B1
Westfields Ct DL10 209 B7
Westfield Sq 8 LS24 189 E6
Westfield Terr
2 Great Preston WF10 200 D7
Tadcaster LS24 189 E6
9 Thornton Dale YO18 96 D5
Westfield Way YO17 215 F4
Westfold YO17 215 E6
WEST GARFORTH 194 B3
Westgarth
Collingham LS22 180 A2
Northallerton DL7 210 D4
West Garth
Cayton YO11 100 B6
Sherburn YO17 124 D8
Ulleskelf LS24 190 B3
West Garth Gdns 23 YO11 100 B6
Westgate
22 Barnoldswick BB18 171 D1
Eaglescliffe TS15 5 D3
Guisborough TS14 8 F6
Malton YO17 215 E6
Pickering YO18 95 E7
Rillington YO17 122 F5
Ripon HG4 214 C5
Tadcaster LS24 189 E6
Thirsk YO7 211 B2
West Gate
Thornton-le-Dale YO18 96 C5
Wetherby LS22 180 B3
Wykeham YO13 98 D6
Westgate Carr Rd YO18 95 D5
Westgate La
Malton YO17 215 D6
Thornton in Lonsdale LA6 103 C5
Westgate Rd 3 DL3 3 B7
West Gn 15 TS9 26 C7
West Gr
Bishop Thornton HG3 139 A2
Swinton YO17 121 B4
West Grove Rd HG1 219 D4
WEST HADDLESEY 203 A5
West Hall La LS29 175 A5
WEST HARLSEY 44 D5
WEST HESLERTON 123 F7
West Heslerton CE Prim Sch YO17 123 F6
Westholme 10 TS15 25 C5
Westholme Bank DL8 58 F2
Westholme Cres 2 HG4 86 C3
Westholme Ct 3 HG4 86 C3
Westholme Dr YO30 224 E1
Westholme Rd 1 HG4 86 C3
WESTHOUSE 103 C4
West Ing La BD23 171 A5
West Ings Cl 4 WF11 202 A3
West Ings Cres 5 WF11 202 A3
West Ings Ct 1 WF11 202 A3
West Ings La 2 WF11 202 A3
West Ings Mews 6 WF11 202 A3
West Ings Way 3 WF11 202 A3
WEST KNAPTON 123 B6
West La
Appleton Wiske DL6 24 A3
Askwith LS21 176 C3
Azerley HG4 112 F3
Bewerley HG3 136 E4
Boston Spa LS23 180 E1
Burniston YO13 54 C1
Burn YO8 203 C6
Burton Fleming YO25 126 E3
Caldwell DL11 1 B4
Cononley BD20 173 C2
Dalton-on-Tees DL2 22 D6
Danby YO21 29 C8
East Layton DL11 20 A8
Embsay BD23 217 D8
Hampsthwaite HG3 161 A4
Hornby DL6 23 F4
Littlethorpe HG4 214 A2
2 Low Bradley BD20 173 E3
Melsonby DL10 20 E7
Mickleby TS13 12 A4
Nether Silton YO7 66 B7
North Deighton LS22 179 F6
Snainton YO13 97 F5
Stillington YO61 143 F7
Sutton BD20 187 E6
Sykehouse DN14 207 F2
Whixley YO26 163 F5
West La Hill LA2 129 A6
Westland Cl 3 BD20 187 F7
Westlands
Bilton-in-Ainsty with Bickerton YO26 181 D5
6 Kirklevington TS15 24 E8
Pickering YO18 96 A7
Stokesley TS9 26 B7
Westlands Ave 1 YO21 208 C7
Westlands Gr YO31 228 F7
Westlands La YO7 211 A4
Westlands Rd DL3 3 B6
Westlands Sch TS17 6 C6
Westlands Way TS18 5 F8
WEST LAYTON 20 A8
West Lea Ave HG2 222 B7
WEST LILLING 145 C4
West Lodge Gdns YO17 215 A4
West Lund 17 YO62 70 B1
West Lund La YO62 94 B8
WEST LUTTON 150 B8
WEST MARTON 171 F5
West Mead WF10 201 A4
Westminster Bsns Ctr YO26 227 C8
Westminster Cl HG3 222 C3
Westminster Cres HG3 222 D2
Westminster Dr HG3 222 D3
Westminster Gate HG3 222 C3
Westminster Gr HG3 222 D3
Westminster Pl YO26 224 B1
Westminster Rd
Pannal HG3 222 C3
York YO30 228 A6
Westminster Rise HG3 222 D2
West Moor La
Finghall DL8 61 E4
Heslington YO10 184 A4
West Moor Rd
Darlington DL2 3 E3
Raskelf YO61 116 E2
Westmoreland St
Darlington DL3 3 C7
1 Harrogate HG1 219 E3
19 Skipton BD23 217 A3
West Mount LS24 189 E5
Westmount Cl HG4 214 B6
WEST NESS 94 B1
West Nooks 25 YO32 166 F5
West Oaks Sch 4 LS23 188 E8
WESTON 176 E2
Weston Cres 7 LS21 176 F1
Weston Dr LS21 176 E1
Weston La LS21 176 F1
Weston Moor Rd LS21 176 E4
Weston Park View LS21 176 E1
Weston Rd LS29 218 B4
Weston Ridge LS21 176 F1
Westover Rd YO12 212 F4
WESTOW 147 B4
West Par LS29 218 C4
West Parade Rd 11 YO12 212 F5
West Park Ave YO12 212 C8
West Park Cres YO12 212 C7
West Park Hospl DL3 3 A7
West Park Rd 13 YO13 75 D5
West Pasture
Kirkbymoorside YO62 70 B1
7 Pickering YO18 95 F6
West Pier YO11 213 B6
Westpit La YO32 167 A7
West Pk Harrogate HG1 219 D1
Selby YO8 232 A4
Westpoint Rd DL1 3 F6
West Rd Carleton BD23 173 A4
12 Filey YO14 101 B3
Melsonby DL10 20 F7
Westridge Cres 1 DL9 40 F5
WEST ROUNTON 24 D2
West Row DL2 4 C7
West Sandgate Terr 19 YO11 213 B6
WEST SCRAFTON 83 F6
Westside Cl YO17 215 B4
Westside Rd
Bransdale YO62 48 B5
Fadmoor YO62 69 E7
West Side Rd YO13 53 A1
West Sq 7 YO11 212 F5
West St
Castleford WF10 200 E4
Eaglescliffe TS15 5 D4
Gargrave BD23 155 D1
Gayles DL11 19 E6
Harrogate HG1 219 C5
Ilkley LS29 218 B4
Muston YO14 100 F2
Normanton South WF6 200 A1
Scarborough YO11 213 A4
Swinton YO17 121 B4
WEST STONESDALE 15 E1
WEST TANFIELD 87 A1
West Terr
Richmond DL10 209 B7
Scarborough YO11 212 F4
15 Whitby YO21 208 D7
West Thorpe YO24 230 D8
West Vale 37 YO14 101 B3
West View
Carleton BD23 173 B4
Darlington DL3 3 A5
Draughton BD23 174 B7
Ilkley LS29 218 B3
Kippax LS25 194 D1
Micklefield LS25 195 A3
North Deighton LS22 180 A6
Ripon HG4 214 D2
Sherburn in Elmet LS25 195 E3
West View Ave 25 LS29 176 C1
Westview Cl
3 Low Bradley BD20 173 E3
York YO26 227 B7
West View Rd 26 LS29 176 C1
West View Terr
Eaglescliffe TS16 5 D4
16 Knaresborough HG5 221 A6
West Villa YO61 144 A4
Westville Ave LS29 218 A4
Westville Cl 6 LS29 218 A4
Westville House Prep Sch LS29 218 D7
Westville Oval HG1 219 C6
Westville Rd LS29 218 A4
Westway Eastfield YO11 99 F7
Harrogate HG2 222 B8
West Way YO61 118 A1
WEST WITTON 59 E3
Westwood Carleton BD23 173 B4
Scarborough YO11 212 F5
Westwood Cl 2 YO11 212 F4
Westwood Dr LS29 218 A2
Westwood Gdns 3 YO11 212 F4
Westwood La
Ampleforth YO62 92 A2
West Tanfield HG4 86 E1
West Wood La YO23 182 E4
Westwood Mews
Carleton BD23 173 B4
12 Dunnington YO19 184 F7
Westwood Rd Ripon HG4 214 A2
Scarborough YO11 212 F4
Westwood Terr YO23 228 B1
Westwood Way LS23 188 E8
Wetherall Rd YO8 204 F5
WETHERBY 180 D4
Wetherby Bsns Ctr LS22 180 B3
Wetherby Bsns Pk LS22 180 C3
Wetherby High Sch LS22 180 C3
Wetherby La LS22 180 D7
Wetherby L Ctr LS22 180 C2
Wetherby Racecourse★ LS22 180 E3
Wetherby Rd
8 Boroughbridge YO51 141 B4
Bramham cum Oglethorpe LS23 188 E6
Harrogate HG2 220 B1
Kirk Deighton LS22 180 B5
Knaresborough HG5 221 D4
Sicklinghall LS22 179 E3
Tadcaster LS24 189 D6
Walton LS23 180 F2
Wetherby LS22 180 B2
York YO26 227 B3
Wethercote La YO7 67 C1
Wet Ings La 15 BD20 187 E6
Wetlands La DL11 18 G7
Weydale Ave YO12 212 E8
Weymouth Ave TS8 7 A7
Weymouth Rd 1 HG1 219 E4
Whaddon Chase TS14 8 F6
Whaites La YO7 115 C5
Whales La DN14 202 E3
Wham La BD24 130 F1
WHARFE 131 A8

Wharfedale YO14 .... 101 A3
Wharfedale Ave HG2 .... 222 A7
Wharfedale Cl 1 BD23 .. 217 B4
Wharfedale Cres
Harrogate HG2 .... 222 B7
Tadcaster LS24 .... 189 E6
Wharfedale Dr
Ilkley LS29 .... 218 C4
Normanton WF6 .... 200 A3
Wharfedale Hospl LS21 .. 176 F1
Wharfedale Nurseries
LS23 .... 188 E8
Wharfedale Pl HG2 ..... 222 A7
Wharfedale View 6
LS29 .... 174 F4
Wharfe Dr YO24 .... 230 D8
Wharfe Gr 8 LS22 ...... 180 B3
Wharfe La
Grassington BD23 .... 134 D3
Kearby with Netherby
LS22 .... 179 B1
Wharfe Pk 2 LS29 ...... 175 A4
Wharfeside Ave BD23 ... 134 D3
Wharfeside La LS29 ..... 218 C5
Wharfe View
Grassington BD23 .... 134 D3
Kirkby Overblow HG3 .... 179 A4
Wharfe View Rd LS29 ... 218 B4
Wharncliffe Pl 14 YO14 .. 101 A3
Wharnscliffe Dr YO30 ... 224 F2
WHARRAM LE STREET .. 149 A4
Wharram Quarry Nature
Reserve* YO17 .... 148 F4
Wharton Ave YO30 ...... 228 B7
Wharton Rd 8 YO41 ..... 168 D2
Whartons Prim Sch The
LS21 .... 177 A2
Whartons The LS21 ..... 177 A1
WHASHTON 20 A5
WHASHTON GREEN 20 A5
Whashton Rd Aske DL10 ... 20 C1
Richmond DL10 .... 209 C8
WHAW 17 B3
Wheatcroft 6 YO32 ..... 167 A6
Wheatcroft Ave YO11 ... 213 B1
Wheatcroft Prim Sch
YO11 .... 213 B1
Wheatdale Rd LS24 ..... 190 B2
Wheatear La TS17 .... 6 A5
Wheatfield La YO32 ..... 225 C8
Wheatfields Wlk YO19 .. 192 A1
Wheatlands
Great Ayton TS9 .... 8 A2
Ilkley LS29 .... 218 C4
Wheatlands Ave 8 BD20 187 E8
Wheatlands Cl 6 TS14 ..... 8 F6
Wheatlands Dr 4 TS13 .... 11 A8
Wheatlands Garth 20
BD20 .... 187 E8
Wheatlands Gr
Harrogate HG2 .... 222 E8
York YO26 .... 227 C6
Wheatlands La
7 Glusburn BD20 .... 187 E8
Roecliffe YO51 .... 140 E4
Wheatlands Rd HG2 ..... 222 E7
Wheatlands Road E HG2 222 E8
Wheatlands Way HG2 ... 222 F8
Wheatley Ave Ilkley LS29 . 218 E3
Normanton South WF6 ... 200 A1
Wheatley Dr YO32 .... 225 C8
Wheatley Gdns 2 LS29 .. 218 E3
Wheatley Gr LS29 .... 218 E3
Wheatley La 3 LS29 ..... 218 E3
Wheatley Rd LS29 .... 218 C3
Wheatley Rise LS29 ..... 218 E3
Wheeldale Cres TS17 ...... 6 B7
Wheeldale Dr YO32 ..... 226 E2
Wheeldale Rd YO22 .... 51 A4
Whelgate YO17 .... 215 C4
Wheelhouse Sq YO12 ... 212 F6
Wheelhouse The 4
YO30 .... 224 B5
Wheels La DN14 .... 204 F3
Wheelwright Cl
Copmanthorpe YO23 ..... 230 B2
Sutton upon Derwent
YO41 .... 185 C1
Wheel Wright Cl YO23 .. 230 B3
Wheelwrights Courts
BD23 .... 154 B3
WHELDALE 201 B5
Wheldale La WF10 ...... 201 B5
Wheldon Infant Sch
WF10 .... 200 F4
Wheldon Rd WF10 .... 201 A5
WHELDRAKE 193 A7
Wheldrake CE Prim Sch
YO19 .... 193 A8
Wheldrake Cl 1 TS14 ...... 8 F7
Wheldrake Ings Nature
Reserve* YO19 .... 193 C7
Wheldrake La
Deighton YO19 .... 184 B1
Escrick YO19 .... 192 B5
WHENBY 145 B8
Whenby Gr YO31 .... 225 F1
Whenby La YO60 .... 145 C6
Whernside TS7 .... 7 C5
Whernside Ave YO31 .... 229 A5
Whessoe Rd DL3 .... 3 C8
Whin Bank YO12 .... 212 D5
Whinbeck Ave WF6 ..... 200 B1
Whinbush La 1 HG3 ..... 138 A1
Whinbush Way DL1 .... 3 F8
Whinchat Tail TS14 .... 8 D6
Whin Cl
3 Strensall YO32 .... 167 B6
York YO24 .... 230 F7
Whincup Ave HG5 .... 221 B6
Whincup Cl 6 HG5 ...... 221 B6
Whincup Gr 7 HG5 ...... 221 B6
WHINFIELD 3 F8
Whinfield 34 LS29 .... 175 C2
Whinfield Bglws 5 HG3 . 138 A1
Whinfield Ct BD23 ...... 216 F3
Whinfield Prim Sch DL1 ... 3 F7
Whinfield Rd DL1 .... 3 E7
Whin Garth YO24 .... 230 F6
Whin Gn YO22 .... 32 A6
Whingroves TS17 .... 6 C8
Whin Hill YO17 .... 147 E1
Whin La
South Milford LS25 ...... 195 D2
Warlaby DL7 .... 64 C5
Whinmoor Hill YO7 ...... 66 C2
Whinney Banks Prim Sch
TS5 .... 6 D8
Whinney La HG3 .... 222 A5
Whinney Mire La LA2 ... 103 E1
Whinny Bank YO61 ...... 117 C8
Whinny Gill Rd BD23 ... 217 B3
Whinny Hagg La YO8 ... 197 A2
Whinny Hill DL9 .... 40 E3
Whinny La YO60 .... 168 A7
Whinnythwaite La YO26 . 181 C8
Whin Rd YO24 .... 230 F6
Whins La
Spofforth with Stockeld
HG3 .... 179 E4
Thorp Arch LS23 .... 180 F1
Whins The YO12 .... 212 A7
Whinstone Prim Sch TS17 .. 6 A5
Whinstone View 13 TS9 .... 8 A2
Whinwath La DL8 .... 87 F4
Whipley Bank HG3 ...... 161 A8
Whipley La HG3 .... 161 A7
Whip-ma-whop-ma-gate
YO1 .... 233 C2
Whipperdale Bank
Leyburn DL8 .... 60 A8
Redmire DL8 .... 38 F1
Whistler Cl YO23 .... 230 C3
Whistler Dr
Castleford WF10 .... 200 F2
Pickering YO18 .... 96 A6
Whiston Dr 18 YO14 .... 101 B3
WHITBY 208 C6
Whitby Archives & Heritage
Ctr* 25 YO21 .... 208 D6
Whitby Ave
Guisborough TS14 .... 8 F6
York YO31 .... 229 A7
Whitby Benedictine Abbey
(rems of)* YO22 .... 208 E7
Whitby Bsns Pk YO22 .... 32 F8
Whitby Com Coll YO21 .. 208 C5
Whitby Dr YO31 .... 229 A7
Whitby Gate YO18 .... 96 D6
Whitby Hospl YO21 ...... 208 D6
Whitby Jet Heritage Ctr*
YO22 .... 208 E7
Whitby L Ctr YO21 ...... 208 C7
Whitby Mus & Pannett Art
Gall* YO21 .... 208 C6
Whitby Pavilion Complex
YO21 .... 208 C8
Whitby Rd
Guisborough TS14 .... 9 A7
Pickering YO18 .... 96 B8
Staithes TS13 .... 13 K2
Whitby Sta YO21 .... 208 D6
Whitby Way DL3 .... 3 A7
Whitby Wizard (Hands-on-
Science)* YO21 .... 208 C8
Whitcliffe Ave HG4 ...... 214 B4
Whitcliffe Cres HG4 ..... 214 B3
Whitcliffe Dr HG4 .... 214 B3
Whitcliffe Gr HG4 .... 214 B3
Whitcliffe Grange DL10 . 209 A7
Whitcliffe La
Littlethorpe HG4 .... 139 D8
Ripon HG4 .... 214 A2
Whitcliffe Pl DL10 ...... 209 A7
Whitcliffe Terr DL10 .... 209 A7
Whitebridge Dr DL1 .... 3 D8
White Bridge Rd YO21 .. 208 B8
White Canons Ct 4
DL10 .... 209 E8
White Canons Wlk 3
DL10 .... 209 E8
Whitecarr La YO18 .... 95 A5
Whitecliffe Cres LS26 ... 194 A1
Whitecliffe Dr 1 LS26 .. 194 A1
Whitecliffe Rise LS26 ... 194 A1
Whitecote La LS25 ...... 195 D2
Whitecross Gdns YO31 .. 228 D7
Whitecross Hill DL8 ...... 87 F3
White Cross Rd YO31 ... 228 D7
White Cross Way YO41 .. 169 A2
Whitefield Bglws DN14 .. 206 F8
Whitefield La DN14 ..... 202 E1
Whitefields Dr DL10 ..... 209 E7
Whitefields Gate 1
DL10 .... 209 E8
Whitefields Wlk 2 DL10 . 209 E8
Whitefriars Cl DL10 ..... 209 F8
Whitefriars Ct 9 BD24 .. 131 D2
White Friars Gdns 6
DL10 .... 209 E8
White Friars Wlk 5
DL10 .... 209 E8
White Gate
Heslerton YO17 .... 123 E6
Sherburn YO17 .... 124 C6
Whitegate Cl 7 TS13 .... 13 K2
White Gate Hill YO11 ... 100 B2
Whitegate La HG4 .... 114 F1
Whitehall Landing YO22 . 208 E5
White Hart Cres 4 DL1 ..... 3 F6
Whitehead Hill 18 YO11 . 213 B6
White Hill La BD20 ...... 172 E1
Whitehill Rd BD22 .... 187 E3
White Hills Croft BD23 .. 216 E6
White Hills La BD23 ..... 216 E6
Whitehorn Rd WF10 ..... 200 F2
White Horse Cl 6 YO32 . 225 F5
White Horse Fold WF10 . 200 F7
White Horse La 9 YO12 ... 99 D6
White Horse Mews 3
HG3 .... 179 E5
White Horse of Kilburn*
YO61 .... 91 B4
Whitehouse Ave LS26 ... 200 B8
Whitehouse Cres LS26 .. 200 B8
White House Croft TS21 .... 5 A7
White House Dale YO24 . 227 F1
Whitehouse Dr LS26 .... 200 B8
White House Dr YO24 ... 227 F1
White House Garth YO8 . 199 D7
White House Gdns 4
YO24 .... 228 A2
White House Gr 1 YO41 . 185 B2
Whitehouse La Great & Little
Preston LS26 .... 200 B8
Swillington LS26 .... 194 B2
White House Rise YO24 . 227 F1
White House Wynd DL6 ... 24 D2
White La BD22 .... 187 F1
White Lands DL10 .... 209 E7
Whitelass Cl YO7 .... 211 B4
White Lee Ave BB8 ...... 186 B1
White Ley Rd WF8 .... 206 C1
White Leys Cl BB18 ..... 171 F1
White Leys Rd YO21 .... 208 A7
Whiteley Yd 18 HG5 ..... 221 A6
White Lilac Cl DL10 ..... 209 E7
White Lodge YO8 .... 232 B4
Whitemoor La YO8 ...... 198 C6
Whiteoak Ave YO61 ..... 143 C8
White Pastures DL10 .... 209 E7
Whitepits La LA2 .... 129 A5
White Point Ave 1 YO21 208 B7
White Point Ct YO21 .... 208 B8
White Point Rd YO21 ... 208 B8
White Rose Ave 3 YO32 225 D3
White Rose Candles*
DL8 .... 60 B4
White Rose Cl
Huby YO61 .... 144 A5
8 Linton-on-Ouse YO30 . 164 F7
Nether Poppleton YO26 .. 224 C1
White Rose Cres DL10 .. 209 E7
Whiterose Dr YO41 ..... 168 D2
White Rose Gr 5 YO32 .. 225 D3
White Rose Way
Nether Poppleton YO26 .. 227 C8
Thirsk YO7 .... 211 D4
Whiterow Rd DL8 .... 82 F7
White Scar Cave* LA6 .. 104 A4
White Sprunt Hill YO17 . 125 A1
White St YO8 .... 232 B6
Whitestone Ct YO7 ...... 211 D3
Whitestone Dr YO31 .... 225 E2
Whitethorn Cl YO31 .... 225 E2
Whitewall YO17 .... 215 D1
WHITEWALL CORNER ... 215 C1
Whitewall Corner Hill
YO17 .... 147 E8
White Wall La HG3 ..... 160 D4
White Way YO13 .... 54 C1
Whiteway Head HG5 .... 221 A4
White Way Heads YO18 ... 51 F4
Whitewood Ctr WF10 ... 200 D3
Whitfield Ave YO18 ...... 96 A6
Whitkirk Pl 17 YO14 .... 101 B3
WHITLEY 207 A7
Whitley Bridge Sta DN14 202 F1
Whitley Cl YO30 .... 225 A1
Whitley & Eggborough Prim
Sch DN14 .... 202 F1
Whitley Farm Cl DN14 .. 207 A8
Whitley Pl WF10 .... 200 E6
Whitley Rd
Elvington YO41 .... 185 A3
Norton-le-Clay YO7 ..... 115 B1
Thornaby TS17 .... 6 B6
WHITLEY THORPE 206 F7
Whitley Thorpe La DN14 . 206 F7
Whit Moor Rd HG3 ..... 158 F5
Whitsundale Cl 4 HG5 .. 221 D5
WHITTINGTON 102 A7
Whittle St 6 YO7 .... 89 B1
Whitton Croft Rd 9
LS29 .... 218 B4
Whitton Pl YO10 .... 229 C4
WHITWELL 42 B6
Whitwell Dr HG4 .... 114 B8
WHITWELL-ON-THE-
HILL 146 E4
Whitwell Rd YO60 ...... 146 E5
WHITWOOD 200 C3
Whitwood Comm La
WF10 .... 200 C3
Whitwood La WF10 ..... 200 C3
Whitworth Way BB18 ... 171 E2
WHIXLEY 164 A5
Whixley Field La YO26 . 164 B4
Whixley La LS22 .... 163 E2
WHORLTON 25 E1
Whorlton Castle (rems of)*
DL6 .... 25 E1
Whorlton La DL6 .... 45 E8
Whyett Bank YO21 .... 28 F6
Wickets The
8 Hutton Rudby TS15 ..... 25 C5
Middlesbrough TS7 .... 7 B6
Widdale Rd HG5 .... 221 D5
Widdowfield St DL3 .... 3 C6
Wide Howe La YO7 ..... 114 E8
Wide La YO14 .... 127 E5
Widgeon Cl 4 YO14 ..... 101 A4
WIGANTHORPE 119 E3
Wigby Cl HG3 .... 140 A2
WIGGINTON 166 D5
Wigginton Prim Sch
YO32 .... 166 D5
Wigginton Rd YO31 .... 233 B4
Wigginton Terr YO31 ... 228 C8
WIGGLESWORTH 153 C4
WIGHILL 181 D1
Wighill Garth LS24 ..... 189 E6
Wighill La LS24 .... 181 F3
Wighill St 25 BD20 ..... 187 E7
Wilberforce Ave YO30 .. 228 B7
WILBERFOSS 185 F5
Wilberfoss CE Prim Sch
YO41 .... 185 E6
Wilcock La BD20 .... 173 F2
Wildair Cl 2 DL2 .... 3 A7
Wild Rd DL1 .... 4 A4
Wilfreds Gr 8 YO8 ...... 198 B4
Wilken Cres TS14 .... 8 F7
Wilkinson Ct HG4 .... 214 B6
Wilkinsons Cl 13 YO13 ... 99 A7
Wilkinsons Ct 22 YO61 . 143 C8
Wilkinson St TS12 .... 9 E7
Wilkinson Way
6 Otley LS21 .... 176 F1
3 Strensall YO32 .... 167 A7
Willance Gr DL10 .... 209 A7
Willans Gr YO26 .... 227 E4
Willaston Cres HG2 ..... 220 A2
Willaston Rd 1 HG1 ..... 220 A3
WILLERBY 99 C2
Willerby Carr La YO12 ... 99 C3
Willgutter La BD22 ..... 187 F1
William Crossthwaite TS17 . 6 B4
William Ct YO10 .... 233 C1
William Jacques Dr YO8 . 198 E2
William Plows Ave YO10 . 228 E2
William Rd YO8 .... 198 B4
William's Hill Ring & Bailey*
DL8 .... 60 E2
Williamson Cl 14 HG4 ... 214 C5
Williamson Dr 8 HG4 ... 214 C5
Williamson Gdns HG4 ... 214 B4
William St 16 BB18 ..... 172 A1
Willins Cl 13 TS15 .... 25 C5
Willis St YO10 .... 228 E3
Willitoft Rd DN14 ...... 199 F6
Willoughby Way YO24 .. 230 B8
Willow Ave LS23 .... 188 E7
Willowbank TS8 .... 7 A5
Willow Bank
14 Brayton YO8 .... 197 D1
York YO32 .... 225 E4
Willow Bank Dr 1 WF8 . 201 C1
Willow Beck Rd DL7 .... 210 D6
Willowbridge Cl 8
WF10 .... 200 D3
Willowbridge La WF10 .. 200 C3
Willow Bridge La YO7 .. 115 F8
Willowbridge Rd WF8 ... 206 C2
Willowbridge Way WF10 200 C3
Willow Brook Cl YO17 .. 215 F4
Willow Chase The TS21 .... 4 F7
Willow Cl
20 Burley in Warfedale
LS29 .... 176 C1
2 Filey YO14 .... 101 B4
5 North Featherstone
WF7 .... 200 E1
Willow Cres
Clifford LS23 .... 188 E7
Richmond DL10 .... 209 D8
Willow Ct Kexby YO41 .. 168 C2
2 North Featherstone
WF7 .... 200 E1
16 Pickering YO18 .... 95 F6
Selby YO8 .... 232 D2
Willowdene La WF8 .... 201 B2
Willow Dr 6 Bedale DL8 ... 63 B3
Eston & South Bank TS6 .... 7 E8
1 North Duffield YO8 ... 199 A7
Willowgarth TS9 .... 25 C5
Willow Garth
Ferrensby HG5 .... 162 F7
Scalby YO12 .... 212 A7
10 Thornton Dale YO18 ... 96 D5
Willow Garth Ave BD20 . 187 E8
Willow Garth La DN6 ... 207 A1
Willowgate 24 YO18 ...... 95 F7
Willow Glade
5 Boston Spa LS23 ...... 188 E7
York YO32 .... 225 F3
Willow Gr
3 Boston Spa LS23 ...... 188 E7
Earswick YO32 .... 226 A7
Harrogate HG1 .... 219 E5
York YO31 .... 228 F7
Willow La
Boston Spa LS23 .... 188 E7
Ferrybridge WF11 .... 201 C4
North Featherstone WF7 .. 200 E1
Sleights YO22 .... 32 B6
Willow Lane E 4 WF7 .. 200 E1
Willow Park Rd YO41 .. 185 F5
Willow Rd
9 Campsall DN6 .... 206 E1
Darlington DL3 .... 3 B6
10 Knottingley WF11 .... 202 A3
Northallerton DL7 ...... 210 D2
Willow Rise
5 Kirkbymoorside YO62 .. 70 B1
Tadcaster LS24 .... 189 D5
Thorpe Willoughby YO8 .. 197 B1
Willows Ave TS8 .... 6 C4
Willows The
7 Acaster Malbis YO32 .. 191 C7
1 Hambleton YO8 .... 196 E1
Middlesbrough TS7 .... 7 C6
8 Strensall YO32 .... 167 B7
Willow Tree Gdns 9
LS29 .... 176 C1
Willow View
1 Catterick DL10 .... 41 D5
Cliffe YO8 .... 198 E3
Willow Way
16 Glusburn BD20 .... 187 E6
16 Sutton-in-Craven BD20 . 187 E6
Willow Wlk 1 HG4 ...... 214 B2
Willy Howe* YO25 ...... 126 C3
Willymath Cl YO13 .... 75 D7
Wilmot Rd LS29 .... 218 C4
WILSILL 137 E3
Wilson's La 5 YO13 ...... 99 A7
Wilson St
Castleford WF10 .... 200 E4
Guisborough TS14 .... 8 F6
Lockwood TS12 .... 9 F7
16 Pontefract WF8 .... 201 B1
Sutton BD20 .... 187 F7
Wilsthorpe Gr 1 YO10 .. 231 F8
Wilstrop Farm Rd YO23 . 230 A2
WILTON 97 A5
Wilton Carr La YO18 ..... 97 A3
Wilton Ings La YO18 ..... 97 A4
Wilton La TS14 .... 8 F7
Wilton Rd LS29 .... 218 A3
Wilton Rise YO24 .... 227 F3
Wimbledon Cl 2 DL1 ...... 3 E6
Wimpole Cl 6 YO30 .... 225 A1
Winchester Ave 3 YO26 . 227 E4
Winchester Gr 1 YO26 .. 227 E4
Winchester Way DL1 ...... 3 F6
Windermere YO24 ...... 230 D7
Windermere Dr WF11 .. 201 F1
Windgate Hill La YO8 .. 197 B6
Windle La BD20 .... 173 D1
Windleston Dr TS3 .... 7 B8
Windmill Gdns YO8 .... 232 B7
Windmill Gr LS24 ...... 189 D5
Windmill La
Norton DN6 .... 206 D1
York YO10 .... 229 B2
Windmill Mdw 13 DN6 .. 206 E2
Windmill Mdws YO41 ... 185 E6
Windmill Rd LS23 ...... 188 F6
Windmill Rise
Aberford LS25 .... 194 F7
Tadcaster LS24 .... 189 D5
York YO26 .... 227 E3
Windmill Way 23 YO32 .. 166 F5
Windrose Cl WF6 .... 200 A2
Windross Sq 11 YO61 ... 143 C8
Windsor Ave
Richmond DL10 .... 209 D8
Skipton BD23 .... 217 A4
Windsor Cl 17 WF6 ..... 200 B1
Windsor Cres
Middlesbrough TS7 .... 7 D6
7 Whitby YO21 .... 208 D6
Windsor Dr
2 Haxby YO32 .... 166 D5
Lockwood TS12 .... 9 F7
Windsor Garth YO24 ... 227 D1
Windsor La HG5 .... 221 B5
Windsor Pl BB18 .... 171 E2
Windsor Rd
24 Catterick Garrison DL9 .. 40 E4
4 Harrogate HG2 .... 220 A1
Ripon HG4 .... 214 C3
Thornaby TS17 .... 6 B7
Windsor St 1 YO23 .... 228 B1
Windsor Terr YO21 ..... 208 D6
Windy Hill LA2 .... 129 B8
WINEWALL 186 B2
Winewall La BB8 .... 186 B2
Winewall Rd 11 BB8 .... 186 A3
WINKSLEY 112 F2
Winksley Banks Rd HG4 . 112 E2
Winksley Gr HG3 .... 219 A4
Winn La YO7 .... 115 C6
Winnow La LS23 .... 188 D8
Winscar Gr 9 YO30 .... 224 E3
WINSLEY 160 D8
Winston Ave BD20 ..... 187 F8
Winston Ct
Northallerton DL6 .... 210 E6
Norton YO17 .... 215 E3
WINTERBURN 155 D5
Winterburn La BD23 ... 155 D5
Winter Gap La BD20 ... 186 D8
Winter Gn 21 HG3 ...... 161 B3
Winterscale Ct YO1 .... 228 D2
Winterscale St YO10 ... 228 D2
Winthropp Cl YO17 .... 215 C5
WINTON 44 C3
Winton Rd DL6 .... 210 E6
WINTRINGHAM 123 C4
Wise House La YO17 ... 215 F7
Wisker La YO32 .... 226 C7
Wisp Hill 12 BD23 ...... 134 E3
WISTOW 197 D6
Wistowgate YO8 .... 197 B8

Wistow Parochial CE Prim Sch YO8 197 D6
Wistow Rd YO8 232 A8
Witch La YO16 127 B2
Witcombe Cl 5 TS17 5 F5
Witham Dr YO32 226 A6
Witherick La HG4 114 B7
Withington Rd 6 YO62 92 F7
Witton Cres DL3 3 A7
Witton Steeps DL8 59 E2
WKM Ind Pk DL1 3 D7
Wobeck La HG4 114 B7
Woburn Cl YO33 167 B8
Woburn Way WF6 200 B1
Woldcroft YO41 185 C2
Wold La YO12 99 D1
WOLD NEWTON 126 A3
Wold Newton Foundation Sch YO25 126 A4
Wold Newton Rd YO25 126 E3
Wold Rd YO17 149 E8
Wold St YO17 215 D3
Wolds Way Lavender* YO17 123 B5
Wold View YO14 100 F2
Wold View Gr 5 YO12 99 E6
Woldview Rd YO41 185 F5
Wolfe Ave YO31 228 F5
Wolsey Ave YO8 197 B8
Wolsey Cl 11 LS25 195 F4
Wolsey Croft LS25 195 F4
Wolsey Dr YO23 231 A3
Wolsey Gdns 12 LS25 195 F4
Wolsey Grange 7 YO8 197 B8
Wolsingham Dr TS5 6 E7
Wolsley St YO10 228 E3
Wolviston Ave YO10 229 C3
WOMBLETON 93 F7
WOMERSLEY 206 C6
Womersley CE Sch DN6 206 C6
Womersley Park Gdns DN6 206 D5
Womersley Rd WF11 202 A2
Wood Acre Cl BD23 134 C3
WOODALE 83 A2
Woodale Cl 14 TS14 8 F7
Woodall Ave YO12 212 F7
Woodall Ct 9 YO8 197 D6
Wood Aven Cl 35 HG3 161 B3
Woodbine Cl 12 TS9 8 A2
Woodbine Terr 9 HG1 219 D3
Woodbridge Ave LS25 194 E5
Woodburn Dr 3 DL8 60 D5
Wood Cl
Bradleys Both BD20 173 D3
Skipton BD23 216 E5
7 Strensall YO32 167 A7
14 Thorpe Willoughby YO8 197 B1
Woodcock Cl
Eston & South Bank TS6 7 F8
9 Haxby YO32 166 F5
Woodcock Dr 8 DL9 40 F2
Woodcrest Rd DL3 3 B4
Woodend WF10 200 C7
Woodend Creative Ctr* 13 YO11 213 A5
Woodend Cres WF10 200 C7
Wood End La DL8 59 D5
Wooden Hill La DL7 210 B2
Woodfield Ave HG1 219 E4
Woodfield Cl HG1 219 E4
Woodfield Dr
Harrogate HG1 219 E4
6 Low Bradley BD20 173 E3
Woodfield Gdns 5 HG1 219 E4
Woodfield Gr HG1 219 E4
Woodfield Pl 6 HG1 219 E4
Woodfield Prim Sch HG1 219 F5
Woodfield Rd HG1 219 F7
Woodfield Sq HG1 219 E4
Woodfield View HG1 219 E4
Woodfield Wlk HG1 219 E4
Woodford Pl 1 YO24 227 D1
Woodgate YO12 212 D5
Wood Gate YO13 74 A1
Woodgate La LS17 178 B2
Wood Gn WF10 200 C3
WOODHALL
Selby 199 B2
Thoralby 58 B5
Woodhall Dr HG1 219 F6
Woodhall Gr
Harrogate HG1 219 F6
Mickletown LS26 200 B6
4 Stockton-on-Tees TS18 5 D8
Woodhall La
Hemingbrough YO8 199 B3
Womersley DN6 206 D6
Woodhead Field La YO62 70 A4
Wood Hill Cl YO51 141 D1
Woodhill View 3 LS22 180 C3
WOODHOUSE 200 A1
Woodhouse Fields Rd YO7 89 C6
Woodhouse Gr 4 YO31 229 A5
Woodhouse La BD23 157 B7
Woodhouse Rd
Guisborough TS14 8 E6
Thorganby YO19 193 A3
Wood La
Acaster Selby YO23 191 B2
Austwick LA2 131 A8
Birkin WF11 202 D6
Gainford DL2 1 D8
10 Grassington BD23 134 E2
Great Preston LS26 200 C7
Howsham YO60 146 F1
Wood La *continued*
Low Coniscliffe & Merrybent DL2 2 E4
Newland YO8 205 A3
Spennithorne DL8 61 A3
Thorp Arch LS23 180 F2
13 Thorpe Willoughby YO8 197 B1
Threshfield BD23 134 B3
Whitwood WF10 200 C3
Woodland Ave YO12 212 D6
Woodland Chase YO30 225 B1
Woodland Cl YO12 212 D6
Woodland Cres 8 LS26 194 A1
Woodland Croft LS23 181 A2
Woodland Ct LS23 180 F2
Woodland Dr Leeming DL7 63 F3
Walton LS23 180 F2
Woodland Gr YO12 212 C6
Woodland Mews LS23 181 A2
Woodland Pl
New Earswick YO32 225 E4
Scarborough YO12 212 C6
Woodland Ravine YO12 212 D6
Woodland Rd DL3 3 B6
Woodland Rise YO12 212 D6
WOODLANDS 220 C1
Woodlands Escrick YO19 192 B5
Ilkley LS29 218 D4
Woodlands Ave
Harrogate HG2 220 B1
Haxby YO32 225 C8
Norton YO17 215 E2
Rillington YO17 122 F5
Tadcaster LS24 189 D5
Woodlands Cl
15 Barlby with Osgodby YO8 198 B4
Goldsborough HG5 163 A3
Harrogate HG2 220 C2
15 Ilkley LS29 175 C2
Sherburn in Elmet LS25 195 F2
Woodlands Com Junior Sch HG2 220 B2
Woodlands Cres HG2 220 C2
Woodlands Croft LS25 200 D8
Woodlands Ct
13 Barlby with Osgodby YO8 198 B4
3 Harrogate HG2 220 B1
Woodlands Dr
14 Barlby with Osgodby YO8 198 B4
Egglescliffe TS15 5 E3
Garforth LS25 194 D3
Harrogate HG2 220 C1
Middlesbrough TS6 7 F8
Scarborough YO12 212 B5
Skipton BD23 216 E5
Woodlands Gn
8 Harrogate HG2 220 B1
Middleton St George DL2 4 C5
Woodlands Gr
Harrogate HG2 220 C2
8 Ilkley LS29 175 C2
Kippax LS25 200 E8
Rillington YO17 122 F5
York YO31 229 A7
Woodlands Hospl (Private) DL1 4 A4
Woodlands La
Hillam LS25 202 B7
14 South Milford LS25 195 F2
Woodlands Rd
Harrogate HG2 220 C2
Rillington YO17 122 F5
Woodlands Rise
1 Harrogate HG2 220 C2
14 Ilkley LS29 175 C2
Norton DN6 206 E1
Woodlands Sch YO12 212 B5
Woodland St 3 BD22 187 B6
Woodlands The TS7 7 D5
Woodlands View
11 Barlby with Osgodby YO8 198 B4
Kippax LS25 200 E8
3 Tadcaster LS24 189 D5
2 Thornton Dale YO18 96 D5
Woodlands Way
Hurworth DL2 3 D1
7 Hurworth-on-Tees DL2 22 D8
Woodlands Wlk
Harrogate HG2 220 C2
Scarborough YO12 212 D6
Skipton BD23 216 E5
Stokesley TS9 26 C8
Woodland Terr DL3 3 B5
Woodland View 5 YO7 89 A1
Woodland Way
8 Airmyn DN14 205 E4
Longnewton TS21 4 F7
York YO32 225 F4
Wood Lea 1 WF11 201 E4
Woodlea Ave YO26 227 C4
Woodlea Bank YO26 227 D4
Woodlea Cres YO26 227 D4
Woodlea Gr YO26 227 D5
Woodleigh Ave LS25 194 C4
Woodleigh Cl 2 YO32 167 A6
Woodleigh Sch YO17 148 A6
Woodley Gr TS7 7 D7
Woodman La LA6 102 B6
Woodman Terr BD23 216 F4
Woodmanwray La HG3 159 C8
Woodpark Ave HG5 221 A7
Wood Park Cl HG2 220 B1
Woodpark Dr HG5 221 A7
Woodpecker Rd 12 LS29 176 C1
WOOD ROW 200 A6
Wood Row LS26 200 A6
Woodrow Ave TS7 7 B6
Woodrow Cres LS26 200 A6
Woodroyd Gdns LS29 218 F3
Woodruff Cl 27 HG3 161 B3
Woodrush TS8 7 B4
Wood's Cl YO13 75 C8
Woods Ct HG2 222 C6
Wood's Gr YO13 75 C8
Woodside
Castleford WF10 201 B4
Harrogate HG1 219 E2
Hutton Rudby TS15 25 C6
5 Leyburn DL8 60 D5
Woodside Ave YO31 229 A6
Woodside Cl 3 YO61 117 D1
Woodside Gr
Allerton Bywater WF10 200 C7
3 Stockton-on-Tees TS18 5 E8
Woodside La BD20 173 C2
Woodside Rd
Ganton YO12 125 A8
Silsden BD20 174 B1
Woodside St WF10 200 C7
Woods La YO26 142 B2
Woodsmill Quay YO1 233 B2
Woods Pl LS29 218 C4
Woodspring Way YO14 127 B8
Wood St Castleford WF10 200 E4
Norton YO17 215 D3
York YO31 228 E6
Woodstock Cl DL6 210 B6
Woodstock Way YO7 211 D3
WOODTHORPE 230 C7
Woodthorpe Prim Sch YO24 230 C7
Woodvale TS8 7 B5
Woodvale Rd DL3 3 B4
Wood View Airmyn DN14 205 E3
Embsay BD23 217 C7
Harrogate HG1 219 C3
Wood View Ave WF10 200 D4
Woodview Cl DN14 207 A7
Woodville DN14 204 C1
Woodville Ave
Middlesbrough TS4 6 F8
3 Scalby YO12 212 D8
Woodville Terr YO8 232 E3
Wood Way YO32 226 A4
Woolcotts Cl 1 TS17 6 A3
Wooldale Dr YO14 101 B4
Wooler St YO12 212 E5
Woolmoor Cl YO7 211 D4
Woolnough Ave YO10 229 B3
Woolpots La YO61 117 B4
Woolsington Dr DL2 4 C4
Worcester Dr YO31 229 B5
Wordsworth App 2 WF8 201 B1
Wordsworth Ave 4 DN6 206 E1
Wordsworth Cl YO13 75 C5
Wordsworth Cres
Harrogate HG2 222 C8
York YO24 230 D7
Wordsworth Dr WF11 201 D3
Workhouse Mus* HG4 214 C6
World of James Herriot* YO7 211 B3
Worsall Rd TS15 5 D2
Worsall Toll Bar TS15 24 B7
Worsendale Rd YO42 169 F2
Worsley Cl TS16 5 E7
Worsley Cres TS7 7 B5
Worsley Ct YO17 215 A3
WORTON 57 F5
Woundales La
Knayton with Brawith YO7 65 F4
Upsall YO7 66 A2
Wrangham Dr 1 YO14 127 A8
WRAY 128 A6
Wray's Ave YO31 225 E1
WRAYTON 102 B3
Wray with Botton Endowed Prim Sch LA2 128 A6
Wrea Head Cl 2 YO13 75 D5
Wreaks La HG4 111 E6
Wreaks Rd Birstwith HG3 160 E6
Harrogate HG1 220 B3
Wrea La 1 YO12 212 F6
WRELTON 71 C1
Wrelton Cliff Rd YO18 95 B8
Wrelton Hall Gdns YO18 71 C1
Wrenbeck Ave 1 LS21 177 A1
Wrenbeck Cl 2 LS21 177 A1
Wrenbeck Dr LS21 177 A1
Wren Croft 5 WF8 201 B2
Wren Hall La YO8 204 E6
Wren La 2 YO8 232 D5
WRESSLE 199 D2
Wressle Sta YO8 199 D2
Wrexham Rd LS29 176 B1
Wreyfield Dr YO12 212 C7
Wrights La WF11 206 B8
Wright St 30 BD20 187 E7
Wycar 1 DL8 63 A2
Wycliffe Ave
Northallerton DL7 210 C2
York YO10 229 B3
Wycliffe Rd DL7 22 E1
WYCOLLER 186 C2
Wycoller Ctry Pk* BB8 186 D2
Wycoller View BB8 186 C3
Wydale La YO13 98 B6
Wydale Rd YO10 229 D4
Wydale Rise YO13 98 A5
WYDRA 160 A1
Wydra La HG3 159 F1
WYKEHAM Malton 122 B6
Seamer 98 E6
Wykeham Abbey* YO13 98 E5
Wykeham Ave TS14 8 E5
Wykeham Carr Rd YO13 98 E3
Wykeham CE Prim Sch YO13 98 E6
Wykeham Dale YO62 93 B8
Wykeham La YO13 98 E7
Wykeham Rd YO26 182 F7
Wykeham St YO12 212 E5
Wykeham Way TS8 7 A6
Wyke La TS7 7 D4
Wylam Ave DL1 3 D7
Wynam La YO41 185 C1
Wynbrook Ct YO13 75 C5
Wynd Cl 12 TS15 25 C5
Wynd The
3 Bedale DL8 63 A3
Burnt Yates HG3 160 F8
Hawes DL8 56 D4
Hutton Rudby TS15 25 D5
Skeeby DL10 20 F1
Wytherstone Gdns* YO62 69 B1
Wyvil Cres LS29 218 E4
Wyville Gr DL8 61 E7
Wyvil Rd LS29 218 E5

X

Xscape* WF10 200 F2

Y

YAFFORTH 43 C1
Yafforth Rd DL7 210 B6
Yall Flat La YO21 29 B6
Yan Brow YO62 70 C3
Yarborough Cl DL10 41 B2
Yarburgh Gr 2 YO26 227 E5
Yarburgh Way YO10 229 C3
Yarde Ave DL10 41 E4
Yarker Bank La DL8 60 C6
Yarlside La BD23 171 B4
YARM 5 D3
Yarm Back La TS18 5 D8
Yarm La TS9 7 D1
Yarm Prim Sch TS15 5 E2
Yarm Rd
Darlington DL1 3 E5
Egglescliffe TS16 5 E5
Hilton TS15 6 C2
Middleton St George DL2 4 C4
Yarm Road Ind Est DL1 3 F5
Yarm Sta TS15 5 E2
Yarrow Dr HG3 161 B3
Yatts Rd YO18 96 A8
Yeadon Wlk 12 DL2 4 C4
Yealand Ave BD24 131 D3
Yearby Cl TS5 6 D7
YEARSLEY 118 C5
Yearsley Cres YO31 228 D7
Yearsley Gr YO31 225 E1
Yearsley Grove Prim Sch YO31 225 F1
Yearsley Moor Bank YO62 118 B7
Yearsley Swimming Pool YO31 228 D8
Yederick Rd YO13 98 B8
YEDINGHAM 97 D2
Yedingham Priory (site of)* YO17 97 D2
Yedmandale Rd
2 East Ayton/West Ayton YO13 99 A7
Hutton Buscel YO13 98 F7
Yeomans Mount 11 HG3 137 B4
Yewbank Cl 3 LS29 218 A4
Yewbank Terr LS29 218 A4
Yewcroft LS29 218 A4
Yewdale Rd HG2 220 A1
Yew Tree Cl
Acaster Malbis YO23 191 C8
Harrogate HG2 222 C4
8 Low Bradley BD20 173 E3
Rufforth YO23 182 C6
Selby YO8 232 C6
13 Sleights YO22 32 A6
Yewtree Dr 1 LA2 128 F8
Yew Tree Gdns HG2 222 B5
Yew Tree La HG2 222 C5
Yew Tree Mews YO19 229 C5
Yew Tree Pk DN14 207 A7
Yew Tree Wlk HG2 222 B6
Yew Wlk The TS21 4 F7
Yiewsley Dr DL3 3 A5
YMCA & L Ctr YO11 213 A7
YMR Exhibition* YO24 233 A2
Yoadwath Bank YO62 70 C3
YOCKENTHWAITE 81 A1
Yoredale Ave
Darlington DL3 3 B6
17 Leyburn DL8 60 D5
Yoredale Dr 4 DL3 3 B6
YORK 233 B3
York Barbican Ctr YO10 233 C1
York Brewery* YO1 233 A2
York Bridge Rd YO61 143 B2
York Castle Mus* YO1 233 C1
York Cl 2 HG5 221 C5
York Coll YO24 230 E6
Yorkdale Ct 4 YO8 196 F1
Yorkdale Dr 3 YO8 196 F1
York Designer Outlet YO19 231 D4
York Dungeon The* YO1 233 B2
York Eco Bsns Ctr YO30 225 A3
Yorkersgate YO17 215 B4
York Garth 1 HG5 221 C5
York High Sch YO24 227 C2
York Hospl YO30 233 B4
York Ind Est LS22 180 C3
York La
Flaxton YO60 167 E8
Knaresborough HG5 221 B5
York Maze* YO19 184 F4
York Minster* YO1 233 B3
York Pl
Harrogate HG1 219 E1
Knaresborough HG5 221 B5
Scarborough YO11 213 A5
York Racecourse (The Knavesmire)* YO24 228 A1
York Rd
Bagby YO7 211 D2
Barlby YO8 198 B5
Bilbrough YO23 182 B2
Bilton-in-Ainsty with Bickerton LS22 181 A4
Boroughbridge YO51 141 B5
37 Burley in Warfedale LS29 176 C1
Cliffe YO8 198 E3
5 Colburn DL9 40 F4
Cottam YO25 151 B2
Dunnington YO19 184 D6
Easingwold YO61 143 C7
Flaxby HG5 163 B5
Green Hammerton YO26 164 B3
Harrogate HG1 219 C2
Haxby YO32 225 D7
Kilham YO25 151 F3
Kirk Hammerton YO26 164 C3
Knaresborough HG5 221 D5
Leavening YO17 147 E2
Long Marston YO26 182 A6
Malton YO17 215 A3
Middlesbrough TS7 7 D6
Naburn YO19 191 D8
North Duffield YO8 199 A8
Riccall YO19 192 A1
Sledmere YO25 150 E1
Sowerby YO7 211 E1
Stillingfleet YO19 191 D4
Strensall YO32 167 A6
Sutton-on-the-Forest YO61 166 C8
Tadcaster LS24 189 F6
Wetherby LS22 180 C3
York YO26 227 C3
York Rise BD23 154 B3
York Road Ind Pk YO17 121 C1
York St John University (Lord Major's Walk Main Campus) YO31 233 B3
York Science Park YO10 229 B2
Yorkshire Air Mus* YO41 184 F3
Yorkshire Coast Coll (Main Campus) YO12 212 B6
Yorkshire Coast Coll (Scarborough Bsns Sch) 20 YO11 212 F5
Yorkshire Coast Coll (Westwood Campus) YO11 212 F5
Yorkshire Dales Falconry & Wildlife Conservation Ctr* LA2 131 A5
Yorkshire Dales Mining Mus* BB18 172 A2
Yorkshire Dales National Park Ctr* BD24 131 D3
Yorkshire Garden World* YO8 203 A5
Yorkshire Lavender* YO60 119 E1
Yorkshire Mus* YO30 233 A3
Yorkshire Mus of Farming* YO19 229 F5
York St
Barnoldswick BB18 171 D1
Castleford WF10 200 E4
Crathorne TS15 24 E6
5 Dunnington YO19 184 E7
12 Glusburn BD20 187 E8
1 Selby YO8 232 C5
York Sta YO24 233 A2
York Steiner Sch YO10 228 D1
York Theatre Royal* YO1 233 B3
York View DL10 209 E8
York Villas WF6 200 A1
YOULTHORPE 169 C2
YOULTON 142 E2
Young Bank La YO62 70 C2
Young's Ct LS25 194 F7
Young's Dr 3 HG3 161 B2
Youngs Way 10 DL10 41 E4
Ypres Rd DL9 209 D1
Yule La YO26 164 C3

Z

Zetland Dr DL10 209 F8
Zetland St DL6 210 D4